THE

WORKS

OF

JOHN JEWEL,

BISHOP OF SALISBURY.

The Parker Society.

Instituted A.D. M.DCCC.XL.

For the Publication of the Works of the Fathers
and Early Writers of the Reformed
English Church.

THE

WORKS

OF

JOHN JEWEL,

BISHOP OF SALISBURY.

THE FIRST PORTION,

CONTAINING,

A SERMON PREACHED AT PAUL'S CROSS.

CORRESPONDENCE WITH DR COLE.

THE REPLY TO HARDING'S ANSWER

OF PRIVATE MASS.—OF COMMUNION UNDER BOTH KINDS.—
OF PRAYERS IN A STRANGE TONGUE.—OF THE SUPREMACY.—OF REAL PRESENCE.—
OF BEING IN MANY PLACES.—OF ELEVATION OF THE SACRAMENT.—
OF ADORATION OF THE SACRAMENT.

EDITED FOR

The Parker Society,

BY THE

REV. JOHN AYRE, M.A.,

OF GONVILLE AND CAIUS COLLEGE, CAMBRIDGE, MINISTER OF ST JOHN'S CHAPEL, HAMPSTEAD.

WIPF & STOCK · Eugene Oregon

Wipf and Stock Publishers
199 W 8th Ave, Suite 3
Eugene, OR 97401

The Works of John Jewel, Bishop of Salisbury
The First Portion
By Jewel, John
ISBN 13: 978-1-60608-062-7
Publication date 12/9/2009
Previously published by Cambridge University Press, 1845

CONTENTS.

ADVERTISEMENT.

THE volume now presented to the members of the Parker Society will be found to contain the challenge Sermon of Bishop Jewel, the correspondence upon it with Dr Cole, and a portion of the subsequent controversy with Dr Harding. It was the hope of the editor that the whole of the reply to Harding might have been published at once. The labour however of verifying so vast a mass of references must have delayed the publication to a late period; and, besides, the book would have overstepped the limits necessarily imposed each year by the amount of subscription to the Society. It was therefore necessary that this volume should close with the eighth article of the Reply, being thus far complete.

The text used is that of the folio of 1611, with which other editions have been collated; viz. "The true copies of the letters between the Reverend Father in God John Bishop of Sarum and D. Cole," 1560, containing also the sermon; "An Answer to Master Jewel's Challenge by Doctor Harding," Lovaine, 1564; "A Reply unto M. Harding's Answer," 1565. The folio of 1609 has also been consulted; and in a few cases, of which due notice is given, the text of one or more of the earlier editions has been adopted when that of 1611 was clearly in error.

The numerous references have been verified; and in cases where only an English translation is found in the text, the original has been subjoined: where, however, a Greek author is cited in a Latin version, it has not been deemed needful, except in cases of discrepancy, to add the Greek.

It would be uncandid in the editor not to confess that he has often met with serious difficulties in this part of his labours. Sometimes general allusions are made to an author or a treatise; and he cannot be always sure that he has referred to the exact passage meant. Sometimes a more precise quotation has defied his endeavours to discover it; in some cases probably from early errors in printing names or numerals. Perhaps, had he been able at all times to obtain the editions of the Fathers which Jewel used, the number of these might have been diminished. But if, after all the care which the editor has endeavoured to exercise, he should, in a work so extensive, embracing such a variety of topics, and studded with such a multiplicity of citations, have fallen occasionally into error, he trusts that none will be found of serious moment; and every inaccuracy he may discover he will be most ready to correct.

Jewel has himself been charged with errors; and the charges have been urged with much vehemence against him by his opponents. But as most of these are stated and insisted on in a subsequent work of Harding's, and as the bishop has replied to them in his Defence of the Apology, it appeared desirable to reserve the consideration of them to the proper opportunity.

As only a portion of Bishop Jewel's works is here presented, it is considered better not to supply an index to it. The folio editions contain two or three indices to the separate works respectively; and much inconvenience has thence been felt by those who have had occasion to consult them. A general index will therefore be compiled when the publication of this author shall be finished; and pains will be taken to facilitate reference to every part and topic. Additional title-pages will also be supplied, so as to render each portion of Jewel's works complete, and to enable the possessor to arrange them in the way most suitable to his inclination.

A memoir of the author will accompany a future volume.

The editor has to acknowledge the kindness of various friends. To the Rev. Josiah Allport, Birmingham, the Rev. W. H. Cox, M.A., Vice Principal of St Mary Hall, Oxford, the Rev. Richard Gibbings, M.A , Rector of Raymunterdoney, Raphoe, and the Rev. Joseph Mendham, M.A., Sutton Coldfield, he is especially indebted; and he begs to tender to those gentlemen his grateful acknowledgements.

J. A.

FEBRUARY, 1846.

CORRIGENDA ET ADDENDA.

PAGE

35 note 6. The reference should rather have been Lib. VI. cap. xv. fol. 257; where *Romanus pontifex superior est et judex conciliorum universalium, etiam congregatorum legitime: quæ ut bene, ita et perperam, injuste, impieque judicare definireque posse demonstratum est.*

84 note 3. *Insert* 3.

85 lines 1, 2. The passage referred to may be found Tertull. Op. Par. 1580. Lib. de Trin. p. 505.

90 line 22 from bottom. See August. Op. Par. 1679–1700. Ad Glor. et cet. Epist. xliii. 4. Tom. II. col. 90.

93 note 2, line 5. *For* 67 *read* 68.

97 note 10. The reference is to Chrysost. Op. Par. 1718-38. De Profect. Evang. Tom. III. p. 309.

113 note 15, line 2, *read* ad calc.

142 lines 34-36. The passage referred to is ... panis, quem ... frangimus, et quem unum in multas partes dividimus, ad &c.—Anselm. Op. Col. Agrip. 1612. In I. Epist. ad Cor. cap. x. Tom. II. p. 140. See page 315, note 11.

— line 35, later, 1565.

193 note 6. *Supply* [6

213 note 6. ...quam nihil firmitatis habeat hæc ratio hinc claret...quæ enim, &c. ipse ad, &c. —Mich. Vehe Assert. Sacr. Axiom. Lips. 1535. Tractat. v. fol. N. 3. 2.

250 note 9. *For* note 20 *read* note 21.

267 note 9. *Add:* But see Hieron. Op. Basil. 1516. Tom. I. fol. 121; where *Crescens in Galliis prædicavit evangelium.* This, however, was not a part of Jerome's work: see Cave, Script. Eccles. Hist. Lit. Oxon. 1740-3. Tom. I. p. 271.

381 note 7. This note should stand: Ergo consistorium Dei et papæ unum et idem est censendum...et breviter excepto peccato quasi omnia de jure potest ut Deus.—Hostiens. Op. Par. 1512. Super Prim. Decretal. De Transl. Episc. fol. 75. 2.

425 note 9. *For* notes 17, 8, *read* 18, 9.

470 note 2. The passage, as Harding has quoted it, may be found Chrysost. Op. Lat. Basil. 1547. In cap. Matt. xxvi. Hom. lxxxiii. Tom. II. col. 669.

A SERMON

PREACHED BY

THE BISHOP OF SALISBURY,

AT

PAUL'S CROSS.

The copie of a Sermon pronounced by the Byshop of Salisburie at Paules Crosse the second Sondaye before Ester in the yere of our Lord. 1560. wherupon *D. Cole* first sought occasion to encounter, shortly setforthe as nere as the authour could call it to remembraunce, without any alteration or addition.

TERTVLLIANUS.

Præiudicatum est aduersus omnes hæreses : id esse verum, quodcunque primum : id esse adulterum quodcunque posterius.

¶ This is a preiudice against all heresies : that that thinge is true, what soeuer was first : that is corrupt, whatsoeuer came after.

Concilium Nicinum.

Εθη ἀρχαῖα κρατείτω.

Mores antiqui obtineant.

[Title-page of Edition of 1560.]

THE

COPY OF A SERMON[1]

PREACHED[2] BY THE

BISHOP OF SARISBURY

AT PAUL'S CROSS,

THE SECOND SUNDAY BEFORE EASTER, IN THE YEAR OF OUR LORD GOD 1560.

WHEREUPON DOCTOR COLE FIRST SOUGHT OCCASION TO ENCOUNTER: SHORTLY SET FORTH, AS NEAR AS THE AUTHOR COULD CALL IT TO REMEMBRANCE, WITHOUT ANY ALTERATION, OR ADDITION.

---

1 Cor. xi. 23.

Ego accepi a Domino, quod et tradidi vobis: quoniam Dominus Jesus in qua nocte tradebatur, accepit panem, etc.

I have received of the Lord that thing which I also have delivered unto you; that is, that the Lord Jesus, in the night that he was betrayed, took bread, &c.

St Paul, after he was once appointed out by God to be his chosen vessel, to carry his name among all people, having occasion to make his abode for a long time in the city of Corinth, began there to instruct the people, to draw them from the follies and errors that they and their fathers had long lived in aforetime, and to lead them to the gospel of Christ, which then God of his mercy had newly shewed unto the world. And therewithal he delivered unto them the sacrament or holy mystery of Christ's last supper, to be practised and continued amongst them, as a most certain pledge and testimony of the same.

But after that, through the wickedness of the Jews, he was driven to depart thence, and to sail into Syria, the false prophets, men full of pride and vain-glory, taking occasion at his absence, sought means to discredit whatsoever he had taught or done, and caused the people not only to mislike the gospel of Christ that they had received at St Paul's hand, but also to missense[3] the sacraments. For as touching the gospel, they were fallen from it into sundry great and horrible heresies, concerning the resurrection and other special points of Christ's religion. And as touching the sacraments, whereas St Paul had appointed them the holy mysteries of the breaking of Christ's body and shedding of his blood, that they should all eat and drink together with fear and reverence in remembrance of his death and passion, and so cleave together in brotherly charity, as being all the members of one body, they, forgetting the very use and institution thereof, made small account of Christ's death, took each man to himself severally his own supper, despised their poor brethren, rent and divided the church of God, and so made the holy sacrament of love and charity to serve them as an instrument of discord and dissension.

Therefore saith St Paul unto them: "Shall I praise you for thus doing? in this thing surely I may not praise you. For I see your congregations and common meetings are not to the better, but to the worse."

For a redress hereof he calleth them back to the first original, and to the institution of Christ, from whence they were fallen. For I, saith he, being amongst you delivered you none other thing than that I had received of the Lord.

[[1] The challenge contained in this sermon was first given at Paul's Cross, Nov. 26, 1559, before Jewel's consecration as bishop of Salisbury. The sermon, with the challenge amplified, was preached at the court, March 17, 1560, and repeated at Paul's Cross, March 31, being the second Sunday before Easter.]

[[2] Pronounced, 1560.]

[[3] Mis-sense: misunderstand, mistake or pervert the sense of.]

That thing he thought meetest for you: and therefore with the same ought you also to be contented.

Thus, whensoever any order given by God is broken or abused, the best redress thereof is to restore it again into the state that it first was in at the beginning.

Thus, when the temple of God at Hierusalem was so shamefully disordered by the priests and Levites, that it was become a cave of thieves, Christ, for reformation thereof, called them back again to the first erection of the temple. *Scriptum est, Domus mea domus orationis vocabitur:* "It is written," saith Christ, "in the scriptures, My house shall be called the house of prayer." Thus was the temple of God used at the beginning, and thus ought it to be used now.

Thus, when Christ was opposed[1] by the scribes and Pharisees in the case of divorce, whether he thought it lawful for a man to put his wife from him for every light cause, and to marry another, he made them answer by the first institution and ordinance of marriage: *A principio non fuit ita: scriptum est, Erunt duo in carne una:* "It was not so," saith Christ, "at the beginning. It is written, They shall be two in one flesh; now therefore they are not two, but one flesh." As if he should have said: This is the ordinance of God my Father, this may not be broken for our[2] pleasure's sake, but must remain in strength and last for ever.

This St Paul, that the Corinthians might the better understand that they had unreverently missensed the Lord's supper, and be the more willing to redress the same, laid Christ's first institution before their eyes as a true pattern, whereby the sooner they might redress it. Look, saith he, "what thing I received of the Lord, the same thing I delivered over faithfully unto you." I gave you not any phantasy[3] or device of mine own, but that thing only that Christ had before delivered me. This rule is infallible: hereby your doings may best be tried. This I judge to be the very true meaning of these words of St Paul. Now, forasmuch as in this last age of the world the same holy sacrament or mystery of Christ's last supper hath been likewise stained with divers foul abuses, and specially for that, notwithstanding it hath pleased Almighty God of his great mercy in these our days to remove away all such deformities, and to restore again the same holy mysteries to the first original, yet there be divers that wilfully remain in ignorance, and not only be unthankful unto Almighty God for his great benefits, but also take pleasure in the errors wherein they have of long time been trained; and that not only the poor and ignorant, but also the rich and such as should be learned and know God; I have thought it good therefore at this time to stand the longer upon the same words of St Paul, that we may the more clearly see the first institution of the holy sacrament, and how far in these latter days we have strayed from it. It was to be hoped, forasmuch as the glorious light of the gospel of Christ is now so mightily and so far spread abroad, that no man would lightly miss his way (as afore in the time of darkness), and perish wilfully.

But we may remember, when the Jews were delivered out of Egypt, and had been wonderfully conducted through the Red sea, and set at liberty, and were passing quietly into the land of promise, a land flowing with milk and honey; yet were there divers weary of their being there, and fain would return again into Egypt to be in bondage, in thraldom, and in misery, as they had been before. We may remember, when the Jews were delivered from idolatry, wherein they and their fathers had long continued, and were brought to the true knowledge and worship of the everliving God of Israel, notwithstanding they were indeed[4] the people of God, yet were there many amongst them that misliked the time, and, as it is reported by the prophet Hieremy,
[Jer. xliv.] cried out against him: *Sermonem, quem locutus es nobis in nomine Domini, non*

[1 Apposed, 1560, 1609.] [2 Your, 1560, 1609.]
[3 Phansie, 1560, 1609.]
[4 In deed, 1560. In the earlier edition many words appear separated into their component parts, which, in that of 1611 and according to modern usage, are printed as respectively but one word; as "an other," "a loud," "in to," "up right." On the other hand, the edition of 1611 presents some, elsewhere distinguished, in a composite form; *e.g.* "asmuch," "somedeal," "willbe." It is not thought necessary to mark all these as they occur: the modern practice has been adopted here, as with the spelling.]

audiemus ex te: sed facientes faciemus omne verbum quod egreditur[5] *ex ore nostro, ut sacrificemus reginæ cœli, et libemus ei libamina: sicut fecimus nos et patres nostri, reges nostri, et principes nostri in urbibus Judæ et in plateis Hierusalem; et saturati sumus panibus, et bene nobis erat, et malum non vidimus.* That is, "We will not hear the word that thou speakest unto us in the name of the Lord, but we will do every thing that shall proceed out from our own mouth, as to burn incense to the queen of heaven, and to offer up drink-offerings unto her; as both we have done, and our fathers and our kings and our princes, in the city of Juda and in the streets of Hierusalem: for then had we plenty of victuals, and were well, and felt no evil."

We remember, when the gospel of Christ was preached by St Paul at Ephesus, and the devil's mouth was thereby stopped, and all his force and power taken from him, yet there was a great number that rose up against Paul, and violently withstood his doctrine, and cried out with main voice against him, *Magna est Diana Ephesiorum;* "Great is Diana the goddess of the Ephesians."

Even so in these days, notwithstanding the comparison may happily[6] seem somewhat odious, whereas the holy communion is restored to the use and form of the primitive church, to the same order that was delivered and appointed by Christ, and after practised by the apostles, and continued by the holy doctors and fathers for the space of five or six hundred years throughout all the whole catholic church of Christ, without exception, or any one sufficient example to be shewed to the contrary; yet are there some this day that refuse it and shun it, and unadvisedly and wilfully run headlong to the mass, of a good zeal, I hope, but not according unto knowledge. For, alas! they understand not what they do: they know not neither the communion, neither the mass: neither will they hearken or inquire to come to knowledge. And so in the midst of the light they remain still in darkness.

Wherefore, as I said afore, I have thought it needful to entreat somewhat hereof at this time, and have good hope through God's grace so to lay forth the whole matter, not with eloquence of words, but with simplicity of the truth, that it may be plain both unto them that have forsaken the mass, for what cause and how justly they have forsaken it, and also unto them that as yet delight in it, what manner of thing it is that they delight in.

I know some man will say, Forasmuch as the sacrament is a holy thing, the ordinance of Christ, the high mystery of his death and of our salvation, to remain in the church for ever; therefore it cannot possibly be abused; and all that we speak this day in this behalf, we speak of malice, and not of truth.

True it is, the sacrament is an holy thing, the ordinance of Christ, the mystery of our salvation; yet is there nothing so good, no ordinance so holy, no mystery so heavenly, but through the folly and frowardness of man it may be abused.

The serpent that was set up by Moses in the wilderness was an holy thing, for it was a sacrament, and a figure of Christ hanging on the cross; yet was it abused. The gospel of Christ is an holy thing; yet St Paul saith to the Philippians, there were some then that preached it for malice and contention, doing thereby service, not unto Jesus Christ, whom they professed in their mouth, but unto their own belly: and thus, being holy in itself, yet was it shamefully abused.

And what thing is there so holy as the name of God? and yet what thing is there so often taken in vain, or so much abused?

But, to come near to our purpose: the sacrament of baptism is an holy thing, yet hath it been abused, and that in the church of God, yea, even at the beginning of the church, even when the apostles of Christ were yet alive, and the blood of Christ as yet fresh and green before their eyes.

In St Paul's time there were some that baptized for the dead; after that, there were some that baptized such as were already dead, and sprinkled them

---

[5 Egredietur, 1560.] [6 happely, 1560: i. e. haply.]

with water, in the name of the Father, of the Son, and of the Holy Ghost, laid their hands over them, and called them by their names, as if they had been alive. Which thing was reproved and forbidden in the council of Carthage[1].

Others there were that baptized children before they were born, being as yet in their mother's womb. Which thing is mentioned and reproved by St Augustine[2].

All these, as may soon appear, were great abuses.

Thus the sacrament of baptism, notwithstanding it were a holy thing, yet was abused.

The sacrament of the breaking of Christ's body and the shedding of his blood is an heavenly mystery, and a[3] holy thing; yet hath it oftentimes been abused, and that in the primitive church, when the religion of Christ seemed to be in highest perfection.

In the time of Tertullian and of St Cyprian, which was a thousand and four hundred years ago, women commonly took the sacrament home with them in their napkins, and laid it up in their chests, and received a portion of it in the morning before other meats[4]. This was an abuse of the sacrament, and therefore was it broken.

In St Cyprian[5] and St Augustine's time, young babes, as soon as they were baptized, received the communion[6]: but that was a great abuse; for, by the doctrine of St Paul, the holy mysteries ought to be given unto none but only unto such as be able to understand the meaning thereof, to judge the Lord's body, and to declare his death. And therefore now infants when they be baptized receive not the communion. In the time of St Hierome, some portion of the holy communion was sent from the church to the new-married man and to his wife, to be received at home[7]. This was a disorder of the sacrament, and therefore now is not used.

St Irenæus saith, that one Marcus, a necromancer, was wont to enchant the cup of the sacrament of Christ's blood; so that the liquor should seem to increase and multiply, and from a little to grow to a great quantity[8]. This also was an horrible abuse of Christ's holy sacraments.

Some of late time have received the communion for their purgation, to clear themselves[9] against some notorious slander. And then the priest changed the words which commonly be used at the ministration, and said thus: *Corpus Domini nostri Jesu Christi sit tibi ad purgationem.* Some others have used to hang the sacrament, as an *Agnus Dei*, before their breasts, for a protection against the assaults of the devil and all other worldly enemies. St Benet ministered the communion unto a woman that was dead[10]; and it may well be

[1 Item placuit, ut corporibus defunctorum eucharistia non detur. Dictum est enim a Domino: Accipite et edite. Cadavera autem nec accipere possunt, nec edere. Cavendum est etiam ne mortuos baptizari posse fratrum infirmitas credat, cum eucharistiam mortuis non dari animadverterit.—Concil. Carth. III. cap. vi. in Concil. Stud. Labb. et Cossart. Lut. Par. 1671-2. Tom. II. col. 1168.]

[2 Perhaps the reference is to the following passage: Nam si ad matris corpus id quod in ea concipitur pertineret, ita ut ejus pars deputaretur; non baptizaretur infans, cujus mater baptizata est aliquo mortis urgente periculo, cum eum gestaret in utero. Nunc vero cum etiam ipse baptizatur, non utique bis baptizatus habebitur.—August. Op. Par. 1679-1700. Cont. Jul. Pelag. Lib. VI. 43. Tom. X. col. 685. See also Corp. Jur. Canon. Lugd. 1624. Decret. Gratian. Decr. Tert. Pars, De Consecr. Dist. iv. cans. 114, 5, 6. cols. 2017, 8.]

[3 An, 1560.]

[4 Non sciet maritus quid secreto ante omnem cibum gustes?—Tertull. Op. Lut. 1641. Ad Uxor. Lib. II. 5. p. 190.

Et cum quædam arcam suam, in qua Domini sanctum fuit, manibus indignis tentasset aperire, igne inde surgente deterrita est, ne auderet attingere.—Cypr. Op. Oxon. 1682. De Laps. pp. 132, 3.]

[5 Cyprians, 1560, 1609.]

[6 Illud vero quod in eadem commemoratur epistola [Cypr. De Laps. p. 132], quamdam parvulam, turbatis in fugam parentibus, nutrici derelictam, atque ab eadem nutrice dæmonum sacrilegiis impactam, postea in ecclesia illatam sibi eucharistiam miris motibus respuisse.—August. Op. Epist. ad Bonif. xcviii. 4. Tom. II. col. 265.]

[7 This seems to be gathered from a passage afterwards quoted.—Hieron. Op. Par. 1693-1706. Epist. xxx. pro Libr. adv. Jovin. Apol. Tom. IV. Pars II. col. 239.]

[8 Καὶ τοιαῦτά τινα εἰπὼν, καὶ ἐξοιστρήσας τὴν ταλαίπωρον, θαυματοποιὸς ἀνεφάνη, τοῦ μεγάλου πληρωθέντος ἐκ τοῦ μικροῦ ποτηρίου, ὥστε καὶ ὑπερεκχεῖσθαι ἐξ αὐτοῦ. καὶ ἄλλα τινα τούτοις παραπλήσια ποιῶν ἐξηπάτησε πολλοὺς, καὶ ἀπηγήοχεν ὀπίσω αὐτοῦ.—Iren. Op. Par. 1710. Cont. Hæres. Lib. I. cap. xiii. p. 61.]

[9 Themself, 1560.]

[10 The author probably referred to the stories nar-

thought that other did so as well as he; for it is forbidden by general consent in two councils, the one holden at Antifrodorum[11], the other at Carthage[12].

No man can lightly deny but these were great abuses. For Christ appointed not the sacrament of his last supper, that women should bear it home and keep it in their chests; nor that it should be sent home to new-married men and women, to be received in several; nor that it should be ministered to babes and infants that knew not what it meant; nor that enchanters or necromancers should thereby avant[13] their detestable practices; nor that men should thereby discharge themselves from slander; nor that it should be hanged before men's breasts, and carried about as a shield against the devil; nor that it should be ministered unto dead men or women, and closed up in their mouths and laid with them in their graves; but that such as bare the name of Christ, and trusted to be saved by his blood, should communicate together, and solace themselves in the remembrance of his death.

Thus[14] Christ himself hath instructed us: "Do this," he saith, "in remembrance of me." This is the very true and lawful use of the holy communion of Christ's body and blood; and all others are abuses.

We see therefore, that, albeit the sacrament be an holy thing and an heavenly mystery, yet that, notwithstanding, it may many ways be abused.

But what need we so many proofs in a thing that is so evident? St Paul himself saw the abuses thereof in his time. St Paul himself, even in the beginning of the church, within forty years after Christ's death, witnesseth that even then there were abuses crept into the sacrament, and therefore reproveth the Corinthians; and for redress thereof calleth them back to the example and first institution of Christ. "That same self thing," saith he, "that I received of the Lord, that I delivered unto you, in such sort as I had received it." Let that be a pattern for you to follow.

Some man perhaps will here reply: Notwithstanding the sacrament in itself, either through the wickedness or through the folly of man, may be, and hath[15] been abused, yet neither was there ever, nor can there be, any such abuse in the mass. For it standeth on four special parts; godly doctrine, godly consecration, godly receiving of the sacrament, and godly prayers. In conclusion, it is so heavenly and so godly a thing, that no folly or wickedness can enter into it.

These things, good brethren, I know have been oftentimes spoken out of such places as this is, and stoutly avouched in your hearing. And therefore, after that the mass had been once abolished by the[16] noble prince of godly memory, king Edward the Sixth; and the next prince, for that she knew none other religion, and thought well of the thing that she had been so long trained in, would needs have it put in ure again through all her dominions; it was forthwith restored, in like manner in all points as it had been used before, without any kind of alteration or change, as I believe, that their very doings therein might stand for proof sufficient, that neither the mass itself, nor any parcel or point thereof, had ever been abused.

But, alas! what if they that most of all other defend the mass, themselves find faults and abuses in the mass? Mark, I pray you, what I say: What if the very maintainers and proctors of the mass confess plainly unto the world, in their books openly printed and set abroad, that there have been, and be, abuses and errors in the mass?

Albertus Pighius, the greatest pillar of that part, in a little treatise that he writeth of the mass, hath these words: *Quod si qui abusus in rem sacratissimam et saluberrimam irrepserunt, ut irrepsisse plerosque non diffitemur, scimus ad quem et ad quos pertineat eosdem corrigere*[17]. That is to say, "If there have certain abuses crept into that holy and wholesome thing, that is, the mass, as I grant there

rated by Gregory the Great.—Gregor. Magni Papæ I. Op. Par. 1705. Dial. Lib. II. capp. xxiii. xxiv. Tom. II. cols. 253, 6. See also P. Mart. Def. Doctr. Vet. et Apost. de Sacros. Euch. Sacr. Tig. 1559. Pars I. Object. xxxviii. p. 171.]

[[11] Non licet mortuis nec eucharistiam nec osculum tradi, nec velo vel pallis corpora eorum involvi.—Concil. Autisiod. [Auxerre,] can. xii. in Concil. Stud. Labb. et Cossart. Tom. V. col. 958.]

[[12] See before, page 6, note 1.]

[[13] Avant: set forward in a boasting way, vaunt.]

[[14] This, 1560.] [[15] Have, 1560.] [[16] That, 1560.]

[[17] Alb. Pigh. Explic. Cathol. Contr. Par. 1586. De Miss. Priv. Controv. VI. fol. 123. 2.]

have crept in very many, yet we know to what man and men the redress thereof doth appertain." Here Pighius granteth simply, without colour, that divers abuses have at sundry times privily crept into the mass. And yet I believe he was no such enemy to the cause, that he would ever have granted so much, specially against the self-same[1] thing that he defended, unless he had known it perfectly to be true. If any man doubt of this man Albertus Pighius, and know not his authority, nor what he was, let him understand that, when I speak of him, I speak of all: for this is he that all the rest have chosen to follow as their captain, the greatest learned man, as it is supposed, and as he himself thought, that ever wrote in that quarrel. He hath found out errors and abuses in the mass, and is not abashed openly to confess the same.

Of these errors I have intended somewhat to entreat at this time; not of all, for that would be an infinite labour, but of so many, and so far forth, as the time shall suffer me.

I will not here enter to speak either of transubstantiation, either of the real presence, either of the sacrifice, either of the common sale or utterance, either of the superstitious ceremonies of the mass, which are for the most part both very vain, and also in manner without number.

Of these things I am content to disadvantage myself at this time, and briefly to touch two or three points, as of the Latin tongue wherein commonly the mass hath been used; of the communion under one kind; of the canon; of the adoration of the sacrament; and of the private mass. And of these things I intend to speak, although not so largely, and with so many words as the cause would require; yet, by God's grace, so simply and so truly, that whoso will be moved with truth or reason shall soon perceive there have been abuses in the mass. And if there were but one of these abuses in it, yet were it worthy to be spoken of, and to be amended. But if we shall plainly see with our eyes that all the errors and disorders, besides[2] a great number else, which I willingly pass by, have been in the mass, O good brethren, let us not then think that so many godly men in these our days have spoken against it without cause.

First, as touching the unknown and strange tongue that hath been used in the mass, St Paul's counsel and commandment is in general, that whatsoever is done or said in the congregation should so be done and said that the hearers may have comfort thereby, and yield thanks unto God, and say, Amen. But the same St Paul saith: "If thou make thy prayer in the congregation with the[3] spirit or noise of strange words, how shall the unlearned man thereunto say, Amen? For he knoweth not what thou sayest. For notwithstanding thy prayer perhaps be good, yet hath the other no comfort or profit by it." And therefore he saith farther: "I had rather[4] utter five words in the congregation with understanding of my meaning, so that the rest may have instruction thereby, than ten thousand words in a strange and unknown tongue."

St Augustine writing upon the Psalms saith thus: *Oportet nos humano more, non avicularum ratione cantare: nam et merulæ, et psittaci, et corvi docentur sonare quod nesciunt*[5]: "We must," saith St Augustine, "in the prayers that we make to God, not chirp like birds, but sing like men. For popinjays, and ravens, and other birds, are taught to sing they know not what."

Justinian, a christian emperor, made a strait constitution, that all bishops and priests should pronounce the words of the ministration with open voice, that the people might say, Amen[6].

[[1] Same self, 1560, 1609.] [[2] Beside, 1560.]

[[3] Thy, 1560.] [[4] Lever, 1560.]

[[5] ... quid hoc sit intelligere debemus, ut humana ratione, non quasi avium voce cantemus. Nam et meruli et psittaci et corvi et picæ et hujusmodi volucres sæpe ab hominibus docentur sonare quod nesciunt.—August. Op. Par. 1679-1700. In Psalm. xviii. Enarr. II. 1. Tom. IV. col. 81.]

[[6] Ad hæc jubemus, ut omnes episcopi pariter et presbyteri non tacito modo, sed clara voce, quæ a fideli populo exaudiatur, sacram oblationem et preces in sancto baptismate adhibitas celebrent, quo majore exinde compunctione in depromendis Domini Dei laudibus audientium animi efferantur. Ita enim et divus apostolus docet, dicens in prima ad Corinthios epistola: Enimvero si solummodo benedicas spiritu, quomodo is qui privati locum implet, dicet ad gratiarum actionem tuam Deo ipsum Amen; quandoquidem quid dicas, non videt? Tu quidem pulchre gratias agis, alter autem non ædificatur. Et rursus in epistola ad Romanos sic inquit: Corde quidem creditur ad justitiam, ore autem fit confessio ad salutem.

And, to pass by all other authorities and examples in this behalf, before the church grew to corruption, all christian men throughout the world made their common prayers, and had the holy communion, in their own common and known tongue. But in the mass, as it hath been used in this latter[7] age of the world, the priest uttereth the holy mysteries in such a language, as neither the people nor oftentimes himself understandeth the meaning. And thus the death of Christ and his passion is set forth in such sort as the poor people can have no comfort or fruit thereby, nor give thanks unto God, nor say, Amen. Of all that holy supper, and most comfortable ordinance of Christ, there was nothing for the simple souls to consider, but only a number of gestures and countenances; and yet neither they nor the priest knew what they meant. Think you this was Christ's meaning when he ordained the communion first? Think you that St Paul received these things of the Lord, and delivered the same to the Corinthians? O good brethren, Christ ordained the holy sacrament for our sakes, that we might thereby remember the mysteries of his death, and know the price of his blood.

Touching the second abuse of the communion under one kind, it would be long to say so much as the place would seem to require. For, besides the institution of Christ, and the words of St Paul, which to a christian man may seem sufficient, it was used throughout the whole catholic church six hundred years after Christ's ascension, under both kinds, without exception. But in one word, to say that may be sufficient for a wise man to consider, Gelasius, an old father of the church, and a bishop of Rome, saith that to minister the communion under one kind is open sacrilege. His words be these: *Divisio unius ejusdemque mysterii sine grandi sacrilegio non potest pervenire*[8]. I trust I shall need no further[9] evidence to prove that the mass in this part hath been abused.

The third point that I promised to speak of is the canon, a thing for many causes very vain in itself, and so uncertain that no man can readily tell on whom to father it. St Paul saith: *Scio cui credidi et certus sum:* "I know whom I have believed, and I am certain." And unto Timothy he saith: *Permane in his quæ didicisti, sciens a quo didiceris:* "Stand stedfastly in such things as thou hast learned, knowing of whom thou hast learned them." Yet many men this day stand to the canon as unto the holiest part of all the mass, and know not of whom they have learned it. Some say Alexander the First made it; some say Leo; some say Gelasius; some say Gregorius the First; Gregorius saith, one Scholasticus; some others say, Gregorius the Third; but Innocentius Tertius, to put the matter quite out of doubt, said plainly it came from Christ and from his apostles[10]. Howbeit, whosoever was[11] the first deviser of it, it forceth not. The substance of it and the meaning is more material; and thereof I think it needful to touch some part in as few words as I may. For notwithstanding I have small pleasure in opening such matters as may seem odious, yet is it behoveful for every man to understand of that thing that was counted so high and holy, what manner a thing it was, and what it contained.

First, the priest in the canon desireth God to bless Christ's body, as though it were not sufficiently blessed already. Further, he saith that he offereth and presenteth up Christ unto his Father[12], which is an open blasphemy. For, contrariwise, Christ presenteth up us, and maketh us a sweet oblation in the sight of God his Father.

His igitur de causis convenit, ut inter ceteras preces et ea quæ in sancta oblatione dicuntur clara voce a religiosissimis episcopis et presbyteris Domino nostro Jesu Christo Deo nostro cum Patre et sancto Spiritu proferantur: scituris religiosissimis sacerdotibus, quod si quid horum neglexerint, et in horrendo judicio magni Dei et Servatoris nostri Jesu Christi de his rationem reddent, neque nos hæc cognoscentes conquiescemus, relinquemusque inulta.—Justin. Princ. Novell. Constit. Basil. 1561. Const. cxxxvii. (al. cxxiii.) pp. 409, 10.]

[[7] Later, 1560.]

[[8] Gelas. in Corp. Jur. Canon. Lugd. 1624. Decret. Gratian. Decr. Tert. Pars. De Consecr. Dist. ii. can. 12. col. 1918; where the last word is *provenire.*]

[[9] Farther, 1560.]

[[10] Credimus igitur, quod formam verborum, sicut in canone reperitur, et a Christo apostoli, et ab ipsis eorum acceperint successores.—Innoc. III. in eod. Decretal. Greg. IX. Lib. III. Tit. xli. cap. 6. col. 1371.]

[[11] Were, 1560.]

[[12] Te igitur, clementissime Pater, per Jesum Christum Filium tuum Dominum nostrum supplices rogamus ac petimus, uti accepta habeas et benedicas hæc dona, hæc munera, hæc sancta sacrificia illibata, in primis quæ tibi offerimus pro ecclesia tua sancta catholica.—Missal. ad Us. ac Consuetud. Sar. Paris. 1527. Canon, fol. 156.]

Moreover, he desireth God so to accept the body of his Son Jesus Christ, as he once accepted the sacrifice of Abel, or the oblation of Melchisedech. It is known that Abel offered up of the fruit of his flock a lamb or a sheep, and that Melchisedech offered unto Abraham and his company, returning from the battle, bread and wine. And think we that Christ the Son of God standeth so far in his Father's displeasure, that he needeth a mortal and a miserable man to be his spokesman to procure him favour? Or think we that God receiveth the body of his only-begotten Son no[1] otherwise than he once received a sheep or a lamb at the hands of Abel? or than Abraham received bread and wine of Melchisedech? If no, why then maketh the priest this prayer in the canon immediately after the consecration? *Supra quæ propitio ac sereno vultu respicere digneris, et accepta habere, sicuti accepta habere dignatus es munera pueri tui justi Abel, et sacrificium patriarchæ nostri Abraham, et quod tibi obtulit summus sacerdos tuus Melchisedech*[2]. That is to say, "Look down with merciful countenance upon these sacrifices (that is, the body of Christ thy Son, and the cup his blood), and vouchsafe to receive them, as thou sometime vouchsafedst to receive the oblations of thy child Abel the just, and the sacrifice of our patriarch Abraham, and that thing that was offered unto thee by thy high priest Melchisedech." Besides this, he desireth God that an angel may come and carry Christ's body away into heaven. This is the prayer that he maketh: *Jube hæc perferri per manus sancti angeli tui in sublime altare tuum*[3]. What a fable is this, that Christ should be borne upon an angel, and so carried up away into heaven! I would not stand so long upon these follies, if force drave me not thereunto. Therefore I leave to speak farther of the canon, giving you occasion by these few things the better to judge of the rest.

The fourth matter that remaineth to be touched is the adoration, a great matter full of danger, and full of jeopardy, and so much the more dangerous, for that it is an honour belonging only unto God, and yet without any warrant of God's word. Christ, that best knew what ought to be done herein, when he ordained and delivered the sacrament of his body and blood, gave no commandment that any man should fall down to it or worship it. St Paul, that took the sacrament at Christ's hand, and, as he had taken it, delivered it to the Corinthians, never willed adoration, or godly honour to be given unto it. The old doctors and holy fathers of the church, St Cyprian, St Chrysostom, St Ambrose, St Hierome, St Augustine, and others, that received the sacrament at the apostles' hands, and (as it may be thought) continued the same in such sort as they had received it, never make mention in any of all their books of adoring or worshipping of the sacrament. It is a very new device, and, as it is well known, came but lately into the church.

About three hundred years past, Honorius, being then bishop of Rome, commanded the sacrament to be lifted up, and the people reverently to bow down to it[4]. After him, Urbanus the Fourth appointed a holy day of "Corpus Christi," and granted out large pardons to the keepers of it, that the people should with better will resort to the church, and keep it holy[5]. This is the greatest antiquity of the whole matter: about three hundred years ago it was first found out, and put in practice; but Christ and his apostles, the holy fathers in the primitive church, the doctors that followed them, and other learned and godly men whatsoever for the space of a thousand and two hundred years after Christ, never heard of it. Once again I say, for the space of a thousand and two hundred years after Christ's ascension into heaven this worshipping of the sacrament was never known or practised in any place within the whole catholic church of Christ throughout the whole world. But after it was once received and put in use, and the people began to worship the sacrament with godly honour, the learned men and school-doctors that then were saw it could not stand without great danger, and confessed that the ignorant sort thereby might soon be led into

---

[1 Non, i.e. none, 1560.]

[2 Missal. ad Us. ac Consuetud. Sar. Par. 1527. Canon. fol. 159.]

[3 Id. ibid.]

[4 Honor. III. in Corp. Jur. Canon. Lugd. 1624. Decretal. Greg. IX. Lib. III. Tit. xli. cap. 10. col. 1378.]

[5 Clem. V. in eod. Clement. Lib. III. Tit. xvi. cols. 240, &c.]

idolatry. Mark, I beseech you, what I say: for I know unto some men it seemeth not possible that there may be any kind of danger in worshipping the sacrament of Christ's body; and therefore some have alleged St Augustine's words in this behalf: *Nemo manducat nisi prius adoret:* "No man eateth Christ's body but first he doth worship it." And again: *Non peccamus adorando, sed magis peccaremus non adorando*[6]*:* "We offend not in worshipping the flesh of Christ, but rather we should offend if we should not worship it." But indeed the school-doctors and learned men saw there might be danger in worshipping the sacrament, and therefore gave warning of it.

John Duns and William Durand say thus: If there remained the substance of bread after consecration, the people would therefore[7] take occasion of idolatry, and, instead of Christ[8] body, would give godly worship unto the bread[9]: and therefore they thought it best to remove away the bread and to bring in transubstantiation, a word newly devised, and never once heard or spoken of before the council of Lateran, holden at Rome in the year of our Lord 1215. But the old doctors and fathers, which first planted the church, and to whom more credit is to be given, write plainly that in the sacrament after consecration there remaineth still very bread and wine in nature and substance as before. And to allege one or two instead of many, St Augustine saith in a sermon, *Ad Infantes: Quod videtis [in mensa], panis est*[10]*:* "That thing that ye see upon the table is bread." Gelasius also saith in like sort: *Non desinit esse substantia panis, vel natura vini;... sed manent in suæ proprietate naturæ*[11]*:* "It leaveth not to be the substance of bread, or the nature of wine; but they remain in the property of their own nature."

Theodoretus, an old doctor of the church, likewise saith: *Christus ea symbola, quæ videntur, corporis et sanguinis sui appellatione honoravit, non naturam transmutans, sed naturæ adjiciens gratiam*[12]*:* "Christ," saith Theodoretus, "honoured the bread and wine which we see with the names of his body and blood; not changing the nature thereof, but unto the same nature joining his grace."

I know not what may be more clearly spoken. St Augustine saith, it is bread; Gelasius saith, it leaveth not to be the substance and nature of bread and wine; Theodoretus saith, Christ honoured the bread and wine with the natures of his body and blood, but yet changed not their nature. Thus the old godly bishops and fathers of the church acknowledge and affirm that bread remaineth in the sacrament after consecration. But Duns and Durand, and some others of the young fathers and doctors, say, If the people worship the sacrament, and bread remain, then must they needs be in great danger of idolatry. Wherefore we may well conclude of them both, forasmuch as it is clear by the old doctors that bread remaineth, that the people, resorting to the mass, and there[13] worshipping the sacrament, must needs be in danger of idolatry.

Farther, they say, Idolatry may be done to the sacrament if a man happen to worship the accidents of the bread, that is to say, the whiteness, or roundness, or other such outward forms or shews of bread, as he seeth with his eye, and give the honour unto that instead of Christ's body. O miserable people, that thus[14] is led to worship they know not what! For, alas, how many of them understand[15] these distinctions, or care for them? How many of them understand after what sort *accidentia* may be *sine subjecto?* or how whiteness is founded in the sacrament? or what is the difference between *substantia* and *accidens?* Or what

---

[6 ... nemo autem illam carnem manducat, nisi prius adoraverit: ... et non solum non peccemus adorando, sed peccemus non adorando.—August. Op. Par. 1679-1700. In Psalm. xcviii. Enarr. 9. Tom. IV. col. 1065.]

[7 Thereof, 1560, 1609.]

[8 Christ's, 1560, 1609.]

[9 Duns reports this as the opinion of Thomas:... si ibi maneret substantia panis, non deberet talis cultus exhiberi propter idololatriam, adorando creaturam: but himself seems to differ: ... non est idololatra, qui adoret Christum in eucharistia: et tamen non potest negari, quin sit ibi creatura aliqua, &c.—Joan. Duns Scot. Op. Lugd. 1639. In Lib. IV. Sent. Dist. xi. Quæst. 3. Tom. VIII. pp. 607, 8.]

[10 August. Op. Serm. cclxxii. ad Infant. Tom. V. col. 1103.]

[11 Gelas. Episc. Rom. adv. Eutych. et Nestor. in Mag. Biblioth. Vet. Patr. Col. Agrip. 1618-22. Tom. V. Pars. III. p. 671; where we find, *et tamen esse non desinit substantia vel natura panis et vini,* and *permanente tamen.*]

[12 Theodoret. Op. Lut. Par. 1642-84. Immut. Dial. I. Tom. IV. p. 18.]

[13 their, 1611.]

[14 This, 1560.]

[15 Understandeth, 1560.]

priest, when he went to mass, ever taught the people to know these things, and to avoid the danger? Undoubtedly, I could never yet perceive by any reading, either of the scriptures or else of other profane writings, but that the people of all ages hath evermore been readier to receive idolatry than to learn the distinctions and quiddities of logic or philosophy.

Thus we see, even by the confession of Duns and Durand, and other their own doctors, that he that goeth to the mass, and worshippeth the sacrament, unless he be learned and take good heed, may soon commit idolatry. The doctrine of itself is new, the profit of it such as the church of God for the space of twelve hundred years was well able to be without it, the jeopardy of it great and horrible, and scarcely possible to be avoided. I speak not these things, good brethren, to the intent to spoil Christ of the honour that is due unto him. I know, and confess, that Christ's blessed body is most worthy of all honour. I know that the flesh of the Son of God is not therefore the less honourable, because it is now become glorious, and sitteth in heaven at the right hand of God his Father. The body of Christ, sitting above all heavens, is worshipped of us, being here beneath in earth. Therefore the priest at the communion, before he enter into the holy mysteries, giveth warning unto the people to mount up with their minds into heaven, and crieth unto them, *Sursum corda:* "Lift up your hearts;" according to the doctrine of St Paul: *Si una surrexistis cum Christo, ea quæ sursum sunt quærite, ubi Christus est sedens ad dextram Patris:* "If ye be risen again with Christ, seek for those things that be above, where as Christ is sitting at the right hand of his Father." And again: *Nostra conversatio est in cœlis, unde Salvatorem exspectamus:* "Our conversation or dwelling is in heaven; from whence we look for our Saviour." Therefore St Augustine spake the words that I before alleged: *Nemo manducat nisi prius adoret*[1]*:* "No man eateth Christ's flesh, but first he doth worship it." The eating thereof and the worshipping must join together. But where we eat it, there must we worship it; therefore must we worship it sitting in heaven. So saith[2] the old doctor and father St Chrysostom: *Ubi cadaver, ibi aquilæ: cadaver Domini corpus est; aquilas autem nos appellat; ut ostendat, oportere illum ad alta contendere, qui ad hoc corpus accedit: aquilarum enim, non graculorum, est*[3] *hæc mensa*[4]. That is to say: "'Wheresoever is the carcase, there be the eagles:' the carcase is Christ's body; us he calleth the eagles, to declare that whosoever will approach near to that body must get aloft. For this is a banquet for eagles, that soar a high, not for jays, that keep the ground." Christ's body is in heaven: thither therefore must we direct our hearts; there must we feed; there must we refresh ourselves; and there must we worship it.

(Col. iii.) (Phil. iii.) ([1 Cor. xvi. 1560.])

(Ad Hedibiam.) So saith St Hierome: *Ascendamus cum eo in cœnaculum magnum stratum: ibi accipiamus ab eo sursum calicem novi testamenti*[5]. "Let us get up," saith St Hierome, "with him into the great dining-chamber that is already prepared, and there let us receive of him above the cup of the new testament."

(In Lucam, cap. xxiv.) So saith St Ambrose: *Non super terram, nec in terra, nec secundum terram te quærere debemus, si volumus invenire*[6]*:* "We may not seek for thee, neither upon the earth, nor in the earth, nor about the earth, if we list to find thee."

And to conclude, so saith Eusebius Emissenus: *Exaltata mente adora corpus Dei tui*[7]*;* that is: "Lifting up thy mind unto heaven, there worship and adore the body of thy God."

Thus did the old catholic fathers worship the body of Christ. Thus may we also worship it safely, and without peril.

[[1] See before, page 11, note 6.]

[[2] Layeth, 1560.]

[[3] *est* omitted, 1560.]

[[4] Chrysost. Op. Par. 1718-38. In Epist. I. ad Cor. Hom. xxiv. Tom. X. p. 216.]

[[5] ... ascendamus cum Domino cœnaculum magnum, stratum atque mundatum: et accipiamus, &c.—Hieron. Op. Par. 1693-1706. Ad Hedib. Epist. Quæst. ii. Tom. IV. Pars. I. col. 172.]

[[6] Ambros. Op. Par. 1686-90. Expos. Evang. sec. Luc. Lib. X. 160. Tom. I. col. 1538; where *supra terram,* and *secundum carnem* are found.]

[[7] The following is probably the passage intended; but, though the sense is the same, the words, it will be seen, are different: ... sacrum Dei tui corpus et sanguinem fide respice, honora, mirare, mente continge, cordis manu suscipe, et maxime haustu interiore assume.—Euseb. Emiss. in Corp. Jur. Canon. Lugd. 1624. Decret. Gratian. Decr. Tert. Pars, De Consecr. Dist. ii. can. 35. col. 1928.]

But to give God's honour to the sacrament is a thing both lately brought into the church, unknown and strange to the ancient doctors; and, as the schoolmen and the greatest maintainers of it have themselves confessed, an occasion of idolatry, and full of danger.

For what if the priest happen not to consecrate? What if he leave out the words of consecration, and never speak them? as it is known that some priests have done many years together. Or what if the priest have no intention or mind to consecrate? What case standeth the poor people then in? or what thing is it that they worship? Christ's body cannot be there without consecration: consecration there can be none, as they themselves have taught, if there miss either pronunciation and[8] utterance of the words, or else purpose to consecrate and intention. And how can the people know with what intention or mind the priest goeth to the mass? or whether he hath duly pronounced the words? or whether he hath consecrated or no? And knowing none of these things, which in very deed is not possible for them to know, how can they be well assured that it is the body of Christ that the priest holdeth up, and whereunto they fall down, and give godly honour? Thus, by their own learning, the people must needs stand still in doubt, and never know certainly what they worship. O good people, think not that I imagine these things of myself. Our own adversaries that stand against us in this cause, even the famoust[9] and best learned of them all, have seen, and written, and confessed the same.

Alexander, a bishop of Rome, writing upon the Master of the Sentences, taketh up the matter on this sort: Forasmuch as the priest's purpose, and his privy doings about the consecration, cannot be known, that therefore no man ought to worship the sacrament when it is holden up, but with this condition, *Si ille consecraverit*[10], that is, if the priest hath consecrated. That is to say, when ye see the sacrament lifted up, ye must say or think thus with yourself: If this priest hath consecrated, then do I worship it; if he hath not consecrated, then do I not worship it. Thus saith Alexander, a bishop of Rome.

But Thomas of Aquine leaveth the matter a little more at large. He saith: *Ista conditio non semper actu requiritur: satis est habere habitum*[11]: that is to say: "It shall not be needful at every time to say or to think thus, whensoever ye kneel down to worship; but it shall be sufficient if ye have a certain readiness in your mind to say or to think so." Yet Holcot, writing likewise upon the Master of the Sentences, saith thus: *Laicus adorat hostiam non consecratam: ista fides sufficit illi ad salvationem: tamen est erronea*[12]: "The layman," saith he, "as it may sometimes happen, worshippeth a wafer that is not consecrate: this faith is sufficient unto him to his salvation, and yet is it a false faith and erroneous." And farther he concludeth in this sort: *Homo potest mereri per fidem erroneam, etiamsi contingat ut adoret diabolum*[13]. By these words we may see, such as will not content themselves to be ordered by God's wisdom, how dangerously they run headlong at the last.

Holcot was not the worst learned man amongst them; yet, to uphold the error that he had once taken in hand to defend, he was driven to confess, that a man may meed[14] at God's hand by an erroneous and false faith, yea, although he worship the devil.

This is the certainty of the doctrine that the people of God of long time hath been led in. In the highest and heavenliest point of religion, that is, in the worshipping of God, they themselves know not what they do. It is true of them that Christ saith to the woman of Samaria: "Ye worship ye know not what."

Alas, is this the honour that is due to Christ? Is this the worshipping of God in spirit and truth? Is this the seeking of Christ in heaven? But some

---

[[8] An, 1560.]

[[9] Famoust: famousest, most famous.]

[[10] Alexander V. See Oudin. De Script. Eccles. Lips. 1722. Tom. III. cols. 1141, 2.]

[[11] ...non tamen oportet, quod hæc conditio semper fit actu explicita: sed sufficit quod habitu teneat illam.—Thom. Aquinat. Op. Venet. 1595. In Lib. III. Sent. Dist. ix. Quæst. i. Art. 2. Tom. VII. fol. 37. 2.]

[[12] Rob. Holkot. sup. Quat. Lib. Sent. Quest. Lugd. 1497. Lib. Tert. Quæst. I. l. vi. YY; where we find *sibi sufficit*, and *et tamen*.]

[[13] ... dixi quod non solum excusatur a peccato: immo tamen meretur quantum mereretur si Christum adoraret.—Id. ibid. l.iiii. MM]

[[14] Meed: deserve.]

man will say, these be trifling and light matters, and prove nothing. Such reports, I know, are given abroad of all that is preached and taught this day, that whatsoever is spoken by any of us is light and childish, and not worth the hearing. But the reporters hereof are they to whom the authority of the old doctors, the authority of the primitive church, the authority of the scriptures, the authority of Christ himself, seemeth light, and not greatly worth the hearing.

Loth I am here to rip up and to open unto you the high mysteries and secrets of their learning, and the force and strength of their reasons. Yet at this time the importunity of them forceth me so to do, that, after ye have once taken as well some taste of their arguments, as ye have of ours, ye may the better and more indifferently judge of both. And let not them that privily and untruly find fault with our reasons be aggrieved, if they hear openly and truly somewhat of their own. And first, to begin with the head, mark ye well and weigh this argument. God made two lights in heaven, the greater light to rule the day, the less light to rule the night; *ergo*, there be two powers to rule the world, the pope, that resembleth the sun, and the emperor, that is far less than he, and is likened unto the moon. And how much the emperor is less, the gloss declareth by mathematical computation, saying that the earth is seven times greater than the moon, and the sun eight times greater than the earth; so followeth it that the pope's dignity is six and fifty times greater than the dignity of the emperor[1]. This is an argument of theirs, used by Innocentius Tertius unto the emperor of Constantinople. *In principio creavit Deus cœlum et terram, non in principiis:* "God created heaven and earth in the beginning," as in one, "not in the beginnings," as in many; *ergo*, the pope hath the sovereignty over all kings and princes[2]. This is an argument of theirs used by pope Bonifacius the Eighth, *Extra de majoritate et obedientia: Unam sanctam. Cum transierit ad Dominum, tolletur velamen:* that is, When the infidel shall come to Christ, the veil of darkness shall be taken from his heart; *ergo*, he that becometh a priest must shave his crown[3]. This is an argument of theirs to be found in Isidorus. There is but one only God; *ergo*, all nations throughout the world must pray to him in one tongue[4]. This is an argument of theirs, made by Gerson, sometime chancellor of Paris. *Ecce duo gladii hic:* "Behold, here be two swords;" *ergo*, the bishop of Rome hath power of both swords, both spiritual and temporal[5]. This is an argument of theirs used by Bonifacius the Eighth, *Extra de majoritate et obedientia*, as above. The bishop of Rome granteth out pardons; *ergo*, there must needs be a purgatory[6]. This is an argument of theirs used by John Fisher, bishop of Rochester. *Euntes docete omnes gentes:* "Go and teach all nations." And again: *Quam speciosi pedes evangelizantium pacem, evangelizantium bona!* "O how beautiful be the feet of them that preach peace, of them that preach good things!" And again: *Calciati pedes in præparationem evangelii pacis:* "Having your feet shod to the preparation of the gospel of peace:" *ergo*, the

De Major. et Obed. cap. Solitæ, et in gloss. ibidem.

Isai. lii.

Eph. vi.

[[1] Ad firmamentum igitur cœli, hoc est, universalis ecclesiæ, fecit Deus duo magna luminaria, id est, duas instituit dignitates, quæ sunt pontificalis auctoritas et regalis potestas. Sed illa, quæ præest diebus, id est, spiritualibus, major est; quæ vero carnalibus, minor: ut quanta est inter solem et lunam, tanta inter pontifices et reges differentia cognoscatur. —Innoc. III. in Corp. Jur. Canon. Lugd. 1624. Decretal. Greg. IX. Lib. I. Tit. xxxiii. cap. 6. col. 426. The gloss adds: Igitur cum terra sit septies major luna, sol autem octies major terra; restat ergo, ut pontificalis dignitas quadragesies septies sit major regali dignitate.—Ibid.]

[[2] Bonifac. VIII. in eod. Extrav. Comm. Lib. I. De Major. et Obed. cap. 1. col. 212; where the words as above quoted are transposed.]

[[3] Quæritur autem, cur, sicut apud antiquos Nazaræos, non ante coma nutritur, et sic tondetur. Sed qui hæc exquirunt, advertant quid sit inter illud propheticum velamentum et hanc evangelii revelationem. De qua dicit apostolus: Cum transieris ad Christum, auferetur velamen.—Isid. Hispal. Op. Col. Agrip. 1617. De Offic. Eccles. Lib. II. cap. iv. p. 401.]

[[4] The editor has not been able to discover the argument referred to in the works of Gerson.]

[[5] Ecce gladii duo hic .... Uterque ergo est in potestate ecclesiæ, spiritualis scilicet gladius et materialis.—Bonifac. VIII. in Corp. Jur. Canon. Extrav. Comm. Lib. I. De Major. et Obed. cap. 1. col. 208.]

[[6] The following is doubtless the argument intended ... non absque maxima sancti Spiritus dispensatione factum sit, quod post tot annorum curricula purgatorii fides et indulgentiarum usus ab orthodoxis generatim sit receptus. Quamdiu nulla fuerat de purgatorio cura, nemo quæsivit indulgentias. Nam ex illo pendet omnis indulgentiarum existimatio. Si tollas purgatorium, quorsum indulgentiis opus erit? His enim, si nullum fuerit purgatorium, nihil indigebimus, &c.—Joh. Roffens. Episc. Assert. Luther. Confut. Antv. 1523. Artic. xviii. fol. 111. 2.]

bishop must wear purple sandals[7]. *Aspergam super vos aquam mundam:* "I will sprinkle upon you clean water;" *ergo*, the priest must sprinkle the people with holy water[8]. *Sine me nihil potestis facere:* "Without me you can do nothing;" *ergo*, the bishop only must consecrate the church, and no man else[9]. All these, with a number more of the like, be their arguments, used by William Durand in his *Rationali Divinorum*. [Ezek. xxxv 1560.]

But let us come near, and see the arguments whereupon the mass is built. *Nolite sancta dare canibus:* "Give not holy things to dogs;" *ergo*, the priest at mass, and other where, may not speak to the people but in a strange tongue[10]. The title of Christ's death was written upon the cross in Greek, Hebrew, and Latin; *ergo*, all common prayers in the church must be used in one of the same tongues, that is, either in Greek, or in Hebrew, or in Latin[11]. These arguments have been used by many, devised first, as may be thought, by master Eckius.

Christ was buried in a shroud of linen cloth; *ergo*, the corporal must be made of fine linen[12]. This argument may be found in Sylvester.

Many of the lay people have the palsy, and many have long beards; *ergo*, they must all receive the communion under one kind[13]. This is a common argument, used in manner by all them that have written in this behalf.

Petra erat Christus: "Christ was the rock;" *ergo*, the altar must be made of stone[14]." *Domini est terra, et plenitudo ejus:* "The earth is the Lord's, and the fulness thereof." And, *Veritas tua in circuitu tuo:* "Thy truth is in thy compass." The money for which Judas sold Christ was round; *ergo*, the host or the sacramental bread must be round[15]. *Calix aureus Babylon in manu mea:* "Babylon is a cup of gold in my hand," saith the Lord; *ergo*, the chalice must be of silver or gold[16]. This is an argument of theirs used by master William Durand. When Virgil saith, *Cum faciam vitula*, he useth *facere* for *sacrificare:* that is, he useth this word "doing," for this word "sacrificing;" *ergo*, when Christ said to his disciples, *Hoc facite in mei memoriam;* "Do this in remembrance of me,"

[[7] Celebraturi igitur pontifices pedes interea, dum dicuntur quinque psalmi in præparatione evangelii pacis, caligis et sandaliis calciantur: quorum pulchritudinem admirabatur propheta, dicens: Quam speciosi pedes evangelizantium pacem, evangelizantium bona. Unde apostolus ad Ephesios: Calciati pedes calciamentis virtutum. Et in evangelio legitur Dominum misisse discipulos suos sandaliis calciatos, calciatos utique in præparatione evangelii pacis.—Durand. Rat. Div. Offic. Lugd. 1565. Lib. III. cap. viii. 2. fol. 69. 2.]

[[8] Rursus tunc sacerdos justus tabernaculum aspergit, dum Dei misericordiam petit. Cyprianus quoque papa ait, quod ideo homines aqua benedicta asperguntur, quia valet ad sanctificationem: unde scriptura per Ezechielem dicit: Aspergam super vos aquam mundam et mundabimini ab omnibus immunditiis vestris, &c.—Id. Lib. IV. cap. iv. 3. fol. 94.]

[[9] Secundo notandum quod solus pontifex potest ecclesias et altaria dedicare ... quoniam gerit imaginem et figuram summi Pontificis Christi spiritualiter dedicantis, sine quo nihil possumus in ecclesia stabilire: unde ipse ait: Sine me nihil potestis facere.—Id. Lib. I. cap. vi. 2. fol. 24. 2.]

[[10] Atque hi etiam verentur, ne si hæc summa mysteria ad tantam ac tam promiscuam multitudinem (quæ est præsentis ecclesiæ facies) lingua vernacula frequenter adferantur et decantentur, fore ut ab impiis et male institutis in canticum et proverbium vertantur; atque ita impingatur in id quod inhibuit Christus, ne scilicet sanctum canibus daretur.—Joh. Eck. Apol. adv. Cal. Buc. Antv. 1542. Lib. Propos. ad Comp. Relig. xxi. fol. 39. This book was submitted to both sides by Charles V.; and Eckius's annotations follow. It is attributed to Gropper: Eckius, however, it is said, ascribed it to Vicelius.]

[[11] This argument in substance may be found Joh. Eck. Enchir. Loc. Com. Col. 1532. cap. xxxiv.]

[[12] Et utrumque horum [corporalium et pallarum] debet esse de panno lineo simplici ... requiruntur adminus duæ et sufficiunt: ut respondeant linteaminibus quibus involutum fuit corpus Christi, quæ pluraliter nominantur: et intellige duæ excepto corporali.—Sylvestr. Summa Summar. Bonon. 1515. fol. 133. 2.

...statuimus, ut sacrificium altaris non in serico panno...quisquam celebrare præsumat: sed in puro linteo...sicut corpus Domini nostri Jesu Christi in sindone linea munda sepultum fuit.—Ex Epist. Eus. et Sylvestr. in Corp. Jur. Canon. Decret. Gratian. Decr. Tert. Pars, De Consecr. Dist. i. can. 46. col. 1091.]

[[13] Quartum [periculum] in barbis longis laicorum.—Joh. Gerson. Op. Antw. 1706. Cont. Hær. de Com. Laic. sub Utr. Spec. Tom. I. Pars. III. col. 466.

...ubi sunt...debiles...fieret injuria sacramento per effusionem liquidi.—Joh. Eck. Enchir. Loc. Com. cap. x. fol. E. 5.]

[[14] Non ergo unguntur altaria nisi lapidea: quia Christus per altare significatus est lapis excrescens in montem, &c.—Durand. Rat. Div. Offic. Lib. I. cap. vii. 28. fol. 34. 2.]

[[15] Hostia autem formatur rotunda: quia Domini in terra, et plenitudo ejus orbis terrarum, et universi qui habitant in eo ... Rursus cum figura rotunda formetur a puncto ad punctum: per hoc innuitur, quod ab ipso sunt omnia, et ad ipsum omnia retorquentur: unde Psal. Veritas tua in circuitu tuo....Panis autem hic formatur in modum denarii: tum quia panis vitæ pro denariis traditus est.—Id. Lib. IV. capp. xxx. 8. xli. 8. fol. 139, 162. 2.]

[[16] ... Urbanus papa ... statuit quod in argenteis vel aureis vasis sacrificetur: vel propter paupertatem in stanneis.... Et nota quod calicis nomen a veteri et novo testamento originem traxit. Hie. xii. Calix aureus Babylon inebrians omnem terram, &c.—Id. Lib. I. cap. iii. 44, 5. fol. 18.]

he meant, sacrifice this in the remembrance of me[1]. This argument is fashioned out by M. Clitovey. And to be short, the angel looked into the grave; *ergo*, the priest must take off the paten and look into the chalice[2]. Pilate washed his hands before the people; *ergo*, the priest must likewise wash his hands when he is at mass[3]. Judas kissed Christ; *ergo*, the priest must kiss the altar[4]. The thief on the cross repented himself of his wicked life; *ergo*, the priest at mass must fetch a sigh, and knock his breast[5]. These, and other like, be their reasons; and whoso listeth to see them may find them, and other more as good as these, in William Durand. Now, good people, judge ye in your conscience indifferently us both, whether of us bringeth you the better and sounder arguments. We bring you nothing but God's holy word; which is a sure rock to build upon, and will never fleet or shrink. And therefore are we able truly to say with St Paul: *Quod accepimus a Domino, hoc tradidimus vobis:* "We have delivered unto you the same things that we have received of the Lord."

For, concerning the last matter that I promised to touch, it cannot be denied by any man, be he never so wilful, but Christ in his last supper ordained a communion, and shewed no manner token of a private mass; as may plainly appear both by the words that he spake, and also by the order of his doings. For he took the bread, brake it, divided it, and gave it to his disciples, and said, "Eat[6] ye all hereof," not unto one alone, but unto the whole. He said farther by way of charge, "Do this;" that is to say, Practise this that I have here done, and that in such form and sort as ye have seen me do it.

St Paul likewise, when he saw that the use of the sacrament was grown to disorder, that every man took his own supper privately to himself, and that thereby both the holy communion and also brotherly love and unity was despised, as it hath been in the west part of the church now a great many of years in this latter times[7], he called them back again to the beginning thereof and to the institution of Christ, as giving them thereby to understand that the sacrament cannot be better used than Christ himself used it. Thus[8] he saith: *Cum conveneritis*[9] *in unum locum, non potestis dominicam cœnam manducare; unusquisque enim præsumit cœnam suam:* "When ye resort together into one place, ye cannot eat the Lord's supper; for every one of you eateth his own supper aforehand." Therefore he saith unto them, *Alter alterum exspectate:* "Tarry ye, and wait one for another," and so receive the holy communion all together. For this is it that I delivered unto you, and the same self thing I received of the Lord.

Here have I briefly shewed the disorder of the private mass, by the first institution of the sacrament, and by the commandment and authority of St Paul. Now will I, by God's grace, also declare and open the same by the examples and whole practice of the primitive church, and by the ancient doctors and other learned fathers that followed after the apostles' time, for the space of six hundred years or more; and I trust ye shall clearly see that for so long time there was no private mass in the catholic church of Christ in any country or coast throughout the world. For all the writers that were within the compass of that time have left behind them witness sufficient of a communion; but not one of them all could ever tell us of any private mass.

Clemens, who, as they say, was scholar to St Peter, writeth thus in an epistle

---

[[1] Quippe verbum *facere* etiam apud secularis literaturæ authores *sacrificare* significat, ut apud Maronem in illo Bucolico carmine....Cum faciam vitula pro frugibus, ipse venito. Quid enim sacrificare, quam facere sacra signat? et qui sacrifici dicuntur, nisi qui sacra faciunt?—Jud. Clichtov. Anti-Lutherus, Col. 1525. Lib. II. cap. xiv. fol. 93.]

[[2] ...diaconus discooperit calicem, et in eum discoopertum intuetur...significans quod angelus Domini lapidem ab ostio monumenti revolvit, et linteamen amovit, et in sepulchro diligenter aspexit.—Durand. Rat. Div. Offic. Lib. IV. cap. li. 1. fol. 194.]

[[3] Tertio, quia ut aiunt quidam, hæc purificatio designat ablutionem manuum, quam Pilatus fecit ad perditionem sanguinis justi super Judæos, &c.—Id. Lib. IV. cap. lv. 3. fol. 203.]

[[4] ... osculatur semel altare per quod repræsentat osculum proditoris, &c.—Id. Lib. IV. cap. xliv. 2. fol. 179.]

[[5] Et hæc verba proferendo sacerdos, paululum expressa voce, percusso pectore silentium interrumpit, repræsentans contritionem et confessionem latronis in illo passionis dominicæ articulo increpantis alterum, et dicentis: Nos digna factis recipimus, &c.—Id. Lib. IV. cap. xlvi. 1. fol. 181. 2.]

[[6] Drink, 1560.] [[7] Time, 1560.]

[[8] This, 1560.] [[9] Convenitis, 1560.]

to St James: *Tot in altare holocausta offerantur, quot*[10] *populo sufficere debeant*[11]: "Let there be so many hosts offered upon the altar as may be sufficient for the people to receive."

Dionysius, an ancient writer, and, as some have thought, disciple unto St Paul, (although the contrary may appear plainly by his own words,) in a little book that he hath made of the whole order of the church in his time, setting forth the manner of the Lord's supper, writeth thus: *Tum sacerdos ad sacram communionem et ipse convertitur, et reliquos ut una communicent hortatur;* that is: "The priest both turneth himself to the communion, and also exhorteth the rest to communicate and receive with him." And farther he saith: *Sumpta demum atque omnibus tradita communione divina, gratias referens, finem mysteriis imponit*[12]; that is: "The priest, when he hath received himself, and delivered the holy communion to all the people, giveth God thanks, and maketh an end of the mysteries." Hitherto we find plain tokens of a communion, but not one word of the private mass.

Justinus Martyr, in his Apology, or defence of the christian faith, sheweth in what sort the Lord's supper was used in his time. *Diaconus*, saith he, *hortatur populum, ut illorum, quæ proposita sunt, velint esse participes;* that is: "The deacon exhorteth the people, that they will be partakers of those things that be laid forth before them." Farther he saith: *Diaconi distribuunt ad participandum præsentium unicuique, ex consecrato pane, et vino et aqua: illis vero, qui non adsunt, deferunt domum*[13]; that is: "The deacons deliver of the consecrate bread and wine and water to every one that is there present: and, if there be any away, they carry it home to them." Here also we find a communion, but no private mass.

St Ambrose rebuketh his people that were then grown negligent in receiving the Lord's supper, and used to excuse the matter for that they thought themselves[14] not worthy: *Si non es dignus quotidie, ergo nec semel dignus es in toto anno*[15]: "If thou be not worthy," saith St Ambrose, "every day, then art thou not worthy once in a year."

And again, the same St Ambrose expounding these words of St Paul, *Alius alium exspectate*, writeth thus: *Exspectandum dicit, ut multorum oblatio simul celebretur, et omnibus ministretur*[16]; that is: "He commandeth them to tarry one for another, that the oblation of many may be celebrate or done together, and so be ministered unto them all." These words also savour altogether of a communion, and nothing of a private mass.

St Hierome, St Augustine, and the Ecclesiastical History witnesseth, that until that time commonly every where, but specially in Rome, the people used to communicate every day[17]. Leo, writing unto Dioscorus the bishop of Alexandria, gave him this advice, that, where the church was so little that it was not able to receive all the whole people to communicate all together, then the priest should minister two or three communions in one day, that, as the people came in and had once filled the church, so they should receive the communion, and afterward give place to others[18]."

St Hierome, writing upon the eleventh chapter of the first to the Corinthians,

[10 Quanta, 1560.]

[11 Clement. Papæ I. Epist. ii. ad Jacob. in Epist. Decret. Sum. Pont. Rom. 1591. Tom. I. p. 16; where the expressions are *tanta in altario* and *quanta*. These decretal epistles are not genuine.]

[12 Dionys. Areop. Op. Antv. 1634. De Eccles. Hierarch. cap. iii. 2. Tom. I. p. 284.]

[13 Just. Mart. Op. Par. 1742. Apol. i. p. 83. The words first quoted do not appear.]

[14 Themself, 1560.]

[15 Qui non meretur quotidie accipere, non meretur post annum accipere.—Ambros. Op. Par. 1686-90. De Sacram. Lib. v. cap. iv. 25. Tom. II. col. 378.]

[16 Id. in I Epist. ad Cor. cap. xi. Tom. II. Appendix, col. 150; where *ut* precedes *et*. This is not a genuine work of St Ambrose.]

[17 ... de eucharistia, an accipienda quotidie, quod Romana ecclesia et Hispaniæ observare perhibentur, &c.—Hieron. Op. Par. 1693-1706. Epist. lii. ad Lucin. Tom. IV. Pars II. col. 579.

Alii quotidie communicant corpori et sanguini Domini, alii certis diebus accipiunt.—August. Op. Par. 1679-1700. Ad Inquis. Januar. Lib. I. seu Epist. liv. 2. Tom. II. col. 124. For testimonies of the frequent and in some places daily communion in the first three ages of the church, see Bingham, Orig. Eccles. Book XIV. chap. ix. 2, 3, 4.]

[18 ... cum solennior festivitas conventum populi numerosioris indixerit, et ad eam tanta fidelium multitudo convenerit, quam recipere basilica simul una non possit, sacrificii oblatio indubitanter iteretur.—Leon. Magn. Op. Lut. 1623. Epist. ad Diosc. lxxxi. 2. col. 436.]

hath these words: *Cœna dominica omnibus debet esse communis, quia ille omnibus discipulis suis qui aderant, æqualiter tradidit sacramenta*[1]; that is: "The supper of the Lord must be common to all the people; for Christ gave his sacraments to all his disciples that were present." I leave out other authorities for shortness sake; for it would be too long to say as much herein as might be said. All these holy doctors and godly fathers give us most perfit[2] evidence of a communion, without mention making of any private mass.

Thus the catholic church of Christ used the holy communion at the beginning. And even thus the most part of christian people throughout the whole world, the Indians, the Mauritanians, the Egyptians, the Persians, the Arabians, the Armenians, the Grecians, and as many as bear the name of Christ, have[3] kept and continued the same amongst themselves, from the first time they received the gospel until this day, and never received or used the private mass.

But what better witness may we use in this behalf, than the very mass-book itself, which is the rule and direction of the mass? If the mass-book itself bear witness against the private mass, then I trust our cause shall appear somewhat better than it hath been taken heretofore.

First by the way, before I enter near into the matter, the prayers that be used in the mass be common as well to the people as to the priest. The priest saith, *Oremus*[4], "Let us pray," and so goeth forth in his collect; and at the end thereof the whole people by the mass-book are taught to say, "Amen." The priest saith, "The Lord be with you:" the people by the mass-book is taught to answer, "And with thy spirit." The priest saith, "Lift up your hearts:" the people by the mass-book should answer, "We lift them up to the Lord." The priest turneth him to the people, and saith, *Orate pro me, fratres et sorores:* "Pray for me, brothers and sisters:" and by the very order of the mass-book the people should know what he saith, and at his request should pray for him. Hereby we see, that whatsoever prayers be used about the ministration of the sacrament, ought to be the common requests of all the people. Therefore saith Justinus, an old godly father and a holy martyr: *Ubi gratias egit præpositus, universus populus acclamat, Amen*[5]; that is: "When the priest hath given thanks, the whole people say, Amen." And Chrysostom likewise saith: *Ne mireris si populus in mysteriis nostris cum sacerdote colloquatur*[6]: "Marvel not," saith Chrysostom, "though the people and the priest in our mysteries talk together." For in the common prayers that be used about the ministration the priest and the people both in voice and heart should join together; and, when the priest hath once done the consecration, and the people should at his hand receive the communion, the mass-book itself biddeth him to break the bread in three parts. And thereof have idle heads of late time fancied out many mystical follies; as though one part thereof were offered for them that be in heaven, the other for them that, they say, be in purgatory, the third for them that be alive[7]. These be phantasies and very follies, without any ground either of the holy scriptures, or of the doctors, or of the old catholic church. But, in very deed, the breaking and dividing of the bread is a remainent of the true and the old communion, that was in use in the time of the doctors of the church and of the holy catholic fathers: for to that end the bread is broken, that it may be divided among the people; and therefore the supper of the Lord is called *Fractio Panis,* that is, "The breaking of bread."

Moreover, the priest by the mass-book is taught to say, *Accipite, edite;* "Take ye, eat ye:" and, *Habete vinculum caritatis, ut apti sitis sacrosanctis mysteriis;* that is: "Have ye the band[8] of charity, that ye may be meet for the holy mysteries." And to whom shall we think the priest speaketh these words? It were

---

[[1] Hieron. Op. Par. 1693–1706. Comm. in Epist. I. ad Cor. cap. xi. Tom. V. col. 997; where the first two words are transposed.]

[[2] Perfect, 1560.] [[3] Hath, 1560.]

[[4] Missal. ad Us. ac Consuet. Sar. Par. 1527. fol. 150.]

[[5] Just. Mart. Op. Par. 1742. Apol. i. p. 83.]

[[6] Chrysost. Op. Par. 1718-38. In Epist. II. ad Cor. Hom. xviii. Tom. X. p.568.]

[[7] Circa quod notandum est, quod in duas medietates frangitur, juxta duplicem prædestinatorum statum, scilicet æternæ gloriæ, et temporalis miseriæ: ideoque una medietas subdividitur in duas partes; quarum una est de prædestinatis, qui purgantur in purgatorio, alia pro illis, qui adhuc vivunt in hoc mundo caduco.—Durand. Rat. Div. Offic. Lugd. 1565. Lib. IV. cap. li. 5. fol. 198.]

[[8] Bond, 1560, 1609.]

too vain a thing for him in the open congregation to speak to himself, and specially in the plural number. Yet were it a great deal more vain for him to speak the same words to the bread and wine, and to say unto them, "Take ye, eat ye," or "Have ye the band of charity, that ye may be meet for the holy mysteries." Therefore it is evident that these words should be spoken to the people, and that in such sort as they might well understand them, and prepare themselves[9] to the communion.

And to conclude, the priest by his own mass-book is bidden to say these words immediately after the *Agnus Dei: Hæc sacrosancta commixtio [et consecratio] corporis et sanguinis Domini nostri Jesu Christi fiat mihi et omnibus sumentibus salus mentis et corporis*[10]; that is to say: "This commixtion and consecration of the body and blood of our Lord Jesus Christ be unto me, and to all that receive it, health of body and soul." Thus in the mass-book itself, which (as I said afore) is the very rule and direction of the mass, if it were used accordingly, we find a communion for the whole congregation to receive together, and no private mass.

Perhaps there may be some that will say, we grant these things be spoken of the communion in the old doctors; but there be as many things or more spoken by them of the private mass, and all that you dissemble and pass by.

I know such replies have been made by divers; but, good brethren, I will make it plain unto you, through God's grace, by the most ancient writers that were in and after the apostles' time, and by the order of the first primitive[11] church, that then there could be no private mass, and that whoso would not communicate with the priest was then commanded out of the congregation. In the canons of the apostles there is a decree made against all such as would be present at the communion, and yet not receive the sacrament: the words be these: *Fideles qui in ecclesiam ingrediuntur, et scripturas audiunt, et communionem sanctam non recipiunt, tanquam ecclesiasticæ pacis perturbatores, a communione arceantur*[12]; that is: "Such christian men as come to the church and hear the scriptures, and receive not the holy communion, let them be excommunicated, as men that disquiet the whole church."

Calixtus, a bishop of Rome, not long after the apostles' time, giveth out the like commandment in the same behalf: his words be these: *Peracta consecratione, omnes communicent, qui noluerint carere ecclesiasticis liminibus: sic enim apostoli statuerunt, et sancta Romana tenet ecclesia*[13]; that is: "When the consecration is done, let every man receive the communion, unless he will be put off from the entry of the church; for this thing have the apostles ordained, and the holy church of Rome continueth the same." St Chrysostom, upon the epistle of St Paul to the Ephesians, sharply rebuketh the people for refraining the holy communion. Thus he saith: *Non est*[14] *dignus communione: ergo nec precibus: qua ratione præco dicit, Abite; tu vero impudenter perstas*[15]: "Thou wilt say," saith St Chrysostom, "that thou art not worthy to receive the communion. Then art thou not worthy to be present at the common prayers. The deacon saith unto you that will not communicate, Get you hence; and yet thou, like an impudent man, standest still."

St Gregory in his dialogues shewed[16] the manner of the communion in his time, to the like purpose: *Diaconus clamat, Si quis non communicat, exeat, et locum cedat alteri*[17]: "The deacon," saith St Gregory, "speaketh out aloud, Whoso will not communicate, let him depart away and give place to others." This was the order of the old time: the deacon gave warning to the people, *Exeunto catechumeni: exeunto pœnitentes*[18]: "Let such as be young novices in the faith go forth: let such as are in their penance go forth:" that they that might not communicate with the rest, should depart from the church, and not be present at the commu-

[9 Themself, 1560.]

[10 Missal. ad Us. ac Consuet. Sar. fol. 161, 2; where we find *omnibusque*.]

[11 First and primitive, 1560.]

[12 Canon. Apost. ix. in Concil. Stud. Labb. et Cossart. Lut. Par. 1671-2. Tom. I. col. 28.]

[13 Anacletus Papa in Corp. Jur. Canon. Lugd. 1624. Decret. Gratian. Decr. Tert. Pars, De Consecr. Dist. ii. can. 10. col. 1917; where *ecclesiasticis carere* and *et apostoli* are found. A note is added to this canon: Tribuebatur Calixto. Restitutum est Anacleto ex aliquot vetustis exemplaribus.]

[14 Es, 1560, 1609.]

[15 Chrysost. Op. In Epist. ad Ephes. cap. i. Hom. iii. Tom. XI. p. 23.]

[16 Sheweth, 1560.]

[17 Cum...ex more diaconus clamaret, Si quis non non communicat, det locum; &c.—Gregor. Magni Papæ I. Op. Par. 1705. Dial. Lib. II. cap. xxiii. Tom. II. col. 253.]

[18 This was a customary proclamation in the ancient liturgies.]

nion. And this order continued still until the time of St Gregory, which was six hundred years after Christ. Who was there then that consecrated the bread and wine, and received altogether to himself alone? where then was the private mass? where then was the single communion all this while?

Yet are there some that whisper in corners, that the mass is a blessed and a catholic thing, and that the holy communion, which now God of his great mercy hath restored to us, is wicked and schismatical; and therefore they murmur against it, therefore they refrain it, and will not come to it.

O merciful God, who would think there could be so much wilfulness in the heart of man? O Gregory! O Augustine! O Hierome! O Chrysostom! O Leo! O Dionyse! O Anacletus! O Sixtus! O Paul! O Christ! If we be deceived herein, ye are they that have deceived us. You have taught us these schisms and divisions, ye have taught us these heresies. Thus ye ordered the holy communion in your time: the same we received at your hand, and have faithfully delivered it unto the people.

And that ye may the more marvel at the wilfulness of such men, they stand this day against so many old fathers, so many doctors, so many examples of the primitive church, so manifest and so plain words of the holy scriptures; and yet have they herein not one father, not one doctor, not one allowed example of the primitive church to make for them. And when I say, no[1] one, I speak not this in vehemency of spirit, or heat of talk, but even as before God, by the way of simplicity and truth; lest any of you should happily be deceived, and think there is more weight in the other side, than in conclusion there shall be found. And therefore once again I say: Of all the words of the holy scriptures, of all the examples of the primitive church, of all the old fathers, of all the ancient doctors, in these causes they have not one.

Here the matter itself that I have now in hand putteth me in remembrance of certain things that I uttered unto you to the same purpose at my last being in this place. I remember I laid out then here before you a number of things that are now in controversy, whereunto our adversaries will not yield. And I said, perhaps boldly, as it might then seem to some man; but, as I myself and the learned of our adversaries themselves do well know, sincerely and truly, that none of all them, that this day stand against us, are able, or shall ever be able, to prove against us any one of all those points, either by the scriptures, or by example of the primitive church, or by the old doctors, or by the ancient general councils.

Since that time it hath been reported in places, that I spake then more than I was able to justify and make good. Howbeit, these reports were only made in corners, and therefore ought the less to trouble me. But if my sayings had been so weak, and might so easily have been reproved, I marvel that the parties never yet came to the light, to take the advantage. For my promise was, and that openly here before you all, that, if any man were able to prove the contrary, I would yield and subscribe to him; and he should depart with the victory. Loth I am to trouble you with rehearsal of such things as I have spoken afore; and yet, because the case so requireth, I shall desire you that have already heard me to bear the more with me in this behalf. Better it were to trouble your ears with twice hearing of one thing, than to betray the truth of God. The words that I then spake, as near as I can call them to mind, were these:

If any learned man of all our adversaries, or if all the learned men that be alive, be able to bring any one sufficient sentence out of any old catholic doctor, or father, or out of any old general council, or out of the holy scriptures of God, or any one example of the primitive church, whereby it may be clearly and plainly proved that there was any private mass in the whole world at that time, for the space of six hundred years after Christ; Or that there was then any communion ministered unto the people under one kind; Or that the people had their common prayers then in a strange tongue that they understood not; Or that the bishop of Rome was then called an universal bishop, or the head of the universal church; Or

[1 Not, 1560.]

that the people was then taught to believe that Christ's body is really, substantially, corporally, carnally, or naturally, in the sacrament; Or that his body is, or may be, in a thousand places or more at one time; Or that the priest did then hold up the sacrament over his head; Or that the people did then fall down and worship it with godly honour; Or that the sacrament was then, or now ought to be, hanged up under a canopy; Or that in the sacrament after the words of consecration there remaineth only the accidents and shews, without the substance of bread and wine; Or that the priest then divided the sacrament in three parts, and afterward received himself all alone; Or that whosoever had said the sacrament is a figure, a pledge, a token, or a remembrance of Christ's body, had therefore been judged for an heretic; Or that it was lawful then to have thirty, twenty, fifteen, ten, or five masses said in one church, in one day; Or that images were then set up in the churches, to the intent the people might worship them; Or that the lay people was then forbidden to read the word of God in their own tongue—if any man alive were able to prove any of these articles by any one clear or plain clause or sentence, either of the scriptures, or of the old doctors, or of any old general council, or by any example of the primitive church; I promised then that I would give over and subscribe unto him.

These words are the very like, I remember, I spake here openly before you all. And these be the things that some men say I have spoken and cannot justify. But I for my part will not only not call in any thing that I then said (being well assured of the truth therein), but also will lay more matter to the same; that, if they that seek occasion have any thing to the contrary, they may have the larger scope to reply against me.

Wherefore, besides[2] all that I have said already, I will say further[3], and yet nothing so much as might be said: If any one of all our adversaries be able clearly and plainly to prove, by such authority of the scriptures, the old doctors, and councils, as I said before, that it was then lawful for the priest to pronounce the words of consecration closely and in silence to himself; Or that the priest had then authority to offer up Christ unto his Father; Or to communicate and receive the sacrament for another, as they do; Or to apply the virtue of Christ's death and passion to any man by the mean of the mass; Or that it was then thought a sound doctrine to teach the people, that the mass, *ex opere operato*, that is, even for that it is said and done, is able to remove any part of our sin; Or that then any christian man called the sacrament his Lord and God; Or that the people was then taught to believe, that the body of Christ remaineth in the sacrament as long as the accidents of the bread remain there without corruption; Or that a mouse, or any other worm or beast, may eat the body of Christ (for so some of our adversaries have said and taught); Or that when Christ said, *Hoc est corpus meum*, this word *hoc* pointeth not the bread, but *individuum vagum*, as some of them say; Or that the accidents, or forms, or shews of[4] bread and wine, be the sacraments of Christ's body and blood, and not rather the very bread and wine itself; Or that the sacrament is a sign or token of the body of Christ that lieth hidden underneath it; Or that ignorance is the mother and cause of true devotion and obedience—these be the highest mysteries, and greatest keys of their religion, and without them their doctrine can never be maintained and stand upright—if any one of all our adversaries be able to avouch any one of all these articles, by any such sufficient authority of scriptures, doctors, or councils, as I have required,—as I said before, so say I now again, I am content to yield unto him, and to subscribe. But I

[2 Beside, 1560.] [3 Farther, 1560.] [4 Or, 1609, 1611.]

am well assured that[1] they shall never be able truly to allege one sentence. And because I know it, therefore I speak it, lest ye happily should be deceived.

All this notwithstanding, ye have heard men in times past allege unto you councils, doctors, antiquities, successions, and long continuance of time, to the contrary. And an easy matter it was so to do, specially before them that lack either leisure or judgment to examine their proofs. On a time Mithridates, the king of Pontus, laid siege to Cyzicum, a town joined in friendship to the city of Rome. Which thing the Romans hearing, made out a gentleman of theirs, named Lucullus, to raise the siege. After that Lucullus was within the sight of the town, and shewed himself with his company upon the side of an hill, thence to give courage to the citizens within that were besieged, Mithridates, to cast them into despair, and to cause them the rather to yield to him, made it to be noised, and bare them in hand, that all that new company of soldiers was his, sent for purposely by him against the city. All that notwithstanding, the citizens within kept the walls, and yielded not. Lucullus came on, raised the siege, vanquished Mithridates, and slew his men[2]. Even so, good people, is there now a siege laid to your walls: an army of doctors and councils shew themselves upon an hill: the adversary, that would have you yield, beareth you in hand that they are their soldiers, and stand on their side. But keep your hold: the doctors and old catholic fathers, in the points that I have spoken of, are yours: ye shall see the siege raised, ye shall see your adversaries discomfited and put to flight.

The Pelagians were able to allege St Augustine as for themselves[3]; yet, when the matter came to proof, he was against them. Helvidius was able to allege Tertullian as making for himself; but in trial he was against him. Eutyches alleged Julius Romanus for himself; yet indeed was Julius most against him. The same Eutyches alleged for himself Athanasius and Cyprian; but in conclusion they stood both against him. Nestorius alleged the council of Nice; yet was the same council found against him[4].

Even so they that have advanced[5] themselves of doctors and councils, and continuance of time in any of these points, when they shall be called to trial to shew their proofs, they shall open their hands and find nothing. I speak not this of arrogancy (thou, Lord, knowest it best, that knowest all things); but, forasmuch as it is God's cause and the truth of God, I should do God great injury if I should conceal it. But to return again to our matter. There be some that say that no mass is private, or to be taken as the action of one private man. For they say, the priest that saith mass here doth communicate with another priest that saith mass some other where, wheresoever it be, the distance being never so great. This commission seemeth very large. For so may the priest that saith mass in England or Scotland communicate with the priest that is in Calicute, or in the farthermost part of India. And by this means should there be no excommunication at all; for the party excommunicate might say, he would communicate with the priest whether he would or no. But [1 Cor. xi.] St Paul glosseth not the matter on this sort, but saith: *Alter alterum exspectate*[6]; that is, "Tarry ye one for another." And again he saith: "When ye come together, ye cannot eat the Lord's supper; for every one of you taketh his own supper aforehand."

Some others say, the priest may communicate for the people, and that is as meritorious unto them as if they had communicated themselves[7]. But what commission hath the priest so to do? or from whom? or what certain knowledge hath he that his receiving of the communion shall be available for the people? For, if it be so, what needed it then Christ to say, *Accipite, bibite ex hoc omnes?* Or, if we may receive the sacrament of Christ's body one for another, why may not we as well be baptized one for another? Why may we not as well confess our faults before the congregation, and receive absolution one for another? Why may we not hear the gospel, and believe one for another? O that these follies,

[1 *That* is omitted, 1560.]
[2 Plutarch. in Lucull.]
[3 Themself, 1560.]
[4 For an account of these heretics see Mosheim; also Hieron. Op. Par. 1693–1706. Adv. Helvid. Tom. IV. Pars II. col. 141.]
[5 Avaunted, 1560, 1609.]
[6 Exspectare, 1560.]
[7 Communicate themself, 1560.]

so weak and so vain, without shew or shadow of any truth, should ever sink into a christian heart, or take place in God's religion! St Paul saith: *Qui manducat et bibit indigne, judicium sibi manducat et bibit:* "Whoso eateth or drinketh unworthily, eateth and drinketh judgment," not unto others, saith St Paul, "but to himself." Again, St Paul saith: "Whoso believeth in him that [Rom. iv.] justifieth the wicked;" not the faith of any other man, but "his own faith is reckoned to him unto justice." St Chrysostom saith, it is the heresy of the Marcionites to think that any one man may receive the sacrament for another; and therefore he maketh light of such disorder of the sacraments, and calleth them *Sacramenta*[8] *vicaria*[9]. Origen saith: *Ille est sacerdos et propitiatio et hostia*[10]. *Est enim Agnus Dei qui tollit peccata mundi: quæ propitiatio ad unumquemque venit per viam fidei*[11]: "He is our priest," saith Origen, "he is our atonement, he is our sacrifice. For he is the Lamb of God that taketh away the sins of the world. Which atonement," saith he, "cometh unto us (not by the application of the mass, but) by the way of faith."

St Augustine likewise saith: *Si non obliviscimur mundi Salvatoris, quotidie nobis Christus immolatur. Ex ipsis reliquis*[12] *cogitationis, id est, ex memoria, Christus nobis quotidie immolatur*[13]: "If we forget not the Saviour of the world, Christ is every day sacrificed unto us. Even by the remainents of our cogitations, that is, by our remembrance of his death, Christ is made a sacrifice unto us every day." It is not therefore neither the faith, neither the doing of the priest, but our own doing, and our own faith, that applieth unto us the virtue and merits of Christ's death.

Some other say that St Peter said mass at Rome, and St James at Hierusalem. And why say they not rather that Christ himself said mass? for that were the near way to bring the mass into credit. Or why say they not sooner that Aaron and his chaplains said mass? For indeed, as it hath been used, the church hath had much more of the robes, of the ceremonies, and of the sacrifices of Aaron, than of the institution or ordinance of Christ. But this have men told you, and with such things as they have found out themselves[14] they have infeoffed and fathered the apostles of Christ. So commonly conjurers and sorcerers make their vaunts, that they have all their books and their cunning from Athanasius, from Moses, from Abel, from Adam, from Raphael the archangel.

Thus the people of God is deceived and mocked, and instead of precious stones driven to take counterfeits. For I assure you, brethren, in the time of Peter and James neither was there any man that ever heard the name of mass (for *missa* was never named until four hundred years after Christ; and yet then was it no private mass neither, but a communion), nor yet were the pieces and parts of the mass, as we in our time have seen them, set together. And what mass could that be, that as yet had neither her own name nor her parts? But forasmuch as they affirm so constantly that St James said mass at Hierusalem, and, whatsoever it were that he said, will needs have it called by the name of a mass, let us compare their mass and St James' mass both together. St James said his mass in the common tongue, as the people might understand him: they say their mass in a strange Latin tongue, that the people should not know what they mean. St James spake out the words of consecration distinctly and plainly: they in their mass suppress the same words and keep them close. St James in his mass ministered the communion unto the people: they in their mass receive themselves[14] all alone. St James in his mass ministered the sacrament unto the people under both kinds: they in their mass

[8 *Vicaria* is omitted, 1560.]

[9 The reference is probably to a passage where Chrysostom, commenting on 1 Cor. xv. 29. condemns the practice of the Marcionites who baptized the dead, living persons being substituted to make answer for them.—Chrysost. Op. Par. 1718-38. In Epist. I. ad Cor. Hom. xl. Tom. X. p. 378.]

[10 Hostilia, 1560.]

[11 ... esse ipsum et propitiatorium, et pontificem, et hostiam quæ offertur pro populo ... Hic est agnus &c. ... quæ tamen propitiatio ad unumquemque credentium per viam fidei venit.—Orig. Op. Par. 1733-59. In Epist. ad Rom. Lib. III. Tom. IV. p. 515.]

[12 Impiis reliquiis, 1560.]

[13 ... cum autem non obliviscimur munus Salvatoris, nonne quotidie nobis Christus immolatur? ... ex ipsis reliquiis cogitationis, id est, ex ipsa memoria, quotidie nobis sic immolatur, quasi, &c.—August. Op. Par. 1679-1700. In Psalm. lxxv. Enarr. 15. Tom. IV col. 801.]

[14 Themself, 1560.]

minister the sacrament unto the people in one kind only. St James in his mass preached and set forth the death of Christ: they in their mass have only a number of dumb gestures and ceremonies which they themselves[1] understand not, and make no manner mention of Christ's death. St James' mass was full of knowledge: their mass is full of ignorance. St James' mass was full of consolation: their mass is full of superstition. When St James said mass, the people resorted to receive the sacrament: when they say mass, the people resorteth to look upon only and to behold the sacrament. And, to conclude, St James in his mass had Christ's institution: they in their mass have well near nothing else but man's invention.

Such difference ye may see between St James' mass and theirs. O that St Paul were now alive, and saw the behaviour and order of the priest[2] at their mass! Think ye that he would take it and account it for the Lord's supper? When he had espied but one fault in the holy communion amongst the Corinthians, straightway he rebuked them, and called them back to Christ's institution. "This," saith he, "I received of the Lord, and the same I gave over unto you."

But if he saw the disorder that we have seen, would he not be moved as much against us now, as he was sometime against the Corinthians? Would he not pull us back to the institution of Christ, as he did them[3]? Would he not say unto us, Did I ever teach you to minister the holy communion in a strange language? Did I ever teach you to receive the communion privately to yourselves[4] alone, and so to disdain and to despise your brethren? Did I ever teach you to minister the communion to the people in one kind? Did I ever teach you to say mass, or to receive the sacrament for the people? Did I ever teach you the idle follies of your canon? Did I ever teach you to offer up the Son of God unto his Father? Did I ever teach you any other propitiatory sacrifice for sin than that Christ once offered upon the cross? Did I ever teach you to minister the Lord's supper, wherein the people should nothing else but look upon and behold your doings, without any kind of knowledge or comfort? Did I ever teach you to lift the sacrament over your head? Did I ever teach the people to fall down thereunto, and to worship they know not what? Be these the things that I delivered you? Be these the things that I received of the Lord? This would St Paul say unto us if he were now alive. Thus would he reprove us, and call us to the standard and original of the first appointing of the holy sacrament.

Our own inventions and phantasies, wherewith we had filled the mass, were so many and so gross, that they quite covered and shadowed the death of Christ, and the holy mysteries of our salvation. Therefore we could not truly say, These things Paul delivered unto us, or these things Paul received of the Lord.

Wherefore, good people and dearly-beloved brethren, forasmuch as we see there have been great and evident abuses and errors in the mass, so plain and so manifest, that no man that hath reason, and will consider them[5], can deny it; let us follow the counsel of St Paul, let us return to the ordinance of Christ, unto the true standard that cannot fail us.

As it is not in the power of man to appoint sacraments, so is it not in the power of man to alter or change sacraments. God will not be worshipped after our phantasies, and therefore so oftentimes he chargeth us in the scriptures: *Non facietis quod bonum videtur in oculis vestris:* "Ye shall not do that thing that seemeth good to you in your own sight:" "Ye shall not turn, neither to the left hand, nor to the right;" but "what thing soever I bid you do, that only shall ye do." "Your thoughts be not my thoughts, neither be your ways my ways. For as far as heaven is from the earth, or the east from the west, so far off be your thoughts from my thoughts, and your ways from my ways, saith the Lord." It is a dangerous thing for a mortal man to control or find fault with the wisdom of the immortal God.

Tertullian, an old father of the church, sheweth us the wilfulness of man's heart after it hath once enterprised to presume a little against God's truth and ordinance: *Præter scripturas faciunt, ut post audacius contra scripturas faciant*[6]

[1 Themself, 1560.]
[2 Priests, 1560.]
[3 Then, 1560.]
[4 Yourself, 1560.]
[5 Therein, 1560.]
[6 Is the following the passage intended? Se

"First," saith he, "they attempt somewhat beside the scriptures, to the intent that afterward they may gather courage and boldness to do contrary to the scriptures." At the end they proceed as far as the scribes and Pharisees, that, for maintenance of their own traditions, despised and brake the commandments of God. For redress therein, there is no better way than to follow St Paul's counsel here, and to have recourse to God's holy word.

St Ambrose saith: *Interrogemus Petrum, interrogemus Paulum, si verum volumus invenire*[7]: "If we will find out the truth, and be put out of doubt," saith St Ambrose, "let us hearken what Peter and Paul will say unto us."

St Cyprian saith: *Hinc schismata oriuntur, quia caput non quæritur, et ad fontem non reditur, et cœlestis Magistri præcepta non servantur*[8]: "Hereof," saith St Cyprian, "arise schisms and divisions, for that we seek not to the head, nor have recourse to the spring, nor keep the commandments of the heavenly Master."

Tertullian saith: *Hæc ratio contra omnem hæresim valet, hoc verum est quod primum fuit*[9]: "This reason," saith he, "is able to confound all manner heresies: that thing is true that was first appointed."

O that our adversaries, and all they[10] that stand in defence[11] of the mass this day, would content themselves[12] to be judged by this rule! O that in all the controversies that lie between us and them they would remit the judgment unto God's word! So should we soon agree and join together: so should we deliver nothing unto the people but that we have received at God's hand.

And if there be any here that have had, or yet have[13] any good opinion of the mass, I beseech you for God's sake, even as ye tender your own salvation, suffer not yourselves[14] wilfully to be led away, run not blindly to your own confusion. Think with yourselves[14], it was not for nought that so many of your brethren rather suffered themselves to die, and to abide all manner extremity and cruelty, than they would be partakers of that thing that you reckon to be so holy. Let their death, let their ashes, let their blood, that was so abundantly shed before your eyes, somewhat prevail with you and move you. Be not ruled by your wilful affections. Ye have a good zeal and mind towards God: have it according unto the knowledge of God. The Jews had a zeal of God, and yet they crucified the Son of God. Search the scriptures: there shall ye find everlasting life. There shall ye learn to judge yourselves[14] and your own doings, that ye be not judged of the Lord. If ever it happen you to be present again at the mass, think but thus with yourselves[14]: What make I here? what profit have I of my doings? I hear nothing; I understand nothing; I am taught nothing; I receive nothing: Christ bade me take; I take nothing: Christ bade me eat; I eat nothing: Christ bade me drink; I drink nothing. Is this the institution of Christ? Is this the Lord's supper? Is this the right use of the holy mysteries? Is this it that Paul delivered unto me? Is this it that Paul received of the Lord? Let us say but thus unto ourselves[15]; and no doubt God of his mercy will open our hearts: we shall see our errors, and content ourselves[15] to be ordered by the wisdom of God, to do that God will have us to[16] do, to believe that God will have us to[16] believe, to worship that God will have us worship. So shall we have comfort of the holy mysteries; so shall we receive the fruits of Christ's death; so shall we be partakers of Christ's body and blood; so shall Christ truly dwell in us, and we in him; so shall all error be taken from us; so shall we join all together in God's truth; so shall we all be able, with one heart and one spirit, to know and to glorify the only, the true, and the living God, and his only-begotten Son Jesus Christ; to whom both with the Holy Ghost be all honour and glory for ever and ever. Amen.

---

credent sine scripturis, ut credant adversus scripturas.—Tertull. Op. Lut. 1641. De Præscript. Hæret. 23. p. 239.]

[7 The editor has not been able to discover the passage referred to.]

[8 Jewel appears in these words to have condensed what Cyprian asserts at considerable length. See Cypr. Op. Oxon. 1682. Ad Pomp. Epist. lxxiv. pp. 214, 5.]

[9 Quo peræque adversus universas hæreses jam hinc præjudicatum sit, id esse verum quodcunque primum; id esse adulterum, quodcunque posterius. Tertull. Op. Adv. Prax. 2. p. 635.]

[10 Them, 1560.] [11 In the defence, 1560.]

[12 Themself, 1560.] [13 Hath, 1560.]

[14 Yourself, 1560.] [15 Ourself, 1560.]

[16 *To* is omitted, 1560.]

THE TRUE COPIES

OF

THE LETTERS

BETWEEN THE

REVEREND FATHER IN GOD

JOHN BISHOP OF SARUM AND D. COLE,

UPON OCCASION OF A SERMON THAT THE SAID BISHOP PREACHED BEFORE THE QUEEN'S MAJESTY, AND HER MOST HONOURABLE COUNCIL. 1560[1].

I TRUST *I shall not need many words to make my entry with you. You have made so large and gentle an offer, that my request, being employed within the compass of the same, shall have an answer (I hope) to my comfort.*

Where in these articles you seem very resolute, and as it is thought so well armed, that you have wherewith to persuade any reasonable man to be in them of your opinion, may it therefore like you to send me the chief places in these matters, not written (for that were too much pains for you), but noted, or, as they term it, quoted, which and where they be; and I promise you, by the faith I bear to God, I shall yield so far as you shall give me cause.

I would wish it might please you to write herein again; for talk will not so well further that you should herein intend. If happily it shall like you to write any more than the places, which ye account will thoroughly prove your opinion, I pray you do it rather dialectice *than otherwise. For the weight of these matters more requireth learning than words.*

If the places that you have in these articles be but such as are already answered by learned men on our side, or but such as Calvin, Bucer, or other of the protestants have laid for themselves[2], then I trust you will lay more weight or reason to them. For such as they be, in them I have already seen. I repute them percase somewhat able to do with young folk, or the simple and unlearned people: other, I ween, weigh them no better than they be worthy.

Yet one thing more I long much to be answered in, why ye rather offer both in your sermon yesterday in the court, and at all other times at Paul's Cross, to dispute in these four points, than in the chief matters that lie in question betwixt the church of Rome and the protestants. It seemeth to me far the nearer way to compass that you would so fain win, if ye began not with such matters, which we deny not but a general council might take order that they should be practised as ye would have it. Marry, the article of the presence of Christ's body and blood in the sacrament; the article of our justification; the value of a christian man's good works; whether the mass used in the church of Rome be tolerable, yea, or no; yea, whether that the mass be not a very sacrifice acceptable to God indeed, and good both for the quick and the dead; whether any scripture forbiddeth a man to desire the blessed apostles and martyrs in heaven to pray for us; whether it be lawful[3] to honour them; and whether it be lawful[3] for us, and good for them, to pray for all christian souls; I ween, if ye had the upper hand but in one of these questions, the world might well think we were

---

[[1] This is the title-page of the edition of 1560: the following heading is in that edition prefixed to the present letter: "The copy of a letter sent from D. Cole to the bishop of Sarum, upon occasion of a sermon that the said bishop had preached in the court before the queen's majesty."]

[[2] Themself, 1560.]

[[3] Lefull, 1560.]

smally to be trusted in all the rest. For we make a plat and plain answer to them, without "if," or "and." So do we not, whether the service ought to be in English or not: Or, whether the people ought to receive in both kinds or no: Or, whether any private mass ought to be said in the church or no.

I have jeoparded to wade thus[4] far with you, for no worse purpose than I have uttered at the beginning. For, of truth, if you shew me good cause why, I shall yield, as I have promised.

Mine adventure in this case shall be so taken, I trust, as no advantage be sought against me, as for breach of any part of my duty one way or other. Wherefore, I pray you, construe my doings by the meaning I had in them.

I have here set in writing the questions that you have so gently offered to be reasonable[5], in such sort in effect as they were reported from your mouth to me.

1. *Whether there remain any substance of bread and wine after the consecration done as the church appointeth?*
2. *Whether it be tolerable that the people should receive under one kind or no?*
3. *Whether it be any offence before God that the common service should be said in a tongue that the people understandeth not?*
4. *Whether it be any offence before God, a priest to say mass, unless one or other receive with him?*

HENRICUS COLE.

18 *Martii.*

THE BISHOP OF SARISBURIE'S[6] ANSWER UNTO THE LETTER AFORE WRITTEN.

I PERCEIVE by your letters that ye were not present yourself at my sermon in the court, but only heard of it by the report of others. And where you desire to be answered in certain points touching the same, considering both my calling, and also the place where I spake, I stand in doubt whether I may safely, without further licence, give a reckoning of my doctrine, being uttered before the prince, the council, and the whole state of the realm, specially to a subject, and such a subject, as misliketh all sermons, and yet will not vouchsafe to hear one. Notwithstanding, forasmuch as I am persuaded that you charitably desire to be resolved, I can also charitably be contented, as a friend with a friend, or a scholar with a scholar, to confer with you herein, reserving alway my former protestation.

Touching the quotations of the special points and grounds that I stand upon, if you had heard the manner of my doctrine yourself, I believe you would not have required them. For your reporter hath altered the whole form of my speaking.

For I stood only upon the negative, which, as you said, when time was, in the disputation that should have been at Westminster, is not possible to be proved.

My offer was this, That if any one, of all those things that I then rehearsed, could be proved of your side by any sufficient authority, either[7] of the scriptures, or of the old doctors, or of the ancient councils, or by any one allowed example of the primitive church, that then I would be content to yield unto you.

I say you have none of all those helps, nor scriptures, nor councils, nor doctors, nor any other antiquity; and this is the negative. Now it standeth you upon to prove but one affirmative to the contrary, and so to require my promise.

The articles that I said could not be proved of your part were these:

That it cannot appear by any authority, either[7] of the old doctors, or of the ancient councils, that there was any private mass in the whole church of Christ at that time.

Or, that there was then any communion ministered in the church to the people under one kind only.

Or, that the common prayers were then pronounced in a strange tongue, that the people understood not.

[[4] This, 1560.] [[5] i. e. to be reasoned upon.] [[6] Salisburies, 1560.] [[7] Other, 1560.]

Or, that the bishop of Rome was then called *Universalis episcopus*, or *caput universalis ecclesiæ*, an universal bishop of the whole world, or else the head of the universal church.

Or, that the people was then taught to believe, that in the sacrament after the consecration the substance of bread and wine departeth away, and that there remaineth nothing else but only the accidents of bread and wine.

Or, that then it was thought lawful to say ten, twenty, or thirty masses in one church in one day.

Or, that the people was then forbidden to pray, or to read the scriptures, in their mother-tongue.

And other more articles a great number I reckoned up then at Paul's Cross, which it were long now to rehearse.

And if any one of all these articles can be sufficiently proved by such authority as I have said, and as ye have borne the people in hand ye can prove them by, I am well content to stand to my promise.

If you say these are but small matters in comparison of others; yet, as small as ye would have them seem now, some men have felt no small smart for them.

And where you marvel why I began not rather with the real presence, with justification, with the value of good works, with the sacrifice of the mass, with praying unto saints, with praying for the dead; although indeed it may seem very much for me to be appointed by others what order I should take in my preaching; yet, to answer the truth, why I passed by these matters at the first, and rather began with other, the cause was, not for that I doubted in any of the premises, but only for that I knew the matters, that you move question of, might at least have some colour or shadow of the doctors. But I thought it best to make my entry with such things, as wherein I was well assured ye should be able to find not so much as any colour at all. And if ye will first grant this to be true, as I believe you will, notwithstanding the people have been long told the contrary, afterward I am well content to travail with you farther in the rest.

Further, I marvel much ye write, that touching a private mass, or the receiving under one kind, or the common prayers to be had in an unknown tongue, or otherwise, ye are not resolved to answer precisely without "if" or "and." For where ye say ye are content to be ordered herein by a general council, first, I would know what general council of any antiquity ever decreed any of those matters against us: unless perhaps ye will say the council of Constance, that of late years pronounced openly, against Christ himself and all the primitive church, that it should be a schismatical disorder if the people should communicate under both kinds. And having no ancient council that ever was to allege in these matters, I marvel how ye can justly say, ye are altogether ordered by councils. And yet farther would I learn, what warrant any general council can have to decree any thing contrary to God's word.

Where ye say, ye have seen master Calvin's and master Bucer's reasons, and have found them very weak, and not able to move any other[1] than young folk and unlearned people; methinketh that answer is so common and so general, that it may serve our turn as well as yours. For we have read Coclæus, Eckius, Pighius, Bunderius, and such others, and have found such reasons and answers in them, as I believe you yourself are not much moved withal.

Where you say, that master Calvin's and master Bucer's reasons have been answered; I grant indeed they have been answered, but not so much by learning, as by other means, as you know. But your reasons have been answered by reason sufficiently; as now, God be thanked, the whole world knoweth.

But, to conclude as I began, I answer that in these articles I hold only the negative, and therefore I look how you will be able to affirm the contrary, and that, as I said afore, by sufficient authority. Which if ye do not, you shall cause me the more to be resolved, and others to stand the more in doubt of the rest of your learning.

20 *Martii.* JOH. SARUM.

[[1] Others, 1560.]

DOCTOR COLE'S SECOND LETTER TO THE BISHOP OF SARUM.

I shall for this time pass over all other parts of your answer, and renew my former suit unto you, in most hearty and humble wise, desiring you to give ear unto me in the same.

Remember, for God's sake, how I began with you, not for other intent than to be instructed why I should be accounted obstinate for standing in contrary opinion with you. Now, when I weigh your answer sent me lately in writing, I think you do mistake my doing, supposing that the same cometh not of such ground as it doth. My letter sent to you declareth in my first entry with you what my meaning was, and whereof it proceeded. I heard by report of many that, both at Paul's and other where, ye openly wished that one man thinking otherwise than you do would charitably talk with you, whom you would with like charity answer, and endeavour to satisfy. And although you had not so protested, yet is it the part of a common and public preacher to perform no less when occasion is given. With which cause I was moved to write as I did, intending, if I might, to learn of you that I knew not, and that could by learning persuade a man not wholly unlearned to yield thereunto, according to the words of my writing and protestation.

But I find not this meaning in your writing sent unto me, wherein you shew yourself disposed only to defend your teaching, as confessed and taken for true, and not to give any account thereof, or to satisfy any that doubteth. And there you bid me allege to the contrary and disprove your saying; which neither reason nor law can drive me to. Reason, because, the doctrine being yet doubtful, and standing upon proof, the teacher should first approve it unto such as doubt. Which the custom of learning in all universities proveth true; where the opponent, when the[2] matter is denied, as your doctrine is by us, allegeth for that part which he would have seem true. And you take on you to disprove that doctrine, which long time hath been received. Evermore, when any man professed a reformation of doctrine, as you do, the reformer hath ever alleged causes why they so did, and so take in hand to prove that they taught, against such as did and would think otherwise.

But because you are a bishop, and spake in such an audience, ye doubt whether you ought to shew cause of that you teach or no, and therefore ye spake by protestation. Whereat I do much marvel; for the person or the place maketh no difference who should prove or disprove. The greater personage you bear, the less cause have ye to be put to answer. You have not yet, I ween, all forgot the trade in Oxford, which you and I were brought up in. In schools of philosophy a master of art is the highest degree; where the master is rather put to oppose than to answer. And likewise in divinity, in ordinary disputation, the doctor opposeth, the meaner man answereth. And what reason should lead you to think that a bishop should not rather shew cause of that he teacheth, than any other? St Paul requireth in a bishop that he be διδακτικὸς, a man before all other meet and able to teach. And it is a rule [1 Tim. iii.] *in bishops, that they be ready to give an account of their belief. And many reasons are there why it should be so.*

You cannot say I am an heretic, or obstinate, and thereby put me off. For I offer to yield in all that ye prove to me. I stand in place and case to learn, and you a man appointed to teach. I come for no other purpose but to learn more than I know. I come to you for counsel in those points ye seem very resolute in: I mean you no harm nor guile. Cast me not off, for God's love, as men do beggars, when they mind to do them no good.

If ye have scriptures, councils, &c. with you, I desire to know them. If ye have none, let me and my fellows alone in your sermons. We trouble you not, nor give you cause to deal so unmerciful with us, as some of your side do[3], as though we were the most unreasonable men in the world.

By law, upon good grounds, no man should be put to reason where matters are

[2 *The* is omitted, 1560.]

[3 Doth, 1560.]

once agreed on. I and my fellows are in bands to avoid such kind of reasoning as ye would put me to. Wherein wise men see, when ye openly provoke us to disprove that ye teach, ye fare as if you should say to one that is bound hand and foot, Come strike me, and thou darest. We are, as I said, in place of learners, and ye in place to teach. We are defendants, and ye the plaintiffs. We continue in the faith we professed sith our baptism, ye pretend a change in the same. We have with us an apostolical church, ye have none yet approved. We make no innovation; for, in rebus novis constituendis, *saith the law,* evidens debet esse utilitas; *and all new attempts are to be suspected.*

Ye seem to mislike in manner all that hitherto hath been received. But ye say, ye bring us again to the primitive church. It is a foul fall in reasoning, to bring that for proof which lieth yet in question, or plainly denied. We are in possession: ye come to put us from it. Ye mean to draw us to you: we desire to know cause why. What reason leadeth you to put a negative in question thereby to grieve your adversary (yet have you none of me, for I seek on you to be taught)? where in law a person assaulted can be put to no more but to defend. Where a negative implieth in it a[1] yea, or affirmation, there the plaintiff is put to his proof. But I protest once again, I come not to dispute, but to learn.

You will happily say, that both our side and yours hath already said even so much in the matters that be in question betwixt us, that, as ye can say no more for your part than hath been said already, no more can we neither, and therefore as good never a whit as never the better. If the reasons, that Calvin, Bucer, and other protestants do[2] make, cannot move you, what availeth any more talk? If the case be such indeed, that neither part can go further, but all is said that maketh for either part; then either let both parts let other alone, until such a general council be assembled as ye will agree to stand by; which will not be, I trow, whiles I live, nor seven years after, for ought I see yet. And yet I see other folk think that not reasonable, because the chiefest points we strive on are already determined.

And here it booteth not to say as ye do of the council of Constance slanderously, till ye had proved that ye say. I am somewhat bold with you in this term—but pardon me, I pray you, this case requireth the same—it booteth not, I say, to say the church hath walked in blindness, so as ye make none account of such determination. Remember, ye have not yet proved the error of one general council.

If it be as you say, all is said that can be; then you and I now should do well to weigh the reasons of both sides. Here if ye say, What weights or balance will ye weigh them by? let us hardly do herein as men do, when the question is, which of two pieces of gold or two pieces of cloth is best; then they take a fine piece of gold or cloth, and that that goeth nearest the best, that ought to be so taken for best. Let you and me weigh your men's reasons and ours by the fathers' weights and balance, and see who reasoneth most like St Augustine, St Basil, St Cyprian, Tertullian, Irenæus, and Dionysius, the councils, and such other weights fit for that purpose.

Thus we see there is yet good cause enough, why men may soberly learn one of another. And if it misfortune that for lack of insight we cannot agree which balance weigheth heaviest, let us borrow eyes of our neighbours. And if ye begin handsomely with me, I mistrust not but men shall at length get more liberty for so good a purpose, when good meaning is well known.

By this ye see I mean no guile, nor attempt no new practice. If ye refuse me at this request, foresee what may be thought. You are not all without enemies, pardy. Some will percase construe ye refuse conscientia imbecillitatis, &c.

Well, if ye send word ye are at a point, and will go no further, then I pray you that of all this encounter there grow no farther breach of amity, or harm other ways. I mean and deal plainly, and trust upon your open promise to go harmless again from you, as I began. Here repeating again my former protestation, that I am not nor will be against any article that learning or reason can shew I ought to believe, being ready without malice to hear and take what may be alleged to drive me to that ye teach; and desiring you herewithal to construe my sayings by the intent I

[1 An, 1560.] [2 Doth, 1560.]

had in them, and also to tender my suit, I shall here make an end, and trouble you no further, unless I see more comfort at your hand.

I had once made ready to be sent you another answer, which upon better advice I thought good to stay. I meant in both one thing; but my first was some deal sour, and would have been as bitter as a medicine, or in time of Lent penance. I strive with nature, the less to offend you; and so I trust you see cause to forgive me, if in any part of my writing I seem over eager.

HENRICUS COLE.

24 *Martii.*

THE ANSWER OF JOHN BISHOP OF SARUM UNTO DOCTOR COLE'S SECOND LETTER.

A In your second letters I find many words to little purpose. It had been
B better for you to have alleged one sufficient authority, whereby I might have learned that I looked for.

C For in my sermon at Paul's, and elsewhere, I required you to bring forth on your part either some scripture, or some old doctor, or some ancient council, or else some allowed example of the primitive church. For these are good grounds to build upon; and I would have marvelled that you brought nothing all this while, saving that I knew ye had nothing to bring.

D But now forasmuch as you seek shifts, and will not[3] come to answer, I count him unwise that knoweth not your meaning.

E Ye ask why ye should be called obstinate. Doubtless I have a better opinion of you, and trust ye be not so. But if a man withstand an open truth, having nothing wherewith to defend himself, I remit him to your own judgment, whether he may be called obstinate or no.

F You put me in remembrance of mine office, that, forasmuch as I am a bishop, I should be διδακτικὸς, that is, ready to yield account of such things as I teach: I thank God, so I do, and have done hitherto to my power, both privately and openly.

G But if this be my duty, and required at my hands, what privilege have you, that you only may not allow one poor sentence to the confirmation of your learning?

H You would have men think I fly answering because I am a bishop. This in logic is called *Paralogismus, a non causa ut causa.*

I I alleged the place and audience where I spake, and not only mine office, for that I thought it might appear some want of discretion to call that doctrine into question which I knew was grounded upon God's word, and authorised and set forth by the queen's majesty, and by the assent of the whole realm.

K But as touching my calling, I am not only ready to answer any man in any thing that I profess, but also upon sufficient allegation, as I have promised, very well content to yield unto you.

L But I beseech you, what reason of your faith in these matters gave you sometime when ye were in place? Scriptures, doctors, councils ye had none, as it now appeareth by your silence.

M Therefore the ground of your persuasion must then needs be, *Nos habemus legem, et*[4] *secundum legem*, &c.

N You know what followeth; for, as truly as God is God, if ye would have vouchsafed to follow either the scriptures, or the ancient doctors and councils, ye would never have restored again the supremacy of Rome after it was once abolished, or the private mass, or the communion under one kind, &c.

O It grieveth you that I should rest upon the negative, and so put you to your proofs. Wherein notwithstanding ye allege against me the custom of the schools, yet ye know, Christ used the same kind of reasoning in his school. As when he said to the Pharisees: *Hoc Abraham non fecit:* "This thing Abraham never

---

[3 *not*, omitted, 1611.] [4 1560 omits *et*.]

did." And again, when he answered them in the case of matrimony, *A principio non fuit sic;* "It was not so from the beginning;" he stood only upon the negative. Wherein if the Pharisees had been able to prove but one affirmative, either that Abraham had done so, or that the law of divorce had been so from the beginning, Christ with his negative might soon have been confounded.

P Even so, when the bishop of Constantinople had taken upon him to be called the universal bishop of the whole church, (which title afterward the bishop of Rome began to usurp to himself, and for the maintenance of the same had[1] oftentimes disquieted and shaken the whole world; but, when the bishop of Constantinople first began to use this style,) Gregory, being then the bishop of Rome, confounded him only with the negative: *Nemo,* said he, *decessorum meorum hoc profano vocabulo uti voluit*[2]*:* "None of my predecessors would ever use this unchristian-like and lewd name." Lib. iv. Epist. 80. And again, Epist. 92: *Sancti ante legem, sancti in lege, sancti sub gratia, omnes perficientes corpus Domini in membris sunt constituti; at nemo se universalem dici voluit*[3]*:* "The holy men before the law, the holy men under the law, the holy men under the grace of the gospel, all together making up one body of the Lord, are placed amongst his members; but none of them would ever suffer himself to be called universal."

I have chosen especially these examples, because they seem to serve me to double purpose. Thus Gregory reasoned then as we do now, only upon negative[4]; and if then the bishop of Constantinople had been able to prove but one affirmative, that any bishop of Rome aforetime had used that style, or that ever any man, either[5] before the law, or under the law, or under the gospel, had suffered himself to be called universal bishop, then had Gregory been confounded.

Q But as touching the custom of the schools, I trust ye have not yet forgotten, that Aristotle giveth order to the opponent in many cases to require an instant; as I do now at your hand. And what is that else, but in the denial to defend the negative, and to drive the adversary to avouch the affirmative? But that will ye not do; and ye know why, although ye dissemble it. But sooner ye require to see our grounds.

R And what better ground can we have on our side, than that doctor Cole, the chiefest man on the other side, can find no ground to stand against us?

S He that will make any innovation, say you, must give a reason of his doings. O master doctor, this reason fighteth most against yourself; for you have misliked and put away the most part of the order of the primitive church, and yet ye never gave any good reason of your doings.

T You say you are in possession. No; ye were sometimes, you are not now. And when you were, ye had no right title nor good evidence, no more than they that sometimes[6] sat in Moses' chair, or they that said, *Nos sumus filii Abraham;* "We are the children of Abraham," and thereby claimed their possession. Therefore ye were *possessores malæ fidei,* and for that cause ye are now justly removed.

V Now, if ye think ye have wrong, shew your evidence out of the doctors, the councils, or scriptures, that ye may have your right and re-entry. I require you to no great pain: one good sentence shall be sufficient.

Aa You would have your private mass, the bishop of Rome's supremacy, the common prayer in an unknown tongue; and for the defence of the same ye have made no small ado. Methinketh it reasonable ye bring some one authority beside your own, to avouch the same withal. Ye have made the unlearned people believe ye had all the doctors, all the councils, and fifteen hundred years on your side. For your credit's sake let not all these great vaunts come to nought.

Bb Where ye say ye are in place of a learner, and gladly come to be taught, you must pardon me, it seemeth very hard to believe. For if you were desirous

---

[[1] Hath, 1560.]

[[2] Gregor. Magni Papæ I. Op. Par. 1705. Epist. Lib. v. Indict. XIII. Ad Eulog. et Anastas. Epist. xliii. Tom. II. col. 771; where we find *nullus umquam, tam profano,* and *consensit.*]

[[3] Id. ibid. Ad Johan. Episc. Constant. Epist. xviii. col. 743; where *sub lege, omnes hi, sunt ecclesiæ, et nemo se umquam,* and *vocari* are read.]

[[4] Upon the negative, 1560, 1609.]

[[5] Other, 1560.]

[[6] Sometime, 1560, 1609.]

to learn, as you would seem, ye would come to the church, ye would resort to the lessons, ye would abide to hear a sermon; for these are the schools, if a man list to learn: it is a token the scholar passeth little for his book, that will never be brought to school.

Cc Ye desire ye may not be put off, but that your suit may be considered. And yet this half-year long I have desired of you, and of your brethren, but one sentence; and still, I know not how, I am cast off, and can get nothing at your hands.

Dd You call for the special proofs of our doctrine, which would require a whole book; whereas, if you of your part could vouchsafe to bring but two lines, the whole matter were concluded.

Ee Yet lest I should seem to fly reckoning, as ye do, or to follow you in discourtesy, I will perform some part of your request, although indeed it be unreasonable.

Ff Against your new device of transubstantiation, besides many others whom I will now pass by, ye have the old father and doctor Gelasius, whose judgment I believe ye will regard the more, because he was sometime bishop of Rome, which see, as you have taught, can never err.

Gg And is alleged in the decrees: his words be plain: *Non desinit esse substantia panis et natura vini*[7]*:* "It leaveth not to be the substance of bread, and the nature of wine."

Hh But, to avoid this authority, some men of your side have been forced to expound these words in this sort: *Non desinit esse substantia, hoc est, non desinit esse accidens:* "It leaveth not to be the substance of bread, that is to say, it leaveth not to be the accidence, or the form, or the shape of bread." A very miserable shift.

Ii Even as right as the scholy expoundeth the text, Dist. iv.: *Statuimus, id est, abrogamus*[8]. Yet doctor Smith of Oxford took a wiser way; for his answer is, that Gelasius never wrote those words, and that they hang not together, and that there is no sense nor reason in them.

Kk Here have you, that after the consecration there remaineth the substance of bread and wine.

Ll Now bring ye but one doctor that will say as ye say, that there remaineth only the accidents, or shapes of bread and wine; and I will yield.

Mm As touching a private mass, Gregory saith in his dialogues, that, before the time of the communion, the deacon was wont in his time to cry unto the people: *Qui non communicat, locum cedat alteri*[9]*:* "Whoso will not receive the communion, let him depart and give place to others."

Nn To break the ordinance of Christ, and to communicate under one kind only, your own doctor Gelasius calleth it *sacrilegium.* And Theophilus Alexandrinus saith: *Si Christus mortuus fuisset pro diabolo, non negaretur illi poculum sanguinis*[10]*:* "If Christ had died for the devil, the cup of the blood should not be denied him."

Oo That the common prayers were used in the common tongue, you have St Basil, St Hierome, St Augustine, St Chrysostom, St Ambrose, and the emperor Justinian: the places be known.

Pp You see I disadvantage myself of many things that might be spoken; for at this present I have no leisure to write books.

Qq Now must I needs likewise desire you, forasmuch as I have followed your mind so far, either to bring me one old doctor of your side, or else to give us leave to think (as the truth is) ye have none to bring.

You desire us to leave talking against you, and no more to deal so unmercifully with you in the pulpits.

Rr O master doctor, call you this unmerciful dealing? when you were in autho-

[7 Gelas. adv. Eutych. in Mag. Biblioth. Vet. Patr. Col. Agrip. 1618-22. Tom. V. Pars III. p. 671. See before, page 11, note 11.]

[8 Corp. Jur. Canon. Lugd. 1624. Decret. Gratian. Decr. Prima Pars, Dist. iv. Gloss. in can. 4. col. 12.]

[9 Gregor. Magni Papæ I. Op. Dialog. Lib. II. cap. xxiii. Tom. II. col. 253. See before, page 19, note 16.]

[10 Si enim et pro dæmonibus crucifigetur...quod erit privilegium aut quæ ratio, ut soli homines corpori ejus sanguinique communicent, et non dæmones quoque, pro quibus in passione sanguinem fuderit?—Theophil. Alex. in Mag. Biblioth. Vet. Patr. Epist. Pasch. ii. Tom. IV. p. 717.]

rity; ye never could call us other than traitors and heretics; and yet, besides all that, used our bodies as you know.

Ss We only tell the people, as our duty is, that you withstand the manifest truth, and yet have neither doctor, nor council, nor scripture for you; and that you have shewed such extremity as the like hath not been seen, and now can give no reckoning why: or if ye can, let it appear.

Tt You say our doctrine is yet in doubt. I answer you, to us it is most certain and out of all doubt. But if you for your part be yet in doubt, reason and charity would ye had been quite resolved and out of doubt before ye had dealt so unmercifully for it with your brethren.

Vv You are bound, you say, and may not dispute; yet, God be thanked, you are not so bound as ye have bound others. But I would wish the queen's majesty would not only set you at liberty in that behalf, but also command you to shew your grounds. But when ye were at liberty, and a free disputation was offered you at Westminster before the queen's most honourable council and the whole estate of the realm, I pray you, whether part was it that then gave over? And yet then you know ye were not bound.

Aaa Ye say ye remain still in the faith ye were baptized in. O good master doctor, stand not too much in that point. You know ye have already forsaken a great number of such things as were thought necessary when ye were baptized; and yet, besides that, how many times have some of you altered your faith within the space of twenty years? Remember yourself, who wrote the book [a]*De Vera Obedientia*[1], against the supremacy of Rome? [b]Who commended it with his preface? [c]Who set it forth with solemn sermons? [d]Who confirmed it with open oath?

[a] Gardiner.
[b] Bonner.
[c] Tonstall.
[d] Cole. And in manner all the rest.

You have *ecclesiam apostolicam,* ye say; and we have none. Howbeit, in

Bbb all these matters that we now entreat of, we have, as you know, and must needs confess, the old doctors' church, the ancient councils' church, the primitive church, St Peter's church, St Paul's church, and Christ's church; and this, I believe, ought of good right to be called the apostles' church. And I marvel much that you, knowing ye have none of all these, yet should say ye have *ecclesiam apostolicam.*

Ccc Where ye say ye make no innovation, it is no marvel; for in manner all things were altered afore to your hands, as may most evidently appear by all these matters that be now in question between us, wherein ye have utterly changed and abolished the order of the old church, and do nothing but the contrary; and what evident profit the church of God hath gotten by it, I think it a hard matter to declare.

Ddd You would have the matter turned over to some general council as we would be content to stand by; howbeit, that you think will not be in your time.

Eee Notwithstanding, I dare boldly say, such a council will be a great while before ye shall be able to find any doctor, or old council to serve your purpose. But though there were never such a council, yet truth will be truth notwithstanding; for the council cannot make the falshood[2] truth, but the thing that is taken to be true, it certifieth only to be true. But what redress can there be looked for of such a council, whereas no man shall be judge, or suffered to speak one way or other, but only such as be openly and justly accused and found faulty, and whereas he, that is himself most out of order, shall be head and reformer of the whole?

Fff Both parties, ye say, have waded so far herein, that now they can go no further; and therefore ye would have either part let other alone. If you of your part would have done so when time was, many a godly man had now been alive.

Ggg Whereas you say, you would have the sayings of both parties weighed by the balance of the old doctors, ye see, that is our only request; and that in the matters ye write of I desire even so to be tried.

Hhh But why throw ye[3] away these balance, and, being so earnestly required, why be ye so loth to shew forth but one old doctor of your side? Ye make me believe ye would not have the matter come to trial, only ye set forth the empty

[[1] First published A. D. 1534. See Strype, Eccles. Memor. Vol. I. Book I. chaps. xxiv. xliv.]

[[2] Falsehead, 1560.]

[[3] You, 1560.]

names of St Augustine, of St Hierome, of St Chrysostom, of St Basil, of St Cyprian, of Tertullian, of Irenæus, of Dionysius, of the councils, &c.; as the apothecaries oftentimes set forth their painted boxes, and nothing in them: you shew me only the names of the doctors, which I knew afore; but ye shew me not one word in them of the private mass, or of the rest of the matters that lie between us. If ye could have found any thing in them for your purpose, I believe you would not have brought them empty. But that is a policy in the time of siege, when the soldiers within begin to want victuals, to throw forth a few loaves over the walls, that the enemy without may think they have store enough, and so give over the siege.

Iii You say I slanderously misreport the late council of Constance. O sir, these words savour too much of your choler, and might better have been spared. I speak more favourably of that council than I might have done.

Kkk For the words of the council be these, speaking namely of the communion under both kinds: *Pertinaciter asserentes oppositum, tamquam hæretici arcendi sunt*[4]; that is: "They that stubbornly defend and maintain the contrary," that is to say, they that stand in defence of that that Christ commanded to be done and the apostles, which all the old catholic doctors and the whole primitive church observed, "ought to be punished so as is meet for heretics." By these words they are called not schismatics, as I said, but stubborn heretics, which is a great deal more odious. You see therefore my report was more gentle than the council deserved.

Lll Whereas you say we could never yet prove the error of one general council, I think your memory doth somewhat deceive you. For, to pass by all other matters, Albertus Pighius, the greatest learned man, as it is thought, of your side, hath found such errors to our hands; for in his *Ecclesia*[5] *Hierarchia*, speaking of the second council holden at Ephesus, which you cannot deny but it was general, and yet took part with the heretic abbat Eutyches against the catholic father Flavianus, he writeth thus: *Concilia universalia etiam congregata legitime, ut bene, ita perperam, injuste, impieque judicare et definire possunt*[6]: "General councils," saith he, "yea, even such as be lawfully summoned, as they may conclude things well, so may they likewise judge and determine things rashly, unjustly, and wickedly."

Mmm And of the two councils holden of late years at Constance and at Basil, where as pope John and pope Eugenius were deposed, he saith plainly that they decreed both against reason, and against nature, and against all examples of antiquity, and against the word of God[7]; and yet both these councils were called general.

Nnn Ye press me sore that, if I write you not a book of my proofs, it will be thought I do it *conscientia imbecillitatis*, "for the distrust of the weakness" of my part. Belike you have forgotten wherefore you with all your company not long since openly refused to enter disputation with us at Westminster. Doubtless the greatest part thought it was (as it was indeed) *conscientia imbecillitatis*, even "for distrust of the weakness" of your part. And what think ye is there now judged of you, that, being so long time required, yet cannot be won to bring one sentence in your own defence?

Ooo I have afore alleged a few reasons of my part, which by order of disputation I was not bound to do: now let the world judge which of us two flieth conference. I protest before God, bring me but one sufficient authority in the matters I have required; and afterward I will gently and quietly confer with you farther at your pleasure.

Ppp Wherefore, forasmuch as it is God's cause, if ye mean simply, deal simply; betray not your right, if ye may save it by the speaking of one word.

[[4] Concil. Constant. in Concil. Stud. Labb. et Cossart. Lut. Par. 1671–2. Sess. XIII. Tom. XII. col. 100; where *oppositum præmissorum.*]

[[5] Ecclesiastica, 1560.]

[[6] Testimonio insuper Ephesinum II. et ipsum universale ..... Testimonio, inquam, hæc sunt errare posse etiam universalia concilia, etiam congregata legitime, &c.—Pigh. Hierarch. Eccles. Assert. Col. 1538. Lib. VI. cap. xiii. fol. 247. 2.]

[[7] Sibi ipsis...totius ecclesiæ caput...subjicientes, adversus rerum ordinem et naturam, contra clarissimam evangelicæ veritatis lucem, contra omnem antiquitatis auctoritatem, atque adeo ipsius orthodoxæ ecclesiæ...indubitatam fidem et sententiam.—Id. ibid. cap. ii. fol. 213. 2.]

3—2

Qqq The people must needs muse somewhat at your silence, and mistrust your doctrine, if it shall appear to have no ground, neither of the old councils, nor of the doctors, nor of the scriptures[1], nor any allowed example of the primitive church to stand upon; and so your fifteen hundred years, and the consent of antiquity and generality, that ye have so long and so much talked of, shall come to nothing. For think not that any wise man will be so much your friend, that in so weighty matters will be satisfied with your silence.

Rrr Whereas you say, I am not altogether without enemies; I assure you, whosoever be enemy unto me, I for my part am enemy unto no man, but only wish that God's truth may be known of all men. But he that is enemy unto me in this behalf, I fear me, is enemy unto some other, whom he would be loth to name.

Sss You suppressed, ye say, your first letters, for that you saw they were too sour. That had been all one to me; for sour words are not enough to quail the truth. Howbeit, to my knowledge, I gave you no evil word to increase that humour. But if ye will still strive against nature, as ye say ye have done now, and conquer the rest of your affections too, I doubt not but we shall soon agree.

Ttt Here I leave, putting you eftsoons gently in remembrance, that, being so often and so openly desired to shew forth one doctor, or council, &c., in the matters afore mentioned, yet hitherto ye have brought nothing; and that, if ye stand so still, it must needs be thought ye do it *conscientia imbecillitatis*, for that there was nothing to be brought.

JOHN SARUM.

20[2] *Martii.*

DOCTOR COLE'S ANSWER TO CERTAIN PARCELS OF THE SECOND LETTERS OF THE BISHOP OF SARUM,

SET FORTH IN SUCH SORT AS IT CAME FROM THE AUTHOR, 8 APRILIS, ANNO 1560.

A *It liketh you thus to say, that your readers may think you touch me very sore, where you discover great[3] untruth in your writing. For my purpose was to be taught, and to this mark only I shot. You, for lack of good matter, answer, I speak not to the purpose: not to your purpose, but to mine.*

B *How oftentimes must I tell you, I come not to teach, but to be taught?*

C *You require that is dangerous for me to do, as you know.*

D *Well railed: you shall find that we have more than all you shall be able to answer, when time shall require.*

E *These words glistered[4] gold-like, and discloseth in you no will to satisfy my demand; I ween, for lack of stuff.*

F *You say much, and prove nothing: your truths be so open, that none seeth them but your own side.*

G *I have no privilege: when reason and law shall will me to do it, you shall find it; now I stand bound to the contrary, as you know.*

H *I must needs think some part of your writings made by some smatterer, as here, for a shew of skill in logic, brought in a place of logic out of all purpose. How frame you this to your purpose? and you shall find me therein true, as I shall happily make you to see, if you drive me to it.*

I *So did I too. Your doctrine against transubstantiation is yet to be proved, and no man bound to believe it. And yet, being as true as you would have it seem, yet may you inform the weak and willing to learn.*

K *That you are required, that you refuse, and make large offer to no purpose.*

L *We brought more than ye were able to answer, all were it no scriptures, nor councils, nor doctors.*

M *This argument would I fain see proved.*

[1 Scripture, 1560, 1609.] [2 29, 1560.] [3 A great, 1560.] [4 Glistereth, 1560.]

N *Stout and bold asseveration maketh no proof in the law.*

O *Here is again one place that I reckon ye put not in yourself; for it maketh quite against you. For Christ proved the Pharisees were not Abraham's children, and that a man may not put away his wife for every cause.*

P *Two purposes against yourself. Gregory proveth a negative; because none of his forefathers ever used the[5] title. As one might say, that you preach is naught, because men in times past taught not so. This part of Gregory serveth no whit to disprove the sovereignty; as Driedo will teach you, if you vouchsafe to read him[6].*

Q *If you read again the place in Aristotle's Topics, you shall there see the better to understand it. He speaketh it where men dispute* dialectice, *in such sort as we do not; and therefore it served[7] not your purpose. But I tell you[8] yet once again, I come not to dispute, but to learn.*

R Ridetur, chorda qui semper aberrat eadem[9].

D. Cole will prove it when it cometh to his turn.

S *In the end of this writing ye shall find mine answer to that you here say. The last answer.*

T *When you meddle with law, you shew your skill. I am still in possession of all that ever I thought; and if you put me out of possession by force, I ought to be restored. Had not the priests in the old law good title to sit in Moses' chair? What, you forget yourself: yes, pardy. The law accounteth no man* malæ fidei possessorem, *after that he hath continued in possession an hundred years. But I pardon you for mistaking the law: it is not your faculty.*

V *I enter no suit against you, and it were folly to shew mine evidence until it may serve and take place. I crave only to be informed, which I cannot obtain.* Patientia.

Aa *When I commence law against you, then this speech may serve you to some purpose.*

Bb *Why I come not to your sermons? This question is captious; and yet you are not herewith discharged, why you should not instruct me. As men choose their wives, so choose they their teachers. St Augustine, St Chrysostom, &c. Sermons tend more to teach than to convince.*

Cc *We stand not in case like: what need so much of one thing?*

Dd *All that I required may be couched in six lines, and, for ought that I see yet, in less too.*

Ee *It is no discourtesy to refuse to do that wherewith I might forfeit my recognizance.*

Ff *I see well ye write much and read little. Gelasius is full answered by Tapper[10],* in articulo de transubstantiatione[11].

Gg *You allege his words otherwise than you find them; which fault I trust groweth on[12] oversight.*

Hh *Shew what they are, that it be not thought that you devise this of your own fantasy.*

Ii *This gloss you mislike, because you understand not the glosser's meaning. It may stand full well.*

[5 That, 1560.]

[6 Deinde manifestum est doctrinam Gregorii in registro non obstare supra dictis, cum et ipse Gregorius ibidem manifeste dicat, Cura totius ecclesiæ et principatus Petro committitur, et tamen universalis pastor non appellatur. Ecce, ubi Gregorius vetat Romanum pontificem non appellari universalem pastorem, ibi et plane asseruit totius ecclesiæ ei curam esse commissam. Aliud ergo appellat universalem pastorem, aliud universalis ecclesiæ pastorem: per universalem pastorem seu episcopum intelligens eum, qui solus esset pastor et episcopus, ita ut alii sint dumtaxat illius vicarii et ministri, et non veri pastores, non veri episcopi, hoc etenim manifeste est falsum. Unde et Romanæ ecclesiæ episcopus vocat se episcopum servum servorum Dei, juxta Salvatoris doctrinam, Qui major est vestrum, erit vester minister. Ceteros episcopos vocat fratres suos, seu coepiscopos, alios autem sacerdotes appellat filios.—Joh. Driedon. a Turnhout De Eccles. Script. et Dogmat. Lov. 1533. Lib. IV. cap. iii. 3. pp. 559, 60.]

[7 Serveth, 1560.] [8 *You* is omitted, 1560.]

[9 Hor. De Art. Poet. 356.] [10 Capper, 1560.]

[11 Et si diligenter expendamus ejus sententiam, non adversatur transubstantiationi, sed magis ei patrocinatur. Dicit quidem, quod non desinit substantia et natura panis et vini, natura, inquam, extrema: hoc est, proprietates et qualitates cum dimensionibus panis et vini naturalibus, quæ utique eorum sunt natura. Quem sensum et ipse explicare videtur, dum dicit panem et vinum in proprietate suæ naturæ permanere, non in suis substantiis, quas aperte dicit divino Spiritu perficiente in divinam transire substantiam.—Ruard. Tapper. Op. Col. Agrip. 1582-3. Art. xiv. Resp. ad Arg. Calv. cont. Trans. Tom. II. p. 211.]

[12 Of, 1560.]

Kk *Soft and fair, you have not read the answer. Read Royard, and you shall see more.*

Ll *At my cue I shall be ready for you.*

Mm *Ye have better stuff than this, I trow. For this is somewhat weak.*

Nn *The decrees, where you learned this of Gelasius, tell*[1] *you how you should understand it.*

Theophilus shall be answered, when I come to dispute with you.

Oo *Whether the Greek and the Latin tongue were then understood*[2] *of the common people, remaineth yet upon proof. Well, I trow St Basil, &c. proveth not very well. Here I remain still in doubt.*

Pp *I pray you, take good leisure, and write effectually.*

Qq *I wis, you know I may not, nor the case I stand in requireth it not. You misreport: I said, If, &c.*

Rr *Men of your side used themselves traitorously to queen Mary; as none of us do now.*

Ss *Not manifest, until it be better proved. You had but the law; you require more than any law will bear against us.*

Tt *I doubted more than I do. You give me good cause to be well confirmed.*

Vv *At Westminster we came to dispute, and we were answered, there was none appointed; where we refused not to write neither. But when our book could not be read*[3]*, as yours was, we refused not utterly to dispute, but only this case, if our book could not be suffered to be read as indifferently as yours was. Now hardly weigh whether you have indifferently reported, that we utterly refused to dispute with you or no.*

Aaa *What one thing am A*[4] *gone from? You say much, and prove little. You mean the old bishop of Winchester, who repented at the hour of his death. And where you mean I condescended to the primacy of king Henry at my first coming home, or I had laboured that matter, you did the like yourself: for in queen Mary's time you subscribed to the articles, some of them we are entered to talk in, to your no less blame than mine. There be in the town that both saw you subscribe, and can bring forth your hand.*

Bbb *To this, and some part of the next article, you shall be answered in the end of this writing, as I before said.*

Ccc *What needeth so much of one thing? this serveth you to seem to say too much.*

Ddd *I grant.*

Eee *Such fond excuses men lay; how true, let other judge.*

Fff *You forget yourself; I say not thus, pardy: look better in the place.*

Ggg *Then begin, if you think the time will serve, or put it over till another time.*

Hhh *All these be but words often repeated, and answered already.*

Iii *Read the place again: I say not so; and then you shall see less cause to complain.*

Kkk *You say, the council at Constance openly pronounced against Christ himself. Wherein, I pray you? Because the fathers there said, Who saith it is of necessity to receive under both kinds, and that the approved custom of the church is sacrilege, to be taken for an heretic; and yet no heretic, but in a wrong opinion. Then belike you can bring in some text, where Christ commanded it should not be received but under both kinds; which you can never do. So is your report of this council very slanderous still. Read* 4. Canonem Concilii Constantiensis.

Lll *You ground your proof upon Pighius' error. For Pighius holdeth the council of Ephesus was general, which the council of Chalcedon denieth. So that I marvel much herein of you, that you allege that for a council which hath no place in the Book of Councils.*

Mmm *Wherein doth Pighius prove the councils of Constance and Basil to have erred? Marry, because they decreed the general council to be above the pope. If ye take these two councils to have erred in this point, you are a greater papist than I am; for I hold herein rather with Gerson. I trow this be one place that you wrote not yourself. Yet I reckon no error proved in any general council by that you have said.*

Nnn *To this I have answered already to you.*

[1 Telleth, 1560.] [2 Understand, 1560.] [3 Ready, 1560.] [4 I, 1560, 1609.]

Ooo *I have answered to this already. What order of disputation dischargeth you of proof? Yet, remember I came not to dispute, but to be taught.*

Ppp *If you refuse to instruct me, unless I bring some proof of*[5] *my part, you bid me to my cost. You bid me to a feast, where, while I should take on me to prove your doctrine naught, I were like to forfeit my recognisance; which you guilefully allure me unto.*

Qqq *God wot, I pass little in these matters what the poor silly souls deem of my doings. Wherein you have no cause to complain, sith they be edified toward you. Wise men, I doubt not, see what just cause I have to do as I do.*

Rrr *You would bear folk in hand that they, that agree not in doctrine with you, are not the queen's friends; which you gather by your own side in queen Mary's reign: but I never brake amity with any man for dissent in religion. I keep still mine old friends, be their religion good or bad.*

Sss *As though mine affection only caused me to dissent from you in religion. Which argument may serve you happily in rhetoric, but no where else, I ween.*

Ttt *This place is above answered.*

Now, forasmuch as you make this a great foundation against us, that we vary from the primitive church, and thereby make the simple souls ween that we were in the wrong side; here, I pray you, shew your opinion, whether we are bound to do all things which we find by sufficient authority were in ure in the primitive church. And because you shall not be herein squeamish, I shall here begin to shew you mine.

I am of the opinion that the council of Constance was in this matter. I think it an error, I am bound to do as the primitive church did, where the church customably used[6] *the contrary. I reckon an example no bond. I deny not but those examples were to be followed, and not to be broken at every man's will and pleasure, until by common assent other order were taken. But if you seek old writers, and find me that the church these six hundred years observed not many things which were practised, and accounted for good, wholesome, and holy in the primitive church, and thereby deem us in error, this were a wrong judgment. For the church of Christ hath his childhood, his manhood, and his hoar hairs; and as that that is meet for a man in one age, is unmeet in another, so were many things meet, requisite, and necessary in the primitive church, which in our days were like to do more harm than good.*

This is no new devised phantasy, but uttered eleven hundred years ago by St Ambrose, without reproach[7]. *I shewed you and read you the place at Westminster (as you may remember), and it were too long to make rehearsal of his words here.*

We might, by taking the contrary opinion herein, be led to think we ought to receive the sacrament evermore after supper, and not fasting. But St Augustine saith, that Christ left this to his church, to take order how, and in what sort, his sacraments should be received and used; wherein he saith it is a marvellous insolent kind of madness to mislike that which is received in the church, where the custom is not against any commandment in the scripture[8]. *St Peter caused (as Damasus saith) a commandment to be given, that no man should come bare-faced to the church. St Clement took order, that the clergy should have all things in common, and to live together*[9], *as in the late reformed order of St Benet's monks doth most godly appear. And not many years since, the said order in all cathedral churches was observed. Yet I ween it were an error to hold of necessity it should be so still, or to say the church were in error, because it hath suffered a contrary custom to creep in. Then, if the custom of the church may break that was in the primitive church commanded, it is less offence to leave undone that was at the beginning practised, and no commandment given for other to follow the*

[5 On, 1560.]

[6 Useth, 1560.]

[7 Ambros. Op. Par. 1686-90. Comm. in Epist. ad Ephes. cap. iv. Tom. II. Appendix, col. 241.]

[8 Nam et hinc quin ita faciendum sit, disputare insolentissimæ insaniæ est...Et ideo non præcepit quo deinceps ordine sumeretur, ut apostolis, per quos ecclesias dispositurus erat, servaret hunc locum.—August. Op. Par. 1679-1700. Ad Inquis. Januar. Epist. liv. 6. 8. Tom. II. cols. 126, 7.]

[9 Clement. Epist. v. in Concil. Stud. Labb. et Cossart. Lut. Par. 1671-2. Tom. I. cols. 115, 6.]

same. Thus much I thought to put you in remembrance of, for such matters as you touch in the 17, 42, 43 *numbers*[1].

HENRICUS COLE.

8 *Aprilis.*

A LETTER SENT FROM THE BISHOP OF SARUM TO DOCTOR COLE;

WHEREIN HE REQUIRETH OF HIM A TRUE AND A FULL COPY OF THE FORMER ANSWER.

I UNDERSTAND by the report of divers, that, appearing of late before the queen's majesty's visitors at Lambeth, and being there demanded of a letter that was then abroad in your name, as[2] answer unto me, whether ye would acknowledge the same as your own, or no; and so much the more, for that ye had used the matter under covert, and sent your copies abroad into all places, even into mine own diocese, and yet not unto me, thereby to discredit me in corners at my first coming, whereof I have the greater cause to complain of your doings; ye made answer, not only that it was your own, but also that it was much abridged, and that the original was twice as much. If it be so, the fault is your own, that would so unadvisedly bestow your writings. As for my part, as they came to me not by your sending, but by very chance, even so did I cause them to be copied out justly and truly, without adding or diminishing of one letter; and according have I made out mine answer to the whole. Now, forasmuch as I understand there be certain both honourable and worshipful that would gladly have our doings to the print, and so published; these shall be to desire you, for the bettering of[3] your own cause, to send me your own copy full and large, as ye say ye gave it out at the first, that I may do as I shall think good, and you have no cause to think yourself injuried if I answer one parcel of your letters, and not to[4] the whole. I pray you, let me hear from you with expedition; for I mean plainly, and therefore have caused the print to stay upon your answer. Thus I bid you farewell. From Shirburne the 22nd of July. Anno 1560.

JOHN SARUM.

Unto this letter doctor Cole, being besides by messenger earnestly required, would make no answer one way or other: therefore, upon his refusal, it was thought good to answer his letters as they were.

THE REPLY OF THE BISHOP OF SARUM TO THE LETTER ABOVE WRITTEN;

WHICH D. COLE, CONTRARY TO EVEN DEALING, HAD GIVEN OUT AND SENT ABROAD, NOT TO THE SAID BISHOP TO WHOM HE WROTE IT, BUT PRIVILY AND SECRETLY UNTO CERTAIN OF HIS OWN FRIENDS.

THERE came to my hands of late by chance a scroll set forth in short broken sentences, containing an answer to the second letters that I had sent unto you before; which, as by certain familiar phrases, by the date, by the subscription of your own name, and by other tokens, appeared to me to be yours; so by the using and ordering of the same, I had some cause to think it should not be yours, and especially, for that, being as it appeared written unto me, it was sent privily abroad unto others, and not to me. For I thought, that you, being a man of this age and credit, would not have been ashamed of your own writings, or would have concealed them from him to whom you had directed them, or have sought for a false light to set forth your matters in; as merchants sometimes use to do, the better to utter their sorry wares.

[[1] Those marked S, Bbb, Ccc.]
[[2] As an, 1560.]
[[3] Yf, 1560.]
[[4] *To* is omitted, 1560.]

Moreover, I saw that your words throughout were heaped up with taunts and scorns, and were somewhat too much stained with choler to have proceeded from a sober grave man, as I ever took you to be.

Thus being uncertain of the truth herein, after I had sent oftentimes to you, to know whether you would avouch it for your own, or no, and could never get word from you, by reason that you shifted yourself, and would not be found; I thought it good to stay myself from answering, until I might get certain knowledge of the author.

At the last, after I had assayed many ways, and could by no means hear from you, having no longer continuance in the city, to stay the untrue reports which I heard were scattered by some of your friends, I could not but before my departure hence make out mine answer unto you, as having cause to think the letters that were brought me should be his in whose name they were given abroad.

First, where you have made your answers several, and set them so far off from the parcels of my letters, I guess you did that of very purpose, that your reader might see your answer, but not see what it was whereunto you answered.

Therefore I have joined my sayings and yours simply and plainly both together, without colour or shadow, that the indifferent reader may have all before his eyes, and so be the better able to judge aright.

SARUM.

In your second letters I find many words to small purpose. It had been far better for you to have alleged one sufficient authority, whereby I might have learned that I looked for.

COLE.

It liketh you thus to say, that your readers may think you touch me very sore; where you discover a great untruth in your writing; for my purpose was to be taught, and to this mark only I shot. You for lack of good matter answer, I speak not to the purpose. Not to your purpose, but to mine. How oftentimes must I tell you, I come not to teach, but to learn?

THE REPLY OF THE BISHOP OF SARUM.

Contrary to the rules of rhetoric, I see you begin to chafe and to inflame all your affections even at the first. Soberness were much fitter for a doctor. But your heats be such, that your friends have shewed me you must be borne withal.

I neither discover, nor cover any untruth in my writing, but, as you know, only utter the very truth. For at Paul's cross I required you, or any of you, to shew the grounds of your religion, if you had any, that by indifferent conference the truth the better might appear. And this had been to your purpose, if ye had meant plainly, and to mine too. But you run away in the mist, and fly the net, lest happily ye should be taken, and so purposely go about to blear your readers' eyes, and to cover the truth; and, having in very deed nothing to allege for yourself, yet ye make a countenance as though ye lacked nothing. And so I grant you follow your purpose, and not mine.

Where you say, ye come only to learn, and not to quarrel, he must needs be your very friend that will believe you. Howbeit, the pretence of a learner may keep your credit for a while, and save you from shewing what ye can say; and therefore I read you, use it still. But by your scoffs and scorns it may appear you come to control, sooner than to learn. God send us both humbleness of heart, that we may content ourselves to be taught!

SARUM.

In my sermons as well at Paul's cross, as elsewhere, I required you to bring forth of your part either some scripture, or some old doctor, or some ancient general council, or else some allowed example of the primitive church; for these are good grounds to build upon. And I would have marvelled that you brought forth nothing all this while, saving that I knew you had nothing to bring.

COLE.

You require that is dangerous for me, as you know.

THE REPLY. SARUM.

If it be dangerous to you because you stand bound, why do you not put it over to some other of your side that is not bound? This shadow will serve well before your friends, that will wink when you bid them, and see no more than you will have them see: but, forasmuch as ye have used this excuse so often, and so few wise men will believe it, I would think it good that now ye would devise some other.

SARUM.

But now, forasmuch as ye seek shifts, and will not come to answer, I account him unwise that knoweth not your meaning.

COLE.

Well railed: you shall find that we have more than all you shall be able to answer, when time shall require.

THE REPLY. SARUM.

This answer, notwithstanding it is bitter, yet, because it is untrue, and beareth more smoke than flame, it moveth me the less. Here I miss in you some part of your courtesy. These matters would be tried by reasoning better than by scolding. By likelihood some other man had moved your choler; for my words be as far from railing as yours are from modesty.

Where you write, that you have more than all we shall be able to answer, if every crack were a good substantial argument, I were confuted. But notwithstanding these terrible threats, yet in conclusion, as your custom is, ye bring nothing.

The arguments, that you say we shall never be able to answer, are sword and fire, such as of late days ye used so plenteously, for lack of others. And yet, as strong and as forcible as they were (God be thanked!), they have been fully answered, to the great and unspeakable comfort of God's people, and to your shame and confusion for ever.

As touching the old doctors and councils, I would ye had a term assigned you *ad exhibendum:* in the mean season, for lack of other witness, ye may write *teste meipso,* as princes do.

SARUM.

Ye ask me, why ye should be counted obstinate? Doubtless I for my part have a better opinion of you, and trust you are not so. But if a man withstand an open truth, having nothing wherewith to defend himself, I remit him to your own judgment, whether he may be counted obstinate, or no.

COLE.

These words glitter[1] gold-like, and disclose in you no will to satisfy my demand; I ween, for lack of stuff.

THE REPLY. SARUM.

It pleaseth you to make yourself merry with these words. I alleged unto you St Augustine, St Ambrose, St Basil, St Chrysostom, St Hierome, Gelasius, Theophilus, and St Gregory; therefore it is untrue that ye say, I had no will to satisfy your demand. Now bring you but one of all these, or any other of your side in the matters that lie now between us, to satisfy my demand, and, as I have said, you shall have the victory.

You say, we lack stuff to prove our purpose. O would to God your stuff

[[1] Glittereth, 1560.]

and ours might be laid together! then should it soon appear how true it is that ye say, and how faithfully ye have used the people of God.

SARUM.

You put me well in remembrance of mine office, that, forasmuch as I am a bishop, I should be διδακτικὸς, that is, ready to yield an account of such things as I teach. I thank God, so I do, and have done to my power, both privately and openly. But if this be my duty, and required at my hands, what privilege have you, that you only may not allow out one sentence to the confirmation of your doctrine?

COLE.

You say much, and prove nothing. Your truth is so open, that no man can see it but your own side. I have no privilege: when reason and law shall will me to do it, you shall find it. Now I stand bound to the contrary, as you know.

THE REPLY. SARUM.

I speak not too much, as yourself can witness. How much I prove, shall rest upon the wisdom and judgment of the reader. Both the truth of our part, and the untruth of your part is so open, that now (God be thanked!) the whole world is able to see it, unless there be some such as have[2] eyes and will not see: yet *Justificata est sapientia Dei a filiis suis.*

Ye say you will speak when reason and law shall will you to do it. Of the law I will say nothing, but only this by the way, because you are a doctor of law; what law have you that can drive a man to prove a negative? or, if ye have no law, what reason have you that I should do it? But methinketh both reason and humanity would ye should have answered me somewhat, specially being so often and so openly required. At the least you should have alleged Augustine, Ambrose, Chrysostom, Hierome, as ye did sometimes allege the decree of the council of Ephesus, the first, for the communion under one kind; which decree never was yet found, nor never will be. Howbeit, because you speak of reason, where as a man hath nothing to say, it is good reason he keep silence, as you do.

SARUM.

You would have men think I fly answering, because I am a bishop. This in sophistry is called *paralogismus, a non causa ut causa.* I alleged the place and audience where I spake, and not only mine office. For I thought it might appear some want of discretion, to call that doctrine into question, which I knew was grounded upon God's word, and authorised and set forth by the queen's majesty, and by the assent of the whole realm.

COLE.

I must needs think some part of your writing made by some smatterer, as here, for a shew of skill in logic, brought in a place of logic out of all purpose. How frame you this to your purpose? and you shall find me therein true, as happily I shall make you to see, if you drive me to it. Your doctrine against transubstantiation is yet to be proved, and no man bound to believe it. And being as true as ye would have it seem, yet may you inform the weak and willing to learn.

THE REPLY. SARUM.

Ye do me too much wrong, that will not allow me thus much logic of mine own. But it was ever your grace to bear the people in hand that all we are altogether unlearned, and know nothing. Which thing if it were true, it were the more to your shame, thus openly to be confounded thorough the whole world by men of so small learning. Howbeit, thus it pleased you to talk, for want of better reason.

[[2] Hath, 1560.]

Ye call me a smatterer in logic, as if yourself were as perfect[1] in logic as Aristotle. And yet I remember well, I understood as much logic as this cometh to, and some deal more, for twenty years ago, ye wis when you, by your own report, were but a simple smatterer in divinity. Neither did I bring it in for a shew of skill, as you say, but to declare your oversight and lack of skill, which appeareth now not only in divinity, but also in logic. For where you say, I brought it in out of all purpose, methink you have forgotten some part of your old rules, and know not what *paralogismus, a non causa ut causa,* meaneth: which is, whensoever in reasoning the very true cause is suppressed, and another cause of purpose set in place. For example, I say, I confer with you under protestation, lest I should seem to call the[2] doctrine into doubt, which I knew to be established by God's word, and by sufficient authority throughout this realm: and you would have it taken that I do it, because I am a bishop. Which indeed is of your side a sophistication, *a non causa ut causa.* So likewise I say, you allege no doctors, nor scriptures, nor general councils, as true it is, because ye have none to allege. But you would make men believe ye dare not allege them, because ye stand bound in recognisance to the contrary. And this of your side is another sophistication, *a non causa ut causa.*

Where you say, ye will shew me that I brought this in out of all purpose, it had been more for your credit, if ye would have done it out of hand. But forasmuch as the fairest shew of your learning hangeth on the future tense, and standeth only upon promise, I trust you will bring forth your old doctors and councils, and perform this both together, which will be ye know when.

The truth of our doctrine against transubstantiation was proved sufficiently, and well allowed, before your doctrine with transubstantiation was ever heard of. For you are not able to shew me not so much as the very name of transubstantiation in any kind of writer, new or old, before the late council of Lateran, which, as you know, was holden in Rome a thousand two hundred and fifteen years after Christ. So long the church of God and the catholic faith was able to stand without your transubstantiation. Which if it were so true, as ye would have men think it, I marvel it could never be known before.

SARUM.

But, as touching my calling, I am not only ready to answer any man in any thing that I profess, but also, upon sufficient allegation, as I have promised, very well content to yield unto you.

COLE.

That you are required, that you refuse, and make large offer to no purpose.

THE REPLY. SARUM.

That you required me I have partly performed, even in my last letters, as you yourself do know right well, and that not altogether from the purpose, as it shall appear. Bring you forth as much of your side; and I will say ye come well to the purpose.

SARUM.

But, I beseech you, what reason of your faith in these matters gave you sometime, when you were in place? Scriptures, doctors, councils, ye had none, as now appeareth by your silence.

COLE.

We brought more than ye were able to answer, all were it not scriptures, nor doctors, nor councils.

THE REPLY. SARUM.

Instead of scriptures, doctors, and councils, ye brought such extremity as the world hath not seen the like, and as you are now loth to hear of; and yet

[1 Perfit, 1560, 1609.] [2 That, 1560.]

it pleased God that the same should be answered sufficiently, with patience and sufferance. But here am I glad ye confess one truth by the way, that ye brought in all that time neither scriptures, nor doctors, nor general councils, of your side; and yet I trow ye were free from recognisance. This I believe passed you unwares, and not of purpose: as your prolocutor[3], in the disputation at Oxford, gave out one truth by chance unadvisedly, as he gave knowledge to the audience in the divinity school of what matters they would dispute. For thus he said, and that in your own hearing: *Viri fratres, convenimus huc hodie disputaturi contra horribilem illam hæresim, de veritate corporis et sanguinis Christi in eucharistia*[4]: "Brethren," said he, "we come hither this day to dispute against that horrible heresy, of the verity of Christ's body and blood in the sacrament." God would have him utter some truth then, as you do now, because he was *pontifex illius anni*. But, forasmuch as you confess ye brought neither scriptures, nor doctors, nor councils, I remit the matter to your own reader to consider what ye brought.

SARUM.

Therefore the ground of your persuasion must then needs be, *Nos habemus legem, et secundum legem, &c.* You know what followeth, that is, "We have a law, and according to our law he must die."

COLE.

This argument I would fain see proved.

THE REPLY. SARUM.

Your whole practice, and the order of your doings for six years together, hath proved it sufficiently. And besides that, a bishop of yours even in that time sitting in judgment upon a poor man in a case of religion, and hearing him allege the scriptures and other authorities for himself, rounded a gentleman in the ear that sat next to him with these words, "Nay, if we strive with them in scriptures and reasoning, we shall never have done. We must proceed against them with the law."

SARUM.

For, as truly as God is God, if ye would have vouchsafed to follow either the scriptures, or the ancient doctors, or the councils, ye would never have restored again either the supremacy of Rome, after it was once abolished, or the private mass, or the communion under one kind, &c.

COLE.

Stout and bold asseveration maketh no proof in the law.

THE REPLY. SARUM.

True and earnest asseveration maketh a proof sufficient in the law, as long as ye have nothing to the contrary, as indeed ye have not, nor never shall have. But without question your terrible guard of bills and halberds, your grinning and scoffing, with other like your demeanour, as ye used in the disputations at Oxford against the martyrs and faithful witnesses of God's truth, and as now your cracks of many things, and bringing forth of nothing, I believe to any wise man maketh but small proof in divinity. But, if ye would have had any wise man mislike my asseveration, ye should have shewed by what scriptures, by what councils, or by what doctors, ye restored these things again.

SARUM.

It grieveth you that I should rest upon the negative, and so put you to your proofs; wherein notwithstanding ye allege against me the custom of the schools, yet you know Christ used the same kind of reasoning

[3 Dr Weston.]

[4 Fox, Acts and Mon. Lond. 1684. Vol. III. p. 38. The words as there reported slightly differ from those given here.]

in his school. As when he said to the Pharisees: *Hoc Abraham non fecit:* "This thing Abraham never did." And again, when he answered them[1] in the case of divorce: *A principio non fuit sic:* "It was not so from the beginning," he stood only upon the negative.

COLE.

Here is again one place that I reckon you put not in yourself; for it maketh quite against you. For Christ proved the Pharisees were not Abraham's children, and that a man may not put away his wife for every cause.

THE REPLY. SARUM.

I see you would fain put me out of credit, as though I were not able to answer your letters without conference. But this I reckon you do for a jolly policy, that, while your reader is looking upon me, he should forget the whole matter that we talk of. If the examples that I allege be against myself, then are you the more beholding to me. For they cannot likely make against me in this case, but they must needs make for you. Yet, I pray you, shew me by all your logic how holdeth this argument of yours:

Christ proved that the Pharisees were not Abraham's children, and that a man may not put away his wife for every cause: *ergo*[2], this matter maketh quite against me[3].

Methinketh here is a very short syllogismus. I marvel where you left your *medius terminus:* you should have squared it better before it had past your hands. As for the allegation, it maketh evidently for me. For, as I said, Christ stood then upon the negative against the Pharisees; as we do now against you.

SARUM.

Even so, when John the bishop of Constantinople had taken upon him to be called universal[4] bishop of the whole church—which title afterward the bishop of Rome began to usurp to himself, and for the maintenance of the same hath oftentimes disquieted and shaken the whole world—but, when the bishop of Constantinople first began to use this title, Gregory, being then bishop of Rome, confounded him only with the negative. *Nemo,* said he, *decessorum meorum hoc profano vocabulo uti voluit*[5]*:* "None of my predecessors (which had continued from Peter downward, for the space of six hundred years after Christ) would ever use this unchristian-like and lewd name." Lib. iv. Epist. 80. And again, Epist. 92: *Sancti ante legem, sancti in lege, sancti sub gratia, omnes perficientes corpus Domini in membris sunt constituti*[5]*:* "The holy men before the law, the holy men under the law, the holy men under the grace of the gospel, all together making up one body of the Lord, are placed amongst his members. But none of them would ever suffer himself to be called universal." I have chosen me specially these examples, because they seem to serve me to double purpose. Thus Gregory reasoned then, as we do now, only upon the negative; and if the bishop of Constantinople had been able to prove but one affirmative, that any bishop of Rome aforetime had used that title, or that ever any man, either[6] before the law, or under the law, or under the gospel, had suffered himself to be called universal bishop, then had Gregory been confounded.

COLE.

D. Cole confesseth that no bishop of

Two purposes against yourself. Gregory proved a negative; because none of his forefathers ever used that title. As one might say, that you preach is naught,

[1 Then, 1560.] [2 Lo, 1560.] [3 Him, 1560.] [4 The universal, 1560.] [5 Gregor. Magni Papæ I. Op. Par. 1705. Epist. Lib. v. Epist. xviii. xliii. Tom. II. cols. 743, 71. See before, page 32, notes 2, 3.] [6 Other, 1560.]

because men in times past taught not so. This part of Gregory serveth no whit to disprove the sovereignty; as Driedo will teach you, if you vouchsafe to read him[7].

Rome before Gregory, that is, for the space of six hundred years after Christ, would ever take upon him the title of universal bishop.

THE REPLY. SARUM.

You say, I bring Gregory against myself. God be thanked, you are able to bring neither Gregory, nor any else, that in any of these matters may but seem to make with you. But if Gregory stand upon the negative, as I do, and as you yourself confess, he maketh sufficiently to my purpose. Now judge you whether these proofs be negatives, or no. *Nemo decessorum meorum hoc profano vocabulo uti voluit.* Or this: *Nemo se universalem dici voluit.* And say not I allege matter against myself[8], unless ye have wherewith to disprove it better.

You answer farther, that one might say the like against us, that we preach this day is naught; because men in times past taught not so: like as Gregory found fault with John the bishop of Constantinople, for that he entitled himself an universal bishop of the whole church; whereas none of his predecessors durst never[9] take that name upon him. Indeed, this answer might have some shew, if men in times past had never taught so as we teach now. But I doubt not but herein your own learning and conscience crieth out against you. For you know that the matters that lie in question between us have been taught, as we now teach them, both by Christ himself, and by his apostles, and by the old doctors, and by the ancient general councils; and that you, having none of these or like authorities, have set up a religion of your own, and built it only upon yourself. Therefore I may justly and truly conclude, that you now teach, and of long time have taught the people, touching the mass, the supremacy, the common prayer, &c., is naught; for neither Christ, nor his apostles, nor the old doctors, Tertullian, Cyprian, St Hierome, St Augustine, St Ambrose, St Chrysostom, &c., ever taught the people so as you have taught them.

You say, this place serveth me nothing against the supremacy. I marvel much you say not, it serveth you to prove the supremacy. Gregory saith, no bishop of Rome until his time, which was six hundred years after Christ, would ever be called the universal bishop.

He saith that Leo his predecessor refused the[10] name, notwithstanding[11] it were offered unto him in the general council of Chalcedon.

He saith, it is a proud and a profane title, and a name meet for antichrist.

He saith, whosoever will take that name upon him is antichrist's forerunner.

He saith, to consent to such a name is the denial of the faith[12]: and yet say you, he speaketh not one word against the supremacy.

Here would I fain be answered one thing by the way: if no bishop of Rome would ever take upon him to be called the universal bishop, or head of the whole church, for the space of six hundred years after Christ, where then was the head of the universal church all that while? or how could it then continue without a head more than now? For now you say it is unpossible. Or, if the church had no universal head in the earth for so long a time after Christ, why do you now furnish out the bishop of Rome's authority, in the hearing of the unlearned, with such a glory and face of antiquity? As if the bishop of Rome had ever been named the head of the church since the time that Peter came first to Rome. But, because yourself were not able to avoid the force of Gregory's words, you did well to turn me over to doctor Driedo.

SARUM.

But, as touching the custom of the schools, I trust ye have not yet forgotten that Aristotle giveth order to the opponent in many cases to require an instant of the respondent, as I do now at your hands. And

[7 See before, page 37, note 6.]

[8 Me self, 1560.]

[9 Ever, 1560, 1609.]

[10 That, 1560.]

[11 Withstanding, 1560.]

[12 In a multitude of places besides those already cited, Gregory inveighs against this title. See Gregor. Magni Papæ I. Op. Epist. Lib. v. Epist. xix. ad Sabin. xx. ad Mauric. Aug. Lib. VII. Epist. xxxiii. ad eund. Tom. II. cols. 747, 9, 881, &c. &c.]

what is that else but in denial to defend the negative, and to drive the adversary to avouch the affirmative?

COLE.

If you read again the place in Aristotle's Topics, you shall see there the better to understand it. He speaketh it where men dispute dialectice, *in such sort as we do not; and therefore it serveth not your purpose. But I tell you yet once again, I come not to dispute, but to learn.*

THE REPLY. SARUM.

I never thought it had been so high a mystery to understand the nature of an instant. Children were wont to have it in their common disputations in the parvise schools in Oxford. If it serve only for them that dispute *dialectice*, and ye (as ye pretend) bear the person only of a learner, and come not to dispute; why then did ye allege against me the custom of the schools, and the disputations[1] of masters of art in the universities? Ye know they use there to dispute only *dialectice*, and none otherwise. And that I speak[2] herein, I speak[2] only upon occasion of your own words. How shall I think ye remember your Aristotle, if ye so soon forget your own letters?

SARUM.

But that ye will not do, and ye know why, although ye dissemble it. But sooner ye require to see our grounds. And what better ground can we have on our side, than that doctor Cole, the chiefest man on the other side, can find no ground to stand against us?

COLE.

Ridetur chorda qui semper aberrat[3] eadem[4]. *Doctor Cole will prove it when it cometh to his turn.*

THF REPLY. SARUM.

Seeing for lack of doctors ye answer me with poets, it shall do well to answer you again with the same. *Decies repetita placebunt*[4]. And yet, when ye come so often with the pretence of desire to be taught, and of your recognisance, if I list to scoff as ye do, why may not I as well say to you, *Ridetur chorda qui semper aberrat*[3] *eadem*[4]? As for the proving hereof, ye do well to take a day. In the mean season give others leave to think the truth.

SARUM.

He that will make any innovation, say ye, must give a reason of his doings. O master doctor, this reason fighteth most against yourself; for ye have misliked and put away the most part of the order of the primitive church, and yet ye never gave good reason of your doings.

COLE.

In the end of my writing ye shall find mine answer to that ye here say. The last answer.

THE REPLY. SARUM.

And there shall you find the reply.

SARUM.

Ye say ye are in possession. No, ye were sometime[5]; ye are not now: and, when ye were, ye had no right, title, or good evidence to claim by, no more than they which sometime sat in Moses' chair, or they that said, *Nos sumus filii Abrahami*[6]: "We are the children of Abraham;"

[1 Disputation, 1560.] [2 Spake, 1560, 1609.] [3 Oberrat, 1560.]
[4 Hor. De Art. Poet. 356, 65.] [5 Sometimes, 1560.] [6 Abraham, 1560.]

and thereby claimed their possession; therefore ye were *possessores malæ fidei;* and for that cause ye are now justly and orderly removed.

COLE.

When ye meddle with law, ye shew your skill. I am still in possession of all that ever I taught; and if you put me out of possession by force, I ought to be restored. Had not the priests in the old law good title to sit in Moses' chair? What! ye forget yourself: yes, perdy. The law accounted[7] *no man* malæ fidei possessorem, *after that he hath continued in possession an hundred years. But I pardon you for mistaking the law; it is not your faculty.*

THE REPLY. SARUM.

I have not so little skill in the law but I understand what are *malæ fidei possessores.* And as now (God's name be praised!) it is well known that ye have been they[8], ye are put out of possession, not by violence of man, but by the very force of God's truth; which so devoureth and consumeth up all error and falsehood[9], as Moses' serpent devoured and swallowed up the famed serpents of the sorcerers: if ye claim to be restored, be not aggrieved to shew your evidence.

Where ye say, the bishops and priests that were in Christ's time had good title to sit in Moses' chair, I grant you they had even as good title as ye had to sit and bear rule in the church of Christ; and therefore your example misliketh me never a whit. Yet ye know, Christ called them *fures et latrones,* "thieves and robbers;" and said unto them, *Vos ex patre diabolo estis:* "Ye are the children of the devil."

Ye say, the law accounteth no man *possessorem*[10] *malæ fidei,* that hath continued in possession one hundred years. Which thing notwithstanding I can be content to grant you to be true in the civil law, yet is it not true in the law of God; and that, as ye know, is proved by divers authorities, even in your own decrees, Dist. 8. There is alleged St Augustine, whose words are these: *Veritate manifestata, cedat consuetudo veritati... Nemo consuetudinem rationi et*[11] *veritati præponat; quia consuetudinem ratio et veritas semper excludit*[12]*:* "After the truth is once found out, let custom give place unto the truth. Let no man set custom before truth and reason; for reason and truth evermore put custom to silence."

Likewise St Gregory; and his words are these: *Si consuetudinem... opponas, advertendum est, quod Dominus dicit, Ego sum [via,] veritas, et vita: non dicit, Ego sum consuetudo... Et certe... quælibet consuetudo quantumvis vetusta, quantumvis vulgata, veritati omnino est postponenda*[13]*:* "If ye lay custom for yourself, ye must remember that Christ saith, 'I am the way, the truth, and the life:' he saith not, I am custom. And doubtless any custom, be it never so ancient, never so common, yet must it needs yield to the truth."

Likewise St Cyprian, whose words be these: *Si solus Christus audiendus est, non debemus attendere, quid aliquis ante nos faciendum putarit, sed quid, qui ante omnes est, Christus prior fecerit. Neque enim hominis consuetudinem sequi debemus, sed veritatem Dei, cum per Esaiam prophetam Deus loquatur, et dicat, Sine causa colunt me docentes mandata et doctrinas hominum*[14]*:* "If only Christ must be heard, we may not weigh what any man hath thought good to do that hath been before us, but what Christ hath first done that is before all men. For we may not follow the customs of man, but the truth of God, specially for that God saith by the prophet Esay, 'They worship me in vain, teaching the commandments and doctrines of men.'" Thus ye see, even by your own decrees, that custom against the truth is a very simple ground to build upon.

And like as ye use to say, *Nullum tempus præscribit regi,* so methinketh of

---

[[7] Accompteth, 1560.] [[8] There, 1560.]
[[9] Falshead, 1560.] [[10] Possessor, 1560.]
[[11] Et rationi, 1560.]
[[12] August. in Corp. Jur. Canon. Lugd. 1624. Decret. Gratian. Decr. Prima Pars, Dist. viii. can. 4. col. 24; where the reading is *manifesta.*—Op. Par. 1679-1700. Tom. IX. col. 112.]
[[13] Gregor. [VII.] in eod. ibid. can. 5; where *dixit* for *dicit.*]
[[14] Cypr. in eod. ibid. can. 9. cols. 25, 6; where we find *putaverit, sequi oportet Dei veritatem,* and *docentes* after *hominum.*—Op. Oxon. 1682. Epist. lxiii. p. 155.]

good right ye ought as well to say, *Nullum tempus præscribit Deo.* Otherwise antichrist shall come and sit in possession of the holy place, and bear himself as if he were God, and that, God knoweth how many hundred years together; and yet at the last he shall be but antichrist, sit he never so high. For prescription of an hundred years cannot make the[1] falsehood to be the truth: nor can any prescription be available in your own law, unless it have *bonum titulum;* and that in religion must needs be the word of God: which word forasmuch as ye have not to allege (as ye yourself know, no man better), all the face of your prescription is but vain; and therefore ye were, as I said, *possessores malæ fidei.* And ye have a rule of your law: *Possessor malæ fidei nulla temporis longinquitate præscribit*[2]. And therefore Christ in the case of divorce[3] rested not upon the custom that was then received, but appealed unto the first institution of marriage, and told the Pharisees then, as we now tell you, *A principio non fuit sic:* "It was not so at the beginning."

Whereas ye say, I mistake your law; I grant it is possible I may so do, as well as you: howbeit I am well assured in this place I mistake it not. I would to God, you, being a doctor of the law, did no worse mistake the scriptures.

SARUM.

Now, if ye think ye have wrong, shew your evidence out of the scriptures, the doctors, or councils, that ye may have your right again, and so re-enter. I require you to no great pains: one good sentence shall be sufficient. Ye would have your private mass, the bishop[4] of Rome's supremacy, the common prayers in an unknown tongue; and for defence of the same ye have made no small ado: methinketh it were reason ye should bring some authority, besides your own, to avouch the same withal. Ye have made the unlearned people believe that ye have all the doctors, all the councils, and fifteen hundred years of your side. For your credit's sake, let not all these great vaunts come to nought.

COLE.

I enter no suit against you; and it were folly to shew my evidence until it may serve and take place. I crave only to be informed, which I cannot obtain. When I commence law against you, then this speech may serve you to some purpose.

THE REPLY. SARUM.

If you will not prosecute your suit, it is reason ye be cast in a non-suit. But ye do best to make a delay, for ye know ye have to do with them that have seen your evidence.

Ye say ye keep your proofs until some better time, when they may serve and take place. When Pompey, a noble gentleman of Rome, was marching forth to fight in the field against his enemy Julius Cæsar, and Cato, an old grave senator, one of the same party, had shewed him he wanted men: "Tush," quoth he, "I shall have men enow[5]; for, as soon as I shall but stamp the ground with my foot, ye shall see spring up a swarm of soldiers." Afterward, when the field was fought, and Pompey discomfited, and began to fly with much dishonour: "O sir," said Cato, "where is now your promise? why stamp ye not the ground? when shall we see your swarm of soldiers[6]?" Even so may I say to you, notwithstanding your great vaunts that ye have made, ye see now ye are discomfited, ye see the field is almost lost: where are now your cracks of doctors and councils? Why stamp ye not your books? why come ye not forth with your evidence? Now ye stand in need of it, now it will serve and take place, if ye have any. But ye learned this policy of your Tully: *Scitum est,* saith he, *causam conjicere in tempus, cum adferre plura, cum velis, non queas:* "When ye have no more to say, it is wisdom to lay the fault in time."

[[1] This, 1560.]

[[2] Bonifac. VIII. in Corp. Jur. Canon. Lugd. 1624. De Reg. Jur. ad calc. Sext. Decretal. Reg. ii. cols. 780-3; where we find *ullo tempore non.*]

[[3] Diverse, 1550.]

[[4] Bishops, 1560.]

[[5] Enough, 1560.]

[[6] Plut. in Pomp.; who however attributes the question to Favonius.]

SARUM.

Where ye say, ye are in place of a learner, and gladly come to be taught, ye must pardon me to say the truth, I reckon your very friends, in this point, will hardly believe you. For if ye were desirous to learn, as ye would seem to be, ye would come to the church, ye would resort to the lessons, ye would abide to hear the sermons; for these are the schools, if a man list to learn. It is a token the scholar setteth little by his book, that will never be brought to school.

COLE.

Why I come not to your sermons? This question is captious; and yet ye are not herewith discharged, why ye should not instruct me. As men choose their wives, so choose they their teachers. St Augustine's and St Chrysostom's sermons tend more to teach than to convince.

THE REPLY. SARUM.

I meant not to be captious, but only to put you in remembrance that your pretence of learning is but feigned, and that you are not indeed so willing to be taught as ye would seem to be. Whensoever ye shall shew me by your law that a man may be required to prove a mere negative, I will be content to confer with you, and to shew you the rest of my proofs.

Ye say, ye choose your teacher as men do their wives: many men are led by folly and fancy in choosing their wives. I would your luck should be better in choosing your teacher. But St Paul prophesied in his time that there should come scholars with tickling[7] ears, and choose themselves teachers according to their own appetites, that should turn away their ears from the truth, and give themselves to the hearing of fables. The prophet Esay saith there were scholars in his time that would say to their teachers: *Loquimini nobis placentia, videte nobis errores. Auferte a nobis viam, declinate semitam, cesset a facie nostra senectus*[8] *Israel.* [Isai. xxx.] That is: "Speak to us[9] such things as may like us, see to us[9] errors, lead us out of the way, bring us out of the path. Let us have no more of the holy God of Israel before our face." And shall I think you choose me for love, as men do their wives? I can as yet little find it in your talk. But because I came near to the matter, and with my negative declared the weakness of your side more than some others did, therefore ye break[10] out first upon me, and laid in a claim without evidence, and, having nothing to say, ye would seem to have somewhat; as women that would seem to be with child sometimes rear up their bellies with a cushion.

SARUM.

Ye desire ye may not be cast off, but that your suit may be considered. And yet this half year long I have desired of you, and all your brethren, but one poor sentence; and still, I know not how, I am cast off, and can get nothing at your hands.

COLE.

We stand not in case like. What need so much of one thing?

THE REPLY. SARUM.

Ye are much beholden to your recognisance: ye make much ado, and yet bring nothing.

SARUM.

Ye call for the special proofs of our doctrine; which thing requireth a whole book: whereas, if ye of your part would vouchsafe to bring but two lines, the whole matter were concluded.

[7 Titlyng, 1560.]
[8 Sanctus, 1560.]
[9 Speak us, see us, 1560; see us, 1609.]
[10 Brake, 1560, 1609.]

COLE.

All that I required may be couched in six lines, and, for ought I see, in less too.

THE REPLY. SARUM.

Let the rest of your truth be tried by this. Ye know that the old father Theodoretus had more than six lines of our side; and therefore D. Clement tare the whole place out of his book, and burnt it, thinking there had been no more copies, lest perhaps it should come to light[1].

Ye know that Occam, one of your own doctors, hath more than six lines against you; and therefore the last pope condemned him as an heretic.

Ye know there is somewhat beside in St Augustine, in St Hierome, in St Chrysostom, &c.; I believe more than Royard or Tapper[2] could ever answer.

Ye know that ye yourself in your last answer granted me, that the examples of the primitive church are of our side; and therefore ye rest upon another point, that the primitive church in the apostles' and old doctors' time was but an infant and a babe in comparison of your church of Rome. Therefore methinketh, saving that it was your pleasure, ye were somewhat overseen to say that all our allegations may be couched in six lines. But, as I have offered you oftentimes, bring ye but two lines of your side; and the field is yours.

SARUM.

Yet, lest I should seem to fly conference and trial, which indeed in this case I most desire, or to follow you in discourtesy, I will perform some part of your request, although indeed it be unreasonable.

COLE.

It is no[3] discourtesy to refuse to do that wherewith I might forget[4] my recognisance.

THE REPLY. SARUM.

Your recognisance doth you good service to save your credit: ye fly away like a faint soldier, and yet hold up your shield as if ye were fighting still.

SARUM.

Against your new device of transubstantiation (besides many others, whom I now pass by) ye have the old father and doctor Gelasius, whose judgment, I believe, ye will regard the more, because he was sometimes a bishop of Rome, which see, as ye have taught, can never err. And is alleged in the decrees: his words be plain: *Non desinit esse substantia panis, et natura vini*[5].

COLE.

I see well ye write much, and read little: Gelasius is full answered by Tapper, in articulo de transubstantiatione[6]. *Ye allege his words otherwise than ye find them: which fault, I trust, groweth of oversight.*

THE REPLY. SARUM.

How are ye so privy to my reading? Wise men avouch no more than they know: ye lacked shift when ye were driven to write thus. I assure you I have not been so slack a student these twenty years, but that, besides other old writers of divers sorts, Greek and Latin, I have not spared to read over even such as have written of your side, as Roffensis, Pighius, Hosmasterus, Eckius, Hosius, and such others; and yet until this day I never set abroad in print twenty lines. But this is your old wont, to make the people think that we read nothing else but two-penny doctors, as ye call them. As, in the disputation at Westminster, ye would seem to stand in doubt whether we were able to understand you or no, when ye

---

[[1] In the Apology, and the Defence of it, Jewel relates this story more particularly.]

[[2] Capper 1560.]

[[3] Not, 1560.]

[[4] Forfeit, 1560, 1609.]

[[5] See before, page 11, note 11.]

[[6] See before, page 37, note 11.]

speak a little Latin; and as of late ye doubted not to say that master doctor Martyr was not able to make a syllogismus: which thing indeed is as true as the rest of your religion.

But I pray you, what had Stephen Gardiner read, when he alleged the third book of St Augustine, *de Sermone Domini in monte;* and yet St Augustine never wrote but two[7]?

What had the same Stephen Gardiner read, when he alleged Theophylactus, and called him Theophilus Alexandrinus, who was before Theophylactus well near five hundred years[8]?

What had doctor Smith of Oxon read, that openly in the disputations there, Anno Dom. 1554, alleged the council of Nice to prove the fancy of your transubstantiation; and when he came to shew the place, was not able to find one word, either[9] in that council or in any other of antiquity, that might seem to make for it[10]?

What had he read, that, being a judge in the same disputations, cried out so bitterly upon the[11] man of God, the archbishop of Canterbury, and that four or five times together, *Ostende mihi qualis corpus fuit? qualis corpus fuit?* and was not able to utter his mind in congrue[12] Latin[13]? This thing I trust ye will record with me; for it was spoken in your own hearing. D. Oglethorp

Your importunity hath caused me, contrary to mine own nature, to utter these things, which otherwise I could have concealed. O, boast not yourself too much of your great reading. When you[14] bring me any old doctor or council for your purpose in the matters that we now talk of, then will I say ye have read much.

As for Gelasius, howsoever it pleaseth D. Tapper to construe him, he saith plainly that in the sacrament there remaineth the substance and nature of bread and wine. But ye say, I allege Gelasius otherwise than I find him; and hereof your friends have made much ado. I see it must be a very small fault that shall escape your eyes. Gelasius' words be these: *Non desinit esse substantia panis vel natura vini.* Which words, having not the book at hand, I reported thus: *Non desinit esse substantia panis et natura vini.* I beseech you, how far went I either from the words or from the meaning of the author? I see it was not for nought that children in the schools were wont to find a difference between these two propositions, *comedi bis panem*[15], and *bis panem comedi.* But I perceive the fault was such that ye were loth to make matter of it. If I had altered any part of the sense and meaning of the writer, I trow I had been like to hear more of it.

I remember what a clapping of hands and stamping of feet ye made at Oxon against that notable godly learned man, the archbishop of Canterbury, for that he, alleging a place out of St Hilary, had changed but one letter, and written *vero* instead of *vere.* Ye triumphed over him, and pointed him to the people, and called him a falsary, a wrester, a corrupter of the doctors[16]. And yet afterward it was found, and will yet appear, that two of your own doctors, Stephen Gardiner and Smith, in their own printed books had changed the same letter, and written *vero,* as well as he.

Howbeit, God be thanked! ye will not give me cause to find such fault with your allegations; for ye are able to allege nothing at all.

But it were too long to shew how many times, and how shamefully, the writers of your side have corrupted the old doctors. Yet, for example sake, of a great number to shew you one or two: how think you[14] by your doctor Pighius, that violently altereth both the words and the meaning of St Augustine? For where St Augustine writeth thus: *Quid tam grate offerri aut ab illo suscipi potest, quam caro sacrificii nostri, corpus effectum sacerdotis nostri?* meaning the sacrifice that Christ offered upon the cross; Pighius putteth in of his own, *a nobis,* which St Augustine had not, and made up the sentence of this sort: *Quid tam grate* De Trin. lib. iv. cap. xiv.

[[7] Cranmer's Answer to a Crafty and Sophistical Cavillation, Book IV. Park. Soc. Ed. pp. 201, 4.]

[[8] Id. ibid. pp. 186, &c.]

[[9] Other, 1560.]

[[10] Fox, Acts and Mon. Lond. 1684. Vol. III. p. 64.]

[[11] That, 1560.]

[[12] Congrue: fitting, proper.]

[[13] Fox, Acts and Mon. Vol. III. p. 41. Oglethorpe was afterwards bishop of Carlisle.]

[[14] Ye, 1560.]

[[15] Bis comedi panem, 1560.]

[[16] Fox, Acts and Mon. Vol. III. p. 46. and Cranmer, Writings and Disputations, Park. Soc. Ed. p. 414.]

offerri a nobis, aut ab illo suscipi potest, quam caro sacrificii nostri, corpus effectum sacerdotis nostri?[1] and so perforce turned it to the pretensed sacrifice of your mass.

How think ye by Stephen Gardiner, that, in his book of the Devil's Sophistry, was not afraid to corrupt the words of the holy prophet[2]? For whereas David had written, *Escam dedit timentibus se;* he doubled the pronoun, and wrote it thus: *Escam se dedit timentibus se*[3]. This must needs appear to be somewhat more than an oversight. But what needeth more examples? Camotensis[4], a doctor of your own, saith in general of all your side: *Vim faciunt scripturis, ut habeant plenitudinem potestatis:* "They wrest," saith he, "the scriptures violently, that they may have the fulness of their power."

SARUM.

But to avoid this authority some men of your side have been driven to expound these plain words of Gelasius in this sort: *Non desinit esse substantia, hoc est, non desinit esse accidens.* Even as right as the gloss expoundeth the text, Dist. 4, *Statuimus, id est, abrogamus*[5].

COLE.

Shew what they are, that it be not thought that ye devise this of your own fantasy. This gloss ye mislike, because ye understand not the glosser's meaning. It may stand full well.

THE REPLY. SARUM.

What if I should say doctor Cole hath expounded it so? If not, then, I pray you, imagine with yourself how ye may be able to shift away Gelasius otherwise. Yet because ye will needs put me to my proofs in a matter that ye know is plain, I pray you take the pains to read Stephen Gardiner, in his book that is answered by the archbishop of Canterbury, Thomas Cranmer; ye shall find these words: "Gelasius," saith he, "speaking of the bread and wine, reciteth not precisely the substance to remain, but saith the substance or nature; which nature he calleth after the property[6]." Here, by this doctor's mind, *substantia* is Latin for property, which, as ye know, is nothing else but *accidens.*

And again in his book that he calleth *Marcus Antonius Constantius,* written in Latin, ye shall find these words: *Quod ait [panem] in sua substantia vel natura manere, vel substantiam sentit accidentium*[7], *vel naturæ proprietatem*[8]. It is a very strange phrase of speech to say *substantia accidentium*[7]. But it is as strange to say, as he saith in another place, *Accidentia sunt substantiarum partes.* Howbeit, after ye had once devised a new religion, it was meet that ye should devise out also some new phrases of speech that never had been heard of afore[9]. And yet is

[[1] Alb. Pigh. Explic. Cathol. Contr. Par. 1586. De Miss. Sacrific. Controv. v. fol. 110; where we find *et* for *aut*, and *posset*. See August. Op. Par. 1679—1700. De Trin. Lib. IV. cap. xiv. 19. Tom. VIII. col. 823.]

[[2] Prophet David, 1560.]

[[3] A Detection of the Deuils Sophistrie, Lond. 1546. fol. 69. 2; where *timentibus eum.*]

[[4] Or Carnotensis, John of Salisbury, bishop of Chartres.]

[[5] Telesph. in Corp. Jur. Canon. Lugd. 1624. Decret. Gratian. Decr. Prima Pars. Dist. iv. can. 4; and Gloss. cols. 11, 2.]

[[6] Gard. in Cranmer, Answer to a Crafty and Sophist. Cavill. Park. Soc. Ed. Book II. p. 292.]

[[7] Accidente, 1560.]

[[8] *Objicitur* 250: Objicitur ex Gelasio adversus Eutychetem, qui scripsit in sacramento eucharistiæ, substantiam et naturam panis et vini minime desinere esse, et facit collationem hujus sacramenti cum Christo, in quo manet salva utraque natura, et divina et humana, sicuti in hoc sacramento natura panis et corpus Christi. *Respondet Catholicus:* Gelasius id agit argumento ab eucharistia ducto, ut ostendat in Christo nullam naturarum confusionem, sed in suæ naturæ finibus eas manere; quod et in eucharistia fieri ostendit, sed illis verbis, quæ commoda interpretatione cum ecclesiastica doctrina consentiant: nam de pane et vino fatetur, quod transeant in divinam substantiam, quod *transire* compositæ dictionis *transubstantiatio* prima pars est, ut transubstantiare sit paris compositionis quasi transnominare; quod verbum *transnominare* et Latinum et elegans est, ac significat, priore nomine posito, aliud substitui, quemadmodum in confirmatione puerorum interdum negligentia, interdum data opera transnominabant pueros; et ad eam rationem *transubstantiare* significat substantiæ permutationem fieri, quam in hoc mysterio videtur definire Gelasius, dicens panem et vinum transire in substantiam divinam: nam quod addit in sua substantia vel natura manere; vel substentiam sentit accidentium, vel naturæ proprietatem, et disjunctive loquitur de natura vel substantia. Confut. Cavill. in Ven. Euch. Sacr. Verit. Par. 1552. fol. 154.]

[[9] Heard afore, 1560.]

not this the grossest part of your learning neither. Now I trust ye see I devised not this of mine own fantasy.

I marvel somewhat that ye say I understand not the glosser's meaning. For methinketh there is not so high nor mystical learning in it, but that a mean learned man may soon reach unto it. But I see it must be a desperate sore but ye will find some salve for it: I pray you, first read the text, and then consider how handsomely the gloss will frame unto it. The text is this: *Statuimus, ut septem hebdomadas plenas ante sanctum pascha omnes clerici* [*id est*] *in sortem Domini vocati a carne jejunent.* Now followeth your gloss: *Statuimus, id est, abrogamus.* And because ye understand the gloss better than I, as ye say, and like it so well, read the text accordingly, and say thus: *Abrogamus ut septem hebdomadas plenas ante sanctum pascha omnes clerici a carne jejunent.* And I believe, whatsoever meaning ye make of it, ye shall make but unhandsome Latin. Now let your reader judge whether of us two better understandeth the glosser's meaning.

SARUM.

Here ye have, that after the words of consecration there remaineth in the sacrament the substance of bread and wine. Now bring ye but one doctor that will say as ye say, that there remaineth only the accidents and shews of bread and wine; and I will yield.

COLE.

Soft and fair: ye have not read the answer. Read Royard, and ye shall see more. At my cue I shall be ready for you[10].

THE REPLY. SARUM.

If Royard's answer had been worth the hearing, ye would not have been ashamed to have alleged his words. At your cue you[10] will be as ready as St George a horseback, evermore riding, and yet evermore standing still: ye will be a very evil auditor, that lay down so little, and reckon so much. But bring somè old council or doctor with you at your cue; or else folk will say, ye have none to bring.

SARUM.

As touching a private mass, Gregory saith in his dialogues, that before the time of the communion the deacon was wont, even in his time, to cry unto the people on this wise: *Qui non communicat, locum cedat alteri*[11]: "Whoso will not receive, let him depart, and give place to others."

COLE.

Ye have better stuff than this, I trow; for this is somewhat weak.

THE REPLY. SARUM.

Whatsoever this stuff seemeth to you, your answer seemeth to me very weak. If ye be no better able to answer this, how will ye be able to answer the rest? It appeareth by these words of St Gregory, that in his time, which was six hundred years after Christ, whoso would not communicate with the priest at the communion, was commanded out of the church. Whereby it is clear they had then a communion, and that all the congregation present received together. Now either shew ye me so much for your private[12] mass, or else say no more, this stuff is weak.

SARUM.

To break the ordinance of Christ, and the people to communicate[13] under one kind only, your own doctor, Gelasius, calleth it *sacrilegium.*

[10 Ye, 1560, 1609.]

[11 Gregor. Magni Papæ I. Op. Par. 1705. Dial. Lib. II. cap. xxiii. Tom. II. col. 253. See before, page 33, note 9.]

[12 Privy, 1560.]

[13 To communicate the people, 1560.]

And Theophilus Alexandrinus of the same matter writeth thus: *Si Christus mortuus fuisset pro diabolo, non negaretur illi poculum sanguinis*[1].

COLE.

The decrees where ye learned this of Gelasius telleth you how ye should understand it. Theophilus shall be answered, when I come to dispute with you.

THE REPLY. SARUM.

Here, I trow, your memory deceived you: ye mean the gloss, and not the decree. For the words of Gelasius in the decree are plain: *Divisio unius ejusdemque mysterii sine grandi sacrilegio non potest pervenire*[2]. And the words that he useth farther[3], *ut integra sacramenta percipiant, aut ab integris arceantur*[4], seem not so much to pertain to the priests as to the people. But ye did well to turn over Theophilus until some other time; for I ween ye had no answer ready made.

SARUM.

That the common prayers were used in the common known tongue, ye have St Basil, St Hierome, St Ambrose, St Augustine, St Chrysostom, and the emperor Justinian, and many others. The places be known.

COLE.

Whether the Greek and Latin tongues were then understood[5] *of the common people, remaineth yet upon proof: well, I trow, St Basil approveth not very well. Here I remain still in doubt.*

THE REPLY. SARUM.

I marvel much that any learned man should doubt at this. For, if the common Greek people understood not the Greek tongue, nor the common Latin people the Latin tongue, then would I fain know what tongue they understood? I can see no great cause why they should forget their own tongue, and learn another. But Arnobius in his time called the Latin tongue *Sermonem Italum*[6], because it was used throughout all Italy.

St Ambrose in his time preached to the people of Italy in Latin; and, as it is to be thought, the people understood him.

St Augustine, in his sermons to the common people in Africa, hath divers times these words: *Nunc loquar Latine, ut omnes intelligatis*[7]*:* "Now will I speak Latin," saith St Augustine to the common people, "that ye may all understand me." St Gregory in his sermons used the Latin tongue to the people; and I trow he spake not all in vain. I marvel why ye doubt not as well whether the common Greek people understood Demosthenes or Æschines; or the common Latin people understood Cicero or Hortensius, when they spake unto them in their mother-tongue.

Now, that the common prayers, in St Basil's, St Ambrose, and St Augustine's time, were in the common vulgar tongue, mark how well it may be proved.

St Basil saith thus of the usage of the common prayer in his time: *Conjunctus sonus virorum, mulierum, parvulorum, tanquam fluctus ferientis littora in nostris ad Deum precibus excitatur*[8]*:* "In our prayers that we make to God we raise up such a sound of the voices of men, women, and children praying together, as if it were the noise of the waves beating against the sea-banks." Whereby it appeareth that, in St Basil's time, men, women, and children, sang in the churches all together.

[[1] Theophil. Alex. in Mag. Biblioth. Vet. Patr. Col. Agrip. 1618-22. Epist. Pasch. ii. Tom. IV. col. 717. See before, page 33, note 10.]

[[2] Provenire, 1560.] [[3] Further, 1560.]

[[4] Gelas. in Corp. Jur. Canon. Lugd. 1624. Decret. Gratian. Decr. Tert. Pars. De Consecr. Dist. ii. can. 12. col. 1918; where for *ut* we find *aut.*]

[[5] Understand, 1560.]

[[6] ... quam...viri...tam sermone Italo explicuere quam Græco.—Arnob. Op. Par. 1580. Adv. Gent. Lib. IV. p. 176.]

[[7] An expression nearly similar to the words here quoted, and one which Jewel afterwards declares that he intended, may be found August. Op. Par. 1679-1700. Serm. clxvii. 4. De Verb. Apost. Tom. V. col. 804.]

[[8] Basil. Op. Par. 1721-30. In Hexaem. Hom. iv. Tom. I. p. 39.]

Chrysostom of his time saith thus: *Ne mireris, si in sacris nostris populus cum sacerdote colloquatur*[9]: "Marvel not," saith he, "if that in our prayers the priest and the people talk together."

Augustine of his time saith thus: *Non est opus loquutione cum oramus, id est, sonantibus verbis, nisi forte sicut sacerdotes faciunt, significandæ mentis suæ causa, non ut Deus, sed ut homines audiant*[10]: "We need not," saith he, "to use words, or sound of voice, when we pray, unless it be as the priests do, to declare their meaning; not to the intent that God may therefore hear them, but that they may be heard of men."

But, because ye be a doctor of law, I would not have you forget Justinian the emperor, the first compiler of your laws. He, if ye be remembered, commanded the bishops that they should set forth the common prayers in open voice, and that, as he saith, *ut majori devotione audientium animi efferantur*[11]: that is, "that the minds of the hearers may be stricken with more devotion." He thought then that the understanding of the prayers should enkindle devotion in the hearts of the hearers. For I believe he had never heard say that ignorance should be the cause of true devotion, as ye boldly avouched in the disputation at Westminster, in the hearing and wondering of the most part of the honourable and worshipful of this realm[12]. I know not by what secret revelation ye learned this first. For your own councils say: *Ignorantia mater est cunctorum errorum*[13]: that is to say, "Ignorance is the mother of all manner errors." And the same words ye have alleged in your own decrees, Distin. 38, and are very agreeable unto Christ's words in the gospel: *Erratis nescientes scripturas:* "Ye are in error, because ye understand not the scriptures." [Matt. xxii.]

Origenes, one of the oldest doctors of the church, saith thus: *Tormentum est diabolo, si quem videat legere sacras literas; possidet enim omnes qui versantur in ignorantia*[14]: "It is a scourge," saith he, "and a torment to the devil, if he see any man read the scriptures; for he hath power upon all them that remain in ignorance[15]."

St Cyril saith: *Pueri nostri legunt sacras literas, et ex eo fiunt religiosissimi*[16]: "Our children," saith he, "read scriptures, and thereof they become devout and holy."

And what needeth more allegations? Your own doctor Lyra saith: *Si populus intelligat rationem sacerdotis, melius reducitur in Deum, et majori devotione respondet, Amen*[17]: that is, "If the people understand the priest, they are better brought to God, and with more devotion they answer, Amen."

It must needs be a miserable cause that is grounded only upon ignorance; for no man hateth the light but he that doth evil. Christ said to the Pharisees: "This is your time, and the power of darkness." If the people had understanding [Luke xxii.] of the truth, they would not suffer you thus to lead them into error as ye do, and have done. But I remember Plinius writeth that, notwithstanding the lion be a marvellous fierce and courageous beast, yet, if ye may once hoodwink him, or make him blind, ye may lead him whither ye list[18]. Thus much by the way I thought good to put you in remembrance, for that the strangeness of your doctrine so required: if ye had as much to shew of your side, I believe, of your courtesy ye would not hide it.

[9 Chrysost. Op. Par. 1718-38. In Epist. II. ad Cor. Hom. xviii. Tom. X. p. 568.]

[10 August. Op. Lib. de Magist. 2. Tom. I. col. 542; where we find *opus est.*]

[11 Justin. Princ. Novell. Constit. Basil. 1561. Const. cxxxvii. (al. cxxiii.) pp. 409, 10. See before, page 8, note 6.]

[12 See account of Cole's speech at this disputation contained in a letter of Jewel to Peter Martyr, printed by Burnet in the collection appended to Vol. III. Book VI. No. 49.]

[13 Concil. Tolet. IV cap. xxiv. in Corp. Jur. Canon. Decret. Gratian. Decr. Prima Pars. Dist. xxxviii. can. 1, where *est* is omitted.]

[14 Super omnia vero eis [dæmonibus] est tormentorum genera, et super omnes pœnas, si quem videant verbo Dei operam dare, scientiam divinæ legis et mysteria scripturarum intentis studiis perquirentem ...possident enim cunctos qui in ignorantia vivunt.—Orig. Op. Par. 1733-59. In Num. Hom. xxvii. 8. Tom. II. p. 378.]

[15 The translation after *ignorantia* is omitted, 1560.]

[16 Cyril. Alex. Op. Lut. 1638. Cont. Julian. Lib. VII. Tom. VI. p. 234.]

[17 Bibl. cum Gloss. Ord. et Expos. N. de Lyr. Basil. 1502. In 1 Cor. xiv. Pars VI. fol. 55. 2; where we find *orationem seu benedictionem sacerdotis,* and *devotius respondet.*]

[18 C. Plin. Secund. Nat. Hist. Lib. VIII. cap. xvi.]

SARUM.

Ye see I disadvantage myself of many things that might be spoken; for at this present I have not leisure to write books.

COLE.

I pray you, take good leisure, and write effectually.

THE REPLY. SARUM.

A doctor of law, and a man of wisdom, should bring more learning and fewer scorns.

SARUM.

Now must I needs desire you, forasmuch as I have followed your mind so far, either to bring me one doctor of your side, or else to give us leave to think ye have none.

COLE.

I wis ye know I may not, nor the case I stand in requireth it not.

THE REPLY. SARUM.

I wis ye know ye cannot, and therefore ye do best to say ye may not.

SARUM.

Ye desire us to leave talking against you, and no more to deal so unmercifully with you in the pulpits. Alas, master doctor, call ye this unmerciful dealing? What was then your dealing, when ye were in place? If ye remember, ye could never vouchsafe to call us other than schismatics, heretics, or traitors, in your pulpits; and yet, besides all that, ye used our bodies as ye know. We only tell the people, as our duty is, that ye withstand the manifest truth, and yet have neither scripture, nor doctor, nor council for you, and that ye have shewed such extremity, as the like hath not been seen, and now can give no reckoning why; or, if ye can, let it appear.

COLE.

Ye misreport me. I said, If men of your side used themselves traitorously to queen Mary, as none of us do now. Not manifest, until it be better proved: ye had but the law: ye require more than any law will bear against us.

THE REPLY. SARUM.

If they were traitors, why did ye burn them as heretics? The matter would be too odious to shew what hath been wrought by men of your side against their princes. But as I then never liked them that drew their sword against their sovereign, even so now I pray God confound them, whosoever they be, that shall first begin the same.

What law ye ministered us in those days, I remit it unto you that are a lawyer. But I am well assured ye shewed us neither divinity nor humanity. But I pray you, what law had ye to imprison such even[1] as had broken no law; and so to keep them in your coal-houses, in stocks and fetters, with all extremity and cruelty, until ye had made a law for them, and to do with them as Cyril saith the Jews did with Christ? *Primum ligant, deinde causas in eum quærunt: prius captum habent, quam accusatum*[2]: "First, they bind him fast," saith Cyril "and then they devise matter against him: they lay hands upon him before any man accuse him."

[[1] Men, 1560.] [[2] Cyril. Alex. Op. Lut. 1638. Comm. in Joan. Evang. Lib. xi. Tom. IV. p. 1025.]

What law had ye to burn the queen's subjects' hands with candles or torches[3], before they were condemned to die by any law?

What law had ye to ascite a man to appear, *peremptorie*, at Rome, within fourscore days, and yet that notwithstanding to keep him still in prison in Oxford; and afterward for not appearing at his day at Rome to condemn him there as obstinate[4]?

Or what law had ye to put the same man to death, against the express words of your own law, after he had subscribed unto you, and was found in no relapse? I trust ye can say somewhat herein, for that you, being then a lawyer, and in commission, had the execution of the[5] law. But I believe, when ye have searched your books through, ye shall find ye had not so much law as they that said: *Nos* [John xix.]
habemus legem, et secundum legem debet mori.

SARUM.

Where ye say, our doctrine is yet in doubt, I assure you to us it is most certain and out of doubt. But if ye, for your part, be yet in doubt, reason and charity would ye had been better resolved, and quite out of doubt, before ye had dealt so unmercifully with your brethren.

COLE.

I doubted more than I do now: ye give me good cause to be well confirmed.

THE REPLY. SARUM.

This is a fair shift of rhetoric, when other help faileth you. Even thus the Pharisees, after they had been long in a mammering, and in doubt of Christ, at the last were fully confirmed and out of doubt, and said unto him: *Jam scimus* [John viii.]
te habere dæmonium. As if they should then have said unto Christ, as you say now to us: We doubted more before than we do now; for now ye give us good cause to be well confirmed. But if I have confirmed you, bringing such proofs as ye are not able to answer, how then, think ye, have others cause to be confirmed at your hands, that have used such extremity, and yet are able to bring nothing at all?

SARUM.

Ye are bound, ye say, and may not dispute: yet are ye not so bound as ye have bound others. But when ye were at liberty, and a free disputation was granted and offered at Westminster, before the queen's majesty's most honourable council, and the whole state of the realm, I pray you, whether part was it that then gave over? And yet then, ye know, ye were not bound, unless it were to silence, because ye had nothing to say.

COLE.

At Westminster we came to dispute, and were answered, that there was none appointed, where we refused not to write neither. But, when our book could not be read as yours was, we refused not utterly to dispute, but only in the case, if our book could not be suffered to be read as indifferently as yours was. Now hardly weigh whether ye have indifferently reported, that we utterly refused to dispute with you, or no.

THE REPLY. SARUM.

Ye could not lightly have gotten so many untruths together without some study. Where ye say, ye were answered, there was no disputation appointed at Westminster; if I should ask you who made you that answer, I reckon ye would be to seek[6]. For I trust ye have not yet forgotten, that ye yourself were the first

[3 Thomas Tomkins, and Rose Allen.—Fox, Acts and Mon. Lond. 1684. Vol. III. pp. 154, 5, 697, 8.]

[4 Archbishop Cranmer.—Ibid. pp. 555, 6.]

[5 That, 1560.]

[6 Seeking, 1560.]

man that began to dispute there that day, and spake there an whole hour together without interruption. But I marvel ye say not that we of our part gave you over, and refused to dispute.

Ye say, ye refused not to write your allegations and answers, as ye had promised to do, and earnestly required it might be so; and yet, contrary to your request and promise, ye could not be gotten, as ye know, to write one line.

Ye say, your book could not be read as ours was; and yet ye know ye had no book there to be read at all, as we had.

As for the indifferent ordering and hearing of the matters, I remit that to them that were the orders[1] of it, of whom ye cannot in any wise complain, but both your own and the hearers' consciences must needs accuse you.

The order of the disputation was, that both parts should the first day bring in their assertion[2] all in writing, and that the next day either party should answer the other's book, and that also by writing; which was your own request, as it will appear by your protestation sent to the council in that behalf. The first day ye came without any book at all, contrary to the order taken, and also, as I have said, to your own request. The second day ye refused to proceed any farther, and stood only upon this point, that, unless ye might have the last word, ye would not dispute. For ye said, whosoever might have that, were like to *discedere*
Dr Skot and Feckenham. *cum applausu;* for these very words two of your own company uttered in Latin, even by the same terms as I do now; otherwise ye said ye would not dispute. Which answer was so vain, that not only the rest of the hearers, but also the bishop, that then was, of York, your own friend, found fault with it, and was ashamed of it, and bade you proceed. In conclusion, contrary to all men's looking for, only upon your refusal, the disputation was suddenly broken off. And I am content to stand to the judgment of all the hearers herein, whether I have reported indifferently, or no.

SARUM.

Ye say, ye remain still in the faith ye were baptized in. O master doctor, stand not too much upon that point. Ye know ye have already forsaken a great number of things that were thought necessary when ye were baptized. And yet, besides that, how many times have some of you altered your faith within the space of twenty years? Remember well yourself, who wrote the book, *De Vera Obedientia,* against the supremacy
Gardiner. of Rome? *Who commended it with his preface? *Who set it forth
* Bonner. * Tunstall. * Doctor Cole, and almost all the rest. in solemn sermons? *Who confirmed it with open oath?

COLE.

What one thing am I gone from? Ye say much, and prove little. Ye mean the old bishop of Winchester, who repented at the hour of his death. And where ye mean I condescended to the primacy of king Henry at my first coming home, or I had laboured the matter, ye did the like yourself: for in queen Mary's time ye subscribed to the articles, some of them we are entered to talk in, to your no less blame than mine. There be in this town that both saw you subscribe, and can bring forth your hand.

THE REPLY. SARUM.

Yes, I think ye are gone from one thing at the least, besides pardons and pilgrimages. I meant not doctor Gardiner to pull him out of his grave, and to torment him, being dead, as ye did master Bucer, master Fagius in Cambridge, doctor Peter Martyr's wife in Oxford[3], and others more; but only that I would not have you build too much upon your constancy, which hitherto hath been found to be even as the pleasure of the prince.

But he repented him, ye say, when he saw he should needs die. I trust he did so; for he had good cause so to do. But if he repented himself of his book that he had written so stoutly against the pope, why did he not recant it in all his

[1 Orderers, 1560, 1609.] [2 Assertions, 1560.] [3 Oxon, 1560.]

life-time? why did he not revoke his error openly? why held he his peace? why dissembled he so deeply for the space of twenty years together?

Ye say, it was only at your first coming home from Italy that ye condescended to the primacy of king Henry. Here must I put you in remembrance that ye continued therein still all king Henry's time out, even until the death of king Edward and the coming in of queen Mary. And if her grace had continued out to have entitled herself the supreme head of the church of England, as she did a great while after her first entry, and that (as it is to be thought) without burden of her conscience, I doubt not then but ye would have talked better with yourself, and continued so still. All this meanwhile ye came to the church, ye said, and heard the common prayers, ye ministered, and received the communion, and in all your doings bare yourself as any other subject of this realm: and thus held out, as I said, for the space of twenty years: I may say to you, this was a good long coming home. Therefore I may well thus conclude, and ye must needs confess the same, that either ye deceived the people then by your example, and conformity of all your doings, allowing that religion for good which in your conscience ye knew to be naught; or else that ye be a dissembler, and deceive the people now, making them, as much as in you lieth, by your example, to think this religion to be naught, which in your conscience and knowledge ye find to be godly and good. So that, whatsoever judgment ye have now, or heretofore have had of this religion, it must needs appear that either ye be now, or else have been, a deceiver of the people. But after ye had laboured the matter better, and, as ye say, had read the doctors, I pray you, what doctor found ye that ever told you, either that the pope ought to have the supremacy of the whole church, or that the prince in his own church ought not to have it?

But I have subscribed, ye say, as well as ye, and my hand is to be seen, and there be some that saw me when I did it. These proofs were needful, if I had denied the fact. But I have confessed it openly, and unrequired, in the midst of the congregation[4]. The arguments that ye made were so terrible; ye concluded altogether with fire and fagot. I confess I should have done otherwise; but, if I had not done as I did, I had not been here now to encounter with you: if ye should now be apposed with the like conclusions, I doubt not but ye would be glad to do as both ye yourself and your fellows have done heretofore.

SARUM.

Ye have *Ecclesiam Apostolicam*, ye say, and we have none: yet ye know, in all these matters that we now entreat of, we have the old doctors' church, the ancient councils' church, the primitive church, St Peter's church, St Paul's church, and Christ's church. And this, I believe, unless ye can bring me good reason to the contrary, may be called the apostles' church. And I marvel much that ye, having, as ye know, none of all these churches, or any shadow or token of them, yet[5] should so boldly say ye have *Ecclesiam Apostolicam*.

COLE.

To this, and some part of the article[6], ye shall be answered in the end of this writing; as I before said.

SARUM.

Where ye say ye make no innovations, it is no marvel: for in a manner all things were altered to your hand[7]; as may most evidently appear by all these matters that be now in question: wherein ye have utterly changed and abolished the order of the primitive church, and do nothing else but the contrary. And what evident profit the church of God hath gotten by it, I think it a hard matter for you to declare.

[4 At Frankfort.] [5 Ye, 1560.] [6 The next article, 1560.] [7 Hands, 1560.]

COLE.

What needeth so much of one thing? This serveth you to seem to say too much.

THE REPLY. SARUM.

This answer is so short, that it concludeth nothing.

SARUM.

Ye would have the matter turned over to some such general council as we would be content to stand unto; howbeit that ye think will not be in your time. Notwithstanding, this I dare boldly say, such a council will be a great while before ye shall find any doctor or old council to serve your purpose. But if there never be such a council, yet truth will be truth, notwithstanding. For the council cannot make falsehood[1] truth; but that thing that it taketh for truth it certifieth only to be true.

COLE.

I grant.

SARUM.

But what redress can there be looked for at such a council, whereas no man shall be judge, or suffered to speak one way or other, but only such as be openly and justly accused and found faulty? and whereas he that is himself most out of order shall be head and reformer of the whole?

COLE.

Such fond excuses men lay: how true, let other men judge.

THE REPLY. SARUM.

Ye know that in your own law there was evermore *Exceptio judicis incompetentis.* And by what law can ye find that a man may be a competent judge in his own cause? If the indifferent using of the matter may be tried by experience, in this your last general council holden at Trident, ye know that not one man of our side, notwithstanding there were a great number of them there, sent thither of purpose by their princes, could be suffered to sit among the rest, or to have a voice, or to yield a reason of his faith. And pope Julius the Third[2] gave out under his brief, that none of them all should be heard there, unless it were, as he said, to recant their errors.

And notwithstanding Pighius himself had confessed there were open errors in the mass[3]; notwithstanding Latomus[4], a doctor of your own, had confessed a great abuse in the communion under one kind[5]; notwithstanding Pius the Second, bishop of Rome, had seen and confessed great abuse in the restraining of priests' marriage[6]; yet in the same council they concluded among themselves, that no manner of thing should be changed at all that had been once received in their church. Therefore these be not fond excuses: the world seeth they be too true.

SARUM.

Both parties, ye say, have waded so far herein, that now they can go no farther, and therefore ye would have either party let other alone.

[1 Falsehead, 1560.]

[2 And the pope, Julius third, 1560, 1609.]

[3 Alb. Pigh. Explic. Cathol. Contr. Par. 1586. Controv. VI. fol. 123. 2.]

[4 Latonus, 1560.]

[5 Latomus fully acknowledges that in the primitive church the sacrament was given to the laity under both kinds; but then he goes on speaking of the change...in quo non est dicendum quod patres aliquid evangelii aut mutaverint aut prætermiserint, sed quod aliquid viderunt Spiritu sancto ecclesiam suam regente, quod prædecessores latuit.—Latom. Op. Lovan. 1550. Cont. Art. M. Luther, Art. iii. fol. 36. 2. See also the discussion on this point of Latomus with Bucer.]

[6 Sacerdotibus magna ratione sublatas nuptias, majori restituendas videri.—Platin. De Vit. Pont. Col. 1551. Pius II. p. 295.]

This ye say now, because ye see ye are called to an audit, and are not able to make your account. But, if ye of your part had been so indifferent when time was, many a godly man had now been alive.

COLE.

Ye forget yourself, I say not so perdy: look better in the place.

THE REPLY. SARUM.

If ye meant not so, it skilleth not greatly; it is to small purpose: consider it well, and ye shall find my conclusion true.

SARUM.

Where ye say, ye would have the sayings of both parties weighed by the balance of the old doctors, ye see that is our special request unto you; and that in the matters you writ[7] of, I desired even so to be tried. But why throw ye away these balance? and, being so oftentimes required, why be ye so loth to shew forth but one old doctor of your side? Ye make folk believe ye would not have the matter come to trial: only ye set forth the empty names of St Augustine, of St Hierome, of St Chrysostom, of St Basil, of St Cyprian, of Tertullian, of Irenæus, of Dionysius, of the councils, &c.; as the apothecaries set forth their painted boxes, and oftentimes nothing in them. Ye shew me only the names of the doctors which I knew before; but ye shew me not one word in them of the private mass, or of the rest of the matters that lie between us. If ye could have found anything in them for your purpose, I believe ye would not have brought them empty.

Ye say, all these matters be already determined. But where, I pray you? or in what general council? This is it that I would so gladly know at your hand; and that, ye say, ye have, and yet so ungently keep it from me.

COLE.

Then begin, if ye think the time will serve, or put it over till another time. All these be but words often repeated, and answered already.

THE REPLY. SARUM.

I have offered and begun in vain; for ye keep yourself off, and will not come to answer. These words, I grant, have been upon good occasion oftentimes repeated; and I think ye would say somewhat to them, if ye were able.

SARUM.

Ye say, I slanderously misreport the late council of Constance. O good master doctor, these words savour too much of your choler, and might better have been spared. I spake more favourably of that council than I might have done. The words of the council be these, speaking namely of the communion under both kinds: *Pertinaciter asserentes oppositum*[8], *tanquam hæretici arcendi sunt*[9]. By these words they, that maintain the manifest ordinance of Christ, and the practice of the apostles, are not called schismatics, as I said, but stubborn and wilful heretics. Ye see, therefore, my report was more favourable than the council deserved.

[7 Write, 1560.] [8 Appositum, 1560.]
[9 Concil. Constant. in Concil. Stud. Labb. et Cossart. Lut. Par. 1671—2. Sess. xiii. Tom. XII. col. 100. See before, page 35, note 4.]

COLE.

Ye say, the council of Constance openly pronounced against Christ. Wherein, I pray you? because the fathers there said, Whoso saith it is of necessity to receive under both kinds, and the approved custom of the church is sacrilege, is to be taken as an heretic; and yet none[1] *heretic, but in a wrong opinion. Then belike ye can bring in some text, where Christ commanded it should not be received but under both kinds, which ye can never do: so is your report of this council slanderous still. Read* 4. Canonem Concilii Constantiensis.

THE REPLY. SARUM.

It grieveth you that I should say the council decreed against Christ; but consider it aright, and ye shall find it. Christ, as ye know, appointed the communion under both kinds, and commanded his disciples to do the same as he had done it. Therefore he that commandeth the contrary, and that under the pain of heresy, pronounceth openly against Christ.

Ye call it an approved custom of the church. Yet[2] remember St Cyprian's words that be alleged in your own decrees: *Christus non dicit, Ego sum consuetudo, sed ego sum veritas*[3]*:* that is to say, "Christ saith not, I am custom, but I am the truth." But if custom might justly prevail against an open and plain truth, I pray you, where was your communion under one kind ever at any time since the beginning of the world allowed for a general custom? Or, being but a particular custom, as it is, and that received only of yourself, in what general council was it ever allowed?

Ye say, your own ordinances may not be broken without the authority of a general council. And dare ye without any such authority, only upon a vain and particular custom, to break the universal ordinance of Christ?

Ye say, men are not to be judged heretics that withstand your order herein, but only to be in a wrong opinion. Here I see that ye and your brethren agree not in judgment both together, and therefore ye shall the less marvel if we disagree from you, and mistrust you both. For Hosius, a doctor of your side, is not afraid to call it heresy, and sacrilege: his words be plain. *Nunc hæresin profert, seque pollicetur ostensurum, omnes esse impios, qui utriusque speciei communionem laicis denegant*[4]. And again: *An autem idem in regno tuo factum non vidimus? ubi calix per summum sacrilegium usurpatur?* And again: *Vellem autem unam mihi terram aliquam ostendi, ubi privata libidine calix usurpari cœptus est, in qua non e vestigio multæ sint aliæ et quidem horribiles hæreses consequutæ*[5]. Thus, to do that thing that Christ and his apostles and all the old fathers did in the primitive church, without exception, this doctor concludeth it to be an horrible heresy.

And if it were taken for no heresy, as ye say it was not, then was your council too much to blame that gave so cruel sentence against the people of Bohemia, for that they thought it necessary to use both kinds, according to the institution of Christ, and pronounced thus against them, *Tanquam hæretici arcendi sunt.* For if they take them for no heretics, they did them great wrong to punish them as heretics. And yet is your doctor Hosius too much to blame to condemn any thing for heresy, without any word of God, and specially without the authority of any old doctor, or any general council.

Ye ask me what text I can bring forth, wherein Christ commanded that the communion should be received under both kinds. The institution of Christ, and his commandment thereunto annexed, as methinketh, is text good enough to him that will be ruled by Christ. I will not ask ye, what text ye can bring wherein Christ hath commanded you to minister the communion in one kind. But this only would I know, what text ye can bring whereby a priest, minis-

---

[1 No, 1560.] [2 Yet ye, 1560, 1609.]

[3 Corp. Jur. Canon. Lugd. 1624. Decret. Gratian. Decr. Prima Pars, Dist. viii. can. 5. col. 24. But the words there are not Cyprian's, though that father is cited in the canon. See before, page 49, note 14.]

[4 Hos. Op. Col. 1584. De Utr. Spec. Comm. Dial. Tom. I. p. 649; where we find *mox* for *nunc*.]

[5 Ibid. p. 656; where the ideas, though not the precise words as above quoted, may be found.]

tering the sacrament, is commanded to receive it in both kinds, more than any other layman. I know your answer; ye must needs say, the institution of Christ. And yet, by your own interpretation, if a priest communicate himself under one kind, Gelasius calleth it *sacrilegium;* which thing I reckon he would not have said, if he had not thought it contrary to the open words and institution of Christ.

Again, what text can ye bring whereby, as touching this point, the priest hath any privilege above the people? If ye can find none, as indeed ye shall never be able, then that that is sacrilege in the priest is also sacrilege in the people.

Again, what text can ye bring whereby Christ hath precisely forbidden any man to baptize only in the name of the Holy Ghost? Undoubtedly ye can find none in all the scriptures, but only Christ's institution. And yet whosoever would decree that such kind of baptism should be used, I trow ye would say he decreed against Christ, because he breaketh the institution of Christ.

Even so doth your council of Constance in the matter we last talked of. Therefore my words are true still; and yet ye (ye must give me leave to say the truth) have concluded with a slander.

Touching the thing itself, ye are so certain of it, that none of you all can tell at what time it first began. But this ye know well, if ye list to be known of it, that it began neither[6] in Christ's time, nor in the apostles' time, nor in the old doctors' time, nor within the compass of seven hundred years after Christ. And therefore if a man should ask you of your communion under one kind, *De cœlo est, an ex hominibus?* ye must needs answer, it came not from heaven, forasmuch as it hath no testimony of God's word, but only crept in (as Stephen Gardiner confesseth) by a superstitious negligence in the people.

SARUM.

Where ye say, ye could never yet find the error of one general council, I trow this escaped you for default of memory. Albertus Pighius, the greatest learned man of your side, hath found out such errors to our hands: namely, in his book that he calleth *Ecclesiastica Hierarchia,* speaking of the second council holden at Ephesus, which ye cannot deny but it was general, and yet took part with the heretic, abbat Eutyches, against the godly man Flavianus, he writeth thus: *Concilia universalia, etiam congregata legitime, ut bene, ita perperam, injuste, impieque judicare ac definire possunt*[7]*;* that is: "General councils, yea, even such as be lawfully summoned, as they may conclude things well, so may they likewise judge and determine things rashly, unjustly, and wickedly."

COLE.

Ye ground yourself upon Pighius' error; for Pighius holdeth the council of Ephesus was general, which the council of Chalcedon denieth. So that I marvel much herein of you, that ye allege that for a council which hath no place in the book of councils.

THE REPLY. SARUM.

In Pighius' words there are two things to be noted. The one is, that he saith a general council may err in faith; the other, that he saith the second council of Ephesus was general. And, forasmuch as ye challenge him only for the latter, I think ye will agree with him in the first; which to my purpose is sufficient.

But here ye cause me to marvel what ye mean to make so little account of Pighius; for he, as ye know, hath been taken for the chiefest champion of your side.

Pighius saith the council of Ephesus was general; and ye say it was not so. Ye must give me leave to say the truth: if the matter come to a *quid*

[6 Nother, 1560.]

[7 See before, page 35, note 6.]

dicunt, Pighius will be taken in the country for a man as well learned and as skilful in the councils as doctor Cole. Ye should not so little esteem the doctors of your own side, lest that, being not able to allege any old doctor, and refusing the new, it may happily be thought ye have neither old nor new. And yet, when ye were before the queen's majesty's commissioners at Lambeth, ye said openly there that Pighius is full of errors. But forasmuch as ye yourself have[1] begun to find fault with your own doctors, I trust hereafter ye will the better bear with us, if we sometime shall do the same. Here ye drive me to use the more words, partly to defend Pighius in his right, and partly to make you see how wilfully ye withstand an open truth, having so little to the contrary. And as ye shall be found true in this, even so am I well content to take you in all the rest.

First, Nicephorus[2], and Evagrius[3], that write the whole story and order of the council of Ephesus, never denied it to be general.

Theodosius the emperor, that summoned the bishops together, as it may appear by his words, took it to be general. For thus he writeth to the council: *Cogitantes non esse tutum absque vestra sancta synodo, et ubique sanctarum ecclesiarum præsulibus, hujusmodi quæstionem de fide*[4] *renovari, necessarium duximus vestram sanctitatem convenire*[5]. These words, *sanctarum ecclesiarum, quæ ubique sunt,* import a generality of all churches through the world. Farther, there was the emperor's authority, the bishop of Rome's legate, (which, as some men think, maketh up all together,) and other bishops of all nations. And how could such a council not be general?

Your doctors of Paris have concluded thus, *Articulo* XXII: *Quod autem magistri nostri dicunt de legitima congregatione, notandum est ad hoc*[6], *ut concilium legitime congregetur, sufficere, quod solemnitas et forma juris solemniter sit servata: quia si quis trahere vellet hoc in disputationem, utrum prælati, qui ibi sedent, habeant rectam intentionem, et utrum sint docti, et utrum habeant scientiam sacrarum literarum, et animum obediendi sanæ doctrinæ, esset processus in infinitum*[7]. That is to say: "Whereas our doctors speak of a lawful council, we must mark, that to this, that the council be lawfully gathered, it shall be sufficient that the solemnity and form of law be solemnly observed. For if we should move question, whether the bishops that sit in council have a godly meaning, and whether they be learned, and whether they have understanding of the scriptures, and whether they mind to submit themselves to sound doctrine, then should we never have done." Thus it is decreed by your doctors, that neither godly meaning, nor learning, nor knowledge of the scriptures, nor obedience unto sound doctrine, is to be weighed in the bishops that rule the council, but only a certain solemnity and form of law.

Dioscorus, that was president of the same council (and his words be reported in the council of Chalcedon) saith thus: *Theodosius confirmavit omnia quæ judicata sunt a sancta et universali synodo generali*[8]: "Theodosius," saith he, "hath confirmed all such things as were determined by this universal and general council." Here ye see, it is called an universal and a general council. And afterward in the same council of Chalcedon ye shall find these words: *Sanctissimæ, et Domino amantissimæ, universali synodo congregatæ in Epheso metropoli*[9]: "To the holy, beloved unto the Lord, the universal council gathered in the mother city of Ephesus."

[[1] Hath, 1560.]

[[2] Niceph. Callist. Hist. Eccles. Lut. Par. 1630. Lib. XIV. cap. xlvii. Tom. II. pp. 546, &c.]

[[3] Evagr. Scholast. in Hist. Eccles. Script. Amst. 1695-1700. Lib. II. capp. ix. x. pp. 266, 7.]

[[4] Fidei, 1609, 1611.]

[[5] Imp. Epist. ad Synod. Ephes. Secund. in Concil. Chalced. in Concil. Stud. Labb. et Cossart. Lut. Par. 1671-2. Tom. IV. cols. 109, 10.]

[[6] Hæc, 1560.]

[[7] The doctors of Paris published a censure upon certain doctrines held by Luther. The 22nd article is as follows: Certum est concilium generale legitime congregatum, universalem repræsentans ecclesiam, in fidei et morum determinationibus errare non posse.—Decret. Fidel. tenend. per Facult. Theol. Paris. in Ord. Digest. xxii. in Coll. Judic. Stud. D'Argent. Lut. Par. 1728-36. Tom. I. p. 414. It is to this and consequent explanations probably that reference is made in the text.]

[[8] Diosc. in Concil. Calched. in Concil. Stud. Labb. et Cossart. Tom. IV. cols. 111, 2; where we find *generali lege*: νόμῳ γενικῷ.]

[[9] Libell. Confess. Eutych. in eod. cols. 133, 4.]

But if perhaps ye doubt of these words, because the one was Eutyches, the other was Dioscorus, by whom they were spoken (howbeit, notwithstanding they were heretics, yet could they not lightly make an open lie in a matter that was so evident), then read ye the old father Liberatus, that was *Archidiaconus Carthaginensis*, and lived under Vigilius, bishop of Rome, at the least a thousand years ago, and writeth the very story of this council: his words be these: *Fit Ephesi generale concilium, ad quod convenerunt Flavianus,...et Eutyches, tanquam judicandi*[10]: "There is appointed," saith he, "at Ephesus a general council, in the which Flavianus and Eutyches made their appearance, as men standing to be judged." Now if ye will say that *generale concilium* is not in English "a general council," then I would it might be put over to some other court. O master doctor, if ye meant nothing else but truth, ye would not do as ye do.

Thus much have I written in the defence of your doctor Pighius, for that I saw him accused of you without cause.

SARUM.

And of the councils holden of late years at Constance and Basil, where as pope John and pope Eugenius were deposed, he saith plainly, that they decreed both against reason, and against nature, and against all examples of antiquity, and also against the word of God[11]. And yet both these councils were called general.

COLE.

Wherein doth Pighius prove the councils of Constance and Basil to have erred? Marry, because they decreed the general council to be above the pope. If ye take these two councils to have erred in these points, ye are a greater papist than I am: for I hold herein rather with Gerson. I trow this be one place that ye wrote not yourself. Yet I reckon no error proved in any general council by that ye have yet said.

THE REPLY. SARUM.

Yes, I assure you, master doctor, I put in this place and all the rest myself alone without conference. And yet, God be thanked, I can find nothing in your writings but such as any man may soon guess it came only from yourself alone. Ye take exception before with that I alleged the council of Basil, and sent me word that no such thing could be found. But now I see ye are better advised.

As touching Pighius, I[12] used his authority herein, as St Paul, to reprove them that denied the resurrection, used the authority of them that baptized for the dead; not for that he thought such baptism well ministered, but only for that it serveth[13] to his purpose. For I shewed you not what I thought myself, but what Pighius your great doctor thought, and what ye yourself must needs think, unless ye will pull down your own doctrine, and set the pope himself and all his adherents upon your top.

But if ye take part with Gerson, as ye say you[14] do, mark how the chief pillar of your building begins to shake.

If the pope be head of the church, as ye say, and the council be but *ecclesia repræsentativa*, that is, "a resemblance of the church," as your canonists and schoolmen say; how can it be but the pope by your own saying (whether Gerson will or nil) must needs be head of the council? for he that is head of the whole must also be head of the part; unless perhaps ye will say, the part is greater than the whole. Of these grants of yours there followeth consequently great inconvenience against yourself.

[[10] Liberat. Breviar. Par. 1675. cap. xii. p. 73.]
[[11] See before page 35, note 7.]
[[12] He, 1560.]
[[14] Ye, 1560.]
[[13] Served, 1560.]

Ye say, The pope is not above the council. *Ergo*, may some other man say, he is much less above the whole church.

Again: The pope is not above the church. *Ergo*, he is not head of the church.

But, all this notwithstanding, ye say the council is above the pope. And yet ye know that even now, whatsoever is decreed in any general council, there is evermore devolution made to the pope, as unto him that is thought to be above the council, and without whom nothing may be concluded.

Have ye forgotten that pope Pius and pope Julius of late years commanded there should no appeal be made from the pope to any council[1]?

Have ye forgotten that the last general council holden at Trident concluded thus at the end, *Salva semper in omnibus sedis apostolicæ auctoritate*[2]; as confessing openly that they took the pope to be above the council?

Have ye forgotten that your own doctors say, *Papa est fons omnis juris:* "The pope is the fountain of all manner law;" and, *Papa habet omnia jura in scrinio pectoris sui*[3]: "The pope hath all law under the secret of his breast?"

Have ye forgotten what it[4] is written in the pope's own decretals, *Extra, de Electione et Electi Potestate: Si totus mundus sentiet in aliquo contra papam, videtur quod standum sit sententiæ papæ*[5]: "If all the world should give sentence in any matter against the pope, it appeareth, for all that, we ought to stand to the determination of the pope?"

Have ye forgotten that it[6] is written in your own councils, *Papa a nemine judicatur:* "The pope is judged of no man?" and a jolly reason joined to the same, *Quia non est discipulus supra magistrum*[7]:" "For there is no scholar above his master?"

Have ye forgotten that that is written in your decrees, *Neque ab Augusto, neque a regibus, neque a toto clero, neque a populo, judex judicabitur*[8]: "The judge," that is to say, the pope, "shall be judged neither[9] by the emperor, nor[5] by kings, nor by the whole clergy, nor by the people?"

And again: *Aliorum hominum causas voluit Deus per homines terminare; sed hujus sedis præsulem suo sine quæstione servavit arbitrio*[10]: "Other men's causes God would have to be determined and ruled by men; but the bishop of this see, out of all doubt, he reserved only to his own judgment.

And again: *Facta subditorum judicantur a nobis, nostra autem a solo Deo*[11]: "The doings of our subjects are judged by us; but our doings are judged only by God."

Have ye[12] forgotten that your schoolmen say, *Papa habet jus infragabile, de quo non licet disputare*[13]: "The pope hath a right that no man may withstand, of which right no man may dispute?"

Have ye forgotten that is written in your decretals, *De Translatione Episcopi*, in the gloss, [*Papa*] *naturam rerum immutat, substantialia unius rei applicando*

[[1] Pii II. Epist. Greg. Heymb. denunc. in Fascic. Rer. Expet. et Fug. Lond. 1690. Tom. II. p. 125. See also Bull. Leon. X. adv. Luth. in Concil. Stud. Labb. et Cossart. Tom. XIV. cols. 396, 7.]

[[2] Concil. Trident. in eod. Sess. VII. Decr. de Ref. Tom. XIV. col. 779. Sess. XXV. De Ref. cap. xxi. col. 917.]

[[3] Bonifac. VIII. in Corp. Jur. Canon. Lugd. 1624. Sext. Decretal. Lib. I. Tit. ii. cap. 1. col. 11; where we find *censetur habere:* some of the words also are transposed.]

[[4] *It* is omitted, 1560, 1609.]

[[5] Corp. Jur. Canon. Lugd. 1624. Decret. Gratian. Decr. Sec. Pars, Caus. IX. Quæst. iii. Gloss. in can. 13. col. 877; where we read *sententiaret in aliquo negotio*, and *quod sententiæ papæ standum esset.*]

[[6] *It* is omitted, 1560.]

[[7] Neque præsul summus a quoquam judicabitur, quoniam scriptum est: Non est discipulus super magistrum.—Concil. Rom. II. sub Silvestr. in Concil. Stud. Labb. et Cossart. Lut. Par. 1671—2. Epil. Tom. I. col. 1542.]

[[8] Innoc. Papa in Corp. Jur. Canon. Decret. Gratian. Decr. Sec. Pars, Caus. IX. Quæst. iii. can. 13. col. 877; where the reading is *neque ab omni clero, neque a regibus.* See also Conc. Rom. II. in Concil. Stud. Labb. et Cossart. cap. xx. Tom. I. col. 1556.]

[[9] Nother, 1560.]

[[10] Aliorum hominum causas Deus voluit homines terminare, sed sedis istius præsulis suo sine quæstione reservavit arbitrio.—Symmach. Papa in Corp. Jur. Canon. ibid. can. 14. col. 877.]

[[11] Anter. Papa in eod. ibid. can. 15. col. 878; where we find *nostra vero judicat Deus.*]

[[12] Yet, 1611.]

[[13] The following may be intended: Cuncta...novit ecclesia, quod ... Romana ecclesia fas de omnibus habeat judicandi: neque cuiquam de ejus liceat judicare judicio.—Gelas. in eod. ibid. can. 17. col. 878.]

alteri: et de nullo potest facere aliquid: et sententiam, quæ nulla est, facit aliquam: quia in his quæ vult, ei est pro ratione voluntas; nec est qui illi dicat, Cur ita facis[14]*?* That is: "He changeth the nature of things, applying the substantial parts of one thing to another; and of nothing he is able to make somewhat. And that that is no sentence, he maketh a good sentence. For in any thing that he willeth, his will standeth instead of reason. And there is no man that may say unto him, Why doest thou thus?"

Have ye forgotten the words of your own councils, *Papa non potest judicari:* "The pope cannot be judged?" and the same fortified with a good reason out of the words of the prophet Esay, who[15] spake in the person of God: *Quia scriptum est, Nunquid gloriabitur securis adversus eum qui secat cum ea*[16]*?* "Shall [Matt. xxviii. xviii.] the axe boast himself against him that heweth with it?" Or have ye forgotten that Hostiensis your own doctor writeth, *Papa est omnia et super omnia*[17]*:* "The pope is all, and above all?" which words St Paul speaketh only of Christ. So reverently the doctors of your side use God's holy scriptures.

Yet I pass by as great a number[18] of the like sentences to the same purpose. Thus ye see, if ye take part with Gerson, a great many of your own friends will fall out with you, and ye will be in hazard to be called an heretic.

Ye see by this, that the council of Constance and Basil, being both general, as Pighius saith, decreed a falsehood[19], and were in error; as ye yourself must needs confess, as well as Pighius, if ye will stand to your own doctrine. And therefore Cardinalis Cajetanus, one of your own side, saith that both these councils were afterward justly abrogate[20]; I think for that they were thought to have decreed amiss. And so both Gerson and you[21], by the judgment of all your brethren, remain still in error. And, when ye have sought out the bottom of your learning, I believe it will be hard for you to find any good sufficient cause why a general council may not as well be deceived[22] as a particular. For Christ's promises, *Ecce ego vobiscum sum;* and, *Ubicunque duo aut tres convenerint* [Isai. x.] *in nomine meo, ibi sum ego in medio illorum,* are made as well to the particular council, as to the general.

Howbeit, whether the council may err or no, ye know it availeth you but little to stand greatly to the defence of councils in these points, unless ye had some council to make for you. But like as the Romans, in old times, worshipped their god Vulcanus with all godly honour, and yet would never vouchsafe to give him a chapel within their town; even so ye, as it appeareth, can content yourselves[23] to honour the councils, and to have them ever in mouth, yet will ye not vouchsafe to take them near to you, and to be ordered by them. And therefore these words of yours are only of office, and of course, that the very countenance ye give the matter might make your reader believe that ye have all the councils of your side, and we have none.

But, alas! what reverence or regard have ye to the councils? The council of Nice appointed three patriarchs to rule the whole church, each of them within his precincts of like authority[24]: ye have broken this council, and given all the whole authority to one alone. The council holden at Eliberis decreed that there should be no kind of image of any thing that is worshipped painted in

---

[[14] Corp. Jur. Canon. Decretal. Greg. IX. Lib. I. De Transl. Episc. Tit. vii. Gloss. in cap. 3. col. 217; where for *alteri* we find *alii*, for *facere aliquid, aliquid facere*, and for *illi, ei.*]

[[15] *Who* is omitted, 1560.]

[[16] Nicol. Papa in eod. Decret. Gratian. Decr. Prima Pars, Dist. xxi. cap. 4. col. 96; where the words of the text quoted are slightly varied.]

[[17] Papa ergo super omnes est.—Hostiens. Op. Par. 1512. Super Quart. Decretal. Qui Fil. Sint Legit. fol. 37. Similar assertions are common in the voluminous works of this author. See Ibid. fol. 39; where many reasons are given in proof, papam esse majorem omnibus christianis; also In Extrav. Decr. Innoc. IV. De For. Comp. fol. 140. 2.]

[[18] A great number, 1560.] [[19] Falsehead, 1560.]

[[20] Cajetan in substance asserted this at the fifth Council of Lateran. See Orat. Cajetan. in Sess. ii. Concil. Later. v. in Concil. Stud. Labb. et Cossart. Tom. XIV. col. 74.]

[[21] Ye, 1560.]

[[22] Decreed, 1560.] [[23] Yourself, 1560.]

[[24] Τὰ ἀρχαῖα ἔθη κρατείτω, τὰ ἐν Αἰγύπτῳ καὶ Λιβύῃ καὶ Πενταπόλει, ὥστε τὸν Ἀλεξανδρείας ἐπίσκοπον πάντων τούτων ἔχειν τὴν ἐξουσίαν, ἐπειδὰν καὶ τῷ ἐν τῇ Ῥώμῃ ἐπισκόπῳ τοῦτο σύνηθές ἐστιν· ὁμοίως δὲ καὶ κατὰ τὴν Ἀντιόχειαν, καὶ ἐν ταῖς ἄλλαις ἐπαρχίαις, τὰ πρεσβεῖα σώζεσθαι ταῖς ἐκκλησίαις.—Concil. Nic. in Concil. Stud. Labb. et Cossart. can. 6. Tom. II. col. 32.]

the church[1]: ye have broken this council, and filled your churches full of images. The council of Antioch decreed that such as came into the church and heard the scriptures read, and abstained from the communion, should be excommunicate from the church[2]: ye have broken this council, and neither do ye read the scriptures in such sort as the people may perceive them, nor once exhort them to the communion. The council of Carthage commanded there should nothing be read in the church, but only the scriptures of God[3] : ye have broken this council, and read such legends and fables unto the people, as ye yourselves[4] know were manifest and open lies. The council of Rome, under pope Nicolas, commandeth that no man be present at the mass of a priest, whom he knoweth undoubtedly to keep a concubine, and that under the pain of excommunication[5]: yet he, whom ye would so fain have to be taken for the head of your church, not only hath broken this council, but also, for a certain ordinary tribute to be yearly paid, giveth his priest[6] free licence and dispensations, under his great seal, openly to keep concubines without controlment. And what need we more examples? Ye make the councils weigh as ye will; when ye list, as heavy as gold; again, when ye list, as light as feathers. Pope Julius the second called a council at Rome, only to overthrow the council of Pisa[7]. And the whole order of St Dominic's friars cried out shame upon the council of Basil, for that the bishops there had taken part with the Scotists against the Thomists touching original sin in our lady[8]. The council of Paris was scoffed at, and jested out of all parts, and until this day kept of no part. For our doctors of England said it had no power to sail over the sea. Egidius of Rome saith it was too heavy to climb over the Alps. Thus much for that ye seem to stand so earnestly to the defence of councils, having in these points not one council to allege for yourself.

SARUM.

Ye press me sore, that, if I write you not a book of my proofs, it will be thought I do it *conscientia imbecillitatis*. Belike ye have forgotten why ye, with all your company, not long since refused to enter into disputation with us at Westminster. Doubtless the greatest part thought it was, as it was indeed, *conscientia imbecillitatis*. And what think you[9] is there now thought in you, that, being so often required, yet cannot be won to bring so much as one poor sentence in your own defence? I have before alleged a few reasons of my part, which by order of disputation I was not bound to do. Now let the world judge whether of us both flieth conference.

COLE.

I have answered to this already. What order of disputations dischargeth you of proof? Yet remember, I came not to dispute, but to be taught.

[[1] Placuit, picturas in ecclesia esse non debere; ne quod colitur et adoratur in parietibus depingatur.—Concil. Elib. in eod. can. 36. Tom. I. col. 974.]

[[2] *Πάντας τοὺς εἰσιόντας εἰς τὴν ἐκκλησίαν τοῦ Θεοῦ, καὶ τῶν ἱερῶν γραφῶν ἀκούοντας, μὴ κοινωνοῦντας δὲ εὐχῆς ἅμα τῷ λαῷ, ἢ ἀποστρεφομένους τὴν μετάληψιν τῆς εὐχαριστίας κατά τινα ἀταξίαν, τούτους ἀποβλήτους γίνεσθαι τῆς ἐκκλησίας.*—Concil. Antioch. I. in eod. can. 2. Tom. II. col. 561.]

[[3] Item placuit, ut præter scripturas canonicas nihil in ecclesia legatur sub nomine divinarum scripturarum.—Concil. Carthag. III. in eod. can. 47. Tom. II. col. 1177.]

[[4] Yourself, 1560.]

[[5] Nullus missam audiat presbyteri, quem scit concubinam indubitanter habere, aut subintroductam mulierem. Unde etiam ipsa sancta synodus hoc capitulum sub excommunicatione statuit.—Concil. Roman. in eod. Tom. IX. col. 1099. See also Nicol. Papa in Corp. Jur. Canon. Decret. Gratian. Decr. Prima Pars, Dist. xxxii. can. 5. col. 156.]

[[6] Priests, 1560.]

[[7] Concil. Lateran. V. in Concil. Stud. Labb. et Cossart. Lut. Par. 1671-2. See especially Bull. Indict. Tom. XIV. cols. 30, &c.; also Bull. Sec. Sess. cols. 63, &c.]

[[8] Nos ... doctrinam illam disserentem gloriosam virginem Dei genetricem Mariam ... nunquam actualiter subjacuisse originali peccato, sed immunem semper fuisse ab omni originali et actuali culpa ... ab omnibus catholicis approbandam fore, tenendam et amplectendam, diffinimus et declaramus, &c.—Concil. Basil. in eod. Sess. xxxvi. Tom. XII. cols. 622, 3.]

[[9] Ye, 1560.]

THE REPLY. SARUM.

Ye have answered me by saying nothing; which I think ye would not have done, if ye had[10] any thing else to answer: from proof in this matter I am sufficiently discharged by the law of impossibility. For as he[11] said openly at Westminster (and once again I put you in remembrance of the same, because it is your own law), it is impossible to prove a negative. All your help is in the shadow and pretence of learning, whereby it appeareth well ye fly disputation. Ye were best to get some better cloke to hide you under; for these be but fig-leaves, and cover not your shame.

SARUM.

I protest before God, bring me but one sufficient sentence or authority in the matters I have required, and afterwards[12] I will gently and quietly confer with you farther at your pleasure. Wherefore, forasmuch as it is God's cause, if ye mean simply, deal simply; betray not your right, if ye may save it by speaking one word.

COLE.

If ye refuse to instruct me unless I bring some proof of my part, ye bid me to my cost. Ye bid me to a feast, where while I should take on me to prove your doctrine naught, I were like to forfeit my recognisance, which ye guilefully allure me unto.

THE REPLY. SARUM.

Ye hide yourself under your recognisance, and think ye walk invisible, as the ostrich, when he hath once couched his head under a little bough, though the rest of his body, which is great and large, stand open and uncovered, yet he thinketh no man can espy him. Although ye be sanded and set aground, yet ye keep up the sail still, as if ye had water at your will.

Ye say ye may not dispute lest ye should forfeit your recognisance. I would wish you to remember yourself, and to let the people understand the truth. Ye know ye are not bound in recognisance for disputing with any man; but for that, being required to disputations by the queen's most honourable council, and the place appointed, and great and worthy audience assembled to the same, ye gave over, as ye know, upon the sudden, and would not dispute at all. And therefore for your disobedience and contempt ye were bound in recognisance.

But, I pray you, were ye thus bound in queen Mary's time too, as well as now? Or, if ye were not bound, how happened it that ye never durst allege one ancient doctor in these matters all that while? Remember your own words: ye said, a little before, that ye brought more than we were able to answer, notwithstanding it were, as ye said, nor scriptures, nor councils, nor doctors. And further[13], I pray you, were all the rest of the doctors of your side, Pighius, Eckius, Hosmasterius, Bunderius, &c., bound in recognisance as well as you[14]? Or, if they were not bound, why were they so dainty of their doctors, that in these matters they could never vouchsafe to allege one? Look better upon your recognisance: I cannot believe ye should be so free to scoff and to scorn, more than either divinity or good humanity would bear withal, and only be forbidden to do that thing which of all good reason ye ought most to do; or that ye should be restrained from the alleging of St Augustine, St Hierome, St Ambrose, St Chrysostom, St Basil, &c., and have a privilege only to allege Aristotle, Horace, the decrees, the decretals, the gloss, Gerson, Driedo, Royard, and Tapper, such men as I never could have thought had been canonized and allowed for doctors of the church. Augustus Cæsar on a time, as he was passing through Rome, and saw certain strange women lulling apes and whelps in their arms, "What," said he, "have the women of these countries none other

[10 Had had, 1560.] [11 Ye, 1560.] [12 Afterward, 1560.] [13 Farther, 1560.] [14 Ye, 1560.]

children?" So may I say unto you that make so much of Gerson, Driedo, Royard, and Tapper, Have the learned men of your side none other doctors? For, alas! these that ye allege are scarcely worthy to be allowed amongst the black guard. Hilarius saith unto the Arrians, *Cedo aliud evangelium:* "Shew me some other gospel;" for this that ye bring helpeth you not. Even so will I say to you, *Cedo alios*[1] *doctores:* "Shew me some other doctors;" for these that ye bring are not worthy the hearing. I hoped ye would have come in with some fresher band. It must needs be some miserable case[2] that can find no better patrons to cleave unto. I know it was not for lack of good-will of your part: ye would have brought other doctors, if ye could have found them.

SARUM.

The people must needs think somewhat of your silence, and mistrust your doctrine, if it shall appear to have no manner of ground, neither of the councils, nor of the doctors, nor of the scriptures, nor any one allowed example of the primitive church, to stand upon. And so your fifteen hundred years, with the consent of antiquity and generality, shall come to nothing.

COLE.

God wot, I pass little in these matters what the poor silly souls deem of my doings, wherein ye have no cause to complain, sith they be edified towards you. Wise men, I doubt not, see what just cause I have to do as I do.

THE REPLY. SARUM.

Now God wot, then are the poor silly souls little beholden to you, that have been so long and so worshipfully maintained by the sweat of their brows; and now, seeing them, as ye say, deceived, and perish before your eyes, ye can hold
[2 Cor. xi.] your peace and let all alone. St Paul said: *Quis infirmatur, et ego non infir-*
[Rom. ix.] *mor? quis offenditur, et ego non uror? Cupio anathema esse a Christo pro fratribus meis.* And so would ye say too, if ye were so sure of the matter as St Paul was, or if ye[3] had the spirit of St Paul. Wise men, ye say, know that ye have just cause to do as ye do. Doubtless; for he that can find nothing to say, hath a reasonable cause to hold his peace: and yet, I think, a mean wise man may see that by the virtue of your recognisance ye might as well have alleged St Augustine and St Hierome, as Royard and Tapper. But ye know, the matter is such, that, if ye once come to allegations, whatsoever ye say, it will be the worse. As for my part, so that both the wise and the unwise may see your errors, and how little ye have to say for yourself, I pass not greatly whether ye confess the same by speaking, or by holding your peace. For, *Qui tacet consentire videtur*[4], as ye yourself are wont to say. O master doctor, deal simply in God's causes, and say ye have doctors when ye have them indeed; and when ye have them not, never lay the fault in your recognisance.

SARUM.

Where ye say I am not altogether without enemies, I assure you, whosoever he be that is enemy unto me, I for my part am enemy unto no man, but only wish that God's truth may be known of all men. But he that is enemy unto me in this behalf, I fear me, is enemy unto some other, whom he would be loth to name.

COLE.

Ye would bear folk in hand, that they that agree not in doctrine with you are not the queen's friends, which ye gather by your own side in queen Mary's

[[1] Alias, 1560.] [[2] Cause, 1560.] [[3] He, 1560.]

[[4] Corp. Jur. Canon. Lugd. 1624. De Reg. Jur. ad calc. Sext. Decretal. Reg. xliii. col. 825.]

reign. But I never brake amity with any man for dissent in religion: I keep still my old friends, be their religion good or bad.

THE REPLY. SARUM.

To the first part thereof I will not say so much as I were able: God soon confound all them that be, or shall be otherwise! If ye love your friends, notwithstanding their religion, ye are more charitable than some of your brethren. For ye remember how unfriendly some of you have used their friends, only for dissent in religion, unless perhaps ye will say ye imprisoned them, and burnt them, even for very love.

SARUM.

Ye suppressed, ye say, your first letters, for that they were too sour. That had been all one to me; for sour words are not enough to quail the truth. Howbeit, to my knowledge, I gave you no ill words to increase that humour. But if ye strive still against nature, as ye say ye have done now, and conquer the rest of your affections too, I doubt not but we shall soon agree.

COLE.

As though mine affection only caused me to dissent from you in religion. Which argument may serve you well in rhetoric, but no where else, I ween.

THE REPLY. SARUM.

When ye shall bring me any such authority as I have required of you, wherefore ye should dissent from us in these points, then will I grant ye dissent not only for affection. If ye be able to bring nothing, I trust ye will pardon me to say as I say. This argument, ye say, would serve me in rhetoric, and no where else. Thus ye write to make your reader believe (as ye have reported in places) that the ground of my sermons is rhetoric, and not divinity. Wherein ye were somewhat to blame for your so light credit. For if ye had heard me yourself, as ye never did, I think ye might have heard somewhat else than rhetoric. But it appeareth ye hunt very narrowly for faults, that account learning for a fault. If I were skilful in rhetoric, as ye would have me appear, only to discredit me with the people; yet can I not understand wherefore that thing should be so faulty in me, that was sometimes commendable in St Augustine, in St Chrysostom, in St Hierome, in Arnobius, in Lactantius, in Cyprian, in Tertullian, and in many other old godly fathers; for all these, as ye know, were great rhetoricians. But as in the book of the Kings, the Assyrians, when they were overthrown by the Jews, cried out, *Dii montium sunt dii illorum:* "The gods of the hills be their gods;" as though Silvanus, or Pan, or Faunus had conquered them, and not the true living God of Israel; even so ye at this time, after ye see yourselves[5] scattered and put to flight, cry out, It is rhetoric and eloquence that hath overthrown you, and not the force of the gospel of Jesus Christ. [1 Kings xx.]

Likewise was Porphyrius wont to say that St Paul persuaded so far, and won so many to the faith of Christ, not for that he had any truth of his side, but only for that with his eloquence and other subtilty[6] he was able to abuse the simplicity of the people. But, alas! small rhetoric would suffice to shew how little ye have of your side to allege for yourself.

SARUM.

Here I leave, putting you eftsoons in remembrance that, being so oft and so openly desired to shew forth one scripture, or one allowed

[5 Yourself, 1560.]

[6 Subtility, 1560.]

example of the primitive church, or one old doctor, or one ancient council, in the matters before named, yet hitherto ye have kept back, and brought nothing; and that if ye stand so still, it may be well[1] thought ye do it *conscientia imbecillitatis,* for that there was nothing to be brought.

COLE.

This place is above answered.

THE REPLY. SARUM.

Doubtless, by saying nothing, as all the rest.

COLE.

Now, forasmuch as ye make this a great foundation against us, that we vary from the primitive church, and therefore make simple souls ween that we were in the wrong side; here, I pray you, shew me your opinion, whether we are bound to do all things which we find by sufficient authority were in ure in the primitive church.

And because ye shall not be herein squeamish, I shall here myself begin to shew you mine. I am of the opinion that the council of Constance was in this matter. I think it an error, I am bound to do as the primitive church did. Where the church customably useth the contrary, I reckon an example, and no bond.

I deny not but these examples were to be followed, and not to be broken at every man's will and pleasure, until by common assent other order were taken.

But if ye seek old writers, and find me that the church this six hundred years observed not many things which were practised, and accounted for good, wholesome, and holy, in the primitive church, and thereby deem us in error, this were a wrong judgment. For the church of Christ hath his childhood, his manhood, and his hoar hairs: and, as to one man that is meet to him in one age is not meet for him in another; so were many things requisite and necessary in the primitive church, which in our days were like to do more harm than good. This is no new-devised fantasy, but uttered 1100 *years ago by St Ambrose, without reproach. I shewed you, and read you the place at Westminster, as ye may remember, and it were too long to make rehearsal of his words here*[2]. *We might, by taking contrary opinion herein, be led to think we ought to receive the sacrament evermore after supper, and not fasting. But St Augustine saith that Christ left this to his church, to take order how and in what sort the sacraments should be received and used. Wherein he saith it is a marvellous insolent kind of madness to mislike that which is received in the church, where the custom is not against any commandment in scripture*[3]. *St Peter caused (as Damasus saith) a commandment, that no woman should come barefaced to the church*[4]. *St Clement took order that the clergy should have all things in common, and so live together*[5], *as in the late reformed order of St Benet's monks doth most godly appear. And not many years since the same order in all cathedral churches was observed. Yet I ween it were an error to hold of necessity it should be so still; or to say, the church were in an error, because it hath suffered a contrary custom to creep in.*

Then, if the custom of the church may break that was in the primitive church commanded, it is no less offence to leave undone that was at the beginning practised, and no commandment given for other to follow the same.

Thus much I thought to put you in remembrance of, for such matters as ye touch in 17, 42, 43, *numbers.*

[[1] Well be, 1560, 1609.]

[[2] See below, page 75, note 8.]

[[3] August. Op. Par. 1679–1700. Ad Inquis. Jan. Lib. I. seu Epist. liv. 6. 8. Tom. II. cols. 126, 7. See before, page 39, note 8.]

[[4] Hic [Linus] ex præcepto B. Petri constituit, ut mulier velato capite in ecclesiam introiret.—Ex Libr. Pontif. Damas. in Concil. Stud. Labb. et Cossart. Lut. Par. 1671–2. Tom. I. col. 72. Hence the reading "man," (see page 39,) which is that of the original editions, is erroneous.]

[[5] Clement. Epist. v. in eod. Tom. I. cols. 115, 6.]

THE REPLY. SARUM.

In the conclusion ye take great advantage to answer many things in one, wherein your words, because they come[6] flowing down in abundance like a stream, they carry[7] away a great deal of slime and baggage with them.

First, where ye grant that ye of your side have varied, and do yet vary from the custom of the primitive church, I cannot but commend your plainness therein in telling the truth.

But where then is your antiquity become? Where be your ancient doctors? Where be the fifteen hundred years that ye have so much talked of? If ye would grant the same in the pulpit openly before the people, that we require the use and order of the primitive church; and that ye, of your part, maintain your private mass, your supremacy, your unknown prayers, and the most part of your religion, contrary to the same; that our doctrine is old, and that yours is new; if ye would but grant this simply and plainly before the people, we would desire no more at your hands.

But ye say, further, that the examples of the apostles and doctors bind you not; that in their time the church was but an infant; and that many things, that were good for her in that age, would be hurtful to her in this age. And thereto, notwithstanding your recognisance, ye allege St Augustine and St Ambrose: wherein I have cause somewhat to marvel at your doings, that now can so frankly bring in your doctors to so small purpose, and afore in matters of weight, touching the greatest part of the contention that standeth between us, durst not once name one doctor for fear of your recognisance. At the last, ye conclude that it were an error to say, we are bound of necessity to follow the use of the primitive church.

To make you a full and a clear answer hereunto, I must needs use this distinction: there were some orders in the primitive church commanded by God; and some other were devised by men, for the better training of the people. Such orders as were commanded by God may not be changed in any case, only because God commanded them: for, as God is everlasting, so is his word and commandment everlasting.

Of the other side, such orders as have been devised by men may be broken, upon some good consideration, only because they were men that devised them; for as men themselves[8] be mortal, so all their wisdoms and inventions be but mortal: as, that the communion should be used in the morning, or at night; that women should come to the church either covered or open-faced, wherein ye say St Peter took order; that the ministers' goods should be all in common, or otherwise, &c. These and other like were things appointed and ordered by men, and therefore were never used in all places of one sort; but, as they were brought in by men, so might they be dissolved and broken by men. In these things, I grant, the examples of the doctors or apostles bind us not. In these things it were an error to say we are bound of necessity to follow the use of the primitive church. These and other like things they be that St Ambrose speaketh of, whom ye at Westminster alleged in the case ye then entreated of, directly making against yourself. And we, when we heard you name him first, marvelled much what ye meant to meddle with him above all others. For as touching the common prayers to be had in a strange tongue (which matter we had then in hand), St Ambrose seemeth of purpose to control both you and your brethren, in manner one whole chapter through, writing upon the fourteenth chap. 1 Cor. And farther, the examples, that he useth in the place where ye alleged him, are these: that the deacon in the primitive church used to preach, and in his time preached not; and that women in the primitive church used to baptize, and in his time baptized not; and that in the primitive church the sacrament of baptism was ministered at all times indifferently, without difference of days, and that in his time it was ministered only upon certain

[6 Came, 1560, 1609.] [7 Carried, 1560, 1609.] [8 Themself, 1560.]

days[1]. And yet in your church, contrary to the order of St Ambrose, both women baptize, and deacons preach, and children are baptized every day without difference of time. Thus ye would seem to follow St Ambrose, and yet allege him in such places where yourself most of all vary from him. But perhaps your mind was occupied, or ye had not then leisure to mark him better.

Hitherto, I think, we agree, that, touching such things as have been ordained by men, we are not bound of necessity to the order of the primitive church.

But of the other part I say, that such things as God hath commanded precisely by his word may never be broken by any custom or consent. And such be the things that we now require at your hands, not devised by men, but commanded by God to last for ever. Unless ye will happily say, as Montanus did, that God hath revealed both more things, and also better things unto you than ever he did unto his apostles; or else, as Manichæus said, that the apostle[2] saw nothing, but only in *speculo et in œnigmate;* or, as your doctor Silvester Prierias saith, *Indulgentiæ non habent auctoritatem ex verbo Dei, sed habent auctoritatem ab ecclesia Romana, quia major est*[3]*:* "Pardons," saith he, "have no ground of God's word, but they have their ground of the church of Rome, which is a great deal more." The cup, which ye have taken from the people, is not a ceremony, but a part of the sacrament; and as good right as ye had to take that part away, so good right had ye to take away also the other, and so to leave the people nothing at all. And therefore the old father Gelasius saith: *Aut integra percipiant, aut ab integris arceantur*[4]*:* "Either let them receive the whole sacrament," that is to say, under both kinds, "or else let them be put from the whole." By which words of the old doctor Gelasius it may appear that, unless both parts of the sacrament be received together, the sacrament is mangled, and not whole.

Again, to pray in such a tongue as the people may understand, and thereby be edified, is not a ceremony to be changed at man's pleasure, but the commandment of God; for Paul, when he had spoken long thereof, concludeth at [1 Cor. xiv.] the end: *Si quis est propheta, aut spiritualis, sciat, quod quæ scribo Domini sunt præcepta:* "If any man be a prophet, or spiritual, let him well know, that the things that I write are the commandments of God." Prayer in the vulgar and known tongue, St Paul saith, is the commandment of God, and not an order taken by man.

Again, for any one man to take upon him to be universal bishop of the whole church, St Gregory saith, it is both against the gospel of Christ, and also against the old canons and ancient orders of the church: his words be these: *Quis est iste, qui contra statuta evangelica, contra canonum decreta, novum sibi nomen usurpare præsumit*[5]*?* "What man is this that taketh upon him this new-fangled name, to be called the universal bishop of the whole church, contrary to the laws of the gospel, and contrary to the decrees of the canons?" And farther he saith: *Consentire in hoc nomen est fidem amittere*[6]*:*" "To agree unto this name is to go from the faith." These things, and other like, because they have their foundation in God's word, may not be changed by any order of the church. For the church, as she is lady of her own laws, so is she but a handmaid to the laws of Christ.

But here would I fain know what smatterer taught you to frame this argument: The church hath power to break some orders:

[[1] Ut ergo cresceret plebs et multiplicaretur, omnibus inter initia concessum est et evangelizare, et baptizare, et scripturas in ecclesia explanare: at ubi omnia loca circumplexa est ecclesia, conventicula constituta sunt, &c...Hinc ergo est, unde nunc neque diaconi in populo prædicant, neque clerici vel laici baptizant, neque quocumque die credentes tinguntur, nisi ægri. Ideo non per omnia conveniunt scripta apostoli ordinationi, quæ nunc in ecclesia est; quia hæc inter ipsa primordia sunt scripta.—Ambros. Op. Par. 1686-90. Comm. in Epist. ad Ephes. cap. iv. Tom. II. Append. col. 241.]

[[2] Apostles, 1560.]

[[3] Veniæ ergo sive indulgentiæ auctoritate scripturæ nobis non innotuere, sed auctoritate ecclesiæ Romanæ, Romanorumque pontificum, quæ major est.—Sylvest. Prier. In Luth. Concl. Dial. in Luth. Op. Witeb. 1552-1580. Tom. I. fol 166. See also Summ. Summar. Bonon. 1515. fol. 335.]

[[4] Gelas. in Corp. Jur. Canon Lugd. 1624. Decret. Gratian. Decr. Tert. Pars, De Consecr. Dist. ii. can. 12. col. 1918.]

[[5] Gregor. Magni Papæ I. Op. Par. 1705. Epist. Lib. v. Ad Mauric. August. Epist. xx. Tom. II. col. 748; where we find *usurpare nomen.*]

[[6] In isto enim scelesto vocabulo consentire, nihil est aliud quam fidem perdere.—Id. ibid. Ad Sabin. Diac. Epist. xix. col. 747.]

Ergo, She hath power to break all orders, where and when she listeth.

As perfit a logician as ye make yourself, yet here ye have made a sophistication, *a secundum quid ad simpliciter;* which, as ye know, in logic is a foul error in reasoning.

But it is a world to consider the reason ye use to prove your purpose withal. For ye say, the church in Christ's and the apostles' time was but an infant, but now she is well stricken in age; therefore she must be otherwise dieted now than she was then. This is not the handsomest comparison that I have heard of. For I never heard before now that Christ and his apostles were called infants; or that ever any man before now took upon him to set them to school. Esay saith that Christ should be *Pater futuri seculi;* that is, "the Father of the world to come," which is the time of the gospel. And St Hierome in your own decrees calleth the apostles *patres*, that is, not infants, but the fathers of the church. And I believe, though ye would study and labour for it, yet would it be very hard for you either to find out any good substantial reason, wherefore ye with your brethren ought to be called the fathers of God's church, or Christ and his apostles ought to be called babes. O that ye would indifferently compare the one with the other! ye should find that, as like as ye and your bishops are to the apostles, so like is your church to the apostles' church. [Isai. ix.]

But if I would grant you your comparison, that Christ and his apostles are unto you as children to old fatherly men; yet how could ye make this argument good by all your logic?

The church is now become old and ancient:

Ergo, The people must pray in a strange language, they know not what.

Or this: The church is old:

Ergo, The people must receive the sacrament but under one kind.

Or this: The church is old:

Ergo, The people may not be exhorted to the holy communion, but only content themselves[7] with a private mass.

If these arguments seem to be good in law, yet I assure you they seem to me very weak either in logic or in divinity: howbeit, of such reasons ye have store enough; as I were able to shew you at large, if need so required. As where ye say:

Quæ sunt potestates, a Deo ordinatæ sunt: "The powers that be are ordered by God:" [Extra de Majoritate et Obedientia, cap. Unam sanctam.]

Ergo, The pope is above the emperor[8].

Spiritualis a nemine judicatur: "The man that is ruled by God's Spirit is judged of no man:" [Ibidem, 1560.]

Ergo, No man may judge the pope[9].

Sancti estote, quoniam ego sanctus sum: "Be you holy, for I am holy, saith the Lord:" [Innocentius, Dist. 82. Proposuisti.]

Ergo, No married man may be a priest[10].

Christ said unto Peter, *Solve pro me et te:* "Pay the tribute money for me and thee:" [Roffensis.]

Ergo, The pope is head of the church[11].

[7 Themself, 1560.]

[8 Oportet autem gladium esse sub gladio, et temporalem auctoritatem spirituali subjici potestati. Nam cum dicat apostolus, Non est potestas nisi a Deo; quæ autem sunt, a Deo ordinata sunt: non autem ordinata essent, nisi gladius esset sub gladio, et tanquam inferior reduceretur per alium in suprema.—Bonifac. VIII. in Corp. Jur. Canon. Extrav. Comm. Lib. I. De Major. et Obed. cap. 1. cols. 208, 9.]

[9 Ergo si deviat terrena potestas, judicabitur a potestate spirituali; sed si deviat spiritualis minor, a suo superiori: si vero suprema, a solo Deo, non ab homine poterit judicari: testante apostolo, Spiritualis homo judicat omnia; ipse autem a nemine judicatur.—Id. in eod. ibid. cols. 210, 1.]

[10 Est enim vetus admodum sacræ legis auctoritas... quod, &c... neque eos ad sacra officia fas sit admitti, qui exercent vel cum uxore carnale consortium: quia scriptum est: Sancti estote quia et ego sanctus sum, Dominus Deus vester... Quo magis hi sacerdotes, vel Levitæ pudicitiam ex die ordinationis suæ servare debent, &c.—Innoc. in eod. Decret. Gratian. Decr. Prim. Pars, Dist. lxxxii. can. 2. cols. 395, 6.]

[11 Quinta subinde prærogativa non parvi ponderis est, quia in solvendo didragmate Christus Petrum solum, præ ceteris omnibus apostolis, sibi tanquam parem adjunxit. Quæ res tam apertum indicium cujusdam præeminentiæ fuit in Petro futuræ, ut inde mox inter ceteros...oborta quæstio fuerit, quis futurus esset major in regno cœlorum.—Joh. Roffens. Episc. Assert. Luther. Confut. Antv. 1523. Artic. xxv. 5. fol. 128. 2.]

Durandus. Ecclesiasticus saith: *In medio ecclesiæ aperuit os suum:* "He opened his mouth in the midst of the congregation:"

Ergo, The priest must turn round at the midst of the altar[1].

Concilium Nicenum secundum sub Iren. *Fecit Deus hominem ad imaginem et similitudinem suam:* "God made man to the image and likeness of himself:"

Ergo, There must be images in the church[2].

Concilium Basil. sub Eugenio. *Papa juratur in fidem apostolicam:* "The pope is sworn to the apostles' faith:"

Ergo, The church cannot err[3].

Concilium Rom. sub Silvestro. *Non est discipulus supra magistrum:* "There is no scholar above his master:"

Ergo, No man may judge the pope[4].

The canonists. *Papa est dominus omnium beneficiorum:* "The pope is lord of all benefits[5]:"

Ergo, He cannot commit simony though he would[6].

Durandus. *Domini est terra et plenitudo ejus:* "The earth is the Lord's, and the fulness thereof:"

Ergo, The communion cake must be made[7] round[8].

Eckius. *Omnis spiritus laudet Dominum:* "Let all spirits praise the Lord:"

Ergo, Ye must have organs in the church[9].

Doctor Cole at Westminster. *Lac vobis potum dedi:* or, *Ignorantia est mater pietatis:* "I gave you milk to drink:" or, "Ignorance is the mother of devotion:"

Ergo, The people must make their prayers in a strange tongue[10].

Logic was good cheap when these arguments were allowed; but these, and a great many others, as good as these, have been made of your side, as ye know. But judge ye whether they seem to you to be of such warrant, that upon the sight of them we may safely break the commandments of God, or no. Very loth I was so much to open the weakness of your side; but, forasmuch as ye write that master Calvin's and master Bucer's reasons be such, as none but young folk and children will be moved with them, your importunity herein hath caused me to do otherwise than I would: therefore out of a great number of like arguments of yours I have laid forth a few; and I believe, neither child, nor young body, nor yourself, will be greatly moved with them.

Where ye say, these things may not be broken by any private authority[11], but only by a general consent; this is but a dilatory plea to defraud your adversary. Ye know all the princes of Christendom are not so soon brought together: in the mean while perhaps ye will say to yourself, as ye know who saith, *Interea fiet aliquid spero.* But forasmuch as ye give such credit to a general consent, I would fain learn at your hand where this custom of yours first began, or by what consent it was ever allowed.

Stephen Gardiner, in his book of the Devil's Sophistry, touching the communion under one kind, imagineth that first some good devout body, for reverence he had to the sacrament, thought himself not worthy to receive the cup, and so abstained. And then followed another, and so another, and after another; and so at length it became, as he saith, a general consent[12].

Thus he imagineth[13], only upon his own guess: for there was never any

---

[1 Debent etiam fieri illæ volutiones et revolutiones ante medium altaris: juxta illud: In medio ecclesiæ aperuit os suum, &c.—Durand. Rat. Div. Offic. Lugd. 1565. Lib. IV. cap. xiv. 11. fol. 111.]

[2 Ὅτε γὰρ ὁ Θεὸς τὸν Ἀδὰμ ἔπλασε ... ἔλεγε, ποιήσωμεν ἄνθρωπον κατ' εἰκόνα καὶ ὁμοίωσιν ἡμῶν ... ὅτι εἰκὼν Θεοῦ ἐστι, τετιμημένος ἐστὶ καὶ εὐπρόσδεκτος. πᾶσα γὰρ εἰκὼν ἐν ὀνόματι Κυρίου, ἢ τῶν ἀγγέλων, ἢ προφητῶν, ἢ ἀποστόλων, ἢ μαρτύρων, ἢ δικαίων γινομένη, ἁγία ἐστίν.—Concil. Nic. II. in Concil. Stud. Labb. et Cossart. Lut. Par. 1671-2. Hadr. Epist. ad Imper. Tom. VII. cols. 112, 3.]

[3 ...quilibet summus pontifex...tenetur...profiteri...fidem catholicam tenere secundum traditiones apostolorum...ipsa [ecclesia] enim errare non potest. —Concil. Basil. in eod. Respons. Synod. iii. Tom. XII. cols. 681, 3.]

[4 Concil. Rom. II. sub Silvestr. in eod. Epil. Tom. I. col. 1542. See before, page 68, note 3.]

[5 Benefices, 1560, 1609.]

[6 Papa non potest committere simoniam. Sic tenent juristæ. Theodoric. de Schismat. inter Urban. et Clem. Lib. I. cap. 22. quoted by Jewel in the *Defence of the Apology;* where see.]

[7 *Made* is omitted, 1560, 1609.]

[8 Durand. Rat. Div. Offic. Lib. IV. cap. xxx. 8. fol. 139. See before, page 15, note 15.]

[9 Eckius in his Enchiridion has a section *De hymnis et antiphonis et psallendi usu;* in which he cites several passages of scripture, but not the one here mentioned.—Joh. Eck. Enchir. Loc. Com. col. 1532. cap. xxxii. fol. M. 3, 4.]

[10 See before, page 57, note 12.]

[11 Authoritate, 1560.]

[12 A Detection of the Deuils Sophistrie, Lond. 1546. fol. 139. 2, &c.]

[13 Imagined, 1560.]

man that so wrote before him: neither was he able to shew nor whence nor where this custom first began, nor how far it went abroad. But if any one man began it first, and so another, why did not the priests and bishops then speak against it? Why did they suffer one singular man only upon a singular fancy to break the general order, that was given by Christ, and observed by general consent thorough the whole church? If it had been stayed at the first in one, it had never passed afterward to so many. If it be a wickedness, as ye say, for one man of his own vain fantasy[14] to alter the general order of the whole church, then ye see, even by Stephen Gardiner's confession, that your general consent, whereunto ye lean so much, proceeded at the first only of wickedness; and, being so, ye remember ye have a rule in your own law: *Quæ a principio male inchoata fuit institutio, temporis tractu non convalescit*[15]; that is: "The thing, that was naught at the beginning, cannot be made good by process of time."

O master doctor, let us lay aside all self-will and contention, and have recourse only unto the truth that God hath revealed to us in his holy word. For thereby shall ye be able to know whether the church do right or no: and thereby shall ye be able to reform her, if she happen to do amiss. For it is possible the church may err; but it is not possible the scriptures may err. And the scriptures of God have authority to reform the church; but I never heard that the church hath authority to reform the scriptures.

Thus Christ reformed the errors of the church in his time, brought in by the scribes and Pharisees, and said unto them, *Scriptum est.* Thus St Paul reformed the Corinthians for misusing the holy communion in his time, and told them: *Quod accepi a Domino, hoc tradidi vobis:* "I delivered you that thing that I received of the Lord." Thus the old father Irenæus, to stay the errors of his time, bade the parties have recourse[16] to the most ancient churches, from whence religion sprang first[17]. Thus saith Tertullian to redress the errors of his time: *Hoc contra omnes hæreticos præjudicat; id esse verum, quodcunque primum; id esse adulterum, quodcunque posterius*[18]: "This saying," saith he, "prevaileth against all heretics, that the thing that was first ordained is to be taken for true; and whatsoever was devised afterward is to be taken for false."

Thus saith St Hierome of the abuses of his time: *Quæ absque testimonio scripturarum quasi tradita ab apostolis asseruntur, percutiuntur malleo verbi Dei*[19]: "The things that are fathered upon the apostles, and have no testimony of the scriptures, are beaten down with the hammer of God's word."

Thus saith St Cyprian to stay the schisms and sects of his time: *Hinc schismata oriuntur, quia caput non quæritur, et ad fontem non reditur, et cœlestis Magistri præcepta non observantur*[20]: "Hereof spring schisms and divisions, for that we have no recourse to the first institution, and go not backward to the spring, and keep not the commandments of the heavenly Master."

Thus saith St Augustine to reform the errors of his time: *Ne audiatur hoc, Ego dico, hoc tu dicis; sed, Hæc dicit Dominus: Ibi quæratur ecclesia*[21]. "Let not these words be heard between us, Thus say I, or, Thus say ye; but, Thus saith the Lord. And there let us seek for the church of God."

Thus saith St Cyprian: *Si ad divinæ traditionis caput et originem revertaris,*

[[14] Fancy, 1560, 1609.]

[[15] This rule, in sense, though with variety of words, is repeatedly enacted in the canon law.—Corp. Jur. Canon. Lugd. 1624. Decret. Gratian. Decr. Sec. Pars, Caus. I. Quæst. i. can. 25; Caus. XVI. Quæst. iii. can. 15. cols. 508, 1147; De Reg. Jur. ad calc. Sext. Decretal. Reg. xviii. cols. 801, 2.]

[[16] Have a recourse, 1560.]

[[17] Et si de aliqua modica quæstione disceptatio esset, nonne oporteret in antiquissimas recurrere ecclesias, in quibus apostoli conversati sunt, &c.—Iren. Op. Par. 1710. Cont. Hær. Lib. III. cap. iv. p. 178.]

[[18] Tertull. Op. Lut. 1641. Adv. Prax. 2. p. 635. See before, page 25, note 9.]

[[19] Sed et alia quæ absque auctoritate et testimoniis scripturarum quasi traditione apostolica sponte reperiunt atque confingunt, percutit gladius Dei.—Hieron. Op. Par. 1693-1706. Comm. in Agg. Proph. cap. i. Tom. III. col. 1690.]

[[20] Hoc eo fit...dum ad veritatis originem non reditur, nec caput quæritur, nec Magistri cœlestis doctrina servatur.—Cypr. Op. Oxon. 1682. De Unit. Eccles. p. 105. This passage should have been cited, page 25, note 8.]

[[21] ... non audiamus, Hæc dicis, hæc dico: sed audiamus, Hæc dicit Dominus ... ibi quæramus ecclesiam.—August. Op. Par. 1679-1700. De Unit. Eccles. cap. iii. 5. Tom. IX. cols. 340, 1.]

cessat omnis error humanus[1]: "If ye will return to the head and beginning of God's ordinance, all errors of man will soon give place."

Theodosius the emperor pronounceth that they only are to be taken for catholic, that follow the doctrine that Peter delivered at the first to the church of Rome[2]; and so examined he the matter by the original.

Wherefore it standeth you now upon, to prove that your private mass, your communion under one kind, your prayers in an unknown tongue, and your supremacy was delivered at the first by Peter to the church of Rome; or else to confess that these things be not catholic.

To conclude, like as the errors of the clock be revealed by the constant course of the sun, even so the errors of the church are revealed by the everlasting and infallible word of God.

But to say, as some of you have said, the church is the only rule of our faith, and, whatsoever God saith in his word, she can never err, is as much as if a man would say: Howsoever the sun goeth[3], yet the clock must needs go true. For God's truth is an everlasting truth, and hangeth not upon the pleasure or determination of men; but, being once true, is true for ever. God open the eyes of our hearts, that we may see it, and rejoice in it, that the truth may deliver us!

Thus much I thought it good to say to your letters, before my departure hence; not for that I knew precisely they were yours, but only because they bare your name. If ye think I have been somewhat long, specially your answers being so short, ye shall remember that a little poison requireth ofttimes a great deal of treacle.

Here once again I conclude as before, putting you in remembrance, that thus long I have desired you to bring forth some sufficient authority for proof of your party, and yet hitherto can obtain nothing. Which thing I must needs now pronounce simply and plainly, because it is true, without if or and, ye do *conscientia imbecillitatis,* because, as ye know, there is nothing to be brought. All these things considered, if I might be so bold with you, I would say friendly to you, as St Augustine saith to St Hierome: *Arripe severitatem christianam, et cane palinodiam*[4].

JOHN SARUM.

18 *May*, 1560.

[[1] Cypr. Op. Ad Pomp. Epist. lxxiv. p. 215; where we find *revertamur*, and the word *omnis* is omitted.]

[[2] Cunctos populos ... in tali volumus religione versari, quam divum Petrum apostolum tradidisse Romanis, religio usque adhuc ab ipso insinuata declarat ... Hanc legem sequentes, Christianorum catholicorum nomen jubemus amplecti: reliquos vero dementes, &c.—Grat. Valent. et Theod. Edict. in Corp. Jur. Civil. a Gothofr. Amst. 1663. Cod. Lib. I. Tit. i. 1. Tom. II. p. 1.]

[[3] Go, 1560.]

[[4] August. Op. Par. 1679-1700. Ad Hieron. Epist. xl. 7. Tom. II. col. 86; where the words are transposed, and others besides those quoted intervene.]

A REPLY

TO

M. HARDING'S ANSWER.

A REPLIE VNTO M. HARDINGS Answer:

By perusing whereof, the discreet and diligent
Reader may easily see the weake and
vnstable grounds of the Roman reli-
gion, which of late hath been ac-
counted Catholike:

By IOHN IEVVEL Bishop of *Sarisburie.*

3. ESDR. 4.

Magna est Veritas, et preualet.

Great is the Truth, and preuaileth.

Ex Edicto Imperatorum Valentin. & Martian, in Concil Chalcedon. Actione 3.

Qui post semel inuentam Veritatem aliud quærit, Mendacium quærit non Veritatem.

After the Truth is once found, whosoeuer seeketh further, he seeketh not for the Truth, but for a lie.

UNTO THE CHRISTIAN READER.

Perusing a certain book lately set forth in the name of M. Harding, and weighing the substance, and parcels of the same, good christian reader, I called to mind these words spoken sometime by Socrates the philosopher, touching his accusers, in his own defence before the judges: "My lords, in what sort your affections have been stirred with mine accusers' eloquence, while ye heard them speak, I cannot tell. But well I wot, for mine own part, I myself[1], whom it toucheth most, was almost persuaded to believe that all they said was true; yea, although it were against myself[1]. So handsomely they can tell their tale, and so likely and so smoothly they convey their matters. Every word they spake had appearance of truth. And yet in good sooth they have scarcely uttered one word of truth." Thus then said Socrates to[2] his accusers. Even so may I say now of M. Harding: for both in truth of matter, and also in probability of utterance, they are much alike. Aristotle, touching the darkness and doubtfulness of natural worldly things, saith thus: *Quædam falsa probabiliora sunt quibusdam veris:* "Certain falsehoods[3] (by means[4] of good utterance) have sometimes more likelihood of truth than truth itself." For truth is many times brought in simple, and naked, in poor array: but falsehood[5] must needs apparel and attire herself with all her furnitures. Thus many times we are deceived, and embrace falsehood[5] instead of truth. And this is the misery of the simple. For neither are they able to teach themselves, nor have they wherewith to discern their teachers. There was never neither error so horrible, but the simple have received it, nor poison so deadly, but the simple have drunken it. In this sort St Hierome saith: "Infidelity was sometime published among the simple under the name of faith[6]." And antichrist shall be adored and honoured instead of Christ.

Plato in Apologia Socratis.

Hieron. contra Luciferianos.

Touching the state and issue of the matter: whereas I, upon just occasion offered, and only in regard of the truth, sometime said in great audience, that in any of these cases here moved our adversaries are not able to allege either any one sufficient clause or sentence out of the scriptures, councils, or ancient fathers, or any certain usage or example of the primitive church, M. Harding hath here alleged and published, not only one, or other, but (as he himself saith, and as it is thought of many) great numbers of such authorities of scriptures, councils, and doctors, both Greek and Latin, and many ancient and evident examples to the contrary. The places are noted, the words are clear: it cannot be denied; and, as it is supposed, all the world is not able to answer it. It seemeth now an undoubted truth, that as well these, as also all other the doctrines and orders of the church of Rome, have been derived directly from Christ himself and his apostles, and have continued the space of fifteen hundred and thirty years at the least. Therefore some have wished my words had been more warily qualified, and uttered with more circumspection. Even this is it that Aristotle said: "The shew of truth beareth often more likelihood, than truth itself." There is no way so easy to beguile the simple as the name and countenance of ancient fathers. The Arian heretics alleged for themselves the ancient father Origen: the Nestorian heretics alleged the council of Nice: the Donatian heretics alleged St Cyprian: the Pelagian heretics alleged St Ambrose, St Hierome, and St Augustine: Dioscorus the heretic alleged Gregorius, Cyrillus, and Athanasius, and complained openly in the council, even in like sort, and as justly, as M. Harding doth now: *Ego defendo dogmata sanctorum patrum. Ego illorum habeo testimonia, non obiter, nec in transcursu, sed*

In Conc. Chalcedon. Action. I.

[1 Meself, 1565.]
[2 Of, 1565.]
[3 Falsheads, 1565.]
[4 Mean, 1565.]
[5 Falshead, 1565.]

[6 Nomine unitatis et fidei infidelitas scripta est.—Hieron. Op. Par. 1693—1706. Adv. Lucifer. Tom. IV. Pars II. col. 299.]

in ipsorum libris posita. Ego cum patribus ejicior[1]*:* "I maintain the doctrine of the holy fathers. I have their witnesses, not uttered by chance, or by the way, but written in their books. I am excommunicate, and cast out, and banished with the fathers." If the devil can shew himself as the angel of light, and if false prophets can come in the name of Christ, much more may some others come in the name and under the colour of certain fathers.

But, good christian reader, for thy better understanding, lest happily thou be deceived, it may please thee to know that these authorities, alleged here by M. Harding, are neither new, nor strange, nor unknown to any man of mean learning; but have been both often brought in, and alleged by others, and also weighed and examined, and thoroughly confuted long ago. Indeed, M. Harding hath added of himself some beauty of his eloquence and majesty of words; and yet not so much, nor such, but it may easily be answered, although not with like eloquence, whereof in these cases there is no need, yet at least with more truth. I trust by indifferent conference hereof thou shalt soon see the ancient fathers, some that never were, by M. Harding surmised and counterfeited; some untruly alleged; some corruptly translated; some perversely expounded; some unaptly and guilefully applied; their words sometimes abridged, sometimes enlarged, sometimes altered, sometimes dissembled; fabulous and unknown authorities newly founded; childish arguments fondly concluded; to be short, infinite untruths, and known untruths, boldly avouched. In consideration

August. de Morib. Manichæ. Lib. ii. cap. xvi.

hereof St Augustine crieth out: *O rerum naturæ obscuritas! quantum tegmen est falsitatis*[2]*!* "O the darkness of natural things! what a covert have lies to lurk in!" Therefore Socrates saith: "We may not believe every argument that is shewed us, upon the sight, but must open it, and search it, and look it through." For oftentimes it seemeth otherwise than it is. It seemeth strong without, and is weak within. King Agesilaus, when he withstood[3] his enemies, of policy, to cover the smallness and weakness of their bodies, had bombasted and embossed out their coats with great quarters, that they might seem big and mighty men, and that his soldiers therewith were much dismayed, after he had overthrown and slain them in the field, pulled off their coats, and stript them, and left them naked; and when he had caused his soldiers to behold the poor, lither, slender, wearish bodies, nothing like that they seemed before, then said he unto them: "Lo, these be they of whom ye stood so much afraid; these be their great bodies, these be their mighty bones[4]". Even so, good reader, if thou stand in fear of these M. Harding's authorities and arguments, and think them terrible and invincible, for that they are embossed and wrought out by art; take them, rip them, open them, search them, weigh them, strip them naked, shake them out, confer them with the places from whence they were taken; consider the causes and the circumstances, what goeth before, what cometh after; mark the story of the time; examine the judgment of other fathers; and thou shalt marvel wherefore thou stoodest so much afraid, or ever thoughtest them to be invincible.

It were above all things to be desired of God, that his heavenly truth might pass forth without these contrarieties and quarrels of judgments; and many godly-wise men are much offended to see it otherwise. But thus it hath been ever from the beginning. Cain was against Abel, Esau against Jacob: the kingdom of darkness was ever against the kingdom of light: the scribes and Pharisees were grieved with Christ: Celsus, Porphyrius, Julianus, Symmachus, were grieved

[Luke ii. 34.]

with the glory of the gospel. Christ himself is the stone of offence, "laid to the resurrection and ruin of many." But through these offences and contentions the truth of God breaketh out, and shineth more glorious.

Blessed therefore be the name of God, that hath offered this occasion. For I have no doubt in God but of this necessary conflict, through his mercy, there shall issue some sparkle to the glory of his holy name. For, as Moses' rod devoured the rods of the sorcerers, even so will the truth of God devour error.

[1 Diosc. in Concil. Chalced. in Concil. Stud. Labb. et Cossart. Lut. Par. 1671-2. Action. I. Tom. IV. col. 181.]

[2 August. Op. Par. 1679—1700. De Mor. Manich. Lib. II. cap. xvi. 38. Tom. I. col. 729.]

[3 Understood, 1565, 1609.] [4 Plut. in Agesil.]

Darkness cannot stand before the light. Tertullian saith: *Scriptura divina hæreticorum fraudes et furta convincit, et detegit:* "The holy scripture discloseth and confoundeth the subtleties and robberies of heretics." And Nehemias saith: "Great is verity, and prevaileth." 1 Esdr. iv.

But M. Harding threatened aforehand that mine answer (be it true, be it false) shall soon be answered. Howbeit, if he will not dissemble, but deal plainly, and lay out the whole, and answer the whole as he seeth I have dealt with him, perhaps it may require him some longer time. But if he dismember my sayings, and cull out my words, and take choice of my sentences, without regard what goeth before or what cometh after; or if he send us over such pretty pamphlets[5] as he lately printed together, and joined with the Turkish news of Malta, I warn him beforehand I may not vouchsafe to make him answer.

Notwithstanding, before he address himself to his second book, I would counsel him, first, to consider better the oversights and scapes of his former book; and further, to think that whatsoever he shall write, it will be examined and come to trial. And let him remember, it is not sufficient to call us sacramentaries and heretics, or to condemn our books for pelf and trash and fardels of lies, before he see them: for these things will now no longer go for arguments. But, before all things, let him write no more untruths; for thereof he hath sent us enough already: let him no more wrest and rack the scriptures: let him no more neither misallege, nor misconstrue, nor corrupt, nor alter the holy fathers: let him no more imagine councils and canons that he never saw: let him no more bring us neither his Amphilochius, nor his Abdias, nor his Hippolytus, nor his Clemens, nor his Leontius, nor any other like childish forgeries, nor his guesses, nor his visions, nor his dreams, nor his fables: let him no more bring one thing for another. And, to be short, let him bring no more contradictions in his own tales, nor be found contrary to himself. Otherwise, the more he striveth, the more he bewrayeth his own cause.

Now, good christian reader, that thou mayest be the better able both to satisfy thine own conscience in these cases, and also to understand as well what is said, as also what is answered of either party, I have laid forth before thee M. Harding's book, without any diminution, fully and wholly, as he himself gave it out. And to every parcel thereof, according to my poor skill, I have laid mine answer; whether sufficient or insufficient, thou mayest be judge. To thee it is dedicated[6], and for thy sake it is written. Here must I say unto thee even as St Hierome saith to his reader in the like case: *Quæso, lector, ut memor tribunalis Domini, et de judicio tuo te intelligens judicandum, nec mihi nec adversario [meo] faveas; neve personas loquentium, sed causam consideres*[7]: "I beseech thee, good reader, that, remembering the judgment-seat of the Lord, and understanding that, as thou dost judge, so thou shalt be judged, thou favour neither me, nor mine adversary that writeth against me; and that thou regard not the persons, but only the cause." Adversus Error. Johan. Hierosolymitani.

God give thee the spirit of understanding, that thou mayest be able to judge uprightly: God give thee eyes to see, that thou mayest behold the comfortable and glorious face of God's truth; that thou mayest know the good, and merciful, and perfit will of God; that thou mayest grow into a full perfit man in Christ, and no longer be blown away with every blast of vain doctrine; but mayest be able to know the only, the true, and the living God, and his only-begotten Son Jesus Christ: To whom both, with the Holy Ghost, be all honour and glory for ever and ever. Amen.

JOHN JEWEL, *Sarisburien.*

From London, the 6th of August, 1565.

[5 Jewel doubtless refers to the letter dated June 12, 1565, which Harding printed from Antwerp. It may be found in Strype, Annals, Vol. I. chap. xlv., and Appendix, No. xxx.]

[6 Dedicate, 1565.]

[7 Hieron. Op. Par. 1693—1706. Epist. xxxviii. Ad Pammach. adv. Error. Johan. Jerosol. Tom. IV. Pars II. col. 311.]

TO THE READER[1].

Whereas Horace saith, "They that run over the sea change the air, not the mind[2];" it is so, reader, that I, passing over the sea out of England into Brabant, have in some part changed also my mind. For whereas, being there, I minded to send this treatise but to one friend, who required it for his private instruction, and never to set any thing abroad; now, being arrived here in Lovaine, I have thought good, by putting it in print, to make it common to many. Yet, to say the truth, hereto I have been pricked more by zealous persuasions of others, than induced by mine own
2 Cor. vi. *liking. For though duty require, be it with shame, or be it with fame, to employ all endeavour to the defence of the catholic faith in these most perilous times much impugned; yet, partly by a certain cowardly judgment, and specially by natural in-*
λαθὲ βιώσας. *clination, I have ever liked more that old counsel uttered by the Greeks in two words, which adviseth a man so to live secretly as it be not known he hath lived. Wherefore, as this labour in that respect deserveth less thank, so for my part it ought less to be blamed. If ought be found amiss, the blame thereof rightly divided between my friends and me, the greater portion shall redound to them, the lesser to me, as on whom the spot of unskill only shall cleave, but the note of undiscretion shall remain to them. For as the defects be mine and none other's, so oversight of setting forth that which was of less sufficiency is to be imputed to them, not to me. Howsoever it be, the meaning of us both is only this, christian reader, hereby to minister unto thee matter of comfort in these sorrowful, of stay in these wavering, of understanding the truth in these erroneous times; withal, to call him back, who in denying these articles hath overrun himself. Wherein I am not altogether void of hope. Our Lord grant the spirit of heresy, pride, stoutness of heart in gainsaying, estimation of himself, and regard of this world, stop not from him the Holy Ghost's working! Would God he may weigh this my doing so indifferently, as my meaning towards him is right wholesome and friendly! But in case that deep wound may not be cured with such salve, yet my trust is it shall do thee good, reader, who art either yet whole, or not so desperately wounded: which if it do, I shall think my labour well requited, and myself to have achieved that reward which I sought.*

Now, this much I have thought good here to warn thee of, that, whereas at the first I appointed this to my private friend only, and not to all in common (though in sundry places I follow the manner of such as mind to publish their writings), I have so both ordered the matter and tempered the style, as I judge it might have been liked of my friend at home, and doubt whether it may bear the light abroad. I see men's stomachs of our time to be very delicate and diverse. Some require sweet junkets, some sour and sharp sauces; some esteem the curiosity of cookery more than the wholesomeness of viands; some can like no dish, be it never so well dight. In this diversity no man can please all: whosoever seeketh it shall find himself deceived. I ween the best way is, if a man herein mind to do ought, to make his provision of the things only which be wholesome. So shall he displease many, hurt none, and please all the good. Whosoever in doing this directeth his whole purpose and endeavour to this end, that he may profit and help all, in my judgment he doth do the duty of an honest and a good man. Verily in this treatise this hath been mine only purpose; and the mean to bring the same to effect hath been such as whereby I studied to profit wholesomely, not to please delicately. How much good I have performed, I know not; my conscience (which is enough) beareth me witness of good-will. What the apostles have planted, in this great barrenness and drought of faith I have desired again to water. God give increase!

If the multitude of allegations brought for confirmation of some these articles shall seem tedious, no marvel. I should mislike the same in another myself. I grant

[[1] Reprinted from Harding's Answer, 1564, and not given in the editions of Jewel's works.]
[[2] Cœlum non animum mutant, qui trans mare currunt.—Hor. Epist. I. xi. 27.]

herein I have not always kept due comeliness. For, simply to say what I think (having leave to return to my former metaphor), soothly in some courses I have over-charged the board with dishes. Marvel not I have done that I discommend myself: to avoid a more reproof in greater respect, I have wittingly done a thing in some degree reprovable. Neither think I greatly to offend, if in this time of spiritual famine I follow the wont of some feast-makers; who, of their neighbours twitted with niggardness, to shew their largess and bounty feast them with lavish. The adversary, as here thou mayest see, hath not spared to irk us with reproach of penury, of scarcity, of lack; I mean, of proofs for maintenance of some good part of our religion. In this case to me it seemed a part of just defence to utter some good store. And the niggard's feast by old proverb is well commended, thou knowest pardy. Neither yet have we emptied all our spence[3]*, as hereafter it shall appear, if need require.*

If some do not allow this consideration, whosoever the same shall blame, him here concluding shortly I answer with Alexander king of Macedons, who to Leonidas, one of his minions, finding fault with spending much frankincense in sacrifices, wrote thus in few: "Frankincense and myrrh to thee we have sent plenty, that now to the gods thou be no more a niggard." Farewell.

At Lovaine, 14 *of June,*
1563.

THOM. HARDING.

[3 Spence: store-room.]

THE PREFACE TO MASTER JEWEL[1].

This heap of articles which you have laid together, master Jewel, the greater it riseth, the less is your advantage. For whereas you require but one sentence for the avouching of any one of them all, the more groweth your number, the more enlarged is the liberty of the answerer. It seemeth you have conceived a great confidence in the cause, and that your adversaries (so it liketh you to term us whom God hath so stayed with his grace as we cannot bear you company in departing from his catholic church) have little or nothing to say in their defence. Else what should move you, both in your printed sermon, and also in your answers and replies to doctor Cole, to shew such courage, to use such amplification of words, so often and with such vehemency to provoke us to encounter, and as it were at the blast of a trumpet to make your challenge? What, feared you reproach of dastardness if you had called forth no more but one learned man of all your adversaries; and therefore, to shew your hardiness, added more weight of words to your proclamation, and challenged all the learned men that be alive?

In the sermon, fol. 46.[2]

Among cowards, perhaps, it serveth the turn sometimes to look fiercely, to speak terribly, to shake the weapon furiously, to threaten bloodily, no less than cutting, hewing, and killing; but among such we see many times sore frays foughten, and never a blow given. With such brags of himself, and reproach of all others, Homer, the wisest of all poets, setteth forth Thersites for the fondest man of all the Grecians that came to Troy. Goliath the giant, so stout as he was, made offer to fight but with one Israelite: "Choose out a man amongst you," quoth he, "and let him come and fight with me, man for man." But you, master Jewel, in this quarrel ask not the combat of one catholic man only, but, as one sure of the victory before proof of fight, cast your glove, as it were, and with strange defiance provoke all learned men that be alive to camp with you.

1 Sam. xvii. Eligite ex vobis virum, et descendat ad singulare certamen.

Now, if this matter shall so fall out as the overthrow appear evidently on our side, and the victory on yours, that is to wit, if we cannot bring one sentence for proof of any one of all these articles out of the scriptures, ancient councils, doctors, or example of the primitive church; yet wise and grave men, I suppose, would have liked you better, if you had meekly and soberly reported the truth. For truth, as it is plain and simple, so it needeth not to be set forth with brag of high words. You remember that old saying of the wise: Simplex veritatis oratio: *"the utterance of truth ought to be simple."*

But if the victory (loth I am to use this insolent word, were it not to follow the metaphor which your challenge hath driven me unto) fall to our side, that is to say, if we shall be able to allege some one sufficient sentence for proof of some one of all these articles; yea, if we shall be able to allege divers and sundry sentences, places, and authorities, for confirmation of sundry these articles; in this case, I ween, you shall hardly escape among sober men the reproach of rashness, among humble men, of presumption, among godly men, of wickedness: of rashness; for what can be more rash than in so weighty matters as some of these articles import, so boldly to affirm that, the contrary whereof may sufficiently be proved? of presumption; for what can be more presumptuous, than in matters by you not thoroughly seen and weighed, to impute ignorance, and unableness to avouch things approved and received by the church, to all learned men alive? of wickedness; for what is more wicked than (the former case standing) so to remove the hearts of the people from devotion, so to bring the church into contempt, so to set at nought the ordinances of the Holy Ghost?

As you follow the new and strange doctrine of Theodorus Beza and Peter Martyr, the prolocutors of the Calvinian churches in France, whose scholar a long time you have been; so you divert far from that prudency, sobriety, and modesty, which in their outward demeanour they shewed in that solemn and honourable assembly

[[1] Reprinted from Harding's Answer, 1564, and not given in the editions of Jewel's works.]
[[2] See before, page 20.]

at Poyssi, in September 1561; *as it appeareth by the oration which Beza pronounced there in the name of all the Calvinists. In which oration, with humble and often protestation, they submit themselves, if cause shall so appear, to better advice and judgment, as though they might be deceived, uttering these and the like words in sundry places: "If we be deceived, we would be glad to know it." Item: "For the small measure of knowledge that it hath pleased God to impart unto us, it seemeth that this transubstantiation," &c. Item: "If we be not deceived." Item: "In case we be deceived, we would be glad to understand it*[3]," *&c. But you, master Jewel, as though you had read all that ever hath been written in these points, and had borne away all that ever hath been taught, and were ignorant of nothing touching the same, and none other beside you had seen ought, and were able to say ought, say marvellous confidently, and that in the most honourable and frequent audience of this realm, that you were well assured that none of your learned adversaries, no, nor all the learned men alive, shall ever be able to allege one sentence for any one of these articles, and that, because you know it, therefore you speak it, lest haply your hearers should be deceived.* In the sermon, fol. 49.[4]

Likewise in your answer to doctor Cole's first letter you say, speaking of these articles, you thought it best to make your entry in your preaching with such things as wherein you were well assured we should be able to find not so much as any colour or shadow of doctors at all. Wherein you withdraw yourself from plainness, so much as you do in your presumptuous challenge from modesty. For, being demanded of doctor Cole why you treat not rather of matters of more importance than these articles be of, which yet lie in question betwixt the church of Rome and the protestants, as of the presence of Christ's body and blood in the sacrament, of justification, of the value of good works, of the sacrifice of the mass, and of such other; not unwitting how much and how sufficient authority may be brought against your side for proof of the catholic doctrine therein, lest all the world should espy your weakness in these points, you answer that you thought it better to begin with smaller matters, as these articles be, because you assure yourself we have nothing for confirmation of them. Thus craftily you shift your hands of those greater points wherein you know scriptures, councils, doctors, and examples of the primitive church to be of our side, and cast unto us, as a bone to gnaw upon, this number of articles of less weight (a few excepted) to occupy us withal: which be partly concerning order rather than doctrine, and partly sequels of former and confessed truths, rather than principal points of faith; in the exact treaty of which the ancient doctors of the church have not employed their study and travail of writing. For many of them being sequels depending of a confessed truth, they thought it needless to treat of them: forasmuch as, a principal point of truth granted, the granting of all the necessary sequels is implied: as in a chain (which comparison St Basil[6] *maketh in the like case) he that draweth the first link after him, draweth also the last link. And for this cause, indeed, the less number and weight of such ancient authorities may be brought for the avouching of them; and yet the things in them expressed be not justly improved by any clause or sentence you have said or uttered hitherto.* Fol. 6.[5] Epist. ad Gregorium fratrem.

Verily, M. Jewel, if you had not been more desirous to deface the catholic church, than to set forth the truth, you would never have rehearsed such a long roll of articles, which for the more part be of less importance; whereby you go about to discredit us, and to make the world believe we have nothing to shew for us in a great part of our religion, and that you be to be taken for zealous men, right reformers of the church, and undoubted restorers of the gospel. As touching the other weighty points, whereupon almost only your school-masters of Germany, Switzerland, and Geneva, both in their preachings and also in their writings treat, you will not yet adventure the trial of them, with making your match with learned men, and in the mean time set them forth by sermons busily among the unlearned and simple people, until such time as you have won your purpose in these smaller matters.

Thus you seem to follow a sleight which king Alexander the Great used to further the course of his conquests; who, as Plutarch writeth, whereas he thought verily In Vita Alexandri Magni.

[3 An Oration made by Master Theodore de Beze, Lond. R. Jugge. foll. B iii. 2, C vi. 2, C viii. &c.]

[4 See before, page 22.]

[5 See before, page 28.]

[6 Basil. Op. Par. 1721—30. Ad Greg. Fratr. Epist. xxxviii. Tom. III. p. 118.]

that he was begotten of a god, shewed himself toward the barbarians very haut and proud; yet among the Greeks he used a more modesty, and spake little of his godhead. For they being rude, and of small understanding, he doubted not but by ways and means to bring them to such belief: but the Greeks, whom he knew to be men of excellent knowledge and learning, of them he judged, as it proved indeed, the matter should be more subtilly scanned, than simply believed. Right so you, M. Jewel, persuading yourself to have singular skill in divinity, among the simple people you utter the weighty and high points of christian religion that be now in question, in such wise as the protestants have written of them, and with vehement affirmations, with misconstrued and falsified allegations, and with pitiful exclamations you lead the seely souls into dangerous errors. But in your writings, which you knew should pass the judgment of learned men, the points of greater importance you cover with silence, and utter a number of articles of less weight for the more part in respect of the chief, though for good cause received and used in the church (I speak of them as they be rightly taken), denying them all, and requiring the catholics, your adversaries, to prove them. Wherein you shew yourself not to fear controlment of the ignorant, but to mistrust the trial of the learned.

Likewise in the holy canon of the mass you find faults where none are, as it may easily be proved, thinking for defence thereof we had little to say. But of the prayer there made to the virgin Mary, the apostles and martyrs, of the suffrages for the departed in the faith of Christ, in your whole book you utter never a word, though you mislike it, and otherwheres speak against it; as all your sect doth. And why? Forsooth, because you know right well we have store of good authorities for proof thereof. And by your will you will not yet strive with us in matters wherein by the judgment of the people, to whom you lean much, you should seem overmatched. And therefore you search out small matters in comparison of the greatest, such as the old doctors have passed over with silence, and for that cannot of our part by ancient authorities be so amply affirmed, at leastway as you think yourself assured. And in this respect you lay on load of blame, contumelies, and slanders, upon the church for maintaining of them. Wherein the mark you shoot at every man perceiveth what it is; even that, when you have brought the catholic church into contempt, and borne the people in hand we are not able to prove a number of things by you denied, for lack of such proofs, as yourself shall allow, in certain particular points of small force (which falsely you report to be the greatest keys and highest mysteries of our religion), then triumphing against us, and despising the ancient and catholic religion in general, you may set up a new religion of your own forging, a new church of your own framing, a new gospel of your own device. Well may I further say, cathedram contra cathedram, *but not, I trow, as St Augustine termeth such state of religion,* altare contra altare: *for whatsoever ye set up, if ye set up any thing at all, and pull not down only, all manner of altars must needs be thrown down.*

Now, being sorry to see the catholic church by your stout and bold brags thus attempted to be defaced, the truth in manner outfaced, and the seely people so dangerously seduced; imbarred of liberty to preach by recognisance, and yet not so discharged in conscience of duty appertaining to my calling; I have now thought good to set forth this treatise in writing, whereby to my power to save the honour of the church, which is our common mother, to defend the truth, in whose quarrel none adventure is to be refused, and to reduce the people from deceit and error, which by order of charity we are bound unto.

For the doing hereof, if you be offended, the conscience of good and right meaning shall soon ease me of that grief. Verily mine intent was not to hurt you, but to profit you, by declaring unto you that truth which you seem hitherto not to have known: for, if you had, I ween you would not have preached and written as you have. Your years, your manner of study, and the party you have joined yourself unto considered, it may well be thought you have not thoroughly seen how much may be said in defence of the catholic doctrine, touching these articles which you have denied.

For the manner of doing, I am verily persuaded that neither you, nor any of your fellows, which of all these new sects by your side professed soever he liketh best, shall have just cause to complain. The whole treatise is written without choler, without gall, without spite. What I mislike in you, and in them of your side, I could not allow in myself. Where truth's cause is treated, human affections, whereby the clear light is dimmed, ought to be laid apart. Glikes, nips, and scoffs, bites, cuts, and girds, become not that stage. Yet, if I shall perhaps sometimes seem to scar or lance a festered bunch that deserveth to be cut off, you will remember, I doubt not, how the meekest and the holiest of the ancient fathers, in reproving heretics, ofttimes have shewed themselves zealous, earnest, eager, severe, sharp, and bitter.

Whose taste soever longeth most after such sauce, in this treatise he shall find small liking. For it is occupied more about the fortifying of the articles denied, than about disproving of the person who hath denied them. Wherein I have some deal followed the latter part of Chilo the wise man his counsel, which I allow better than the first: Ama, tanquam osurus; oderis tanquam amaturus: *"Love as to hate; hate as to love."*

If any man that shall read this be of that humour as shall mislike it as being cold, low, flat, and dull, and require rather such verdure of writing as is hot, lofty, sharp, and quick, which pleaseth best the taste of our time; understand he that, before I intended to put this forth in print, I thus tempered my style for these considerations. First, whereas a certain exercise of a learned man, of five or six sheets of paper, spread abroad in the realm in defence of some of these articles by M. Jewel denied, was fathered upon me, which indeed I never made sentence of, and therefore a storm imminent was mistrusted; that, by changing the hue, which many know me by that know me familiarly, in case it should come to the hands of many, as it was likely, I might escape the danger of being charged with it, and nevertheless satisfy my friend's request, and in some part also my conscience, and do good. Secondly, that I thought meek, sober, and cold demeanour of writing to be most fitting for such kind of argument. Thirdly, and specially, that my heart served me not to deal with M. Jewel, mine old acquainted fellow and countryman, otherwise than sweetly, gently, and courteously. And indeed here I protest that I love M. Jewel, and detest his heresies.

And now, sir, as I love you, right so I am desirous of your soul health, which you seem either to forget or to procure by a wrong way. Bethink yourself, I pray you, whether the way you walk in be not the same, and you the man, that Salomon, moved with the Spirit of God, speaketh of: "There is a way that seemeth to a man Prov. xvi.
right; and the end of it leadeth to damnation." Certain it is you are deceived, and maintain untruth, as it shall appear by this treatise. Herein you sustain the evil of human infirmity. Marry, when deceit is by plain truth detected, then to dwell and continue in error, that proceedeth not of human weakness, but of devilish obstinacy. But you, M. Jewel, as many men think, and I trust, are not yet swallowed up of that gulf. Fain would I do you good, if I wist how. I fear me, your sore is putrefied so far as oil and lenitives will not serve now, but rather vinegar and corrosives. You remember, I doubt not, what Cicero saith, that medicine to profit most which causeth the greatest smart; and what Salomon also, "The wounds of a friend to be Prov. xxvii.
better than the kisses of an enemy."

The best salve any man can minister unto you, verily I think, is, to exhort you to humility, and to denying of yourself. For if you could be brought to humble yourself, and to deny yourself, doubtless you should see in yourself that you see not. If you were humble, you would not be so puffed up, and swell against your mother the church; you would not contemn her whom you ought to honour. You would not rejoice, like the accursed Cham, to shew her unseemliness, if by corruption of times Gen. ix.
any perhaps be grown. For by authority and public consent, say what ye will, none is maintained. If you would deny yourself to be the man you be not, you should better see who and what you be indeed. Deny yourself to be so well learned as you seem to esteem yourself, and you will be ashamed to make such strange cracks and vaunts of your being well assured of that you have preached and written touching these articles wherein you are deceived. Deny yourself to be a bishop, though you have put on the bishop of Salisbury his white rochet, and you shall be content and think it meet also to give a reckoning of the doctrine which you preach openly before the high estates, and therefore confer with D. Cole and with meaner men also, which In the beginning of the first answer to D. Cole.
more insolently than reasonably you refused to do: and by such conference you shall be advertised of your error. Deny your private judgment, and estimation of your long study in divinity, which you acknowledge in your replies, and of your

great cunning in the same, and you shall evidently see and remember that your time hath been most bestowed in the study of humanity and of the Latin tongue, and concerning divinity your most labour hath been employed to find matter against the church, rather than about serious and exact discussing of the truth; and that, in comparison of that holy and learned father B. Fisher and others, whom you jest and scoff at, and seek to discredit by fond arguments of your own framing upon them by you fathered, you are, touching the sound and deep knowledge of divinity, scantly a smatterer.

In the sermon, fol. 31.[1]

Again, deny yourself to be so great a man, but that you may take advertisement of a man of meaner calling; deny yourself to be so honourable, but that it may stand with your honesty to abide by your promise in a most honest manner by your own prepensed offer made; you may easily learn how to redress that hath been done amiss, you may see your own infirmities, defects, oversights, and ignorances plainly, as it were in a glass, all self-love and blind estimation of yourself set apart; you may, with the favour of all good men, with the winning of your own soul, and many others, whom you have perilously deceived, and to the glory of God, be induced to yield to the truth, to subscribe to the same, and to recant your errors. Wherein you should do no other thing than, these articles, which you deny, by us with sufficient proofs and testimonies avouched, you have already freely and largely offered. Which thing, that it may be done, God give you the grace of his holy Spirit, to humble your heart, to deny yourself, and to make a greater accompt of your everlasting salvation than of your worldly interest!

THOMAS HARDING.

[[1] See before, page 14.]

AN ANSWER

TO

M. HARDING'S PREFACE.

It misliketh you much, M. Harding, that, in so many and sundry cases by me moved, wherein standeth the greatest force of your religion, I should say you and others of that part are utterly void, not only of the scriptures, but also of the old councils and ancient fathers; and that in such an audience I should so precisely and so openly discover the wants and weakness of your side. And therefore, "The greater my heap riseth, the less," say you, "is mine advantage."

Whereunto I may easily reply, the larger is mine offer, the more will your discreet reader mislike the insufficiency of your answer; and, the more enlarged is your liberty, the less cause have you to complain.

"Wise men," ye say, "would more have liked greater modesty." Verily, the men that you call wise would have thought it greatest modesty to have dissembled and said nothing. But what may the same wise men think of your modesty, that, having so often made so large and so liberal offers of so many doctors, are not able in the end to shew us one?

Neither "look we so fiercely, nor shake we the sword so terribly," as you report us. This was evermore your and your fellows' special and peculiar commendation; who, besides your fierce and cruel looks, and besides the shaking and terror of your sword, have also hewn, and cut, and slain, and filled your hands with the blood of your brethren.

Wherefore ye should not take it in such grief, that, only for distinction's sake, by so civil and courteous a name we call you our "adversaries." For, finding you armed with sword and fire, and imbrued with our blood, we might well have spared you some other name. That I said, ye have no such assurance of the ancient fathers as ye have borne us in hand, and as your friends upon your credit have believed, I said it not, neither of ambition, as you expound it, nor of malice; but forced thereto by your importunity, and with great grief of mind.

Therefore ye did me the greater wrong to say, "I came vaunting, as Goliath, and throwing forth my glove like a challenger, and proclaiming defiance to all the world." In these words, M. Harding, wise men may find some want of your modesty. For whoso avoucheth the manifest and known truth, and saith that you both have been deceived yourselves, and also have deceived others, ought not therefore to be called Goliath. And notwithstanding you have adventured yourself to be the noble David, to conquer this giant, yet, forasmuch as ye have neither David's sling in your hand, nor David's stones in your scrip, and therefore not likely to work great masteries, ye may not look that the ladies of Israel with their lutes and timbrels will receive you in triumph, or sing before you, "David hath conquered his ten thousands." He rather is Goliath, that setteth his face against the heavens and his foot in emperors' necks, and openeth his mouth awide to utter blasphemies, that soundeth out these words into all the world: "I cannot err: I have all laws, both spiritual and temporal, in my breast: I am above all general councils: I may judge all men; but all the world may not judge me, be I never so wicked: I am king of kings, and lord of lords: I can do whatsoever Christ himself can do: I am all, and above all: all power is given to me, as well in heaven as in earth[2]." Ye know whose words these be, by whom they

Extra. de Constit. Licet. De Electio. et Elect. Potestate, Significasti. ix. qu. 3. Nemo. De Majorit. et Obedient. Unam Sanctam. In Glossa. In Concil. Latera. Sub Julio.

[2 The following are the passages referred to by the author:

Bonifac. VIII. in Corp. Jur. Canon. Lugd. 1624. Sext. Decretal. Lib. I. Tit. ii. cap. 1. col. 11. See before, page 67.

Aiunt in conciliis statutum non inveniri: quasi Romanæ ecclesiæ legem concilia ulla præfixerint: cum omnia concilia per Romanæ ecclesiæ auctoritatem et facta sint, et robur acceperint, &c.—Paschal. in eod. Decretal. Greg. IX. Lib. I. Tit. vi. cap. 4. cols. 111, 2.

Nemo judicabit primam sedem justitiam temperare desiderantem. Neque enim ab Augusto, &c.—Innocent. Papa in eod. Decret. Gratian. Decr. Sec. Pars, Caus. IX. Quæst. iii. can. 13. col. 877. See before, page 68.]

are spoken, by whom they are defended, and to whom they are applied. This seemeth to be the very express and lively image of Goliath; that Goliath, I say, whom now you see knocked in the forehead and falling down, not with force of worldly power, but only with that little rough despised stone of God's everlasting and heavenly word. Touching that most worthy and learned father, sometime your master, D. Peter Martyr, whom ye would seem somewhat to commend, not for his doctrine, from which you have so suddenly fallen away, but only for his modesty, it cannot be doubted but he, being at Poissy in that worthy assembly, in the presence of the king, and of other the princes and nobles of that realm, both did and spake that might stand with the truth of the cause, and also might well become his own person. But, being demanded his judgment in these cases, he would have answered even as we do, and would much have marvelled that any learned man would say the contrary. Not long sithence, ye made the pulpits ring that your mass and all other your whole doctrine was assured unto you by Christ and his apostles, and that for the same ye had the undoubted continuance and succession of fifteen hundred years, the consent of all the old councils, doctors, and fathers, and all antiquity, and the universal allowance of the world[1]. Thus ye doubted not then to say, without fear of controlment of God or man. Many thousands thought ye dealt simply, and would not deceive them, and therefore were easily led to believe you.

In this case christian duty and charity required that the truth and certainty of your tales should be opened, that the simple might understand ye had deceived them, and that of all that your so large talk and countenance of antiquity you were, as you well know, utterly able to avouch nothing. Whereas it so much offended[2] you that I should so precisely avouch the negative, and require you to prove your affirmative, whereof ye would seem so well assured, it may please you to consider that St Gregory, writing against John the bishop of Constantinople, that had entitled himself the universal bishop of the whole world, rested[3]
Lib. iv. Epist. 13. himself likewise upon the negative. His words be these: *Nemo decessorum meorum hoc superbo vocabulo uti consensit: nemo Romanorum pontificum hoc singularitatis nomen assumpsit*[4]: "None of my predecessors ever consented to use this arrogant name: no bishop of Rome ever took upon him this name of singularity." St Augustine, when he had reckoned up all the bishops of Rome before his time,
Aug. Epist. 165. added thereto by a negative: *In hoc ordine successionis nullus Donatista episcopus invenitur*[5]: "In this order of succession there is found no bishop that was a Donatist." Yet neither St Augustine nor St Gregory was ever condemned for Goliath. By the like negative you, M. Harding, yourself say, although untruly,
In the 3 Article, and in the 15 Division. as you[6] do many other things besides, that "neither M. Jewel, nor any one of his side, is able to shew that the public service of the church in any nation was ever, for the space of six hundred years after Christ, in any other tongue than in Greek or Latin." And yet we may therefore not call you either Goliath, or Thersites, or by any other like uncourteous name. You say, "I take presumptuously upon me to have read all things, and to be ignorant of nothing;" only because I say you in these cases can allege nothing. And why so? Can no man descry your wants and disclose your untruths without presumption? You say ye have

---

Iste [summus pontifex] omnia judicat etiam auctoritate, quia supra omnes auctoritatem habet: et ipse a nemine judicatur, quia nullus habet auctoritatem super ipsum.—Gloss. in eod. in Extrav. Comm. Lib. I. De Major. et Obed. cap. 1. col. 211.

...sicut in Jerusalem illa quæ in cœlis est...unus tantum dominus est Jesus Christus: ita in hac Jerusalem illius filia...unus tantum princeps est, vicarius Christi et pontifex maximus, cui omnes...obedire debent, &c....accingere, pater sancte, gladio tuo... binos enim habes...accingere, potentissime, et accingere super femur tuum, id est super universas humani generis potestates...regna, sacerdos et rex...Is namque idem, quem imitari debes, et rex regum est, &c. —Orat. Cajetan. in Sess. ii. Concil. Later. v. in Concil. Stud. Labb. et Cossart. Lut. Par. 1671—2, Tom. XIV. cols. 73, 5.

Quapropter Bernardus ad Eugenium tamquam ad summum hierarchicum in cœlo ecclesiæ virum, in quo erat omnis potestas supra omnes potestates, tam cœli quam terræ, recte scripserat: Tibi data est omnis potestas, &c.—Orat. Steph. Arch. Patrac. in Sess. x. in eod. col. 269.]

[1 Of all the world, 1565, 1609.]

[2 Offendeth, 1565.]

[3 Resteth, 1565.]

[4 Gregor. Magni Papæ I. Op. Par. 1705. Epist. Lib. v. Indict. XIII. Ad Eulog. et Anastas. Epist. xliii. Tom. II. col. 771. See before, page 32, note 2.]

[5 August. Op. Par. 1679—1700. Ad Gen. Epist. liii. 2. Tom. II. col. 121.]

[6 Ye, 1565, 1609.]

the consent of all doctors, of all ages, and of all times, of your side: shall we, therefore, say that you vaunt yourself of your knowledge, or that you know all things, and are ignorant of nothing? You say, ye "have all the doctors:" I say, and true it is, ye have not one doctor. The difference of these sayings standeth only in this, that the one is true, the other untrue; that your affirmative cannot be proved, my negative cannot be reproved. But touching vaunt of reading and knowledge, there is no difference.

Howbeit, forasmuch as this negative so much offendeth you of our side, let us hardly turn it of your side; and let us say so as it may best like you to have us say, that it cannot appear by any sufficient clause or sentence, either of the scriptures, or of the old doctors, or of the ancient councils, or by any example of the primitive church, either that the priest then received the holy communion together with the people, or that the sacrament was then ministered unto the people under both kinds, or that the public prayers were ever said in the vulgar or known tongue, or that the whole people thereto said "Amen," within the space of six hundred years after Christ. Let us say, further, that Christ himself and all his apostles said private mass, and received the holy sacrament severally alone; that all the ancient fathers ministered the half communion only under one kind; that all the common prayers were every where said in a strange learned tongue, utterly unknown unto the people. This offer is free and liberal. And what can you desire more? But perhaps it shameth you to say so much. For, albeit some of you have often said it, yet the untruth thereof is manifest, and sheweth itself.

Only ye wish, I "had used some greater modesty." And would you that I should have said, "Ye have one ancient doctor directly and plainly of your side," and so in that place and in that presence, for modesty's sake, to have avouched open untruth, as you and others had done before? O, M. Harding, in these cases a mean way is no way. Accursed is that modesty that drowneth the truth of God. Chrysostom saith: *Veritatem negat, qui eam non libere prædicat*[7]: "He is a renouncer of the truth, that dareth not freely say[8] the truth." xi. Quæst. 3, Nolite.

Ye say, I "have sought up certain small questions of light importance, wherein the ancient doctors have not travailed," as not daring to enter into matters of greater weight. Howbeit it seemeth overmuch for you to limit and appoint each man what he should preach at Paul's Cross. Neither is it much material whether these matters be great or small, but, whether you, by colour of the same, have deceived the people.

But would ye have us now at last believe that your mass, your transubstantiation, your real presence, your adoration, your sacrificing of the Son of God, and your supremacy of Rome, be so small matters? Ye told us not long sithence, there were no other matters so great as these. And may we think that your religion is now greater, now smaller; and increaseth and vadeth[9], and waxeth and waneth, as doth the moon? Verily pope Nicolas would have joined your transubstantiation to the creed, and would have made it the thirteenth article of our faith[10]. And pope Boniface the eighth saith that "to be subject to the church of Rome is of the necessity of salvation[11]." And pope Nicolas saith: "Whosoever denieth the authority and pre-eminence of that see is an heretic[12]." Extr. de Majorit. et Obed. Unam Sanctam. Dist. 22, Omnes.

Notwithstanding, how great or small these matters be, it forceth not. Indeed, you had learned them in very small time; and, as now, ye avouch them with very small proofs. And how small and light soever you would now have them to appear, yet for the same ye have made no small ado. Nothing ought to be taken for small, wherewith so great multitudes of God's people may be deceived.

[7 ...non solum ille proditor est veritatis, qui, &c. ...sed etiam ille, qui non libere veritatem pronunciat, &c.—Chrysost. in Corp. Jur. Canon. Lugd. 1624. Decret. Gratian. Decr. Sec. Pars, Caus. XI. Quæst. iii. can. 86. col. 952.]

[8 To say, 1565, 1609.]

[9 Vadeth: goeth away, fadeth.]

[10 The author doubtless refers to the confession imposed on Berengarius.—Ibid. Decr. Tert. Pars. De Consecr. Dist. ii. can. 42. cols. 1932, 3.]

[11 Porro subesse Romano pontifici, omni humanæ creaturæ declaramus, dicimus, diffinimus, et pronunciamus omnino esse de necessitate salutis.—Bonifac. VIII. in eod. Extrav. Comm. Lib. I. De Major. et Obed. cap. 1. col. 212.]

[12 Qui autem Romanæ ecclesiæ privilegium ab ipso summo omnium ecclesiarum capite traditum auferre conatur, hic proculdubio in hæresim labitur, et cum ille vocetur injustus, hic est proculdubio dicendus hæreticus.—Nicol. II. in eod. Decr. Prim. Pars, Dist. xxii. can. 1. col. 100.]

The matters wherewith Christ charged the Pharisees were not so great. Yet Christ saith unto them: "Ye strain a gnat, and swallow a camel." St Paul saith: "A little leaven soureth a whole lump of dough." A hair is small, yet we read it hath choked a big man. Plato saith: "Robbery is no less in a small matter than in a great." The ciniphes[1] were but small, yet are they reckoned among the great plagues of God.

Matt. xxiii.

1 Cor. v.

They that first began to maintain that arrogant presumptuous title of universal bishop, which now the bishop of Rome challengeth wholly to himself, said it was but a small matter. But Gregory saith: *Alia sunt frivola, et innoxia: alia sunt frivola, et noxia:* "Some things are small, and do no hurt: some things are small, and do great hurt."

Greg. Lib. vi. Epist. 30.

And comparing the same with the pride of antichrist, who should call himself, *Deus,* (that is to say, God,) he saith thus: *Si spectes quantitatem vocis, duæ sunt syllabæ: si pondus iniquitatis, est universa pernicies*[2]*:* "If ye weigh the quantity of the word, it standeth in two syllables; if the weight of the wickedness, it is an universal destruction."

Ibid.

Though these matters were small, yet the untruths and errors that thereof have risen are not small. Remove the same; and your greatest religion will fall to nothing.

To conclude, if these matters be great, they are the more worthy to be considered; if they be small, there is the less hurt in leaving of them, and the more wilfulness in defending of them: verily, the whole world is weary of them. Christ saith: *Qui in modico iniquus est, et in majori iniquus est:* "He that is wicked in the small, is also wicked in the great."

Luke xvi.

You say, "We fly[3] and forbear the judgment of the learned, and shake out these things with great admiration only amongst the simple;" as Alexander the king of Macedonia made himself a god, and had much talk of his father Jupiter amongst the barbarians; but amongst the Greeks, that were wise and able to judge, and knew him well enough, he was content to talk of other matters.

This comparison, M. Harding, is odious, and savoureth overmuch of your choler. We hunt not for any admiration or opinion of Godhead among the people. "We preach not ourselves, but Christ Jesus."

But thus the Pharisees said of Christ himself: "These rascals are accursed, they have no learning, they know not the law." Amongst them will he be: there he reigneth like a prince: there he seeketh to be made a God. Here might I eftsoons put you in remembrance of him that hath so long abused and mocked the whole world, both princes and subjects, as well learned as unlearned, accounting them all as wild and barbarous, and hath suffered himself openly to be proclaimed and published by the name of God. The words be known: *Dominus Deus noster papa*[4]*:* "Our Lord God the pope:" and again: *Constat papam a pio principe Constantino Deum appellatum; et Deum ab hominibus judicari non posse, manifestum est*[5].

[John vii.]

Extra. Jo. 22. Cum inter. In Glossa.

Dist. 96. Satis evidenter.

Alexander stood in some awe and reverence of the wise; but this man despiseth both wise and unwise, learned and unlearned, and all the world.

It was somewhat out of season for you in this place to entreat of the validity of your canon, and so earnestly to labour to prove it faultless, before any man had begun to touch it, or to prove it faulty. It is supposed that some part thereof was devised by Leo; and afterward augmented by Gelasius; and after that by one whom St Gregory calleth Scholasticus[6]; and after again by Gregorius himself; and that at last, about eight hundred and fifty years after Christ, it was

Gregor. Lib. vii. Epist. 63.

[[1] Exod. viii. 17, 18. σκνίφες. Septuag.]

[[2] ...alia sunt frivola valde innoxia, atque alia vehementer nociva...Si quantitatem sermonis attendimus, duæ sunt syllabæ: si vero pondus iniquitatis, universa pernicies.—Gregor. Magni Papæ I. Op. Par. 1705. Epist. Lib. VII. Indict. xv. Ad Mauric. August. Epist. xxxiii. Tom. II. col. 881.]

[[3] Flee, 1565.]

[[4] Extrav. Joan. XXII. ad calc. Sext. Decretal. Par. 1585. Tit. xiv. Gloss. in cap. 4. col. 153. Latterly, the word *Deum* has been omitted.]

[[5] ...pontificem, quem constat, &c. nec posse Deum, &c.—Nicol. Papa in Corp. Jur. Canon. Lugd. 1624. Decret. Gratian. Decr. Prima Pars, Dist. xcvi. can. 7. col. 467.]

[[6] The epistle referred to is doubtless that directed Ad Martinum Scholasticum.—Gregor. Magni Papæ I. Op. Epist. Lib. IX. Indict. II. Epist. lviii. Tom. II. col. 975.]

brought to some perfection, and made up by pope Sergius; as now it is more closely pronounced, and more reverently used, than either the epistle or the gospel. The Canon, 1565.

But whether there be any fault therein, or none, I leave that to you, M. Harding, to be better considered by yourself. Your doctor Durand saith thus: *Cum [sacerdos]... oraverit pro hostia transubstantianda, eamque ... transubstantiatam Patri obtulerit, ... orat pro ipsius acceptatione*[7]: "When the priest hath prayed for the transubstantiation of the host, and hath offered the same, being transubstantiate, unto God the Father, afterward he prayeth that God will favourably accept it." Durand. Lib. iv. part. 2.

St Paul saith: "Christ is the Mediator between God and man." But here by your canon, contrariwise, the priest is made a mediator between God and Christ. 1 Tim. ii. The priest a mediator between God and Christ.

And now[8] yourself, M. Harding, at your mass, and in the highest secrets of your canon, desire God the Father to look favourably upon Jesus Christ his own Son at your request. Your words be plain and evident: no interpretation or shift is able to salve them. Now, if it be meet you should entreat God the Father to be merciful unto Christ his Son, and to behold him favourably for your sake, then may you say there is no fault in all your canon.

You seem to complain that I leave out prayer for the dead, and invocation of saints; and that thing you amplify largely with many words. And yet, I think, you would not have us believe that these points of your religion be greater than your sacrifice, or than your mass.

Verily, touching the first, I heard once, when you yourself blew down the paper walls, as ye then called them, and utterly quenched all the painted fires of purgatory. For the other St Chrysostom saith: *Homines utuntur atriensibus. In Deo nihil est tale; sine mediatore exorabilis est*[9]: "Men use porters and ushers. But in God there is no such thing; he is easy to be entreated, yea, without a mediator." Again he saith: *Nihil tibi opus est patronis apud Deum. Neque enim tam facile Deus audit, si alii pro nobis orent, quam si ipsi oremus, etsi pleni simus omnibus malis*[10]: "Thou needest no attorney to speak to God. For God doth not so soon hear us, when others pray for us, as when we pray for ourselves, yea, although we be full of all sin." St Ambrose likewise saith: *Isti*[11] *se non putant reos, qui honorem nominis Dei deferunt creaturæ, et relicto Domino, conservos adorant... Nam et ideo ad reges per tribunos et comites itur: quia homo utique est rex, et nescit quibus debeat rempublicam credere. Ad Deum autem, quem ... nihil latet, (omnium enim merita novit,) [ad] promerendum suffragatore non est opus, sed mente devota. Ubicunque enim talis loquutus fuerit ei, respondebit illi*[12]: "These men think they do no ill, giving the honour of God unto a creature; and, leaving the Lord, adore their fellow-servants. For therefore we have access to kings by knights and marshals; for that the king is a mortal man, and knoweth not to whom he may commit his kingdom. But God knoweth all men's merits, and there is nothing privy from him. Therefore to obtain his favour we need no spokesman, but a devout mind. Wheresoever such a one shall speak, God will answer him." In a sermon preached in St Mary's church in Oxford. Chrysost. de Pœniten. Hom. 4. Chrysost. de profectu Evangelii. Ambros. in i. cap. ad Roman.

Whereas ye untruly say, we lay on load of slanders, to deface the church, you may remember that there were sometime that charged St Stephen, St Paul, and Christ himself, in like sort; for that they seemed likewise to speak unreverently against the church. And against the prophet Jeremy they cried out, even as you do now: "The temple of God, the temple of God." Jer. vii.

But he defaceth not the church, that defaceth the defacers of the church, and wipeth off the soil of your errors, that her face may shine, and appear more glorious. When Christ mourned over the city and temple of Hierusalem; or when he said, "Ye have made my father's house a den of thieves;" and when Esay said, "O how is this beautiful city (that then was the church of God) become an harlot!" or when the prophet Jeremy said, "Who will give abundance Isai. i. Jer. ix.

[7 Durand. Rat. Div. Offic. Lugd. 1565. Lib. iv. cap. xliii. 9. fol. 178.]

[8 Yowe, i.e. you, 1565, you, 1609.]

[9 Chrysost. Op. Par. 1718-38. De Pœnit. Hom. iv. Tom. II. p. 307.]

[10 The editor has not succeeded in finding the passage meant.] [11 Iste, 1611.]

[12 Ambros. Op. Par. 1686-90. Comm. in Epist. ad Rom. cap. i. v. 22. Tom II. Append. col. 33; where we find *regem, aut comites*, and *opus est*.]

of water unto mine eyes, that I may mourn day and night for the sins of my people?" we may not think, that Christ, Esay, and Jeremy, were defacers of the church. He hindereth not health, that sheweth the disease. He despiseth not the church, that setteth Christ before the church. The church is our mother: but Christ saith: "Whoso loveth his father or mother more than me is not meet to be my disciple." He despiseth not his mother, that lamenteth the captivity of his mother, and delivereth her from the hands of thieves.

Matt. x.

"But we have set up altar against altar;" or rather, as you say, "We have overthrown altars, and all together;" and so have erected a new church, a new gospel, and a new religion of our own. Verily, M. Harding, we have overthrown nothing but that God's good will was should be overthrown. Christ saith: "Every plant that my heavenly Father hath not planted shall be rooted up." An altar we have, such as Christ, and his apostles, and other holy fathers had, which of the Greeks was called ἱερὰ τράπεζα, "the holy table;" and of the Latins, *mensa dominica*, "the table of the Lord;" and was made, not of stone, but of timber; and stood not at the end of the quire, but in the midst of the people, as many ways it may appear. And other, or better altar, than Christ and these holy fathers had, we desire to have none; and specially any such altar as hath been purposely set up against the altar of Christ.

Matt. xv.

But you of your side have said, "Here is Christ, and there is Christ;" and so have erected up, not only altar against altar, and church against church, but also Christ against Christ. So Leo seemeth to say of you: *Ecclesiæ nomine armamini; sed contra ecclesiam dimicatis*[1]: "Ye arm yourselves with the name of the church; and yet ye fight against the church." So saith Nazianzene: "Ye strive for Christ against Christ himself[2]."

Matt. xxiv.

Leo in Epist. ad Palæstinos.

Nazianzenus In Apologeti.

But you seem to set light of mine age, and to disable my knowledge in divinity; as though it were much pertinent unto these matters either to calculate mine age, or else to examine the order of my study. I may say with Origen: *Gratias ago Deo, quod ignorantiam meam non ignoro:* "I thank God that I am not ignorant of mine ignorance." But whatsoever want either is, or is surmised to be in me, it ought not to prejudice the truth of God.

And yet I see no great cause why any man should seek so greatly to disadvantage me in respect of mine age or study. For it is well known that I, although unworthy of that degree, proceeded bachelor in divinity, in the university of Oxford, one whole year and more before M. Harding. Indeed, I grant I could not read all the councils, and old fathers of the church, both Greeks and Latins, in seven days, as M. Harding could[3]. And yet so much had I read, that I marvelled M. Harding would ever enterprise so much to abuse the names of the holy fathers.

Anno Domini 1551. anno Edvardi VI. quinto.

But knowledge oftentimes is vain, and puffeth up the mind. God make us learned to the kingdom of God, that we may humble all our knowledge to the obedience of faith!

It rejoiceth me much that ye say ye love me, and in respect of our old friendship and love have thus written to me. Howbeit our old private friendship needed not so many public witnesses. Ye say, "ye will follow the latter part of Chilo's counsel:" *Oderis, tanquam amaturus:* "Hate so as afterward thou mayest love."

Between which your two sayings, of hating and loving, I know not how, you include a plain contradiction: unless ye will say, ye can hate and love in one respect both together. But I take it in the best sense, wherein I doubt not but ye meant it.

Howbeit, touching your friendly advice, I may answer you likewise with another piece of Chilo's counsel: *Obsequendum est amico usque ad aras:* "A man may follow his friend's counsel, so it be not either against God, or against his

---

[[1] Leon. Magni Op. Lut. 1623. Ad Palæst. Episc. Epist. lxxiii. 8. col. 444; where for *sed* we find *et*.]

[[2] Ὑπὲρ Χριστοῦ δὲ ἀγωνιεῖταί τις οὐ κατὰ Χριστόν;—Gregor. Naz. Op. Par. 1778—1840. Orat. ii. 85. Tom. I. p. 53.]

[[3] Alluding to Harding's sudden change of religion on the accession of queen Mary, which he professed was grounded on the study of the fathers.]

conscience." The people of Alexandria said unto Timotheus: *Etsi non communicamus tecum, tamen amamus te*[4]: "Although we communicate not with you, yet we love you notwithstanding." Ye promise to deal herein without either gall or bitterness; "for that," as you say, "glikes, nips, and scoffs, bites, cuts, and girds (these be your words) become not your stage." And doubtless such kind of dealing, as it is most commendable in itself, so it seemeth most fitting for them that travail in God's cause[5]. Christ saith: "Learn of me; for I am meek and gentle." Liberatus. Cap. xvi. Matt. xi.

But whose words then be these, M. Harding? from what spirit have they proceeded? upon what stage were they spoken? these words, I say, wherewith ye seem so much, and so often, to solace yourself, and to refresh your spirits: "Goliath, Thersites, rash, presumptuous, wicked, unlearned, ignorant, peevish, Lucians, scoffers, coggers, foisters, pert, insolent, vaunters, braggers, sectaries, schismatics, heretics, sacramentaries, new masters, new fanglers, false reporters, slanderers of the church, terrible seducers, the enemies of the sacrifice, the enemies of the church, the ministers of the devil, sitters in the chair of pestilence, monsters, heathens, publicans, Turks, infidels, antichrists, and forerunners of antichrist?" Terms used commonly by M. Harding through his whole book.

These words be yours, M. Harding, not only for that they be uttered by you, but also for that they pertain directly and properly unto yourself. With these and other like pearls ye have thoroughly beset your whole book, that it might the more glitter in the eye of your reader. Herewith your stage is fully fraught[6]. Some man would think it were *Vetus Comœdia;* so faithful ye seem to be in keeping your promise. If ye utter such words of pure love and friendship, what then may we look for if ye once begin to hate? They say, the scorpion embraceth lovingly with his feet, but smiteth his poison with his tail. Thus ye suffer the tempests of your affections sometime[7] to blow you out, and to toss you off from the shore. In a man of professed gravity reasons had been more convenient than reproaches. Such eloquence might better become some of your younger Jannizers; who, as their friends say here, have not yet learned to speak otherwise.

As for these words, and these stages, they may not well chase us away from the gospel of Christ. It is not needful for us to hear your good reports, but it is most needful for us to speak the truth.

The advertisement that you allege out of Salomon, "There is a way that unto a man seemeth right; but the end thereof leadeth unto damnation," is common, and toucheth us both, as well you as me; or rather, somewhat more you than me. Ye were once deceived before, by your own confession. But they that have indifferently weighed the causes and suddenness of your change, have thought ye are as much, or rather much more, deceived now.

Mark, I beseech you, M. Harding, what ye were lately, and what ye would now seem to be; what way ye trode then, and what way ye tread now. The difference is no less than is between light and darkness, life and death, heaven and hell. So great a change would require some good time of deliberation.

But if you[8] be thoroughly changed, as you say, and if ye be touched indeed, either with the zeal of God, or with the love of your brethren, be not then ashamed to tell us what things God hath done for you. Let your reader understand, that you yourself sometime were that man of whom Salomon speaketh; that you sometime were in a way that seemed right, and yet the end thereof led to damnation; that you sometime bent your whole heart and study to deface the church of God; that you preached so many years together directly contrary to your conscience; that you sometime wittingly, and willingly, and of purpose and malice, deceived God's people; that you sometime were the minister of the devil, a Turk, an heathen, an infidel, a forerunner of antichrist; and that from this rueful state ye were suddenly changed, not by reading, or conference of the scriptures, or ancient fathers, but only for that ye saw the prince was changed.

[4 Liberat. Brev. Par. 1675. cap. xvi. p. 108; where we have *vel si non tibi communicamus*, &c.]
[5 Causes, 1565.]
[6 Freight, 1565, fraight, 1609.]
[7 Sometimes, 1565.]
[8 Ye, 1565.]

Thus must ye deal, M. Harding, if ye deal truly. So will your friends think ye dissemble not now, as you did before, but are moved only of true zeal and pure conscience. Certainly either, as we say, ye are now deceived; or, at the least, as yourself must needs grant, not long sithence ye were deceived. And St Augustine saith: *Hoc est erroris proprium, ut quod cuique displicet, id aliis quoque oportere existimet displicere*[1]: "This is the very nature of error, that, whatsoever misliketh any man, he thinketh all others should likewise mislike the same."

Augustin. de Gen. contra Manichæ.

Such is the misery of Adam's children: their heart is evermore inclined unto ill and error. Hereof false prophets oftentimes take occasion to say: "Good is ill; and ill is good: light is darkness; and darkness is light." And oftentimes the people is wilfully led away, and cannot abide to hear sound doctrine, but turn[2] their ears to hear fables.

Therefore Salomon's counsel is wise and good. And for that cause we trust not our own eyes to choose our way; but we call unto God, with the prophet David, "O Lord, shew us the way, that we may walk in:" we seek unto him that saith, "I am the way, the truth, and the life." "I am the light of the world: whoso followeth me walketh not in darkness, but hath the light of life." And we thank God, that with his day-spring from above hath visited us, and directed our feet into the way of peace—into the same way that Christ hath shewed us, and the holy apostles and ancient catholic fathers have trodden before us.

Psal. cxliii. John xiv. John viii.

Touching your exhortation to humility, and the denial of my learning, which, I trust, of your part proceedeth from a meek and humble spirit, I may safely deny that thing that I never avouched. It cannot shame me to say that St Hierome said: *Dicam illud Socraticum, Hoc tantum scio, quod nihil scio*[3]: "I will say, as Socrates sometime said, This thing only I know, that I know nothing." In these cases, as I seek no praise, so I fear no reproach. Whatsoever want is in me, there be others that can supply it. Howbeit I never understood but verity and humility might well stand together.

Hieron. in Præf. in Abdiam.

Where you say, whatsoever skill or knowledge I have, or had, I have evermore bent it only to the reproach and slander of the church, it is no great mastery, M. Harding, to speak ill. But I trust God himself, that judgeth justly, judgeth otherwise. If there be in me, I say not any talent, but only any mite of a talent, my prayer unto God is, and ever was, it may be bestowed wholly to the honour and comfort of his church.

And yet may not you, M. Harding, neither set such store by yourself, nor so much abase and discredit others, as though, besides you and your fellows, there were no man meet to be counted learned. When the Jews, in contempt of all others, boasted themselves to be the only stock and blood of Abraham, St Paul, by an humble kind of presumption, doubted not in all respects to compare with them in this wise: "Hebrews they be; and so am I. Israelites they be; and so am I. The seed of Abraham they be; and so am I." Again he saith: "Thus do I, and thus will I do, that in the things whereof they glory they may be found to be as we are." I will force this comparison no further. Such contention is but vain. O M. Harding, this saying is common unto us both: "By the grace of God we are that we are." O that his grace be not in us in vain!

2 Cor. xi. 1 Cor. xv.

For my part, both at your request, and also without your request, I utterly deny my learning. And touching my bishopric, if that in any part happen to grieve you, I deny it too: I deny mine estimation; I deny my name; I deny myself[4]. Only the faith[5] of Christ, and the truth of God, I cannot deny. Or with this faith, or for this faith, I trust I shall end. I cannot withstand the Spirit of God. I cannot say the consent of all the ancient catholic fathers was an heap of errors and a link of heresies. Although you, M. Harding, could deny all together at an instant, and upon the sudden, yet bear with others that cannot so easily do the same.

[[1] The following is perhaps the passage meant: Est autem hoc erroris proprium, ut quod cuique displicet, hoc etiam Deo displicere arbitretur.—August. Op. Par. 1679-1700. De Gen. cont. Manich. Lib. II. 24. Tom. I. col. 675.]

[[2] Turneth, 1565.]

[[3] ...saltem Socraticum illud habeo: Scio, quod nescio.—Hieron. Op. Par. 1693—1706. In Abd. Proph. Præfat. Tom. III. cols. 1455, 6.]

[[4] Meself, 1565.] [[5] Father, 1609, 1611.]

Touching D. Fisher, I scoffed neither at him, nor at any others. Only I laid out the imperfection of certain their arguments; which if they were weak, and many ways faulty, the fault was not mine: I made them not. D. Fisher's argument was this: "We are sure there is purgatory:" *Ergo*, "The pope's pardons be good and available[6]." I shall be forced, in perusing your book, to disclose many like infirmities and follies in your arguments, M. Harding. Yet, notwithstanding, I will not scoff. But happy are you, that may call us "gospellers," "new masters," "patriarchs," and I know not what, and to write what you list, without scoffing. In the end of your foretalk, which is before the shewing of your book, ye think all the world singeth *Sanctus, sanctus,* and receiveth you with *Ozanna:* and therefore ye will everybody to come and subscribe. Howbeit, it seemeth this request is very sudden, and out of season. You should first have shewed us both whereunto we should subscribe, and also your authorities and reasons wherewith ye would force us to subscribe. But the old learned father Tertullian saith thus of the Valentinian heretics: *Habent artificium, quo prius persuadent, quam doceant: veritas autem docendo suadet, non suadendo docet*[7]*:* "These heretics have a kind of cunning, and a policy, whereby they persuade us first, and teach us afterward: but the truth persuadeth us by teaching, and not teacheth us by persuading."

Polydo. de Invent. Rer. Lib. viii. Cap. 1.

Tertul. adversus Valentinian. Lib. i.

King Agesilaus, the better to embolden his soldiers to the fight, with a certain juice wrote this word, "Victory," in the palm of his hand; and afterward, being at his service, as the manner then of the heathens was, he laid his hand so written closely and secretly upon the heart of the sacrifice, and so printed it with the said word, "Victory;" and immediately shewed the same unto his captains and soldiers, as if it had been written by the gods. The simple soldiers, not understanding this policy, and thinking the whole matter had indeed been wrought by miracle, grew full of courage, not doubting but their gods, that had written "Victory," would also give them victory.

By like policy, and to like purpose, it seemeth you, M. Harding, would beguile your reader, and that you lack in strength would win by policy, and that you want in reasons would gain in words; that the simple may think you have the victory, because you have written "victory" with your pen.

But you are not yet equal with the credit of Pythagoras. It is not sufficient for your scholars to say, *Ipse dixit;* "M. Harding hath said it." Every man will not think it is so, because you can write it, or print it, or say it is so. As for myself[8], I will say with St Hierome: *Cupio discere, et discipulum me profiteor, dummodo doceant:* "I would fain learn, and make a vow to be their scholar, so they would teach me." First, ye should have given us leave to have perused your whole book. And when we had well weighed your untrue allegations, your vain constructions, your new petite doctors, your corruptions, your forgeries, your dreams, your fables, and the huge multitude of your untruths, then hardly ye should have called us to subscribe.

Howbeit, M. Harding, this is no force sufficient to subdue the world. It was not thought ye had been so weakly appointed. It is not enough for you thus odiously to upbraid us in your anger, and to call us new masters and heretics. That lesson might have served you long ago, before ye were espied. It behoveth you now to have some stronger arguments, specially fighting against God.

For my part, notwithstanding I were thoroughly persuaded long before, yet am I now some deal the more satisfied by these your travails. For touching your want of scriptures, councils, doctors, and examples of the primitive church, I am well and fully confirmed by the slenderness of your proofs.

And I doubt not but some of these that now be about you, being, I trust, not frowardly carried away with wilful malice, but having the fear of God, and a reverent zeal to do the best, although perhaps not knowledge sufficient to judge what is best, after they shall understand some part of your dealing herein, will, by God's grace, begin somewhat to forethink themselves of their journey, and to cast some doubts of your credit. St Augustine saith: *Juris forensis est, ut qui in*

August. in Joan. Tract. 7.

[6 Polyd. Verg. De Invent. Rer. Amst. 1671. Lib. VIII. cap. i. pp. 475, 6; where Fisher's words are quoted. See before, page 14, note 6.]

[7 Tertull. Op. Lut. 1641. Adv. Valentin. 1. p. 289; where we have *persuadeant quam edoceant,* and *docendo persuadet.*]

[8 Meself, 1565.]

precibus mentitus sit, illi ne prosit, quod impetravit[1]: "The law is this, that whoso hath made a false suggestion shall lose whatsoever he have gotten by the same."

Chrysostom. de Laudibus Pauli, Hom. 5.

O M. Harding, credit without truth is no credit. Your work is over weak: it hath no foundation: it cannot stand. Chrysostom telleth you: "Such is the nature of error, it vadeth of itself, and will come to ground without resistance[2]."

Ecclus. iv.

John ix.

Remember the place ye sometime stood in: remember from whence ye are fallen: remember the causes of your fall. It is no shame to rise again. God is able to restore you. The wise man saith: "There is confusion that bringeth grace and glory." God hath endued you largely with great gifts. Turn the same to the obedience of the faith of Christ. As there is wisdom in seeking the victory, so there is wisdom in giving place. Follow the same counsel ye give others. Deny your own learning: deny your own estimation: deny yourself. "Give the glory unto God."

[[1] August. Op. Par. 1679–1700. In Johan. Evang. cap. i. Tractat. vii. 11. Tom. III. Pars II. col. 346; where we find *Juris enim*, and *mentitus fuerit, non illi.*]

[[2] *Τοιοῦτον γὰρ ἡ πλάνη, καὶ μηδενὸς ἐνοχλοῦντος καταῤῥεῖ.*—Chrysost. Op. Par. 1718–38. De Laud. Paul. Apost. Hom. IV. Tom. II. p. 499.]

THE TABLE OF THE ARTICLES TREATED ON IN THIS BOOK.

---

1. THAT there was any private mass in the world at that time, for the space of six hundred years after Christ.

2. Or that there was then any communion ministered unto the people under one kind.

3. Or that the people had then[3] common prayer in a strange tongue that they understood not.

4. Or that the bishop of Rome was then called an universal bishop, or the head of the universal church.

5. Or that the people was then taught to believe that Christ's body is really, substantially, corporally, carnally, or naturally in the sacrament.

6. Or that his body is or may be in a thousand places, or more, at one time.

7. Or that the priest did then hold up the sacrament over his head.

8. Or that the people did then fall down and worship it with godly honour.

9. Or that the sacrament was then, or now ought to be, hanged up under a canopy.

10. Or that in the sacrament, after the words of consecration, there remain only the accidents and shews, without the substance, of bread and wine.

11. Or that the priest then divided the sacrament in three parts, and afterward received himself all alone.

12. Or that whosoever had said, the sacrament is a figure, a pledge, a token, or a remembrance of Christ's body, had therefore been judged for an heretic.

13. Or that it was lawful then to have thirty, twenty, fifteen, ten, or five masses said in one day.

14. Or that images then were set up in the churches, to the intent the people might worship them.

15. Or that the lay people was then forbidden to read the word of God in their own tongue.

16. Or that it was then lawful for the priest to pronounce the words of consecration closely and in silence to himself.

17. Or that the priest had then authority to offer up Christ unto his Father.

18. Or to communicate and receive the sacrament for another, as they do.

19. Or to apply the virtue of Christ's death and passion to any man by the mean of the mass.

20. Or that it was then thought a sound doctrine to teach the people that mass *ex opere operato*, that is, even for that it is said and done, is able to remove any part of our sin.

21. Or that then any christian man called the sacrament his Lord and God.

22. Or that the people was then taught to believe that the body of Christ remaineth in the sacrament as long as the accidents of the bread remain there without corruption.

23. Or that a mouse, or any other worm or beast, may eat the body of Christ (for so some of our adversaries have said and taught).

24. Or that when Christ said, *Hoc est corpus meum*, this word *Hoc* pointed not the bread, but *Individuum vagum*, as some of them say.

25. Or that the accidents, or forms, or shews of bread and wine be the sacraments of Christ's body and blood, and not rather the very bread and wine itself.

26. Or that the sacrament is a sign or token of the body of Christ that lieth hidden underneath it.

27. Or that ignorance is the mother and cause of true devotion and obedience.

[[3] There, old editt.]

OF PRIVATE MASS.

THE FIRST ARTICLE.

THE BISHOP OF SARISBURY.

If any learned man of our adversaries, or if all the learned men that be alive, be able to bring any one sufficient sentence out of any old catholic doctor or father, or out of any old general council, or out of the holy scriptures of God, or any one example of the primitive church, whereby it may clearly and plainly be proved that there was any private mass in the whole world at that time, for the space of six hundred years after Christ, &c.,—The conclusion is this: as I said before, so say I now again, I am content to yield and to subscribe.

M. HARDING. THE FIRST DIVISION.

[AN ANSWER TO MASTER JEWEL'S CHALLENGE, BY D. HARDING.

OF MASS WITHOUT A NUMBER OF OTHERS RECEIVING THE COMMUNION WITH THE PRIEST AT THE SAME TIME AND PLACE, WHICH THE GOSPELLERS CALL PRIVATE MASS. ARTICLE I.—HARDING'S ANSWER, 1564.]

Every mass is public, concerning both the oblation and also the communion, and none private. For no man offereth that dreadful sacrifice privately for himself alone, but for the whole church of Christ in common. The communion, likewise, of the sacrament is a public feast by Christ through the ministry of the priest in the same, (1) *prepared for every faithful person; from partaking whereof none is excluded, that, with due examination having before made himself ready, demandeth the same. And so being common by order of the first institution, and by* (2) *will of the ministers, it ought to be reputed for common, not private.*

[*No mass private in itself, but in respect of circumstances.* Harding's Answer, 1564.]

The first untruth. For there is no such preparation.

The second untruth. There appeareth no such will in the minister.

That others do so commonly forbear to communicate with the priest, it is through their own default and negligence, not regarding their own salvation. Whereof the godly and careful rulers of faithful people have sithence the time of the primitive church always much complained.

THE BISHOP OF SARISBURY.

There appeareth small hope that M. Harding will deal plainly in the rest, that thus maketh his first entry with a cavil. For whereas the matter is known and agreed upon, it is great folly to pick quarrel upon the word. "Every mass," saith he, "is common, and none private." If it be so, then hath he already concluded fully on our side; for if there be no private mass at all, then was there no private mass in the primitive church, which was my first assertion.

But M. Harding, as may be gathered by his manner of proofs, is not yet well resolved, neither what is private, nor what is mass. For in the twenty-second article of his book, entreating of the accidents of bread and wine, to the intent to avoid the gross absurdities that follow transubstantiation, he saith: "These matters were never taught in open audience, but privately disputed in the schools, and set abroad by learned men in their private writings." There he calleth that thing private, that is disputed in open audience, in the hearing of five hundred or more, and is set abroad to the knowledge of the world; and here the thing, that is done by the priest and his boy alone in a corner, he calleth common.

Page 182, b[1].

M. Harding maketh common private, and private common.

[[1] The reference here, and in other similar marginal notes, is to the original edition of Harding's Answer, 1564.]

Thus he maketh words to sound what him listeth, sometime common to be private, sometime private to be common, at his pleasure.

And as touching mass, sometime he maketh it the sacrifice, sometime the communion, sometime the prayers; and so seemeth not yet well to know upon what ground to stand.

His first reason is this: the sacrifice of the priest is common; therefore the mass is common. Here might be demanded, who gave the priest authority to make his[2] sacrifice? and without authority how can he make it? But if his sacrifice be common, why doth he give it these private titles; this for the living, this for the dead, this for a friend, this for himself? These reasons be answered afterward more at large.

His second reason is this: it is a feast, and therefore it is common; and thus he salveth one error with another. For, if it be a feast, how is it received by one alone? If it be received by one alone, how can it seem to be a feast? But he saith, "it is prepared for all." Verily it is but small provision to serve so many. The priest himself knoweth this is untrue: he prepareth for himself, and not for others; he speaketh to himself, and not unto the congregation; he receiveth himself alone, and not with his brethren. Therefore in this respect we must needs say the mass is private, and not common.

The third reason, touching the will of the minister, is very uncertain. For neither can the priest, by his willing, alter natures, or make that thing common which is private; nor can any man certainly know what thing the priest willeth. For what if his will be to work necromancy or sorcery, as it is reported of pope Hildebrand? Or what if his will be to poison somebody, as Henry the emperor was poisoned in the communion-bread[3], pope Victor in the chalice[4]? Or what if his will be to work feigned miracles, as Lyra saith many are wrought in the open church by the priest, to mock the people[5]? Doubtless, if the priest's will may be known either by his words, or by his doings, or by his gesture, or by his provision, or by the quantity of his bread and wine, or by his whole usage and practice, it may soon be seen his will is to make a private banquet, and not a common. Hermanus Contractus. Nicolaus Lyra in xiv. cap. Danielis

These be very weak foundations to build upon. Of the same M. Harding might rather and far better have gathered the contrary. For, if it be the common sacrifice of the whole church, it should be offered by the whole church, as St Ambrose saith: *Ut multorum oblatio simul celebretur*[6]; "That the oblation of many may be made together." Ambros. 1 Cor. xi.

If it be a common feast of the whole church, it should be received commonly of the whole church. And therefore St Hierome saith: *Dominica cœna omnibus debet esse communis:* "The Lord's supper must be common to all;" and that not for these simple shifts that M. Harding and his fellows have devised. St Hierome's reason is this: *Quia Dominus omnibus discipulis, qui aderant, æqualiter tradidit sacramenta*[7]: "Because the Lord gave the sacraments equally to all the disciples that were present." These words be plain: "equally," and "to all the disciples." And therefore saith St Hierome, according to this example, the Lord's supper must be common. Hier. 1 Cor. xi.

M. HARDING. THE SECOND DIVISION.

Therefore in this respect we do not acknowledge any private mass, but leave that term to Luther's school, where it was first devised and so termed by Satan himself, seeking how to withdraw his novice Luther from the love and estimation of that most blessed sacrifice, by reasoning with him against the same, in a night vision; as himself recordeth in a little book which he made, De missa angulari et unctione sacerdotali[9]. The[8] third untruth.

[2 This, 1565, 1609.]

[3 Henry VII.—Naucler. Chronic. Tubing. 1516. Vol. II. Gen. xliv. fol. 246. The chronicle of Hermannus Contractus ends at an earlier period.]

[4 Victor III.—Id. ibid. Gen. xxxvii. fol. 164.]

[5 Et similiter aliquando fit in ecclesia maxima deceptio populi in miraculis fictis a sacerdotibus vel eis adhærentibus propter lucrum temporale.—Bibl. cum Gloss. Ord. et Expos. N. de Lyra, Basil. 1502. Pars IV. fol. 330. 2.]

[6 Ambros. Op. Par. 1686-90. Comm. in Epist. I. ad Cor. cap. xi. vv. 33, 4. Tom. II. Append. col. 150.]

[7 Hieron. Op. Par. 1693-1706. Comm. in Epist. I. ad Cor. cap. xi. Tom. V. col. 997.]

[8 1565 omits *the*.]

[9 Luth. Op. Witeb. 1558. De Miss. Priv. et Unct. Sacerd. Tom. VII. fol. 226, &c.]

THE BISHOP OF SARISBURY.

This tale against that godly man doctor Luther is scornful and slanderous, blazed abroad by Pighius, Hosius, Staphylus the runagate[1], and such others, only of wilful malice and hatred of the truth; and therefore not worthy to be answered. Doctor Luther sheweth what terrible tentations the devil layeth to trap man withal, taking occasion sometime of well-doing, sometime of evil, sometime of truth, sometime of falsehood[2]. And, for example, he sheweth that the devil on a time assaulted him, not in visible form, but by dreadful suggestions in his conscience, as it were, thus calling him to remembrance: "These many years thou hast said mass, thou hast shewed up bread and wine to be worshipped as God, and yet now thou knowest it was a creature and not God: thereof followed idolatry; and thou wert[3] the cause thereof." All these things he saw to be true by the testimony and light of his own conscience, and therefore confessed he had offended, and yielded himself unto God. The devil's purpose was to lead him to despair; but God mercifully delivered him. And this is doctor Luther's whole and only meaning in that place, that no man of himself is able to withstand such assaults and tentations of the enemy, but only by the power and mercy of God. This, good reader, is that "School of Satan," this is that wonderful tragedy, whereat M. Harding maketh such horrible exclamations. If he think it so heinous a matter for a godless[4] man to be vexed by the devil, perhaps he will also find some fault with Christ, that was carried by the devil into the mount; or with St Paul, that had the angel of Satan to buffet him; or with a great number of his portuise saints, whose legends are full of visions of devils, with other like childish fables. As for Luther, the doctrine that he taught in his school touching this point is the very gospel of Christ; and therefore it increaseth and entereth into the hearts of men, and the lies and slanders of the enemies shall never be able to prevail against it.

Matt. iv.
2 Cor. xii.

M. HARDING. THE THIRD DIVISION.

Yet we deny not but[5] the fathers of some ancient councils, and sithence likewise St Thomas and certain other school-doctors, have called it sometimes a private mass, but not after the sense of Luther and his scholars, but only as it is contrary to public and solemn, in consideration of place, time, audience, purpose, rites, and other circumstances: the variety and change of which, being things accidentary, cannot vary or change the substance or essential nature of the mass. M. Jewel, an earnest professor of the new doctrine of Luther and of the sacramentaries, calleth, as they do, that a private mass whereat the priest, having no company to communicate with him, receiveth the sacrament alone.

Concil. Valen. cap. 4[6]. *Concil. Tilburien*[7]. *Decretal. Lib.* iii. *tit.* 41. *cap.* 2[8]. *De consecrat. Dist.* 1. *ex Aug. quod quidam Greg. tribuunt*[9]. *Greg. ex Regist. Lib.* ii. *ad Casterium. cap.* 9.[10]
3. *Parte Summæ Quæst.* 83. [*responsione ad* 12. *argumentum articuli* 5. Harding's Answer, 1564.]

[*What the Lutherans call private mass.* Harding's Answer, 1564.]

THE BISHOP OF SARISBURY.

M. Harding by a rhetorical correction upon better advice putteth himself in remembrance that there is mention made of peculiar and private masses, as he saith, "in certain ancient councils, and in the school-doctors." He might have named Stephen Gardiner, and Albertus Pighius[11], that wrote the defence of private mass, and he himself acknowledgeth abuses and errors in the same. Yet will he not, I trow, confess that either of them both was the disciple of Satan.

In the bishops' book. Alb. Pighius in Locis Communib. de Privata Missa.

Here M. Harding standeth upon terms, and saith, "The mass is called private in respect of place, time, audience, and other circumstances." And even such be

[1 Renegate, 1565.] [2 Falsehead, 1565.]
[3 Were, 1565.] [4 Godly, 1565, 1609.]
[5 But that, 1565, and Harding's Answer, 1564.]
[6 Harding's Answer, 1564, has Vasen.; which is probably the right reading. See Concil. Vasens. II. in Concil. Stud. Labb. et Cossart. Lut. Par. 1671, 2. can. 3. Tom. IV. col. 1680. This council, however, was held A.D. 529.]
[7 Triburien. 1565, and Harding's Answer, 1564.]
[8 Concil. Tribur. in Corp. Jur. Canon. Lugd. 1624, Decretal. Greg. IX. Lib. III. Tit. xli. cap. 2. col. 1365.]
[9 August. in eod. Decret. Gratian. Decr. Tert. Pars, De Consecr. Dist. i. can. 51, col. 1903.]
[10 Gregor. Magni Papæ I. Op. Par. 1705. Epist. Lib. II. Indict. x. Ad Castor. Epist. xii. Tom. II. col. 577.]
[11 Alb. Pigh. Explic. Cathol. Præc. Contr. Par. 1586. Controv. VI. fol. 123. 2.]

their private masses for the most part, said in side aisles, alone, without company of people, only with one boy to make answer; so private, that the people of God is thereby deprived and robbed of all comfort. And thus it seemeth Thomas understandeth the private mass; for thus he saith: *In missis privatis sufficit, si unus sit præsens, scilicet minister, qui populi totius personam gerit*[12]: "In private masses it is sufficient if there be one present, I mean the clerk that standeth instead of the whole people." Part. 3. Quæst. 83. Art. 5.

Touching the allegations in the margin, the school-doctors are all of very late years; the place of St Augustine is forged, and not St Augustine's; the place of St Gregory nothing to purpose, not once naming private mass; the councils, that are called so ancient, were all at the least seven hundred years after Christ, and so without the reach of my compass.

But to agree upon terms and not to fly the name of mass, although it be very seldom, and for the most part never, found in the old catholic writers; that we call the common or public mass, where as the priest and people receive the holy communion together, which was the ancient order of the apostles and holy fathers in the primitive church. But where as the priest receiveth the sacrament himself alone, without distribution made unto others, that we call the private mass, yea, although the whole parish be present and look upon him. For a thing may be private, although it be done by the public minister, and for the people, and in the midst of all the people. And thus Thomas of Aquine seemeth to take these words, private and common. "First," saith he, "the people is prepared to receive by the common prayer of all the people, which is the Lord's prayer; and also by the private prayer which the priest offereth specially for the people[13]." Here the prayer is called private, notwithstanding it be made by the priest for the people and in the midst of the congregation. Public mass. Private mass. 3 Part. Quæst. 183. Art. 4 In explanatione Missæ Romanæ.

M. HARDING. THE FOURTH DIVISION.

Against this private mass, as he termeth it, he inveigheth sore in his printed sermon, which he preached at Paul's Cross, the second Sunday before Easter, in the year of our Lord 1560, *as he intituleth it; shunning the accustomed name of Passion Sunday*[14], *lest, as it seemeth, by using the term of the catholic church he should seem to favour any thing that is catholic. In which sermon he hath gathered together, as it were into one heap, all that ever he could find written in derogation of it in their books by whom it hath been impugned.*

THE BISHOP OF SARISBURY.

Mark, gentle reader, how small occasions this man taketh hold at, contrary to this[15] promise, to serve his intemperate humour of speaking evil. What, thinketh he that all folk are heretics that name the days otherwise than they be named in his portuise? So may he soon condemn the Greeks and (the church of Rome only excepted) all other Christians throughout the world, who, as I reckon, never had the name of Passion Sunday in their calendar or use of speaking. So may he condemn all such as call *Parasceve,* Good Friday; or the Italians, that, contrary to the portuise, call the first week in Lent the carnival. Indeed, the portuise calleth that day not only Passion Sunday, but also the Sunday Judica, and taketh the one name to be as catholic as the other. God be thanked, we are not ashamed of Christ's passion, as having nothing to glory in but only the cross of Christ and his passion: neither do we refuse your fantasies because they be catholic, as you surmise, but because they be your own, devised by yourself of late days, many of them contrary to God's holy word, and are not catholic. Dominica Judica. Gal. vi.

Invectives I made none, neither do we use the pulpit to that purpose, but soberly and far otherwise than M. Harding seemeth to use his pen. I spake of

[12 ...in missis tamen privatis sufficit unum habere ministrum, qui gerit personam totius populi catholici.—Thom. Aquinat. Op. Venet. 1595. Summ. Theol. Tert. Pars, Quæst. LXXXIII. Art. v. Tom. XII. fol. 280. 2.]

[13 ... et primo præparatur populus ad percipiendum, primo quidem, per orationem communem totius populi (quæ est oratio dominica ...) et etiam privatam, quam specialiter sacerdos pro populo offert, &c.—Id. ibid. Art. iv. fol. 278. 2.]

[14 The Sunday before Palm Sunday was usually so called.]

[15 His, 1565.]

the abuses of Christ's last supper, having thereto occasion of these words of St Paul: "The thing that I received of the Lord, the same have I delivered unto you;" who in his time seemeth to find fault with the Corinthians for the same. Neither is the supper of Christ so privileged, but it may be abused, as appeareth by the very confession of our adversaries, who deny not but that there be abuses and errors cropen into the private mass.

1 Cor. xi.

Albertus Pighius de Privata Missa.

M. HARDING. THE FIFTH DIVISION.

Although[1] *he pretend enmity against private mass in word, yet indeed whosoever readeth his sermon, and discerneth his spirit, shall easily perceive that he extendeth his whole wit and cunning utterly to abolish the unbloody and daily sacrifice of the church,* (4) *commonly called the mass. Which, as the apostles themselves affirm in Clement their scholar and fellow, being unbloody, hath succeeded in place of the bloody sacrifices of the old law, and is by Christ's commandment frequented, and offered in remembrance of his passion and death, and to be used all times until his coming*[3]. *But whatsoever he or all other the forerunners of antichrist speak or work against it, all that ought not to overthrow the faith of good and true christian men, having for proof thereof, beside many other places of holy scripture, the figure of Melchisedech that was before the law, the prophecy of Malachi in the law, and lastly, and most plainly the* (5) *institution of Christ in the new testament; which he left to the apostles, the apostles to the church, and the church hath continually kept and used through the whole world until this day.*

The fourth untruth. For[2] the old fathers never commonly called it so.

Pro sacrificio cruento rationale et incruentum ac mysticum sacrificium instituit, quod in mortem Domini per symbola corporis et sanguinis ipsius celebratur. Clemens, Constitutionum Apostolicarum, Lib. vi. cap. 23.

The fifth untruth. For[2] Christ speaketh not one word of any sacrifice.

[*Proofs for the mass briefly touched.* H. A. 1564.]

Touching doctors, they have with one consent in all ages, in all parts of the world, from the apostles' time forward, both with their example and also testimony of writing, confirmed the same faith. They that have been brought up in learning, and yet through corruption of the time stand doubtful in this point, let them take pains to travail in study, and they shall find by good ancient witness of the priests and deacons of Achaia, that (6) *St Andrew the apostle, touching the substance of the mass, worshipped God every day with the same service as priests now do, in celebrating the external sacrifice of the church. They shall find by witness of Abdias, first bishop of Babylon, who was the apostles' scholar,* (7) *and saw Christ our Saviour in flesh, and was present at the passion and martyrdom of St Andrew, that St Matthew the apostle celebrated mass in Ethiopia, a little before his martyrdom*[4]. *They shall find by report of an ancient council general, that St James wrote a liturgy, or a form of the mass*[5]. *They shall find that Martialis, one of the seventy-two disciples of Christ and bishop of Bourdeaux in France, sent thither by St Peter, served God in like sort*[6]. (8) *They shall find in Clement the whole order and form of the mass, set forth by the apostles themselves, and the same celebrated by them after our Lord was assumpted, before they went to the ordering of bishops, priests, and the seven deacons, according to his institution*[7], *and the same right so declared by Cyrillus, bishop of Jerusalem,* In Mystagogicis orationibus. *They shall find the same most plainly treated of,* (9) *and a form of the mass, much agreeable to that is used in these days, in writing set forth by St Dionyse, whom St Paul converted to the faith, of whom it is mentioned in the Acts of the Apostles, who had conference with St*[8] *Peter, Paul, and John the Evangelist, and much acquaintance with Timothy.*

The sixth untruth. For[2] St Andrew said the communion, and not the mass.

The seventh untruth. For[2] this Abdias never saw Christ in the flesh: it is a very legend of lies.

Abdiæ Li. 7. *Historiæ Apostol.*

Concilium Constantinopol. in Trullo, cap. 32.

Epist. ad Burdegali.

The eighth untruth. For[2] there is no manner, token, or shew of private mass.

Constit. Apostol. 8. *cap. ult.*

The ninth untruth. For[2] it is the very form of the communion, and nothing like the private mass.

In Eccles. Hierarch. cap. 3. *Acts* xvii.

* *Thus do I give thee, good christian reader, but a taste as it were of proofs, without allegation of the words, for confirmation of thy faith concerning the blessed mass,*

*Faith confirmed without words. St Paul saith: "Faith cometh by hearing."

[[1] And though, Harding's Answer, 1564.]

[[2] In all these places, 1565 omits *for*.]

[[3] Const. Apost. in Concil. Stud. Labb. et Cossart. Lut. Par. 1671-2. Lib. VI. cap. xxiii. Tom. I. col. 403.]

[[4] Abd. Apost. Hist. Par. 1571. Lib. VII. fol. 94. 2.]

[[5] Concil. Quinisext. in Concil. Stud. Labb. et Cossart. can. 32. Tom. VI. col. 1158.]

[[6] Martial. ad Burdegal. Epist. i. cap. iii. in Biblioth. Patr. per M. de la Bigne, Tom. III. col. 3.]

[[7] Const. Apost. in Concil. Stud. Labb. et Cossart. Lib. VIII. cap. xlvi. Tom. I. col. 509.]

[[8] *St* is omitted, Harding's Answer, 1564.]

out of the scriptures, apostles, and apostolic men. (10) *I do further refer thee to Justinus, the martyr and philosopher, to Irenæus, the martyr and bishop of Lyons, who lived with the apostles' scholars; to the old bishop and martyr Hippolytus, that lived in Origen's time, who, in his oration* De consummatione mundi, *extant in Greek, maketh Christ thus to say at the general judgment unto bishops:* Venite, pontifices, qui pure mihi sacrificium die nocteque obtulistis, ac pretiosum corpus et sanguinum meum immolastis quotidie[10]: "*Come, ye bishops, that have purely offered sacrifice to me day and night, and have sacrificed my precious body and blood daily.*" (11) *Finally, I refer them, instead of many, to the two worthy fathers Basil and Chrysostom, whose masses be left to the posterity at this time extant.* (12) *Amongst all, Cyrillus Hierosolymitanus is not to be passed over lightly, who at large expoundeth the whole mass used in Hierusalem in his time, the same which now we find in Clement, much like to that of Basil and Chrysostom, and, for the canon and other principal parts, to that is now also used in the Latin church*[11].

Lib. iv. contra hæres. cap. 32.

In mystagogicis orationibus.

The[9] tenth. A burden of untruths.

The eleventh untruth. For[2] they contain the very order of the communion.

The twelfth untruth. For[2] it is the very express order of the communion. It is no private mass.

As for the other doctors of the church that followed the apostles and those apostolic men, many in number, excellent in learning, holy of life, to shew what may be brought out of their works for proof of this matter, that the oblation of the body and blood of Christ in the mass is the sacrifice of the church, and proper to the new testament, it would require a whole volume; and therefore, not being moved by M. Jewel's challenge to speak specially thereof, but as it is private after their meaning, and many good treatises in defence of this sacrifice being set forth already in print, at this present I will say nothing, thinking hereof as Sallust did of Carthago, that great city, that it were better to keep silence than to speak few[12].

THE BISHOP OF SARISBURY.

God grant unto all his people the spirit of wisdom and understanding, that they may be able to discern the spirits, whether they be of God, or no; that they may take heed of false prophets, and give ear to the voice of the Prince of pastors, and fly the voice of strangers, and beware of blind guides that so often have deceived them!

Isai. xi. 1 John iv. Matt. vii. John x. Matt. xxiii.

Here M. Harding a little overmuch inflameth his choler, and whom he listeth he calleth the enemies of the sacrifice, and the forerunners of antichrist, and what not, even with the same spirit that the Pharisees sometime said, Stephen had spoken against the holy temple; or, Christ had uttered blasphemy against God. I will not answer heat with heat, but in such kind of eloquence will rather give place.

Forerunners of antichrist. Acts vi. Matt. xxvi.

As touching the matter, M. Harding knoweth that St Gregory calleth him the forerunner of antichrist, not that saith, Christ hath made a full sacrifice for sin once for all upon the cross, but that vaunteth himself above his brethren, as did Lucifer, and nameth himself an universal bishop over the whole church of Christ[13]. Such a one St Gregory calleth the forerunner of antichrist.

Ad Constantian. Aug. ep. 78. Lib. iv. Ad Mauritium Imperat. Lib. vii. Epist. 197.

And whereas he calleth us at his pleasure the enemies of the holy sacrifice, wo were unto us if we had not that sacrifice. We know that Christ is that Lamb of God that hath taken away the sins of the world, and that there is no name or sacrifice under heaven whereby we can be saved, but only the name and sacrifice of Jesus Christ. And because we know that this sacrifice is sufficient, therefore we fly to no sacrifice made by man.

John i. Acts iv.

"The sacrifice," saith M. Harding, "commonly called the mass." But why sheweth he not of whom it is so called? Verily, neither the Hebrews in their tongue, nor the Greeks in their tongue, nor Christ, nor his apostles, nor Tertullian, nor St Cyprian, nor Origen, nor Lactantius, nor St Hierome, nor St Augustine,

Commonly called the mass.

[9 1565 omits *the*.]

[10 Hippol. De Consum. Mund. Par. 1556. p. 56.]

[11 Cyril. Hieros. Par. 1720. Cateches. Myst. v. pp. 325, &c.]

[12 Nam de Carthagine silere melius puto, quam parum dicere.—Sallust. in Bell. Jugurth.]

[13 Sed in hac ejus superbia quid aliud nisi propinqua jam antichristi esse tempora designatur?—Gregor. Magni Papæ I. Op. Par. 1705. Epist. Lib. v. Indict. XIII. Epist. xxi. Ad Const. August. Tom. II. col. 751. Id. Lib. VII. Indict. XV. Epist. xxxiii. Ad. Maur. August. col. 881. This passage is afterwards quoted.]

in any books undoubtedly known for theirs, nor his own doctors, Clement, Abdias, Hippolytus, ever used the name of mass. Therefore it is marvel that he would say the sacrifice is so commonly called the mass. If it might have pleased him to say that he himself and his fellows so call it, he had done right.

But here is brought in a whole troop of doctors in a rank; Melchisedech, Malachias, Clemens the apostles' fellow, the deacons of Asia, Abdias the apostles' disciple, and bishop of Babylon, that saw Christ in the flesh, St Andrew, St James, Martialis, Dionysius, who had conference with Peter, Paul, and John, Irenæus, Justinus Martyr, Hippolytus Martyr, Basil, Chrysostom, Cyril of Jerusalem, and all the rest of the doctors, in all ages and in all parts of the world. And who would not be afraid to see such an army come against him? Howbeit, gentle reader, be of good cheer. All this is but a camisado[1]: these be but vizards: they be no faces. They are brought in, like mummers, for a shew, and say nothing. That M. Harding lacked in weight, he would needs make up in tale, and so useth this only as a flourish before the fight; and, as a stream blown up with wind and weather carrieth with it much froth and filth by the very rage and drift of the water, even so M. Harding in this place flowing and wandering over the banks with *copia verborum*, by the violence and force of his talk carrieth a great deal of error and untruth along before him. Notwithstanding, thus hath he given thee, good christian reader, as he saith, a taste of his proofs

For confirmation of faith.

without allegation of any words for confirmation of thy faith concerning the mass. Miserable is that faith, that in so weighty matters can be confirmed with bare names by hearing nothing. I marvel that M. Harding ever durst either to allege such authorities, as he knoweth the most hereof be, or thus openly to mock the world. For, briefly to touch Melchisedech, Malachias, and the institution of

Gen. xiv.

Christ, what weight can there appear in these reasons? Melchisedech brought forth bread and wine to banquet Abraham and his army, being weary of the

Mal. i.

chase: or, Malachias prophesied that all the nations of the world should be turned

Matt. xxvi.

unto God, and should offer unto him a pure sacrifice: or, Christ ordained his last supper amongst his disciples, and bade them do the same in his remembrance: *Ergo*, there was private mass in the church. Who ever made any such arguments in any school? What, will M. Harding make folk believe that Melchisedech, Malachias, or Christ, said private mass? Or doth he think that these reasons must be taken because he speaketh the word?

But he will say, Melchisedech and Malachias signified the sacrifice of the new testament. We deny it not. But did they signify a sacrifice done by one man alone, in a strange language, the people looking on him, and no man knowing what he meaneth? Why may we not think rather they signified the sacrifice of the holy communion, where as the whole people doth lift up their hands and hearts unto heaven, and pray, and sacrifice together, rejoicing in the cross of Christ, and so celebrating the Lord's death until he come? For the sacrifice that is prophesied by Malachy, as it is expounded by Tertullian[2], St Hierome[3], and other holy fathers, is the sacrifice of prayer, and contrite heart; as hereafter in the seventeenth article it shall further appear.

Touching the witnesses here alleged, first, I marvel that M. Harding would ever bring them forth, but much more that he would thus set them out, with such circumstances of commendation, as that they saw Christ in the flesh, or that they were the apostles' fellows. For he knoweth well that many of them are little worthy of such credit, as partly being ever doubted of, and suspected to be written, not by them whose names they bear, but by heretics, to whom M. Harding seemeth now to fly for aid; partly also obscure, unknown, unacquainted, not read, not seen, not heard of in the world before this time. But most of all, I marvel that he would ever hazard his cause on these witnesses, who, as he himself very well knoweth, will speak against him. And therefore he hath here

[[1] Camisado: a night attack in which the soldiers wore shirts over their armour.]

[[2] Sic itaque sacrificia spiritalia laudis designantur, &c.—Tertull. Op. Lut. 1641. Adv. Jud. 5. p. 211. ...sacrificium mundum, scilicet simplex oratio de conscientia pura.—Id. Adv. Marc. Lib. IV. 1. p. 502.]

[[3] ... thymiama, hoc est, sanctorum orationes Domino offerendas.—Hieron. Op. Par. 1693-1706. In Mal. Proph. cap. i. Tom. III. col. 1813. Other authorities to the same effect will be hereafter cited.]

cunningly suppressed their words, and hath only made a muster of their names, but would suffer them to say nothing. Clemens.

And that thou, good reader, mayest have a taste hereof, and see the faithfulness of these men's dealing, let us first consider Clemens, who, as it is reported here, was the apostles' fellow. The title of the book seemeth to be *De apostolicis traditionibus:* that is, "Of orders taken and devised by the apostles of Christ for the better government of the church." A worthy book, no doubt, and in all ages to be had in great price, if men had been persuaded it had been written indeed by Clement. But St Hierome by the report of Eusebius maketh mention only of one epistle of Clement's that he thought worthy to be received; which epistle, notwithstanding, is not now to be found[4]. One other epistle of Clement's he speaketh of, but he saith it was never allowed by the church[5]. And further St Hierome saith: "Certain other books there are reported to be abroad in the name of Clement, as the disputation of Peter and Appion; which books were never in use amongst our fathers, neither contain they pure and apostolical doctrine[6]." Thus much St Hierome.

Clement.

Hier. de Ecclesiast. Scriptorib.

Books counterfeited in St Clement's name.

Now, whence then cometh M. Harding's Clement? It was found very lately in the Isle of Candy, by one Carolus Capellius, a Venetian, written in Greek, and in these countries never heard of nor seen before[7].

Petrus Crab, in 1 Tom. Concil.

Here the reader, be he never so simple, yet must he think thus much with himself: Clemens was bishop of Rome, as it is thought, next after St Peter; and were the bishop of Rome's books, and such books, so strange, so holy, and of such weight, kept in Candy, so far off from Italy, in an island in the sea, and not in Rome? written in Greek, and not in Latin? And could such a worthy work devised by all the apostles, and set forth by the apostles' fellow, be laid up in secrecy for the space of a thousand five hundred years and more, and no man miss it? Thus much the reader may soon consider with himself, be he never so simple.

But what if this book were never written by St Clement? What if it were written by no honest man? What if it were written by an heretic? Verily, it was a common practice in old times, to set wicked books abroad under the names and titles of the apostles, and other godly fathers. Leo, sometime bishop of Rome, writeth thus: *Apocryphæ ... scripturæ, quæ sub nominibus apostolorum multarum habent seminarium falsitatum, non solum interdicendæ, sed etiam penitus auferendæ atque ignibus tradendæ sunt*[8]*:* "Secret scriptures, which, bearing the names of the apostles, contain a nursery and occasion of much falsehood[9], are not only to be forbidden, but also utterly to be taken away and to be committed to the fire." By this we see, that the apostles' names were borrowed sometimes to avouch heresies and wicked doctrine.

Decretal. Leon. i. Can. xv.

As touching Clemens, Gelasius writeth thus, and, for that he was bishop of the same see, it is the more likely he should know the truth: *Pauca quæ ad memoriam venerunt, et catholicis vitanda sunt, decrevimus esse subdenda. In primis, Ariminensem synodum a Constantino Cæsare Constantini filio congregatam mediante Tauro præfecto ex tunc...et...in æternum, confitemur esse damnatum*[10]. *Item itinerarium nomine Petri apostoli, quod appellatur sancti Clementis, libri octo apocryphi*[11]*:* "We

Dist. 15. Sancta Romana.

[4 It was not printed until 1633, being found in the Codex Alexandrinus, brought to England in 1628.]

[5 Scripsit....... ad ecclesiam Corinthiorum valde utilem epistolam. ... Fertur et secunda ejus nomine epistola, quæ a veteribus reprobatur.—Hieron. Op. Catal. Script. Eccles. xv. Tom. IV. Pars. II. col. 107.]

[6 Ἤδη δὲ καὶ ἕτερα πολυεπῆ καὶ μακρὰ συγγράμματα ὡς τοῦ αὐτοῦ χθὲς καὶ πρώην τινὲς προήγαγον, Πέτρου δὴ καὶ Ἀπίωνος διαλόγους περιέχοντα. ὧν οὐδ' ὅλως μνήμη τις παρὰ τοῖς παλαιοῖς φέρεται. οὐδε γὰρ καθαρὸν τῆς ἀποστολικῆς ὀρθοδοξίας ἀποσώζει τὸν χαρακτῆρα.—Euseb. Eccles. Hist. in Hist. Eccles. Script. Amst. 1695-1700. Lib. III. cap. xxxviii. pp. 88, 9.]

[7 Epitome apostolicarum constitutionum, quas octo libris constare aiunt, nuper in Creta insula repertis, inventore et interprete Carolo Capellio Veneto.—Crabb. Concil. Col. Agrip. 1551. Tom. I. p. 27. See, for the works imputed to Clement, Patr. Apostol. a Coteler. Amst. 1724. Tom. I.]

[8 Leon. Magni Op. Lut. 1623. Ad Turrib. Epist. xciii. cap. xv. col. 489; where we find *auferendæ sunt atque ignibus concremandæ.*]

[9 Falsehead, 1565.]

[10 Damnatam, 1565, 1609.]

[11 Gelas. in Corp. Jur. Canon. Lugd. 1624. Decret. Gratian. Decr. Prim. Pars, Dist. xv. can. 3. cols. 56, 7; where we find *a catholicis, credimus, Constantio,* for *Constantini, damnatam,* and *apocryphum.*]

Abdias. have thought good (saith Gelasius) to note certain books which are come to knowledge, and ought to be avoided of catholic people. First, the council holden at Ariminum, gathered by Constantinus the emperor, the son of Constantinus, by mean of Taurus the lieutenant, from thenceforth and for ever we judge worthy to be condemned. Likewise the journal of Peter the apostle, bearing the name of Clement, eight books are secret (unlawful) writings." Thus we see divers books of Clement condemned by name, and but one epistle only allowed for good; and this volume, here alleged by M. Harding, containing eight books, as it is noted by Peter Crab, fully agreeing in number of books with the other condemned by Gelasius. To be short, cardinal Bessarion, alleging a[1] parcel of the same book of Clement, that hath been hidden so long, writeth thus of it: *Licet ...hæc Clementis verba inter apocryphas scripturas commemorari soleant, placet tamen eis inpræsentiarum tanquam veris assentiamus*[2]: "Albeit the words of Clement be accounted amongst secret (unlawful) writings, yet for once we are content to receive them, as if they were true." Thus M. Harding's Clement is disallowed by Eusebius, and by St Hierome, mistrusted by Bessarion, condemned by Gelasius, kept forth-coming in close prison for the space of a thousand and five hundred years: yet must we now, without refusal, stoop unto him, and take him as the apostles' fellow.

Petrus Crab, 1. Tom. Concil.

Bessar. de Sacrament. Eucharistiæ.

Abdias.

One other of these witnesses is Abdias, and he is brought in with all his titles: the bishop of Babylon, planted there by the apostles; one that was conversant with Christ, and heard him preach, and saw him in the flesh, and was present at the martyrdom of St Andrew; with all other circumstances that may gather credit among the simple. Of this Abdias somewhat must be spoken, and so much the more, for that his name is so glorious. He was sought out, and found, and set abroad of very late years, under the name of Abdias, by one Wolphgangus Zazius, a man that taketh great pains to force men to believe it is the very self-same Abdias that he maketh himself to be; and therefore he saith, he was one of the lxxii. disciples, ordered bishop by the apostles, and that St Luke the evangelist, writing the Acts of the Apostles, borrowed many whole stories, word by word, out of him[3]. Then was St Luke very unthankful, that never once made mention of his author.

But whosoever or whatsoever this Abdias were, his own words do so bewray him, that a blind man may see it was not he. He maketh many shameless lies, that he was present with Christ, and at the most part of the apostles' doings; and yet were the apostles then, according to Christ's commandment, gone into the whole world, some into Italy, some into Asia Minor, some into Scythia, some into India, some into Ethiopia, and were many thousand miles asunder. In his fable of Iphigenia he saith, that the people took her brother Beor, being then christened by St Matthew, and made him king, and that he reigned afterward in Ethiopia the space of lxiii. years[4]; and further maketh mention of Egesippus[5], that lived above one hundred and threescore years after Christ. If Abdias were alive all this while, he might be likened to *Johannes de temporibus*, who, as the French story recordeth, lived in France above three hundred years[6]. A liar must be circumspect, and mindful what he say. If he saw Christ in the flesh, it is not likely he ever saw Egesippus, that was so long after Christ: if he saw Egesippus, it is not likely he ever saw Christ. Thus if he report truth in the one, he lieth in the other; and so, whether he lie, or say truth, he cannot be Abdias.

Mark xvi.

Abdias in vita Matthæi.

Gaguinus. Paul. Æmil.

Touching the substance of his book, it is nothing else, for the more part of it, but a vain peevish tale, laid out with falsehood[7], wicked doctrine, and curious conference and talk with devils; things far unmeet for that gravity and majesty of the apostles of Christ, as it may soon appear unto the reader.

[1 1565 and 1609 omit *a*.]

[2 Bessar. De Sacram. Eucharist. in Biblioth. Patr. per M. de la Bigne, Par. 1624. Tom. VI. col. 482.]

[3 ... ut vel Abdiam hæc ex Luca sumpsisse, vel Lucam ex Abdia, &c.—Abd. Apost. Hist. Par. 1571. Præfat. Wolfg. Laz. fol. i. v.]

[4 Id. Lib. VII. fol. 95. 2.]

[5 Id. Lib. VI. fol. 73.]

[6 Gaguin. De. Orig. et Gest. Franc. Lugd. 1497. Lib. VI. fol. 36. 2. Paul. Æmyl. De Reb. Gest. Franc. Par. 1544. Lib. V. fol. 105. The individual referred to is said to have died at the age of 361, in the reign of Louis VII.]

[7 Falsehead, 1565.]

It may be gathered by St Augustine in sundry places, that some part of this book was written by certain heretics, named the Manichees, and avouched by them as the very true story of the apostles. For he reporteth the fables of St Thomas, of St Matthew, of St Andrew, of the lion that slew the man that had stricken St Thomas, of the dog that brought the same man's hand unto the table, of Maximilla, wife unto Egis, and other like tales, even in such order as they be set forth by this Abdias[8].

Abdias. Martialis.

August. contra Faustum, Lib. xi. et Lib. xxii. cap. 80.

Against one Adimantus he writeth thus: "They (that is, the Manichees) read secret scriptures, which they themselves[9] say are pure and perfect; in which scriptures it is written that St Thomas cursed a man, and that afterward a lion slew him, &c.[10] And in another place he saith: *Attendite qualia sint quæ scribuntur de Maximilla, uxore Egetis: illam noluisse viro debitum reddere: donasse et supposuisse Eucliam ancillam, et alias similes fabulas*[11]: "Behold what things they be that be written of Maximilla, wife unto Egis; that she (being once christened) would no more yield duty unto her husband, but set Euclia her maid in her own place; and other like fables."

August. contra Adimantum, cap. 16.

Aug. de Fide, contra Manichæos. cap. 30.

All these and such like tales, thus disallowed by St Augustine, are reported by M. Harding's Abdias in great sooth. I thought it not amiss to speak hereof the more at large, for that I saw a book so full of tales, so lately found out, without any good shew of credit, to be fathered upon the apostles' disciple, and sent into the world with such a countenance. St Augustine seemeth in divers places to have given his judgment of the same. Writing against the adversary of the law and prophets, he hath these words: "He hath brought forth witnesses out of secret scriptures, under the names of the apostles John and Andrew; which writings, if they had been theirs, they had been received of the church[12]." The like judgment hereof seemeth to be given by Gelasius, who also saith that "such writings, according to an ancient custom, and by a singular provision, were not read in the church of Rome, for that they were thought to be written by heretics[13]."

August. contra Adversarium Legis et Prophetarum, Lib. i. cap. xx.

Dist. 15. Sancta Romana.

Thus is this Abdias a book, as it is apparent, full of manifest lies, and, as it may be supposed by St Augustine and Gelasius, written and favoured by heretics, and refused of the church: upon such a one, good reader, M. Harding will have thee to stay thy faith.

As for the rest of these new witnesses, although I mind to take no great exception against them, yet M. Harding knoweth there is scarcely one of them but may be doubted of.

Martialis was lately found in France, in the city of Lemovica[14], in an arch of stone under the ground, so corrupt and defaced that in many places it could not be read, and was never seen in the world at any time before[15].

Martialis.

Dionysius, although he be an ancient writer, as it may many ways well appear, yet it is judged by Erasmus, John Colet, and others many, grave and

Dionysius.

Erasm. contra Parisienses.

[[8] Aliud est ipsos libros non accipere ...... quod denique nos ipsi de vestris et aliorum hæreticorum, si quos suos et proprios habent, vel de iis qui appellantur apocryphi ...... Legunt scripturas apocryphas Manichæi, a nescio quibus sutoribus fabularum sub apostolorum nomine scriptas: .... Ibi tamen legunt apostolum Thomam, &c.—August. Op. Par. 1679-1700. Cont. Faust. Lib. xi. cap. ii. Lib. xxii. cap. lxxix. Tom. VIII. cols. 218, 9, 409.]

[[9] Themself, 1565.]

[[10] Ipsi autem legunt scripturas apocryphas, quas etiam incorruptissimas esse dicunt, ubi scriptum est apostolum Thomam maledixisse homini, &c.—Id. Cont. Adimant. Lib. cap. xvii. 2. Tom. VIII. col. 137.]

[[11] Adtendite ..... qualia sint quæ accipitis de Maximilla uxore Egetis: quæ cum nollet marito debitum reddere ... illa supposuerit marito suo ancillam suam Eucliam nomine, &c.—Id. De Fid. cont. Manich. Lib. cap. xxxviii. Tom. VIII. Append. col. 33. This is most probably not a genuine work of Augustine. It has been attributed to Evodius.]

[[12] Sane de apocryphis iste posuit testimonia, quæ sub nominibus apostolorum Andreæ Johannisque conscripta sunt. Quæ si illorum essent, recepta essent ab ecclesia, &c.—Id. Contr. Advers. Leg. et Proph. Lib. I. cap. xx. 39. Tom. VIII. col. 570.]

[[13] Sed ideo secundum antiquam consuetudinem singulari cautela in sancta Romana ecclesia [gesta sanctorum martyrum] non leguntur: quia et eorum, qui conscripsere, nomina penitus ignorantur; et ab infidelibus aut idiotis superflua aut minus apta, quam rei ordo fuerit, scripta esse putantur: sicut cujusdam Quirici, &c.—Gelas. in Corp. Jur. Canon. Lugd. 1624. Decret. Gratian. Decr. Prima Pars, Dist. xv. can. 3. col. 56.]

[[14] Limoges.]

[[15] Præfat. ad Hist. Marc. Episc. ad calc. Abd. Hist. Apost. fol. 153. 2. See also Not. adcalc. Mart. Epist. in Biblioth. Patr. per M. De la Bigne, Par. 1624. Tom. III. cols. 15, 6.]

learned men, that it cannot be Areopagita, St Paul's disciple, that is mentioned in the Acts[1].

Liturgia Jacobi.

St James' liturgy hath a special prayer for them that live in monasteries; and yet it was very rathe[2] to have monasteries built in all St James' time[3].

Liturgia Chrysostomi, edita a Claudio du Sanctes.

Chrysostom's liturgy prayeth for pope Nicolas by these words: *Nicolai sanctissimi et universalis papæ longa sint tempora*[4]: "We pray God send Nicolas, that most holy and universal pope, a long time to live." But pope Nicolas, the first of that name, was the second pope after pope Joan the woman, in the year of our Lord eight hundred fifty and seven, almost five hundred years after Chrysostom was dead. And likewise in the same liturgy there is a prayer for the empire and victory of the emperor Alexius[4]. And the first emperor of that name was in the year of our Lord a thousand and fourscore, after the decease of Chrysostom seven hundred years. Now it were very much for M. Harding to say Chrysostom prayed for men by name seven hundred years before they were born. I trow that were prophesying, and not praying.

Pope Joan.

Thou seest, christian reader, what doctors here be brought, as M. Harding saith, to ground thy faith and salvation upon. If he could have brought any better, I trow he would have spared these. But such doctrine, such doctors. These doubtful authorities, I trust, will set men's consciences out of doubt.

M. Hard. witnesses against himself.

Now, notwithstanding it be something troublesome, yet shall it not be from the purpose, for trial of these men's faithful dealing, to examine some of M. Harding's own witnesses, and to hear what they will depose. All these, as it is said, avouch the sacrifice, otherwise called the mass; and not only these, but also all others, of all ages and times, and that in a manner in the self-same order and form that now is used.

Fol. 11, a. lin. 1.

Here M. Harding much abuseth both his own learning, and also the trust and credit that many have in him. For he knoweth well that the apostles had neither the form, nor the order, nor the name of mass.

Dumb witnesses. M. Harding allegeth witnesses against himself.

Howbeit, if all these bear witness to the mass, why speak they not? Why come they forth so dumb? What, have they nought to say in this behalf? Or is their word not worth the hearing? Or are they so old that they cannot speak? Or must we needs believe M. Harding without evidence?

But what if neither Clement, the apostles' fellow, nor Abdias, nor St James, nor Basil, nor Chrysostom, nor any other of all these here alleged, speak one word of private mass? What if they have not so much as the name of mass? What if they testify plainly against M. Harding's mass? What if they testify fully and roundly with the holy communion? It were great shame for M. Harding to fly from his own witnesses, and very much for me to stand to be tried by them that are brought in such a throng to depose against me.

Liturgia Jacobi.

Dishes and cups.

And to begin first with St James,—the order of his liturgy, which M. Harding calleth mass, standeth thus: *Sacerdos* [*ait*], *Nullus eorum qui orare non possunt nobiscum ingrediatur....Diaconus* [*ait*], *Cum timore, et fide, et dilectione accedite: Populus* [*respondet*], *Benedictus qui venit in nomine Domini....Deinde impertit clero: cum autem attollunt diaconi discos et calices ad impertiendum populo, diaconus ait,... Domine, benedic*[5]. Which words may be turned thus: "The priest saith, Let not one of them that may not pray enter in with us. The deacon saith, With reverence and faith and love approach ye near. The people answereth, Blessed is he that cometh in the name of the Lord. After this he ministereth unto the clergy. But when the deacons take up the dishes and cups, to minister unto the people, the deacon saith, Lord, bless." Here, by the order of St James' mass, the people answereth the priest in their own tongue; provision is made for

[1 Erasm. Op. Lugd. Bat. 1703-6. Declar. ad Cens. Facult. Theol. Paris. Tit. xxii. 91. Tom. IX. cols. 916, 7.]

[2 Rathe: soon, early.]

[3 Pro iis qui in virginitate et castitate, in monasteriis, ac in venerando connubio degunt.—S. Jacob. Miss. in Lit. Sanct. Patr. Par. 1560. fol. 3. The Greek text is, Ὑπὲρ τῶν ἐν παρθενίᾳ καὶ ἁγνείᾳ καὶ ἀσκήσει καὶ ἐν σεμνῷ γάμῳ διαγόντων.—p. 14.]

[4 Chrysost. Miss. in eod. fol. 20.—Et pro imperio in victoria ... Alexii magni imperatoris et porphyrogeniti.—Ibid. These passages are not in the Greek text.]

[5 S. Jacob. Miss. in eod. foll. 2. 2, 7; where the first address is ascribed to the deacon, and the words are transposed *nobiscum non possunt;* where also we find *timore Dei et fide ac,* &c.]

the whole congregation in dishes and cups; they be called to receive the communion; and they do receive all together. Now let M. Harding be judge, whether St James bear record to the private mass or to the communion.

Abdias, although he report many untrue tales, yet he reporteth not one word of private mass, but much to the contrary. Writing the life of St Thomas, and shewing in what sort he ministered the holy communion, he saith thus: *Eucharistiam divisit his quos supra memoravimus* [*id est, populo*][6]: "He divided the sacrament unto the people, of whom we spake before." And again, in the life of St Matthew, who, as M. Harding beareth us in hand, without all question said mass in Ethiopia, he writeth thus: *Cumque respondissent Amen, et mysteria Domini celebrata* [*essent*], *et missam suscepisset omnis ecclesia*[7]: "When they had answered Amen, and the mysteries of the Lord had been celebrate, and the whole church had received the communion." Where the whole church answereth the priest, and receiveth the communion together, I reckon M. Harding will hardly call that a private mass.

Abdias in Vita S. Thom. Apost.

Abdias in Vita S. Matt. Apost.

Justinus Martyr, another of M. Harding's witnesses, in his second apology unto the emperor Antoninus, declaring the innocency of the christian people that then lived under great persecution, and shewing the manner of their assemblies, writeth thus: "Before the end of our prayers we kiss each of us one another. Then is there brought unto him that is the chief of the brethren bread, and a cup of wine and water mingled together, which having received he praiseth God and giveth thanks a good space; and, that done, the whole people confirmeth his prayer, saying Amen. After that they that among us be called deacons give unto every of them that be present part of the bread, and likewise of the wine and water, that are consecrate with thanksgiving, and carry the same home unto them that happen to be absent[8]." Here is a full communion, and no private mass.

Justin Martyr in 2 Apologia.

ἐπευφημεῖ.

Dionysius, another of the witnesses, and, as M. Harding saith, the apostles' scholar, openeth the whole order of the ministration in his time, writing namely and purposely of that matter. "The priest," saith he, "beginneth the holy psalmody; and the whole body of the church singeth[9] with him. Then followeth in order the reading of the holy scriptures, which is done by the ministers. After that, the *catechumeni*," that is, they that are newly come unto the religion of Christ and are not yet baptized, "and *energumeni*," that is, such as are molested with evil spirits, "and such others as are enjoined to penance, are commanded forth. And so there remain such as are meet to have the sight and communion of the holy things[10]." It followeth: "And, shewing forth the gifts of the holy sacraments, he goeth to the communion himself, and likewise exhorteth others[11]." And a little after that: "The priest, uncovering the bread that came covered and in one cake or loaf, and dividing the same into many portions, and likewise dividing the unity of the cup unto all, mystically and by way of a sacrament he fulfilleth and divideth unity[12]." It followeth again: "Then the minister, receiving himself and distributing the holy communion unto others, in the end concludeth with holy

Dionys. Eccles. Hierar. Cap. 3.

τὰς δωρεὰς τῶν θεουργιῶν ὑποδείξας.

συμβολικῶς.

τῆς θεαρχικῆς κοινωνίας μεταδούς.

[6 Abd. Apost. Hist. Par. 1571. Lib. IX. fol. 118.]

[7 Id. Lib. VII. fol. 94. 2.]

[8 Ἀλλήλους φιλήματι ἀσπαζόμεθα παυσάμενοι τῶν εὐχῶν· ἔπειτα προσφέρεται τῷ προεστῶτι τῶν ἀδελφῶν ἄρτος καὶ ποτήριον ὕδατος καὶ κράματος. καὶ οὗτος λαβὼν, αἶνον καὶ δόξαν ... ἀναπέμπει· καὶ εὐχαριστίαν ὑπὲρ τοῦ κατηξιῶσθαι τούτων παρ' αὐτοῦ ἐπὶ πολὺ ποιεῖται· οὗ συντελέσαντος ... πᾶς ὁ παρὼν λαὸς ἐπευφημεῖ λέγων, ἀμήν ... οἱ καλούμενοι παρ' ἡμῖν διάκονοι, διδόασιν ἑκάστῳ τῶν παρόντων μεταλαβεῖν ἀπὸ τοῦ εὐχαριστηθέντος ἄρτου καὶ οἴνου καὶ ὕδατος, καὶ τοῖς οὐ παροῦσιν ἀποφέρουσι.—Just. Mart. Op. Par. 1742. Apol. I. pp. 82, 3.]

[9 Signeth, 1611.]

[10 Ὁ μὲν ἱεράρχης ... ἀπάρχεται τῆς ἱερᾶς τῶν ψαλμῶν μελῳδίας, συναδούσης αὐτῷ τὴν ψαλμικὴν ἱερολογίαν ἁπάσης τῆς ἐκκλησιαστικῆς διακοσμήσεως. ἑξῆς δὲ, διὰ τῶν λειτουργῶν ἡ τῶν ἁγιογράφων δέλτων ἀνάγνωσις ἀκολούθως γίνεται· καὶ μετὰ ταύτας, ἔξω γίγνονται τῆς ἱερᾶς περιοχῆς οἱ κατηχούμενοι, καὶ πρὸς αὐτοῖς οἱ ἐνεργούμενοι, καὶ οἱ ἐν μετανοίᾳ ὄντες, μένουσι δὲ οἱ τῆς τῶν θείων ἐποψίας καὶ κοινωνίας ἄξιοι.—Dionys. Areop. Op. Antv. 1634. De Eccles. Hierarch. cap. iii. 2. Tom. I. pp. 283, 4.]

[11 ... καὶ τὰς δωρεὰς τῶν θεουργιῶν ὑποδείξας, εἰς κοινωνίαν αὐτῶν ἱερὰν αὐτός τε ἔρχεται, καὶ τοὺς ἄλλους προτρέπεται.—Id. ibid. p. 284.]

[12 ... τὸν γὰρ ἐγκεκαλυμμένον καὶ ἀδιαίρετον ἄρτον ἀνακαλύψας, καὶ εἰς πολλὰ διελὼν, καὶ τὸ ἑνιαῖον τοῦ ποτηρίου πᾶσι καταμερίσας, συμβολικῶς τὴν ἑνότητα πληθύνει, καὶ διανέμει, παναγεστάτην ἐν τούτοις ἱερουργίαν τελῶν.—Id. ibid. 3. p. 299.]

Hippolyt. Martyr. thanksgiving, together with all the whole holy company of the church[1]." I believe M. Harding himself will say here is yet but bare witness for his private mass.

Liturgia Basil. In the liturgy of St Basil, which is also brought for a witness in this matter, the priest prayeth thus: "All we receiving of one bread and of one cup," &c. It followeth: "The priest divideth the holy bread into four parts: the quire singeth the communion; and so they communicate all[2]." Et sic communicant omnes.

Liturgia Chrysostomi. Another witness is Chrysostom. His liturgy, or (as M. Harding delighteth to speak) his mass, is thus ordered: "After that the priest hath communicate with the ministers, then the great door is set open, the priest sheweth forth the cup unto the people, saying, With the fear of God, and faith, and love approach ye near. The deacon saith: Come ye near in peace. The people answereth: In the name of the Lord." Again, "The deacons receive the communion. Afterward, the mysteries be carried unto a place where the people must communicate[3]."

Ignatius ad Philadelphien. Ignatius, another witness, writing unto the people of Philadelphia, hath these words: *Unus panis pro omnibus fractus est, et unus calix omnibus dividebatur*[4]: "One bread was broken for all, and one cup was divided unto all."

What needeth it me to discourse further of the rest? By these few, I doubt not, it may soon appear how faithfully these men allege the catholic fathers, only amazing the reader with naked names. Here we see such as cannot communicate are commanded[5] forth; the whole church prayeth, singeth, and receiveth the holy sacraments all together. Such masses they be that the old catholic fathers can witness of. And of other mass they know none. M. Harding himself confesseth, that in the primitive church the people received the communion every day.

Yet, notwithstanding, for his private mass he allegeth the names of doctors of the primitive church. And so, like a crafty apothecary, in his marks or papers he hath the mass, but in his boxes he hath the communion.

But he will say, he alleged all these doctors by way of digression to another purpose, to prove the sacrifice. First, there is very small proof in such witnesses as say nothing; and, besides that, it is a simple kind of rhetoric to use so large digressions from the matter, before ye once enter into the matter. And as touching the sacrifice, if you have any at all, you have it only of the institution of Christ; otherwise you have none. But we are sure we have Christ's institution. Wherefore it followeth we have the sacrifice that Christ appointed.

Hippolytus Martyr. Touching Hippolytus, the bishop and martyr, that, as M. Harding saith, lived in Origen's time, and is now extant in Greek, it is a very little book, of small price and as small credit, lately set abroad in print, about seven years past; before never acquainted in the world. Such be M. Harding's ancient authorities for his mass. It appeareth it was some simple man that wrote the book, both for the phrases of speech in the Greek tongue, which commonly are very childish, and also for the truth and weight of the matter. He beginneth the first sentence *ἐπειδὴ γάρ.* of his book with *enim*, which a very child would scarcely do. He hath many vain guesses of the birth and life of antichrist: he saith, and soothly avoucheth, that antichrist shall be the devil and no man, and shall only bear the shape of a man; yet St Paul calleth antichrist "the man of sin." Besides this, he hath a further fantasy, that antichrist shall subdue the kings of Egypt, Africa, and Ethiopia, and that he shall build up again the temple of Hierusalem, and that St John, that wrote the books of Apocalypse, or Revelations, shall come again

2 Thess. ii. Revelabitur homo peccati.

[1 Μετασχὼν δὲ καὶ μεταδοὺς τῆς θεαρχικῆς κοινωνίας, εἰς εὐχαριστίαν ἱερὰν καταλήγει μετὰ παντὸς τοῦ τῆς ἐκκλησίας ἱεροῦ πληρώματος.—Id. ibid. p. 300.]

[2 Basil. Miss. in Lit. Sanct. Patr. Par. 1560. foll. 12, 13.]

[3 At ille partitur portionem sanctam in quatuor partes ... jubet archidiaconus ut diaconi accedant: et accedentes suscipiunt, ut fecerunt sacerdotes ...... [diaconus] dicit populo, Cum Dei timore accedite. Populus respondet, Benedictus qui venit in nomine Domini ...... et sic feruntur ad locum mysteria ubi populus debet communicare.—Chrysost. Miss. in eod. foll. 20. 2, 21. The Greek text differs considerably; the former part agreeing more closely with the quotation as made by Jewel.]

[4 Μία γὰρ σὰρξ τοῦ Κυρίου ἡμῶν Ἰησοῦ Χριστοῦ, καὶ ἓν ποτήριον εἰς ἕνωσιν τοῦ αἵματος αὐτοῦ.—Ignat. ad Philad. cap. iv. in Patr. Apostol. Oxon. 1838. Tom. II. p. 378.]

[5 Commandeth, 1565.]

with Elias and Enoch to reprove antichrist[6]. And all this saith he without either warrant of the scriptures, or authority of the church. And writing that book, namely upon the prophet Daniel, he allegeth the Apocalypse of St John in the stead of Daniel; which is a token either of great ignorance or of marvellous oblivion. Moreover, he saith that the souls of men were from the beginning, which is an heresy; with other dreams and fantasies many more. This is M. Harding's catholic doctor. Concerning the place of him here alleged: *Venite, pontifices, qui pure mihi sacrificium die nocteque obtulistis, ac pretiosum corpus et sanguinem meum immolastis quotidie*[7]; if he will precisely build upon the words, then must all other priests stand back, and have no place in heaven, but bishops only. For although they offer up, as M. Harding saith, the daily sacrifice, yet it is well known, according to the nature and use of the word, they are priests only, and not bishops. If he will make reckoning of this word *quotidie*, "daily," then where shall the bishop of Rome and his cardinals stand, that scarcely have leisure to sacrifice once through the whole year? And if it be Christ himself that they offer up unto the Father, as they say, how is the same Christ offered up unto Christ himself? How is Christ both the thing that is offered, and also the party unto whom it is offered? But there is no inconvenience to a man in his dream. And if it be the mass that Hippolytus here speaketh of, how is it offered both day and night? For Hostiensis saith: "It is not lawful by the canons to say mass in the night-season, saving only the night of Christ's nativity[8]." Hostien. in Summa, de Celebratione Missarum.

But the meaning of Hippolytus seemeth to be this, that all faithful people in this respect be priests and bishops, like as St Peter also calleth them, and that every of them by faith maketh unto God a pure sacrifice, and both day and night as it were reneweth and applieth unto himself that one and everlasting sacrifice of Christ's precious body, once offered for all upon the cross. Thus are the words of Hippolytus plain and without cavil; and thus shall Christ's calling be very comfortable. 1 Pet. ii.

M. HARDING. THE SIXTH DIVISION.

Now, this presupposed, that the mass standeth upon good and sufficient grounds for the stay of all true Christian men's belief, let us come to our special purpose, and say somewhat of private mass, as our adversaries call it.

THE BISHOP OF SARISBURY.

The grounds he here speaketh of be his doctors, such as he hath already brought forth, laid up in great secrecy and hidden from all the world by the space of one thousand years and more, and now of late found out by chance—some in islands in the sea, some in arches under the ground, some so defaced with mould and canker that it was hard to guess their meaning, some full of impudent lies and fables, one parcel not agreeing with another, some devised and written by heretics, and ever mistrusted and condemned of the church; yet every of these, as M. Harding well knoweth, fully reporting the holy communion, and manifestly testifying against private mass. These be M. Harding's great[9] grounds. Now judge thou, gentle reader, what worthy building may stand upon the same. Doubtless this beginning is very simple.

M. HARDING. THE SEVENTH DIVISION.

The chief cause why they storm so much at[10] *private mass is for that the priest receiveth the sacrament alone, which thing they express with great villany of words. Now in case the people might be stirred to such devotion as to dispose themselves worthily to receive their housel every day with the priest, as they did in the primitive* Private mass proceeded first of the negligence and misdoing of the people.

[6 Hippol. De Consum. Mund. Par. 1556. pp. 3, 14, 22, 6, 7, 8, 30, &c.]

[7 Ibid. p. 56.]

[8 Hostiens. sup. Tert. Decretal. Par. 1512. De Celebr. Miss. fol. 157. See also Telesp. Papa in Corp. Jur. Canon. Lugd. 1624. Decret. Gratian. Decr. Tert. Pars, De Consecr. Dist. i. can. 48. col. 1902; which is referred to by Hostiensis; also Decretal. Gregor. IX. Lib. III. Tit. xli. Gloss. in cap. 3, cols. 1365, 6; which contains the substance of what he says.]

[9 Greatest, 1565, 1609.]

[10 Against, Harding's Answer, 1564.]

church, when they looked hourly to be caught and done to death in the persecution of paynims, that they departed not hence sine viatico, *without their voyage provision, what should these men have to say? In this case perhaps they would find other defaults in the mass; but against it in this respect only, that it is private, they should have nothing to say at all. So the right of their cause dependeth of the misdoing of the people, which if they would amend, these folks should be driven either to recant or to hold their peace. To other defaults of the mass, by them untruly surmised, answer shall be made hereafter. Now touching this.*

Lack of devotion cause of private mass.

Where no fault[1] *is committed, there no blame is to be imputed. That oftentimes the priest at mass hath no compartners to receive the sacrament with him, it proceedeth of lack of devotion of the people's part, not of envy or malice of his part.*

The thirteenth untruth. For[2] they invite no man.

The feast is common: (13) *all be invited: they may come that list: they shall be received that be disposed and proved: none is thrust away that thus cometh: it may be obtruded to none violently, ne offered to none rashly. Well, none cometh. This is not a sufficient cause why the faithful and godly priest, inflamed with the love of God, feeling himself hungry and thirsty after that heavenly food and drink, should be kept from it, and imbarred from celebrating the memory of our Lord's death, according to his commandment, from his duty of giving of thanks*[3] *for that great benefit, from taking the cup of salvation and calling upon the name of God; for these things be done in the mass.* [*Psal.* cxvi. H. A. 1564.]

THE BISHOP OF SARISBURY.

God be thanked! both our life and manner of teaching, notwithstanding these slanderous reports, is void of villany. Or if there had been any defect in us, this man of his courtesy should not have supplied it with another villany.

M. Harding confesseth that in the primitive church there was no private mass. M. Harding Articul. 15. Divis. 7. Fol. 155. b.

Here M. Harding granteth that the people in the primitive church received the holy communion every day, and so consequently unawares he confesseth that in the primitive church was no private mass, which, as he saith, came in afterward by the negligence and undevotion of the people. It is great pity that so good a thing, as it is supposed, should have no better beginning. One special principle of these men's doctrine is to imbar the people from reading and understanding of the scriptures, and to suffer them to know nothing; for that, as some of them have said, they be dogs and swine, and therefore should not precious stones be laid before them. Yet now must their negligence be the rule of Christ's religion. This is laid as the ground and foundation of the whole cause, and therefore it ought the better to be considered.

Eckius, Pighius, Hosius, and others, have often cried out amain in their books and pulpits, "Where was your religion before Luther first began to preach?" So may we likewise say, And where was your private mass, which is the crown of your kingdom, before your people first began to grow negligent and to want devotion? Some have said the church is governed by the pope, some by the general councils, some by the Holy Ghost. M. Harding saith better, it is not amiss that the church be governed by the negligence and undevotion of the people.

"Charity," say they, "is cold, and the people is careless." But therefore hath God appointed pastors and ministers to oversee and control the people, and not to suffer them to perish in their negligence. Were it a matter of tithes or other payments, the people should be called upon, and not suffered in any wise to be negligent; neither should their negligence stand for excuse. How much less should it be suffered, when the case toucheth God! The bishops and fathers in the second council holden at Barcara[4] in Spain decreed thus: "If any man resort unto the church, and hear the scriptures, and for negligence or wantonness withdraw himself from the communion of the sacrament, and in the reverend mysteries do break the rule of discipline; we decree that such a one[5] be put out of the catholic church, until he have done penance and shewed the fruits of his

Ex editamento Conc. Brac. 2. cap. 84. Seu ex Synod. Græco collecto. Pro luxuria sua.

[1 Default, H. A. 1564.]
[2 *For* is omitted, 1565.]
[3 Giving thanks, H. A. 1564.]
[4 Bracara, 1565, 1609.]
[5 Such one, 1565.]

repentance, that, having obtained pardon, he may be received again to the holy communion[6]."

Thus the godly fathers in old time did not flatter and favour the people's negligence in this case, as M. Harding and his fellows do; but exhorted, warned, reproved, rebuked them[7], called them malapert and impudent, that would be present and not receive, and excommunicated them for their negligence. But these men, contrariwise, turn away their faces from their brethren, and suppress their voice, and will not be heard, and speaking[8] nothing but in an unknown tongue, and find no fault with the people, but rather make them believe that they receive for them, and apply Christ's death unto them by their mass, and that the very hearing thereof is sufficient for them and meritorious; and thus, as much as in them lieth, they increase the negligence of the people, and discourage them from the holy communion.

Chrysost. in Epist. ad Ephes. Hom. 3.

The people is taught nothing, they understand nothing, they hear nothing, and, saving only a few childish and unseemly gestures, they see nothing, neither comfort, nor memory of Christ, nor benefit of his passion. And this is the cause of their negligence; therefore they stand thus back and withdraw themselves[9].

The cause of the people's negligence.

Howbeit, what needeth M. Harding thus to charge the people with negligence and undevotion? The pope himself and his cardinals do scarcely communicate once in the year, but are as negligent and as undevout therein as the most part of the people.

The pope and his cardinals as negligent as the people.

"The feast," saith M. Harding, "is common: all are invited: they shall be received that be disposed and proved." If this feast be common, it must needs be common to very few; for the provision is very little to serve many. That all be called in the Latin mass, it is a great and manifest untruth: for neither the priest nor the deacon, either by word or by gesture, calleth them; nor have they any preparation for them if they were called. Yet are these men not ashamed to say, "They shall be received that be disposed and proved."

Every man ought humbly to prepare and dispose his heart before he presume to hear or receive any thing that toucheth God. For God is Spirit, and we are flesh; God in heaven, and we in earth. Pythagoras, being but an heathen, was wont to say: *Non loquendum de Deo sine lumine:* "We ought not to speak of God without light," that is, without premeditation and good advisement who it is of whom we speak. And the pagans, in their sacrifices, were wont to remember their priest with these words, *Hoc age;* the meaning whereof was, "Dispose thy mind: it is God unto whom thou speakest." The wise man saith: "Before thou pray prepare thine heart, and be not as a man that tempteth God." Likewise in old times they that were called *catechumeni* were warned aforehand to prepare their hearts, that they might worthily receive baptism, as it is decreed under the name of Clement, whose words be these: "Let him prepare himself in all things, that after three months ended upon the holy day he may be baptized[10]." St Augustine also exhorteth the catechumeni likewise to dispose their minds against their[11] time of their baptism[12]. Thus ought every man to examine and prepare himself before he hear God's word, before he presume to open his mouth to pray unto God, before he receive the sacrament of baptism, and namely before he come to the holy communion. And therefore the priest giveth warning unto the people with these words: "Lift up your hearts;" which words, as St Augustine saith, were commonly used in the holy mysteries[13].

Preparation of the mind before the communion.

Ecclus. xviii.

Clem. Epist. 3.

August. Tract. 10 & 11 in Johan.

August. de bono Perseverantiæ, Lib. ii. cap. xiii.

[6 Si quis intrat ecclesiam Dei, et sacras scripturas non audit, et pro luxuria sua avertit se a communione sacramenti, et in observandis mysteriis declinat constitutam regulam disciplinæ; istum talem projiciendum de ecclesia catholica esse decernimus, donec pœnitentiam agat, et ostendat fructum pœnitentiæ suæ; ut possit communionem percepta indulgentia promereri.—Capit. Mart. Epist. Brac. 83. in Concil. Stud. Labb. et Cossart. Lut. Par. 1671-2. Tom. V. col. 914.]

[7 Chrysost. Op. Par. 1718-38. In Epist. ad Ephes. cap. i. Hom. iii. Tom. XI. pp. 21, &c.]

[8 Speak, 1565, 1609.] [9 Themself, 1565.]

[10 Accedat autem, qui vult, ad sacerdotem suum ... ac semetipsum in omnibus probet, ut tribus mensibus jam consummatis, in die festo possit baptizari. —Clem. in Epist. Decret. Sum. Pont. Rom. 1591. Epist. iii. Tom. I. p. 22.]

[11 The, 1565, 1609.]

[12 August. Op. Par. 1679-1700. In Johan. Evang. Tractat. x. 10. xi. 1. Tom. III. Pars ii. cols. 373, 4, 5.]

[13 Id. De Don. Persev. cap. xiii. 33. Tom. X. col. 839.]

The negligence of the people.

[a] Senten. Lib. iv. Dist. 17. [b] Innocent. III. in Concil. Lateran. cap. 21. Hugo de potestate Ecclesiæ.

But I think M. Harding here by these words, "prepare" and "dispose," meaneth private confession, which many have used as a rack of men's consciences to the maintenance of their tyranny. Peter Lombard[a] saith, without it there is no way to heaven[1]. Innocentius the third[b] commandeth that whosoever is not confessed neither be suffered to come into the church being alive, nor to be buried when he is dead[2]. Hugo writeth thus: "I am bold to say, whosoever cometh to the communion unconfessed, be he never so repentant and sorry for his sins, certainly he receiveth unto his judgment[3]." So violent the late writers have been in exacting things of their own devices. Otherwise the old fathers, notwithstanding sometime they speak of confession, yet they require it with more modesty, and many of them require no such thing at all.

Chrysostom. de Pœnitentia. Ἀμάρτυρον ἔστω τὸ δικαστήριον. Chrysost. in Psal. l. Hom. 2. Chrysost. de Lazar. Hom. 4. De Pœnitentia, Dist. 1. Quidam Deo.

Chrysostom saith: "Let the court (where thou yieldest thyself guilty) be without witness: let God alone see thee[4]." And again: "If thou be ashamed to shew thy sins to any man, then utter them every day in thy heart. I say not, go confess thy sins unto thy fellow-servant, that may upbraid thee with them; but confess them unto God, that is able to cure them[5]." And again, thus he imagineth God to speak unto a sinner: *Mihi soli dic peccatum tuum privatim, ut sanem ulcus*[6]*:* "Open thy sin privately to me alone, that I may heal thy wound." And Theodorus, sometime archbishop of Canterbury, saith: *Græci et totus oriens confitetur soli Deo*[7]*;* "The Greeks and all they of the east confess themselves[8] only to God." Thus much I thought good to touch hereof, lest it should be thought there is none other way for a man to prove and dispose himself but only by auricular confession. The meaning of these words of St Paul, "Let a man examine himself," standeth in two points, in faith and repentance. Faith containeth the truth of our belief; repentance concerneth the amendment of our life: which kind of examining endureth all our life long. But to say or think we are all examined and disposed one only day in the year, and that of custom, not of holiness, and not one day before nor one day after, it is childish, it is superstitious, it is Jewish, it is no persuasion meet for the people of God. If Chrysostom were alive, he would cry out: *O præsumptionem! O consuetudinem*[9]*!* "O what presumption! O what a custom is this!" And St Ambrose would say: "If thou be not worthy every day to receive, then art thou not worthy once in the year[10]."

Chrysos. ad Pop. Antioch. Hom. 61. Ambros. de Sacram. Lib. v. cap. iv.

But grant it, that charity and devotion is fainted in the people: may we yet think that the same resteth whole and sound in the clergy? or that the devotion of the priests aboundeth more now than it did in the primitive church? For then the priest ministered the holy communion but once in a day; unless the multitude of the communicants had been so great that it required double ministration[11]. But now the priest may say two, three, or more masses in one day, yea, although he have no man to receive with him. I would it were not as the prophet saith: *Qualis populus, talis sacerdos:* "As the people is, such is the priest." Verily Bonifacius, talking of the change of the holy cups, which in the

Leo Epist. 81. Isai. xxiv. Bonifacius de Con. Dist. 1. Vasa.

[1 Ex his aliisque pluribus indubitanter ostenditur, oportere Deo primum, et deinde sacerdoti offerri confessionem: nec aliter posse perveniri ad ingressum paradisi, si adsit facultas.—Pet. Lomb. Libr. Sent. Col. Agrip. 1576. Lib. IV. Dist. xvii. D. fol. 374.]

[2 Omnis utriusque sexus fidelis, postquam ad annos discretionis pervenerit, omnia sua solus peccata confiteatur fideliter, saltem semel in anno ... alioquin et vivens ab ingressu ecclesiæ arceatur, et moriens christiana careat sepultura.—Concil. Lat. IV. in Concil. Stud. Labb. et Cossart. cap. xxi. Tom. XI. cols. 172, 3.]

[3 The work referred to is probably that of Hugh de Fleury, *De regia Potestate et sacerdotali Dignitate,* printed in a Latin translation by Baluze, Miscellanea, Tom. IV. Paris, 1683, where sentiments similar to the above may be found, pp. 41, 54.]

[4 Chrysost. Op. De Pœnit. Hom. iv. Tom. II. p. 307.]

[5 Si confunderis alicui dicere, quia peccasti, dicito ea quotidie in anima tua. Non dico ut confitearis conservo tuo, ut exprobret: dicito Deo, qui curat ea.—Id. Op. Lat. Basil. 1547. In Psal. Quinquag. Hom. ii. Tom. I. cols. 744, 5.]

[6 Id. Op. Par. 1718-38. De Laz. Conc. iv. Tom. I. p. 758.]

[7 Quidam Deo solummodo confiteri debere peccata dicunt, ut Græci.—Theod. in Corp. Jur. Canon. Lugd. 1624. Decret. Gratian. Decr. Sec. Pars, De Pœnit. Dist. i. can. 90. col. 1718.]

[8 Themself, 1565.]

[9 Chrysost. Op. Lat. Basil. 1547. Hom. lxi. Tom. V. col. 403. See also Op. Par. 1718-38. In Epist. ad Ephes. cap. i. Hom. iii. Tom. XI. pp. 22, 3.]

[10 Ambros. Op. Par. 1686-90. De Sacram. Lib. v. cap. iv. 25. Tom. II. col. 378. See before, page 17, note 15.]

[11 Leon. Magn. Op. Lut. 1623. Epist. ad Diosc. lxxxi. 2. col. 436. See before, page 17, note 18.]

old times had been treen[12], and in his time were made of gold: "Then," said he, "we had treen cups and golden priests; but now we have golden cups and treen priests[13]." St Bernard complaineth thus of the state of the clergy in his time: "O Lord, wickedness hath proceeded from the elder judges thy vicars, which seem to rule thy people. We cannot now say, 'as the people is, so is the priest;' for the very people is not so (wicked) as is the priest[14]." And the same St Bernard, in the synod holden at Rheims in France, in the presence of the pope spake these words: *Nunc non habemus mercenarios pro pastoribus, nec lupos pro mercenariis; sed pro lupis habemus diabolos*[15]: "Now have we not hirelings (to rule the flock) instead of shepherds, nor wolves instead of hirelings; but instead of wolves we have devils."

Bernardus de Conversione Pauli.

Bernardus in Concilio Remensi.

Johannes Vitalis, a cardinal of Rome, likewise complaineth: "And of the priests of this age (saith he) the prophet Esay hath written thus: 'The pastors themselves[16] are void of understanding: they have all followed their own way, every one, even from the highest to the lowest[17].'" Wherefore, if want of devotion and looseness of life may breed negligence in the people, why may not the like want, and as great looseness, breed the like negligence in the priests? And if negligence be excuse sufficient, to warrant the people to communicate but once in the year, why may not the same negligence cause the priests to say mass but once in the year? For it is not the love of God, as you surmise, neither the hunger or thirst of heavenly food, that maketh the priest say[18] mass, but order of foundation, custom, hire or wages for his labour.

Johan. Vitalis Cardinalis, in Speculo. Isai. lvi.

Now let us view the weight of M. Harding's reasons: "The people is negligent and undevout; *ergo*, the priest may say mass alone." This argument is very weak. But the next that is gathered of the same is much weaker: "The people is negligent now; *ergo*, there was private mass in the primitive church." For this only was my denial; and this hath M. Harding taken in hand to prove. It is called *petitio principii*, where as one weak thing is proved by another, as weak as it. So might M. Harding say: The people will not hear the word of God; *ergo*, the priest may go into the pulpit, and preach alone. "For Christ's supper (as St Augustine saith) is a sermon; and the priest therein preacheth and uttereth the death of the Lord[19]."

August. de Trin. Lib. iii. Cap. 4.

Again, if only the negligence of the people have enforced private mass, how then came it into colleges, monasteries, cathedral churches, yea, even into the very holy church of Rome, where as be such numbers of clerks, vicars, monks, priests, and prebendaries, that the emperor Justinian was fain to stay the increase of them[20]; all idle, all in study and contemplation, all void from worldly cares, all confessed, all in clean life, all prepared? Wherefore have they private mass? Yea, wherefore have they so many masses severally, at divers altars, and many of them at one time? Wherefore do not they communicate together, as it appeareth they did in the primitive church? Doubtless this groweth not of the negligence of the people.

Authen. Collat. prima ut determinatus sit numerus Clerico.

As for the people, they are not so negligent nor undevout, as M. Harding here chargeth them. They are God's people, glad to be instructed, and desirous to follow; and, wheresoever the gospel is received, ready to give testimony thereof,

[12 Treen: made of tree, wooden.]

[13 ... Bonifacius ... respondit: Quondam sacerdotes aurei ligneis calicibus utebantur: nunc e contrario lignei sacerdotes aureis utuntur calicibus.—Ex Conc. Trib. in Corp. Jur. Canon. Decret. Gratian. Decr. Tert. Pars, De Consecr. Dist. i. can. 44. col. 1900.]

[14 ... egressa est iniquitas a senioribus judicibus, vicariis tuis, qui videntur regere populum tuum. Non est jam dicere, Ut populus, sic sacerdos; quia nec sic populus, ut sacerdos.—Bernard. Op. Par. 1690. In Conv. S. Paul. Serm. i. 3. Vol. I. Tom. III. col. 656.]

[15 Id. ad Cler. in Concil. Remens. Serm. Vol. II. Tom. V. cols. 735, 6; where, however, the exact words, as above quoted, are not found. The Benedictine editor does not consider this address a genuine work of Bernard.]

[16 Themself, 1565.]

[17 Sed e contra de sacerdotibus moderni temporis: Ipsi pastores ignoraverunt intellectum, omnes in viam suam declinaverunt, unusquisque a summo usque ad novissimum.—Vital. Specul. Moral. Tot. Script. Venet. 1594. De Prælat. et Sacerd. fol. 235. 2.]

[18 To say, 1565.]

[19 The following is probably the passage intended: ... potuit tamen significando prædicare Dominum Jesum Christum, aliter per linguam suam, aliter per epistolam, aliter per sacramentum corporis et sanguinis ejus.—August. Op. Par. 1679-1700. De Trin. Lib. III. cap. iv. 10. Tom. VIII. col. 798.]

[20 Corp. Jur. Civil. Amst. 1663. Auth. Collat. I. Tit. iii. Novell. iii. cap. 1. Tom. II. p. 7.]

and to increase the same by the holy communion of Christ's body and blood, in great companies, and whole congregations all together.

But what ill luck is this, that they whom M. Harding so often condemneth for heretics can be so devout, and he and his catholics thus remain without devotion? Let the people be taught; let them hear the holy ministration in their own tongue that they may understand the holy mysteries, and feel comfort and sweetness in the same; let them see examples of diligence in the clergy; then will they be no longer negligent. Then should M. Harding perforce give over his private mass, as seeing that the whole right of his cause hangeth only of the negligence and misdoing of the people.

M. HARDING. THE EIGHTH DIVISION.

But the enemies of this holy sacrifice say that this is against the institution of Christ. God forbid the institution of Christ should not be kept!

But it is a world to see how they cry out for the institution of Christ, by whom it is most wickedly broken. For, whereas in Christ's institution concerning this sacrament three things are contained, which he himself did, and by his commandment gave authority to the church to do the same, the consecration, the oblation, and the participation, wherein consisteth the substance of the mass; they, having quite abrogated the other two, (14) *and not so much as once naming them in their books of service, now have left to the people nothing but a bare communion, and that after their own sort: with what face can they so busily cry for Christ's institution, by whom in the chief points the same is violated?*

[*Three essentials of the mass,* H. A. 1564.]

The fourteenth untruth. The sacrifice is specially named in the communion book. And in the mass itself consecration is not named.

Of consecration and oblation, although much might be said here against them, I will at this time say nothing. Concerning participation, the number of communicants together in one place, that they jangle so much of as a thing so necessary, that without it the mass is to be reputed unlawful, (15) *is no part of Christ's institution. For Christ ordained the sacrament, after consecration and oblation done, to be received and eaten; and for that end he said:* Accipite, manducate, bibite: "*Take, eat, drink.*" *Herein consisteth his institution.*

The fifteenth untruth. For St Basil thinketh the number is part of Christ's institution, *Exercitationis ad pietatem* Sermone 4[1].

Now as for the number of communicants[2], *how many should receive together in one place, and in what place, what time, sitting at table (as some would have it), standing or kneeling, fasting or after other meats; and whether they should receive it in their hands or with their mouths, and other the like orders, manners, and circumstances; all these things pertain to the ceremony of eating, the observation whereof dependeth of the church's ordinance, and not of Christ's institution. And therefore St Augustine, writing to Januarius, saith:* Salvator non præcepit, quo deinceps ordine sumeretur, ut apostolis, per quos dispositurus erat ecclesiam, servaret hunc locum[3]: "*Our Saviour gave not commandment in what order it should be received, meaning to reserve that matter* unto*[4] *the apostles, by whom he would direct and dispose his church.*"

[*Number of communicants, place, time, with other rites, be not of Christ's institution,* H. A. 1564.]

Epist. 118.

*The apostles used and ordained the communion of a number, and never any private receiving of the priest alone.

Wherefore the receiving of the sacrament being the institution of Christ, and the manner, number, and other rites of receiving[5], (16) *not fixed nor determined by the same, but ordered by the church's disposition, whether many or few, or but one in one place receive, for that respect the ministration of the priest is not made unlawful.*

The sixteenth untruth. Christ appointed a number, although no certain fixed number.

THE BISHOP OF SARISBURY.

It liketh M. Harding to call us wicked, and the enemies of the sacrifice; and to say we jangle of the institution of Christ, and yet ourselves break Christ's institution. I must here protest in the name of many, we are not enemies of the sacrifice and cross of Christ, but of the errors, abuses, and sacrilege of the mass, which now are maintained to the open derogation of the sacrifice and cross of Christ.

[1 Et quemadmodum spiritualis lex non pauciores quam duodecim esse vult mysticum pascha comedentes: sic, &c.—Basil. Op. Lat. Basil. 1540. Exerc. ad Piet. Serm. iv. Tom. III. p. 425.]

[2 Of the communicants, H. A. 1564.]

[3 August. Op. Par. 1679-1700. Ad Inquis. Januar. Lib. I. seu Epist. liv. 8. Tom. II. col. 127. See before, page 39, note 8.]

[4 To, H. A. 1564.]

[5 The receiving, H. A. 1564.]

As touching Christ's institution, forget not, good christian reader, that M. Harding confesseth there are three things therein contained, which, as he saith, Christ himself did, and by his commandment gave authority to his church to do; the consecration, the oblation, and the participation. Here he leaveth quite out the annunciation of Christ's death, thinking perhaps it is no matter essential of Christ's institution. Of these three (he saith) we have broken two, the consecration and oblation, and so have only a bare communion.

Conse-cration. 1 Cor. xi. Ye shall shew forth the Lord's death.

But whereby may it appear to M. Harding that we have thus broken Christ's institution? Is it because we communicate together with the people? or because we minister the sacrament under both kinds? or because we shew forth the death of Christ? or because we do that Christ did, and commanded us to do?

Concerning consecration, he doth great wrong to charge us with the breach thereof, before he himself, and others of his side, be better resolved wherein standeth consecration. For Scotus and Innocentius tertius, and certain others say, that this word *Benedixit*, "He blessed," worketh consecration. The common opinion is, that it is wrought by these words, "This is my body." Some think that Christ spake these words twice, first secretly to himself, and afterward openly, that the apostles might understand him[6]. Cardinal Bessarion, bishop of Tusculum, writeth thus: "The Latin church, following Ambrose, Augustine, and Gregory, thinketh that consecration standeth in these words, 'This is my body;' but the Greek church thinketh the consecration is not wrought by these words, but by the prayer of the priest, which followeth afterward; and that according to St James, St Chrysostom, and St Basil[7]." By these it appeareth that they themselves[8] of that side are not yet fully agreed upon their own consecration.

Consecration. Tho. et Bonaven. in 4 Sent. Bessar. de Sacramento Eucharistiæ.

Howbeit, by whatsoever words consecration is made, it standeth not in the abolishing of natures, as M. Harding teacheth; nor in precise and close pronouncing of certain appointed words; but in the converting of the natural elements into a godly use; as we see in the water of baptism. For Christ said not, "Say ye this," or, "By these words go and transubstantiate or change natures." But thus he said: "Do this in my remembrance." And so: "The bread that we break is the communication of Christ's body;" and, "As often as we eat of that bread, we do declare and publish the Lord's death." This is well noted and opened by St Augustine: "Put the words of God (saith he) unto the element; and it is made a sacrament. For what power is there so great of the water (in baptism), that it toucheth the body and washeth the heart, saving by the working of the word? Not because it is spoken, but because it is believed; and this is the word of faith, which we preach[9]." "The word of faith, which we preach," saith St Augustine, not the word which we whisper in secret, is the word of consecration.

In the tenth article. 1 Cor. x. 1 Cor. xi. August. in Johan. Tract. 80. Accedat verbum ad elementum, et fit sacramentum.

With what honest countenance then can M. Harding say that we have no consecration? We pronounce the same words of consecration that Christ pronounced: we do the same that Christ bade us do: we proclaim the death of the Lord: we speak openly in a known tongue; and the people understandeth us: we consecrate for the congregation, and not only for ourselves[10]: we have the element: we join God's word unto it; and so it is made a sacrament. Yet, saith M. Harding, we have no consecration. And can he think that a priest of his side doth consecrate, that whispereth his words closely, and that in a strange tongue, in such sort as no man heareth or understandeth him; that oftentimes

[6 For the various opinions see Joan. Duns Scot. Op. Lugd. 1639. In Lib. IV. Sent. Dist. VIII. Quæst. ii. Tom. VIII. pp. 422, 3; Innoc. III. Op. Col. 1575. Myst. Miss. Lib. IV. cap. vi. Tom. I. p. 377; Thom. Aquinat. Op. Venet. 1595. In Lib. IV. Sent. Dist. VIII. Quæst. ii. Art. 1. Tom. VII. foll. 42, 3; Bonavent. Op. Mogunt. 1609. In Lib. IV. Sent. Dist. VIII. Pars II. Art. i. Quæst. 1. Tom. V. pp. 94, 5.]

[7 Alii enim hoc facere alia existimantes, Latini Ambrosium, Augustinum, Gregorium, aliosque doctores suos secuti ... illa Domini verba id facere manifestissime asseverant, Hoc est corpus meum, &c.... Græci vero ... cum Jacobo fratre Domini, Basilio, et Chrysostomo sentientes, ... non illis Salvatoris nostri verbis Christi corpus et sanguinem confici putant, sed quibusdam quæ sequuntur precibus sacerdotum. —Bessar. De Sacram. Eucharist. in Biblioth. Patr. per M. De la Bigne, Par. 1624. Tom. VI. col. 467.]

[8 Themself, 1565.]

[9 Unde ista tanta virtus aquæ, ut corpus tangat et cor abluat, nisi faciente verbo; non quia dicitur, sed quia creditur? ... Hoc est verbum fidei quod prædicamus.—August. Op. In Johan. Evang. cap. XV. Tractat. lxxx. 3. Tom. III. Pars II. col. 703.]

[10 Ourself, 1565.]

himself knoweth not neither the words of Christ, nor the sense of the words, nor the use, nor the end of the sacrament; that exhorteth no man; that speaketh to no man; that,, if he do consecrate, doth consecrate only for himself, and not for others; that doth neither that Christ did, nor that Christ commanded to be done? If we consecrate not, can he think that such a one doth consecrate?

And whereas he saith further, that we have no manner of oblation[1] in our communion, he should not himself speak manifest untruth, having taken upon him, as he saith, to reform falsehood[2]. For he knoweth we offer up unto God in the holy communion ourselves, our souls, our bodies, and alms for the poor, praises and thanksgiving unto God the Father for our redemption, and prayer from a contrite heart, which, as the old catholic fathers say, is the sacrifice of the new testament[3]. To conclude, we offer up as much as Christ commanded us to offer. Indeed, we offer not up Christ's body to be a propitiatory sacrifice for us unto his Father: for that sacrifice is once wrought for all upon the cross; and there is none other sacrifice left to be offered for sin.

Tertull. contra Marcionem, Lib. iv. et adversus Judæos. Eusebius de Demonstratione, Lib. i. Heb. x.

But, saith M. Harding, we make no mention of any sacrifice in all our ministration; therefore we break Christ's institution. This reason impeacheth Christ himself as well as us; for Christ himself in his whole ministration spake not one word of any sacrifice, no more than we do. Therefore, by M. Harding's logic, Christ himself brake his own institution.

Hereof he concludeth that we have nothing but a bare communion; which conclusion is as true as the premises. God's name be blessed, we have a holy communion, to the great comfort of the godly. But in M. Harding's mass there is neither communion, nor any other consolation at all; but only a number of light and bare gestures and ceremonies, far unmeet for so grave a purpose. But what should move this man thus scornfully to jest at the holy ministration, and to call Christ's ordinance "a bare communion?" Others call it the mystical supper; others the holy distribution: bare or naked, no man, I trow, durst ever to call it, but M. Harding. One of his own doctors, comparing consecration and communion together, saith thus: *Communio sacra major est in effectu sanctitatis quam consecratio*[4]: "The holy communion in effect of holiness is more than consecration." And again: *Consecratio...est propter communionem: ergo, communio majus [est consecratione]*[5]: "Consecration is for communion. Therefore is communion greater than consecration."

M. Harding jesteth at the ordinance of Christ.

Alexander de Hales, 4 q. 35. mem. 2.

Ibid. sol. 2.

A little before, M. Harding said, in Christ's institution three things are contained, consecration, oblation, participation. Immediately after, as a man that had suddenly forgotten himself, he saith: "The number of the communicants together in one place, that they jangle so much of as a thing so necessary, is no part of Christ's institution." It is no marvel though he can so ill agree with the old catholic doctors, that falleth thus out so suddenly with himself. For, if participation be not necessary, how is it a part of Christ's institution? If it be a part of Christ's institution, how is it not necessary? He would fain convey Christ's institution and his mass both under one colour. But they are contraries; the one of them bewrayeth the other. As for the priest, he taketh no part of the sacrament with others, which is the nature and meaning of this word "participation," but receiveth all alone. Thus it appeareth, by M. Harding's own confession, that private mass, having no participation of the priest with others, and therefore no participation at all, is no part of Christ's institution.

M. Harding hath forgotten himself.

I grant certain circumstances, as fasting, sitting, standing, kneeling, and other like ceremonies about the holy ministration, are left to the discretion of the church. But this is a very simple argument: "Certain circumstances may be

---

[1 Manner oblation, 1565.]

[2 Falsehead, 1565.]

[3 Tertull. Op. Lut. 1641. Adv. Jud. 5. p. 211; Adv. Marc. Lib. IV. 1. p. 502. See before, page 110, notes 1, 2.

Τὸ γὰρ ἐν παντὶ τόπῳ θυμίαμα καὶ θυσίαν ἀναφερέσθαι Θεῷ, τί ἕτερον παρίστησιν, ἢ ὅτι μὴ ἐν Ἱεροσολύμοις, μηδ' ἀφωρισμένως ἐν τῷδε τῷ τόπῳ, ἐν πάσῃ δὲ χώρᾳ, καὶ ἐν πᾶσι τοῖς ἔθνεσι μέλλουσι τὸ δι' εὐχῶν θυμίαμα, καὶ τὴν οὐ δι' αἱμάτων, ἀλλὰ δι' ἔργων εὐσεβῶν καθαρὰν ὠνομασμένην θυσίαν τῷ ἐπὶ πᾶσιν ἀναφέρειν Θεῷ;—Euseb. Pamph. De Demonstr. Evang. Par. 1628. Lib. I. cap. vi. p. 17.]

[4 Etsi communio sacra sit major in effectu sanctitatis, tamen, &c.—Alex. Alens. Theol. Summ. Col. Agrip. 1622. Pars IV. Quæst. x. Membr. v. Art. i. 2. Resol. p. 262.]

[5 Id. ibid.]

altered; *ergo*, the priest may receive alone." Christ himself hath already determined the case. For albeit he have appointed no certain number of communicants, yet hath he by special words appointed a number. For these very words, "Take ye, eat ye," "drink ye all," "divide ye among yourselves," "do ye this Matt. xxvi. Luke xxii.
in my remembrance," "ye shall set forth the Lord's death;" these very words, I 1 Cor. xi.
say, cannot be taken of one singular man, but necessarily import a number.

Yet, saith M. Harding, St Augustine's words be plain: *Salvator .... non præcepit,* August. Epist. 118. ad Januarium.
quo deinceps ordine sumeretur; ut apostolis, per quos dispositurus erat ecclesiam, servaret hunc locum[6]*:* "Christ gave no commandment in what order it should be received; to the intent he might leave that matter to his apostles, by whom he would dispose his church." "Therefore," saith M. Harding, "the number of communicants is at liberty; and the priest may receive alone."

St Augustine in that place speaketh not one word of any number, but only of the time of receiving, whether it might seem convenient to minister the communion after supper, as Christ did to his disciples, and some used then to do; as appeareth by the words that follow: *Nam si hoc ille monuisset, ut post cibos alios* August. in eadem epist. ad Januarium 118.
semper acciperetur, credo quod eum morem nemo variasset[6]*:* "For, if Christ had commanded that the sacrament should ever be received after other meats, I believe no man would have changed that order." It is wrong dealing to bring one thing for another, to allege number instead of time, and of St Augustine's words to conclude that St Augustine never meant. For that St Augustine requireth a number of communicants, it appeareth by that immediately in the same place he allegeth the words of St Paul: *Quapropter, fratres, cum convenitis* 1 Cor. xi. Invicem exspect.
ad manducandum, invicem exspectate: "Wherefore, brethren, when ye meet together to eat (the communion), wait one for another." Which words M. Harding thought best cunningly to dissemble. In other places St Augustine[7], like as also August. de Serm. Dom. in Monte, Lib. ii. In Johan. Tract. 26. Hieron. ad Lucinium. Idem in Apolog. advers. Jovinian.
St Hierome[8] and others, witnesseth that the whole people daily received together; and generally, entreating of the holy communion, he speaketh evermore of a number, and never of one alone.

Now whereas M. Harding saith, "Christ left such matters to the determination of the church," and to that purpose seemeth to allege, as others do, these words of St Paul, *Cetera cum venero disponam;* "Touching the rest, I will take order 1 Cor. xi.
when I come;" this kind of doctrine unto the old fathers seemed very dangerous. For St Augustine saith: *Omnes...insipientissimi hæretici, qui se Christianos vocari* August. in Johan. Tract. 97.
volunt, audacias figmentorum suorum [hac]...occasione evangelicæ sententiæ colorare conantur, ubi Dominus ait, Adhuc multa habeo vobis dicere, sed [ea] non potestis portare modo[9]*:* "The most peevish heretics that be, that would fain be called Christians, do colour the bold enterprises of their fantasies by occasion of this saying of the gospel, where as the Lord saith, 'Yet have I many things to say unto you; but ye are not able now to bear them.'"

But if the church have determined this matter for private mass, as M. Harding saith, in what council, at what time within six hundred years after Christ, and in what place was it determined? Who was witness of the doing? Who was president? Who was present? This is it that the reader would fain learn. And M. Harding thinketh it best to prove it by silence. Howbeit it is already confessed that private mass came in, not by Christ, or by any of his apostles, or by the authority of the church, but only by the undevotion and negligence of the people.

It is wonderful to see how handsome constructions these men make of these words of St Paul: "Touching the rest I will take order when I come." For upon these words they build their private mass, even in such form as it is now used in. As if St Paul should say thus: "At my coming I will take order that ye shall have mass in a strange tongue; that ye shall receive alone; that ye shall not look and wait one for another, notwithstanding any my former commandment;

[6 See p. 122.]

[7 Id. De Serm. Dom. in Mont. Lib. II. 25. Tom. III. Pars II. col. 209.

Id. In Johan. Evang. cap. vi. Tractat. xxvi. 15. Tom. III. Pars II. col. 500.]

[8 Hieron. Op. Par. 1693-1706. Epist. lii. ad Lucin. Tom. IV. Pars II. col. 579.

Id. Epist. xxx. ad Pammach. pro Libr. adv. Jovin. Tom. IV. Pars II. col. 239.]

[9 August. Op. In Johan. cap. xvi. Tractat. xcvii. 3. Tom. III. Pars II. col. 738.]

that ye shall not need to meet together; that one shall receive for all the rest; and so at my coming I will undo whatsoever hitherto I have ordained."

M. Harding's argument. I may not now dissemble the value of M. Harding's argument: "Christ (saith he) ordained the sacrament, after consecration and oblation done, to be received and eaten; *ergo*, the number of communicants together is no part of Christ's institution."

What, thought M. Harding that none but children and fools should read his book? For how loosely hang these parts together! The sacrament must be received after consecration; *ergo*, the number of communicants is not necessary. There is not one piece hereof, that either is true in itself or agreeth with other.

For touching consecration, if he will precisely follow the words of the evangelists, which wrote the story, "Christ first took the bread, and blessed it, and brake it, and gave it, and said, Take ye, eat ye;" and afterward, this being said and done, he added the words of consecration, "This is my body;" thus the evangelists witness, contrary to M. Harding, that the receiving was first, and the consecration afterward. Matt. xxvi. Luke xxii. 1 Cor. xi.

M. Harding concludeth against himself. Concerning the force of M. Harding's argument, it concludeth directly against himself. For if Christ instituted the sacrament to the intent it should be first consecrate, and then received of a company, it must needs follow that receiving with company is part of Christ's institution; as it is also avouched by Cardinal Bessarion, the bishop of Tusculum. His words be these: *Hoc...ipse ordo rerum poscebat: primum consecrare, deinde frangere, postea distribuere: quod nos in præsentia facimus*[1]: "This the very natural course of things required; first to consecrate, then to break, and after to distribute; which thing we also do at this day." And Gabriel Biel: *Consecratio ad usum, qui est manducatio, tanquam ad finem quodammodo proximum ordinatur: quia Christus accepit panem, benedixit,* [*et*] *dedit discipulis, ut manducarent*[2]: "Consecration is ordained for a use, which is the eating, as it were for an end. For Christ, after he had taken the bread, blessed it, and gave it to his disciples to eat." Bessar. de Sacrament. Eucharistiæ. Biel. Lect. 26.

Biel. Lect. 38. And again: *Consecratio non est semper finis consecrationis, sed potius usus fidelium. Ad hoc enim consecratur corpus et sanguis Christi, ut fideles illis utantur manducando*[3]: "Consecration is not the end of consecration, but rather the use of the faithful. For to that end is the body and blood of Christ consecrate, that the faithful may use them in eating." Thus M. Harding frameth arguments against himself.

M. HARDING. THE NINTH DIVISION.

M. Harding refuseth Christ's example. *But if they allege against us the example of Christ, saying that he received not it*[4] *alone, but did communicate with his twelve apostles, and that we ought to follow the same; I answer, that we are bound to follow this example,* quoad substantiam, non quoad externam ceremoniam; *"for the substance, not for the outward ceremony," to the which pertaineth the number and other rites, as is aforesaid. Christ's example importeth necessity of receiving only;* (17) *the other rites, as number, place, time, &c., be of congruence and order.* (18) *In which things the church hath taken order, willing and charging that all shall communicate that be worthy and disposed. And so it were to be wished, as oftentimes as the priest doth celebrate this high sacrifice, that there were some who, worthily disposed, might receive their rights with him, and be partakers sacramentally of the body and blood of Christ with him. But in case such do lack, as we have seen that lack commonly in our time, yet therefore the continual and daily sacrifice ought not to be intermitted. For sith this is done in the remembrance*[5] *of Christ's oblation once made on the cross for the redemption of all mankind, *therefore it ought daily to be celebrated throughout the whole church of Christ for the better keeping of that great benefit in remembrance; and that though none receive*

The seventeenth untruth. For number is not only of congruence, but also of institution. The eighteenth untruth. The church of Rome hath taken no such order. *A weak reason.

[1 Bessar. De Sacram. Eucharist. in Biblioth. Patr. per M. De la Bigne, Par. 1624. Tom. VI. col. 484; where we find *primo* for *primum*.]

[2 Gab. Biel. Sacr. Canon. Miss. Expos. Lugd. 1517. Lect. xxxvi. fol. 61; where we find *ejus manducatio, postquam accepit,* and *discipulis suis.*]

[3 ... consecratio non est simpliciter finis consecrantis; sed &c....sanguis: ut fideles eorum, &c.—Id. ibid. Lect. xxxviii. fol. 65. 2.]

[4 It not, H. A. 1564.]

[5 In remembrance, H. A. 1564.]

with the priest. And it is sufficient in that case if they that be present be partakers of those holy mysteries spiritually, and communicate with him in prayer and thanksgiving, in faith and devotion, having their mind and will to communicate with him also sacramentally when time shall serve. This is only M. Harding's gloss.

THE BISHOP OF SARISBURY.

Here is great pain taken to prove that christian men, in the ministration of Christ's supper, are not bound to follow the example of Christ; all learning also shewed to beguile the simple with a vain distinction of *substantia* and *accidens*. St Hilary, writing of the lewd dealing of the Arians used in racking of the scriptures, saith thus of them: *Aut ita scribuntur fides, ut volunt; aut ita ut volunt, intelliguntur*[6]: "Their faiths must either be so written as they will, or else they must be construed and taken as they will." Hilar. ad Constant August.

The question that lieth between us standeth not in this point, whether we ought to do every thing that Christ did; but whether we ought to do that thing that Christ both did himself, and also commanded us to do, and was afterward practised by the apostles and holy fathers, that had the spirit of understanding, and knew Christ's meaning, and was never broken, until the negligence and undevotion of the people, as M. Harding confesseth, brought in the contrary.

Christ said not, Do this in Hierusalem, or in this parlour, or after supper, or at this table, or being so many together, or standing or sitting; but he said thus, "Do ye this:" that is, take ye bread: bless it: break it: give it "in my remembrance." This is not a ceremonial accident, but the very end, purpose, and substance of Christ's institution. And therefore St Paul saith: "The bread that we break is the participation of the Lord's body; and all we are one bread and one body, as many as are partakers of one bread." Matt. xxvi. Luke xxii. 1 Cor. x.

Yet saith M. Harding, "We are bound to follow Christ's example in things that be of the substance of the sacrament, not in things that be of order and congruence." Here unawares he seemeth to confess that his mass, whatsoever substance it bear, yet is void both of good order and also of congruence. But what wicked wilfulness may this be! To minister the sacraments of Christ as Christ himself did, and commanded to be done, is called an accident ceremonial, that may well be changed; but for the priest to speak in a strange unknown tongue, to turn his face from the people, to minister unto himself alone, and to use an infinite sort of childish ceremonies, which neither Christ nor his apostles ever either used or thought of; all these are holden for things substantial, and of importance, and be defended as necessary, and may not be changed. Such power have these men to change accidence into substance, and substance into accidence, when they list.

"The church," saith M. Harding, "hath charged and ordered that no man that is worthy and disposed shall be refused." O miserable is that church, where as no man, no, not so much as one, is well disposed! Here in few words he condemneth the whole church of Rome, even the whole college of cardinals; amongst whom, as he saith, there is not one well disposed and worthy; and therefore they all withdraw themselves from the communion. But Chrysostom saith: "If thou be not worthy to receive the communion, then art thou not worthy to be present at the prayers[7]." Therefore M. Harding should drive his unworthy people from the church, and not suffer them to hear his mass. Chrysost. ad Popul. Antiochen. Hom. 61.

They imagine that any man, be he never so great a sinner, may pray to God, and have free access to the throne of Majesty: only they think a sinner may not receive the holy communion. But it is written: "Let him depart from his wickedness, whosoever calleth upon the name of the Lord." Whosoever is a member of Christ, and may boldly call God his Father, may also be bold to receive the communion. Hebr. iv. 2 Tim. ii.

If M. Harding wish indeed that the people would prepare themselves, and

[6 ... dum aut ita fides scribuntur ut volumus, aut ita ut nolumus intelliguntur.—Hilar. Op. Par. 1693. Ad Constant. August. Lib. II. 4. col. 1227.]

[7 Ὀυκ εἶ τῆς θυσίας ἄξιος, οὐδὲ τῆς μεταλήψεως; οὐκοῦν οὐδὲ τῆς εὐχῆς.—Chrysost. Op. Par. 1718-38. In Epist. ad Ephes. cap. i. Hom. iii. Tom. XI. p. 23.]

Daily Sacrifice.

communicate with the priest, as he pretendeth, why doth he not exhort and move the people? Why doth he not provide for them? Why doth he rather defend his sole receiving contrary to his own wishing, and contrary to the example of Christ, as he himself confesseth? Doubtless there are many godly men among the people, and oftentimes more virtuously disposed a great deal than the priest. Neither is it of their unworthiness that they abstain so often, nor of their worthiness that they receive once in the year, but only of custom.

"But if the people be slack, yet must the priest do the daily sacrifice," saith M. Harding; that is, he must offer up Christ unto his Father for the sins of the world. Herein appeareth the wanton folly of this people. That they may do, and are commanded to do, they will not do; but that they cannot do, that they will needs do. The matter being so weighty, and not yet thoroughly believed, it had been good for M. Harding to have made proof thereof by the authority of St Augustine, St Hierome, or some other old catholic doctor, within the compass of six hundred years; but he bringeth forth only an article or decree of his own making. "Sith this is done," saith he, "in the remembrance of Christ's oblation once made on the cross for the redemption of mankind, therefore it ought daily to be celebrated throughout the whole church."

Daily sacrifice. Daily bread.

Lest any error grow hereof, it is to be noted, that these words, "daily sacrifice," and "daily bread," are sometimes used in the holy fathers, and both applied unto the body of Christ, but far otherwise, and to other purpose, than M. Harding meaneth, as it shall soon appear. The old fathers call that the daily sacrifice that Christ made once for all upon the cross, for that, as Christ is a priest for ever, so doth the same his sacrifice last for ever; not that it is daily and really renewed by any mortal creature, but that the power and virtue thereof is infinite in itself, and shall never be consumed. So saith St Augustine: *Tibi hodie Christus est, tibi quotidie resurgit*[1]: "To thee this day is Christ; and to thee daily he riseth again." So likewise saith St Hierome: *Quotidie nobis Agnus occiditur, et pascha quotidie celebratur*[2]: "Unto us every day the Lamb is slain; to us every day the Easter-feast is kept." And in like sort writeth Germanus, a later writer: *Panis quotidianus est Christus, qui est, et ante fuit, et manet in secula*[3]: "Our daily bread is Christ, which is now, and was before, and endureth for ever." Thus in Christ's behalf is that most precious sacrifice everlasting.

De Verb. Dom. in Evan. secundum Lucam. Serm. 28. Hieron. in 1 ad Corint. cap. v. Germanus in Eccles. rerum Theoria.

Likewise the same one sacrifice is everlasting, not only in itself, for that the virtue thereof is daily effectual in us, and endureth for ever; but also of our behalf, in that we do daily offer up unto God our sacrifices of praises and thanksgiving for that so merciful and wonderful work of our redemption. And this kind of daily sacrifice, beside a great number of other old doctors, the godly father Irenæus hath taught us to make. His words be these: *Sic et...nos quotidie offerre vult munus ad altare frequenter sine intermissione. Est ergo altare in cœlis: illuc enim preces et oblationes nostræ diriguntur*[4]: "Even so hath God willed us daily to offer up our sacrifice at the altar without ceasing. Therefore our altar is in heaven; for thither our prayers and oblations are directed." Thus is that sacrifice once offered upon the cross rightly called our daily sacrifice, in like phrase of speech as is this of Tertullian: *Nos sabbatum non septeno quoque die celebramus, sed omni die*[5]: "We keep the sabbath, not every seventh day, but every day." But M. Harding's fantasy, that is, that the ministration of the sacraments is the daily sacrifice, includeth a manifest untruth. For afterward he granteth himself, that upon Good Friday there is no such oblation made, and that (as he saith) by the order of the apostles. And again, he knoweth that the Grecians in the Lent time never used to consecrate, but only upon Saturdays and Sundays; as it appeareth by the sixth council holden at Con-

Iren. Lib. iv. Cap. xxxiv.

Tertul. adversus Judæos.

Articul. 2. Divis. 23, Fol. 44 b.

Sexta Synod. Constant. cap. 52.

[1 August. Op. Par. 1679-1700. Serm. lxxxiv. 3. Tom. V. Append. col. 153; where we find *est Christus*. The Benedictine editors say, Totus exscriptus est ex Ambrosii Lib. v. de Sacram. cap. iv.]

[2 Hieron. Op. Par. 1693-1706. Comm. in I Epist. ad Cor. cap. v. Tom. V. col. 983; where we find *celebramus*.]

[3 Germ. Const. Rer. Eccles. Theor. in Biblioth. Vet. Patr. Stud. Galland. Venet. 1765-81. Tom. XIII. p. 226.]

[4 Iren. Op. Par. 1710. Lib. IV. cap. xviii. pp. 251, 2; where *nostræ* follows *preces*.]

[5 Unde nos intelligimus magis sabbatizare nos ab omni opere servili semper debere, et non tantum septimo quoque die, sed per omne tempus.—Tertull. Op. Lut. 1641. Adv. Jud. 4. p. 209.]

stantinople[6], and by the council of Laodicea[7]. And of the use of the Latin church therein in his time, St Ambrose writeth thus: "*Omni...hebdomada offerendum est, etiamsi non quotidie peregrinis, incolis tamen vel bis in hebdomada*[8]: "Every week we must celebrate the oblation, although not every day unto strangers, yet for the inhabitants, yea, sometimes twice in the week." I trow M. Harding will not say that the thing that is one day left undone, or that is only done upon the Saturdays and Sundays, or, as St Ambrose saith, twice in the week, is notwithstanding done every day.

Daily Sacrifice.

Concil. Laodic. can. 49. Ambros. in 1 ad Tim. cap. ii. Non quotidie.

Yet it is well to be thought, that both St Ambrose and other learned bishops in the Latin church, and the fathers in the council of Constantinople and Laodicea for the Greek church, understood what was the daily sacrifice.

Verily that sacrifice that Christ once made upon his cross endureth for Good Friday, and all days in the Lent, and every day in the year, and for ever; and therefore is justly called our daily sacrifice.

M. HARDING'S REASONS.

"Christ's death must be kept in remembrance; *ergo*, the priest is bound to say daily mass, yea, although there be no man to receive with him." Alas! how holdeth this poor argument? Or how may we make it good? Is there none other mean to remember Christ's death, but only by saying private mass? Or is not every one of the people bound to remember the same as deeply and as often as the priest? It is a very simple sequel, only upon remembrance of Christ's death to found the mass. Doubtless the mass, as it is now used, utterly drowneth and defaceth all manner remembrance of the death of Christ.

But, to put a little more weight to this silly reason, whereas M. Harding saith, "The priest ought daily to sacrifice, yea, although there be no man to receive with him;" I will say further in his behalf, if this sacrifice be so necessary, as it is supposed, then is the priest bound to sacrifice every day, yea, although he himself receive not. For the sacrifice and the receiving are sundry things, as it is also noted in a late council holden at Toledo in Spain: *Quidam sacerdotes uno die plurima offerunt sacrificia, et in omnibus se oblationibus a communione suspendunt*[9]; "Certain priests there be that every day offer many sacrifices, and yet in every sacrifice withhold themselves from the communion." Thus hath M. Harding found his daily sacrifice, and lost his private mass.

De Con. Dist. 2. Relatum est.

ANOTHER REASON.

"The receiving with company is no substantial part of Christ's institution; *ergo*, we are not bound therein to follow Christ's example." First, this antecedent is false, as it is already proved. And, if it were no part of the substance of Christ's institution, yet are we nevertheless bound to his example, because he hath commanded us so to do.

If Christ's example have no more weight of our side, let us turn the same to M. Harding's side, and see how handsomely it will conclude: "Christ ministered the communion to his disciples all together; *ergo*, the priest may receive alone."

Consider, good reader, what credit these men deserve to have, that are thus fain to shun and fly the example of Christ. St Paul, to rectify the Corinthians, thought no way better than to call them back to Christ's example. For thus he saith: "That I received of the Lord, the same have I delivered unto you." Likewise saith St Hierome: *Dominica cœna omnibus debet esse communis, quia ille omnibus discipulis suis qui aderant æqualiter tradidit sacramenta*[10]; "The Lord's

1 Cor. xi.

Hieron. in 1 Cor. xi.

[6 Ἐν πάσαις τῆς ἁγίας τεσσαρακοστῆς τῶν νηστειῶν ἡμέραις, παρεκτὸς σαββάτου καὶ κυριακῆς, καὶ τῆς ἁγίας τοῦ εὐαγγελισμοῦ ἡμέρας, γινέσθω ἡ τῶν προηγιασμένων ἱερὰ λειτουργία.—Concil. Quinisext. can. 52. in Concil. Stud. Labb. et Cossart. Lut. Par. 1671-2. can. 52. Tom. VI. cols. 1166, 7.]

[7 Ὅτι οὐ δεῖ τῇ τεσσαρακοστῇ ἄρτον προσφέρειν, εἰ μὴ ἐν σαββάτῳ καὶ κυριακῇ μόνον.—Concil. Laod. in eod. can. 49. Tom. I. col. 1505.]

[8 Ambros. Op. Par. 1686-90. Comm. in I. Epist. ad Tim. cap. iii. Tom. II. Append. col. 295.]

[9 Relatum est nobis quosdam de sacerdotibus ... si in uno die plurima per se offerant sacrificia, in omnibus se oblationibus a communione suspendant.—Concil. Tolet. XII. c. 5. in Corp. Jur. Canon. Lugd. 1624. Decret. Gratian. Decr. Tert. Pars, De Consecr. Dist. ii. can. 11. col. 1917.]

[10 Hieron. Op. Comm. in Epist. I. ad Cor. cap. xi. Tom. V. col. 997.]

Communio.

supper must be common to all." And that he proveth by Christ's example; "because Christ gave the sacraments equally to all his disciples that were present."

But whose example followeth M. Harding when he saith his private mass? When did either Christ or any of his disciples, or any one of the old catholic doctors, minister in that sort? If he follow none of these, let him not blame others if they refuse to follow him.

M. HARDING. THE TENTH DIVISION.

M. Jewel, and many other of that side, think to have an argument against private mass of the word communio, *as though the sacrament were called a communion in consideration of many receivers together. [So he calleth that a communion, which is for the whole congregation to receive together*[1].] *And therefore in his sermon oftentimes he maketh an opposition between private mass and*[2] *the communion; and, alleging divers places where mention is of a communion, inferreth of each of them an argument against private mass. But this argument is weak, and utterly unlearned, as that which proceedeth of ignorance.* (19) *For it is not so called because many, or, as M. Jewel teacheth, the whole congregation communicateth together in one place; but because of the effect of the sacrament, for that by the same we are joined to God, and many that be divers be united together, and made one mystical body of Christ, which is the church; of which body, by virtue and effect of this holy sacrament, all the faithful*[3] *be members one of another, and Christ is the head. Thus divers ancient doctors do expound it; and specially Dionysius Areopagita, where, speaking of this sacrament, he saith:* Dignissimum hoc sacramentum sua præstantia reliquis sacramentis longe antecellit, atque ea causa illud merito singulariter communio appellatur. Nam quamvis unumquodque sacramentum id agat, ut nostras vitas in plura divisas in unicum illum statum, quo Deo jungitur[4], colligat, attamen huic sacramento communionis vocabulum præcipue ac peculiariter congruit[5]; "*This most worthy sacrament is of such excellency, that it passeth*[6] *all other sacraments; and for that cause it is alonely called the communion. For albeit every sacrament be such as gathereth our lives, that be divided asunder many ways, into that one state, whereby we are joined to God, yet the name of communion is fit and convenient for this sacrament specially and peculiarly, more than for any other." By which words, and by the whole place of that holy father, we understand that this sacrament is specially called the communion, for the special effect it worketh in us, which is to join us nearly to God; so as we be in him, and he in us, and all we that believe in him, one body in Christ. And for this indeed we do not communicate alone. For, inasmuch as the whole church of God is but one house, as St Cyprian saith,* Una est domus ecclesiæ, in qua agnus editur[7]; "*There is one house of the church wherein the Lamb is eaten;" and St Paul saith to Timothy that this house of God is "the church of the living God;" whosoever doth eat this Lamb worthily doth communicate with all christian men, of all places and countries, that be in this house, and do the like. And therefore St Hierome, a priest, shewing himself loth to contend in writing with St Augustine, a bishop, calleth him a bishop of his communion. His words be these:* Non enim convenit, ut ab adolescentia usque ad hanc ætatem in monasteriolo cum sanctis fratribus labore desudans, aliquid contra episcopum communionis meæ scribere audeam, et eum episcopum, quem ante cœpi amare, quam nosse[8]; "*It is not meet (saith he) that I, occupied in labour from my youth until this age in a poor monastery with holy brethren, should be so bold as to write any thing against a bishop of my communion, yea, and that bishop whom I began to love ere that I knew him." Thus we see that St Hierome and St Augustine were of one* (20)

[In his sermon, fol. 41. H. A. 1564.]

The nineteenth untruth. For of communicating together it was called *communio*.

[*Why the sacrament is called a communion.* H.A. 1564.]

Eccles. Hierarc. cap. iii.

De Cœna Dom.

1 *Tim.* iii.

Inter Epistolas Augustini, Epist. 14.

The twentieth untruth, rising of the ambiguity, or doubtful taking of this word, 'communion'

[1 The sentence between brackets is only in Harding's Answer.]

[2 And communion, H. A. 1564.]

[3 Faithfuls, H.A. 1564.]

[4 Jungimur, H. A. 1564.]

[5 Dionys. Areop. Op. Antv. 1634. De Eccles. Hierarch. cap. iii. 1. Tom. I. p. 282.]

[6 Passeth far, 1565, and H. A. 1564.]

[7 Cypr. Op. Oxon. 1682. De Cœn. Dom. (Arnold.) p. 42.]

[8 Hieron. in August. Op. Par. 1679-1700. Epist. lxxii. 4. ad August. Tom. II. col. 163.]

communion, and did communicate together, though they were far asunder; the one at Bethlehem in Palestina, the other at Hippo in Africa. Thus there may be a communion, though the communicants be not together in one place. Communio.

THE BISHOP OF SARISBURY.

Whereas of the nature of this word *communio*, which is most commonly used in all the old fathers, I took occasion to say that the priest ought to communicate with the people, for that otherwise it cannot justly be called a communion; M. Harding maketh answer, as a man well brooking his own learning, "that this reason is weak and unlearned, as proceeding altogether of ignorance." Here, to leave all contention of learning, and only to have regard unto the truth, if the very nature of this word *communio* import not a thing to be common, as it is supposed, much less may it, as I judge, import a thing to be private. Communio.

It is named *communio*, saith M. Harding, of the effect that it worketh in us, because by the same we are joined unto God, not because many communicate together in one place. And for proof hereof he allegeth the authority of Dionysius: wherein he doth great wrong to that good old father, alleging his authority for the mass, that never spake word of the mass.

It is granted of all, without contradiction, that one end of all sacraments is to join us unto God; as Dionysius saith here of the holy communion, and Paul likewise of the sacrament of baptism: "Ye are all the children of God by faith in Christ Jesus; for as many of you as are baptized in Christ have put on Christ." And Chrysostom saith that "by baptism we are made bone of Christ's bones, and flesh of Christ's flesh[9]." Gal. iii. Chrysost. in Epist. ad Ephes Hom. 20.

Another end is to join us all together. And so likewise writeth St Paul of baptism: *Nos omnes in unum corpus baptizati sumus:* "All we are baptized into one body." And therefore saith St Augustine: *In nullum ... nomen religionis, seu verum seu falsum, coagulari homines possunt, nisi aliquo signaculorum vel sacramentorum visibilium consortio colligentur*[10]: "Men cannot be brought into any name of religion, be it true or false, unless they be joined together with the band of visible signs or sacraments." 1 Cor. xii. Contra Faust. Manich. Lib. xix. cap. xi.

And notwithstanding Dionysius speaketh plainly of both these ends, yet it pleaseth M. Harding in his allegation only to name the one, and to conceal the other, and by the affirmation of the one untruly to conclude the denial of the other. And, as touching the latter of these two ends, the same Dionysius, in the same chapter that M. Harding here allegeth, writeth thus: *Sancta illa unius et ejusdem panis, et poculi communis, et pacifica distributio unitatem illis divinam, tanquam una enutritis, præscribit*[11]: "That holy, common, and peaceable distribution of one bread, and one cup, preacheth unto them a heavenly unity, as being men fed together." And Pachymeres the Greek paraphrast, expounding the same place, hath these words: *τὸ γὰρ ὁμοδίαιτον καὶ ὁμότροπον ἔτι εἰς μνήμην ἄγει τοῦ κυριακοῦ δείπνου*[12]: "For that common diet and consent farther bringeth us into the remembrance of the Lord's supper." Whatsoever M. Harding have said, I reckon it will hereby appear unto the indifferent reader, that these words do sufficiently declare both the common receiving of the sacrament, and also the knitting and joining of many together. Dionys. Eccles. Hierar. cap. iii. ὁμοτροπίαν αὐτοῖς ἔνθεον ὡς ὁμοτρόφοις νομοθετεῖ. Pachymeres Paraphrastes.

Now let us examine this reason: the communion hath his name of the effect, for that it joineth us unto God; *ergo*, saith M. Harding, it signifieth not the communicating of many together. Surely this argument is very weak: I will not say it is "unlearned," or "proceedeth of ignorance." He should need a new logic, that would assay to make it good.

Nay, it may much better be replied, What effect can this sacrament have, or whom can it join to God, but only such as do receive it? or, what effect can the sacrament of baptism work, but only in them that receive baptism? Without

[9 Πῶς οὖν ἐκ τῆς σαρκὸς αὐτοῦ ἐσμεν, καὶ ἐκ τῶν ὀστῶν αὐτοῦ; ... ὅπερ δηλοῦν βούλεται, τοῦτό ἐστιν, ὅτι ὥσπερ ἄνευ συνουσίας ἐκεῖνος γεγέννηται ἐκ Πνεύματος ἁγίου, οὕτω καὶ ἡμεῖς γεννώμεθα ἐν τῷ λουτρῷ.—Chrysost. Op. Par. 1718-38. In Epist. ad Ephes. cap. v. Hom. xx. Tom. XI. p. 147.]

[10 August. Op. Cont. Faust. Lib. XIX. cap. xi. Tom. VIII. col. 319.]

[11 Dionys. Areop. Op. De Eccles. Hierarch. cap. iii. 3. Tom. I. p. 285.]

[12 Pachym. Paraph. in eod. cap. iii. 3. p. 317.]

Communio.

all question, the effect that Dionysius meant standeth not in this, that one man saith a private mass and receiveth the sacrament alone; but in this, that the people prayeth and receiveth the holy communion together, and thereby doth openly testify that they be all one in Christ Jesus and all one amongst themselves. And therefore Chrysostom saith: *Propterea in mysteriis alter alterum amplectimur, ut unum multi fiamus*[1]: "For that cause in the time of the mysteries we embrace one another, that, being many, we may become one."

Chrysost. ad popul. Antioch. Hom. 61.

Howbeit, in plain speech, it is not the receiving of the sacrament that worketh our joining with God. For whosoever is not joined to God before he receive the sacraments, he eateth and drinketh his own judgment. The sacraments be seals and witnesses, and not properly the causes of this conjunction. Otherwise our children that depart this life before they receive the communion, and all the godly fathers of the old testament, should have no conjunction with God. Wherefore St Augustine saith: "No man may anywise doubt but every faithful creature is then made partaker of Christ's body and blood, when in baptism he is made the member of Christ; and that he is not put off from the fellowship of that bread and that cup, although before either he eat that bread or drink of that cup he depart this world, being in the unity of Christ's body. For he is not deprived from the partaking and benefit of the sacrament, so long as he findeth in himself that thing that the sacrament signifieth[2]." Likewise St Cyprian: *Nos ipsi corpus Christi effecti, [et] sacramento, et re sacramenti, capiti nostro conjungimur et unimur*[3]: "We ourselves, being made the body of Christ, both by the mean of the sacrament, and also by the thing itself of the sacrament, or represented by the sacrament, are joined and united unto our Head."

Rom. iv.

August. in Serm. ad Infantes. Beda 1 Cor. x.

Cypr. de Cœna Domini.

But St Cyprian saith: "The whole church is but one house, in which the Lamb is eaten[4]." And St Hierome, notwithstanding he dwelt in Bethlehem, so many miles off from St Augustine, being then at Hippo in Africa, yet he calleth him a bishop of his communion[5]: *Ergo*, saith M. Harding, the priest that saith mass alone in Rome communicateth together with another priest that saith mass alone in India. Here St Cyprian and St Hierome are violently drawn in and forced to witness the thing that they never knew; and so M. Harding, as his manner is, concludeth a falsehood[6].

Cypr. de Cœna Domini.

Inter Epistolas August. Epist. 14.

The holy communion was so often and so generally frequented amongst all Christians in the primitive church in all their assemblies and congregations, that at length the very company and fellowship of them was called *communio*, taking name of that action that was most solemnly used among them at their meetings. And therefore, to give somewhat more credit to M .Harding's words, St Augustine saith: *Mulier illa est communionis nostræ*[7]: "That woman is of our communion." Likewise again: [*Donatus*] *non nisi in sua communione baptismum esse credit*[8]: "Donatus thinketh there is no baptism but only in his communion." And St Hierome, writing unto Damasus bishop of Rome, hath these words: *Ego, nullum primum nisi Christum sequens, beatitudini tuæ, id est, cathedræ Petri, communione consocior*[9]: "I, following no chief but only Christ, am joined by communion to thy holiness, that is to say, to Peter's chair." In these places this word, *communio*, signifieth not the ministration of sacraments, but a side, a part,

August. in Epist. ad Eusebium. August. Retract. Lib. i. cap. xxi. Hieron. ad Damasum.

[1 Possibly the following may be the passage meant: ... hoc nos pascimur, huic nos unimur, et facti sumus unum Christi corpus.—Chrysost. Op. Lat. Basil. 1547. Ad Pop. Ant. Hom. lx. Tom. V. col. 396. See also Hom. lxi. col. 400.]

[2 Nulli est aliquatenus ambigendum, tunc unumquemque fidelium corporis sanguinisque dominici participem fieri, quando in baptismate membrum Christi efficitur; nec alienari ab illius panis calicisque consortio, etiamsi antequam panem illum comedat et calicem bibat, de hoc seculo in unitate corporis Christi constitutus abscedat. Sacramenti quippe illius participatione ac beneficio non privatur, quando ipse hoc quod illud sacramentum significat invenit.—Ven. Bed. Op. Col. Agrip. 1612. Ad Cor. I. cap. x. Tom. VI. col. 365. See also Fulgent. Op. Par. 1623. ad calc. Epist. de Baptism. Æthiop. col. 587. This seems to be the conclusion by Fulgentius from a sermon of Augustine which he transcribes.]

[3 Cypr. Op. Oxon. 1682. De Cœn. Dom. (Arnold.) p. 44; where we find *corpus ejus*, and *connectimur* for *conjungimur*.]

[4 Id. ibid. p. 42.]

[5 See before, page 130, note 7.]

[6 Falsehead, 1565.]

[7 ... in illam feminam ... quæ communionis est nostræ.—August. Op. Par. 1679-1700. Epist. xxxv. 4. ad Euseb. Tom. II. col. 67.]

[8 Id. Retract. Lib. I. cap. xxi. 1.; where we find *ejus* for *sua*, and *baptisma Christi esse credatur*.]

[9 Hieron. Op. Par. 1693-1706. Ad Damas. Epist. xiv. Tom. IV. Pars II. col. 19.]

or a fellowship, or consent in articles of religion. And in this sense St Hierome called St Augustine a bishop of his communion, that is, of his faith, of his mind, of his doctrine, of his religion. Communio.

Here may be noted, by the way, that St Hierome saith not, St Augustine is a bishop of my mass, but "of my communion." For M. Harding knoweth that neither of them both ever said private mass, and therefore could not communicate the one with the other in saying mass.

But, for clearer answer to the words of St Hierome, the communion or fellowship of the church standeth in sundry respects. For we communicate together either in consent of mind, as it is written of the apostles, "They had all one heart and one mind;" or in knowledge of God, as Christ prayeth for his apostles unto his Father, "That they may be one, as thou and I be one;" and St Paul to the Philippians, "I thank my God alway that ye are come to the communion of the gospel;" or in one Christ, as Paul saith, "There is now no bondman, there is now no freeman; but all are one in Christ Jesus." To be short, we communicate in spirit, in prayers, in love; we are all washed with one blood, we are all fed with one body, we have all one hope of our vocation; and all together "with one heart and one voice," be we never so far asunder, "do glorify God the Father of our Lord Jesus Christ." Acts iv. John xvii. Phil. i. Gal. iii. Rom. xv.

And this is that only house wherein the Lamb is eaten[10], grounded upon the foundation of the apostles and prophets. In this house we dwell, M. Harding; here we walk together with consent; here we eat that Lamb of God, being all brothers and members of one body, and all one in Christ Jesus[11]. God restore you once again into the same house, that you may open the eyes of your heart, and see from whence you are fallen! Cypr. de Cœna Domini. Psal. lv. Rev. ii.

Where you say, two divers priests saying mass may communicate together, notwithstanding they be in sundry countries, it may soon be granted. For they communicate together in wickedness, in breaking of God's commandment, and in deceiving of the people; even in like sort as the wicked children communicate in wickedness with their wicked fathers, as Christ seemeth to say to the Pharisees: "At your hands shall be sought for all the just blood that hath been spilt, from the blood of Abel the just unto the blood of Zachary." "Fill ye up the measure of your fathers." Matt. xxiii. Luke xi.

1 Now, these things noted, we may the better take the view of M. Harding's arguments.

2 "The whole church," saith he, "through the world is but one house; *ergo*, the priest may say private mass."

3 "The faithful that be far asunder do communicate together in consent of mind; *ergo*, they do communicate in receiving the sacraments."

"St Augustine and St Hierome did communicate in faith and doctrine; *ergo*, they did communicate together in saying mass."

If St Paul might have had some conference with M. Harding, and have found out these reasons, he would never have found such fault with the Corinthians, neither would he have written thus unto them: *Invicem exspectate*, "Wait ye all one for another." Which words even Hugo Cardinalis expoundeth thus: *Ut una sit mensa: Non habeat quilibet* [*mensam*] *suam*[12]: "Let there be one table for all; and let not every man have his sundry table." Hugo Cardinalis.

But who can better expound St Hierome's words than St Hierome himself? Thus he writeth unto Theophilus, against John bishop of Hierusalem: *Quod scribit, nos tecum pergere Romam, et ecclesiæ communicare ei, a qua videmur communione separati, non necesse est ire tam longe: et hic in Palæstina eodem modo ei jungimur. Et ne hoc quod procul sit: in viculo Bethlehem presbyteris ejus, quantum in nobis est, communione sociamur*[13]: "Whereas he writeth that I am going with thee to Rome, to communicate with the church there, from which we be divided by communion, it is nothing needful to go so far. For being here in Palestine we are joined to the same church in like manner. And let him not make matter that Hier. adversus Johan. Hierosolymitan.

[10 See before, page 130, note 6.]

[11 Jesu, 1565.]

[12 Hug. de S. Char. Op. Col. Agrip. 1621. Epist. I. ad Cor. cap. xi. Tom. VII. fol. 105. 2. O.]

[13 Hieron. Op. Ad Theoph. Epist. xxxix. adv. Johan. Jerosol. Tom. IV. Pars II. col. 339.]

Communio. it is so far off: for being here in the little town of Bethlehem, as much as in us lieth, we join in communion with the priests of Rome." He saith, "as much as in us lieth," whereby he excepteth only the use of the sacraments together.

As much as in us lieth. For otherwise they had communicated thoroughly in all things; and these words, "as much as in us lieth," should not have needed.

The error of these M. Harding's reasons is called, *Fallacia æquivocationis*, that is, a falsehood[1] in reasoning, rising by the crafty handling of one word that hath two or more significations; whereby one thing is laid forth in shew, and another is concluded. This word *communio*, being one, importeth two things, consent in religion and the ministration of the holy mysteries: the one is spiritual, the other corporal; the one requireth circumstance of place, the other requireth no place. Therefore to say St Hierome and St Augustine, being so far asunder, did communicate in religion; *ergo*, they did communicate in breaking and receiving the sacrament, hath no more order in sequel than if M. Harding would reason thus: St Hierome and St Augustine did communicate in spirit; *ergo*, they did also communicate in body; or thus: Their spirits were together; *ergo*, their

2 Kings v. bodies were together. So might he as well say, the spirit of Elizæus was with Giezi his man upon the way; *ergo*, the body of Elizæus was with Giezi upon the

1 Cor. v. way; or: The spirit of Paul was with the Corinthians; *ergo*, his body was with the Corinthians.

By this argument M. Harding might very directly have concluded against himself: The whole church of God is but one house, and all the members of the same do communicate together in faith and spirit: hereof we may found the major: Every particular church ought to be a resemblance of the whole church, and this particular communion ought to be a resemblance of that general communion: that general communion is common to all, and every member receiveth his part; *ergo*, the particular communion ought to be ministered commonly unto all, and every member to receive his part.

Or thus: The ministration of the holy communion representeth the conjunction

Cyprian. ad Magnum. and fellowship that we have in faith; and, as St Cyprian saith, "That christian men are joined together with unseparable charity, the Lord's sacraments do declare[2]." But christian people, being assembled in one church, do communicate in faith all together; *ergo*, being so assembled, they ought to communicate in sacraments all together.

But M. Harding, of the nature of this word *communio*, seemeth to fashion out far other arguments.

It is called *communio*, saith he; *ergo*, it may be private.

It is called *communio*; *ergo*, it may be received of one alone.

It is called *communio*; *ergo*, the priest may receive it without communicants.

O M. Harding, weigh your arguments better before you send them thus abroad. You shall less offend God and your own conscience: you shall less deceive your brethren; and children shall take less occasion to wonder at you.

Now, to add a little more hereunto, touching the nature of this word *communio*, wherein you so uncourteously charge all others with ignorance and lack of learning, as it pleaseth you to do throughout your whole book; I think it not amiss to shew you what certain writers, both old and new, have thought and written in that behalf. I need not here to allege the words that St Paul useth

1 Cor. x. touching the holy communion: "We are all one bread, all one body, as many as

Hieron. 1 Cor. xi. do communicate of one bread;" neither that St Hierome saith: "The Lord's

Chrysost. 1 Cor. Hom. 27. supper must be common[3];" neither that Chrysostom: "The thing that is the Lord's they make private; but the Lord's things are not this servant's or that

August. in Johan. Tract. 26. servant's, but common to all[4];" neither that St Augustine saith: *Hunc...cibum et potum societatem vult intelligi corporis et membrorum suorum*[5]: "He would have

---

[[1] Falsehead, 1565.]

[[2] Denique unanimitatem christianam, firma sibi atque inseparabili caritate connexam, etiam ipsa dominica sacrificia declarant.—Cypr. Op. Oxon. 1682. Epist. lxix. ad Magn. p. 182.]

[[3] Hieron. Op. Par. 1693-1706. Comm. in Epist. I. ad Cor. cap. xi. Tom. V. col. 997.]

[[4] Τὸ γὰρ κυριακὸν ἰδιωτικὸν ποιοῦσιν ... τὰ γὰρ τοῦ Δεσπότου οὐχὶ τοῦδε μέν ἐστι τοῦ οἰκέτου, τοῦδε δὲ οὐκ ἔστιν, ἀλλὰ κοινῇ πάντων.—Chrysost. Op. Par. 1718-38. In Epist. I. ad Cor. Hom. xxvii. Tom. X. p. 244.]

[[5] August. Op. Par. 1679-1700. In Johan. Evang. cap. vi. Tractat. xxvi. 15. Tom. III. Pars II. col. 500.]

us to understand that this meat and drink is the fellowship of his body and of his members;" neither that Chrysostom saith: *Quidnam appello communicationem? Idem ipsum corpus sumus. Quidnam significat panis? corpus Christi. Quid fiunt qui accipiunt? corpus Christi*[6]: "What call I the communication, or communion? We are all one self-same body. What signifieth the bread? the body of Christ. And what are they made that receive it? the body of Christ." Although these fathers by these words do manifestly declare that the holy mysteries in their time were divided commonly to the whole people, yet will I take no advantage thereof; for that M. Harding will reply, they come not precisely to the nature of this word *communio*.

Commu- nio.

Chrysost. 1 Cor. Hom. 24. Significat.

Therefore I will note one or two others, and such as M. Harding cannot deny but they speak directly to the matter. Pachymeres, a Greek writer, the paraphrast upon Dionysius, hath these words: ταύτην δὲ καὶ κοινωνίαν λέγει, διὰ τὸ τότε κοινωνεῖν τοὺς ἀξίους πάντας τῶν μυστηρίων[7]: "Therefore," saith he, "hath this father Dionysius called it the communion, for that then all they that were worthy did communicate of the holy mysteries." Thus Pachymeres, a man of late years, wrote upon the same book of Dionysius; and we may safely think he understood his author's mind as well as M. Harding. He saith *communio* is so called of that we do communicate together; but M. Harding thinketh otherwise, and constantly saith it is not so.

Pachymeres in Dionys. cap. iii. Κοινωνία. Dicitur communio, quia omnes communicant

Haimo, writing upon St Paul's epistles, saith thus: *Calix appellatur communicatio, quasi participatio, quia omnes communicant ex illo*[8]: "The cup is called the communication, which is as much as participation, because all do communicate of it."

Haimo in 1 ad Cor. x.

Hugo Cardinalis saith thus: *Post hoc dicatur communio, quæ...appellatur, ut [omnes] communicemus*: "Afterward let the communion be said, which is so called, that we should all communicate." And he saith further: *Vel dicitur communio, quia in primitiva ecclesia populus communicabat quolibet die*[9]: "Otherwise," saith he, "it is called the communion, for that the people in the primitive church did communicate every day."

Hugo Cardinalis in Speculo Ecclesiæ.

Gerardus Lorichius: *Dicitur communio, quia concorditer de uno pane et uno calice multi participamus; et communio participationem et communicationem significat*[10]: "It is called *communio*, because we do communicate together agreeably of one bread and one cup; and this word *communio* is as much as participation, or receiving of parts."

De Missa Publica Proroganda.

Micrologus[11]: *Non potest proprie dici communio, nisi plures de eodem sacrificio participent*[12]: "It cannot justly be called a communion, unless many do receive together of one sacrifice."

Micrologus de Eccles. Observation. apud Cassand. de Liturgiis, cap. xxii.

If M. Harding will not believe us, yet I hope he will believe some of these. They be all his own. It were much for him to say, they be all ignorant and unlearned, and not one of them understood what he wrote. Certainly their age will give it them; they are no Lutherans. St Basil reporteth an ecclesiastical decree or canon, that at the receiving of the holy communion, which he calleth *mysticum pascha*, there ought to be twelve persons at the least, and never under[13].

Basil. Exercit. ad Pietat. Serm. 4.

M. HARDING. THE ELEVENTH DIVISION.

What if four or five of sundry houses, in a sickness time, being at the point of death, in a parish, require to have their rights ere they depart? The priest, after that he hath received the sacrament in the church, taketh his natural sustenance and dineth, and then, being called upon, carrieth the rest a mile or two to the sick: in each

[6 Chrysost. Op. In Epist. I. ad Cor. Hom. xxiv. Tom. X. p. 213.]

[7 Pachym. Paraph. in Dionys. Areop. Antv. 1634. De Eccles. Hierarch. cap. iii. Tom. I. p. 315.]

[8 Haym. in Paul. Epist. Interp. 1528. Ad Cor. I. cap. x. fol. yii. 2. where *Appellatur et ipse calix, &c.*]

[9 Expos. Miss. Hug. Card. Nuremb. 1507. fol. ult. where we find *qualibet.*]

[10 Dictum est missam esse communionem, qua concorditer, &c....et ex uno calice, &c.—Ger. Lorich. De Miss. Pub. Prorogand. 1536. Lib. II. cap. iii. p. 214.]

[11 Micrologus saith, 1565.]

[12 Microl. de Eccles. Observat. in Cassandr. Op. Par. 1616. cap. xxvi. p. 55; where we find *nec proprie communio dici potest.*]

[13 Basil. Op. Lat. Basil. 1540. Exerc. ad Piet. Serm. iv. Tom. III. p. 425. See before, page 122, note 1.]

The twenty-first untruth. M. Harding saith, the priest doth communicate, and not communicate both together; which is a contradiction in nature.

house none being disposed to receive with the sick, he doth that he is required. (21) *Doth he not in this case communicate with them? And do not they communicate one with another, rather having a will to communicate together in one place also, if opportunity served? Else, if this might not be accounted as a lawful and good communion, and therefore not to be used, the one of these great inconveniences should wittingly be committed;* (22) *that either they should be denied that necessary victual of life at their departing hence, which were a cruel injury, and a thing contrary to the examples and godly ordinances of the primitive church; or the priest, rather for company's sake than of devotion, should receive that holy meat after that he had served his stomach with common meats; which likewise is against the ancient decrees of the church. Even so the priest that receiveth alone at mass doth communicate with all them that do the like in other places and countries.*

The twenty-second untruth. This order was taken, not for every sick party, but for persons excommunicate.

THE BISHOP OF SARISBURY.

He that seeth no mark must shoot by aim. What, saith M. Harding, if four or five men of sundry houses within one parish be at the point of death, and require their rights, and the priest have dined? Hereupon he thinketh may be grounded an argument invincible for his mass. But what if the priest were fasting? Should he then say four masses to serve all four? And what if no man happen to be sick? Then hath M. Harding lost a good argument. Alas! must he leave all the old doctors and holy fathers, and beg at death's door, to get somewhat to help his mass? In this case, saith M. Harding, either the priest must communicate after he hath dined, which is against the canons; or the sick man must receive alone, which is proof sufficient for the mass; or else he must pass without that necessary victual, which were a cruel injury and a thing contrary to the primitive church. To answer these points, if the priest, notwithstanding his dinner, communicate with the sick, then hath M. Harding yet found no private mass. And it appeareth by St Augustine and certain old canons, that in the primitive church both the priest and people sometimes communicated together after supper[1].

August. ad Januarium, Epist. 118. Conc. Carthagin. 3. can. 6.

And why is this provision thought so necessary? Or why is it counted so cruel an injury if the sick man pass without it? Shall no man be saved that so departeth? Indeed that were a cruel injury. Infinite numbers of children and others depart this life in God's mercy, without that victual. In the primitive church this order was thought expedient, not for the sick, (for they in their health received[a] daily[2], and in their sickness had the sacrament ordinarily sent[b] home unto them[3],) but for persons excommunicate and enjoined to penance, who upon great and notorious crimes could not be suffered to communicate with the rest of the faithful, sometimes during their whole life, but only when they should depart the world. This extremity was used for terror of others; and such reconciliation was thought necessary at the end for solace of the party, that he should not utterly be swallowed up in despair, but might perceive he was received again amongst the faithful, and so depart comfortably as the member of Christ. And therefore it was decreed by the council of Carthage, "That, if any man after such reconciliation had recovered his health again, he should nevertheless not be received to the communion of the church, but only be admitted to the common prayers[4]." Thus far forth, and in this case, this provision was counted necessary in the end.

[a] August. de Sermon. Domini in Monte, cap. xii.
[b] Just. Martyr, Apol. 2.

Concil. Carth. 6. can. 13.

Howbeit, I confess, sometimes it was otherwise used, and at last grew to such superstition, that it was thrust into men's mouths after they were dead; as we may see by the council of Carthage forbidding the same[5]. But if the people

Concil. Carth. 3. can. 6.

[[1] August. Op. Ad Inquis. Januar. seu Epist. liv. 9. Tom. II. col. 127.

Concil. Carthag. III. cap. 29. in Concil. Stud. Labb. et Cossart. Lut. Par. 1671-2. Tom. II. col. 1171.]

[[2] Id. De Serm. in Mont. Lib. II. cap. xii. See before page 125, note 7.]

[[3] Just. Mart. Op. Par. 1742. Apol. I. p. 83. See before, page 115, note 8.]

[[4] Si vero desperatus, communione sumpta et oblatione percepta, iterum convalescat, sit inter eos qui orationibus tantum communicant.—Concil. Carthag. VI. cap. 13. in Concil. Stud. Labb. et Cossart. Tom. II. col. 1597.]

[[5] Concil. Carthag. III. cap. 6. in eod. Tom. II. col. 1168. See before, page 6, note 1.]

would now communicate every day, as they did then, or at least oftener than they do now, then should not this matter seem so necessary at the end as it is here pretended; and so had M. Harding lost another argument.

But let us grant M. Harding his whole request: let his priest come and minister to the sick. What maketh all this for his private mass? The members of these arguments hang together like a sick man's dream, not one piece like another. For if here be a mass, which of the two is it that saith this mass? Is it the sick man or the priest? The priest hath dined, and therefore may not; the sick man is no priest, and therefore cannot. Here would M. Harding fain find a mass, but he can find no man to say his mass, and so hath hitherto found no mass at all. And thinketh he to prove his mass by that thing that is no mass?

Again, grant we this action of the priest not only to be a private mass, but also, the necessity of the sick considered, to be lawful: yet could not this precedent make it lawful to be done openly in the church, where as is no such case of necessity. The circumstances of place, of time, of cause, of end, of manner of doing, be not like. In case of necessity a dispensation was granted to the priests of Norway to consecrate the mystical cup without wine; for that wine being brought into that country by mean of the extreme cold cannot last[6]. Yet was it never thought lawful for all other priests in all churches generally to do the same. Volatter Lib. vii

M. HARDING. THE TWELFTH DIVISION.

Now, if either the priest, or every other christian man or woman, might at no time receive this blessed sacrament, but with more together in one place, then, for the enjoying of this great and necessary benefit, we were bound to condition of a place. And so the church, delivered from all bondage by Christ, and set at liberty, should yet for all that be in servitude and subjection under those outward things which St Paul calleth infirma et egena elementa, *"weak and beggarly ceremonies," after the English bible's translation. Then when[7] St Paul, blaming the Galatians, saith, "Ye observe days, and months, and times;" for this bondage he might likewise blame us, and say, Ye observe places. But St Paul would not we should return again unto[8] these which he calleth elements; for that were Jewish. And to the Colossians he saith: "We be dead with Christ from the elements of this world." Now, if we except those things which be necessarily required to this sacrament by Christ's institution, either declared by written scriptures, or taught by the Holy Ghost, (23) as bread and wine mingled with water for the matter, the due words of consecration for the form, and the priest rightly ordered, having intention to do as the church doth, for the ministry; all these elements and all outward things be subject unto[8] us, and serve us, being members of Christ's church. In consideration whereof St Paul saith to the Corinthians:* Omnia enim vestra sunt, &c.: *"All things are yours, whether it be Paul, either Apollo, either Cephas; whether it be the world, either life, either death; whether they be present things, or things to come; all are yours, and ye Christ's, and Christ is God's.*

[*Necessity of many communicants together, contrary to the liberty of the gospel.* H. A. 1564.]

Gal. iv.

Even so St Paul calleth them, πτωχὰ στοιχεῖα.

[*Col. ii.* H. A. 1564.]

[*Similiter et calicem miscens ex vino et aqua, et sanctificans, tradidit eis, dicens, Bibite, &c. Clemens in Canone Liturgiæ, Lib. viii. Apostol. Constitut. c. xvii* [9]. H. A. 1564.]

The twenty-third untruth. The mingling of wine and water together is neither catholic nor necessary. Scotus.

[*1 Cor. iii.* H. A. 1654.]

THE BISHOP OF SARISBURY.

"If it be lawful neither for the priest nor for any other christian man or woman to receive alone, then," saith M. Harding, "we must needs condition of a place to receive together." Here these words, "every other christian man or woman," that he hath taken in by the way, are an overplus and quite from the purpose. For the question is moved, not of "any other man or woman," but of the mass, and only of the priest that saith the mass. Now, to condition of a place, saith M. Harding, were as bad as to observe months and days, which thing St Paul utterly forbiddeth: it were a very Jewish ceremony: it were an element Gal. iv.

[6 Norvegiæ Innocentii VIII. pont. concessione permissum sine vino calicem sacrificare, quod ob immensa frigora vinum in ea regione importatum acescat.—Volaterr. Comm. Urb. Par. 1603. Lib. VII. col. 248.]

[7 Where, H. A. 1564.] [8 To, H. A. 1564.]

[9 Const. Apost. in Concil. Stud. Labb. et Cossart. Lib. VIII. cap. xii. Tom. I. col. 479.]

of this world, and so a miserable servitude of the church. But from such bondage Christ hath delivered us.

I know not well whether M. Harding scoff and dally herein for his pleasure, or speak soothly as he thinketh. If he dally, it becometh not the matter; if he speak soothly and as he thinketh, then he hath not well advised himself, neither from what servitude Christ by his blood hath delivered us, nor of what liberty St Paul speaketh. Certain it is, Christ hath not delivered us from honest civil policies, without which no state, neither ecclesiastical nor civil, can be maintained, but from the curse of the law, wherein we rested under sin, and from the ceremonies and ordinances given by Moses, which for that they were weak, according to the imperfection of that time, therefore St Paul calleth them the elements of this world.

Gal. iii.

Here M. Harding seemeth by the way to touch the English translation of the bible, which calleth such elements "beggarly ceremonies," himself being not able to translate it better. And yet if he were well apposed, I think he would hardly yield any great difference between the Greek word πτωχὰ, and the Latin word *egena*, and this English word "beggarly:" which word if it seem too homely, yet St Hierome in his exposition is as homely, calling it *vilem intelligentiam traditionum*[1]. And yet the prophets abase it further. Hieremy calleth such ceremonies so abused, and others devised by men, chaff, swill, dross, and dreams: Esay, filth: Zachary, curses; Ezechiel, man's dung, and other like.

Beggarly ceremonies.

πτωχά.

Egena.

Hieron. ad Gal. cap. iv.

From this servitude, saith Paul, God hath delivered you. Now are ye free, and no more bond; now are ye the children and heirs of God. From this liberty the Galatians were fallen away to the servile observation of circumcisions, washings, and other ceremonies of the law. Therefore of this liberty and of this bondage St Paul speaketh, and of none other.

Gal. iv.

To condition of a place, saith M. Harding, were mere Jewish; for, as St Paul saith to the Galatians, "Ye observe months and days," so might he say unto you, "Ye observe places." Thus he saith, as though he himself had no choice of place to say his mass in. He moveth talk of place, whereof we had no question; but the number of communicants, whereof St Paul so plainly speaketh, he thought best to salve with silence. If these men account all utter things to be worldly elements, then must they take away the bread and wine in the holy ministration, the water in baptism, the words of the gospel, the whole ministry, and all kind of civil policy. All these be utter creatures, given to us by God to be used freely, without servile observation or subjection of conscience. For God hath appointed these things for us, not us for them.

M. Harding shifteth number into place.

But will our adversaries now at last defend the liberty of the church, or complain of bondage? O good reader, they deal not simply: they dissemble: they mean it not. They have defiled the Lord's sacraments with a multitude of superstitious and childish ceremonies, and have annexed unto the same a deep charge of God's high displeasure, and burden of conscience. They teach the people of God in this sort: O touch not this, O taste not this. They burden the people's consciences with choice of meats. They restrain lawful matrimony, the restraint whereof is a yoke intolerable, and a snare of men's lives, and, as St Paul calleth it, "the doctrine of devils." They hear St Augustine complain, that by mean of such traditions, which he calleth men's presumptions, the church of Christ was in worse case in his time than ever was the synagogue of the Jews[2]. They hear others of late years likewise complain much of the same[3]. Yet would they never, nor yet will they yield, that any one of all their vain ceremonies be released, no not now, having had, as they call it, a general council for that purpose. And can these men stand forth to complain of bondage? Or will they restore us the liberty of the church?

Col. ii.

1 Cor. vii.

1 Tim. iv.

August. ad Januarium, Epist. 118.

Bernardus Clarevallen. Gerson Cancellari. Parisien.

[1 ... Judæorum traditiones, et secundum litteram vilem intelligentiam, &c.—Hieron. Op. Par. 1693-1706. Comm. Lib. II. in Epist. ad Gal. cap. iv. Tom. IV. col. 270.]

[2 ... ipsam tamen religionem, quam paucissimis et manifestissimis celebrationum sacramentis misericordia Dei esse liberam voluit, servilibus oneribus premunt, ut tolerabilior sit conditio Judæorum, qui ... legalibus tamen sarcinis, non humanis præsumtionibus subjiciuntur.—August. Op. Par. 1679-1700. Ad Inquis. Januar. seu Epist. lv. 35. Tom. II. col. 142.]

[3 Such complaints are frequently made. See Bernard. Op. Par. 1690. Apol. ad Guillelm. Abbat. cap. xii. 28. Vol. I. Tom. II. col. 538; &c. See also Joh. Gerson. Op. Antw. 1706. Lib. de Vit. Spirit. Anim. Lect. IV. Coroll. xi. Tom. III. Pars. I. cols. 44, 5.]

Howbeit M. Harding hath well disclosed himself herein, that this liberty is nothing else but to do what him listeth, and his bondage nothing else but to be subject unto God. For he addeth immediately, that the mingling and blending of water and wine together, and the intention of the priest, are things necessarily required to the consecration of this sacrament. Of the first hereof, the superstition only excepted, no man maketh any great account. Indeed, St Cyprian and certain old fathers speak of it, and force it much[4]; and Justinus Martyr calleth it ποτήριον ὕδατος καὶ κράματος[5], "The cup of water and mixture." But neither Christ nor any of his disciples ever gave commandment of it; neither was it at any time in the church universally received, or accounted necessary. For Scotus[6] and Innocentius[7] witness that the Greek church in their time used it not. Wherefore it cannot be judged catholic. And touching the necessity thereof, Scotus saith in plain words: *Huic...vino apponere aquam non est simpliciter necessarium de necessitate sacramenti*[8]. Here we see these doctors agree not. M. Harding saith: "This mixture is necessary to the sacrament." Scotus saith: "It is not necessary."

Mingling of water and wine.

M. Harding's liberty.

Cypr. contra Aquarios.

Justin. in Apol. 2.

Joh. Scotus in iv. Sent. Dist. xi. Quæst. 6.

Innocentius de Officio Miss. Part. iii. cap. iv.

The mingling of wine and water is not necessary.

Now, to reveal the secrets of M. Harding's mysteries touching the same; that one drop or two must be poured on the ground; how much thereof must be put to the wine, that there may be made a convenient mixture; what becometh afterward of the same water; whether it be turned into a thin phlegm, or into Christ's blood by mean of mixture, or into a sacrament of ablution to wash the rest away, it would require longer talk, and not necessary at this present. Neither would I now have moved one word hereof, saving that this man thus vaunteth himself to be the restorer of christian liberty.

Whereas he saith, "The priest must have intention to do that the church doth;" unless he be well assured of the church's doing herein, he cannot be sure of his own intention; and so must he say mass with intention to do he knoweth not what. Now it appeareth that the church is not yet resolved upon one intention. For the intention of the church of Rome is to work the transubstantiation of bread and wine: the Greek church had never that intention, as is[9] plain by the council of Florence[10]. The intention of the church of Rome is to consecrate with Christ's words: the intention of the Greek church is to consecrate with prayers[11]. And whether of these churches shall the priest follow with his intention? This is the very dungeon of uncertainty. The heart of man is unsearchable. If we stay upon the intention of a mortal man, we may stand in doubt of our own baptism.

The intention of the priests[7].

Concil. Florent. Sess. ultima.

Bessarion de Sacramento Eucharistiæ.

Christ hath delivered us from the elements of this world; *ergo*, the priest may say private mass. We are forbidden to observe months and days; *ergo*, the priest may receive alone.

M. Harding's arguments.

Thus he reasoneth, as if St Paul's words were written that he might thereby prove what himself listeth. Indeed, the bread, the wine, the water, and the priest himself, are worldly creatures, and therefore subject unto christian liberty no less than place or time. Yet may not M. Harding therefore have the communion ministered without either priest, or bread, or wine; neither baptism ministered without water. Christ hath delivered us from the subjection and superstitious using of the creatures, but not from the creatures themselves. Otherwise by the same form of reason M. Harding might as well have concluded thus: Apollo, Paul, Peter, life, and things to come, are worldly creatures; for so saith St Paul; even as M. Harding hath alleged, "All things are yours, whether it be Paul, or Apollo, or Peter, or the world, or life, or things to come:" but Christ hath delivered us from worldly creatures; *ergo*, Christ hath delivered us

1 Cor. iii.

[4 Cypr. Op. Oxon. 1682. Ad Cæcil. Epist. lxiii. pp. 148, &c.]

[5 Just. Mart. Op. Par. 1742. Apol. I. p. 82.]

[6 Joan. Duns Scot. Op. Lugd. 1639. In Lib. IV. Sent. Dist. xi. Quæst. 7. Schol. Tom. VIII. p. 688.]

[7 Innocent. III. Op. Col. 1575. Myst. Miss. Lib. IV. cap. xxxii. Tom. I. p. 390.]

[8 Priest, 1565.]

[9 It is, 1565, 1609.]

[10 Concil. Florent. Sess. xxv. in Concil. Stud. Labb. et Cossart. Lut. Par. 1671-2. Tom. XIII. col. 492.]

[11 Græci vero ... non illis Salvatoris nostri verbis Christi corpus et sanguinem confici putant, sed quibusdam quæ sequuntur precibus sacerdotum.—Bessar. De Sacram. Eucharist. in Biblioth. Patr. Per M. De la Bigne, Par. 1624. Tom. VI. col. 467.]

Intention. from Paul, Apollo, Peter, from the world, from life, and from things to come. Such arguments M. Harding hath brought to prove his mass.

M. HARDING. THE THIRTEENTH DIVISION.

Again, whereas the ancient and great learned bishop Cyrillus teacheth plainly and at large the marvellous uniting and joining together of us with Christ, and of ourselves into one body by this sacrament; seeing that all so united and made one body be not for all that brought together into one place, for they be dispersed abroad in all the world; thereof we may well conclude, that to this effect the being together of communicants in one place is not of necessity. His words be these, much agreeable to Dionysius Areopagita afore mentioned: Ut igitur inter nos et Deum singulos uniret, quamvis corpore simul et anima distemus, modum tamen adinvenit, consilio Patris et sapientiæ suæ convenientem. Suo enim corpore credentes per communionem mysticam benedicens, et secum, et inter nos, unum nos corpus efficit. Quis enim eos, qui unius sancti corporis unione in uno Christo uniti sunt, ab hac naturali unione alienos putabit? Nam si omnes unum panem manducamus, unum omnes corpus efficimur: dividi enim atque sejungi Christus non patitur[1]: "*That Christ might unite every one of us within ourselves, and with God, although we be distant both in body and also in soul, yet he hath devised a mean covenable*[2] *to the counsel of the Father, and to his own wisdom. For in that he blesseth them that believe, with his own body through the mystical communion, he maketh us one body both with himself, and also between ourselves. For who will think them not to be of this natural union, which with the union of that one holy body be united in one Christ? For if we eat all of one bread, then are we made all one body; for Christ may not be divided nor done asunder.*" *In Joan. Lib. xi. cap. xxvi.*

Thus we see after this ancient father's learning, grounded upon the scriptures, that all the faithful[3]*, blessed with the body of Christ, through the mystical communion, be made one body with Christ, and one body between themselves. Which good blessing of Christ is of more virtue, and also of more necessity, than that it may be made frustrate by condition of place, specially where as is no wilful breach nor contempt of most seemly and covenable order.*

THE BISHOP OF SARISBURY.

As I can easily yield in part that these two fathers, Cyrillus and Dionysius, agree together, as it is here avouched; so, if M. Harding can prove that this same Cyrillus ever said private mass, or in any of all his works once used the name of mass, I will as gladly yield unto the whole. But, if Cyrillus never spake word of the mass, how is he here brought in to prove the mass? Howbeit these men know it is an easy matter to mock the ignorant with the glorious name of catholic fathers.

Cyrillus saith that as many as believe in Christ, whether they be far or near, Jews or Gentiles, free or bond, they are all one body in Christ Jesus[4]. This thing neither is denied, nor in any point toucheth the private mass. We confess that Christ by the sacrament of regeneration, as Chrysostom saith, hath made us flesh of his flesh, and bone of his bones[5]; that we are the members, and he is the head. We confess also, that all the faithful are one body, all endued with one spirit. And be that distance never so great, yet are we one another's members. Chrysost. in Epist. ad Ephes. Hom. 20.

This marvellous conjunction and incorporation is first begun and wrought by faith; as saith Paulinus unto St Augustine: *Per fidem nostram incorporamur in Christo Jesu Domino nostro*[6]: "By our faith we are incorporate or made one body with Jesus Christ our Lord." Afterward the same incorporation is assured Paulin. et Theras. ad August. Epist. 31.

[1 Cyril. Alex. Op. Lut. 1638. Comm. in Joan. Evang. Lib. XI. cap. xi. Tom. IV. pp. 998, 9. See also Op. Cyril. in Evang. Joan. G. Trapezont. trad. Par. 1508. Lib. XI. cap. xxvi. fol. 181; from which the passage is cited; *convenientem* being put for *congruentem*.]

[2 Covenable (or convenable, H. A. 1564): agreeable.]

[3 Faithfuls, H.A. 1564.]

[4 Jesu, 1565.]

[5 Chrysost. Op. Par. 1718-30. In Epist. ad Ephes. cap. v. Hom. xx. Tom. XI. p. 147. See before, page 131, note 8.]

[6 Paulin. et Theras. in August. Op. Par. 1679-1700. Ad August. Epist. xxv. 1. Tom. II. col. 36; where we find *qua adcorporamur*.]

unto us, and increased in our baptism; so saith St Augustine: *Ad hoc baptisma valet, ut baptizati Christo incorporentur, et membra ejus efficiantur*[7]: "To this availeth baptism, that men, being baptized, may be incorporate into Christ, and made his members." And for that we are very unperfect[8] of ourselves, and therefore must daily proceed forward, that we may grow into a perfect[9] man in Christ, therefore hath God appointed that the same incorporation should be often renewed and confirmed in us by the use of the holy mysteries. Wherein must be considered that the said holy mysteries do not begin, but rather continue and confirm, this incorporation. First of all, we ourselves must be the body of Christ, and afterward we must receive the sacrament of Christ's body; as it is well noted by St Augustine: *Corpus... Christi si vis intelligere, apostolum audi dicentem fidelibus, Vos estis corpus Christi, et membra:...mysterium vestrum in mensa Domini positum est: mysterium Domini accipitis. Ad id, quod estis, respondetis, Amen.... Audis,...corpus Christi, et respondes, Amen. Esto membrum corporis Christi, ut verum sit Amen tuum*[10]: "If thou wilt understand the body of Christ, hear what St Paul saith to the faithful: 'Ye are the body and the members of Christ:' your mystery is set on the Lord's table; ye receive the mystery of the Lord. To that thing that ye are ye answer, Amen. Thou hearest, The body of Christ, and sayest, Amen. Be thou a member of Christ's body, that thy Amen may be true."

August. de Baptismo Parvulorum. De Consecr. Dist. 4. Ad hoc.

Aug. in Sermone ad Infantes. Citatur a Beda in 1 Cor. x.

Neither may we think that Christ's body must grossly and bodily be received into our bodies. St Cyprian saith: "It is meat not for the belly, but for the mind[11]." And St Augustine saith: *Crede, et manducasti*[12]: "Believe in Christ, and thou hast eaten." And Cyrillus, that is here alleged, writeth thus against the objections of Theodoretus: "We do not maintain the eating of a man unreverently, drawing the minds of the faithful unto gross and profane imaginations; neither do we submit these things unto man's fantasy, that be received only by pure and tried faith[13]." Therefore saith Athanasius: "It is spiritual meat, and spiritually is digested in us[14]."

Cypr. de Cœn. Dom. De Consecr. Dist. 2. Ut quid August. Cyrillus contra objectiones Theodoreti.

Athanasius in illa verba, Si quis dixerit verbum.

Thus is Christ set forth unto us in that most holy supper, not to be received with the mouth, (for that, as Cyrillus saith, "were a gross and profane imagination;") but to be embraced with a pure and a single faith; and, as Athanasius saith, to be eaten as spiritual food, and spiritually to be digested into all his members. Thus are we all one body and one spirit in Christ; for that Christ is in all us, and all we in him. And because the holy ministration representeth the same unto our eyes, therefore St Augustine calleth it "the mystery of unity[15]." Thus doth the holy communion knit and join us together, be we in number never so many, and in distance never so far asunder. For therein we profess that we are all servants in one house, and resort all to one table, and feed all of one spiritual food, which is the flesh and blood of the Lamb of God. Which thing Paulinus seemeth very well and in plain manner to open unto St Augustine by these words: *Non mirum, si et absentes adsumus nobis, et ignoti nosmet novimus, cum unius corporis membra simus, unum habeamus caput, una perfundamur gratia, uno pane vivamus, una incedamus via, eadem habitemus* [*in*] *domo*[16]: "It is no marvel though we, both being absent, are nevertheless present together; and, being

August. de Con. Dist. 2. Quia passus.

Paul. Epist. ad Aug. 33.

[7 August. in Corp. Jur. Canon. Lugd. 1624. Decret. Gratian. Decr. Tert. Pars, De Consecr. Dist. iv. can. 143. col. 2030; where we have *baptismus*, and *habeantur*.]

[8 Unperfite, 1565.]

[9 Perfite, 1565.]

[10 Ven. Bed. Op. Col. Agrip. 1612. Ad Cor. I. cap. x. Tom. VI. col. 364; where *amen respondetis*.]

[11 ... non dentes ad mordendum acuimus, sed fide sincera panem ... frangimus.—Cypr. Op. Oxon. 1682. De Cœn. Dom. (Arnold.) p. 44. The same idea frequently occurs, but the exact words are not found in the treatise referred to.]

[12 August. in Corp. Jur. Canon. Decret. Gratian. Decr. Tert. Pars, De Consecr. Dist. ii. can. 47. col. 1936.]

[13 Ἀρ' οὖν, ὡς ἕτερόν τινα υἱὸν...διαβεβαιούμενος...οὐκ ἀνθρωποφαγίαν ἡμῶν ἀποφαίνει τὸ μυστήριον, παριστὰς ἀνοσίως εἰς ἐξιτήλους ἐννοίας τῶν πιστευσάντων τὸν νοῦν· καὶ λογισμοῖς ἀνθρωπίνοις ὑποφέρειν ἐπιχειρῶν, ἃ μόνως καὶ ἀζητήτῳ πίστει προσλαμβάνεται;—Cyril. Alex. Op. Lut. 1638. Apolog. adv. Orient. Anath. xi. Def. Cyril. Tom. VI. p. 193.]

[14 Ἀλλ' αὔτη [ἡ σὰρξ] ὑμῖν καὶ τὸ ταύτης αἷμα παρ' ἐμοῦ πνευματικῶς δοθήσεται τροφὴ, ὥστε πνευματικῶς ἐν ἑκάστῳ ταύτην ἀναδίδοσθαι.—Athanas. Op. Par. 1698. Epist. iv. 19, ad Serap. Tom. I. Pars II. p. 710.]

[15 Qui accipit mysterium unitatis, &c.—August. in Corp. Jur. Canon. Decret. Gratian. Decr. Tert. Pars, De Consecr. Dist. ii. can. 36. col. 1929.]

[16 Paulin. et Theras. in August. Op. Par. 1679-1700. Ad August. Epist. xxx. 2. Tom. II. col. 54; where the reading is *nec mirum*.]

unacquainted, yet know one another; seeing we be the members of one body, and have one head, and are poured over by one grace, and live by one bread, and walk one way, and dwell in one house." I thought it good to accompany Cyrillus with these other ancient fathers, for the better understanding of his meaning.

Hereof M. Harding seemeth to reason thus: By the communion all faithful are joined both unto God, and also between themselves; *ergo*, the priest may say private mass. Little thought that good father that his words should ever be thus used, or so violently forced to such conclusions. But let us drive this argument a little further, that the inconvenience and the error may the better appear.

Only the priests in their private masses receive the communion; *ergo*, for that action and time only the priests are made one body of Christ. And then further, that body of Christ is the whole church; *ergo*, the priests by their private masses are made the whole church.

But that thou mayest plainly see, christian reader, wherein M. Harding was thus deceived, thou must understand that Cyrillus taketh his reason, as far as it toucheth the communion of the sacrament, as we use to say in schools, *ab effectis*, and not *a causis*. But M. Harding turneth it quite contrary; as if it were taken *a causis*, and not *ab effectis*. And that Cyrillus so reasoneth, it is soon seen. For the receiving of the sacrament is not the efficient cause that we are made one body in Christ, but a token and testimony, or, as St Paul saith, the "seal" and confirmation of that effect. For Judas received the sacrament as well as Peter did; yet was not Judas a member of Christ's body, as Peter was. And many infants, and others faithful and godly be very members of that body; and yet by occasion of death, or otherwise, never receive the sacrament of Christ's body.

Rom. iv. Signaculum.

And notwithstanding M. Harding hath thus altered his author's meaning, yet shall he very hardly thereof in good order conclude his mass. But he may of the same very well and directly conclude the communion. For if the communion, in that it is received of many, be a testimony and a declaration that all faithful are one body in Christ, as Cyrillus meaneth, then ought the same communion to be received together of many; otherwise it is no such testimony or declaration as is supposed. The antecedent or first proposition hereof is proved by sundry old fathers. St Cyprian saith: "With what love and concord all faithful Christians are joined together, the Lord's sacrifice doth declare[1]." And Anselmus, a man of latter years: *Frangimus et dividimus panem in multas partes, ad designandam unionem caritatis accipientium:* "We break and divide the bread into many parts, to declare the unity of the love of them that receive it." Here note, Anselmus saith, this declaration of unity standeth in receiving of the sacraments, and not only in looking on. Neither doth Cyrillus say, They that hear mass, but "they that receive the mystical benediction, are one body with[2] Christ, and also between themselves[3]." Like as St Paul also saith: "The bread that we break is the communication of the Lord's body. And we, being many, are all one bread and one body, as many as be partakers of one bread." Whereunto agree these words of St Hierome spoken in the behalf of Christ: *Benedic hæreditati tuæ, quam per corporis et sanguinis mei mysterium in ecclesia congregasti:* "Bless thine inheritance, which thou hast gathered together in the church by the mystery of my body and blood." And Dionysius: "The common and peaceable distribution of one and the same bread and cup prescribeth a godly concord unto them, as unto men fed together with one food[4]." And thus, as M. Harding hath truly said, Cyrillus and Dionysius agree in one, but both together against him; both utterly condemning his private mass.

Cyprian. ad Magnum.

Anselm. in 1 Cor. x. Accipientium.

Cyril. in Johan. Lib. xi. cap. xxvi. 1 Cor. x.

Hier. in Eccles. cap. iii.

De Eccles. Hierarch. cap. iii. ὡς ὁμοτρόφοις.

M. HARDING. THE FOURTEENTH DIVISION.

And therefore that one may communicate with another, though they be not together in one place (which M. Jewel denieth, with as peevish an argument of the use of excommunication, as any of all those is, that

[*Many may communicate together, not being in one place together.* H. A. 1564.]

[1 See before, p. 134, note 2.]
[2 Body both with, 1565.]
[3 See before, page 140, note 1.]
[4 Dionys. Areop. Op. Antv. 1634. De Eccles. Hierarch. cap. iii. 3. Tom. I. p. 285. See before, page 131.]

[Sermon, fol. 51. H. A. 1564.] *he scoffeth at some catholic writers for*), (24) *and that it was thought lawful and godly by the fathers of the ancient church, near to the apostles' time, it may be well proved by divers good authorities.* The twenty-fourth untruth. [5] For there appeareth no such thing in any ancient father.

THE BISHOP OF SARISBURY.

I used the pulpit as a place of reverence, and not of scoffing. Only I thought good to lay out the weakness of sundry reasons alleged on your side, that the people might see upon how slender grounds your religion standeth. And thus I did, having just occasion thereunto of the unjust reports moved in corners by you and others, whereby you bear the people in hand that all our doctrine was light and childish, and not worth the hearing. Therefore that the people, having taken some taste of the arguments on both parts, might be the better able to judge of both, I shewed forth this argument of pope Innocentius: "The sun is greater than the moon;" *ergo*, "The pope is greater than the emperor;" and the gloss in the margin upon the same: "The sun is seven and fifty times greater than the moon;" *ergo*, "The pope is seven and fifty times greater than the emperor[6]." And likewise the argument of pope Bonifacius the eighth: *In principio creavit Deus cœlum et terram, non in principiis*: "In the beginning, and not in sundry beginnings, God made heaven and earth;" *ergo*, "The pope hath the sovereignty over all kings and princes[7]." He that sheweth the weakness of these arguments and such other, deserveth not therefore by and by to be called a scoffer. De Major. et Obed. cap. Solitæ. De Major. et Obed. Unam Sanctam.

Further, touching excommunication, I said thus: If the priest that saith mass in Lovaine may communicate with the priest that saith mass in Calicute, (which is M. Harding's greatest ground for his private mass,) then hath the church, so far forth as toucheth the priests, lost the whole use of excommunication. For the party excommunicate, being a priest, might say, he would say mass, and so receive the communion, even with the bishop of whom he were excommunicate, whether he would or no. This saying M. Harding hath condemned for peevish, by his authority only, and not by reason. Excommunication.

Indeed, the church of Rome, as it hath lost the whole use of the holy communion, so hath it also the[8] whole use of excommunication. For these two words be of contrary natures, and the one of them hath his name of the losing of the other. In the primitive church, as all the godly were freely received to the holy mysteries, so by the authority of the Spirit of God the apparent wicked and ungodly were removed, and that with great discretion, according to the enormity and quality of the faults; as it is specially noted by Gregorius Neocæsariensis, in a canon touching the same[9]. The greatest offenders were utterly excluded from the congregation, as men not meet to be in the company of the godly. Others were suffered to enter into the temple, and to hear the sermon; but at the beginning of the prayers they were removed, as men not meet to pray with their brethren. Others were suffered to be present at the prayers, but at the beginning of the communion were willed to depart. The rest were the godly that remained still, and heard the sermon, and continued in prayer, and received the holy mysteries all together. The order hereof is declared by Cassiodorus out of Socrates: *Stant...rei, et velut in lamentationibus constituti: et cum sacra celebratio fuerit adimpleta,...communionem non percipiunt*: "They stand wofully, and as it were men in lamentation and in heaviness; and when the holy celebration is ended, they receive not the communion." It followeth: *Constituto vero tempore, velut quoddam debitum exsolventes,...cum populo communionem participant*[10]: "At the time appointed, as if they had discharged a certain debt, they communicate together with the people." Thus the offenders were put from the communion; and all the rest received together. And therefore it is decreed by the canons of the apostles, "That all faithful, that enter into the church, and hear the scriptures, Gregorius Neocæsariensis. Lugentes. Audientes. Precantes. Hist. Trip. Lib. ix. cap. xxxv. Canon. Apost. Canon. 9.

[[5] 1565 omits *for*.]

[[6] Innoc. III. in Corp. Jur. Canon. Lugd. 1624. Decretal. Greg. IX. Lib. I. Tit. xxxiii. cap. 6. col. 426; and Gloss. ibid. See before, page 14, note 1.]

[[7] Bonifac. VIII. in eod. Extrav. Comm. Lib. I. De Major. et Obed. cap. 1. col. 212. See before, page 14, note 2.]

[[8] Also lost the, 1565.]

[[9] Gregor. Neocæs. Thaumat. Op. Par. 1621. Epist. Canon. can. xi. p. 41.]

[[10] Hist. Trip. Par. Lib. IX. cap. xxxv. fol. T. v.; where we have *dum enim sacra*, and *percipientes*. The passage is found in Sozomen, Hist. Eccles. Lib. VII. cap. xvi.]

Excommunication.

and do not continue out the prayers, nor receive the communion, should be excommunicate, as men working the trouble and disorder of the church[1]." And the people said unto Timotheus, being a bishop of the Arians, and nevertheless a man of mild and gentle nature, and shunning his company for the one, and yet loving him for the other: "Although we communicate not with thee, yet we love thee notwithstanding[2]."

Now if M. Harding's principle stand for good, that the priest saying his private mass may receive the communion with all others in other places that do the like, then can no priest be excommunicate. For, notwithstanding neither any other priest, nor any of the people will receive with him, yet may he say a private mass, and by M. Harding's new device straightway communicate with them all.

But, for better declaration of this matter, it is commonly taught in schools that *privatio præsupponit habitum*, that is, that the losing of a thing first presupposeth the having of the same; for no man can lose that thing that he hath not. Therefore to say there is excommunication from the sacraments, where as is no communion of the sacraments; or that he is put from the Lord's table, that neither is at nor coming to the table; or that he is excommunicate, that is only forbidden to hear mass; or that the people doth sufficiently receive the sacraments by the mouth of the priest; verily, this kind of learning in the primitive church would have seemed not only peevish, but also fantastical and mere frantic. Thus the bishop of Rome (as it is said) useth to excommunicate locusts, snakes, caterpillars, and other like worms; and conjurers use to excommunicate their devils; as though these creatures, saving the force of their authority, were otherwise meet enough to receive the communion.

M. HARDING. THE FIFTEENTH DIVISION.

Eccles. Hist. Lib. v. cap. xxiv.

Irenæus, writing to Victor bishop of Rome, concerning the keeping of Easter, as Eusebius Cæsariensis reciteth, to the intent Victor should not refrain from their communion which kept Easter after the custom of the churches in Asia founded by St John the Evangelist, sheweth that, when bishops came from foreign parts[3] *to Rome, the bishops of that see used to send to them, if they had been of the catholic faith, the sacrament to receive; whereby mutual communion between them was declared. Irenæus his words be these:* Qui fuerunt ante te presbyteri, etiam cum non ita observarent, presbyteris ecclesiarum (cum Romam accederent) eucharistiam mittebant[4]: "*The priests (by which name in this place bishops are understanded) that were afore thy time, though they kept not Easter as they of Asia did, yet, when the bishops of the churches there came to Rome, did send them the sacrament.*" (25) *Thus those bishops did communicate together before their meeting in one place.*

Græca sic habent: aliter quam Ruffini versio vulgata.

The twenty-fifth untruth. [5]For Irenæus saith not, they did communicate together.

THE BISHOP OF SARISBURY.

This story is common and known to many. The west church in keeping of Easter-day followed St Peter: the east church followed St John, and kept it otherwise. Hereof grew contention, and brake out into cruel heats: Victor the bishop of Rome on the one side, and Polycarpus the bishop of Smyrna on the other side; both godly men, and both martyrs. Each part would have the other to yield. Victor, being a man of a fiery nature, was minded to excommunicate the whole church of Asia, and all others whatsoever, that in keeping of Easter-day would not follow the church of Rome. Irenæus, the bishop of Lyons, hearing thereof, wrote unto him a sharp letter out of France, willing him in any wise to proceed no further; for that it might tend to such a breach as would not afterward be recovered. Among other words he saith thus, as it is here alleged: "The

---

[1 Canon. Apost. 9. in Concil. Stud. Labb. et Cossart. Lut. Par. 1671-2. Tom. I. col. 28.]

[2 Liberat. Brev. Par. 1675. cap. xvi. p. 108. See before, page 99, note 4.]

[3 Parties, H. A. 1564.]

[4 Ἀλλ' αὐτοὶ μὴ τηροῦντες οἱ πρὸ σοῦ πρεσβύτεροι, τοῖς ἀπὸ τῶν παροικιῶν τηροῦσιν ἔπεμπον εὐχαριστίαν.—Euseb. in Hist. Eccles. Script. Amst. 1695-1700. Lib. v. cap. xxiv. p. 157. The version of Ruffinus is: Immo potius et omnes presbyteri qui fuerunt ante te omnibus semper qui non ita observabant presbyteris ecclesiarum eucharistiam solenniter transmittebant.]

[5 1565 omits *for*.]

priests that were (in Rome) before thee, notwithstanding they kept not the Easter as they of Asia do, yet they sent the sacrament unto the priests of those churches when they came to Rome." Hereof M. Harding concludeth; *ergo*, "These bishops did communicate before they met together;" and noteth also by the way in the margin, that the Greek in Eusebius differeth from the common translation of Ruffinus. And yet is the same translation alleged and used in the book of councils among the decrees of Victor[6]. But, if M. Harding had marked the matter well, he should have seen that his own translation in English varieth also somewhat from the Greek. Concil. Tom. I. inter Decreta Victoris.

In this short story three things specially may be noted. First, that Irenæus, a bishop of France, durst to write so roughly to the bishop of Rome, without any style of superiority, only calling him and all others before him bishops of Rome by the name of priests.

Secondly, that so notable learned men and martyrs of Christ, agreeing otherwise in the substance of religion, yet notwithstanding, in certain small matters of no great weight, contended and strived so extremely and so long, and could in no wise be reconciled. Which thing well considered, M. Harding hath less cause to triumph, if God have suffered any such sparkle of dissension in the special members of his church in these days.

Thirdly, where was then that great superiority of the bishop of Rome, when, notwithstanding his threats and commandments, the church of this island of Britain, well near until seven hundred years after Christ, in the keeping of Easter-day followed the manner of the Greek church, without any regard therein had to the church of Rome[7]? Beda. Eccl. Hist. Lib. iii. cap. xxv.

But to the matter: "These bishops," saith M. Harding, "communicated together before they met." If he mean in faith and religion, it is not denied; if in the use of the sacraments, it is not proved. In my judgment, this word *eucharistia*, in this place of Irenæus, signifieth not the sacrament already consecrate, but rather other common bread, wherewith one bishop used then to present another, as with a special token of consent in religion and christian concord; which bread the receiver afterward, if he thought it good, might use at the holy ministration. In that sense, it seemeth, Paulinus wrote unto St Augustine: *Panem unum sanctitati tuæ caritatis gratia misimus, in quo etiam Trinitatis soliditas continetur. Hunc panem [tu] eulogiam esse facies dignatione sumendi*[8]. "In token of mutual love I have sent unto thee one loaf of bread, in which also the soundness of the holy Trinity is contained. This loaf you shall cause to be a loving present of my behalf, vouchsafing to receive it." And in the next epistle following: *Quinque panes misimus tibi, pariter et filio nostro Licentio. Non enim potuimus in benedictione secernere, quem cupimus eadem nobis gratia penitus annectere*[9]: "Five loaves have I sent unto thee, and unto my son Licentius. For I could not sever him in blessing, whom I desire thoroughly to join with us in grace." Hereby it may appear that this bread was not the sacrament; and namely by that Paulinus writeth in another place: *Panem unum, quem unanimitatis indicio misimus caritati tuæ, rogamus [ut] accipiendo benedicas*[10]: "I pray you to take and bless this one loaf, which I have sent unto you in token of unity." If it had been already consecrate, he would not have desired St Augustine to have blessed it. Paulin. ad August. Epist. 35. Paulin. ad August. Epist. 36. Paulin. ad August. Epist. 31.

But Irenæus useth this word *eucharistia*, which is taken for the sacrament. I answer: It might so be called, for that it was prepared for the sacrament. Howbeit, herein I will not strive. Tertullian nameth it *hospitalitatis contesseratio*[11], and seemeth to speak it of the sacrament; which thing being also granted in this place of Irenæus, let us now see M. Harding's reasons. Tertull. de Præscr. adversus Hæreticos.

[[6] Decret. Victor. in Crabb. Concil. Col. Agrip. 1551. Tom. I. p. 96.]

[[7] Bæd. Hist. Eccles. Cant. 1722. Lib. III. cap. xxv. pp. 131, &c.]

[[8] Paulin. et Theras. in August. Op. Par. 1679-1700. Ad Alyp. Epist. xxiv. 6. Tom. II. col. 36; where for *caritatis* we have *unitatis*.]

[[9] Id. in eod. ad Roman. Epist. xxxii. 3. col. 59; where we read *panes quinque tibi, &c. Licentio misimus*, and *a* for *in*.]

[[10] Id. in eod. ad August. Epist. xxv. 5. col. 38.]

[[11] Tertull. Op. Lut. 1641. De Præscr. Hæret. 20. p. 238.]

The bishop of Rome, saith he, sent the sacrament unto them that came out of Asia; *ergo*, there was private mass.

This conclusion is far fet[1], and hangeth loosely. For I might demand, Which then of the three said mass? He that sent the sacrament, or he that received it, or else the messenger that brought it? It were a strange matter to see a mass, and yet no man to say mass. Verily Irenæus hath not one word, neither of the communion, nor of the mass, unless M. Harding will say that *mittere* is Latin to "communicate," or *mittere eucharistiam* is Latin to "say mass."

Mittere eucharistiam.

If it were common bread, then was it but a present: if it were the sacrament, then was it to be received, not straight upon the way, or perhaps late in the night, or in the inn, at the common table among other meats, but afterward at his pleasure in his congregation. Thus we see this place first is doubtful; and, being never so plain, yet it proveth nothing for private mass. But immediately after followeth a manifest mention, in what order the bishops used then to communicate together; which thing M. Harding thought better to dissemble. *Cum res ita haberent, communicabant inter se mutuo, et in ecclesia Anicetus concessit eucharistiam Polycarpo*[2]: "The matters between them thus standing, they communicated together; and Anicetus in the church granted the sacrament or the ministration of the sacrament unto Polycarpus."

τούτων οὕτως ἐχόντων, ἐκοινώνησαν ἑαυτοῖς· καὶ ἐν τῇ ἐκκλησίᾳ παρεχώρησεν ὁ Ἀνίκητος τὴν εὐχαριστίαν τῷ Πολυκάρπῳ.

Here mark, good christian reader, then they communicated, saith Irenæus, when they met in the church, and not before they met together, as M. Harding saith. Anicetus, as Irenæus saith, received the sacrament with Polycarpus in the church, and not, as M. Harding seemeth to say, in his inn or hostery.

Now, the truth of the matter standing thus, what hath M. Harding here found for his private mass?

M. HARDING. THE SIXTEENTH DIVISION.

Justinus the martyr likewise, describing the manner and order of christian religion of his time, touching the use of the sacrament, saith thus: Finitis ab eo qui præfectus est gratiis et orationibus, et ab universo populo facta acclamatione, diaconi, quos ita vocamus, unicuique tunc[3] temporis præsenti panis, et aquæ, et vini consecrati, dant participationem, et ad eos qui non adsunt deferunt[4]: "*When the priest hath made an end of thanks and prayers, and all the people thereto have said* Amen, *they which we call deacons give to every one then present bread and water and wine, consecrated, to take part of it for their housel, and for those that be not present they bear it home to them." Thus in that time they that served God together in the common place of prayer, and some others that were absent, letted from coming to their company by sickness, business, or otherwise,* (26) *communicated together, though not in one place; and no man cried out of breaking the institution of Christ.*

Apolog. 2.

The twenty-sixth untruth. For[5] Justinus speaketh not one word of communicating together.

And because M. Jewel is so vehement against private mass, for that the priest receiveth the sacrament alone, and triumpheth so much, as though he had won the field, making himself merry with these words, indeed without a cause[6], "*Where then was the private mass? Where then was the single communion all this while?" (he meaneth for the space of six hundred years after Christ, as there he expresseth;) I will bring in good evidence and witness, that long before St Gregory's time that he speaketh of, yea, from the beginning of the church, faithful persons, both* *men and women, *received the sacrament alone, and were never therefore reproved as breakers of Christ's institution. And ere I enter into the rehearsal of the places which I am able to shew for this purpose, one question I demand of M. Jewel: If they which remained at home, of whom Justinus Martyr writeth, received the communion by themselves alone lawfully, why may not the priest do the same in the church, serving God in most devout wise in the holy sacrifice of the mass, lacking compartners without any his default? Have the sacramentaries any religion*

[*In his sermon, fo. 43, H. A. 1564.*]

* M. Harding bringeth one thing for another; sole receiving instead of private mass; men and women instead of the priest.

[1 Fet: fetched.]

[2 Euseb. in Hist. Eccles. Script. Amst. 1695-1700. Lib. v. cap. xxiv. p. 157.]

[3 Tum, H. A. 1564.]

[4 Just. Mart. Op. Par. 1742. Apol. i. p. 83.]

[5 1565 omits *for*.]

[6 Without cause, 1565, 1609, and H. A. 1564.]

to condemn it in the priest and to allow it in lay-folk? What is in the priest that should make it unlawful to him more than to the people? Or may a layman or woman receive it kept a long time; and may not a priest receive it forthwith, so soon as he hath consecrated and offered? And if case of necessity be alleged for the lay, the same may no less be alleged for the priests also, wanting compartners without their default: for otherwise the memory and recording of our Lord's death should not according to his commandment be celebrated and done. Well, now to these places.

THE BISHOP OF SARISBURY.

Good reader, behold not the names of these fathers here alleged, but rather weigh their sayings. M. Harding hath brought them for his mass; but they witness clearly and fully against his mass; and of all others, none more pregnant or plain than Justinus Martyr: whereof thou hast good occasion to consider how faithfully these men demean themselves in the allegation of the doctors. Justinus, touching this matter, writeth thus: "Towards the end of the prayers, each of us with a kiss saluteth other. Afterward, unto him that is the chief among the brethren is delivered bread, and a cup mingled with wine and water, which he having received rendereth praise and glory unto the Father of all things, in the name of the Son and the Holy Ghost, and yieldeth thanks a great space, for that he is thought worthy of these things. Which being orderly done, the people blesseth or confirmeth his prayer and thanksgiving, saying, Amen, &c. This ended, they that among us be called deacons deliver to every of them that be present the bread, wine, and water, which are consecrate with thanksgiving, and carry of the same to them that be absent[7]." Here is set forth the whole and plain order of the holy ministration used in the church at that time. The priest prayeth and giveth thanks in the vulgar tongue: the whole congregation heareth his words, and confirmeth the same, saying, Amen. The holy communion is ministered to the people in both kinds; and all the whole church receiveth together. I marvel much wherein M. Harding can liken any part hereof to his private mass, unless it be for that, as he said before every private mass is common, so he will now say, every communion is private.

Justin. Martyr in Apologia 2.

πᾶς ὁ λαὸς ἐπευφημεῖ λέγων, Ἀμήν.

The order of the holy ministration in Justinus' time.

Let us a little compare Justine's mass and M. Harding's mass both together. And, to pass by all other circumstances of difference, in Justine's mass all the people did receive: in M. Harding's mass none of the people do receive. In Justine's mass none abstained: in M. Harding's mass all abstained[8]. In Justine's mass a portion was sent to the absent: in M. Harding's mass there is no portion delivered; no, not unto the present. With what countenance then can any man allege the authority of Justine to prove the antiquity of private mass?

Justine's communion and M. Harding's mass compared together.

"M. Jewel triumpheth," saith M. Harding, "and maketh himself merry, as if he had won the field." No, no; M. Jewel triumpheth not, but giveth all triumph, victory, and glory unto God, that will subdue all them that withstand his truth, and make his enemies his footstool.

Psal. cx.

"I will bring good evidence and witness," saith M. Harding, "that, from the beginning of the church, faithful persons, both men and women, received the sacrament alone." I have no great cause to doubt these witnesses; for, excepting only the fable of Amphilochius, and John the Almoner, which were not worth the reckoning, I alleged all the rest in mine own sermon. I knew them, and had weighed them, and therefore I alleged them. That certain godly persons, both men and women, in time of persecution, or of sickness, or of other necessity, received the sacrament in their houses, it is not denied, neither is it any parcel of this question.

But if M. Harding could have proved that any man or woman in the primitive church ever said private mass, then had he answered somewhat to the purpose.

He seemeth to reason thus: Some received the sacrament alone; *ergo*, there was private mass.

[[7] Just. Mart. Op. Apol. i. pp. 82, 3. See before, page 115, note 8.]   [[8] Abstain, 1565.]

The folly of this argument will the better appear by the like:

Women received the sacrament alone; *ergo*, women said private mass.

But, saith M. Harding, it was lawful for laymen to receive alone: why then was it not lawful for the priest? If he could have proved his mass by priests, he would never have sought help at laymen's hands. Howbeit, this doubt is soon answered. For he knoweth by his own learning that it is lawful for a priest to say mass; yet is it not lawful for a layman to do the same. Of the other side, it is lawful (as he saith) for the layman to receive in one kind; yet is not the same lawful for the priest. But if he will needs take a precedent of laymen for priests to follow, let him rather reason thus: This manner of private receiving at home was not lawful for the laymen, for it was abolished by godly bishops in general council[1]; *ergo*, it was not lawful for the priest to say private mass.

Concil. Cæsaraugust. cap. 3.

M. HARDING. THE SEVENTEENTH DIVISION.

Proofs for private mass.

Lib. ii. ad Uxorem.

Tertullian, exhorting his wife, that, if he died before her, she marry not again, specially to an infidel, shewing that, if she did, it would be hard for her to observe her religion without great inconvenience, saith thus: Non sciet maritus quid secreto ante omnem cibum gustes? Et si sciverit, panem, non illum credit[2] esse qui dicitur[3]: *"Will not thy husband know what thou eatest secretly before all other meat? And if he do know, he will believe it to be bread, and not* (27) *him who it is called." He hath the like saying in his book* De Corona Militis[5]; *which place plainly declareth unto us the belief of the church then in three great points, by M. Jewel and the rest of our gospellers utterly denied. The one, that the communion may be kept; the second, that it may be received by*[6] *one alone, without other company; the third, that the thing, reverently and devoutly before other meats received, is not bread, as the infidels then and the sacramentaries now believe, but he who it is said to be of christian people, or who it is called, that is,* (28) *our Maker and Redeemer, or, which is the same, our Lord's body. And by this place of Tertullian, as also by divers other ancient doctors, we may gather that in the times of persecution the manner was, that the priests delivered to devout and godly men and women the sacrament consecrated in the church, to carry home with them, to receive a part of it every morning fasting, as their devotion served them, so secretly as they might, that the infidels should not espy them, nor get any knowledge of the holy mysteries. And this was done because they might not assemble themselves in solemn congregation, for fear of the infidels amongst whom they dwelt. Neither should the case of necessity have excused them of the breach of Christ's commandment, if the sole communion had been expressly forbidden, as we are borne in hand by those that uphold the contrary doctrine. And Origen*[7]*, that ancient doctor, and likewise St Augustine*[8]*, do*[9] *write of the great reverence, fear, and wariness, that the men and women used in receiving the sacrament in a clean linen cloth, to carry it home with them for the same purpose. St Cyprian writeth of a woman that did the like, though unworthily, after this sort:* Cum quædam arcam suam, in qua Domini sanctum fuit, manibus indignis tentasset aperire, igne inde surgente, deterrita est, ne auderet attingere[10]*: "When a certain woman went about to open her chest, wherein was the holy thing of our Lord, with unworthy hands, she was frayed with fire that rose from thence, that she durst not touch it." This place of St Cyprian*

The twenty-seventh untruth. For[4] the translation is wilfully corrupted; "it" violently turned into "him."

The twenty-eighth untruth. For[4] the sacrament was never called our Maker or Redeemer by any of the old fathers.

[*Origen. in Exod. Hom. xiii.* H. A. 1564.]

[*August. Hom. 26. in Lib. l. Hom. et Sermon. cclii. de Tempore.* H. A. 1564.]

In Ser. de Lapsis.

[1 Eucharistiæ gratiam si quis probatur acceptam in ecclesia non sumpsisse, anathema sit in perpetuum.—Concil. Cæsaraug. can. 3. in Concil. Stud. Labb. et Cossart. Lut. Par. 1671-2. Tom. II. cols. 1009, 10.]

[2 Credet, 1565, and H. A. 1564.]

[3 Tertull. Op. Lut. 1641. Ad Uxor. Lib. II. 5. p. 190.]

[4 1565 omits *for*, and *is*.]

[5 Id. De Coron. 3. p. 121.]

[6 Of, H. A. 1564.]

[7 ...nostis...quomodo cum suscipitis corpus Domini, cum omni cautela et veneratione servatis, ne ex eo parum quid decidat, &c.—Orig. Op. Par. 1733-59. In Exod. Hom. xiii. 3. Tom. II. p. 176.]

[8 August. Op. Par. 1679—1700. Serm. ccc. 2. Tom. V. Append. col. 504. See below, page 151, note 12. The Benedictine editors attribute this sermon to Cæsarius.

Omnes viri, quando ad altare accessuri sunt, lavant manus suas, et omnes mulieres nitida exhibent linteamina, ubi corpus Christi accipiant.—Id. Serm. ccxxix. 5. Tom. V. Append. cols. 376, 7. This also is ascribed to Cæsarius.]

[9 Doth, 1565, and H. A. 1564.]

[10 Cypr. Op. Oxon. 1682. De Laps. pp. 132, 3.]

reporteth the manner of keeping the sacrament at home, to be received of a devout christian person alone at convenient time. The example of Serapion, of whom Dionysius Alexandrinus writeth, recited by Eusebius, confirmeth our purpose of the single communion. This Serapion, one of Alexandria, had committed idolatry, and, lying at the point of death, that he might be reconciled to the church before he departed, sent to the priest for the sacrament. The priest, being himself sick and not able to come, gave to the lad that came of that errand, parum eucharistiæ, quod infusum jussit seni præberi, *"a little of the sacrament, which he commanded to be poured into the old man's mouth." And when this solemnity was done (saith the story), as though he had broken certain chains and gyves, he gave up his ghost cheerfully*[11].

Eccles. Hist. Lib. vi. cap. xliv.

THE BISHOP OF SARISBURY.

M. Harding shooteth fair, but far from the mark. To prove private mass in the primitive church, for lack of priests he allegeth Tertullian's wife, certain women out of Cyprian, and Serapion's boy; not the fittest people that might have been found to say mass. And yet, that the folly might the more appear, he hath besides given a special note in the margin of his book, by these words, "Proofs for private mass:" whereof I conceive some hope that he mindeth no more to slip away under the colour of single communion, as he hath done hitherto; but simply and plainly, as he hath here noted unto the world, to stand upon the bare terms of private mass. For else his note was not worth the noting.

As touching Tertullian, we must remember that the faithful in that time, for fear of the tyrants under whom they lived, were often driven to pray asunder. Wherefore, when they might privily assemble together, besides that they presently received there, they reserved certain portions of the mysteries to be received afterward in their houses at home, to put them daily the better in remembrance that they were the members of one church.

This manner of the church considered, Tertullian, being a priest, as St Hierome writeth of him[12], and having a wife, wrote unto her an exhortation, that if it should please God to take him first from the world, that she would remain still unmarried, or at the least not match with any heathen; shewing her the dangers that thereof might ensue, that she should be suffered neither to keep the solemn feasts, nor to watch, nor to pray with the congregation. Among other things he saith thus: "And will not thy husband know what thou eatest before other meats? And if he know it, he will believe it to be bread, but not that bread that it is called."

Hieron. de Eccles. Scrip. Tertullian a married priest.

Tertul. Lib. ii. ad Uxorem.

Here M. Harding, as if the gospel of Christ were become odious unto him, in scorn and disdain calleth us gospellers, by the name of that gospel that he so wilfully hath forsaken, returning to his old vomit. And out of these words of Tertullian three things, he saith, he will teach us; of which three things notwithstanding his private mass is none. Of the first we have to speak otherwhere. Of the second there is no question. In the third M. Harding hath manifestly corrupted both the words and meaning of Tertullian. He saith, "The thing that we receive is no bread;" but so Tertullian saith not. His words be these: "Thy husband will think it (only) bread, and not that bread that it is called"—that is to say, the sacrament of Christ's body, or the mystery of any holy thing, as christian men believe of it: like as Chrysostom also saith of the water of baptism: *Ethnicus cum audit lavacrum baptismi, persuadet sibi simpliciter esse aquam*[13]: "A heathen, when he heareth of the bath of baptism, believeth it is nothing else but plain water."

Gospellers.

Chrysost. in 1 ad Cor. Hom. 7.

But that the thing which our bodily mouth receiveth is very bread, both the scriptures and also the old catholic fathers have put it out of doubt. St Paul five times in one chapter nameth it bread.

1 Cor. xi.

Cyrillus saith: "Christ unto his faithful disciples gave pieces of bread[14]." And

Cyril. in Johan. Lib. iv. cap. xiv.

[11 Euseb. in Hist. Eccles. Script. Amst. 1695—1700. Lib. VI. cap. xliv. pp. 200, 1.]

[12 Hieron. Op. Par. 1693—1706. Catal. Script. Eccles. Tom. IV. Pars II. col. 115.]

[13 Chrysost. Op. Par. 1718-38. In Epist. I. ad Cor. Hom. vii. Tom. X. p. 51.]

[14 Τοῖς γὰρ ἤδη πεπιστευκόσι διακλάσας τὸν ἄρτον ἐδίδου.—Cyril. Alex. Op. Lut. 1638. In Joan.

In Sermone ad Infantes: citatur a Beda. 1 Cor. x.

St Augustine saith: "The thing that ye see is bread, as your eyes bear you witness[1]." I pass by Gelasius, Theodoretus, Chrysostom, Origen, Justinus Martyr, Irenæus, Clemens, and others, who all together with one consent have confessed that in the sacrament there remaineth the nature and substance of bread. Wherefore it is much presumed of M. Harding, to say there remaineth no bread, specially having nothing to bear him in his author here alleged.

Tertullian falsified by M. Harding. Ludov. Vives De Civit. Dei, Lib. ii. cap. xiii. John xix. Petrus Crini. Lib. xiii. cap. vi. Codrus Urceus, Serm. 8. Judg. xii.

Yet for advantage he hath also falsified Tertullian, englishing these words, *illum panem*, "him," as if it were the person of a man; as Thomas Valois, writing upon St Augustine, *De Civitate Dei*, hath turned this word *apex*, which was the tuft or crest of the flamen's hat, into a certain chronicler that wrote stories[2]; or as the divines of late years, upon the gospel of St John, of this Greek word *lonche*, which signifieth a spear, have made *Longinus*, the blind knight[3]. If Tertullian had not meant *illum panem*, "that bread," he would not have said *illum* at all, but rather *illud*, referring the same unto *corpus*. A small difference between "him" and "it." So was there small difference between "sibboleth" and "shibboleth." Yet was it sufficient to descry the traitor.

And, whereas M. Harding thus hardly and violently, contrary to the phrase and manner of speech, and, as it may be doubted, contrary to his own knowledge and conscience, hath translated *illum panem*, "him," so as, to my remembrance, never did man before, meaning it was the very person of a man that the woman had in her hand, and did eat before other meats; Cyrillus saith: *Non asseveramus anthropophagiam*[4]: "We teach not our people to eat the person of man."

Cyril. contra Objectiones Theodoreti.

But who can better expound Tertullian's mind than Tertullian himself? In his book *De Corona Militis*, speaking of the same matter, he calleth it *sacramentum eucharistiæ*[5], "the sacrament of thanksgiving." And against Marcion he writeth thus: *Christus non reprobavit panem, quo corpus suum repræsentat*[6]: "Christ refused not the bread wherewith he representeth his body." And St Augustine likewise saith: *In sacramentis videndum est, non quid sint, sed quid significent*[7]: "Touching sacraments, we must consider, not what they be indeed, but what they signify." So also saith St Chrysostom: *Ego non aspectu judico ea quæ videntur, sed mentis oculis corpus Christi video*[8]: "I judge not those things which are seen, after the outward appearance; but with the eyes of my mind I see the body of Christ."

Tertull. de Coron. Militis. Tertull. contra Marcion. Lib. i. August. contra Maximinum, Lib. iii. cap. xxii. Chrysost. in 1 Cor. Hom. 7.

This is the thing that the husband, being an[9] heathen, could not see: for, believing not in Christ, he could not understand that the bread should be the sacrament or mystery of Christ's body.

And that this was the very meaning of Tertullian, it may well appear by the words that immediately follow: "The husband," saith he, "will doubt whether it be poison or no; and therefore will dissemble and bear for awhile, that at length he may accuse his wife for poisoning before a judge, and do her to death, and have her [10]dowry[11]."

Sine gemitu, sine suspicione panis, an veneni.

Touching St Augustine and Origen, the portion so taken was to be used with reverence, as being the sacrament of Christ's body: and so ought we also reverently to have and to order the water of baptism, the book of the gospel, and all

Evang. Lib. IV. cap. ii. Tom. IV. p. 360. The Latin version is, Fragmenta panis dedit.]

[1 Quod ergo videtis, panis est et calix; quod vobis etiam oculi vestri renuntiant.—August. Op. Par. 1679—1700. Ad Infant. Serm. cclxxii. Tom. V. cols. 1103, 4.]

[2 Testante apice. apex hic est proprium nomen scriptoris historiographi Romanorum.—August. de Civ. Dei, cum Comm. Thom. Valois et Nic. Triveth, Basil. 1479. Comm. in Lib. II. cap. xv. fol. 8. 2.

Id. de Civ. Dei, per Joan. Lud. Vivem. Basil. 1522. Lib. II. cap. xiii. p. 48.]

[3 Unde ridiculus error vulgi e sacra historia emersit, Longinum temere credentis pro lancea, &c.—Pet. Crinit. De Honest. Discipl. Lugd. 1543. Lib. XIII. cap. vi. p. 206.

Ant. Codr. Urc. Serm. &c. Par. 1515. Serm. x. fol. 72.]

[4 Cyril. Alex. Op. Lut. 1638. Apolog. adv. Orient. Anath. xi. Def. Cyril. Tom. VI. p. 193. See before, page 141, note 13.]

[5 Tertull. Op. Lut. 1641. De Coron. 3. p. 121.]

[6 Sed ille quidem...reprobavit...nec panem, quo ipsum corpus, &c.—Id. Adv. Marcion. Lib. II. 14. pp. 439, 40.]

[7 Hæc enim sacramenta sunt, in quibus non quid sint, sed quid ostendant semper adtenditur.—August. Op. Cont. Maxim. Lib. II. cap. xxii. 3. Tom. VIII. col. 725.]

[8 Chrysost. Op. Par. 1718—38. In Epist. I. ad Cor. Hom. vii. Tom. X. p. 51. Gr. ἀκούω σῶμα Χριστοῦ.]

[9 A, 1565.]

[10 Dower, 1565.]

[11 Tertull. Op. Ad Uxor. Lib. II. 5. p. 190.]

other things that be of God; as the Jews were also commanded to keep their manna reverently in a golden pot. "Tell me," saith St Augustine, "whether of these two things trow ye to be the greater, the body of Christ (meaning thereby the sacrament of Christ's body), or the word of Christ? If ye will answer truly, ye must needs say, that the word of Christ is no less than the body of Christ. Therefore look, with what diligence ye take heed, when the body of Christ is ministered unto you, that no part thereof fall unto the ground; even so with like diligence must ye take heed that the word of God, being once received, be not lost from a pure heart[12]." Likewise St Chrysostom touching the same: *Si...hæc vasa sanctificata ad privatos usus transferre sic periculosum est, in quibus non est verum corpus Christi, sed mysterium corporis Christi continetur*[13]: "If the matter be so dangerous, to put these sanctified vessels unto private uses, wherein is contained not the very body of Christ, but the mystery or sacrament of Christ's body," &c. All these authorities do declare, that the sacraments of Christ ought discreetly and reverently to be used.

1 Q. i. Interrogo vos. Idem de Temp. The word of Christ is no less than the body of Christ.

Chrysost. in Opere Imper. Hom. 11. The very body of Christ is not contained in the holy vessels.

The story that St Cyprian reporteth[14], as it sheweth the manner of keeping of the sacrament, so it seemeth also to shew that God was offended with the same: the like whereof hath often been seen in the water of baptism and in other holy things, as appeareth by Nicephorus[15], and others in sundry places. Therefore this authority serveth M. Harding to small purpose, unless it be to prove that, as God was then displeased with sole receiving in private houses, so he is now displeased with sole receiving in the mass.

Cypr. de Lapsis, Serm. 5.

Niceph. Lib. xiv. cap. xvii.

Concerning the story of Serapion, here are interlaced many fair words for increase of credit, that it was written by Dionysius Alexandrinus and recited by Eusebius, as though the sick man had only desired his housel before he departed, and nothing else. But the special matter, whereupon the story is grounded, is passed by. Eusebius recordeth in plain words, that the book wherein Dionysius wrote this story was entitled *De Pœnitentia*[16]. Whereby he giveth to understand that the sacrament then was not generally sent home to all men's houses, but only unto them that were excommunicate and might not receive in the congregation among the faithful, and now lay in despair of life.

Euseb. Lib. vi. cap. xlv.

The case stood thus: Serapion, in the time of persecution, for fear of death, had offered sacrifice unto an idol. The faithful, being therewith sore offended, put him out of their congregation and gave him over to Satan. He, being thus left as an heathen and an idolater, might[17] neither resort to the common church, nor pray, nor receive the holy communion or any other spiritual comfort among his brethren. So hard the church was then to be entreated for them that had fallen back into idolatry. After he had made all means, and had with tears besought his brethren, and was no way considered, through heaviness of mind he began to droop and fell sick, and for three days lay speechless and without sense. The fourth day being somewhat revived, he said to them that were about him: "O how long will ye keep me here? Send for one of the priests (that I may be restored before I depart)."

His mind was tormented with consideration of the state he stood in, for that he had forsaken God. The priest, being sick himself, in token he was restored, and might depart as a member of Christ, sent unto him the sacrament by his boy. The rest that M. Harding addeth, "And this solemnity being done, saith the story, as though he had broken certain chains and gyves, he gave up the

Ruffin. Lib. vi. cap. xxxiv.

[12 Interrogo vos, fratres, vel sorores, dicite mihi, quid vobis plus esse videtur, verbum Dei an corpus Christi? Si verum vultis respondere, hoc utique dicere debetis, quod non sit minus verbum Dei, quam corpus Christi. Et ideo, quanta solicitudine observamus, quando nobis corpus Christi ministratur, ut nihil ex ipso de nostris manibus in terram cadat, tanta solicitudine observemus, ne verbum Dei, quod nobis erogatur, dum aliud aut cogitamus aut loquimur, de corde nostro pereat.—August. in Corp. Jur. Canon. Lugd. 1624. Decret. Gratian. Decr. Sec. Pars, Caus. I. Quæst. i. can. 94. col. 540. Op. Serm. ccc. 2. Tom. V. Append. col. 504.]

[13 Chrysost. Op. Op. Imperf. in Matt. Hom. xi. Tom. VI. p. lxiii; where we find *corporis ejus*.]

[14 Cypr. Op. Oxon. 1682. De Laps. pp. 132, 3.]

[15 The story referred to is of the water miraculously disappearing, when a Jew who had been before baptized approached.—Niceph. Call. Hist. Eccles. Lut. Par. 1630. Lib. XIV. cap. xvii. Tom. II. pp. 471, 2.]

[16 Euseb. in Hist. Eccles. Script. Amst. 1695—1700. Lib. VI. cap. xliv. pp. 200, 1; where καταβροχθίσας. See the next page.]

[17 Mought, 1565.]

Receiving with the hand.

spirit cheerfully"—all this is set to, either by Ruffinus[1] or by some other, I know not by whom, and is no part of the story. For neither doth Dionysius nor Eusebius in the original make any mention either of solemnity, or of chains or gyves, or of cheerfulness of Serapion's departing, but only thus: "And swallowing down a little, straightways he yielded up the ghost." As for his joyful departure, I doubt nothing. But any great solemnity there could not be between a man in that case, and a boy alone, specially having no such outward pomp as hath been used of late, to make it solemn.

μικρὸν ... καταβροχθήσας, εὐθέως ἀπέδωκε τὸ πνεῦμα.

Now must I desire thee, gentle reader, to have an eye a little backward to M. Harding's note, given thee for a remembrance in the margin by these words, "Proofs for private mass;" which note must needs be in the foot and conclusion of all his arguments. Therefore of these stories, here by him reported, we must conclude thus: Tertullian's wife, and the woman of whom Cyprian speaketh, received the sacrament alone; *ergo*, Tertullian's wife and the other woman said private mass. Or thus: Serapion's boy ministered the sacrament to his master; *ergo*, Serapion's boy said private mass. For if the conclusion be otherwise, we conclude one thing for another. And indeed M. Harding may as certainly say, This action was a mass, as he can say, Serapion's boy was a priest.

M. HARDING. THE EIGHTEENTH DIVISION.

Of keeping the sacrament secretly at home, and how it might be received of devout persons alone without other company, I ween none of the ancient doctors wrote so plainly as St Basil, in an epistle that he wrote to a noble woman called Cæsaria, which is extant in Greek, where he saith further that this manner began not in his time first[2], but long before. His words be these: Illud autem, in persecutionis temporibus necessitate cogi quempiam, non præsente sacerdote aut ministro, communionem propria manu sumere, nequaquam esse grave, supervacaneum est demonstrare, propterea quod longa consuetudine et ipso rerum usu confirmatum est. Omnes enim in eremis solitariam vitam agentes, ubi non est sacerdos, communionem domi servantes, a seipsis communicant. In Alexandria vero, et in Ægypto, unusquisque eorum qui sunt de populo plurimum habet communionem in domo sua... Semel enim sacrificium sacerdote consecrante et distribuente, merito participare et suscipere, credere oportet. Etenim et in ecclesia sacerdos dat partem, et accipit eam is qui suscipit cum omni libertate, et ipsam admovet ori propria manu. Idem igitur est virtute, sive unam partem accipiat quisquam a sacerdote, sive plures partes simul[3]: *"As concerning this, that it is no grievous offence for one to be driven by necessity, in times[4] of persecution, to receive the communion with his own hand, no priest nor deacon being present, it is a thing superfluous to declare, for that by long custom and practice it hath been confirmed and taken place. For all they which live a solitary life in wilderness, where no priest is to be had, keeping the communion at home, do communicate with* (29) *themselves alone. And in Alexandria and in Egypt every one of the people, for the most part, hath the communion at home in his house. For when as the priest hath[6] once consecrate and distribute the host, it is reason we believe that we ought to be partakers of it; and he that taketh it receiveth it without all scruple of conscience, and putteth it to his mouth with his own hand. And so it is of one virtue, whether any body take one part of the priest, or more parts together."*
Thus[7] far St Basil. In this saying of Basil it is to be noted: first, that necessity 1.
here hath respect to the lack of priest and deacon, so as (30) *in that case the*
sacrament might be received of a faithful person with his own hand. And that for 2.
the ratifying of so doing he allegeth continuance of custom, which for us, in this
point of the sole receiving, may in more ample wise be alleged. Again, that holy 3.

The twenty-ninth untruth. For[5] M. Harding hath corrupted the translation. The words "with themselves alone" are not in St Basil.

The thirtieth untruth. For[5] St Basil saith the communicant received with his own hand, even in the presence of the priest.

[1 Cumque esset completa solemnitas, velut catenis quibusdam vinculisque diruptis, lætiorem jam spiritum reddidit.—Hist. Eccles. Par. Lib. VI. cap. xxxiii. fol. 74. 2.]

[2 First in his time, H. A. 1564.]

[3 Basil. Op. Par. 1721—30. Ad Cæsar. Epist. xciii. Tom. III. pp. 186, 7. The Benedictine editors add, *καὶ ὅτε βούλεται μεταλαμβάνει δι' ἑαυτοῦ*, on manuscript authority.]

[4 In the times, H. A. 1564.]

[5 1565 omits *for*.]

[6 Doth, H. A. 1564.]

[7 This, H. A. 1564.]

eremites, living in wilderness apart from company, and also the devout people of Alexandria and Egypt, received the communion alone in their cells and houses.
4. *Furthermore, that the host, once consecrated of the priest, is algates*[8] *to be received,*
5. *whether of many together or one*[9] *alone, by him it seemeth not to force. Finally,*
that, whether a man take at the priest's hand the blessed sacrament in one piece or more pieces, and receive them at convenient times, when devotion best serveth, the virtue, effect, and power thereof is one. By which authority reservation is avouched. Doubtless, where he speaketh so precisely and particularly of sundry cases touching the order of receiving, if he had been of M. Jewel's opinion, that the sacrament may not be received of one, without a certain number of communicants together, he would not so have passed over that matter in silence, much less written so plainly of the contrary. Now that the communion, thus kept in wilderness and in Egypt, places of extreme heat, where wine in small quantity[10]*, as is for that purpose convenient, cannot be long kept from souring and changing his nature, was in the form of bread only, and not also of wine, I defer to note it here, because it pertaineth to the treatise of the next article.*

Receiving with the hand.

[*Reservation of the sacrament.* H. A. 1564.]

THE BISHOP OF SARISBURY.

This place of St Basil we might have safely passed over without prejudice of our cause, as touching other things impertinent, and not once making mention of the mass. Yet, seeing it hath pleased M. Harding thus to colour and to emboss out this ancient father, as if he alone of all others spake most plainly of his side, having, notwithstanding, both in this very self-same place and also in other words immediately before, which M. Harding thought best of purpose to dissemble, manifest record against private mass, I may not well utterly leave him in silence.

First, the case being supposed lawful for the people, both men and women, to take some portion of the sacrament home with them, and to receive it alone secretly, and at their pleasures; to make further doubt, whether the party so having it might touch it and receive it with his own hands, was a very nice question and meet for a gentlewoman, as Cæsaria was, to demand. And so it seemed also to St Basil, as may appear by his answer. For whosoever hath considered the old fathers, shall find this matter fully debated by the continual practice of the church.

St Cyprian sheweth that in his time the people received the holy mysteries of the deacons with their hands; and that one, that had committed idolatry, and afterward came to receive the communion amongst the faithful, opened his hand and found the sacrament turned into ashes[11].

Cypr. Serm. 5, de Lapsis.

The like manner of receiving is recorded also by Tertullian[12].

Tertull. Lib. ii. ad Uxorem.

Dionysius, bishop of Alexandria, hath these words in an epistle unto Sistus, the bishop of Rome, touching the same, speaking of one that had received the communion in the church: "After he had heard the thanksgiving, and had sounded Amen with the rest, and had been at the table, and had reached forth his hand to receive the holy food[13]," &c.

Euseb. Lib. vii. cap. viii. Reached forth his hand.

Clemens of Alexandria thus uttereth the manner of the church there: "When certain have divided the sacrament, as the order is, they suffer every of the people to take part of it[14]."

Clem. Alex. Strom. Lib. i.

Novatus the heretic, when he ministered the communion to the people, used to swear them by that they had in their hands, that is to say, by the sacrament, that they would no more return to Cornelius[15].

Euseb. Lib. vi. cap. xlii.

[8 Algates: however, at all events.]

[9 Or of one, 1565, and H. A. 1564.]

[10 Quantie, H. A. 1564.]

[11 Et alius qui et ipse maculatus, sacrificio a sacerdote celebrato, partem cum ceteris ausus est latenter accipere: sanctum Domini edere et contrectare non potuit; cinerem ferre se apertis manibus invenit.—Cypr. Op. Oxon. 1682. De Laps. p. 133.]

[12 See before, page 148, note 3.]

[13 Εὐχαριστίας γὰρ ἐπακούσαντα, καὶ συνεπιφθεγξάμενον τὸ ἀμὴν, καὶ τραπέζῃ παραστάντα, καὶ χεῖρας εἰς ὑποδοχὴν τῆς ἁγίας τροφῆς προτείναντα· κ. τ. λ.—Euseb. in Hist. Eccles. Script. Amst. 1695—1700. Lib. VII. cap. ix. p. 208.]

[14 Ἢι καὶ τὴν εὐχαριστίαν τινὲς διανείμαντες, ὡς ἔθος, αὐτὸν δὴ ἕκαστον τοῦ λαοῦ λαβεῖν τὴν μοῖραν ἐπιτρέπουσιν.—Clement. Alex. Op. Oxon. 1715. Stromat. Lib. I. Tom. I. p. 318.]

[15 Euseb. Lib. VI. cap. xliii. p. 199.]

Receiving with the hand.

St Augustine, writing against certain letters of Petilian, saith thus: "I speak of him whose crosse[1] of peace ye received at the ministration, and in whose hands ye laid the sacrament[2]." I leave the story between St Ambrose and the emperor Theodosius[3], and other sundry like authorities to the same purpose.

August. contra Literas Petiliani, Lib. ii. cap. xxiii. Theodoret. Lib. v. cap. xvii. Col. ii.

Yet, because many have been superstitiously led and simply seduced herein by the doctrine of them that say, "O taste not this, O touch not this," which are nothing else (as St Paul saith) but "commandments and doctrines of men, having a shew of wisdom in superstition, and abasing of the mind;" I think it not amiss to note one special place out of the council of Constantinople concerning the same. The words of the council be these: "We do in no wise admit them, that instead of their hand make to themselves instruments of gold or of any other matter, for the receiving of the holy communion, as men more regarding a dead metal than the image of God. And if any priest receive such persons with such instruments unto the communion, let him be excommunicate, and him likewise that bringeth them[4]."

Conc. Constantin. vi. cap. 101.

But if this gentlewoman's doubt were not, whether a layman might safely touch the sacrament, but only whether it were lawful for any such one to minister the same unto his own mouth, St Basil saith it is no question. Custom already hath made it good. "For," saith he, "both the eremites in the wilderness, and every of the people in Egypt and Alexandria, for the more part, have the sacrament at home, and each of them doth minister it unto himself. Yea, even in the church, after that the priest hath distributed a portion of the sacrament, he that hath received it putteth it to his mouth with his own hand, without any remorse or doubt of conscience; and whether he receive one portion of the priest, or more, the effect and strength thereof is all one[5]." This is the very meaning of St Basil: albeit, for plainness sake, reserving the sense, I have somewhat altered the words. But much I marvel how M. Harding can gather hereof his private mass.

Basilius ad Cæsariam patriciam.

Touching his five special notes, if we grant them thoroughly every one, yet is he nothing near[6] his purpose. For his mass is none of them.

The eremites' sole receiving, as it nothing hindereth us that deny not the fact, so it nothing furthereth him, unless he will have laymen and women to do so still.

The reason that St Basil maketh of custom and continuance, being well considered, is very weak, both for many other good and just causes, and also for that the same custom, as it was never universally received, so upon better advice, by order of the church, it was clean abolished. For wise men in God's causes have evermore mistrusted the authority of custom.

The heretics in old time named *Aquarii*, that in the holy ministration used water only and no wine, notwithstanding they manifestly brake Christ's institution, as our adversaries do now, yet they upheld their doings therein by long custom. But St Cyprian being then alive wrote thus against them: *Victi ratione opponunt consuetudinem, quasi consuetudo sit major veritate*[7], &c.: "Being overcome with reason, they defend themselves[8] by custom, as though custom were better than the truth." "We may not prescribe of custom, but we must overcome with reason[9]." "Custom without truth is the mother of error[10]."

Ad Jubaian. De Hæreticis Baptizan. Cypr. ad Quirinum. Cypr. ad Pompeium contra Epistolam Stephani.

[1 Cosse (i. e. kiss), 1565.]

[2 ...ego illum commemoro...cui pacis osculum inter sacramenta copulabatis, in cujus manibus eucharistiam ponebatis.—August. Op. Par. 1679—1700. Cont. Lit. Petil. Lib. II. cap. xxiii. 53. Tom. IX. col. 233.]

[3 Theodor. in Hist. Eccles. Script. Amst. 1695—1700. Lib. v. cap. xviii. pp. 220, &c.]

[4 Τοὺς γὰρ ἐκ χρυσίου ἢ ἄλλης ὕλης ἀντὶ χειρός τινα δοχεῖα κατασκευάζοντας πρὸς τὴν τοῦ θείου δώρου ὑποδοχὴν, καὶ δι' αὐτῶν τῆς ἀχράντου κοινωνίας ἀξιουμένους, οὐδαμῶς προσιέμεθα, ὡς προτιμῶντας τῆς τοῦ Θεοῦ εἰκόνος τὴν ἄψυχον ὕλην καὶ ὑποχείριον. εἰ δέ τις ἁλῷ τῆς ἀχράντου κοινωνίας μεταδιδοὺς τοῖς τοιαῦτα δοχεῖα προσφέρουσιν, καὶ αὐτὸς ἀφοριζέσθω, καὶ ὁ ταῦτα ἐπιφερόμενος.—Concil. Quinisext. can. 101. in Concil. Stud. Labb. et Cossart. Lut. Par. 1671-2. Tom. VI. col. 1186.]

[5 See before, page 152.]

[6 The near, 1565.]

[7 Proinde frustra quidam qui ratione vincuntur, consuetudinem nobis opponunt; quasi consuetudo major sit veritate.—Cypr. Op. Oxon. 1682. Ad Jubaian. Epist. lxxiii. p. 203.]

[8 Themself, 1565.]

[9 Non est autem de consuetudine præscribendum, sed ratione vincendum.—Id. Ad Quint. Epist. lxxi. p. 194.]

[10 Nam consuetudo sine veritate vetustas erroris

But be it that both the reason were good, and the custom, that long sithence hath been abolished, had remained still; yet is not M. Harding able out of this place precisely and undoubtedly to prove his private mass. For if a man should say, it may possibly be that these eremites did not minister several[11] each man to himself alone, but one of them unto the rest of the eremites dwelling in the wilderness, as it appeareth diversely they had times to meet and to pray together; or, that the householders in Egypt and Alexandria ministered not only to themselves, but also to their whole several families, as it is written of Hippolytus Martyr, that, being a layman, he received the communion of Justinus, being a priest, and bare it home, and ministered the same to his wife, his children, and his servants[12]—if a man would thus say, perhaps M. Harding would better bethink himself of his conclusions. This sense may seem to stand very well with St Basil's words; notwithstanding M. Harding, in his translation into English, hath openly falsified the same. For whereas it is written in the Greek, and so likewise in the Latin, "They receive of themselves," which may well be understanded, ἀφ' ἑαυτῶν μεταλαμβάνουσι. that one of them received of another for want of a priest, he hath otherwise wrested it to come to his tune, and hath turned it thus: "They do communicate with themselves alone;" wherein albeit I will not greatly strive, yet neither this word "alone," nor these words "with themselves," can be found either in the Greek or in the Latin[13].

This long allegation of St Basil's words, with all the furniture thereof, may shortly be gathered into this reason: These eremites being no priests received alone; *ergo*, these eremites being no priests said private mass.

Further, M. Harding saith: This sole receiving was allowed by custom; *ergo*, private mass likewise is lawful by custom.

This reason goeth round against himself. For it may be well replied: This sole receiving was an abuse, and therefore was abolished by the church notwithstanding custom; *ergo*, private mass likewise is an abuse, and ought to be abolished notwithstanding custom.

Now let us see, whether these very self words of St Basil here alleged by M. Harding make any thing for the holy communion. And what authority can be against us, if M. Harding's own authorities, yea, as himself vaunteth, the most manifest and plainest of all his authorities, be found with us? For trial hereof we must resort, not into the wilderness, where as was neither priest nor deacon, as it is confessed, but unto the churches that were in St Basil's time. So shall we soon see whether the ministration then used were a communion or a private mass.

St Basil in the same place saith thus: "We do communicate four times in the week; upon the Sunday, Wednesday, Friday, and Saturday[14]." If we may found any thing upon words, he saith, "We communicate:" he saith not, "We say mass." And thus, saith St Basil, "we do four times in the week." Then had they not the daily sacrifice, whereupon private mass is grounded. He much misreckoneth himself, that saith, that thing is daily done, which is done but four times in seven days. Basil. ad Cæsariam patriciam. No daily sacrifice.

Moreover St Basil saith: "After the priest hath once consecrate and divided the sacrifice, we must think that we ought to receive and to be partakers of it *accordingly. For in the church the priest giveth part; and the communicant receiveth it with all freedom of conscience, and with his own hand putteth it to his mouth. Therefore is the virtue all one, whether it be one portion only that he receiveth of the priest, or more together[15]." τελειώσαντος. *εἰκότως.

Here mark well, good reader, how many ways St Basil overthroweth M. Harding's mass.

---

est.—Id. Ad Pomp. Epist. lxxiv. p. 215. For Cyprian's reproof of the heretics above referred to see Ad Cæcil. Epist. lxiii. pp. 154, 5.]

[11 Severally, 1565, 1609.]

[12 Pet. de Natal. Catalog. Sanct. Lugd. 1519. Lib. VII. cap. lvi. foll. 141, 2.]

[13 See before, page 152.]

[14 Ἡμεῖς μέντοιγε τέταρτον καθ' ἑκάστην ἑβδομάδα κοινωνοῦμεν, ἐν τῇ κυριακῇ, ἐν τῇ τετράδι, καὶ ἐν τῇ παρασκευῇ, καὶ τῷ σαββάτῳ.—Basil. Op. Par. 1721—30. Ad Cæsar. Epist. xciii. Tom. III. p. 186.]

[15 Id. ibid. p. 187.]

1. St Basil saith: We do communicate: M. Harding in his mass doth not communicate.

2. St Basil divideth and distributeth: M. Harding divideth indeed, but distributeth nothing.

3. In St Basil's mass the people receiveth: in M. Harding's mass the people receiveth not.

4. In St Basil's mass each man receiveth with his own hand: in M. Harding's mass no man receiveth, no, not with the priest's hand.

5. In St Basil's mass the people, besides that they received presently there, had portions also delivered them to receive at home: in M. Harding's mass there is no portion delivered unto the people, no, not so much as presently to be received in the church.

6. In St Basil's mass each man receiveth and eateth for himself: in M. Harding's mass the whole people eateth by the mouth of the priest. O what meaneth M. Harding, to bring such witnesses for his mass as do so openly witness against his mass? Who may trust him in the dark, that thus dealeth in the light?

M. HARDING. THE NINETEENTH DIVISION.

It appeareth evidently by witness of St Hierome also, that this custom of receiving the communion privately at home continued among christian men at Rome, not only in time of persecution, but also afterward when the church was at rest and peace; so as the case of necessity cannot here serve them for maintaining[1] *of their strange negative in this point. These be his words:* Scio Romæ hanc esse consuetudinem, ut fideles semper Christi corpus accipiant, quod nec reprehendo, nec probo. Unusquisque enim in suo sensu abundat. Sed ipsorum conscientiam convenio, qui eodem die post coitum communicant, et, juxta Persium, noctem flumine purgant[2]: quare ad martyres non[3] audent? quare non ingrediuntur ecclesias? An alius in publico, alius in domo Christus est? Quod in ecclesia non licet, nec domi licet. Nihil Deo clausum est, et tenebræ quoque lucent apud Deum. Probet se unusquisque, et sic ad corpus Christi accedat[4]: *"I know this custom is at Rome, that christian folk receive the body of Christ daily, which I do neither reprove nor allow. For every man hath enough in his own sense. But I appose their conscience, which do communicate that same day as they have done wedlock-work, and, as Persius saith, 'do rince night-filth with running water.' Why dare they not*[5] *go to martyrs' shrines? Why go not they into the churches*[6]*? What, is there one Christ abroad, and another Christ within the house? Whatsoever is not lawful in the church, neither at home is it lawful. To God nothing is hidden: yea, darkness also shineth before God. Let every one examine himself, and so come to the body of Christ." St Hierome reproveth this in the Romans, that, whereas St Paul ordained that for cause of prayer married folk should at times forbear their carnal embracings, they, notwithstanding that, though they had*[7] *doing with their wives, yet received their rights nevertheless daily. And yet, what day they had so done, they durst not go to churches where martyrs' tombs were, there to receive our Lord's body. For it is to be understanded for better knowledge hereof, that such as knew themselves to have done any uncleanness were afraid in old*[8] *time to come to*[9] *martyrs' sepulchres. For there commonly by miracle such things were bewrayed, and many times by open confession of the parties, whether they would or no. Erasmus in his scholies upon this place of St Hierome saith thus: "Of this place we gather, that in the old time every one was wont to receive the body of Christ at home in his house, that would." He saith further:* Idem videtur innuere Pau-

In Apolog. adversus Jovin.
[*Rom.* xiv. 1565, and H. A. 1564.]

Hereof speaketh St Hierome, ad Vigil.[10] *S. Aug. Epistola* 137[11], *and Severus Sulpitius in Vita S. Martini, Dial.* iii. *cap* 7[12].

Erasmus speaketh of private receiving, but not one word of private mass.

[[1] Maintenance, H. A. 1564.]
[[2] Pers. Sat. ii. 16.]
[[3] Martyres ire non, 1565, H. A. 1564.]
[[4] Hieron. Op. Par. 1693—1706. Epist. xxx. pro Libr. adv. Jovin. Apol. Tom. IV. Pars II. col. 239; where *ire* is inserted.]
[[5] Why dare not they, 1565, and H. A. 1564.]
[[6] Into churches, H. A. 1564.]
[[7] Had had, H. A. 1564.]
[[8] In the old, 1565, and H. A. 1564.]
[[9] To the, H. A. 1564.]

lus, cum ait: An domos non habetis ad manducandum[13]? "*St Paul (saith he) seemeth to mean the same thing where he saith: 'Have ye*[14] *not houses to eat in?'" Thus Erasmus gathereth proof of private, or, as M. Jewel jesteth, single communion, out of the scriptures; and he was as well learned in them as M. Jewel is. Yet herein I leave Erasmus to his own defence. By this we may understand, that in the ancient times of the church the receiving of the communion of one by himself alone *was well allowed. And though it was done but by one faithful person at once in one place, yet was it called a communion both of St Basil, and also of St Hierome, clean contrary to M. Jewel's sense. It is to be judged that they knew the institution of Christ so well as he or any other of these new masters, and that their conscience was such as, if Christ's ordinance therein had been broken, they would not have winked at it, ne with their ungodly silence confirmed such an ungodly custom. Verily, for excuse of this sole receiving, necessity cannot justly be alleged.*

*St Hierome reproveth this custom. Thus he saith: "That is not lawful in the church is not lawful at home."

THE BISHOP OF SARISBURY.

How often will M. Harding allege the old doctors against himself? Here he bringeth in St Hierome; and the first words that he could find for his purpose were these: "I know the custom at Rome is this, that the christian people there receive the body of Christ every day[15]." It seemeth this custom grew first from Peter, and was planted in Rome. A man may here well demand, when the custom was that the people[16] should communicate daily together, where then was the custom of private mass?

Hier. in Apologa adversus Jovinianum.

Where was then the private mass?

Besides this, M. Harding, to prove the custom of the people's receiving at home, hath alleged St Hierome, that earnestly reproveth that custom, and would not have them receive at home. St Hierome's words be these: "Why dare they not go to the temples built in the remembrance of martyrs? Why go they not to the church? What, is there one Christ abroad, and another Christ at home?" If the people did well, why doth St Hierome thus reprove them? If they did ill, why doth M. Harding thus allow them?

Here M. Harding interlaceth other matter of the office of wedlock, the word[17] of Persius the pagan poet, and the superstitious ceremony of the heathens, as I take it, little pertaining unto his mass. Whereas the whole people received the holy mysteries every day, the man and wife, remembering sometimes what they had done between themselves, and thinking themselves for the same not to be in so clean state of life as the rest were, for that cause forbare the church for the time; and, having the sacrament sent unto them, received it privately at home. Unto this superstition St Hierome himself gave great occasion, many times both writing and speaking unseemly of the state of marriage, in defence whereof St Augustine wrote a book against Jovinian, entitled, *De Bono Conjugii*[18]; and St Hierome afterward was driven to make his answer by way of purgation unto Pammachius for the same. In this error were divers of the old learned fathers. Tertullian saith: "I allow not marriage; for fornication and that stand both in one thing[19]." Origen saith: "No man can offer the continual sacrifice, that is to say, the sacrifice of prayer, unless he be a virgin[20]." St Hierome saith: "It is good not to touch a woman; therefore it is ill to touch a woman[21]." Upon occasion of

Tertull. in Exhortatione ad Castitatem.
Origen. in Numeros, Hom. 23.
Hieron. adversus Jovin. Lib. i.

[10 Hieron. Op. Adv. Vigilant. Tom. IV. Pars II. col. 286.]

[11 August. Op. Par. 1679—1700. Ad Cler. Eccles. Hipp. Epist. lxxviii. 3. Tom. II. col. 184.]

[12 Reference is probably made to the stories related Div. Martin. Vit. ad calc. Abd. Apost. Hist. Par. 1571. Dial. iii. foll. 242, 3.]

[13 Ex hoc loco colligimus olim domi suæ quemque corpus Christi sumere solere, qui voluisset. Idem, &c.—Hieron. Op. Basil. 1516. Schol. Erasm. Epist. Præced. Tom. III. fol. 51.]

[14 You, H. A. 1564.]

[15 See before, page 156, note 4.]

[16 The whole, 1565.]

[17 Words, 1565.]

[18 August. Op. De Bono Conjugali Lib. Tom. VI. cols. 319—40.]

[19 ...inquis...unas nuptias destruis. Nec immerito, quoniam et ipsæ ex eo constant, quo et stuprum.—Tertull. Op. Lut. 1641. De Exh. Cast. 9. p. 670.]

[20 Unde videtur mihi quod illius est solius offerre sacrificium indesinens, qui indesinenti et perpetuæ se devoverit castitati.—Orig. Op. Par. 1733-59. In Num. Hom. xxiii. 3. Tom. II. p. 358.]

[21 Si bonum est mulierem non tangere, malum est ergo tangere.—Hieron. Op. Par. 1693—1706. Adv. Jovin. Lib. I. Tom. IV. Pars II. col. 149. See also Epist. xxx. pro Libr. adv. Jovin. Apol. col. 237.]

which error, the people sometime[1] forbare the churches where martyrs were buried. Wherein M. Harding's translation swerveth much from the original. For instead of "churches," he hath translated, "martyrs' shrines," as though the bones of holy men had then been shrined, and offerings made unto them, as of late years hath been used.

M. Harding corrupteth St Hierome.

True it is, Almighty God, for the testimony of his doctrine and truth, hath oftentimes wrought great miracles even by the dead carcases of his saints, in witness that they had been his messengers and the instruments of his will. But as these were good inducements at the first to lead the people to the truth, so afterward they became snares, to lead the same people into error; and that even in the time of the old fathers above eleven hundred years ago. St Augustine saith: "I know many worshippers of graves and images, that drink and quaff disorderly over the dead, and offer meat unto their carcases, and bury themselves[2] over the buried, and make account, that even their very drunkenness and gluttony is a religion that pleaseth God[3]." Gelasius saith: "It is reported that with procession they furnish up their churches, built in the name of dead men, and the same, for ought that I can learn, while they were alive not altogether good faithful men[4]." St Martin on a time came to a chapel built in the name of a holy martyr: but afterward he learned by revelation that the same martyr had been sometime a common thief, and for a robbery had been put to death, and by error of the people was honoured for a saint[5]." Likewise St Augustine saith: "Some there be that carry about martyrs' bones to sale; and yet it may well be doubted whether ever they were martyrs or no[6].

August. de Morib. Eccles. et Manich. cap. xxxiv. Idem Confession. Lib. vi. cap. ii. Gelasius, can. 2. De Con. Dist. 1. Placuit. Sulpitius in Vita Martini.

De Opere Monachorum, cap. xxviii.

Thus much briefly and by the way of the reliques and miracles of martyrs' bones; for that M. Harding upon so small occasion seemeth to touch them in such sort, as if he would have them shrined and set up again.

Heb. xiii.

As for the matrimony of the godly, as St Paul saith, "It is clean and honourable in all estates." And therefore St Chrysostom saith: "Use thy marriage with sobriety, and thou shalt be the chief in the kingdom of heaven[7]." And the same Chrysostom, expounding these words of St Paul, "Marriage is honourable," writeth thus: "Here he toucheth the Jews, that reckon the marriage-bed to be unclean, and that a man rising from the same cannot be in clean life. But, O you most unkind and most insensible Jews, the thing is not filthy that God hath granted of nature unto man, &c.[8]"

Chrysost. ad Heb. Hom. 7.

Chrysost. ad Heb. Hom. 8.

Touching Erasmus, M. Harding hath already refused his authority, and turned him over to his own defence. Where he saith, "Every man was wont in old times to receive the sacrament severally at home," it would much better have sounded of M. Harding's side, if Erasmus had said: "Every man was wont then to say mass severally at home." And albeit in that short note upon St Hierome he seem to understand these words of St Paul, "Have ye not houses to eat and drink in?" of the private receiving of the sacrament; yet otherwhere, writing of purpose and good deliberation upon the same, he saith, St Paul meant it only of common meats, and not of the sacrament. In his paraphrase he expoundeth it thus: *Hic unanimitatis christianæ mysterium agitur*, &c.: "Here is practised the mystery of

Paraphrasis Erasm. in 1 Cor. xi.

[1 Sometimes, 1565.]

[2 Themself, 1565.]

[3 Novi multos esse sepulcrorum et picturarum adoratores: novi multos esse, qui luxuriosissime super mortuos bibant, et epulas cadaveribus exhibentes, super sepultos seipsos sepeliant, et voracitates ebrietatesque suas deputent religioni.—August. Op. Par. 1679—1700. De Mor. Eccles. Lib. I. cap. xxxiv. 75. Tom. I. col. 713. See also Confess. Lib. VI. cap. ii. Tom. I. cols. 119, 20.]

[4 ...hoc sumus tamen judicio detestabiliore permoti, quia in quocunque nomine defunctorum, et (quantum dicitur) non omnino fidelium, constructiones ædificatas sacris processionibus audacter instituere memorantur.—Decret. Gelas. Papæ I. in Crabb. Concil. Col. Agrip. 1551. cap. 27. Tom. I. p. 968.

Corp. Jur. Canon. Lugd. 1624. Decret. Gratian. Decr. Tert. Pars, De Consecr. Dist. i. can. 26. cols. 1895, 6.]

[5 Div. Martin. Vit. ad calc. Abd. Apost. Hist. Par. 1571. Lib. I. foll. 194, 5.]

[6 Alii membra martyrum, si tamen martyrum, venditant.—August. Op. De Op. Monach. cap. xxviii. 36. Tom. VI. col. 498.]

[7 Μετὰ συμμετρίας τῷ γάμῳ χρῶ, καὶ πρῶτος ἐν τῇ βασιλείᾳ ἔσῃ.—Chrysost. Op. Par. 1718-38. In Epist. ad Hebr. cap. iv. Hom. vii. Tom. XII. p. 80.]

[8 Ἐνταῦθα καὶ Ἰουδαίους αἰνίττεται, ὅτι βδελυρὰν ἡγοῦντο τὴν κοίτην. καὶ ὃς ἂν ᾖ, φησὶν, ἀπὸ κοίτης, οὐκ ἔστι καθαρός. οὐκ ἔστι βδελυρὰ τὰ ἀπὸ φύσεως, ὦ ἄγνωμον καὶ ἀναίσθητε Ἰουδαῖε, ἀλλὰ τὰ ἀπὸ προαιρέσεως.—Id. ibid. cap. xiii. Hom. xxxiii. p. 305.]

christian unity, and not provision made for the belly. For that ought ye to do in your private houses, and not in the public congregation. If ye would fill your bellies, have ye not houses, where ye may do it by yourselves alone?" And again: "If any man be so greedy of meat that he cannot tarry, let him eat at home[9]." Thus, saith M. Harding, "Erasmus gathereth the private mass out of the scriptures." M. Harding is over quick in his conclusions: he maketh himself sure of the consequent, before he see the antecedent: for Erasmus hath not one word there, neither of private mass, nor of single communion. How then can he get that of Erasmus, that Erasmus himself hath not? Neither is this any necessary form of reason: Men received the sacrament in their houses; *ergo*, they received the sacrament alone. For they might receive in their several houses with their wives and families all together, as it is already proved by the example of Hippolytus Martyr. And St Hierome saith: "The sacrament was sent home to the man and wife[10]." Otherwise it might be said: God commanded that every man should eat the Easter lamb in his house; *ergo*, God commanded that every man should eat that lamb alone. Howbeit I make small account of this matter, as nothing touching the private mass, but only shew the feebleness of these conclusions.

Hieron. in Apologia adversus Jovinianum.

Yet saith M. Harding: "Both St Hierome and St Basil call it the communion, notwithstanding it were privately received: which is clean contrary to M. Jewel's sense." But neither St Hierome nor St Basil ever called it the mass, and that little furthereth M. Harding's[11] sense. They call it a "communion," not for that he that received it communicated with others in other places, as M. Harding guesseth, but for that it was a portion of the holy communion ministered and divided openly in the congregation to be received of the faithful.

The communion.

The reason that M. Harding hereof gathereth must needs be this: The husband and his wife received the sacrament at home; *ergo*, the priest said private mass. He must needs be very simple that will be led by such single proofs. St Hierome's plain words necessarily import the contrary. For if this were the custom in Rome for the space of four hundred years, that the people should communicate every day, then must it needs follow that during that time there was no custom there of private mass.

No private mass in Rome.

M. HARDING. THE TWENTIETH DIVISION.

Damasus, bishop of Rome in St Hierome's time, writeth, In libro Pontificiali[12], *that Milciades, pope and martyr, ordained that the sacrament in sundry portions consecrated by a bishop should be sent abroad among the churches for cause of heretics, that the catholic people of the churches (which word here signifieth as the Greek word* παροικία *doth, so as it is not necessary to understand that the sacrament was directed only to the material *churches, but to the people of the parishes) might receive the catholic communion, and not communicate with heretics. Which, doubtless, must be understanded of this private and single communion in each catholic man's house, and that where heretics bare the sway, and priests might not be suffered to consecrate after the catholic usage. Else, if the priests might without let or disturbance have so done, then what need had it been for Milciades to have made such a provision for sending abroad hosts sanctified for that purpose by the consecration of a bishop? The place of Damasus hath thus:* Milciades fecit, ut oblationes consecratæ per ecclesias ex consecratu episcopi (propter hæreticos) dirigerentur[13]:" "*Milciades ordained that consecrated hosts should be sent abroad amongst the churches, prepared by the consecration of a bishop." The two words,* propter hæreticos, *"for heretics," added by Ado, the writer of martyrs' lives, openeth the meaning and purport of that decree.*

A heap of simple guesses without sense or savour.

*A church by M. Harding's judgment signifieth a private house.

M. Harding otherwise reporteth these words than he findeth them.

[9 Erasm. Op. Lugd. Bat. 1703-6. Paraph. in Epist. I. ad Cor. cap. xi. Tom. VII. cols. 896, 7.]

[10 See before, page 156, note 4.]

[11 M. Harding, 1565.]

[12 Pontificali, 1565, and H. A. 1564.]

[13 See below, page 160, note 4.]

THE BISHOP OF SARISBURY.

1. This guess is one of the weakest of all the rest; and therefore M. Harding hath staid it up on[1] every side with other guesses, that one guess might help another. The first guess is, what Damasus should mean by these words, *propter hæreticos.*

2. The next guess is, that this order was taken by Milciades against certain heretics, that in the holy ministration kept not the catholic church[2].

3. The third guess is, that this word *ecclesia* must needs signify the people of the parishes, and not the material church.

4. The fourth guess is, that the sacrament was then consecrate in little round cakes, as of late hath been used.

5. The fifth guess is, that the sacrament was sent to every several house, which must have been an infinite labour to the deacon that carried it, and wondrous painful.

6. The sixth guess is, that first every husband received the sacrament in his house alone, and so the wife, and so the servants, and so likewise the children, every one severally by himself alone: which thing I reckon M. Harding himself thinketh not very likely. So many guesses are here in a throng heaped together: which if I deny altogether, M. Harding is hardly able to prove; if I grant him altogether without exception, yet all are not able to prove his private mass.

In Libro Concil. impresso Colon. Anno 1551.

First, in this place of Damasus neither is there mention of any mass, nor any perfect[3] sense or reason in the words. For thus it is written: *Milciades fecit ut oblationes consecratæ per ecclesias ex consecratu episcopi dirigerentur, quod declaratur fermentum*[4]*:* "Milciades caused that the oblations consecrate by the churches by the consecration of the bishop should be directed, which is declared leaven." Neither is there any kind of thing either going before or following after, whereby we may guess the meaning. It is much to see so learned a man as M. Harding is, so scanted of authorities, that he is thus driven to prove his mass by such places as be utterly void of sense and reason. But a man must use such weapons as may be gotten.

M. Harding allegeth authorities without sense or reason.

The two words, *propter hæreticos,* that are patched in by Ado, a man of late years, as they do nothing help the sense, so have they no help of the story of that time. For a man may well demand of Ado, this new doctor, what were these strange unknown heretics without name, that you at the last for a shift have espied out? where began they? where dwelt they? what taught they? how long continued they? who maintained them? who confuted them? what councils[5] condemned them? For it seemeth somewhat strange, that there should be companies and routs of heretics in the world, that no man ever knew but doctor Ado.

M. Harding addeth of himself, beside his author.

And whereas M. Harding putteth in of his own, besides his book (for Damasus hath no such thing, nor any other thing like), that these new-found heretics in the ministration "kept not the catholic usage," he should have shewed, for his credit's sake, what other usage they kept that was not catholic; for his word is not yet canonized. The world will believe neither him nor Ado without some proof.

Ecclesia, a private house.

πaροικία.

Further, to increase absurdities, he saith by these words, *per ecclesias,* is meant not the material church, but the people of the church: that is to say, in plainer terms, *ecclesia* is not a church, but a private house. I grant the Greek word *παροικία,* out of which our English word "parish" seemeth to have been taken, signifieth a congregation, or meeting of neighbours, or a company dwelling within some space together, whether it be in compass more or less. So saith Eusebius: "Dionysius writeth unto Basilides, the bishop of the divisions of Pentapolis[6]." [a]Athanasius saith that Demetrius took upon him the bishopric of Alexandria, and *τῶν παροικιῶν,* of the divisions in Egypt[7]. In these places and certain others that

Euseb. Lib. vii. cap. xxv. τῷ κατὰ Πεντάπολιν παροικιῶν ἐπισκόπῳ.

[a] Athanas. in Epist. de Sententia Dionys. adversus Arian.

[1 One, 1611.] [2 Usage, 1565.]

[3 Perfite, 1565.]

[4 Decret. Milciad. in Crabb. Concil. Col. Agrip. 1551. Tom. I. p. 217; where for *Milciades* we have *hic.*] [5 Council, 1565.]

[6 Euseb. in Hist. Eccles. Script. Amst. 1695—1700. Lib. VII. cap. xxvi. p. 226; where we find τῶν for τῷ.]

[7 There is probably a mistake in the reference. The word is often used by Athanasius: thus...τῇ ἑκάστου τῶν ἀδικηθέντων παροικίᾳ.—Athanas. Op. Par. 1698. Apol. contr. Arian. 36. Tom. I. Pars II. p. 155; where see note.]

might be alleged out of Basil, Nazianzene, and other Greek fathers, this word παροικία seemeth to signify a bishopric, or a diocese, and not a several parish. [b]And therefore Irenæus thus writeth unto Victor bishop of Rome: "The priests of Rome (meaning thereby the bishops there) sent the sacrament τοῖς ἀπὸ τῶν παροικιῶν, to them that came out of other dioceses or divisions[8]." And Eusebius thus writeth of Hippolytus: Ἑτέρας πως καὶ αὐτὸς ἐπίσκοπος παροικίας[9]· "He being bishop of another division." Thus much touching this word παροικία, being moved thereto by the strange interpretation of M. Harding. Certainly, I think he himself will say that, sithence the church was once in peace, neither this word *ecclesia*, nor this word *parochia*, ever signified a private house, in any kind of writer or in any time.

[b] Euseb. Hist. Lib. v. cap. xxvi.

But, saith M. Harding, Ado's heretics (for Damasus speaketh of none) bare all the sway, and would not suffer the catholic people to communicate in the church: therefore we must needs understand here private houses. Alas! when did heretics ever bear such sway in the church of Rome? Or if they did at any time, as it is untrue, unless he mean the sovereign heretics, the pope and his cardinals, yet may we think that the catholics were so weak in the common church, being all together, and so strong in their own houses, being alone? Or were these heretics able to withstand a whole congregation, and not able to withstand one single man by himself?

Sovereign heretics.

Mark well, good reader, how handsomely M. Harding's arguments hang together. He must needs think thee to be very unsensible, that hopeth thou wilt yield to such guesses.

To leave a great number of other like absurdities, M. Harding's arguments are framed thus: The sacrament was received in private houses (albeit there appeareth no such thing by Damasus); *ergo*, one man received alone. Surely then had that man a very empty house: he might well sing, *Tanquam passer solitarius in tecto*. It is more likely that, being a godly man, he would desire his wife and family to receive with him, as I have said before.

Again: The sacrament was sent among the parishes; *ergo*, there was private mass. The force of this reason may soon be seen. But who said this mass, whether it were the messenger or the receiver, I leave it to M. Harding to consider. He might better have concluded thus: The bishop sent the mysteries abroad for the people to communicate; *ergo*, he meant a communion, and no private mass.

Further, he saith, this was done in time of necessity, because of heretics: and yet by the same he defendeth the mass used now without any such necessity; and that in the church of Rome, where, he saith, can be no heretics.

To conclude, this manner of sending abroad the sacrament was afterward abolished by the council holden at Laodicea[10].

Concil. Laodicen. cap. 14.

Thus is M. Harding driven to go by guess, to imagine strange heretics, for shew of some antiquity to allege vain decrees without sense, to avouch such orders as he knoweth were long sithence condemned, and to comment the same with his own glosses.

M. HARDING. THE TWENTY-FIRST DIVISION.

Here have I brought much for private and single communion, and that it hath not only been suffered in time of persecution, but also allowed in quiet and peaceable times, even in the church of Rome itself, (31) *where true religion hath ever been most exactly observed above all other places of the world, and* (32) *from whence all the churches of the west have*[12] *taken their light; as the bishops of all Gallia, that now is called France, do acknowledge in an epistle sent to Leo the pope, with these words:* Unde religionis nostræ, propitio Christo, fons et origo manavit[13]: "*From the apostolic see, by the mercy of Christ, the fountain and spring of our religion hath come.*"

The thirty-first untruth. For[11] Rome is now become the "mother of fornication." Rev. xvii.

Epist. proxima post 51. *inter Epist. Leonis.*

The thirty-second untruth. For the faith of the west church came not first from Rome.

[8 Euseb. Lib. v. cap. xxiv. (al. xxvi.) p. 157. See before, page 144, note 4.]

[9 ...ἑτέρας που καὶ αὐτὸς προεστὼς ἐκκλησίας.—Id. Lib. VI. cap. xx. p. 181. But in Stephens's edition, Lut. Paris. 1544, cap. xxi. ἑτέρας που καὶ αὐτὸς ἐπίσκοπος παροικίας.]

[10 Concil. Laod. can. 14. in Concil. Stud. Labb. et Cossart. Lut. Par. 1671-2. Tom. I. col. 1500.]

[11 1565 omits *for*.]

[12 Hath, H. A. 1564.]

[13 Epist. Episc. Gallor. cap. v. in Leon. Magn. Op. Lut. 1623. col. 371.]

THE BISHOP OF SARISBURY.

M. Harding pretendeth private mass, and concludeth single communion.

M. Harding useth a strange kind of logic: he pretendeth private mass, and concludeth single communion. And why might he not as well plainly and without colour conclude his private mass? Doubtless the wise reader may soon gather thus: If he could find it, he would not conceal it.

This talk of the church of Rome in this place was needless, as nothing serving to private mass. Yet is it generally confessed by all men, that Rome is the eldest church that we know founded in this west part of the world; and that the churches of France and other countries at the beginning had both the confirmation of doctrine, and also other great conference and comfort, from thence: like as also the church of Rome had from Hierusalem, and Antioch, and other great churches in the east. But that the first that ever preached the gospel in France were sent from Rome, I reckon it not so easy to be proved. For some say that
Nathaniel. Nathaniel, whom Christ commendeth to be the true Israelite, preached at Trire
Lazarus. Saturninus. and Bituriges[1]; Lazarus, whom Christ raised, at Marseilles; Saturninus at Tolouse; long before Peter came to Rome. St Paul, as it is thought, after his delivery
2 Tim. iv. under Nero, went into Spain, sent Titus into Dalmatia, and Crescens into Galatia,
Epiphanius contra Alogos. or, as Epiphanius readeth it, into Gallia[2]; Joseph of Arimathæa came into England. And yet it appeareth not that any of these were sent by commission from Rome. But why doth M. Harding thus out of season rush into the commendation of the church of Rome that was so long ago? It had been more to purpose to have viewed the state of the same church as it standeth now. But as one once said, "Ye shall not now find Samnium in Samnio," because the city of Samnium was sacked and rased up and utterly overthrown; even so I heard M. Harding sometime say, he had sought for the church of Rome in Rome itself, and yet could not find the church of Rome. The bishops, cardinals, and priests do neither teach, nor exhort, nor comfort, nor any other part of their duties: the people, as it is already confessed, is careless and void of devotion. St Bernard saith: *O Domine, sacerdotes tui facti sunt tonsores; prælati, Pilati; doctores, seductores*[3]: "O Lord, thy priests are become shearers; thy prelates, Pilates; thy doctors, deceivers." If a church[4] cannot err, then may we say of it, as Euripides sometimes[5] said of the city of Athens: ὦ πόλις, πόλις, ὡς εὐτυχῆς εἶ μᾶλλον, ἢ καλῶς φρονεῖς: "O city, city, thy luck is far better than thy wit."

M. HARDING. THE TWENTY-SECOND DIVISION.

More could I yet bring for confirmation of the same, as the example of St Hilaria the virgin in the time of Numerianus; of St Lucia in Diocletian's time done to martyrdom; of St Maria Ægyptiaca, and[6] *St Ambrose: of which every one, as ancient testimonies of ecclesiastical histories and of Paulinus*[7] *do declare, at the hour of their departure hence to God, received the holy sacrament of the altar for their voyage provision alone. But I judge this is enough; and if any man will not be persuaded with this, I doubt whether with such a one a more number of authorities shall any thing prevail.*

THE BISHOP OF SARISBURY.

Now M. Harding hieth himself unto the end of his authorities; and for speed is content to pass by the stories of Hilaria, Lucia, Maria Ægyptiaca, and others, written, I suppose, in *Legenda Aurea;* of whom, as it appeareth, he is certain that they said mass a little before their departure hence. The like is also
Paulinus, in Vita Ambros. avouched for certain of St Ambrose, lying in his death-bed. But this thing seemeth marvellous in my judgment, that, notwithstanding St Ambrose were bishop in Milan two and twenty years and more, being also so holy a man as

[1 Treves and Bourges.]

[2 Οὐ γὰρ ἐν τῇ Γαλατίᾳ, ὥς τινες πλανηθέντες νομίζουσιν, ἀλλὰ ἐν τῇ Γαλλίᾳ.—Epiph. Op. Par. 1622. Adv. Hær. Lib. II. Tom. I. p. 433.]

[3 See Catalog. Test. Verit. Gen. 1608. cols. 1379, 80.]

[4 Such a church, 1565.]

[5 Sometime, 1565, 1609.]

[6 And of, H. A. 1564.]

[7 Ambros. Op. Par. 1686-90. Tom. II. Append. col. xii. The passage will be more fully given hereafter.]

few the like in those days, yet M. Harding cannot learn that ever he said private mass but only when he lay breathless in his death-bed.

M. HARDING. THE TWENTY-THIRD DIVISION.

Now that I have thus proved the single communion, I use their own term, I desire M. Jewel to reason with me soberly a word or two. How say you, sir? Do you reprove the mass, or do you reprove the private mass? I think, whatsoever your opinion is herein, your answer shall be, you allow not the private mass. For as touching that the oblation of the body and blood of Christ done in the mass is the sacrifice of the church, and proper to the new testament, (33) *commanded by Christ to be frequented according to his institution; if you deny this, make it so light as you list, all those authorities which you deny us to have for proof of your great number of articles will be found against you; I mean doctors, general councils the most ancient, the examples*[9] *of the primitive church, the scriptures; I add further, reason, consent universal and uncontrolled, and tradition. If you deny this, you must deny all our religion from the apostles' time to this day; and now in the end of the world, when iniquity aboundeth, and charity waxeth cold, when the Son of Man coming shall scarcely find faith in the earth, begin a new. And therefore you, M. Jewel, knowing this well enough, whatsoever you do in deed, in word, as it appeareth by the little book you have set forth in print, you pretend to disallow, yea, most vehemently to improve, the private mass.*

The thirty-third untruth. For[8] Christ never commanded or named any such sacrifice.

Great words without ground.

THE BISHOP OF SARISBURY.

Hitherto M. Harding hath brought doctors without reason: now he bringeth reason without doctors. And "how say you, sir? (saith he) do you reprove the mass, or do you reprove private mass?" I trust he hath not so soon forgotten whereof he hath discoursed all this while. Neither doth the matter rest upon that point, what I list to allow or disallow, but what he can prove or not prove by the scriptures, and by the ancient councils and fathers.

But mark well, good christian reader, and thou shalt see how handsomely M. Harding conveyeth and shifteth his hands to deceive thy sight. First, he hath hitherto forborne both the name, and also the proof of private mass, and only hath used the words of "sole receiving" and "single communion;" and so hath taken pains to prove that thing that was never denied; and that thing that we deny, and wherein the whole question standeth, he hath left utterly untouched. Now he demandeth, whether I reprove the mass, or the private mass. What meaneth this, that private mass, and sole receiving, be so suddenly grown in one? Surely M. Harding well knoweth that the nature of these words is not one: neither whosoever receiveth alone doth therefore of necessity say private mass. This so sudden altering of terms may breed suspicion.

That he further interlaceth of the "sacrifice of the new testament," is another conveyance to blind thy sight, as utterly nothing making to this purpose.

For neither doth the sacrifice import private mass; nor doth sole receiving imply the sacrifice. Yet for short answer, we have that only sacrifice of the new testament, that is, the body of Jesus Christ upon the cross, that "Lamb of God that hath taken away the sins of the world:" the virtue of which sacrifice endureth for ever. To this everlasting sacrifice the sacrifice that is imagined in the mass is mere injurious.

And whereas M. Harding saith, "If you deny this, you must deny all our religion from the apostles' time until this day;" these be but empty words, without weight, and prove nothing.

In my little book, saith he, I disallow the private mass. If he find fault with my book for that it is little, he might consider it is but a sermon, and therefore no reason it should be great. Yet is it a great deal longer than either Hippolitus Martyr, or the fable of his Amphilochius, of whom, notwithstanding their shortness, he maketh no small account. And where he saith, I disallow private

[[8] 1565 omits *for*.] [[9] Example, H. A. 1564.]

mass; I disallow that thing that infinite numbers of godly and learned men have disallowed, and that M. Harding himself, not long sithence, openly and earnestly disallowed, both in schools and pulpits, until he was suddenly persuaded to the contrary only by the alteration of the state. Of these two words, "private mass," I can no better say, than St Gregory sometime said of that antichrist should be called *Deus*, God: *Si quantitatem vocis perpendimus, sunt duæ syllabæ; sin pondus iniquitatis, universa pernicies*[1]: "If we weigh the quantity of the word, they are but two syllables; but if we weigh the weight of wickedness, it is an universal destruction."

Lib. vi. Epist. 30.

M. HARDING. THE TWENTY-FOURTH DIVISION.

Upon this resolution, that the mass, as it is taken in general, is to be allowed; I enter further in reason with you, and make you this argument: if private mass, in respect only of that it is private, after your meaning, be reprovable, it is for the single communion, that is to say, for that the priest receiveth the sacrament alone. But the single communion is lawful, yea, good and godly; ergo, *the private mass in this respect, that it is private, is not reprovable, but to be allowed, holden for good and holy, and to be frequented. If you deny the first proposition, or major, then must you shew for what else you do reprove private mass, in respect only that it is private, than for the*[2] *single communion. If you shew any thing else, then do you digress from our purpose, and declare that you reprove the mass. The minor you cannot deny, seeing you*[3] *see how sufficiently I have proved it. And so the private mass, in that respect only it is private, is to be allowed for good, as the mass is.*

THE BISHOP OF SARISBURY.

Out of all these former authorities of Tertullian's wife, monks in the wilderness, laymen, women, and boys, M. Harding gathereth this conclusion, which, as he would have folk think, standeth so soundly on every side that it cannot possibly be avoided.

The private mass is single communion:
Single communion is lawful;
Ergo, private mass is lawful.

This syllogism unto the unskilful may seem somewhat terrible, as a visard unto a child that cannot judge what is within it. But M. Harding that made it knoweth it is vain, and worth nothing. And that it may the better appear, I will open the error by another like.

The ministration of private mass is a single communion:
Single communion is lawful for a woman;
Ergo, the ministration of private mass is lawful for a woman.

It is all one kind of argument, of like form, and like terms. And as this is deceitful, so is the other likewise deceitful. The error is in the second proposition, which is called the minor; and that shall ye soon see, if you turn the same minor, and make it an universal, and say thus in M. Harding's argument:

All manner single communions be lawful:

Or in the other argument,

All manner single communions are lawful for a woman. So shall ye soon find out the folly.

Further, *medius terminus*, that holdeth and knitteth the argument, must agree with the *subjectum* and *prædicatum*, in circumstance of time, of place, of person, of subject, and part of subject; with which circumstances a thing may be lawful, and without the same may be unlawful. For example, it is thought lawful for a woman to baptize at home; but it is not thought lawful for a woman to baptize in the open church: yet is the thing all one, but the circumstance of place being changed changeth the whole. Again: it is lawful for a priest to minister the sacrament in the forenoon, and in the church; but it is not lawful for a priest to minister the sacrament after he hath dined, or in his bed: yet was it

[1 Gregor. Magni Papæ I. Op. Par. 1705. Epist. Lib. VII. Indict. xv. Ad Mauric. August. Epist. xxxiii. Tom. II. col. 881. See before, page 96, note 2.]

[2 1565, 1609, and H. A. 1564, omit *the*.]

[3 Seeing that you, H. A. 1564.]

lawful for St Ambrose and others so to receive the sacrament. We see, therefore, there is great matter in alteration of the circumstance.

These things perhaps may seem over curious, and therefore I pass them by, giving[4] thee nevertheless, gentle reader, to understand that without consideration hereof thou mayest be deceived. Set the head in his natural place between the shoulders; and there is a man: set the same head in the breast, or otherwhere out of his place; and there is a monster.

Now, touching M. Harding's syllogism, thou mayest see that the minor or second proposition is not true, as they term it, *simpliciter*, and without exception. For the single communion was never so taken for lawful, but only in consideration of circumstances and cases of necessity; which cases being either removed or better examined, the same kind of single communion is no longer thought lawful. Therefore thou mayest thus say to M. Harding: "How say you, sir? Do you allow the examples that ye[5] have brought to prove your mass by, or do you not allow them? If you allow them, why then suffer ye not women to carry home the sacrament, and to keep it in chests and napkins, as they did of old? If you allow them not, because they were abuses, why then seek you to prove your mass by the same, and so to establish one abuse by another?" Now let us look a little back to the note that M. Harding set out in the margin for our remembrance, by these words, "Proofs for private mass." That it might seem lawful for a priest to say private mass, he hath brought in examples of laymen, women, sick folk, and boys. Alas! doth M. Harding think it was the manner in old times that lay-people should say mass? Or was there no priest all this while in the world, for the space of six hundred years, that women and children must come forth to prove these matters? Or was there no difference then between sole receiving and private mass? Or shall we think that women and boys did then consecrate the holy mysteries, or offer up Christ's body, or make sacrifice for quick and dead, or apply Christ's death unto others? Where is M. Harding's logic become? Where is the sharpness of his wit?

But mark, good christian reader, how far he swerveth from that he hath taken in hand. I demand of the open church: he answereth me of private houses. I demand of priests: he answereth me of women, boys, and laymen. I demand of the mass: he answereth me of that thing that himself granteth is no mass. I demand of the right use of the holy supper that ought to stand: he answereth me of abuses that be abolished. I demand of the usage that then was ordinary: he answereth of necessity, and cases extraordinary. Judge thou therefore, how well and substantially he hath hitherto performed his promise.

How aptly M. Harding answereth to the question.

M. HARDING. THE TWENTY-FIFTH DIVISION.

Marry I deny not but that it were more commendable, and more godly on the church's part, if many well disposed and examined would be partakers of the blessed sacrament with the priest. But, though the clergy be worthily blamed for negligence herein, through which the people may be thought to have grown to this slackness and indevotion, yet, that notwithstanding, this part of the catholic religion remaineth sound and faultless. For as touching the substance of the mass itself, by the single communion of the priest, in case of the people's coldness and negligence, it is nothing impaired. Else, if the public sacrifice of the church might not be offered without a number of communicants receiving with the priest in one place, then would the ancient fathers in all their writings somewhere have complained of the ceasing of that, which everywhere they call Quotidianum et juge sacrificium, "*The daily and continual sacrifice:*" *of which their opinion is, that it ought* (34) *daily to be sacrificed, that the death of our Lord and the work of our redemption might always be celebrated, and had in memory, and we thereby shew ourselves, according to our bounden duty, mindful and thankful. But verily the fathers nowhere complain of intermitting the daily sacrifice, but very much of the slackness of the people, for that they came not more often unto this holy and wholesome banquet: and yet they never compelled*

The undevotion of the people groweth of the negligence of the clergy.

The thirty-fourth untruth. For[6] the fathers say not so, but plainly the contrary.

[[4] Doing, 1565, 1609.] [[5] You, 1565.] [[6] 1565, omits *for*.]

them thereto; but, exhorting them to frequent it worthily, left them to their own conscience.

THE BISHOP OF SARISBURY.

The painter that pourtrayed out in colours Medea killing her own child, by the skill he had in painting, made to appear in her face two contrary affections; for in the one side he expressed extreme fury, that bade her kill, and in the other side motherly love and pity, that bade her not kill[1]. Such two contrary affections we may here see in M. Harding, both painted and set out in one face. For notwithstanding, for his credit's sake, he advance[2] his mass, and deface the holy communion with all that he is able; yet here again, for conscience sake, of the other side he confesseth that the communion is the better, and so rippeth up all that he hath sewed before, and willeth others to assent unto him before he can assent unto himself. God's name be blessed, that is thus able to force out his truth even by the mouths of them that openly withstand his truth! But neither should he in such disdain, and so often, call us new masters and gospellers, for defending that himself knoweth and confesseth to be the better: nor, after the holy communion was once restored, should he have drawn the people again to the private mass; that is, by his own confession, from the better to the worse.

Concil. Nicen. ii. Action. iv.

M. Harding confesseth that the communion is better than his mass.

"But," saith M. Harding, "in case of negligence of the people, if the priest receive alone, the substance of the mass is not impaired." This difference in terms of substance and accidents, in Christ's institution, is newly found out, and hath no warrant neither of the scriptures nor of the old fathers. Howbeit Christ's example in doing, and commandment to do the same, may not be taken for a shew or accident, but for the effect and substance of his supper. "Do this," saith Christ, the same that you have seen me do: take, bless, break, divide, "in my remembrance." Which words St Chrysostom expoundeth thus: *Hoc facite in memoriam beneficii mei, salutis vestræ*[3]*:* "Do this in remembrance of my benefit, and of your salvation." This is no accident, or light fantasy, that may be left at our pleasure, but the very substantial point of that sacrament which we are specially commanded "to continue until he come;" and for want whereof St Paul saith, "That supper is not the Lord's supper."

Matt. xxvi.

Ad Populum Antiochen. Hom. 61.

1 Cor. xi.

Certainly Alexander of Hales, and Humbertus, two of M. Harding's own scholastical doctors, are full against him in this point. Alexander saith: "Consecration is for the communion; therefore of both the communion is the greater[4]." Humbertus saith: *Hoc quotiescunque feceritis, id est, benedixeritis, fregeritis, distribueritis, in mei memoriam facietis: quia quodlibet horum trium, si sine reliquis fiat...perfectam memoriam Christi non repræsentat*[5]*:* "As often as ye shall this do, that is to say, as often as ye shall bless, break, and distribute, ye shall do it in my remembrance: for whatsoever one thing of these three things be done without the rest, it representeth not the perfect[6] remembrance of Christ." And thinketh M. Harding that the sacrifice, whereof neither Christ nor his disciples ever spake one word, is the substance of his supper; and the mystical distribution in remembrance of his death, whereof he gave us such a strait commandment, in so manifest and so plain words, is no part of the substance?

Par. iv. q. 35. m. 2. Sol. 2.

Humbert. contra Libell. Nicetæ Monachi. Ex Cassandro.

The allegation of which sacrifice to this purpose is mere vain. The old fathers never complained of ceasing thereof, because they knew it could never cease. For the strength and virtue of Christ's sacrifice resteth in itself, and not in any diligence or doing of ours. "Christ[7], being a priest after the order of Melchisedech, hath offered up one sacrifice for all upon his cross, full and perfect[6];" therefore we need none other: "one and everlasting;" therefore it

Heb. vii. & x.

[1 ...μέλλουσα τοῖς τέκνοις ἐπιφέρειν τὸ ξίφος, ἐλέῳ καὶ θυμῷ μερίζει τὸ πρόσωπον.—Aster. Relat. in Concil. Nic. II. Act. iv. in Concil. Stud. Labb. et Cossart. Lut. Par. 1671-2. Tom. VII. col. 209.]

[2 Avance, 1565.]

[3 Chrysost. Op. Par. 1718-38. In Epist. ad Ephes. cap. i. Hom. iii. Tom. XI. p. 22.]

[4 Alex. Alens. Theol. Summ. Col. Agrip. 1622. Pars IV. Quæst. x. Membr. v. Art. i. 2. p. 262. See before, page 124.]

[5 Humbert. cont. Nicet. in Mag. Biblioth. Vet. Patr. Col. Agrip. 1618-22. Tom. XI. p. 333; where for *hoc* we find *hæc, et distribueritis,* and *Christi memoriam non repræsentant.*]

[6 Perfite, 1565.]

[7 Christs, 1611.]

needeth no renewing: "by privilege given to himself only;" therefore it cannot be wrought by any other. Daily sacrifice.

This sacrifice notwithstanding is revived, and freshly laid out before our eyes, in the ministration of the holy mysteries; as it is well recorded by sundry of the old godly fathers. St Augustine saith: "Was not Christ once offered in himself? Yet, that notwithstanding, by way of a sacrament he is offered every day unto the people, not at Easter only, but also every day; and he saith no untruth, that, being demanded the question, saith, 'Christ is offered.' For if sacraments had not a certain likeness of the things whereof they be sacraments, then should they indeed be no sacraments. And of this likeness many times they bear the names of the things themselves: as the sacrament of Christ's body, by a certain manner of speech, is the body of Christ[8]." Likewise again he saith: *Cum...non obliviscimur munus Salvatoris, nonne Christus quotidie nobis immolatur?... Ex ipsis reliquiis cogitationis, et ex ipsa memoria, quotidie nobis sic immolatur, quasi quotidie nos innovet*[9]: "When we forget not the gift of our Saviour, is not Christ daily offered unto us? Through the remnants of our cogitation, and by way of our very memory, Christ is so offered unto us every day as if he daily renewed us." And again likewise he saith: *Holocaustum Dominicæ passionis...eo tempore offert quisque pro peccatis suis, quo ejusdem passionis fide dedicatur, et Christianorum fidelium nomine baptizatus imbuitur*[10]: "At that time doth every man offer up the sacrifice of Christ's passion for his sins, when he is endued with the faith of Christ's passion, and, being baptized, receiveth the name of faithful Christians."

August. Epist. 23. ad Bonifacium.

August. in Psal. lxxv.

August. in Epist. ad Rom. sub finem.

Thus is the sacrifice of Christ's passion expressed in the holy ministration; and yet not as M. Harding imagineth, by any action there done by the priest alone, but by the communion and participation of the people; as St Augustine also otherwhere witnesseth: *Dum frangitur hostia, et sanguis...in ora fidelium funditur, quid aliud quam Dominici corporis in cruce immolatio...designatur*[11]? "While the oblation is broken, and the blood" (that is, the sacrament of the blood) "is poured into the mouths of the faithful, what other thing is there expressed or signified but the sacrificing of the Lord's body upon the cross?"

De Con. Dist. 2. ex Sentent. Prosperi. Designatur.

This sacrifice of Christ on his cross is called the "daily sacrifice," not for that it must be renewed every day, but for that, being once done, it standeth good for all days, and for ever. What force then is there in this reason: "The fathers never complained of ceasing of the daily sacrifice; *ergo*, they had private mass?" For it may be answered in one word, they had the holy communion every day, and therefore they complained not. Howbeit, neither is the holy communion that daily sacrifice itself, but a memory of the same: neither was the communion then ministered every day. For proof whereof I would wish M. Harding to mark this epistle, sent from the council of Alexandria in the defence of one Macarius, who was charged by his enemies that he had forcibly entered into the church, and broken the cup of the holy ministration. They make his defence in this manner: "The place where they say the cup was broken was no church, nor any priest at that time near thereabout; and, touching the day, it was no Sunday. Seeing then there was no church in that place, nor ministration of the sacraments, nor the day required the same, what manner cup was it then, or when, or where was it broken[12]?" It appeareth plainly by these words of the

Epist. Synod. Conc. Alex.

[[8] Nonne semel immolatus est Christus in seipso, et tamen in sacramento non solum per omnes paschæ solemnitates, sed omni die populis immolatur, nec utique mentitur, qui interrogatus eum responderit immolari? Si enim sacramenta quamdam similitudinem earum rerum, quarum sacramenta sunt, non haberent, omnino sacramenta non essent. Ex hac autem similitudine plerumque etiam ipsarum rerum nomina accipiunt. Sicut ergo secundum quemdam modum sacramentum corporis Christi corpus Christi est, &c.—August. Op. Par. 1679—1700. Epist. ad Bonifac. xcviii. 9. Tom. II. col. 267.]

[[9] Id. in Psal. lxxv. Enarr. 15. Tom. IV. col. 801; where we read *quotidie nobis Christus*, and *id est* for *et.*]

[[10] Id. Epist. ad Rom. Expos. Inch. 19. Tom. III. Pars II. col. 937; where *holocausto.*]

[[11] Id. in Lib. Sent. Prosp. in Corp. Jur. Canon. Lugd. 1624. Decret. Gratian. Decr. Tert. Pars, De Consecr. Dist. ii. can. 37. col. 1930; where *cum frangitur*, and *dum sanguis.*]

[[12] Καὶ γὰρ ὁ τόπος ἐκεῖνος ἐν ᾧ κεκλᾶσθαι τὸ ποτήριόν φησιν, οὐκ ἦν ἐκκλησία, πρεσβύτερος οὐκ ἦν ὁ τὸν τόπον παροικῶν, ἡμέρα καθ' ἣν Μακάριον τοῦτο πεποιηκέναι φασὶν, οὐκ ἦν κυριακή. μήτε τοίνυν ἐκκλησίας οὔσης ἐκεῖ, μήτε τοῦ ἱερουργοῦντος, μήτε τῆς ἡμέρας ἀπαιτούσης, ποῖον ἢ πότε ἢ ποῦ τὸ ποτήριον κέκλασται μυστικόν;—

Daily sacrifice.

council, that they had no ministration of the sacraments at that time in Alexandria but only upon the Sundays. And yet no man ever complained of the ceasing of the daily sacrifice notwithstanding. For they knew that the sacrifice of Christ's death is daily, and for ever, and can never cease.

Communion only upon the Sunday.

M. HARDING. THE TWENTY-SIXTH DIVISION.

St Ambrose witnesseth, that the people of the east had a custom in his time to be houseled but once in the year. And he rebuketh sharply such as follow them, after this sort: Si quotidianus est cibus, cur post annum illum sumis, quemadmodum Græci in oriente facere consueverunt[1]? *"If it be our daily meat (saith he), why takest thou it[2] but once in the year; as the Greeks are wont to do in the east?" St Augustine uttereth the same thing almost with the same words[3]. And in the second book,* De sermone Domini in Monte, *the twelfth chapter, expounding the fourth petition of our Lord's prayer, "Give us this day our daily bread," shewing that this may be taken either for material bread, either for the sacrament of our Lord's body, or for spiritual meat, which he alloweth best, would that, concerning the sacrament of our Lord's body, they of the east should not move question, how it might be understanded to be their daily bread, which were not daily partakers of our Lord's supper,* (35) *whereas, for all that, this bread is called daily bread. There he saith thus:* Ut ergo illi taceant, neque de hac re sententiam suam defendant, vel ipsa auctoritate ecclesiæ [sint contenti], quod sine scandalo ista faciunt, neque ab eis qui ecclesiis præsunt facere prohibentur, neque non obtemperantes condemnantur[5]: *"Wherefore, that they hold their peace, and stand not in defence of their opinion, let them be content at leastway with the authority of the church, that they do these things without offence thereof taken, neither be forbidden of those that be over the churches, neither be condemned when they disobey." Here we see, by St Augustine, that they of the orient, who so seldom received the sacrament, were holden (for all that) christian[6] people, by the authority of the church: none offence thereof was taken, neither were they inhibited of their custom; and, though they obeyed not their spiritual governors, moving them to receive more often, yet were they not condemned, nor excommunicated.*

[*Lib. vi. De Sacra. c. iv.* 1565, and H. A. 1564.]

[*De Verbis Domini secund. Lucam. Hom.* 28. 1565, and H. A. 1564.]

The thirty-fifth untruth. For St Augustine saith: "Hic[4] in illis partibus non intelligitur quotidianus panis."

THE BISHOP OF SARISBURY.

Ambros. Lib. v. de Sacram. cap. iv.

M. Harding findeth small force herein to prove that he seeketh for. St Ambrose rebuketh the slackness of some of his people that received so seldom, and wisheth them to communicate daily all together. Wherein he quite overthroweth the private mass.

As for St Augustine, I must needs say he hath taken wrong, and is ill used at M. Harding's hand, as being by violence and perforce made both to suppress that he would say, and also to say that he would not say; and yet in the end saith not one word for private mass, but plainly to the contrary. First, he would have St Augustine say, that the sacrament of Christ's body, to them of the east, was their daily bread, yea, although they daily received it not. This matter of itself is not weighty. Yet St. Augustine saith far otherwise, not in any other of his books, but even in the self-same sentence wherehence M. Harding had these words. For he addeth immediately: *Unde probatur, non hunc in illis partibus intelligi quotidianum panem. Nam magni peccati crimine arguerentur, qui ex illo non accipiunt quotidie*[7]: "Whereby it appeareth that they of the east understand not the sacrament to be their daily bread. For then were they guilty of great sin that do not daily receive it." But touching private mass, he saith thus even

August de Serm. Dom. in Mont. cap. xii.

M. Harding falsifieth St Augustine's mind.

The sacrament is not the daily bread.

Epist. Synod. Concil. Alex. in Concil. Stud. Labb. et Cossart. Lut Par. 1671-2. Tom. II. col. 548.]

[[1] Ambros. Op. Par. 1686-90. De Sacram. Lib. v. cap. iv. 25. Tom. II. col. 278; where we find *panis* for *cibus*, and *consuerunt*.]

[[2] Takest it, H. A. 1564.]

[[3] August. Op. Par. 1679—1700. Serm. lxxxiv. 3. Tom. V. Append. col. 152.]

[[4] 1565 omits *hic*.]

[[5] August. Op. De Serm. Dom. in Mont. Lib. II. cap. vii. 25, 6. Tom. III. Pars II. cols. 209, 10; where we have *suam sententiam, ecclesiastica,* and *damnantur.*]

[[6] For christian, H. A. 1654.]

[[7] August. Op. ibid. 26. col. 210; where *ex eo.*]

in the same place: *Panis quotidianus...[potest accipi] pro sacramento corporis Christi, quod quotidie accipimus*[8]: "The daily bread may be taken for the sacrament of Christ's body, which we receive every day." St Augustine saith the people then received the sacrament every day: whereof it followeth necessarily, that the private mass was then said never a day.

Daily sacrifice.

The sacrament received every day.

But the Grecians' custom was to receive once only in the year; *ergo*, the priest at other times received alone. No, saith St Augustine, this custom or negligence was not universal among all the people of Græcia, but among a certain of them only. For thus he saith: *Plurimi in orientalibus partibus non quotidie...communicant*[9]: "Many in the east parts do not daily communicate." Wherein may be well implied that some daily did communicate: otherwise the exception of many had been in vain. And that the rest did daily communicate, it may plainly appear by these words of St Augustine in the same place: *Vel...auctoritate ecclesiæ [sint contenti], quod sine scandalo ista faciant*: "Let them hold themselves content with the authority of the church, that they may thus do without offence." These words do necessarily import that the rest received the communion, and yet, that notwithstanding, were not offended with the negligence of their brethren that received not. For if the negligence had been general, and the whole people had abstained all together, as they do now in the church of Rome, there had been no cause at all why one of them in that respect should be offended with another.

Plurimi.

Augustinus.

In the Greek church some received the communion every day.

Now touching the matter itself, Jesus Christ, the Son of God, is our daily and everlasting food, not to be removed and renewed after certain days, as the shew-bread of the Jews, but to stand before the mercy-seat of God for ever. "Our daily bread," saith Germanus, "is Christ, that is, and was before, and continueth for ever[10]." Likewise St Augustine saith: "Not the bread that passeth into our body, but the bread of everlasting life, which sustaineth the substance of the soul[11]."

Germ. in Rerum Eccles. Theoria.

August. de Verbis Dom. secund. Luc. Serm. 28.

A sacrament of this food is the bread that Christ commanded to be blessed, broken, and delivered in his remembrance: which also may be called the daily bread; not for that it is daily received, but for that there is no day excepted, but it may be received every day. And that in such places, where as the sacrament was not daily received of the people, it was not received privately and daily of the priest, for continuance of the daily sacrifice, as M. Harding surmiseth, it appeareth well by sundry good records. And, to leave [a]St Basil, *Ad Cæsariam Patritiam*[12]; the [b]council of Laodicea[13]; the [c]council of Constantinople holden in Trullo[14]; and the synodal [d]epistle sent from the bishops of the east part, in the defence of Macarius[15]; St Augustine saith: *Hujus rei sacramentum... alicubi quotidie, alicubi certis intervallis dierum, in dominico præparatur, et de mensa dominica sumitur*[16]: "The sacrament of this thing is prepared, or consecrate in the church, and received of the Lord's table, in some places every day, in some places upon certain days." Likewise also saith St Ambrose: "Every week we must celebrate the oblation, although not every day unto strangers, yet unto the inhabitants at least twice in the week[17]." St Augustine saith: "The sacrament was ministered at certain days:" St Ambrose saith: "Sometimes twice in the week," and not every day. But what record hereof can be plainer than the council of Toledo? The words in English be these: "There be sundry

Ambros. de Sacram. Lib. v. cap. iv.

The sacrament called the daily bread.

[a] Basil. ad Cæsariam.
[b] Conc. Laod. cap. 49.
[c] Conc. Constantinop. cap. 52.
[d] Conc. Alex. Epist. Synod.
August. in Johan. Tract. 26.

Ambros. in Epist. ad Tim. i. c. iv.

Concil. Tolet. iv. cap. 9.

[[8] Id. ibid. 25. col. 209.]

[[9] Id. ibid. 20. col. 210.]

[[10] Germ. Const. Rer. Eccles. Theor. in Biblioth. Vet. Patr. Stud. Galland. Venet. 1765-81. Tom. XIII. p. 226. See before, page 128, note 3.]

[[11] Non iste panis qui vadit in corpus, sed ille panis vitæ æternæ, qui animæ nostræ substantiam fulcit.—August. Op. Serm. lxxxiv. 3. Tom. V. Append. col. 152. See also Ambros. Op. De Sacram. Lib. v. cap. iv. 24. Tom. II. col. 378.]

[[12] Basil. Op. Par. 1721-30. Ad Cæsar. Epist. xciii. Tom. III. p. 186. See before, page 155, note 14.]

[[13] Concil. Laod. can. 49. in Concil. Stud. Labb. et Cossart. Tom. I. col. 1505. See before, page 129, note 7.]

[[14] Concil. Quinisext. in eod. can. 52. Tom. VI. cols. 1166, 7. See before, page 129, note 6.]

[[15] Epist. Synod. Concil. Alex. in eod. Tom. II. col. 548. See before, page 167, note 12.]

[[16] August. Op. In Johan. Evang. cap. vi. Tractat. xxvi. 15. Tom. III. Pars II. col. 500; where *in dominica mensa præparatur.*]

[[17] Ambros. Op. Comm. in I. Epist. ad Tim. cap. iii. Tom. II. Append. col. 295. See before, page 129.]

priests in Spain, that, touching the prayer that the Lord taught, and commanded daily to be said, say the same only upon the Sunday, and upon no day else[1]." Hereof we may very well gather that, if the priests in Spain said the Lord's prayer only upon the Sunday, forsomuch as the communion is never ministered without the Lord's prayer, therefore the priests in Spain ministered not the communion but only upon the Sunday.

The communion ministered only upon the Sunday.

These things well considered, the weakness of M. Harding's guesses may the better appear. For where he saith, "Some of the people withdrew themselves[2];" *ergo*, "no man did receive;" or, "Many abstained;" *ergo*, "the priest received alone;" these reasons be of no value, neither are worthy of any answer. For of the same premises the contrary will rather follow. St Augustine saith, "Many in the east part abstained:" hereof we may well gather; *ergo*, some abstained not: otherwise he should have said, All abstained, and not some. Then further, Some abstained not; *ergo*, some received with the priest. So did not the priest receive alone. And so hath not M. Harding yet found his private mass.

M. HARDING. THE TWENTY-SEVENTH DIVISION.

In x. cap. ad Heb. Homil. 17.

St Chrysostom, many times exhorting his people to prepare themselves to receive their rights, at least at Easter, in one place saith thus: "What meaneth this? The most part of you be partakers of this sacrifice but once in the year, some twice, some oftener. Therefore this that I speak is to all, not to them only that be here present, but to those also that live in wilderness. For they receive the sacrament but once in the year, and peradventure but once in two years. Well, what then? Whom shall we receive? Those that come but once, or that come often, or that come seldom? Soothly, we receive them that come with a pure and a clean conscience, with a clean heart, and, to be short, with a blameless life. They that be such, let them come always; and they that be not such, let them not[3] *come, not so much as once. Why so? Because they receive to themselves judgment, damnation, and punishment*[4]*." The ancient doctors, specially Chrysostom and Augustine, be full of such sentences.*

THE BISHOP OF SARISBURY.

It is needless to answer such places as make no shew of proof. Chrysostom, as M. Harding well knoweth, hath neither here, nor elsewhere, either the name or the sense of private mass. Only he exhorteth the people to examine and prepare themselves, and so to come worthily to the Lord's supper. Now, if M. Harding think he may found his mass upon this place, he may also presume the like of St Paul, that, where he said, *Probet seipsum homo*, "Let a man examine himself," he meant to erect private mass.

M. HARDING. THE TWENTY-EIGHTH DIVISION.

[The people's forbearing the communion is no cause why the priest should not say mass. H. A. 1564.]

The thirty-sixth untruth. M. Harding is able to shew no such case.

Now to this end I drive these allegations, leaving out a great number of the same sense. Although many times the people forbare to come to the communion, so as many times (36) *none at all were found disposed to receive, yet the holy fathers, bishops, and priests, thought not that a cause why they should not daily offer the blessed sacrifice, and*

[1 Nonnulli sacerdotum per Hispanias reperiuntur, qui dominicam orationem, quam Salvator noster docuit et præcepit, non quotidie, sed tantum die dominica dicunt.—Concil. Tolet. IV. cap. x. in Concil. Stud. Labb. et Cossart. Lut. Par. 1671-2. Tom. V. col. 1708.]

[2 Themself, 1565.]

[3 Let not them, H. A. 1564.]

[4 Τί οὖν ἐστι; πολλοὶ τῆς θυσίας ταύτης ἅπαξ μεταλαμβάνουσι τοῦ παντὸς ἐνιαυτοῦ, ἄλλοι δὲ δὶς, ἄλλοι δὲ πολλάκις. πρὸς οὖν ἅπαντας ἡμῖν ὁ λόγος ἐστὶν, οὐ πρὸς τοὺς ἐνταῦθα δὲ μόνον, ἀλλὰ καὶ πρὸς τοὺς ἐν τῇ ἐρήμῳ καθεζομένους. ἐκεῖνοι γὰρ ἅπαξ τοῦ ἐνιαυτοῦ μετέχουσι, πολλάκις δὲ καὶ διὰ δύο ἐτῶν. τί οὖν; τίνας ἀποδεξόμεθα; τοὺς ἅπαξ; τοὺς πολλάκις; τοὺς ὀλιγάκις; οὔτε τοὺς ἅπαξ, οὔτε τοὺς πολλάκις, οὔτε τοὺς ὀλιγάκις, ἀλλὰ τοὺς μετὰ καθαροῦ συνειδότος, τοὺς μετὰ καθαρᾶς καρδίας, τοὺς μετὰ βίου ἀλήπτου. οἱ τοιοῦτοι ἀεὶ προσίτωσαν· οἱ δὲ μὴ τοιοῦτοι μηδὲ ἅπαξ. τί δήποτε; ὅτι κρίμα ἑαυτοῖς λαμβάνουσι, καὶ κατάκριμα, καὶ κόλασιν, καὶ τιμωρίαν.—Chrysost. Op. Par. 1718-38. In Epist. ad Hebr. cap. x. Hom. xvii. Tom. XII. p. 169.]

celebrate mass. Which thing may sufficiently be proved, whether M. Jewel, that maketh himself so sure of the contrary, will yield and subscribe, according to his promise, or no. Of the daily sacrifice, these words of Chrysostom be plain: Quid ergo nos? Nonne per singulos dies offerimus? Offerimus quidem, sed ad recordationem facientes mortis ejus: et una est hostia, non multæ, &c.[5] *"Then what do we? Do we not offer every day? Yes, verily we do so, but we do it for recording of his death. And it is one host, not many." Here I hear M. Jewel say, though against his will, "I grant the daily sacrifice, but I stand still in my negative, that it cannot be shewed there was ever any such sacrifice celebrated without a communion," that is, as they will have it, without some convenient number to receive the sacrament in the same place with the priest. For proof of this, these be such places as I am persuaded withal. The better learned men, that be of more reading than I am, have other, I doubt not.*

[*In x. cap. ad Hebr. Hom.* 17. H. A. 1564.]

[*By order of the last communion book, no communion may be said or had, without three do communicate with the minister at least, of how small number soever the parish be.* H. A. 1564.]

THE BISHOP OF SARISBURY.

Here M. Harding notably betrayeth himself, laying forth, for a countenance, a few of Chrysostom's words, and the same nothing to the matter, hewing and mangling them as him listeth best, requiring also subscription, as upon sufficient proof; and yet, in the same place and with one breath, himself secretly confessing the insufficiency and weakness of his proof.

These words of St Chrysostom, as they make nothing for private mass, so do they very well declare what the old fathers meant by these words, "oblation" and "sacrifice," in the holy ministration. Chrysostom compareth the sacrifices of the Jews in the law with the sacrifice of Christ in the gospel. He saith, the sacrifices of the law were many and unperfect[6], and therefore daily renewed; this of the gospel is one and perfect[7], and therefore everlasting: and resembleth the same unto a sovereign salve, which, being once laid on the wound, healeth it up thoroughly, and needeth no more laying on[8].

Chrysost. ad Heb. Hom. 17.

He saith further, that we of the gospel have a sacrifice also, and that daily, but in remembrance of that sacrifice once made upon the cross. And although we sacrifice in sundry places, yet, saith he, the sacrifice is but one, because it hath relation unto that one sacrifice of Christ. And therefore he addeth: *Quomodo una est hostia, et non multæ? Quia semel oblata est, oblata est in sancta sanctorum. Hoc autem sacrificium exemplar illius est*[8]. "How is it one oblation, and not many? Because it was once offered, it was offered into the holy place; but this sacrifice (meaning the ministration of the sacrament) is an example of that." And what he meaneth by this word *exemplar*, he sheweth a few lines before: *Quæ formam tantum alicujus habent, exemplar ostendunt, non autem virtutem; sicut in imaginibus exemplar hominis habet imago, non etiam virtutem*[9]: "The things that bear only a likeness shew the samplar of some other thing, but not the power of the same: as an image sheweth the pattern of a man, but not the power of a man." Hereof St Chrysostom concludeth thus: "The thing that we do is done in remembrance of that thing that was done before. For Christ said, Do this in my remembrance[10]." Hereby it appeareth in what sense the old fathers used these words, "oblation" and "sacrifice."

Chrysost. ad Hebr. Hom. 17.

Exemplar.

But what doth all this further M. Harding's private mass? Or, if it further it not, what doth it here? It is but a faint conclusion to say,

Chrysostom had the daily sacrifice;

Ergo, Chrysostom had private mass.

Soothly, good reader, if it had liked M. Harding to have given thee leave to read the next lines following in Chrysostom, thou mightest easily have seen the whole order of the holy ministration in his time. For thus he saith unto the people: *Per singulos dies intras in ecclesiam*[11]: "Thou comest daily to the church." Whereby we see the priest was not in the church alone. Then, touching the

M. Harding nippeth Chrysostom's words.

[5 Id. ibid. p. 168.]
[6 Unperfite, 1565.]
[7 Perfite, 1565.]
[8 Chrysost. Op. ibid.] [9 Id. ibid.]
[10 Τοῦτο εἰς ἀνάμνησιν γίνεται τοῦ τότε γενομένου. τοῦτο γὰρ ποιεῖτέ, φησιν, εἰς τὴν ἐμὴν ἀνάμνησιν—Id. ibid. p. 169.]
[11 Id. ibid. p. 170.]

Vocat sanctos.

Sancta sanctis.

receiving, he saith: "The deacon at that hour calleth the holy, and by that voice, as it were, beholdeth the people's spots. For like as in a flock where as be many sound sheep, and many infected, the one must needs be sundered from the other; even so fareth it in the church. For some are sound, and some are sick. And by that voice the deacon divideth these from them. For that voice of his falling into our ears, as it were a hand, removeth and shutteth forth some, and other some it taketh in, and presenteth them to the congregation[1]." I send thee not unto other places of Chrysostom, which be both many more and far plainer than this, but only unto this same place, out of which M. Harding hath picked as much as he thought good.

Chrysostom saith: "The people resorted daily to the church; the deacon sundered them with his voice, the sound from the sick; the one part to receive, the other to abstain; the one part he shut out at the time of the holy communion, the other he brought in and presented to the congregation." This was the ordinary practice of the church in Chrysostom's time: where we see plainly by his own report that he received not alone.

Yet saith M. Harding, "For proof of this, these following be such places as I am persuaded withal." By this cold conclusion he cutteth off credit from all that he hath hitherto said, as not making shew sufficient to win his purpose, and so condemneth his note made in the margin, which was, "Proofs for private mass;" and layeth all the burden of his grounds upon these other guesses that hereafter follow. Verily hitherto, for any thing that may appear by his book, notwithstanding his long time, his much reading, and great conference with all his fellows, he hath not yet found either the name of private mass in any old catholic writer, or the sole receiving of the priest. If he will have the world to believe him, and subscribe, he must leave his guesses, and bring some sound and substantial proofs.

M. HARDING. THE TWENTY-NINTH DIVISION.

Soter, bishop of Rome, about the year of our Lord 170, *who suffered martyrdom under Antoninus Verus, the emperor, for order of celebrating the mass, made this statute or decree:* Ut nullus presbyterorum... solennia celebrare præsumat, nisi duobus præsentibus, sibique respondentibus, [et] ipse tertius habeatur; quia cum pluraliter ab eo dicitur, Dominus vobiscum, et illud in secretis, Orate pro me; apertissime convenit, ut ipsius respondeatur salutationi[2]: *This hath been ordained, "that no priest presume to celebrate the solemnity of the mass, except there be two present, and answer him, so as he himself[3] be the third. For whereas he saith (as by way of speaking to many), Our Lord be with you, and likewise in the secrets, Pray you for me; it seemeth evidently convenient, that answer be made to his salutation accordingly." Which ancient decree requireth not that all people of necessity be present,* (37) *much less that all so oftentimes should communicate sacramentally; which thing it requireth neither of those two that ought to be present. If of the bare words of this decree a sufficient argument may not be made for our purpose, inducing, of the affirmation of that one thing there specified, the denial of that other thing we speak of, which manner of argument is commonly used of our adversaries; then more weight may be put unto it in this case; for that, whereas the receiving of Christ's body is a far greater matter than to answer the priest at mass, if that holy bishop and martyr had thought it so necessary, as that the mass might not be done without it, doubtless of very reason and convenience he would and should have specially*

De Con. Dist. 1. *can. Hoc quoque statutum.*

The thirty-seventh untruth. For all that were present were willed either to communicate, or to depart. A bare collection.

[1 Διὰ τοῦτο καὶ ὁ διάκονος ἐπιφωνεῖ τότε τοὺς ἁγίους καλῶν, καὶ διὰ τῆς φωνῆς ταύτης μωμοσκοπῶν ἅπαντας, ὥστε μὴ προσελθεῖν τινα ἀπαράσκευον. καθάπερ γὰρ ἐπὶ ποίμνης, ἔνθα πολλὰ μὲν ὑγιαίνει πρόβατα, πολλὰ δὲ ψώρας ἀναπέπλησται, ἀνάγκη ταῦτα διείργεσθαι ἀπὸ τῶν ὑγιαινόντων· οὕτω καὶ ἐν τῇ ἐκκλησίᾳ, ἐπειδὴ τὰ μέν ἐστιν ὑγιαινὰ πρόβατα, τὰ δὲ κεκακωμένα, διὰ τῆς φωνῆς ταύτης διείργει ταῦτα ἐκείνων...ἡ γὰρ φωνὴ ἐκείνη εἰς τὴν ἀκοὴν ἐμπίπτουσα τὴν ἡμετέραν, καθάπερ χεὶρ, τοὺς μὲν ὠθεῖ καὶ ἐκβάλλει, τοὺς δὲ εἰσάγει καὶ παρίστησιν.—Id. ibid. pp. 170, 1.]

[2 Soter. in Corp. Jur. Canon. Lugd. 1624. Decret. Gratian. Decr. Tert. Pars, De Consecr. Dist. i. can. 61. col. 1907; where we find *aptissime.*]

[3 H. A. 1564, omits *himself.*]

spoken of that, rather than of the other. But for that he thought otherwise, he required only of necessity the presence of two, for the purpose above mentioned. Epistles decretal.

THE BISHOP OF SARISBURY.

Some say, this decree was made by pope Anacletus; some others say, by Soter; and so they seem not to be yet thoroughly resolved upon the author[4]. (Polydorus de inventoribus rerum.) But if we had not good cause to doubt of the authority of these decrees and epistles decretal, we would the less doubt of their doctrine. It was evermore the common practice of deceivers to blaze their doings by the names of such as they knew to be in estimation in the world. For, to pass by Homer, Hesiod, Cicero, Plautus, and such others counted learned and famous among the heathens, in whose names many counterfeit books were set abroad, St Paul himself willeth the Thessalonians not to suffer themselves to be drawn from their faith, "neither by spirit, nor by talk, nor by letters[5] as sent from him." (2 Thess. ii.) By which last words he signifieth that letters sometimes were falsified and set abroad in his name. So were there given out gospels in the name of Peter, Thomas, and other the apostles; and other matters of small weight in the names of Augustine, Hierome, Ambrose, Cyprian, and other like. This was unto some a common pastime; and many godly fathers complain much of it.

Wherefore we ought the less to marvel if the like have happened unto Anacletus, Evaristus, Soter, and such others as followed immediately in Rome after the apostles' time.

Gratian sheweth that the decretal epistles have been doubted of among the learned[6]. (Dist. 19, de Epist.) And doctor Smith, although his authority be not great, declared openly at Paul's cross, that they cannot possibly be theirs whose names they bare. (Anno secundo Edwardi sexti.) And, to utter some reasons shortly for proof thereof, these decretal epistles manifestly deprave and abuse the scriptures, as it may soon appear unto the godly reader upon the sight. They maintain nothing so much as the state and kingdom of the pope; and yet was there no such state erected in many hundred years after the apostles' time: they publish a multitude of vain and superstitious ceremonies, and other like fantasies, far unlike the apostles' doctrine: they proclaim such things as M. Harding knoweth to be open and known lies.

Anacletus, that was next after Peter, willeth and straitly commandeth, (Dist. 97. Juxta Sanctorum.) that all bishops once in the year do visit the entry of St Peter's church in Rome, which they call *Limina Petri*[7]. Yet was there then no church yet built there in the name of Peter: for pope Cornelius saith (as he is alleged) that (In Decretal. Cornelii.) he first took up St Peter's body, and buried the same in Apollo's church in Rome, at the least one hundred and forty years after that Anacletus was dead[8]. Pope Antherus maketh mention of Eusebius Alexandrinus, and Felix[9], which lived a long time after him; and therefore was it not possible for him to know them. Fabianus writeth of the coming of Novatus into Italy[10]; and yet it is clear by St Cyprian and by Eusebius, that Novatus came first into Italy in the time of Cornelius, which was next after him[11]. (Cypr. Lib. i. Epist. 3. Euseb. Lib. vi. cap. xlii.) And, to leave a number of other conjectures, which may be hereafter more aptly touched some other where, neither St Hierome, nor Gennadius, entreating of the ecclesiastical writer[12], nor Damasus, writing purposely of the lives of the bishops of Rome before him, ever made any mention, either of such epistles, or of any such decrees; which they would not have dissembled, if there had been any such extant, or known in their time.

[4 Polyd. Verg. De Invent. Rer. Amst. 1671. Lib. v. cap. xii. p. 356.]

[5 Letter, 1565, 1609.]

[6 De epistolis vero decretalibus quæritur, an vim auctoritatis obtineant, &c.—Decret. Gratian. Decr. Prim. Pars, Dist. xix. col. 79.]

[7 ...omnes episcopi...annue circa Idus Maii sanctorum principum apostolorum Petri et Pauli liminibus præsententur, &c.—Anacl. et Zach. in eod. Dist. xciii. can. 4. col. 441.]

[8 Postea vero beati apostolorum principis Petri accepimus corpus, et...posuimus illud...in templo Apollinis, &c.—Cornel. Epist. i. in Concil. Labb. et Cossart. Lut. Par. 1671-2. Tom. I. col. 669.]

[9 Ant. Epist. in eod. Tom. I. col. 630.]

[10 ...supervenit Novatus ex Africa, et separavit de ecclesia Christi Novatianum, &c.—Fabian. Epist. i. in eod. Tom. I. 637.]

[11 The places referred to are Euseb. in Hist. Eccles. Script. Amst. 1695—1700. Lib. vi. cap. xliii. pp. 197, &c.; and Cypr. Op. Oxon. 1682. Epist. ad Cornel. lix. pp. 126, &c. It may be sufficient to add that Pearson places the death of Fabian, Jan. 20, 250, and the arrival of Novatus in Rome, Jan. 251. Annal. Cypr. pp. 18, 27.]

[12 Writers, 1565.]

Thus have I briefly given a taste of these decretal authorities, that the reader may the better understand of what credit they ought to be.

Now touching the matter, that by this decree of Soter, bishop of Rome, it should then be lawful for the priest there to say mass, having only two others in his company, the state and story of the time considered, it seemeth very unlikely.

1. For both St Augustine[1] and St Hierome[2], who lived two hundred and fifty years after Soter, have recorded that the people of Rome, even in their time, used to receive the communion together every day; which practice can hardly stand with that is here imagined.

August. Epist. 118. ad Januarium. August. in Joh. Tract. 26. Hieron. in Apologia adversus Jovinianum.

The words also themselves[3] imply a manifest contrariety. For this word *solennia*, which here is used, seemeth to import a solemn company or resort of the

2. people. And yet this Soter, requiring to this action only the company of three persons, nevertheless calleth it *Missarum solennia.*

3. As touching the causes mentioned in this decree, which are, that the priest may seem conveniently and aptly to say in the plural number, "The Lord be with you," and, "Brethren, pray you for me;" it may well be doubted whether *Dominus vobiscum*, or *Orate pro me fratres*, were any part of the liturgy of Rome in Soter's time. For Damasus, which was bishop of Rome two hundred and fifty years after that, writeth unto St Hierome, that things were done with such simplicity in the church of Rome in his time, that upon the Sunday there was nothing else but some epistle of the apostle, or some chapter of the gospel read openly unto the people[4]; which whether he meant of the holy ministration or no, I leave further to be considered.

Damas. in Epist. ad Hieron.

4. Further, this same Soter requireth that both these two, and as many others as be present, make answer unto the priest; wherein is included both nearness of place for the people to stand in and to hear, and also a common known tongue; which both are contrary to M. Harding's mass.

5. Moreover, touching these two, whose presence is required, question is moved by the canonists, whether they ought to be two clerks or two laymen; or one clerk and one layman; or one man and one woman. The resolution whereof is that they must be two clerks[5].

De Con. Dist. 1. Hoc quoque. In Glossa.

6. Howbeit the matter is otherwise determined, that, if the mass be public, there must needs be two at the least; but, if it be a private mass, that then one is sufficient[6].

Summa Angeli Missa 38.

7. Gerson likewise saith that the priest may well say, *Dominus vobiscum*, although there be but one present at his mass. For it may be presumed, saith he, that the priest speaketh not only unto that one, but also unto the whole church[7]. Thus we see, notwithstanding Soter's determination, the number of two for a shift may well be abridged.

Gerson contra Floretum. Lib. iv.

8. Pope Innocentius hath yet another fetch to help the matter. He saith, though there be but one there, yet may the priest nevertheless say, *Dominus vobiscum;* because it may be thought there be angels there to supply men's rooms[8].

Innocent. Lib. ii. cap. xx. de Off. Miss.

9. Again, that there were any such secrecies in the mass in the time of Soter, it

---

[1 August. Op. Par. 1679—1700. Ad Inquis. Januar. Lib. I. seu Epist. liv. 2. Tom. II. col. 124. See before, page 17, note 17.

Id. ibid. In Joan. Evang. cap. vi. Tractat. xxvi. 15. Tom. III. Pars II. col. 500. See before, page 169.]

[2 Hieron. Op. Par. 1693—1706. Epist. xxx. ad Pammach. pro Libr. adv. Jovin. Tom. IV. Pars II. col. 239. See before, page 156.]

[3 Themself, 1565.]

[4 ...qui tantæ apud nos simplicitatis indago est, ut tantum in die dominica apostoli epistola una recitetur, et evangelii capitulum unum dicatur, &c.—Damas. Epist. iii. ad Hieron. in Concil. Stud. Labb. et Cossart. Lut. Par. 1671-2. Tom. II. col. 868.]

[5 Satis videtur, quod debent esse duo clerici.—Corp. Jur: Canon. Lugd. 1624. Decret. Gratian. Decr. Tert. Pars, De Consecr. Dist. i. Gloss. in can. 61. col. 1907.]

[6 Quarto debent esse saltem duo præsentes celebrationi missarum. De Cons. dist. i. Hoc quoque. et hoc verum in missa publica. sed in missa privata potest dici uno præsente servitore solum, qui respondeat in persona totius populi.—Clavas. Summ. Angel. Hagen. 1509. Missa 38. fol. 213. 2.]

[7 Quæritur hic utrum semper debeat sacerdos dicere *Dominus vobiscum*. Solutio. Dicendum quod sic posito casu, quod non esset nisi unus in missa sua, quia loquitur toti ecclesiæ.—Floret. Lugd. 1499. Lib. IV. fol. 88.]

[8 Pie quoque credendum est, et sacris auctoribus comprobatur, quod angeli Dei comites assistant orantibus, &c.—Innocent. Pont. Max. III. Op. Col. 1575. Myst. Miss. Lib. II. cap. xxv. Tom. I. p. 344.]

were very hard for M. Harding to prove. For then every piece of the mass was spoken aloud, that the people might hear it, and say *Amen.* And indeed to say unto the people, "Pray for me, brethren and sisters," as it is now used in the mass, unless the people may hear and understand the same, it is a mockery. And yet Durandus saith: [*Sacerdos*] *ante secretellam... volvens se ad populum dicturus, Orate fratres,* &c. *debet dicere, Dominus vobiscum sub silentio*[9]: "The priest before the little secret turning himself to the people to say, Brethren, pray for me, must say, The Lord be with you, under silence." Durand. Lib. iv.

Now saith M. Harding, "Soter's decree is not that these two should communicate with the priest, but only requireth their presence; *ergo*, it is likely the priest received alone; which is an argument much used among our adversaries." But what if these two will not come, neither to communicate, nor to be present at all? Verily, by M. Harding's mind the priest's devotion ought not to stay for want of company. For these be his very words a little before: "Well, none cometh: this is not a sufficient cause why the faithful and godly priest, inflamed with the love of God, feeling himself hungry and thirsty after the heavenly food and drink, should be kept from it[10]," &c. This is a cause sufficient, saith Soter: it is no sufficient cause, saith M. Harding. The judgment hereof I refer unto the reader. Page 12.

Touching the force of the argument, wherewith he chargeth us by the name of his adversaries, I trust there doth already appear some difference between our proofs and his guesses. But the argument that he meaneth, and not very plainly uttereth, is called in the schools *argumentum ab auctoritate negative;* which is thought to be good, whensoever proof is taken of God's word, and is used not only by us, but also by St Paul, and by many of the catholic fathers. St Paul saith: "God said not unto Abraham, In thy seeds all nations shall be blessed, but, In thy seed, which is Christ." And thereof he thought he made a good argument. Gal. iii.

Likewise saith Origen: "The bread which the Lord gave unto his disciples, saying unto them, Take, and eat, he deferred not, nor commanded to be reserved until the next day[11]." Such arguments Origen and other learned fathers thought to stand for good, whatsoever misliking M. Harding hath found in them. This kind of proof is thought to hold in God's commandments, for that they be full and perfect[12], and God hath specially charged us that we should neither put to them nor take from[13] them; and therefore it seemeth good unto them that have learned of Christ, *Unus est magister vester Christus:* "Christ only is your master;" and have heard the voice of God the Father from heaven, *Ipsum audite:* "Give ear unto him." But unto them that add to the word of God what them listeth, and make God's will subject unto their will, and break God's commandments for their own traditions' sake, unto them it seemeth not good. To conclude, if this manner of reasoning be good, why doth M. Harding reprove it? If it be naught, why doth he use it, and that even in the same place where he doth reprove it? Orig. in Levit. Hom. 5. Matt. xxiii. Matt. xvii. Matt. xv.

But, saith M. Harding, Soter required[14] only the presence of two, and these two were not commanded to communicate; *ergo*, the priest did receive alone; and so there was undoubtedly private mass. But mark well a little, good reader. If these two were bound to communicate with the priest, then, notwithstanding this decree, M. Harding hath not yet found his private mass. Then consider this decree written in the name of pope Calixtus: *Peracta consecratione, omnes communicent, qui noluerint ecclesiasticis carere liminibus. Sic enim et apostoli statuerunt, et sancta Romana tenet ecclesia*[15]: "The consecration being done, let all communicate, unless they will be removed from the church. For so the apostles appointed; and so holdeth the holy church of Rome." By this decree these two were bound either to communicate with the priest, or to depart forth of the church. If they did communicate, then hath M. Harding here no private mass: De Con. Dist. 2. Peracta. De Con. Dist. 1. Episcopus Deo.

[9 Durand. Rat. Div. Offic. Lugd. 1565. Lib. IV. cap. xiv. 9. fol. 110; where we have *sub silentio: Dominus vobiscum.*]

[10 See before, page 118.]

[11 Nam et Dominus panem, quem discipulis dabat, et dicebat eis, Accipite et manducate, non distulit, nec servari jussit in crastinum.—Orig. Op. Par. 1733-59. In Levit. Hom. v. 8. Tom. II. p. 211.]

[12 Perfite, 1565.] [13 Fro, 1565.]

[14 Requireth, 1565.]

[15 Anaclet. [tribuebatur Calixto] in Corp. Jur. Canon. Decret. Gratian. Decr. Tert. Pars, De Consecr. Dist. ii. can. 10. col. 1917. Ibid. Dist. i. can. 59. col. 1907.]

if they departed forth, then could the priest say no mass at all; for Soter at least requireth the presence of two.

Again, the argument that M. Harding gathereth out of this decree,

Three persons were present;

Ergo, two of them did not receive,

is utterly unsensible and void of reason. Rather he might have concluded thus:

Soter willeth that two be present;

Ergo, much more he willeth that the same two do communicate.

It may also stand with reason, and with the common practice of the church at that time, that these two, whose presence Soter requireth, were priests or deacons, or otherwise of the clergy, and that over and beside the company of the people; as indeed it is determined by the gloss[1]. And so this decree of Soter agreeth with another decree of Anacletus made to the like purpose, that is, "That the bishop at the ministration have about him a certain number of deacons, subdeacons, and other ministers, besides the common multitude of the lay-people[2]:" and likewise with another decree of the same Soter, that is, "That every priest making the sacrifice have by him another priest to assist him, and to make an end of the ministration, if any qualm or sickness happen to fall upon him[3]." And this assistance of the priest is required, notwithstanding the presence of others, either of the clerks or of the laity.

De Con. Dist. 1. Hoc quoque. In Glossa. De Con. Dist. 1. Episcopus Deo. De Con. Dist. 1. Ut illud.

Now being priests or clerks, and being present at the ministration, the law specially constrained them to receive the holy communion with the minister, as it appeareth by this decree written in the canons of the apostles: "If any bishop, or priest, or deacon, or any other of the clerks, after the oblation is made, do not communicate, either let him shew cause thereof, that, if it be found reasonable, he may be excused; or, if he shew no cause, let him be excommunicate[4]."

Canon. Apost. Can. 9.

Thus whosoever these two were, whose presence Soter required, whether they were of the laity or of the clergy, the law constrained them to receive together with the priest; and therefore M. Harding hath hitherto found a communion, and no manner token or inkling of his private mass.

M. HARDING. THE THIRTIETH DIVISION.

In a council holden at Agatha, a city of France, then called Gallia, about the time of Chrysostom, an old decree of Fabianus, bishop of Rome and martyr, and also of the council Elibertine, in the time of St Sylvester, Anno Domini 314, *was renewed, that all secular christian folk should be houseled three times every year, at Easter, Whitsuntide, and Christmas*[5]. *It was there also decreed that they should hear the whole mass every Sunday, and not depart before the priest had given blessing*[6]. *So they were bound to hear mass every Sunday, and to receive the communion but thrice in the year. The self-same order was decreed in the council of Orleans*[7]. *Then of like, specially in small towns and villages, they had mass without the communion of many together sometimes.*

Ex Con. Agath. Can. 31. *Missas die dominico secularibus totas audire, speciali ordine præcipimus: ita ut ante benedictionem sacerdotis egredi populus non præsumat: quod si fecerint, ab episcopo publice confundantur.*

De Con. Dist. 1. *Cum ad celebrandas Missas.*

Private Mass proved by likelihood.

THE BISHOP OF SARISBURY.

M. Harding knoweth well that these decrees which he here allegeth could never be found written, neither in the council holden at Agatha in France, nor at

M. Harding allegeth councils that cannot be found.

[1 Gloss. in can. 61. ibid.]

[2 Episcopus Deo sacrificans testes secum habeat ...In solemnioribus quippe diebus aut septem, aut quinque, aut tres diaconos... et subdiaconos, atque reliquos ministros secum habeat.—Anaclet. in eod. ibid. Dist. i. can. 59. ibid.]

[3 ...necessarium duximus instituere, ut...habeat quisque... sacrificans post se vicini solaminis adjutorem: ut, si aliquo casu ille...turbatus fuerit, vel ad terram elisus, a tergo semper habeat, qui ejus vicem exequatur intrepidus, et officium inceptum adimpleat.—Ex Decret. Soter. in eod. ibid. can. 58. col. 1906.]

[4 Εἴ τις ἐπίσκοπος, ἢ πρεσβύτερος, ἢ διάκονος, ἢ ἐκ τοῦ καταλόγου τοῦ ἱερατικοῦ, προσφορᾶς γενομένης μὴ μεταλάβοι, τὴν αἰτίαν εἰπάτω. καὶ ἐὰν εὔλογος ᾖ, συγγνώμης τυγχανέτω. εἰ δὲ μὴ λέγει, ἀφοριζέσθω. κ. τ. λ.—Canon. Apost. 8. in Concil. Stud. Labb. et Cossart. Lut. Par. 1671-2. Tom. I. col. 25.]

[5 Ex Concil. Agath. c. 18. in Corp. Jur. Canon. Lugd. 1624. Decret. Gratian. Decr. Tert. Pars, Dist. ii. can. 19. col. 1920.]

[6 Ex. Concil. Agath. c. 47. in eod. ibid. Dist. i. can. 64. col. 1908.]

[7 Ex Concil. Aurel. I. c. 28. in eod. can. 65. ibid.]

the other council holden at Eliberis, now called Granado, in Spain; but were set forth many hundred years after in the name of those councils, by one Gratian, a man of great diligence, as may appear by his gathering, but of no great judgment, as we may see by his choice. Yet here M. Harding shuffleth a great many of them together, that the one may the better countenance the other. [To hear mass.]

But let us receive the authority of these decrees, and grant there was no error committed by Gratian in his gathering; yet will they stand M. Harding in small stead. For, as in many other matters they utterly cast him, so they nothing relieve him for his mass. For thus it is concluded by both these councils: *Qui in natali Domini, paschate, et pentecoste non communicant, catholici non credantur, nec inter catholicos habeantur*[8]: "They that receive not the communion at Christmas, Easter, and Whitsuntide, let them not be taken nor reckoned for catholic people." It appeareth by these general councils, that in the whole church of Rome, saving only a few massing priests, there is not one man worthy to be accounted catholic. [De Con. Dist. 2. Sæcularis.]

And to draw near to the purpose, whoso will narrowly view the points of these decrees shall soon see they cannot stand with the very form and order of the church of those days. For, besides that I have already proved by the authority of St Hierome and St Augustine, that the holy communion was then ministered unto the people in Rome every day, Fabianus also, bishop of Rome, which is likewise brought forth here for a witness, hath plainly decreed, not that the people should hear mass every Sunday, as it is soothly warranted by M. Harding, but that they should receive the communion every Sunday. His words be plain: *Decernimus ut in omnibus dominicis diebus altaris oblatio ab omnibus viris et mulieribus fiat, tam panis, quam vini*[9]: "We decree that every Sunday the oblation of the altar be made of all men and women, both of bread and of wine." Here, besides that in these words is included the receiving of the communion every Sunday, may be noted also by the way that, by this authority of Fabian, men and women made the sacrifice of the altar, and that of bread and wine, and therefore after the order of Melchisedech. Therefore St Bernard saith: *Non solus [sacerdos] sacrificat,...sed totus conventus fidelium*[10]: "Not only the priest sacrificeth, but also the whole company of the faithful." These things well considered, the sense that M. Harding would so fain wring out of these decrees will seem unlikely. [Inter Decreta Fabiani, cap. 7.] [Bernard. in Serm. in die Purific. Tom. ii.]

Moreover, when did St Augustine, St Hierome, St Chrysostom, or any other learned father or doctor of that age, ever use this manner of speech, *audire missas*, "to hear mass?" Certainly this phrase was so far unacquainted and unknown in that world, that the very originals of these decrees have it not, but only have these words, *tenere missas*, "to hold mass;" as may be seen in the book of councils, noted purposely in the margin[11]. The Italians this day seem to speak far better. For of them that hear mass, and understand not what they hear, they say, *videre missas*, that is, not to hear, but "to see mass." [Con. Agath. can. 31.]

And, forsomuch as M. Harding seemeth to delight himself with this kind of speech, "to hear mass," to the intent he may make some simple body believe that the people, hearing that they understand not, are nevertheless well and devoutly occupied, and therein follow the order of the primitive church; I will also demand of him, what learned doctor or ancient father ever took hearing in that sense. Surely Christ in the godly joineth hearing and understanding both together. Thus he saith: *Audite et intelligite*: "Hear ye and understand ye." And the wise man saith: "If thou give thine ear, thou shalt receive knowledge." And God himself in the Deuteronomy saith: "Thou shalt read the words of this law in the presence of all the people of Israel, &c. that they hearing may learn, and fear the Lord your God, and may keep and fulfil all the words of this law." [To hear mass.] [Hearing.] [Matt. xv.] [Ecclus. vi.] [Deut. xxxi.]

[8 Ex Concil. Agath. c. 18. in eod. ibid. Dist. ii. can. 19. col. 1920; where we read *pascha* and *communicaverint*.]

[9 Decret. Fabian. in Concil. Stud. Labb. et Cossart. Tom. I. col. 650.]

[10 Bernard. Op. Par. 1690. De Purif. B. Mar. Serm. v. 16. Vol. II. Tom. vi. col. 961. The Benedictine editor ascribes this sermon, though with some hesitation, to Guerricus.]

[11 Concil. Agath. in Crabb. Concil. Col. Agrip. 1551. cap. 47. Tom. I. p. 618; where on *missas tenere* in the decree is a marginal note *audire*.]

To hear mass. And in the book of Kings it is written thus: *Loquere nobis Syriace, nam audimus:* "Speak to us in the Syrian tongue; for we hear it." That is to say: "For we understand it." And to that use hath God endued us with the sense of hearing,
2 Kings xviii. that thereby we might learn and attain knowledge. And therefore Aristotle calleth hearing the sense of understanding: for hearing, void of all manner
Cic. in Tusc. Quæst. understanding, is no hearing. Cicero saith: *In illis linguis quas non intelligimus, quæ sunt innumerabiles, surdi profecto sumus*[1]: "In the tongues that we understand not, which are innumerable, we are doubtless deaf, and hear nothing." By this it appeareth that the simple people, hearing mass in a strange language, is deaf, and heareth no mass at all.

De Auctoritate et Consen. Tut. et Cur. Non multum. The emperor Justinian likewise[2] saith: *Non multum interest, [utrum] abfuerit tutor, cum negotium contraheretur, an præsens ignoraverit, quale esset quod contrahebatur*[3]: "There is no great difference, whether the tutor were absent when the bargain was made (in the behoof of his pupil), or being present understood
De Verbor. et Rer. Significat. not the manner of the bargain." Likewise also in another place he saith: *Coram Titio aliquid facere jussus, non videtur præsente eo fecisse, nisi is intelligat*[4]: "He that is commanded to do a thing in the presence of Titius seemeth not to do it in his presence, unless he understand it." Upon the which words Alciat writeth
Andr. Alciat. thus: *Quid...opus erat ejus præsentiam adhibere, qui quod agatur non intelligat? Siquidem aiebat Epicharmus philosophus, mentem esse, quæ videt, non oculos. Qui igitur animo non adest, abesse videtur*[5]: "What needeth his presence, that understandeth not what is done? For the philosopher Epicharmus saith: 'It is the mind that seeth, and not the eyes.' Therefore he that is not present with his mind (to understand what is done) may be taken for absent."

I have alleged these authorities rather than other, for that in them we may see the very light and sense of nature. How then can M. Harding think he may steal away invisible under the cloke of these words, "of hearing mass?" Verily in the savour and judgment of common reason, it is as strange and as fond a
To hear mass. To see the sermon. speech to say, I will hear mass, as it is to say, I will see the sermon. For what is there in the mass that the unlearned can hear? The oblation that they imagine is an outward action or doing, and therefore is to be seen, and not to be heard: the consecration, as they use it, is spoken in silence, and may not in any wise be heard: their communion is none at all, and therefore cannot be heard.
Fol. 12. b. These be the three substantial parts, whereof, as M. Harding saith, the whole mass consisteth. How then can he say, the unlearned man heareth mass, that heareth not one part of the mass?

If by this word "mass" he understand the prayers that be said in the mass, the unlearned understandeth them not, and therefore heareth them not. Chrysostom, speaking of him that heareth the prayers in a strange unknown tongue, saith thus:
Chrysost. in 1 Cor. Hom. 35. *Tu recte oras: Spiritu scilicet concitatus sonas: sed ille nec audiens nec intelligens ea quæ dicis, parvam ex ea re utilitatem capit*[6]: "Thou prayest well; for thou soundest out words, being moved by the Spirit; but the unlearned, neither hearing nor understanding what thou sayest, hath thereby but small profit.

1 Cor. xiv. Likewise saith St Paul: *Qui loquitur lingua, non hominibus loquitur, sed Deo; nullus enim audit:* "He that speaketh with tongue speaketh not unto men, but unto God; for no man heareth him." M. Harding saith: "The unlearned heareth the mass and other prayers, yea, although he understand not one word that is spoken." But St Paul and St Chrysostom say: "The unlearned heareth not, because he understandeth not." God saith unto the wicked, and not unto the
Isai. vi. Matt. xiii. godly: "Ye shall hear with your ears, and shall not understand."

Now let us see what M. Harding gathereth out of these two councils. "Then of like (saith he), specially in small towns and villages, they had mass without the
Of like. communion of many together." "Of like" was never good argument in any schools.

Thou seest, good reader, the best that here can be had is but a guess, and, as it

[1 Cic. Tusc. Disp. Lib. v. 40; where *his*.]

[2 1565 omits *likewise*.]

[3 Corp. Jur. Civil. Amst. 1663. Digest. Lib. XXVI. Tit. viii. 14. Tom. I. p. 375.]

[4 Id. ibid. Lib. L. Tit. xvi. 209. Tom. I. p. 785.]

[5 Alciat. De Verb. Signif. Lugd. 1530. Comm. Lex ccix. p. 233; where we have *mentem eam esse, quæ videat, non autem oculos.*]

[6 Chrysost. Op. Par. 1718-38. In Epist. I. ad Cor. Hom. XXXV. Tom. X. p. 326. σὺ μὲν γὰρ καλῶς εὐχαριστεῖς, Græce.]

shall afterward appear, a very simple and a blind guess. It is a wonder to see so great a matter, and so single proofs. You have taught the people that in your mass Christ himself is presently and really sacrificed for the sins of the world; that all that ever he did or suffered for our sakes is lively expressed in the same[7]; and that all kings, princes, and other estates must needs stoop unto it. And yet was the same, for the space of six hundred years, to be found only in poor towns and villages, and that only by guess and blind conjecture, and none otherwise? Or could it never all that while once enter into any city or good town? And, being so good a thing, can no man tell us who published it and said it first?

To hear mass.

Innoc. III. in Prolog. De Offic. Miss. Durand. Lib. iv. Rupert. De Missa.

But what if the very words of these councils, whereupon M. Harding hath founded his mass, make manifest proof against his mass? The words be these: "All secular christian folk be bound to receive the communion at the least thrice in the year." This relaxation or privilege is granted only unto the secular Christians. Whereof it followeth necessarily, that all ecclesiastical persons, as priests, deacons, clerks, and others whatsoever of that sort, were not excepted, but stood still bound to receive orderly, as they had done before; and that was at all times, whensoever there was any ministration. And so by the plain words of these councils the priest received not alone; neither hath M. Harding yet found out his private mass.

But that the whole matter may the better appear, not by guess or aim, but by the very ecclesiastical order of that age, we must understand that these and such other like decrees were made, not for the greatest part of the people, that in those days used to communicate in all their assemblies, but for a few, that were negligent and haled back. For otherwise the general order doth well appear by all the ecclesiastical records of that time.

And whereas M. Harding hath taken exception of small towns and villages, which he guesseth had then the private mass, it was decreed and straitly ordered in a council holden at Gerunda in Spain, that all little churches in the country should conform themselves unto the great cathedral churches that were in cities and towns, as well for order of the communion, as also for singing, and other ministration[8]. But, by M. Harding's own grant, there was no private mass then in cathedral churches. It followeth therefore necessarily (this council of Gerunda standing in force), that there was no private mass then in towns or villages.

Con. Gerund. can. 1. De Con. Dist. 2. [Institutio Missarum, 1565.]

And that the people did then commonly receive the sacrament every Sunday, it appeareth by most certain and undoubted proofs. The council holden at Matiscona in Italy hath this canon: *Decrevimus, ut omnibus dominicis diebus altaris oblatio ab omnibus viris et mulieribus offeratur*[9]: "We have decreed that every Sunday the oblation of the altar be offered of all, both men and women." Likewise the council holden at Antisiodorum: [*Decernimus*] *ut unaquæque mulier, quando communicat, dominicalem suum habeat. Quod si non habuerit, usque in alium diem dominicum non communicet*[10]: "We decree that every woman, when she doth communicate, have her dominical. If she have it not, let her not communicate until the next Sunday." Likewise Carolus Magnus, a long while after, among other his ecclesiastical laws, writeth thus: *Ut populi oblationes sacerdotibus in ecclesia offerant, et in die dominico communicent*[11]. "That the people offer their oblations unto the priests in the church, and receive the communion upon the Sunday." By these councils and decrees it appeareth plainly, without guess or gloss, that the people used commonly in all that time, and long after, to communicate the holy mysteries every Sunday. Therefore M. Harding must yet seek further for his private mass.

Concil. Matiscon. ii. cap. 4.

Concil. Antis. cap. 42.

Lib. vi. cap. 162. Ex Cassandr.

[7 Innoc. Pont. Max. III. Op. Col. 1575. Prolog. Myst. Miss. Tom. I. p. 318.

Durand. Rat. Div. Off. Lugd. 1565. Lib. IV. cap. i. 11. fol. 87.

Rupert. De Div. Offic. 1526. Lib. I. cap. xvii. pp. 15, &c.]

[8 Institutio missarum sicut in metropolitana ecclesia agitur, ita in Dei nomine in omnibus provinciis tam ipsius missæ ordo, quam psallendi, vel ministrandi consuetudo servetur.—Ex Concil. Gerund. cap. i. in Corp. Jur. Canon. Lugd. 1624. Decret. Gratian. Decr. Tert. Pars, De Consecr. Dist. ii. can. 31. col. 1925.]

[9 Concil. Matiscon. II. can. 4. in Concil. Stud. Labb. et Cossart. Lut. Par. 1671-2. Tom. V. col. 981.]

[10 Concil. Autis. in eod. can. 42. Tom. V. col. 961; where we have *si qua non*. The dominical is there explained to be a napkin in which the eucharist was to be received. It was, however, more probably, a veil. See Bingham, Orig. Eccles. Book XV. chap. V. 7.]

[11 Ex Leg. Car. Magn. Lib. VI. cap. 162. in Cassandr. Op. Par. 1616. Liturg. cap. xxvii. p. 61; where we find *dominica*.]

M. HARDING. THE THIRTY-FIRST DIVISION.

Missa signifieth the communion.

In that council of Agatha we find a decree, made by the fathers assembled there, whereof (38) *it appeareth that priests oftentimes*[1] *said mass without others receiving with them. And thus*[3] *much it is in English: "If any man will have an*[4] *oratory or chapel abroad in the country, beside the parish churches, in which lawful and ordinary assembly is, for the rest of the holy days, that he have masses there, in consideration of weariness of the household, with just ordinance we do*[5] *permit. But at Easter, Christ's birth, Epiphany, the Ascension of our Lord, Whitsunday, and the*[5] *Nativity of St John Baptist, and if there be any other special feasts, let them not keep their masses, but in the cities and parishes. And as for the clerks, if any will do, or have their masses, at the aforesaid feasts, in chapels, unless the bishop so command or permit, let them be thrust out from communion*[6]*." By this decree we learn that then masses were commonly said in private chapels at home, at such times as the people were not accustomed to be houseled. For when by commandment and common order they received their rights, as in the aforenamed feasts, then were the priests prohibited to say masses in private oratories or chapels, without the parish churches. And hereof we may plainly understand that in such places priests customably said masses of their own and of the householders' devotion, when none of the household were disposed to receive with them. The like decree is to be found,* Concilii Arvernensis, cap. 14[7]; Concil. Constantinopol. Generalis in Trullo, cap. 31[8].

Can. 21.

The thirty-eighth untruth. For[2] there appeareth no such thing, but rather the contrary.

THE BISHOP OF SARISBURY.

This objection, being all one with the former, may the sooner be discharged by the former answer.

Missa used for the communion.

Notwithstanding, here we may learn by the way, that the old fathers, when they use this word *missa*, mean not thereby a private mass, as M. Harding would fain have it taken, but a communion. These be the words: "At Easter, Christmas, Epiphany, the Ascension of our Lord, Whitsunday, and at the Nativity of St John the Baptist, let them hold their masses, *teneant missas*, in cities or parishes." Now it is known and confessed by M. Harding, that in great parishes and cities, at their solemn feasts, they used to have general communions for all the whole people, and no private mass.

Missa used for any assembly of the people.

Notwithstanding, for avoiding of error, it is also further to be marked, that this same word *missa*, in the old writers, sometime signifieth no mass at all, neither private nor common, but only a resort and meeting of the people together in place and time of prayer; as it may sundry ways appear, and namely by old translations out of the Greek into Latin touching the same. For that the Greek writer uttereth by the word that signifieth an assembly or meeting of the people, the same doth the Latin interpreter oftentimes translate by this word *missa*. For example, Sozomenus in Greek writeth thus: ἐκκλησιάζοντος τοῦ λαοῦ[9]; that is: "When the people came together;" that doth Epiphanius translate into Latin thus: *Cum populus...congregaretur ad missas*[10]: "When the people came to mass." Likewise Socrates writeth thus in the Greek: καθ' ἑαυτοὺς ἐκκλησιάζειν[11]; that is to say: "To have a congregation or assembly by themselves;" that doth Epiphanius translate into Latin thus: *Apud seipsos missarum celebrare solennia*[12]; that is: "Among

Soz. Lib. vii. cap. v. Epiphan. in Trip. Hist. Lib. ix. cap. ix. Socr. Lib. v. cap. xv. Epiph. in Trip. Lib. vii. cap. xxxi.

[1 Oftimes, H. A. 1564.] [2 1565 omits *for.*]

[3 This, 1565, and H. A. 1564.]

[4 And, H. A. 1564.]

[5 H. A. 1564 omits *do* and *the.*]

[6 Si quis etiam extra parochias, in quibus legitimus est ordinariusque conventus, oratorium in agro habere voluerit; reliquis festivitatibus, ut ibi missas teneat propter fatigationem familiæ, justa ordinatione permittimus: pascha vero, natale Domini, epiphania, ascensionem Domini, pentecostem, et natalem S. Joannis Baptistæ, vel si qui maximi dies in festivitatibus habentur, non nisi in civitatibus aut in parochiis teneant. Clerici vero, si qui in festivitatibus, quas supra diximus, in oratoriis, nisi jubente aut permittente episcopo, missas facere aut tenere voluerint, a communione pellantur.—Concil. Agath. can. 21. in Concil. Stud. Labb. et Cossart. Lut. Par. 1671-2. Tom. IV. col. 1386.]

[7 Concil. Arvern. in eod. can. 15. Tom. IV. col. 1806.]

[8 Concil. Quinisext. in eod. can. 31. Tom. VI. col. 1155.]

[9 Sozom. in Hist. Eccles. Script. Amst. 1695-1700. Lib. VII. cap. v. p. 576.]

[10 Hist. Trip. Par. Lib. IX. cap. ix. fol. R. 8.; where we find *dum.*]

[11 Sozom. Lib. VI. cap. xv. p. 534. There appears to be an error in the reference to Socrates.]

[12 Hist. Trip. Lib. VII. cap. xxxi. fol. P. 3.; where *semetipsos.*]

themselves to celebrate the solemnity[13] of the mass." In these and many other like places, which I purposely pass by, it must needs be confessed, that *missa* cannot any way be taken for the mass, but only for an assembly of the people. For which cause all manner of common prayers many times are called *missa*, as may be seen in Cassianus, an ancient writer, and sometime scholar to St Chrysostom, *In Canone Divinarum Orationum*[14], and in Honorius and others, sufficient only to be touched. But amongst all other significations, it cannot be found that this word *missa* in any old writer was ever taken for the private mass, notwithstanding any thing by M. Harding yet alleged.

Cass. Lib. iii. cap. xii.

Missa in the old writers never taken for private mass.

Now, if a man would say that this council of Agatha, that is here brought in, by this word *missa* meant nothing else but ordinary prayers, in which signification the old writers, as I have proved, have often taken it, and so dispensed with them that dwelt far from the church, only to have such ordinary prayers at home, and for the holy communion to resort to the parish churches, perhaps M. Harding should not find much to reply against it. If he will say, I force and rack this exposition only of myself[15], without precedent, it may please him to remember that the same practice is yet continued until this day in many parishes within this realm; and that the law itself determineth a difference between *ecclesia parochialis* and *ecclesia baptismalis*[16].

16. Quæst. i. Quidam abbas.

But let this word *missa* in these decrees be taken for the mass, that is to say, for the ministration of the sacraments; yet is not M. Harding much therefore the nearer[17] to prove his purpose. For, alas! what a simple reason is this: "Upon principal holy days the priest received the sacrament solemnly in the common church, with all the whole parish; *ergo*, at other times he received alone!" Or how hangeth this argument: "At certain times all the people received together; *ergo*, at other times the priest received alone?" Or this: "The priest ministered the sacraments in a chapel; *ergo*, he said private mass?" What leadeth M. Harding thus to say? What, was there no company at all in the chapel to communicate with the priest? Verily it is provided by the decree itself, that there should be a lawful and an ordinary company[18]. And that in such companies, yea, and in men's several houses, they had the communion ministered, it is evident by the preface of the council of Gangra against the heretic Eustachius. These be the words: *In domibus conjugatorum ne orationes quidem debere celebrari persuaserunt, in tantum ut easdem fieri vetent; et oblationibus, quæ in domibus factæ fuerint, minime communicandum esse decernant*[19]: "They have persuaded the people that prayers may not be made in married men's houses; and that so far forth that they forbid any such prayers to be made, and determine that no man may communicate of the oblations made in houses." Here we have not only the communion, but also the ordinary use of the communion in private houses.

Can. 21. In quibus est legitimus ordinariusque conventus.

In Præfatione Con. Gangren.

Now let M. Harding shew us as much for the ordinary use of private mass, or for any private mass at all, and that without his surmises and guesses; and then let him hardly require subscription.

Thou mayest see, good reader, these be but very poor helps. In his former allegation he sought his mass in little towns and villages; now he hunteth for it in private men's houses, and yet cannot find it. They say, they have had the use and possession of their private mass these fifteen hundred and three-score years and more. Wherefore it is much to be marvelled, that of so long continuance of time, of so many doctors and councils, they have so slender proofs to bring for it.

Yet, for clearer answer unto M. Harding's blind guesses, it appeareth by the plain words of the same council of Agatha, that in those days the people received the holy communion together with the priest, and not the priest by himself alone. The words are these: *Lapsi in hæresim, agentes pœnitentiam, cum catechumeni egredi*

Con. Agathen. can. 60.

[13 Solemnities, 1565, 1609.]

[14 Cass. Op. Lips. 1733. De Diurn. Orat. Lib. III. cap. xi. p. 47.]

[15 Meself, 1565.]

[16 Corp. Jur. Canon. Lugd. 1624. Decret. Gratian. Decr. Sec. Pars, Caus. XVI. Quæst. i. cans. 44, 5, 6, and Gloss. cols. 1112, 3.]

[17 Neare, 1565, 1609.]

[18 See before, page 180, note 6.]

[19 Concil. Gangr. in Concil. Stud. Labb. et Cossart. Præfat. Tom. II. col. 416.]

commonentur, discedant[1]: "They that have fallen into some heresy, and do penance for the same, when the novices (that be not yet christened) be commanded to depart out of the church, let them depart also." They were commanded forth, not to the intent they should not hear mass, but that they should not communicate with the rest. For it is well known both to M. Harding, and also to others, that all such as were newly entered into the faith of Christ, but were not yet baptized, and were called *catechumeni*, after the sermon was ended, were commanded out of the church before the distribution of the holy mysteries; and so likewise were the penitents, that they should not communicate with the rest of their brethren: which is a manifest and undoubted proof that the rest of the brethren that remained still did communicate all together. And so it followeth in the same canon: *Hoc si observare voluerint, constituto tempore admittendis ad altare observatio relaxetur*[2]: "If they will do thus, after a time appointed, their penance shall be released, and they shall be admitted again unto the altar" (which was the communion-table), there to receive together with the congregation, and no more to be commanded forth. Hereunto agreeth another canon set forth in the name of Siricius, touching the same case, by these words: "Certain that after their penance have gone back again, like dogs unto their vomit, we decree that they shall join in prayer only with the faithful within the church; and that they may be present at the celebration of the mysteries, although they be not worthy; but that they be kept off from the banquet of the Lord's table, to the intent that, by this advertisement being corrected, they may both amend themselves[3], and also shew example unto others[4]." Here we may plainly see that the rest received, and those[5] that had offended sat by and received not, for example unto others. But what example could that have been, if they had abstained all together?

Epist. Decret. Siricii.

Offenders kept from the Lord's table.

M. HARDING. THE THIRTY-SECOND DIVISION.

M. Harding proveth his mass by a childish fable.

*John the Almoner began to be in estimation in the year of our Lord 610.

Now let us see what examples of the old fathers we have for the private mass. Leontius, a Greek bishop of a city in the east church, called Neapolis, writeth[6] *the life of St John the holy patriarch of Alexandria, who for his great charity was commonly called* Eleemosynarius*, *that is, the alms-giver*[7], *telleth this story, whereby it appeareth that at that time private mass was used. Though the translator, through ignorance of the time he lived in, turned this life into Latin of mean eloquence, yet, for truth's sake, I will not let to recite that which I take for my purpose, as I find it:* Malitiam reservantem quendam industrium contra alium principem audiens hic magnus Johannes, monuit eum sæpe, et suasit ad concordiam, et non potuit eum convertere ad pacem. Semel ergo ad eum mittit, et adducit eum sanctus, quasi pro republica, et facit missas in oratorio suo, nullum habens [secum] nisi ministrum suum. Cum ergo sancta benedixisset patriarcha, et orationem dominicam inchoasset, cœperunt dicere tantum tres illi, Pater noster. Et cum pervenissent ad sermonem quo dicitur, Dimitte nobis debita nostra, sicut et nos dimittimus debitoribus nostris; innuit domestico patriarcha, ut taceret. Siluit ergo et patriarcha, et remansit princeps solus dicens versum, Dimitte nobis, sicut et nos dimittimus. Et statim conversus sanctus, dicit ei mansueta voce, Vide in quam terribili voce dicas Deo, Quoniam sicut ego dimitto, ita et tu dimitte mihi. [Et] tanquam ab igne statim cruciatum ferens prædictus princeps, cecidit in faciem ad pedes sancti, dicens, Quæcunque jusseris, domine, faciet servus tuus. Et reconciliatus est inimico suo...cum omni veritate[8]. *This*

[1 In pœnitentium loco standi et orandi humilitatem ita noverint observandam, ut etiam ipsi [lapsi], cum catechumeni, &c. abscedant.—Concil. Agath. in eod. can. 60. Tom. IV. col. 1393.]

[2 Id. ibid. where *altarium.*]

[3 Themself, 1565.]

[4 De his...qui acta pœnitentia, tanquam canes ac sues ad vomitus pristinos et ad volutabra redeuntes... De quibus...id diximus decernendum, ut sola intra ecclesiam fidelibus oratione jungantur, sacræ mysteriorum celebritati, quamvis non mereantur, intersint; a dominicæ autem mensæ convivio segregentur, ut hac saltem districtione correpti, et ipsi in se sua errata castigent, et aliis exemplum tribuant, &c.—Siric. Epist. i. 5. in eod. Tom. II. col. 1019.]

[5 These, 1565.] [6 Writing, H. A. 1564.]

[7 Almose-giver, 1565, and H. A. 1564.]

[8 Leont. Vit. S. Joan. Eleemosyn. cap. xii. 73, in Bolland. Act. Sanctor. Antv. 1643. Jan. 23. Tom. II. p. 513; where we read *quemdam illustrium, ergo mittit et adducit eum sanctus, tres tantum illi, pervenisset,* and *in quali terribili hora quid dicas.*]

story soundeth thus in English: "This great patriarch John, hearing that a nobleman bare malice to another nobleman, warned him oftentimes of it, and treated with him to be at accord; but he could not bring him to be at peace. Wherefore on a day this holy father sent for the nobleman, and caused[9] *him to come to him, as though it were about some matter of the commonweal. At that time* (39) *he saith mass in his chapel, having none other body with him, but his servant. When the patriarch had consecrated the sacrament, and had begun to say our Lord's prayer, they three only began*[11] *to say, 'Our Father,' and so forth. When they were come to these*[12] *words, 'Forgive us our trespasses, as we forgive them that trespass against us,' the patriarch made a beck to his servant to hold his peace. Then the patriarch held his peace also; and the nobleman remained alone saying forth the verse, 'Forgive us as we forgive.' Then the holy father, turning himself towards*[13] *him, by and by saith with a mild voice, Consider with how terrible words thou sayest to God, that, as I forgive, so forgive thou me also. Whereat the said nobleman, as though he had felt the torment of fire, forthwith fell down on his face at the holy father's feet, saying, My lord, whatsoever thou biddest me thy servant to do, I will do it. And so he was reconciled unto his enemy without all dissembling."*

The thirty-ninth untruth. For[10] there was never private mass said in Alexandria, neither before this time, nor at any time sithence.

Here M. Jewel will grant, I trow[14]*, that this was a private mass. The place was private; the audience not public, nor common; the purpose touching the nobleman was private; the communion also private, I mean for the patriarch's part alone; for, beside that the story maketh no mention of any other communicants, he could not be assured of that nobleman to communicate with him. For whereas he could by no means before bring him to forgive his enemy, he had but a small conjecture he should bring it to pass now. And again, though he had conceived no distrust of his reconciliation upon this holy policy, yet we may doubt whether the patriarch forthwith, without further and more mature probation and examination, which St Paul in this case requireth, would have admitted him to receive our Lord's body so upon the sudden. Now for the servant, it is a strait case that so holy and so great a patriarch, and bishop of so populous a city as Alexandria was, understanding that mass could not*[15] *be celebrated without breach of Christ's institution (as M. Jewel holdeth opinion), except he have a number to communicate with him in the same place, should have none of his spiritual flock with him at so weighty a matter of conscience, but one only, and him his own household servant. He was not so simple as not to think that the servant might be letted from receiving by some sudden pang coming upon him, or with some cogitation and conscience of his own unworthiness suddenly coming to his mind. If either this, or any other let had chanced, in what case had the patriarch been then? He had been like, by M. Jewel's doctrine, to have broken Christ's institution, and so God's commandment, through another's defect, which were strange. But I judge that M. Jewel, who harpeth so many jarring arguments against private mass upon the very word "communion," will not allow that for a good and lawful*[a] *communion, where there is but one only to receive with the priest. Verily it appeareth by his sermon, that all the people ought to receive, or to be*[b] *driven out of the church. Now therefore to another example of the private mass.*

Private mass: private fable.

[1 Cor. xi. H. A. 1564.]

[a] Order was taken, that at the receiving of the communion there should be twelve persons at the least, and never under. S. Basil, *Exercitationis ad Pietatem. Sermon.* iv.[16]

[b] This decree, as it is supposed, was made by Anacletus and Calixtus immediately after the apostles' time. De Consecr. Dist. i. Episcopus[17].

THE BISHOP OF SARISBURY.

This is the best proof of all others. A short answer may well serve it: for, being but a little viewed, it is able to answer itself. There is neither authority in the tale, nor weight in the matter. The translation is peevish, and all without the compass of six hundred years.

St Augustine saith, that certain heretics in his time, named the Donatists, that they might the rather prevail in disputation against St Augustine, and other

August. Epist. 152

[9 Causeth, 1565, and H. A. 1564.]
[10 1565 omits *for*.]
[11 Begun, 1565, and H. A. 1564.]
[12 Those, H. A. 1564.]
[13 Toward, H. A. 1564.]
[14 I trow, will grant, H. A. 1564.]
[15 Can not, H. A. 1564.]
[16 See before, page 122, note 1.]
[17 Anaclet. in Corp. Jur. Canon. Lugd. 1624. Decret. Gratian. Decr. Tert. Pars, De Consecr. Dist. i. can. 59. col. 1907.]

John the Almoner.

Christians, and that the world might understand they had some company of their side, therefore, for a shew, subscribed their articles with the names of certain that were dead, and oftentimes such as never were Donatists[1]. Such a policy methinketh M. Harding hath here begun to practise. For what is this Leontius that wrote this story? Or who ever heard of his name before? I trow, he hath raised up one of the seven sleepers to help him to mass. He should have shewed us, as his manner is, what this strange doctor was; what books he wrote, where, when, in what age, and in what credit he lived. If he had said, this John the Almoner lived above six hundred years after Christ, and this Leontius, that wrote his life, a great while after that, this one circumstance would have answered the matter wholly. For, notwithstanding the rest of this tale were true, yet my assertion standeth still good, that, within the space of six hundred years after Christ, M. Harding is not able to find his private mass.

M. Harding rangeth without the compass of 600 years.

Vincentius, in his book that he calleth *Speculum*, writeth thus: "After Gregory was dead, Bonifacius ruled the church of Rome. This Bonifacius obtained of the emperor Phocas, that the church of Rome should be the head of all churches, and that because the church of Constantinople wrote itself by that title. The next year after that, Augustine, that was called the Englishman's bishop, died. The year following, John the Almoner was in great fame, at which time also Mahomet first spread his religion in Arabia[2]." The same computation of years appeareth in Freculphus, Sabellicus, Palmerius, and others. Wherefore M. Harding might well have spared this tale, as nothing else but bewraying his want of better matter, and proving that his mass is of the very age of Mahomet.

Vincent. in Spec. Lib. xxiii. cap. xvii.

An. Dom. 610.

But to leave both the advantage of the time, and also the exception against the author, let us consider the likelihood of the doing; and, if John the Almoner said this private mass in his chapel, how safely he might so do by the order of the holy canons, which to break, Damasus saith, is blasphemy against the Holy Ghost[3]. M. Harding's Leontius saith: "John the Almoner said mass in his oratory at home, being sure of no more company, but of one of his own household servants alone." But pope Soter, as it is before alleged by M. Harding, straitly commandeth that no priest presume to celebrate the sacrament "without the company of two together[4]." [a]And again, that no priest dare to minister without the company of some other priest[5]. And in the [b]council holden at Orleans it is decreed thus: "It is lawful for every christian man to have a chapel in his house; but to have mass said there it is not lawful[6]." And in the [c]council holden at Laodicea: "It is not lawful for bishops or priests to minister the oblations at home[7]." Likewise [d]pope Felix: "It is not lawful to minister the communion at home, but upon exceeding great necessity[8]." The same order was taken in the council of Acon[9], and in sundry other councils. Which decrees being so many, and so strait, it is not likely that John the Almoner, being so holy a man, would wilfully break them all without cause.

25 Quæst. i. Violatores.

De Consecr. Dist. i. Hoc quoque.

[a] De Consecr. Dist. i. Et illud.

[b] De Consecr. Dist. i. Unicuique

[c] Conc. Laodicen. cap. 58.

[d] Inter Decret. Felicis Papæ, Decret. 4.

[1 ... ita ut volentes gloriari de multitudine coepiscoporum suorum, inter aliquorum absentium nomina etiam mortui nomen insererent.—August. Op. Par. 1679-1700. Ad Donatist. Concil. Zertens. Epist. cxli. 1. Tom. II. col. 456.]

[2 Post quem [Sabinianum] Bonifacius Romanæ ecclesiæ 64. præsidet. Hic obtinuit apud Phocam imperatorem, ut ecclesia Romana caput esset omnium ecclesiarum, quia ecclesia Constantinopolitana scribebat se esse primam omnium ecclesiarum...Anno sequenti Augustinus primus Anglorum episcopus moritur...Anno sequenti Alexandriæ Joannes episcopus claruit, qui ob eximiam in Christum liberalitatem nomen Eleemosynarii habere meruit.—Vincent. Spec. Maj. Duac. 1624. Tom. IV. Lib. XXII. cap. cvii. p. 896.]

[3 Violatores canonum voluntarii graviter a sanctis patribus judicantur: et a sancto Spiritu...damnantur: quoniam blasphemare Spiritum sanctum non incongrue videntur, &c.—Damas. in Corp. Jur. Canon. Lugd. 1624. Decret. Gratian. Decr. Sec. Pars, Caus. xxv. Quæst. i. can. 5. col. 1439.]

[4 Soter in eod. ibid. Decr. Tert. Pars, De Consecr. Dist. i. can. 61. col. 1907. See before, page 172, note 2.]

[5 Ex Decret. Soter. in eod. ibid. can. 58. col. 1906. See before, page 176, note 3.]

[6 Unicuique fidelium in domo sua oratorium licet habere, et ibi orare: missas autem ibi celebrare non licet.—Ex Concil. Aurel. c. 3. in eod. ibid. can. 33. col. 1897.]

[7 Ὅτι οὐ δεῖ ἐν τοῖς οἴκοις προσφορὰς γίνεσθαι παρὰ ἐπισκόπων ἢ πρεσβυτέρων.—Concil. Laod. can. 58. in Concil. Stud. Labb. et Cossart. Lut. Par. 1671-2. Tom. I. col. 1505.]

[8 ...de missarum celebrationibus, non alicubi quam in sacratis Domino locis absque magna necessitate fieri debere, liquet omnibus, &c.—Felic. IV. Epist. i. 1. in eod. Tom. IV. col. 1651.]

[9 Concil. Aquisgr. cap. 84. in eod. Tom. VII. col. 1361.]

John the Almoner.

Neither indeed, if M. Harding will thoroughly behold the matter, shall he find here any mass spoken of at all, neither bread, nor wine, nor consecration, nor oblation, nor elevation, nor altar, nor vestiment, nor any other thing to the mass belonging.

And if we agree there was mass said there, yet may there grow another doubt, which of these three said that mass, I mean the bishop, or the gentleman, or the servant. For here is no more noted, but that they said the Lord's prayer all three together; which verily is not the manner of private mass: for there the priest, as he receiveth alone, so he saith the *Pater noster* himself alone. But in the communion, as the people said the Lord's prayer all together, as it is noted by St Gregory[10], so they received all together. Thus M. Harding bringeth a witness for the mass, that saith nothing for the mass. The law saith: *Qui mutum exhibet, nihil exhibet*[11]: "He that presenteth a dumb body presenteth no body."

Gregor. Lib. vii. Epist. 63. De Verbor. et Rer. Significat. Apud Labeon.

But he will reply, Here is the very name of the mass, *et facit missas.* And to make the more appearance, M. Harding helpeth it forth with a pretty false translation of his own. For whereas it is written in the Latin, *Cum benedixisset sancta;* he translateth it thus: "When he had consecrate the sacrament." And likewise these words, *Post finem orationum,* he translateth thus: "After he had done the prayer of consecration[12]:" notwithstanding he knew right well that in these words there is no mention at all, neither of any sacrament, nor of any consecration. And thus, *vocat ea quæ non sunt, tanquam sint:* "he calleth things that be not, as though they were;" and yet is not afraid of *lex Cornelia de falsis.* But this I trow, he himself will confess, is no sincere nor plain dealing. Yet will he say, here is the very word *missa.* It is well known that *missa* is no Greek word; and therefore Leontius, whatsoever he were, in his Greek tongue could not use it. As for the translator, seeing he was not able to write true Latin, we may well think he had simple skill in the Greek.

M. Harding corrupteth and falsifieth his translation.

Rom. iv.

But grant we there be no error in the word, yet will it not necessarily follow that *missa* in this place importeth the mass. For, as I have already proved by sundry authorities, *missa* is oftentimes used for any kind of prayer; as it may further appear by an epistle of Chromatius and Heliodorus, sent unto St Hierome, touching Gregory, the bishop of Corduba[13]; and by the words of the council of Cabilon[14]. Which thing also very well agreeth with the custom and order of the church of Alexandria at that time, whereof Nicephorus writeth thus: *Quarta hebdomadis die, et ea quæ parasceve dicitur, Alexandrini scripturas legebant, doctoribus eas interpretantibus: omniaque, quæ ad synaxin pertinent, peragebant, præter divinorum mysteriorum perceptionem. Atque eam illi antiquitus habuere consuetudinem*[15]: "At Alexandria they read the scriptures upon Wednesdays and Fridays; and the doctors or preachers expound the same. And they do all things that appertain unto the communion, saving only the receiving of the holy mysteries. And this custom there they have had of old."

Chromatius. De Con. Dist. i. Solent plures.

Nicephor. Lib. xii. cap. xxxiv.

Touching these words, *benedicere sancta,* they do no more signify the "consecration of the sacrament," as M. Harding hath translated it, than these words, *extollite manus vestras in sancta,* do signify the lifting up of hands to the sacrament. Chrysostom in his liturgy useth the same manner of speech to a far other purpose. For, after the communion is ended, and the people ready to depart forth, he writeth thus: *Sacerdos benedicit sancta, et exuit.* Here if M. Harding will take *benedicere sancta* for consecration, there must needs follow

Benedicere sancta.

Chrysost. in Liturg. ad finem.

[10 In the epistle referred to there is nothing to the point: in that following, Gregory speaks of the custom in the Greek church of all the people repeating together the Lord's prayer. Sed et dominica oratio apud Græcos ab omni populo dicitur, apud nos vero a solo sacerdote.—Gregor. Magni Papæ I. Op. Par. 1705. Epist. Lib. IX. Indict. ii. Ad Johan. Syracus. Epist. xii. [ant. Lib. VII. Epist. lxiv.] Tom. II. col. 941.]

[11 Apud Labeonem Pithanon ita scriptum est... qui mutum...exhibet, non potest videri ejus præstare præsentiam.—Corp. Jur. Civil. Amst. 1663. Digest. Lib. L. Tit. xvi. 246. Tom. I. p. 787.]

[12 See below, page 188.]

[13 Epist. Chromat. et Heliod. ad Hieron. in Usuard. Martyrol. Antv. 1583. fol. 2. 2. This epistle is not genuine, and is therefore not inserted in the editions of Jerome.]

[14 Ex Concil. Cabilon. in Corp. Jur. Canon. Decret. Gratian. Decr. Tert. Pars, Dist. i. can. 50. cols. 1902, 3.]

[15 Niceph. Callist. Eccles. Hist. Lut. Par. 1630. Lib. XII. cap. xxxiv. Tom. II. p. 296.]

John the Almoner.

a great inconvenience, that there were two consecrations in one communion; yea, and one consecration after all was ended. It may appear that Chrysostom by these words meant a solemn prayer to conclude the whole. For it followeth immediately: "O thou that art the fulfilling of the law and prophets, Christ our God, thou that hast fulfilled all the dispensation of the Father, fill our hearts with joy and gladness now and for ever[1]." This Chrysostom calleth *benedicere sancta;* and the same seemeth to be the meaning of this Leontius, whatsoever he were. And notwithstanding all these things were granted, yet is not M. Harding able thereof necessarily to import his private mass.

But saith he: "The place was private; the audience was private; the purpose was private: only one nobleman, only one servant, all was private." And further he saith: "It was a very strait case, that so holy a bishop, in so populous a town, could find no man to communicate with him, but his own servant only." Yea, doubtless, it was a very strait case, that a nobleman should be driven to help the priest to mass; a strait case for M. Harding to run to Alexandria, a thousand miles beyond all Christendom, to seek his mass, and that not in open church neither, but only in a private oratory; a strait case, that for the space of six hundred years after Christ, and more, there was not one private mass to be found in the whole church of Rome; a very strait case, that M. Harding is thus forced to leave St Augustine, St Hierome, St Chrysostom, and all other the godly-learned fathers, and to take[2] up of the dust Hippolytus, Abdias, Leontius, and other like new doctors, without name or credit, such as never were thought worthy to be alleged or named before.

Yet he forceth his guesses further: "The nobleman came unlooked for: the servant might have had some sudden pang, or some conscience of his unworthiness; and so the priest perforce must have received alone." Here to answer guess with guess, even so might the priest also himself have had some sudden pang or qualm—as indeed it is specially presumed by the law, that it may so happen[3]—or else some sudden conscience of his own unworthiness; and so had there been no mass at all. Alas! these guesses be too light in so great a matter.

De Consecr. Dist. i. Ut illud.

Here further for his pleasure he saith: "M. Jewel harpeth many jarring arguments." Of my arguments I make no vaunt: if they sound well in God's ears, they are well in tune. God be thanked, we lead not the people by aims and guesses: we rear up no new doctors: we cumber not the people's ears with lies and fables, as M. Harding doth: we bring forth neither women nor boys to prove the communion, as these men are driven to do to prove their mass.

Moreover, he saith in scorn, as his manner is, "that we would have all the people, that will not receive, to be driven out of the church." O M. Harding, how long will you thus wilfully pervert the ways of the Lord? You know, this is neither the doctrine, nor the practice of our church. Howbeit, the ancient doctors have both taught so, and also practised the same. Anacletus saith: "After the consecration is ended, let all receive, unless they will be thrust from the church[4]." And Calixtus saith further: "For so is it appointed by the apostles, and so is it observed in the church of Rome[5]."

De Consecr. Dist. i. Episcopus.

De Consecr. Dist. ii. Peracta.

Now saith M. Harding: "The place was private; *ergo*, there was a private mass." A child may soon see that this reason hath no hold. For touching that the place was private, St Gregory saith thus of one Cassius, the bishop of Narnium: "He said mass" (which is, he ministered the communion) "in an oratory within his palace, and with his own hand he gave the body of the Lord and peace unto them all[6]." The like hereof we may see in the preface before the council of Gangra[7]. And in the tripartite story it is written thus: "Gregory

Gregor. Hom. 37. In Evang.

In Præfatione in Concilium. Gangr.

Hist. Trip. Lib. ix. cap. viii.

[1 Liturg. Sanct. Patr. Par. 1560. Chrysost. Miss. fol. 22.]

[2 Rake, 1565, 1609.]

[3 Ex Decret. Soter. in Corp. Jur. Canon. Lugd. 1624. Decr. Tert. Pars, De Consecr. Dist. i. can. 58. col. 1906.]

[4 Anaclet. Epist. i. in eod. ibid. can. 59. col. 1907.]

[5 Id. [al. Calixt.] in eod. ibid. Dist. ii. can. 10. col. 1917.]

[6 ...in Episcopii oratorio missas fecit, et manu sua corpus dominicum pacemque omnibus tribuit.—Gregor. Magni Papæ I. Op. Par. 1705. In Evang. Lib. II. Hom. xxxvii. 9. Tom. I. col. 1633.]

[7 Concil. Gangr. in Concil. Stud. Labb. et Cossart. Lut. Par. 1671-2. Præfat. Tom. II. col. 416.]

Nazianzene at Constantinople in a little oratory, *συναγωγὰς ἐποιεῖτο*, made assemblies of the people[8]." Here we see the action was common, and a full communion ministered, notwithstanding the place were private. John the Almoner.

Again he saith, There were but three;

Ergo, But one did receive.

This reason holdeth as the former.

Consider now, gentle reader, how aptly M. Harding answereth to the purpose. I demand the authority of St Augustine, St Hierome, or some other catholic ancient father: he answereth me with a childish fable. I demand of the usage of the open church: he answereth me with a private oratory, as though at that time there had been no churches built. I demand what was done in the face and sight of the people: he answereth me what he supposeth was done in a corner. I demand of him undoubted truth and certainty: he answereth me by conjecture and blind guess.

I believe he would not willingly have hindered his own cause. If he could have found better matter, doubtless he would have brought it forth. Is this the antiquity, is this the universality, that they so much talk and glory of? Is this the common consent of all the world?

Thus then, gentle reader, standeth my answer to this tale. First, that it was forbidden by many decrees, to minister the sacrament in private houses, and therefore unlikely that John the[9] Almoner, being a godly man, would presume to do the contrary.

Secondly, that this word *missa*, used here by the rude and utterly unlearned interpreter, doth not necessarily import the mass.

Thirdly, that M. Harding, the better to furnish out the matter, hath violently, and of purpose, falsified the translation.

Fourthly, that, notwithstanding here were granted the celebration of the sacrament, yet it cannot be forced thereof that the priest received alone.

Fifthly, that, although this were proved a private mass, yet hath M. Harding utterly misreckoned himself, and so gotten nothing. For it was without the compass of six hundred years.

Last of all, hereunto I add, that the place, where these things are imagined to be done, was ill chosen, and very unlikely to serve this purpose. For M. Harding is not able to prove, that in the city of Alexandria was ever any one private mass said, either before that time, or ever sithence.

M. HARDING. THE THIRTY-THIRD DIVISION.

Amphilochius, bishop of Iconium, the head city of Lycaonia, to whom St Basil dedicated his book De Spiritu Sancto, *and another book intitled* Ascetica, *writing the life of St Basil, or rather the miracles through God's power by him wrought, which he calleth " worthy of record, true, and great miracles," specially such as were not by the three most worthy men, Gregory Nazianzene, Gregory Nyssene, and holy Ephrem, in their epitaphical or funeral treatises, before mentioned; amongst*[10] *other things, reporteth a notable story, wherein we have a clear testimony of a private mass. And for the thing that the story sheweth, as much as for any other, of the same Amphilochius he is called* cœlestium virtutum collocutor, et angelicorum ordinum comminister; *" a talker together with the heavenly powers, and a fellow-servant with orders of angels." The story is this: The holy bishop Basil besought God in his prayers, he would give him grace, wisdom, and understanding, so as he might offer the sacrifice of Christ's blood-shedding,* propriis sermonibus, *with prayers and service of his own making; and that, the better to achieve that purpose, the Holy Ghost might come upon him. After six days he was in a trance, for cause of the Holy Ghost's coming. When the seventh day was come, he began to minister unto God, that is to wit, he said mass every day. After certain*[11] *time thus spent, through faith and prayer, he began to write with his own hand,* mysteria ministrationis, *the mass, or the service of the mass. On a night*

A fabulous tale under the name of Amphilochius.

[*Memorabilia, et vera ac magna miracula, in præfatione.* H. A. 1564.]

[8 Gregorius Nazianzenus...in parvo oratorio sacra celebrabat.—Hist. Trip. Par. Lib. IX. cap. viii. fol. R. 7. See also Socr. in Hist. Eccles. Script. Amst. 1695-1700. Lib. v. cap. vii. p. 216.]

[9 1565 omits *the*.] [10 Among, H. A. 1564.]

[11 After a certain, 1565, and H. A. 1564.]

our Lord came unto him in a vision with the apostles, and laid bread to be consecrated on the holy altar; and, stirring up Basil, said unto him: Secundum postulationem tuam, repleatur os tuum laude, &c.: "*According to thy request, let thy mouth be filled with praise, that with thine own words thou mayest offer up to me sacrifice." He, not able to abide the vision with his eyes, rose up with trembling, and going to the holy altar, began to say that he had written in paper thus:* Repleatur os meum laude, et hymnum dicat gloriæ tuæ, Domine Deus, qui creasti nos, et adduxisti in vitam hanc, et ceteras orationes sancti ministerii: "*Let my mouth be filled with praise, to utter an hymn to thy glory, Lord God, which hast created us, and brought us into this life;" and so forth, the other prayers of the mass. It followeth in the story:* Et post finem orationum, exaltavit panem, sine intermissione orans, et dicens, Respice, Domine Jesu Christe, &c.: "*After that he had done the prayers of consecration, he lifted up the bread, praying continually, and saying, Look upon us, Lord Jesus Christ, out of thy holy tabernacle, and come to sanctify us, that sittest above with thy Father, and art here present invisibly with us; vouchsafe with thy mighty hand to deliver to us, and by us to all thy people,* sancta sanctis, *thy holy things to the holy. The people answered, One holy, one our Lord Jesus Christ, with the Holy Ghost, in glory of God the Father. Amen."*

The people answered; yet was there no people there.

Now let us consider what followeth, pertaining most to our purpose: Et dividens panem in tres partes, unam quidem communicavit timore multo, alteram autem reservavit consepelire secum, tertiam vero imposuit columbæ aureæ, quæ pependit super altare[1]: "*He divided the bread into three parts, of which he[2] received one at his communion with great fear and reverence; the other he reserved, that it might be buried with him; and the third part he caused to be put in a golden pix that was hanged up over the altar, made in the[3] form and shape of a dove." After this, a little before the end of this treatise, it followeth how that St Basil, at the hour that he departed out of this life, received that part of the host himself, which he had purposed to have interred with him in his grave, and immediately, as he lay in his bed, gave thanks to God, and rendered up the ghost[4].*

The burying of the sacrament.

Seven years after he had seen this vision.

That this was a private mass, no man can deny. Basil received the sacrament alone; for there was no earthly creature in that church with him. The people that answered him were such as Christ brought with him. And that all this was no dream, but a thing by the will of God done indeed, though in a vision, as it pleased Christ to exhibit, Amphilochius plainly witnesseth; declaring how that one Eubulus, and other[5] the chief of that clergy, standing before the gates of the church, whiles this was in doing, saw lights within the church, and men clothed in white, and heard a voice of people glorifying God, and beheld Basil standing at the altar, and for this cause at his coming forth fell down prostrate at his feet[6]. Here M. Jewel and his consacramentaries do stagger, I doubt not; for grant to a private mass they will not, whatsoever be brought for proof of it. And therefore some doubt to avoid this authority must be devised. But whereof they should doubt, verily I see not. If they doubt any thing of the bringing of the bread and other necessaries to serve for consecration of the host, let them also doubt of the bread and flesh that Elias had in the pond of Carith. Let them doubt of the bread and pot of water he had under the juniper-tree in Bersabee. Let them doubt of the pot of pottage brought to Daniel, for his dinner, from Jewry into the cave of lions at Babylon, by Abacuk the prophet. But perhaps they doubt of the authority of Amphilochius that wrote this story. It may well be that they would be glad to discredit that worthy bishop. For he was that vigilant pastor and good governor of the church, who first with Letoius, bishop of Melite, and with Flavianus, bishop of Antioch, overthrew and utterly vanquished the heretics called Messaliani, otherwise Euchitæ[7], the first parents of the sacramentary heresy; whose opinion was, that the holy eucharisty, that is, the blessed sacrament of the altar, doth neither good nor evil, neither profiteth ought nor hurteth.

The forcing of this fable.

Christ and his apostles bring bread from heaven.

[1 *Kings* xvii. 1 *Kings* xix. *B. & Dr.* 1565, 1609, and H. A. 1564.]

[*Theodor. in Hist. Eccles. Lib.* iv. *cap.* xi. 1565, 1609, and H. A. 1564.]

[εὐχῖται. i. *precatores*, H. A. 1564.]

Rather the first parents of hypocritical and idle monks.

[1 Amphiloch. Op. Par. 1644. In Vit. S. Basil. pp. 175, 6.]

[2 Be, H. A. 1564.]

[3 H. A. 1564 omits *the*.]

[4 Id. ibid. p. 224.]

[5 Others, H. A. 1564.]

[6 Id. ibid. pp. 176, 7.]

[7 Theodor. in Hist. Eccles. Script. Amst. 1695-1700. Lib. iv. cap. xi. pp. 163, 4.]

Even as our sacramentaries do ascribe all to faith only, and (40) *call the most worthiest sacrament none other but tokening-bread, which of itself hath no divine efficacy or operation. Therefore I wonder the less, I say, if they would Amphilochius his authority to be diminished. But for this I will match them with great Basil, who esteemed him so much, who loved him so entirely, who honoured him so highly, with the dedication of so excellent works. I will join them also with the learned bishop Theodoretus, who seemeth to give him so sovereign praise, as to any other bishop he writeth his stories of, never naming him without preface of great honour, now calling him* admirandum, "*the wonderful;*" *at another time* sapientissimum, "*the most wise;*" *and most commonly* laudatissimum, "*most praise-worthy*[9]." *If they doubt of Basil himself, whether he were a man worthy to obtain by his prayer of God such a vision, it may please them to peruse what Gregorius Nyssenus, what holy Ephrem of Syria, and specially what Gregory Nazianzene wrote of him; which two Gregories be not afraid to compare him with Elias, with Moses, with St Paul, and with whosoever was greatest, and for virtue of most renown. Whereby without all envy he hath obtained of all the posterity to be called* magnus, *Basil the great, much more for desert of virtue and learning, than those other for merit of chivalry, the great Charles, the great Pompey, the great Alexander. If they deny the whole treatise, and say, that it was never of Amphilochius' doing, that were a shift indeed, but yet the worst of all and furthest*[10] *from reason and custom of the best learned; and much like the fact of king Alexander, who, being desirous to undo the fatal knot at Gordium, a town in Phrygia, hearing that the empire of the world was boded by an old prophecy to him that could unknit it, not finding out the ends of the strings, nor perceiving by what means he could do it, drew forth his sword and hewed it in pieces, supplying want of skill with wilful violence. For the authority of this*[11] *treatise this much I can say. Beside that it is set forth in a book of certain holy men's lives printed in Colen, and beside very great likelihood appearing in the treatise itself; it is to be seen in the library of St Nazarius in the city of Verona in Italy, written in vellum, for three hundred years past, bearing the name of Amphilochius, bishop of Iconium.*

[The fortieth untruth. For[8] we never called it so. The glorious painting of a shadow.]

[*Theodor. Lib.* v. *Eccles. Hist. c. xvi.* 1565, 1609, and H. A. 1564.]

[*In Monodia.* 1565, 1609, and H. A. 1564.]

[Set abroad lately with other fables.]

THE BISHOP OF SARISBURY.

If this serve not the turn, nothing, I trow, will ever serve. The authority of St Basil and Amphilochius is so great, the matter so clear, the wonder so strange, the antiquity so ancient, the fable so likely, the dream so plain: the original hereof at Verona in Italy, in the library of Nazarius, kept as a relique, fair written in vellum, above three hundred years ago, Basil a worthy bishop, Ephrem a holy father, Amphilochius a man that had conference with the heavenly powers. Not one shew or circumstance left out that may serve to win credit. And what should need so much ado, if there were not some suspicion in the matter? He that never saw this book, nor knoweth the contents thereof, happily by such circumstances and colours may be deceived.

But I myself[12] have had this unknown doctor in my poor library these twenty years and more, written likewise in vellum, as true, as fair, and of as good record in all respects as that other of Verona, indeed not under the name of Amphilochius, but no doubt[13] very ancient, as it may soon appear. For the same author, in the same book, hath written also the life of Thomas Becket, who lived at the least seven hundred years after that Amphilochius, this writer, was dead. Therefore that story, written by him of one that was to come so many hundred years after him, must needs be a prophecy, and not a story.

The very names of old godly fathers are worthy of much honour. But, as it is well known, many vain tales have been covered under the name of old fathers. The life of St Basil hath been set forth fully and faithfully by sundry old worthy writers, as by his own brother Gregorius[14] Nyssenus, by his dear friend

[8 1565 omits *for*.]
[9 Id. in eod. Lib. v. cap. xvi. p. 218.]
[10 Farthest, H. A. 1564.]
[11 His, H. A. 1564.]
[12 Meself, 1565.]
[13 Doubts, 1565.]
[14 Georgius, 1611.]

The fable of Amphilochius.

Gregory Nazianzene, by Gregorius Presbyter, by Socrates, by Theodoretus, by Sozomenus, by Nicephorus, touched also in divers places by Chrysostom. And notwithstanding of late years he that wrote *Vitas Patrum,* and Jacobus de Voragine, and Vincentius *in Speculo,* who seem to entitle this book by the name of Amphilochius, have furnished the same with many unsavoury vain tales; yet was there none of them so impudent, once to make any mention of this peevish fable of M. Harding's mass.

But forsomuch as the glorious name of this holy father is here brought in to bear witness to these matters, and that in the night season in a dream, and a vision, with the visible appearance of Christ and his apostles; and the great[1] stay of M. Harding's cause resteth hereupon, and many are amazed with the strangeness hereof, and many are led away as though it were matter of good truth; and specially, for that the book is not commonly to be had, and it would be chargeable to send to Verona into Italy for a copy; suffer me therefore, good christian reader, to give thee some taste of the same, that thou mayest be able of thyself[2] to judge further, and to see by what doctors M. Harding proveth his private mass.

The contents of M. Harding's Amphilochius. Tert. Lib. v. contra Marcionem.

To pass over the idle talk and conference with devils, the visions, the dreams, the fables, and other fantastical vanities, which are the whole contents and substance of this new book, Tertullian hath a good discreet saying: *Furibus aliqua semper excidere solent in indicium*[3]*:* "The thief evermore leaveth somewhat behind him that he may be known by." Let us therefore compare M. Harding's Amphilochius with Socrates, Sozomenus, Gregory Nazianzene, Gregory Nyssen, and other old writers of approved credit, that have of purpose written St Basil's life.

Socrat. Lib. iv. cap. xxi. Sozom. Lib. vi. cap. xvii. Nazianz. in Vit. Basil. Gregor. Presbyter in Vit. Nazianzeni.

Socrates and Sozomenus say that Basil in his youth was Libanius' scholar: M. Harding's Amphilochius saith Basil was Libanius' school-fellow[4].

Nazianzene and Gregorius Presbyter say that Basil, continuing at Cæsarea, was well acquainted with Eusebius the bishop there, before he went into Pontus: M. Harding's Amphilochius saith, that at his return from Pontus, which was soon after, Eusebius knew him not, neither had ever spoken with him or seen him before[5].

M. Harding's Amphilochius saith Basil was bishop of Cæsarea in the time of the emperor Julianus, whereupon also are founded a great many fond fables:

Nazianz. in Vit. Basil.

Nazianzene, his nearest friend, saith, he was chosen bishop there a long while after, in the time of the emperor Valens, and was not bishop there at all during the whole time of Julianus[6].

M. Harding's Amphilochius telleth a long tale, how that St Mercury, being then dead, and a saint in heaven, at the commandment of our lady, took his own spear out of his chapel where it was kept, and went out with the same into the field, and slew the emperor Julian, and that the same spear was found bloody afterward: Nazianzene, Socrates, Theodoretus, and Sozomenus say it could never be known by whom he was slain[7].

Nazianz. in Orat. 2. contra Julian. Socrat. Lib. iii. cap. xviii. Theod. Lib. iii. cap. xxv. Sozom. Lib. vi. cap. ii. Theod. Lib. iii. cap. ii. Sozom. Lib. vi. cap. xvi.

M. Harding's Amphilochius saith, Basil foretold the death of Julian: Theodoretus saith, it was one Julianus Sabba that foretold it, and not St Basil[8].

M. Harding's Amphilochius saith, the emperor Valens yielded and gave place unto Basil: Sozomenus saith, the emperor continued still his purpose, and would not yield[9].

[1 Greatest, 1565.] [2 Theeself, 1565.]

[3 ...furibus solet aliquid excidere de præda in indicium.—Tertul. Op. Lut. 1641. Adv. Marcion. Lib. v. 4. p. 582.]

[4 Socrat. in Hist. Eccles. Script. Amst. 1695-1700. Lib. IV. cap. xxvi. p. 198.
Sozom. in eod. Lib. VI. cap. xvii. p. 535.
Amphiloch. Op. Par. 1644. In Vit. S. Basil. p. 158.]

[5 Gregor. Nazianz. Op. Par. 1778-1840. Vit. Gregor. Tom. I. p. cxxxviii. Orat. xliii. 28. Tom. I. pp. 792, 3.
Amphiloch. Op. In Vit. S. Basil. p. 174. But in this edition Leontius is substituted for Eusebius.]

[6 Amphiloch. Op. In Vit. S. Basil. pp. 175, 9, &c.
Gregor. Nazianz. Op. Orat. xliii. 31, 7. Tom. I. pp. 794, 5, 9.]

[7 Amphiloch. Op. In Vit. S. Basil. pp. 181, 2.
Gregor. Nazianz. Op. Sec. in Julian. Orat. v. 13. Tom. I. pp. 155, 6.
Socrat. Lib. III. cap. xxi. p. 160.
Theodor. Lib. III. cap. xxv. p. 146.
Sozom. Lib. VI. cap. ii. p. 518.]

[8 Amphiloch. Op. In Vit. S. Basil. pp. 182, 3.
Theodor. Lib. VI. cap. xxiv. pp. 145, 6.]

[9 The account given by Amphilochius, in Vit. S.

The fable of Amphilochius.

M. Harding's Amphilochius saith, Nazianzenus was present at St Basil's burial: Nazianzene himself, that ought to know it best, saith he came afterward, and was not present[10].

Nazianz. in Monodia. Gregor. Presbyter in Vita Nazianz.

Gregorius Presbyter saith, Nazianzene came a great while after that Basil was buried. M. Harding's Amphilochius is so impudent that he saith, Nazianzenus came in all haste, and saw the blessed body, and fell upon it when it was buried[11]. Whereby it seemeth that this Amphilochius was not very wise nor circumspect in his talk. For if Nazianzene saw St Basil's body, how was it buried? If it were buried, how could he see it?

Again, M. Harding's Amphilochius saith, Gregory Nazianzene ruled the apostolic see for the space of twelve years[12]. By the apostolic see he must needs mean either Rome or Constantinople. If he mean Rome, Nazianzene was never bishop there: if he mean Constantinople, where indeed he was bishop, yet was that never called the apostolic see; and so, whatsoever he meant, he made a lie.

Now judge thou indifferently, good christian reader, whether Amphilochius the bishop of Iconium, St Basil's special and nearest friend, writing of him that he knew so well, could possibly so many ways be deceived. If M. Harding had known him better, I think he would have spared this authority. Howbeit Ulpian saith: *Etiam monstra et portentosi partus prosunt*[13]: "Even monsters and ill-shapen children may go for children."

De Verbor. et Rer. Significat. Quæret aliquis.

To come to the matter, M. Harding's Amphilochius thus telleth on his tale: Basil, saith he, being once made bishop, besought God that he might offer up the unbloody sacrifice with his own words: he fell in a trance, came again to himself, and so ministered every day. On a certain night Christ with his apostles came down to him from heaven, brought bread with him, awoke Basil, and bade him up and offer the sacrifice. Up he arose, was straight at the altar, said his prayers as he had written them in his paper, lifted up the bread, laid it down again, brake it in three parts, received one, reserved another to be buried with him, hung up the third in a golden dove. And all this was done, Christ and his apostles being still present, who came purposely from heaven to help Basil to say[14] mass.

We may now the better believe Homer, that Jupiter with his gods went down sometime for his pleasure to banquet in Ethiopia; or that an [a]angel evermore ministered the sacrament unto Marcus that holy monk[15]; or that [b]angels came from heaven to consecrate Amphilochius bishop of Iconium[16]; [c]or that the Holy Ghost was sent from heaven to Remigius with a box of holy oil[17]; [d]or that, when holy Arnulphus began matins at midnight, and said, *Domine labia*, &c. and all his monks were asleep, a number of angels supplied the lack, and answered him, *Et os meum annuntiabit laudem tuam*[18].

[a] Sozom. Lib. vi. cap. 29. [b] Niceph. Lib. xi. cap. 20. [c] Paulus Æmilius. Gaguinus. [d] Henricus Herfordien. cap. 49.

M. Harding falsifieth his own fable.

But M. Harding layeth on more weight, and forceth this fable to his purpose; and, albeit in the whole tale there is not once the name of mass, yet is he content to take pains cunningly to falsify the text, and seven times together to translate it only by the name of mass. For with him *offerre sacrificium* is "to say mass;" likewise *ministrare Deo* is "to say mass;" and *ministerium ministrationis* is "the service of the mass." For as Midas, whatsoever he touched, had power to

---

Basil. pp. 185, &c. does not much differ from that of Sozomen. But perhaps the story pp. 206, &c. may be meant: there, however, the emperor's mind is said to have remained obstinate.

Sozom. Lib. VI. cap. xvi. pp. 534, 5. Sozomen admits ἀμέλει ἀποθανόντος μὲν τοῦ υἱέος, οὐκέτι αὐτὸν [Βασίλειον] ἠνώχλησεν.]

[10 Amphiloch. In Vit. S. Basil. pp. 224, 5.

Gregor. Nazianz. Op. Epist. lxxvi. Tom. II. p. 65.]

[11 Ibid. Vit. Gregor. Tom. I. p. clvii.

Amphiloch. In Vit. S. Basil. p. 224.]

[12 Id. ibid. p. 158.]

[13 Et magis est ut hæc [portentosum vel monstrosum] quoque parentibus prosint: &c.—Ulpian. in Cod. Jur. Civil. Amst. 1663. Digest. Lib. L. Tit. xvi. 135. Tom. I. p. 782.]

[14 1565 and 1609 omit *say*.]

[15 Sozom. Lib. VI. cap. xxix. p. 553.]

[16 Niceph. Callist. Eccles. Hist. Lut. Par. 1630. Lib. XI. cap. xx. Tom. II. p. 138.]

[17 Gaguin. De Orig. et Gest. Franc. Lugd. 1497. Lib. I. fol. 2. 2. Paul. Æmyl. De Reb. Gest. Franc. Par. 1544. Lib. I. fol. 6.]

[18 Henricus Herfordiensis, or de Hervordia, wrote Chronicon Generale, which, it would seem, has never been printed entire. See Oudin. Comm. de Script. Eccles. Ant. Lips. 1722. Tom. III. cols. 973-5.]

The fable of Amphilochius.

turn the same into gold; so M. Harding, whatsoever he toucheth, hath a special power to turn the same into his mass.

But let us a little view the circumstances, and weigh the likelihoods of this matter. Basil besought God that he might make the sacrifice with his own words. And shall we think he had more fancy to his own words than he had to the words of Christ? He awoke, stood up, and suddenly was at the altar at midnight. What, shall we think he was the sexton there, or lay all night, like Eli or Samuel, in the church; and yet, being so famous a bishop, had no man to attend upon him?

The golden dove.

He divided the bread, and laid up the third part of it "in a golden dove" that hung over the altar: and yet, by his own tale, his golden dove then was not yet ready made. For it followeth immediately in the next lines: "After Basil had done these things, and had communed with Eubulus and others, the next day he sent for a goldsmith, and made a dove of pure gold." It behoveth a liar to be mindful what he saith. If this dove were made before, how was it made afterward? If it were not made before, how could it then hang over the altar? Or how could Basil put his bread in it before it was made? And to what end was that bread so kept in the dove? And wherein, or where was the other third part kept, that Basil thus reserved purposely to be buried, or as M. Harding termeth it, to be interred with him? Wherein M. Harding's Amphilochius both uttereth words of manifest blasphemy, and also shamefully belieth that holy father, and doth him great and open injury. It was but fondly done by St Benet, as Gregory reporteth of him, to cause the sacrament to be laid upon a dead man's breast[1]; and likewise it was as fondly done of others, that ministered the sacrament unto the dead, and gave it into their mouths; which thing is namely forbidden by the council of Carthage[2].

Dialogorum, Lib. ii. cap. 24.

Conc. Carthag. iii. can. 6.

The burying of the sacrament.

But the sacrament being, as M. Harding would have the world believe, no bread, nor wine, and so no sacrament at all, but only the natural and real body of Christ, it were horrible blasphemy to bury it, and as a dead thing to lay it in the grave.

Further, as this doctor saith, St Basil had this dream or vision, and reserved this portion of the sacrament, immediately after he was made bishop of Cæsarea; and after that, as it is clear by other stories, continued bishop there seven years at the least. Now judge thou, gentle reader, what kind of bread that would have been, after seven years keeping, to be given to a sick man in his death-bed. So many absurdities and contrarieties may easily be found in the very shew and sight of this childish fable.

The sacrament reserved seven years.

Yet saith M. Harding: "Here doth M. Jewel with his consacramentaries stagger, and knoweth not what to say." Yea verily, M. Harding, we are astonied to consider the wonderful and just judgments of God, that any man should so wilfully renounce God's known truth, and be thus utterly given over to follow lies; or so much to presume of his own wit and eloquence, that he thinketh himself able to over-rule and lead all the world with a fable. As for axes or instruments to hew up this knot, we need none. Every child may see the ends. It openeth and looseth itself. Christ cometh with his apostles down from heaven to hear mass. The apostles sing mass by note; Christ playeth the clerk's part, and attendeth the priest; Amphilochius writeth Thomas Becket's life seven hundred years before he was born; St Basil lieth all night in the vestry; he hangeth up a golden dove first, and maketh it afterward: he keepeth a portion of the sacrament seven years together; he receiveth the same in his death-bed, and is buried, or (as M. Harding delighteth rather to say) is interred with it; besides a multitude of other like follies and fables. This is that wonderful Gordius' fatal knot, that can never be opened without an axe.

The true Amphilochius.

And although M. Harding's Amphilochius were a manifest and an impudent liar, yet I confess, and it is well known, that the true Amphilochius of Iconium was a godly and a worthy bishop, stout and courageous in suppressing the Messalians,

[[1] Gregor. Magni Papæ I. Op. Par. 1705. Dial. Lib. II. cap. xxiv. Tom. II. col. 256.]

[[2] Concil. Carth. III. cap. 6. in Concil. Stud. Labb. et Cossart. Lut. Par. 1671-2. Tom. II. col. 1168.]

the first parents, as M. Harding here saith, of the sacramentary heresies[3]. Howbeit the rest of his brethren, and he himself elsewhere saith, Berengarius was the first father of that heresy. For afterward in the fifth article he writeth thus: "Berengarius first began openly to sow the wicked seed of the sacramentary heresy." So it appeareth that M. Harding neither is resolved in the heresy, nor can tell when it first began. Notwithstanding, the seed that he called[4] wicked was first sown, neither by the Messalians, nor by Berengarius, but by Christ himself and by his apostles.

The true Amphilochius.

M. Harding much forgetteth himself.

Indeed the Messalians, whom Amphilochius suppressed, were heretics, the fathers of many idle swarms yet remaining in the world. They were named in Greek ψαλλιανοὶ, or εὐχίται, of their long counterfeit praying. St Augustine saith: "They prayed so much, or so fast, that a man that knew it not would not think it possible. They thought it unlawful for a monk to labour for his living, and therefore became monks, that they might be free from labour[5]." Thus far St Augustine.

The first fathers of idle monks.

Aug. ad Quod-vult-Deum.

Theodoretus saith: *Orationi vacantes, maximam diei partem dormiunt*[6]: "They give themselves to contemplation, and sleep the most part of the day." St Augustine saith: *Tanquam conservatricem evangelii prædicant pigritiam*[7]: "They highly commend sloth, as if it were the maintenance of the gospel." For these causes Amphilochius, being the archbishop of Lycaonia, and Flavianus the bishop of Antioch, withstood them, and drave them from their dioceses; and Letoius, being an earnest and a zealous man, utterly consumed and burnt their monasteries, or rather, as Theodoretus termeth it, their dens of thieves[8].

Theod. Hæret. Fabular. Lib. iv.

De Opere Monach. cap. xxii.

Theodoretus, Lib. iv. cap. xi.

μᾶλλον δὲ ληστρικὰ σπήλαια.

These were the Messalians, not the open maintainers of any error touching the mystical supper; neither doth either St Augustine or Epiphanius report any such matter of them.

Indeed Theodoretus saith, they had certain secret instructions among themselves, that sacraments did at all neither further nor hinder; meaning thereby as well the sacrament of baptism as the sacrament of Christ's body; into which error they were led, for that they gave all perfection and holiness to their prayers, and in respect thereof refused the communion of their brethren.

But, whereas M. Harding saith, this is also our doctrine, and that we teach the people the sacrament of Christ's body to be nothing else but tokening-bread; his own conscience knoweth it is a slander, and will be required of him in the day of the Lord. Our doctrine is, that the sacraments of Christ unto the godly are the instruments of the Holy Ghost, and unto the wicked are increase of further judgment. Like as St Augustine also saith: *Sacramentum...sumitur quibusdam ad vitam, quibusdam ad exitium. Res vero ipsa, cujus est sacramentum, omni homini ad vitam, nulli ad mortem, quicunque ejus particeps fuerit*[9]: "The sacrament is received of some unto life, of some unto destruction. But the thing itself (that is, the body of Christ), whereof it is a sacrament, is received of all men to life, and of no man to destruction, whosoever be partaker of it." Here St Augustine maketh great and manifest difference between the body of Christ and the sacrament of the same. And this is not the Messalian monks' heresy, but St Augustine's and the catholic faith.

August. in Joh. Tract. 26.

"Now, to deny that ever this was Amphilochius' doing, that (saith M. Harding) were a shift indeed." Thus he is bold to say, I believe, for that he never considered the whole book. For otherwise he might soon have seen it is but a rude gathering out of the tripartite story, in many places word by word, without discretion, with interlacing of lies and fables of his own, without shame. Neither can M. Harding justly prove that ever Amphilochius wrote St Basil's life. For, notwithstanding a clause in Nazianzene's *Monodia* touching the same, as it is now

Amphilochius never wrote St Basil's life.

[[3] Heresy, 1565, 1609.]

[[4] Calleth, 1565, 1609.]

[[5] Tantum enim orant, ut eis qui hoc de illis audiunt incredibile videatur...Dicuntur Euchitæ opinari, monachis non licere sustentandæ vitæ suæ causa aliquid operari, atque ita se ipsos monachos profiteri, ut omnino ab operibus vacent.—August. Op. Par. 1679-1700. Lib. De Hæres. 57. Tom. VIII. col. 19.]

[[6] Theodor. Op. Lut. Par. 1642-84. Hæret. Fab. Lib. IV. cap. xi. Tom. IV. p. 243.]

[[7] August. Op. De Op. Monach. cap. xxii. 26. Tom. VI. col. 493; where we have *prædicantes*.]

[[8] Theodor. in Hist. Eccles. Script. Amst. 1695-1700. Lib. IV. cap. xi. pp. 163, 4; where σπήλαια ληστρικά.]

[[9] August. Op. In Johan. Evang. cap. vi. Tractat. xxvi. 15. Tom. III. Pars II. col. 500; where we read *sacramentum est*, and *nulli ad exitium*.]

The fable of Amphilochius. extant in Latin, yet must he understand that the said clause was thrust in by Volaterane the translator, a man that hath perverted and altered a great part of that book, as by conference to any learned man may appear, and is not to be found in the Greek[1]. But false translation maketh no proof.

But, "This book is found at Verona in Italy:" he might as well have said, at Falsona. "It is written in vellum." This is but a simple allegation. A calf's skin is no sufficient warrant of truth: lies have been written in letters of gold.

The allegation of the book called ἀσκητικὰ, which M. Harding saith St Basil dedicated to Amphilochius, rather hindereth, than furthereth[2] his matter. For Nazianzenus, reckoning up all St Basil's books, passeth that book by, as none of his[3]. And Sozomenus saith, it was ever doubted of, and thought of many never to be written by St Basil, but rather by an heretic named Eustathius[4], a book full of superstition and wicked doctrine, and namely condemned by the council of Gangra[5].

Nazianz. in Monodia. Sozom. Lib. iii. cap. xiii.

Præfat. in Concil. Gangrense.

Eubulus.

But, "Eubulus is witness of these things:" he peered in at the crevice[6], and espied what was done. Certainly a meet witness for such a matter. I have heard sometime a man without a name; but here we have found a name without a man. M. Harding's Amphilochius ever maketh this Eubulus the chiefest man about St Basil in all his affairs; yet neither doth Basil in any of all of[7] his epistles, or other works, nor Nazianzene, nor Socrates, nor Sozomenus, nor Gregorius Nyssenus, nor Gregorius Presbyter, once make mention of any such. Thus much for the credit of M. Harding's Amphilochius.

But, if all this were good record and matter of truth, yet were it but a miracle, but a vision, and perhaps but a dream, but one man's fact, but once done, not in the day-time, but at midnight, and that without company, and without witness. If this Eubulus, which doubtless was nobody, had not espied it, nobody should ever have heard of it.

Now, as touching the very mass, that St Basil said indeed, we may soon learn the order of it without any dream or vision. St Basil himself, in the liturgy that beareth his name, plainly declareth the whole order in this sort: "The priest speaketh thus aloud unto the people: the whole people maketh answer: 'One is holy, one is the Lord, one Jesus Christ in the glory of the Father'." "Then," saith St Basil, "the quire singeth the communion; and so they communicate all together[8]."

Liturgia Basilii.

Here may we clearly see the very order and usage of St Basil's mass. Here was no sole receiving, no single communion, no private mass: the whole people prayed aloud together with the priest, and received the communion all together.

And what if M. Harding's own Amphilochius, notwithstanding all his fables, say the same? Can any man desire more substantial witness? Verily his words be plain, that there was people in the church with St Basil, and received the communion at his hand. For thus saith St Basil, even as it is here written by this Amphilochius: "Vouchsafe, O Lord, to give unto us, and by us unto all the people, holy things unto the holy: the people answereth, One is holy, &c." I shuffle not these words, but leave them even as this Amphilochius hath written them, and M. Harding himself hath here alleged them.

St Basil's mass is a communion, and no mass.

Now mark, good reader, what help M. Harding hath here found for his private mass. M. Harding's own Amphilochius saith, "The holy things were given unto all the people:" M. Harding saith, "St Basil received alone." M. Harding's own

[1 Basil. Op. Lat. Basil. 1540. Monod. Gregor. Nazianz. per Raph. Volater. conv. p. 1. The names of Gregory Nyssen and Amphilochius are here mentioned as biographers of Basil, for which there is no kind of warrant in the Greek text, which merely says: Εἰ δὲ τοσοῦτον ἀπήντηκα τοῦ καιροῦ δεύτερος, καὶ μετὰ τοσούτους ἐπαινέτας, κ. τ. λ.—Gregor. Nazianz. Op. Par. 1778-1840. Orat. xliii. 2. Tom. I. p. 771.]

[2 Further, 1611.]

[3 Gregor. Nazianz. Op. Orat. xliii. 67. Tom. I. pp. 821, 2.]

[4 Sozom. in Hist. Eccles. Script. Amst. 1695-1700. Lib. III. cap. xiv. p. 424.]

[5 The ascetic rules and practices for which Eustatius was censured are enumerated Concil. Gangr. Præfat. in. Concil. Stud. Labb. et Cossart. Lut. Par. 1671-2. Tom. II. cols. 413-6.]

[6 Creavie, 1565.] [7 1565 omits *of*.]

[8 *Et voce magna.* Sancta sanctis. *Populus respondet.* Unus sanctus, unus Dominus, unus Jesus Christus in gloria Dei Patris cum Spiritu Sancto. Amen. *Et cantant cantores communionem: et sic communicant omnes.*—Liturg. Sanct. Patr. Par. 1560. S. Basil. Miss. fol. 13. The Greek text differs.]

Amphilochius saith, "There was people in the church:" M. Harding saith, "There was no people there."

The fable of Amphilochius.

"But this people," saith M. Harding, "was Christ and his apostles." No doubt, a strange kind of people. And Basil, being so notable a man for his eloquence, was not able to utter his mind in his own mother-tongue, but said, "All the people;" and yet saw no people there at all; and, "Give this to all," and yet knew there was nobody there to give unto. Thus may we conclude, according to M. Harding's own construction, that that people was no people; that Christ, no Christ; that Eubulus, no Eubulus; that Amphilochius, no Amphilochius; that Basil, no Basil; that dove, no dove; and that mass, no mass at all. Such be the proofs of private mass.

M. Harding and his Amphilochius cannot agree.

M. HARDING. THE THIRTY-FOURTH DIVISION.

Now one place more for proof of private mass, at the winding up of this matter, and then an end of this article. (41) *This place is twice found in Chrysostom, in an homily upon the Epistle to the Ephesians, and more plainly in an homily* Ad Populum Antiochenum, *where he hath these very words:* Multam video rerum inæqualitatem. In aliis quidem temporibus cum puri frequenter sitis, non acceditis: in pascha vero licet sit aliquid a vobis patratum acceditis. O consuetudinem! O præsumptionem! Sacrificium frustra quotidianum. Incassum assistimus altari. Nullus qui communicetur[10]: *"I see great inequality of things among you. At other times, when as for the most[11] part ye are in clean life, ye come not to receive your rights. But at Easter, though ye have done some things[12] amiss, yet ye come. O what a custom is this! O what a presumption is this! The daily sacrifice is offered in vain. We stand at the altar for nought. There is not one that will[13] be houseled."*

The forty-first untruth. For[9] private mass is never found in Chrysostom.

Homil. 61. *ad Popul. Antioch.*

Here is to be noted, whereas Chrysostom saith, the daily sacrifice was celebrated in vain, and the priests stood at the altar in vain; it is not to be understanded of the sacrifice in itself, as though it were in vain and frustrate; but this is to be referred to the people: it was in vain for their part that should have received their communion with the priests, who waited daily for them, and cried out as the manner was, Sancta sanctis, *"Holy things for the holy;" and after that they had received the bread themselves, shewing the chalice to the people, said:* Cum timore Dei, [et fide,] et dilectione accedite[14]: *"Come ye up to receive with the fear of God, with faith, and charity." But all was in vain.* (42) *For none came; so cold was their devotion in that behalf. Now if Chrysostom had cause to complain of the people's slackness in coming to the communion, in that great and populous city of Antioch, where the scriptures were daily expounded and* (43) *preached, where discipline and good order was more straitly exacted, where in so great number some of likelihood were of more devotion than others; what is to be thought of many little towns and villages through the world, where little preaching was heard, where discipline slacked, where, the number of the faithful[15] being small, and they occupied altogether in worldly affairs, few gave good example[16] of devotion to others? Doubtless in such places was much less resort of the people at the mass-time to receive the sacrament with their priests. And whereas, lest this place might seem plainly to avouch the having of mass without a number communicating with the bishop or priest, for avoiding of this authority the gospellers answer, by way of conjecture, that in Chrysostom's time the priests and deacons communicated together daily with the party that offered the sacrifice, though none of the people did; we tell them that this poor shift will not serve their purpose. For though they say some sufficient number ever communicated with him that celebrated the daily sacrifice in that great and famous church of Antioch, where many priests and deacons were,*

[*A true declaration of Chrysostom's place,* H. A. 1564.]

[*In Missa Chrysost.* H. A. 1564.]

The forty-second untruth. For[9] there came many both of the people and also of the clergy.

The forty-third untruth. For[9] there was no such daily preaching, as shall appear.

M. Harding seeketh up his mass in little towns and villages.

[9 1565 omits *for*.]

[10 Chrysost. Op. Lat. Basil. 1547. Ad Pop. Antioch. Hom. lxi. Tom. V. col. 403. Op. Par. 1718-38. In Epist. ad Ephes. cap. i. Hom. iii. Tom. XI. pp. 22, 3.]

[11 More, H. A. 1564.]

[12 Thing, H. A. 1564.]

[13 Woll, H. A. 1564.]

[14 Chrysost. Op. Par. 1718-38. Liturg. Tom. XII. pp. 795, 7.]

[15 Faithfuls, 1565, and H. A. 1564.]

[16 Ensample, H. A. 1564.]

which neither, being denied, they shall never be able to prove; what may be said or thought of many thousand other less[1] *churches through the world, where the priest that said mass had not*[2] *in readiness a sufficient number of other priests and deacons to receive with him, so to make up a communion? Of such churches it must be said that either the sacrifice ceased, and that was not done which* (44) *Christ commanded to be done in his remembrance, which is not to be granted; or that the memory of our Lord's death was oftentimes celebrated of the priests in the daily oblation, without tarrying for others to communicate with them, and so had these churches private masses, as the churches now-a-days have. Now to conclude, of this most evident place of Chrysostom, every child is able to make an invincible argument against M. Jewel for the private mass, as they call it, in this sort. By report of Chrysostom, the sacrifice in his time was daily offered, that is to say, the mass was celebrated; but many times nobody came to communicate sacramentally with the priests,* (45) *as it is before proved;* ergo, *there were masses done without other receiving the sacrament with the priests. And then further;* ergo, *private masses in Chrysostom's days were not strange: and then yet one step further, there to stay;* ergo, *M. Jewel, according to his own promise and offer, must yield, subscribe, and recant*—unto a guess.

The forty-fourth untruth. For[3] Christ commanded no such daily sacrifice.

Private mass proved by a simple collection.

The forty-fifth untruth. For[3] this is not yet proved.

THE BISHOP OF SARISBURY.

Now is M. Harding come (as he saith) to the winding up of his clew; meaning thereby, as may be thought, that the substance of all that he hath alleged hitherto hangeth only by a twined thread.

This conjecture is taken out of certain words of Chrysostom; and the whole force thereof standeth only upon this word *nemo*, which is in English "nobody." Chrysostom's words be these: "We do daily offer the sacrifice," or, as M. Harding delighteth rather to say, "we do daily say mass; and there is nobody to communicate[4]; *ergo*," saith he, "Chrysostom received alone." And so have we without question a plain private mass.

Chrysost. ad Populum Antiochen. Hom. 61.

Here would I first know, whether M. Harding will rest upon the bare words of Chrysostom, or rather qualify them somewhat, and take his meaning. If he press the words so precisely as he seemeth to do, then did not Chrysostom himself communicate. For he was some body; and the plain words be, "Nobody doth communicate." By which words doubtless Chrysostom himself is excluded as well as others. And so there was no sole receiving, nor any receiving at all, and therefore no private mass.

If he will rather take Chrysostom's meaning, it appeareth, his purpose was to rebuke the negligence of the people, for that, of so populous a city, they came to the holy communion in so small companies; which companies he, in a vehemency of speech, by an exaggeration in respect of the whole, calleth "nobody." The like manner of speech is used also sometimes in the scriptures. St John saith of Christ: *Testimonium ejus nemo accipit:* not for that nobody at all received his witness; for his disciples and many others received it; but for that of a great multitude very few received it. In like phrase Chrysostom himself saith otherwhere: *Nemo divina sapit, nemo contemnit ea quæ in terra sunt, nemo attendit ad cœlum*[5]*:* "Nobody savoureth godly things: nobody despiseth the things of this world: nobody hath regard to heaven." In these words M. Harding must needs confess that Chrysostom, instead of few, by heat of speech and by way of comparison, said, "nobody."

John iii.

Chrysost. ad Hebræos, Hom. 12.

And albeit this only answer, compared with the manner of Chrysostom's eloquence, which commonly is hot and fervent, and with the common practice of the church then, may suffice a man more desirous of truth than of contention; yet I have good hope it may be proved, notwithstanding M. Harding's *nemo*, that Chrysostom neither was alone, nor could be alone at the holy ministration, and therefore could say no private mass. For, if the whole company of the lay-people would have forsaken him, yet had he company sufficient of the priests and

[[1] Lesser, 1565, and H. A. 1564.]
[[2] Had not always, H. A. 1564.]
[[3] 1565 omits *for*.]
[[4] See before, page 195.]
[[5] Chrysost. Op. Par. 1718-38. In Epist. ad Hebr. cap. vii. Hom. xii. Tom. XII. p. 126.]

deacons, and others of the quire. And, if the whole quire would have forsaken him, yet had he company sufficient of the lay-people, as it may be clearly proved.

That there was then a great number to serve in the ministry, it may diversly well appear.

Ignatius calleth *presbyterium*, "the sacred college, the council and company of the bishop[6]."

Ignat. ad Trall. τὸ ἱερὸν σύστημα.

Chrysostom himself in his liturgy saith thus: "The deacons bring the dishes with the holy bread unto the holy altar: the rest carry the holy cups[7]." By which words appeareth both a number of the ministry, and also provision for them that would receive.

Chrysost. in Lit.

Cornelius writeth that in the church of Rome there were forty and six priests, seven deacons, seven subdeacons, forty and two acolutes, exorcists, readers, and other officers of the church, fifty and two, widows, and other afflicted people that there were relieved, a thousand five hundred[8].

Epist. Corn. ad Fab. Antioch. ex Euseb. Lib. vi. cap. xlii.

Nazianzene complaineth of the number of the clergy in his time, that they seemed to be more than the rest of the people[9]. And therefore the emperor Justinian afterward thought it needful to abridge the number, and to make a law, that in the great church at Constantinople, where Chrysostom was bishop, there should not be above the number of threescore priests, one hundred deacons, forty women, fourscore and ten subdeacons, one hundred and ten readers, and five and twenty singers[10]. Hereby we may see that Chrysostom, being at Antioch, in so populous a city, although he had none of the lay-people with him, yet could not be utterly left alone.

Nazianz. in Apologet. καὶ εἰσὶ σχεδόν τι πλείους κατ' ἀριθμὸν, ἢ ὁπόσων ἄρχουσι.

In Authent. Collat. prima, Tit. Ut determinatus sit numerus clericorum.

Now, if we say that some of these priests, deacons, or other, communicated with the bishop, "I tell them," saith M. Harding, boldly, and with a solemn countenance, which must needs make good proof, "this is but a poor shift, and will not serve their purpose." But if it be true, it is rich enough: if it agree with Chrysostom's own meaning, it is no shift; and therefore sufficiently served[11] our purpose.

And because he sitteth so fast upon the bare words, and reposeth all his hope in *nemo*, if we list to cavil in like sort, we might soon find warrant sufficient to answer this matter, even in the very plain words of Chrysostom. For thus they lie: *Frustra assistimus altari:* "In vain we stand at the altar." "We stand," saith he, and not "I stand;" and therefore includeth a number, and not one alone. Howbeit our shifts are not so poor: we need not to take hold of so small advantages.

It is proved[12] by the canons of the apostles, "that, if any bishop, or priest, or deacon, or any other of the quire, after the oblation is made, do not receive, unless he shew some reasonable cause of his so doing, that he stand excommunicate[13]." There was then neither such number of altars, nor such chevisance[14] of masses, as hath been sithence. All the priests received together at one communion. The like law in the church of Rome was afterward renewed by pope Anacletus[15].

Canon. Apost. can. 9. ἐκ τοῦ καταλόγου ἱερατικοῦ.

De Consecr. Dist. 1. Episcopus.

The council of Nice decreeth thus: *Accipiant diaconi secundum ordinem, post presbyteros, ab episcopis, vel a presbytero communionem*[16]: "Let the deacons in order, after the priests, receive of the bishops, or of the priest, the holy communion."

Concil. Nicen. can. 14.

Likewise the council of Carthage: *Accipiant* [*diaconi*]...*ex ordine eucharistiam post presbyteros, eis dante...episcopo, vel presbytero*[17]: "Let the deacons receive

Concil. Carthag. vi. cap 18.

[6 Τί δὲ πρεσβυτέριον ἀλλ' ἢ σύστημα ἱερὸν, σύμβουλοι καὶ συνεδρευταὶ τοῦ ἐπισκόπου; Ignat. Op. Ed. Voss. 2da, Lond. 1680. p. 162. Epist. ad Trall. Interpolat.]

[7 Diaconi discos cum panibus sanctis deferunt ad sanctum altare: reliqui portant sanctos calices.—Ord. Lit. B. Joan. Chrysost. in Cassandr. Op. Par. 1616. Liturg. cap. vii. p. 18. Different copies of the liturgy ascribed to Chrysostom differ exceedingly.]

[8 Euseb. in Hist. Eccles. Script. Amst. 1695-1700. Lib. VI. cap. xliii. p. 198.]

[9 Gregor. Nazianz. Op. Par. 1778-1840. Orat. ii. 8. Tom. I. p. 15.]

[10 Corp. Jur. Civil. Amst. 1663. Authent. Collat. I. Tit. iii. Novell. iii. cap. 1. Tom. II. p. 7.]

[11 Serveth, 1565.] [12 Provided, 1565, 1609.]

[13 Canon. Apost. 8. in Concil. Stud. Labb. et Cossart. Lut. Par. 1671-2. Tom. I. col. 25.]

[14 Chevisance: enterprise, achievement, bargain.]

[15 Anaclet. in Corp. Jur. Canon. Lugd. 1624. Decret. Gratian. Decr. Tert. Pars, De Consecr. Dist. i. can. 59, col. 1907.]

[16 Concil. Nicen. can. 18. in Concil. Stud. Labb. et Cossart. Tom. II. col. 37.]

[17 Concil. Carthag. VI. in eod. cap. 18. Tom. II. col. 1598; where *aut* for *vel*.]

the communion in order after the priests, either the bishop or the priest ministering it."

Concil. Laod. can. 59. So the council of Laodicea: "It is lawful only for the priests of the church to enter into the place where the altar standeth, and there to communicate[1]."

Concil. Tolet. iv. cap. 17. So the council of Toledo: "Let the priests and deacons communicate before the altar, the clerks in the quire, and the people without the quire[2]."

Nic. Cusan. ad Cler. et Lit. Bohem. Nicolaus Cusanus, writing unto the clergy and learned of Bohemia, hath these words: *Hoc est ... singulariter attendendum, quod sacerdotes nunquam sine diacono celebrabant: et in omni missa diaconus de manu sacerdotis accipit eucharistiam sub specie panis, et sacerdos de manu diaconi calicem*[3]: "This thing is specially to be noted, that the priest did never celebrate without a deacon; and that in every mass the deacon received the sacrament in the kind of bread at the priest's hand, and the priest the cup at the deacon's hand."

But what needeth much proof, in a case that is so plain? Chrysostom himself, in the liturgy that commonly beareth his name, followeth the same order. Chrysost. in Lit. "After that the priests have received," saith he, "the archdeacon commandeth the deacons to come forth; and they, so coming, receive as the priests did before[4]." This was the very order of Chrysostom's mass, touching the clergy, and that by the witness of Chrysostom himself.

Now let M. Harding judge uprightly, whether these shifts be so poor as he would make them.

But if the whole clergy had been so negligent, that not one of them all, being so many, and so straitly charged, would have communicated with the priest, as M. Harding seemeth to condemn them all, only upon his own word, without any evidence; yet let us see whether M. Harding's *nemo* were able of necessity to shut out all the rest of the people.

Chrysostom in divers places seemeth to divide the whole multitude into three sorts, whereof some were "penitent," some "negligent," and some "devout." The "penitent" were commanded away, and might not communicate: the "negligent" some time departed of themselves, and would not communicate: the "devout" remained, and received together. Now that the "devout" remained still with Chrysostom the whole time of the holy mysteries, it is plain by the very same place that M. Harding here allegeth for his purpose. For thus Chrysostom saith unto Chrysost. ad Popul. Antioch. Hom. 61. the people: "Thou art come into the church, and hast sung praises unto God with the rest, and hast confessed thyself[5] to be one of the worthy, in that thou departedst not forth with the unworthy[6]." By these words he sheweth that some were worthy, and some unworthy; that the unworthy departed, and the worthy remained. And again in the same homily he saith: "The deacon, standing on high, calleth some to the communion, and putteth off some; thrusteth out some, and bringeth in some[6]." Chrysostom saith: "Some are called," and "some are brought in," to receive with the priest. Where then is now M. Harding's *nemo?* Verily, if there were "some people" with the priest, then was there no place for "nobody." If "nobody" received, then is it not true that Chrysostom saith, that "some received."

Here of a false principle M. Harding, as his wont is, guesseth out the like conclusion: "If there were so few communicants in that populous city of Antioch, where the scriptures were daily expounded and preached, then it is likely in country churches there were none at all." This argument hangeth only by likelihood, as

[1 ... καὶ μόνοις ἐξὸν εἶναι τοῖς ἱερατικοῖς εἰσιέναι εἰς τὸ θυσιαστήριον, καὶ κοινωνεῖν.—Concil. Laod. in eod. can. 19. Tom. I. col. 1500.]

[2 ... sacerdos et Levita ante altare communicent, in choro clerus, extra chorum populus.—Concil. Tolet. IV. in eod. cap. 18. Tom. V. col. 1711.]

[3 Nic. de Cusa Op. Basil. 1565. Ad Cler. et Lit. Bohem. Epist. vii. pp. 854, 5; where we find *celebrarunt, et in omni missa diaconus de manu diaconi calicem, ut glo. in cap. pervenit* 93. *distin. ponit causam, et ita præceptum fuit servari.*]

[4 Chrysost. Miss. in Lit. Sanct. Patr. Par. 1560. fol. 21. See before, page 116, note 3.]

[5 Theeself, 1565.]

[6 Ita scilicet et tu venisti, cecinisti Deo laudem, cum omnibus es confessus de dignis esse, cum indignis non secedendo.—Chrysost. Op. Lat. Basil. 1547. Ad Pop. Antioch. Hom. lxi. Tom. V. col. 403. ... stans erectus ... hos quidem vocat, hos autem arcet ... hos quidem pellit et ejicit, hos autem introducit et assistit.—Id. ibid. col. 405. Op. Par. 1718-38. In Epist. ad Ephes. cap. i. Hom. iii. Tom. XI. p. 23. In Epist. ad Hebr. cap. x. Hom. xvii. Tom. XII. pp. 170, 1.]

do the rest of his making; and being set in order, it standeth thus: There was no private mass in the great city of Antioch; *ergo*, there was private mass in the country. Surely, good reader, this is a very country argument, whatsoever it seem to M. Harding.

And further, whereas to advance the city, and to abase the country, he saith, "The people in cities were daily taught by open sermons;" herein he must needs be content that his guess give place unto the truth. For Chrysostom himself saith far otherwise. Thus he speaketh unto the people in the city: *Dum per hebdomadam semel vocamus vos, et ignavi estis, et alii quidem non advenitis, alii autem præsentes sine lucro disceditis; quid non faceretis, si nos hoc continuo faceremus*[7]? "Whereas, being called by us but once in the week, yet ye be slothful, and some of you come not at all, and other some, being present, depart without profit; what would ye not do, if we should call you every day?" I note not this for that I mislike with daily preaching, but for that untruth so boldly presumed should not pass untouched. Chrysost. in Act. Hom.45. Idem in Matt. Hom. 5.

Yet saith M. Harding: "In small country churches, either the priest let cease the daily sacrifice, or else he received alone. But the daily sacrifice ceased not; for then that had been left undone that Christ commanded to be done; *ergo*, there was private mass." O M. Harding, is it not possible your doctrine may stand without lies? So many untruths in so little room, without shame of the world, without fear of God? Where did Christ ever command you to make your sacrifice? By what commission? By what words? Where did Christ will you to do it every day? Where did Christ ever call it the daily sacrifice? Or where ever learned you that the remembrance of Christ's death pertaineth more to the priest than to the people? And if your mass be that sacrifice, who ever commanded your priest to say your daily mass? What law, what decree, what decretal, what legantine, what provincial? Or what priest ever was there that said it daily?

Peccham in his provincial was never so strait. He saith no more but thus: *Statuimus,...ut quilibet sacerdos, quem canonica necessitas non excusat, conficiat omni hebdomada saltem semel*[8]: "We ordain that every priest, unless he be excused by some canonical necessity, do consecrate every week once at the least." There is odds between once a week and once a day. And Linwood, writing upon the same, allegeth these words of St Augustine's: *Quotidie eucharistiæ communicare nec laudo nec vitupero*[9]: "As for receiving the communion every day, I neither praise it nor dispraise it." Innocentius the third noteth, that there were priests in his time that would scarcely say mass at four times in the year[10]. And Thomas of Aquine thinketh it sufficient for a priest, that is not charged with cure, to say mass only upon principal feasts[11]. It is also written in *Vitis Patrum*, that a certain holy man, being made priest, would notwithstanding never say mass while he lived. Yet was there none of these ever charged with foreslowing[12] or ceasing the daily sacrifice, or leaving undone that thing that Christ had commanded to be done. De Celebr. Miss. can. Altissimus. De Con. Dist. 2. Quotidie. Extr. de Celebr. Miss. Dolentes. In Summ. Parte ult. Quæst.lxxxii. Art. 1.

Concerning the priest's sole receiving, which is grounded only upon itself, without further proof, verily I see no cause but that Nicolaus de Cusa, being a cardinal of Rome, ought to carry as good credit herein as M. Harding, with all his guesses. He saith, and willeth his words to be specially noted, as it is before touched, that in those days the priest did never receive without the deacon[13]. Yet hath M. Harding a certain surmise by himself, that the priests in the country received alone. Nicol. de Cusa, ad Cler. et Lit. Bohem.

[7 Id. In Act. Apost. Hom. xliv. Tom. IX. p. 335. See also In Matt. Hom. v. Tom. VII. p. 72.]

[8 Provincial. seu Const. Angl. Antw. 1525. Lib. III. De Celebr. Miss. fol. 168.]

[9 Id. ibid.; where *communionem accipere*. See August. Op. Par. 1679-1700. De Eccles. Dogm. cap. xxiii. Tom. VIII. Append. col. 78.]

[10 Sunt et alii, qui missarum solemnia vix celebrant quater in anno.—Innoc. III. in Corp. Jur. Canon. Lugd. 1624. Decretal. Greg. IX. Lib. III. Tit. xli. cap. 9. col. 1377.]

[11 ... unde sacerdoti, etiam si non habeat curam animarum, non licet omnino a celebratione cessare, sed saltem videtur, quod celebrare teneatur in præcipuis festis, &c.—Thom. Aquinat. Op. Venet. 1595. Summ. Theol. Pars III. Quæst. lxxxii. Art. 10. Tom. XII. fol. 276.]

[12 Foreslowing: putting off.]

[13 Nic. de Cusa Op. Ad Cler. et Lit. Bohem. Epist. vii. pp. 854, 5. See before, page 198, note 3.]

But what a wonderful case is this! The mass that we must needs believe is so ancient, so universal, so catholic, so holy, so glorious, cannot be found, neither in churches, nor in chapels, nor in secret oratories, nor in private houses, in town or city; but must be sought out in some petty parish in the country, and that by conjecture only, and by guess, and by such records as directly condemn the whole order of the mass, and will suffer no man to be present thereat, but only such as will receive!

Chrysost. ad Ephes. Hom. 3.

For thus saith Chrysostom: "If thou stand by and do not communicate, thou art malapert, thou art shameless, thou art impudent. Thine eyes be unworthy the sight hereof, unworthy be thine ears. O, thou wilt say, I am unworthy to be partaker of the holy mysteries. Then art thou unworthy to be partaker of the prayers: thou mayest no more stand here than a heathen that never was christened." And, touching himself, he saith: "In vain we come to offer the daily sacrifice: in vain we stand at the altar[1]:" meaning thereby, as may appear, that, if he said private mass for lack of company, it was in vain. Here M. Harding, seeing that his mass, even by his own authority, is shrewdly cracked, and left for vain, assayeth to salve it as well as he may.

"The mass," saith he, "is not in vain in itself, but unto the people that will not come." This is a gloss beside the text; yet let us take it as it were true. But if hearing of the mass be a thing pleasant unto God, and meritorious unto the people; if Christ be there offered indeed for the sins of the world; if the priest alone may receive for all the rest; if it be sufficient for the people to communicate spiritually, as M. Harding hath avouched; then is not the saying of the mass in vain, no, not unto the people; no, although they never would communicate. Chrysostom saith, "It is in vain:" M. Harding saith, "It is not in vain." And yet, to see a greater contradiction, M. Harding himself in this place saith: "It is in vain unto the people." And yet the same M. Harding hath said before: "It is commanded by councils: it is sufficient for the people to communicate in spirit: it is not in vain unto the people."

Division ix. fol. 13. b.[2]

If M. Harding will stand unto the authority of Chrysostom, let him not dissemble, but speak plainly unto the people, as Chrysostom spake. Let him say to them that come to hear his mass: "If ye receive not, ye are shameless, ye are impudent, ye are not worthy to be partakers of the common prayers: depart ye from the church; ye have no more place here than Turks and heathens; your eyes be unworthy to see these things, unworthy be your ears; our masses cannot profit you; they are not meritorious for you; they please not God; they provoke his anger; they are all in vain." This is Chrysostom's sense and plain meaning; and this is a fair winding up of M. Harding's clew.

Now let us examine this invincible argument, wherewithal every child, as M. Harding vaunteth, is able to prove the private mass.

The major is this: "The sacrifice in Chrysostom's time was daily offered."

The minor is this: "But many times no man came to communicate with the priest."

The conclusion: *ergo*, "There was private mass."

Here the major is apparent false; the minor proved at adventures, only by blind guess, and so not proved at all: therefore the conclusion must needs follow after as it may. Unless M. Harding look better to it, I trow it will prove but a childish argument.

Concil. Constan. vi. can. 52. Aug. Tract. 26. Basil. ad Cæsar.

As for the major, it is plain by the sixth council of Constantinople[3], by St Augustine upon St John[4], by St Basil *Ad Cæsariam Patriciam*[5], by the epistle of the council of Alexandria in the defence of Macarius[6], and by the council

[1 ... εἰκῇ θυσία καθημερινὴ, εἰκῇ παρεστήκαμεν τῷ θυσιαστηρίῳ...πᾶς γὰρ ὁ μὴ μετέχων τῶν μυστηρίων ἀναίσχυντος καὶ ἰταμῶς ἑστηκώς...ἀνάξιός εἰμι, φησίν· οὐκοῦν καὶ τῆς κοινωνίας ἐκείνης τῆς ἐν ταῖς εὐχαῖς...ἀνάξιοι καὶ ὀφθαλμοὶ τῶν θεαμάτων τούτων, ἀνάξιαι καὶ ἀκοαί.—Chrysost. Op. Par. 1718-38. In Epist. ad Ephes. cap. i. Hom. iii. Tom. XI. pp. 23, 4.]

[2 See before, pages 126, 7.]

[3 Concil. Quinisext. can. 52. in Concil. Stud. Labb. et Cossart. Lut. Par. 1671-2. Tom. VI. cols. 1166, 7.]

[4 August. Op. Par. 1679-1700. In Johan. Evang. cap. vi. Tractat. xxvi. 15. Tom. III. Pars II. col. 500.]

[5 Basil. Op. Par. 1721-30. Ad Cæsar. Epist. xciii. Tom. III. p. 186.]

[6 Epist. Synod. Concil. Alex. in Concil. Stud. Labb. et Cossart. Tom. II. col. 548.]

holden at Laodicea[7], and by sundry other authorities to that purpose before alleged, that the sacrifice was not daily offered, as M. Harding imagineth. Communion.

Touching the minor, it is not proved, but hangeth, as I have said, only by guess. M. Harding himself saw that this is but[8] a slender proof: "Chrysostom ministered every day; *ergo*, he received alone;" and therefore he sought further to find his single communion in the country. But Chrysostom saith: "There is nobody to communicate." By this it may appear, as I have already said, that Chrysostom himself did not communicate, unless we will say Chrysostom was "nobody," and so "nobody" received alone, and "nobody" himself said M. Harding's private mass. And therefore "nobody" may come forth and justly require me to subscribe. Thus, the major being false, the minor not proved, the conclusion not following, thou seest, good christian reader, what invincible force M. Harding hath brought to reprove[9] his mass. Concil. Laod. can. 49.

But because he seemeth to set somewhat by the winding up of his clew, it shall not be from the purpose to unwind it again, and to lay it abroad, and to consider the stuffing of it, and to see how closely and handsomely it is wound together.

1. First, there is not one thread of the holy scriptures in all this clew, but the plain example of Christ and his apostles quite refused.

2. Secondly, the private mass is founded upon the negligence, and, as M. Harding calleth it, the undevotion of the people.

3. Thirdly, there is a way devised, how two priests, saying their masses in divers countries, may communicate together in breaking bread, be the distance between them never so great; and that without any manner warrant of scripture or doctor.

4. Fourthly, lay-people, women, sick folks, and boys, that received or ministered the sacrament alone, are brought in for this purpose, as though it had been lawful then for women or boys to say mass.

5. Fifthly, because St Ambrose, St Augustine, St Hierome, St Chrysostom, St Basil, and such others would not serve, there is brought in a great number of petty doctors, all of doubtful credit, and many of them long sithence misliked and condemned by the church.

6. Sixthly, the matter is made good by visions, dreams, and fables.

7. Seventhly, there are alleged canons of councils not extant in any council, gathered without great judgment by one Gratian, and yet none of them neither proving nor once naming the private mass.

8. Eighthly, because M. Harding could not find his mass in the whole church of Rome, within the space of six hundred years after Christ, he hath therefore made search at Alexandria in Egypt, at Antioch in Syria, at Cæsarea in Cappadocia, a thousand miles beyond the limits of all Christendom, where as was never private mass said, neither then, nor before that time, nor never sithence.

9. Ninthly, for that he stood in despair of cathedral and other like great churches, he hath sought out chapels, cells, oratories, and private houses; and, because he had no hope to speed in towns or cities, he hath sought out the little churches in the country.

10. Tenthly, notwithstanding all this inquiry, he hath not yet found neither the name of private mass, nor any priest that ever ministered and received alone.

11. To be short, the whole substance of his proofs hangeth only upon his own surmise, without any certainty or appearance of truth.

These be the contents of M. Harding's clew, and thus substantially hath he proved the antiquity and universality of his mass.

Now, good reader, to give thee only a taste of some part that may be said of our side; first, it is apparent that Christ our Saviour, at his last supper, ministered the holy communion, and no private mass, and bade his disciples to do the same in his remembrance.

Likewise St Paul willed the Corinthians one to wait and tarry for another in the holy ministration, and to conform themselves to Christ's example. Where-

[7 Concil. Laod. in eod. can. 49. Tom. I. col. 1505.] [8 Put, 1611.] [9 Prove, 1565, 1609.]

Communion.

Hieron. in 1 Cor. xi. Ambros. 1 Cor. xi.

upon St Hierome saith, as it is before alleged: "The Lord's supper must be common unto all; for the Lord delivered the sacraments equally unto all the disciples that were present[1]." And St Ambrose likewise, expounding these words, *Invicem exspectate*, "Wait one for another," saith thus: "That the oblation of many may be celebrate together, and may be ministered unto all[2]."

Can. Apost. can. 9. De Con. Dist. 2. Peracta. De Con. Dist. 1. Episcopus. De Con. Dist. 2. Si non. De Con. Dist. 2. Si quis.

In the canons of the apostles it is decreed that, if any man resort unto the church, and hear the scriptures, and abstain from the communion, he stand excommunicate, as one that troubleth the congregation[3].

The like decrees are found under the names of Calixtus[4], Anacletus[5], Martinus[6], Hilarius[7], and others; by which it is certain that the whole church then received together.

a Clem. Epist. 2.

[a]Clemens, as M. Harding calleth him, the apostles' fellow, writeth thus: "Let so many hosts be offered upon the altar as may be sufficient for the people[8]."

b Aug. de Serm. Dom. in Mont. Lib. ii. c August. in Psal. x.

[b]St Augustine saith of the congregation in his time: "Every day we receive the sacrament of Christ's body[9]." [c]And, opening the same more particularly, he saith thus: *Unde... confido in eis, quibus heri communicasti, et hodie communicas, et cras communicabis*[10]? "What trust can I have in them, with whom thou didst communicate yesterday, and dost communicate to-day, and wilt communicate again to-morrow?"

d Clement. Strom. Lib. i.

[d]Clemens Alexandrinus saith: "After that certain, as the manner is, have divided the sacrament, they give every of the people leave to take part of it[11]."

Chrysost. in 1 Cor. Hom. 27.

St Chrysostom plainly describeth the very order of the communion that was used in his time, by these words: "The spiritual and reverend sacraments are set forth equally to rich and poor: neither doth the rich man enjoy them more, and the poor man less: they have all like honour, and like coming to them. The sacraments being once laid forth (as then the manner was for the people to receive) are not taken in again, until all the people have communicate, and taken part of that spiritual meat; but the priests stand still, and wait for all, even for the poorest of them all[12]."

Chrysost. 2 Cor. Hom. 18.

Again he saith: "There are things wherein the priest differeth nothing from the people; as when we must use the fearful mysteries. For we are all of one worthiness to receive the same[13]."

Gregor. Dial. Lib. ii. cap. xxiii.

St Gregory saith that even in his time the order was, that in the time of the holy communion the deacon should stand up and say aloud unto the people: *Si quis non communicat, det locum*[14]: "If there be any body that is not disposed to communicate, let him give place."

Missa.

This Latin word *missa*, in the time of Tertullian and St Cyprian, signified a dimissing, or a licence to depart, and was specially applied unto the communion upon this occasion that I must here declare. They that were then named *catechumeni*, that is to say, novices of the faith, and not yet christened, were suffered to be present at the communion until the gospel was ended. Then the deacon commanded them forth, pronouncing these words aloud: *Catechumeni exeunto*: or thus: *Ite, missa est*: "Go ye forth, ye have licence to depart." Of this dimis-

Isidor. in Lex.

[1 Hieron. Op. Par. 1693-1706. Comm. in Epist. I. ad Cor. cap. xi. Tom. V. col. 997. See before, page 18.]

[2 Ambros. Op. Par. 1686-90. Comm. in Epist. I. ad Cor. cap. xi. Tom. II. Append. col. 150. See before, page 17.]

[3 Canon. Apost. 9. in Concil. Stud. Labb. et Cossart. Lut. Par. 1671-2. Tom. I. col. 28.]

[4 Anaclet. in Corp. Jur. Canon. Lugd. 1624. Decret. Gratian. Decr. Tert. Pars, De Consecr. Dist. ii. can. 10. col. 1917.]

[5 Id. in eod. ibid. Dist. i. can. 59. col. 1907.]

[6 Ex Concil. Mart. Brach. cap. 83. in eod. ibid. Dist. ii. can. 18. col. 1920.]

[7 Hilar. in eod. ibid. can. 15. col. 1919.]

[8 Clement. Papæ I. Epist. ii. ad Jacob. in Epist. Decret. Sum. Pont. Rom. 1591. Tom. I. p. 16. See before, page 17.]

[9 ... quod [sacramentum] quotidie accipimus.—August. Op. Par. 1679-1700. De Serm. Dom. in Mont. Lib. II. cap. vii. 25. Tom. III. Pars II. col. 209.]

[10 Id. In Psalm. x. Enarr. 5. Tom. IV. cols. 61, 2.]

[11 Clem. Alex. Op. Oxon. 1715. Strom. Lib. I. Tom. I. p. 318. See before, page 153, note 14.]

[12 Chrysost. Op. Par. 1718-38. In Epist. I. ad Cor. Hom. xxvii. Tom. X. pp. 240, &c. The homily expresses at large what is here asserted; but the precise words do not appear in it.]

[13 Ἔστι δὲ ὅπου οὐδὲ διέστηκεν ὁ ἱερεὺς τοῦ ἀρχομένου· οἷον, ὅταν ἀπολαύειν δέῃ τῶν φρικτῶν μυστηρίων. ὁμοίως γὰρ πάντες ἀξιούμεθα τῶν αὐτῶν.—Id. In Epist. II. ad Cor. Hom. xviii. Tom. X. p. 568.]

[14 Gregor. Magni Papæ I. Op. Par. 1705. Dial. Lib. II. cap. xxiii. Tom. II. col. 253.]

sing or departing forth of the *catechumeni* and others, the service itself was then called *missa*[15]. The rest remained still in the church, and received the communion together with the priest. Further, the breaking of the bread, which even now is used in the mass itself, signifieth a distribution of the sacrament unto the people, as St Augustine saith unto Paulinus: *Ad distribuendum comminuitur*[16]; "It is broken, to the end it may be divided." Moreover, the priest himself in his mass saith thus: "This holy mixture and consecration, &c. be unto me, and to all that shall receive it, unto salvation[17]." Thus the very name of the mass, the very breaking of the bread, the very gestures and words that the priest useth at his mass, bear manifest witness against private mass.

Commu-nion.

The breaking of the bread.

August. ad Paulin. Epist. 59.

Here I leave out a great number of councils, and canons, and old fathers, as Justinus Martyr, Dionysius, Tertullian, Epiphanius, and Eusebius, with sundry other ancient writers, both Greeks and Latins; thinking it sufficient by these few to have given a taste of the rest.

Our proofs hang not upon conjecture, or uncertain guesses: we pray not aid of sick folk, women, boys, and children, for the proof of the holy communion; as M. Harding is driven to do for proof of his mass: we seek not out secret oratories or privy chapels: we forge no new doctors, such as the world never knew before; as these men do for lack of others: we allege neither dreams, nor visions, nor fantastical fables.

We rest upon the scriptures of God, upon the authority of the ancient doctors and councils, and upon the universal practice of the most famous cities and churches of the world.

These things well compared and weighed together, judge thou now, gentle reader, whether M. Harding have hitherto just cause either to blow up the triumph with such courage, or to require any man to subscribe.

[15 Isidor. Hisp. Op. Col. Agrip. 1617. Orig. Lib. VI. cap. xix. p. 51.]

[16 August. Op. Ad Paulin. Epist. cxlix. 16. Tom. II. col. 509.]

[17 Missal. ad Us. ac Consuet. Sar. Par. 1527. fol. 161. 2. See before, page 19.]

OF

COMMUNION UNDER BOTH KINDS.

THE SECOND ARTICLE.

THE BISHOP OF SARISBURY.

OR that there was then any communion ministered unto the people under one kind.

[OF COMMUNION UNDER ONE KIND. ARTICLE II. H. A. 1564.]

M. HARDING. THE FIRST DIVISION.

This being a sacrament of unity, every true christian man ought in receiving of it to consider how unity may be achieved and kept, rather than to shew a straitness of conscience about the outward forms of bread and wine to be used in the administration of it; and that so much the more, how much the end of every thing is to be esteemed more than that which serveth to the end. Otherwise herein the breach of unity is so little recompensed by the exact keeping of the outward ceremony, that, according to the saying of St Augustine, "whosoever taketh the mystery of unity, and keepeth not the bond of peace, he taketh not a mystery for himself, but a testimony against himself[1]." *Therefore they have great cause to weigh with themselves, what they receive in this sacrament, who, moved by slender reasons made for both kinds, do rashly and dangerously condemn the church for giving of it under one kind to all that do not in their own persons consecrate and offer the same in remembrance of the sacrifice once offered on the cross. And that they may think the church to stand upon good grounds herein, may it please them to understand, that the fruit of this sacrament, which they enjoy that worthily receive it, dependeth not of the outward forms of bread and wine, but redoundeth of the virtue of the flesh and blood of Christ. And whereas under either kind* (46) *whole Christ is verily present (for now that he is risen again from the dead, his flesh and blood can be sundered no more, because he dieth no more), this healthful sacrament is of true christian people with no less fruit received under one kind than under both.* [*And as this spiritual fruit is not any thing diminished to him that receiveth one kind, so it is not any whit increased to him that receiveth both*[2].] *The sacramentaries, that believe not the truth of Christ's body and blood in this holy sacrament, I remit to sundry godly treatises made in defence of the right faith in that point. I think it not necessary here to treat thereof, or of any other matter which M. Jewel hath not as yet manifestly touched in his sermon.*

The forty-sixth untruth, proceeding only of the gross error of transubstantiation.

[*Rom.* vi. H. A. 1564.]

THE BISHOP OF SARISBURY.

The former article of private mass, by M. Harding's own confession, proceedeth not from God, but from the negligence of the people: but the abuse of the communion under one kind, from whence soever it first proceeded, standeth now only upon the wilfulness of the priests, who, seeing and knowing the institution and commandment of Christ, yet notwithstanding have devised ways, against their own knowledge, violently to repel the same. And that the whole case may the better appear, the question that standeth between us is moved thus: "Whether

[1 Qui accipit mysterium unitatis, et non tenet vinculum pacis, non mysterium accipit pro se, sed testimonium contra se.—August. in Corp. Jur. Canon. Lugd. 1624. Decret. Gratian. Decr. Tert. Pars, Dist. ii. can. 36. col. 1929. Op. Par. 1679-1700. Serm. cclxxii. Tom. V. col. 1104.]

[2 The sentence between brackets is found only in H. A. 1564.]

the holy communion at any time, within the space of six hundred years after Christ, were ever ministered openly in the church unto the people under one kind." For proof whereof M. Harding hath here brought in women, children, sick folks, infants, and madmen, that these have sometimes received the one kind, some in their private houses, some in their death-beds, some otherwise, as he did before for proof of his private mass. If in all this long treaty he have brought any one example, or proof sufficient, of the ministration in one kind openly used in any church, it is good reason he be believed. But if he, after all these vaunts, having published such a book as all the world (as it is supposed) is not able to answer, have hitherto brought no such, neither example nor proof; then may we justly think there is nothing to be brought at all, but that by his eloquence and fair speech he seeketh to abuse the simplicity and ignorance of his reader. Difference between priest and lay.

The council of Basil[3], above one hundred and thirty years past, made no conscience to grant the use of both kinds unto the kingdom of Bohemia; and this council now presently holden at Trident[4], upon certain conditions, hath granted the same to other kingdoms and countries; and, were it not they should seem to confess the church of Rome hath erred, they would not doubt to grant the same freely to the whole world. None of them all can tell, neither when, nor where, nor how this error first began. Some think it sprang only of a certain superstition and simplicity of the people[5]. But whence soever it first began, as Tertullian writeth of the frowardness that he saw in certain of his time, it must now needs be maintained and made good against the truth. His words be these: *Consuetudo initium ab aliqua ignorantia vel simplicitate sortita in usum per successionem corroboratur, et ita adversus veritatem vendicatur. Sed Dominus noster Christus veritatem se, non consuetudinem, cognominavit... Viderint ergo, quibus novum est, quod sibi vetus est. Hæreses non tam novitas, quam veritas revincit. Quodcunque adversus veritatem sapit, hoc erit hæresis*[6], *etiam vetus consuetudo*[7]: "Custom, either of simplicity, or of ignorance, getting once an entry, is inured and hardened by succession, and then is defended against the truth. But Christ our Lord called himself the truth, and not custom. Let them take heed therefore, unto whom the thing seemeth new, that in itself is old. It is not so much the novelty of the matter, as the truth, that reproveth an heresy. Whatsoever savoureth against the truth, it is an heresy, be the custom thereof never so old." Concil. Basil. Concil. Trident. S. Gardiner in the Devil's Sophistry. Tertull. de Virg. Vel.

To come near the matter: "Unity," saith M. Harding, "is the substance of this sacrament: and whoso receiveth not the same in unity, receiveth a testimony against himself." As this is true, and avouched by St Augustine, and of our part not denied, so is it also true that St Ambrose writeth: *Indignus est Domino, qui aliter mysterium celebrat, quam ab eo traditum est. Non enim potest devotus esse, qui aliter præsumit, quam datum est ab auctore*[8]: "He is unworthy of the Lord, that doth otherwise celebrate the mystery than it was delivered of the Lord. For he cannot be devout, that taketh it otherwise than it was given of the author." But this excuse, under the pretence and colour of unity, seemeth to import some default. For what, think these folk that unity cannot stand without the breach of Christ's institution? or that the apostles and holy fathers, that ministered the communion under both kinds, were not in unity? or that there was never unity in the church for the space of a thousand four hundred and more years after Christ, until the council of Constance, where this matter was first concluded? Herein standeth that mystical unity, that one bread is broken unto all, and one cup is delivered unto all equally, without difference; and that, as Chrysostom saith, in the reverend sacrifice there is no difference between the priest and the people, but all is equal[9]. But our adversaries have herein forced a Ambros. 1 Cor. xi. Chrysost. in 2 Cor. Hom. 18.

[[3] Concil. Basil. Sess. xxx. in Concil. Stud. Labb. et Cossart. Lut. Par. 1671-2. Tom. XII. cols. 600, 1.]

[[4] Concil. Trident. in eod. Sess. xxii. Decr. sup. Pet. Conc. Cal. Tom. XIV. col. 861.]

[[5] A Detection of the Deuils Sophistrie, Lond. 1546. fol. 139. 2, &c.]

[[6] *Hæreses*, 1611.]

[[7] Tertull. Op. Lut. 1641. De Virg. Vel. 1. p. 192.]

[[8] Indignum dicit esse Domino, &c.—Ambros. Op. Par. 1686-90. Comm. in I. Epist. ad Cor. v. 27. Tom. II. Append. col. 149.]

[[9] Chrysost. Op. Par. 1718-38. In Epist. II. ad Cor. Hom. xviii. Tom. X. p. 568. See before, page 202, note 13.]

Whole Christ in either part.

difference between the priest and the people without cause, and say, there must needs be such a difference.

Johan. Sleidan. Lib. ix. Gerson. in Tract. con. Hær. Com. Laic. sub Utr. Spec. Gab. Biel.

And when the French king, who until this day receiveth still in both kinds, had moved his clergy wherefore he might so do more than others, they made him answer, "For that kings are anointed as well as priests[1]." Gerso[2] saith that, if laymen should communicate under both kinds as well as priests, *dignitas sacerdotis non esset supra dignitatem laicorum*[3]: "the dignity of the priest should not be above the dignity of laymen." And Gabriel Biel extolleth the priest above our lady, and All-hallows, because he may communicate under both kinds, and they cannot[4]. And so have they altered the sacrament of equality and unity, and made it a sacrament of difference and dissension.

"The fruit of the sacrament," saith M. Harding, "hangeth not of the forms of bread and wine." This is a strange form of speech unto the ignorant, that knoweth not what these forms mean. Beware, good reader; for under this word there lieth a snare. St Paul five times in one place calleth it bread; but this man saith it is the "form," the "appearance," and "shew of bread," but he would have thee believe that indeed it is no bread.

1 Cor. xi.

We know well the fruit of the sacrament standeth not, neither in the forms, nor in the bread or wine, which are outwardly received with the bodily mouth, but in the flesh and blood of Christ, which only are received spiritually into the soul.

He addeth further: "Whole Christ is under either kind; therefore he that receiveth in one kind only hath no wrong." If any ancient doctor had said the same, it might the rather have been believed. But M. Harding, of false principles of his own, thinketh he may boldly gather the like conclusions. These toys are sufficient to please vain fantasy; but they are not sufficient to content a godly conscience. But doth M. Harding so surely know that whole Christ is in either kind; and did Christ himself not know it? Or, if Christ did know it, was not he able to break his own ordinance, and to provide for this inconvenience, as well as others? We know, and it is our belief, that Christ's whole humanity, both flesh and blood, is in heaven. But that the same humanity of Christ is in the sacrament in such gross sort as is supposed by our adversaries, notwithstanding many bold vaunts thereof made, yet was it hitherto never proved. And although this matter be moved by M. Harding out of season, as being no part of this question, yet I think it not amiss briefly to signify by the way what the old catholic fathers have thought of it.

Lib. Epist. Epist. 146.

Consentius demandeth this question of St Augustine: "Whether the body of Christ, being now in heaven, have in it blood or no[5]?" Here to leave St Augustine's answer, it is easy for any man to consider, if Consentius had been persuaded, as M. Harding would seem to be, that Christ's body hath blood in[6] the sacrament, he would never have moved this question of the body of Christ that is in heaven. To leave these new fantasies, whereof it doth not appear that ever the old catholic doctors made any report, we must understand that the bread is the sacrament of Christ's body, and the wine is the sacrament of his blood. So saith

Beda in Luc. cap. xxii. Lib. vi.

Beda: *Panis ad corpus Christi mystice, vinum refertur ad sanguinem*[7]: "The bread in mystical manner hath relation to the body of Christ: the wine hath relation unto his blood." So likewise saith St Paul: "The bread that we break, is it not the communication of the body of Christ? And the cup of the blessing which we bless, is it not the communication of the blood of Christ?" St Paul saith not each part is in other; but each hath a peculiar signification by itself.

[1 ... deinde Galliæ regibus administrari totam: et cum inter disputandum theologis hoc ipsum rex objicit, illos respondere, unctos esse reges æque ac sacerdotes, &c.—Sleidan. de Stat. Relig. Comm. Argent. 1566. Lib. IX. fol. 155.]

[2 Gerson, 1565.]

[3 ... tanta esset dignitas laicorum circa sumptionem corporis Christi, sicut et sacerdotum.—Gerson. Op. Antw. 1706. Contr. Hær. de Com. Laic. sub Utr. Spec. Tom. I. Pars III. col. 467.]

[4 Biel discusses at length the communicating under one kind.—Gab. Biel. Sacr. Canon. Miss. Expos. Lugd. 1517. Lect. lxxxiv. See particularly fol. 182. 2; which perhaps is the passage referred to.]

[5 August. Op. Par. 1679-1700. Ad Consent. Epist. ccv. 2. Tom. II. col. 767.]

[6 Blood in it in, 1565.]

[7 Ven. Bed. Op. Col. Agrip. 1612. In Luc. Evang. cap. xxii. Lib. VI. Tom. V. col. 424; where for *panis* and *vinum*, we find *hic* and *illud*.]

But if it were so as M. Harding and certain others of late days have grossly imagined, yet notwithstanding the people, taking but one kind only, receiveth injury; as M. Harding may see by Alexander of Hales, and Durandus, and other of his own doctors. Alexander's words be these: *Licet illa sumptio, quæ est in accipiendo sub una specie, sufficiat, tamen illa quæ est sub duabus est majoris meriti*[8]: "Although that order of receiving the sacrament which is under one kind be sufficient, yet the other which is under both kinds is of greater merit." And immediately after: *Sumptio sub utraque specie, quem modum sumendi tradidit Dominus, est majoris efficaciæ, et [majoris] complementi*[9]: "The receiving under both kinds, which order the Lord delivered, is of greater strength, and of greater fulness." And the same Alexander again saith: *Totus Christus non continetur sub utraque specie sacramentaliter; sed caro tantum sub specie panis, [et] sanguis...sub specie vini*[10]: "Whole Christ is not contained under each kind by way of sacrament, but the flesh only under the form of bread, and the blood under the form of wine." The like might be reported out of Durandus and others. Here M. Harding's own doctors confess that the people, receiving under one kind, receiveth not the full sacrament, nor the blood of Christ by way of sacrament; and that their doing therein is of less strength and merit than the doing of the priest. Wherefore M. Harding, in saying, "The people receiving only under one kind taketh no injury," doth the people double injury.

Whole Christ in either part.

Alex. iv. Quæst. liii. Memb. i.

Alex. iv. Quæst. xl. Memb. iii. Art. 2.

But to pass over these scholastical subtle points, it behoveth us to know that Christ the Son of God appointed the sacrament of his body to be given in bread, and the sacrament of his blood to be given in wine. These be the holy mysteries of Christ's body and blood. We may not here account what may be in either of them by the drift of vain fantasy; but rather we ought to consider what Christ in the first institution hereof did, and what he commanded to be done. Neither do we here condemn the church, as it pleaseth M. Harding unjustly to charge us; but we wish and pray to God that his whole church may once be reformed after the example and institution of Christ; without whom the church is no church, neither hath any right or claim without his promise, nor any promise without his word.

Now, whereas M. Harding saith, "The reasons that we make for the maintenance of Christ's institutions[11] are so slender;" if he had first weighed his own, perhaps he would the more favourably have reported ours. I mean not the reasons that others of that side have taken of men's beards, of fear of the palsy and shaking, or other diseases, or inconveniences that may happen; but even of the same that he hath here planted in the first rank and entry of his cause. The first is this:

"It is a sacrament of unity; therefore, if it be abused, we may seek no redress."

The second is this: "The fruit of the sacrament dependeth not of the forms of bread and wine; therefore we may break Christ's institution."

The third is this: "Whole Christ," as M. Harding saith, "is in either part of the sacrament; therefore there is no wrong done in barring the people from one kind." Certainly these reasons seem very slender, and specially to countermand the plain word of God. The sentence that St Basil useth in this case is very terrible: "Whoso forbiddeth the thing that God commandeth, and whoso commandeth the thing that God forbiddeth, is to be holden accursed of all them that love the Lord[12]."

Basil. Moral. Summ. cap. 14.

M. HARDING. THE SECOND DIVISION.

Now, concerning the outward forms of bread and wine, (47) their use is employed in signification only, and be not of necessity, so as grace may not be obtained by worthy receiving of the sacrament, unless both kinds be ministered. Therefore in

The forty-seventh untruth. For the bread and wine signify

[8 Alex. Alens. Theol. Summ. Col. Agrip. 1622. Pars IV. Quæst. XI. Membr. ii. Art. iv. 3. p. 406; where we find *illa tamen*.]

[9 Id. ibid.]

[10 Id. Pars IV. Quæst. x. Membr. vii. Art. iii. 2. Resol. p. 350.]

[11 Institution, 1565.]

[12 ...qui prohibet nos facere quod a Domino præceptum est; vel rursum imperat quod Dominus fieri prohibuit; execrabilis debet esse, qui ejusmodi est, omnibus qui diligunt Deum.—Basil. Op. 1520. De Inst. Mon. Reg. cap. xiv. fol. 165.]

Whole Christ in either part.

consecrating of the sacrament, according to Christ's institution, both kinds be necessary; forasmuch as it is not prepared for the receiving only, but also for renewing and stirring up of the remembrance of our Lord's death. So inasmuch as the sacrament serveth the sacrifice, by which the death and oblation of Christ is represented, both the kinds be requisite; that, by divers and sundry forms, the blood of Christ, the body and blood of Christ: the whiteness, the roundness, and other outward forms signify nothing. *shed for our sins, and separated from his body, may evidently be signified. But inasmuch as the faithful people do receive the sacrament, thereby to attain spiritual grace and salvation of their souls; diversity of the forms or kinds, that be used for the signification only, hath no further use nor*[1] *profit. But by one kind, because in it whole Christ is exhibited, abundance of all grace is once given; so as by the other kind thereto over added (which giveth the same, and not another Christ) no further augmentation of spiritual grace may be attained. In consideration of this, the catholic church, taught by the Holy Ghost all truth, whiles in the daily sacrifice the memory of our Lord's death and passion is celebrated, for that it is necessary therein, to express most plainly the shedding and separating of the blood from the body that was crucified, hath always to that purpose diligently used both kinds of bread and wine; but in distributing of the blessed sacrament to christian people hath used liberty*[2] *(which Christ never imbarred by any commandment to the contrary),* The forty-eighth untruth. For[3] the church never thus ministered the sacrament unto the people in any open congregation within the space of six hundred years. *so as it hath (48) ever been most for the behoof and commodity of the receivers; and hath ministered sometimes both kinds, sometimes one kind only, as it hath been thought most expedient, in regard of time, place, and persons.*

THE BISHOP OF SARISBURY.

Here is much talk, and no proof. I grant, the priest, if he minister the communion orderly, and as he should, doth renew the memory of Christ's passion, according to his own commandment: "Do this in my remembrance." Yet all this concludeth not directly, that therefore Christ's ordinance may be broken. Neither is it yet so clearly proved, that the priest in his mass rèpresenteth the separation of Christ's blood from his body. For, beside that there is no ancient doctor here alleged for proof hereof, I might well demand by what words, by what gesture, or to whom doth he represent this separation? His words be strange, his gesture secret: the people neither heareth nor seeth ought, nor knoweth what he meaneth. And being granted, that the separation of Christ's body and blood is represented in the holy mysteries, yet how knoweth M. Harding that the priest ought more to represent the same than the people? Doubtless Christ's blood was shed indifferently for all the faithful, as well for the people as for the priest; between Chrysost. in. 2 ad Cor. Hom. 18. whom and the people, as I have before shewed out of St Chrysostom, in this case there is no difference[4]. For whereas M. Harding taketh the name of sacrifice for some shew of proof in this matter, it behoveth him to know that not only the portion received by the priest, but also the portion that is distributed unto the people, is of the old fathers called a sacrifice. St Augustine hath these Retract. Lib. ii. words: "In Carthage the manner was that hymns should be said at the altar out of the book of Psalms, either when the oblation was made, or when the thing that was offered was divided unto the people[5]."

By these plain words we may see that both the priest and people received one sacrifice. And Clemens (as M. Harding calleth him, the apostles' fellow) saith Clemens. Epist. 2. thus: *Tanta in altario holocausta offerantur, quanta populo sufficere debeant*[6]: "Let there be so many sacrifices offered at the altar, as may suffice for the people."

And, whereas it is further said that the priest, by receiving both parts in several, expresseth, as it were, unto the eye, how Christ's body and blood were done asunder; the scriptures and ancient fathers have taught us otherwise, that not any gesture of the priest, but the very ministration of the holy communion,

---

[1 Ne, 1565, 1609, and H. A. 1564.]

[2 Her liberty, H. A. 1564.]

[3 1565 omits *for*.]

[4 Chrysost. Op. Par. 1718-38. In Epist. II. ad Cor. Hom. xviii. Tom. X. p. 568. See before, page 202, note 13.]

[5 ... Hilarius ... morem, qui tunc esse apud Carthaginem cœperat, ut hymni ad altare dicerentur de psalmorum libro, sive ante oblationem, sive cum distribueretur populo quod fuisset oblatum,...lacerabat.—August. Op. Par. 1679-1700. Retract. Lib. II. cap. xi. Tom. I. col. 45.]

[6 Clement. Papæ I. Epist. ii. ad Jacob. in Epist. Decret. Sum. Pont. Rom. 1591. Tom. I. p. 17.]

and the whole action of the people, expresseth unto us the manner and order of Christ's death. St Paul saith: "As often as ye shall eat this bread, and drink this cup, ye shall declare the Lord's death until he come." And this St Paul writeth, not only to the priests, but also to the whole congregation of the Corinthians. And in like sort writeth St Augustine touching the same: *Cum frangitur hostia, et sanguis de calice in ora fidelium funditur, quid aliud quam dominici corporis in cruce immolatio, ejusque sanguinis de latere effusio designatur*[7]? "When the oblation is broken, and the blood from the cup is poured into the mouths of the faithful, what thing else is there signified, but the offering of the Lord's body upon the cross, and the flowing of his blood from his side?" Thus it is clear that the separation of Christ's body and blood is represented as well by the people as by the priest. Wherefore to devise a difference without cause, and of the same to conclude an error, it is double folly.

1 Cor. xi.

De Con. Dist. 2. Cum frangitur.

"The diversity of forms and kinds," saith M. Harding, "serveth for signification only, and hath no further use nor[8] profit." Notwithstanding this saying were otherwise true, yet the issue thereof seemeth dangerous. It is our part to be obedient, and not to discuss or rectify God's commandments, and to say, any thing that Christ the Son of God hath appointed us to do is utterly void of use and profit. As for the liberty of the church that is here claimed, if we should demand where and when it was granted, perhaps the charter would not be found. The liberty of the church is not to be against God, nor to control any his ordinance. Neither hath M. Harding yet proved that the church within six hundred years after Christ, in open congregation and assembly of people (which is the state of this question), ever used any such kind of liberty.

In these words M. Harding hath privily couched sundry arguments, which of what value or force they be, I pray thee, gentle reader, to understand.

1. The first is this: The priest consecrateth the sacrament; therefore the people is not bound to receive in both kinds.

2. The second is this: The priest offereth the sacrifice, and representeth the separation of Christ's body and blood; *ergo*, it is sufficient for the people to receive in one kind.

3. The third is this: The church hath her liberty; *ergo*, she is not bound to Christ's institution.

Alas, how slenderly hang these things together! Yet these are the arguments that (as it is supposed) are never able to be answered.

M. HARDING. THE THIRD DIVISION.

[*Matt. xxvi.* H. A. 1564.]

[*Christ's words bind not the laity to receive both kinds,* H. A. 1564.]

Ante passionem nobis solis præcepit hoc facere, inquiunt apostoli apud Clementem. Lib.viii. Const. Apostolicarum. cap. ult.[9]

As touching the words of Christ, Bibite ex hoc omnes, *"Drink ye all of this;" they pertain to the apostles only, and to their successors. For to them* (49) *only he gave commandment to do that, which he did in his supper, as Clement saith, to them only saying, Do this in my remembrance, he gave commission to consecrate, offer, and to receive the sacrament in remembrance of his death and passion, by the same words ordaining them priests of the new testament. Wherefore this belongeth not to the lay-people, neither can it justly be*[10] *gathered by this place, that they are bound of necessity, and*[a] *under pain of deadly sin, to receive the sacrament under both kinds.*

The forty-ninth untruth. For these words pertained as well to the people as to the priests, as shall appear.

[a] Here M. Harding altereth the case.

THE BISHOP OF SARISBURY.

When I read the words of M. Harding's, I am stricken with horror to consider the terrible judgment of God. It is much to be feared that he that is led away of this sort offendeth not of ignorance—for so were the fault the more pardonable—but against the manifest known truth, and against the Spirit of God. For whereas Christ saith, "Drink ye all of this;" if he will follow the letter, the words

[7 August. Lib. Sent. Prosp. in Corp. Jur. Canon. Lugd. 1624. Decret. Gratian. Decr. Tert. Pars, De Consecr. Dist. ii. can. 37. col. 1930.]

[8 Ne, 1565, 1609.]

[9 Const. Apost. in Concil. Stud. Labb. et Cossart. Lut. Par. 1671-2. Lib. VIII. cap. xlvi. Tom. I. col. 509.]

[10 Be justly, H. A. 1564.]

be plain that all should drink. If he will leave the letter, and take the meaning, St Paul hath opened it. For, writing unto the whole congregation at Corinth, he saith thus: "As often as ye shall eat this bread, and drink of this cup, ye shall declare the Lord's death until he come." If he doubt St Paul, yet the very practice and continual order of the primitive church fully declareth what Christ meant: and they say, *Consuetudo est optima interpres legis*[1]: "Custom is the best interpreter of the law." If he will take neither the words of Christ, nor Christ's meaning, then I know not how to deal with him.

1 Cor. xi.

Once again he bringeth forth Clement, the apostles' fellow. And what Clement? Verily, even the same that ministered and delivered the holy communion to the faithful that then were in Rome under both kinds, as appeareth by the long usage of that church, even as Christ delivered it to his disciples; and M. Harding is not able to shew that the same Clement ever ministered otherwise. He seeth and knoweth that the word *Omnes* is against him; the meaning against him; the practice of the church against him; his own Clement against him: yet he beareth his countenance so as if all were with him. To be short, if Christ, when he said, "Drink ye all," meant not that all should drink; why did St Paul and all the apostles, and the whole primitive church, expound it and practise it as though he had meant so? And if he meant so, why doth M. Harding deceive the world, and say he meant not so?

But Clement saith, "Christ spake these words, 'Do this in my remembrance,' only unto the apostles." "Therefore," saith M. Harding, "these words, 'Drink ye all,' pertain to the apostles only, and to their successors." Understand, good reader, that Clement, in the place here alleged, speaketh not one word, either of one kind or of both; but only saith thus: "That Christ appointed his apostles to the office of the holy ministration," which he calleth "the spiritual oblation[2]." Therefore thou mayest see that M. Harding, shewing thee one thing for another, and of the same concluding what him liketh, cannot seem to deal plainly.

Spiritualis hostia.

The argument that hereof is gathered standeth thus: Clement saith that Christ gave only unto his apostles the office of the ministry, and authority to offer the spiritual sacrifice; *ergo*, these words, "Drink ye all of this," pertain nothing to the people. Here is a very faint conclusion. For by force of this reason he may take from the people both parts of the sacrament, as well as one, and so leave them no sacrament at all.

M. HARDING. THE FOURTH DIVISION.

The fiftieth untruth. For[4] they changed not, but restored the old custom.

And this understood they which above one[3] hundred years past, (50) *changing the old custom of the church of receiving the communion under one kind, by their private authority would needs usurp the cup also. For, seeing themselves not to have sufficient proof and warrant for their doing, of these words, "Drink ye all of this," the better to bolster up their new-fangled attempt, they thought it better to allege the words of Christ in St John: "Except ye eat the flesh of the Son of man, and drink his blood, ye shall not have life in you;" which words, for all that, our new masters of forty years[5] past will to be understanded of the spiritual, and not of the sacramental eating. [Which place although it be taken for the sacramental eating][6], as it may be, and is taken for both, of the doctors viewed apart; yet in all that chapter there is no mention of the cup nor of wine at all. Wherefore they, that cry so much on the institution and commandment of Christ, cannot find in all the scriptures neither commandment where he gave charge the sacrament so to be given, neither so much as any example where Christ gave it under both kinds to any other than to the apostles. Whereas, contrariwise, it may be shewed of our part that the sacrament was given under one kind only to the two disciples that went to Emmaus; for that the bread which Christ there took, blessed, brake, and*

John vi.

Luke xxiv.

[1 Corp. Jur. Civil. Amst. 1663. Digest. Lib. I. Tit. III. 37. Tom. I. p. 79. This law is afterwards more fully given.]

[2 Ὃς [Χριστὸς] γενόμενος ἄνθρωπος δι' ἡμᾶς καὶ τὴν πνευματικὴν θυσίαν προσφέρων τῷ Θεῷ αὐτοῦ καὶ Πατρὶ πρὸ τοῦ πάθους ἡμῖν διετάξατο μόνοις τοῦτο ποιεῖν· κ. τ. λ.—Const. Apost. in Concil. Stud. Labb. et Cossart. Lut. Par. 1671-2. Lib. VIII. cap. xlvi. Tom. I. col. 509.]

[3 An, H. A. 1564.]

[4 1565 omits *for.*]

[5 These forty, H. A. 1564.]

[6 The words between brackets are found only in H. A. 1564.]

gave to them, was not simple and common bread, but the sacrament of the body and blood of Christ: for so [a]*Chrysostom*[7], [b]*Augustine*[8], [c]*Bede*[9], *and* [d]*Theophylact*[10], *with one accord do witness. It appeareth also, that the communion under one kind was used at Hierusalem among Christ's disciples, by that St Luke writeth in the Acts of the Apostles of the breaking of the bread. If M. Jewel here think to avoid these places by their accustomed figure,* Synecdoche, *among his own sect happily it may be accepted; but among men of right and learned judgment that shift will seem over weak and vain. Now to conclude, touching the sixth chapter of St John, as thereof they can bring no one word mentioning the cup or wine, for proof of their both kinds; so it sheweth, and not in very obscure wise, that the form of bread alone is sufficient, whereas Christ saith,* Qui manducat panem hunc, vivet in æternum: *"He that eateth this bread shall live for ever."*

[a] *In Matth. hom.* 17. [b] *De Consensu Evangel. lib. iii. cap. xxv.* [c] *In Lucam.* [d] *In Lucam.* *Acts ii.*

THE BISHOP OF SARISBURY.

In these words M. Harding chargeth not only us, but also the apostles of Christ, and all the fathers of the primitive church, with great oversight; who in their times ministered the holy sacrament unto the vulgar people, as it is now supposed by these men, without any example of Christ, and without commission.

Touching the institution of Christ, I have already said so much as unto a quiet mind may seem sufficient. Yet for further declaration I would demand of M. Harding, what thing he requireth to Christ's institution: if words, Christ's words be plain; if example, Christ himself ministered in both kinds; if authority, Christ commanded his disciples, and in them all other ministers of his church, to do the like; if certainty of his meaning, the apostles endued with the Holy Ghost so practised the same, and understood he meant so; if continuance of time, he bade the same to be continued until he come again. If neither the words, nor example, nor commandment of Christ, nor the understanding and practice of the apostles can warrant us Christ's institution, alas, what warrant then have they, that, being utterly void of all these things, only stay themselves, as it is confessed by the best of that side, by the simple devotion of the people[11]? When Christ had delivered both kinds unto his disciples, he said unto them: "This do ye," the same that ye see I have done. But where did Christ ever say, Minister unto yourselves one way, and another way unto the people; or, Receive ye in both kinds, and let all the rest receive in one?

S. Gardiner in the Devil's Sophistry.

Although these things be plain and evident of themselves[12], yet, that the folly of these men may the better appear, it shall be good to hear the report of one of their own doctors touching these matters. One Gerardus Lorichius, in a book that he wrote, *De Missa Publica Proroganda*, hath these words: *Sunt pseudocatholici, qui reformationem ecclesiæ quoquo modo remorari non verentur. Hi ne laicis altera species restituatur, nullis parcunt blasphemiis. Dicunt enim, Christum solis apostolis dixisse, Bibite ex eo omnes. Atqui verba canonis habent, Accipite et manducate ex hoc omnes. Hic dicant, oro, num et hoc ad solos dictum sit apostolos... Ergo, laicis et a specie panis est abstinendum: Quod dicere est hæresis, et blasphemia pestilens, et execrabilis: Consequitur ergo, utrumque verbum dictum esse ad omnem ecclesiam*[13]: "They be false catholics," saith this man, "that are not ashamed by all means to hinder the reformation of the church. They, to the intent the other kind of the sacrament may not be restored unto the lay-people, spare no kind of blasphemies. For they say, that Christ said only unto his apostles, 'Drink ye all of this.' But the words of the canon (of the mass) be these: 'Take and eat ye all of this.' Here, I beseech them, let them tell me whether they will have these words also only to pertain unto the apostles. Then must the lay-people abstain from the other kind of the bread also. Which thing

Ger. Lorich. in 7. Parte Canonis.

[7 Chrysost. Op. Par. 1718-38. Opus Imperf. in Matt. Hom. xvii. ex cap. vii. Tom. VI. p. lxxxviii.]

[8 August. Op. Par. 1679-1700. De Consens. Evang. Lib. III. cap. xxv. 72. Tom. III. Pars II. cols. 141, 2.]

[9 Ven. Bed. Op. Col. Agrip. 1612. In Luc. Evang. cap. xxiii. Lib. VI. Tom. V. col. 446.]

[10 ... μεταλαμβάνουσι τοῦ εὐλογημένου ἄρτου.—Theophyl. Op. Venet. 1754-63. In Luc. Comm. cap. xxiv. Tom. I. p. 495.]

[11 A Detection of the Deuils Sophistrie, Lond. 1546. fol. 139. 2, &c.]

[12 Themself, 1565.]

[13 Ger. Lorich. De Miss. Pub. Prorogand. 1536. Lib. II. cap. ii. Sept. Pars Canon. p. 177.]

to say is an heresy, and a pestilent and a detestable blasphemy. Wherefore it followeth, that each of these words was spoken unto the whole church." Thus far Lorichius, an earnest defender of transubstantiation, of the pope's supremacy, and of private mass; lest M. Harding should say he were one of Luther's scholars, and so except against him, as being a party. And Julius, sometime bishop of Rome, hearing of certain that used to dip the bread in the wine, and so to deliver it to the people, had no way to reform them, but only by Christ's institution. For thus he saith: *Quod pro complemento communionis intinctam tradunt eucharistiam populis, nec hoc prolatum ex evangelio testimonium receperunt:* "Whereas for accomplishment of the communion they dip the sacrament and deliver it unto the people, they have not received this witness of the gospel." He addeth further: *Seorsum enim panis, et seorsum calicis commendatio memoratur*[1]*:* "For the delivery of the bread and the delivery of the cup are mentioned asunder." And thus he speaketh of the ministration of the sacrament, that is due not only to the priests, but also to the people.

De Con. Dist. 2. Cum omne.

The learned men of Bohemia saw they could have no hold of Christ's institution; and therefore, to maintain their "new-fangled attempt," as it pleaseth M. Harding to term it, they were fain to take the words of Christ out of the sixth chapter of John: "Unless ye eat the flesh of the Son of man, and drink his blood, ye shall have no life in you." But "these words in the sixth chapter of St John," saith M. Harding, "our new masters will have expounded of the spiritual, not of the sacramental eating." Of the Bohemians I cannot see why they should be called "new-fangled." Their request was none other but that they might continue the order of the primitive church, which Thomas of Aquine saith had continued in divers churches from the apostles until his time, for the space of a thousand and three hundred years, without controlment[2]. And it may ill become a christian man, and a scholar of the apostolic see, to call the doing of Christ and of his disciples "new-fangled." Touching their reasons made in this behalf, I need not to speak. God's name be blessed, they have prevailed with the best-learned of the world. Whatsoever their premises seem to M. Harding, their conclusion was this, that no mortal creature should presume to disallow the ordinance of the immortal God.

Part. iii. Qu. 80. Art. 12.

"But our new masters," saith M. Harding, "must needs have these words of St John expounded of the spiritual eating." If it be either the violence of nature, or the manner of his catholic doctrine, that driveth M. Harding thus to taunt, he must be borne withal; notwithstanding it agreeth not with his promise. As touching the understanding of the words of Christ in the sixth of St John, they are not all new masters that have so taken them. For, to leave St Augustine, Origen, and others of that age, Nicolas Lyra, a man of latter[3] years, saith, the said words of Christ must needs be taken spiritually, and none otherwise. Thus he saith: *Ista intelligi debent de manducatione et potatione spirituali; quia sequitur, Qui manducat meam carnem, et bibit meum sanguinem, in me manet, et ego in eo. Quod B. Augustinus exponens ait: Hoc est manducare illam escam, et bibere illum potum, in Christo manere, et Christum manentem in se habere: quod nihil aliud est, quam esse in caritate Christi*[4]*:* "These words must be taken of the spiritual eating and drinking. For it followeth: 'He that eateth my flesh and drinketh my blood dwelleth in me, and I in him.' Which thing St Augustine expounding saith thus: This is the eating of that food, and the drinking of that drink, for a man to dwell in Christ, and

Nicol. Lyra in Psal. cxi.

[[1] Jul. Papa in Corp. Jur. Canon. Lugd. 1624. Decret. Gratian. Decr. Tert. Pars, De Consecr. Dist. ii. can. 7. col. 1915, where in the text *recipit.*]

[[2] The author most probably refers to those expressions of Aquinas which imply that the communion in one kind was customary in some, not in all churches; *e.g.* Contra est multarum ecclesiarum usus, in quibus populo communicanti datur corpus Christi communicanti sumendum, non autem sanguis.—Thom. Aquinat. Op. Venet. 1595. Summ. Theol. Pars III. Quæst. lxxx. Art. 12. Tom. XII. fol. 267. See also below, page 261.]

[[3] Later, 1565.]

[[4] Bibl. cum Gloss. Ord. et Expos. N. de Lyra, Basil. 1502. Psal. cx. Replic. Pars III. fol. 254; where we find, *de qua manducatione et potatione intelligi debet videlicet de spirituali; quia, &c.*]

to have Christ in him dwelling; which thing is nothing else but to be in the love of Christ." Here we see that Nicolas Lyra, a man that lived two hundred years ago, and therefore no very "new master," expoundeth these words of the spiritual eating.

Yet M. Harding saith, "the same place may be taken also of the sacramental eating." But Lyra thinketh no, and therefore addeth further: [*Hoc verbum*] *nihil directe pertinet ad sacramentalem vel corporalem manducationem... Nam hoc verbum fuit dictum diu antequam sacramentum eucharistiæ esset institutum. Ex illa igitur litera de sacramentali communione non potest fieri argumentum efficax*[5]. "These words pertain not directly unto the sacramental or corporal eating. For it was spoken long before the sacrament was ordained. Therefore out of this letter there cannot be made any good argument for the sacramental communion." Nicol. Lyra in Psal. cxi.

Likewise one Michael Væhe, one of late years, a man of M. Harding's own side, touching the same matter writeth thus: *Infirmum est argumentum: quæ enim de spirituali manducatione dicta sunt, ille ad sacramentalem torquet*[6]: "This," saith he, "is but a weak reason; for the words that be spoken of spiritual eating he applieth to the sacramental eating." Here may M. Harding see, besides St Augustine, Origen, and other old catholic fathers, whose words I have not alleged, what men he hath called "new masters." Nicolas Lyra was an Englishman, and lived two hundred years before Luther. Michael Væhe was of late years, and wrote namely against Luther. Verily, if Christ and his apostles were now conversant in the world, unless they would forsake their own doctrine, they should be called "new masters" too, as well as others. Mich. Væhe, Tract 5. contra Lutherum.

And notwithstanding these words in the sixth chapter of St John be spoken and taken of the spiritual eating, as it is already proved, yet are they oftentimes by the old fathers applied unto the sacrament; but undirectly, as it is above noted by Lyra. To allege the places specially, being so many, and not unknown unto the learned, it would be tedious. Christ's being at Emmaus, and the disciples' breaking of bread at Hierusalem, because it hath pleased M. Harding to bring them twice, shall be afterward answered in their places.

The reasons that M. Harding hath here gathered be these: In the sixth chapter of St John there is no mention made of the cup or wine; *ergo*, the people may receive under one kind. This reason is very weak; for he may as well conclude of the same words; *ergo*, the priest may receive under one kind; which he himself saith is against Christ's institution. He might far better have concluded the contrary. The lay-people, being faithful and godly, by faith and in their hearts do indeed and verily drink the blood of Christ: therefore they may drink the sacrament of the same. And as Eckius, a doctor of that side, saith: "The people drinketh in the person of the priest[7]." Therefore they may drink in their own person as well and without danger. Eckius in Locis Communibus.

Another reason is this: It doth not appear that Christ ever ministered in both kinds but only to his disciples; *ergo*, the people may receive in one kind. I marvel what luck M. Harding hath to such conclusions. For what necessary sequel can there be, either from the apostles to the people, or from both kinds to one kind, or from an affirmative to a negative? The sum of the reason standeth thus: The apostles are commanded to receive both kinds; *ergo*, the people is not commanded to receive both kinds. The weakness whereof is evident, and sheweth itself. It will much rather and better follow thus: The people is commanded to receive as the apostles received, for there is expressed no difference. The apostles received in both kinds; *ergo*, the people is commanded to receive in both kinds. And thus, notwithstanding it be here stoutly avouched that we have neither example nor institution, yet I trust it doth well appear that we have both the example of Christ that ministered the sacrament in both kinds, and also Christ's institution, that bade his disciples to do the same.

[5 Id. ibid.; where *hoc verbum* follows *manducationem*, and *fuerit* is found for *esset*.]

[6 The editor has not been able to meet with the works of this writer.]

[7 ... in cujus [sacerdotis] persona totus populus quadam spiritali sumptione sanguinem Christi bibere gaudenter debet credere.—Joh. Eck. Enchir. Loc. Com. Col. 1532. cap. x. fol. E 5.2.]

M. HARDING. THE FIFTH DIVISION.

Thus our adversaries have nothing to bring out of the scriptures against the use of the catholic church, in ministering the communion under one kind. And yet they cease not crying out upon the breach of Christ's express commandment. And M. Jewel, for his part, in his first answer to D. Cole, saith, that the council of Constance pronounced openly against Christ himself. But forasmuch as they are so hot in this point, I will send them to Martin Luther himself, their patriarch, that either by his sobriety in this matter they may be somewhat colded, or by his and his scholars' inconstancy herein be brought to be ashamed of themselves. Though the places be well known, as oftentimes cited of the catholic writers of our time against the gospellers, yet here I think good to rehearse them, that the unlearned may see how themselves make not so great a matter of this article as some seem to bear the people in hand it is[1]. *Luther writeth to them of Bohemia these very words:* Quoniam pulchrum quidem esset, utraque specie eucharistiæ uti, et Christus hac in re nihil tanquam necessarium præcepit; præstaret pacem et unitatem, quam Christus ubique præcepit, sectari, quam de speciebus sacramenti contendere[2]: "*Whereas it were a fair thing (saith he) to use both kinds of the sacrament, yet, for that Christ herein hath commanded nothing as necessary, it were better to keep peace and unity, which Christ hath every where charged us withal, than to strive for the outward kinds of the sacrament." Again his words be these, in a declaration that he wrote of the sacrament:* Non dixi, neque consului, neque est intentio mea, ut unus aut aliquot episcopi propria auctoritate alicui incipiant utramque speciem porrigere, nisi ita constitueretur et mandaretur in concilio generali[2]: "*Neither have I said, nor counselled, nor my mind is, that any one or more bishops begin by their own authority to give both kinds (of the sacrament) to any person, unless it were so ordained and commanded in a*[3] *general council.*

[*Luther and his offspring doth not necessitate communion under both kinds.* H. A. 1564.]

THE BISHOP OF SARISBURY.

It grieveth M. Harding that we should say the council of Constance decreed against Christ himself; and therefore he sendeth us to Luther himself, that, seeing his inconstancy, we may be ashamed of ourselves[4]. And thus with one poor syllable he thought it good merrily to refresh himself: and yet touching inconstancy, wherein he so triumpheth against D. Luther, he seemeth utterly to have forgotten himself. For it is known to the world, that D. Luther in all his life never changed but once, and that from manifest error to the open confessed truth. But M. Harding, upon how good occasions I will not say, hath changed his doctrine and whole faith twice within the space of two years. And so much would I not now have touched, saving only to put him in remembrance of himself.

That the determination of the council of Constance was against Christ, besides Gerardus Lorichius, a doctor of M. Harding's own school, who affirmeth it in vehement words, what can there be so plain, as that St Paul writeth unto the Corinthians, "That I received of the Lord, the same have I delivered unto you?" After, he mentioneth each kind apart, and sheweth that, as Christ took the bread, so he also took the cup; and that the apostles received both at Christ's hands, not only for themselves, but also to the use and behoof of the people. Therefore, whereas M. Harding crieth so often against us, that the delivery of the cup unto the people is no part of Christ's institution, if he had considered these things well, or had conferred herein with the old catholic fathers, he would have better advised himself. For instead of many, for shortness sake, to allege but one, St Cyprian's words in this matter be very plain: *Quidam vel ignoranter*

De Miss. Publica Proroganda.

1 Cor. xi.

Cypr. Lib. ii. Epist. 3.

[1 In much of what Harding alleges under this article, he does little more than copy Hosius. See Hos. Op. Col. 1584. De Express. Dei Verb. Tom. I. pp. 625, &c. De Utr. Spec. Com. pp. 644, &c.]

[2 Luther afterward speaks of his earlier opinion in these terms: Hactenus ego stultus sensi, pulchrum fore, si pro laicis utraque species sacramenti porrigenda statueretur concilio generali.—Luth. Op. Witeb. 1552-80. De Captiv. Babyl. Tom. II. fol. 63. 2.

These passages are extracted almost literally from Hosius, De Utr. Spec. Com. p. 649.]

[3 H. A. 1564 omits *a*.]

[4 Ourself, 1565.]

vel simpliciter, in calice dominico sanctificando et plebi ministrando, non hoc faciunt, quod Jesus Christus Dominus et Deus noster, hujus sacrificii auctor et doctor, fecit et docuit[5]: "Some there be that, in sanctifying the cup, and delivering it unto the people, do not that thing that Jesus Christ our Lord and God, the author and teacher of this sacrifice, both did and taught." And addeth further: "If any man be in this error, seeing the light of the truth, let him return again unto the root and unto the original of the Lord's tradition[6]." And after in the same epistle: "We keep not the thing that is commanded us, unless we do the same that the Lord did[7]." In these few words St Cyprian saith, "The Lord both did it, and taught it to be done." He calleth it "the Lord's tradition:" he calleth it "the Lord's commandment." And here cannot M. Harding steal away in the mist, and say, St Cyprian meant all this of the cup that the priest consecrateth for himself. For his very words be plain to the contrary: *In calice dominico sanctificando, et plebi ministrando:* that is, "In sanctifying the Lord's cup, and ministering it unto the people." And if St Cyprian might well write thus against the heretics called *Aquarii*, which in the holy ministration would use no wine, but instead thereof did consecrate water, and ministered it unto the people; much more may we say the same against our adversaries, which consecrate and minister unto the people no cup at all. Wherefore at the end of the same epistle he concludeth with these words: "Not to do that thing that the Lord did, what is it else than to cast off his word, and to despise his discipline, and to commit not worldly but spiritual robbery and adultery, while as a man from the truth of the gospel stealeth away both the sayings and doings of the Lord, and corrupteth and defileth God's commandments? So is it[8] written in the prophet Jeremy: 'What is chaff in comparison of corn? Therefore will I upon these prophets, saith the Lord, that steal my words each one of them from his neighbour, and deceive my people in their lies and in their errors[9].'"

Ad originem traditionis dominicæ. Quod mandatum est.

Jer. xxiii.

The words that Luther wrote to them of Bohemia, and the others here reported, were written by him before God had appointed him to publish the gospel; and therefore are no more to be alleged against him for that he wrote afterward, as note of inconstancy, than M. Harding's sermons, preached openly in the time of king Edward, are to be alleged against that he writeth now.

M. HARDING. THE SIXTH DIVISION.

Thus he wrote before he had[10] *conceived perfect*[11] *hatred against the church. But after that he had been better acquainted with the devil, and of him, appearing unto him sensibly, had been instructed with arguments against the sacrifice of the mass,* (51) *that the memory of our redemption by Christ wrought on the cross might utterly be abolished, he wrote hereof far otherwise:* Si quo casu concilium ... statueret ... minime omnium nos velle [mus] utraque specie potiri: imo tunc primum in despectum...concilii...vellemus aut una...aut neutra, et nequaquam utraque potiri, et eos plane anathema habere, quicunque talis concilii auctoritate ... potirentur utraque[12]: "*If in any case the council would so ordain, we would in no wise have both the kinds; but even then, in despite of the council, we would have one kind, or neither of them, and in no wise both, and hold them for accursed whosoever by authority of such a council would have both." These words declare what spirit Luther was of. They shew him like himself. Whosoever*

[*Of his conference with the devil he writeth Libello de missa angulari.* H. A. 1564.]

The fifty-first untruth, joined with a slander. Never man spake more reverently of the oblation of Christ upon the cross.

[5 Cypr. Op. Oxon. 1682. Ad Cæcil. Epist. lxiii. p. 148, where two words are transposed, *sacrificii hujus*.]

[6 ... si quis in isto errore adhuc teneatur, veritatis luce perspecta ad radicem atque originem traditionis dominicæ revertatur.—Id. ibid.]

[7 ... invenimus non observari a nobis quod mandatum est, nisi eadem quæ Dominus fecit, nos quoque faciamus.—Id. ibid. p. 152.] [8 It is, 1565.]

[9 ... non hoc idem facere quod fecerit Dominus, quid aliud est, quam sermones ejus abjicere, et disciplinam dominicam contemnere, nec terrena sed spiritalia furta et adulteria committere; dum quis de evangelica veritate furatur Domini nostri verba et facta, et corrumpit atque adulterat præcepta divina? Sicut apud Hieremiam scriptum est: Quid est, inquit, paleis ad triticum? propter hoc ecce ego ad prophetas, dicit Dominus, qui furantur verba mea unusquisque a proximo suo, et seducunt populum meum in mendaciis suis et in erroribus suis.—Id. ibid. p. 157.]

[10 Before that he had, H. A. 1564.]

[11 Perfite, 1565, and H. A. 1564.]

[12 Luth. Op. Form. Miss. pro Eccles. Witemb. Tom. II. fol. 386; where for *una* we find *alterutra, ac plane eos, autoritate talis concilii,* and *utraque potirentur.*]

readeth his books with indifferent judgment shall find that, sithence the apostles' time, never wrote man so arrogantly, ne so despitefully against the church, nor so contrarily to himself. Which marks be so evident, that whosoever will not see them, but suffereth himself to be carried away into error, hatred of the church, and contempt of all godliness, either by him or by his scholars, except he repent and return, he is guilty of his own damnation, utterly overthrown, and sinneth inexcusably, as one condemned by his own judgment. [Tit. iii. H. A. 1564.] *But for excuse hereof, in his book of the Captivity of Babylon, he confesseth that he wrote thus, not for that he thought so, nor for that he judged the use of one kind unlawful, but because he was stirred by hatred and anger so to do. His words do sound so much plainly:* Provocatus, imo per vim raptus[1]: "*I wrote this (saith he) otherwise than I thought in my heart, provoked, and by violence pulled to it, whether I would or no." Here I doubt not but wise men will regard more that Luther wrote when his mind was quiet and calm, than when it was enraged with blustering storms of naughty affections*[2].

THE BISHOP OF SARISBURY.

There is nothing so easy as to speak ill. There was nothing further off from Luther's mind, than, upon any determination of any council, to minister the sacrament under one kind, and so to break Christ's institution into halves. But he thought it not meet that God's truth immortal should hang of the authority of a mortal man, and stand for true no further than it should please a man to allow of it. Notwithstanding, such interest and authority the pope hath claimed to himself, forcing the world to believe, as he himself writeth, that "he hath all right and law in the closet of his breast[3]." And one Sylvester Prierias, governor of pope Leo's palace, was not ashamed nor afraid to write these words: *A doctrina Romanæ ecclesiæ et Romani pontificis sacra scriptura robur et auctoritatem trahit*[4]: "The holy scripture taketh strength and authority of the church and bishop of Rome." This was the thing that D. Luther misliked, and thought intolerable. And therefore he said he would have God's word received only because it is God's word, and spoken by him, not because it is authorised by a council; and if the council would allow the ministration in one kind, then, he said, he would use both, because Christ in his institution appointed both. But if the bishops in the council would agree upon both kinds, as a matter standing wholly in their pleasures, as though they had full power to control or to ratify the will of God, then, he said, he would have no regard unto the authority of such a council, that setteth itself above God, but rather would use one kind only, or none at all. For this cause M. Harding reproveth Doctor Luther so bitterly, and calleth him arrogant, because he would not have God's will subject to the will of man.

Extr. de Const. Licet Roman.

Sylvest. Prier. Magist. Palatii.

Yet it appeareth that St Paul in the like case did the like. For, notwithstanding he had circumcised Timothy, yet, when he saw certain come in that would needs force the same upon Titus also, and so make it necessary, he withstood them stoutly, and would not yield. Thus he writeth: "Neither was Titus, that then was with me, compelled to be circumcised, for the coming in of certain false brethren, which came upon us to try out our liberty that we have in Christ Jesus[5], to the intent to bring us into bondage. Unto whom we gave no place by yielding, no, not for any time, that the truth of the gospel might remain among you."

Acts xvi.

Gal. ii.

Eusebius in his story saith, there was an old law in Rome, that no emperor should consecrate a god, unless the same god had been first allowed by the council. Tiberius being emperor, when he heard of the wonderful works that

Euseb. Lib. ii. cap. ii.

[1 The whole passage will shew Luther's real meaning: Nam quo tempore sermonem de eucharistia edebam, in usu communi hærebam...At nunc, provocatus et exercitatus, imo per vim raptus in hanc harenam, dabo libere, quæ sentio.—Id. De Captiv. Babyl. Tom. II. fol. 64. 2.]

[2 This passage is almost literally from Hosius, Op. Col. 1584. De Utr. Spec. Com. Tom. I. p. 649.]

[3 Bonifac. VIII. in Corp. Jur. Canon. Lugd. 1624. Sext. Decretal. Lib. I. Tit. ii. cap. 1. col. 11. See before, page 68.]

[4 Quicunque non innititur doctrinæ Romanæ ecclesiæ ac Romani pontificis, tanquam regulæ fidei infallibili, a qua etiam sacra scriptura robur trahit et autoritatem, hæreticus est.—Sylvest. Prier. In Luth. Concl. Dial. in Luth. Op. Witeb. 1552-80. Tom. I. fol. 159. 2.]

[5 Jesu, 1565.]

were wrought by Christ in Jewry, thought therefore he was a God, and promoted a bill unto the council, that Christ might be proclaimed and taken for a God. But the council was otherwise bent, and would allow him for no God[6]. Tertullian laugheth at their folly. His words be these: *Apud vos de humano arbitrio divinitas pensitatur. Nisi homini Deus placuerit, non erit Deus. Homo jam Deo propitius esse debet*[7]: "Amongst you the divinity and state of God is weighed by man's judgment. Unless God please man, God (amongst you) shall be no God. Now therefore man must be good and favourable unto his God." The like folly seemeth to be in them that think God's truth is no truth, unless the consent of a council allow it to be truth. To this same purpose Luther wrote a book unto the knights of the order of Russia, after they had obtained from the pope a dispensation to marry, notwithstanding their vow. He chargeth them, "that in any wise they marry not by warrant of that dispensation; otherwise (he saith) they offend God, and be worse than adulterers, as having more regard unto man than unto God; and having God's own dispensation, as if it were not sufficient, would seek further for the dispensation of a man.

Tertull. in Apologet.

Ad Nobiles Ordinis Teutonici.

Luther wrote not this in the despite of any godly council, no more than the prophet Esay, when he said: *Inite concilium, et dissipabitur:* "Go, gather your council; and it shall be broken." But he could not suffer to see God's glory so defaced, that a company of men should presume to allow or disallow his truth, as if it were not true in itself, but must fall or stand only at their pleasure.

Isai. viii.

The rest that followeth is nothing else but unseemly slander. But God be blessed, that hath delivered that godly man from lying tongues!

But Luther, saith M. Harding, was contrary unto himself. Even so Marcion the heretic charged St Paul that he spake against the ceremonies, and yet himself shaved his head at Cenchreæ, and observed the ceremonies; that he would not circumcise Titus, and yet had circumcised Timotheus; that he would sometime defend the law, and sometime reprove the law; and so was evermore contrary to himself. And he that had M. Harding's spirit perhaps would no more doubt to find fault with St Paul for inconstancy than with Luther. If Luther were ever contrary to himself, yet might no man worse charge him in that behalf than M. Harding. But Luther evermore followed God's calling, and never returned back unto his vomit, neither fought against his own conscience, nor against the manifest known truth. And therefore, although he were contrary unto himself, as passing from error unto truth, yet was he not contrary unto God.

Acts xxi.

M. HARDING. THE SEVENTH DIVISION.

Now to put this matter, that Luther judged it a thing indifferent whether one receive the sacrament under one kind or both, more out of doubt, Philip Melancthon, his scholar, and nearest of his counsel, writeth: Sicut edere suillam, aut abstinere a suilla, sic alterutra signi parte uti medium esse[8]: "*That, as it is a thing indifferent to eat swine's flesh, or to forbear swine's flesh, so it is also to use which part of the sign a man listeth." By the word "sign," he meaneth the sacrament, liking better that strange word, than the accustomed word of the church, lest he might perhaps be thought, of the brethren of his sect, in somewhat to join with the catholics.*

In Locis Communibus.

Bucer also is of the same opinion, who, in the conference that was had between the catholics and protestants, for agreement in controversies of religion at Ratisbone, confirmed and allowed this article by his full consent, with these words: Ad controversiam, quæ est de una aut utraque specie, tollendam, cum primis conducturum, ut sancta ecclesia liberam faceret potestatem sacramentum hoc in una vel in utraque specie sumendi; ea tamen lege, ut nulli per hoc detur occasio, quem usum tantopere retinuit ecclesia, temere condemnandi, aut invicem judicandi[9]: "*That the controversy for the one or both kinds may be taken*

[[6] Euseb. in Hist. Eccles. Script. Amst. 1695-1700. Lib. II. cap. ii. pp. 31, 2.]

[[7] Tertull. Op. Lut. 1641. Apologet. 5. p. 6; where we find *arbitratu, deus non erit*, and *debebit*.]

[[8] Hosius confesses that in later editions of the Common-places Melancthon left out these words.]

[[9] Hosius, from whom Harding transcribed the passage, did not mean to attribute these words to Bucer. They are, with some difference of expression, those of the article itself proposed at the con-

A Sign. *away, it shall be very well done that holy church made it free to receive this sacrament in one or both kinds; yet under such condition as hereby no occasion be given to any body rashly to condemn the use which the church hath so long time kept, nor to judge another*[1]*." Soothly he which would have it free and at liberty to receive the sacrament under one or both kinds, and holdeth opinion that the old custom of the one kind only is not to be condemned, seemeth plainly enough to confess that nothing hath been instituted or commanded of Christ touching this matter, as necessary to salvation.*

Thus we may see plainly that they, which have divided themselves from the mystical body of Christ, that is, his church, who were of greatest learning and judgment, make it a matter indifferent (as it is indeed of itself left to the liberty of the church) whether the sacrament be ministered under one kind or both. And thus[2] *much hath been confessed against M. Jewel and his sect, not only by the learned adversaries of the church in our time, but also by a learned man of Bohemia, above six-score years past. His name is John Przybram, of whose writings some are set forth in print. This learned man, whereas he endeavoured to prove the use of both kinds of the words of Christ written by St John, "Except ye eat the flesh of the Son of man, and drink his blood, ye shall not have life in you," at length uttereth these words according to the eloquence of his time:* Veruntamen hic Deum timens, et mores impios aliorum præcavens, fateor, quod quaslibet personas de ecclesia communioni fidelium sub utraque specie repugnantes damnare aut hæreticare non intendo[3]: *"But here, having the fear of God before mine eyes, and being well ware I follow not the wicked conditions of others, I grant that, what persons soever of the church repine against the communion of the faithful people under both kinds, I intend not to condemn them, nor to hold them for heretics." But if it be the commandment of God that the sacrament be received of all under both kinds, why should he be forbidden by the fear of God to condemn those that withstand that order of communion, seeing that whosoever goeth against God's commandment is worthy to be condemned? Therefore by his testimony the use of one or both kinds is indifferent*[4].

In Li. Profession. Fidei Catholicæ, cap. xix.

Thus we are able to allege Luther, Melancthon, Bucer, and that learned Bohemian, for the indifferency of the communion to be ministered[5] *either under one kind or both: whereby I mean not that the use of the sacrament is so left to every man's liberty as he that listeth may require both kinds, and another may content himself with one kind. Not so. Every man is bound to follow the order of the church; but the church is not bound of necessity, by God's commandment, to minister it under both kinds to the laity.*

THE BISHOP OF SARISBURY.

To prove that the half communion is a thing indifferent, he bringeth forth the authority of Melancthon, Bucer, and a certain learned man of Bohemia; some of them falsely alleged, and some without any allegation at all. Neither doth he bring them to the intent to take them for his authors, and to follow them; for they, neither in their books, nor in the order of their churches, ever consented to the breach of Christ's institution. But herein he bewrayeth his want of old doctors; for, having the authority of them, he would never have alleged any of these.

In Melancthon he misliketh much the manner of his speech, in that he calleth the sacrament a sign: "which word," as he saith, "is strange, and not the accustomed word of the church." Saving that he seeketh occasions and quarrels without cause, as his wont is, otherwise he knoweth that a sacrament hath been called a sign in all times and ages of the church.

---

ference. See Lib. Propos. ad Comp. Relig. xxi. in Joh. Eck. Apol. adv. Col. Buc. Antv. 1542. foll. 38, 9. The following is the opinion of Bucer: Porro constituto consensu doctrinæ, si populus invitaretur ad hunc usum, et usus restitueretur, esset jam concordia. quia enim persecutio cessasset, et doctrina sincera proponeretur, etiamsi non subito mutarent suam consuetudinem singuli, in usu tamen discordia publica non esset, &c.—Acta Coll. Ratisp. Hab. per M. Bucer. Argent. 1541. Artic. Protest. De Us. Integr. Sacr. fol. 37.]

[1 One another, 1565, and H. A. 1564.]

[2 This, H. A. 1564.]

[3 Duo de Sept. Sacr. Tractat. duor. Bohem. ad calc. Cochl. Hist. Hussit. Mogunt. 1549. p. 511.]

[4 The preceding paragraphs with the authorities are taken from Hosius, Op. Col. 1584. De Utr. Spec. Com. Tom. I. p. 650.]

[5 Minister, H. A. 1564.]

Petrus Lombardus thus defineth a sacrament: *Sacramentum est signum rei sacræ*[6]: "A sacrament is the sign of a holy thing." And as it is thought, the very substance and nature of a thing cannot be better known than by the definition. St Augustine saith: [*Signa*] *cum ad res divinas adhibentur, sacramenta vocantur*[7]: "Signs, when they be applied to godly things, be called sacraments." And again, writing of the difference that is between the sacraments of the old law and of the new, he saith thus: *In signis diversis eadem fides*[8]: "The signs being divers, the faith is one." And writing against one Adimantus, he saith: *Non dubitavit Dominus dicere, Hoc est corpus meum, cum daret signum corporis sui*[9]: "The Lord doubted not to say, This is my body, when he gave the sign of his body." Likewise saith Chrysostom: *Si mortuus Jesus non est, cujus symbolum ac signum hoc sacrificium est*[10]? "If Jesus died not, whose token and whose sign is this sacrifice?" And lest any man should be deceived in the meaning of this word "sign," St Augustine himself hath expounded it thus: *Signum est res, præter speciem, quam ingerit sensibus, aliud quiddam faciens ex se in cognitionem venire*[11]: "A sign is a thing, that, besides the sight itself which it offereth unto the senses, causeth of itself some other certain thing to come into knowledge." Hereby it may appear that this word "sign" is not so strange as M. Harding would have it seem, nor so unaccustomed unto the church. Although it mislike him that we should do as the old fathers did, yet he might give us leave to use such words and phrases as the old fathers used.

A Sign.

Lib. iv. Dist. 1.

August. de Doctrina Christiana, Lib. iii. cap. vi.

In Johan. Tract. 45.

August. contra Adimantum, cap. xii.

Chrysost. in Mat. Hom. 83.

August. de Doctrina Christiana, Lib. ii. De Con. Dist. 2. Signum est.

"But," saith he[12], "Melancthon and Bucer accounted it a[13] thing indifferent." Indeed these godly-learned men, when they saw that, through the malice of their adversaries, they could not obtain that Christ's institution might universally be received, yet they desired at the least it might be left free, without restraint, for every church to do therein as they should think good, and that without murmur or offence of others. And thus far forth their desire was it might be judged free; not that they thought Christ had not ordained the sacrament to be ministered unto the people in both kinds, or that in itself it is indifferent, but that the faithful of God might indifferently and freely use it without controlment, and that it should not be judged heresy to do as Christ hath commanded.

So the godly fathers at the beginning, when they could not persuade the princes of the world, with their people, to receive the gospel, yet they thought they were gainers, and gave God thanks, when they might have place and liberty for themselves freely and with quiet conscience to meet together, and to preach the gospel.

This liberty M. Harding cannot like withal. He would have it free for the whole church to determine of it; but not for every church particular. This is a shift to deceive the ignorant. For he knoweth well that all other churches throughout the world, from the first planting of the gospel until this day, do still minister the holy communion in both kinds, as Christ commanded; and that Christ's institution was never openly and by consent broken, but only in the church of Rome; which church also is not universal, but mere particular; and that the same breach, in the same church of Rome, sprang not of any consent of bishops, or other learned men, but, as it is proved before, only of the simple devotion of the people. And doth M. Harding think the people may safely break Christ's institution without any general council, and may not safely return again to the same without a general council? Verily there needeth no council, where as nothing is done by council.

[6 Pet. Lombard. Lib. Sentent. Col. Agrip. 1576. Lib. IV. Dist. i. B. fol. 330. 2; where the words are transposed.]

[7 These words do not occur in the place indicated. See however August. Op. Par. 1679-1700. Ad Marcellin. Epist. cxxxvii. 7. Tom. II. col. 412; where for *adhibentur* we find *pertinent.*]

[8 Id. In Johan. Evang. cap. x. Tractat. xlv. 9. Tom. III. Pars II. col. 598.]

[9 Id. Cont. Adimant. Lib. cap. xii. 3. Tom. VIII. col. 124; where the words are transposed: *Non enim Dominus dubitavit,* and *signum daret.*]

[10 Εἰ γὰρ μὴ ἀπέθανεν ὁ Ἰησοῦς, τίνος σύμβολα τὰ τελούμενα;—Chrysost. Op. Par. 1718-38. In Matt. Hom. lxxxii. Tom. VII. p. 783.]

[11 August. in Corp. Jur. Canon. Lugd. 1624. Decret. Gratian. Decr. Tert. Pars, De Consecr. Dist. ii. can. 33. col. 1926; where we find *aliud aliquid ex se faciens.* Op. De Doctr. Christ. Lib. II. cap. i. 1. Tom. III. Pars I. col. 19.]

[12 He saith, 1565.]

[13 It as a, 1565.]

Nestorius.

Touching the indifferency of this matter, whereupon M. Harding hath built this whole treaty, and in what sort the breach of Christ's institution may seem a thing indifferent, I know no better answer than that is already made by St Cyprian, who in the like case maketh answer thus: *Si quis de antecessoribus meis... non hoc observavit et tenuit, quod nos Dominus... exemplo et magisterio suo docuit, potest simplicitati ejus de indulgentia Domini venia concedi: nobis vero non poterit ignosci, qui nunc a Domino admoniti et instructi sumus, &c.*[1]: "If any of my predecessors have not followed and kept that thing which the Lord, by his example and commandment, hath taught us, he for his simplicity may be pardoned; but if we wilfully offend, there is no pardon for us, that are already warned and instructed of the Lord. We give God thanks, that, whiles he instructeth us what we shall do for the time to come, he forgiveth us that is past, because we have erred of simplicity." Thus far forth the breach of God's ordinance may be borne withal, by the judgment of St Cyprian. But he addeth further: *Post inspirationem vero, et revelationem factam, qui in eo quod erraverat perseverat, prudens et sciens, sine venia ignorantiæ peccat, præsumptione... atque obstinatione... superatus*[2]: "After that God hath once opened and revealed (his truth) whoso continueth still in his error, willingly and wittingly offendeth, without hope of pardon, as being overcome with presumption and wilfulness."

Cypr. Lib. ii. Epist. iii.

Cypr. ad Jubaianum, de Hæreticis Baptizandis.

M. HARDING. THE EIGHTH DIVISION.

And whereas it was ministered in both kinds at Corinth, as it appeareth by St Paul, and in sundry other places, as we find most evidently in the writings of divers ancient fathers, yet the church hath been moved by divers and weighty causes to take order that the people should receive their communion under one kind, not only in the council of Basil, but also in that of Constance, and long before them, above a thousand years, in (52) *the first council of Ephesus, as many do probably gather, and namely Urbanus Regius, a doctor of Luther's school, confesseth in his book* De Locis Communibus[4]. *One cause, and not the least, was, that thereby the heresy of Nestorius might the rather be extinguished, who, amongst other errors, held opinion* (53) *that under the form of bread in the sacrament is contained the body of Christ without his blood; and under the form of the wine, his blood only without his body. Many other causes moved those fathers to take that order, for the avoiding of many inconveniences, dangers, and offences, which might happen in the use of the cup, as unreverence of so high a sacrament, whereof christian people at the beginning had a marvellous care and regard; the loathsomeness of many that cannot brook the taste of wine; the difficulty of getting, and impossibility of keeping wine from corruption, in countries situated near to the north pole, in that clime where is known to be great extremity of cold; beside a number of the like. So that it had been besides*[5] *reason to have bound all to the necessity of both kinds.*

[*Causes moving the church to communicate under one kind.* H. A. 1564.]

The fifty-second untruth. For[3] there was no such canon touched, or once moved in that council.

The fifty-third untruth. For[3] Nestorius never dreamed of any such folly.

Weighty considerations wherefore Christ's institution should be broken.

THE BISHOP OF SARISBURY.

He granteth that St Paul at Corinth, and sundry other holy fathers in their several churches, ministered the sacrament in both kinds. He might as well have said, all the apostles, and all the holy fathers, saving for hindering of his cause. "But the church afterward upon good causes (as it is here alleged) took order to the contrary, and namely to confute the heretic Nestorius."

Here must thou mark, good christian reader, the question is, whether M. Harding's half communion were ever ministered openly to the people in the church within the space of six hundred years after Christ. For proof hereof he allegeth that this order was allowed in the councils of Constance and Basil;

[1 Cypr. Op. Oxon. 1682. Ad Cæcil. Epist. lxiii. pp. 156, 7; where for *meis* we find *nostris.*]

[2 Id. Ad Jubai. Epist. lxxiii. p. 204; where *cum ratione superetur.*]

[3 1565 omits *for.*]

[4 Nestorius Constantinopolitanus episcopus laicos sub utraque specie communicavit, Ephesina synodus restitit.—Urban. Reg. Op. Norib. 1562. Loc. Com. xii. fol. 318. 2. See also Hos. Op. Col. 1584. De Utr. Spec. Com. Tom. I. p. 645.]

[5 Beside, H. A. 1564.]

the former whereof was begun and holden in the year of our Lord a thousand four hundred and fourteen[6], and the same neither general, nor ever generally received. And what force can he find herein to prove his purpose? "It is also probably gathered," saith M. Harding, "that the same order was taken a thousand years before, in the first council of Ephesus." Here he is driven utterly to leave his learning, and, as he commonly doth, only to hold by bare guess. But if this new device were brought in to confute the heretic Nestorius, why then took it place first in the councils of Constance and Basil, a thousand years after that Nestorius was dead, and his heresy quite forgotten? If it were so ordered in the council of Ephesus, why is there no act or mention thereof extant in that council, nor any learned man within a thousand years after, to record the same?

Nestorius. Anno 1414.

"But Urbanus Regius, a doctor of Luther's school, confesseth it." First, Urbanus Regius departed this life not above twenty years ago; and therefore is a very young witness to testify a thing done so long before. Besides this, the book of Common-places that is abroad in his name is nothing else but a heap of things gathered together by long reading, as the manner of students is, out of divers and sundry books, and that as well of the one side as of the other, only for help of memory and increase of knowledge. Neither was that book ever corrected or published by him, but only delivered to the printer as it was, by his widow, after his death, as appeareth by Pomeranus, that dedicated that book to the prince of Mensburg[7]. And therefore these collections do witness his diligence, but not his judgment. As touching that note concerning the council of Ephesus, it may be thought he had it out of Alardus, or Michael Væhe, or some other like writer of this age.

"Nestorius, amongst other errors," saith M. Harding, "held opinion, that, under the form of bread in the sacrament is contained the body of Christ without his blood, and, under the form of wine, the blood only without his body." Why should this man thus delight himself to uphold one falsehood[8] with another? First he saith, "The council of Ephesus decreed against both kinds." This is untrue, and was never yet proved. Next, some cause must be devised that should lead the fathers to that decree: which, as it is here surmised, was this error of Nestorius. A cause that never was is good enough to prove the effect that never was. Thus is M. Harding driven not only to forge new doctors, and new decrees of councils, but also to imagine new heresies such as were never heard of before; even in like sort, and to like purpose, as by some it is supposed that Aristotle sometime imagined strange and monstrous opinions to be taught by Democritus, Parmenides, Melissus, and other old philosophers; not because they had ever taught or written so indeed, but to the end to find occasion of talk, and the better to set abroad his own learning. If it be true that is surmised by Nestorius, then M. Harding's whole defence standeth but upon an heresy: if it be untrue, as indeed it is, then it standeth upon an open falsehood[8]: and so, whether it be true or false, it hath a very weak foundation.

As for Nestorius, it is known he was a wicked and a blasphemous heretic, and was worthily condemned by sundry holy fathers and councils. Philastrius, Epiphanius, and St Augustine, have written namely of his errors: the council of Ephesus, the council of Chalcedon, Cœlestinus, Gelasius, Leo, bishops of Rome, Cyrillus bishop of Alexandria, have ripped up and condemned all the branches of his heresies. Yet none of them all ever charged Nestorius with this new heresy of M. Harding's making. If there had been in it any shew of truth, M. Harding, as he is eloquent, would have laid out all the circumstances, when this strange error first began, where, and how long it continued, who wrote against it, and by whom and in what council it was condemned. Verily this great silence declareth some want. It must needs be a very strange heresy, that never had neither beginning nor ending, nor defender nor reprover, nor mouth to utter it, nor ear to hear it, nor pen to write it, nor time to last in, nor place to

[6 Fourteenth, 1565.]
[7 Urban. Reg. Op. Epist. Loc. Theol. a J. F. Pomer. fol. 298. 2.]
[8 Falsehead, 1565.]

rest in. And if all this had been true of Nestorius, yet had it been no reason that, for any one man's private error, Christ's institution should be broken.

But that the vain folly and manifest falsehood[1] of these men may appear, understand, good reader, that where as Nestorius dwelt, and his heresy took place, in those countries they have evermore kept Christ's institution in both kinds; but in these countries, where as neither the name of Nestorius was ever heard of, but only unto a few, nor his heresy ever received, there have they made great provisos against Nestorius, yea, a thousand years after Nestorius was dead.

The rest of the causes which he calleth so weighty, are scarcely worth any answer. "Some men do loathe wine; some people can hardly get, some can hardly keep wine; *ergo*, there must be made a law general, that the whole world shall communicate in one kind." If the conclusion had been, that such as have these impediments or wants might so communicate, it had been more tolerable. For, as it is well noted by Pomponius, "Laws must touch things that happen commonly and for the most part, not things that happen to few, or seldom[2]." Otherwise the like reason may be made for the priests: some priests, by mean of disease, can taste no wine; some in certain countries can hardly get, some can hardly keep wine; therefore it were well provided that all priests should minister under one kind. Certainly, where as wine may be provided for the priest, there may also wine be provided for the people: for it were strange to hear that a cart or a whole ship should come laden[3] only with one bottle of wine into a country.

De Legib. et Senatuscons. et Longa Consuetud. Ἐπὶ τὸ πλεῖστον ἐκ παραλόγου.

Some say that the priests in Russia, for lack of wine, used to consecrate in metheglen: some other say that Innocentius the Eighth, for the like want, dispensed with the priests of Norway to consecrate without wine[4]. It were no reason to bind the whole church to the necessity or imbecility of a few. For otherwise the same want and impossibility, that M. Harding hath here found for the one part of the sacrament, may be found also for the other. For Arrianus *de rebus Indicis*, and Strabo in his Geography, have written, that there be whole nations and countries that have no bread[5]. Therefore it should seem necessary by this conclusion, that, in consideration of them, the whole church should abstain from the other portion of the sacrament also, and so have no sacrament at all.

Corn. Agrip. de Vanit. Scient. Volaterranus.

Arrianus, Lib. viii. Strabo.

M. HARDING. THE NINTH DIVISION.

Now in very deed, if we would grant our[6] adversaries, which in no wise we do[7] grant, that it hath been commanded of Christ the lay-people should communicate under both kinds, by these words, "Drink ye all of this;" yet, this notwithstanding, the exact straitness of God's ordinance may without sin in cases be omitted, in such things which be not necessarily to be observed of themselves, or of the prescript of the law of nature; so that great and weighty causes (the rule of charity exactly observed) require the same. For evident proof of this, we have examples both of the old, and also of the new testament. Did not God command that none should eat of the shew-bread but the priest[8] only? David ate thereof; and yet Christ cleareth him of all blame. The law of circumcision, so straitly commanded, was for the space of forty years by the people of Israel quite omitted, whiles they passed from Egypt to the land of promise; and God found no fault with them for it. God gave the law of keeping holy the sabbath-day without exception. The Machabees notwithstanding sticked not to arm themselves against Antiochus, and to spend

Lev. xxiv. 1 Sam. xxi. Mark ii. Gen. xvii. and xxxiv. Exod. xx. 1 Macc. ii.

[1 Falsehead, 1565.]

[2 Jura constitui oportet, ut dixit Theophrastus, in his quæ ἐπὶ τὸ πλεῖστον, id est, *ut plurimum*, accidunt, non quæ ἐκ παραλόγου, id est, *ex inopinato*. —Pompon. in Corp. Jur. Civil. Amst. 1663. Digest. Lib. I. Tit. iii. 3. Tom. I. p. 78.]

[3 Loaden, 1565.]

[4 Innocentius octavus (Volaterrano teste) concessit Norwegiis, ut liceret illis sine vino sacrificare calicem.—H. Corn. Agrip. De Incert. et Vanit. Scient. Col. 1584. De Cær. cap. lx. fol. N. 4. See before, page 137, note 6.]

[5 The Ichthyophagi are doubtless meant.—Arrian. Lib. Hist. Ind. cap. xxix. Strabon. Geograph. Lib. xv.]

[6 To our, 1565, and H. A. 1564.]

[7 Do not, 1565, 1609, and H. A. 1564.]

[8 Priests, 1565, and H. A. 1564.]

that day in the field in their defence, having no scruple of conscience for breach of that law. Many the like examples we find in the old testament. But let us come to the new testament, and to the sacraments of the time of grace. In due consideration of which, we may find that Christ hath scarcely commanded any outward thing, the moderation, qualifying, and ordering whereof he hath not left to his church, as, according to the condition of the time, it hath been seen most expedient for the common preferment and edifying of the same: so that notwithstanding there be no swerving from the scope and principal intent, and no creature defrauded of that good which by the outward things is to be attained.

Touching the sacrament of baptism, though nothing be said of the teaching of them that should be baptized, neither of the dipping of them into the water, which Christ's charge in this behalf given seemeth plainly to require: "Go you," saith he to his apostles, "and teach all nations, baptizing them," &c.; and yet the church hath not feared to baptize infants, that be without capacity of teaching; and for the due administration of this sacrament too many have[9] *thought pouring or sprinkling of water upon them sufficient: though this be not spoken of, I say, it is much to be considered to this purpose, that the apostles sticked not for a time to alter and change the very essential form of words with which Christ would this sacrament to be ministered. For, whereas he commanded them to baptize in the name of the Father, and of the Son, and of the Holy Ghost, they baptized in the name of Jesus Christ* (54) *only, intending thereby to make that to be of more fame and celebrity.*

Matt. xxviii.

[Acts viii. H. A. 1564.]

The fifty-fourth untruth. A foul depravation of the scriptures.

So, to return to the sacrament of the body and blood of Christ, whereof we treat, no man can deny but many things were at the institution of it done by the example of Christ, and by him commanded, which now be not observed; and yet in that respect no fault is found. Christ washed the apostles' feet, and gave them an express commandment to do the same, with these most plain words: "If I, that am your Master and Lord, have washed your feet, you also ought to wash one another's feet: for I have given you an example, that, as I have done, you do so likewise;" which commandment of Christ, according to the outward letter, verily bindeth no less than these words: "Drink ye all of this;" yet this commandment is not kept, but clean grown out of use: though it appear by St Bernard, who calleth it Magnum Sacramentum[10], *"a great sacrament," and long before, by report of St Cyprian, that Christ did not only wash his apostles' feet, but commanded also by solemn request, and ordained that the apostles afterward should do the same*[11]. *Whether this ordinance of Christ hath been abolished, for that it should not be thought a rebaptization, as it may be gathered of St Augustine*[12], *or for any other cause, it forceth not greatly. But this is much to be marvelled at, that this, so earnestly commanded, is so quietly and with such silence suffered undone, and in the ministration of the sacrament the use of the cup so factiously and with so much crying out required. Neither in many other rites and ceremonies we do not as Christ did. Christ celebrated this sacrament after that he had supped: we do it in the morning and fasting. Christ sat at the table with his twelve apostles: neither sit we at a table, neither think we it necessary to observe such number. Christ brake the bread: we think it not necessary to break the host that is to be delivered to the faithful participants. Here is to be noted, that St Cyprian, rebuking them which thought sprinkling or pouring of water not to be sufficient for baptism, declareth that the sacraments be not to be esteemed according to*[13] *their extreme and rigorous observation, or administration of all the extern elements, but rather according to the integrity and soundness of faith of the giver and of the receiver; and that divine things, used in a compendious sort, confer and give nevertheless to the right believers their whole virtue*[14], Lib. iv. Epist. 7. *Many other commandments of God concerning outward things might here be rehearsed; which notwithstanding by little and little in the church have been omitted; as the forbearing of*

John xiii.

In Serm. de Cœna Domini.

In Serm. de Unctione Chrismatis.

Ad Januarium. cap. xviii.

[9 To many, hath, 1565, and H. A. 1564.]

[10 Bernard. Op. Par. 1690. In Cœn. Dom. Serm. 4. Vol. I. Tom. III. col. 891. See below, page 225, note 6.]

[11 Cypr. Op. Oxon. 1682, De Unct. Chrism. (Arnold.) p. 46.]

[12 August. Op. Par. 1679-1700. Ad Inq. Januar. seu Epist. lv. 33. Tom. II. col. 141.]

[13 Unto, H. A. 1564.]

[14 Cypr. Op. Ad Magn. Epist. lxix. pp. 185, 6.]

In the name of Christ only.

strangled things and blood; which was commanded by God in the old testament, and, according to the pleasure and advice of the Holy Ghost, decreed by the apostles in the new testament. Yet, forasmuch as concerneth outward things, both this and many other the like have in process of time grown out of observation, and have without any scruple of conscience been abrogated.

THE BISHOP OF SARISBURY.

The best stay, that these men can lay hold upon, is to deny Christ's institution. And therefore M. Harding saith here, "In nowise we do not grant it;" which is an argument of good courage, but of small proof. But he addeth further, if it were Christ's institution, yet notwithstanding, by the authority of the church, and upon good consideration, it might be broken. His reasons be these: in the old testament, David did eat the shew-bread, notwithstanding it were forbidden; the people in the wilderness ceased from circumcision, notwithstanding it were commanded; the Machabees fought and defended themselves upon the sabbath-day, notwithstanding God had appointed that day to rest. In the new testament, we baptize infants that can receive no teaching; and sometime we think it sufficient to sprinkle them, or to pour them over; and the apostles, contrary to Christ's institution, baptized in the name of Jesus only. If M. Harding could have brought any such example or authority as was required, such poor helps should not have needed. For these allegations are partly true, partly false, partly not agreeable to that we have in hand, neither in place, nor in time, nor in the end, nor in the manner of doing, nor in other circumstances, and therefore make little to this purpose.

1 Sam. xxi. Josh. v. 1 Macc. ii.

1 Sam. xxi. David took of the shew-bread: but he was forced thereto by extremity of famine; neither did he ever decree that it should be lawful for all others to do the like.

Josh. v. The people ceased from circumcision in the wilderness: but they had God's special dispensation so to do, as it is noted by Lyra, for that they were in continual travel from place to place; and people being newly circumcised could abide no labour[1]: yet made they made no law that circumcision should quite be abolished.

1 Macc. ii. Matt. xii. Dion. The Machabees might lawfully defend themselves upon the sabbath-day. For, as Christ expoundeth the law: "Man is not made for the sabbath; but the sabbath is made for man." And therefore the Jews did ill, that being besieged upon the sabbath-day, as Dion saith, stood still, and yielded themselves unto their enemies[2]. Yet did not the Machabees proclaim that it should be lawful upon the sabbath to go to the field.

Ezek. xvi. Touching baptism, first we teach the fathers, and afterward we baptize them and their children; and this is no breach of Christ's commandment. For after we be once become God's people, God hath promised, "that he will be our God, and the God of our children;" and by the prophet Ezechiel he saith, "Your children be my children." They that sprinkled them that they baptized used both the word and also the element or kind of water that was commanded: neither doth it appear that Christ gave any commandment of dipping the party into the water. But these men take quite away from the people both the element and kind of wine, and also the words of consecration.

M. Harding falsifieth the words of St Luke. Last of all, in that he saith, "The apostles, contrary to the institution, baptized in the name of Christ *only*," beside[3] the mere sophistication of the matter, he also falsifieth the words, putting that behind that St Luke set before.

And that thou mayest the better perceive the fraud, I must do thee, christian reader, to understand that, in the time of the apostles, some that were baptized received the Holy Ghost in sensible signs, and were able immediately, some to

---

[1 Populus enim Israel movebat castra quacumque hora nubes movebatur præbens eis ducatum: et quia incertus erat eis motus nubis; ideo dispensative factum est quod illi qui fuerunt nati in deserto remanserunt incircumcisi usque ad tempus istud: quia periculosum esset de novo circumcisos itinerare seu portari in itinere.—Bibl. cum Gloss. Ord. et Expos. N. de Lyra, Basil. 1502. Jos. cap. v. Pars II. fol. 8. 2.]

[2 Dion. Cass. Hist. Rom. Libb. xxxvii. xlix.]

[3 Besides, 1565.]

speak sundry tongues, some to work other miracles. Some others received[4] no such miracle, but baptism only; as they of Samaria, that were baptized by Philip. Therefore, saith St Luke, "Peter and John prayed for them, that they also might receive the Holy Ghost in visible signs, as well as others. For the Holy Ghost, until that time, was come upon none of them, but only they were baptized in the name of the Lord Jesus;" by this word "only" excluding nothing else but the outward miraculous gifts of the Holy Ghost.

Washing of feet.

Acts viii.

Only.

But M. Harding transporteth[5] and shifteth St Luke's words at his pleasure, and placeth this word "only" in the end, and thereby excludeth the essential form of baptism, as if they had been baptized in the name of Christ only, and so not in the name of the Father and of the Holy Ghost. This error must needs hold by the canvassing of the scriptures.

To baptize in the "name of Christ," is to baptize according to the order, institution, and commandment of Christ. Neither do these words, "in the name of Christ," import that baptism was ministered in the name of Christ only, and in none other name beside; no more than these words, "Paul the servant of Jesus Christ," do import that Paul was the servant of Christ only, and so not the servant of God the Father, nor of the Holy Ghost; or these words that Paul spake unto the keeper, "Believe in the Lord Jesus," do discharge him from believing in the other two Persons of the holy Trinity. Doubtless he must be very bold with the scriptures of God, that will presume hereby to prove, either that the apostles altered the essential form of baptism, or that they proclaimed them heretics, that in baptizing would follow Christ's institution.

Acts xvi.

The objection of washing of feet is common, and hath been often answered. "St Bernard calleth it a sacrament[6]." I grant. But St Bernard is a doctor but of late years; and therefore his authority herein must weigh the lighter. Neither doth he so call it according to the nature and common definition of a sacrament. For neither was there any certain element namely chosen, nor any special words appointed to make it a sacrament, nor any promise of grace thereto annexed. Only he calleth it a sacrament by a general kind of taking. And in that meaning St Hilary saith, "The sacrament of prayer:" "the sacrament of fasting:" "the sacrament of fulness:" "the sacrament of thirst:" "the sacrament of weeping[7]." And St Bernard in another place in like sort saith, "The sacrament of a painted cross[8]." And in this place he saith that the washing of feet betokeneth the washing and purging of venial sins, which signification he calleth a sacrament.

In Serm. de Cœn. Dom.

Hilar. in Matt. can. 5, 11, 12, 13. Hilar. de Trin. Lib. x. Bernard de bonis defendendis.

But Christ saith: "I have given you an example, that, as ye have seen me do, ye also do the like." "Therefore," saith M. Harding, "this commandment bindeth as well as the other, Drink ye all of this." How may a man trust M. Harding in the dark, that will thus deceive him in the light? For he knoweth that the washing of feet was neither institution of Christ, nor any part of the sacrament, nor specially appointed to be done by the apostles, nor the breach thereof ever deemed sacrilege, as Gelasius writeth of this disorder of the half communion[9]. Whether the apostles for any time after Christ's resurrection observed it or no, it appeareth not. Neither is there anything, to my remembrance, written of it. As we may perceive by St Paul, it was an office more belonging unto women than unto men. And it seemeth by St Augustine, that this ceremony in the church had relation unto some other cause, and not unto the institution of Christ, neither to the example or practice of the apostles. For thus he writeth unto his friend Januarius touching the same: "If thou demand,

De Con. Dist. Comperimus.

1 Tim. v.

August. ad Januar. Epist. 118.

[[4] Receive, 1611.]

[[5] Transposeth, 1565, 1609.]

[[6] ... habemus ejus sacramentum pedum ablutionem.—Bernard. Op. Par. 1690. In Cœn. Dom. Serm. 4. Vol. I. Tom. III. col. 891.]

[[7] De orationis autem sacramento, &c.—Hilar. Op. Par. 1693. Comm. in Matt. cap. v. 1. col. 630.

... virtus interjecta verborum sacramentum et esuritionis et satietatis absolvit.—Id. ibid. cap. xii. 2. col. 668.

Quamquam ad fidei sacramentum, &c.—Id. ibid. cap. xiii. 6. col. 676.

Qui sacramentum fletus, sitis atque esuritionis ignorat, &c.—Id. De Trin. Lib. x. 24. col. 1052.]

[[8] Hujus rei sacramentum est, quod in dedicatione ecclesiarum depictas in pariete cruces oleo sancto pontifex linit.—Bernard. Op. Gaufrid. Abbat. Declam. ex Bern. xlvii. 58. Vol. II. Tom. v. col. 306.]

[[9] Gelas. in Corp. Jur. Canon. Lugd. 1624. Decret. Gratian. Decr. Tert. Pars, De Consecr. Dist. ii. can. 12. col. 1918.]

Washing of feet. upon what consideration this ceremony of washing feet began first, notwithstanding I have well thought of it, yet can I find nothing that seemeth more likely than this; for that the bodies of them that had appointed to be baptized (at Easter), being ill cherished by reason of the Lenten fast, would have had some loathsomeness in the touching, unless they had been washed at some time before; and that therefore they chose this day chiefly to that purpose, upon which day the Lord's supper is yearly [1]celebrated[2]." Here St Augustine saith, it was the fulsomeness of the bodies, and loathsomeness of the senses, that first began this ceremony, and not the institution or commandment of Christ. But, as touching the ministration of the communion in both kinds, it is most certain that the apostles used it, and that Christ commanded it to be used still until his coming.

With what indifferent judgment then can M. Harding thus compare these things together; a sacrament with no sacrament; an institution with no institution; a thing that in the primitive church was everywhere used with that thing whereof no proof can be made that upon Christ's commandment it was ever used? Neither did Christ therefore so abase himself to wash his disciples' feet, to the intent they according to the letter should do the same; but in himself to shew them a perfect[3] example of humility. For they were yet in a deep dream that Christ should come like a king with all worldly majesty, and that they should be princes, and sit with him to rule the world. Therefore, to break them out of this sleep, he took upon him this vile and servile office, that they might see that his coming was to serve them, and therefore might learn humility by his example, one of them to serve another. In like manner Christ set a child before his disciples, and willed them all to be as children. He bade them to shake off the dust from their shoes, and to carry neither rod nor scrip about them, and to salute no man upon the way; not that they should practise these things according to the rigour of the words, but to the intent that by the same they might be induced to a deeper understanding. Such was the sacrament and meaning of the washing of feet.

Matt. xx. Matt. xviii. Matt. x. Matt. viii.

The reasons that follow are of like value. For Christ said not, Do this after supper, or sitting, or at a table, or being so many together. Neither did the apostles ever so understand his words. But, when he had ministered the sacrament unto his apostles in both kinds, he bade them do the same that he had done; and so they understood his words, and ministered the sacrament unto the people in both kinds accordingly.

The words of St Cyprian here alleged are spoken of sprinkling, or pouring on water over them that were baptized; which is but a ceremony, and therefore ought to be at liberty, and is not of the substance of baptism. Neither doth it follow: We may break a ceremony; *ergo*, we may break the substance of Christ's institution. This reason rather maketh against M. Harding and his fellows. For if "ceremonies should be used freely and without rigour," as St Cyprian saith, why then be they so precise in their oil, their balm, their lights, and other things of like value, that, be the abuse thereof never so great, yet they will remit nothing? And, if they be so precise and so earnest in ceremonies and devices of their own, how much more ought we to be earnest in matters touching the essential form of the institution of Christ?

M. HARDING. THE TENTH DIVISION.

I trust no man will gather of that I have said here, that it is none offence to do against God's commandment. My meaning is far otherwise. Neither say I that this saying of Christ in Matthew, "Drink ye all of this," or that in John, "Except ye eat the flesh of the Son of man, and drink his blood, ye shall not have life in you," or other commandments of Christ, be not to be kept; but this is that I say, and that

---

[1 Celebrate, 1565.]

[2 Si autem quæris, cur etiam lavandi mos ortus sit: nihil mihi de hac re cogitanti probabilius occurrit, nisi quia baptizandorum corpora, per observationem quadragesimæ sordidata, cum offensione sensus ad fontem tractarentur, nisi aliqua die lavarentur: istum autem diem potius ad hoc electum, quo cœna dominica anniversarie celebratur.—August. Op. Par. 1679-1700. Ad Inquis. Januar. seu Epist. liv. 10. Tom. II. col. 127.]

[3 Perfite, 1565.]

every catholic man saith, that the universal church doth better understand which are the commandments of Christ, and how they ought to be kept, than Berengarius, Wickleffe, Hus, Luther, Zuinglius, Calvin, Cranmer, Peter Martyr, or any their scholars and followers, which now be sundry sects. As for example, God hath thus com-
Matt. v. *manded: "Thou shalt not swear;" and, "Thou shalt not kill;" and, "If*
Exod. xx. *thine eye cause thee to offend, pull him out and cast him away from thee." Whereas certain sects of heretics, as namely they which be called Waldenses and Picardi*[4]*, by their construction hereof have maintained opinion that no oath ought to be given or made in no case or respect; likewise that in no case or respect a man may do another to death; and also that, after the outward letter of the gospel, sometime a man is bound to pull out his eye and cast it from him; which thing hath been done by some of the Picardes, as it is reported, as though else God's commandment were not kept; this hath so been understanded by the catholic church, confessing nevertheless these to be God's commandments, as in time, in place, and in certain cases, a man might and ought, without breach of commandment, both swear and kill, and likewise keep his eye in his head, and therein offended*[5] *God nothing at all. So the catholic church understandeth, "Drink ye all of this," to be Christ's commandment, and of necessity to be observed; but of priests only—I mean of necessity, and that when in the sacrifice of the church is celebrated the memory of Christ's death—which in that degree be the successors of the apostles, to whom that commandment was specially given when they were consecrated priests of the new testament; who so did*
Mark xiv. *drink indeed, as St Mark witnesseth:* Et biberunt ex eo omnes: *"And they drank all of it." To these only, and to none other, the (55) catholic church hath ever referred the necessity of that commandment. Else if the necessity of it should pertain to all, and because Christ said, "Drink ye all of this," if all of every state and condition ought to drink of this cup of necessity*[7]*, how is it come to pass that our adversaries themselves (who pretend so strait a conscience herein) keep from it infants and young children, until they come to good years of discretion; specially whereas the custom of the primitive church was that they also should be partakers of this sacrament*[8]*, as it may plainly be seen in St Dionyse, Cyprian, Augustine, Innocentius, Zosimus, and other ancient fathers? What better reason have they to keep the infants from the cup, than the anabaptists have to keep them from their baptism? If they allege their impotency of remembering the*[9] *Lord's death, the anabaptists will likewise allege their impotency of receiving and understanding doctrine, that Christ's institution in this behalf seemeth to require.*

The fifty-fifth untruth. For[6] the catholic or universal church never understood it so; but only the church of Rome, which is both late and mere particular.

Thus the adversaries of the church themselves do agnise[10] *that the use of the cup in the sacrament pertaineth not to all of necessity. So have they neither godly charity to join with the church, neither sufficient reason to impugn the church.*

THE BISHOP OF SARISBURY.

The best defence to colour disobedience is to improve[11] God's commandment. Therefore saith M. Harding, "The half communion is no breach of Christ's institution. For Christ never commanded that the whole communion should be ministered unto the people in both kinds. And that (saith he) the church knoweth better than Luther, or Cranmer, or such others." Whatsoever ordinary light the church hath, she hath it not of herself, but of God's holy word, that is a lantern Psal. cxix.
unto her feet. And it is no christian modesty to make such boasts of the gifts of God. God's holy "Spirit bloweth where it thinketh good." Daniel alone saw John iii.
the innocency of Susanna: the judges and elders saw it not. Paphnutius alone Hist. Sus. Sozom. Lib.
was heard against all the rest of the Nicene council[12]. St Hierome alone is re- i. cap. xxii.
ceived against all the whole council of Chalcedon[13]. And forasmuch as M. Harding xxxvi. Quæst. ii. Tria legit.
delighteth himself with odious comparisons without cause, why may[14] not a man

[4 See Mosheim, Cent. XIII. Part II. chaps. ii. v.]
[5 Offend, 1565, 1609, and H. A. 1564.]
[6 1565 omits *for*.]
[7 Of necessity ought to drink of the cup, H. A. 1564.]
[8 See before, page 6.] [9 Our, H. A. 1564.]
[10 Agnise: acknowledge.]
[11 Improve: reprove, disprove.]
[12 Sozom. in Hist. Eccles. Script. Amst. 1695-1700. Lib. I. cap. xxiii. pp. 356, 7.]
[13 Hieron. in Corp. Jur. Canon. Lugd. 1624. Decret. Gratian. Decr. Sec. Pars, Caus. XXXVI. Quæst. ii. can. 8. cols. 1882, 3. See also can. 4. col. 1881.]
[14 Might, 1565.]

likewise say, The primitive church in the time of the apostles and other catholic doctors and old councils, that ministered the whole sacrament unto the people in both kinds, understood Christ's institution as well as did afterward the council of Constance, in which council, holden fourteen hundred years after Christ and more, it was determined that the laity should content themselves only with the half communion in one kind? But therefore hath God given his holy scriptures, that the church should be directed, and never err. And St Augustine saith: *Dominus semper veraciter judicat: ecclesiastici autem judices, sicut homines, plerumque falluntur*[1]:" The Lord always judgeth truly; but the ecclesiastical judges, for that they be men, are oftentimes deceived.

August. contra Cresc. Gram. Lib. ii. cap. xxi.

The examples of killing, swearing, pulling out of eyes, eating of blood and strangled things, that are here brought in, stand more for a countenance, than for proof of the matter. Touching the first, God saith unto the private man: "Thou shalt not kill;" but unto the magistrate he saith: "Thine eye shall not spare: thou shalt not suffer the wicked sorcerer to live." This case was never doubtful; or if it were, let M. Harding shew in what council it was determined. Touching oaths, it is forbidden that any shall swear unadvisedly or without just cause, and so to abuse the name of God; but otherwise to swear before a judge, in the way of judgment, justice, and truth, God himself hath commanded.

Exod. xx. Lev. xx. Deut. xviii. Jer. iv. Matt. v.

The pulling out of the eye is an allegory, wherein by a figure or manner of speech one thing[2] is conceived of another, and Christ's meaning is, that whoso will follow him must pull out and cast from him his affections, his goods, and his friends, for the gospel's sake, yea, though he love them as his eyes. And if the Picard took it otherwise, it was an error of simplicity, much like the error of Origen[3], and certain others, who, as it is written of them, grossly, and according to the letter, gelded themselves for the kingdom of heaven; or the error of the bishop of Rome, who, upon small occasion of these words, *Ecce duo gladii hic*, "Behold here be two swords," claimeth unto himself both the spiritual and also the temporal sword, and so the whole jurisdiction of all the world[4].

Euseb. Lib. vi. cap. vii. De Major. et Obed. Unam Sanctam.

[Acts xv. 1565.]

The forbearing of blood and strangled meats began among the faithful in the time of the apostles, not as of God's commandment, or to continue for ever, but only of charity, to bear with the weakness of the Jews, until they might grow to a perfect[5] knowledge in Christ; during which weakness this charitable order among the rest of the faithful Christians continued still, as may appear by Tertullian, by Arnobius, by Eusebius, by Œcumenius, and others[6]: but after that the Jews were thoroughly persuaded that all creatures of God were clean, this forbearing, which began only for their sakes, had an end.

But how can M. Harding apply these things to his purpose? Or how can he hereby warrant the manifest breach of Christ's institution? The church in every of these orders was directed and guided by God's word. Touching killing, God saith unto the magistrate: "Thou shalt not suffer the wicked to live." Touching swearing, God saith: "Thou shalt swear in truth, in judgment, and in justice." Touching pulling out of our eyes, St Paul saith: "No man ever hated his own flesh, but doth nourish and cherish it." And touching blood and strangled meats, Christ saith: "The thing that entereth into the mouth defileth not the man." And St Paul saith: "Every creature of God is good." Therefore the church in these cases devised no new thing of herself, nor brake any of God's ordinances, but only followed the word of God.

Jer. iv. Eph. v.

Now of the other part, let M. Harding shew what word of God the church of Rome had to follow in the ordering of the half communion. Where did Christ or his apostles ever say, Let not the people receive the whole sacrament as it was ordained at the first, but let it be sufficient for them to receive one portion? If there be no such commandment to be shewed, then be not these cases like.

[[1] August. Op. Par. 1679-1700. Cont. Cresc. Donatist. Lib. II. cap. xxi. 26. Tom. IX. cols. 422, 3; where we read *ille* for *Dominus, judicet,* and *fallantur.*]

[[2] Things, 1609, 1611.]

[[3] Euseb. in Hist. Eccles. Script. Amst. 1695-1700. Lib. VI. cap. viii. pp. 169, 70.]

[[4] Bonifac. VIII. in Corp. Jur. Canon. Lugd. 1624. Extrav. Comm. De Major. et Obed. Lib. I. cap. 1. col. 208.]

[[5] Perfite, 1565.]

[[6] Tertull. Op. Lut. 1641. De Monogam. 5, p. 676; De Pudicit. 12. p. 728. For further authorities, see Bingham, Orig. Eccles. Book XVII. chap. v. 20.]

And if the cases be not like, why doth M. Harding deceive the world, and compare them thus together as though they were like? What, troweth he there is no difference between obeying God's commandment, and breaking God's commandment? Or thinketh he, because it was lawful for Abraham, having God's commandment, to have slain his son Isaac, that therefore it was lawful for him to slay Ismael also, having no commandment? It is a dangerous doctrine to say, the church is omnipotent, and may allow or disallow God's commandments without difference, at her pleasure. For, as it is discreetly noted by the emperors Valentinian and Martian, "Whosoever, after the truth is once found, seeketh further, he seeketh for a lie, and not for the truth[7]."

Gen. xxii.

In Edict. Imp. Valent. et Mart. in Chalced. Con. Act. iii.

"But to minister unto the vulgar lay-people in both kinds," saith M. Harding, "was not Christ's institution." Thus he saith, and saith it often, and only saith it. Other authority than his own he bringeth none. The reason that moveth him, I ween, is this; for that there was no lay-people at that banquet with Christ, but the apostles only. But this reason would spoil the lay-people not of one part only, but of all together. Surely one Lorichius, a doctor of M. Harding's own side, saith thus: *Ipsius sacramenti institutio vult, ut omnes una manducemus et bibamus*[8]: "The very institution of the sacrament willeth that we all eat and drink together." M. Harding's doctor saith: "It is Christ's institution." M. Harding himself saith: "It is not Christ's institution." Whether of them two a man may believe, I leave it to others. Howbeit in the mean time, while these doctors can better agree, it cannot be denied but Christ ministered unto his disciples the whole sacrament in both kinds, and gave them in charge, in plain express words, to do the same. But of the half communion in one kind Christ neither gave them charge, nor spake any one word at all. If M. Harding will reply, that Christ's words in this case be doubtful, and may be diversly taken, yet is that objection already answered. For the law saith: *Si de interpretatione legis quæratur, in primis inspiciendum est quo jure civitas retro in hujusmodi casibus usa fuerit. Optima enim est legum interpretatio consuetudo*[9]: "If question happen to be moved touching the meaning of a law, first of all we must see what order hath been used in the like cases in times past. For the custom and practice of the people is the best expounder of the law." Now it appeareth plainly that the custom and practice of the purest church in the time of the apostles, and others old catholic fathers, was, to minister unto the people in both kinds; whereof we may conclude that the same was Christ's institution and very meaning. But if M. Harding will apply the authority of custom unto his purpose, for that the common practice of the church of Rome for a few late years hath been to the contrary, that therefore this was Christ's meaning, this objection is also soon answered. For both law and common reason saith: *In ambiguo sermone non utrumque dicimus, sed id duntaxat quod volumus*[10]: "In a doubtful speech we speak not both the things (that may be gathered), but that thing only that we mean." Now, if Christ meant both the order that was practised by the apostles and old fathers, and also the contrary order, that of late hath been practised in the church of Rome; then had Christ, at one time, and in the uttering of one sentence, not only two, but also divers and contrary meanings, and so, by M. Harding's judgment, Christ must needs construe his own words in this wise: "Drink ye all of this;" I mean, let priests only drink of this. "Drink ye all;" I mean, some may not drink. "Drink ye all;" I mean contrary, drink ye not all. And when I say, "Do ye the same that I have done," my meaning is otherwise, do not the same that I have done. O M. Harding! it is an old saying: *Maledicta glossa quæ corrumpit textum:* "Cursed be that glossing construction that destroyeth the text."

De Miss. Pub. Prorogand.

De Legibus et Senatusconsult. et Longa Consue. Si de.

De Rebus Dubiis. In ambiguo.

Ye say, "The priests are bound of necessity to receive both kinds, but the lay-people is not bound." And so ye conclude that Christ ordained two sundry

[7 Quisquis enim post veritatem repertam aliquid ulterius discutit, mendacium quærit.—Edict. Valent. et Marc. Imp. in Concil. Chalced. Act. III. in Crabb. Concil. Col. Agrip. 1551. Tom. I. p. 863.]

[8 Sed major profecto ejus rei causa est, ipsius sacramenti institutio, quæ vult &c.—Ger. Lorich. De Miss. Pub. Prorogand. 1536. Lib. II. cap. iii. p. 214.]

[9 Callistr. in Corp. Jur. Civil. Amst. 1663. Digest. Lib. I. Tit. iii. 37. Tom. I. p. 79; where we find *ejusmodi* and *interpres*.]

[10 Paul. in eod. Digest. Lib. XXXIV. Tit. v. 3. Tom. I. p. 487.]

communions, the one not like the other; the one for the priests, the other for the people. And therefore by your advice we must correct St Hierome, that saith, "The Lord's supper must be common to all[1];" and likewise Chrysostom, that saith, "In the holy mysteries there is no difference between the priest and the people[2]." For it is now otherwise agreed that the Lord's supper may not be common unto all, and that in the mysteries there must be a difference between the priest and the people.

Hieron. 1 Cor. xi. Chrysost. 2 Cor. xviii.

The objection that is made of keeping children from the communion is but childish, and nothing to the matter. For in so doing we divide not the mysteries, nor break any part of Christ's institution; no more than when, by order of excommunication, we remove the wicked from the whole use of the sacrament. For notwithstanding it appear by St Augustine, St Cyprian, and others, that infants in the primitive church in sundry places were admitted to the holy communion[3], yet afterward, upon good advice, they were justly removed from it; because that, being in that age, they were not thought able to examine and prove themselves according to the doctrine of St Paul, and so to eat of that bread, and to drink of that cup. In like sort in the law of Moses, notwithstanding all men-children were commanded to be circumcised, yet none were admitted to eat the passover but only such as could demand what it meant.

"The church," saith M. Harding, "is the interpreter of God's mind. The church knoweth that this was not Christ's institution." Verily, if the church know it now at last, she hath been long in learning this lesson. For the old catholic church, as it is well known, took it far otherwise, and that following the plain words of God, whereby God's ordinary way is to reveal his mind; and because Christ ministered unto his disciples in both kinds, and commanded them to do the same, therefore that church understood him, even as his words sounded, and ministered unto the people the whole communion in both kinds.

Now, whereas M. Harding saith, "The church of Rome of late years hath more secret intelligence of God's mind than the elder church had at any time before;" methinketh he imagineth Christ thus to say to his apostles: "Do the same to others that ye have seen me do to you. For a time it shall be lawful: after it shall not be lawful. Now it is my institution: the time shall come when it shall be no longer my institution. After fourteen hundred years there shall be a certain council of five hundred bishops and eight hundred monks and friars: there shall be terrible contention whether the pope be above the council, or the council above the pope. One pope shall be deposed: another shall be erected against him; and so two popes at one time. The one shall excommunicate and curse, and seek all means to depose the other. Kings and princes shall be in parts. The whole world shall be troubled. Then shall these matters be concluded. That I command, they shall break: that I bind, they shall loose." Unless M. Harding give such exposition to Christ's words, he cannot be greatly relieved by them. Thus have we reason sufficient to open the error of M. Harding's church, and godly charity to join with the old catholic church of the apostles and holy fathers, which, we doubt not, was the church of God.

M. HARDING. THE ELEVENTH DIVISION.

And although herein we could be content infants not to be spoken of, yet it may easily be proved that the communion under both kinds hath not ever been general. And as we do not condemn it, but confess it might be restored again by the authority of the church lawfully assembled in a general council, upon mature deliberation before had, and a wholesome remedy against the inconveniences thereof provided; even so are we able to shew good authority for the defence of the one kind now used in the church.

THE BISHOP OF SARISBURY.

M. Harding would have us put God's word to daying, and none otherwise to be obedient to Christ's commandment, than if a few bishops gathered at

[[1] Hieron. Op. Par. 1693-1706. Comm. in Epist. I. ad Cor. cap. xi. Tom. V. col. 997.]

[[2] Chrysost. Op. Par. 1718-38. In Epist. II. ad Cor. Hom. xviii. Tom. X. p. 568.]

[[3] See before, p. 6.]

Trident shall allow it. But we may answer such a council as king Agesilaus sometime answered the Macedonians, through whose country he desired to have passage against his enemies. For when they had sent him word that the matter was great, and that therefore they would well consider of it: "Let them consider," said he, "while they list; but in the mean time I will pass through." If the council, upon advice, will restore again the whole communion, why then doth pope Leo call it "the heresy of the Greeks and of the Bohemians[4]?" Or why doth Gerson entitle his book, *Contra hæresim communicandi laicos sub utraque specie?* "Against the heresy of communicating the lay-people under both kinds?" I trow, councils be not called to restore the world to heresies. The great inconveniences, that M. Harding would have a general council to make provisos for, are noted by Gerson, the greatest promoter of the council of Constance, and are these:

Emmaus.

In Bulla Leonis x. Gerson.

The liquor might[5] be shed:
It cannot be carried about without danger:
In winter it would soon sour, and turn to vinegar:
In summer it would putrefy, and breed worms:
It would be loathsome for men to drink:
In some countries it is hard to be gotten:
The lay-people should touch the cup:
Some of them have beards, some have palsies:
The dignity of the priest and layman should be all one[6].

These and other like inconveniences are such as Christ and his apostles never knew; yet the council that is now holden at Trident, upon mature and solemn deliberation, hath pronounced and published: "If any man will say that these be not just causes why the people should stand content with the half communion, accursed be he[7].

And notwithstanding the bishops in that council have already yielded that certain countries and kingdoms may use the whole communion, according to Christ's institution[8], yet have they added so fond conditions unto the same, that all men may see they sit there only for a countenance to mock the world.

M. HARDING. THE TWELFTH DIVISION.

And because M. Jewel beareth the world in hand nothing can be brought for it of our side, some places I will allege here that seem to me very evidently to prove that the use of both kinds hath not always been thought necessary to all persons, and that the communion under one kind hath been practised and holden for good within the six hundred years after Christ, that he would so fain bind us unto.

*Here may be alleged, first, the example of our Lord himself, out of the twenty-fourth chapter of St Luke, which is spoken of before, where it is declared that he gave the sacrament unto[9] the two disciples at Emmaus under *the form of bread only; which place ought to have the more weight of authority, in a catholic man's judgment, because it is brought by the council of * Constance, and also by the council of Basil, for proof of the communion under one kind. That it was the sacrament, the ancient doctors do affirm it plainly; and the words, conferred with the words of our Lord's supper, do agree. And that it is not needful of our own head to add thereto the administration of the cup, as our adversaries do by their figure* Synecdoche, *it appeareth by that those two disciples declared to the twelve apo-*

[*Proofs for communion under one kind.* H. A. 1564.]

*S. Luke nameth neither 'form' nor 'only.'

*In the year of our Lord 1414.

[4 ...hæresin etiam Græcorum et Bohemicam expresso continentes, &c.—Bull. Leon. Papæ X. adv. Luth. in Concil. Stud. Labb. et Cossart. Lut. Par. 1671-2. Tom. XIV. col. 391.]

[5 Mought, 1565.]

[6 Primum periculum in effusione. Secundum in deportatione de loco ad locum. Tertium in vasorum sordidatione ... Quartum in barbis longis laicorum. Quintum in conservatione pro infirmis; quoniam posset in vase acetum generari ... addito quod in æstate bibliones aut muscæ generarentur...quandoque etiam putresceret, aut fieret velut abominabile ad bibendum :...Sextum damnum esset in sumptuositate vini, saltem apud multas partes in quibus vix invenitur vinum, &c.—Gerson. Op. Antw. 1706. Contr. Hær. de Com. Laic. sub Utr. Spec. Tom. I. Pars III. cols. 467, 8.]

[7 Si quis dixerit, sanctam ecclesiam catholicam non justis causis et rationibus adductam fuisse, ut laicos, atque etiam clericos non conficientes, sub panis tantummodo specie communicaret, aut in eo errasse, anathema sit.—Concil. Trident. in Concil. Stud. Labb. et Cossart. Sess. XXI. can. 2. Tom. XIV. col. 847.]

[8 See before, page 205, note 4.]

[9 To, H. A. 1564.]

Emmaus. *stles, assembled together in Hierusalem, how they knew our Lord* in fractione panis, *"in breaking of the bread" to them, which cannot be taken for the wine. And as soon as they knew him in breaking of the bread, he vanished away from their sight, ere that he took the cup into his hands, and blessed it, and gave it unto them,* (56) *as it appeareth evidently enough to St Augustine, to Bede, and to all other that be not wilfully opinative.*

The fifty-sixth untruth. For[1] neither S. Augustine, nor Beda, nor any other ancient father, hath any such word, but rather the contrary.

Again, what need is it to use violence in this scripture, and join unto it a patch of our own device, by so simple a warrant of a figure, sith that, according to the mind of the learned fathers, Christ gave here to the two disciples, not a piece of the sacrament, but the whole sacrament? as it is proved by the effect of the same; and the effect presupposeth the cause. For St Augustine confesseth by that sacrament of bread (so he calleth it), Unitate corporis... participata, removeri... impedimentum inimici, ut Christus possit[2] agnosci[3]; *"That thereby they were made partakers of the unity of Christ's body, that is to say, made one body with Christ, and that all impediment or let of the enemy, the devil, was taken away, so as Christ might be acknowledged." What more should they have gotten, if they had received the cup also?* [*De Consensu Evangelistarum. Lib. iii. cap. xxv.* H.A. 1564.]

THE BISHOP OF SARISBURY.

If I would speak only by authority, and prove nothing, as M. Harding's wont is, I might answer all this matter in three words:

First, that the bread that Christ brake at Emmaus was common table-bread, and not the sacrament.

Secondly, that, albeit some writers seem to call it the sacrament, yet none of them saith it was ministered in one kind; as M. Harding by his slender guesses would seem to gather.

Thirdly, although he were able to prove that Christ so ministered at that time, and in that place, yet were all this nothing to prove his purpose. For we join issue of the people; he answereth of the priests. I speak of the church; he speaketh of an inn. And to conclude, by this example it appeareth that Christ himself received in one kind; which one thing overthroweth all that M. Harding hath built.

And because he maketh himself so sure and certain that Christ at Emmaus ministered the sacrament, it may please him to remember, that even the same doctors that he hath here alleged, and divers others of late years, upon good consideration have said it was not the sacrament. St Augustine saith the breaking of bread there was hospitality, and entertaining of strangers. His words be these: *Quia hospitalitatem sectati sunt, eum, quem in... expositione scripturarum non agnoverunt, in panis fractione cognoscunt*[4]: "Because they were given to hospitality, they knew him in the breaking of bread, whom they knew not in the expounding of the scriptures." Which thing St Gregory uttereth in plainer manner: *Mensam [igitur] ponunt, [panes] cibos[que] offerunt, et Deum, quem in scripturarum expositione non cognoverant, in panis fractione cognoscunt*[5]: "They lay the table, and set forth bread and meat, and God, whom they knew not in the expounding of the scriptures, they know in the breaking of bread." It were hard to say, the setting forth of bread and meat upon a table in an hostery was the ministration of the sacrament. And, to leave Beda and others, that follow the same exposition, Dionysius, one of late years, and therefore led away with many errors, according to the weakness of that time, saith thus: *Accepit panem et benedixit: non tamen in suum corpus convertit, sicut in cœna; sed ut moris est benedicere cibum*[6]: "He took bread and blessed it; but he turned it not into his body, as he did at his supper; but only as the manner is, to say grace, or to bless the meat."

Aug. in Caten. in xxiv. Luc.

Greg. in Evangel. Hom. 23.

Dionys. in xxiv. Lucæ.

[1 1565 omits *for*.]

[2 Posset, 1565, and H. A. 1564.]

[3 August. Op. Par. 1679-1700. De Consens. Evang. Lib. III. cap. xxv. 72. Tom. III. Pars II. col. 142.]

[4 August. in Caten. Aur. in Thom. Aquinat. Op. Venet. 1595. Sup. Luc. xxiv. Tom. XV. fol. 209. 2; where *cognoverunt*. Op. Quæst. Evang. Lib. II. Quæst. li. Tom. III. Pars II. col. 276; where the reading is *cognoverant*.]

[5 Gregor. Magni Papæ I. Op. Par. 1705. In Evang. Lib. II. Hom. xxiii. Tom. I. col. 1538; where we find *scripturæ sacræ*.]

[6 Dionys. Carthus. in Nov. Test. Col. 1532. In Evang. Luc. Enarr. cap. xxiv. Art. 50. Tom. I. fol. 271. 2.]

So likewise saith Antonius Julianus: *Accepit panem... benedixit... fregit, et porrigebat illis, sicut consueverat... ante passionem*[7]: "He took bread, blessed it, brake it, and gave it unto them, as his manner was before his passion." Lyra saith they knew him, for that "he brake the bread so even as if he had cut it with a knife[8]." By these writers it appeareth it was common bread that Christ gave to his disciples, and not the sacrament.

Emmaus.

Anton. Julianus in Postilla majori. Nicol. Lyra.

And whereas M. Harding allegeth St Augustine to the contrary, if he had considered the words of one William Wideford, a doctor of his own side, which he useth against Wickliffe, I reckon, either he would have better advised himself, or else would have refused his own doctor. Wideford's words be these: *Hic dico, quod non habetur ex textu, vel ex glossa Lucæ* xxiv, *vel per antiquos doctores, quod ille panis, quem [Christus] fregit post resurrectionem...fuit consecratus, vel...sacramentalis...Ideo inepte...et consequenter dico, quod falso allegat auctoritatem Augustini*[9]: "This I say, it cannot be gathered neither by the text of St Luke, nor by the gloss, nor by the ancient doctors, that the bread that Christ brake after his resurrection was the consecrate or sacramental bread. And therefore I say that foolishly, and by consequence that falsely, he allegeth St Augustine to this purpose."

Wil. Wideford contra Wiclevum.

"The two councils of Constance and Basil thus understood the words of St Luke; and that," saith M. Harding, "in a catholic man's judgment ought to weigh much." The former of these two councils was holden but of late days, above fourteen hundred years after Christ, and the weight of them is already determined by others. For all the Dominick friars, and all others that held with Thomas of Aquine, which thought themselves to be the best learned that were then alive, utterly refused the council of Basil, and said it was never lawfully called together[10].

Ludovic. Vives in xx. de Civit. Dei, cap. xxvi.

And Albertus Pighius saith that both these councils, as well that of Basil as the other of Constance, "decreed against the order of nature, against the manifest scriptures, against the authority of all antiquity, and against the catholic faith of the church[11]."

Pigh. in Hierarch.

Those be the two councils that M. Harding would have to weigh so deeply in a catholic man's conscience. Neither can it justly be replied, that any of these were Lutherans. For the Dominick friars were a hundred years before Luther ever preached; and Albertus Pighius wrote namely and of purpose against Luther. Verily these councils seem over light to weigh down all the old councils of grave and catholic fathers that were before them. Touching the authority of councils, because they seem oftentimes to vary, Gelasius thought it best to take up the matter thus: *In gestis conciliorum, quotiescunque discors sententia invenitur, illius concilii sententia magis teneatur, cujus antiquior et potior extat auctoritas*[12]: "Whensoever contrariety in sentence is found in the acts of councils, let the sentence of that council be taken that hath the elder and better authority." If this determination of Gelasius be good, there is no cause why these two so late councils should weigh down any catholic man's conscience, specially against so many contrary councils as have been before. Doubtless it is a marvellous case, that either of these two councils should at last see that thing in the words of St Luke that the council of the apostles could not see.

Dist. 50. Domino Sancto.

Yet, to help M. Harding forthward, let us grant St Augustine understood these words of the sacrament. Indeed, he calleth it in the same place *sacramentum panis*, "the sacrament of bread;" meaning thereby that the substance of bread in the same remaineth still; but he calleth it not, "the form or shadow of bread," as M. Harding doth. But let us grant it was the sacrament.

Now have an eye, good reader, to M. Harding's fingers, and mark how he juggleth with St Augustine's words. St Augustine saith, *Per sacramentum panis*

Aug. de Consens. Evang. Lib. iii. cap. xxv.

[7 Postill. Maj. Lugd. 1525. Fer. ii. post Pasch. Evang. fol. 173.]

[8 Sic enim frangebat panem ac si scinderetur cum cultello... cognoverunt eum per modum fractionis panis.—Bibl. cum Gloss. Ord. et Expos. N. de Lyra, Basil. 1502. Luc. cap. xxiv. Pars V. fol. 182. 2.]

[9 Wilh. Wodford. adv. Johan. Wiclef. in Fascic. Rer. Expet. et Fug. Lond. 1690. Tom. I. p. 198.]

[10 August. De Civit. Dei, per Joan. Lud. Vivem, Basil. 1522. Comm. in Lib. xx. cap. xxvi. p. 702.]

[11 Pigh. Hierarch. Eccles. Assert. Col. 1538. Lib. VI. cap. ii. fol. 213. 2. See before, page 35, note 7.]

[12 Isidor. in Corp. Jur. Canon. Lugd. 1624. Decret. Gratian. Decr. Prima Pars, Dist. l. can. 28. col. 251; where we find *quotiescumque in gestis, magis teneatur sententia*, and *aut antiquior, aut potior*.]

...*unitate corporis...participata*[1]: these plain words it liketh M. Harding to English thus: "Thereby they were made partakers of the unity of Christ's body, that is to say, made one body with Christ's[2]." Alas! this was no part of St Augustine's mind. Beware, good reader; this man seeketh ways to deceive thee. Lyra himself confesseth that these words of St Augustine have *mysticam interpretationem*, "a mystical understanding;" and may not be taken neither of the sacrament, nor of Christ's natural body, but of his body mystical, which is the church; and that whosoever is partaker or member of the church knoweth Christ; whosoever is without the church knoweth not Christ. But who can better report the same than St Augustine himself? His words be these, plain and clear, and in the same place; howbeit M. Harding thought good to dissemble them: *Nec quisquam se Christum agnovisse arbitretur, si ejus corporis particeps non est, id est, ecclesiæ; cujus unitatem in sacramento panis apostolus commendat, dicens, Unus panis, unum corpus multi sumus*[3]: "Let no man think he knoweth Christ, unless he be partaker of his body, that is to say, of the church; the unity of which church the apostle commendeth in the sacrament of bread, saying, 'We being many, are one bread, and one body.'" The church was that body whereof the two disciples were made partakers and members, and so came to the knowledge of Christ.

Now, notwithstanding we have granted that St Augustine expoundeth this place of the sacrament, yet doth not St Augustine say that Christ ministered the half sacrament to his disciples in one kind only. But saith M. Harding, "Luke speaketh only of the bread; *ergo*, there was no wine."

This argument may be good in M. Harding's divinity; but it is of small force in good logic.

"As for your synecdoche, whereby of the part ye understand the whole," saith M. Harding, "it is but a patch of your device, and will not serve." Yet St Augustine, St Gregory, Bede, Julianus, Dionysius, Lyra, Wideford, and others that understand these words of St Luke of hospitality, must needs crave the warrant of a figure, and, under the name of bread, must needs conceive meat and wine also; otherwise there had been a very simple and a dry feast. Now, if M. Harding can allow them the figure of synecdoche, why may not he as well allow us the same? It is a manner of speech commonly used in all the scriptures.

"But Christ straightway vanished from their sight upon the breaking of the bread, and therefore had no leisure to deliver the other portion: neither is there any mention made of the cup." O what miserable straits these men be driven into! To make up their tale, they are glad to say that Christ lacked leisure. "But there is nothing written of the cup." I grant. Neither is there anything there written that Christ did consecrate the bread. And this place is privileged above all others. We must conceive no more of it than is spoken. Then was there a sacrament without consecration. Neither is there anything there written, that either Christ himself or the disciples did eat the bread. Thus hath M. Harding, with much ado, found out at last, not a communion of one kind, that he sought for, but a communion of no kind at all. And so have we a sacrament without sacrament, and a communion without communion.

What shall I say further? If I grant M. Harding his whole demand, yet hath he won nothing against me, but very much against himself. For the question is moved of lay-people: M. Harding bringeth examples of Christ and two disciples, who were of the number of the seventy and two that were sent abroad to preach the gospel; and therefore it may well be thought they were ministers, and not of the lay sort. Lyra and others think the one of them was St Luke himself[4]. Epiphanius thinketh it was Nathaniel[5]. Therefore M. Harding may well gather hereof, that priests may receive in one kind; which thing he will in no wise grant:

Lyra in Luc. cap. xxiv. Epiph. contra Saturnil.

[1 August. Op. Par. 1679–1700. De Consens. Evang. Lib. III. cap. XXV. 72. Tom. III. Pars II. col. 142; where *ad* for *per*.]

[2 Christ, 1565, 1609.]

[3 Id. ibid. col. 141; where *ne* for *nec*, and *commendat apostolus*.]

[4 Alius dicitur fuisse Lucas evangelista: propter quod et nomen suum tacuit.—Bibl. cum Gloss. Ord. et Expos. N. de Lyra, Basil. 1502. Luc. cap. xxiv. Pars V. fol. 182.]

[5 ... *ὁ Λουκᾶς διαβεβαιοῦται αὐτὸν τὸν Σωτῆρα μετὰ τὸ ἀναστῆναι ... ὤφθαι κατὰ τὴν ὁδὸν τοῖς περὶ τὸν Ναθαναὴλ καὶ τὸν Κλεόπαν.*—Epiph. Op. Par. 1622. Adv. Hær. Lib. I. Tom. I. p. 67.]

but he can conclude nothing against the people. Such luck hath he to allege matter against himself.

M. HARDING. THE THIRTEENTH DIVISION.

Here might be alleged the place of the Acts in the second chapter, where mention is made of the communion of breaking of the bread, the cup not spoken of; which the heretics called Waldenses did confess that it must be understanded of the sacrament, In confessione ad Uladislaum[6]; *and likewise the place of the twentieth chapter, and specially that of the twenty-seventh chapter of the Acts,* (57) *where Chrysostom and other fathers understand the bread that St Paul, in peril of shipwreck, took, gave thanks over, brake, and ate, to be the holy sacrament*[8].

The fifty-seventh untruth. For[7] Chrysostom understandeth it of common meat.

THE BISHOP OF SARISBURY.

He thought it not good to recite the words, as knowing they would not greatly serve his purpose. "That the two former places were meant of the sacrament, it appeareth," saith he, "not only by the Waldenses, but also by the exposition of the old fathers." Yet could none of them, in either of these places, ever find out the half communion in one kind. "But here is no mention of the cup; *ergo* (saith M. Harding), the communion was ministered in bread alone." A learned man, before he conclude so unadvisedly, should foresee what would follow. M. Harding granteth, as shall hereafter appear, that if a priest do communicate in one kind alone, he committeth sacrilege; for so it is determined by Gelasius. Now let us lay these two verities of M. Harding's both together. The first is, if a priest minister in one kind, he committeth sacrilege: the second is, the apostles were priests, and ministered only in one kind; for here is no manner mention of the cup. These both be M. Harding's premises. Hereof it must necessarily follow, and cannot be avoided, that the apostles of Christ committed sacrilege. But what will not these men grant, to win their purpose?

M. Harding's conclusion, that the apostles of Christ committed sacrilege.

The weight of M. Harding's argument is taken, as they name it in schools, *ab auctoritate negative;* and, unless it be in consideration of some other circumstance, it is so simple, that a very child may soon answer it. For as he saith here, "There is no mention made but of breaking of bread; *ergo,* there was no cup;" so might he also say, There is no mention made but of breaking of bread; *ergo,* there was not Christ's body. Or thus: Jacob went down into Egypt with threescore and ten souls; *ergo,* in his company he had no bodies. Certainly, as the soul in that place importeth the whole man, even so in the other place the breaking of bread importeth the whole ministration.

Gen. xlvi.

As for the breaking of bread in the twenty-seventh of the Acts, which place (as it is avouched) Chrysostom understandeth of the sacrament, verily M. Harding was therein much overseen. For the text is clear: if St Paul gave the sacrament, being at that time in the ship, he gave it only unto infidels, that knew not Christ. And Chrysostom's exposition, even in the same place, is plain to the contrary. For thus he enlargeth St Paul's words, that he spake to the mariners: *Obsecro vos, ut sumatis cibum: hoc enim ad salutem vestram fuerit: hoc est, ne forsan fame pereatis, cibum sumite*[9]: "I pray you take some sustenance; it is behoveful for you that ye so do. That is to say, take some meat, lest perhaps ye die for hunger." Now let M. Harding either say these words are spoken of the sacrament, or confess that he hath made untrue report of his doctor.

M. Harding misreproveth[10] St Chrysostom.

M. HARDING. THE FOURTEENTH DIVISION.

It is not to be marvelled at, albeit St Paul delivered to the Corinthians the institution of our Lord's supper under both kinds, that yet, upon occasion given, and

---

[6 Profess. Fid. Fratr. Wald. ad Ulad. in Fascic. Rer. Expet. et Fug. Lond. 1690. Tom. I. p. 170.]

[7 1565 omits *for*.]

[8 Et Paulus navigans non solum benedixit panem, sed de manu sua porrexit Lucæ et ceteris discipulis suis. Quod autem de manu porrigitur, nec animalibus dandum est, nec infidelibus porrigendum; quia non solum sanctificatum, sed etiam sanctificatio est, &c.—Chrysost. Op. Par. 1718–38. Opus Imperf. in Matt. Hom. xvii. ex cap. vii. p. lxxxviii; which passage favours Harding's notion: but see Chrysostom again as referred to in the next note.]

[9 Id. In Act. Apost. Hom. liii. Tom. IX. p. 401.]

[10 Misreporteth, 1565, 1609.]

The fifty-eighth untruth. For St Paul never ministered the communion so. *when condition of time so required,* (58) *he ministered the communion under one kind; sith that (without doubt) he took that holy mystery under one kind for*[1] *the whole sacrament, as we perceive by his words, where he saith,* Unus panis, et unum corpus, multi sumus, omnes qui de uno pane participamus: *"One bread, and one body, we (being many) are, all that do participate of one bread."* (59) *Where he speaketh nothing of the cup. And likewise by his words, where he speaketh disjunctively, as the Greek and the true Latin text hath:* Quicunque manducaverit panem, vel biberit calicem Domini indigne, reus erit corporis et sanguinis Domini: *"Whosoever eateth the bread or drinketh of the cup of our Lord unworthily, he shall be guilty of the body and blood of the*[2] *Lord." Whereon dependeth an argument of the contrary, that whosoever eateth*[3] *this bread worthily, or drinketh this cup worthily, he eateth and drinketh righteousness and life.*

1 Cor. x.

The fifty-ninth untruth. For immediately before he saith: "The cup of blessing which we bless, is it not the communion of Christ's blood?"

1 Cor. xi. H. A. 1564.

THE BISHOP OF SARISBURY.

"It is no marvel," saith M. Harding, "though St Paul ministered sometimes in one kind." But it is much to be marvelled that any christian man durst ever thus boldly to publish open error under the name of St Paul. What would not these men take in hand to prove, that dare thus to allege St Paul himself against himself, and that without any testimony, or word of St Paul? "Yes, marry," saith M. Harding, "St Paul saith, 'We being many are one bread, and one body;' and speaketh nothing of the cup." Here, by the way, M. Harding chargeth St Paul with manifest sacrilege. For it is already confessed by all them of that side, that it is sacrilege if a priest, such as St Paul was, do minister and receive the sacrament under one kind.

M. Harding chargeth St Paul with sacrilege.

"But," he saith, "there is nothing spoken of the cup." What may we think hereof? Whether is this man himself blind, or thinketh he all others to be blind? Is there nothing there spoken of the cup? O good christian reader, mark the dealing of this man, and beware of him. Unless thou consider well the places that he allegeth, he may soon deceive thee. Thus lie St Paul's words: "The cup of the blessing, which we bless, is it not the communication of the blood of Christ? The bread that we break, is it not the communication of the body of Christ? For we, being many, are one bread and one body, all that be partakers of one bread." Here St Paul distinctly nameth both parts together, and the cup before the bread. "Yet," saith M. Harding, "there is nothing spoken here of the cup." If he hath[4] dealt faithfully herein, thou mayest trust him further for the rest. Verily St Hierome noteth it thus: *Ideo de calice primum dixit, ut posset postea de pane latius disputare*[5]: "Therefore St Paul spake first of the cup, that he might afterward entreat more at large of the bread."

1 Cor. x.

M. Harding misreporteth St Paul's words.

Hieron. in 1 Cor. x.

"Further," saith M. Harding, "St Paul useth a disjunctive, as appeareth both by the Greek, and also by the true Latin text." Such diligence and circumspection in searching the scriptures for defence of a truth is much to be commended. For there may be oftentimes[6] great weight in one letter, as appeareth by sundry disputations between the Christians and the Arians. But this man seeketh so narrowly only to find some covert for his error. St Hierome, Anselmus, Haimo[7], and many others, both in the text and in the exposition of the same place, use the copulative. Notwithstanding, to grant M. Harding his disjunctive, yet, if he be so skilful in the digest, as in other places of his book he would seem to be, he might soon remember that the very discretion of the law hath determined, that sometimes disjunctives stand instead of copulatives, sometimes copulatives instead of disjunctives: *Sæpe ita comparatum est, ut [et] conjuncta pro disjunctis accipiantur, et disjuncta pro conjunctis*[8].

De Verb. et Rerum Significatione.

[1 1565 omits *for*.]

[2 Our, H. A. 1564.]

[3 Either eateth, H. A. 1564.]

[4 Have, 1565, 1609.]

[5 Hieron. Op. Par. 1693-1706. Comm. in Epist. I. ad Cor. cap. x. Tom. V. col. 995; where *ideo primum calicem nominavit, ut posset de pane, &c.*]

[6 Oft-times, 1565.]

[7 Id. Comm. in Epist. I. ad Cor. cap. xi. Tom. V. col. 998.

Anselm. Op. Col. Agrip. 1612. In I. ad Cor. cap. xi. Tom. II. p. 148.

Haym. in Paul. Epist. Interp. 1528. Ad Cor. I. cap. xi. fol. z. ii.]

[8 Paul. in Corp. Jur. Civil. Amst. 1663. Digest. Lib. L. Tit. xvi. 53. Tom. I. p. 778.]

But if M. Harding have so good eye to one little disjunctive, and mean uprightly, why doth he so blindly pass by so many copulatives in the self-same place altogether? For St Paul saith: "As often as ye shall eat of this bread, and drink of this cup;" and again: "Let a man examine himself, and so eat of that bread, and drink of that cup;" and again: "He that eateth and drinketh unworthily eateth and drinketh his own damnation:" here be four copulatives together. And by these it were good reason that M. Harding should expound his disjunctive; specially for that St Paul, recording the institution, useth a copulative; and the order of the primitive church, and the exposition of St Hierome and others, is agreeable to the same. In such cases Tertullian hath given a good rule: *Oportet secundum plura intelligi pauciora. Sed proprium hoc est omnium hæreticorum. Nam quia pauca sunt, quæ in sylva invenire*[9] *possunt, pauca adversus plura defendunt, et posteriora adversus priora suscipiunt*[10]*:* "It is meet that we expound the fewer places according to the more. But this is the very cast of all heretics. For because there be few things to be found in the wood, or in the multitude, therefore they defend a few things against many, and things lately devised, against the first." Thus doth M. Harding, as we plainly see; "and this," saith Tertullian, "is the very cast of all heretics.

1 Cor. xi.

Likewise also the cup.

Tertull. adv. Praxeam.

M. HARDING. THE FIFTEENTH DIVISION.

For this purpose we have a notable place in the Hebrew gospel of St Matthew, which St Hierome saith he saw in the library of Cæsarea, and translated it. This place is cited by St Hierome in his book, De Ecclesiasticis Scriptoribus, in Jacobo fratre Domini: *the words touching the communion, that St Hierome rehearseth, agree thoroughly with those of St Luke xxiv. chap.* Mattheus sic refert: Dominus autem, &c.: "*Matthew reporteth thus: When our Lord had given his shroud unto the bishop's servant, he went to James, and appeared to*[11] *him; for James had made an oath that he would not eat bread from that hour he drank of the cup of the*[12] *Lord, until he saw him raised from the dead." It followeth a little after:* Afferte, ait Dominus, mensam et panem. Statimque addit: Tulit panem, et benedixit, et[13] fregit, ac[14] dedit Jacobo Justo, et dixit ei, Frater,... comede panem tuum, quia resurrexit Filius hominis a dormientibus[15]: "*Bring the table, and set on bread, quoth our Lord; and by and by it is added, He took bread, and blessed it, and brake it, and gave it to James the just, and said unto him, My brother, eat thy bread; for the Son of man is risen again from the dead." No man can doubt but this was the sacrament. And wine was there none given, for anything that may be gathered. For it is not likely that St James had wine in his house then; forasmuch as Egesippus, who was not long after him, witnesseth of him, that he never drank wine but at our Lord's supper*[16].

THE BISHOP OF SARISBURY.

What shall need long answer to him that allegeth nothing? Here is no word spoken of the sacrament, no more than when Christ did eat of the broiled fish and of the honeycomb. And other proof thereof there is none brought, but words and boldness. For shew and countenance of somewhat there is brought forth the gospel of St Matthew, and that written in Hebrew, as though St Matthew had written two gospels, in two sundry tongues; and not only two, but also divers. I know it is thought of some that St Matthew wrote his gospel in Hebrew; and, by report of Theophylactus, St John the evangelist translated the same into Greek[17]. But that there should be any contrariety or diversity of story, or matter, as M. Harding seemeth to mean, I have not heard.

Luke xxiv.

[9 Inveniri, 1565, 1609.]

[10 Tertull. Op. Lut. 1641. Adv. Prax. 20. p. 651; where we have *cum oporteat*, and *inveniri.*]

[11 Unto, H. A. 1564.] [12 Our, H. A. 1564.]

[13 Ac, H. A. 1564.] [14 Et, H. A. 1564.]

[15 Evangelium quoque quod appellatur secundum Hebræos, et a me nuper in Græcum Latinumque sermonem translatum est, quo et Origenes sæpe utitur, post resurrectionem Salvatoris refert: 'Dominus autem cum dedisset sindonem servo sacerdotis, ivit ad Jacobum, et apparuit ei. Juraverat enim Jacobus, se non comesturum panem ab illa hora qua biberat calicem Domini, donec videret eum resurgentem a dormientibus.' Rursusque post paululum: 'Afferte, ait, &c.... additur ... ac fregit, et, &c.'—Hieron. Op. Catal. Script. Eccles. 2. Tom. IV. Pars II. col. 102.]

[16 See the next page, note 4.]

[17 Ὁ τοίνυν Ματθαῖος πρῶτος πάντων ἔγραψε τὸ εὐαγγέλιον Ἑβραΐδι φωνῇ ... μετέφρασε καὶ τοῦτο Ἰωάννης ἀπὸ τῆς Ἑβραΐδος γλώττης εἰς τὴν Ἑλληνίδα, ὡς λέγουσι.—Theophyl. Op. Venet. 1754-63. In Matt. Comm. Præfat. Tom. I. p. 2.]

Hieron. de Eccles. Script.

But St Hierome, in the place here alleged, as he not once nameth the sacrament, so he speaketh not one word of St Matthew. Which thing addeth some more distrust to M. Harding's dealing. St Hierome only nameth the gospel of the Hebrews, which, he saith, he himself translated both into Greek and Latin, and is often alleged by Origen[1]. But Eusebius accounteth it for no gospel, but only among the bastard scriptures[2].

Euseb. Lib. iii. cap. xxiv.

Howbeit, whatsoever the credit of the book be, thus it is written: "Christ took bread, and blessed it, and brake it." "Here," saith M. Harding, "no man can doubt but it was the sacrament." I see well he would fain have it so. Yet is there here, neither by the Hebrews' gospel, nor by St Hierome, any word[3] spoken of the sacrament. Neither had St James vowed that he would not minister or receive the communion, but that he would eat no common bread before he had seen Christ risen again from the dead. As for the blessing of the bread, it was not a thing peculiar to the sacrament, but a general manner that Christ observed, whensoever he used God's creatures, as it may appear throughout the story of the gospels. That Christ should then minister the sacrament, it is but M. Harding's guess. No old writer ever saw so much before, no, not St Hierome, that wrote the story. Yet M. Harding, as though he had learned it in the third heaven, saith, "It is so plain, that no man may doubt of it."

But be it the sacrament; *ergo*, saith M. Harding, "there was but one kind." And how may that be proved? Now must one guess help another. "For it is likely," saith M. Harding, "that there was no wine in the house." And why so? "Because St James drank no wine." If guesses go for arguments, this matter is done: howbeit, it seemeth a very silly guess, to say: "St James drank no wine;" *ergo*, he had no wine in his house.

Egesippus. Abd. Lib. vi.

Verily the same Egesippus, that saith St James never drank wine, saith also that "he never was anointed, never ware woollen cloth, never eat flesh in all his life[4]." Hereof, by M. Harding's logic, we may conclude that he had neither ointment, nor woollen cloth, nor flesh in his house. Yet is there here another greater inconvenience. St Hierome saith that St James continued bishop in Hierusalem the space of thirty years, until the seventh year of Nero[5]: if it be true that is here avouched, that in all his life he never drank wine but only at Christ's last supper, then must it follow that, being bishop in Hierusalem the space of thirty years, he never said mass; which thing M. Harding may not well grant: or else that he consecrated in one kind; which thing by Gelasius is adjudged sacrilege. Which way soever M. Harding turn himself, into one of these inconveniences he must needs fall.

Hieron. de Eccles. Script.

Again, if here be mention indeed of the sacrament, and no wine to be had in St James's house, then did Christ himself receive in one kind, to whose example, as these men say, bishops and priests are bound to stand. Therefore let them no longer defraud the people, but, by Christ's example, let both bishops and priests content themselves with the half communion, as well as others.

M. HARDING. THE SIXTEENTH DIVISION.

But because perhaps our adversaries will cast some mist over these allegations to darken the truth with their cloudy glosses, which be clear enough to quiet and sober wits, that give ear to the Holy Ghost, speaking to us by the mouth of the church; I will bring forth such witnesses and proofs for this purpose out of ancient fathers, as by no reason or sophistical shift they shall be able to avoid. Many of the places that I alleged in the article before this for private communion, may serve to this[6] purpose very well; and therefore I will not let to recite some of them here also.

[1 See the preceding page, note 15.]

[2 Ἤδη δ' ἐν τούτοις τινὲς καὶ τὸ καθ' Ἑβραίους εὐαγγέλιον κατέλεξαν ... ταῦτα μὲν πάντα τῶν ἀντιλεγομένων ἂν εἴη.—Euseb. in Hist. Eccles. Script. Amst. 1695-1700. Lib. III. cap. XXV. p. 78.]

[3 Any one word, 1565, 1609.]

[4 Vinum et siceram non bibit, sed neque animal manducavit ... Oleo non est perunctus ... Neque enim laneo utebatur indumento, sed tantum sindone.—Abd. Apost. Hist. Par. 1571. Lib. VI. fol. 73.]

[5 Triginta itaque annos Ierosolymorum rexit ecclesiam, id est, usque ad septimum Neronis annum, &c.—Hieron. Op. Par. 1693-1706. Catal. Script. Eccles. 2. Tom. IV. Pars II. col. 102.]

[6 His, H. A. 1564.]

THE BISHOP OF SARISBURY.

God wot, it were great wrong to cast a mist over darkness. But M. Harding having alleged such matter for his half communion, as he himself seeth may be easily answered, and William Wideford, a doctor of his own learning, saith, "is foolishly and falsely brought in to serve this turn[7];" yet he would not pass it over without some bravery. But now will he bring in such authorities, so clear, so forcible, and so invincible, as cannot possibly be avoided. Howbeit, God be thanked, these authorities be neither so weighty, nor so strange. I knew them all, and had weighed them well before I spake anything in that behalf. Here he doubleth a great many things before by him alleged for his private mass, indeed, serving as well to the one purpose as to the other. Wil. Wideford, contra Wiclevum.

M. HARDING. THE SEVENTEENTH DIVISION.

Melciades, that constant martyr of Christ, and bishop of Rome, ordained that sundry hosts, prepared by the consecrating of a bishop, should be sent abroad among the churches and parishes, that christian folk, who remained in the catholic faith, might not through heretics be defrauded of the holy sacrament[8]. *Which can none otherwise be taken than for the form of bread only; because the wine cannot so conveniently be*[9] *carried abroad from place to place, in small quantity, for such use, much less any long time be kept without corruption.*

THE BISHOP OF SARISBURY.

This argument hangeth only upon lack of carriage. For if it were possible to devise a way that the sacrament might be carried about in both kinds, then were this guess soon answered. For otherwise Melciades speaketh not one word of the communion in one kind. Now that the carriage of both kinds is not unpossible[10], the examples of antiquity do well declare. St Hierome writeth thus of Exuperius, the bishop of Tolouse in France: *Nihil illo ditius, qui corpus Domini [in] canistro vimineo, sanguinem portabat in vitro*[11]: "There was no man richer than he, that carried the Lord's body in a wicker basket, and his blood in a glass." Likewise Justinus Martyr, declaring the order of the church in his time, saith thus: *Illis, quæ cum gratiarum actione consecrata sunt, unusquisque participat: eadem ad eos qui absunt, diaconis dantur perferenda*[12]: "Of the things that be consecrate (that is, the bread, water, and wine) every man taketh part: the same things are delivered to the deacons to be carried unto them that be away." Here have we found not only a possibility, but also a common usage and practice, of carrying the sacrament in both kinds. This is the first invincible argument that all the world cannot answer. Hieronym. ad Rusticum. Justinus Martyr in Apologia ii.

M. HARDING. THE EIGHTEENTH DIVISION.

[Can. 14. H. A. 1564.] *The council of Nice decreed, that in churches where neither bishop nor priest were present, the deacons themselves bring forth and eat the holy communion*[13]. *Which likewise cannot be referred to the form of wine, for cause of souring and corruption if it be long kept.* This canon is neither found in the Greek, nor extant in the first edition, nor alleged by Gratian.

THE BISHOP OF SARISBURY.

This latter clause (*Ipsi proferant et edant*), "Let them bring it forth themselves and eat," neither is in the Greek, nor in the decrees, nor in the former edition of the councils. Certain words somewhat like are found in Ruffinus in this sort: *Præsentibus presbyteris, diaconi ne dividant eucharistiam, sed illis agentibus solum ministrent. Si vero presbyter nullus sit in præsenti, tunc demum etiam ipsis liceat* Ruffinus, Libro i. cap. vi.

[7 Et ideo inepte adducit hoc ad propositum.—Wilh. Wodford. adv. Johan. Wiclef. in Fascic. Rer. Expet. et Fug. Lond. 1690. Tom. I. p. 198.]

[8 Decret. Melciad. in Crabb. Concil. Col. Agrip. 1551. Tom. I. p. 217. See before, page 160.]

[9 Conveniently be so, H. A. 1564.]

[10 Impossible, 1565, 1609.]

[11 Hieron. Op. Ad Rust. Monach. Epist. xcv. Tom. IV. Pars II. cols. 777, 8; where we find *portat.*]

[12 Just. Mart. Op. Par. 1742. Apol. i. p. 83.]

[13 Quod si non fuerit in præsenti vel episcopus vel presbyter, tunc ipsi proferant, et edant.—Concil. Nicen. in Crabb. Concil. Edit. ii. can. 14. Tom. I. p. 255. These words do not appear Edit. i., nor in Corp. Jur. Canon. Lugd. 1624. Decret. Gratian. Decr. Prima Pars, Dist. xciii. can. 14. col. 444; where the canon of Nice is quoted.]

dividere[1]: "In the presence of the priests let not the deacons divide or minister the sacrament, but only serve the priests in their office. But if there be no priest present, then let it be lawful for the deacons to minister." Here is very small help for M. Harding's purpose; unless perhaps he will say that *proferre* or *dividere* is "to minister in one kind." But if he think this a very fond translation, as it is indeed, then this authority might have been spared.

M. Harding upon occasion of these words would have men believe, that the deacon, in the absence of the priest, went to the pix, and took out the sacrament and received it. But Ruffinus speaketh not one word neither of taking forth of the sacrament, nor of the receiving of the deacon, but of dividing or ministering to the people. And his meaning seemeth to be this, that, in the absence of the priest, the deacon might consecrate, and so serve the people. Which thing, notwithstanding it seem in some part contrary to another canon of
Canon 18. the same council[2], namely in the presence of a priest, yet that it was so used in the primitive church, it appeareth by most manifest and certain proofs. St Ambrose imagineth St Laurence, being a deacon, thus to say unto Sixtus the bishop,
Ambr. Offic. Lib. i. cap. xli. when he saw him led to his martyrdom: *Experire... utrum idoneum ministrum elegeris, cui commiseris dominici sanguinis consecrationem*[3]: "O father, try whether thou have chosen a fit minister unto whom thou hast committed the consecration of the Lord's blood." By these words we see that deacons then used to conse-
Eutropius. crate. Therefore Eutropius was not well advised, when he without cause corrupted and altered St Ambrose's words, and for *Dominici sanguinis consecrationem*, read, *Dominici sanguinis dispensationem*. For it followeth immediately in St Ambrose: *Et consummandorum consortium sacramentorum*[3]: that is, "The fellowship of perfecting[4] the sacraments."

Folio 356. Authen. De Eccl. Diver. Capitulis. And the emperor Justinian in his Authentics, *De ecclesiasticis diversis capitulis:* "Let the bishop appoint unto the women that be under his government such priest or deacon as they shall choose to make answer[5] unto them, or to minister unto them the holy oblation[6]."

The same also may evidently be gathered by the second canon of the council
Concil. Ancyran. can. 2. Ancyrane: the words be: *Diaconi similiter, qui immolaverunt, honorem quidem habeant: cessare vero [debent] ab omni sacro ministerio, sive a pane sive a calice offerendo, vel prædicando*[7]: "Let the deacons that have offered (unto idols) keep their estate still. But they must give over all holy ministry, both of offering the bread and wine, and also of preaching."

This part of the deacon's office was afterward in sundry decrees abrogated.
Bergomen. in Honorio. First, Bergomensis in the life of Honorius saith: "It was decreed by Zosimus bishop of Rome, that the deacon should not minister in the presence of the bishop or priest[8]." And long before that time order was taken in the council holden at Arle in France, that deacons should not minister the sacrament at all.
Concil. Arelat. I. cap. 15. The words be: *De diaconis, quos cognovimus multis locis offerre, placuit [id] minime fieri debere*[9]: "Touching deacons, of whom we hear say that they make the oblation in many places, we have thought it good that they do so no more."

M. Harding will not deny but these be proofs sufficient, that the deacons in those days used to minister the holy communion. Therefore the meaning of the council of Nice is not that the deacon should go to the pix, and take the sacrament reserved, as M. Harding seemeth to gather upon a false text, being neither in the Greek, nor in the former setting forth of the councils, nor alleged by

---

[1 Et ne diaconi... illis [presbyteris] præsentibus eucharistiam dividant, sed, &c.... licere, &c.—Hist. Eccles. Par. Lib. x. cap. vi. fol. 108.]

[2 ... qui [diaconi] potestatem non habent offerendi, &c.—Concil. Nicen. in Crabb. Concil. Col. Agrip. 1551. Edit. i. can. 18. Tom. I. p. 256.]

[3 Ambros. Op. Par. 1686-90. De Offic. Ministr. Lib. I. cap. xli. 214. Tom. II. col. 55; where we read *commiseris*, and *cui consummandorum*. See Not. in loc. for the various reading of Eutropius.]

[4 Perfiting, 1565.] [5 Answers, 1565.]

[6 *Ταῖς δὲ γυναιξὶν, ὃν ἂν αὐταὶ ἐπιλέξωνται εἴτε πρεσβύτερον εἴτε διάκονον, εἰς τὸ ποιεῖν αὐταῖς τὰς ἀποκρίσεις, ἢ τὴν ἁγίαν αὐταῖς κοινωνίαν φέρειν, ὁ ὁσιώτατος ἐπίσκοπος, ὑφ' ὃν εἰσίν.*—Corp. Jur. Civil. Amst. 1663. Auth. Coll. IX. Tit. vi. Novell. cxxiii. 36. Tom. II. p. 175. See also Just. Princ. Novell. Const. Basil. 1561. Const. cxxiii. p. 365.]

[7 Concil. Ancyr. in Crabb. Concil. Ed. i. cap. 2. Tom. I. p. 199.]

[8 Censuit item diaconum præsente episcopo vel presbytero eucharistiæ sacramentum ministrare non debere.—J. P. Bergom. suppl. Chronic. Par. 1538. Lib. IX. Honor. fol. 218. 2.]

[9 Concil. Arel. I. in Crabb. Concil. cap. 15. Tom. I. p. 287; where *diaconibus*.]

Gratian; but that the deacon, in the absence of the priest, might consecrate the holy mysteries, and deliver the same unto the people, as may well be gathered by the words of Ruffine. But let us grant M. Harding, that the sacrament was reserved; yet hath he gotten very small advantage for his half communion. For if he would say thus: The sacrament was reserved;

Ergo, it was reserved in one kind,

the sequel of his argument would be too weak. No logic could make it good.

I grant the holy mysteries were sometimes kept in the primitive church upon sundry occasions; but they were kept in both kinds, as manifestly appeareth by Nicephorus[10], and by the first epistle of complaint sent by Chrysostom unto Innocentius[11]. This being true, as it cannot be denied, that the sacrament was reserved in both kinds, what then hath M. Harding gotten by this invincible argument for his half communion in one kind?

Nicephor. Lib. xiii. cap. xix.

Chrys. Epist. i. ad Innocentium.

M. HARDING. THE NINETEENTH DIVISION.

Where oftentimes we find it recorded of the fathers, that christian people in time of persecution received of the priests at church in fine linen cloths the sacrament in sundry portions, to bear with them, and to receive it secretly in the morning before other meat, as their devotion served them; for the same cause, and in respect[12] of other circumstances, it must of necessity be taken only for the kind or form of bread. The places of Tertullian and St Cyprian be known. Tertullian, writing to his wife, exhorteth her not to marry again, specially to an infidel, if he die before her; for that, if she do, she shall not be able at all times, for her husband, to do as a christian woman ought to do. "Will not thy husband know," saith he, "what thou eatest secretly before all other meat? And in case he do know it, he will believe it to be bread, not (60) *him who it is called[13]." St Cyprian writeth in his sermon,* De Lapsis, *that, when a woman had gone about with unworthy hands to open her coffer where the holy thing of our Lord was laid up, she was made afraid with fire that rose up from thence, as she durst not touch it[14]. Which doubtless must be taken for that one kind of the sacrament.*

Lib. ii. ad Uxorem.

The sixtieth untruth. Standing in the false translating of Tertullian.

THE BISHOP OF SARISBURY.

The matter that hangeth in question between us is, whether the people, being assembled together in the church, at any time within the space limited received the communion under one kind. M. Harding answereth me, not of the order of the church, but of several men and private houses. Thus he flieth that thing that should be proved; and the thing that needeth no proof, as nothing pertinent unto the matter, he proveth only by[15] conjecture. In the place of Tertullian he useth a manifest corruption; as I have already shewed.

M. Harding falsifieth Tertullian.

His conjectures be these: "Women received the sacrament in a linen cloth: Tertullian's wife received it at home before meats: St Cyprian saith, a woman kept it at home in a chest; *ergo*, the sacrament was ministered in one kind." These be cold guesses, and no proofs. To say, They had the bread; *ergo*, they had not the wine, is a very faint reason, and hangeth only of ignorance, for that M. Harding knoweth not in what order these things were kept. But that women and others kept the sacrament and carried it about them, and that in both kinds, it is evident, and cannot be denied.

Gregory Nazianzene thus writeth of his sister Gorgonia: *εἴ πού τι τῶν ἀντιτύπων τοῦ τιμίου σώματος καὶ αἵματος ἡ χεὶρ ἐθησαύρησεν, τοῦτο καταμιγνῦσα τοῖς δάκρυσι*[16], &c. "If her hand had laid up any portion of the tokens of the precious body and of the blood, mingling it with her tears," &c. Here Nazianzene, contrary to M. Harding's judgment, saith, she had laid up both parts. And what should I stand

Nazian. in Funere Gorgoniæ.

[10 Niceph. Callist. Hist. Eccles. Lib. XIII. cap. xix. Tom. II. p. 391.]

[11 Ἀλλ' ἔνθα τὰ ἅγια ἀπέκειντο εἰσελθόντες οἱ στρατιῶται ... πάντα τε ἑώρων τὰ ἔνδον, καὶ τὸ ἁγιώτατον αἷμα τοῦ Χριστοῦ...εἰς τὰ τῶν προειρημένων στρατιωτῶν ἱμάτια ἐξεχεῖτο.—Chrysost. Op. Par. 1718-38. Ad Innocent. Epist. i. Tom. III. p. 519.]

[12 Respects, H. A. 1564.]

[13 Tertull. Op. Lut. 1641. Ad Uxor. Lib. II. 5. p. 190. See before, page 148.]

[14 Cypr. Op. Oxon. 1682. De Laps. pp. 132, 3.]

[15 To, 1565.]

[16 Gregor. Nazianz. Op. Par. 1778-1840. In Laud. Gorgon. Orat. viii. 18. Tom. I. p. 229; where we find ἢ τοῦ αἵματος, and ἐθησαύρισεν.]

Amphilochius. long to heap examples? M. Harding's own Amphilochius, of whom he seemeth to make so great account, among other his fables, whereof he hath good store, saith that a certain Jew came and received among the faithful, and privily carried part of either kind home with him[1]: how or wherein, it is not written. Yet will it not follow: M. Harding cannot tell wherein the Jew carried home the wine; therefore Amphilochius' tale is not true.

Now, if M. Harding had his own request, yet is he far off from his purpose. For if he would reason thus: One woman received the half sacrament in one kind at home; *ergo*, the people received in like sort openly in the church (which is the thing that should be proved), this argument would hardly hold.

To be short, these three examples here alleged are nothing else but mere abuses of the sacrament. And therefore, as it appeareth by St Cyprian, God shewed himself by miracle to be offended with it, fraying the woman that so had kept it with a flame of fire[2]. And it was decreed in the council holden at Cæsaraugusta in Spain, that, if any man received the sacrament, and eat not the same presently in the church, he should be accursed for ever[3]. Thus M. Harding's reasons hold only by guess, grounded upon abuse, and, being granted, yet are not able to prove his purpose.

Cyprian. de Lapsis Serm. 5.

Concil. Cæsaraugust. cap. 3.

M. HARDING. THE TWENTIETH DIVISION.

The examples of keeping the holy sacrament under the form of bread only, to be in a readiness for the sick and for others in time of danger, that they might have their necessary victual of life, or voyage provision, with them at their departure hence, be in manner infinite. Here one or two may serve instead of a number. For though M. Jewel maketh his vaunt that we have not one sentence or clause for proof of these articles, which he so defaceth with his negative; yet I will not accumulate this treatise with tedious allegation of authorities. St Ambrose, at the hour of death, received the communion under one kind, kept for that purpose, as it appeareth by this testimony of Paulinus, who wrote his life. And because it may be a good instruction to others to die well, I will here recite his words: "At the same time as he departed from us to our Lord, from about the eleventh hour of the day, until the hour that he gave up the ghost, stretching abroad his hands in manner of a cross, he prayed. We saw his lips move, but voice we heard none. Horatus, a priest of the church of Vercels, being gone up to bed, heard a voice three times of one calling him, and saying to him, Arise and haste thee; for he will depart hence by and by. Who, going down, gave to the saint our Lord's body, which taken and swallowed down, he gave up the ghost, having with him a good voyage provision, so as the soul, being the better refreshed by the virtue of that meat, may now rejoice with the company of angels, whose life he led in the earth, and with the fellowship of Elias[4]."

THE BISHOP OF SARISBURY.

It is no vaunt to say the truth. Neither did I deny that ever any one man received the communion in one kind. For I knew all these examples, and the weight of them. Neither is it so hard a matter for a man to know them. But this is the only thing that I denied: "That you are not able to bring any one sufficient authority or example that ever the whole people received the communion in the open church under one kind." Hereupon resteth that strange negative, wherewithal ye are so grieved. This is it that ye should prove, and

---

[[1] Amphiloch. Op. Par. 1644. In Vit. S. Basil. pp. 177, 8.]

[[2] Cypr. Op. Oxon. 1682. De Laps. pp. 132, 3.]

[[3] Concil. Cæsaraug. can. 3. in Concil. Stud. Labb. et Cossart. Lut. Par. 1671-2. Tom. II. cols. 1009, 10. See before, page 148, note 1.]

[[4] Sed eodem tempore quo migravit ad Dominum, ab hora circiter undecima diei usque ad illam horam, in qua emisit spiritum, expansis manibus in modum crucis oravit: nos vero labia illius moveri videbamus, vocem autem non audiebamus. Honoratus etiam sacerdos ecclesiæ Vercellis cum in superioribus domus se ad quiescendum composuisset, tertio vocem vocantis se audivit, dicentisque sibi: Surge, festina, quia modo est recessurus. Qui descendens, obtulit sancto Domini corpus: quo accepto ubi glutivit, emisit spiritum, bonum viaticum secum ferens; ut in virtute escæ anima refectior, angelorum nunc consortio, quorum vita vixit in terris, et Eliæ societate lætetur. —Ambros. Op. Par. 1686-90. Vit. Sanct. Ambros. a Paul. 47. Tom. II. Append. col. xii.]

yet hitherto have not proved. Ye say, ye will not accumulate examples, as though ye had enow[5] to spare. Yet have ye gotten together sick folk, women, infants, madmen, conjectures, guesses, miracles, and fables; and have spared nothing that might be found, although it made nothing to your purpose. Such is the store of your examples. Paulinus.

Touching Paulinus, that (as it is supposed) wrote this life of St Ambrose, I will say nothing as of myself[6], but only refer you to Erasmus, whose judgment ye would seem sometime not to mislike. Thus he saith: *Idem est artifex qui tam multa contaminavit in scriptis Hieronymi et Augustini*[7], &c. "It is the same craftsman that hath corrupted so many things in the writings of St Hierome and St Augustine, a man even made to such purpose[8]. He had the story of St Ambrose's life written by some other. Unto the same he set a jolly preface of his own: he wove in a great many talks between parties, and thereunto framed a conclusion, and patched on a sort of miracles. Compare the very phrase and manner of speech of the true Paulinus with this fellow's rags," &c. Erasm. in præfatione in Ambrosium.

This is that Paulinus whom M. Harding hath chosen for his author.

Touching the matter, if it be granted, it neither relieveth M. Harding's purpose, nor hindereth ours. For, if St Ambrose straight upon receiving of the bread yielded up the spirit, and therefore did not receive the cup, which thing notwithstanding is not yet proved, yet will it not follow that this was the common order of the church. What example of dying well M. Harding hath here found, I cannot see: unless he mean that the sacrament, only because it is received, hath power to work salvation, and to cause a man to die well; which is a dangerous doctrine, and by M. Harding already refused. For as much as may appear by the Articulo xx. story, neither did St Ambrose in that case call for the sacrament, nor utter any kind of word, nor understood what he received; but only lay speechless, and, as soon as he had swallowed the bread down, gave up the ghost. But this Paulinus in the same story noteth one special sentence of St Ambrose, much had in remembrance and commended by St Augustine in his old age, and here dissembled by M. Harding, whereof a man may take great comfort, and indeed learn a good lesson to die well. For he said lying in his death-bed: *Non sic vixi, ut pudeat inter vos vivere; nec mori timeo, quia bonum habemus Dominum*[9]: "Neither have I so lived, that I am ashamed longer to live amongst you; nor am I afraid to die, for that we have a gracious Lord."

M. HARDING. THE TWENTY-FIRST DIVISION.

Eccl. Hist. Lib. vi. c. xliv. *Dionysius Alexandrinus, about the year of our Lord* 200, *as Eusebius Cæsariensis reciteth, manifestly declareth how that an old man, called Serapion, was houseled under one kind at his end. This Serapion, after that he had lain speechless three days, sent for the sacrament. The priest, for sickness not able to come himself, gave to the lad that came of that errand a little of the sacrament, commanding him to wet it, and so, being moisted, to pour it into the old man's mouth.* Ἀποβρέξαι κελεύσας καὶ τῷ πρεσβύτῃ κατὰ τοῦ στόματος ἐπιστάξαι. *Thus*[10] *much is expressed by the words there, as the Greek is to be construed. The lad, being returned home, moisted with some liquor that divine meat to serve the old man withal, lying now panting for desire to be dismissed*[11] *hence, and to haste him away to heaven, and poured it into his mouth. For that this old man's mouth and throat had long been dry by force of his sickness, the priest, who had experience in that case, providently gave warning to moist the sacrament with some liquor, and so together to pour it into his mouth. Which was so done by the lad, as Dionysius*

[5 Enough, 1565.] [6 Meself, 1565.]

[7 Ambros. Op. Basil. 1555. D. Erasm. Cens. Tom. I. fol. B. 2; where he proceeds: Hieronymianis, et Augustinianis, natus ad hunc ludum. Habebat historiam Ambrosianæ vitæ, ei attexuit præfationem (ut vides) lepidam, intertexuit interlocutiones, addidit coronidem, et affinxit aliquot prodigia...Conferat qui volet Paulini stylum cum hujus assutis pannis, &c.]

[8 A purpose, 1565.]

[9 Non ita inter vos vixi, ut pudeat me vivere: nec timeo mori, quia Dominum bonum habemus.—Ambros. Op. Vit. Sanct. Ambros. a Paul. 45. Tom. II. Append. col. xii.]

[10 This, H. A. 1564.]

[11 Dimissed, 1565, and H. A. 1564.]

expresseth[1]. *Now, if the form of wine had then also been brought by the lad to be ministered, there had been no need of such circumstance to procure the old man a moisture to swallow down that holy food. And that this was the manner of ministering the sacrament to old men at their departing, it appeareth by record of Theodoretus, who writeth in his ecclesiastical story, how one Bassus, an arch-priest, ministered unto an old man called Simeones, of great fame for his holiness. "Bassus," saith he, "as he visited his churches, chanced upon holy Simeones, that wonder of the world, lying sic , who through feebleness was not able to speak nor move. When Bassus saw he should die, he giveth him his rights before: but after what sort, it is to be marked.* Spongia petita Simeoni os humectat atque eluit, ac tum ei divinum obtulit sacramentum: *he calleth for a sponge (saith Theodoretus), and therewith moisteth and washeth Simeones' mouth, and then giveth him the holy sacrament*[2]." *If at that time the receiving of the sacred cup had been in use, such procuring of moisture for the better swallowing down of the sacrament under one*[3] *kind had been needless.*

The burying of the sacrament.

Amphilochius, that worthy bishop of Iconium in Lycaonia, of whom mention is made in the article afore this, writeth in the life of St Basil, that, a little before he gave up his ghost, he received a portion of the holy sacrament, which long before he had caused[4] *to be kept, to the intent it might be put in his grave with him at his burial*[5]*; which no man can cavil to be any other than the form of bread only.*

THE BISHOP OF SARISBURY.

M. Harding, rather than he would seem to answer nothing, answereth one thing for another. The question is of the usage and order of the church: his answer is of Serapion's death-bed, as though there had been no churches yet erected in those days.

This Serapion, for open idolatry by him committed, was excommunicate from the church, and utterly cut off from the company of the faithful, and that in such extreme sort, for the greater terror of others, that during his life he should never be admitted again. Notwithstanding which extremity, upon good proofs and tokens of repentance, lest the party should be utterly swallowed up with despair, the church oftentimes with charitable discretion remitted some part of that rigour; as may appear by St Cyprian, St Augustine, and others, and by Dionysius that wrote this story.

August. Epist. clxxx.

St Augustine, speaking of the times of persecution: "Do not we consider," saith he, "in what multitudes the people in such danger[6] resorteth to the church, some desiring they may be baptized, some that they may be reconciled from excommunication, some that they may be admitted to shew their repentance (for their open crimes); every man desiring comfort, every man desiring the participation of the sacrament? In which case, if there be no minister to be had, what misery then followeth them that depart this life either unbaptized or else bound (in their sins)[7]!" Likewise St Cyprian saith: "In this extreme case of death, the party excommunicate should not tarry to be reconciled by the bishop (in the presence of the church, as the order was then), but discharge himself before any deacon, and so depart unto the Lord in peace[8]." Therefore the priest,

[1 Euseb. in Hist. Eccles. Script. Amst. 1695-1700. Lib. VI. cap. xliv. pp. 200, 1.]

[2 Σπογγιὰν τοίνυν αἰτήσας, καὶ ταύτῃ τὸ στόμα διαβρέξας, καὶ ἀποκλύσας, προσήνεγκεν αὐτῷ τῶν θείων μυστηρίων τὰ σύμβολα.—Theodor. Op. Lut. Par. 1642-84. Relig. Hist. xxvi. Tom. III. p. 880.]

[3 The one, H. A. 1564.]

[4 Willed, H. A. 1564.]

[5 Amphiloch. Op. Par. 1644. In Vit. S. Basil. p. 224. See before, page 188.]

[6 Dangers, 1565, 1609.]

[7 An non cogitamus, cum ad istorum periculorum pervenitur extrema, nec est potestas ulla fugiendi, quantus in ecclesia fieri soleat ab utroque sexu atque ab omni ætate concursus, aliis baptismum flagitantibus, aliis reconciliationem, aliis etiam pœnitentiæ ipsius actionem, omnibus consolationem et sacramentorum confectionem et erogationem? Ubi si ministri desint, quantum exitium sequitur eos, qui de isto seculo vel non regenerati exeunt vel ligati!—August. Op. Par. 1679-1700. Ad Honorat. Epist. ccxxviii. 8. Tom. II. col. 833.]

[8 ... si incommodo aliquo et infirmitatis periculo occupati fuerint, non expectata præsentia nostra, apud presbyterum ... vel si presbyter repertus non fuerit, et urgere exitus cœperit, apud diaconum quoque, exomologesin facere delicti sui possint; ut manu eis in pœnitentia imposita veniant ad Dominum in pace.—Cypr. Op. Oxon. 1682. Ad Presb. et Diac. Epist. xviii. pp. 40, 1.]

understanding the state the old man Serapion, being excommunicate, stood in, and being not able for sickness to go himself, lest he should depart comfortless in desperation, in token that he was reconciled unto the church, sent unto him the sacrament by the lad, and sent it not in one kind only, but in both. For such was the order of the church then, as it appeareth well by the story of Exuperius[9], and by Justinus[10], and others. And the boy that carried the sacrament, for more ease of the old man in that case, was warned by the priest to moist the bread in the sacramental wine that he brought with him, like as Bassus also did unto Simeones; whom M. Harding highly commendeth for his holiness, notwithstanding he were the founder of the Messalians[11], and therefore, as he afterward saith, the first parent of the sacramentary heresy. And what hath M. Harding herein found for his half communion? He will say, the boy was commanded to dip the bread; and Bassus was fain to wash Simeones' mouth; *ergo,* he[12] received in one kind. Verily Serapion's boy were soon able to answer this argument. For what sequel is this in reason: The sick man's mouth was dry; *ergo,* he could not receive the cup? Who would make such reasons but M. Harding? Of this ground he might better reason thus: The sick man's mouth was dry; *ergo,* he could not receive the bread. In my judgment, the scouring of the sick man's mouth hath small force to take from him the sacrament of Christ's blood, and so to prove the half communion.

Hieronym. ad Rusticum. Justinus, Apologia ii.

Theodoret. Lib. iv. cap. xi.

As for the fable of M. Harding's Amphilochius, it were great wrong to answer it otherwise than as a fable. For thus it is: The bread had been kept by the space of seven years, or more; St Basil in his death-bed called for it, and received it, to the intent, as M. Harding saith, it might be buried with him. The former part hereof, to say, either that the sacrament was kept the space of seven years, or that at the end of so long time it was fit to be received of a sick man in his death-bed, is mere folly. But to say, as M. Harding here saith, that the body of Christ, being now immortal and glorious, and at the right hand of God, may be laid in the grave and buried, is manifest and wicked blasphemy. Abdias saith that St Matthy the apostle, when he was stoned to death, desired that two of the first stones might be buried with him, for a witness against them that so used him[13]: who, although he be full of like fables, yet hath he some reason in his fables; but M. Harding's Amphilochius hath none at all.

Now for view of M. Harding's proofs, good reader, consider this: I demand of the laity: he answereth of St Ambrose and St Basil, which were bishops. I demand of the whole people: he answereth of several men. I demand of the usage of the church: he answereth of persons excommunicate, that were without the church. I demand of sufficient and certain proofs: he answereth me by guesses and fables. And these be his invincible arguments, that no man can answer.

M. HARDING. THE TWENTY-SECOND DIVISION.

It hath been a (61) *custom in the Latin church from the apostles' time to our days, that on Good Friday, as well priests as other christian people, receive the sacrament under the form of bread only, consecrated the day before, called the day of our Lord's supper, commonly Maunday Thursday, and that not without signification of a singular mystery; and this hath ever been judged a good and sufficient communion.*

The sixty-first untruth, without any colour or shew of truth.

THE BISHOP OF SARISBURY.

This may well be called a Good Friday's argument, it cometh in so naked without witness. Indeed M. Tonstal saith, it hath been used of old in the Latin church[14]; but he durst not say from the time of the apostles, as M. Harding

Tonstal. De Euchar.

[9 Hieron. Op. Par. 1693-1706. Ad Rust. Monach. Epist. xcv. Tom. IV. Pars II. col. 778.]

[10 Just. Mart. Op. Par. 1742. Apol. i. p. 83.]

[11 Theodoret. in Hist. Eccles. Script. Lib. IV. cap. xi. p. 163.]

[12 They, 1565, 1609.]

[13 Matthias autem petiit illos duos lapides consepeliri sibi, in testimonium illis.—Gest. S. Matthiæ, ad calc. Abd. Apost. Hist. Par. 1571. fol. 131. 2.]

[14 ...sciendum est, Græcorum ecclesiam, in quadragesima eucharistiam non consecrare, nisi in sabbatis et dominicis diebus. Ceteris vero diebus utuntur

here saith. Yet, for augmentation of matter of his side, I will say further; the first council Arausicane[1], holden sometime in France, and Innocentius the first[2], have added hereto the holy Saturday, which now is called Easter Eve, and say it is a tradition of the church that in those two days the sacrament in any wise be not ministered. The like whereof is written by Socrates of Good Friday, and the Wednesday before[3].

Concil. Araus. i. Socr. Lib. v. cap. xxi. Innoc. i. cap. 4.

The singular mystery hereof M. Harding holdeth secret as a mystery. Innocentius saith: "It is because the apostles ran their way that day, and hid themselves[2]." Thomas of Aquine[4] and Gerson[5] say: "Because, if any had consecrate that day while Christ lay dead, the body had been without blood, and the blood without the body." Others say: "If the sacrament that mean while had been kept, it would have been dead in the pix."

Thom. iii. Par. de Euch. q. 76. Art. 2. Gerson contra Floret. Lib. iv. Thom. iii. Par. q. 81. Art. 4. Innoc. iii. Hugo Cardinal in Evang. secundum Lucam, cap. xxiv. Eleganter.

Hugo Cardinalis saith: *Quinta feria duæ hostiæ consecrantur, et altera in crastinum reservatur, quod eleganter fit*[6], *&c.*; "Upon Shire[7] Thursday two hosts be consecrate, and the one of them is reserved until the next day; which thing is very trimly done. For Christ's passion is the truth; and the sacrament is a figure of the same. Therefore when the truth is come, the figure giveth place." These be the greatest mysteries that I could ever learn touching this matter.

"But this," saith M. Harding, "was ever counted a good communion." I grant. But ye have not yet proved that this was your half communion. For if ye say, they consecrated the day before; *ergo*, they received in one kind only the day after, this would be no formal argument. For the Greek church all the Lent long used to consecrate the sacrament only upon Saturdays and Sundays, as it is noted in the council of Constantinople[8]; and upon other days they used the communion of things consecrate before; and yet had they never until this day the communion under one kind. Yet, notwithstanding, unto this manner of the Greek church [a]M. Tonstal resembleth the observation of Good Friday in the Latin church[9]. So far is M. Harding off from proving his purpose by Good Friday.

Sexta Synoda Constantin. can. 52. τῇ θείᾳ λειτουργίᾳ τῶν προηγιασμένων. [a] Tonstal. De Euchar.

M. HARDING. THE TWENTY-THIRD DIVISION.

And that in the Greek church also, even in the time of Chrysostom, the communion under the form of bread only was used and allowed, it appeareth by this notable story of Sozomenus, a Greek writer; which because it is long, I will here rehearse it only in English, remitting the learned to the Greek. "When John, otherwise named Chrysostom, governed the church of Constantinople very well, a certain man of the Macedonian heresy had a wife of the same opinion. When this man had heard John in his sermon declare how one ought to think of God, he praised his doctrine, and exhorted his wife to conform herself to the same judgment also. But when as she was led by the talk of noble women, rather than by her husband's good advertisements, after that he saw counsel took no place, 'Except,' quoth he, 'thou wilt bear me company in things touching

Histor. Eccles. Lib. viii. cap. v. in Græco.

---

liturgia ante consecratorum ... qualis mos ab antiquo in die parasceves in Latinorum etiam ecclesiis servari solitus est.—Tonstal. De Verit. Corp. et Sang. Dom. in Euchar. Lut. 1554. Lib. I. fol. 47. 2.]

[1 ... in biduo isto, id est, parasceve et sabbato, sacramenta penitus non celebrari.—Concil. Araus. I. in Crabb. Concil. Col. Agrip. 1551. Tom. I. p. 624.]

[2 ... constat, apostolos biduo isto ... propter metum Judæorum se occuluisse ... non dubium est ... eos jejunasse biduo memorato, ut traditio ecclesiæ habeat, isto biduo sacramenta penitus non celebrari. —Innoc. Papæ I. Epist. i. 4. in eod. Tom. I. p. 453.]

[3 Αὖθις δὲ ἐν Ἀλεξανδρείᾳ τῇ τετράδι καὶ τῇ λεγομένῃ παρασκευῇ ... πάντα τὰ συνάξεως γίνεται, δίχα τῆς τῶν μυστηρίων τελετῆς.—Socrat. in Hist. Eccles. Script. Amst. 1695-1700. Lib. v. cap. xxii. p. 235.]

[4 Unde si tunc fuisset hoc sacramentum celebratum sub speciebus panis, fuisset corpus Christi sine sanguine, et sub speciebus vini sanguis sine corpore, sicut erat in rei veritate.—Thom. Aquinat. Op. Venet. 1595. Summ. Theol. Tert. Pars. Quæst. lxxvi. Art. 2. Tom. XII. fol. 245. 2. See also Quæst. lxxxi. Art. 4. foll. 272, 3.]

[5 Nota quod si quis in triduo confecisset, panis fuisset conversus in corpus mortuum; non in vivum, cum anima esset actualiter separata a corpore.—Floret. Lugd. 1499. Lib. IV. fol. 97. 2.]

[6 Hugon. de S. Char. Op. Col. Agrip. 1621. In Evang. sec. Luc. cap. xxiii. Tom. VI. fol. 272. Hugo proceeds: Congruum est enim ut ea die qua veritas est exhibita, cesset omnino figura.]

[7 See Brand, Pop. Antiq. with Sir H. Ellis's note. Vol. I.]

[8 Concil. Quinisext. can. 52. in Concil. Labb. et Cossart. Lut. Par. 1671-2. Tom. VI. cols. 1166, 7. See before, page 129, note 6.]

[9 See above, page 245, note 14.]

God, thou shalt have no more to do with me, nor live any longer[10] *with me.' The woman, hearing this, promising feignedly that she would agree unto it, conferreth the matter with a woman-servant that she had, whom she esteemed for trusty, and useth her help to deceive her husband. About the time of the mysteries, she, holding fast that which she had received, stooped down, making resemblance to pray. Her servant, standing by, giveth to her secretly that which she had brought with her in her hand. That, as she put her teeth to it to bite it, hardeneth into a stone. With that the woman, sore astonied, fearing lest some evil should happen unto her therefore, which came by the power of God, ran forthwith to the bishop, and, bewraying herself, sheweth him the stone, having yet in it the prints of her bit, representing a strange matter and a wondrous colour; and so with tears of her eyes besought forgiveness, promising her husband she would consent and agree to him. If this seem to any incredible (saith Sozomenus), that stone is witness, which to this day is kept among*
κειμήλια. *the jewels of the church of Constantinople*[11]*." By this story it is clear the sacrament was then ministered under one kind only. For, by receiving that one form, this woman would have persuaded her husband that she had communicated with him, and with that holy bishop. Else, if both kinds had then been ministered, she should have practised some other shift for the avoiding of the cup, which had not been so easy.*

THE BISHOP OF SARISBURY.

I may not disgrace the credit of this story; albeit in Sozomenus and Nicephorus[12], of both whom the same is recorded, there be sundry things that may well be filed. But I see no cause yet wherefore M. Harding should blow the triumph. For in all this long rehearsal there is not one word spoken of the communion under one kind. The bread so changed into a stone, and kept for a memory among the jewels there, was a witness of the woman's dissimulation, and not of M. Harding's half communion. "Yet," saith he, "by this story it is clear the sacrament was then ministered under one kind only. For by receiving that one form, the woman would have persuaded her husband that she had communicated with him. Else, if both kinds had then been ministered, she would have practised some other shift for the avoiding of the cup, which had not been so easy." Now truly here is but a cold conclusion, hanging wholly (as it may appear) only upon the sleight of a woman's wit. For as this woman had devised to deceive her husband in the bread, why might she not as well devise to deceive him in the cup? Why might she not take the cup, and feign that she drank, and yet drink nothing? Doubtless such dissimulation is sooner wrought in the cup than in the bread; and she, that durst so to dissemble in the one part of God's sacraments, would little fear to dissemble in the other.

Here we see the certainty of M. Harding's guesses. He reapeth the thing that was never sown, and gathereth of his authors the thing that was never spoken.

But touching the truth of this whole matter, if a man list only to go by guess, as M. Harding doth, why may he not thus imagine with himself: If this woman would thus dissemble in a case so dangerous, what needed her to take the bread at her maid's hand, and specially at that time, in that place, and in the sight of

[10 Further, H. A. 1564.]

[11 Ἰωάννης δὲ ἄριστα τῆς Κωνσταντινουπόλεως ἐκκλησίας ἐπιτροπεύων ...... ἀνήρ τις τῆς Μακεδονίου αἱρέσεως τοιαύτῃ γυναικὶ συνῴκει· περιτυχὼν δὲ αὐτῷ διδάσκοντι ὅπως χρὴ περὶ Θεοῦ δοξάζειν, ἐπαινέτης ἦν τοῦ δόγματος, καὶ τὴν γυναῖκα ὁμοφρονεῖν αὐτῷ παρεκάλει· ἐπεὶ δὲ τῇ πρὸ τούτου συνηθείᾳ καὶ ταῖς ὁμιλίαις τῶν γνωρίμων γυναικῶν ἡττᾶτο, καὶ πολλάκις νουθετῶν ὁ ἀνὴρ οὐδὲν ἤνυεν, εἰ μὴ, φησὶ, κοινωνήσεις μοι τῶν θείων, οὐδὲ τοῦ βίου κοινωνὸς ἔσῃ μοι τοῦ λοιποῦ· ἐνταῦθα δὲ ἡ γυνὴ συνθεμένη τοῦτο ποιεῖν, κοινοῦται τινὶ τῶν θεραπαινίδων ἣν ἡγεῖτο πιστὴν, καὶ παραλαμβάνει συνεργὸν ἐς ἀπάτην τοῦ ἀνδρός· περὶ δὲ τὸν καιρὸν τῶν μυστηρίων· ἴσασι δὲ οἱ μεμυημένοι ὃ λέγω· ἡ μὲν, ὅπερ ἐδέξατο κατέχουσα, ὡς εὐξομένη ἀπέκυψε· παρεστῶσα δὲ αὐτῇ ἡ θεράπαινα, λάθρα δέδωκεν ὃ μετὰ χεῖρας ἦλθε φέρουσα. τὸ δὲ πρὸς τοῖς ὀδοῦσι λίθος ἐπήγνυτο· περιδεὴς δὲ γενομένη ἡ γυνὴ μή τι πάθοι, θεῖον οὕτω πρᾶγμα ἐπ' αὐτῇ συμβὰν, δρομαία ἐπὶ τὸν ἐπίσκοπον ἐλθοῦσα, ἑαυτὴν κατεμήνυσε. καὶ τὸν λίθον ἐπέδειξεν, εἰκόνα φέροντα τοῦ δήγματος, ἀγνῶτα δὲ τὴν ὕλην, καὶ παράξενόν τι δεικνύντα χρῶμα· σὺν δάκρυσί τε συγγνώμην αἰτήσασα, ὁμοφρονοῦσα τῷ ἀνδρὶ συνῆν. ἀλλὰ τάδε μὲν εἴτῳ μὴ πιθανὰ δοκεῖ, μάρτυς αὐτὸς ὁ λίθος, εἰσέτι νῦν ἐν τοῖς κειμηλίοις τῆς ἐκκλησίας Κωνσταντινουπόλεως φυλαττόμενος.—Sozom. in Hist. Eccles. Script. Lib. VIII. cap. v. pp. 617, 8.]

[12 Niceph. Callist. Hist. Eccles. Lut. Par. 1630. Lib. XIII. cap. vii. Tom. II. pp. 363, 4.]

the whole people? Or how could she so openly receive it without suspicion? Or why might she not have brought it in a napkin secretly about herself? The burden was not great: her feigning and hypocrisy had been the easier. And thus much to answer one guess by another.

But that there was no such dismembering of the holy communion at that time, we may well understand both by St Basil, Nazianzene, Gregory Nyssene, and others of that age, and also by these plain words of Chrysostom: *Est ubi nihil differat sacerdos a subdito: ut quando fruendum est horrendis mysteriis*[1]: "In some cases there is no difference between the priest and the people; as when they must enjoy the reverend mysteries." Besides that, the Greek church never had this half communion, neither before that time nor never sithence. And therefore pope Leo the tenth calleth the use of the whole sacrament, according to Christ's institution, the Bohemians' and the Grecians' heresy[2].

Chrysost. in 2 Cor. Hom. 18.

M. HARDING. THE TWENTY-FOURTH DIVISION.

The place of St Basil's epistles ad Cæsariam *cannot be avoided by no shift nor sophistry of the gospellers. These be his words: "All they which live the solitary life in wilderness, where is no priest, keeping the communion at home, communicate themselves. And in Alexandria and in Egypt each*[3] *of the people for the most part hath the communion in his house*[4]*."*

Here I might ask M. Jewel, how they could keep wine consecrated in small measures, as should serve for every man's housel apart, in those countries of extreme heat, specially in wilderness, where they had neither priest, nor deacon, as in that place St Basil writeth; for lack of whom they kept it in store a long time, that they might not be destitute of it at need. Again, here I might ask him, whether it was the form of bread only, or of wine also, which christian men, and specially women, were wont devoutly to receive of the priests in their clean linen or napkins, to bear home with them, taking great heed that no fragments of it fell down to[5] *the ground, as both Origen*[6]*, and also St Augustine*[7] *do witness. I think he will confess that linen cloth is not a very fit thing to keep liquor in.*

Bread and wine shifted suddenly into forms.

[*Vide articulum priorem*, H. A. 1564.]

THE BISHOP OF SARISBURY.

The gospellers, whom M. Harding so often upbraideth with that name, as if he himself had no part in God's gospel, have little need to avoid that thing whereby they see themselves nothing hindered. For the question is moved of the whole congregation: answer is made of several persons. We speak of the order of churches: M. Harding answereth of forests and wilderness. Verily, if he could find any thing to purpose in the church, he would not thus hunt the mountains; neither would he fly[8] for aid into Egypt, if he could find any near at home.

The ground of this argument is the impossibility of keeping wine, which M. Harding hath hitherto uttered by the name of form. Now that it is come to souring, he calleth it wine. There is cunning in shifting of terms. But if there be no wine there remaining, as these men would persuade the world, what shall we call it then that thus standeth in danger of souring? Certainly Christ's blood will not sour; and forms of wine, without substance, cannot sour: either of these both can as well abide the hot country as the cold. But Gelasius saith, "There remaineth in the sacrament[9] the nature and substance of bread and wine[10]."

Of preserving wines in hot countries I will not reason. Notwithstanding, I remember Macrobius saith that, as the country of Egypt is extreme hot, so the wines of the same be extreme cold[11], and therefore, as it may be supposed, the

Macrobius.

[1 Chrysost. Op. Par. 1718-38. In Epist. II. ad Cor. Hom. xviii. Tom. X. p. 568. See before, page 202, note 13.]

[2 See before, p. 231.]

[3 Each one, H. A. 1564.]

[4 Basil. Op. Par. 1721-30. Ad Cæsar. Epist. xciii. Tom. III. pp. 186, 7. See before, page 152.]

[5 On, H. A. 1564.]

[6 Orig. Op. Par. 1733-59. In Exod. Hom. xiii. 3. Tom. II. p. 176. See before, page 148, note 7.]

[7 August. Op. Par. 1679-1700. Serm. ccxxix. 5. Tom. V. Append. cols. 376, 7. See before, page 148, note 8.]

[8 Flee, 1565.] [9 Sacraments, 1565, 1609.]

[10 Gelas. Episc. Rom. adv. Eutych. et Nestor. in Mag. Biblioth. Vet. Patr. Col. Agrip. 1618-22. Tom. V. Pars III. p. 671.]

[11 A. Macrob. Saturn. Lib. VII. cap. viii.]

more durable. And although the country of Naples be very hot, yet the wines thereof have been preserved the space of forty or fifty years, as it is mentioned by Plutarch, Athenæus, and others. Howbeit, this is not much material. But as the wine is in danger of souring, so is the bread in danger of moulding, as appeareth by sundry cautels of the mass therefore provided. Yet one question would well be here demanded. If the wine in the mountains of Egypt could not be kept in small quantities a few days, how then could the wine that Christ changed out of water in Cana of Galilee be kept at Orleance in France[12], as a relique, for the space of fifteen hundred and thirty years, ever sithence that time, until this day, and that still without souring? But let us yield that wine in the mountains could not be kept; yet might[13] it well be had, and kept in churches, at the least during the time of the communion; and that to this purpose is sufficient.

Plut. in Lucull. Athen. Lib. i.

Vinum Architriclini.

The keeping of liquor in a linen cloth was M. Harding's conceit, more to solace himself withal, than much making to the matter. For otherwise, as the women received the bread in a cloth, so might they receive the wine in a vial, or some other like thing. And that they so did, it may well be gathered by the story of Gorgonia, Nazianzene's sister[14], by Exuperius, of whom St Hierome writeth[15]; and by the fable of the Jew, in M. Harding's own Amphilochius[16]. And for that M. Harding maketh such sport with "keeping liquor in a cloth," it was decreed in the council holden at Altisiodorum, "That the priest should put his oil in a chrismatory, and in linen," by these words: *Ut...chrisma...chrismario et linteo imponant*[17]. I doubt not but M. Harding thinketh a linen cloth will hold wine as well as oil.

Naz. in Funere Gorg. Hieron. ad Rusticum. Narbonen.

Concil. Altisiodor. can. 6.

M. HARDING. THE TWENTY-FIFTH DIVISION.

Though I might bring a great number of other places for the use of one kind, which, after the most common rule of the church, was the form of bread; yet here I will stay myself[18], *putting the reader in mind that the communion hath been ministered to some persons under the form of wine only, and hath been taken for the whole sacrament; specially to such, as for driness of their throat, at their death, could not swallow it down under the form of bread. Whereas it appeareth by St Cyprian, and also by St Augustine, that the sacrament was given to infants in their time*[19]. *We find in St Cyprian, that, when a deacon offered the cup of our Lord's blood to a little maid-child, which, through default of the nurse, had tasted of the sacrifices that had been offered to devils, the child turned away her face, by the instinct of the divine Majesty (saith he), closed fast her lips, and refused the cup. But yet, when the deacon had forced her to receive a little of the cup, the yeax*[20] *and vomit followed, so as that sanctified drink in the blood of our Lord gushed forth of the polluted bowels. If the sacrament had been given to this infant under the form of bread before, she would have refused that no less than she did the cup, that the deacon then would not have given her the cup. And that this may seem the less to be wondered at, Johannes Teutonicus, that wrote scholies upon Gratian, witnesseth that, even in his time, the custom was in some places to give the sacrament to infants, not by delivering to them the body of Christ, but by pouring the blood into their mouths*[21]*; which custom hath been, upon good consideration, abrogated in the church of Rome, and kept in the Greek church, as Lyra writeth upon St John*[22].

Sermone 5 de Lapsis.

De Consecrat. dist. 4, can. 4. Si qui apud illos Hæreticos.

[12 See Becon's Works, Lond. 1560-4. *Monstrous Merchandise of the Romish Bishops.* Vol. III. fol. 188.]

[13 Mought, 1565.]

[14 Gregor. Nazianz. Op. Par. 1778-1840. In Laud. Gorgon. Orat. viii. 18. Tom. I. p. 229.]

[15 Hieron. Op. Par. 1693-1706. Epist. xcv. ad Rust. Monach. Tom. IV. Pars II. cols. 777, 8.]

[16 Amphiloch. Op. Par. 1644. In Vit. S. Basil. pp. 177, 8.]

[17 Concil. Antisiodor. can. 6. in Crabb. Concil. Col. Agrip. 1551. Tom. II. pp. 184, 5.]

[18 Meself, 1565.]

[19 Cypr. Op. Oxon. 1682. De Laps. p. 132. August. Op. Epist. ad Bonif. xcviii. 4. Tom. II. col. 265. See before, page 6, note 6.]

[20 Yeax: hiccough.]

[21 Hoc de adultis: quia parvulis non datur corpus Christi.... nisi forte ubi consuetudo est, quod infunditur per ora eorum sanguis Christi, non corpus secundum quosdam.—Gloss. in August. in Corp. Jur. Canon. Lugd. 1624. Decret. Gratian. Decr. Tert. Pars, De Consecr. Dist. iv. can. 28. col. 1985.]

[22 Dicunt Græci quod hoc sacramentum est tantæ

THE BISHOP OF SARISBURY.

Whatsoever plenty of such examples M. Harding hath, if he had any better he might well have spared these. Here he saith: "Some old men, for their age and drithe[1], were suffered to communicate of the cup only, as being not able to swallow the bread." A little before he said that "St Ambrose, lying in his death-bed, received the bread only[3];" and that "St Basil, in the like case, received the sacrament, being then stale and dry, of seven years' keeping, and that alone, without wine[4]." Seneca saith: *Proprium est luxuriæ, gaudere perversis:* "It is the property of wantonness to delight in things out of order."

M. Harding is against himself, and speaketh contrary[2].

Infants, saith M. Harding, received in one kind, and thereto he allegeth the authority of St Cyprian; which although it made with him to this purpose, touching children, yet to other great purposes it maketh directly against him. For first, by that place of St Cyprian, the holy communion was thought so necessary to all the faithful, that children and infants were not excluded[5]; which plainly overthroweth the private mass. Besides that, the whole people received in both kinds, as it is manifest by St Cyprian's words; which thing is contrary to M. Harding's half communion.

Cypr. Serm. 5. de Lapsis.

M. Harding allegeth S. Cyprian against himself.

All this he granteth touching the people—wherein only I joined issue—and maketh his whole plea upon an infant; and yet of infants, as he knoweth, I spake nothing. If all that he saith were proved true, yet hath he gotten but an infant of his side. But what if this infant received both kinds? Verily there is nothing in Cyprian to the contrary. And it appeareth by St Hierome, St Augustine[6], and other old writers, that they that were baptized, as well children as others, immediately received the holy mysteries in both kinds. St Hierome, speaking of one Hilarius, saith thus: *Non [potest] baptisma tradere sine eucharistia*[7]: "He cannot minister baptism without the sacrament of thanksgiving." St Cyprian's words touching this matter be these: *Ubi...solemnibus adimpletis calicem diaconus offerre præsentibus cœpit, et accipientibus ceteris, locus ejus advenit, faciem suam parvula, instinctu divinæ Majestatis, avertere*[8], &c. "After the solemnity (of the consecration) was done, and the deacon began to minister the cup unto them that were present, and among others that received her turn was come, the child, by the power of God's divine majesty, turned away her face, &c." Hereby we may well gather, that, like as the priest, the deacons, and the people received, even so the child received too, without any manner innovation or difference.

August. de Eccl. Dogmat. Lib. i. cap. lii. Hieron. contra Lucif.

He will say, There is mention made but only of the cup: therefore the child received not the other kind. This guess is over slender: yet is it an ordinary argument with M. Harding. But it seemeth he doth not well consider the inconvenience that thereof may follow. For so may he as well conclude that the priest himself, and the deacons, and the whole people, received only of the cup. For there is no mention at all made of the other portion.

"If the bread had been offered to the child, she would as well have refused that as she did the cup." This is another guess, without any necessary sequel. This effect followed when God would have it; of whose doings we can give no reason.

Lyra and Teutonicus lived at the least thirteen hundred years after Christ; wherefore their authority in this case must needs seem the less. Yet, for ought that I can see, Lyra is untruly alleged, as writing to another purpose. Teutonicus in his gloss in the same place manifestly corrupteth St Augustine's text. For whereas St Augustine speaketh namely of children, and calleth them *parvulos*, "little ones," he saith in his gloss, *Hoc intellige de adultis*[9]: "Understand this of

---

necessitatis, quod pueris debet dari sicut baptismus: quod est falsum: quia in sumente hoc sacramentum requiritur actualis devotio et reverentia: quæ non sunt in pueris.—Bibl. cum Gloss. Ord. et Expos. N. de Lyra, Basil. 1502. Johan. cap. vi. Pars V. fol. 206. 2.]

[[1] Drithe: driness.]

[[2] Contraries, 1565, 1609.]

[[3] See before, page 242.]

[[4] See before, page 244.]

[[5] See the preceding page.]

[[6] August. Op. Par. 1679-1700. Lib. de Eccles. Dog. cap. xxii. Tom. VIII. Append. col. 78. It is this passage (falsely attributed to Augustine) upon which, as recited in Gratian, the gloss before mentioned (see the preceding page, note 20.) is made.]

[[7] Hieron. Op. Par. 1693-1706. Adv. Lucifer. Tom. IV. Pars II. col. 302; where *neque* for *non*.]

[[8] Cypr. Op. Oxon. 1682. De Laps. p. 132.]

[[9] See the preceding page, note 20.]

men of ripe years." Then, to confirm his error, he allegeth a custom, but he knoweth not where; and proveth it also, but he knoweth not by whom. For thus he avoucheth it: *Secundum quosdam;* that is, "As some men say." Which was never good witness in any court. Wherefore M. Harding might have spared these doctors, without any prejudice of his cause.

M. HARDING. THE TWENTY-SIXTH DIVISION.

Can. 76. *The fourth council of Carthago decreed, if a man in sickness (who was enjoined public penance) do demand his housel, and ere he die fall in a phrensy, or become speechless, that the sacrament be poured into his mouth*[10]. *To take this for* Can. 11. *the form of wine, we are moved by the decree of the eleventh council Toletane; where it is said, that "the weak nature of man is wont at the point of death to be so far oppressed with drouth, that it may be refreshed by no means, unless it be sustained*[11] *with comfort of drink." Then it followeth: "Which thing we see to be so at the*[12] *departing of many, who, being very desirous to receive their voyage provision of the holy communion, when the sacrament was given them, have cast it up again; not that they did this through infidelity, but for that they were not able to swallow down the sacrament delivered to them, but only a draught of our Lord's cup*[13]." *Howsoever this be taken, it is plain by this council, as by many other ancient councils and doctors, that the manner of the catholic church hath been to minister the sacrament to the sick under one kind.*

THE BISHOP OF SARISBURY.

These authorities answer themselves[14]. Being every way granted, yet is M. Harding never the nearer[15]. The whole matter we stand upon is the open order and usage in the church. For proof hereof, here are brought in lunatics and madmen. It were a strange sight to see a church full of such people. The substance of his argument resteth only upon this guess, That the bread cannot be poured into the sick man's mouth: and yet he may learn by the third council of Concil. Carthage[16], and by the abridgement of the council of Hippo[17], that the sacra- Carthag. iii. cap. 6. ment was then put into dead men's mouths. Neither can I see what necessity is in this reason: The man is frantic, or lieth speechless, which was the suggestion of that council; *ergo*, he cannot receive the sacramental bread. If there be danger in the receiving, there is none more than in the cup.

The canon of the council of Toledo here alleged is not an exposition of this council of Carthage, as M. Harding thinketh; but a declaration of a canon made in the first council of Toledo, as it is plain by these words: *In collatione nostri* Concil. Tolet. xi. cap. 11. *cœtus relectus est canon Toletani concilii primi, in quo præceptum est, ut si quis acceptam a sacerdote eucharistiam non sumpserit, velut sacrilegus propellatur*[18]. "In the conference of our council there was read a canon of the council of Toledo, wherein it was ordered, that if any man received not the sacrament delivered to him by the priest, the same should be excommunicate, as a wicked doer." This decree seemed very strait, specially for that a godly man, by mean of sickness, or other weakness of nature, might happen to refuse, or not to receive down the sacrament, but to cast it up against his will. Therefore the council, by way of declaration, determineth thus: That, if any man happen so to do by force of sickness, he shall not stand in danger of the law.

[10 Is qui pœnitentiam in infirmitate petit, si casu, dum ad eum sacerdos, invitatus, venit, oppressus infirmitate obmutuerit, vel in phrenesim versus fuerit ... Et si continuo creditur moriturus, ... infundatur ori ejus eucharistia.—Concil. Carth. IV. can. 76. in Crabb. Concil. Col. Agrip. 1551. Tom. I. p. 440.]

[11 Unneth sustained, 1565, 1609, and H.A. 1564.]

[12 1565, 1609, and H. A. 1564 omit *the*.]

[13 Solet enim humanæ naturæ infirmitas, in ipso mortis exitu prægravata, tanto siccitatis pondere deprimi, ut nullis ciborum illationibus refici, sed vix tantundem illati delectetur poculi gratia sustentari. Quod etiam in multorum exitu vidimus, qui, optatum suis votis sacræ communionis expetentes viaticum, collatam sibi a sacerdote eucharistiam rejecerunt. Non quod infidelitate hæc agerent, sed quod propter [al. præter] dominici calicis haustum, traditam sibi non possent eucharistiam deglutire.—Concil. Tolet. XI. cap. 11. in eod. Tom. II. p. 269.]

[14 Themself, 1565.]

[15 Neare, 1565, 1609.]

[16 Concil. Carthag. III. cap. 6. in eod. Tom. I. p. 427.]

[17 Concil. Hippon. Abbrev. 5. in eod. Tom. I. p. 433.]

[18 Concil. Tolet. xi. cap. 11. in eod. Tom. II. p. 269.]

Hereupon M. Harding concludeth thus: "It is plain by this council, and by many other councils and doctors," &c. Other council or doctor here is none named. This council neither maketh any law touching this matter, nor declareth any order or manner of public ministration, but only excuseth the invincible necessity and weakness of nature.

Si quis acceptam eucharistiam non sumpserit. Collatam a sacerdote eucharistiam rejiciunt.

But touching the manner and order of the church, the same council in the self-same[1] place saith, that the whole sacrament was offered even to the sick: that the sick did sometime of infirmity cast it up again[2]; which is a good argument that they did receive it; and that infants did sometime the like: whereof we may gather that infants then received the sacrament, and that in such sort as others did.

All these things considered accordingly, M. Harding might well conclude thus against himself: It was granted of special favour unto lunatics and madmen, and other sick persons, that, in consideration of their weakness, they might communicate under one kind without danger of the law. Therefore the rest, that were not so excepted, communicated under both kinds, and that by the very force of the law.

M. HARDING. THE TWENTY-SEVENTH DIVISION.

Now, whereas some say that the sacrament, to be given under the form of bread, was first dipped in the blood of our Lord, and would have so used now also for the sick, and that it is so to be taken for the whole and entire sacrament, as though the sacrament under the form of bread were not of itself sufficient; let them understand that this was an old error, condemned above twelve hundred years past by Julius the first, that great defender of Athanasius; who hereof, in an epistle to the bishops through Egypt, wrote thus: Illud vero quod pro complemento communionis intinctam tradunt eucharistiam populis, nec hoc prolatum ex evangelio testimonium receperunt, ubi apostolis corpus suum Dominus commendavit et sanguinem. Seorsum enim panis, [et] seorsum calicis commendatio memoratur[3]. *"Whereas some deliver to the people the sacrament dipped, for the full and whole communion, they have not received this testimony pronounced out of the gospel, where our Lord gave his body and his blood. For the giving of the bread is recorded apart by itself, and the giving of the cup apart likewise by itself." And whereas some afterward, in the time of Vitellianus, would have brought in again this abrogated custom, it was in like manner condemned and abolished,* In tertio Concilio Braccarensi, Can. 1.[4]

De Con. dist. 2. can. Cum omne crimen.

THE BISHOP OF SARISBURY.

There have been many great abuses about the holy mysteries, not only of late years in the church of Rome, whereof we justly complain, but also in the primitive church, even from the apostles' time. For some there were that ministered in water only; some that ministered milk instead of wine; some bruised grapes into the cup, and so ministered; some ministered bread and cheese together; some dipped the sacrament of Christ's body in the sacrament of his blood[5]. But neither this folly, whereof Julius speaketh, nor any other like old folly, was ever renewed by any of us. Indeed M. Harding, and all the rest of that side, have used to break the bread, and to dip the third part of it into the wine, and for the same have devised a solemn mystery. For some of them say, "It signifieth Christ's rising from the dead;" some, "the faithful that be yet alive;" some others, "the blessed that be in heaven[6]." And yet M. Harding knoweth

De Con. Dist. 2. Cum Omne. Aug. ad Quod-vult-deum.

[[1] Same self, 1565.] [[2] See before, page 251.]

[[3] Jul. Papa in Corp. Jur. Canon. Lugd. 1624. Decret. Gratian. Decr. Tert. Pars, De Consecr. Dist. ii. can. 7. col. 1915; where the text has *recipit*, also *corpus suum, et sanguinem commendavit.*]

[[4] Concil. Brac. III. cap. 1. in Crabb. Concil. Col. Agrip. 1551. Tom. II. p. 272.]

[[5] Audivimus ... quosdam ... lac pro vino ... dedicare: alios quoque intinctam eucharistiam populis... porrigere: quosdam etiam expressum vinum...offerre: &c.—Jul. Papa in Corp. Jur. Canon. Decret. Gratian. Decr. Tert. Pars, De Consecr. Dist. ii. can. 7. col. 1914.

Artotyritæ...offerunt ... panem et caseum. Aquarii...aquam offerunt in poculo sacramenti.—August. Op. Par. 1679-1700. Lib. de Hæres. capp. xxviii. lxiv. Tom. VIII. cols. 10, 20, 1.]

[[6] See, for a variety of notions, Durand. Rat. Div. Offic. Lugd. 1565. Lib. IV. cap. li. 21, 2. foll. 196, 7. cap. liv. 9. fol. 201. 2.]

that Julius calleth it "a schismatical ambition, and a practice contrary to the apostles' doctrine."

We, both herein and in all other cases like, follow only Christ's institution: who, as the evangelists have written, and as Julius also recordeth, first gave the bread apart, and afterward the wine likewise apart; and said not only, "Eat this," but also by express words, "Drink this." Yet Ivo saith that, for danger of shedding, sometimes the bread is dipped into the cup, and so delivered to the people[7]. Ivo de Div. Offic. Cassandr.

This Julius here alleged standeth fully of our side; and therefore I marvel that M. Harding would seek comfort at his hand. For where he saith, *Porrigunt eucharistiam populis;* "They deliver the sacrament unto the people;" he importeth a communion: where he reproveth the error of dipping, and rectifieth the same by Christ's institution, and commandeth both kinds to be given apart, he signifieth the whole communion expressly in both kinds; and so quite overthroweth whatsoever M. Harding hath hitherto builded[8]. Julius commandeth both kinds, contrary to M. Harding's doctrine.

M. HARDING. THE TWENTY-EIGHTH DIVISION.

Now I refer me to the judgment of the reader, of what opinion soever he be, whether, for proof of the communion under one kind, we have any word, sentence, or clause at all, or no; and whether these words of M. Jewel in his sermon be true or no, where he saith thus: "It was used throughout the whole catholic church, six hundred years after Christ's ascension, under both kinds, without exception." That it was so used, yea, six hundred years, and long after, we deny not; but that it was so always, and in every place used, and without exception, that we deny; and upon what grounds we do it, let M. Jewel himself be judge. If some of our allegations may be with violence wrested from our purpose, verily a great number of them cannot; the authority of the ancient fathers who wrote them remaining inviolated. Wherefore it followeth that, after the judgment of these fathers, whereas Christ instituted this blessed sacrament, and commanded it to be celebrated, and received in remembrance of his death, (62) *he gave no necessary commandment, either for the one, or for both kinds (beside and without the celebration of the sacrifice), but left that to the determination of the church. Now that the church, for the avoiding of unreverence, perils, offences, and other weighty and important causes, hath decreed it *in two general councils, to be received of the lay-people in*[11] *one kind only, we think it good, with all humbleness, to submit ourselves to the church herein; which church Christ commandeth to be heard and obeyed, saying, "He that heareth not the church, let him be to thee as a heathen and as a publican." In doing whereof we weigh advisedly with ourselves the horrible danger that remaineth for them who be authors of schism and breakers of unity.*

The question is of the open ministration in the church.

[*Fol.* 16, *in the end*[9]. H. A. 1564.]

The sixty-second untruth. For[10] Christ's institution pertaineth as well to the people, as to the priest.

*These councils were holden fourteen hundred and fourteen years after Christ.

Matt. xviii.

THE BISHOP OF SARISBURY.

Good christian reader, now that M. Harding hath said so much as he is able, it behoveth thee, as thou wilt judge indifferently between us both, so to consider and mark well the very state and issue of the matter, wherein the whole question lieth. The negative of our side, which so much troubleth him, is this: "That, for the space of six hundred years after Christ, it cannot be found in any old doctor, or council, that ever the holy communion was ministered to the people, in the church, or any open assembly, in one kind only, as it is now ministered in the church of Rome." The issue therefore of the whole matter between us standeth upon the order and usage of the church.

M. Harding, for proof hereof, hath brought certain particular examples of drouth, infirmities, sickness, age, inevitable necessities, and impossibilities, and weakness of nature. Verily, good reader, I looked for other proofs at M. Harding's hands. For all these, and other like things, I knew before. He hath alleged Christ's breaking of bread at Emmaus; the allegation whereof to

[7 ... quem [populum] intincto pane, non auctoritate, sed summa necessitate timoris sanguinis Christi effusionis, permittitur communicare.—Ivo. de Div. Offic. in Cassandr. Op. Par. 1616. Liturg. cap. xxxi. p. 76.]

[8 Built, 1565.] [9 See before, page 9.]

[10 1565 omits *for*.]

[11 Under, H. A. 1564.]

Wil. Wideford. this purpose, one of his own doctors saith, is mere folly[1]. He hath alleged two women, three sick folk in their death-beds, persons excommunicate, infants, phrenetics, and madmen.

He allegeth napkins, chests, chambers, mountains, and wilderness; and, for further proof, hath brought conjectures, guesses, lies, and fables. He allegeth abuses that long sithence have been condemned. He allegeth scriptures, doctors, and councils, plainly and directly against himself.

He is learned, and hath read much: he is eloquent, and can utter much: yea, he is able to make nothing to appear somewhat, and a little to seem much.

He hath had good conference with as many as he thought meet, either within this realm, or without. He hath seen whatsoever hath been written by Cochlæus, Eckius, Pighius, Hofmeister, Michael Væhe, Hosius, Staphylus, and such other of that sort. He hath had five whole years and more to order and digest his book. It toucheth him very near that any man should be so bold to say, "They have defrauded the people of half the sacrament, and yet can allege nothing for it." He sheweth himself much offended, and therefore spareth not his familiar terms, "heretics, schismatics, adversaries of the church, God's enemies, and such like." Yet, having so much learning, so much eloquence, so much conference, so much study, so much leisure, being so affected, and so offended, yet hath he not hitherto brought one word, either of ancient council, or of old doctor, to prove that thing that is denied; that is, "That the sacrament was ever ministered unto the people in one kind, openly in any congregation, or in the open order and usage of any church." Yet were there churches then erected; yet were there priests and people then; yet was the holy ministration then openly used in form and order, and learned men to record the same. All this notwithstanding, M. Harding hath hitherto found nothing in the open ministration, in the congregation and assembly of the people, whereby to prove his half communion. Wherefore there is no cause yet shewed to the contrary but M. Jewel may say now as he truly before said in his sermon, "The whole communion was used throughout the whole catholic church under both kinds six hundred years after Christ's ascension, in all congregations and churches, without exception."

"But Christ hath left these matters to the discretion and determination of the church." By what record may that appear? M. Harding's word is no charter. Or if it be true, where did the church ever so determine of it, within the compass of six hundred years? St Augustine in this case is very reasonable. His words

Ad Casul. be these: *Ubi auctoritas deficit, ibi consuetudo majorum pro lege tenenda est*[2]: "Where authority faileth, there the custom of our elders must hold for a law." But having God's word, and Christ's institution, we want no authority.

"The authority of the church is great." I grant; but the causes that moved the church of Rome to break Christ's institution, "as the keeping of the wine, beards, and palsies, and such like," are not great; notwithstanding M. Harding enlarge them much, and call them "important and weighty causes." The two councils of Basil and Constance, where this matter was first concluded, as they were at the least fourteen hundred years after Christ, and therefore not to be alleged in this case against my assertion; so the authority of them both hangeth

Lud. Vives in xx. Lib. de Civ. Dei, cap. xxvi. yet in question. For the Thomists say the council of Basil came unlawfully together, and that therefore all their determinations were in vain[3]. And Pighius saith the other council of Constance "concluded against nature, against the scriptures, against antiquity, and against the faith of the church[4]." These be the two councils that M. Harding would have us yield unto.

"We are bound to hear the church," saith M. Harding. But much more are we bound to hear God. This saying of St Cyprian is worthy deeply to be noted: *Non jungitur ecclesiæ, qui ab evangelio separatur*[5]: "He hath no fellowship with the

---

[[1] Wilh. Wodford. adv. Joan. Wiclef. in Fasc. Rer. Expet. et Fug. Lond. 1690. p. 198. See before, page 233.]

[[2] In his enim rebus de quibus nihil certi statuit scriptura divina, mos populi Dei vel instituta majorum pro lege tenenda sunt.—August. Op. Par. 1679-1700. Ad Casul. Epist. xxxvi. 2. Tom. II. col. 68.]

[[3] Id. de Civit. Dei, per Joan. Lud. Vivem. Basil. 1522. Comm. in Lib. xx. cap. xxvi. p. 702. See before, page 233.]

[[4] Pigh. Hierarch. Eccles. Assert. Col. 1538. Lib. vi. cap. ii. fol. 213. 2.]

[[5] Nec ecclesiæ jungitur, qui &c.—Cypr. Op. Oxon. 1682. De Laps. p. 129.]

church that is divided from the gospel." And likewise, writing against certain that abused the cup of Christ, ministering therein water instead of wine, he giveth this lesson to all bishops and others, touching the reformation of the church: *Religioni ...nostræ congruit, et timori, et ipsi loco, et officio sacerdotii nostri,...custodire traditionis dominicæ veritatem; et quod prius apud quosdam videtur erratum, Domino monente, corrigere: ut cum in claritate sua et majestate cœlesti venire cœperit, inveniat nos tenere quod monuit, observare quod docuit, facere quod fecit*[6]: "It behoveth the religion that we profess, and our reverence towards God, and the very place and office of our priesthood, to keep the truth of the Lord's tradition, and by the Lord's advertisement to correct that thing that by certain hath been amiss; that when he shall come in his glory and majesty, he may find us to hold that he warned us, to keep that he taught us, to do that he did."

Gelasius.

Cypr. ad Cæcil. Lib. ii. Epist. 3.

M. HARDING. THE TWENTY-NINTH DIVISION.

[*Gelasius his canon, guilefully by M. Jewel alleged, truly examined,* H. A. 1564.]

Now for answer to M. Jewel's place alleged out of Gelasius, which is the chief that he and all other (the adversaries of the church) have to bring for their purpose in this point, thus[7] *much may be said. First, that he allegeth Gelasius untruly, making him to sound in English otherwise than he doth in Latin. M. Jewel's words be these: "Gelasius, an old father of the church, and a bishop of Rome, saith, that to minister the communion under one kind is open sacrilege." But where saith Gelasius so? This is no sincere handling of the matter. And because he knew the words of that father imported not so much, guilefully he reciteth them in Latin, and doth not English them; which he would not have omitted, if they had so plainly made for his purpose. The words of Gelasius be these:* Divisio unius ejusdemque mysterii sine grandi sacrilegio non potest pervenire[8]: "*The division of one and the same mystery cannot come without great sacrilege." Of these words he cannot conclude Gelasius to say, that to minister the communion under one kind is open sacrilege. Gelasius rebuketh and abhorreth the division of that high mystery, which under one form, and under both, is* unum idemque, "*one and the same:" not one under the form of bread, and another under the form of wine; not one in respect of the body, and another in respect of the blood; but* unum idemque, "*one and the self-same." The words afore recited be taken out of a fragment of a canon of Gelasius, which is thus, as we find in Gratian:* Comperimus autem, quod quidam, sumpta tantum...corporis sacri portione, a calice sacrati cruoris abstineant. Qui proculdubio (quoniam nescio qua superstitione docentur adstringi) aut integra sacramenta percipiant, aut ab integris arceantur; quia divisio unius ejusdemque mysterii sine grandi sacrilegio non potest pervenire[8]; *which may thus be Englished: "But we have found that some, having received only the portion wherein is the holy body, abstain from the cup of the sacred blood; who without doubt (forasmuch as I know not with what superstition they be taught to be tied) either let them receive the whole sacraments, or let them be kept from the whole; because the division of one and the same mystery cannot come without great sacrilege."*

De Con. dist. 2. *can. Comperimus.*

Gelasius untruly translated by M. Harding.

Here might be said to M. Jewel, Shew us the whole epistle of Gelasius from whence this fragment is taken, that we may weigh the circumstance, and the causes why he wrote it, conferring that goeth before, and that followeth; and we will frame you a reasonable answer. But it is not extant; and therefore your argument, in that respect, is of less force.

THE BISHOP OF SARISBURY.

Neither are we the adversaries of the church, nor Gelasius the chiefest that we bring for our purpose. We follow Christ, as he hath commanded us, whom it became Gelasius also to follow. But it is a world to see into how many faces and fashions M. Harding is fain to turn himself to avoid this authority of Gelasius. He leaveth the whole rout of his own company, and is glad to run alone. He expoundeth Gelasius by Leo, as though they wrote both of one thing. And yet

---

[6 Id. ad Cæcil. Epist. lxiii. p. 157; where *atque officio*.]

[7 This, 1565, and H. A. 1564.]

[8 Gelas. in Corp. Jur. Canon. Lugd. 1624. Decret. Gratian. Decr. Tert. Pars, De Consecr. Dist. ii. can. 12. col. 1918; where *sacri cruoris, obstringi*, and *provenire*.]

Gelasius. others of his own side say that Leo wrote of heretics, and Gelasius of catholics; Leo of the people, Gelasius of the priests. He complaineth that the rest of Gelasius is not to be found, as though it were suppressed by some of us; and yet it is thought the pope hath it whole in his library[1]. He deviseth new causes of unity of the mystery, such as Gelasius never knew. He concludeth at the last, that this breach of Christ's institution, and ministration under one kind, that is now universally used in the church of Rome, was first brought in and practised by the Manichees, which were in old time wicked and horrible heretics.

In Pontif. ut citatur in i. Tom. Concil. Vita Gelasii.

He saith I have guilefully alleged Gelasius; and, to the intent it might the sooner appear, he hath noted it specially in the margin. But, if M. Harding himself had meant no guile, he would have shewed plainly wherein I have been guileful, or what I might have gotten by this guile, or what advantage I might have lost by plainer dealing. For guile without cause is mere folly, and no guile. But I recited the words in Latin, and had forgotten to English them. Now surely that is but a simple guile, and might well have been spared out of the margin.

But my words be these: "Gelasius saith that to minister the sacrament in one kind is open sacrilege." And what guile can he find herein? This word "sacrilege," and "the refusing of the cup," are both specially named by Gelasius. There remain only these words, "To minister the sacrament;" and there, saith M. Harding, lieth the guile. Howbeit, therein, as it shall well appear, I say nothing but that Gelasius saith, and M. Harding himself would have him say. For thus saith Gelasius, "The division of the mystery," whereby he meaneth the sacrament, "is sacrilege:"

The priest, ministering in one kind, committeth sacrilege.

But the priest that ministereth in one kind divideth the mystery;

Ergo, the priest that ministereth in one kind committeth sacrilege.

This argument is perfect[2], and formal, and founded upon Gelasius' words. I trow this is no guileful dealing.

Unum et Idem.

Hugo Cardinal. 1 Cor. xi.

Hieron. ad Ephes. Lib. ii. cap. iv.

Durand. Lib. iv. cap. xxiv.

The unity of the mystery that M. Harding hath here fantasied, that either part is in other, and therefore harpeth so often, as it were by reports, upon these words, *Unum et idem*, is but his own voluntary. He is not able to allege either Gelasius, or any other old father that ever expounded *unum* and *idem* in that sort. He calleth it "one mystery," as Hugo Cardinalis saith (although otherwise a very gross writer), *propter unitatem institutionis*[3], "for the unity of the institution," and for that the bread and wine, being sundry portions, have both relation unto one Christ. And for that cause, by St Hierome's judgment, St Paul saith, *Una fides, unum baptisma*[4]; "One faith, one baptism:" and for that also, that being, as I said, two sundry portions, yet they make not two sundry sacraments, but one only sacrament. And therefore Durandus, a late writer, seemeth to say well: *In multis locis communicatur cum pane et vino, id est, cum toto sacramento*[5]: "In many places they communicate with bread and wine; that is," saith he, "with the whole sacrament." Of which words the reader, be he never so simple, may easily gather that the communion in one kind is but the half sacrament, and so the division of one mystery, and so, further, the self-same thing that Gelasius calleth sacrilege.

M. HARDING. THE THIRTIETH DIVISION.

But for avoiding that[6], *our adversaries would hereof conclude, it is to be understanded, that this canon speaketh against the heretics named Manichæi, who, in the*

[[1] Hic fecit 5. libros adversus Nestorium et Eutychem, qui hodie in bibliotheca et archivo ecclesiæ continentur. Fecit et hymnos, &c.—Decret. Gelas. Ex Libr. Pontif. in Crabb. Concil. Col. Agrip. 1551. Tom. I. p. 964.]

[[2] Perfite, 1565.]

[[3] The passage intended is probably the following: Unum quidem ex unitate institutionis, et principaliter signati.—Hugon. de S. Char. Op. Col. Agrip. 1621. In Epist. I. ad Cor. cap. xi. fol. 104. 2. Hugo is not however in this place speaking of the two kinds.]

[[4] Unus est Dominus, et unus est Deus: quia Patris et Filii dominatio una divinitas est. Propterea et fides una dicitur: quia similiter in Patrem, et in Filium, et in Spiritum sanctum credimus. Et baptisma unum: eodem enim modo et in Patrem, et in Filium, et in Spiritum sanctum baptizamur. Et ter mergimur, ut Trinitatis unum appareat sacramentum, &c.—Hieron. Op. Par. 1693-1706. Comm. in Epist. ad Ephes. Lib. II. cap. iv. Tom. IV. Pars. I. cols. 361, 2.]

[[5] This passage is afterwards (see below, page 261) assigned to another chapter. Both references are probably erroneous. See, however, Durand. Rat. Div. Offic. Lugd. 1565. Lib. IV. cap. liv. 12, 13. fol. 202. 2; where the receiving under one kind is said not to be *plenum*, or *completum sacramentum*.]

[[6] Of that, H. A. 1564.]

time of Leo the first, about forty years before Gelasius, went about to spread their heresy in Rome, and in the parts[7] *of Italy. Their heretical opinion was, that Christ took not our flesh and blood, but that he had a fantastical body, and died not, nor*[8] *rose again truly and indeed, but by way of phantasy. And therefore, at the communion, they abstained from the cup; and, the better to cloke their heresy, came to receive the sacrament in form*[9] *of bread, with other catholic people. Against whom Leo saith thus:* Abdicant enim se sacramento salutis nostræ[10], &c.; "*They drive themselves away from the sacrament of our salvation. And, as they deny that Christ our Lord was born in truth of our flesh, so they believe not that he died, and rose again truly. And for this cause they condemn the day of our salvation and gladness (that is, the Sunday) to be their sad fasting day. And whereas, to cloke their infidelity, they dare to be at our mysteries, they temper themselves so in the communion of the sacraments, as in the mean time they may the more safely keep them privy. With unworthy mouth they receive Christ's body; but to drink the blood of our redemption, utterly they will none of it. Which thing we would advertise your holiness of, that both such men may be manifested by these tokens unto you, and also that they, whose devilish simulation and feigning is found, being brought to light, and bewrayed of the fellowship of saints, may be thrust out of the church by priestly authority." Thus far be Leo his words.* *Serm. 4. de quadragesima.*

Gelasius, that succeeded forty years after Leo, employed no less diligence than he did, utterly to vanquish and abolish that horrible heresy. Of whom Platina writeth, that he banished so many Manichees as were found at Rome, and there openly burned their books[11]. *And because this heresy should none elsewhere take root, and spring, he wrote an epistle to Majoricus and Joannes, two bishops, amongst other things warning them of the same. Out of which epistle this fragment only is taken: whereby he doth both briefly shew what the Manichees did for cloking of their infidelity, as Leo saith; and also, inasmuch as their opinion was that Christ's body had not very blood, as being fantastical only, and therefore superstitiously abstained from the cup of that holy blood, giveth charge and commandment, that either forsaking their heresy they receive the whole sacraments, to wit, under both kinds, or that they be kept from them wholly. Here the words of Leo afore mentioned, and this canon of Gelasius conferred together, specially the story of that time known, it may soon appear to any man of judgment, against whom this fragment of Gelasius was written. Verily, not against the church for ministering the communion under one kind, but against the detestable Manichees, who, going about to divide the mystery of the body and blood of Christ, denying him to have taken very flesh and blood, so much as in them lay, loosed Christ, whereof St John speaketh, and would have made frustrate the whole work of our redemption.* *1 John iv.*

THE BISHOP OF SARISBURY.

To avoid the inconvenience growing of this authority, M. Harding is driven to avoid the company of Pighius, Hosius, Tapper, D. Cole, and all others his fellows of that side, and to say that Gelasius wrote this decree against the Manichees; notwithstanding all they say, he wrote it against certain superstitious priests. D. Cole referreth himself unto the construction of the gloss there written[12]. The words thereof be these: "There were certain priests that consecrated the body and blood of Christ in due order, and received the body, but abstained from the De Con. Dist. 2. Comperim. In Glossa.

[7 Parties, H. A. 1561.]

[8 Ne, 1565, 1609, and H. A. 1564.]

[9 The form, 1565, and H. A. 1564.]

[10 Abdicant enim se sacramento salutis humanæ, et Christum Dominum nostrum, sicut in veritate carnis nostræ denegent natum, ita vere mortuum et resurrexisse non credunt. Et ob hoc diem salutis et lætitiæ nostræ sui jejunii mœrore condemnant. Cumque ad tegendum infidelitatem suam nostris audeant interesse mysteriis, ita in sacramentorum communione se temperant, ut interdum tutius lateant: ore indigno Christi corpus accipiunt; sanguinem autem redemptionis nostræ haurire omnino declinant. Quod ideo vestram volumus scire sanctitatem, ut vobis hujuscemodi homines et his manifestentur indiciis, et quorum deprehensa fuerit sacrilega simulatio, notati et proditi a sanctorum societate sacerdotali auctoritate pellantur.—Leon. Magn. Op. Lut. 1623. Serm. iv. De Quadrag. col. 108.]

[11 Gelasius autem Manichæos in urbe deprehensos exilio damnat, eorumque libros apud basilicam divæ Mariæ publice comburit.—Plat. De Vit. Sum. Pont. Col. 1551. Gelas. I. p. 61.]

[12 See before, pages 38, 56.]

blood. Against them Gelasius writeth[1]." This guess of that glosser for many good causes seemeth unlikely: for, first, it cannot be shewed by any story, neither where nor when any such priests were that so abstained; and again, Gelasius seemeth to write of them that should be taught, not of them that should teach; of them that should be removed from the sacraments, not of the priests that should remove them; of the sacrilege and wickedness of the fact, not of the difference of any persons.

But the gloss saith notwithstanding: "The priest[2] consecrated both the body and the blood, and received the body, and abstained from the blood." Here would I fain learn of D. Cole, what then became of the cup. The priest drank it not: that is certain; for the gloss saith so. Again, the people drank it not; for so saith the gloss also, and, be it true or false, it must be defended.

Then must it needs follow that Christ's blood was consecrate to be cast away. D. Cole might have foreseen that this gloss would soon be taken against himself. Now let us see of this very self gloss what may be concluded of our side. The sacrament of Christ's blood was not thrown away: the priest received it not; *ergo*, it followeth, of very fine force, it was received by the people. Thus D. Cole, seeking to prove that the people received not in both kinds, himself unawares necessarily proveth that the people received in both kinds. Wherefore M. Harding's conjecture carrieth more substance of truth. For the very story and conference of time will soon give the advised reader to understand, that Gelasius wrote this decree against the Manichees.

Heretics, the first authors of the half communion.

Thus much therefore hath M. Harding gotten hereby, that now it appeareth that the first authors of his half communion were a sort of heretics. They held that Christ never received flesh of the blessed virgin, neither was born, nor suffered, nor died, nor rose[3] again. Which errors are manifestly convinced by the sacraments. For they are sacraments of Christ's body and blood; therefore whoso receiveth the same confesseth thereby that Christ of the virgin received both body and blood. So saith St Chrysostom: *Si mortuus Christus non est, cujus symbolum et signum hoc sacramentum est*[4]*?* "If Christ died not indeed, tell me then, whose token or whose sign is this sacrament?" Tertullian also by a like argument taken of the sacrament reproveth Marcion, that held that Christ had no body, but only a shew and a phantasy of a body: [*Christus*] *acceptum panem, et distributum discipulis, corpus suum illum fecit, dicendo, Hoc est corpus meum, hoc est, figura corporis mei. Figura autem non esset, nisi veritatis esset corpus. Ceterum vacua res, quod est phantasma, figuram capere non potest*[5]*:* "Christ, having received the bread, and giving the same to his disciples, made it his body, saying, 'This is my body,' that is to say, a figure of my body. But it could not be a figure, unless there were a body of a truth. For a void thing, as is a phantasy, can receive no figure at all." Thus the sacraments do plainly testify that Christ received not a phantasy or shew of a body, but a very body indeed. Therefore the Manichees abstained from the holy cup, as it appeareth by Leo: notwithstanding St Augustine in one place, writing namely against the Manichees, seemeth to signify the contrary. These be his words: *Sacramentum panis et calicis ita laudatis, ut in eo nobis pares esse volueritis*[6]*:* "Ye so commend the sacrament of the bread and of the cup, that therein you would make yourselves equal with us." Neither were they indeed able to shew any simple cause, why they should more shun the one portion than the other. For the sacrament of the bread no less confounded their error than the sacrament of the cup. And as they thought that Christ's body was no body, but only a phantasy, so they likewise thought that Christ's blood was no natural blood, but only a phantasy. But if they would

Chrysost. in Matt. Hom. 83.

Contra Marcion. Lib. iv.

Contr. Faust. Manich. Lib. xx. cap. xiii.

[1 Erant quidam sacerdotes, qui ordine debito consecrabant corpus et sanguinem Christi: corpus sumebant, sed a sanguine abstinebant, &c.—Corp. Jur. Canon. Lugd. 1624. Decret. Gratian. Decr. Tert. Pars, De Consecr. Dist. ii. Gloss. in can. 12. col. 1917.]

[2 These priests, 1565.]

[3 Arose, 1565.]

[4 Chrysost. Op. Par. 1718-38. In Matt. Hom. lxxxii. Tom. VII. p. 783.]

[5 Tertull. Op. Lut. 1641. Adv. Marcion. Lib. iv. 40. p. 571; where we have *illum suum fecit, hoc est &c. dicendo, non fuisset* and *posset.*]

[6 August. Op. Par. 1679-1700. Contr. Faust. Lib. xx. cap. xiii. Tom. VIII. col. 342; where *panis et calicis sacramentum, quod ita laudastis, ut &c.*]

not believe Leo or Augustine, that Christ had one body, how much less would they believe M. Harding that Christ hath two bodies, the one in the bread, the other in the cup, and each wholly in the other! Gelasius.

M. HARDING. THE THIRTY-FIRST DIVISION.

And therefore M. Jewel doth us great wrong in wresting this canon against us; forasmuch as we do not divide this divine mystery, but believe stedfastly with heart, and confess openly with mouth, that, under each kind, the very flesh and blood of Christ, and whole Christ himself is present in the sacrament; (63) *even as Gelasius believed. Upon this occasion, in the parties of Italy, where the Manichees uttered their poison, the communion under both kinds was restored, and commanded to be used again; whereas before* (64) *of some the sacrament was received under one kind, and of some under both kinds. Else, if the communion under both kinds had been taken for a necessary institution and commandment of Christ, and so generally and inviolably observed everywhere and always without exception; what needed Gelasius to make such an ordinance of receiving the whole sacraments, the cause whereof by this*[8] *parenthesis* (quoniam nescio qua superstitione docentur adstringi) *plainly expresseth? Again, if it had been so inviolably observed of all until that time, then the Manichees could not have covered and cloked their infidelity, as Leo saith, by the*[9] *receiving the communion with other catholic people under one kind. For whiles the catholics went from church, contented with the only form of bread, it was uncertain whether he that came to receive were a Manichee or a catholic. But after that, for descrying of them, it was decreed, that the people should not forbear the communion of the cup any more, the good catholic folk so received, and the Manichees by their refusal of the cup bewrayed themselves. Whereby it appeareth, that the communion under one kind, used before, by the commandments of Leo and Gelasius was forbidden, to the intent thereby the Manichees' heresy might the better be espied, rooted out, and clean abolished.*

The sixty-third untruth. For[7] Gelasius never believed so.

The sixty-fourth untruth. For[7] no catholic congregation ever received the sacrament in one kind.

Thus because we do not divide the mystery of the[10] *Lord's body and blood, but acknowledge, confess, and teach, that Christ took of the virgin Mary very flesh and very blood indeed, and was a whole and perfect*[11] *man, as also God, and delivered the same whole flesh to death for our redemption, and rose again in the same for our justification, and giveth the same to us to be partakers of it in the blessed sacrament to life everlasting; that decree of Gelasius cannot seem against us justly to be alleged; much less may he seem to say or mean, that to minister the communion under one kind is open sacrilege.*

THE BISHOP OF SARISBURY.

Here M. Harding complaineth, we do him wrong to allege this canon against him; for that he believeth, even as Gelasius did, that whole Christ is in each part of the sacrament. It is very much to allege Gelasius' faith without his words, or to found any new faith, as this is, without some kind of proof. This is M. Harding's gross error, and not Gelasius', or any other of the catholic fathers' faith. If the holy fathers had so believed, they had words, and were able to utter it. If this had been the faith of the catholic church, it had not been kept so long in silence.

As for Gelasius, his own words are sufficient to declare his faith. Thus he writeth against Nestorius and Eutyches: *Sacramenta, quæ sumimus, corporis et sanguinis Christi, divinæ res sunt; propter quod et per eadem divinæ efficimur consortes naturæ. Et tamen esse non desinit substantia vel natura panis et vini*[12]: "The sacraments of Christ's body and blood, that we receive, are a godly thing; and therefore by the same we are made partakers of the divine nature. Yet there letteth not to be the substance or nature of bread and wine." This was Gelasius' faith touching these portions of the sacrament.

Gelas. contr. Eutych.

Now hath M. Harding devised another mystery of the wonderful conjunction

[7 1565 omits *for*.]
[8 His, H. A. 1564.]
[9 Their, H. A. 1564.]
[10 Our, H. A. 1564.]
[11 Perfit, 1565, and H. A. 1564.]
[12 Gelas. Episc. Rom. adv. Eutych. et Nestor. in Mag. Biblioth. Vet. Patr. Col. Agrip. 1618–22. Tom. V. Pars III. p. 671; where we find *divina res est*.]

of God and man in Christ, whereof Gelasius spake not one word in this place, neither was it any thing to his purpose to speak of it. Besides this, he imagineth Gelasius to give a law, that no man should divide that mystery; whereas it never lay in the power of man to divide it. Neither had that been a division, but an utter dissolution of the mystery.

Thus, so he may seem to say somewhat, he weigheth not greatly what he say, examining each thing, as St Augustine saith, *non in statera æqua divinarum scripturarum, sed in statera dolosa consuetudinum suarum*[1]: "Not in the just balance of the holy scriptures, but in the deceitful and false beams of his own customs."

August. contr. Epist. Parmen. Lib. iii. cap. ii.

Of the cup he maketh the bread: of the bread he maketh the cup: of one he maketh both: of both he maketh one: of one mystery he maketh another: and thus they deal, even as Irenæus writeth of the heretic Valentinus: *Ordinem et textum scripturarum supergredientes, et quantum in ipsis est, solventes, membra veritatis transferunt, et transfingunt, et alterum ex altero facientes, seducunt multos, ex his quæ aptant ex dominicis eloquiis male composito phantasmati*[2]: "Overrunning the order and text of the scriptures, and, as much as in them lieth, dismembering the limbs of the truth, they alter and transpose matters, and, making one thing of another, they deceive many by that they gather out of the Lord's words, and join to their ill-favoured phantasy."

Irenæus, Lib. i.

The mystery whereof Gelasius speaketh is the holy sacrament, which, albeit it stand of two parts, yet is it one sacrament, and not two. The Manichees divided the same, taking one part, and leaving the other. And this is it that Gelasius calleth sacrilege.

Here it is further surmised that Leo and Gelasius, by their decrees, restored the catholic people again to the use of both kinds. This is utterly untrue, and may be guessed by M. Harding, but cannot any way be proved.

The decrees of Leo and Gelasius be abroad, and may be known. But where are these decrees? In what books are they written? Or who ever made mention of them? Verily these godly fathers reproved the Manichees for their sacrilege, and not the catholics; and commanded such as had offended to correct their faults, and not such as were faultless.

"But how could the Manichees have been known," saith M. Harding, "unless the catholic people among whom they received, had communicated[3] in one kind?" This question is out of course. I might better say: "Nay, how could the Manichees have been known, if they and the catholics had received in one kind both alike?" For this is the token that Leo would have them known by: *Sanguinem redemptionis nostræ haurire detrectant*[4]: "They refuse to drink the blood of our redemption." By these words it is clear that the cup was offered orderly unto them, as unto others; but they refused it.

Thou seest, good christian reader, that M. Harding, notwithstanding he be driven to leave his own fellows, to shift one mystery for another, to imagine new laws and new decrees, that were never heard of, to change himself into sundry forms, and to seek all manner holes to creep out at, yet at last hath found by the authority of Leo, whom he himself allegeth, that the catholic people received the whole communion under both kinds, according to Christ's institution; and that the patrons and founders of his half communion were old wicked heretics, named the Manichees; that the same is the division of one whole entire mystery; and therefore by the authority of Gelasius may well be called open sacrilege.

Now, to shew what might be said of our side were labour infinite. For our doctrine taketh no authority of private folk, of women, of forcelets[5], of napkins, of sick bodies, of death-beds, of miracles, of fables, of children, and of madmen, which be the only grounds of all that M. Harding seemeth hitherto able to say; but of Christ's institution, of the scriptures, of the practice of the apostles,

---

[1 August. Op. Par. 1679—1700. Contr. Epist. Parmen. Lib. III. cap. ii. 9. Tom. IX. col. 61.]

[2 Iren. Op. Par. 1710. Cont. Hæres. Lib. I. cap. viii. p. 36.]

[3 Communicate, 1565]

[4 See before, page 257, note 10.]

[5 Forcelets. Little or no information is supplied as to this word by lexicographers; but the meaning may be conjectured from Whitaker's Latin version of Jewel's work, made a few years after its publication, where, for "forcelets and napkins," we find "linteis atque lineis."]

of the usage of the primitive church, of old canons, of ancient councils, of catholic fathers, Greeks and Latins, old and new, even of Clemens, Abdias, and Amphilochius, which are M. Harding's peculiar doctors. St Chrysostom saith: "In the receiving of the holy mysteries there is no difference between priest and people[6]." Dionysius saith: "The unity of the cup is divided unto all[7]." Ignatius saith: "One cup is divided unto the whole church[8]." St Augustine saith: "We drink all together, because we live all together[9]." But to reckon up the authorities of antiquity, as I said, it would be infinite.

Chrysost. in 2 Cor. Hom. 18. Eccl. Hier. cap. iii. Ignat. ad Philad. De Consecr. Dist. 2. Quia passus.

The scholastical doctors of very late years have seen and testified that M. Harding's doctrine is but new. Thomas of Aquine saith: *In quibusdam ecclesiis provide observatur, ut populo sanguis... non detur*[10]: "In certain churches it is providently observed, that the blood be not given to the people." "In certain churches," he saith, not in all churches.

Thom. Par. iii. Quæst. 80. Art. 12.

Likewise Durandus: *In multis locis communicatur cum pane et vino, id est, cum toto sacramento*[11]: "In many places they communicate with bread and wine, that is to say, with the whole sacrament." "In many places," he saith, but not in all places. Likewise Alexander de Hales, a great school-doctor: *Ita fere ubique a laicis fit in ecclesia*[12]: "Thus the lay-people in the church for the most part do." "For the most part," he saith, but not in all parts. And Linwood in his Provincials: *Solis... celebrantibus sanguinem sub specie vini consecrati sumere, in hujusmodi minoribus ecclesiis est concessum*[13]: "It is granted only unto the priests that celebrate in such small churches, to receive the blood under the form of wine." He excepteth only "the small country churches," not the greater churches in cities and towns. All these doctors lived within the space of three hundred years past. So long it was before M. Harding's doctrine could grow general.

Durand. Lib. iv. cap. xlii. Alex. Par. iv. Quæst. 55. Membr. 1. Linwood de Summ. Trin. et Fide Cathol.

Antoninus saith, that king William the Conqueror, that lived a thousand years after Christ, caused his whole army to communicate, and that, as the order was then, under both kinds[14]. Haimo, that was not long before him, saith: *Appellatur ... calix communicatio propter participationem; quia omnes communicant ex illo*[15]: "The cup is called the communication, because of the participation; for that every man receiveth of it." Thus is our doctrine confirmed, not only by the old doctors, but also by the new.

Antoninus. Haimo in 1 Cor. xi.

Wherefore M. Harding, thus maintaining the open abuse of the holy mysteries, offendeth against Christ's institution, against the scriptures, against the perfection of the sacrament, against the confirmation of the new testament, against the tradition and practice of the apostles, against the ancient councils, against the canons, against the doctors, both old and new. The apostles of Christ, being full of the Holy Ghost, so took Christ's words as we take them now. And St Hierome saith: *Quicunque ... aliter scripturam intelligit, quam sensus Spiritus sancti flagitat, quo conscripta est, licet de ecclesia non recesserit, tamen hæreticus appellari potest*[16]: "Whosoever understandeth the scriptures otherwise than the sense of the Holy Ghost requireth, by which Holy Ghost the scriptures were written, although he be not yet departed from the church, yet he may well be called an heretic." If M. Harding will say, "That was true then, and this is true now;" then may we answer him as St Hilary did the Arians: *Veritas ergo temporum erit*

Hieron. ad Galat. Lib. iii. cap. v. Hilar. ad Const. August.

[6 Chrysost. Op. Par. 1718-38. In Epist. II. ad Cor. Hom. xviii. Tom. X. p. 568. See before, page 202, note 13.]

[7 ... τὸν ἑνιαῖον τοῦ ποτηρίου πᾶσι καταμερίσας.—Dionys. Areop. Op. Antv. 1634. De Eccles. Hierarch. cap. iii. Tom. I. p. 299.]

[8 Ignat. ad Philad. cap. iv. in Patr. Apostol. Oxon. 1838. Tom. II. p. 378. See before, page 116, note 4. But Jewel quotes the interpolated epistle: ἓν ποτήριον τοῖς ὅλοις διενεμήθη.]

[9 ... simul bibimus, quia simul vivimus.—August. in Corp. Jur. Canon. Lugd. 1624. Decret. Gratian. Decr. Tert. Pars, De Consecr. Dist. ii. can. 36. col. 1929.]

[10 Thom. Aquinat. Op. Venet. 1595. Summ. Theol. Tert. Pars, Quæst. lxxx. Art. 12. Tom. XII. fol. 267. 2; where *provide* precedes *in*.]

[11 See before, page 256, note 5.]

[12 ... sicut fere ubique fit a laicis in ecclesia.—Alex. Alens. Theol. Summ. Col. Agrip. 1622. Pars IV. Quæst. XI. Membr. ii. Art. iv. 3. p. 106.]

[13 Provincial. seu Const. Angl. Antw. 1525. Lib. I. De Summ. Trin. foll. 7, 8.]

[14 Northmanni... mane dominico corpori et sanguini communicaverunt.—Antonin. Chron. Lugd. 1586. Tit. XVI. Var. Hist. Undec. Sæc. cap. v. 1. Pars II. fol. 623.]

[15 Haym. in Epist. Interpr. 1528. Ad Cor. I. cap. x. fol. yii. 2. See before, page 135.]

[16 Hieron. Op. Par. 1693-1706. Comm. in Epist. ad Galat. Lib. III. cap. v. Tom. IV. Pars I. col. 302.]

magis, quam evangeliorum[1]*:* "Then truth must be as pleaseth the time, not as pleaseth the gospel." And further, as St Augustine answered the Donatists: *Si aliud declamas, aliud recitas, nos post vocem Pastoris nostri, per ora prophetarum, et os proprium,* [*et*] *per ora evangelistarum, nobis apertissime declaratam, voces vestras non admittimus, non credimus, non accipimus*[2]*:* "If ye preach any otherwise, or tell us any other tale, after we have once heard the voice of our Shepherd, most plainly declared unto us by the mouths of his prophets, by his own mouth, and by the mouths of his evangelists, touching your voices, we take them not, we believe them not, we receive them not."

August. de Unit. Eccles. cap. xi.

But, forasmuch as this is a mystery of unity, God grant unto us such humility of mind, that we may all submit ourselves unto his holy word, that we may join together in holy and perfect[3] unity; and, as I alleged before out of St Cyprian, "by his advertisement redress that thing wherein certain have erred; that, when he shall come in his glory and in his heavenly majesty, he may find us to hold that he warned us, to keep that he taught us, to do that he did! Amen[4]."

Cypr. ad Cæcil. Lib. ii. Epist. 3.

[1 ... facta est fides temporum potius quam evangeliorum.—Hilar. Op. Par. 1693. Ad Constant. August. Lib. II. 4. col. 1227.]

[2 August. Op. Par. 1679-1700. Lib. De Unit. Eccles. cap. xii. 32. Tom. IX. col. 359; where *Si autem aliunde clamas vel recitas,* and *per os.*]

[3 Perfit, 1565.]

[4 Cypr. Op. Oxon, 1682. Ad Cæcil. Epist. lxiii. p. 157. See before, page 255.]

OF PRAYERS IN A STRANGE TONGUE.

THE THIRD ARTICLE.

THE BISHOP OF SARISBURY.

Or that the people had their common prayers then in a strange tongue, that they understood not.

To furnish out this article, M. Harding hath laid together a great heap of stories, antiquities, observations of writers, erections, propagations, canons, and orders of the church, cosmography, situation of countries, corruptions and changes of tongues; which things he might better have used to some other purpose. Now they serve him more for shew of learning than for substance of proof. He hath bestowed upon this treaty, whatsoever he could either devise of himself, or find in others, adding besides all manner of beauty and force unto the same, both with weight of sentence, and also with colour of words. Howbeit, great vessels be not always full; and the emptier they be, the more they sound. The wise reader will be weighed with reason, and not with talk. As I said at the beginning, one good sentence were proof sufficient. And if there be any one such in this whole book, I will yield according to promise. If there be none, then must M. Harding consider better of the matter, and begin again. Howbeit he hath done that was the part of a good orator, that the learned may say, he hath shewed learning and eloquence; the unlearned may think, he hath said some truth.

[OF THE CHURCH SERVICE IN LEARNED TONGUES, WHICH THE UNLEARNED PEOPLE IN OLD TIME IN SUNDRY PLACES UNDERSTOOD NOT.—Article III. Harding's Answer, 1564.]

M. HARDING. THE FIRST DIVISION.

If you mean, M. Jewel, "by the people's common prayers," such as at that time they commonly made to God in private devotion, I think they uttered them in that tongue which they understood; (65) *and so do christian people now for the most part; and it hath never been reproved by any catholic doctor. But if by the common prayers you mean the public service of the church, whereof the most part hath been pronounced by the bishops, priests, deacons, and other ecclesiastical ministers, the people to sundry parts of it saying Amen, or otherwise giving their assent; I grant some understood the language thereof, and some understood it not; I mean, for the time you refer us unto, even of six hundred years after Christ's conversation here in earth.*

The sixty-fifth untruth. For under the subjection of the bishop of Rome the people for the most part pray[5] in Latin.

For about nine hundred years past, (66) *it is certain the people in some countries had their service in an unknown tongue, as it shall be proved of our own country of England.*

The sixty-sixth untruth For[6] this certainty will never be proved.

THE BISHOP OF SARISBURY.

The disorder of prayer that M. Harding hath here taken in hand to defend is not only repugnant to the scriptures of God, but also contrary to the sense of nature. For if birds and beasts could speak, as Democritus the philosopher sometime thought, and as Lactantius, a christian writer, seemeth partly to say they do[7]; yet, being birds and beasts, and void of reason, they would not speak they know not what. Wherefore, seeing this abuse appeareth contrary to God and nature, and now also is misliked and condemned by the common judgment of

Lactant. Inst. Lib. iii. cap. x.

[5 Prayeth, 1565.]

[6 1565 omits *for*.]

[7 Cum enim suas voces propriis inter se notis discernunt atque dinoscunt, colloqui videntur.—Lactant. Op. Lut. Par. 1748. Div. Inst. Lib. iii. cap. x. Tom. I. p. 211.]

all people; therefore it behoveth M. Harding to leave his guesses, and soundly and effectually seek[1] to prove it.

Two special things he hath confessed in this treaty, which quite overthrow his whole purpose: the one is, "that the prayers in the primitive church were said in the common known tongue;" the other is, "that it were good even now, that the people understood their own prayers." This is the plain song, and may well stand for the ground: the rest is altogether descant and vain voluntary, and the most part out of tune.

This distinction of common prayers, whereof he imagineth some to be made openly by the minister of the church, some severally by every of the people in private devotion, is both unperfect[2], and also needless. For the secret prayers, that the faithful make severally by themselves, have evermore been called "private," and never "common." And in this sense Thomas of Aquine thinketh that a prayer made in such sort by the priest, and in the church, may be called private[3].

Par. iii. Quæst. 183. Art. 4.

He thinketh "that the people uttered their secret prayers in the tongue that they understood," and so, he saith, "christian people do now for the most part." The former part hereof is undoubtedly true. But for the second, "that christian people do so now," God's name be blessed that hath brought it so to pass, not by M. Harding or his catholic doctors, but by such as they have withstanded for the same, and called heretics!

"Touching the public service pronounced by the priest, whereunto the people said Amen; some," saith M. Harding, "understood the language thereof, and some understood it not." Here unawares he implieth a repugnance in reason, and a manifest contradiction. For if some of the people understood it not, how could all the people say Amen? St Paul's words be plain: "How shall the unlearned say Amen to thy thanksgiving? For he knoweth not what thou sayest." This runneth directly against M. Harding: all the people gave their assent, and said Amen to the common prayers in the church; *ergo*, all the people understood the common prayers. The allegation of the church of England in the time of Augustine, whereof M. Harding maketh himself so sure, and saith with such affiance, "It shall be proved," when it shall hereafter come to proof indeed, shall prove nothing.

M. Harding implieth a contradiction.

As concerning the distinction of private and common prayers, between which M. Harding would also have a difference of speech, undoubtedly the tongue, that is godly and profitable, and will stir the mind in private devotion, is also godly and profitable, and likewise able to stir the mind in the open church. And I marvel what reason can lead any man to think the contrary.

M. HARDING. THE SECOND DIVISION.

Here M. Harding wandereth vainly from the purpose.

But to speak first of antiquity and of the compass of your six[4] hundred years, it is evident by sundry ancient records, both of doctors and of councils, specially of the council Laodicene in Phrygia Pacatiana, holden by the bishops of the lesser Asia, about the year of our Lord 364, that the Greek churches had solemn service in due order and form, set forth with exact distinction of psalms, and lessons, of hours, days, feasts, and times of the year, of silence and open pronouncing, of giving the kiss of peace to the bishop, first by the priests, then by the lay-people, of offering the sacrifice, of the only ministers coming to the altar to receive the communion, with divers other seemly observations[5].

Also[6] the Latin churches, they had their prayers and service also, but in such fixed order long after the Greeks. For Damasus the pope first ordained that psalms should be sung in the church of Rome alternatim, "*interchangeably or by course,*" *so as now we sing them in the quire, and that in the end of every psalm should be said,* Gloria Patri, et Filio, et Spiritui sancto, sicut erat, &c.; *which he caused to*

[1 To seek, 1565, 1609.]

[2 Unperfit, 1565.]

[3 Thom. Aquinat. Op. Venet. 1595. Summ. Theol. Tert. Pars, Quæst. lxxxiii. Art. 4. Tom. XII. fol. 278. 2. See before, page 107, note 13.]

[4 First six, H. A. 1564.]

[5 Concil. Laod. in Concil. Stud. Labb. et Cossart. Lut. Par. 1671-2. See especially cans. 16-19. Tom. I. col. 1500.]

[6 As for, 1565, 1609, and H. A. 1564.]

In Rescripto Hieronymi ad 2 Epist. Damasi Papæ ad Hieronymum Presbyterum.

Singing.

be done by counsel of St Hierome, that the faith of the 318 *bishops of the Nicene council might with like fellowship be declared in the mouths of the Latins. To whom Damasus wrote by Bonifacius the priest to Hierusalem, that Hierome would send unto him* Psallentiam Græcorum, "*The manner of the*[7] *singing of the Greeks," so as he had learned the same of Alexander, the bishop in the east. In that epistle, complaining of the simplicity of the Roman church, he saith that there was on*[8] *the Sunday but one epistle of the apostle, and one chapter of the gospel rehearsed, and that there was no singing with the voice heard, nor the comeliness of hymns known among them*[9].

About the same time St Ambrose also took order for the service of his church of Milan, and made holy hymns himself. In whose time, as St Augustine writeth, "*when Justina, the young emperor Valentinian's mother, for cause of her heresy, wherewith she was seduced by the Arians, persecuted the catholic faith, and the people thereof occupied themselves in devout watches more than before time, ready to die with their bishop in that quarrel; it was ordained that hymns and psalms should be sung in the church of Milan, after the manner of the east parts*[10]*; that the good folk thereby might have some comfort and spiritual relief in that lamentable state and continual sorrows. Thereof the churches of the west forthwith took example, and in every country they followed the same*[11]." *In his second book of Retractations he sheweth, that in his time such manner of singing began to be received in Africa*[12]. *Before this time had Hilarius also, the bishop of Poitiers in France, made hymns for that purpose, of which St Hierome maketh mention*[13].

Lib. Confessionum.

cap. xi.

In 2 Proœmio Commentariorum Epist. ad Galat.

THE BISHOP OF SARISBURY.

We may well suffer M. Harding to wander at large in matters that relieve him nothing. If it were lawful for others so to do, it were no great mastery to write books. Many matters be here heaped together, touching order of service, distinction of psalms, lessons, hours, days, feasts, the giving of peace, the form of communion, singing in the church, when it began in Græcia, when in Rome, when in Milan, when in Africa, when in France, and when in other places. These be none of the matters that lie in question. And therefore, as they nothing further M. Harding to this purpose, so in other respects they hinder him sundry ways. For in the same council of Laodicea[14] it is decreed, like as also in the council of Carthage[15], "that nothing be read in the church unto the people, saving only the canonical scriptures." Therefore the lessons there mentioned were not taken out of the Festival, or *Legenda Aurea*, as hath been used in the church of Rome; but out of the chapters of the holy bible, as it is now used in the church of England. The peace given to the bishop was not a little table of silver or somewhat else, as hath been used in the church of Rome, but a very kiss[16] indeed, in token of perfect[17] peace and unity in faith and religion. So Justinus Martyr saith, speaking of the time of the holy ministration: "We salute each other with a [16]kiss[18]." So likewise Chrysostom and others.

Concil. Laod. can. 59. Concil. Carth. iii. can. 47.

In Apol. 2. ἀλλήλους φιλήματι ἀσπαζόμεθα.

[[7] H. A. 1564, omits *the*.]

[[8] In, 1565, and H. A. 1564.]

[[9] Hieron. Op. Par. 1693-1706. Epist. Damas. ad Hieron. et Hieron. ad Damas. Tom. V. Append. cols. 415, 6. Both these epistles are considered spurious by the Benedictine editor.]

[[10] Parties, 1565, and H. A. 1564.]

[[11] Nimirum annus erat, aut non multo amplius, cum Justina, Valentiniani regis pueri mater, hominem tuum Ambrosium persequeretur hæresis suæ caussa, qua fuerat seducta ab Arianis. Excubabat pia plebs in ecclesia, mori parata cum episcopo suo... Tunc hymni et psalmi ut canerentur secundum morem orientalium partium, ne populus mœroris tædio contabesceret, institutum est; et ex illo in hodiernum retentum, multis jam ac pene omnibus gregibus tuis, et per cetera orbis imitantibus.—August. Op. Par. 1679-1700. Confess. Lib. IX. cap. vii. 15. Tom. I. col. 162.]

[[12] Id. Retract. Lib. II. cap. xi. Tom. I. col. 45.]

[[13] Hieron. Op. Comm. Lib. II. in Epist. ad Gal. Præf. Tom. IV. Pars I. cols. 255, 6.]

[[14] Ὅτι οὐ δεῖ ἰδιωτικοὺς ψαλμοὺς λέγεσθαι ἐν τῇ ἐκκλησίᾳ, οὐδὲ ἀκανόνιστα βίβλια, ἀλλὰ μόνα τὰ κανονικὰ τῆς καινῆς καὶ παλαιᾶς διαθήκης.—Concil. Laod. can. 59. in Concil. Stud. Labb. et Cossart. Tom. I. col. 1507.]

[[15] Concil. Carth. III. can. 47. in eod. Tom. II. col. 1177. See before, page 70, note 3.]

[[16] Cosse, 1565.]

[[17] Perfit, 1565.]

[[18] Just. Mart. Op. Par. 1742. Apol. i. p. 82.]

Where he saith that the church of Rome, being as then plain and simple, learned the psalmody and other ecclesiastical music, and the singing of *Gloria Patri* at the end of every psalm, of St Hierome and the bishops of the east, he doth us well to understand that then Rome is not the mother of all these things, neither is so to be taken.

But where he further saith Damasus ordained that the psalms should be sung "interchangeably and in sides, and even so as they be now sung in the quire," meaning, as it seemeth, that only the priests and clerks sung, and the people sat still; it is an open and a manifest untruth. For it is certain many ways that the whole people then sung the psalms all together.

[a] Confessionum, Lib. ix. cap. vii.
[b] Nazianz. in Funeb. Orat. de Basil. τὴν ἀκοὴν προσβαλούσῃ τῇ ψαλμωδίᾳ κατεβροντήθη.
[c] In Psal. lxv.
[d] Theodor. Lib. ii. cap. xxiv.

St Augustine saith [a]that "St Ambrose took that order in Milan in time of persecution and great danger, for the solace of the people[1]." [b]Nazianzenus expresseth the terrible sound of the people so singing together in this wise: "When the emperor Valens was entered into the church where St Basil preached, and was stricken with the psalmody, as if it had been with a thunder, &c.[2]" [c]The like hath St Hilary, writing upon the psalms[3]. [d]The like hath Theodoretus of one Flavianus and Theodorus, that first devised this order of singing in the city of Antioch[4].

Basil. in Epist. ad Cler. Neocæsarien.
Ἀντιψάλλουσιν ἀλλήλοις.
Dist. 92. In Sancta Romana.

But none plainer than St Basil: his words be these: "The people rise before day, and hie them to the house of prayer, and there, after that in mourning, and in heaviness, and continual tears, they have confessed themselves unto God, standing up from their prayers, they begin the psalmody, and, being divided into two parts, they sing together, the one part answering to the other. And this order," he saith, "was agreeable to all the other churches of God[5]." Certainly it seemeth that St Gregory in his time thought singing in the church to be a thing fitter for the multitude of people than for the priest. For he expressly forbiddeth the priest to sing in the church[6]; but I do not remember that ever he forbade the people.

Hereof we may gather that Damasus divided the whole people into two parts, and willed them to sing the psalms in their own known tongue, the one part making answer by course to the other; saving only the sides, nothing like to that is now used in M. Harding's quires.

M. HARDING. THE THIRD DIVISION.

Much might be alleged for proof of having service in the Greek and in the Latin churches, long before the first six hundred years were expired, which is not denied. The thing that is denied by M. Jewel is this, that, for the space of six hundred years after Christ, any christian people had their service, or common prayers, in a tongue they understood not; which they of his side bear the world in hand to be a heinous error of the church, and a wicked deceit of the papists. And I say, as I said before, that (67) *the service was then in a tongue which some people understood, and some understood not; I mean the Greek tongue, and the Latin tongue; for*[7] *that it was, within the six hundred years, in any other barbarous or vulgar tongue, I never read; neither, I think, M. Jewel, nor any the best learned of his side, is able to prove. To be the better understanded, I call all tongues barbarous and vulgar beside the Hebrew, Greek, and Latin.*

The sixty-seventh untruth. For M. Harding is not able to shew one nation that understood not their common service.

[*Usage of church service in any vulgar tongue within 600 years after Christ cannot be proved.* H. A. 1564.]

The gospel and the faith of Christ was preached and set forth in Syria and Arabia

---

[1 See the preceding page, note 11.]

[2 Gregor. Nazianz. Op. Par. 1778-1840. In Laud. Basil. Orat. xliii. 52. Tom. I. p. 808.]

[3 Hilar. Op. Par. 1693. Tractat. in Psal. lxv. 4. col. 174.]

[4 Theodor. in Hist. Eccles. Script. Amst. 1695-1700. Lib. II. cap. xxiv. p. 107.]

[5 ... ὅτι τὰ νῦν κεκρατηκότα ἔθη πάσαις ταῖς τοῦ Θεοῦ ἐκκλησίαις σύνῳδά ἐστι καὶ σύμφωνα. ἐκ νυκτὸς γὰρ ὀρθρίζει παρ' ἡμῖν ὁ λαὸς ἐπὶ τὸν οἶκον τῆς προσευχῆς, καὶ ἐν πόνῳ καὶ θλίψει καὶ συνοχῇ δακρύων ἐξομολογούμενοι τῷ Θεῷ, τελευταῖον ἐξαναστάντες τῶν προσευχῶν, εἰς τὴν ψαλμῳδίαν καθίστανται. καὶ νῦν μὲν διχῇ διανεμηθέντες, ἀντιψάλλουσιν ἀλλήλοις.—Basil. Op. Par. 1721-30. Ad Cler. Neoc. Epist. ccvii. Tom. III. p. 311.]

[6 Qua de re præsenti decreto constituo, ut in hac sede sacri altaris ministri cantare non debeant, &c.—Gregor. in Corp. Jur. Canon. Lugd. 1624. Decret. Gratian. Decr. Prim. Pars, Dist. xcii. can. 2. cols. 435, 6.]

[7 1565 omits *for*.]

by Paul; in Egypt by Mark; in Æthiopia by Matthew; in Mesopotamia, Persia, Media, Bactra, Hyrcania, Parthia, and Carmania, by Thomas; in Armenia the greater by Bartholomew; in Scythia by Andrew; and likewise in other countries by apostolic men, who were sent by the apostles and their next successors: as in France by Martialis, sent by Peter; by Dionysius, sent by Clement; by Crescens, as Clement and Hierome writeth; and by Trophimus, St Paul's scholar; and by Nathaniel, Christ's disciple; of whom he at Arelate[10], *and this at Bourges and Treveres, preached the gospel, as some record: in our countries here of Britain, by Fugatius, Damianus, and others, sent by Eleutherius the pope and martyr, at the request of king Lucius, as Damasus writeth in* Pontificiali[11]. *Other countries, where the Greek and Latin tongue was commonly known, I pass over of purpose. Now, if M. Jewel, or any of our learned adversaries, or any man living, could shew good evidence and proof, that the public service of the church was then in the Syriacal or Arabic, in the Egyptian, Æthiopian, Persian, Armenian, Scythian, French, or Britain tongue; then might they justly claim prescription against us in this article, then might they charge us with example*[12] *of antiquity, then might they require us to yield to the manner and authority of the primitive church.* (68) *But that doubtless cannot appear, which if any could shew, it would make much for the service to be had in the vulgar tongue.*

Barbarous tongue.

Constit. Apost. Lib. vii. cap. xlvi[8]. *Lib. de Scriptor. Ecclesiasticis*[9]. *Temporib. Antonini Commodi. Anno Do.* 181.

The sixty-eighth untruth. For doubtless it will soon be shewed.

THE BISHOP OF SARISBURY.

M. Harding, being now out of his digression, foundeth himself upon this principle, that some people understood the common prayers, and some understood them not. But, if it might have pleased him to shew any one kind of people that understood them not, it had been sufficient. But he sheweth none, neither here, nor elsewhere. Therefore we may conjecture, his store of such things is not great.

He granteth that the service was commonly said in the Greek and in the Latin tongue. All other tongues he condemneth for barbarous; by what authority, I cannot tell. For in the[13] respect of God, "there is neither Jew nor gentile, nor Greek nor barbarous, nor any other distinction of tongues; but all are one in Christ Jesus[14]." Otherwise any tongue, unto him that understandeth it not, appeareth barbarous; and in that sense St Paul saith: "Unless I understand the meaning of the speech, I shall be barbarous unto him that speaketh; and he that speaketh shall be likewise barbarous unto me:" like as Anacharsis the philosopher also said: "The Scythian is barbarous at Athens; and the Athenian is barbarous among the Scythians." And so the priest that prayeth in an unknown tongue, whether it be Greek or Latin, is barbarous unto the people; and, if he be ignorant, and himself understand not his own prayers, he is barbarous also unto himself. As for the Latin tongue, which M. Harding so favourably excepteth, it hath no such special privilege above others. St Paul, making a full division of the whole world, nameth some Greeks, and some barbarous, and so leaveth out the Latins among the barbarous. The same division Strabo also followeth in his Cosmography. For thus he saith: *Barbaræ sunt omnes nationes, præter Græcos*[15]: "All nations be barbarous, beside the Greeks." Afterward the Romans misliking herewithal, as they increased the state of their empire, so first they excepted themselves, and in continuance, all other nations, that would become provinces, and be subject unto them. And therefore pope Nicolas the first made a piteous exclamation against the Greek emperor Michael, that seemed to deface the Latin tongue with that odious name: *Appellatis Latinam linguam barbaram, ad injuriam ejus qui fecit eam*[16]: "Ye call the Latin tongue barbarous, in despite of him that

Gal. iii.

1 Cor. xiv.

Strabo, Cosmograph. Lib. i. and iv.

Epist. Nicol. i.

[8 Const. Apostol. in Concil. Stud. Labb. et Cossart. Lut. Par. 1671-2. Lib. VII. cap. xlvii. Tom. I. cols. 450, 1.]

[9 Hieron. Op. Par. 1693-1706. Catal. Script. Eccles. Tom. IV. Pars II. cols. 101, &c. There appears however here no mention of Crescens.]

[10 Arles.]

[11 Hic [Eleutherius] accepit epistolam a Lucio Britannico rege, ut Christianus efficeretur per ejus mandatum.—Decr. Eleuth. Ex Lib. Pontif. in Crabb. Concil. Col. Agrip. 1551. Tom. I. p. 91. Little credit is to be attached to this story.]

[12 The example, H. A. 1564.]

[13 1565 omits *the*.] [14 Jesu, 1565.]

[15 Strabon. Geograph. Lut. Par. 1620. Libb. I. XIV. pp. 66, 662.]

[16 ...ut linguæ Latinæ injuriam irrogaretis, hanc ... barbaram et Scythicam appellantes, ad injuriam &c.—Nicol. Papæ I. ad Michael. Imp. Epist. in Crabb. Concil. Tom. II. pp. 748, 9.]

Strabo, Cosmograph. Lib. i.

Beda, 1 Cor. xiv.

made that tongue." Great Alexander's modesty is much commended, who, as Strabo saith, would never sort his subjects by Greeks and barbarous, but rather by the difference of good and ill. "For many Greeks," said he, "be ill people; and many barbarous be good[1]." The like modesty might well have served M. Harding in this place. For many that know the Greek and the Latin tongues be notwithstanding ungodly; and many be godly, that know them not. Therefore it is very discreetly said by Beda: *Barbara est lingua, quæ Deum laudare non potest*[2]*:* "The[3] tongue is barbarous, that cannot serve[4] God."

Acts ii.

M. Harding maketh a long discourse of the apostles' and other apostolic men's travels throughout the world. If he had shewed to what end, we might the better have known his purpose. If he will say, "The apostles preach in sundry countries; *ergo*, the people had their common prayers in an unknown tongue," this argument will hardly hold. For to that end God gave unto them the gift of tongues, that they might deal with all nations in their own languages.

Here are we required to shew some evidence, that in the primitive church the public service was in the Syriacal, or Arabic, or Egyptian, or any other barbarous tongue; and it is stoutly presumed that we are able to shew none. Whatsoever we can shew, this is no indifferent dealing.

M. Harding requireth others to shew, being himself able to shew nothing.

In the fifteenth division.

For M. Harding, being required of me to shew but one sentence of proof for his side, and having as yet shewed nothing, suddenly altereth the whole state of the cause, and shifteth his hands, and requireth me to shew. Which thing although I be not bound to do by any order of disputation, yet, that it may appear that we deal plainly, and seek nothing but the truth, I am content, only in one example or two, presently to follow his will, referring the rest to another place more convenient for the same.

Hieron. in Epit. Paul.

August. de Catechiz. Rud. cap. ix.

And, forasmuch as the first tongue that he nameth amongst others, is the Syriacal, let him read St Hierome, describing the pomp of Paula's funeral. These be his words: *Tota ad funus ejus Palæstinarum urbium turbà convenit:... Hebræo, Græco, Latino, Syroque sermone, psalmi in ordine personabant*[5]*:* "At her funeral all the multitude of the cities of Palestine met together. The psalms were sung in order, in the Hebrew, Greek, Latin, and Syrian tongue." Here may he see that in one city four several nations, in their common service, used four several tongues, among which tongues is the Syriacal; which thing M. Harding thinketh all the world cannot shew. St Augustine, willing the priests to apply their studies to correct the errors of their Latin speech, addeth thereto this reason: *Ut populus ad id quod plane intelligit, dicat, Amen*[6]*:* "That people[7], unto the thing that they plainly understand, may say, Amen." This of St Augustine seemeth to be spoken generally of all tongues. M. Harding himself, at the end of his treaty, confesseth that the Armenians, Russians, Æthiopians, Sclavons, and Moscovites, have from the beginning of their faith, in their public service, used evermore their own natural country tongues. Wherefore, by M. Harding's own grant, we may justly claim prescription, and charge him with antiquity, and require him to yield to the authority of the primitive church.

M. HARDING. THE FOURTH DIVISION.

[Fol. 168. H. A. 1564.]

Wherefore, M. Jewel in his sermon, which he uttered in so solemn an audience, and hath set forth in print to the world, saith more than he is able to justify, where he speaketh generally thus: "Before the people grew to corruption (whereby he meaneth the first six hundred years after Christ) all christian men throughout the world made their common prayers, and had the holy communion, in their own common and known tongue[8]*." This is soon spoken, sir; but it will not by you be so soon proved.*

[1 Πολλοὺς γὰρ καὶ Ἑλλήνων εἶναι κακοὺς, καὶ τῶν βαρβάρων ἀστείους, κ. τ. λ.—Strabon. Geogr. Lut. Par. 1620. Lib. I. p. 66.]

[2 The passage does not appear in Bede in the place referred to. See however August. Op. Par. 1679-1700. In Psalm. cxiii. Serm. i. 5. Tom. IV. col. 1257; where we find, *Non est enim lingua vestra, sed barbara, quæ Deum laudare non novit.*]

[3 That, 1565.] [4 Praise, 1565, 1609.]

[5 Hieron. Op. Par. 1693-1706. Ad Eustoch. Epist. lxxxvi. Epit. Paul. Tom. IV. Pars II. cols. 687, 8.]

[6 August. Op. De Catechiz. Rud. cap. ix. 13. Tom. VI. col. 272.]

[7 That the people, 1565, 1609.]

[8 See before, page 9.]

THE BISHOP OF SARISBURY.

Ephrem's Homilies

That M. Jewel there said is proved sufficiently, unless M. Harding be able to bring some example, one or other, to prove the contrary. Neither is the matter so hard of our side to be proved. Thomas of Aquine and Nicolas Lyra, M. Harding's own witnesses, for some good part, will prove it for me.

M. HARDING. THE FIFTH DIVISION.

Indeed we find, that whereas holy Ephrem, deacon of the church of Edessa, wrote many things in the Syriacal tongue, he was of so worthy fame and renown, that (as St Hierome witnesseth) his writings were rehearsed in certain churches openly, post lectionem scripturarum[9], *"after the scriptures had been read;" whereof it appeareth to Erasmus that nothing was wont then to be read in the churches, beside the writings of the apostles, or at least of such men as were of apostolic authority*[10]. *But by this place of St Hierome it seemeth not that Ephrem's works were used as a part of the common service; but rather as homilies, or exhortations, to be read after the service, which consisted in manner wholly of the scriptures. And whether they were turned into Greek, or no, so soon, it is uncertain.*

Lib. de Scriptorib. Ecclesiast.

THE BISHOP OF SARISBURY.

M. Harding, contrary to the order of rhetoric, would confute our side, before he confirm his own. But I marvel much to what end he should thus allege Ephrem, unless it be to heap matter against himself. For will he thus frame his reason:

"Ephrem wrote sundry things in his own mother tongue;"

Ergo, the people had their service in a strange tongue?

Will he have this to be allowed, and go for an argument? If there were nothing else here to be gathered, yet hath he touched two things expressly against himself. The one is, that nothing was then read in the church, saving only the scriptures, or other matters of apostolic authority; which thing is also straitly commanded by the council of Carthage[11]. Yet M. Harding in his church, even in the public service, readeth lessons and legends of childish fables.

Concil. Carth. iii. can. 47.

The other is, that Ephrem's homilies were pronounced unto the people in the vulgar tongue: yet M. Harding himself pronounceth gospels, epistles, and homilies, and all whatsoever, unto the people in a strange tongue.

But, to avoid this inconvenience, he saith: "The homilies were no part of the service." First, how is he sure of that? Certainly, the Latin homilies be read in the matins, and accounted part of the Romish service. Again, what necessary sequel is this:

The people understood Ephrem's homilies:

Ergo, his homilies were no part of the service?

Or what leadeth him to think it was profitable for the people to hear and understand Ephrem, and yet was not profitable for them to hear and understand Peter, Paul, or Christ? To be short, he confesseth that Ephrem's writings were exhortations to the Greek people, and yet doubteth whether they were translated into the Greek or no; and so he endeth in uncertainty, and concludeth nothing.

Now let us see, whether the same Ephrem will conclude any thing of our side. First, Theodoretus saith: "He was utterly ignorant of the Greek tongue[12]." Which thing is also confirmed by M. Harding's own Amphilochius. For, in the conference that was between him and Basil, he saith: "He spake by an interpreter, as being not able to speak Greek himself[13]." Yet was the same Ephrem a minister in the church, being, as St Hierome saith, a deacon[14], and, as some

Theodor. Lib. iv. cap. xxix.

Amphiloch.

Hieron. de Eccles. Script.

[9 Hieron. Op. Catal. Script. Eccles. 115. Tom. IV. Pars II. col. 126.]

[10 Hinc apparet non nisi apostolicas litteras olim legi solitas in templis, aut certe virorum apostolicæ auctoritatis, cum hodie monachorum somnia, imo mulierculorum deliramenta legantur inter divinas scripturas.—Hieron. Op. Basil. 1516. Erasm. Schol. in Catal. Script. Eccles. Tom. I. fol. 141.]

[11 Concil. Carth. III. can. 47. in Concil. Stud. Labb. et Cossart. Lut. Par. 1671-2. Tom. II. col. 1177.]

[12 Παιδείας γὰρ οὐ γεγευμένος Ἑλληνικῆς.—Theodor. in Hist. Eccles. Script. Amst. 1695-1700. Lib. IV. cap. xxix. p. 192.]

[13 Amphiloch. Op. Par. 1644. In Vit. S. Basil. p. 202.]

[14 Hieron. Op. Catal. Script. Eccles. 115. Tom. IV. Pars II. col. 126.]

St Hierome's translation.

others write, the archdeacon of the church of Edessa. Now let M. Harding shew us in what other tongue he could minister the ecclesiastical service, but in his own. If he think this conjecture to be weak, let him understand further, that, as Theodoretus reporteth, the same Ephrem made hymns and psalms in the Syrian tongue[1]; and that the same were sung at the solemn feasts of martyrs; and that, as Sozomenus saith plainly, the same hymns and psalms were sung in the churches of Syria[2].

Theodor. Lib. iv. cap. xxix. φαιδροτέρας τῶν νικηφόρων μαρτύρων... πανηγύρεις ποιεῖ.

M. HARDING. THE SIXTH DIVISION.

Neither St Hierome's translation of the scriptures into the Dalmatical tongue (if any such was by him made at all) proveth that the service was then in that vulgar tongue. That labour may be thought to have served to another purpose. But of the translation of the scriptures into vulgar tongues, I shall speak hereafter, when I shall come to that peculiar article. Verily the handling of this present, and of that, hath most things common to both. Thus, that the people of any country had the church service in their vulgar and common tongue, beside the Greek and the Latin tongue, we leave as a matter stoutly affirmed by M. Jewel, but faintly proved; yea, nothing at all proved.

See the fifteenth division of this article.

THE BISHOP OF SARISBURY.

M. Harding seemeth to doubt whether St Hierome translated the scriptures into the Sclavon tongue, or no. Yet Stanislaus Hosius, one of the greatest of that side, maketh it very certain, and putteth it quite out of doubt. His words be plain: *In Dalmaticam linguam sacros libros Hieronymum vertisse constat*[3]: "It is certainly known that St Hierome translated the scriptures into the Sclavon tongue." And likewise Alphonsus de Castro: *Fatemur,... olim sacros libros in linguam vulgarem fuisse translatos, beatumque Hieronymum in linguam Dalmaticam eos vertisse*[4]: "We confess that in old times the scriptures were translated into the vulgar tongue, and that St Hierome turned them into the Sclavon tongue." Neither ever wist I any man that made doubt hereof, but M. Harding. "But, being granted," saith he, "that St Hierome so translated the scriptures, yet that proveth not that the service was then in the vulgar tongue." Good sir, much less it proveth that the service was then among the Sclavons in the Latin tongue. He saith further: "That labour may be thought to have served to another purpose." But to what other purpose, he sheweth not. Surely whatsoever is thought hereof by M. Harding, M. Eckius, one of his own doctors, confesseth that the same St Hierome, that translated the scriptures into the Sclavon tongue, procured also that the common service there should be said in the Sclavon tongue[5]. And it may well be thought, his translation could serve to no better purpose. I grant St Chrysostom[6], and Origen[7], in their sermons, exhort the people to read the scriptures in their houses at home; which purpose also, no doubts, was very godly. But such private reading at home excludeth not the open reading in the church. Chrysostom saith, it was the reader's duty openly in the church to pronounce the scriptures[8]. And St Augustine saith unto the people: "The apostle St Paul witnesseth that this psalm, which ye have heard, pertaineth to that grace of God, whereby we are made Christians; therefore I have caused the same lesson to be read unto you[9]." I think M. Harding will grant that these lessons that St Chry-

Hosius de Sacro Vernacule Legendo.

Alph. de Hæres. Lib. i. cap. xiii.

Eck. de Missa Latine Dicenda.

Chrysost. in Matt. Hom. 2. et in Gen. Hom. 28. Orig. in Levit. Hom. 9. Chrysost. in Act. Apost. Hom. 19. Aug. in Psal. xxxi.

[[1] Theodor. in Hist. Eccles. Script. Amst. 1695–1700. Lib. IV. cap. xxix. p. 192.]

[[2] Sozom. in eod. Lib. III. cap. xvi. p. 428.]

[[3] Cum præsertim Dalmatica lingua sacros libros Hieronymum vertisse constet, &c.—Hos. Op. Col. 1584. De Sacr. Vernac. Leg. Tom. I. p. 664.]

[[4] Alf. de Castr. Adv. Omn. Hæres. Col. 1539. Lib. I. cap. xiii. fol. 28. 2.]

[[5] Identidem [ut in lingua sua rem divinam facerent] aliqui de lingua Sclavonica altissima testantur, a Hieronymo impetratum.—Joh. Eck. Enchir. Loc. Com. Lugd. 1572. cap. xxxvii. p. 339.]

[[6] Chrysost. Op. Par. 1718–38. In Matt. Hom. ii. Tom. VII. pp. 30, 1. Id. in cap. ix. Gen. Hom. xxix. Tom. IV. p. 281.]

[[7] Orig. Op. Par. 1733–59. In Levit. Hom. ix. 5. Tom. II. p. 240.]

[[8] Chrysost. Op. In Act. Apost. Hom. xix. Tom. IX. p. 160.]

[[9] Hunc autem psalmum ad eam gratiam pertinere, qua Christiani sumus, testatus est apostolus Paulus: unde ipsam lectionem vobis legi voluimus.—August. Op. Par. 1679-1700. In Psalm. xxxi. Enarr. ii. 2. Tom. IV. Pars I. col. 171.]

sostom and St Augustine speaketh of, were uttered in such a tongue as the people might understand. For else Origen saith: *Alioqui non fuisset necessarium, legi hæc in ecclesia, nisi ex his ædificatio aliqua audientibus præberetur*[10]: "Otherwise it had not been necessary for these things to be read in the church, unless some profit might come thereof unto the hearers." St Hierome's translation.

"Yet notwithstanding," saith M. Harding, "these matters be stoutly affirmed by M. Jewel, and faintly proved." My proofs were taken out of the manifest words of St Paul, St Ambrose, St Augustine, St Chrysostom, Arnobius, Gregory, and others like; notwithstanding it please M. Harding to call them so faint. Let us therefore see the weighty reasons that he and others of his side have made for the contrary. M. Harding seemeth to reason thus: Orig. in Levit. cap. vii.

Ephrem made homilies in the Syrian tongue;

And, St Hierome translated the bible into the Sclavon tongue;

Ergo, the common service was in the Latin or Greek tongue.

Cardinal Otho saith: "There were three tongues written in the title of the cross; the Greek, the Hebrew, and the Latin;" Otho Cardinal. in Stat. Synod. August.

Ergo, in one of these three tongues the people must have their common service[11].

Eckius saith: "Christ prayed secretly, being in the mount alone;" Eckius de Miss. Lat. Dicenda.

Ergo, the service must be in an unknown tongue[12].

These and such-like arguments be brought by them. I leave it unto the discreet reader to judge their force.

M. HARDING. THE SEVENTH DIVISION.

Now concerning the two learned tongues, Greek and Latin; and first the Greek. That the service was in the Greek tongue, and used in the Greek church, I grant. And, to shew what is meant by the Greek church, the learned do understand all the christian people of that country which properly is called Græcia, of Macedonia, Thracia, and of Asia the less[13], *and the countries adjoining. The provinces that were allotted to the patriarch of Alexandria in Egypt, and to the patriarch of Antiochia in Syria, are of the old writers called sometime by the name of the oriental, or east church, sometime of the Greek church. Thus*[14] *much by us both confessed, M. Jewel, and agreed upon, I say that, if I can shew that the people of some countries of the Greek church,* (69) *which all had their common prayers and service in the Greek tongue, for the more part understood not the Greek tongue, more than Englishmen now understand the Latin tongue; then I have proved that I promised to prove, that some peoples, I mean whole nations, understood not their service, for that they had it in an unknown tongue.* The sixty-ninth untruth. For it is certain that sundry of the east nations had not their service in the Greek tongue, as shall appear.

THE BISHOP OF SARISBURY.

M. Harding, first having divided the whole world into two churches, the Greek and the Latin, afterward maketh offer to prove his purpose. Whereof it may be gathered, that he hath hitherto proved nothing. This division of the church neither is greatly material, nor of our part much denied; albeit many ways it seemeth unperfect[15]. For the great churches of Æthiopia, India, and Scythia, planted by St Matthew, by St Thomas, and by St Andrew, besides Arabia, Syria, Persia, Media, Armenia, and a great number of other countries, which never were neither of the Greek church nor of the Latin, are here quite left out. The division of the church into Greek and Latin.

Two propositions M. Harding hath here chosen to prove. The one is, that all the Greek church had the common service wholly and thoroughly in the Greek tongue: the other is, that some whole countries in the Greek church understood not the Greek tongue.

If both these propositions be proved soundly and substantially, without surmise

[10 Orig. Op. In Levit. Hom. v. 12. Tom. II. p. 214; where *alioquin nec*, &c.]

[11 Lingua Latina, cui veluti divino instrumento in ipsa crucis ara sacris usibus dedicato, ecclesia occidentalis religionem christianam fert acceptam, in sacramentorum administratione ... retineatur, et exclusa revocetur.—Statut. Synod. August. Othon. Card. Præs. cap. 15. in Crabb. Concil. Col. Agrip. 1551. Tom. III. p. 872.]

[12 Christus in silentio oravit et secrete et secedens a discipulis.—Joh. Eck. Enchir. Loc. Com. cap. xxxvii. p. 343.]

[13 Lesser, H. A. 1564.]

[14 This, H. A. 1564.] [15 Unperfite, 1565.]

Asia the Less.

or guess, then it behoveth me to yield. But, good reader, mark them well both, and consider the proofs. For if he fail in either of these, he proveth nothing, as I hope it will appear.

M. HARDING. THE EIGHTH DIVISION.

Now, how well I am able to prove this, I refer it to your own consideration. The less[1] *Asia, being a principal part of the Greek church, had then the service in the Greek tongue. But the people of sundry regions and countries of the less*[1] *Asia then understood not the Greek tongue;* ergo, *the people of sundry regions and countries had then their service in an unknown tongue. The first proposition, or* major, *is confessed as manifest: no learned man will deny it; and if any would, it may easily be proved. The second proposition, or* minor, *may thus be proved: Strabo, who travelled over all the countries of Asia, for perfect*[2] *knowledge of the same, near about the time of St Paul's peregrination there, who also was born in the same, in his 14th book of Geography writeth, that, whereas within that* Cherronesus *(that is, the strait between sea and sea) there were sixteen nations, by report of Ephorus;* (70) *of them all only three were Greeks, all the rest barbarous*[3]. *Likewise Plinius, in the sixth book* Naturalis Historiæ, cap. 2, *declareth, that* (71) *within the circuit of that land were three Greek nations only, Dores, Iones, Æoles; and that the rest were barbarous*[4]: *amongst whom the people of Lycaonia was one, who, in St Paul's time, spake before Paul and Barnabas in the Lycaonical tongue.*

A fallax, or a deceitful argument.

[All people of the Greek church understood not the Greek service. H. A. 1564.]

The seventieth untruth, misreporting Strabo's words.

The seventy-first untruth, misreporting the words of Pliny.

[Acts xiv. 1565, 1609, H. A. 1564.]

The scripture itself reporteth a diversity of language there and thereabout, as it appeareth by the second chapter of the Acts; where the Jews gathered together in Hierusalem, for keeping of the feast of Pentecost, wondering at the apostles for their speaking with so many sundry tongues, amongst other provinces different in language they reckon Pontus, and Asia, Cappadocia, Phrygia, and Pamphilia: which two provinces are of all attributed unto the less[1] *Asia: which maketh a good argument, that all Asia the less*[1] *had not only*[5] *the Greek tongue. And therefore so many of them as were of other language, having the service in Greek, had it in a tongue they understood not. They that will seem to search the cause why that land had so great diversity of languages, impute it to the often change of conquests, for that it was overcome and possessed of divers nations; of which every one coveted, with enlarging their empire, to bring into the countries subdued their laws, their customs, and their language. Now, this being proved by good and sufficient authority, that in Asia, of sixteen nations, three only were Greeks, it followeth that the other thirteen, having their service in Greek, had it not in their own, but in a strange tongue. For else, if they had all naturally spoken Greek, why should not they have been called Greeks? Thus we see, it is no new thing, proceeding of a general corruption in the church, some peoples to have the service in an unknown tongue.*

THE BISHOP OF SARISBURY.

Take heed, good reader: M. Harding hath here thrown a great mist of learning, to dazzle thy sight. Unless thou eye him well, he will steal from thee. Thus he frameth his *syllogismus:* The less Asia, being a principal part of the Greek church, had then the service in the Greek tongue; but sundry countries of the same Asia understood not the Greek tongue; *ergo,* they had their service in an unknown tongue.

The disclosing of M. Harding's fallax.

Here is a fair gloss. But be not deceived. M. Harding knoweth well enough, it is but a fallacy, that is to say, a deceitful argument, named in the schools, *Ex meris particularibus,* or, *A non distributo, ad distributum.* Unless he amend the major, and make it an universal, and say thus, All Asia the less had the service in the Greek tongue, it can in no wise hold. That Asia the less had the service in Greek, it is doubted of no man, nor learned, nor unlearned. But that all Asia the less had throughout in all parts the same service, if it be denied, M. Harding

[1 Lesser, H. A. 1564.]
[2 Perfite, 1565, and H. A. 1564.]
[3 See below, page 272, note 7.]
[4 See below, page 274.]
[5 One only, H. A. 1564.]

with all his learning is not able to prove it; and therefore he did better to turn it over without any proof at all. Asia the Less.

The minor is this: "Sundry nations in Asia the less understood not the Greek." And to prove this M. Harding hath directed all his drift. But to what end? For neither is it denied by any of us, nor is it any part of our question. And yet notwithstanding is not M. Harding able to prove it with all his guesses.

He allegeth the Acts of the Apostles, where as mention is made of sundry languages, and, among the same, certain provinces of this Asia specially named for their difference in speech. But what if answer were made, that all there rehearsed were not divers tongues, but rather certain differences in one tongue? Certainly, Beda seemeth plainly so to say. His words be these: "'Verily this man was with him, for he is of Galilee:' not for that the people of Galilee, and the people of Hierusalem, used sundry tongues; but for that every province (of Jewry), having a peculiar manner of utterance in their speech, could not avoid the same[6]." And hereunto he applieth this story of the Acts of the Apostles. Acts ii. Bed. in Luc. cap. xxi. Lib. vi. Ex Hieron. in Matt. cap. xxvi.

But, saith M. Harding: "There must needs be greater difference between these countries of Asia, and that because of often overthrows and conquests that there had happened." The conjecture is good. But the greatest conquerors that came there were the Macedonians, the Thebans, and other Grecians, who (no doubt) planted there the Greek tongue, as it may soon appear to any man that can with judgment consider of it. St Paul unto the Ephesians, the Galathians, and the Colossians, dwelling all in this same Asia the less, wrote in Greek. And St Luke, writing of St Paul's being and preaching at Ephesus, saith, it came so to pass, *ut omnes qui habitabant in Asia audirent sermonem Domini Jesu, Judæi simul et Græci:* "that all they that dwelt in Asia heard the word of the Lord Jesus, both Jews and Greeks." St Luke, that had travelled over that whole country with St Paul, knew none other nation there, but Jews and Greeks: M. Harding hath a guess, there should be some other barbarous people also; but what they were, or whereabout they dwelt, or what tongue they spake, he cannot tell. Verily Polycarpus was bishop of Smyrna: Gregorius was bishop in Pontus: St Basil was bishop of Cæsaria in Cappadocia; Amphilochius bishop of Iconium in Lycaonia; Gregorius, St Basil's brother, bishop of Nyssa in Caria, or Thracia. All these, in sundry countries within Asia the less, preached openly in the Greek tongue; and the vulgar people understood them. Acts xix. Acts xix.

"Yet," saith M. Harding, "Strabo, being born in the same country, and living under the emperors Augustus and Tiberius, in the time of St Paul, writeth in his Geography, that, whereas there were then sixteen sundry nations in Asia the less, three only of them were Greeks, and the rest barbarous." I know not whether M. Harding be unwittingly deceived himself, or wilfully go about to deceive others. But well I know that this is no part of Strabo's meaning. For Strabo speaketh not this of his own time, but of the time of Ephorus, that lived well near five hundred years before him. This Ephorus reporteth that in his time there were but three Greek nations as yet entered into Asia, but all the rest then were barbarous[7]. And therefore Apollodorus saith, that before the battle of Troy no people of the Greeks at all ever came over to dwell there[8]. For, if Strabo had meant this of his own time, to what end should he allege the record of Ephorus, that lived so many hundred years before him, for proof of that thing that he had so diligently viewed and seen himself? and specially, seeing his purpose is not to follow, but to reprove Ephorus; as it well appeareth by his words. As for Apollodorus, thus he saith of him: "He seemeth not discreetly to deal herein; for he disordereth and falsely allegeth the words of Homer[9]." And unto this construction of Strabo very well agreeth the place of Plinius here alleged, and con- Strabo, Geogr. Lib. xiv. Strabo, Lib. xiv. eodem loco. τὰ...τοῦ ποιητοῦ ταράττων καὶ καταψευδόμενος.

[6 *Vere et hic cum illo erat, nam et Galilæus est.* Non quod alia lingua Galilæi atque alia loquerentur Hierosolymitæ, qui utrique fuerunt Hebræi; sed quod unaquæque provincia et regio suas habendo proprietates, vernaculum loquendi sonum vitare non possit. Unde in Actibus apostolorum, &c.—Ven. Bed. Op. Col. Agrip. 1612. In Luc. Evang. cap. xxii. Lib. VI. Tom. V. col. 431. See also Hieron. Op. Par. 1693-1706. Comm. Lib. IV. in Matt. cap. xxvi. Tom. IV. Pars I. col. 133.]

[7 Φήσαντος δὲ τοῦ 'Εφόρου, διότι τὴν χεῤῥόνησον κατοικεῖ ταύτην ἑκκαίδεκα γένη, τρία μὲν 'Ελληνικά, τὰ δὲ λοιπὰ βάρβαρα, κ. τ. λ.—Strabon. Geograph. Lut. Par. 1620. Lib. XIV. pp. 677, 8.]

[8 Id. ibid.]

[9 Id. ibid. p. 663.]

Asia the Less. cludeth manifestly against M. Harding, as it appeareth by the very words: *In omni [eo] tractu proditur tres tantum gentes Græcas jure dici, Doricam, Ionicam, Æolicam: ceteras barbarorum esse*[1]: "In which whole circuit it is written that only three nations be rightly called Greeks; and that the rest are of the barbarians." In that he saith, *proditur*, "it is written;" he meaneth by Ephorus, Apollodorus, or such others as had lived long before. In that he saith, *ceteras barbarorum esse*, "the rest be of the barbarians;" he meaneth that they had arrived thither, not out of Græcia, as had the other three, but out of other countries that were barbarous. But in that he saith, *tres tantum gentes Græcas jure dici*, "that only three nations be rightly, or naturally, called Greeks;" he must needs mean that the rest were called Greeks also, although not so rightly and naturally as the other: for else the exception of this word *jure*, that is, "rightly or naturally," had been in vain. And thus M. Harding, seeking to prove that the people of Asia were no Greeks, allegeth Plinius, by whose words it appeareth necessarily that they were Greeks.

Plin. Hist. Nat. Lib. vi. cap. ii.

M. Harding falsifieth Strabo's mind.

But M. Harding will force the matter further: "Strabo saith that, these three nations excepted, the rest were barbarous; *ergo*, they understood no Greek." And hereupon resteth his whole proof. But this is another falsification of Strabo's mind. For Strabo calleth them barbarous that understood and spake Greek. And what better witness can we herein have than Strabo himself? Thus he writeth: *Barbarismum in his dicere consuevimus, qui male loquuntur Græce; non autem in illis, qui Carice loquuntur. Sic etiam barbariloquos et barbari sermonis homines eos accipere debemus, qui male Græca pronuntiant:* "We take a *barbarismus*, or a barbarous manner of speech, to be in them that speak the Greek disorderly, and not in them that speak a strange tongue, as is the tongue of the Carians. So we ought to take them to be barbarous, or men of barbarous speech, that ill-favouredly pronounce the Greek." Thou mayest see, good reader, with what faith M. Harding allegeth the authority of old writers. He would prove by Strabo, that these people spake no Greek, because they were barbarous: and Strabo himself saith, notwithstanding they were barbarous, yet they spake Greek. Now therefore, seeing the *syllogismus* itself, as I have said, is a fallacy, the major false, the minor false, and neither of them any way proved, and Strabo and Pliny falsely alleged; to gather hereof, that these people had their service in an unknown tongue, must needs seem a strange conclusion.

Lib. xiv. Geogr.

M. Harding's syllogism.

M. HARDING. THE NINTH DIVISION.

Here perhaps M. Jewel, or some other for him, replieth, and saith that the people of Asia commonly, beside their own proper language, spake the Greek tongue also; and allegeth for the same purpose[2] *St Hierome, who saith:* Galatas, excepto sermone Græco, quo omnis oriens loquitur, propriam linguam eandem...habere, quam Treviros[3]: "*That the Galathians, beside the Greek language, which all the orient or the east speaketh, have their own peculiar tongue, the very same that they of Trevers have.*" *Lo, saith this replier, St Hierome affirmeth all the orient to speak the Greek tongue;* ergo, *the service in Greek to them was not strange and unknown.*

In Proœmio 2 Lib. Comment. Ep. ad Galatas.

To this I answer, St Hierome meaneth that some of all countries of the orient, or east, spake Greek, as the learned men, gentlemen, merchants, all of liberal education, and such other as had cause to travel those countries. To be short, it was without doubt very common, as being their only learned tongue for all sciences, and the tongue that might best serve to travel withal from country to country within the east, right so as the Latin tongue serveth to the like intents for all nations of the west. And he meaneth not that all and singular persons, of what degree and[4] *condition soever they were, all uplandish people, tillers of the ground, herdmen, and women, spake Greek. For, if it had been so, then had they not had peculiar and proper tongues. For it is not for their simple heads (for the most part) to bear*

[1 C. Plin. Secund. Nat. Hist. Par. 1685. Lib. VI. cap. ii. Tom. I. p. 651.]

[2 For that purpose, H. A. 1564.]

[3 Hieron. Op. Par. 1693–1706. Comm. Lib. II. in Epist. ad Gal. Præf. Tom. IV. Pars I. cols. 255, 6.]

[4 Or, H. A. 1564.]

away two languages. In that St Hierome calleth the Galathians' tongue propriam linguam, *a proper and a peculiar tongue to that nation, he doth us to understand the same to pertain to all in particular, that is, to every one of that province, and the Greek to all in general, in respect of other nations there, so as not of necessity it be understanded of every one.*

THE BISHOP OF SARISBURY.

M. Harding overmuch paineth himself to prove that thing that no wise man will deny him. For how can it seem likely that the whole east, which is in a manner the one half part of the world, containing so many and so sundry nations, should speak all one tongue; seeing we ourselves, in this one little kingdom of England, have the use of five tongues, and not one of them understanding another? I marvel that M. Harding alleged not the fables of Herodotus, that *bek*, in the Phrygians' tongue, signifieth bread; *kiki*, in the Egyptians' tongue, an ointment; *achmach*, one of the guard; or *alila*, or *urotal*, in the Arabic tongue, and such-like[5]. For these might have stand him instead of good proofs, that all the nations of the whole east part of the world spake not Greek. Herod.

And although we agree with him in the principal, that in the east part were used sundry languages, and likewise that the Greek tongue was commonly used among the learned; yet his distinction of all in general, and all in particular, that he hath here devised to shift off St Hierome, seemeth very homely and home-made. For how can it be a general, unless it include every particular? By M. Harding's construction, we must take all for some, or all not for the tenth part of all; and by this rhetoric, less than half is as much as all; and so all is not all. Thus M. Harding's general is a mere particular; and to conclude, his general is no general. So weakly and so loosely his answer standeth.

As touching the Galathians, of whom St Hierome saith, that beside their own natural tongue they had also the use of the Greek, because, as Apollodorus saith, "They of all others arrived last into that country[6]," it is likely they kept their own barbarous speech longer than others. But like as, whether they of[7] all sorts spake Greek or no, as M. Harding saith, of necessity it cannot be proved, so indeed it forceth nothing: for he cannot prove thereby, that they that understood not the Greek had their service in the Greek. Yet is this the major, and the ground of the whole, which M. Harding so closely dissembleth and passeth by. Strabo, Geogr. Lib. xiv.

M. HARDING. THE TENTH DIVISION.

Tract. in Joan. 117. *St Augustine, speaking of the title written by Pilate on the cross, saith thus: "It was in Hebrew, Greek, and Latin,* Rex Judæorum. *For these three tongues were there in pre-eminence before all other";* Hebræa, propter Judæos, in Dei lege gloriantes; Græca, propter gentium sapientes; Latina, propter Romanos multis ac pene omnibus jam tunc gentibus imperantes[8]: "*The Hebrew for the Jews, that gloried in the law of God; the Greek for the wise men of the gentiles; the Latin for the Romans, bearing rule at that time over many, and almost over all nations." Now where he saith here, that the Greek tongue was in pre-eminence* propter gentium sapientes, "*for the wise men of the gentiles," he discusseth fully the doubt that might seem to rise of St Hierome's saying, and sheweth that the Greek tongue was common, not to all the vulgar people of the whole orient, but to the wise men only, and that for the attaining of learning. And for this it is to be noted, that the scripture reporteth the vulgar tongue of the Lycaonians to have been uttered in the hearing[9] of Paul and Barnabas; not by the magistrates, or other the chief, but by the vulgar people.* Turbæ levaverunt vocem suam Lycaonice dicentes, &c. Act. xiv[10]. *And so St Hierome is to be understanded to speak in that place, not of all men of the nations of the east, but rather of a great number, and of*

[5 Herod. Lib. II. capp. ii. xxx. xciv. Lib. III. cap. viii.]

[6 Strabon. Geograph. Lut. Par. 1620. Lib. XIV. p. 678.]

[7 They all of, 1565.]

[8 August. Op. Par. 1679-1700. In Johan. Evang. cap. xix. Tractat. cxvii. 4. Tom. III. Pars II. col. 98.]

[9 In hearing, H. A. 1564.]

[10 Act. 2, H. A. 1564.]

some persons of all nations. For else, if all the east had spoken Greek, the soldiers that buried Gordianus the younger emperor apud Circeium Castrum, "*at Circey Castle*[1]," *near to the land of Persia, would not have written his title of honour upon his sepulchre in Greek and Latin, in the Persians', Jews', and Egyptians'*[2] *tongues,* ut ab omnibus legeretur[3], "*that it might be read of all,*" *as Julius Capitolinus writeth: which is an argument that all the east spake not, nor*[4] *understood not the Greek tongue. As likewise that Epiphanius writeth, where he saith thus: "Most of the Persians, after the Persical letters, use also the Syrians' letters; as with us many nations use the Greek letters, yea, whereas in every nation in manner they have letters of their own. And others some much esteem the profound*[5] *tongue of the Syrians, and the tongue that is about Palmyra, both the tongue itself, and also the letters of the same. Books also have been written of Manes in the Syrians' tongue*[6]." *Again, if all the east had spoken Greek, sundry the holy fathers would not have been so envious to the commonweal of the church as to hide their singular works from the reading of all, which they wrote in barbarous and vulgar tongues, to the commodity only of their brethren that understood the same: Antonius, that wrote seven notable epistles to divers monasteries of apostolic sense and speech, as St Hierome witnesseth, in the Egyptian tongue*[7]. *Likewise holy Ephrem of Edessa, Bardesanes of Mesopotamia, who wrote very excellent works in the Syriacal tongue. Even so did Isaac of Antioch, and Samuel of Edessa, priests, write many goodly works against the enemies of the church in the same tongue, as Gennadius recordeth*[8]. *But what shall we speak of all the east? Neither all the less*[9] *Asia, and the countries there adjoining, spake not Greek one generation before the coming of Christ. For if all had spoken Greek, Mithridates, that renowned king of Pontus, had not needed to have learned two and twenty languages of so many nations he was king over, to make answer to suitors, to appoint them orders and laws, and in open audience to speak to them in so many languages without an interpreter, as Pliny writeth*[10]. *Here, if these twenty-two nations of twenty-two sundry tongues had also beside their own language spoken Greek, and understanded the same, Pliny would not have uttered that word,* sine interprete, "*without an interpreter:*" *and likewise that king had taken vain labour in learning those tongues, where one might have served his turn.*

In Gordianis.

Lib. ii. Hæres. 66.

Lib. de Ecclesiast. Script.

Natural. Hist. Lib. vii. cap. xxiv.

Near to this king's dominion, in the shore of the sea Euxinus, in the land of Colchis, there stood a city named Dioscurias, so much haunted of strangers, that, as Pliny writeth by record of Timosthenes, it was resorted unto of three hundred nations of distinct languages; and that the Romans, for the better expedition of their affairs there, had at length lying in the same one hundred and thirty interpreters[11]. *Now, if all the orient had spoken Greek, as St Hierome's words seem to import, the Romans should not have needed to have maintained there, to their great charges, so great a number of interpreters, to be their agents there. But for proof that all the orient spake not Greek, what need we allege profane writers? The known place of the Acts maketh mention of sundry nations there that had distinct languages, the Parthians, Medians, and Elamites, &c. Act. ii.*

Lib. vi. Natural. Hist. cap. v.

To conclude, they that, to maintain their strange opinion of the universal understanding of the service used of old time in the east church, say and affirm that all

---

[1 Circesium, now Kerkesia, the Carchemish of scripture.]

[2 The Egyptians, 1565, and H. A. 1564.]

[3 Jul. Capitol. in Hist. August. Script. Lat. Min. Hanov. 1611. Gord. III. p. 378.]

[4 Ne, 1565, 1609, and H. A. 1564.]

[5 Most profound, H. A. 1564.]

[6 Χρῶνται γὰρ οἱ πλεῖστοι τῶν Περσῶν μετὰ Περσικὰ στοιχεῖα καὶ τῷ Σύρῳ γράμματι, ὥσπερ παρ' ἡμῖν πολλὰ ἔθνη τοῖς Ἑλληνικοῖς κέχρηνται· καί τοί γε ὄντων σχεδὸν κατὰ ἔθνος ἰδίων γραμμάτων. ἄλλοι δὲ δῆθεν τὴν βαθυτάτην τῶν Σύρων διάλεκτον σεμνύνονται, τήν τε κατὰ τὴν Παλμύραν διάλεκτον, αὐτήν τε καὶ τὰ αὐτῶν στοιχεῖα, κ.τ.λ.—Epiph. Op. Par. 1622. Adv. Hær. Lib. II. Hær. lxvi. 13. Tom. I. p. 629.]

[7 ... misit Ægyptiace ad diversa monasteria apostolici sensus sermonisque epistolas septem.—Hieron. Op. Par. 1693—1706. Catal. Script. Eccles. 88. Tom. IV. Pars II. col. 123. Ibid. 33, 115. cols. 111, 2, 26.]

[8 Gennad. Illustr. Vir. Catal. 68, 84, in Hieron. Op. Tom. V. cols. 41, 4.]

[9 Lesser, H. A. 1564.]

[10 C. Plin. Secund. Nat. Hist. Par. 1685. Tom. II. p. 42.]

[11 Id. Lib. VI. cap. v. Tom. I. p. 657.]

the orient spake Greek, seem much to diminish the majesty, utility, and necessity of the miraculous gift of tongues, which the Holy Ghost gave in the primitive church for the better furtherance of the gospel. For, if all in those parties had spoken Greek, the gift of tongues had been in that respect needless. Hitherto of the Greek, (72) *and of the service in that language.* The seventy-second untruth. For he hath not hitherto spoken one word of the service.

THE BISHOP OF SARISBURY.

This labour may well be called *vanitas vanitatum*. For it is a great token of idleness to be so earnest and so copious in proving that thing that no man denieth. And yet he forceth the matter so, as if all the right of his cause lay upon it. He might as well have proved that the Indians, Arabians, Ethiopians, Tartarians, understood no Greek. It is a lewd kind of logic so stoutly to prove that thing that needeth no proof, and to leave the thing that should be proved. The title of the cross written in three sundry languages, as it testifieth that the nations of the east part of the world spake not all one tongue, which thing is not of any wise man denied, so it proveth plainly against M. Harding, that the death of Christ should be published in all tongues. For, as Albertus[12] and Lyra, M. Harding's own doctors, have witnessed, writing upon the same, therefore was the title by God's special provision drawn in the three principal languages, *ut omnes qui de diversis orbis partibus ... venerant, possent illum legere*[13]: "that all they, that were then come to Hierusalem out of sundry parts of the world, might be able to read it." St Hierome likewise saith, the same title was so written *in testimonium universarum gentium*[14]; "for the witness of all nations." For it was the will of God that every tongue should confess that Christ is the Lord in the glory of the Father. Albert. et Lyr. in xix. cap. Johan. Hieron. in Esai. Lib. vii. cap. xx.

Wherein M. Harding much abridgeth the glory of the cross of Christ, that would the title thereof to pertain only to the wise and learned of the Greeks. For Albertus and Lyra say: "It was so written that all might read it." And as St Hierome saith: "For witness of all nations." Neither can we find that there was any great number of philosophers present at Christ's death, to read that title. As for St Augustine, by these words, *sapientes Græcorum*[15], he understandeth all the Greeks. For, as all the Jews generally gloried of the law, even so all the Greeks generally gloried in their wisdom. And St Paul saith generally of them both: *Judæi signum quærunt, Græci sapientiam:* "The Jews call for signs and miracles; and the Greeks call for knowledge." And therefore one of the philosophers said: In old times there were seven wise men among the Greeks, but now there are not so many fools; for that they all gloried in their wisdom. 1 Cor. i.

The people of Lycaonia spake unto Paul and Barnabas, *Lycaonice; ergo,* saith M. Harding, "they spake no Greek." But what if St Luke had said, they spake *Ionice, Æolice,* or *Dorice,* which tongues were adjoining fast upon Lycaonia; would he therefore conclude, they spake no Greek? Verily, if a man by way of contention would say, the Lycaonical tongue was a corruption or difference of the Greek tongue, and not a several tongue of itself, M. Harding should have much ado to prove the contrary. Doubtless, they worshipped Jupiter and Mercury, that were the gods of the Greeks, and had the Greek sacrifice, as it manifestly appeareth by the words of St Luke; and it may be credibly gathered that Paul and Barnabas spake to them in Greek. Howbeit, whether it were so or otherwise, saving that M. Harding maketh the matter so certain, it importeth nothing. Acts xiv.

But this one thing, good reader, I give thee further to consider. These Lycaonians, as M. Harding confesseth, and as plainly appeareth by St Luke, being yet infidels, made their prayers unto their idols, Jupiter and Mercury, in their own tongue. And may it any wise seem likely, that the same, being afterward become Christians, made their prayers unto Almighty God, and to Christ his Acts xiv.

[[12] Et hoc etiam facit et pertinet ad universalem mundo faciendam tituli manifestationem.—Albert. Magn. Postill. super Joan. Evang. Hagen. 1504. cap. xix. fol. 153.]

[[13] Bibl. cum Gloss. Ord. et Expos. N. de Lyra, Basil. 1502. Johan. cap. xix. Pars V. fol. 239; where *partibus orbis*.]

[[14] Hieron. Op. Comm. Lib. VII. in Isai. Proph. cap. xix. Tom. III. col. 187.]

[[15] August. Op. Par. 1679-1700. In Johan. Evang. cap. xix. Tractat. cxvii. 4. Tom. III. Pars II. col. 798. See before, page 275.]

Son, in a strange tongue? If it behove idolators to understand their own prayers, much more it behoveth the people of God to do the like. Certainly, if the same Lycaonians were now alive, they would reprove M. Harding's error in their own tongue.

The blazing of the young emperor Gordian's grave with five sundry languages, like as it was needless in this place, as all the rest, the matter being confessed, even so it weigheth very much against M. Harding's side. For if the barbarous soldiers, of their duty and allegiance towards their prince, thought his death worthy to be published in so many tongues; what may then be thought of them that cannot suffer the death of Christ to be published in any one tongue? And if they so furnished a mortal man's memory, as Capitolinus saith, *ut ab omnibus legeretur*[1], "that it might be read of all men;" why then do these men so hide and bury the immortal memory of the glory of Christ, that, saving themselves, they would have it to be read and seen of no man?

The allegation of the Persians' and Syrians' letters; of the tongue used about Palmyra; of epistles written in the Egyptians' tongue by Antonius, in the Syrian tongue by Bardesanes, Ephrem, Isaac, and Samuel; of Mithridates the king of Pontus, that was able to answer two and twenty nations, that were his subjects, without an interpreter; of the resort of three hundred sundry nations unto the city called Dioscurias in Colchis; and once again, of the miracle of tongues and diversity of languages in the Acts of the Apostles, hath some shew and ostentation of learning, and serveth well either to fill up room, or else to reprove and control St Hierome, for that he saith, "All the east part of the world speaketh Greek;" for against us, that neither write so nor speak so, it maketh nothing.

We know that by mean of the great empire that the Greeks had gotten over many countries and kingdoms in all the east, and partly also for that the barbarous nations whom they had subdued had great pleasure in their philosophy and other skilful knowledge, the Greek tongue was learned of many, and carried about into all places of that part of the world; and that Cicero therefore saith: *Græca leguntur in omnibus fere gentibus*[2]; "The Greek tongue is read in manner amongst all nations." And St Augustine likewise: *Quos Paulus dixit Græcos, eos etiam gentium nomine significavit; eo quod hæc lingua maxime excellit in gentibus*[3]: "Whom Paul called Greeks, them also he uttered by the name of the gentiles; for that the same tongue chiefly excelleth among the gentiles." And yet we doubt not but there were other natural tongues and speeches too, besides the Greek; as the Egyptian, the Syrian, the Arabic, the Persian, the Bactrian, the Indian, the Armenian, the Scythian, and many others. And if I list here to dally for pleasure, and vainly to carry away the reader from the purpose, as M. Harding doth, I could say that Themistocles, a gentleman of Athens, before he presented himself unto the great king of Persia, first learned to speak the Persians' tongue; that the Nestorian heretics translated their books into the Persian, Armenian, and Syrian tongue[4]; that St Augustine saith that St Hierome understood the Hebrew, the Greek, the Chaldee, the Latin, the Persian, the Arabic, and the Median tongue[5]; and that St Chrysostom saith: "So many tongues and voices there be of the Scythians, of the Thracians, of the Romans, of the Persians, of the Moors, of the Indians, of the Egyptians, and of a thousand nations beside[6];" with many other authorities to like purpose, to avouch the thing that M. Harding so earnestly proveth, and no man denieth, that the nations of the east part of the world had several tongues, and spake not all one only tongue.

Cic. pro Archia.

Plut. in Them.

Liberat. cap. x.

August. ad Cyrill. cit. a Petro Crinito, Lib. vi. cap. vi.

Chrysost. in 1 Cor. xiv. Hom. 35.

[[1] See before, page 276, note 3.]

[[2] Cic. Pro Arch. Poet. 5.]

[[3] The following passage, if not that intended, asserts the same fact:...Græci, quorum lingua in gentibus præeminet.—August. Op. Par. 1679-1700. De Civ. Dei, Lib. VIII. cap. x. 2. Tom. VII. col. 199.]

[[4] ... in tantum studii gesserunt, ut ipsa eorum volumina malitiose in Syrorum linguam, et Armeniorum, atque Persarum transferrent.—Liberat. Brev. cap. x. in Crabb. Concil. Col. Agrip. 1551. Tom. II. p. 105.]

[[5] Quod ipse etiam Augustinus in libro ad Cyrillum de Hieronymo testatur: qui eum scribit non Hebraicam modo, Græcamque et Chaldaicam, sed Latinam, Persicam, Arabicam, ac Medam percepisse: etsi plerique affirmant, hunc ipsum librum minime Augustino adscribendum.—Pet. Crinit. De Honest. Discipl. Lugd. 1585. Lib. VI. cap. vi. p. 209. See also Aug. Op. Ad Cyril. Epist. xviii. Tom. II. Ap. col. 18.]

[[6] Τουτέστι, τοσαῦται γλῶσσαι, τοσαῦται φωναὶ, Σκυθῶν, Θρᾳκῶν, Ῥωμαίων, Περσῶν, Μαύρων, Ἰνδῶν, Αἰγυπτίων, ἑτέρων μυρίων ἐθνῶν.—Chrysost. Op. Par. 1718-38. In Epist. I. ad Cor. Hom. XXXV. Tom. X. p. 324.]

Let M. Harding therefore consider better who they be that, as he saith, "deny the majesty, utility, and necessity of the gift of tongues." For we confess that the knowledge thereof is necessary, not only for the furtherance, but also for the continuance of the gospel; neither do we doubt but, by what tongues the heathens were converted unto God, by the same tongues they made their petitions unto God; the contrary whereof M. Harding by his silence confesseth he cannot prove. Which notwithstanding, he passeth over the matter by these words: "Hitherto of the Greek, and of the service in that language:" and so endeth this piece of his treaty with a pretty untruth, having indeed proved somewhat of the tongue; but of the service, whereupon his whole cause resteth, not one word at all.

Which thing that it may the better appear, let us lay together the parts and members of his argument. His major is this: "All Asia the less had the service in the Greek tongue;" the minor: "But many countries of the said Asia understood not the Greek tongue;" the conclusion; "*ergo*, many countries had their service in an unknown tongue." The minor he warranteth but by guess only, and none otherwise; although both St Luke in the nineteenth of the Acts, and also the very story of the times following, be to the contrary. The major he toucheth not at all. Therefore his *syllogismus* halteth down right of one side, and concludeth only upon the minor. And thus M. Harding shoreth up his strange doctrine with a strange major, a strange minor, and a strange conclusion. M. Harding's syllogismus.

M. HARDING. THE ELEVENTH DIVISION.

Now concerning the Latin tongue, which is the learned tongue of the west. That the Latin church, or the west church (for so it is called), had the service in Latin, I grant. The chief regions and countries of the Latin church, within the foresaid six hundred years, were these: Italy, Afric, Illyric, both Pannonies (now called Hungary), and Austria, Gallia (now France), and Spain. The country[7] of Germany, Pole, and Swethen, and those north parts, received the faith long sithence. The countries of Britain here had received the faith in most places, but were driven from the open profession of it again by the cruel persecution of Diocletian the emperor; at which persecution St Alban with many others suffered martyrdom.

After that these countries had been instructed in the faith, as things grew to perfection, they had their service accordingly; no doubt such as was used in the churches, from whence their first apostles and preachers were sent. And because (73) the first preachers of the faith came to these west parts[9] from Rome, directed some from St Peter, some from Clement, some others afterward from other bishops of that see apostolic; they planted and set up, in the countries by them converted, the service of the church of Rome, or some other very like, and that (74) in the Latin tongue only, for ought that can be shewed to the contrary. Wherein I refer me only to the first six hundred years. Now that such service was understanded of those peoples, that spake and understood Latin, no man denieth. For to some nations that was a native and a mother tongue, as the Greek was to the Grecians.

The seventy-third untruth. For[8] the first preaching of the faith in these west countries came not first from Rome.

The seventy-fourth untruth. For the first preachers themselves spake no Latin.

THE BISHOP OF SARISBURY.

I find no fault with M. Harding's cosmography; but I trow, cosmography in this case maketh small proof. His proof for the Latin service hangeth upon two points. The first is, that all the faith of the west part of the world came only from the bishops of Rome. The second is, that the planters of the same faith ministered the common service every where in the Latin tongue. He knoweth well that either of these points is untrue, and will never be proved. And somewhat to touch hereof by the way, St Paul saith "that he himself had filled all places with the gospel of Christ, even as far as Illyricum;" and that not from Rome, but from Hierusalem; and promiseth that he would pass by Rome into Spain, as, by report of some, afterward he did: and Theodoretus saith that

The faith came not first from Rome.

M. Harding wittingly and willingly avoucheth untruth. Rom. xv.

Theodor. de Cur. Græc. Affect.

[[7] Countries, 1565, and H. A. 1564.] [[8] 1565 omits *for*.] [[9] Parties, 1565, and H. A. 1564.]

Paul came into this island, now called England, and here planted the gospel[1]. The like is commonly surmised, by the writers of the British chronicles, of Joseph of Arimathæa. And, although conjectures in such antiquities be often uncertain and dark, yet it may seem very likely that the religion of Christ came first into this island, not from Rome, but from the Greeks; both for that, in the keeping of Easter-day, we followed the church of Græcia, and not the church of Rome; and also for that, when Augustine was sent in hither by Gregory, we would in no wise acknowledge or receive the bishop of Rome[2]. As for Lazarus, Nathaniel, Saturninus, that preached first in France, I have said before. Aventinus saith Lucius, St Paul's companion, went into Germany[3]; and St Paul saith, Titus went into Dalmatia.

Beda in Hist. Angl. Lib. ii. Galfrid. Lib. viii. cap. iv. Aven. in Hist. Boior. 2 Tim. iv.

It is known that the church of Rome, for certain other causes, and namely for the great state and renown of that city, even from the beginning was notable above all others, and was careful in enlarging the glory of Christ, and yielded many martyrs unto God. Yet may we not think that all things therefore came from Rome. For Tertullian calleth Hierusalem *matrem et fontem religionis*[4], "the mother and the spring of religion." And St Augustine saith: *Fides orta est a Græcis*[5]; "The faith sprang first from the Greeks."

Tertul. cont. Marc. Lib. ii. August. Epist. 178.

Now that he further saith, the planters of the faith in all these west countries made the common prayers every where in the Latin tongue; besides that it is manifestly false, as, God willing, hereafter shall well appear, it hath not, no not so much as any likelihood or shew of truth.

For, good reader, consider this reason: "The planters of the faith came from Rome; *ergo*, they kept every where the order of Rome." If this argument would hold, then would I likewise reason thus: The church of Rome was first planted by them that came from Græcia, or from Hierusalem; *ergo*, Rome keepeth the order of Græcia, or of Hierusalem. But M. Harding, presuming this of himself, without other proof, that the churches of these countries followed the order of the church of Rome, concludeth further; "*ergo*, they had their service in Latin, as had the church of Rome." Every child seeth that this is a *fallax*, or a deceitful argument, called, *A secundum quid ad simpliciter*. He might as well have said thus: They followed the order of the church of Rome; *ergo*, they had their exhortations and sermons in Latin; for so had the church of Rome. But is M. Harding so unadvised, or so negligent in his matters, that he seeth not how aptly his own argument reboundeth upon himself? Verily, of this ground we may in good form and truly reason thus: These churches of the west followed the order of the church of Rome: (this he himself hath taken as an undoubted truth.)

M. Harding's reason against himself.

But the church of Rome had the service in the natural known tongue; (which thing he himself also granteth.)

Ergo, these churches of the west had the service in the natural known tongue.

This argument is sound and perfect[6], and without *fallax*.

Again, he might easily have seen that of his own position and principle another necessary argument might soon grow against him in this wise:

All churches, that received their faith from Rome, kept the orders of the church of Rome:

But the church of England followed not the orders of the church of Rome;

[1 ... ταῖς [ὁ Παῦλος] ἐν τῷ πελάγει διακειμέναις νήσοις τὴν ὠφέλειαν προσήνεγκε.—Theodor. Op. Lut. Par. 1642-84. In Psalm. cxvi. Tom. I. col. 871. See also Id. Græc. Affect. Cur. Serm. ix. Tom. IV. p. 610. There however Britain is merely mentioned generally among the nations that had received the gospel.]

[2 Bæd. Hist. Eccles. Cant. 1722. Lib. II. cap. ii. pp. 79, 80.

Galfrid. Mon. Brit. Reg. Gest. Par. 1517. Lib. VIII. cap. iv. foll. 93, 4.]

[3 Ejus [Pauli] commilito et cognatus Lucius Cyrenensis in Vindelicia, et Rhætiis, provinciisque Histro conterminis, christianæ pietatis sementem fecit. —Avent. Annal. Boior. Basil. 1580. Lib. II. p. 86.]

[4 Tribui Judæ Christus fuit: ut scirent Hierosolymis esse ... matricem religionis, et fontem, non puteum, salutis.—Tertull. Op. Lut. 1641. Adv. Marcion. Lib. IV. 35. p. 562.]

[5 ... Græcis ubi fides orta est.—August. Op. Par. 1679-1700. Alterc. cum Pascent. seu Epist. xx. 6. Tom. II. Append. col. 41. This disputation is judged spurious by the Benedictine editors, who are disposed to ascribe it to Vigilius of Thapsus.]

[6 Perfite, 1565.]

as it is most manifest by the keeping of the Easter-day, and by refusing of the bishop there, as it is already proved; *ergo*, the church of England received not her faith from the church of Rome. If M. Harding had better advised himself, he would not have built upon these grounds.

M. HARDING. THE TWELFTH DIVISION.

[*M. Jewel's allegations soluted.* H. A. 1564.]

M. Jewel, alleging for the having of the prayers and service in a vulgar tongue (as for England in the English, for Ireland in the Irish, for Dutchland in the Dutch tongue, &c.) authorities and examples of the churches where, in the time of the primitive church, the Greek and Latin tongue was the usual and common tongue of the people, bringeth nothing for proof of that which lieth in controversy. "Arnobius," saith he, "called the Latin tongue sermonem Italum[7]*: St Ambrose in Milan, St Augustine in Afric, St Gregory in Rome preached in Latin; and the people understood them[8]." What then? No man denieth you this. "St Basil also speaketh of a sound, which the men, women, and children made in their prayers to God, like the sound of a wave striking the sea-banks[9]." What can you conclude of this necessarily, M. Jewel? All this may be understanded of the sounding that one word, Amen, answered at the prayers' end; which is done now by the quire, and may be done by the people also in the lower part of the church. For St Hierome leadeth us so to think; who, commending the devotion of the people of Rome, saith in like manner:* Ubi sic ad similitudinem cœlestis tonitrui Amen reboat, et vacua idolorum templa quatiuntur[10]? *Where else are the churches and the sepulchres of martyrs with so fervent devotion and with so great company resorted unto (which words go before)? where doth Amen give so loud a sound like the thunder-clap out of the air, so as the temples, emptied of idols, shake with it, as at Rome?*

Hexameron, Hom. 4.

In 2 Proœmio Comment. ad Galatas.

"The people speaketh with the priest at the mystical prayers[11]," saith Chrysostom, alleged by M. Jewel. What then? So was it long before, even in the apostles' time, as we read in Clement[12], and likewise in St Cyprian[13], in Cyrillus Hierosolymitanus[14], and many other[15]. So is it now. For he shall find in the old fathers, that to Per omnia secula seculorum, *(which Chrysostom speaketh of,) to* Dominus vobiscum, *(so light as they make of it,) to* Sursum corda, *and to* Gratias agamus Domino Deo nostro, *the people answered* (75) *as now also they answer,* Amen, Et cum spiritu tuo, Habemus ad Dominum, Dignum et justum est.

Constitut. Apostolicarum, Lib. viii. cap. xvi.
In Orationibus Mystagogicis.

The seventy-fifth untruth. For[16] it is not so now. M. Harding knoweth, the people now answereth not the priest.

THE BISHOP OF SARISBURY.

Here M. Harding taketh in hand to answer the authorities by me alleged, and that with this special note of remembrance in the margin: "M. Jewel's allegation solved[17]." It appeareth, his solutions be very short. For whatsoever authority be alleged, it is sufficient for him to say, "What then?" For whereas I said, the common service and ministration in the churches of Rome and Milan, and other places within Italy, was pronounced unto the people in Latin, for that then the Latin tongue was the common natural speech of that country, and that therefore Arnobius calleth the same Latin tongue *sermonem Italum;* and further said that, long after that time, St Ambrose in Milan, St Augustine in Africa, and St Gregory in Rome preached unto the vulgar people in Latin, and in the same tongue ministered the common prayers; all this is soon answered; for M. Harding saith, "What then?"

[7 Arnob. Op. Par. 1580. Adv. Gent. Lib. IV. p. 176.]

[8 See before, page 56.]

[9 Basil. Op. Par. 1721-30. In Hexaem. Hom. iv. Tom. I. p. 39.]

[10 Hieron. Op. Par. 1693-1706. Comm. Lib. II. in Epist. ad Gal. Præf. Tom. IV. Pars I. cols. 255, 6.]

[11 Chrysost. Op. Par. 1718-38. In Epist. II. ad Cor. Hom. xviii. Tom. X. p. 568.]

[12 Const. Apost. in Concil. Stud. Labb. et Cossart. Lut. Par. 1671-2. Lib. VIII. cap. xii. Tom. I. col. 483.]

[13 Cypr. Op. Oxon. 1682. De Orat. Domin. p. 152.]

[14 Cyril. Hieros. Op. Par. 1720. Catech. Myst. v. 4, 5. pp. 326, 7.]

[15 Others, 1565, and H. A. 1564.]

[16 1565 omits *for*.] [17 Soluted, 1565, 1609.]

Basil. Hex. 4. I alleged the saying of St Basil, that "the sound of men, women, and children, praying in the church together, seemed like the sound of the waves beating against the sea-banks[1];" the saying of St Hierome, "that the noise of the people, sounding out Amen together, was like the sound of a thunder[2];" likewise the saying of Chrysostom: *Communes preces et a populo et a sacerdote fiunt, et omnes unam dicunt orationem...Bene precatur sacerdos populo, et bene precatur populus sacerdoti, &c.*[3]: "Common petitions be made together, both of the people and of the priest: all together say one prayer. The priest wisheth well unto the people, and the people unto the priest." But, "What then?" saith M. Harding. Why, "What then?" Thinketh M. Harding that the authority of Arnobius, St Ambrose, St Augustine, St Basil, St Hierome, St Chrysostom, and other holy fathers is so light, that he is able to blow them all away with these two vain syllables, "What then?" He will say: "I grant you the prayers were used in the Greek and Latin tongue; but ye have not proved the same of any other tongue that was barbarous." I have already proved the same of the Syrian tongue; which is neither Greek nor Latin, and therefore, by M. Harding's judgment, mere barbarous. Hereafter, God willing, I shall shew the like, largely and at full, of other tongues. In the mean season, it may stand M. Harding in good stead, if it shall please him to shew these privileges granted unto the Greek and Latin tongue, and how they be specially sanctified above others, that in them only we may make our common petitions unto God, and in other tongues we may not make them. Touching the place of St Basil, and the other of St Chrysostom, M. Harding answereth so as though he had no great regard what he say. For he avoucheth that thing for true, that the simplest of all the people knoweth to be apparent false, that is, "that the people now answereth the priest in the time of the holy mysteries, as they did in Chrysostom's time." "The people," saith he, "answered then, as now also they answer." He taketh no shame to say, "The people answered[4] the priest;" and yet knoweth that the people answereth not the priest. Thus, by this resolution, he answereth that answereth nothing. He answereth that knoweth not, neither what is demanded, nor what to answer. To be short, he answereth that holdeth his peace; and so, answering and not answering, in M. Harding's judgment, is all one thing. But St Chrysostom saith: *Et cum spiritu tuo, nihil aliud est, quam ea, quæ sunt eucharistiæ, communia sunt omnia. Neque enim ille solus gratias agit, sed populus omnis*[3]: "The Lord be with thy spirit" (which words the whole people answereth unto the priest), "is nothing else to say, but the things that pertain to thanksgiving are all common: for it is not the priest only that giveth thanks, but also all the people." Likewise St Ambrose: *Imperitus nescit finem orationis, et non respondet Amen, id est, Verum sit, ut firmetur benedictio. Per hoc enim impletur confirmatio precis, cum respondetur Amen, et omnia dicta rei testimonio in audientium animis confirmantur*[5]: "The ignorant knoweth not the end of the prayer, and answereth not Amen, that is to say, So be it, that the blessing may be confirmed. For thereby the confirmation of the prayer is fulfilled, when Amen is answered, and all the words that be spoken, by the testimony of the thing itself, are confirmed in the minds of the hearers." Thus in Chrysostom's time the whole people and the priest in their common service talked and prayed together.

Hieron. in secundo Prœmio ad Galat.

Chrysost. ii. Cor. Hom. 18.

The privilege of the Greek and Latin tongue.

M. Harding avoucheth open untruth.

Chrysost. in ii. ad Cor. Hom. 18.

Ambros. in i. Cor. xiv.

M. HARDING. THE THIRTEENTH DIVISION.

As for the place he allegeth out of St Augustine upon the psalms, it maketh nothing for his purpose. St Augustine's words be these, otherwise than he reporteth them: Quid hoc sit, intelligere debemus, ut humana ratione, non quasi avium voce, cantemus. Nam et merulæ, et psittaci, et corvi, et picæ, et hujuscemodi volucres, sæpe ab hominibus docentur sonare, quod

In Psalm. xviii. in Expositione secunda.

[1 See before, page 281, note 9.]

[2 See before, page 281, note 10.]

[3 Chrysost. Op. Par. 1718-38. In Epist. II. ad Cor. Hom. xviii. Tom. X. p. 568.]

[4 Answereth, 1565.]

[5 Imperitus enim...nescit finem &c. verum; ut confirmetur benedictio. Per hos enim impletur confirmatio precis, qui respondent, Amen; ut omnia dicta veri testimonio in audientium mentibus confirmentur.—Ambros. Op. Par. 1686-90. Comm. in Epist. I. ad Cor. cap. xiv. v. 16. Tom. II. Append. col. 157.]

nesciunt[6]: *"Having prayed to God," saith St Augustine, "that he make us clean of our privy sins, &c., we ought to understand what this is, that we may sing with man's reason, not with voice, as birds do. For ousels, popinjays, ravens, and pies, and such the like birds ofttimes be taught of men to sound they know not what." These words are to be taken of the understanding of the sense, not of the tongue, which the service is sung in. For the people of Hippo, where he was bishop, understood the Latin tongue meanly. Which sense cannot rightly and safely be attained of the common people, but is better and more wholesomely taught by the preaching of the learned bishops and priests.* A bare gloss. For St Augustine speaketh of praying, and not of preaching.

THE BISHOP OF SARISBURY.

First he saith St Augustine's words be otherwise than I report them. I assure thee, good reader, if this great error had been worth the shewing, it had never been suffered thus to pass in silence.

But to shift off St Augustine's words, here is brought in a gloss plain contrary to the text. "For this comparison," saith M. Harding, "between men and birds, must be taken, not of the words, but of the sense and understanding." And what reason leadeth him thus to say? Verily, birds are utterly void of reason, and neither understand the words they be taught to speak, nor the meaning of the words. And yet must we, only upon this simple warrant, needs believe that St Augustine compareth birds with men in understanding?

St Augustine's meaning is plain, as is the meaning of other godly fathers in this behalf, that the people should know what they pray, and so sing with reason agreeable to a man, and not chatter with voice as birds do. For if they sing or pray they know not what, he saith that, for their sound of voice and want of sense, they may be well compared with ousels or popinjays. This is the very drift of St Augustine's meaning. Birds by skill may be trained to record and sound men's words, although they have no understanding of them; as Plinius[7] writeth of the raven that was taught to say, *Ave Cæsar imperator;* "All hail, emperor Cæsar;" another that had learned to say, *Salve victor Antoni;* "All hail, Antonius the conqueror." And Cælius Rhodiginus writeth, that cardinal Ascanius had a popinjay that could pronounce distinctly all the articles of the creed[8]. With such birds let us compare such men as pray they know not what. "They be taught to sound words, but understand not the meaning of them: neither sing they with reason agreeable to a man." Whether these words agree aptly to my purpose or no, let M. Harding himself be the judge. Certainly he shall have much to do, to rack them to serve for his purpose. Unless perhaps he will reason thus: St Augustine exhorteth men to know what they pray; *ergo,* they may pray in an unknown tongue; or thus: St Augustine willeth men not to sing or chatter like birds; *ergo,* they may pray they know not what. Cæl. Rhod. Lib. iii. cap. xxxii.

And if we receive M. Harding's gloss of "sense and understanding," yet standeth he in case as he did before. For if the people understand not the words, much less can they understand the sense and meaning of the same words. Aristotle saith, hearing is the peculiar sense of learning; and therefore they that hear never can never learn. And Cicero saith: *Sententia constare non potest, si verba semoveris:* "Remove the words; and their meaning cannot stand." Therefore this shift helpeth nothing; unless he think this is a good argument: The people ought to understand the meaning of their prayers; *ergo,* they need not to understand the words. St Augustine's meaning appeareth in the next words that immediately follow: *Scienter...cantare naturæ hominis divina voluntate concessum est*[9]: "To sing with understanding is granted through God's will unto the nature of man." And therefore thus he exhorteth the people: *Carissimi, quod consona voce cantavimus, sereno etiam corde nosse et tenere debemus*[10]: "Dearly beloved, that we have sung Cic. de Orat. August. in Psal. xviii.

[6 August. Op. Par. 1679-1700. In Psalm. xviii. Enarr. II. 1. Tom. IV. col. 81. See before, page 8.]

[7 C. Plin. Secund. Nat. Hist. Par. 1685. Lib. x. cap. lx. Tom. II. p. 436.]

[8 Cæl. Rhodig. Lect. Antiq. 1599. Lib. III. cap. xxxii. col. 134.]

[9 August. Op. In Psalm. xviii. Enarr. II. 1. Tom. IV. col. 81.]

[10 Id. ibid. cols. 81, 2; where we find, *ac videre debemus.*]

Justinian's Constitution.

Basil. in Psal. xxviii.

together with tuneable voice, we must understand and keep with pure heart." But this can we not do, unless we understand what we pray. Therefore St Basil saith: *Lingua cantet; mens autem scrutetur sensum eorum quæ dicuntur*[1]: "Let thy tongue sing; but let thy mind search out the meaning of the things that thou speakest."

M. HARDING. THE FOURTEENTH DIVISION.

De Ecclesiasticis diversis capitulis. Constitutione 123. Greg. Haloandro interprete. Nam in veteri translatione nihil tale habetur.

μετὰ φωνῆς.

[*Justinian's ordinance truly declared.* H. A. 1564.]

The commandment of Justinian the emperor[2], *which M. Jewel allegeth, that bishops and priests should celebrate the holy oblation, or sacrifice, which we call the mass, not closely, but with utterance and sound of voice, that they might be heard of the people, maketh nothing for the service to be had in the English tongue in the church of England, or in any other vulgar tongue in the church of any other nation; but requireth only of the bishops and priests open pronouncing, vocal, not mental; speaking, not*[3] *whispering with the breath only, in the celebration of the holy sacrifice, and other service. Wherein he agreeth with St Augustine, who, in his book* De Magistro, *saith that, "when we pray, there is no need of speaking, unless perhaps we do as priests do, who when they pray (in public assembly) use speaking for cause of signifying their mind, that is, to shew that they pray, not to the intent God, but men may hear, and with a certain consent through putting in mind (by sound of voice) may be lifted up unto God*[4]*." Thus*[5] *much St Augustine there. And this is the right meaning of that constitution.* (76) *And thus he ordained for the Greek church only, and thereto only it is to be referred, for that some thought the sacrifice should be celebrated rather with silence,* (77) *after the manner of the church of Rome, specially at the consecration. And as that constitution pertained to the Greeks, and not to the Latins, so was it not found in the Latin books, until Gregorius Haloander, of Germany, of late years translated the place. And where M. Jewel allegeth this commandment of Justinian against the having of the service in a learned tongue, unknown to the common people; it is to be noted how he demeaneth himself not uprightly, but so as every man may thereby know a scholar of Luther, Calvin, and Peter Martyr. For whereas, by the allegation of that ordinance, he might seem to bring somewhat that maketh for the blessed sacrifice of the church, commonly named the mass, he dissembleth the word of the sacrifice which Justinian putteth expressly,* τὴν θείαν προσκομιδὴν, id est, divinam oblationem, *"the divine or holy oblation," and termeth it otherwise in his replies, by the name of "common prayers*[6]*;" and in his sermon, by the name of "the words of the ministration*[7]*," refusing the word of the church, no less than he refuseth to be a member of the church. Thus through foisting and cogging their die, and other false play, these new perilous teachers deceive many poor souls, and rob them of the sure simplicity of their faith. And where was this commandment given? In Constantinople, the chief city of Greece, where the Greek tongue was commonly known.*

Cap. i.

The seventy-sixth untruth. For it touched the whole empire.

The seventy-seventh untruth. For the priests in Rome prayed aloud, as appeareth by St Hierome, Leo, Ambrose, &c.

THE BISHOP OF SARISBURY.

The gloss that M. Harding hath here imagined, wherewith to defeat this good emperor's whole purpose, may seem somewhat unto the ignorant.

"Justinian," saith he, "speaketh of the open utterance and sound of voice, and agreeth with St Augustine's place, *De Magistro;* therefore it nothing toucheth prayers to be had in the vulgar tongue." Here is a very vulgar conclusion, as, I trust, hereafter it shall appear. Good christian reader, if it shall please thee only to peruse these words of the emperor Justinian, and of St Augustine, by us alleged, I will make thee judge and arbitrour of the whole.

St Augustine saith: "We need no utterance of voice, to pray unto God. For the sacrifice of justice is sanctified in the temple of our mind, and in the secret

---

[[1] Basil. Op. Par. 1721—30. Hom. in Psalm. xxviii. Tom. I. p. 123.]

[[2] Justin. Princ. Novell. Constit. Basil. 1561. Const. cxxxvii. (al. cxxiii.) pp. 409, 10. See before, page 8, note 6.]

[[3] Nor, H. A. 1564.]

[[4] August. Op. Par. 1679—1700. Lib. de Magist. 2. Tom. I. col. 542. See before, page 57.]

[[5] This, 1565, and H. A. 1564.]

[[6] See before, page 57.]

[[7] See before, page 8.]

Justinian's Constitution.

chamber of our heart[8]." As Clemens Alexandrinus also saith: "God looketh not for the voices of our tongues to declare our meaning; for before our creation he knoweth what thoughts would come into our minds[9]." And therefore God saith in the prophet Esay: *Antequam clament, ego exaudiam;* "I will hear them, yea, before they cry."

Clement. Strom. Lib. vii.
Isai. lxv.

Hereupon St Augustine demandeth this question: "Wherefore then doth the priest lift up his voice and pray aloud in the open assembly in the church?" He answereth: "Not that God, but that men may hear him; that the people by the sound of his voice, and understanding his meaning, may be put in mind, and by consent be joined together, and be lifted up to God[10]." This is the very meaning and mind of St Augustine, agreeing fully with these words of St Cyprian: "The priest before prayer prepareth the minds of his brethren, saying thus, 'Lift up your hearts;' to the intent they may be put in mind they ought to think of nothing else but of the Lord. For not the sound of voice, but the mind and understanding, must pray unto the Lord with pure intention[11]."

Cypr. de Orat. Dominica.

"All this," saith M. Harding, "pertaineth to the sense and understanding of the prayer, and nothing to the vulgar tongue." And doth he think the people can understand the prayer without understanding of the tongue? St Augustine, if he were alive, would be ashamed to see such a comment upon his words. He saith further: "The priest lifteth up his voice, not that the people may understand him, but only for a token, to shew that he prayeth." And thus he maketh the minister of God worse than a brasen trumpet, which "if it give no certain sound," as St Paul saith, "no man can prepare himself to war." This is the just judgment of God, that whoso seeketh to blind others shall be given over and become blind himself.

1 Cor. xiv.

And, notwithstanding St Augustine's mind, concerning the speaking of the priest, be plain in itself, yet afterward in the same book he openeth it in this manner more at large: *Constat inter nos, verba esse signa; at signum, nisi aliquid significet, non est signum*[12]: "We are agreed upon this, that the words we speak be tokens. But a token, unless it betoken something, is no token." Now if the priest, after M. Harding's construction, utter his words, which are the tokens of his meaning, in an unknown tongue, and the people understand not what is tokened; according to St Augustine's meaning, he speaketh, and yet saith nothing; and sheweth tokens, and yet tokeneth nothing. Further, St Augustine's words be clear: "The priest in the assembly speaketh aloud, *significandæ mentis causa, ut homines audiant*[13], &c. to the end to declare his mind, that men may hear him, and by the sound of his voice be put in remembrance." But M. Harding saith: "No: the priest speaketh not aloud, to the intent to declare his mind, neither that men may hear him, nor be put in remembrance, but only to give a token that he prayeth." And thus by his gloss he utterly destroyeth the text.

August. de Magistro.

Now let us resolve both St Augustine's and Justinian's words into their causes; which is an infallible way of understanding. The end of them both is, according to the doctrine of St Paul, that the people may say, Amen. Then further: The people must answer Amen unto the prayer; then they must[14] understand the prayer. Yet further: The people must understand the prayer; then must the priest utter the same prayer, both with a loud voice, and also in the people's vulgar tongue. Let us again resolve it forward. The priest, by M. Harding's judgment, may pray openly in a strange tongue; then he needeth not to speak aloud. He speaketh not aloud; then cannot the people understand him.

The resolution of M. Harding's reason.

[8 Ubi putas sacrificium justitiæ sacrificari, nisi in templo mentis et in cubilibus cordis?—August. Op. Lib. de Magist. 2. Tom. I. col. 542.]

[9 Ὅθεν τὰς πολυφώνους γλώσσας οὐκ ἀναμένει ὁ Θεὸς...ἣν [φωνὴν] καὶ πρὸ τῆς δημιουργίας εἰς νόησιν ἥξουσαν ἠπίστατο.—Clement. Alex. Op. Oxon. 1715. Strom. Lib. VII. 7. Tom. II. p. 856.]

[10 See preceding page, note 4.]

[11 Ideo et sacerdos ante orationem præfatione præmissa, parat fratrum mentes dicendo, Sursum corda; ut dum respondet plebs, Habemus ad Dominum, admoneatur nihil aliud se quam Dominum cogitare debere...quando intentione sincera Dominum debeat non vocis sonus, sed animus et sensus orare.—Cypr. Op. Oxon. 1682. De Orat. Domin. p. 152.]

[12 Constat ergo inter nos verba signa esse. Constat. Quid signum, nisi aliquid significet, potest esse signum?—August. Op. Lib. de Magist. 3. Tom. I. col. 542.]

[13 See preceding page, note 4.]

[14 Must they, 1565, 1609.]

Justinian's Constitution.

The people understandeth not the priest; then can they not say, Amen. Thus M. Harding must needs conclude his gloss with the open breach of St Paul's doctrine.

M. Harding uttereth two untruths in one sentence.

M. Harding saith further: "This law took place only in Constantinople, and not in the church of Rome;" and so he coucheth two manifest untruths together in one sentence. But what? will he say, Justinian was not emperor of Rome, or had nothing to do in the church of Rome? Verily, he writeth himself the emperor of Rome, of France, of Almaine, and Germany, &c.; and deposed two bishops of Rome, Silverius and Vigilius[1]: whereof it may appear he had somewhat to do in the church of Rome.

In ii. Tom. Concil. in Vita Vigilii.

De Legatis Præs. Con. Tab. Bon. Poss. Pe. Lib. i. Generaliter.

Touching this constitution the law saith: *Generaliter dictum generaliter est accipiendum*[2]*:* "The thing that is spoken generally must be taken generally." And it is commonly said: *Ubi lex non distinguit, nos distinguere non debemus:* "Where the law maketh no distinction, there ought we to make no distinction." And what reason hath M. Harding, or what witness more than his own, that this only law took no place in the church of Rome? Certainly the rest of the same Novel Constitutions were made not only for Constantinople, or for Rome, but also for the whole empire. And the emperor Justinian in the same title saith thus: "Whatsoever things, touching this matter, were needful for this imperial city of Constantinople, we have comprised in a special law for the same[3]." But what needeth many words? The emperor himself calleth the constitution that concerneth the clergy a law general, by these words: *κοινῷ τε καὶ γενικῷ νόμῳ ... περὶ χειροτονίας*, &c. *διετυπώσαμεν*[4]: "We have enacted by a general and a common law." And in the code, entreating namely of bishops and clerks, he hath these words: *Et hoc non solum in veteri Roma, vel in hac regia civitate, sed et in omni terra, ubicunque Christianorum nomen colitur, obtinere sancimus*[5]*:* "This law we will have to take place, not only in the city of old Rome, or in this imperial city (of Constantinople), but also in all the world, wheresoever the name of Christians is had in honour."

De Eccles. diversis capitulis. *ταῦτα εἰδικῷ περιελάβομεν νόμῳ.* In Auth. Coll. i. Ut definitus sit numer. Cler. In Cod. de Episc. et Cler. Generaliter.

Leo de Jejun. vii. Men. Serm. 6. Ambros. de Sacram. Lib. iv. cap. v. August. in Psal. liv. Hieron. in Præf. Lib. ii. ad Galat.

And how can M. Harding make himself so sure that the church of Rome was never subject to this law? Certainly, both by Leo bishop of Rome[6], and also by St Ambrose, bishop of Milan[7], and other holy fathers, it appeareth otherwise. St Augustine saith of the church of Rome: *Unum psalmum cantamus, unum Amen respondemus*[8]*:* "We sing one psalm, and we answer one Amen." St Hierome saith: "Even in Rome, at the end of the prayer, the people so sounded out Amen, as if it had been a thunder-clap[9]."

Again, if this constitution served only for the Greek church, and only the priests there spake aloud, and the others of the Latin church spake in silence; how then doth M. Harding expound this law of Justinian by the words of St Augustine, who, as he supposeth, did the contrary, and was never subject unto that law? Or how can he make contrarieties agree together? Hath he so soon forgotten himself? Or will he expound speaking by silence, or singing out by whispering?

M. Harding forgetteth himself.

To conclude, Justinian saith, "These constitutions were general;" M. Harding alone saith, "They were not general:" Justinian saith, "They took place in all the world;" M. Harding alone saith, "They took place only in Constantinople." St Ambrose, St Augustine, St Hierome, Leo, and others say, "They were observed in the church of Rome;" M. Harding alone saith, "They were never observed in

---

[1 Ex Lib. Pontif. in Crabb. Concil. Col. Agrip. 1551. Tom. II. pp. 3, &c.]

[2 Generalia generaliter intelligenda sunt.—Corp. Jur. Civil. Amst. 1663. Digest. Lib. XXXVII. Tit. v. 1. Gloss. Tom. I. p. 528.]

[3 Ὅσα μὲν οὖν ἐχρῆν περὶ τοῦ τοιούτου τρόπου, κατὰ τὴν ἁγιωτάτην μεγάλην ἐκκλησίαν τῆς βασιλευούσης ἡμῶν ταύτης πόλεως......τούτῳ τῷ εἰδικῷ περιελάβομεν νόμῳ.—Id. Auth. Coll. I. Tit. vi. Novell. vi. 8. Tom. II. p. 14. This was in older editions assigned to Novell. cxxiii.]

[4 Id. Auth. Coll. I. Tit. iii. Nov. iii. Præfat. Tom. II. p. 6; where ἡγεμονικῷ νόμῳ.]

[5 Id. Cod. Lib. I. Tit. iii. 52. Tom. II. p. 22; where *vetere*.]

[6 Hoc enim ore sumitur, quod fide creditur: et frustra ab illis Amen respondetur, a quibus contra id quod accipitur disputatur.—Leon. Magn. Op. Lut. 1623. Serm. vi. de Jejun. Sept. Mens. col. 248.]

[7 ...non otiose dicis tu: Amen...Dicit tibi sacerdos: Corpus Christi; et tu dicis: Amen.—Ambros. Op. Par. 1686-90. De Sacram. Lib. IV. cap. v. 25. Tom. II. col. 372.]

[8 August. Op. In Psalm. liv. Enarr. 16. Tom. IV. col. 510.]

[9 Hieron. Op. Par. 1693-1706. Comm. Lib. II. in Epist. ad Gal. Præf. Tom. IV. Pars I. cols. 255, 6.]

the church of Rome." If he will thus deceive us in plain things, how may we then trust him in doubtful things? Justinian's Constitution.

Gregorius Haloander, whom M. Harding seemeth to touch with corruption of these laws, was a learned man and a faithful translator; and for his diligence deserved thanks, and therefore needeth no excuse. He addeth nothing more than is to be found in the original. In M. Harding's old translation, even in this same very title, *De ecclesiasticis diversis capitulis,* there wanteth a whole leaf or more at the beginning, that is found extant in the Greek. Gregorius Haloander.

Touching "cogging and foisting," I marvel M. Harding, being so grave a man, would borrow ruffians' terms to scoff withal. As for the sacrifice of Christ upon the cross, which is represented unto us in the holy communion, we believe it with our hearts, and confess it with our mouths. Concerning this word *oblatio,* he knoweth well, I translated not the place, but only touched it: neither had I then any manner occasion to speak of the sacrifice, but only of prayers; which thing also I did without any cogging, or any other sleight, following these very words of Justinian: καὶ τὰς ἄλλας προσευχὰς μετὰ φωνῆς...προσφέρειν: that is to say: "To offer up other prayers also with loud voice." Neither did I avouch any untruth by Justinian; as M. Harding hath here done by Justinian and St Augustine both together. I know the holy ministration is named of the holy fathers sundry ways: "The supper of the Lord;" "the Lord's table;" "the communion;" "the mystery;" "the sacrament;" "the mystical table;" "the thanksgiving;" "the oblation;" and "the sacrifice." Neither is there any of these names, but we use indifferently, as occasion serveth.

Now, forsomuch as M. Harding taketh occasion, for that I passed this place of Justinian so shortly over, only touching it with one word, as the time then forced me; I think it not amiss, for the better contentation of the reader, to lay it out fully, as it lieth. His words be these: "We command all bishops and priests to minister the holy oblation, and the prayer at the holy baptism, not under silence, but with such voice as may be heard of the faithful people; to the intent that thereof the hearts of the hearers may be stirred to more devotion, and honour-giving to God the Lord. For so the holy apostle teacheth, saying in the first epistle to the Corinthians: 'For if thou only bless with the spirit, how shall he that supplieth the room of the ignorant, say Amen (to God) at thy thanksgiving? For he knoweth not what thou sayest. Thou givest thanks well; but the other is not edified.' For these causes therefore it behoveth that the prayer at the holy oblation, and also other prayers, be offered with loud voice of the holy bishops and priests unto our Lord Jesus Christ, with the Father and the Holy Ghost. And let the holy priests understand, that if they neglect any of these things, they shall make answer therefore at the dreadful judgment of the great God and our Saviour Jesus Christ. And yet nevertheless we, understanding the same, will not pass it over, nor leave it unpunished[10]." Auth. Const. cxxiii. 1 Cor. xiv. τῷ Θεῷ.

Here we see, it is lawful for a godly prince to command bishops and priests; to make laws and orders for the church; to redress the abuses of the sacraments; to allege the scriptures; to threaten and punish bishops and priests, if they offend.

Now if these words of Justinian make not for us, and that without foisting or cogging, much less make they for M. Harding, unless he will form his reasons thus:

[[10] Πρὸς τούτοις κελεύομεν πάντας ἐπισκόπους τὲ καὶ πρεσβυτέρους, μὴ κατὰ τὸ σεσιωπημένον, ἀλλὰ μετὰ φωνῆς τῷ πιστοτάτῳ λαῷ ἐξακουομένης τὴν θείαν προσκομιδὴν καὶ τὴν ἐπὶ τῷ ἁγίῳ βαπτίσματι προσευχὴν ποιεῖσθαι, πρὸς τὸ κἀντεῦθεν τὰς τῶν ἀκουόντων ψυχὰς εἰς πλείονα κατάνυξιν καὶ τὴν πρὸς τὸν Δεσπότην Θεὸν διανίστασθαι δοξολογίαν. οὕτως γὰρ ὁ θεῖος ἀπόστολος διδάσκει, λέγων ἐν τῇ πρὸς Κορινθίους πρώτῃ ἐπιστολῇ, Ἐπεὶ ἐὰν εὐλογήσῃς τῷ πνεύματι, ὁ ἀναπληρῶν τὸν τόπον τοῦ ἰδιώτου πῶς ἐρεῖ τὸ ἀμὴν τῷ Θεῷ ἐπὶ τῇ σῇ εὐχαριστίᾳ; ἐπειδὴ τί λέγεις οὐκ οἶδε. σὺ μὲν γὰρ καλῶς εὐχαριστεῖς, ἀλλ' ὁ ἕτερος οὐκ οἰκοδομεῖται...διὰ ταῦτα τοίνυν προσήκει τὴν ἐπὶ τῇ ἁγίᾳ προσκομιδῇ καὶ τὰς ἄλλας προσευχὰς μετὰ φωνῆς παρὰ τῶν ὁσιωτάτων ἐπισκόπων τὲ καὶ πρεσβυτέρων προσφέρεσθαι τῷ Κυριῷ ἡμῶν Ἰησοῦ Χριστῷ, τῷ Θεῷ ἡμῶν, σὺν τῷ Πατρὶ καὶ ἁγίῳ Πνεύματι· γινωσκόντων τῶν ὁσιωτάτων ἱερέων, ὡς εἴ πέρ τι τούτων παρίδοιεν, καὶ τῇ φοβερᾷ κρίσει τοῦ μεγάλου Θεοῦ καὶ σωτῆρος ἡμῶν Ἰησοῦ Χριστοῦ ἀπολογήσονται, καὶ οὐδὲ ἡμεῖς ταῦτα γινώσκοντες ἐφησυχάσομεν, ἢ ἀνεκδίκητα καταλίπωμεν.—Corp. Jur. Civil. Auth. Coll. IX. Tit. XX. Novell. cxxxvii. 6. Tom. II. pp. 196, 7.]

Examples. The priest must speak aloud;
Ergo, he may speak in an unknown tongue.
Or thus: The people must hear the prayer, and answer, Amen;
Ergo, they need not to understand it.

To be short: whereas, to the intent to bring God's truth out of credit, and to make it odious among the ignorant, he saith, we have "refused to be the members of the church of God;" this is only a bitterness of talk, inflamed with malice, whereof it seemeth he wanteth no store, and neither furthereth his cause among the wise, nor hindereth ours. If we be no members of the church, that wish all the people everywhere to understand what they pray, to join their hearts together, and to be lifted up unto God; what then be they that wish all the church to be drowned in ignorance, and the people to know nothing? If St Paul were now alive, he would answer him as sometime he answered Elymas. For certainly he himself knoweth "that he wilfully perverteth the manifest way of the Lord." Acts xiii.

M. HARDING. THE FIFTEENTH DIVISION.

That emperor had dominion over some nations, that understood not the Greek commonly. Yet no man can tell of any constitution that ever he made, for service there to be had in their vulgar and barbarous tongue. So many nations having been converted to the faith, the common people whereof understood neither Greek nor Latin; if the having of the service in their vulgar tongue had been thought necessary to their salvation, the fathers, that sticked not to bestow their blood for their flocks, would not have spared that small pain and travail to put their service in vulgar tongues. If it had been necessary, it had been done: if it had been done, it had been mentioned by one or other.

It appeareth by Arnobius upon the Psalms[1], *by Epiphanius writing against heresies*[2], *and by St Augustine in his books,* De Doctrina Christiana[3], *that by account of the antiquity there were seventy-two tongues in the world. Cicero saith, that they be in number infinite*[4]. *Of them all,* (78) *neither M. Jewel, nor any one of his side, is able to shew that the public service of the church in any nation was ever, for the space of six hundred years after Christ, in any other than in Greek and Latin.*

Psal. civ. Lib. I. Contra Hæres. Hæres. 39. In Tuscul. Quæst.

The seventy-eighth untruth. For it shall appear that we are able to shew manifest examples to the contrary.

THE BISHOP OF SARISBURY.

Arnobius, St Augustine, and Epiphanius say there be threescore and twelve sundry languages in the world: Cicero saith they be infinite. Here must I note by the way, that Cicero's words well alleged do utterly confound M. Harding's doctrine of hearing that thing that the hearers understand not, in such sort as he maintaineth the hearing of mass. For thus he saith: *In his linguis, quas non intelligimus, quæ sunt innumerabiles, surdi profecto sumus*[4]: "In those tongues that we understand not, which be innumerable, certainly we be deaf." By which words M. Harding might perceive that the simple people, hearing him at his mass, is stark deaf, and heareth nothing. "Yet," saith M. Harding, "is not M. Jewel able to shew that ever the public service was in any other tongue than in Greek or Latin." And thus, being required by me to shew any one example, that the people had their common service in a strange tongue; and, as it appeareth, not able to shew any, he altereth cunningly the whole case, and willeth me to shew. Which thing notwithstanding I might justly refuse to do, by the order of any schools, yet I am well content to yield to his request, both for the goodness and pregnancy of the cause, and also specially, good christian reader, for the better contentation of thy mind; not doubting, but of thyself[5] thou wilt be able

Cicero in Tusc. Quæst.

[1 Arnob. Comm. in Psalm. in Mag. Biblioth. Vet. Patr. Col. Agrip. 1618-22. Psalm. civ. Tom. V. Pars III. p. 286.]

[2 Epiph. Op. Par. 1622. Adv. Hær. Lib. I. Hær. xxxix. 7. Tom. I. pp. 288, 9.]

[3 August. Op. Par. 1679-1700. De Doctr. Christ. Lib. II. capp. iv. v. 5, 6. Tom III. Pars I. col. 21. This may be the passage intended; but Augustine speaks here merely of the diversity of languages, without mentioning any number.]

[4 Cic. Tusc. Disp. Lib. V. 40.]

[5 Theeself, 1565.]

to find some distrust and want in M. Harding's side; who, notwithstanding so many words, and so great vaunts, yet is able to shew nothing. Examples.

And to avoid multitude of words, the case being plain, Eckius saith: "The Indians had their service in the Indian tongue[6]." Durandus saith: "The Jews that were christened had their service in the Hebrew tongue[7]." Yet was neither of these tongues either Greek or Latin. Eckius in Locis Communibus. Durand. Lib. iv. cap. i.

Nicolas Lyra[8] and Thomas of Aquine[9] say: "The common service in the primitive church was in the common vulgar tongue." Nicol. Lyra, et Thomas in 1 ad Cor. xiv.

By these few it may appear, it was but a bravery that M. Harding said: "Neither M. Jewel, nor any of[10] that side, is able to shew that the public service was in any other tongue than in Greek or Latin." For it is easy to be shewed, even by the doctors of his own side.

But what if Doctor Harding himself have in plain words confessed the same? Although he have wantonly denied Christ, yet, I trow, he will not deny himself. Consider, good reader, his own words, hereafter following in this self-same article. "But St Paul, say they, requireth that the people give assent, and conform themselves[11] unto the priest, by answering Amen to his prayer made in the congregation." Hereunto M. Harding answereth thus: "Verily, in the primitive church this was necessary, when the faith was a-learning; and therefore the prayers were made then in a common tongue, known to the people." Fol. 69. Divis. 28.

What can there be more plainly spoken? Here M. Harding not only confesseth that the common prayers were pronounced in a common tongue, known to the people, but also further saith the same at that time was necessary, and avoucheth it with his warrant, "verily." Now, quite contrary, as a man that had utterly forgotten himself, he saith the common service was never said but either in the Greek tongue or in the Latin, and therein he offereth stoutly to stand against M. Jewel, and all others of this side; which thing is easy for him to do, seeing he dareth to stand so stoutly against himself. Verily his sayings cannot stand both together. If he be true in the one, in the other he must needs be false. M. Harding contrary to himself.

Yet, good christian reader, for thy better satisfaction, it may please thee to know that in the primitive church the common service was not ministered by one man alone, but by the priest and whole congregation all together, as may appear by the general consent of the old fathers. Clemens Alexandrinus saith: *In orationibus veluti unam vocem habent communem, et unam mentem*[12]: "In the (common) prayers they have all, as it were, one voice and one mind." St Chrysostom saith: "Not only the priest giveth thanks to God, but also all the people. And what dost thou marvel to see the priest and people in the prayers talk together[13]?" And here, to leave St Augustine, St Hierome, St Basil, Nazianzenus, Dionysius Areopagita, with many other like fathers; Isidorus, describing the order of the church in his time, writeth thus: *Oportet, ut quando psallitur, ab omnibus psallatur: [et] cum oratur, [ut] omnibus oretur: cumque lectio legitur, facto silentio, æque audiatur a cunctis*[14]: "When they sing, they must sing all together: when they pray, they must pray all together; and when the lesson is read, silence being commanded, they must hear all together." Clement. Alex. Strom. Lib. vii. Chrysost. in 2 ad Cor. Hom. 18. Isidor. de Eccl. Offic. cap. x.

It were very much for M. Harding to say, all these things were done in a learned tongue, and that the vulgar people in every country understood either

---

[6 Non negamus tamen Indis australibus permissum, ut in lingua sua rem divinam facerent, &c.—Joh. Eck. Enchir. Loc. Com. Lugd. 1572. cap. xxxvii. p. 339.]

[7 Rursus in primitiva ecclesia divina mysteria Hebraice celebrabantur.—Durand. Rat. Div. Offic. Lugd. 1565. Lib. IV. cap. i. 10. fol. 87.]

[8...in primitiva ecclesia benedictiones et cetera communia fiebant in vulgari.—Bibl. cum Gloss. Ord. et Expos. N. de Lyra, Basil. 1502. Ad Cor. I. cap. xiv. Pars VI. fol. 55. 2.]

[9...quare non dantur benedictiones in vulgari?... Dicendum est, quod hoc forte fuit in ecclesia primitiva, &c.—Thom. Aquinat. Op. Venet. 1595. In I. ad Cor. cap. xiv. Lect. iii. Tom. XVI. fol. 84.]

[10 Any one of, 1565.]

[11 Themself, 1565.]

[12 Clement. Alex. Op. Oxon. 1715. Stromat. Lib. VII. 6. Tom. II. p. 848.]

[13 Chrysost. Op. Par. 1718-38. In Epist. II. ad Cor. Hom. xviii. Tom. X. p. 568. See before, page 282.]

[14 Isidor. Hispal. Op. Col. Agrip. 1617. De Offic. Eccles. Lib. I. cap. x. p. 393; where we find *oretur ab omnibus: quando lectio.*]

Examples.

the Greek, or the Latin. Yet, for that nothing seemeth hard for him to say, let us see what the old fathers will report in that behalf. I have already shewed by Theodoretus, Sozomenus, and St Hierome, that the service was in the Syrian tongue[1].

Orig. contra Celsum, Lib. viii.

Old father Origen's words, in my judgment, seem very plain. Writing against one Celsus, a wicked heathen, he saith thus: *Græci quidem Græce Deum nominant et Latine Romani, et singuli item nativa et vernacula lingua Deum precantur, et laudibus pro se quisque extollit. Ille enim qui est linguarum omnium Dominus, audit quavis lingua orantes, idque non secus, quam si unam vocem exciperet e variis linguis expressam. Deus enim cum præsit machinæ universi, non est quasi unus aliquis, qui linguam vel Græcam vel barbaram sit sortitus, ut ceteras nesciat*[2]*:* "The Greeks name God in the Greek tongue, and the Latins in the Latin tongue; and all several nations pray unto God, and praise him in their own natural and mother-tongue. For he, that is the Lord of all tongues, heareth men praying in all tongues none otherwise than if it were one voice pronounced by divers tongues. For God, that ruleth the whole world, is not as some one man, that hath gotten the Greek or Latin tongue, and knoweth none other."

Ambros. in 1 Cor. xiv.

St Ambrose, speaking of the Jews that were converted to Christ, saith thus: *Hi ex Hebræis erant, qui aliquando Syria*[3] *lingua, plerunque Hebræa in tractatibus et oblationibus utebantur*[4]*:* "These were Jews, which in their sermons and oblations used sometime the Syrian tongue, and sometime[5] the Hebrew."

Basil. in Epist. ad Cler. Neoc.

St Basil, writing unto the learned men of Neocæsaria, and shewing in what order the people used to resort to the house of prayer in the night season, and to sing psalms in sides, and to pray together, towards the end thereof hath these words: *Tanquam ab uno ore, et ab uno corde, confessionis psalmum offerunt Domino, et verba pœnitentiæ eorum quisque proprie ascribit sibi*[6]*:* "As it were from one mouth, and from one heart, they offer up unto the Lord the psalm of confession, and the words of repentance every of them applieth particularly unto himself." Hereby it is plain that the people in St Basil's time sung the psalms together, and understood what they sung.

And lest M. Harding should slip away, as his wont is, and say, "All this was done in the Greek tongue, and not in any tongue barbarous," St Basil hath already prevented him. For immediately he addeth further as it followeth: *Horum gratia si nos fugitis, fugietis etiam Ægyptios, et utrasque Lybias, et Thebanos, et Palæstinos, et Arabas, et Phœnices, et Syros, et eos qui ad Euphratem incolunt, et in universum omnes, quibus vigiliæ, et orationes, et communes psalmodiæ in honore habentur*[7]*:* "If ye flee us for thus singing and praying together, then must ye flee the Egyptians, and both the countries of Lybia, and the Thebans, and the Palestines, and the Arabians, and the Phœnicians, and the Syrians, and the borderers of Euphrates; and generally ye must flee all them that have watchings, and prayers, and common psalmody in estimation." I trow, M. Harding will not say all these nations spake Greek or Latin.

Hieron. ad Heliod. Epitaphium Nepotiani.

St Hierome, writing unto Heliodorus of the death of Nepotianus, seemeth to avouch the same. These be his words: *Nunc passionem Christi, et resurrectionem ejus cunctarum gentium et voces et literæ sonant. Taceo de Hebræis, Græcis, et Latinis, quas nationes ... suæ ... crucis titulo Dominus dedicavit.... Bessorum feritas et pellitorum turba populorum, qui mortuorum quondam inferiis homines immolabant, stridorem suum in dulce Christi fregerunt melos, et totius mundi una vox est Christus*[8]*:* "Now both the voices and letters of all nations do sound out Christ's passion and resurrection. I leave the Jews, the Greeks, and the Latins, which nations the Lord hath dedicate with the title of his cross. The savage nature of the Bessians, and people that for their wildness go clad in skins, which some-

[1 See before, pages 269, 70.]

[2 Orig. Op. Par. 1733-59. Cont. Cels. Lib. VIII. 37. Tom. I. pp. 769, 70.]

[3 Syra, 1565.]

[4 Ambros. Op. Par. 1686-90. Comm. in Epist. I. ad Cor. cap. xiv. v. 19. Tom. II. Append. col. 157; where *Syra*, and *aut* for *et*.]

[5 Sometimes, 1565.]

[6 Basil. Op. Par. 1721-30. Ad Cler. Neoc. Epist. ccvii. Tom. III. p. 311.]

[7 Id. ibid.]

[8 Hieron. Op. Par. 1693-1706. Ad Heliod. Epist. xxxv. Epit. Nepot. Tom. IV. Pars II. col. 268; where we read *crucis fregerunt*, and *Christus est*.]

times made sacrifices of men's bodies, have turned their barbarous speech into the sweet harmony of Christ. Christ is now the voice of the whole world." Examples.

Æneas Sylvius saith, that when Cyrillus and Methodius had converted the Sclavons unto God, which was about the year of our Lord eight hundred and three-score, and were suitors that they might minister the common prayers and other service unto them in their common Sclavon tongue, and great stay was made therein by the pope and his cardinals, a voice was heard, as it had been from heaven: *Omnis spiritus laudet Dominum; et omnis lingua confiteatur ei:* "Let every spirit praise the Lord; and let every tongue acknowledge him;" and that thereupon they were suffered to use their own tongue [9]. Æneas Sylv. Hist. Bohem. cap. xiii.

Touching this matter, Innocentius the third hath decreed thus; and whether it make for the purpose or no, let M. Harding himself be judge. His words be these: *Quoniam in plerisque partibus, intra eandem civitatem atque diœcesim, permisti sunt populi diversarum linguarum, habentes sub una fide varios ritus et mores; districte præcipimus, ut pontifices hujuscemodi civitatum sive diœcesium provideant viros idoneos, qui secundum diversitates rituum et linguarum divina illis officia celebrent, et ecclesiastica sacramenta ministrent* [10]: "For so much as in many places, within one city and one diocese, there be nations mingled together of many tongues, having divers orders and customs under one faith; we do therefore straitly command, that the bishops of such cities or dioceses provide meet men to minister the holy service, according to the diversity of their manners and tongues." Extra de Offic. Judicis Ordinarii. Quoniam in plerisque. Rituum et linguarum.

Here might I allege much more out of divers writers, even out of Abdias himself, whom M. Harding so much esteemeth. But I will only note the complaint of one John Billet concerning this case, and so make an end. His words be these: *In primitiva ecclesia prohibitum erat, ne quis loqueretur [linguis] nisi esset qui interpretaretur. Quid enim... prodesset loqui, nisi intelligeretur?... Inde etiam inolevit laudabilis consuetudo,...ut pronuntiato literaliter evangelio, statim [in] vulgari ...populo exponeretur. Quid autem nostris temporibus est agendum, ubi nullus, vel rarus invenitur legens, vel audiens, qui intelligat?... Videtur ergo potius esse tacendum, quam psallendum* [11]: "It was forbidden in the primitive church that no man should speak with tongues, unless there were some present to expound it. For what should speaking avail without understanding? And hereof grew a laudable custom, that, after the gospel was read literally, it should straightway be expounded in the vulgar tongue. But what shall we do in our days, when as there is either none at all, or very seldom, that readeth or heareth, and understandeth? It seemeth it were better now to hold their peace than so to sing." Johan. Billet in Summa de Div. Offic.

Here have I alleged, for proof of our purpose, of the old fathers, Clemens Alexandrinus, Origen, St Basil, St Hierome, Theodoretus, Sozomenus, and Isidorus; of the latter writers, Æneas Sylvius, Innocentius Tertius, John Billet, Thomas of Aquine, Lyra, Durandus, and Eckius. Therefore I trust M. Harding will no more deny but we are able to shew somewhat that the common service, in the primitive church, was in some other tongue, and not only in Greek or Latin. Now, if M. Harding be able to shew any such sufficient example of his side, I will yield, according to promise.

M. HARDING. THE SIXTEENTH DIVISION.

For further answer to the authority of Justinian's ordinance, we hold well with it. Good men think it meet, the service to [12] *be uttered now also with a distinct and audible voice, that all sorts of people, specially so many as understand it, may the more be stirred to devotion, and thereby the rather be moved to say Amen, and give their assent to it, through their obedience and credit they bear to the church, assuring themselves the same to be good and healthful, and to the glory of God.*

[9 Æn. Sylv. Op. Basil. 1571. Hist. Bohem. cap. xiii. p. 91.]

[10 Innoc. III. in Corp. Jur. Canon. Lugd. 1624. Decretal. Greg. IX. Lib. I. Tit. xxxi. cap. 14. col. 413; where *hujusmodi*, and *diœcesum*.]

[11 Joan. Beleth. Div. Offic. Explic. ad calc. Durand. Rat. Div. Offic. Lugd. 1565. Procem. fol. 489. 2; where we find *si non* for *nisi*, *hinc illa laudabilis inolevit consuetudo, secundum literam, quid vero de nostris temporibus dicemus, si vix, ac ne vix quidem inveniatur qui quæ legerit vel audierit intelligat*, and *tacendum potius esse*.]

[12 *To* is omitted, H. A. 1564.]

Africa.

Saunce Bell. Paternoster.

And for that purpose we have commonly seen the priest, when he sped him to say his service, to ring the saunce[1] *bell, and speak out aloud,* Pater noster; *by which token the people were commanded silence, reverence, and devotion.*

THE BISHOP OF SARISBURY.

Cic. pro Cœl.

Cvpr. in Orat. Domin.

I must needs answer M. Harding, as Cicero sometime answered his adversary: *Mimi ergo exitus est, non fabulæ*[2]: "This gear goeth by gesture, and not by speech." St Cyprian, declaring the order of the church in his time, saith: *Sacerdos ante orationem...parat animos fratrum, dicendo, Sursum corda*[3]: "The priest before the prayers prepareth the hearts of the brethren, saying thus unto them, 'Lift up your hearts.'"

Chrysost. in 2 ad Cor. Hom. 18.

Sueton. in August.

Plut. in Catone.

1 Cor. xiii.

The deacons in St Chrysostom's and Basil's time used to call upon the people with these words: *Oremus; Attendamus:* "Let us pray;" "Let us give ear:" like as also the priest in the heathen sacrifices was wont to command silence, and to say to the multitude, *Favete linguis.* This was done in the church of Christ, as St Cyprian saith, to put the people in remembrance that in their prayers they should think of nothing else but only of the Lord. And therefore Chrysostom saith: "The priest in the holy ministration speaketh unto the people, and the people unto the priest[4]." But M. Harding, for ease and expedition, hath devised a shorter way, to teach the people by a bell-rope. He turneth his back unto his brethren, and speaketh out two words aloud, *Pater noster;* and causeth the *sanctus* bell to play the part of a deacon, to put the people in remembrance that now they must pray. If any other man would say so much, he were a scoffer: M. Harding speaketh it, and it is good earnest, and cause sufficient to avoid Justinian's law. Augustus Cæsar warned his son-in-law Tiberius, *Ut ore, non digito loqueretur;* "That he should speak with his mouth, and not with his finger." And Cato was wont to say, when he saw two augurs meet together, "He marvelled that either of them could abstain from smiling; for that their whole profession and occupation stood in mocking of the people." I will not apply this to M. Harding, notwithstanding he seem to profess the like. God grant his bell may remember him to fear God, lest he himself be left "as a sounding piece of brass, or as a tinkling cymbal."

M. HARDING. THE SEVENTEENTH DIVISION.

Now to say somewhat touching the common prayers, or service of the churches of Africa, where St Augustine preached in Latin, as you say, and I deny not; and thereof you seem to conclude that the common people of that country understood and spake Latin, as their vulgar tongue. That the African churches had their service in Latin, it is evident by sundry places of St Augustine in his exposition of the Psalms, in his books De Doctrina Christiana, *and in his sermons, and most plainly in an epistle that he wrote to St Hierome, in which he sheweth that the people of a city in Africa was greatly moved and offended with their bishop, for that, in reciting the scriptures, for part of the service to them he read out of the fourth chapter of Jonas the prophet, not* cucurbita, *after the old text, which they had been accustomed unto, but* hedera, *after the new translation of St Hierome*[5]. *Now, as I grant that some understood it, so I have cause to doubt whether some others understood it, or no. Nay, rather I have great probability to think they understood it not. For the bewraying of Hannibal's ambassadors to the Romans by their Punical language, whereof Titus Livius writeth*[6], *and likewise the conference betwixt Sylla the noble man of Rome, and Bocchus king of Numidia, had by mean of interpreters adhibited of both parts*[7], *as Sallust recordeth in* Bello Jugurthino, *declareth that the tongue of Africa was the Punical tongue before the Romans' conquest. Now, the same people remaining there until St Augustine's time, what should move us to judge that they forgot*[8] *their own native and mother-tongue, and learned anew the*

[*All people of the Latin church understood not the Latin service.* H. A. 1564.]

Lib. xxiii. Belli Punici.

[1 Saunce: a corruption of Sanctus.]

[2 Cic. Pro M. Cœl. 10; where *est jam exitus.*]

[3 Cypr. Op. Oxon. 1682. De Orat. Domin. p. 152. See before, page 285, note 11.]

[4 Chrysost. Op. Par. 1718-38. In Epist. II. ad Cor. Hom. xviii. Tom. x. p. 568.]

[5 August. Op. Par. 1679-1700. Ad Hieron. Epist. lxxi. 5. Tom. II. col. 161.]

[6 Tit. Liv. Hist. Lib. XXIII. cap. xxxiv.]

[7 Parties, H. A. 1564.]

[8 Forgat, 1565, 1609, and H. A. 1564.]

Latin tongue? I confess that many understood and spake Latin, by reason of the Romans' common resort thither, of their laws there executed, of their garrisons there abiding, and specially of the great multitude of Latin people thither sent to inhabit, deductis coloniis, *by Augustus the emperor first, then by Adrianus, and afterward by Commodus, who would have had the great city Carthago, newly re-edified, to be called after his own name,* Alexandria Commodiana, *as Lampridius writeth*[9]. *These Roman colonies, that is to wit, multitudes of people sent to inhabit the country, placed themselves about the sea-coasts in the chief cities, in Carthago, Utica, Hippo, Leptis, &c. and thereabout. And by these*[10] *means the Roman or Latin speech spread abroad there, and became to be very common, as that which remained still among the inhabitants that were of the Roman kind, and was learned by long use and custom of others dwelling amongst them, specially in the cities where the Romans bare the sway and government. For these considerations I think the Latin tongue was there very common. But that it was common to the inward parties of the country also, and to the uplandish people, amongst whom the old accustomed language is longest kept, as experience teacheth; it is not likely. For though the nobility and cities change their language, to be the more in estimation, yet the common and base people of the country fall not so soon to a change. In this realm of England, after William Conqueror's time, by occasion of great resort*[11] *of Frenchmen hither, and of our countrymen into France, also of the French laws, and special favour by the princes borne, and preferments bestowed upon them*[12] *that spake French, the most part of the nobility, lawyers, merchants, captains, soldiers, and wealthy folk, had skill in the understanding and speaking of the French tongue; but yet the common and uplandish people spake little or nought at all: whereof grew this proverb in England of old time, "Jack would be a gentleman, but Jack can no French." The like may be thought of the Latin tongue in Africa.* Africa.

What shall we think of the uplandish people there, when as Septimius Severus the emperor, yea, after the apostles' time, had not very good skill in the Latin tongue, but in the Punical tongue, and that being born at Leptis? Of whom Aurelius Victor saith thus in Epitome: Latinis literis sufficienter instructus,... Punica lingua promptior, quippe genitus apud Leptim provinciæ Aphricæ[13]: "*Severus was learned in the Latin letters sufficiently, but in the Punical tongue he was readier, as being born at Leptis, within the province of Africa." Here the Latin tongue is attributed to instruction and teaching, and the Punical tongue to nature. Ælius Spartianus, writing the life of this Severus to Diocletian, sheweth that when his sister, a woman of Leptis, came to Rome to him,* vix Latine loquens, *her brother the emperor was ashamed of her, and blushed at her, for that she could scantly speak Latin, and therefore commanded her away home again to her country; for these be the very words of Spartianus*[14]. *Now if such noble personages lacked the Latin speech in the chief part of Africa, it is soon understanded what is to be deemed of the common and vulgar people abroad in the country.*

Let us come down lower, even to St Hierome's time. St Hierome, writing to a noble young Roman virgin, called Demetrias, being in Africa, exhorting her to keep herself in that holy state of virginity, saith thus: Urbs tua quondam orbis caput[15]: "*Thy city, once the head of the world, is become the sepulchre of the Roman people. And wilt thou take a banished husband, thyself being a banished woman in the shore of Lybia? What woman shalt thou have there to bring thee to and fro?"* Stridor Punicæ linguæ procacia tibi Fescennina cantabit[16]: "*The jarring Punical tongue shall sing thee bawdy songs at thy wedding." Lo, in St Hierome's time they of Africa spake the Punical tongue, and that by the sea-side, where the Romans of long time had made their abode. Of this may be gathered, that the Latin speech was not in the further parts*[17] *within the country very common. St Augustine in sundry places of his works sheweth that the people of Africa, called Punics, spake the Punical tongue, acknowledging a likeness and*

De Verbis Domini secundum Luc. Serm. 35.

[9 Æl. Lamprid. in Hist. August. Script. Min. Hanov. 1611. Commod. cap. xvii. p. 284.]

[10 This, H. A. 1564.]

[11 Resorts, 1565, and H. A. 1564.]

[12 Those, H. A. 1564.]

[13 Aurel. Vict. Epit. cap. xx. in eod. p. 762; where *eloquentia* for *lingua.*]

[14 Æl. Spart. in eod. Sever. cap. xv. p. 299.]

[15 Caput, etc. H. A. 1564.]

[16 Hieron. Op. Par. 1693-1706. Ad Demetr. Epist. xcvii. Tom. IV. Pars II. col. 786.]

[17 Farther parties, 1565, and H. A. 1564.]

Africa. *cousinage, as it were, to be between that and the Hebrew tongue*[1]. *But most evident witness for the Punical tongue is to be found in his forty-fourth epistle,* Ad Maximum Madaurensem; *in which he answereth him soberly for his scoffing and jesting at certain Punical words in derogation of the Christians. After wondering that he, being an African born, and writing to Africans, should find fault with the Punical names and words, and after commendation of the tongue, for that many things have right wisely been commended to memory by great learned men in books of the Punical language, at length concluded against him thus:* Pœniteat te certe ibi natum, ubi hujus[modi] linguæ cunabula recalent[2]: *"In good sooth thou mayest be sorry in thy heart that thou wert*[3] *born there, where the cradles of such a tongue be warm again." By which words he seemeth to charge him with an unnatural grief and repenting that he was born in that country where they speak Punic ere they creep out of their cradles: whereby it appeareth the mother-tongue of those parts*[4] *of Africa which he speaketh of to be the Punical, and not the Latin.*

To conclude, if they had all spoken Latin, and not some the Punical tongue, St Augustine would never have written, Punici Christiani baptismum,... salutem;.... eucharistiam, vitam vocant[5]: *"That those Christians which speak the Punical tongue, call baptism in their language, health or salvation; and the eucharist, life." Wherefore we see that there were Latin Christians and Punical Christians in Africa, of whom all understood not the Latin service.*

Lib. i. de Peccatorum Meritis et Remissione, cap. xxiv.

THE BISHOP OF SARISBURY.

Here M. Harding, as his wont is, taketh needless pains without profit, to prove that thing that is not denied. I said that at the city of Hippo in Africa, where St Augustine was bishop, the common service of the church was pronounced in Latin, and that no marvel, for that the whole people there understood and spake the Latin tongue. For answer whereof, reply is made, and that by guesses and likelihoods, that the whole people of Africa, in all the mountains and uplandish countries, was never trained up in the Latin tongue. Which thing neither is denied by me, nor anywise toucheth this question. For it is easy to be known by St Augustine, St Hierome, and others, in infinite places, that the people of that country had a natural tongue of their own, distinct from all others, and several only to themselves[6]. And therefore to prove the same in such earnest sort, by Titus Livius, by Sallust, by Aurelius Victor, by Ælius Spartianus, by St Augustine, and by St Hierome, it was only spending of time without winning of matter. St Augustine saith, *eucharistia* in the Punic tongue was called "life;" and *baptismus*, in the same tongue, was called "health;" and rehearseth these words, *mammon*[7] and *iar*[8], and other like words, and certain proverbs, used in the same tongue. St Hierome saith that *alma*, in the Punic tongue, signifieth "a virgin," according to the Hebrew[9]. Quintilian saith that this word *mappa* was borrowed of the Punics, and made Latin, as *rheda* and *petoritum* were borrowed of the Gauls[10]. Neither is there any reason to lead us but that they had other words and sentences of their own sufficient to express their minds.

August. de Verbis Dom. sec. Luc. Serm. 35. August. in Psal. cxxiii. Hieron. in Isai. Lib. iii. cap. vii. Lib. i. cap. ix.

But after the Romans had once subdued them, the better to stablish and confirm their empire, they forced them to receive both the Roman laws, and also the Roman tongue; as they had done before in several countries within Italy, and in other places more. Which thing unto some seemed so grievous, that, as it is reported by Cato, Turrhenus, the last king of Etruria, notwithstanding he were content to yield his country to the Romans, yet could never be won to yield his

Ex. Orig. Caton.

[1 August. Op. Par. 1679-1700. Serm. cxiii. 2. Tom. V. col. 568.]

[2 Id. Ad Max. Madaur. Epist. xvii. 2. Tom. II. col. 21.]

[3 Were, 1565, and H. A. 1564.]

[4 Parties, 1565, and H. A. 1564.]

[5 Id. De Pecc. Mer. et Remiss. Lib. i. cap. xxiv. 34. Tom. X. col. 19; where for *eucharistiam* we read *sacramentum corporis Christi.*]

[6 Themself, 1565.]

[7 Id. Serm. cxiii. 2. Tom. V. col. 568.]

[8 Id. In Psalm. cxxiii. Enarr. 8. Tom. IV. col. 1407.]

[9 Lingua quoque Punica, quæ de Hebræorum fontibus manare dicitur, proprie virgo *alma* appellatur.—Hieron. Op. Par. 1693-1706. Comm. Lib. iii. in Isai. Proph. cap. vii. Tom. III. col. 71.]

[10 M. Fab. Quinctil. Inst. Orat. Lib. i. cap. v. 57.]

tongue[11]. For the better performance hereof, they had it enacted by a law, that the judge in every province should hear, and determine matters, and pronounce sentence only in Latin, as it appeareth by these words: *Decreta a prætoribus Latine debent interponi*[12]. By mean whereof St Hierome saith: "The Punic tongue in his time was much altered from that it had been before[13]."

Africa.

De Re Judic. &c. Decreta.

Hieron. in Præfat. in Lib. ii. Comm. ad Gal.

All these things be confessed, and nothing touch this case, nor serve to any other purpose but only to amaze the ignorant reader with a countenance of great learning.

But that the whole people of the city of Hippo, where the service was ministered in the Latin tongue, understood and spake Latin, who can witness better than St Augustine himself, that was then bishop of Hippo? And to pass over that he reporteth of himself, that, being born in Tagasta, a city of Africa, he learned the Latin tongue *inter...blandimenta nutricum*[14], "as he was playing under his nurse," signifying thereby that his nurses understood and spake Latin; in his book, *De Catechizandis Rudibus*, he writeth thus: "Let them know there is no voice that soundeth in God's ears but the devotion of the mind. So shall they not scorn at the head priests and ministers of the church, if they happen, in making their prayers unto God, to speak false Latin, or not to understand the words that they speak, or to speak them out of order[15]." He addeth further; *Non quod ista corrigenda non sint, ut populus ad id, quod plane intelligit, dicat, Amen:* "Not for that such faults should not be amended, to the end that the people, to the thing that they plainly perceive, may say Amen." Here St Augustine willeth that the priests utter their Latin service distinctly and truly, that the people may understand them. Again he saith thus: *Volens etiam causam Donatistarum ad ipsius humillimi vulgi, et omnino imperitorum, atque idiotarum notitiam pervenire, et eorum, quantum fieri posset per nos, inhærere memoriæ, psalmum, qui eis cantaretur, per Latinas literas feci*[16]: "Being desirous that the cause of the Donatists should come to the knowledge of the lowest sort, and of them that be utterly ignorant and void of learning, and as much as in us lay, might be fixed in their memory, I wrote a psalm for them to sing in the Latin tongue." And Possidonius, writing St Augustine's life, saith, that Valerius, that was bishop of Hippo before St Augustine, for that he was a Greek born, and had small skill in the Latin tongue, was the less able to preach unto the people, and to discharge his duty there[17].

August. Confess. Lib. i. cap. xiv.

De Catechiz. Rud. cap. ix.

Retract. Lib. i. cap. xx.

Possid. in Vita August. cap. v.

I doubt not but by these few words it may well appear that the people of Hippo understood the Latin, albeit not in such good order as they that had learned it at the school; and therefore would oftentimes speak amiss, placing one word for another, and gender for gender, and case for case; as for example, *dolus* for *dolor*. St Augustine saith: *Multi fratres imperitiores Latinitatis loquuntur sic, ut dicant, dolus illum torquet, pro eo quod est, dolor*[18]. And for that cause, in his sermons unto the people, he submitteth oftentimes[19] himself unto their capacity. For thus he speaketh unto the people: *Sæpe...et verba non Latina dico, ut vos intelligatis*[20]: "Many times I utter words that be no Latin, that ye may understand me." And again he saith: *Ego dicam ossum: sic enim potius loquamur. Melius est, [ut] nos reprehendant grammatici, quam non intelligant populi*[21]:

August. in Johan. Tractat. vii.

August. in Psal. cxxiii.

August. in Psal. cxxxviii.

[11 M. Caton. Orig. Lib. Basil. 1530, p. 13.]

[12 Tryphonin. in Corp. Jur. Civil. Amst. 1663. Digest. Lib. XLII. Tit. i. 48. Tom. I. p. 618; where *interponi debent.*]

[13 ...quum et Aphri Phœnicum linguam nonnulla ex parte mutaverint.—Hieron. Op. Comm. Lib. II. in Epist. ad Gal. Præf. Tom. IV. cols. 255, 6.]

[14 August. Op. Confess. Lib. I. cap. xiv. 23. Tom. I. col. 78.]

[15 Noverint etiam non esse vocem ad aures Dei, nisi animi affectum: ita enim non arridebunt, si aliquos antistites et ministros ecclesiæ forte animadverterint, vel cum barbarismis et solœcismis Deum invocare, vel eadem verba quæ pronuntiant non intelligere, perturbateque distinguere. Non quia ista minime corrigenda sunt, ut &c.—Id. De Catechiz. Rud. cap. ix. 13. Tom. VI. col. 272.]

[16 Id. Retract. Lib. I. cap. xx. Tom. I. col. 31.]

[17 Valerius...exsultabat...ut sibi...homo concederetur...qui posset verbo Dei...ecclesiam...ædificare: cui rei se homo natura Græcus, minusque Latina lingua et litteris instructus, minus utilem pervidebat. —August. Vit. Auct. Possid. cap. v. Tom. X. Post-append. col. 260.]

[18 August. Op. In Johan. Evang. cap. i. Tractat. vii. 18. Tom. III. Pars II. col. 349.]

[19 Oft times, 1565.]

[20 Id. In Psalm. cxxiii. Enarr. 8. Tom. IV. col. 1407.]

[21 Habeo in abscondito quoddam ossum. Sic &c...reprehendant nos, &c.—Id. In Psalm. cxxxviii. Enarr. 20. Tom. IV. col. 1545.]

Africa. "I will say *ossum*, for your better understanding; although it be no Latin word, And so hardly let us speak. For better is it that the grammarians find fault with us, than the people should not understand us." Hereby it is plain, that at the city of Hippo, whereof I specially spake, the common service of the church was pronounced and ministered in the Latin tongue; for that the whole people there universally understood and spake Latin.

M. HARDING. THE EIGHTEENTH DIVISION.

And whereas St Augustine, as you allege him[1] *without shewing the place (as your manner is, whereby you may easily deceive the reader), hath these words in his sermons to the common people divers times:* Nunc loquar Latine, ut omnes intelligatis: *"Now will I speak Latin, that you may all understand me;" of that saying, if any such be, may be gathered that sometime*[2] *he spake in the Punical tongue to the Punical Christians, not understanding the Latin; but now among the Latin Africans that were of the Roman kind, and understood not the Punic, he would speak Latin, that all such should understand him.*

Whoso desireth further to be persuaded that the people of Africa, called Pœni, spake and understood their own Punical tongue, and not the Latin tongue; as likewise the people of Spain, named Iberi, *spake that language which was proper to them; let him read Titus Livius,* De bello Macedonico. *For there he recordeth, that when those of Africa, or of Spain, and the Romans came together for parle and talk, they used an interpreter.*

And Ulpianus, the lawyer, a great officer about Alexander Severus, the emperor, at the beginning of christian religion, writeth, that Fidei commissa *may be left in all vulgar tongues, and putteth for examples the Punical, and the French, or rather Gallical tongue*[3]. *In l. fidei commissa. ff. d. leg. 3.*

THE BISHOP OF SARISBURY.

I see there is no pardon to be hoped for at M. Harding's hands. Because I noted not in what book and chapter this place is to be found, therefore he beareth men in hand, I seek means to deceive the reader. If this poor quarrel may stand for proof, then is it no hard matter, by the same logic, to conclude the like against him. For M. Harding ofttimes useth the authority of St Augustine and other fathers, without any noting of the places, as his own book is best witness; *ergo*, M. Harding seeketh means to deceive his reader.

But in my judgment better it is not to note the places at all, than falsely to note them, as M. Harding's manner is to do: as where he untruly allegeth the decree of the council of Ephesus against Nestorius, for the communion in one kind[4]; which decree neither is to be found in that council, nor ever was recorded or mentioned by any old father; or where he allegeth the decree of the first council of Nice for the supremacy of the bishop of Rome, himself confessing that the same decree was burnt, I know not how, and could never yet be seen until this day. Verily, this is a ready way to deceive the reader. I pass by other
Fol. 23. a. petite faults; as that he allegeth the sixth book of Ambrose[5], *De Sacramentis*,
Fol. 18. b. instead of the fifth; or the xxxiv. chapter of the sixth book of Eusebius[6], instead
Cont. Arch. Cant. Lib. iv. of the xliv.: or that Stephen Gardiner allegeth Theophilus Alexandrinus, instead of Theophylactus; or the third book of St Augustine, *De Sermone Domini in monte*, whereas St Augustine never wrote but two[7]. The place wherewith M.
De Verb's Apost. Serm. 25. Harding findeth himself grieved is to be found in St Augustine, *De Verbis apostoli:* the words be these: *Proverbium notum est Punicum; quod quidem Latine vobis*

[1 See before, page 56, note 7.]

[2 Sometimes, 1565, 1609, and H. A. 1564.]

[3 Fidei commissa quocunque sermone relinqui possunt: non solum Latina, vel Græca, sed etiam Punica, vel Gallicana.—Ulp. in Corp. Jur. Civil. Amst. 1663. Digest. Lib. XXXII. De Leg. et Fid. Lib. III. 11. Tom. I. p. 450.]

[4 See before, page 220.]

[5 See before, page 168.]

[6 See before, page 149, in which place in the original edition of Harding's answer the error noted by Jewel is found.]

[7 See before, page 53.]

[8 August. Op. Par. 1679-1700 Serm. clxvii. 4. De Verb. Apost. Tom. V. col. 804.]

dicam, quia Punice non omnes nostis[9]: "There is a common proverb in the Punic tongue, which I will report unto you in Latin, because ye do not all understand the Punic." Here it is plain that the Latin tongue was known to all the hearers, and the Punic tongue only unto some. And therefore in another sermon unto the people he saith thus: *Omnes novimus, Latine non dici sanguines, aut sanguina*[9]: "We do all know" (reckoning himself with the people) "that these words, *sanguines*, or *sanguina*, are no Latin:" and again, as I have before reported, touching a Latin psalm that he made[10] for the common people, he writeth thus: "Being desirous that the cause of the Donatists should come to the knowledge of the lowest sort, and of them that be utterly ignorant and void of learning, and, as much as in us lay, might be fixed in their memory, I wrote a psalm for them to sing in the Latin tongue[11].

Africa.

August. in Psal. l.

Retract. Lib. i. cap. xx.

This long rehearsal of all these authorities, saving that M. Harding gave the occasion, was utterly needless. Notwithstanding, hereby it is evident that the people there understood the Latin, wherein their service was ministered; and therefore had not their service in any unknown tongue. Now, if M. Harding were able to shew that other cities or provinces of the same country, where the Latin tongue was not known, had notwithstanding the Latin service, it would very well serve his purpose. Otherwise, the argument, that he would seem to fashion hereof, is marvellous strange. For thus, as it appeareth, he would conclude: Some people in Africa spake the Punic tongue; *ergo*, they had their service in the Latin tongue. For other argument that he can here gather, I see none. The rest of Titus Livius, *de bello Macedonico;* or of Ulpian, *de fidei commissis*, is utterly out of season, and therefore not worthy to be answered.

M. HARDING. THE NINETEENTH DIVISION.

Thus[12] *much or more might here be said of the language of the people of Gallia, now called France, which then was barbarous and vulgar, and not only Latin; and* (79) *yet had they of that nation their service then in Latin, as all the west church had. That the common language of the people there was vulgar, the use of the Latin serving for the learned, as we must needs judge, we have first the authority of Titus Livius; who writeth, that a Galloes, or, as now we say, a Frenchman, of a notable stature, provoked a Roman to fight with him, man for man, making his challenge by an interpreter*[13]. *Which had not been done in case the Latin tongue had been common to that nation. Next, the place of Ulpianus before mentioned*[14]. *Then the record of Ælius Lampridius, who writeth that a woman of the order of the Druids cried out aloud to Alexander Severus, Mammæa her son, the emperor, as he marched forward on a day with his army,* Gallico sermone, *"in the Gallical tongue," these words boding his death, which right so shortly after followed:* Vadas: nec victoriam speres; ne militi tuo credas[15]: *"Go thy way, and look not for the victory; trust not thy soldiers*[16]*." Lastly, the witness of St Hierome, who, having travelled over that region, and therefore being skilful of the whole state thereof, acknowledgeth the people of Treveres, and of that territory, to have a peculiar language diverse from Latin and Greek*[17].

The seventy-ninth untruth, boldly avouched, but no way proved.

Ab Urbe condita, lib. vii.

In Vita Alexandri Mammææ.

In Procemio 2. Commen. ad Galatas.

If all that I have brought here touching this matter be well weighed, it will seem probable, I doubt not, that all sorts of people in Africa understood not the service which they had in the Latin tongue. And no less may be thought of Gallia and Spain. And so far it is proved against M. Jewel's stout assertion, that within his six hundred years after Christ some christian people had their common prayers and service in a tongue they understood not.

An easy proof without promises.

[9 Id. in Psal. l. Enarr. 19. Tom. IV. col. 472; where we find *nec* for *aut.*]

[10 Had made, 1565.]

[11 Id. Retract. Lib. I. cap. xx. Tom. I. col. 31. See before, page 295.]

[12 This, 1565, and H. A. 1564.]

[13 Tit. Liv. Hist. Lib. VII. cap. xxvi.]

[14 See before, page 296, note 3.]

[15 Æl. Lamprid. in Hist. August. Script. Lat. Min. Hanov. 1611. Alex. Sever. cap. lx. p. 355; where *nec te militi.*]

[16 Soldier, H. A. 1564.]

[17 Hieron. Op. Par. 1693-1706. Comm. Lib. II. in Epist. ad Gal. Præf. Tom. IV. cols. 255, 6. See before, page 274.]

France.

THE BISHOP OF SARISBURY.

A short answer may serve, where nothing is objected. This guess standeth upon these two points. The first is this: "The people of Gallia understood not the Latin tongue." The second is this: "That, notwithstanding, the same people had their service in Latin:" whereof the conclusion followeth; *ergo*, they had service in an unknown tongue. The major hereof is proved, with much ado, by Titus Livius, by Ulpianus, by Ælius Lampridius, and by St Hierome. He might as well have added the story of Brennus; Cæsar's Commentaries; Quintilian, that nameth two mere French words, *rheda* and *petoritum*[1]; and Cicero, who in his oration *pro Fonteio*, and elsewhere, calleth the men of the country *Barbaros*. Thus M. Harding taketh great pains to prove that thing that is confessed, and needeth no proving.

Quint. Lib. i. cap. ix. Cic. pro Font.

But the minor, which is utterly denied, and wherein standeth all the doubt, and without proving whereof he proveth nothing, he passeth over closely, and proveth by silence. If the matter be doubtful, it hath the more need of proof: if it be plain and out of doubt, it is the sooner proved. Surely, to say without any kind of proof or evidence, only upon M. Harding's bare word, "The people of Gallia had the Latin service," it is but a very simple warrant. For what learning, what authority, what conjecture, what guess hath he, so to say? Some hold that Joseph of Arimathæa, Philip the apostle, Nathaniel, and Lazarus, were the first that ever opened the gospel in France. But these four neither came from Rome, nor, to my knowledge, ever spake the Latin tongue: they came from Hierusalem out of Jewry, and spake the Hebrew tongue. Therefore, I reckon, M. Harding will not say that any of these four erected there the Latin service.

The best that he can make hereof is but a guess and a likelihood; for thus he saith: "It will seem probable, I doubt not." But I assure thee, good reader, it will prove nothing, I doubt not. For weigh the probability of these reasons: "The people of Gallia had a speech peculiar to themselves[2], and spake no Latin;" *ergo*, they had the Latin service. Or thus: "The first preachers in Gallia came from Hierusalem, and spake the Hebrew tongue;" *ergo*, they ministered the service and common prayers in the Latin tongue. These be M. Harding's probabilities, wherewith he doubteth not this matter is proved.

But once again, let us view the main reason: the major, "The people of Gallia understood no Latin;" the minor, "The same people had the Latin service;" the conclusion, *ergo*, They had service in an unknown tongue.

Here, M. Harding, we do utterly deny your minor; which unless ye prove otherwise than ye have hitherto begun, very children may see that your conclusion cannot follow. Ye should not so stoutly have said, ye have so thoroughly proved the matter, having indeed as yet proved nothing.

But that the service in the churches of Gallia was not said in such order as M. Harding guesseth, but in a tongue known unto the people, it is evident by Severus Sulpitius, in the life of St Martin. The people of the city of Tours in France, then called Gallia, upon the vacation of the bishopric were desirous to have St Martin to be their bishop; notwithstanding there were others that thought him a very simple man, and in all respects unworthy of any bishopric. In this contention the matter fell out in this wise, as Sulpitius sheweth: *Cum fortuito*[3] *lector, cui legendi eo die officium erat, interclusus a populo defuisset, turbatis ministris, dum exspectatur, qui non aderat, unus e circumstantibus, sumpto psalterio, quem primum versum invenit arripuit: Psalmus autem hic erat: Ex ore infantium et lactentium perfecisti laudem, &c. Quo lecto, clamor populi tollitur,* [*et*] *pars adversa confunditur*[4]: "Whereas by chance the reader, whose office was to read in the church that day, was shut out by mean of the throng, and the ministers were troubled, looking about for him that was not there, one of the company took the psalter, and read that verse that came next to hand. The verse of the psalm was this: 'Out of the mouth of infants and sucklings thou

Sulp. in Vita Mart.

[1 M. Fab. Quinctil. Inst. Orat. Lib. I. cap. v. 57.]

[2 Themself, 1565.]

[3 Fortuitu, 1565, 1609.]

[4 Sulp. Div. Mart. Vit. ad calc. Abd. Apost. Hist. Par. 1571. Lib. I. foll. 193, 4; where *fortuitu*.]

has wrought praise.' As soon as that verse was read, the people made a shout; and the contrary part was confounded. Here we see the practice of the church of Gallia. The reader pronounced the scriptures; and the people understood them. Whether it were in the vulgar tongue, or in the Latin, it was a tongue known unto the people. Therefore M. Harding might have better advised himself before he thus assured the world that "the people of Gallia had their service undoubtedly in an unknown tongue." France.

M. HARDING. THE TWENTIETH DIVISION.

And thus all his allegations brought for proof of his saying in this behalf be answered, the place of St Paul to the Corinthians excepted.

THE BISHOP OF SARISBURY.

If vain guesses without proof, if the corruption of St Augustine, if the falsifying of the emperor Justinian's law, may stand for an answer, then are my allegations fully answered.

M. HARDING. THE TWENTY-FIRST DIVISION.

[*The antiquity of the Latin service in the church of England.* H. A. 1564.]

Which ere I answer, I will, according to my promise, prove that about nine hundred years past, yea, a thousand also, and therefore some deal within his six hundred years, even in St Gregorius'[5] *time, the service was in an unknown tongue in this land of England, then called Britain, and begun to be called England, at least, for so much as sithence and at these days is called by the name of England. Beda, an Englishman, that wrote the ecclesiastical story of the English nation in the year of our Lord* 731, *and of their coming to*[6] *Britain about* 285, *recordeth that St Augustine and his company, who were sent hither to convert the English people to the faith of Christ, which the Britons had here*[7] *professed long before, having a safe-conduct granted them by king Ethelbert to preach the gospel where they would, said and sung their service in a church, builded of old time in the honour of St Martin, adjoining on the east side of the head city of Kent, whiles the Romans dwelt in Britain. The words of Beda be these:* In hac (ecclesia) . . . convenire primo, psallere, orare, missas facere, prædicare, et baptizare cœperunt[8]: "*In this church they began first to assemble themselves together, to sing, to pray, to say mass, to preach, and to baptize." It is plain that this was the service. And, no doubt, they resorted to it, who "believed and were of them baptized, wondering (as Beda*[9] *saith) at the simplicity of their innocent life, and sweetness of their heavenly doctrine*[10]*." In English it was not, for they had no skill of that tongue, as Beda*[9] *sheweth*[11], Lib. I. cap. xxiii. *And therefore, ere they entered the land, they took with them, by commandment of St Gregory, interpreters out of France*[12]. *Which interpreters served for open preaching, and private instruction, exhortation, and teaching. In singing and saying the service there was no use of them.*

Lib. i. Hist. Ecclesiast. cap. xxvi.

They were Italians, and spake no English; neither was this the ordinary service of the English church.

Lib. i. cap. xxv.

THE BISHOP OF SARISBURY.

Here is a great bulk, and no corn. If empty words might make proof, then had we here proof sufficient. First, I will examine every of these guesses particularly by themselves, and in the end will shew the true story of this island, as it may be gathered by Tertullian, Origen, Chrysostom, Theodoretus, and such other old writers.

And lest any man be deceived by ambiguity of names, this Augustine, whom M. Harding calleth "Saint," and some others, "the apostle of England," was not that great learned father and doctor of the church, whom we worthily call St Au-

[5 Gregory's, H. A. 1564.]

[6 In to, H. A. 1564.]

[7 Here had, H. A. 1564.]

[8 Bæd. Hist. Eccles. Cant. 1722. Lib. I. cap. xxvi. p. 61; where *primo convenire.*]

[9 Bede, 1565, and H. A. 1564.]

[10 ...baptizabantur, mirantes simplicitatem innocentis vitæ, ac dulcedinem doctrinæ eorum cœlestis. —Id. ibid.]

[11 ...gentem, cujus ne linguam quidem nossent. —Id. ibid. cap. xxiii. p. 59.]

[12 Acceperunt...præcipiente...Gregorio, de gente Francorum interpretes.—Id. ibid. cap. xxv. p. 60.]

England. Augustine. gustine, but another of the same name, as far unlike him in learning and holiness, so also two hundred years behind him in course of age; a man, as it was judged by them that saw him and knew him, neither of apostolic spirit, nor any way worthy to be called a saint, but an hypocrite, a superstitious man, cruel, bloody, and proud above measure. And notwithstanding he withdrew the English nation from their gross idolatry, wherein he had no great travail, yet it is certain he planted not religion in this realm; for it was planted here, and had grown, and continued still four hundred years and more, before his coming. But it is thought of many that he corrupted the religion that he found planted here before with much filth of superstition; and therefore Galfridus saith that the bishops, and learned men of this island, would none either[1] of him, nor of the pope, that sent him[2].

Galf. Monem. Lib. viii. cap. iv.

And that it may the better appear what a one this Augustine was, and what opinion the faithful people of this realm had of him, I will rehearse a short story that is written by Beda in that behalf. "The bishops of this country," saith Beda, "before they would go to the council where as Augustine should be president, first went unto a holy wise man that lived an anchor's life, and desired his counsel, whether that, at Augustine's preaching, they should leave the traditions that they had so long used, or no. He answered, 'If he be a man of God, follow him.' 'But how shall we know,' said they, 'whether he be a man of God, or no?' He answered again, 'If he be gentle and lowly of heart, it is likely enough that he carrieth the yoke of the Lord, and offereth unto you to carry the same. But if he be disdainful and proud, then it is certain he is not of God; neither ought you to regard what he saith.' Then said the bishops again, 'But how may we know whether he be disdainful and proud, or no?' 'Provide ye,' saith this holy man, 'that he may be in the council sitting before you come. Then, if he arise up from his chair at your coming, and salute you, know you that he is the man of God, and therefore hearken to him. But if he disdain you, and will not once move his place, specially seeing you are the more in number, then set you as little by him, and disdain him too.' And as this holy man had told them, so did they. When they came into the council-house, Augustine sate still and would not move. Whereupon they refused him, and would not hear him, as a man disdainful and proud of heart, and therefore no man of God. Upon which refusal, Æthelbertus the king raised his power, and slew great numbers of the Britons, and a thousand and two hundred godly religious men, even as they were at their prayers[3]." Hitherto Beda. Wherefore the authority of this Augustine's doings must needs seem the less, yea, although it were all true that M. Harding reporteth of him. And further, I trust, it will be proved, that the things that M. Harding allegeth stand without the compass of six hundred years[4]; and therefore, notwithstanding they were true, yet cannot greatly further his purpose. This Augustine, upon his arrival into England, had a place allotted him in Kent. There he and his company sung, and prayed, and said mass (this mass was a communion, as shall appear), and preached, and baptized. In what language, it is not noted by Beda. But be it in Latin. Hereof M. Harding formeth up this argument:

Beda, Lib. ii. cap. ii.

[1 Neither, 1565.]

[2 Galfrid. Mon. Brit. Reg. Gest. Par. 1517. Lib. VIII. cap. iv. foll. 93, 4.]

[3 ...qui ad præfatum ituri concilium, venerunt primo ad quemdam virum sanctum ac prudentem, qui apud eos anachoreticam ducere vitam solebat, consulentes, an ad prædicationem Augustini suas deserere traditiones deberent. Qui respondebat: Si homo Dei est, sequimini illum. Dixerunt: Et unde hoc possumus probare? At ille: Dominus, inquit, ait: Tollite jugum meum super vos, et discite a me, quia mitis sum et humilis corde. Si ergo Augustinus ille mitis est et humilis corde, credibile est quia jugum Christi et ipse portet, et vobis portandum offerat: sin autem inmitis ac superbus est, constat quia non est de Deo, neque nobis ejus sermo curandus. Qui rursus aiebant: Et undè vel hoc dinoscere valemus? Procurate, inquit, ut ipse prior cum suis ad locum synodi adveniat, et si vobis adpropinquantibus adsurrexerit, scientes quia famulus Christi est, obtemperanter illum audite: sin autem vos spreverit, nec coram vobis adsurgere voluerit, cum sitis numero plures, et ipse spernatur a vobis. Fecerunt ut dixerat. Factumque est, ut venientibus illis sederet Augustinus in sella. Quod illi videntes, mox in iram conversi sunt, eumque notantes superbiæ, cunctis quæ dicebat contradicere laborabant...... Siquidem post hæc...rex...Aedilfrid...maximam gentis perfidæ stragem dedit......Exstinctos in ea pugna ferunt, de his qui ad orandum venerant, viros circiter mille ducentos, et solum quinquaginta fuga esse lapsos.—Bæd. Hist. Eccles. Cant. 1722. Lib. II. cap. ii. pp. 80, 1.]

[4 A better opportunity will occur in the Defence of the Apology of examining the chronology of this period.]

Augustine and his company prayed together in Latin, for that they were strangers newly sent in out of Italy, and understood not the English tongue; England.

Ergo, The English people had the Latin service.

M. Harding should not thus mock the world. He knoweth well, a child would not make such reasons. For Augustine was no parish priest, ne served no cure, but only had a place severally appointed to himself. Neither did any Englishman resort to his service, unless it were to see the strangeness of his doings. He might as well reason thus:

The Jews this day in Venice have their service in the Hebrew tongue;

Ergo, The people of Italy have their service in the Hebrew.

Hitherto, I trow, this matter is but simply proved.

M. HARDING. THE TWENTY-SECOND DIVISION.

Whereas St Augustine, after that the English nation had received the faith, and he had been archbishop[5] *over them, having found, the faith being one, diversity of customs in divers churches, one manner of masses in the holy Roman church, another in that of France; for this and certain other purposes sent two of his clergy, Laurence and Peter, to Rome, to be advertised, amongst other things, what order, manner, and custom of masses, it liked St Gregory the churches of the English nation should have. Hereunto that holy father answered, that what he espied either in the Roman or French, or any other church, that might be most acceptable to Almighty God, he should choose out and gather together, and commend the same to the church of England, there to be left in custom to continue.* Lib. I. cap. xxvii[6]. *If it had then been thought necessary the service of the mass to be in English, or if it had been translated into the English tongue, it is not to be thought that Bede, who declareth all things concerning matters of religion so diligently, specially professing to write an ecclesiastical story, would have passed over that in silence. And if the mass had been used in the English tongue, the monuments and books so much multiplied among the churches would have remained in some place or other. And doubtless some mention would have been made of the time and causes of the leaving such kind of service, and of the*[7] *beginning the new Latin service. As certain of St Gregory's works, turned into English by Bede himself, have been kept, so as they remain to this day.*

THE BISHOP OF SARISBURY.

Here was a short victory. Peter and Paul could never so easily conquer kingdoms. But this matter stood not so much in winning the unfaithful, as in killing the godly. After that was once done, straightways Augustine had the conquest, and was out of hand made archbishop, and wrote to Rome both thereof, and also for resolution of certain questions[8], meet, as he saith, for that rude people of England; as, whether a woman might be baptized while she were great with child, or after her delivery; and how long after she should forbear the church; with certain other secret questions, touching both man and wife, so childish, and so rude, that a man may well doubt whether Augustine were ruder or the people. Among other things, he demanded counsel touching the mass, for that in divers countries he had seen divers orders of masses: and yet, good reader, of them all he had seen no private mass. For the mass in Rome at that time was a communion, as I have already shewed, and as it appeareth by these words, which the deacon pronounced at every mass aloud unto the people: "He that receiveth not the communion, let him give place." The difference stood in addition of certain ceremonies. For the countries abroad, as we may judge, kept still that simple order that they had first received. But the church of Rome was ever altering. For Gregory himself, unto whom this Augustine writeth,

Beda, Lib. i. cap. xxvii.

[[5] Been made archbishop, H. A. 1564.]

[[6] Sed mihi placet, sive in Romana, sive in Galliarum, seu in qualibet ecclesia, aliquid invenisti quod plus omnipotenti Deo possit placere, sollicite eligas, et in Anglorum ecclesia...institutione præcipua, quæ de multis ecclesiis colligere potuisti, infundas.—Bæd. Hist. Eccles. Lib. I. cap. xxvii. p. 63.]

[[7] H. A. 1544, omits *the*.]

[[8] Id. ibid. pp. 62, &c.]

England.

Plat. in Vit. Pont. Sabell. Ennead. viii. Lib. v.

added the Introite, and the anthems, and Alleluia, and willed the Introite to be doubled twice, and the *Kyrie eleeson* nine times, and added also a certain portion to the canon[1]. Of these, and other like differences, Augustine demandeth; and of the same Gregory maketh answer. Hereof M. Harding guesseth thus: "It appeareth not by Beda the service was in English;" *ergo*, the service was in Latin. What kind of logic have we here? Or how may this reason hold? It concludeth *ab auctoritate negative.* I believe M. Harding himself will not allow it. By the like form of reasoning a man might as well say: It appeareth not by Beda that the preachers instructed or exhorted the English people in English; *ergo*, they instructed and exhorted the English people in Latin. Yet again he guesseth further: There is no book to be found of the English service in that time; *ergo*, the service was in Latin. O what folly is this! Who is able to shew any book written in English a thousand years ago? Or if it could be shewed, yet who were able to understand it? There is no book to be found of the prayers that the Druids made in France, or the Gymnosophistæ in India; and will M. Harding thereof conclude that therefore the Druids, or the Gymnosophistæ, prayed in Latin? Such regard he hath to his conclusions.

M. HARDING. THE TWENTY-THIRD DIVISION.

St Gregory himself is a witness of right good authority unto us, that this land of England, which he calleth Britain[2] *in his time, that is almost a thousand years past, had the common prayers and service in an unknown tongue, without doubt in Latin, much in like sort as we have of old time had till now. His words be these:* Ecce ..., [omnipotens Dominus] pene cunctarum ... gentium[3] corda penetravit: ecce, in una fide orientis limitem occidentisque conjunxit: ecce, lingua[4] Britanniæ, quæ nihil[5] aliud noverat, quam barbarum frendere, jamdudum in divinis laudibus Hebræum cœpit Halleluia resonare[6]." "*Behold, our Lord Almighty hath now pierced the hearts almost of all nations: behold, he hath joined the borders of the east and the west in one faith together: behold, the tongue of Britain, that could nothing else but gnash barbarously, hath begun now of late in divine service to sound the Hebrew Halleluia.*"

Expositionis in Job. Lib. xxvii. cap. vi.

THE BISHOP OF SARISBURY.

St Gregory in that place upon Job speaketh not one word, neither of the Latin, nor of the English service. Only he sheweth the mighty power of God, that had converted all the world to the obedience of his gospel. These be his words: *Omnipotens ... Dominus coruscantibus nubibus cardines*[7] *maris operuit: qui emicantibus prædicatorum miraculis, ad fidem etiam terminos mundi perduxit. Ecce enim pene cunctarum jam gentium corda penetravit: Ecce, in una fide orientis limitem occidentisque conjunxit*[6]: "The Almighty Lord with his shining clouds hath covered the corners of the sea; for he hath brought the ends of the world unto the faith, at the sight of the glorious miracles of the preachers. For behold, he hath well near pierced through the hearts of all nations, and hath joined together the borders of the east and the west in one faith." Now, saith M. Harding, "Gregory is a witness of right good authority, that this realm of England had the service in an unknown tongue." Verily, Gregory's authority in this case were right good, if he would say the word. "But," saith M. Harding, "St Gregory reporteth that the English people, in the praising of God, pronounced the Hebrew Halleluia;" *ergo*, he is witness to the Latin service. This argument may be perfected[8] and made thus: The English people in their prayers said Halleluia: Halleluia is an Hebrew word; *ergo*, the English people had the Latin service.

Gregor. in Job. Lib. xxvii. cap. vi.

[1 Plat. de Vit. Pont. Col. 1551. Gregor. I. p. 73. Sabell. Rapsod. Hist. Par. 1509. Ennead. VIII. Lib. v. Pars III. fol. 35. 2.]

[2 Brittanie, 1611.]

[3 Jam gentium, H. A. 1564.]

[4 Linguæ, 1611.]

[5 Nil, H. A. 1564.]

[6 Gregor. Magn. Papæ I. Op. Par. 1705. Moral. Lib. XXVII. in cap. xxxvi. B. Job. cap. xi. 21. Tom. I. col. 862.]

[7 Cardinis, 1611.]

[8 Perfited, 1565.]

England.

This is another *syllogismus* of M. Harding's. God wot he might have made it better. Of St Gregory's words he might rather have concluded thus:

The people of England in their prayers pronounced the Hebrew Halleluia; *ergo*, they had the Hebrew service.

Which doubtless in the English churches had been very strange; and yet as much reason in that, as in the Latin. As for these Hebrew words, *Halleluia, Amen, Sabaoth*, and other like, they may as well be used in the English service as in the Latin; and at this day are used, and continued still in the reformed churches in Germany; and therefore can import no more the one than the other.

M. HARDING. THE TWENTY-FOURTH DIVISION.

He lived in the year of our Lord 640.

Bede, in the end of his second book, sheweth, that one James, a deacon of the church of York, a very cunning man in song, soon after the faith had been spread abroad here, as the number of believers grew, began to be a master or teacher of singing in the church, after the manner of the Romans[9]. *The like he writeth of one Eddi, surnamed Stephanus, that taught the people of Northumberland to sing the service after the Roman manner; and of Putta, a holy man, bishop of Rochester, commending him much for his great skill of singing in the church, after the use and manner of the Romans, which he had learned of the disciples of St Gregory*[10].

Anno Dom. 668. Anno 668.

Marvellous proofs.

These be testimonies plain and evident enough, that, at the beginning, the churches of England had their divine service in Latin, and not in English. One place more I will recite out of Bede, most manifest of all other, for proof hereof. In the time of Agatho the pope, there was a reverend man called John Archicantor, that is, chief chaunter or singer, of St Peter's church at Rome, and abbat of the monastery of St Martin there; Benedict, an abbat of Britain, having builded a monastery at the mouth of the river Murus, (Bede so calleth it), sued to the pope for confirmations, liberties, franchisies, privileges, &c., as in such case hath been accustomed. Among other things, he obtained this cunning chaunter John, to come with him into Britain to teach song.

Anno 680.

Because Bede's ecclesiastical story is not very common, I have thought good here to recite his own words, thus Englished: "This abbat Benedict took with him the foresaid John, to bring him into Britain, that he should teach in his monastery the course of service for the whole year, so as it was done at St Peter's in Rome. John did as he had commandment from[11] *the pope, both in teaching the singing men of the said monastery the order and rite of singing and reading with utterance of their voice, and also of writing and pricking those things that the compass of the whole year required in the celebration and keeping of the holy days; which be kept in the same monastery till this day, and be copied out of many round about, on every coast. Neither did that John teach the brethren of that monastery only; but also many other made all the means they could to get him to other places, where they might have him to teach*[12]." *Thus*[13] *far Bede. I trow, no man will think that this Roman taught and wrote the order and manner of singing, and pronouncing the service of the churches of this land, in the English tongue. If it had been deemed of the learned and godly governors of christian people then a necessary point to salvation, to have had the service in the English, no man had been so apt and fit to have translated it, as he, who in those days had, by special grace of God, a singular gift to make songs and sonnets in English metre,*

[9 Reliquerat autem [Paulinus] in ecclesia sua Eburacensi Jacobum diaconum...Qui quoniam cantandi in ecclesia erat peritissimus...crescente numero fidelium, etiam magister ecclesiasticæ cantionis juxta morem Romanorum seu Cantuariorum multis cœpit existere.—Bæd. Hist. Eccles. Cant. 1722. Lib. II. cap. xx. p. 102.]

[10 Id. ibid. Lib. IV. cap. ii. p. 143.]

[11 Of, H. A. 1564.]

[12 Accepit et præfatum Johannem Abbatem Brittaniam perducendum; quatenus in monasterio suo cursum canendi annuum, sicut ad sanctum Petrum Romæ agebatur, edoceret: egitque Abba Johannes ut jussionem acceperat pontificis, et ordinem videlicet ritumque canendi ac legendi viva voce præfati monasterii cantores edocendo, et ea quæ totius anni circulus in celebratione dierum festorum poscebat, etiam literis mandando: quæ hactenus in eodem monasterio servata, et a multis jam sunt circumquaque transcripta. Non solum autem idem Johannes ipsius monasterii fratres docebat, verum de omnibus pene ejusdem provinciæ monasteriis ad audiendum eum, qui cantandi erant periti, confluebant. Sed et ipsum per loca in quibus doceret, multi invitare curabant.—Id. ibid. Lib. IV. cap. xviii. p. 161.]

[13 This, 1565, and H. A. 1564.]

England. *to serve religion and devotion. His name was Cednom, of whom Bede* [*Cednom*, 1565, and H. A. 1564.] *writeth marvellous things: how he made divers songs containing matter*

Anno 680. *of the holy scripture with such exceeding sweetness, and with such a grace, as many, feeling their hearts compunct and pricked with hearing and reading of them, withdrew themselves from the love of the world, and were enkindled with the desire of the heavenly life. "Many," saith Bede, "of the English nation attempted after him to make religious and godly poetries, but none could do comparably to him. For he was not (saith he, alluding to St Paul's words) taught of men,* [*Gal. i.* 1565. and H. A. 1564.] *neither by man, that art of making godly songs; but received from God that gift freely. And therefore he could make no wanton, trifling, or vain ditties, but only such as pertained to godly religion, and might seem to proceed of a head guided by the Holy Ghost*[1]." Lib. IV. cap. xxiv. *This divine poet Cednom, though he made many and sundry holy works, having their whole argument out of holy scripture, as Bede reporteth, yet never made he any piece of the service*

The eightieth untruth. For[2] his examples reach nothing so far.

to be used in the church. Thus the faith hath continued in this land, among the English people, from the fourteenth year of the reign of Mauritius [*The first entry of the English service*, H. A. 1564.] *the emperor, almost these thousand years; and until the late king Edward's time the English service was never heard of, at leastway, never in the church of England, by public authority, received and used.*

THE BISHOP OF SARISBURY.

I little thought M. Harding would so much have bewrayed his want, to prove his matter by pipers and poets, and specially being all without the compass of

Beda, Lib. ii. cap. xiv. Beda, Lib. iv. cap. xxi. Beda, Lib. iv. cap. i.

six hundred years. For it is plain by Beda, that this James, the deacon, lived under king Edwin, about the year of our Lord six hundred and forty[3]; Putta and Edda, in the year six hundred and sixty-eight[4]; John the arch-chaunter, and Cednom, or Cedman (for so his name is read in Beda, written in parchment), in the time[5] of pope Agatho, in the year six hundred and eighty, in whose name

Dist. xix. Sic omnes.

this decree is written: *Sic omnes sanctiones apostolicæ sedis accipiendæ sunt tanquam ipsius divina voce Petri firmatæ*[6]: "All the constitutions of the apostolic see must be received so as if they were confirmed by the very heavenly voice of St Peter." Unto such a tyranny the church of Rome at that time was grown. And the gloss upon the same saith: *Papa sanctitatem* [*suam*] *recipit a cathedra*[7]: "The pope receiveth his holiness of his chair." Therefore herein M. Harding hath somewhat misreckoned himself. Although all the rest were certain, yet these witnesses come too late to make good proof.

"Yet," saith M. Harding, "these testimonies be plain and evident enough, that at the beginning the churches of England had their divine service in Latin, and not in English." These be very dumb testimonies. For neither James the deacon, nor John the arch-chaunter, nor Cednom, nor Putta, nor Beda himself, ever said so. Therefore this matter is proved by M. Harding's guess, and not by the words of the witnesses.

The force of his reason seemeth to weigh thus:

These musicians taught the clerks of England to sing their service after the Roman manner;

Ergo, They had the Latin service.

The substance of this argument may the better appear by some other like:

[[1] Cujus [Caedmonis] carminibus multorum sæpe animi ad contemptum seculi et appetitum sunt vitæ cœlestis accensi. Et quidem et alii post illum in gente Anglorum religiosa poemata facere tentabant; sed nullus eum æquiparare potuit. Namque ipse non ab hominibus, neque per hominem institutis canendi artem didicit; sed divinitus adjutus gratis canendi donum accepit. Unde nihil unquam frivoli et supervacui poematis facere potuit; sed ea tantummodo quæ ad religionem pertinent, religiosam ejus linguam decebant.—Id. ibid. Lib. IV. cap. xxiv. p. 170.]

[[2] 1565 omits *for*.]

[[3] Id. ibid. Lib. II. capp. xiv. xx. pp. 95, 101, 2. Bede states that it was after the death of Edwin that Paulinus quitted York, leaving James the deacon there.]

[[4] Id. ibid. Lib. IV. cap. ii. p. 143.]

[[5] Id. ibid. Lib. IV. capp. xviii. xxiv. pp. 161. 70. The dates assigned in the edition quoted are almost exactly those which Jewel gives.]

[[6] Agath. Papa in Corp. Jur. Canon. Lugd. 1624. Decret. Gratian. Decr. Prim. Pars, Dist. xix. can. 2. col. 82; where we find *apostolicæ sedis sanctiones, divini Petri voce*, and *firmatæ sint*.]

[[7] Ibid. col. 81.]

England.

Triptolemus taught all nations to plough the[8] ground after the manner of the Athenians;

Ergo, he taught all nations in the Athenian tongue.

Or: Abraham taught the Egyptians arithmetic and astronomy;

Ergo, Abraham taught the Egyptians in the Chaldee tongue.

For doth M. Harding believe it is not possible to learn the Roman music without the Roman speech; or that the note cannot be taught without the ditty? Verily, I reckon him no good musician that will say so. By the like reason he might say: Damasus besought St Hierome to send to him *Græcorum psallentiam*[9], "the music of the Greek church," to the intent to practise the same in the church of Rome; *ergo*, Damasus used the Greek service in the church of Rome. Damasus ad Hieron.

But Beda himself is best able to expound his own meaning. Having occasion to entreat of Adrianus and Theodorus, that came into England the year of our Lord 668, he writeth thus: *Sonos cantandi in ecclesia, quos eatenus in Cantio tantum noverant, ab hoc tempore per omnes Anglorum ecclesias discere cœperunt*[10]: "From that time they began to learn throughout all the churches of England the sounds of singing, or the notes of music, which before that time were known only in Kent." Beda saith: "They learned the sounds, or notes, or harmony," and maketh no mention of the tongue or ditty. But let M. Harding's conclusions stand for good:

These musicians taught the clerks of England to sing after the Roman manner;

Ergo, they had the Latin service;

and doth he not see that he concludeth fully with me, and directly against himself? Certainly, if the Roman music import the Latin service, then may I well reason thus: The churches of England had not the Roman music before James the deacon of York, which lived in the year of our Lord 640; *ergo*, before that time the churches of England had not the Latin service. Which thing overthroweth all that M. Harding hath hitherto spoken, and standeth very well with my assertion. No Latin service in England within six hundred years.

Again, where he saith that "John, the arch-chaunter, that lived in the year of our Lord 680, taught the clerks of England to pronounce the Latin tongue;" it may thereof well be gathered, that before that time they could not pronounce the Latin tongue; and so before that time had not the Latin service.

Now, forsomuch as M. Harding saith, By mean of the arrival and conquest of the Englishmen, who then were infidels, the faith was utterly banished out of this realm, and remained only in a few Britons, and Augustine at his coming restored the same again, and therefore is called of some the Englishmen's apostle; I think it necessary therefore shortly to touch somewhat of the state of the church within this land, both before the entry of our English nation, and also in the first time of our being here. Gildas saith that Joseph of Arimathea, that took down Christ from the cross, being sent hither by Philip the apostle, out of France, began first to preach the gospel in this realm, in the time of Tiberius the emperor[11]. Nicephorus saith that Simon Zelotes about the same time came into this island, and did the like[12]. Theodoretus saith that St Paul, immediately after his first delivery in Rome, under the emperor Nero, preached the gospel in this island, and in other countries of the west[13]. Tertullian saith the island of Britain was subject unto Christ in his time[14]. And Origen witnesseth the like of the same island in his time[15]; at which time Lucius, the king of this realm, was baptized, and received the gospel, and sent to Rome to Eleutherius, the bishop there, for

Gildas. Anno Dom. 38.

Niceph. Lib. ii. cap. iv. Anno 38.

Theod. de Curandis Græcorum Affect. Lib. ix.

Tertull. Adv. Jud. Anno 230.

Orig. in Ezech. Hom. 4. Anno 240.

[[8] Their, 1565.]

[[9] See before, p. 265, note 9.]

[[10] Bæd. Hist. Eccles. Cant. 1722. Lib. IV. cap. ii. p. 143; where *Cantia*.]

[[11] Gild. Sap. De Excid. Brit. Pars I. 6. in Biblioth. Vet. Patr. Stud. Galland. Venet. 1765-81. Tom. XII. p. 194. But Gildas does not mention Joseph of Arimathea. See Stillingfleet's Works. Lond. 1709-10. Orig. Brit. chap. i. Vol. III. pp. 4, &c.]

[[12] ...καὶ πρὸς ἑσπέριον ὠκεανὸν εἰσβαλὼν, καὶ τὰς Βρετανικὰς νήσους εὐαγγελισάμενος.—Niceph. Call. Hist. Eccles. Lut. Par. 1630. Lib. II. cap. xl. Tom. I. p. 202.]

[[13] See before, page 280, note 1. Jewel, it may be added, cited Theodoret and other authors here named, on the authority of the Magdeburg Centuriators. See Eccles. Hist. Basil. 1564-74. Cent. I. Lib. II. col. 23.]

[[14] Tertull. Op. Lut. 1641. Adv. Jud. 7, p. 213.]

[[15] Orig. Op. Par. 1733-59. In Ezech. Hom. iv. Tom. III. p. 370.]

England.

his advice touching the ordering of his church and realm. Helena, being an Englishwoman, wife unto Constantius the emperor, and mother unto Constantinus, is notably praised for her faith and religion by St Ambrose[1], by Eusebius[2], by Sozomenus[3], and others.

Ambros. de Obit. Theod. Euseb. de Vit. Constant. Lib. iii. Soz. Lib. ii. cap. i. Chrysost. Adv. Gent. Tom. v. Beda, Lib. ii. cap. ii.

Chrysostom saith, that in his time the island of Britain had received "the power of the gospel[4]."

Now let us consider in what state this realm stood, touching religion, at the coming of Augustine, at which time M. Harding surmiseth the whole faith was utterly decayed. First, Beda saith there were among the Britons seven bishops, and one archbishop, and one and twenty hundred monks, about Bancor; and, as he further avoucheth, *plures viri doctissimi*, "many more great learned men," that utterly refused to receive this Augustine with his new religion[5].

Beda, Lib. i. cap. xxvi.

As touching the English nation, it appeareth by Beda, that the queen herself was christened, and had St Martin's church appointed her freely to pray in with her company[6]. Whereof it may be thought, the king was no great enemy unto the faith; and therefore the like also may well be thought of a great number of the people.

Thus much shortly of the first planting of the religion of Christ within this island, and of the continuance of the same from the time of Joseph of Arimathea until the coming in of Augustine. Now, touching the common prayers that they used among themselves all that while.

First, it were very much for M. Harding to say that St Paul, or Joseph of 1.
Arimathea, or Simon Zelotes, being all Hebrews born, took order that the service here should be ministered unto the people in the Latin tongue.

Again, Eleutherius, the bishop of Rome, for general order to be taken in the 2.
realm and churches here, wrote his advice unto Lucius the king in this sort: *Suscepisti...in regno Britanniæ, miseratione divina, legem et fidem Christi. Habetis penes vos in regno utramque paginam: ex illis, Dei gratia, per concilium regni vestri, sume legem, et per illam, Dei patientia, vestrum rege Britanniæ regnum. Vicarius vero Dei estis in regno* [*illo*][7]: "Ye have received in the kingdom of Britain, by God's mercy, both the law and faith of Christ. Ye have both the new testament and the old. Out of the same, through God's grace, by the advice of your realm, take a law, and by the same, through God's sufferance, rule you your kingdom of Britain. For in that kingdom you are God's vicar." He willeth him to order matters according to the law of God. Now the law of God willeth the service so to be said as the people may understand it, and give consent unto it by saying Amen: but the people of this realm could not have said Amen unto the Latin service; therefore no man can well think that king Lucius appointed the common service to be said in that tongue.

Further, it may well be judged that the greatest furtherers of religion within 3.
this realm were Grecians, and for order of the church had instructions evermore from the Greek church, and not from Rome; as it may appear by the keeping of the Easter-day, and by other good conjectures mentioned by Beda. Now, if the Grecians had refused the common vulgar tongue of this country, doubtless they would have appointed their own Greek tongue for the public ministration, and not the Latin.

Gregor. in Job. Lib. xxvii. cap. vi. Ecce lingua Britanniæ, quæ nil aliud noverat, quam barbarum frendere.

Again, M. Harding allegeth St Gregory, that the tongue of this nation was 4.
never otherwise taught, but only to roar out their barbarous language[8]: how then can he so suddenly say that, from the time of Joseph of Arimathea, they had evermore the service in the learned Latin tongue?

Besides this, St Gregory, writing unto Augustine, "willeth him, of the sundry 5.

[1 Ambros. Op. Par. 1686-90. De Obit. Theodos. Orat. 40, &c. Tom. II. cols. 1209, &c.]

[2 Euseb. in Hist. Eccles. Script. Amst. 1695-1700. De Vit. Constant. Lib. III. capp. xlii. &c. pp. 415, &c.]

[3 Sozom. in eod. Lib. II. capp. i. ii. pp. 360, &c.]

[4 Καὶ γὰρ αἱ Βρετανικαὶ νῆσοι...τῆς δυνάμεως τοῦ ῥήματος ᾔσθοντο. καὶ γὰρ κἀκεῖ ἐκκλησίαι καὶ θυσιαστήρια πεπήγασιν.—Chrysost. Op. Par. 1718-38. Cont. Jud. et Gent. Tom. I. p. 575.]

[5 Bæd. Hist. Eccles. Cant. 1722. Lib. II. cap. ii. pp. 79, 80. Bede does not mention the archbishop here.]

[6 Id. ibid. Lib. I. cap. xxvi. p. 65.]

[7 This epistle may be seen in Sammes Britan. Ant. Lond. 1676. p. 261. The author took it, he declares, from a MS. preserved among the records of London, being that used by Jewel. We find there *suscepistis, miseratione divina in regno*, and *potentia vestrum reges*.]

[8 Gregor. Magn. Papæ I. Op. Par. 1705. Moral. Lib. XXVII. in cap. xxxvi. B. Job. cap. xi. 21. Tom. I. col. 862.]

others[9] that he had seen in divers countries, to take such as he could judge might do most good[10]." But M. Harding granteth that, at the first planting of the faith, it is necessary the common prayers be ministered in the known tongue; therefore it must needs be thought that Augustine, coming hither, as it is supposed, to plant the faith, judged that thing best that M. Harding saith was necessary, and so ministered the common prayers in the known tongue. England.

And to conclude, it was most meet that Augustine, being purposely sent hither from Rome, should conform his church here to the church of Rome. But the service in the church of Rome was ministered then in the vulgar tongue, as it is many ways easy to be proved; therefore it behoved Augustine likewise, in the churches of this country, to see the service ministered in the vulgar tongue.

Howbeit, it seemeth by M. Harding's conclusion, that he maketh his account only from the fourteenth year of the emperor Mauritius, which was in the year of our Lord five hundred four-score and sixteen: "Sithence which time," he saith, "until the time of king Edward the sixth, there was never in this realm other than the Latin service." I may not greatly blame this division. For of the six hundred years after Christ, whereupon I join with him in issue, liberally and of his own accord he giveth me back five hundred four-score and sixteen, and of so great a number reserveth unto himself but only four poor years, and yet is not very certain of the same. But if Marianus Scotus' account be true, that Augustine came into this realm, not the fourteenth year of the emperor Mauritius, but four years after, which was just the six hundredth year after Christ[11], then he reserveth not one year at all unto himself, but yieldeth me back all together. Surely Abbas Urspergensis writeth thus: "Gregorius, in the year of our Lord six hundred and three, having sent in Augustine and Mellitus, converted England to the faith[12]." All this hitherto maketh with me, unless M. Harding will say, the people of this country had christian service before they were christened.

Anno 596.

Marian. Scot.

Anno 600.

Abbas Urspergen. in Vita Mauritii. Anno 603.

M. HARDING. THE TWENTY-FIFTH DIVISION.

Now, touching the scripture by M. Jewel, and by all them of that side alleged, for the service to be had in the vulgar tongue. In the fourteenth chapter of the first epistle to the Corinthians, St Paul treateth of the use of tongues, so as it was in the primitive church a special gift. As the faithful folk came together to pray, and to hear God's word, some one man suddenly stood up, and spake in the congregation with tongues of many nations, Spiritu insusurrante, *as Chrysostom saith, that is, "by inspiration, or prompting of the Spirit," so as neither others that were present, neither himself, after the opinion of Chrysostom, understood what he said. That gift the apostle did not forbid, for that every gift of God is good, and nothing by him done in vain, but dehorted the Corinthians from the vain and ambitious use of it; and therefore did much extenuate the same, and preferred prophesying, that is, the gift to interpret and expound scriptures, far before it. It was not in the church but in the apostles' time, or a very short while after them, and that altogether by miracle, the Holy Ghost being the worker of it.*

As concerning the order of the common prayers, and public service, in such sort as we have now, and that age had not, St Paul mentioneth nothing, neither speaketh one word in that whole chapter, but of the use of the miraculous gift, as is said before. And therefore his sayings out of that chapter be not fitly alleged of M. Jewel, and the rest of our adversaries, against the manner of prayers and service of the church, now received, and of long time used, which in the west is uttered in the Latin tongue, not by way of miracle, or peculiar gift, but according to the institution and ordinance of the church. Profecto enim cœlum ecclesia tum fuit: *"In very deed," saith Chrysostom, "the church then was a heaven, when as the Holy Ghost administered all things, moderated all the heads of the church, taught[13] each one with his*

The place of St Paul to the Corinthians maketh not for the service in the English tongue.

The eighty-first untruth. For sundry doctors, both old and new, allege these words to this self-same purpose.

In 1 Cor. xiv. Hom. 37.

[9 Orders, 1565, 1609.]

[10 See before, page 301, note 6.]

[11 Marian. Scot. Chronic. Basil. 1559. Lib. II. Ætas vi. col. 372.]

[12 Anno Domini DCIII. Gregorius missis doctoribus, Augustino, Mellito, Johanne, aliisque pluribus, Anglos ad Christum convertit.—Chronic. Abbat. Ursperg. Argent. 1537. Anni Maurit. p. 157.]

[13 Caught, 1565, 1609, and H. A. 1564.]

England.

inspiration. As for now, we keep but the steps only of those things. We speak two or three of us, and that asunder, and, one holding his peace, another beginneth. But these be but signs only and memorials of things. And so when we have begun (he meaneth Dominus vobiscum), et cum spiritu tuo, *the people answereth; meaning to signify thereby, that so in old time they spake, not of their own wisdom, but of the instinct of the Spirit of God*[1].*" Thus*[2] *much Chrysostom of the heavenly manner of the primitive church in the apostles' time. Now, if in these days the manner were like, if it pleased the Holy Ghost to pour upon us the like abundance of grace, as to do all things for us, to rule the heads of all faithful people, to carry each one of us with his divine inspiration, and, when we came to church together for comfort and edifying, to give into our hearts, and put into our mouths by daily miracle what we should pray, and what we should preach, and how we should handle the scriptures; in this case no catholic christian man would allow the unfruitful speaking with strange and unknown tongues, without interpretation, to the let and hinderance of God's word to be declared, and to the keeping of the people only in gazing and wondering, from saying Amen, and giving their assent to the godly blessing and thanksgiving. But the order of the church now is far otherwise. We have not those miraculous gifts, and right well may we do without them. For the speaking with tongues was instead of a sign or wonder, not to them that believed, but to the unbelievers. And signs be for the unfaithful: the faithful have no need of them. In churches, I mean where ancient order is kept, whiles the service is sung or said, the ministers do not speak with tongues, or with a tongue, in such sort as St Paul understood; but they do read and rehearse things set forth and appointed to them. St Paul rebuketh them, who, speaking with tongues, letted the preachers, so as the people present might not be edified. The Latin service is not so done in the church, as the exposition of the scriptures be thereby excluded. In the apostles' time they came to church, to the intent they might profitably exercise the gifts God gave them, and by the same, specially by the gift of prophesying, edify one another, and teach one another. Now-a-days they come not together to church*[3]*, one to teach another, and to expound the scriptures in common; but to pray, and to hear the opening of God's word, not one of another, without order, but of some one, to wit, the bishop, priest, curate, or other spiritual governor and teacher.*

THE BISHOP OF SARISBURY.

We may safely grant some part of M. Harding's long talk without prejudice of our cause. Indeed St Paul, in the place alleged, spake of the gift of tongues, as it was a special miracle, enduring only for a while, not gotten by labour or study, but freely inspired by the Spirit of God.

But the Latin tongue, saith M. Harding, as it is now commonly used in the Roman service, is not given by any such prompting of the Holy Ghost, nor is now any miracle at all. Therefore the place of St Paul cannot be applied unto it. We grant well, it is no miracle, as it is now used, nor any way savoureth of the Spirit of God. But this is a great miracle, to see either any man so wicked, that so will use it; or so impudent, that so will defend it; or so patient, that so will suffer it. This verily is a marvellous miracle.

M. Harding seemeth hereof to reason of this sort: St Paul forbade the Corinthians to use the special miracle and gift of God, without profiting the congregation; *ergo*, now having the Latin tongue without miracle, we may minister the service therein, although the congregation have no profit by it. This reason is strange, and holdeth as simply as the rest. Yet hath he given special advertisement in the margin, that this place of St Paul serveth nothing

[1 Καὶ γὰρ οὐρανὸς ἡ ἐκκλησία τότε, τοῦ Πνεύματος πάντα δημαγωγοῦντος καὶ τῶν προεστώτων ἕκαστον κινοῦντος, καὶ ἔνθουν ποιοῦντος. ἀλλὰ νῦν τὰ σύμβολα κατέχομεν τῶν χαρισμάτων ἐκείνων μόνον. καὶ γὰρ καὶ νῦν δύο ἢ τρεῖς λέγομεν, καὶ ἀνὰ μέρος, καὶ ἑτέρου σιγῶντος ἕτερος ἄρχεται. ἀλλὰ σημεῖα ταῦτα μόνον ἐστὶν ἐκείνων καὶ ὑπομνήματα. διὸ ἐπειδὰν ἀρξώμεθα λέγειν, ὁ λαὸς ἀντιφθέγγεται, τῷ πνεύματί σου, δεικνὺς ὅτι τὸ παλαιὸν οὕτως ἔλεγον, οὐκ οἰκείᾳ σοφίᾳ, ἀλλὰ τῷ Πνεύματι κινούμενοι.—Chrysost. Op. Par. 1718-38. In Epist. I. ad Cor. Hom. xxxvi. Tom. X. p. 339.]

[2 This, 1565, and H. A. 1564.]

[3 To church together, H. A. 1564.]

to our purpose. If this note be so certain, and so authentical as he would seem to make it, then were the doctors, both new and old, that took it otherwise, not well advised. For Lyra, writing upon the same, saith thus: *Si populus intelligat orationem...sacerdotis, melius reducitur in Deum, et devotius respondet, Amen. Ideo dicit Paulus, Si tu sacerdos benedixeris spiritu, et populus non intelligat, quid proficit populus simplex et non intelligens? Quapropter in primitiva ecclesia benedictiones et cetera omnia fiebant in vulgari*[4]*:* "If the people understand the prayer of the priest, they are the better brought unto God, and with greater devotion they answer, Amen. Therefore St Paul saith, 'If thou, being a priest, bless with thy spirit, and the people understand thee not, what profit then hath the people, being simple, and not understanding thee?' Therefore in the primitive church both the blessings, and all other things, were done in the vulgar tongue." The vulgar tongue, saith Lyra, was used in the primitive church, upon occasion of these words of St Paul. In the council of Acon, it is written thus: *Psallentium in ecclesia Domino mens concordare debet cum voce, ut impleatur illud apostoli, Psallam spiritu, psallam et mente*[5]*:* "The voice and mind of them that sing unto the Lord in the church must agree together." The reason thereof is taken out of this place of St Paul: "I will sing with my spirit, I will sing with my mind." Chrysostom saith, St Paul driveth the whole tenor of this matter unto the profit of the hearers. These be his words: *Est autem quod Paulus dicit hujusmodi: Nisi dixero quod percipi facile clareque a vobis possit, sed linguarum munere prœditum me esse tantum ostendam, nullum ex his, quæ non intelligetis, fructum facientes abibitis. Nam quæ utilitas esse possit ex voce non intellecta?*[6] "St Paul's saying standeth thus: Unless I utter my words so as they may clearly and plainly be perceived of you, but only shew myself[7] to have the gift of tongues, ye shall have no fruit of those things that ye know not. For what profit can ye get of a voice that ye cannot understand?" And again, the same Chrysostom saith further[8]: *Sic et vos, nisi significantem vocem dederitis, verba (quod dicitur) vento, hoc est, nemini facietis:* "Even so you, unless you give a sound that may be known, as the proverb is, ye shall throw forth your words into the wind, that is to say, ye shall speak to no man."

Lyra in 1 Cor. xiv.

Concil. Aquisgr. cap. 132.

Chrysost. in 1 Cor. Hom. 35.

So likewise the emperor Justinian, where he commandeth all bishops and priests to minister the sacraments and other prayers aloud and with open voice, he avoucheth the same by this place of St Paul. For thus he saith: *Sic enim divinus apostolus docet, dicens, Si solum spiritu benedixeris, qui implet locum idiotæ, quomodo dicet Amen super tuam benedictionem? Non enim intelligit quid dicas*[9]*:* "So the holy apostle saith: 'If thou only bless or pray with thy spirit, how shall he that supplieth the room of the unlearned say Amen unto thy blessing? For he knoweth not what thou sayest'." It appeareth by these authorities, notwithstanding M. Harding's note, that St Paul maketh somewhat for our purpose.

De Eccles. Div. Capit.

Howbeit, we build not our proofs upon the miracle and gift of tongues, that lasted but for a while; but upon these express and plain words of St Paul, which no man can deny: "He that speaketh with tongue speaketh not unto men, but unto God; for no man heareth him. If the trumpet give an uncertain voice, who shall prepare himself unto the war? Even so you, unless ye utter such words as have signification, how shall it be known what we[10] say? For ye shall speak into the wind. I will pray with my spirit, I will pray with my mind: I will sing with my spirit, I will sing with my mind. If thou bless with thy spirit, how shall the ignorant say Amen unto thy thanksgiving? For he knoweth not what thou sayest. In the church I had liefer to speak five words with my mind, so that I may instruct others, than ten thousand words with my tongue. Let all things be done to the profit of the people." These words be evident: the exposition of Lyra, of the council of Acon, of Chrysostom, and

1 Cor. xiv.

[[4] Bibl. cum Gloss. Ord. et Expos. N. de Lyra, Basil. 1502. Ad Cor. I. cap. xiv. Pars VI. fol. 55. 2; where we read *ideo dicit:* Ceterum si benedixeris. *i. tu sacerdos vel episcope.* Spiritu. *i. absque hoc quod populus intelligat...quid proficit, &c. propterea quod in primitiva, &c.* and *cetera communia.*]

[[5] Concil. Aquisgr. cap. 132. in Crabb. Concil. Col. Agrip. 1551. Tom. II. p. 698.]

[[6] Chrysost. Op. In Epist. I. ad Cor. Hom. XXXV. Tom. X. p. 323.]

[[7] Meself, 1565.]

[[8] Farther, 1565.]

[[9] See before, page 287, note 10.]

[[10] Ye, 1565, 1609.]

Justinian, is plain. And yet must we, upon M. Harding's warrant, needs believe that all this maketh nothing for the English service to be had in the church of England.

M. HARDING. THE TWENTY-SIXTH DIVISION.

The eighty-second untruth. The altars to[1] communion tables stood in the midst of the church, as shall appear.

And forasmuch as all the people cannot hear the priest's prayers at the altar (which hath from the apostles' time hitherto ever been a place to celebrate the holy oblation at), turning himself for the most part to the east, according to the[2] *apostolic tradition, in what tongue soever they be uttered, for distance of the place they remain in, it is no inconvenience, such admitted into the quire, as have better understanding of that is said or sung, that the rest remain in seemly wise in the nether part of the church, and there make their humble prayers to God by themselves in silence, in that language they best understand, conforming themselves to the priest's blessing and thanksgiving, through faith and obedience, with their brethren in the quire, and giving assent to the same, understanding some good part of that is done, as declared by often preaching, and by holy outward ceremonies, perceivable to the senses of the simplest.*

The people taught by ceremonies.

THE BISHOP OF SARISBURY.

Communion tables or altars.

There have been altars, saith M. Harding, even from the apostles' time, and that even as it is used now, far off from the body of the church. Neither could the people beneath hear the priest standing about[3] at the altar, or understand what he meant, but only were instructed by holy reverend ceremonies, and gave consent unto all that was said by the priest, and yet knew not what he said.

This man could never utter so many untruths together without some special privilege. For first, where he saith, The apostles in their time erected altars, it is well known, that there was no christian church yet built in the apostles' time. For the faithful, for fear of the tyrants, were fain to meet together in private houses, in vacant places, in woods and forests, and in caves under the ground. And may we think that altars were built before the church? Verily Origen, that lived two hundred years after Christ, hath these words against Celsus: *Objicit nobis, quod non habeamus imagines, aut aras, aut templa*[4]: "Celsus chargeth our religion with this, that we have neither images, nor altars, nor churches."

Orig. contra Cels. Lib. iv.

Likewise saith Arnobius, that lived somewhat after Origen, writing against the heathens: *Accusatis nos, quod nec templa habeamus, nec imagines, nec aras*[5]: "Ye accuse us, for that we have neither churches, nor images, nor altars."

Arnobius, Lib. ii.

And Volaterranus and Vernerius testify, that Sixtus, bishop of Rome, was the first that caused altars to be erected[6].

Volaterranus. Vernerius.

Therefore M. Harding was not well advised, so confidently to say that altars have ever been, even sithence the apostles' time.

Neither afterward, when altars were first used, and so named, were they straightway built of stone; as Durandus and such others say they must needs be, and that, *quia petra erat Christus*[7]: "because Christ was the stone." For Gerson saith that Sylvester, bishop of Rome, first caused stone altars to be made, and willed that no man should consecrate at a wooden altar, but himself only, and his successors there[8]. And notwithstanding both for continuance and steadiness such altars were used in some places, as it appeareth by Gregorius Nyssenus[9],

Durand. Lib. iv. Gerson. contra Floret. Lib. iv.

Gregor. Nyss. de Sancto Baptismate. August. ad Bonifacium, Epist. I.

[1 Or, 1565, 1609.]

[2 H. A. 1564, omits *the*.]

[3 Above, 1565.]

[4 Μετὰ ταῦτα δὲ ὁ Κέλσος φησὶν, ἡμᾶς βωμοὺς καὶ ἀγάλματα καὶ νεὼς ἱδρύσθαι φεύγειν.—Orig. Op. Par. 1733-59. Cont. Cels. Lib. VIII. 17. Tom. I. pp. 754, 5.]

[5 The following is probably the passage intended: In hac enim consuestis parte crimen nobis maximum impietatis affigere, quod neque ædes sacras venerationis ad officia construamus, non deorum alicujus simulacrum constituamus, aut formam; non altaria fabricemus, non aras, &c.—Arnob. Op. Par. 1580. Adv. Gent. Lib. VI. p. 194.]

[6 Several authors name Sixtus II. as having introduced the use of consecrated altars. See Stella, Vit. Pontif. Basil. 1507. fol. B.]

[7 Durand. Rat. Div. Offic. Lugd. 1565. Lib. I. cap. vii. 28. fol. 34. 2. See page 15, note 14.]

[8 Postea Silvester papa statuit ut omnia altaria essent lapidea, et quod nullus super illud altare ligneum [in ecclesia Lateranensi] nisi solus Romanus pontifex celebret.—Floret. Lugd. 1499. Lib. IV. De Sacr. Euchar. fol. 94. 2.]

[9 Gregor. Nyss. Op. Par. 1638. In Bapt. Christ. Tom. III. pp. 369, 70.]

St Basil's brother; yet it is plain by St Augustine, that in his time in Africa they were made of timber. For he saith that "the Donatists in their rage wounded the priest, and brake asunder the altar-boards[10]." And again he saith that "the deacon's duty was to carry or remove the altar[11]:" which thing cannot be expounded of a heap of stones, but only of the communion table. And therefore St Chrysostom commonly calleth it ἱερὰ τράπεζα, "the holy board," and St Augustine, *mensa Domini*, "the Lord's table," as other fathers also do in infinite places[12].

Communion tables or altars.

August. In Quæst. Vet. et Nov. Test. Quæst. 101.

And notwithstanding it were "a table," yet was it also called "an altar;" not for that it was so indeed, but only by allusion unto the altars of the old law. And so Irenæus calleth Christ "our altar[13]," and Origen calleth our heart "our altar[14]:" not that either Christ or our hearts be altars indeed, but only by a metaphor or a manner of speech. Such were the altars that were used by the old fathers immediately after the apostles' time.

Iren. Lib. iv. cap. xxxiv. Orig. in Matt. Tract. 25.

Now, whether it may seem likely that the same altars stood so far off from the hearing of the people as M. Harding so constantly affirmeth, I refer myself[15] to these authorities that here follow.

Eusebius thus describeth the form and furniture of the church in his time: *Absoluto templo, ac sedibus excelsissimis ad honorem præsidentium et subselliis ordine collocatis ornato, et post omnia sancto sanctorum, videlicet altari, in medio constituto &c.*[16]: "The church being ended and comely furnished with high thrones for the honour of the rulers, and with stalls beneath set in order, and last of all, the holy of holies, I mean the altar, being placed in the midst." Eusebius saith not, the altar was set at the end of the quire, but in the midst of the church among the people.

Euseb. Lib. x. cap. iv. Ex Oratione Panegyrica in Encæniis.

St Augustine likewise saith thus: *Christus quotidie pascit: mensa ipsius est illa in medio constituta. Quid causæ est, o audientes, ut mensam videatis, et ad epulas non accedatis*[17]? "Christ feedeth us daily; and this is his table here set in the midst. O my hearers, what is the matter that ye see the table, and yet come not to the meat?" In the council of Constantinople it is written thus: *Tempore diptychorum cucurrit omnis multitudo cum magno silentio circumcirca altare, et audiebant*[18]: "When the lesson or the chapter was a reading, the people with silence drew together round about the altar, and gave ear." And to leave others, Durandus, examining the cause why the priest turneth himself about at the altar, yieldeth this reason for the same: *In medio ecclesiæ aperui os meum*[19]: "In the midst of the church I opened my mouth." And Platina noteth that Bonifacius, bishop of Rome, was the first that in the time of the ministration divided the priest from the people[20].

August. de Verb. Dom. sec. Johan. Serm. 42.

Concil. Constant. v. Act. i.

Durand. Lib. v. Platina.

To leave further[21] allegations, we see by these few that the quire was then in the body of the church, divided with rails from the rest, whereof it was called *cancelli*, "a chancel," and commonly of the Greeks *presbyterium*, for that it was a place specially appointed unto the priests and ministers, and shut up from all others, for disturbing the holy ministery; as it appeareth notably by the story of St Ambrose, that willed the emperor Theodosius himself to depart forth[22], and by

Theod. Lib. v. cap. xviii.

[10 ... stantem ad altare ... lignis ... ejusdem altaris effracti immaniter ceciderunt.—August. Op. Par. 1679-1700. De Corr. Donatist. seu Epist. clxxxv. 27. Tom. II. col. 654.]

[11 Nam utique [Romanæ ecclesiæ diaconi] et altare portarent et vasa ejus, &c.—Id. Quæst. ex Utroq. (Vet. et Nov. Test.) Mixt. Quæst. ci. Tom. III. Append. col. 92. These questions are not a genuine work of Augustine.]

[12 For the names given by Chrysostom, Augustine, and other fathers to the communion table, see Bingham, Orig. Eccles. Book VIII. chap. vi. 14.]

[13 Est ergo altare in cœlis.—Iren. Op. Par. 1710. Contr. Hær. Lib. IV. cap. xviii. (olim xxxiv). 6. p. 252.]

[14 Altare ergo quod votum significat, est hominis cor,... votum... posuisti super cor tuum, quasi super quoddam altare.—Orig. Op. In Matt. Comm. Ser. 18. Tom. III. p. 842.]

[15 Meself, 1565.]

[16 Euseb. in Hist. Eccles. Script. Amst. 1695-1700. Lib. x. cap. iv. Orat. Paneg. p. 312.]

[17 August. Op. Serm. cxxxii. 1. Tom. V. 645.]

[18 Concil. Constant. sub Menna, Act. v. in Concil. Stud. Labb. et Cossart. Lut. Par. 1671-2. Tom. V. col. 185.]

[19 Durand. Rat. Div. Offic. Lib. IV. cap. xiv. 11. fol. 111. See before, page 78, note 1.]

[20 Divisit et populum a clero dum celebraretur.—Plat. De Vit. Pont. col. 1551. Bonifac. II. p. 66.]

[21 Farther, 1565.]

[22 Theodor. in Hist. Eccles. Script. Lib. v. cap. xviii. pp. 222, 3.]

Naz. in Vita Basil. De Con. Dist. ii. Sacerdotum. Concil. Laod. cap. 19.

Nazianzenus in the life of St Basil[1], and by a decree under the name of Clemens[2], and by the council of Laodicea concerning the same[3]; and, as it may be gathered by St Chrysostom, at certain times of the service was drawn with curtains[4].

Even at this day in the great churches at Milan, Naples, Lyons, Mentz, and Rome, and in the church of St Laurence in Florence, the priest at his service standeth towards the west, and so hath his face still upon the people. And therefore Durandus saith: "In such places the priest needeth not to turn himself round when he saith, *Dominus vobiscum*, and saluteth the people."

And whereas M. Harding imagineth that the people for distance of place could not hear what the priest said, a man that hath considered the old fathers with any diligence may soon see he is far deceived. For Chrysostom saith: "The deacon at the holy mysteries stood up, and thus spake unto the people: *Oremus pariter omnes:* 'Let us pray all together[5].'" And again he saith: "The priest and the people at the ministration talk together. The priest saith, 'The Lord be with you:' the people answereth, 'And with thy spirit[6].'" Justinian the emperor commanded that the priest should so speak aloud at the holy ministration, "as the people might hear him[7]." Clemens Alexandrinus saith: *Est ergo, quod est hic apud nos altare, terrestris congregatio eorum, qui sunt dedicati orationibus; qui veluti unam vocem habent communem, et unam mentem*[8]: "The altar that we have is an earthly congregation of men given to prayers, which have, as it were, both voice and mind common together." And, to leave rehearsal of others, Bessarion saith: *Sacerdote...verba illa ... pronunciante, assistens populus in utraque parte respondet, Amen*[9]: "The priest speaking these words, the people standing by, at each part of the sacrament, or on every side, saith Amen."

Chrysost. in Epist. ad Ephes. Hom. 3. Chrysost. in 2. ad Cor. Hom. 18. Clement. Stromat. Lib. vii. Bessar. de Sacram. Euch.

Now judge thou, good reader, what truth may seem to be in that M. Harding addeth hereto, that the people, remaining in seemly wise in the nether part of the church, was instructed by certain ceremonies and tokens shewed in the quire, and gave assent and said Amen unto the priest praying at the altar, although they understood no part of his prayer. Certainly St Paul saith: *Quomodo dicet Amen ad tuam gratiarum actionem? quandoquidem nescit quid dicas:* "How shall he say Amen, and give assent unto thy thanksgiving? For he knoweth not what thou sayest." So saith St Augustine, *ut populus ad id, quod plane intelligit, dicat Amen*[10]: "that the people, unto that they plainly understand, may say Amen." Likewise St Ambrose: *Imperitus ... audiens, quod non intelligit, nescit finem orationis, et non respondet Amen; id est, Verum, ut confirmetur benedictio. Per hos enim impletur confirmatio precis, qui respondent Amen; ut omnia dicta veri testimonio in audientium mentibus confirmentur*[11]: "The unlearned, hearing that he understandeth not, knoweth not the end of the prayer, neither saith Amen, that is to say, It is true; that the priest's blessing may be confirmed. For by them that answer Amen the prayer is confirmed; whereby is meant, that whatsoever is spoken by the testimony of the truth be made good in the minds of the hearers." Seeing therefore that neither altars were erected in the apostles' time; nor the communion table, that then was used, stood so far off from the body of the church; nor the people gave assent to that they understood not; so many untruths being found in M. Harding's premises, we may well and safely stand in doubt of his conclusion.

1 Cor. xiv. August. de Catechiz. Rud. cap. ix. Ambros. in 1 Cor. cap. xiv.

M. HARDING. THE TWENTY-SEVENTH DIVISION.

Whereas you, M. Jewel, allege St Paul for your purpose, and make him to say thus, otherwise than he wrote, "If thou make thy prayer in the congre- [12 Fol. 15, H. A. 1564.] 1 Cor. xiv.

[1 Gregor. Naz. Op. Par. 1778-1840. In Laud. Basil. Orat. xliii. 27. 52. Tom. I. pp. 792, 808, 9.]

[2 Clemens Papa in Corp. Jur. Canon. Lugd. 1624. Decret. Gratian. Decr. Tert. Pars, De Consecr. Dist. ii. can. 30. col. 1925.]

[3 Concil. Laod. can. 19. in Concil. Stud. Labb. et Cossart. Lut. Par. 1671-2. Tom. I. col. 1500.]

[4 Ὅταν ἴδῃς ἀνελκόμενα τὰ ἀμφίθυρα, κ.τ.λ.—Chrysost. Op. Par. 1718-38. In Epist. ad Ephes. cap. i. Hom. iii. Tom. XI. p. 23.]

[5 Id. ibid.]

[6 Id. in Epist. II. ad Cor. Hom. xviii. Tom. X. p. 568.]

[7 See before, page 287, note 10.]

[8 Clement. Alex. Op. Oxon. 1715. Stromat. Lib. VII. 6. Tom. II. p. 848.]

[9 Bessar. de Sacram. Euch. in Biblioth. Patr. per M. de la Bigne, Par. 1624. Tom. VI. col. 481.]

[10 August. Op. Par. 1679-1700. De Catechiz. Rud. cap. ix. 13. Tom. VI. col. 272.]

[11 Ambros. Op. Par. 1686-90. Comm. in Epist. I. ad Cor. cap. xiv. v. 16. Tom. II. Append. col. 157.]

[12 See before, page 8.]

gation with thy spirit, or noise of strange words, how shall the unlearned man thereunto say Amen? For he knoweth not what thou sayest;" you bombast this text with your own counterfeit stuffing. The translation authorised by king Edward and his council is truer, and followeth the Greek nearer, which hath thus: "When thou blessest with the spirit, how shall he that occupieth the room of the unlearned say Amen at thy giving of thanks, seeing he understandeth not what thou sayest?" Here the apostle St Paul speaketh of blessing or thanksgiving with the spirit; which spirit, what it is, it is not easy to declare, after the judgment of your own patriarch John Calvin[13]. *St Ambrose taketh it for the spirit we have received in baptism, that doth incline and move us to prayer*[14]*: St Thomas for the Holy Ghost given to us, for reason, and for the power imaginative*[15]*: Erasmus for the voice itself*[16]*: Isidorus Clarius for the power of pronouncing or utterance*[17]*: some for the breath that passeth the throat; some for the intention: St Augustine very subtlely* pro apprehensione quæ ideas concipit, et signa rerum[18]: *Calvin in his Institutions,* De Oratione, cap. 15, *for the sound of the mouth that is caused of the breath of a man's throat, and rebounding of the air*[19]*: Chrysostom for the spiritual gift, or the gift of the Holy Ghost to speak with tongues*[20]*: which Calvin himself, sitting in judgment, as it were, upon this doubtful matter, alloweth best, and condemneth the mind of all others, and also his own, though unawares*[21]*, as it seemeth; and so he would condemn your noise of strange words likewise, if he heard it. This text, being so doubtful of itself in sense, so put out of tune by your noise of strange words, wherewith you descant upon the word "spirit," so violently applied by your new-fangled exposition, maketh little to the condemnation of the Latin service in the Latin church, specially seeing that St Paul meaneth by that miraculous speaking with tongues, used or rather abused among the Corinthians, a far different manner of speaking from that speaking whereby the priest uttereth the common service.*

The priest, I grant, saying his service to his parish, speaketh with a tongue; but such manner of speaking is not that which St Paul meant. For the priest understandeth it for the better part, if he be learned; and (83) *the people be not utterly ignorant, because of often preaching, long custom, solemn feasts, and sundry ceremonies. And therefore your argument, gathered out of that text, concludeth nothing against having the service in the learned Latin tongue, not perfectly*[22] *understanded of the unlearned people. Verily, if you admit the exact judgment of St Augustine concerning this place of St Paul, then must you seek for other scriptures and proofs of your English service. For, as he discusseth this point learnedly, by "the tongue" St Paul meaneth not the Latin, Greek, or Hebrew, among the unlearned people, or any other alien or strange tongue, but only, and that by way of metaphor, "any manner of utterance whereby the signs of things are pronounced before they be understanded." And by "the spirit" he understandeth not a noise of strange words, after your strange interpretation; but, as it is here "in a certain proper and peculiar manner taken, a power of the soul*

The eighty-third untruth. For the simple people understandeth not one word or syllable of the Latin tongue.

Vide Augustinum, Lib. xii. de Genes. ad Litteram, c. vii. viii. et ix. to. 3.

[[13] Quid sit autem spiritus, non ita facile est explicatu.—Calvin. Op. Amst. 1667-71. In Epist. I. ad Cor. cap. xiv. 14. p. 195. Calvin recites the opinions of Ambrose and Augustine, and others mentioned in this place.]

[[14] Spiritus autem qui datur in baptismo, scit quid oret animus, dum loquitur, aut perorat lingua sibi ignota.—Ambros. Op. Comm. in Epist. I. ad Cor. cap. xiv. v. 14. Tom. II. Append. col. 157.]

[[15] Spiritu, i. in lingua, quæ non intelligatur, seu imaginatione et motus a Spiritu sancto.—Thom. Aquinat. Op. Venet. 1595. In I. ad Cor. cap. xiv. Lect. iii. Tom. XVI. fol. 84.]

[[16] Orabo spiritu... Precabor voce.—Erasm. Op. L. Bat. 1703-6. Paraphr. in Epist. ad Cor. I. cap. xiv. 15. Tom. VII. col. 903.]

[[17] Per spiritum intelligit hic vim illum pronuntiandi.—Bibl. Sacr. adject. Schol. Auct. Isid. Clar. Venet. 1557. Ad Cor. I. cap. xiv. fol. 473.]

[[18] August. Op. De Gen. ad Litt. Lib. XII. capp. viii. ix. 19, 20. Tom. III. Pars I. cols. 302, 3. The exact words of the text are not given; but the notion will be found in these chapters.]

[[19] Spiritus voce singulare linguarum donum significans, &c.—Calvin. Op. Inst. Lib. III. cap. xx. 33. p. 237. Calvin does not in this place express the opinion attributed to him. In the place quoted above, note 11, he says: Probabilior est eorum opinio, qui spiritum gutturis interpretantur, hoc est flatum. He then mentions an objection to this interpretation and proceeds: Adducor ut in sensu hujus verbi assentiar Chrysostomo, qui exponit, sicuti prius, de spirituali dono.—Ibid. pp. 195, 6.]

[[20] Τὸ καὶ τῷ πνεύματι, τουτέστι, τῷ χαρίσματι, καὶ τῇ διανοίᾳ προσεύχεσθαι.—Chrysost. Op. In Epist. I. ad Cor. Hom. xxxv. Tom. X. p. 325.]

[[21] Unwares, 1565, and H. A. 1564.]

[[22] Perfitely, 1565, and H. A. 1564.]

inferior to the mind, which conceiveth the similitudes of things, and understandeth them not[1]." *And things so uttered be uttered with the tongue and spirit, whether it be in English or Latin, or any other language.*

And, sir, although the people understand not in most exact wise what the priest saith in the Latin service, yet have they commodity and profit thereby, so far as it pleaseth God to accept the common prayer of the church, pronounced by the priest for them.

THE BISHOP OF SARISBURY.

Here M. Harding hath found a sport to pass the time withal. He maketh M. Calvin a patriarch, and setteth him on high in judgment to condemn all the world. St Paul's meaning is bombasted and brought out of tune with a noise of strange words. And in this point he doubleth, and sheweth copy, and playeth round about merrily with his own fantasy. Wherein he may not be much offended if I say unto him, as St Hierome said sometime unto St Ambrose, for his commentaries upon St Luke: *Verbis ludis: sententiis dormitas*[2]*:* that is: "Your words be pleasant; but your senses be half asleep."

Ruffinus.

For that I saw these words of St Paul, "If thou bless with thy spirit," might seem doubtful, and divers expositions rising thereupon, I thought it meet, for the more ease of the unlearned, to open what St Paul might seem to mean by this word "spirit," in that place; and, following the judgment of sundry old fathers, I called it a sound or noise of unknown words. This is it that M. Harding here so pleasantly calleth "stuffing, and bombast, and a strange new-fangled interpretation." Wherein he sheweth himself to be somewhat short-witted, as may soon appear. For within a few lines after, expounding these words of St Paul, *Quam decem millia verborum in lingua,* he himself useth the like bombast and the very same stuffing.

Verily, if he will utterly condemn all manner paraphrase, or adding of other words for declaration of that seemeth hard or doubtful in the text, then must he needs condemn not only the Septuagints, but also all other interpreters of the scriptures. Hereof Origen, weighing in what sort the apostle St Paul allegeth the words of the prophet David, writeth thus: *Sed...quod dixit apostolus, Sicut scriptum est,...Non est justus quisquam, non est intelligens, non est requirens Deum; non iisdem sermonibus invenitur in psalmo, sed alii permutantur, alii assuuntur, alii relinquuntur. Quod a studiosis quibusque si observetur diligentius, puto dari in hoc apostolicam auctoritatem, ut cum scripturæ testimoniis utendum fuerit, sensum magis ex ea quam verba capiamus*[3]*:* "But whereas St Paul saith, 'As it is written, There is not one just man, there is not one of understanding, there is not one that seeketh after God;' this place is not found in the psalm by these words, but some words are altered by St Paul, and some others are added unto, and some are left out. Which thing if the reader advisedly consider, I think that herein the apostle's authority is declared, that, when we have need to use the testimony of the scriptures, we rather take the meaning thereof than the words." Origen saith St Paul both altered the words of the prophet, and added to, and took fro; yet, I trust, M. Harding will not say St Paul bombasted or stuffed the scriptures.

Orig. in Epist. ad Rom. cap. iii. Lib. iii.

Perhaps he will reply, St Paul, by this word "spirit," meant not a strange tongue, or a noise of unknown words; and therefore this stuffing is counterfeit. And because M. Harding saith so, perhaps the simple reader will so believe it. But, if the old doctors and fathers so expound it, then all this strange mirth and triumph might have been spared.

St Ambrose openeth St Paul's meaning, and sheweth what he understood by

[1 ...propterea translato verbo linguam appellavit quamlibet signorum prolationem priusquam intelligantur......qui modo proprio vocatur spiritus, vis animæ quædam mente inferior, ubi corporalium rerum similitudines exprimuntur.—August. Op. Par. 1679-1700. De Genes. ad Litt. Lib. XII. capp. viii. ix. 19, 20. Tom. III. Pars I. cols. 302, 3.]

[2 Ante paucos dies quorundam in Matthæum et Lucam commentarios vos legisse dixistis: e quibus alter et sensibus hebes esset; et alter in verbis luderet, in sententiis dormitaret.—Ruffin. Invect. in Hieron. Op. Par. 1693-1706. Lib. II. Tom. IV. Pars II. col. 432.]

[3 Orig. Op. Par. 1733-59. Comm. in Epist. ad Rom. Lib. III. 2. Tom. IV. pp. 504, 5; where we find *eisdem*, *assumuntur*, and *ab studiosis*.]

this word "spirit," in this wise: *Si [tu] benedixeris spiritu, hoc est, si laudem Dei lingua loquaris ignota audientibus*[4]: "If thou bless with thy spirit, that is to say, if thou utter the praise of God in a tongue unknown unto the hearers." This, I trow, is no bombast, nor counterfeit stuffing: it is St Ambrose[5] interpretation. Ambros. in 1 Cor. cap. xiv.

Likewise St Chrysostom, expounding the same words, saith thus: *Si tu benedixeris spiritu, &c. Est quod dicit hujusmodi: si peregrina lingua gratias agas, quam nec intelligas ipse, nec ceteris idem interpreteris, plebeius non potest subjicere, Amen*[6]: "'If thou bless with thy spirit, &c.' The meaning hereof," saith St Chrysostom, "is this: if thou give thanks unto God (or pray) in a strange tongue, which neither thou knowest thyself[7], nor canst expound unto others, the unlearned cannot say, Amen. This," Chrysostom saith, "is St Paul's very meaning." M. Harding saith: "No: it is a strange new-fangled interpretation." Chrysost. in 1 Cor. xiv. Hom. 35.

Erasmus in his paraphrase turneth it thus: *Si tu decantes laudes Dei sermone omnibus incognito*[8]: "If thou sing out the praises of God in a tongue unknown unto all thy hearers." Dionysius the Carthusian likewise saith thus: *Si tu benedixeris spiritu, id est, non verbis quæ ab aliis intelligantur, sed tantum lingua*[9]: "If thou bless with thy spirit, that is to say, not with such words as others may understand, but only with the[10] tongue." Erasm. in 1 Cor. xiv. Dionys. Carthus. in 1 Cor. xiv.

Anselmus saith: *Spiritus meus [orat,] id [est], flatus oris mei orat, dum loquor in oratione*[11]: "My spirit prayeth, that is, the breath of my mouth prayeth, so long as I continue speaking." Whatsoever opinion M. Harding have of Erasmus, yet, I trow, of his modesty he will not say that either Dionysius the Carthusian, or St Ambrose, or St Chrysostom, or Anselmus, devised new-fangled expositions, or descanted upon St Paul, or set his text out of tune. Anselm. in 1 Cor. xiv.

"But," he saith, "the place of St Paul is doubtful; St Ambrose, St Augustine, St Chrysostom, Isidorus, Erasmus, and Thomas of Aquine understood it diversely." And will he therefore conclude thus: These fathers mistook St Paul's sense; *ergo*, St Paul had no sense? Or: Divers doctors touching this place had divers judgments; *ergo*, we must have no judgment? Or must we follow none of them, because some were deceived? Or must we follow them all together, because they were doctors? Indeed they dissented somewhat in the taking of this word "spirit," as it is evident; but whether it were the Holy Ghost that St Paul meant thereby, or imagination, or reason, or the gift of tongues, or the sound of the mouth, or the power of utterance, or the voice itself, it is certain and confessed by these and all other doctors and fathers, that St Paul spake of "an unknown tongue," and, as St Gregory saith, *de strepitu oris*[12], "of the babbling of the mouth;" and so consequently of "a noise of strange words," wherewith M. Harding's tender ears are so much offended. Hug. Card. citat. Greg.

Now, forasmuch as it is avouched, that these words of St Paul make nothing for our purpose, let us a little examine one or two of M. Harding's reasons, and see how well he applieth the same to his purpose. The first is this: St Paul entreateth of the miraculous gift of tongues; *ergo*, his words make nothing against the Latin service.

Again: St Paul willeth, that the priest utter the common prayers in the congregation in such language as the unlearned may be edified thereby, and answer Amen; *ergo*, M. Harding seemeth to say, the priest may utter the common prayers in an unknown tongue. Surely these arguments would make a strange noise in the schools, and set all logic quite out of tune. But if St Paul's words make nothing against the Latin service, as it is now used, what is it then that

[4 Ambros. Op. Par. 1686-90. Comm. in Epist. I. ad Cor. cap. xiv. v. 16. Tom. II. Append. col. 157.]

[5 Ambroses, 1565, 1609.]

[6 Chrysost. Op. Par. 1718-38. In Epist. I. ad Cor. Hom. xxxv. Tom. X. p. 325.]

[7 Theeself, 1565.]

[8 ... si tu laudes Dei decantas sermone omnibus ignoto, &c.—Erasm. Op. L. Bat. 1703-6. Paraphr. in Epist. ad Cor. I. cap. xiv. 16. Tom. VII. col. 903.]

[9 Dionys. Carthus. in Nov. Test. Col. 1532. In I. ad Cor. Enarr. cap. xiv. Art. 14. Tom. II. fol. 57; where we have *hoc est*, and *solum lingua*.]

[10 Thy, 1565.]

[11 Anselm. Op. Col. Agrip. 1612. In I. Epist. ad Cor. cap. xiv. Tom. II. p. 160. These commentaries are wrongly attributed to Anselm, archbishop of Canterbury: they are the work of another Anselm, of Laon.]

[12 ... quia dicit Gregorius, Quid prodest strepitus oris, &c.?—Hugon. de S. Char. Col. Agrip. 1621. Epist. I. ad Cor. cap. xiv. Tom. VII. fol. 112. 2.]

The learned Latin tongue.

St Paul condemneth? Why concludeth he thus: "How shall the ignorant say Amen at thy thanksgiving? For he knoweth not what thou sayest." Why setteth he the whole difference in knowing, and not knowing? Or what misliketh he else, but the sound or noise of a strange tongue, whereby he thinketh the people in nowise can be edified? If all this be nothing, as M. Harding saith, then let him turn the whole course of St Paul's words, and say thus: "Pray thou in a strange unknown tongue, that the people may say Amen. For so may they say, although they know not what thou prayest."

The allegation of "the learned Latin tongue," which M. Harding so often useth, may serve rather to astonish[1] the simple, than to make any good sufficient proof. So the subtle old heretics, Marcus and Heracleon, as it is reported by St Augustine and Arnobius, used in their prayers certain Hebrew, and other strange unknown words, to the intent to amaze their hearers with admiration, and the more to commend and set forth their treachery[2].

August. ad Quod-vult-Deum. [Arnobius, 1565.]

No tongue is to be accounted learned in itself, but only in respect of some other thing, and, as the learned term it, *per accidens*, that is, either for the eloquent manner of utterance, or for the substance of learned matter therein contained, or for the learning and knowledge of the speaker. But the Latin service, besides that it is not eloquent in itself (as indeed it needeth not to be), sometimes it holdeth not good congruity, but is utterly void of reason. Wherein let this one example stand for many. In the praises of the blessed virgin it is written thus: *Cujus Dominus humilitatem respiciens, angelo nuntiante, concepit Redemptorem mundi.* By the learning of this learned tongue we are taught it was not our lady, but our Lord, that was mother unto Christ; for so it falleth out in construction: "Our Lord conceived the Redeemer of the world." The substance of the matter therein contained is sometimes vain and full of fables, sometimes wicked and idolatrous; the priests that utter this tongue, for the most part such as are hardly able to make it learned. Pope Zachary saith that a priest in his time baptized a child by these words: *In nomine patria, et filia, et spirita sancta*[3]. And St Augustine saith that divers priests in his time, in their common Latin service, where as the people understood the Latin tongue, uttered barbarisms and solœcisms, that is to say, spake false Latin[4]; and further saith: *Multa in illis reperiuntur contra catholicam fidem*[5]: "In the same prayers many things are found contrary to the catholic faith." Such is this tongue, that M. Harding here so highly commendeth to be so learned.

De Consecr. Dist. iv. Retulerunt.

August. de Catechiz. Rud. cap. ix.

De Consecr. Dist. iv. Si non.

But grant we the Latin tongue to be eloquent, copious, and learned above all others. Yet think these men that God's ears be so curious, or so dainty, that he can abide no prayer, but only in a "learned language?" Verily, St Paul requireth no brag of learning to be uttered in the congregation, but only plain speech and understanding, "that the simple may be edified."

Caligula, the emperor, set golden loaves, and all other services of whole gold before his guests, and bade them eat. Indeed, they had a glorious sight to look upon. Yet had they nothing neither to eat nor to drink, for contentation of nature. Even so would M. Harding set his glittering service of Greek, Hebrew, and Latin before the people, and bid them feed. A goodly shew, no doubt, to gaze and to wonder at. But, alas! nothing have they there either to receive or to taste of; either to move them to repentance, or to comfort and quiet their conscience. It is notably well said by St Augustine: *Quid ... prodest clavis aurea, si aperire quod volumus non potest? aut quid obest lignea, si hoc potest? quando nihil quærimus, nisi aperire*[6] *quod clausum erat*[7]: "What availeth a golden key, if it cannot open

August. de Doct. Christ. Lib. iv. cap. xi.

[[1] Astonne, 1565.]

[[2] August. Op. Par. 1679-1700. Lib. de Hæres. 14, 16. Tom. VIII. col. 8.]

[[3] Retulerunt nuntii tui, quod fuerit ... sacerdos, qui Latinam linguam penitus ignorabat, et dum baptizaret ... diceret: Baptizo te in nomine patria, et filia, et spiritu sancta.—Zach. Papa in Corp. Jur. Canon. Lugd. 1624. Decret. Gratian. Decr. Tert. Pars, De Consecr. Dist. iv. can. 86. col. 2010.]

[[4] Aug. Op. De Catechiz. Rud. cap. ix. 13. Tom. VI. col. 272.]

[[5] Id. in Corp. Jur. Canon. Decret. Gratian. Decr. Tert. Pars, De Consecr. Dist. iv. can. 72. col. 2004; where we read *eis*. See also Op. De Bapt. contr. Donatist. Lib. VI. cap. XXV. 47. Tom. IX. col. 176.]

[[6] Patere, 1565, parere, 1609.]

[[7] Id. De Doctr. Christ. Lib. IV. cap. xi. 26. Op. Tom. III. Pars I. col. 74; where *nisi patere quod clausum est.*]

that we would have opened? Or what hurteth a wooden key, if it be able to open? Seeing we desire nothing, but that the thing that is shut may be opened."

"The people," saith M. Harding, "is not utterly ignorant what the priest saith. They understand him, although not perfectly[8], nor in exact wise, yet they understand him." Thus he doubteth and staggereth between perfect and unperfect[9], as not having yet well measured the people's understanding. For to say the ignorant perfectly[8] understand the Latin tongue were against the manifest truth: to say they understand no part thereof at all were directly against St Paul; for he requireth understanding. Therefore M. Harding divideth the matter, and saith: "They understand the Latin tongue, although not exactly or perfectly[8]:" that is to say, they understand neither the scriptures, nor the prayers, nor any one thing that is spoken, nor sentence, nor word, nor syllable, nor letter. They hear the priest speak, and know not what he saith. They see him turn and gesture, and know not what he meaneth. This, saith M. Harding, is the understanding of the Latin tongue. But, alas! is this the understanding that St Paul requireth, "that the people may be edified, and answer Amen?" And what pleasure hath he in abridging and bridling the understanding of God's people? Why should they not rather understand perfectly[8] what the priest saith? Why should there be any imperfection in godly things? St Paul wisheth that we may all grow unto a perfect[9] man in Christ Jesus[10]; and St Augustine wisheth that the people may say Amen "to that they plainly and perfectly[8] understand[11]." Eph. iv. August. de Catechiz. Rud. cap. ix.

M. HARDING. THE TWENTY-EIGHTH DIVISION.

But St Paul, say they, requireth that the people give assent and conform themselves unto the priest, by answering Amen to his prayer made in the congregation.

Verily, in the primitive church this was necessary, when the faith was a-learning. And therefore the prayers were made then in a common tongue known to the people, for cause of their further instruction; who, being of late converted to the faith, and of painims made Christians, had need in all things to be taught. But after that the faithful people was multiplied and increased in great numbers, and had been so well instructed in all points of religion, as by their own accord they conformed themselves to the ministers at the common prayers; in the Latin church the service was set out in Latin; and it was thought sufficient, part of the people in the quire to answer for the whole[12]. And this hath been esteemed for a more expedite and convenient order, than if it were in the vulgar tongue of every nation.

THE BISHOP OF SARISBURY.

Whoso will maintain an untruth, ought to be circumspect and to remember well how his tales may stand together. M. Harding a little before wrote thus: "Cicero saith, tongues be in number infinite. Of them all, neither M. Jewel, nor any one of his side is able to shew that the public service of the church in any nation was ever, for the space of six hundred years after Christ, in any other tongue than in Greek or Latin." Now, contrariwise, either of forgetfulness what he hath said before, or of some better[13] advice, he saith thus: "Verily in the primitive church this was necessary, when the faith was a-learning; and therefore the prayers were made then in a common tongue known to the people, for cause of their further instruction." By these words he utterly overthroweth that he so confidently said before, and very well confirmeth my assertion. M. Jewel may now take his ease: for M. Harding himself is able to prove against himself, that in the primitive church the service was ministered in the common tongue; and that he confirmeth for a verity, and saith: "It was necessary so to be, and could not be otherwise." These sayings of M. Harding's, being directly contrary, cannot possibly stand both together. If the one be true, the other of necessity must needs be false. M. Harding contrary to himself.

The reason that he gathereth in this place standeth upon the diversity of

[8 Perfitely, 1565.]
[9 Perfit and unperfit, 1565.]
[10 Jesu, 1565.]
[11 August. Op. De Catechiz. Rud. cap. ix. 13. Tom. VI. col. 272.]
[12 Whole people, H. A. 1564.]
[13 Some other better, 1565.]

times. Then, saith he, the people was ignorant, and needed of all things to be taught. Now they are instructed and understand the faith, and are increased in multitude. Therefore it is better now for expedition the service be said in a strange language, and that only the clerk make answer to the priest instead of the whole congregation.

Thus saith M. Harding, not by the authority of St Ambrose, St Augustine, St Hierome, St Chrysostom, or any other like old catholic doctor, but only by warrant of late doctors, Thomas of Aquine and Nicholas Lyra, the former of which two lived at the least twelve hundred years after Christ. His reason in short is thus: The people now is instructed; *ergo,* they ought to have their service in a strange tongue.

If M. Harding mind to persuade the world, he had need to bring other arguments. But what if the people be not instructed? What if they know nothing, no, not the articles of the christian faith? What if there be no man to instruct them? What if the priest be even as is the people, and "the blind lead the blind?" Yet, I trow, M. Harding will not alter his new decree; but his strange service must continue still. Verily, the understanding of God is the soul and life of God's church; and, as it was necessary at the first planting thereof, so is it always necessary for the continuance of the same. St Hilary saith: *Ecclesiæ, in quibus verbum Dei non vigilat, naufragæ fiunt*[1]*:* "The churches, wherein God's word is not watchful, suffer wreck." Neither did St Paul say, Let this order hold for the time, while the faith is a-learning, as M. Harding would have him say; but
1 Cor. xiv. thus he saith: *Hæc quæ scribo Domini sunt mandata. Omnia ad ædificationem fiant:* "The things that I write are the commandments of the Lord. Let all things be done to edify." The edifying of the people, which is the final cause hereof, continueth still; therefore ought the understanding of the people, which is the efficient cause hereof, to continue still.

M. HARDING. THE TWENTY-NINTH DIVISION.

I grant they cannot say Amen to the blessing or thanksgiving of the priest, so well as if they understood the Latin tongue perfectly[2]*. Yet they give assent to it, and ratify it in their hearts, and do conform themselves unto the priest, though not in special, yet in general; that is to wit, though not in every particular sentence of praise and thanksgiving, or in every several petition, yet in the whole. For, if they come to church with a right and good intent, as the simple do no less than the learned; their desire is to render unto God glory, praise, and honour, and to thank him for benefits received, and withal to obtain of him things behoveful for them in this life and in the life to come. And without doubt this godly affection of their minds is so acceptable to God, as no understanding of words may be compared with it. This requisite assent, and conforming of themselves to the priests*[3]*, they declare by sundry outward tokens and gestures; as by standing up at the gospel, and at the preface of the mass; by bowing themselves down and adoring at the sacrament; by kneeling at other times, as when pardon and mercy is humbly asked, and by other like signs of devotion in other parts of the service.*

THE BISHOP OF SARISBURY.

Yet once again M. Harding would make the world believe that the ignorant people understandeth the Latin tongue, although not perfectly[2]; and that they may in general give their consent unto whatsoever the priest saith, although they know not one word what he saith. And so between St Paul and M. Harding there appeareth a plain contrariety. For St Paul saith: "The unlearned cannot say Amen to thy prayer, because he knoweth not what thou sayest." "Yes," saith M. Harding, "although he know not what thou sayest, yet may he nevertheless say Amen." But hereto he layeth his correction: "I grant," saith he, "they can-

---

[[1] ... ecclesiæ, intra quas verbum Dei non vigilaverit, naufragæ sunt.—Hilar. Op. Par. 1693. Comm. in Matt. cap. viii. 1. col. 644.]

[[2] Perfitely, 1565, and H. A. 1564.]

[[3] Priest, 1565, and H. A. 1564.]

not say Amen to the blessing and thanksgiving of the priest, *so well* as if they understood the Latin tongue."

O M. Harding, who taught you thus to qualify the people's duties? Why do you thus openly deceive your brethren? Why teach you them to say Amen, to edify themselves, to be thankful, and to conform their hearts unto God, *not so well*, but in worse wise, as you yourself confess, than you know they are bound to do? Your own tongue confesseth against yourself, that you lead the people of God from the better unto the worse.

I know the humble affection and devotion of the heart is more precious before God than any understanding or sound of words. For that indeed is the praying in spirit and truth. And therefore God complaineth of the contrary: John iv.
"This people draweth near unto me with their lips, saith the Lord; but their Matt. xv.
heart is far from me." Hereof M. Harding gathereth this reason:

The people is devout and godly disposed;

Ergo, they must have their prayers in a strange tongue.

I would M. Harding would consider, and reform his reasons better. This is too simple: it needeth no answer. Certainly, if the simple people be so devout and so reverently disposed in the darkness, without any teaching or understanding, much more would they reverently and devoutly dispose themselves, if they heard the godly prayers, and understood them.

Kneeling, bowing, standing up, and other like, are commendable gestures and tokens of devotion, so long as the people understandeth what they mean, and applieth them unto God, to whom they be due. Otherwise they may well make them hypocrites; but holy or godly they cannot make them. Cœlestinus writeth thus unto the bishops of France: *Docendi...potius sunt, quam illudendi: nec impo-* Inter Decreta Cœlest. Pap. I.
nendum est eorum oculis, sed mentibus infundenda præcepta sunt[4]: "The people must rather be taught than mocked: neither must we deceive their eyes, but must pour wholesome precepts into their hearts."

M. HARDING. THE THIRTIETH DIVISION.

And whereas St Paul seemeth to disallow praying with tongue[5] *in the common assembly, because of want of edifying, and to esteem the utterance of five words or sentences with understanding of his meaning, that the rest might be instructed thereby, more than ten thousand words in a strange and unknown tongue; all this is to be referred to the state of that time, which was much unlike the state of the church we be now in. The tongue of the prayers which St Paul speaketh of was utterly strange and unknown, and served for a sign to the unbelievers. The Latin tongue, in the Latin church, is not altogether strange and unknown. For beside the priest, in most places, some of the rest have understanding of it, more or less; and now we have no need of any such sign. They needed instruction: we be not ignorant of the chief points of religion. They were to be taught in all things: we come not to church specially and chiefly to be taught at the service, but to pray, and to be taught by preaching. Their prayer was not vailable for lack of faith, and therefore was it to be made in the vulgar tongue, for increase of faith. Our faith will stand us in better stead, if we give ourselves to devout prayer. They, for lack of faith, had need of interpretation, both in prayers, and also in preaching, and all other spiritual exercises: we, having sufficient instruction in the necessary rudiments of our faith, for the rest have more need, by earnest and fervent prayer, to make suit unto God for an upright, pure, and holy life, than to spend much time in hearing for know-*
Contra Anomæ. Hom. 3. *ledge. Concerning which thing Chrysostom hath this saying:* Profecto The words of Chrysostom much abused.
si orare cum diligentia insuescas, nihil est quod doctrinam tui conservi desideres, quum ipse Deus sine ullo interprete mentem abunde luce afficiat[6]: "*Verily, if thou use to pray diligently, there is nothing why thou shouldest desire teaching of thy fellow-servant; seeing God himself doth abundantly lighten thy mind, without any interpreter.*"

[[4] Cœlestin. Papæ I. ad Episc. Gall. Epist. ii. 1. in Crabb. Concil. Col. Agrip. 1551. Tom. I. p. 526.]

[[5] Tongues, 1565, and H. A. 1564.]

[[6] Chrysost. Op. Par. 1718-38. De Incompr. contr. Anom. Hom. iii. Tom. I. p. 469.]

THE BISHOP OF SARISBURY.

Here M. Harding, by counterpoints, and by sundry circumstances of difference, compareth the state of the primitive church and his church of Rome together; and thereof would seem to prove that St Paul's words, which St Paul himself calleth *mandata Domini*, "the Lord's commandments," stood good only for that time present, and for no time afterward: as if he would say, God's will were mutable, or his commandments hold only for term of years.

I grant, there appear great notes of difference between the order of the primitive church, and the order that now is in the church of Rome. For, to leave all that M. Harding hath here touched by way of comparison, and to note that may seem near to this purpose, the rulers there wished and laboured that the people might abound in knowledge: here their whole labour and study is that the people may abound in ignorance. There the ministers spake with sundry tongues, that the people of all nations might understand them: here the minister speaketh in a strange tongue, to the intent that no man may understand him. There the simple and the ignorant were made eloquent: here the bishops, and cardinals, and greatest learned, are made dumb. And, to prosecute no further, there appeared in the primitive church the undoubted works of the Holy Ghost, and the very tracts and steps of Christ's feet; and Iren. Lib. iii. cap. iii. therefore Irenæus, and other old fathers, in cases of doubt, appealed evermore Tertull. Adv. Prax. to the order and example of that church[1]. And Tertullian saith: *Hoc adversus omnes hæreses valet, id esse verum, quodcunque prius; id esse adulterinum*[2], *quodcunque posterius*[3]: "This mark prevaileth against all heresies: that is the truth that was used first; that is false and corrupt that was brought in afterward." And therefore the holy fathers in the council of Nice made this general shout, Concil. Nicen. and agreed upon the same: *τὰ ἔθη ἀρχαῖα κρατείτω*[4]: "Let the ancient orders hold still;" referring themselves thereby to the use and order of the primitive church. Contrariwise, Valentinus, Marcion, and other like heretics, thought themselves wisest of all others; and therefore utterly refused, as M. Harding and his fellows Iren. Lib. iii. cap. ii. now do, to stand to the apostles' orders. Thus Irenæus writeth of them: *Dicent se non solum presbyteris, sed etiam apostolis...sapientiores* [*esse, et*] *sinceram veritatem invenisse*[5]: "They will say that they are wiser not only than other priests, but also than the apostles, and that they have found out the perfect[6] truth." I say not, M. Harding is so wickedly minded as Valentinus or Marcion was; but thus I say: He utterly refuseth to stand to the apostles' orders, and followeth other late devised fantasies; and therein undoubtedly doth even as the old heretics Marcion and Valentinus did.

Now let us consider M. Harding's reasons:

1. "The state," saith he, "of the primitive church was far unlike the state of the church we be now in;"

Ergo, we are not bound to St Paul's commandments.

2. Again he saith: "Some one or other in a parish understandeth somewhat of the Latin tongue:

3. "The people is sufficiently instructed in religion.

4. "They come together now, not so much to be instructed, as to pray;"

Ergo, they ought to have their service in a strange tongue.

O, what meaneth M. Harding thus to deal? Loth I am to make the comparison; but true it is: very children do not use to reason in so childish sort. He knoweth well that commonly neither any one of the whole parish understandeth the Latin tongue, nor oftentimes the priest himself. He knoweth that the people of his church is not instructed in religion, nor no man suffered to instruct them. And, notwithstanding both these parts were granted true, yet could he not any way conclude, that therefore the people should have their

[[1] Iren. Op. Par. 1710. Contr. Hær. Lib. III. cap. iii. pp. 175, &c.]

[[2] Adulterum, 1565.]

[[3] Tertull. Op. Lut. 1641. Adv. Prax. 2. p. 635. See before, page 25, note 9.]

[[4] Concil. Nic. can. 6. in Concil. Stud. Labb. et Cossart. Lut. Par. 1671-2. Tom. II. col. 32. See before, page 69, note 24.]

[[5] Iren. Op. Contr. Hær. Lib. III. cap. ii. 2; where *dicentes*, and *invenisse veritatem*.]

[[6] Perfit, 1565.]

service in a strange unknown tongue. Thus neither is the antecedent true; nor doth the consequent thereof follow. Now judge thou, good christian reader, whether these proofs bear weight sufficient to lead thy conscience.

He saith prayers in the common vulgar tongue were necessary in the primitive church, for breeding of the faith. But what thing can he breed[7] by prayers in a strange tongue? What knowledge, what faith, what charity? The apostles were not void of faith; yet they said unto Christ: "O Lord, increase our faith." Luke xvii. Christ, speaking of the latter days, saith thus: "When the Son of man shall Luke xviii. come, he shall scarcely find faith in the world." Doubtless, the thing that was good to rear the faith is also good to repair the faith; and that was then necessary to increase faith, is also necessary now to continue faith.

But to what end doth he allege the words of Chrysostom[8]? Did that good Chrysost. contra Anom. Hom. 3. father ever minister the common service unto the people in a strange tongue? M. Harding knoweth, the people understood Chrysostom, what he prayed, and answered him in their own tongue, and prayed with him all together. Or did Chrysostom ever check the people for their knowledge, or discourage them from reading the scriptures? Certainly he oftentimes rebuketh them for not reading, Chrysost. 1 Thess. Hom. 3. and willeth them to buy the scriptures, to read the scriptures, and to confer at home with their families of the scriptures[9]. And whereas M. Harding, to with- Chrysost. in Matt. Hom. 2. draw the people's hearts from reading, saith the scriptures are dark and dan- Chrysost. in Psal. xliii. gerous, and no man able to wade in them without a guide; St Chrysostom Chrysost. ad Coloss. Hom. 9. contrariwise, to encourage the people to read the scriptures, saith they be plain and easy, and that the ignorant and simple man, by prayer unto God, may attain the knowledge of them, without any master or teacher, by himself alone. For these be his words, even as M. Harding hath alleged them: *Profecto si orare cum* Chrysost. contra Anom. Hom. 3. *diligentia insuescas, nihil est, quod doctrinam conservi tui desideres, cum ipse Deus, sine ullo interprete, mentem tuam abunde luce afficiat*[10]: "If thou use to pray diligently, there is no cause why thou shouldest desire the teaching of thy fellow-servant; for God himself will abundantly lighten thy mind, without any interpreter." The like saying he hath often otherwhere. Declaring the story of queen Candace's chamberlain, he writeth thus: *Fieri non potest, ut is qui divinis* Chrysost. in Gen. Hom. 35. *scripturis magno studio ferventique desiderio vacat, semper negligatur: licet enim desit nobis hominis magisterium, tamen ipse Dominus superne intrans corda nostra, illustrat mentem, rationi jubar suum infundit, detegit occulta, doctorque fit eorum quæ ignoramus*[11]: "It cannot be that any man, with great study and fervent desire reading the scriptures, should still be left destitute. For, although we lack the instruction of man, yet will God himself from above enter into our hearts, and lighten our mind, and cast a beam of light into our reason, and open things that be hidden, and become our teacher of such things as we know not." Therefore this place of Chrysostom standeth M. Harding in small stead, unless it be by the countenance of an ancient doctor to make the simple believe he hath said somewhat. The reason that he gathereth hereof is this: The unlearned man, be he never so simple, may read the scriptures in his own vulgar tongue, and understand the same without a teacher; *ergo*, the common service ought to be ministered unto the lay-people in an unknown tongue.

M. HARDING. THE THIRTY-FIRST DIVISION.

I would not here that any man should lay to my charge the defence of ignorance, as though I envied the people any godly knowledge. I wish them to have all heavenly knowledge, and to be ignorant of nothing necessary to their salvation. Yea, Num. xi. *even with my very heart I wish with Moses,* Quis tribuat, ut omnis populus prophetet, et det Dominus illis Spiritum suum! *"O that all the people could*

[7 Be bred, 1565.]

[8 See before, page 319.]

[9 Chrysost. Op. Par. 1718-38. In II. Epist. ad Thess. cap. ii. Hom. iii. Tom. XI. p. 528.
Id. in Matt. Hom. ii. Tom. VII. pp. 29, &c.
Id. Expos. in Psalm. xliii. Tom. V. p. 145.
Id. in Epist. ad Col. cap. iii. Hom. ix. Tom. XI. p. 390.]

[10 Id. De Incompr. contr. Anom. Hom. iii. Tom. I. p. 469.]

[11 Id. in Gen. cap. xiv. Hom. xxxv. Tom. IV. pp. 349, 50.]

General Councils.

prophesy, and were learned in God's holy word, and that our Lord would give them his Spirit!" But all the common people to understand the priest at the service, I think wise and godly men judge it not a thing so necessary, as for the which the ancient order of the church, with no little offence, public and universal authority not consulted, should be condemned, broken, and quite abrogated, by private advice of a few.

If default were in this behalf justly found, it is known to whom the redress pertaineth. Concerning the state of religion, in all ages the general council representing the universal church for all sores hath ordained wholesome remedies. Where they be not heard, of whom Christ said, "He that heareth you heareth me, and he that despiseth you despiseth me;" it is to be feared that, concerning the service, the new learned boldness is not so acceptable to God as the old simple humility. It were good the people, having humble and reverent hearts, understood the service: I deny not. [*Luke* x. H. A. 1564.]

THE BISHOP OF SARISBURY.

M. Harding wisheth unto the people "all manner of knowledge that is godly and heavenly, and necessary for their salvation." Only his Latin service he would in no wise have them know. Whereby he seemeth privily to grant that his Latin service neither is godly, nor heavenly, nor necessary for the people's salvation.

He would that "all the people were learned in God's holy word." And notwithstanding he know there is no man to instruct them, yet may he not suffer them either to read the scriptures, or to understand any part of their common prayers. I trow, he would have them learn only by revelation.

"If any fault were justly found," saith M. Harding, "the redress thereof belongeth to the general council." I grant, the very name of a council is great, and weigheth much. But if there were none other possible way to seek redress, then most miserable were the church of God. If Christ and his apostles would have waited for a general council, the gospel had been unpreached, and the church unplanted, until this day. "It were good," saith M. Harding, "the people understood the service: I deny not." Forget not this, good reader: That the people understood their service, M. Harding himself confesseth it were good. And why so? Doubtless because he is forced to see and say, that it would redound to the glory of God, and to the great comfort and profit of the people. Therefore he saith, "It were good." Whereof we may well gather this argument of the contrary: Then that the people in this brute sort is kept still in ignorance, not understanding any portion of their common service, by M. Harding's own confession, it is ill. And is it not lawful to do that is good, to redress that is ill, to seek God's glory and the comfort of his people, without consent of a general council?

It appeareth well God is not bound to such orders. He hath oftentimes restored his church, and reformed abuses and heresies, by particular conference within several realms and countries; as we see by these private councils holden at Carthage under St Cyprian[1]; at Neocæsaria in Pontus[2]; at Ancyra in Galatia[3]; at Gangra in Paphlagonia[4]; and by other like, without any consent of a general council. So likewise saith St Ambrose against Secundus and Palladius: "The bishops of the east part, and so the bishops of the west, have ever used severally to assemble themselves together, as occasion was offered, and to reform their churches by themselves, without troubling the whole world[5]."

Cypr. Tom. ii. In i. Tom. Concil.

In Concil. Aquil. in Collatione cum Palladio.

But, saith M. Harding, Christ himself hath by special words commended the authority of councils: *Qui vos audit, me audit:* "He that heareth you heareth me, and he that despiseth you despiseth me." We deny not the truth of these words: notwithstanding it is plain Christ spake there no more of a council

Luke x.

[1 Cypr. Op. Oxon. 1682. Concil. Carthag. pp. 229, &c.]

[2 Concil. Neocæs. in Crabb. Concil. Col. Agrip. 1551. Tom. I. pp. 220, &c.]

[3 Concil. Ancyr. in eod. Tom. I. pp. 197, &c.]

[4 Concil. Gangr. in eod. Tom. I. pp. 287, &c.]

[5 Ambrosius episcopus dixit: Interim quia superioribus temporibus concilium sic factum est, ut orientales in orientis partibus constituti, haberent concilium, occidentales in occidente; nos in occidentis partibus constituti, convenimus ad Aquileiensium civitatem, &c.—Concil. Aquil. in eod. Tom. I. p. 397.]

than of any one private man having commission from him, and doing his commandment; whereunto the whole council is bound to yield, no less than others, and without which the council, be it never so general, is no council. But where did ever Christ give commandment that the service should be said in a strange unknown tongue? Or where did any general council ever decree it? Once again I ask M. Harding, and gently desire his answer, Where did any general council, from the beginning of the world, ever decree that the people should hear their service in a strange unknown tongue? If there be any such council, why doth he not shew it? If there be none, nor never were any, why doth he thus mock the world with the name of a council? General Councils.

Cicero saith very well of himself: *Nihil nobis opus erat lege, de quibus nihil esset actum legibus:* "To restore me from exile I needed no law, against whom there was nothing done by law." So may we likewise say, we need no council to restore God's truth, that was taken away from us without a council. Every prince is bound in the whole to see the reformation of his own church and country. Neither will God hold him excused if he say, I will tarry till all other princes and the whole world do the like. Josue, that noble prince, when he had assembled all the tribes of Israel before him, thus he spake unto them: *Si malum vobis videtur, ut serviatis Domino, optio vobis datur: ego autem, et domus mea, serviemus Domino:* "If ye think it ill to serve the Lord, ye shall have your choice; but I and my house will serve the Lord." It pleased God to plant his church in this realm, three hundred years before the first general council was holden at Nice[6]. "The Lord's hand is not shortened." He is likewise able now to reform the same by his holy word, without tarrying for a general council. Cicero de Legib. Lib. iii. Josh. xxiv. Polyd. Gild. Theod. Isai. lix.

Howbeit, the world may see these be but pretexts and vain shifts, without any simple meaning. They have now had a council of long continuance: they have heard the great complaints of all christian kingdoms and countries, namely touching their common service. M. Harding himself confesseth, "It were good the people understood it." Yet notwithstanding the council saith, No, it were ill; it were not good; and can in no wise abide it. And so either the council condemneth M. Harding; or else M. Harding condemneth his council. But Christ saith unto us: "Let the dead bury their dead: come thou, and follow me." Matt. viii.

M. HARDING. THE THIRTY-SECOND DIVISION.

Yet all standeth not in understanding. St Augustine saith notably: Turbam non intelligendi vivacitas, sed credendi simplicitas tutissimam facit[7]: *"That, as for the common people, it is not the quickness of understanding, but the simplicity of believing, that maketh them safest of all." And in another place:* Si propter eos solos Christus mortuus est, qui certa intelligentia possunt ista discernere, pene frustra in ecclesia laboramus[8]: *"If Christ," saith he, "died only for them which can with certain or sure understanding discern those[9] things (concerning God), then is the labour we take in the church in manner in vain." God requireth not so much of us, how much we understand, as how much we believe, and through belief how much we love. And when we shall all appear before Christ, in that dreadful day of judgment,* (84) *we shall not be required to give an account of our understanding, but (faith presupposed) of our charity.* *Contra Manicheos Epist. Fundamenti, cap. iv.* *Ad Euodium Epist.* 102. The eighty-fourth untruth. For it is written: 'He that knoweth not shall not be known.' 1 Cor. xiv. [38.]

THE BISHOP OF SARISBURY.

Whereas M. Harding saith, "All standeth not in understanding;" if he mean thereby profound knowledge and deep conceiving of mysteries, as St Augustine also meant, it may well be granted. Otherwise, as touching the public service, as Chrysostom saith, "Unless the unlearned understand what thou prayest, he is not edified, neither can he give consent unto thy prayer; thou throwest thy words Chrysost. in 1 Cor. Hom. 35.

[6 Polyd. Verg. Angl. Hist. Basil. 1555. Lib. II. pp. 37, 8. See also before, pages 280, 305.]

[7 August. Op. Par. 1679-1700. Lib. Contr. Epist. Manich. quam voc. Fund. cap. iv. 5. Tom. VIII. col. 153.]

[8 Id. ad Evod. Epist. clxix. 4. Tom. II. col. 604.]

[9 These, 1565, and H. A. 1564.]

into the wind, and speaketh[1] in vain[2]." And therefore the very substance of the public prayer resteth in the understanding of the hearer.

No man may justly presume of that M. Harding saith: "We shall not render
Rom. xiv. 2 Cor. v. account of our knowledge." For at that terrible day of the Lord we shall assuredly render account of our wilful ignorance. Christ himself, unto whom God
Matt. xv. hath given all judgment, saith: "If the blind lead the blind, both shall fall into
John iii. the pit." And again: "This is the condemnation of the world: light is come into the world; and men love the darkness more than the light." This (saith Christ) is the condemnation of the world. And the wise man saith, the wicked
Wisd. v. at that terrible time shall make their moan on this sort: *Aberravimus a via veritatis, et justitiæ lumen non fulsit nobis, et sol intelligentiæ non exortus est nobis:* "We strayed from the way of the truth; and the light of justice shined not before us; neither did the sun of understanding arise unto us." Chrysostom oftentimes
Chrysost. in Matt. Hom. 2. complaineth of the people's negligence in this behalf: *Non sum, inquis, monachus: uxorem habeo et filios, et curam domus. Hoc illud est quod omnia quasi una quadam peste corrumpit, quod lectionem divinarum scripturarum ad solos putatis monachos pertinere, &c.*[3]: "Thou wilt say, I am no monk: I have wife, and children, and charge of household. This is it that, as it were with a pestilence, infecteth all together, that ye think the reading of the holy scriptures belongeth only unto
In eadem hom. monks." He addeth further: *Multo est gravius atque deterius, superfluam esse putare legem Dei, quam illam omnino nescire. Hæc enim verba sunt, quæ de diabolica prorsus meditatione promuntur*[4]: "The fault is greater, and more grievous, to think God's law is superfluous (and not needful for thee), than to be ignorant whether there be any such law, or no. For these words come even from the persuasion of
In eadem. the devil." Again he saith: *Hæc diabolicæ inspirationis operatio est, non sinentis nos aspicere thesaurum, ne divitias acquiramus. Propterea ille suadet, nihil omnino esse commodi divinas audire leges, ne quando ex auditu sequi videat actionem*[5]: "This is the working of the devil's inspiration: he would not suffer us to see the treasure, lest we should get the riches. Therefore he counselleth us, that it utterly availeth nothing to hear the laws of God, lest that, upon the hearing, he may see our doing follow." Here we see the doctrine of simple ignorance, which M. Harding so stiffly maintaineth, is called by Chrysostom, "The devil's study:" "The devil's judgment:" "The devil's inspiration." And where he saith, "God will call us to no reckoning of our knowledge, or lack of knowledge;" Chrysostom plainly
Chrysost. ad Heb. Hom. 17. avoucheth the contrary, by these words: *Dices, Non legi: Non est hæc excusatio, sed crimen*[6]: "Thou wilt say, I have not read the scriptures: this is no excuse, but a sin."

Christian simplicity is not wilful ignorance, that is to say, to believe every
Matt. x. fable that is told, and to examine and know nothing. As Christ saith, "Be ye
Col. ii. simple as doves;" so he also saith, "Be ye wise as serpents." "Take heed ye be
1 Cor. xiv. not deceived." St Paul saith: "He that knoweth not shall not be known." Chry-
Chrysost. in Joh. Hom. 16. sostom hereof writeth thus: *Paulus ait, Verbum Christi inhabitet in vobis abundanter. Sed quid ad hæc respondent fucis stultiores? Benedicta omnis anima simplex: Et, Qui simpliciter ambulat, in fiducia ambulat. Hoc videlicet omnium malorum est causa, quod non multi scripturarum testimonia in opportunis rebus sciunt adducere. Non enim eo loco simplex pro stulto, aut pro eo qui nihil novit, intelligendus est; sed pro homine non malo, nec versuto. Nam si ita intelligeretur, supervacaneum fuisset dicere, Estote prudentes, sicut serpentes*[7]: "St Paul saith, 'Let the word of God dwell in you abundantly.' But what will these fools say hereto? O, say they, Blessed is the simple soul: and, He that walketh simply walketh surely. This is the very cause of all mischief, that in cases of necessity there be not many able to allege the scriptures. For a simple man, in that place, may not be taken for a fool, or a man that knoweth nothing; but for a man that meaneth no ill, or worketh no fraud. For if it were to be taken so, it had been

---

[[1] Speakest, 1565, 1609.]

[[2] Chrysost. Op. Par. 1718-38. In Epist. I. ad Cor. Hom. xxxv. Tom. X. cols. 323, 5, 6. The words are not precisely as cited; but the sense is identical.]

[[3] Id. In Matt. Hom. ii. Tom. VII. p. 30.]

[[4] Id. ibid.]

[[5] Id. ibid. p. 32.]

[[6] Id. in Epist. ad Hebr. cap. x. Hom. xvii. Tom. XII. p. 170.]

[[7] Id. in Joan. Hom. xvii. Tom. VIII. pp. 102, 3.]

in vain for Christ to say, 'Be ye wise as serpents.'" Therefore M. Harding, in the defence of ignorance, thus assuring the world that God will not be offended with want of knowledge, deceiveth the people of God, and saith not the truth. The reason that M. Harding hereof gathereth standeth thus:

The people, as St Augustine saith, cannot attain profound knowledge; and God beareth with their simplicity;

Ergo, They ought to have their service in a strange tongue.

M. HARDING. THE THIRTY-THIRD DIVISION.

[*The benefit of prayer uttered in a tongue not understanded.* H. A. 1564.]

Now, though the people know not the Latin tongue, and albeit it were better they had the service in their own vulgar tongue, for the better understanding of it; yet as it is, forasmuch as (85) *it consisteth in manner altogether of the scriptures, that great profit cometh both to the reader and to the hearer of it, Origen sheweth at large in the twentieth homily upon Josue. Because it were over long to bring all that he saith there to this purpose, the sum of the whole may thus be abridged: First, that the heavenly powers and angels of God, which be within us, have great liking in our utterance of the words of the scripture. "Though we understand not the* (86) *words we utter with our mouth, yet those powers," saith he, "understand them, and thereby be invited, and that with delight, to help us." And speaking of the powers that be within us, to whom charge of our souls and bodies is committed, he saith that, "if the scriptures be read of us, they have pleasure therein, and be made the stronger toward taking heed to us, yea, and that if we speak with tongues, and our spirit pray, and our sense be without fruit." And there he allegeth to that purpose the common place of St Paul to the Corinthians, calling it "marvellous, and in a manner*[9] *a mystery," shewing how the spirit prayeth, the sense being without fruit. After this he declareth the evil powers and our ghostly enemy*[10] *the devil, by our reading and hearing of the scriptures, to be driven from us. "As by enchantments," saith he, "snakes be staid from doing hurt with their venom; so, if there be in us any serpent of contrary power, or if any snake wait privily to mischief us, by virtue of the holy scripture rehearsed (so that for weariness thou turn not away thy hearing) he is put away*[11]*." St Augustine confirmeth the same doctrine, where he saith:* Psalmus dæmones fugat, angelos in adjutorium invitat[12]: *"The psalm (read devoutly, or heard) putteth devils to flight, and provoketh angels to help." At length Origen shewing how by meat or drink we find remedy for sore eyes, though we feel no benefit forthwith in eating or drinking, he concludeth his special part of comparison*[13] *with these words: "In this wise we must believe also of the holy scripture, that it is profitable, and doth good to the soul,* etiamsi sensus noster ad præsens intelligentiam non capit, *although presently our sense do not attain the meaning or understanding; because our good powers by these words be refreshed and fed; and the contrary, that is, our adversary powers, are weakened, and put to flight." At length, making objection to himself on the behalf of his hearers, as though they should lay this doctrine to his charge, for excuse of taking further pains in preaching and expounding the scriptures to them, thereto he answereth, and saith: "No, no, we have not said these to you for that cause, neither have we uttered these things to you for excuse, but to shew you,* in scripturis sanctis

The eighty-fifth untruth. For[8] in the Romish service there are infinite vanities, besides the scriptures.

The eighty-sixth untruth. For Origen speaketh of the ignorance of the allegory, not of the words.

In Prologo Psalmorum.

St Augustine speaketh of uttering the psalms in a known tongue.

[8 1565 omits *for*.]

[9 In manner, 1565 and H. A. 1564.]

[10 Enemies, H. A. 1564.]

[11 ...cœlestes virtutes et angeli Dei, qui nobiscum sunt...libenter et grate accipiunt, si semper verba scripturæ...ex nostro ore promamus; quia etsi nos non intelligimus quæ de ore proferimus, illæ tamen virtutes quæ nobis adsunt intelligunt, et velut carmine quodam invitatæ adesse nobis, et ferre auxilium delectantur...Constat ergo multas esse virtutes intra nos, quibus vel animarum nostrarum vel corporum cura permissa est, quæ...cum scripturæ leguntur a nobis, delectantur, et validiores erga nostri diligentiam fiunt, si linguis loquamur, et spiritus noster oret, sensus autem noster sine fructu sit. Dixit enim et hoc sanctus apostolus, et mirum quodammodo mysterium humanis auribus protulit, &c....Si quis vestrum aliquando perspexit præcantationibus sopitum serpentem...ita etiam lectionis divinæ virtute, si quis intra nos est contrariæ potestatis serpens, si quis ad insidiandum coluber latet, si patienter feras, si non tædio fatigatus avertas auditum, scripturæ carminibus et divini sermonis assiduitate depellitur.—Orig. Op. Par. 1733-59. In Lib. Jes. Nav. Hom. xx. 1. Tom. II. p. 444.]

[12 August. Op. Par. 1679-1700. In Lib. Psalm. Prolog. Tom. IV. fol. h. 2; where *ad adjutorium*. The Benedictine editor says of this prologue: Ipsa est Basilii ad ejus commentarium in Psalmos præfatio ex interpretatione Rufini.]

[13 Of the comparison, H. A. 1564.]

Origen.

esse vim quandam, quæ legenti etiam sine explanatione sufficiat[1]: "*That in the holy scriptures there is a certain power or strength, which is sufficient for one that readeth it, yea, without any expounding of it." This sufficiency he referreth, I think, to the procuring of the good powers to help us, and to the driving away the malice of evil[2] powers, our ghostly enemies, that they hurt us not.*

THE BISHOP OF SARISBURY.

M. Harding altereth his judgment.

It appeareth M. Harding is not so certain of his doctrine, but he may alter and vary without discredit. He held before for certain, that the ignorant people understandeth the Latin tongue, although not perfectly[3], or in exact wise. Now he seemeth to be resolved otherwise, that they understand it not at all. These contrary sayings will hardly stand together, unless he mean, the people's understanding, and no understanding, is all one thing.

Orig. in Jos. Hom. 23. περὶ Ἀρχῶν. Lib. iii. cap. iii. Orig. in Num. Hom. 20.

Origen, as he is here alleged, saith: "That the very reading or hearing of God's word profiteth much, and rejoiceth the angels both within and about us, although we understand it not." For better understanding hereof, I must briefly note certain particular opinions that this godly father had of angels and heavenly powers. And to leave much that might be said, he held thus; that angels have their offices allotted unto them diversly, some over trees, some over herbs, some over other things; that some have power to teach grammar, some logic, some rhetoric, some other sciences; and that some others are appointed to guide and guard us in this life, and shall appear before God, at the general judgment, to yield account of our doings[4]. By these it may appear what Origen meaneth by the angels that, as he saith, "be about us."

M. Harding wresteth Origen from his purpose. Orig. in Esai. Hom. 2.

His saying is very comfortable unto the simple mind, that delighteth in God's word, although oftentimes not understanding the deep sense of it. Of reading the scriptures his purpose was to speak, and not of having the service or prayers in a strange tongue. Wherefore M. Harding was the more to blame, thus to wrest his author to a wrong purpose. Origen oftentimes exhorted the people to the reading of the scriptures. Upon Esay the prophet he writeth thus: *Utinam... omnes faceremus illud quod scriptum est, Scrutamini scripturas*[5]*:* "I would we would all perform that is written, Search the scriptures."

Orig. in Jos. Hom. 20.

In this place upon Josue he layeth this objection against himself: "It may be said, The scriptures be hard." He answereth: "Yet, that notwithstanding, if thou read them, they shall do thee good. For the Lord Jesus Christ, if he find us occupied in the scriptures, and exercised in the study thereof, not only vouchsafeth himself to be refreshed and fed in us, but also, seeing such a banquet prepared, bringeth with him his Father unto us[6]." In the end he concludeth thus: *Hæc... idcirco diximus, ne fastidium capiamus audientes scripturas, etiamsi* [*eas*] *non intelligamus*[7]*:* "These things have I said, that we loathe not to hear the scriptures, although we understand them not." And thus much Origen spake, not of the grammatical or plain understanding of the scriptures, that riseth of the letter, but of the allegory, or profound sense, whereunto the unlearned cannot well attain. For so he expoundeth his own meaning, writing upon the gospel of St Matthew:

Orig. in Matt. Tract. xxvi.

Etiam illi salvantur, qui literam evangelii, hoc est, simplicem narrationem, sequuntur.

[[1] Solent medici præbere interdum cibum aliquem, interdum etiam potum dare, verbi gratia ad discutiendam caliginem visus: nec tamen in edendo ipso cibo, vel in potando sentimus quia utile est, et prodest oculis, &c....Hoc ergo modo credendum est etiam de scriptura sancta, quia utilis est, et animæ prodest, etiamsi sensus, &c. quoniam...et bonæ virtutes quæ nobis adsunt, reficiuntur in his sermonibus et pascuntur, et contrariæ torpescunt his meditationibus et effugantur. Sed fortasse dicitur ab auditoribus: Hæc nobis idcirco dicis, ut te ab officio disputationis excuses...Non ista de causa hæc diximus, nec excusantes nos ista protulimus; sed ut ostenderemus in scripturis, &c.—Orig. Op. Par. 1733-59. In Lib. Jes. Nav. Hom. xx. 2. Tom. II. pp. 444, 5.]

[[2] Of the evil, H. A. 1564.] [[3] Perfitely, 1565.]

[[4] Orig. Op. In Lib. Jes. Nav. Hom. xxiii. 3. Tom. II. p. 451.]

Id. De Princip. Lib. III. cap. iii. 2, 3, &c. Tom. I. pp. 143, &c.

Id. in Num. Hom. xx. 4. Tom. II. p. 351.]

[[5] Id. in Isai. Hom. ii. 2. Tom. III. p. 109.]

[[6] Quid dico quia divinæ virtutes pascantur... Ipse Dominus noster Jesus Christus si nos inveniat his vacantes, et hujuscemodi studiis et exercitiis operam dantes, non solum pasci et refici dignatur in nobis; verum etiam si has epulas apud nos viderit apparatas, Patrem secum dignatur adducere.—Id. in Lib. Jes. Nav. Hom. xx. 1. Tom. II. p. 444.]

[[7] Id. ibid. 2. ibid.; where *intelligimus.*]

Sola enim narratio simplex sufficit simplicioribus ad salutem[8]: "Even they be saved that follow the letter, that is to say, the plain story of the gospel. For only the simple story is sufficient unto the salvation of the simple." So far forth may the unlearned have profit by reading of the scriptures, although he further understand them not. So likewise saith St Augustine: *Qui diligit legem Dei, etiam quod in ea non intelligit honorat*[9]: "Whoso loveth the law of God honoureth in it even that thing that he understandeth not." Likewise he confesseth of himself, that, at his first entry into the faith of Christ, he received great profit by reading the epistle of St Paul unto the Romans, "although he were not then able thoroughly to conceive the meaning of it[10];" and further, that, by the counsel of St Ambrose, he read the prophet Esay; and, although he fully understood him not, yet was he thereby made the meeter to receive the grace of God[11]. The like also writeth St Hierome, by way of prophecy of the latter days, before the coming of Christ: *In adventu...Messiæ...populus elevabitur, et prophetabit, qui sub magistris ante fuerat consopitus, et ibunt ad montes scripturarum: Ibi invenient montes Mosen et Josue filium Naue, montes prophetas, montes novi testamenti, apostolos et evangelistas: et cum ad tales montes confugerit, et in hujusmodi montium fuerit lectione versatus, si non invenerit qui eum doceat,... tamen illius studium comprobabitur, quod confugerit ad montes*[12]: "At the coming of Messias the people shall be lifted up, and shall prophesy, that before lay asleep under their masters; and they shall go to the mountains of the scriptures, and there shall they find mountains, Moses, and Josue the son of Naue, the mountains of the prophets, the mountains of the new testament, the apostles, and the evangelists. And when they shall flee to such mountains, and shall be occupied in the reading thereof, if they find not one to teach them, yet shall their endeavour and good-will be allowed, for that they have fled unto the mountains." Thus[13] may the simple have profit by the reading of the scriptures, albeit he fully understand them not. Thus be the angels delighted: thus is the devil molested and grieved with the same; as Origen himself witnesseth by these words: [*Dæmonibus*] *super omnia...est tormentorum genera, et super omnes pœnas, si quem videant verbo Dei operam dare, scientiam divinæ legis et mysteria scripturarum intentis studiis perquirentem*[14]: "Unto the devils it is a grief above all kinds of torment, and above all pains, if they see any man labour the word of God, seeking with earnest mind the knowledge of God's law, and the mysteries of the scriptures."

Origen.

Aug. in Psal. cxix.

Aug. Confess. Lib. vii. cap. xii.

Aug. Confess. Lib. ix. cap. v.

Hieron. in Nahum. cap. iii.

Orig. in Num. Hom. 27.

St Augustine, as M. Harding allegeth him, saith: "The psalm chaseth away devils[15]." But St Augustine giveth not such power unto a psalm pronounced only with the lips, in a strange unknown tongue, but unto a psalm understanded, and believed, and pronounced from the heart. For to say, The word of God, only because it is written or spoken, is available of itself without understanding, as M. Harding seemeth to say, is a superstitious and a Jewish kind of folly. Chrysostom saw and reproved the superstition thereof in his time by these words: *Quidam sacerdotes partem aliquam evangelii alligant circa collum. Dic, sacerdos insipiens: Nonne quotidie evangelium in ecclesia legitur, et auditur ab hominibus? Cui ergo in auribus posita evangelia nihil prosunt, quomodo eum poterunt circa collum suspensa salvare?... Ubi est virtus evangelii? In figuris literarum, an in intellectu sensuum*[16]? "Certain

August. in Prolog. in Librum Psalm.

Chrysost. in Matt. in Op. Imp. Hom. 43.

[8 Litteram autem evangelii qui sequuntur, id est, simplicem narrationem ipsius, salvantur: quoniam et ipsa sola evangelii narratio, &c.—Id. in Matt. Comm. Ser. 27. Tom. III. p. 847.]

[9 Qui enim diligit Dei legem, etiam, &c.—August. Op. Par. 1679-1700. In Psalm. cxviii. Serm. xxxi. 5. Tom. IV. col. 1360.]

[10 Probably the passage is intended in which Augustine says: Avidissime arripui ... præ ceteris apostolum Paulum: &c.—Id. Confess. Lib. VII. cap. xxi. 27. Tom. I. col. 143; though it was not till afterwards that he attained a spiritual understanding of the scripture.—Id. ibid. Lib. VIII. cap. xii. 29. col. 156.]

[11 Et insinuavi...Ambrosio...ut moneret quid potissimum mihi de libris tuis legendum esset, quo percipiendæ tantæ gratiæ paratior aptiorque fierem. At ille jussit Isaiam prophetam...Veruntamen ego primam hujus lectionem non intelligens...distuli repetendum, &c.—Id. ibid. Lib. IX. cap. v. 13. Tom. I. col. 162.]

[12 Hieron. Op. Par. 1693-1706. Comm. in Naum Proph. cap. iii. Tom. III. col. 1590; where we find *Christi* for *Messiæ*, *elevabitur et properabit populus*, *ibit*, *ibique inveniet*, *Jesum*, *hujuscemodi*, and *tunc et illius*.]

[13 This, 1565.]

[14 Orig. Op. In Num. Hom. xxvii. 8. Tom. II. p. 378.]

[15 See before, page 325, note 12.]

[16 Phylacteria alligant circa collum, quidam vero partem aliquam evangelii scriptam. Dic &c.—Chrysost. Op. Par. 1718-38. Opus Imperf. in Matt. Hom. xliii. ex cap. xxiii. Tom. VI. p. clxxxiv.]

Origen. priests there be that bind a piece of the gospel about their necks. Tell me, thou foolish priest, is not the gospel every day read and heard of men in the church? If the gospel do not profit a man being put in his ear, how then can it profit him being tied at his neck? For wherein resteth the power of the gospel? In the form of the letters, or in the understanding of the sense?" So may we say unto M. Harding: Wherein resteth the power of the psalms, wherewith the devil is vanquished? in the bare sound of the words, or in the sense and meaning of the same? Certainly St Augustine saith: The word of God worketh in our hearts, *non quia dicitur, sed quia creditur*[1]: "Not because it is spoken, but because it is believed." Likewise saith St Basil: *Non qui ore profert verba psalmi, psallit Domino, sed quicunque de puro corde proferunt psalmodiam*[2]: "He singeth not unto the Lord that uttereth the words of the psalm, but they that from a pure heart pronounce the psalmody." Likewise Origen: *Fiduciam habet ad Deum, non propter...verba orationis vel psalmi, quamvis videantur bene composita, et de scripturis electa, sed quia...altare cordis sui bene construxit*[3]: "He that prayeth hath trust in God, not for the words of his prayer, or of the psalm, although they seem to be well made, and chosen out of the scriptures, but because he hath well made up the altar of his heart." This was Origen's whole and only purpose. He exhorteth not the people to hear service in a strange language. Neither is M. Harding able to shew that there was any such service in the whole church of God, either then in Origen's time, or within four hundred years after him. Only he encouraged the people to read the scriptures, yea, although they were not able to reach the bottom of them, as it plainly appeareth by his own words following: *In scripturis sanctis est vis quædam, quæ legenti etiam sine explanatione sufficiat*: "In the holy scriptures there is a certain virtue sufficient for the reader, yea, although they be not expounded." And therefore he allegeth these words of St Paul, "My spirit prayeth, but my sense is without fruit;" not to warrant M. Harding's strange order of prayer, which neither St Paul nor Origen himself ever knew; but only to shew, that as God of his mercy helpeth our weakness in praying, so likewise in reading the scriptures he helpeth our weakness in understanding. St Paul saith: *Quid oremus quemadmodum oporteat, nescimus: sed ipse Spiritus postulat pro nobis gemitibus inenarrabilibus*: "We know not what to pray as it is meet for us to pray; but the Spirit of God entreateth for us with sighs that cannot be expressed." "Thus," saith Origen, "the angels of God delight to see us praying. Thus they delight to see us reading." But if they delight only to see us pray, or hear in a strange tongue we know not what, as M. Harding would gather, then are they the angels of darkness, and not of God.

August. Tract. lxxx. in Joh.

Basil. in Psal. xxix.

Orig. in Matt. Tract. xxv.

1 Cor. xiv.

Rom. viii.

Out of this place of Origen M. Harding gathereth these reasons: "The angels are delighted to hear us read or pray, although we of our weakness know not thoroughly what we speak;" *ergo*, the people in Origen's time had the common service in a strange tongue. The error or fraud hereof may the better appear by that I have afore[4] declared. It is called *fallacia ab amphibologia*, that is, of the doubtful taking of one word. For this word, "understanding," hath two significations. For we understand the words, and we understand the meaning of the words. Origen saith: "The people understood not the meaning of the scripture[5];" *ergo*, saith M. Harding, they understood not the words of the scripture[5]. Again, Origen saith: "They had no full and perfect[6] understanding;" *ergo*, saith M. Harding, they had no understanding at all. And therein standeth the falsehood[7] of his argument. And again, the words that Origen writeth of reading the scriptures, M. Harding applieth the same to the common service; and so violently and perforce altereth and depraveth Origen's meaning, and concludeth one thing for another. And thus this good father is drawn in to prove that thing that he never neither knew, nor did, nor willed to be done.

[1 August. Op. Par. 1679-1700. In Johan. Evang. cap. xv. Tractat. lxxx. 3. Tom. III. Pars II. col. 703.]

[2 Basil. Op. Par. 1721-30. Hom. in Psalm xxix. Tom. I. pp. 126, 7.]

[3 Orig. Op. Par. 1733-59. In Matt. Comm. Ser. 18. Tom. III. p. 842.]

[4 Before, 1565.]

[5 Scriptures, 1565, 1609.]

[6 Perfite, 1565.]

[7 Falsehead, 1565.]

M. HARDING. THE THIRTY-FOURTH DIVISION.

I trust, wise, godly, and stedfast men, who be not carried about with every wind of doctrine, will be moved more with the authority of Origen, a man always in the judgment of all the christian world accounted most excellently learned, than with the scorning of Calvin, who, speaking of the ancient Latin service used in England and France, saith: Ad ecclesiam ex sono non intellecto nullus penitus fructus redit[8]: *that, "of the sound not understanded, no fruit at all returneth to the church;" using that word of despite that might better be spoken by a minstrel of his pipe and tabret, than by a preacher of the divine service. Neither hereof with any milder spirit speaketh his disciple and subminister, Theodoret[9] Beza, the hot minister of the deformed churches of France:* Quæcunque...preces ab aliquo concipiuntur eo idiomate, quod ipse non intelligat, pro Dei ludibrio sunt habendæ[10]: *"What prayers soever be made," saith he, "of any man in a tongue that he understandeth not, they be to be taken for a mockery of God." Whosoever here alloweth Calvin and Beza, condemned of the church, must condemn Origen, for this point never reproved or[11] touched of any, that have not spared him wheresoever they could charge him with any error. If all prayers made in an unknown tongue be a mocking to[12] God, as Beza saith, then were the prayers uttered by miracle in the primitive church with tongues, which the utterers themselves understood not, after the mind of Chrysostom, a mocking of God; for I see nothing whereby they are excluded from his* (87) *general saying and universal proposition. Verily this teaching of Beza is not sound: I ween, if he were out of the protection of his deformed churches, and convented before a catholic bishop to give an account of this doctrine, he would step back and revoke that rash saying again. For else he should seem to grant that God gave at the beginning of the church the gift of tongues to be mocked withal; which were very absurd and blasphemous. St Paul wisheth that all the Corinthians spake with tongues, but rather that they prophesied.*

In Institutionib.

Confessionis ca. iv. sectione 16.

The eighty-seventh untruth. For[13] this general saying of Chrysostom is untruly reported.

THE BISHOP OF SARISBURY.

I marvel much what soundness of doctrine M. Harding can mean, having thus taken upon him to be the proctor of ignorance; or how he can well commend others for constancy and stedfastness, finding himself with so light winds so often removed; or wherefore he should so highly commend that old father Origen, at whose hands he findeth so small relief.

That he thus bitterly chargeth that godly-learned father, John Calvin, for saying thus, "Of the unknown service there redoundeth no manner profit to[14] the church;" it toucheth many others more, and not him only. St Augustine saith thus: *Si [Moses mihi] Hebræa voce loqueretur, frustra pulsaret sensum meum, nec inde mentem meam quicquam tangeret*[15]: "If Moses should speak unto me in the Hebrew tongue (for that I understand it not), he should beat my senses in vain; neither should there any thing thereof enter into my mind." St Chrysostom saith: *Nisi dixero quod percipi facile clareque a vobis possit, sed linguarum munere præditum me esse tantum ostendam, nullum ex his quæ non intelligitis fructum facientes abibitis, credo. Nam quæ utilitas esse ex voce non intellecta potest*[16]*?* "Unless I speak that you may plainly and clearly understand, but only shew myself[17] to have the gift of tongues, ye shall depart away, having no fruit of those things that ye understand not. For of a voice that ye know not what profit can ye have?" Again he saith: *Et vos, nisi significantem sonum dederitis . . . verba vento, hoc est, nemini facietis*[18]: "And you, unless ye utter a sound with understanding, ye shall speak to the wind, that is to say, ye shall speak to nobody." And to pass by all others, Nicolas Lyra saith thus: *Si tu sacerdos benedixeris...spiritu, id est,*

August. Confess. Lib. xi. cap. iii.

Chrysost. in 1 Cor. xiv. Hom. 35.

No fruit.

Speak to the wind.

Nicol. Lyra in 1 ad Cor. xiv.

[8 Calvin. Op. Amst. 1667-71. Inst. Lib. III. cap. xx. 33. p. 237; where *quam* for *ecclesiam*.]

[9 Theodore, 1565, 1609, and H. A. 1564.]

[10 Bez. Tractat. Theolog. Genev. 1570-3. Confess. cap. iv. 16. Vol. I. p. 11.]

[11 Nor, H. A. 1564.]

[12 Of, 1565, 1609, and H. A. 1564.]

[13 1565 omits *for*.]

[14 Unto, 1565, 1609.]

[15 August. Op. Confess. Lib. XI. cap. iii. 5. Tom. I. col. 197.]

[16 Chrysost. Op. Par. 1718-38. In Epist. I. ad Cor. Hom. XXXV. Tom. X. p. 323.]

[17 Meself, 1565.]

[18 Chrysost. ibid.]

The Latin church. The Psalms.

absque hoc quod populus intelligat,...quid proficit populus simplex et non intelligens[1]? "If thou, being the priest, do bless with thy spirit, that is to say, if the people understand thee not, what profit hath the simple people thereby, not understanding thee?" Therefore, as M. Harding saith M. Calvin in this point was a scorner, so might he as well have said, St Augustine, St Chrysostom, Nicolas Lyra, and others, are all scorners.

No profit.

"If all prayers," saith M. Harding, "made in a strange tongue be a mocking of God, as Beza saith, then were the prayers uttered by miracle in the primitive church with tongue which the utterers themselves understood not, after the mind of Chrysostom, a mocking of God." This exposition of Chrysostom is very strange, and agreeth with few others; and yet is the same here by M. Harding untruly reported. For Chrysostom saith not, that whosoever in the primitive church uttered the prayers with tongue understood not himself what he said; but plain the contrary. For thus he saith: *Linguis loquens se ipsum ædificat: quod quidem fieri non potest, nisi quæ loquatur norit*[2]: "He that speaketh with tongues profiteth himself; which cannot be unless he understand what he saith." And he addeth further: *Et hactenus quidem disputat de illis, qui ea, quæ loquuntur, intelligunt*[3]: "Hitherto St Paul disputeth of them that understand what they say." Hereby it is plain that M. Harding's general proposition is not generally true. "But others," Chrysostom saith, "there were that abused the gift of tongues, and knew not themselves what they said[4]." And whether this were a mocking of God or no, let M. Harding judge. Chrysostom saith: "It was a confusion of the church, a bragging and ostentation of themselves, without consideration either of themselves or of others; that such a one was Simon Magus; that such were the Jews that betrayed themselves unto the devil[5]." And St Augustine compareth them unto ousels, pies, and ravens, that cry and chatter they know not what[6]. Therefore I doubt not but M. Beza's exposition will stand, both before God, and also before any good catholic bishop.

Chrysost. 1 Cor. xiv. Hom. 35.

Eadem homilia.

M. HARDING. THE THIRTY-FIFTH DIVISION.

If our new masters condemn the Latin service in the Latin church, for that the people understand it not; thereof it must[7] *follow, that the English service, so much of it as consisteth of David's Psalms, which is the most part, be also condemned. The like may be said of other nations. For how many shall we find, not of the people only, but also of the best learned men, that understand the meaning of them, in what tongue soever they be set forth? St Hilary compareth the book of Psalms to a heap of keys, that be to open the doors of every house of a great city, laid together: amongst*[8] *whom it is hard to find which key serveth which lock; and without the right key no door can be opened*[9]. *St Augustine likeneth the people of Africa, singing the psalms which they understood not, to ousels, popinjays, ravens, pies, and such other birds, which be taught to sound they know not what*[6]; *and yet they understood the tongue they sung*[10] *them in. And therefore he exhorteth them to learn the meaning of them at his preaching, lest they should sing not with human reason (as it*[11] *is before recited), but with voice only, as birds do.*

[*Præfat. in Psalmos.* 1565, and H. A. 1564.]

[1 Bibl. cum Gloss. Ord. et Expos. N. de Lyra, Basil. 1502. Ad Cor. I. cap. xiv. Pars VI. fol. 55. 2. See before, page 309, note 4.]

[2 Chrysost. Op. Par. 1718-38. In Epist. I. ad Cor. Hom. XXXV. Tom. X. p. 322.]

[3 Id. ibid.]

[4 Καὶ γὰρ ἦσαν τὸ παλαιὸν καὶ χάρισμα εὐχῆς ἔχοντες πολλοὶ μετὰ γλώττης...ὁ νοῦς δὲ οὐκ ᾔδει τὸ λεγόμενον.—Id. ibid. p. 325.]

[5 ...σύγχυσις ἔσται...τὸ μὲν γὰρ καὶ ἐπίδειξιν ἔχει μόνον, κ.τ.λ....τοιοῦτος ἦν ὁ Σίμων, ὃς ἐπειδὴ πρὸς δόξαν εἶδε κενὴν, οὐδὲ τὸ ἑαυτοῦ χρήσιμον εἶδε. τοιοῦτοι καὶ Ἰουδαῖοι, οἳ διὰ ταύτην τῷ διαβόλῳ τὴν οἰκείαν προέπιον σωτηρίαν.—Id. ibid. pp. 325, 6.]

[6 See before, pages 282, 3.]

[7 Must it, 1565, 1609 and H. A. 1564.]

[8 Among, 1565, 1609 and H. A. 1564.]

[9 Nam liber omnis [psalmorum] similis est urbi pulcræ atque magnæ, cui ædes complures diversæque sint, quarum fores propriis clavibus diversisque claudantur: quæ cum unum in locum congestæ permixtæque sint, volenti unamquamque ædem aperire, maximam ignaro afferant difficultatem, ut clavem uniuscujusque ædis inveniat.—Hilar. Op. Par. 1693. Prolog. in Lib. Psalm. 24. col. 13.]

[10 Sang, 1565, and H. A. 1564.]

[11 H. A. 1564 omits *it*.]

THE BISHOP OF SARISBURY.

All our matter is fully answered and confuted; for M. Harding hath called us "new masters," even with the same authority and spirit that Haman said unto king Darius, "the Jews troubled his country, and professed and used a new law." Certainly our doctrine is Christ's doctrine, and hath the testimony, not only of the law and the prophets, but also of the ancient councils and old fathers.

The Psalms.

Esth. iii. 8.

The greatest proof for the Latin service, that M. Harding can find, standeth upon the bare name of the Latin church. And yet in that whole church this day there is not one nation that either speaketh or understandeth the Latin tongue. Let M. Harding only leave his portuise, and Latin service; then hath he no further cause to brag of his Latin church. For, as it now fareth, his service taketh not name of his church, but his church of his service. Verily, as it is meet the service should be in Latin in the Latin church; so is it meet the service should be in English in the English church.

We grant, the psalms be hard, as it is alleged, for the deep senses, and high mysteries, and secret prophecies of Christ and of his church therein contained. Besides that, M. Harding hath found out a bunch of keys in St Hilary wherewith to shut out all the people. Notwithstanding the right use of keys is rather to open than to shut. Chrysostom saith: *Clavis...est verbum scientiæ scripturarum, per quam aperitur hominibus janua veritatis*[12]: "The key is the word of knowledge of the scriptures, by the which the gate of the truth is opened unto men." And Tertullian likewise saith: *Clavis est interpretatio legis*[13]: "The key is the exposition of the law." And therefore Christ saith: "Wo be unto you, ye scribes and Pharisees, that shut up the kingdom of God before men; for ye enter not yourselves, neither suffer others that would enter." And thus they do, saith Tertullian, *Docentes potius præcepta et doctrinas hominum*[14]; "Teaching rather the commandments and doctrines of men." But if there be so many keys bound together, what if M. Harding have missed in his choice, and have taken one key for another?

Chrysost. in Op. Imp. in Matt. cap. xxiii.

Tertul. contra Marc. Lib. iv.

Matt. xxiii.

His reason standeth thus: The simple people understandeth not the deep meaning of the psalms; *ergo*, they understand nothing in the psalms. By this key M. Harding may happen to shut out himself. This is a false kind of reasoning, which in the schools is called *A secundum quid ad simpliciter*. For albeit the people understand not all the high mysteries of the scriptures, yet it followeth not that therefore they understand nothing in the scriptures. For in the scriptures there is both strong meat for men, and also milk for children; "and in the same," saith St Gregory, "the elephant may swim, and the lamb may wade afoot[15]."

Greg. in Epist. ad Leand.

And if the psalms be hard in the vulgar tongue, be they therefore easy in the Latin tongue? Or if the psalms be dark, must the people therefore have their service in Latin?

Verily it appeareth both by David himself, and also by sundry old fathers, that the simplest of all the people were able to understand the psalms. David exhorteth "young men and maids, old men and children, to praise the name of the Lord." Children were able to receive Christ with psalms, and to sing aloud, "Blessed is he that cometh in the name of the Lord;" and applied the same aptly unto Christ. St Hierome saith: "The poor husbandman sung the psalms at his plough[16]." St Basil exhorteth the artificer "to sing psalms in his

Psal. cxlviii.

Matt. xxi.

Hieron. ad Marcell.

Basil. in Psal.

[12 Chrysost. Op. Opus Imperf. in Matt. Hom. xliv. ex cap. xxiii. Tom. VI. p. clxxxvi.]

[13 Quam vero clavem habebant legis doctores, nisi interpretationem legis?—Tertull. Op. Lut. 1641. Adv. Marcion. Lib. IV. 27. p. 549.]

[14 Id. ibid.]

[15 Quasi quidam...est fluvius...in quo et agnus ambulet, et elephas natet.—Gregor. Magn. Papæ I. Op. Par. 1705. Ad Leandr. cap. iv. De Expos. Lib. Job. Tom. I. cols. 5, 6.]

[16 Quoquumque te verteris, arator stivam tenens, alleluia decantat. Sudans messor psalmis se avocat, &c.—Hieron. Op. Par. 1693-1706. Paul et Eustoch. ad Marcell. Epist. xliv. Tom. IV. Pars II. col. 552.]

The Psalms.

shop[1]." Apollinaris turned the psalms into Greek verses, that children might learn them in the schools[2]. St Chrysostom saith unto the father: "Teach thy child to sing the psalms[3]." St Augustine saith: "Psalms were purposely made that young men and children might learn to sing them[4]." Protogenes in the stead of poets' fables, and other like things, gave David's psalms to children to expound[5]. And that every of these understood what they sung, it may appear by these words of St Augustine: *Simul et cantare videmur, et quod ad animæ utilitatem pertinet, docemur*[6]: "Both we seem to sing, and also withal are taught that thing that is profitable for our soul." Therefore, if any in Africa sung they knew not what, St Augustine compareth them to ravens or popinjays. But will M. Harding thereof conclude thus: They that know not what they sing, sing like ravens or popinjays; *ergo*, the people ought to have their service in a strange tongue?

Chrysost. ad Coloss. Hom. 9. Prolog. in Psal. Theod. Lib. iv. cap. xix. In Prolog. in Psal.

M. HARDING. THE THIRTY-SIXTH DIVISION.

The rest of the scriptures whereof the service consisteth is, though not altogether so obscure as the psalms, yet verily darker and harder than that the common people's gross and simple wits may pierce the understanding of it by hearing the same pronounced of the minister in their mother-tongue. And by this reason we should have no service at all gathered out of the scriptures for default of understanding.

THE BISHOP OF SARISBURY.

The people, saith M. Harding, is gross and simple, and cannot understand the scriptures by hearing the same in their mother-tongue; *ergo*, they must hear it pronounced in the Latin tongue: I trow, that they may the better understand it. This seemeth to be a very simple argument, and a gross ungentle opinion of the simplicity of the people. God is not partial, neither hideth his truth from the simple, because he is simple; but from the proud and reprobate, because he is wilful; and specially chooseth the simple of the world to confound the wise. The simplest and grossest of all them that M. Harding meaneth is able to hear the voice of the shepherd, and to follow him; but the stranger, of whom he hath been deceived by double doctrine, he doubteth him, and refuseth him, and will not follow.

James iv. Psal. xxxiv. 1 Cor. i. John x.

M. HARDING. THE THIRTY-SEVENTH DIVISION.

And whereas of the service in the vulgar tongue the people will frame lewd and perverse meanings of their own lewd senses; so of the Latin service they will make no constructions either of false doctrine or of evil life. And as (88) *the vulgar service pulleth their minds from private devotion to hear and not to pray, to little benefit of knowledge, for the obscurity of it; so the Latin giveth*[7] *them no such motion; they occupy themselves, whiles the priest prayeth for all and in the person of all, in their private prayers, all for all, and every one for himself.*

The eighty-eighth untruth. For the vulgar service increaseth devotion, as by sundry authorities it shall appear.

THE BISHOP OF SARISBURY.

He that understandeth what he heareth read, saith M. Harding, hath his mind wandering, and is drawn abroad with vain imaginations. But whoso understandeth not one word at all, neither what he heareth, nor what he speaketh himself, hath his mind closely fixed upon that he speaketh. Thus M. Harding,

---

[[1] τὰ δὲ τῶν ψαλμῶν λόγια καὶ κατ' οἶκον μελῳδοῦσι, καὶ ἐπὶ τῆς ἀγορᾶς περιφέρουσι.—Basil. Op. Par. 1721-30. Hom. in Psalm. i. Tom. I. p. 90.]

[[2] This work is still extant. It may be seen in Biblioth. Patr. per M. de la Bigne, Par. 1624. Tom. VIII. pp. 163, &c. See Cave, Script. Eccles. Hist. Lit. Oxon. 1740-3. Vol. I. p. 225.]

[[3] Δίδαξον αὐτὸν ᾄδειν ψαλμοὺς, κ. τ. λ.—Chrysost. Op. Par. 1718-38. In Epist. ad Col. cap. iii. Hom. ix. Tom. XI. p. 392.]

[[4] Propterea ergo psalmorum nobis per modulos apta sunt carmina, ut qui vel ætate puerili, vel adolescentes sunt moribus, quasi cantilena quadam psallentes delectari videantur.—August. Op. Par. 1679-1700. In Lib. Psalm. Prolog. Tom. IV. fol. h. 2.]

[[5] Theodor. in Hist. Eccles. Scrip. Amst. 1695-1700. Lib. IV. cap. xviii. p. 172.]

[[6] August. Op. In Lib. Psalm. Prolog. Tom. IV. fol. h. 2; where *videamur, utilitatem animæ*, and *doceamur*.]

[[7] Giving, 1565, and H. A. 1564.]

as he hath made a new divinity, so is he also bold to make a new philosophy. For, naturally, the mind, understanding what it heareth or readeth, and being attentive unto the same, hath less cause to wander and stray abroad. St Basil saith: *Lingua psallat; mens autem scrutetur sensum eorum quæ dicis: ut psallas spiritu, et psallas etiam mente*[8]: "Let thy tongue sing; and let thy mind search out the meaning of that thou speakest, that thou mayest sing with thy spirit, and sing also with thy mind."

The Psalms.

Basil. in Psal. xxviii.

But forasmuch as M. Harding saith the understanding of the priest is a hindrance unto private devotion, in favour whereof he utterly defaceth the public prayers; it shall behove us to consider what the old fathers have thought in that behalf. Chrysostom thereof writeth thus: *Non æque exoras, cum solus Dominum obsecras, atque cum fratribus tuis. Est enim in hoc plus aliquid, videlicet concordia, conspiratio, copula amoris, et caritatis, et sacerdotum clamores. Præsunt enim ob eam rem sacerdotes, ut populi orationes, quæ infirmiores per se sunt, validiores illas complexæ simul in cœlum evehantur*[9]: "Thou dost not so soon obtain thy desire when thou prayest alone unto the Lord, as when thou prayest with thy brethren. For herein there is somewhat more, the concord, the consent, the joining of love and charity, and the cry of the priests. For to that end the priests are made overseers, that they, being the stronger sort, may take with them the weaker prayers of the people, and carry them up into heaven." Likewise again he saith: *Quod quis apud se ipsum precatus accipere non poterit, hoc cum multitudine precatus accipiet. Quare? Quia etiamsi non propria virtus, tamen concordia multum potest*[10]: "The thing that a man cannot obtain praying by himself alone, praying together with the multitude he shall obtain. And why so? For although not his own worthiness, yet the concord and unity prevaileth much." Thus then stood the order of Christ's church: the whole multitude gave ear unto the priest, and at the end of his prayer lifted up their voices unto heaven all together, and said, Amen; which voice oftentimes was so great, that, as it is aforesaid, St Hierome likeneth it unto a thunder-clap; St Basil, unto the roaring of the sea. At that time M. Harding's private devotion, as it is now used in his church, would have been called private superstition. And whereas he thus strangely saith, devotion is hindered by understanding; his own doctor, Nicolas Lyra, saith otherwise, and condemneth him: *Si populus intelligat orationem... sacerdotis, melius reducitur in Deum et devotius respondet Amen*[11]: "If the people understand the prayer of the priest, they are the better reduced unto God, and with more devotion they answer, Amen." The emperor Justinian, where he commandeth all bishops and priests to minister the service with a loud voice, giveth this reason withal: *Ut mentes audientium ad majorem animi compunctionem, et ad reddendam Domino gloriam excitentur*[12]: "That the minds of the hearers may be stirred up to more devotion, and to render praise unto the Lord." And St Basil saith: *Tanquam ab uno ore et uno corde confessionis psalmum offerunt Domino; et verba pœnitentiæ eorum quisque proprie ascribit sibi*[13]: "As it were from one mouth, and from one heart, they offer up unto the Lord the psalm of confession, and the words of repentance every of them applieth particularly unto himself." So likewise it is written in the prologue before St Augustine upon the psalms: *Quomodo debite potest Deo psallere, qui ignorat quid psallat*[14]? "How can he sing duly (or devoutly) unto God, that knoweth not what he singeth?" It is thought by these, notwithstanding M. Harding's contrary and private judgment, that the understanding of the public service is no hindrance unto devotion; and their authority in this case may serve, unless M. Harding will condemn them altogether, as he doth others, for "new masters."

Chrysost. de Incomp. Dei Nat. Hom. 3.

Chrysost. in 2 ad Thess. Hom. 4.

Lyra in 1 Cor. xiv.

In Novell. de Eccles. Diversis Capitulis. εἰς πλείονα κατάνυξιν.

Basil. ad Cler. Neoc.

Prolog. in Aug. super Psal.

[8 Basil. Op. Par. 1721-30. Hom. in Psalm. xxviii. Tom. I. p. 123.]

[9 Chrysost. Op. De Incompr. contr. Anom. Hom. iii. Tom. I. p. 469.]

[10 Id. In II. Epist. ad Thess. cap. iii. Hom. iv. Tom. XI. p. 535.]

[11 Bibl. cum. Gloss. Ord. et Expos. N. de Lyra, Basil. 1502. Ad Cor. I. cap. xiv. Pars VI. fol. 55. 2.]

[12 Justin. Princ. Novell. Constit. Basil. 1561. Const. cxxxvii. pp. 409, 10. See also before, page 287, note 10.]

[13 Basil. Op. Ad Cler. Neoc. Epist. ccvii. 3. Tom. III. p. 161.]

[14 August. Op. Præf. cujusd. Recent. in Comm. August. Tom. IV. fol. h. 2; where *Deo psallere potest*, and *quid psallat ignorat*.]

Prayers, common and private.

M. HARDING. THE THIRTY-EIGHTH DIVISION.

The eighty-ninth untruth. For the service in the vulgar tongue never was cause of schism or heresy.

(89) *The nations that have ever had their service in the vulgar tongue, the people thereof have continued in schisms, errors, and certain Judaical observances, so as they have not been reckoned in the number of the catholic church: as the Christians of Moscovia, of Armenia, of Prester John his land in Æthiopia. Bessarion, asking by way of a question of the Greeks his countrymen, what church that is against the which hell-gates shall never prevail, answereth himself, and saith:* Aut...Latina aut Græca est ecclesia: tertia enim dari non potest: siquidem aliæ omnes hæresibus sunt plenæ, quas sancti patres et generales synodi condemnarunt[1]: "*Either it is the Latin or the Greek church; for there is no third that can be granted. For all other churches be full of heresies, which the holy fathers and general councils have condemned." Wherefore of these churches no example ought to be taken for service in the vulgar tongue; as neither of the churches of Russia, and Moravia, and certain other, to whom, above six hundred years past, it was granted to have the mass in the Sclavons' tongue, through special licence thereto obtained of the see apostolic by Cyrillus and Methodius, that first converted them to the faith. Which manner of service, so many of them as be catholic, for good causes have left, and used*[2] *the Latin, as other Latin churches do. Concerning the rest yet keeping their Sclavon tongue, beside other errors and defaults, for which they are not herein to be esteemed worthy to be followed, we may say of them the words of Gregory Nazianzene:* Privilegia paucorum non faciunt legem communem: "*The privileges of a few make not a thing lawful in common.*"

[Such nations as use church service in their own tongue continue in schisms. H. A. 1564.]

In Epistola ad Græcos.

THE BISHOP OF SARISBURY.

This argument seemeth to hold thus: Service in the vulgar tongue is cause of schisms and errors; *ergo*, within six hundred years after Christ it was ministered in some place in a tongue unknown unto the people. The force of this conclusion is evident: a very child may soon see through it. If the antecedent were true, then should the Jews, the Greeks, and the Latins, which evermore had their service in the vulgar tongue, for that cause have been full of schisms and errors. St Augustine, St Hierome, and other fathers, say that pride and wilfulness of mind[3], Tertullian saith that knowledge of philosophy and affiance of learning, hath caused division and heresies in the church, and therefore calleth the philosophers the patriarchs of heretics[4]. The bishops in the council of Toledo say thus: *Ignorantia est mater omnium errorum*[5]: "Ignorance is the mother of all error." But that the understanding of the common service was ever thought the cause of schism or error in the church, I think it was never either written or spoken by any old doctor, either Greek or Latin, or Jew or Gentile. Epiphanius reckoneth up four-score sundry heresies that had been before his time[6]; St Augustine reckoneth four-score and nine[7]. Yet do they not say that any one of all those heresies ever sprang of understanding the common service. No man would say thus but M. Harding: neither will M. Harding thus say, when, faction and contention laid apart, he shall either say that he knoweth, or have regard to that he saith.

Tertull. contra Hermog.

Concil. Tolet. iv. cap. 24.

Epiph. De Hæres. August. ad Quod-vult Deum.

Touching the Christians, which be in infinite numbers in Moscovia, Armenia, Ethiopia, and elsewhere, whom upon very short advice he hath condemned altogether for schismatics, if he would have credit given unto his tale, it would have behoved him both to have declared their particular errors and heresies, and also substantially to have proved that their vulgar service gave occasion unto the same.

[1 Bessar. ad Græc. Epist. in Odor. Raynald. Cont. Baron. Annal. Eccles. Luc. 1747-56. Tom. X. p. 369; where *ecclesia est*, and *omnes aliæ*.]

[2 Use, H. A. 1564.]

[3 August. Op. Par. 1679-1700. De Bapt. contr. Donatist. Lib. III. 27. Tom. IX. col. 120.]

[4 ... hæreticorum patriarchæ philosophi.—Tertull. Op. Lut. 1641. Adv. Hermog. 8. p. 269.]

[5 Ignorantia mater cunctorum errorum.—Concil. Tolet. IV. cap. 24. in Crabb. Concil. Col. Agrip. 1551. Tom. II. p. 201.]

[6 Epiph. Κατὰ Αἱρεσέων Ὀγδοήκοντα. Op. Par. 1622. Tom. I. p. 1.]

[7 August. Op. Lib. de Hær. Tom. VIII. cols. 4, 5. Augustine here reckons up 88 heresies.]

"The Christians of Russia and Moravia," saith M. Harding, "afterward upon good causes received the Latin service." Howbeit of all these good causes he uttereth none. But after Cyrillus and Methodius by long preaching and great pains had converted them to the faith of Christ, and, for the better continuance of that they had begun, were desirous that the people so converted might have their common service in their mother-tongue, and the matter stood in suspense at Rome, in the consistory, before the bishop there and his cardinals, a voice was heard by an angel from heaven: *Omnis spiritus laudet Dominum: et omnis lingua confiteatur ei*[8]: "Let every spirit praise the Lord; and let every tongue make confession unto him." By this story it appeareth, the angel of God from heaven was author that these nations should have their service in their common tongue. Now if M. Harding be able to shew that either evangelist, or angel, or voice from heaven, ever willed them to leave their own natural speech, and to use the Latin, then may he say they had good causes so to do. Bessarion's authority in this case cannot seem great, both for other sundry causes, which I leave, and also for that he lived at the least fourteen hundred years after Christ; and, being out of his own country, and created cardinal, and bishop of Tusculum, he manifestly flattered the bishop of Rome.

Æn. Sylv. Hist. Bohem. cap. xiii.

M. HARDING. THE THIRTY-NINTH DIVISION.

Wherefore to conclude, seeing (90) *in six hundred years after Christ the service of the church was not in any other than in the Greek and Latin tongue, for that any man is able to shew by good proof, and the same not understanded of all people; seeing the authorities by M. Jewel alleged import no necessary argument, nor direct commandment of the vulgar tongue, but only of plain and open pronouncing, and that where the tongue of the service was understanded; seeing the church of the English nation had their service in the Latin tongue, to them unknown, well near a thousand years past; seeing the place of St Paul to the Corinthians either pertaineth not to this purpose, or, if it be so granted, for the diversity of states of that and of this our time, it permitteth a diversity of observation in this behalf, though some likeness and resemblance yet reserved; seeing great profit cometh to the faithful people having it so as they understand it not; finally, seeing the examples rehearsed herein to be followed be of small authority in respect either of antiquity or of true religion; as the bold assertion of M. Jewel is plainly disproved, so the old order of the Latin service in the Latin church, whereof England is a province, is not rashly to be condemned; specially whereas,* (91) *being first committed to the churches by the apostles of our country, and the first preachers of the faith here, it hath been authorised by continuance almost of a thousand years without control or gainsaying, to the glory of God, the wealth of the people, and the*[10] *procuring of help from heaven always to this land.*

The ninetieth untruth. For[9] the contrary is sufficiently proved in the fifteenth division of this article. A heap of untruths laid together.

The ninety-first untruth. For the first preachers of the faith in this island were Greeks and Hebrews, and not Latins.

And to add hereunto thus[11] *much last of all, though it might be granted that it were good the service were in the vulgar tongue, as in English for our country of England; yet doubtless good men and zealous keepers of the catholic faith will never allow the service devised in king Edward's time, now restored*[12] *again, not so much for the tongue it is in, as for the order itself and disposition of it, lacking some things necessary, and having some other things* (92) *repugnant to the faith and custom of the catholic church.*

The ninety-second untruth, joined with a slander. For[9] our service containeth nothing contrary to the faith.

THE BISHOP OF SARISBURY.

Here, M. Harding, it appeareth ye begin to mislike your own dealing, that, after so many words, and so great a countenance of learning, ye should be found so nakedly and so unsensibly to deceive the people. And therefore, having no manner authority of ancient council or doctor to allege against the English tongue in the church of England, yet, lest in the end, having said so much, ye

[8 Æn. Sylv. Op. Basil. 1571. Hist. Bohem. cap. xiii. p. 91.]
[9 1565 omits *for*.]
[10 H. A. 1564 omits *the*.]
[11 This, 1565 and H. A. 1564.]
[12 Restore, 1611.]

should seem to say nothing, ye begin to find fault with the order of our service, and, without any manner of proof, ye say there are many things therein contained contrary to the catholic faith; and so, contrary to your own knowledge, ye maintain one untruth by another.

You know that we serve God according to his holy word, and the order of his primitive church. For, as Tertullian saith the christian people did in his time:
Tertull. in Apolog. *Coimus ad divinarum scripturarum commemorationem, si quid præsentium temporum qualitas aut præmonere cogit, aut recognoscere. Certe fidem sanctis vocibus pascimus, spem erigimus, fiduciam figimus*[1]*:* "We meet together to hear the rehearsal of the holy scriptures, if the state of the present time do force us either to forewarn anything, or else to call anything to remembrance. Verily we feed our faith with those holy words, we confirm our hope, we assure our trust." We minister the holy sacraments in pure and reverent sort: we baptize in the name of God the Father, the Son, and the Holy Ghost: we receive the sacrament of Christ's body and blood from the holy table: we make our humble confession and fall to the ground, and pray all together, with one heart, and one voice, in spirit and truth; and specially we pray for you, and for such others, that ye may consider from whence ye are fallen, and repent yourselves, and return to God: we excommunicate open offenders: we receive again them that shew themselves penitent: we instruct our youth in the faith of Christ: we make collections and provide charitably for the poor. Of all these things what one thing is contrary to the
Wisd. i. catholic faith? O M. Harding, it is written: "The mouth that lieth destroyeth
Matt. xii. the soul." And Christ saith: "The blasphemy against the Holy Ghost shall never be forgiven, neither in this life, nor in the life to come."

Now, good christian reader, for the better contenting of thy mind, I beseech thee to look back and to consider the whole substance of all that M. Harding hath laid in for proof of this article, what weight it beareth, and how well it serveth to his purpose. He hath entreated largely of singing in the quire, at what time and where it first began, and likewise hath proved, by a great long discourse of situation of countries and diversity of tongues, that neither all the east part of the world understood the Greek, nor all the people of Africa, Mauritania, Spain, and France, understood the Latin; which labour in this case was nothing needful. But that all the nations of the east part had their service in the Greek tongue, and that all the people of Africa, Mauritania, Spain, and France, had their service in the Latin tongue, (which thing only stood in question, and therefore was only to be proved,) he hath hitherto utterly left unproved. Touching the public service within this island, the story of Augustine of Rome, and Edda, and Putta, and other poets and singing-men, as I have shewed, standeth him in small stead. Contrary to his own knowledge, he saith that the fourteenth chapter of St Paul to the Corinthians cannot necessarily be applied to this purpose. And further he saith, that even from the apostles' time the priest evermore made his prayers in the quire, far off from the hearing of the people; that the ignorant people understandeth the Latin tongue, although not in most exact wise, or perfectly[2]; that they are now better instructed in the articles of the faith than they were in the time of the apostles; that it is sufficient for them now to be taught by gestures and ceremonies; and that they have great profit by hearing their service, although they know not what they hear. Again, he saith that the Greek and Latin be learned tongues, and therefore all the service of the church, throughout the whole world, ought to be ministered in one of them; that all the psalms and all other scriptures are hard, and far pass the capacity of the people; that understanding of the matter causeth the mind to wander; and, to be short, that prayer in the common tongue hath evermore bred schisms and divisions in the church. He hath openly falsified Strabo, Justinian, Origen, Chrysostom, and others, and hath forced them to say the thing they never meant.

This is the whole summary of all that he had to say. Hereof he would seem to conclude, that within the first six hundred years after Christ the common service was ministered openly in a tongue unknown unto the people; albeit, he

[[1] Tertull. Op. Lut. 1641. Apologet. 39. p. 34; where *literarum divinarum*.] [[2] Perfitely, 1565.]

hath hitherto alleged neither scripture, nor council, nor decree, nor doctor, nor example, or practice of the primitive church, to prove the same.

Of the other side, it is sufficiently proved of our part, that the fourteenth chapter to the Corinthians must of necessity belong to the use of common prayers; and that in the primitive church the service was everywhere ministered in the vulgar tongue; and that the priest and the people prayed all together[3]. I have proved, not only that the nations that understood Greek or Latin had their service in the Greek or Latin tongue, but by Theodoretus, Sozomenus, St Ambrose, and St Hierome, that the Syrians had their service in the Syrian tongue[4]; by St Basil, that the Egyptians had their service in the Egyptian tongue, the Lybians, the Thebans, the Palestines, the Arabians, and the Phœnicians, each of them in their own tongue[5]; by Origen, that all barbarous people had their service in their several barbarous tongues[5]; by Sulpitius, that the people of France, then called Gallia, had their service in the French tongue[6]. St Hierome saith: *Vox quidem dissona, sed una religio. Tot pene psallentium chori, quot gentium diversitates*[7]: "The voice is divers; but the religion is all one. There be well near so many companies of people singing as there be diversities of nations." To be short, I have proved by St Chrysostom, and by Lyra, and others, that there can no manner profit redound unto the people of prayers made in a strange tongue.

Justinian, Lyra, et Thom.

Hieron. ad Marcell.

Seeing therefore M. Harding's doctrine standeth upon so simple grounds, as I have shewed, and serveth only to maintain ignorance, and the kingdom of darkness, it is now thy part, gentle reader, to judge indifferently between us, both how justly he hath coloured the same with such a face of antiquity, and also how truly and substantially he hath answered my assertion.

[3 See before, pages 287, 9, 308, 9.]
[4 See before, pages 268, 70, 90.]
[5 See before, page 290.]
[6 See before, page 298.]
[7 Paul. et Eustoch. ad Marcell. Epist. xliv. in Hieron. Op. Par. 1693-1706. Tom. IV. Pars II. col. 551.]

OF THE SUPREMACY.

THE FOURTH ARTICLE.

THE BISHOP OF SARISBURY.

Univer-sal bishop.

Or that the bishop of Rome was then called an universal bishop, or head[1] of the universal church.

[OF THE POPE'S PRIMACY.—Article IV. H. A. 1564.]

M. HARDING. THE FIRST DIVISION.

By what name soever the bishop of Rome was called within six hundred years after Christ's ascension, this is clear, that his primacy, that is to say, supreme power and authority over and above all bishops, and chief government of all Christ's flock, in matters pertaining to faith and christian religion, was then (93) *acknowledged and confessed. Which thing being so, whether then he were called by either of those names that you deny, or no, it is not of great importance. And yet for the one of them, somewhat, and for the other, an infinite number of good authorities may be alleged. But thereof hereafter.*

The ninety-third untruth. For there was no such power confessed. Not one at all.

THE BISHOP OF SARISBURY.

Touching these glorious names and titles, wherewith the bishop of Rome hath long sithence furnished and beautified his estate, M. Harding seemeth in part willingly to yield; claiming nevertheless the supreme power and universal authority unto the see of Rome, and that even from the apostles' time: notwithstanding it was as easy a matter for Christ to give Peter the power and title both together, as to give him the power alone, without the title. But to avoid error that might grow by mistaking of words, him we call "the universal bishop," or "the head of the universal church," that hath authority above all general councils, and fulness of power to expound the scriptures; to whose determinations the whole church of God must of necessity submit itself without contradiction; whom neither emperor, nor king, nor clergy, nor the whole universal people, in anywise may control whatsoever he do; unto whom all appeals ought to lie from all places of the world; and who, wheresoever he happen to be, hath the full jurisdiction of a bishop[2]. That ever any such superiority, or universal power, was given by Christ to the see of Rome, it will be too much for M. Harding well to prove.

Extra. de Elect. et Elect. Potest. Solitæ. De Major. et Obed. Unam Sanctam. ix. Quæst. iii. Nemo.

But whereas the bishop there so ambitiously craveth to be known and taken for the universal bishop, and head of the universal church, happy is he if he do the duty of one particular bishop, and be found but a member of Christ's church. St Gregory saith: *Adversus quem ... portæ prævalent inferorum, ille neque petra dicendus est, supra quam Christus ædificat ecclesiam, neque ecclesia, neque pars ecclesiæ*[3]: "He against whom the gates of hell do prevail (as they have often against the bishop of Rome), neither may be called the rock, whereupon Christ doth build his church, nor the church, nor any part of the church."

Greg in Cat. in Matt. cap. xvi.

[[1] The head, 1565, and H. A. 1564.]

[[2] Paschal. in Corp. Jur. Canon. Lugd. 1624. Decretal. Gregor. IX. Lib. I. Tit. vi. De Elect. et Elect. Potest. cap. 3. cols. 110, &c.

Innoc. III. in eod. ibid. Lib. I. Tit. xxxiii. De Major. et Obed. cap. 6. cols. 424, &c.

Bonifac. VIII. in eod. Extrav. Comm. Lib. I. De Major. et Obed. cap. 1. cols. 202, &c.

Innoc. in eod. Decret. Gratian. Decr. Sec. Pars, Caus. IX. Quæst. iii. can. 13. col. 877.

See also before, page 93, note 1.]

[[3] There appears to be an error in the reference to Gregory: the passage in the Catena assigns it to Origen.—Thom. Aquinat. Op. Venet. 1595. Caten. Aur. in Matt. cap. xvi. Tom. XV. fol. 60. 2; where *ædificat Christus*. See also Orig. Op. Par. 1733-59. Comm. in Matt. Tom. XII. Tom. III. p. 526.]

Certainly, touching these vain titles, the same ancient father St Gregory saith: *Ego...fidenter dico,...Quisquis se universalem sacerdotem vocat, vel vocari desiderat, in elatione sua antichristum præcurrit*[4]: "I speak it boldly, Whosoever either calleth himself the universal bishop, or desireth so to be called, in his pride he is the forerunner of antichrist." De Jure Divino. Greg. Lib. iv. Epist. 34.

M. HARDING. THE SECOND DIVISION.

Now concerning the chief point of this article, which is the primacy of the pope, Peter's successor. First, it hath been set up and ordained by God, so as it standeth in force jure divino, *by God's law, and not only by man's law, the scriptures leading thereto. Next, commended to the world by decrees of councils, and confirmed by edicts of christian emperors, for avoiding of schisms. Furthermore, confessed and witnessed by the holy fathers. Again, found to be necessary by reason. Finally, used and declared by the event of things, and practice of the church. For proof of all this, so much might easily be said as should serve to a whole volume.* A heap of untruths.

THE BISHOP OF SARISBURY.

Here M. Harding saith he will trip and dance lightly over this article. And therefore, notwithstanding he would seem to hold *de jure divino*, that is, by the scriptures; yet for haste he allegeth not any one word of the scriptures, as of himself, but only upon the report and credit of others. Howbeit pope Zosimus, in all that long contention he had with the bishops of Africa, touching these matters, never alleged any word of the scriptures, but only the council of Nice[5], which he himself had falsified. And Meltiades, writing hereof to the bishops of Spain, seemeth to claim only by custom, and not by any right of God's word[6]. Zosim. in Concil. Aphri. Melt. in Epist. ad Episcop. His.

Nevertheless, sithence that time, they have found out sundry places of the scriptures to avouch their title, and have forced the same to serve their purpose. Christ saith, "All power is given to me." Hereof Stephanus, the bishop of Patraca, concludeth thus: *Ergo in papa est omnis potestas, supra omnes potestates, tam cœli, quam terræ*[7]: "Therefore in the pope is all power above all powers, as well of heaven as of earth." Some others there be that reason thus: "Peter entered into the grave before John: Peter drew his net full of fish: unto Peter Christ said, Confirm thy brethren; *ergo*, the pope is head of the church[8]." Bonifacius the eighth saith: *In principio creavit Deus cœlum et terram, non in principiis*[9]: "God made heaven and earth in the beginning, and not in the beginnings, as in many." And again: *Spiritualis omnia dijudicat*[10]: "He that is spiritual judgeth all things;" *ergo*, the bishop of Rome ought to have an universal power over all the world. By these and other like authorities of the scriptures they conclude, that the pope holdeth his authority not by any ordinance of man, but *de jure divino*, that is, even by the right of God's undoubted law. And therefore pope Bonifacius determineth the matter in this wise to hold for ever: *Declaramus, dicimus, definimus, pronuntiamus, omnino esse de necessitate salutis omni humanæ creaturæ, subesse Romano pontifici*[11]: "We declare, say, determine, and pronounce, that undoubtedly it standeth upon the necessity of salvation, for every mortal creature to be subject to the bishop of Rome." Likewise saith the gloss upon the same: *Quicquid salvatur, est sub summo pontifice*[12]: "Whatsoever is saved is John xvii. Matt. xxviii. In Concil. Later. sub Leon. Reg. Pol. Adver. Hen. viii. Regem. Angliæ. De Major. et Obed. Unam Sanctam. I Cor. ii. DeMajor.&c. ut supra. Gloss.ibidem

[[4] Gregor. Magni Papæ I. Op. Par. 1705. Epist. Lib. VII. Indict. xv. Ad Mauric. August. Epist. xxxiii. Tom. II. col. 881.]

[[5] This contention, which was not ended by the death of Zosimus, may be seen in Concil. Carthag. VI. cap. 3. in Crabb. Concil. Col. Agrip. 1551. Tom. I. p. 494; Concil. Afric. in eod. pp. 500, &c. See also Baron. Annal. Eccles. Rom. 1607. Tom. V. pp. 446, &c.]

[[6] Melciad. Epist. Decret. in Crabb. Concil. Tom. I. p. 218. Melciades in this epistle certainly refers to a supposed authority given by Christ (Matt. xvi.) to Peter over the rest of the apostles, and of right descending from him to the Roman pontiffs.]

[[7] Orat. Steph. Arch. Patrac. in Sess. x. Concil. Later. v. in Concil. Stud. Labb. et Cossart. Lut. Par. 1671-2. Tom. XIV. col. 269. See before, pages 93, 4, note 2.]

[[8] Reg. Pol. Card. Brit. ad Henric. VIII. pro Eccles. Unit. Def. Ingolst. 1587. Lib. II. pp. 186-9.]

[[9] Bonifac. VIII. in Corp. Jur. Canon. Extrav. Comm. Lib. I. De Major. et Obed. cap. 1. col. 212.]

[[10] Id. in eod. ibid. col. 211. See before, page 77, note 9.]

[[11] Id. in eod. ibid. col. 212. See before, page 95, note 11.]

[[12] Gloss. in eod. ibid. col. 205.]

De Jure Divino.

under the highest bishop." If these claims be good, it is no hard matter to hold by scriptures.

Matt. xvi. Mark viii. Luke ix. 1 Cor. x.

But forasmuch as they seem to make greatest account of these words of Christ, "Thou art Peter; and upon this rock I will build my church;" therefore, for answer hereunto, understand thou, good christian reader, that the old catholic fathers have written and pronounced not any mortal man, as Peter was, but Christ himself, the Son of God, to be this rock. Gregorius Nyssenus saith: *Tu es Petrus, &c.*[1]: "'Thou art Peter; and upon this rock I will build my church.' He meaneth the confession of Christ; for he had said before: 'Thou art Christ, the Son of the living God.'" So saith St Hilary: *Hæc est una felix fidei petra, quam Petrus ore suo confessus est*[2]: "This is that only blessed rock of faith, that Peter confessed with his mouth." Again he saith: "Upon this rock of Peter's confession is the building of the church[3]." So Cyrillus: *Petra nihil aliud est, quam firma et inconcussa discipuli fides*[4]: "The rock is nothing else, but the strong and assured faith of the disciple." So likewise Chrysostom: *Super hanc petram, id est, in hac fide et confessione, ædificabo ecclesiam meam*[5]: "Upon this rock, that is to say, upon this faith and this confession, I will build my church." Likewise St Augustine: *Petra...erat Christus, super quod fundamentum etiam...ædificatus est Petrus*[6]: "Christ was the rock, upon which foundation Peter himself was also built." And addeth further besides: *Non me ædificabo super te, sed te ædificabo super me*[7]: Christ saith unto Peter: "I will not build myself[8] upon thee, but I will build thee upon me." All these fathers be plain; but none so plain as Origen. His words be these: *Petra est, quicunque est discipulus Christi:... et super talem petram construitur omnis ecclesiastica doctrina... Quod si super unum illum Petrum tantum existimas ædificari totam ecclesiam, quid dicturus es de Johanne filio tonitrui, et apostolorum unoquoque? Num audebimus dicere, quod adversus Petrum unum non prævalituræ sint portæ inferorum?...An soli Petro dantur a Christo claves regni cœlorum?*[9] "He is the rock, whosoever is the disciple of Christ; and upon such a rock all ecclesiastical learning is built. If thou think that the whole church is built only upon Peter, what then wilt thou say of John the son of the thunder, and of every of the apostles? Shall we dare to say, that the gates of hell shall not prevail only against Peter? Or are the keys of the kingdom of heaven given only unto Peter?" By these few it may appear, what right the pope hath to claim his authority by God's word, and, as M. Harding saith, *de jure divino*. Indeed, touching the same words of St Matthew, St Hierome writeth thus: *Istum locum episcopi et presbyteri non intelligentes, aliquid sibi de Pharisæorum assumunt supercilio*[10]: "Bishops and priests, not understanding this place, take upon them some part of the proud looks of the Pharisees." And again he saith: *Noverint episcopi, se magis consuetudine, quam dispositionis dominicæ veritate, presbyteris esse majores*[11]: "Let bishops understand that they are greater than the priests, more of custom than of the truth of God's ordinance." By this it appeareth, that the bishop of Rome holdeth by custom, and not, as M. Harding saith, *de jure divino*.

Greg. Nyss. in Test. Delect. ex Vet. Test. — Hilar. de Trin. Lib. ii. — Hilar. de Trin. Lib. vi. — Cyril. de Trin. — Chrysost. in Matt. Hom. 55. — Aug. de Verb. Dom. secund. Matt. Ser. 13. — Orig. in Matt. Tract. i. — Mark iii. — Hier. in Matt. cap. xvi. Lib. iii.

As for the decrees of councils, the edicts of princes, the sayings of holy fathers, the necessity of reason, and the practice of the church, how justly they be avouched by M. Harding, they shall be severally examined as they come.

[1 Tu es Petrus, et super hanc petram ædificabo ecclesiam meam, super confessionem videlicet Christi, quia dixerat: Tu es Christus, filius Dei viventis.—Gregor. Nyss. Op. Par. 1638. Test. de Advent. Dom. adv. Jud. Tom. II. p. 162. But this work is not genuine.]

[2 ...una hæc felix fidei petra Petri ore confessa, &c.—Hilar. Op. Par. 1693. De Trin. Lib. II. 23. col. 800.]

[3 Super hanc igitur confessionis petram ecclesiæ ædificatio est.—Id ibid. Lib. VI. 36. col. 903.]

[4 Cyril. Alex. Op. Lut. 1638. De Sanct. Trin. Dial. IV. Tom. V. Pars I. p. 507.]

[5 ...καὶ ἐπὶ ταύτῃ τῇ πέτρᾳ οἰκοδομήσω μου τὴν ἐκκλησίαν, τουτέστι, τῇ πίστει τῆς ὁμολογίας.—Chrysost. Op. Par. 1718-38. In Matt. Hom. liv. Tom. VII. p. 548.]

[6 August. Op. Par. 1679-1700. In Johan. Evang. cap. xxi. Tractat. cxxiv. 5. Tom. III. Pars II. col. 822.]

[7 Super me ædificabo te, non me super te.—Id. De Verb. Evang. Matt. xiv. Serm. lxxvi. 1. Tom. V. col. 415.]

[8 Meself, 1565.]

[9 Orig. Op. Par. 1733-59. Comm. in Matt. Tom. XII. 10, 11. Tom. III. pp. 524, 5.]

[10 Hieron. Op. Par. 1693-1706. Comm. Lib. III. in Matt. cap. xvi. Tom. IV. Pars I. col. 75.]

[11 Id. in Epist. ad Tit. cap. i. Tom. IV. Pars I. cols. 413, 4; where *episcopi noverint*.]

M. HARDING. THE THIRD DIVISION.

Epistles decretal.

But I, in this treatise, seeking to avoid prolixity, having purposed to say somewhat to this number of the other articles, and knowing this matter of the primacy to be already largely and learnedly handled of others, will but trip (as it were) lightly over at this time, and not set my fast footing in the deep debating and treating of it. Trip.

[*The pope's primacy not of man, but of God's ordinance.* H. A. 1564.] [*The first proof of the pope's primacy, scripture expounded.* H. A. 1564.] *First, as concerning the right of the primacy*[12] *by God's law, by these ancient authorities it hath been avouched. Anacletus, that holy bishop and martyr, St Peter's scholar, and of him consecrated priest, in his epistle to the bishops of Italy, writeth thus:* In novo...testamento, post Christum, &c.[13]*: "In the new testament, the order of priests began, after our Lord Christ, of Peter; because to him bishopric was first given in the church of Christ, where as our Lord said unto him, 'Thou art Peter; and upon this rock I will build my church; and the gates of hell shall not prevail against it; and unto thee I will give the keys of the kingdom of heaven.' Wherefore this Peter received of our Lord, first of all, power to bind and to loose; and first of all he brought people to the faith, by virtue of his preaching. As for the other apostles, they received honour and power in like fellowship with him, and willed him to be their prince, or chief governor."* [*Matt.* xvi. H. A. 1564.]

In another epistle to all bishops, alleging the same text, for the primacy of the see of Rome, speaking of the disposition of churches committed to patriarchs and primates, saith thus most plainly: "This holy and apostolic church of Rome hath obtained the primacy, not of the apostles, but of our Lord and[14] *Saviour himself, and hath gotten the pre-eminence of power over all churches, and over the whole flock of christian people, even so as he said to blessed Peter the apostle, 'Thou art Peter; and upon this rock,'" &c.*[15]

THE BISHOP OF SARISBURY.

The authorities here alleged are full of fog and false ground, and can abide no fast footing; and therefore M. Harding trippeth them so lightly over.

Touching this epistle of Anacletus, and other like epistles decretal, I will only give a taste, and leave the judgment thereof unto the reader.

First, one Petrus Crab, the compiler of the councils, complaineth much that the examples from whence he took them were wonderfully corrupted, and not one of them agreeing with another, and expresseth the same by these words: *Exemplarium intolerabilis nimiaque differentia et depravatio*[16]. In Admon. ad Lect. ante Decret. Lib.

Again, Gratian himself, upon good advice, is driven to say that all such epistles ought to have place rather in debating of matter of justice in the consistory than in determining and weighing the truth of the scriptures[17]. Dist. xx. Decret.

Besides this, neither St Hierome, nor Gennadius, nor Damasus, nor any other old father ever alleged these epistles, or made any account of them; nor the bishops of Rome themselves, no, not when such evidence might have stood[18] them

[12 The pope's primacy, H. A. 1564.]

[13 In novo, &c. Dominum a Petro sacerdotalis cœpit ordo, quia ipsi primo pontificatus in ecclesia Christi datus est, dicente Domino ad eum: Tu es (inquit) Petrus, et super hanc petram ædificabo ecclesiam meam, et portæ inferi non prævalebunt adversus eam, et tibi dabo claves regni cœlorum. Hic ergo ligandi atque solvendi potestatem primus accepit a Domino, primusque ad fidem populum virtute suæ prædicationis adduxit. Ceteri vero apostoli cum eodem pari consortio honorem et potestatem acceperunt, ipsumque principem eorum esse voluerunt. —Anaclet. Epist. ii. in Crabb. Concil. Col. Agrip. 1551. Tom. I. p. 61.]

[14 H. A. 1564, omits *and.*]

[15 Hæc vero sacrosancta Romana et apostolica ecclesia non ab apostolis, sed ab ipso Domino Salvatore nostro primatum obtinuit, et eminentiam potestatis super universas ecclesias ac totum christiani populi gregem assecuta est, sicut ipse beato Petro apostolo dixit: Tu es Petrus, &c.—Id. Epist. iii. in eod. Tom. I. p. 63.]

[16 ... vetustissima exemplaria ... adeo depravata fuere, ut...restitui minime potuerint.—Ad Lect. in eod. Tom. I. fol. a. 4. See also fol. a. 3. 2.]

[17 Apparet, quod divinarum tractatores scripturarum, etsi scientia pontificibus præemineant, tamen, quia dignitatis eorum apicem non sunt adepti, in sacrarum quidem scripturarum expositionibus eis præponuntur; in causis vero definiendis secundum post eos locum merentur.—Corp. Jur. Canon. Lugd. 1624. Decret. Gratian. Decr. Prim. Pars, Dist. xx. col. 88.]

[18 Stand, 1565.]

Epistles decretal.

in best stead, namely in their ambitious contention for the superiority over the bishops of Africa.

The contents of them are such, as a very child of any judgment may soon be able to descry them.

Clem. Epist. 1. Hier. de Eccles. Scrip.

Clemens informeth St James of the order and manner of St Peter's death[1]: yet it is certain, and Clement undoubtedly knew it, that James was put to death seven years before St Peter[2].

Anth. Epist. 1.

Antherus maketh mention of Eusebius, bishop of Alexandria, and of Felix, bishop of Ephesus: yet was neither Eusebius nor Felix neither bishop nor born all the time that Antherus lived[3].

Marcell. Epist. 2. ad Orient.

Marcellinus saith: "The emperor might not attempt to presume any thing against the gospel[4]:" yet was there then no emperor alive that understood Christ, or knew the gospel.

Marcell. Epist. 2.

Marcellus writeth to the emperor Maxentius, and chargeth him straitly with the authority of Clement[5]: yet was Maxentius an infidel, a cruel tyrant, and a persecutor of the church, and neither knew nor cared for the name of Clement.

Zeph. Epist. 1. Luke x.

Zephyrinus saith: "Christ commanded his apostles to appoint the three-score and twelve disciples[6]:" yet St Luke saith Christ himself appointed them.

Luke iii. Meltiad. Epist. 1.

St Luke saith: "John the Baptist gave this counsel to the soldiers, Be ye contented with your wages[7]," &c.: yet Meltiades quite altereth the whole story, and nameth Christ instead of John.

It would be tedious and needless to open all: these few notes may suffice for a taste.

Anacl. Epist. 1. Iren. Lib. iii. cap. iii.

Now touching this Anacletus, whom M. Harding hath furnished with his titles, as though it were the very true Anacletus indeed: first, he saith, Clemens was his predecessor[8]: contrariwise Irenæus, that lived immediately afterward, and Eusebius say, Anacletus was predecessor unto Clement[9]. Whereby it may appear, that Anacletus wrote this epistle after that he himself was dead.

Dist. xciii. Juxta Sanctorum.

He maketh mention of St Peter's church: yet was there no church built in the name of Peter within three hundred years after Anacletus[10].

Anacl. Epist. 3.

Again, he allegeth the decrees and canons of the old fathers: his words be these: *Hæc ab antiquis apostolis et patribus accepimus*[11]: "These things have we received of the old apostles and ancient fathers." As if the apostles had been long before him: notwithstanding, St John the apostle was yet alive, and Anacletus himself was one of the oldest fathers.

Although by that I have thus shortly touched, the likelihood hereof may soon appear, yet I beseech thee, good christian reader, consider also these and other like phrases and manners of speech, which in these epistles are very familiar, and may easily be found: *Persecutiones patienter portare: Peto ut pro me orare debeas: Episcopi obediendi sunt, non insidiandi: Ab illis omnes Christiani se cavere debent.* Here is not so much as the very congruity and natural sound of the Latin tongue. And shall we think that, for the space of three hundred years and more, there was not one bishop in Rome that could speak true Latin? and specially then, when all the whole people there, both women and children, were

---

[1 Clement. Epist. i. ad Jacob. in Crabb. Concil. Col. Agrip. 1551. Tom. I. pp. 31, 2.]

[2 Jerome says that James was put to death in the seventh year of Nero, Peter in the fourteenth.—Hieron. Op. Par. 1693-1706. Catal. Script. Eccles. 1, 2. Tom. IV. Pars II. cols. 101, 2.]

[3 Anter. Epist. Decret. in Crabb. Concil. Tom. I. p. 110. See before, page 173.]

[4 Non licet imperatori...aliquid contra mandata divina præsumere.—Marcellin. Epist. ii. in eod. Tom. I. p. 187. Marcellinus was put to death in the persecution of Diocletian and Maximian.]

[5 Marcell. Epist. ii. ad Maxent. in eod. Tom. I. p. 208.]

[6 ...illi discipuli...quos Dominus ad adjumentum apostolorum eligi præcepit, id est, septuaginta duo.—Zephyrin. Epist. i. in eod. Tom. I. p. 97.]

[7 Unde et Dominus in evangelio militibus interrogantibus respondit, &c.—Melciad. Epist. Decr. in eod. Tom. I. p. 219.]

[8 ...Clemens antecessor noster.—Anaclet. Epist. i. in eod. Tom. I. p. 54.]

[9 *Μετὰ τοῦτον* [*Ἀνέγκλητον*]...*τὴν ἐπισκοπὴν κληροῦται Κλήμης*.—Iren. Op. Par. 1710. Lib. III. cap. iii. 3. p. 176. See also Euseb. in Hist. Eccles. Script. Amst. 1695-1700. Lib. III. capp. xiii. xv. p. 70.]

[10 Anaclet. et Zach. in Corp. Jur. Canon. Lugd. 1624. Decret. Gratian. Decr. Prim. Pars, Dist. xciii. can. 4. col. 441. See before, page 173, note 7.]

[11 Anaclet. Epist. ii. in Crabb. Concil. Tom. I. p. 61; where *hæc a sanctis patribus*.]

able to speak it naturally, without a teacher? Verily, the pope himself saith: *Falsa Latinitas vitiat rescriptum papæ*[12]: "False Latin putteth the pope's own writ out of credit."

Epistles decretal.

Extr. de Rescrip. Ad Audien.

As for the substance and contents of these epistles, they touch nothing, neither of the state of the church in that time, nor of doctrine, nor of persecution, nor of heresy, nor of the office of the ministers, nor of any other thing, either agreeable unto that age, or in any wise greatly worthy to be considered.

All their drift is, by falsifying of the scriptures, and by all other means, only to stablish the state and kingdom of the see of Rome. Anacletus thus interlaceth the words of Christ: *Super hanc petram, id est, super ecclesiam Romanam, ædificabo ecclesiam meam*[13]: "Upon this rock, that is to say, upon the church of Rome, I will build my church." And again: *Romana ecclesia cardo et caput [est]... omnium ecclesiarum... Ut enim cardine ostium regitur, ita hujus sanctæ sedis auctoritate omnes ecclesiæ... reguntur*[14]: "The church of Rome is the hook and the head of all churches. For, as the door is ruled by the hook, so all churches are ruled by the authority of this holy see (of Rome)." Pope Stephanus saith: *Hæc sacrosancta domina nostra Romana ecclesia*[15]: "This holy our lady the church of Rome."

Anacl. Epist. 1.

Anacl. Epist. 3.

Dist. lxx. Oportebat.

And what needed M. Harding to allege only Anacletus, being so well stored of sundry others? For pope Evaristus, Alexander, Sixtus, Telesphorus, Higinus, Pius, Anicetus, Soter, Eleutherius, Victor, and all the rest of the ancient bishops of Rome, whose names have been abused to this purpose, agree in one. All they are made to say: "We are the universal bishops: we are the heads of the universal church: all appeals ought of right to lie to us: we cannot err: we may not be controlled; for it is written, The scholar is not above his master." If these authorities were sufficient, then were the case clear of M. Harding's side. But he saw they were forged, and full of untruth; and therefore he thought it best to trip so lightly over them. As for Anacletus himself, that was Peter's scholar, and the rest of the ancient bishops of Rome, they were holy men and godly fathers, and lived in continual persecution, and were daily taken and put to death, and had no leisure to think upon these ambitious and vain titles.

M. HARDING. THE FOURTH DIVISION.

St Gregory, writing to Mauritius the emperor against John the bishop of Constantinople, ambitiously claiming and usurping the name of an universal bishop, proveth the bishop of Rome, succeeding in Peter's chair, to be primate, and to have charge over all the church of Christ, by scriptures, thus: Cunctis evangelium scientibus liquet, &c.[16]: "*It is evident to all that know the gospel, that the cure and charge of the whole church hath been committed, by the word of our Lord, to the holy apostle Peter, prince of all the apostles. For to him it is said: 'Peter, lovest thou me? Feed my sheep.' To him it is said, 'Behold, Satan hath desired to sift you, as it were wheat, and I have prayed for thee, Peter, that thy faith fail not. And thou, being once converted, strengthen thy brethren.' To him it is said, 'Thou art Peter; and upon this rock will I*[17] *build my church; and the gates of hell shall not prevail against it. And unto thee I will give*

[Epist. xxxii. H. A. 1564.]

John xxi. Luke xxii. Matt. xvi.

M. Harding cutteth off and corrupteth the words of St Gregory; for it followeth immediately: "Tamen Petrus universalis apostolus non vocatur."

[12 Corp. Jur. Canon. Decretal. Gregor. IX. Lib. I. Tit. iii. cap. 11. cols. 39, 40.]

[13 ...ut majores...quæstiones semper ad sedem deferantur apostolicam, super quam Christus universam construxit ecclesiam, dicente ipso, &c.—Anaclet. Epist. i. in Crabb. Concil. Tom. I. p. 58.]

[14 Id. Epist. iii. in eod. Tom. I. p. 64; where *hæc vero apostolica sedes cardo, &c., et sicut cardine,* and *sic hujus.*]

[15 Ex Concil. Steph. Papæ III. in Corp. Jur. Canon. Decret. Gratian. Decr. Prim. Pars, Dist. lxxix. can. 3. col. 378.]

[16 Cunctis, &c. liquet, quod voce dominica sancto et omnium apostolorum Petro principi apostolo totius ecclesiæ cura commissa est. Ipsi quippe dicitur: Petre, amas me? pasce oves meas. Ipsi dicitur: Ecce Satanas expetiit cribrare vos sicut triticum: et ego pro te rogavi, Petre, ut non deficiat fides tua. Et tu aliquando conversus confirma fratres tuos. Ipsi dicitur: Tu es Petrus, et super hanc petram ædificabo ecclesiam meam, et portæ inferi non prævalebunt adversus eam. Et tibi dabo claves regni cœlorum: et quodcumque ligaveris super terram, erit ligatum et in cœlis; et quodcumque solveris super terram, erit solutum et in cœlo. Ecce claves regni cœlestis accepit; potestas ei ligandi ac solvendi tribuitur; cura ei totius ecclesiæ et principatus committitur, et tamen universalis apostolus non vocatur.—Gregor. Magni Papæ I. Op. Par. 1705. Epist. Lib. v. Indict. XIII. Ad Mauric. August. Epist. xx. Tom. II. col. 748.]

[17 I will, H. A. 1564.]

the keys of the kingdom of heaven: and whatsoever thou bindest upon earth shall be bound also in heaven, and whatsoever thou loosest on earth shall be loosed also in heaven.' Behold, he receiveth the keys of the heavenly kingdom: the power of binding and loosing is given to him: the charge of the whole church and principality is committed to him." Thus far Gregory. But because our adversaries, though without just cause, refuse the witness of the bishops of Rome in this article, as unlawful witnesses in their own cause, were they never so holy martyrs, or learned confessors; they may understand, we are able to allege sundry other authorities to the confirmation hereof, that be above all exception.

Cura ei totius ecclesiæ et principatus committitur.

THE BISHOP OF SARISBURY.

If St Gregory were now alive, he would charge M. Harding with open injury; not only for altering his whole meaning, but also for mangling and maiming his very words. M. Harding, to prove that the bishop of Rome was called the universal bishop, allegeth these words of St Gregory: *Ecce, Petrus claves regni cœlorum accipit. Et potestas ei ligandi solvendique tribuitur. Cura ei totius ecclesiæ et principatus committitur*: "Behold, Peter receiveth the keys of the kingdom of heaven. To him is given power both to bind and loose[1]. The charge and chief rule of the church is committed unto him." "Thus far Gregory," saith M. Harding. And why no farther? Was he stayed with the choincouch[2], and forced to break off his tale in the midst? But mark well, gentle reader, and thou shalt see St Gregory set to school, and kept in awe, and not suffered to utter one word more than M. Harding will give him leave. The next words that immediately follow in the same sentence are these: *Tamen [Petrus] universalis apostolus non vocatur*: "Yet Peter is not called the universal apostle." M. Harding saith: "The bishop of Rome was called the universal bishop." But St Gregory, even in the self-same sentence that M. Harding hath here so hastily broken off, saith: "Peter himself, being the apostle of Christ, yet was not called the universal apostle." And would M. Harding have the world believe that the pope's power is greater and more universal than St Peter's? These words M. Harding thought good to nip off in the midst. Such is his dealing in the allegation of the ancient fathers. If I list to use his own terms, I might well call this foisting, or cogging, or I know not what. Certainly the holy fathers, in the council of Constantinople, say thus: *Non convenit orthodoxis, ita circumtruncatas sanctorum patrum voces deflorare. Hæreticorum potius hoc proprium est*[3]: "It is not meet for catholic men thus to chop and to pare the sayings of the holy fathers. It is rather the very property of heretics."

Greg. Lib. iv. Epist. 32.

Petrus universalis apostolus non vocatur.

Concil. Constant. viii. Action. viii.

M. Harding will say, Gregory misliked this name of universal bishop only in John, the bishop of Constantinople, that so ambitiously and so greedily sought for it, and yet nevertheless claimed the same unto himself, as a title only belonging to the see of Rome; and that we therefore do wrongfully rack St Gregory, forcing his words otherwise than he ever meant. For answer hereunto, it shall behove us to consider both what St Gregory hath written in general of this title, and also what special claim he hath laid unto it for himself.

Greg. Lib. vi. Epist. 30.

Thus therefore generally he writeth of it: *Ego...fidenter dico... Quisquis se universalem sacerdotem vocat, vel vocari desiderat, in elatione sua antichristum præcurrit, quia superbiendo se ceteris præponit*[4]: "I speak it boldly, Whosoever calleth himself universal bishop, or desireth so to be called, is in his pride the forerunner of antichrist, because in his pride he setteth himself before others."

Greg. Lib. iv. Epist. 34.

Hac in re a fratre et consacerdote meo contra evangelicam sententiam, &c.[5]:

[1 To loose, 1565, 1609.]

[2 Choinecouch, (or choinecough, 1609): the cough usually called chin-cough.]

[3 Sext. Synod. Constant. Actio VIII. in Crabb. Concil. Col. Agrip. 1551. Tom. II. p. 321. See also Concil. Stud. Labb. et Cossart. Lut. Par. 1671-2. Tom. VI. col. 758.]

[4 Gregor. Magni Papæ I. Op. Par. 1705. Epist. Lib. VII. Indict. XV. Ad Mauric. August. Epist. xxxiii. Tom. II. col. 881.]

[5 Qua in re a prædicto fratre, &c., contra beatum quoque Petrum apostolum, et contra omnes ecclesias, contraque statuta canonum agitur...Sed in hac ejus superbia quid aliud nisi propinqua jam antichristi esse tempora designatur? Quia illum videlicet imitatur, qui spretis in sociali gaudio angelorum legionibus ad culmen conatus est singularitatis erumpere, dicens: Super astra cœli exaltabo solium meum, sedebo in monte testamenti, in lateribus aquilonis, et ascendam super altitudinem nubium, et ero similis Altissimo.—Id. Epist. Lib. v. Indict. XIII. Ad Constant. August. Epist. xxi. Tom. II. col. 751.]

"Herein my brother and fellow-bishop doth against the meaning of the gospel, against St Peter the apostle, against all churches, and against the ordinance of the canons. In this pride of his what other thing is there tokened, but that the time of antichrist is even at hand? For he followeth him, that, despising the equality of joy among the angels, laboured to break up to the top of singularity, saying thus, I will advance[6] my throne above the stars of heaven: I will sit in the mount of the testament, even in the corners of the north: I will get me up above the light of the clouds, and will be like unto the Highest." Again: *Rex superbiæ in foribus est, &c.*[7]: "The king of pride is even in the gates; and, a horrible thing to speak, an army of priests is made ready. For now they play the soldiers, and bear their heads on high, that were ordained to be captains of humility."

Isai. xiv.

Greg. Lib. iv. Epist. 38. Sacerdotum est paratus exercitus. Ita in manuscriptis, melius quam exitus.

Again: "I would have all men to be great and honourable, so that their honour be no derogation to the honour of God. For whoso will be honoured against God shall not be honourable unto me[8]." Again: "Neither may you say, that the using of this title is nothing; for, if we bear this matter quietly, we overthrow the faith of the whole church[9]." "The agreeing unto this wicked title is the loosing of the faith[10]." Thus therefore St Gregory judgeth generally of the name of "universal bishop;" which name notwithstanding the bishops of Rome have sithence chosen and taken to themselves: that is to say, "that it is vain and hurtful; the confusion, the poison, and utter and universal destruction of the church; the corruption and loosing the faith; against the holy canons; against St Peter the apostle; against the very sense and meaning of the gospel; against all the churches of God, and against God himself; that never good or holy man would use such titles; that whosoever useth them in so doing followeth Lucifer, and is the very forerunner and messenger of antichrist."

Greg. Lib. vi. Epist. 28.

Greg. Lib. vi. Epist. 24.

Greg. Lib. iv. Epist. 39.

Perhaps M. Harding will say, this name belonged peculiarly and only to the bishop of Rome; and therefore Gregory reproved John the bishop of Constantinople, for that he so presumptuously, and by way of intrusion, claimed the same as a right and interest that was not his. But St Gregory calleth the same title of universal bishop, [a]*Typhum superbiæ*[11], [b]*Nomen novum*[12], [c]*Vocabulum temerarium, Stultum*[13], [d]*Superbum, Pompaticum*[14], [e]*Perversum*[15], [f]*Superstitiosum, Profanum*[16], [g]*Scelestum*[17], [h]*Nomen erroris*[18], [i]*Nomen singularitatis*[19], [k]*Nomen vanitatis*[20], [l]*Nomen hypocriseos*[21], [m]*Nomen blasphemiæ*[22]: that is to say, "A puff of arrogancy, a new name, a rash, a foolish, a proud, a pompous, a perverse, a superstitious, an ungodly, and a wicked title, a name of error, a name of singularity, a name of vanity, a name of hypocrisy, and a name of blasphemy." And doth M. Harding think, or would he have the world believe, that St Gregory would ever take these names and titles from John the bishop of Constantinople, to the intent to lay them upon his own see of Rome? Or is it likely that M. Harding knoweth St Gregory's mind better than ever St Gregory knew it himself?

[a] Lib. vi. Epist. 2.
[b] Lib. iv. Epist. 32.
[c] Lib. iv. Epist. 38.
[d] Lib. iv. Epist. 32.
[e] Lib. iv. Epist. 39.
[f] Lib. vi. Epist. 24.
[g] Lib. iv. Epist. 39.
[h] Lib. iv. Epist. 38.
[i] Lib. iv. Epist. 32.
[k] Lib. iv. Epist. 39.
[l] Lib. iv. Epist. 39.
[m] Lib. iv. Epist. 39.

[6 Avance, 1565.]

[7 Rex superbiæ prope est, et, quod dici nefas est, sacerdotum ei præparatur exercitus [*olim* exitus]: quia cervici militant elationis, qui ad hoc positi fuerant, ut ducatum præberent humilitatis.—Id. ibid. Ad Johan. Episc. Epist. xviii. col. 744.]

[8 Omnes magnos esse et honorabiles cupio, quorum tamen honor honori omnipotentis Dei non detrahat. Nam quisquis se contra Deum honorari appetit, mihi honorabilis non est.—Id. Lib. VII. Indict. xv. Ad Cyriac. Episc. Epist. xxxi. col. 879.]

[9 Vos tamen eamdem causam nullam esse dicere non debetis: quia si hanc æquanimiter portamus, universæ ecclesiæ fidem corrumpimus.—Id. ibid. Ad Anastas. Episc. Epist. xxvii. col. 873.]

[10 Id. Lib. v. Indict. XIII. Ad Sabin. Diac. Epist. xix. col. 747. See before, page 76, note 6.]

[11 *Al.* typum.—Id. Lib. VII. Indict. xv. Ad Cyriac. Episc. Epist. xxxi. col. 878.]

[12 Id. Lib. v. Indict. XIII. Ad Mauric. August. Epist. xx. col. 748.]

[13 Id. ibid. Ad Johan. Episc. Epist. xviii. cols. 742, 3.]

[14 Id. ibid. Ad Mauric. August. Epist. xx. col. 748.]

[15 Id. ibid. Ad Johan. Episc. Epist. xviii. col. 743.]

[16 Id. Lib. VII. Indict. xv. Ad Anastas. Episc. Epist. xxvii. col. 873.]

[17 Id. Lib. v. Indict. XIII. Ad Sabin. Diac. Epist. xix. col. 747.]

[18 Id. ibid. Ad Johan. Episc. Epist. xviii. col. 742.]

[19 Id. ibid. Ad Mauric. August. Epist. xx. col. 749.]

[20 ...ille [Johannes] in sua vanitate confirmatus esse videretur.—Id. ibid. Ad Sabin. Diac. Epist. xix. col. 746.]

[21 ...spero in...Deum quia hypocrisin illius [Johannis] superna majestas solvet.—Id. ibid.]

[22 Id. ibid. Ad Mauric. August. Epist. xx. col. 749.]

Verily, St Gregory not only misliketh these titles in others, but also disclaimeth the same from himself, and from his see of Rome for ever. For thus he writeth,
Greg. Lib. iv. Epist. 32. and his words be plain: *Nullus [Romanorum pontificum]...hoc singularitatis nomen assumpsit*[1]: "None of the bishops of Rome ever received this name of singu-
Greg. Lib. iv. Epist. 36. larity." *Nullus...decessorum meorum hoc tam profano vocabulo uti consensit*[2]: "None of my predecessors ever consented to use this ungodly name." *Nos hunc honorem nolumus oblatum suscipere*[3]: "We, being bishops of Rome, will not take this honour being offered unto us."

And the reason that he forceth against the bishop of Constantinople may
Greg. Lib. iv. Epist. 38. serve as well against the bishop of Rome. For thus he saith: *Quid tu Christo, universalis...ecclesiæ capiti, in extremi judicii dicturus es examine, qui cuncta ejus membra tibimet conaris universalis appellatione supponere*[4]? "What answer wilt thou make unto Christ, that indeed is the head of the universal church, at the trial of the last judgment, that thus goest about, under the name of universal bishop, to subdue all his members unto thee?" This is the very definition of an universal bishop. Thus the bishop of Rome attempteth to subdue the whole church of God and all the members of Christ unto himself. Therefore by St Gregory's judgment he is the forerunner of antichrist. And writing unto Eulo-
Greg. Lib. vii. Epist. 30. gius the patriarch of Alexandria, he useth these words: *Sanctitas vestra...mihi [sic] loquitur,...Sicut jussistis: quod verbum jussionis, peto, a meo auditu removete; quia scio quis sim, et qui sitis: loco...mihi fratres estis, moribus patres*[5]: "Your holiness writeth thus unto me, As you commanded. This word of commanding, I beseech you, take away from my hearing. For I know both what I am, and also what you are. In place (or dignity) ye are my brethren, in life and manners
Ibidem. ye are my fathers." Again he saith: *Ecce in præfatione epistolæ*[6], *&c.*: "Behold, even in the very preface of the epistle that you sent unto me, you have written the name of that presumptuous title, calling me the universal pope, notwithstanding I have forbidden it. I beseech your holiness to do it no more. For you do defraud yourself when you give another more than reason would." The self-same meaning M. Harding might have found twice written, even in the same place of St Gregory that he here allegeth, if it had pleased him to consider, either what went before, or else what followed immediately after. Before, he
Greg. Lib. iv. Epist. 32. writeth thus: *Non mea causa, sed Dei est...Nec solus ego, sed tota turbatur ecclesia. Quia piæ leges, quia venerandæ synodi, quia ipsa...Domini nostri Jesu Christi mandata superbi atque pompatici cujusdam sermonis inventione turbantur*[7]: "It is God's cause, it is not mine: neither only I, but also the whole church is troubled. For both the godly laws, and the reverend councils, and the very commandments of our Lord Jesus Christ, are cumbered with the device of this proud pompous title." Immediately after it followeth thus: *Nunquid ego in hac re, piissime domine, propriam causam defendo*[8]? "O my most gracious sovereign, do I herein defend mine own right?" By these it may appear that St Gregory, being bishop of Rome, would not suffer the name of universal bishop to be given, neither to any other bishop, nor to himself.

And whereas St Gregory saith, "The charge and chiefty of the whole church is committed unto Peter;" in the sense it is spoken in, we deny it not. St Paul
2 Cor. xi. likewise saith of himself in like sense: *Incumbit mihi quotidiana cura omnium ecclesiarum*: "There lieth upon me the daily charge of all churches;" and
2 Cor. xi. further saith: "I reckon myself[9] to be nothing inferior in travail to the highest apostles." And will M. Harding hereof reason thus?

Peter had the charge of the whole church;

[1 Id. ibid.; where *nomine uti consensit.*]

[2 Id. ibid. Ad Eulog. et Anastas. Episc. Epist. xliii. col. 771.]

[3 Id. ibid.]

[4 Id. ibid. Ad Johan. Episc. Epist. xviii. col. 742; where *tu quid*, and *es dicturus.*]

[5 Id. Lib. VIII. Indict. I. Ad Eulog. Episc. Epist. xxx. col. 919; where we find *vestra beatitudo*, and *qui sum qui estis.*]

[6 Ecce, &c., quam ad me ipsum qui prohibui direxistis, superbæ appellationis verbum, universalem me papam dicentes, imprimere curastis. Quod peto dulcissima mihi sanctitas vestra ultra non faciat: quia vobis subtrahitur quod alteri plus quam ratio exigit præbetur.—Id. ibid.]

[7 Id. Lib. v. Indict. XIII. Ad Mauric. August. Epist. xx. col. 748; where *non causa mea*, and *non solus.*]

[8 Id. ibid.; where *hac in re.*]

[9 Meself, 1565.]

Ergo, the pope is an universal bishop.

Certainly, St Gregory saith: "Peter himself, notwithstanding he received the whole charge, yet is he not called the universal apostle[10]." And can the pope be that thing that St Peter himself could not be?

Greg. Lib. iv. Epist. 32. Tamen universalis apostolus non vocatur.

St Gregory driveth his reason thus: If this title of universality might belong to any man, it should chiefly belong unto St Peter: but it belongeth not unto St Peter; therefore it can belong to no man.

Hereby it is plain that the bishop of Rome challengeth this day a title that St Peter never had, that no holy nor godly man would ever take upon him, that St Gregory utterly refused and detested, and called blasphemy. And yet will he seem to maintain his estate by the authority of this holy father! If St Gregory were now alive, he would cry out, as he did to the emperor Mauritius: *O tempora! O mores!*[11] "O what a time is this! O what manners are these!" Thus much is M. Harding furthered by the authority of St Gregory.

Greg. Lib. iv. Epist. 32.

M. HARDING. THE FIFTH DIVISION.

St Cyprian, declaring the contempt of the (94) *high priest Christ's*[12] *vicar in earth to be cause of schisms and heresies, writeth thus to Cornelius, pope and martyr:* Neque enim aliunde hæreses obortæ sunt[13], &c.: "*Neither have heresies or schisms risen of any other occasion than of that the priest of God is not obeyed, and that one priest for the time in the church, and one judge for the time instead of Christ, is not thought upon. To whom if the whole brotherhood*[14] (95) (*that is, the whole number of christian people, which be brethren together, and were so called in the primitive church*) *would be obedient according to God's teachings; then no man would make ado against the college of priests; no man would make himself judge, not of the bishop now, but of God, after God's judgment, after the favour of the people declared by their voices at the election, after the consent of his fellow-bishops; no man, through breach of unity and strife, would divide the church of Christ; no man, standing in his own conceit, and swelling with pride, would set up by himself abroad, without the church, a new heresy.*"

The ninety-fourth untruth. For St Cyprian speaketh these words of every several bishop, not only of the bishop of Rome.

Secundum magisteria divina.

The ninety-fifth untruth, standing in the manifest corruption and falsifying of St Cyprian.

THE BISHOP OF SARISBURY.

If M. Harding's cause were true, he would not avouch it with such untruth, and so often corruption of the holy fathers. If St Cyprian, writing this epistle to Cornelius the bishop of Rome, once name him either the high priest, or Christ's vicar-general in earth, or universal bishop, or head of the universal church; or say that the whole brotherhood of all christian people ought to be obedient unto him, as M. Harding untruly and contrary to his own knowledge expoundeth it; or if either his words or his purpose of writing may seem any way to lead to that end; then may M. Harding seem to have some honest colour for his defence. Otherwise we may justly say, he racketh the doctors, and forceth them to speak what him listeth to serve his turn.

First, it is certain, that in all that epistle St Cyprian never gave unto Cornelius any such ambitious title, but only calleth him by the name of brother. For thus he saluteth him: "Cyprian unto his brother Cornelius sendeth greeting;" and maketh his entry in this wise: "Dear brother, I have read your letters[15]." Thus St Cyprian, being bishop of Carthage, claimeth brotherhood and equality with the pope. One special occasion of his writing unto Cornelius was this amongst others: Cornelius, being bishop of Rome, and having excommunicate certain

Cypr. Lib. i. Epist. 3.

[10 Id. ibid.]

[11 Id. ibid.]

[12 Christ, 1611.]

[13 Neque, &c., aut nata sunt schismata, quam inde quod sacerdoti Dei non obtemperatur, nec unus in ecclesia ad tempus sacerdos, et ad tempus judex vice Christi cogitatur. Cui si secundum magisteria divina obtemperaret fraternitas universa, nemo adversum sacerdotum collegium quidquam moveret; nemo post divinum judicium, post populi suffragium, post coepiscoporum consensum, judicem se jam non episcopi, sed Dei faceret; nemo dissidio unitatis Christi ecclesiam scinderet; nemo sibi placens ac tumens seorsim foris hæresim novam conderet.—Cypr. Op. Oxon. 1682. Ad Cornel. Epist. lix. p. 129.]

[14 Brotherhead, 1565, and H. A. 1564.]

[15 Cyprianus Cornelio fratri, salutem. Legi literas tuas, frater carissime.—Id. ibid. p. 126.]

One Bishop.

notorious wicked men, and afterward being threatened and ill used at their hands, began to faint, and to be weary of his office. St Cyprian, hearing thereof, wrote comfortably unto him, and willed him in any wise to proceed, and to deal boldly, and not to yield, considering it was God's cause, and not his own. Among other words he saith thus: *Christiani non ultra aut durare aut esse...possumus, si ad hoc ventum est, ut perditorum minas et insidias*[1] *pertimescamus*[2]*:* "We can no longer continue or be christian men, if we, being bishops, once begin to shrink at the threats and fetches of the wicked."

Upon occasion hereof he sheweth what hurt and confusion of sects and schisms ensueth in any province or diocese, where as the bishop's authority and ecclesiastical discipline is despised. "For every bishop," saith St Cyprian, "within his own diocese is the priest of God, and for his time is a judge appointed in the place of Christ; and, as the church is one, so ought he likewise to be but one[3]." And thus he writeth generally of the authority of all bishops, and not only of the authority of the bishop of Rome. And notwithstanding he directeth his epistle only to Cornelius, yet are all his reasons general, and touch both himself, being bishop of Carthage, and also all other bishops whatsoever.

Now therefore to draw that thing by violence to one only bishop, that is generally spoken of all bishops, it is a guileful fetch to mislead the reader, and no simple or plain dealing. But M. Harding seemeth to ground his error upon the mistaking of these words of St Cyprian, *unus sacerdos*, and *fraternitas universa*[3]*;* that is, "one bishop," and "the whole brotherhood." For whereas St Cyprian saith, "There must be one bishop in a church;" he imagineth there must be one bishop to rule over the whole universal church.

The occasion of M. Harding's error.

And whereas again St Cyprian saith, "The whole brotherhood must obey one bishop;" he gathereth that all christian people throughout the whole world, which he untruly calleth "the whole brotherhood," must be obedient unto one universal bishop. And thus he buildeth one error upon another. But mistaking of the doctor maketh no sufficient proof.

It may soon appear St Cyprian meant that, for the avoiding of schisms and divisions, there ought to be only one bishop within one diocese, and not one bishop to rule over all the world. For thus he expoundeth his own meaning: *Cum post primum esse non possit quisquam, qui post unum, qui solus esse debet, factus est, jam non secundus ille, sed nullus est*[4]*:* "Seeing that after the first bishop is chosen there can be none other, whoso is made bishop after that one, which must needs be alone, is now not the second bishop, but indeed is no bishop."

vii Quæst. i. Factus est.

So likewise, when the heretic Novatus had by wicked practice divided the people of Rome into sects, and had solemnly sworn them that gave ear unto him, that they should no more return unto Cornelius the bishop there, and so had rent one bishopric into two, and made two bishops in one city; Cornelius, complaining thereof unto Fabius, the bishop of Antioch, and informing him of the same, writeth thus unto him: *Novatus nescit, unum episcopum in catholica ecclesia esse debere*[5]*:* "Novatus knoweth not that there ought to be but one bishop in a catholic church;" not meaning thereby the whole universal church throughout the world, but only his own particular church of Rome.

Euseb. Lib. vi. cap. xliii.

So when Chrysostom, the bishop of Constantinople, saw Sisinius bear himself as bishop within the same city, he said unto him: "One city may not have two bishops[6]."

Socr. Lib. vi. cap. xxii.

So likewise St Hierome saith that, notwithstanding the power of all priests by the authority of God's word be one and equal, "yet men, by policy to avoid contention, appointed one priest in every city[7]," to order and to direct his brethren.

Hieron. in Epist. ad Tit. cap. i.

[1 Insidia, 1609, 1611.]

[2 Id. ibid.; where we find *nec Christiani*, and *atque insidias*.]

[3 Id. ibid. p. 129.]

[4 Id. in Corp. Jur. Canon. Lugd. 1624. Decret. Gratian. Decr. Sec. Pars, Caus. VII. Quæst. i. can. 5. col. 818; where we find *secundus esse non possit: quisquis post*, &c., *debeat*, and *non jam*. Op. Ad Anton. Epist. lv. p. 104.]

[5 Euseb. in Hist. Eccles. Script. Amst. 1695-1700. Lib. VI. cap. xliii. p. 198.]

[6 ...οὐ δύναται ἡ πόλις δύο ἐπισκόπους ἔχειν.—Socrat. in eod. Lib. VI. cap. xxii. p. 270.]

[7 Postquam vero unusquisque eos quos baptizaverat suos putabat esse, non Christi, in toto orbe decretum est, ut unus de presbyteris electus super-

The Universal Brotherhood.

Thus was the unity of the whole church preserved; thus were all churches as one church, and all bishops as one bishop: for whoso dissented from one dissented from all. So saith St Cyprian: *Ecclesia... cohærentium sibi invicem sacerdotum glutino copulatur*[8]: "The church is coupled and joined in one by consent of bishops agreeing together."

Likewise again he saith: *Hanc unitatem firmiter tenere et vendicare debemus, maxime episcopi, qui in ecclesia præsidemus; ut episcopatum quoque ipsum unum et indivisum probemus*[9]: "This unity must we keep and defend, specially that be bishops and bear rule in the church, that we may declare indeed that our bishopric is one, and not divided." And therefore St Hierome saith: *Episcopi noverint... in commune debere [se] ecclesiam regere*[10]: "Let bishops understand that they ought to govern the church in common, or as all in one."

Cypr. Lib. iv. Epist. 9. Cypr. de Simplicitate Prælatorum.

Hieron. ad Tit. cap. i.

In this sense is every bishop for his time, as St Cyprian saith, in the stead of Christ, and to every such Christ saith: "He that heareth you heareth me; and he that despiseth you despiseth me." And therefore Ignatius saith: "The bishop in his church is the form of God the Father of all; and, so much as is possible, resembleth (in his office) Christ our God[11]." For this cause St Cyprian saith: "Hereof spring schisms and heresies; for that the priest of God (in every several diocese) is not obeyed[12]." As likewise again he saith to like purpose: *Qui cum episcopo non sunt, in ecclesia non sunt*[13]: "They that be not with the bishop be not in the church." So likewise Ignatius: "They that be of Christ are with the bishop[14]."

Luke x.

Ignat. ad Trall. τοῦ πατρὸς τῶν ὅλων τύπος.

Cypr. Lib. i. Epist. 3.

Cypr. Lib. iv. Epist. 9.

Ignat. ad Philad. ὅσοι... Χριστοῦ... εἰσὶν οὗτοι [καὶ] μετὰ τοῦ ἐπισκόπου εἰσίν.

Thus St Cyprian spake these words generally of the authority of all bishops in their several dioceses, and not of any special authority of the bishop of Rome, as it is here untruly affirmed by M. Harding.

But he will reply, St Cyprian saith, *universa fraternitas*, that is, "the whole brotherhood ought to be obedient to that one bishop:" and that whole brotherhood must needs be the whole company of all christian people. Notwithstanding this exposition seem very large, yet, if St Cyprian himself had not opened his own meaning otherwise, perhaps some man, either of simplicity or of ignorance, might so take it. But St Cyprian, that doubtless best knew his own mind, understandeth these words, *fraternitas universa*, not of all the universal company of all christian people throughout all the world, as M. Harding doth, but of the whole brotherhood within every several and particular diocese. For thus he writeth in the next epistle following: *Fere per provincias universas tenetur, ut ad ordinationes rite celebrandas ad eam plebem, cui præpositus ordinatur, episcopi ejusdem provinciæ proximi quique conveniant, et episcopus deligatur plebe præsente, &c. Quod et apud nos factum vidimus in Sabini collegæ nostri ordinatione; ut de universæ fraternitatis suffragio . . . episcopatus ei deferretur*[15]: "This order is in manner kept in all provinces, that, unto the due ordering or installing of a bishop, the bishops of the same province that dwell nearest come together to the people of that city, unto which a new bishop is appointed; and that the bishop be chosen in the presence of the people. Which thing we saw done in the election and ordering of our fellow-bishop Sabinus, that the bishopric was bestowed upon him by the consent and voices of the *whole brotherhood*." Here *universa fraternitas* undoubtedly is used for the whole faithful company of one city. In like manner he writeth unto Cornelius of certain that were returned from schisms and errors unto the unity of the church: *Merito illos revertentes summo... gaudio et clerus et plebis*

Fraternitas universa.

Cypr. Lib. i. Epist. 4.

Cypr. Lib. ii. Epist. 12.

poneretur cæteris, ad quem omnis ecclesiæ cura pertineret.—Hieron. Op. Par. 1693-1706. Comm. in Epist. ad Tit. cap. i. Tom. IV. Pars I. col. 413.]

[[8] Cypr. Op. Oxon. 1682. Ad Florent. Pup. Epist. lxvi. p. 168; where we find *copulata, sit* having preceded.]

[[9] Id. De Unit. Eccles. p. 108; where for *hanc* we have *quam*, and *atque indivisum.*]

[[10] Hieron. Op. Comm. in Epist. ad Tit. cap. i. Tom. IV. Pars I. col. 414.]

[[11] Ignat. ad Trall. cap. iii. in Patr. Apostol. Oxon. 1838. Tom. II. p. 326. See also Not. in loc. which exhibits the reading of the interpolated epistle —that here quoted.]

[[12] Cypr. Op. ad Cornel. Epist. lix. p. 129. See before, page 347, note 13.]

[[13] Id. ad Florent. Pup. Epist. lxvi. p. 168; where *non sint in ecclesia non esse.*]

[[14] Ignat. ad Philad. cap. iii. in Patr. Apostol. pp. 376, 8; where εἰσιν precedes Χριστοῦ.]

[[15] Cypr. Op. Ad Cler. et Pleb. Hisp. Epist. lxvii. p. 172; where we find *apud vos factum videmus.*]

The Universal Brotherhood.

fraternitas omnis excepit[1]: "When they came again, both the clergy and the *whole brotherhood* of the people worthily received them with great joy." So likewise the emperor Honorius writeth unto Bonifacius: "If two bishops through ambition and contention happen to be chosen, we will that neither of them be allowed as bishop; but that he only remain in the apostolic see, whom out of the number of the clergy godly discretion, and the consent of the *whole brotherhood*, shall choose by a new election[2]."

Rescr. Honor. ad Bonif. Quem universitatis consensus elegerit.

In these places M. Harding cannot deny but these words, *universa fraternitas, omnis fraternitas,* and *universitatis consensus,* must needs be taken for one whole particular brotherhood within one province or diocese. In the same sense Origen saith: *Qui vocatur ... ad episcopatum, ... vocatur ... ad servitutem totius ecclesiæ*[3]: "He that is called unto a bishopric is called unto the service of the *whole church.*" Likewise again he saith: *Plus a me exigitur, quam a diacono; plus a diacono, quam a laico: qui vero totius ecclesiæ arcem obtinet, pro omni ecclesia reddet rationem*[4]: "There is more required of me (being a priest) than of a deacon; more of a deacon, than of one of the people; but he that keepeth the watch or castle of the *whole church* (which is every bishop in his diocese) shall yield a reckoning for the whole."

Orig. in Esai. Hom. 6.

Orig. in Hier. Hom. 7.

In these places every particular church is called the *whole church.* And therefore Ignatius saith: *Quid aliud est episcopus, quam quidam obtinens principatum et potestatem supra omnes*[5]? "What is a bishop, but one having all rule and power over all?"

Ignat. ad Trall. τί...ἐστιν ἐπίσκοπος ἄλλο, ἢ πάσης ἀρχῆς καὶ ἐξουσίας ἐπέκεινα πάντων κρατῶν;

These things well weighed, besides the manifest corruption and falsifying of St Cyprian's both words and mind, I doubt not but the weakness also of M. Harding's reason may soon appear. For upon this place of St Cyprian untruly reported, he would seem to reason thus: There must be one bishop in one church or diocese; *ergo,* there must be one bishop over all the world. Or thus: The whole brotherhood in every diocese ought to hearken only to one bishop; *ergo,* all christian people throughout the world ought to be in subjection to the bishop of Rome. These arguments bewray themselves, and therefore need no further opening.

All this notwithstanding, if M. Harding will say, St Cyprian's words must needs import one universal bishop, and the same of necessity must be the bishop of Rome; let him then vouchsafe to read the epistle that the same St Cyprian wrote unto Florentius Pupianus. There shall he find that St Cyprian, even in like form and order, speaketh these self-same words of himself, being, as M. Harding knoweth, the bishop of Carthage in Africa, and not the bishop of Rome. His words be these: *Unde schismata et hæreses obortæ sunt, et oriuntur, [nisi] dum episcopus, qui unus est, et ecclesiæ præest, superba quorundam præsumptione contemnitur, et homo dignatione Dei honoratus ab hominibus indignis judicatur*[6]? "Wherehence have schisms and heresies sprung heretofore, and whereof spring they now, but that the bishop, which is one and governeth the church, by the presumptuous disdain of certain is despised, and a man preferred by God's allowance is examined and judged by unworthy men?" All this St Cyprian speaketh plainly, and namely of himself, being bishop of Carthage. Therefore it is great oversight to force the same only to the bishop of Rome, and stoutly to say it can be applied unto none other.

Cypr. Lib. iv. Epist. 9.

M. HARDING. THE SIXTH DIVISION.

Athanasius forged.

Of all other authorities, that of Athanasius and of the bishops of Egypt and Lybia, gathered together in a synod at Alexandria, is to be regarded; who, making

---

[[1] Id. ad Cornel. Epist. li. p. 95; where *plebs et fraternitas.*]

[[2] At si duo contra fas temeritate certantes fuerint ordinati, nullum ex his futurum penitus sacerdotem; sed illum solum in sede apostolica permansurum, quem ex numero clericorum nova ordinatione divinum judicium et universitatis consensus elegerit.—Rescr. Honor. ad Bonif. Pap. Rom. in Crabb. Concil. Col. Agrip. 1551. Tom. I. p. 491.]

[[3] Orig. Op. Par. 1733-59. In Isai. Hom. vi. 1. Tom. III. p. 116.]

[[4] Id. in Jerem. Hom. xi. 3. Tom. III. p. 189.]

[[5] Ignat. Interp. Epist. ad Trall. in Cotel. Patr. Apost. Amst. 1724. cap. vii. Vol. II. p. 63; where ἐπίσκοπος; ἀλλ' ἤ.]

[[6] Cypr. Op. Oxon. 1682. Ad Florent. Pup. Epist. lxvi. p. 167; where *inde,* and *indignus ab hominibus.*]

humble suit to Felix, then bishop of Rome, for aid and succour against the Arians, through the whole epistle confessing the supreme authority of that apostolic see, utter these very words: Vestræ apostolicæ sedis imploramus auxilium, &c.[7] *"We humbly beseech you of the help of your apostolic see; because (as verily we believe) God hath not despised the prayers of his servants offered up to him with tears, but hath constituted and placed you and your predecessors, who were apostolic prelates, in the highest tower or supreme state, and commanded them to have cure and charge of all churches, to the intent you help and succour us, and that defending us (as to whom judgment of bishops is committed) you forslow not through negligence to deliver us from our enemies."*

In primo tomo Conciliorum.

In summitatis arce constituit.

Now, if the apostolic church of Rome hath obtained the primacy and pre-eminence of power over all churches, and over the whole flock of christian people, of our Lord and[8] Saviour himself[9], as Anacletus saith; if it be evident to all that know the gospel, that the cure and charge of the whole church hath been committed to the holy apostle Peter, prince of all the apostles, by the word of our Lord[10], as Gregory witnesseth; if the whole brotherhood[12] (that is to say, all christian folk) ought to obey the one high priest or bishop of God, and the one judge that is Christ's vicar, or instead[13] of Christ for the time, according to the precepts and teachings of God[14], as Cyprian writeth; if it be God that hath placed and ordained the bishop of Rome in the highest state of the church[15], as Athanasius, with all the fathers of that Alexandrine council, recordeth; if this, I say, be true, then is it easily seen upon how good ground this doctrine standeth, whereby it is affirmed that the bishop of Rome his primacy hath his force by God's law, and not only by man's law, much less by unjust usurpation. The scriptures, by which as well these as all other holy and learned fathers were led to acknowledge and confess the primacy of Peter and his successors, were partly such as Anacletus and Gregory here allegeth, and Cyprian meaneth (as it appeareth by his third treatise, De Simplicitate Prælatorum[16],) *and sundry more of the new testament, as to the learned is known; of which to treat here largely and pithily, as the weight of the matter requireth, at this time I have no leisure; neither if I had, yet might I conveniently perform it in this treatise, which otherwise will amount to a sufficient bigness; and that matter thoroughly handled will fill a right great volume. Wherefore, referring the readers to the credit of these worthy fathers, who so understood the scriptures, as thereof they were persuaded the primacy to be attributed to Peter's successor by God himself, I will proceed, keeping my prefixed order.*

Anacletus forged.

St Gregory nipped. For[11] the next words immediately following are these: "Tamen Petrus universalis apostolus non vocatur."

St Cyprian's mind twice falsified in one place.

Whereas the pre-eminence of power and authority, which to the bishop of Rome by special and singular privilege God hath granted, is commended to the world by many and sundry councils, for avoiding of tediousness I will rehearse the testimonies of a few. Among the canons made by three hundred[17] and eighteen bishops at the Nicene council, which were in number seventy, and (96) *all burnt by heretics in the east church, save twenty, and yet the whole number* (97) *was kept diligently in the church of Rome in the original itself, sent to Sylvester the bishop there from the council, subscribed with the said three hundred and eighteen fathers' hands,—the forty-fourth canon, which is of the power of the patriarch over the metropolitans and bishops, and of the metropolitan over bishops, in the end hath this decree:* Ut autem cunctis ditionis suæ nationibus, &c.[18]: *"As the patriarch beareth rule over all nations of his jurisdiction,*

[*The 2 proof, councils,* H. A. 1564.]

Vide Francisc. Turrianum, Lib. iii. Charact. Dogmat.

The ninety-sixth untruth, joined with folly, as shall appear.

The ninety-seventh untruth. For there was no such original kept in the church of Rome.

[7 Vestræ, &c.: quia (ut credimus) non despexit Deus preces cum lacrymis sibi oblatas servorum suorum, sed ob id vos predecessoresque vestros, apostolicos videlicet præsules, in summitatis arce constituit, omniumque ecclesiarum eis curam habere præcepit, ut nobis succurratis, nosque tuentes, cui omne episcoporum judicium est commissum, liberare ab hostibus nostris non negligatis.—Epist. Ægypt. ad Felic. in Crabb. Concil. Tom. I. p. 355.]

[8 *And* is omitted, 1565, 1609, and H. A. 1564.]

[9 Anaclet. Epist. iii. in Crabb. Concil. Tom. I. p. 63. See before, page 341, note 15.]

[10 Gregor. Magni Papæ I. Op. Par. 1705. Epist. Lib. v. Indict. xiii. ad Mauric. August. Epist. xx. Tom. II. col. 748. See before, page 343, note 16.]

[11 1565 omits *for*.]

[12 Brotherhead, 1565, and H. A. 1564.]

[13 In the stead, H. A. 1564.]

[14 Cypr. Op. Ad Cornel. Epist. lix. p. 129. See before, page 347, note 13.]

[15 See before, note 7.]

[16 Cypr. Op. De Unit. Eccles. pp. 106, &c.]

[17 The three hundred, H. A. 1564.]

[18 ...est tamen patriarcha iis omnibus qui sub potestate ejus sunt, sicut ille qui tenet sedem Romæ, caput est et princeps omnium patriarcharum; quan-

Athanasius forged.

The ninety-eighth untruth. For there was no prince or province christened in St Peter's time.

and giveth laws to them; and as Peter, Christ's vicar, at the beginning set in authority over religion, over the churches, and over all other things pertaining to Christ, was (98) *master and ruler of christian princes, provinces, and of all nations; so he, whose principality or chiefty is at Rome, like unto Peter, and equal in authority, obtaineth the rule and sovereignty over all patriarchs." After a few words it followeth there: "If any man repine against this statute, or dare resist it, by the decree of the whole council he is accursed."*

Julius, that worthy bishop of Rome, not long after the council of Nice, in his epistle that he wrote to the ninety Arian bishops, assembled in the council[1] *at Antioch against Athanasius, bishop of Alexandria, reproving them for their unjust treating of him, saith of the canons of the Nicene council, then fresh in their remembrance, that they command,* non debere præter sententiam Romani pontificis ullo modo concilia celebrari, nec episcopos damnari[2]: "*that, without the authority of the bishop of Rome, neither councils ought to be kept, nor bishops condemned:" again, that nothing be decreed without the bishop of Rome,* cui hæc et majora ecclesiarum negotia tam ab ipso Domino, quam ab omnibus universorum conciliorum fratribus, speciali . . . privilegio contradita sunt[3]: "*to whom these and other the weighty matters of the churches be committed by special privilege, as well by our Lord himself as by all our brethren of the whole universal councils." Among other principal points which he reciteth in that epistle of*[4] *the Nicene council's canons, this is one:* Ut omnes episcopi[5], &c.: "*That all bishops who sustain wrong in weighty causes, so often as need shall require, make their appeal freely to the see apostolic, and flee*[6] *to it for succour, as to their mother, that from thence they may be charitably sustained, defended, and delivered. To the disposition of which see the ancient authority of the apostles and their successors, and of the canons, hath reserved all weighty or great ecclesiastical causes and judgments of bishops."*

Athanasius and the whole company of bishops of Egypt, Thebaida, and Lybia, assembled together in council at Alexandria, complaining in their epistle to Felix the pope of great[7] *injuries and griefs they sustained at the Arians, allegeth the determination of the Nicene council touching the supreme authority and power of that see apostolic over all other bishops:* Similiter et a supradictis patribus est definitum consonanter[8], &c.: "*Likewise (say they) it hath been determined by common assent of the aforesaid*[9] *fathers (of Nice) that, if any of the bishops suspect the metropolitan or their fellow-bishops of the same province, or the judges, that then they make their appeal to your holy see of Rome, to whom by our Lord himself power to bind and loose by special privilege above other hath been granted."* Matt. xvi. *Thus*[10] *much alleged out of the canons of the Nicene council, gathered partly out of Julius' epistle, who wrote to them that were present at the making of them (which taketh away all suspicion of untruth), and partly out of Athanasius and others, that were a great part of the same council.*

THE BISHOP OF SARISBURY.

A scarecrow, stuffed with straw and set upright, may seem afar off to be a man. Even so a forger of lies and fables, pricked up in the apparel of ancient

---

doquidem ipse est primus, sicut Petrus, cui data est potestas in omnes principes christianos, et omnes populos eorum, ut qui sit vicarius Christi Domini nostri super cunctos populos et universam ecclesiam christianam, et quicumque contradixerit, a synodo excommunicatur.—Concil. Nicen. can. Interp. F. Turrian. cap. 39 (al. 44) in Concil. Stud. Labb. et Cossart. Lut. Par. 1671-2. Tom. II. col. 303.]

[[1] In council, H. A. 1564.]

[[2] Rescript. Jul. Papæ I. contr. Orient. in Crabb. Concil. Col. Agrip. 1551. Tom. I. p. 309.]

[[3] Id. in eod. p. 310.]

[[4] Out of, H. A. 1564.]

[[5] Ut omnes episcopi, qui in quibusdam gravioribus pulsantur vel criminantur causis, quoties necesse fuerit, libere apostolicam appellent sedem, atque ad eam quasi ad matrem confugiant, ut ab ea (sicut semper fuit) pie fulciantur, defendantur et liberentur. Cujus dispositioni omnes majores ecclesiasticas causas, et episcoporum judicia, antiqua apostolorum eorumque successorum atque canonum auctoritas reservavit.—Id. cap. 2. in eod. p. 311.]

[[6] Fly, H. A. 1564.]

[[7] The great, H. A. 1564.]

[[8] Similiter, &c., ut si quisquam episcoporum aut metropolitanum aut comprovinciales vel judices suspectos habuerit, vel vestram sanctam Romanam interpellet sedem, cui ab ipso Domino potestas ligandi ac solvendi speciali est privilegio super alios concessa.—Epist. Ægypt. ad Felic. in eod. Tom. I. p. 356.]

[[9] Foresaid, 1565, and H. A. 1564.]

[[10] This, 1565, and H. A. 1564.]

names, may seem to the ignorant an old catholic father. No marvel though this authority like M. Harding best above all others; for it is most vain and shameless above all others, and therefore meetest to help up a shameless doctrine. It is no new practice in the church of Rome to forge evidence in the name of old fathers, as, God willing, hereafter it shall better appear. But as for this epistle and certain others that are carried about under the name of that godly bishop Athanasius, I will only rip up the stuffing, and open some part of the contents of them, and so will not refuse M. Harding himself to be the judge. Athanasius forged.

First, that they were never written in Greek, and therefore not by Athanasius, it may appear by sundry tokens, and namely by the allusion of these two Latin words, *vertex* and *vertuntur*: [*Romana sedes*] *est* . . . *sacer vertex, in quo omnes vertuntur*[11]. The Latin is rude and barbarous, and many times utterly void of sense. The manner of utterance is childish and babbling, empty of matter, and full of words without measure. The substance of the whole is nothing else but flattering and advancing[12] of the see of Rome, farced up, and set out with lies without shame.

The author hereof, speaking of the church of Rome, saith: *Inde ecclesiæ sumpsere prædicationis exordium*[13]: "From Rome the churches received the first preaching of the gospel." But God himself saith: *Ex Sione exibit lex, et verbum Domini de Hierusalem*: "From Sion the law shall proceed, and the word of the Lord from Hierusalem." And therefore Tertullian calleth Hierusalem "the mother of religion[14]." And Nicephorus saith, that Simon Zelotes ran over all Africa, and preached the gospel[15]. Eusebius saith, that St Mark the evangelist first erected congregations, and taught the gospel at Alexandria[16]. And Nicephorus saith further, that St Mark went preaching over all Egypt, and Lybia, and Cyrene, and Pentapolis, and the whole country of Barbary, in the time of the emperor Tiberius[17], which was at the least six years before Peter came to Rome. St Augustine saith, the religion of Christ was first brought into Africa out of Græcia, and not from Rome[18]. Therefore that M. Harding's Athanasius saith, the church received from Rome the first preaching of the gospel, is an open flattery, and a manifest untruth. Isai. ii. Mic. iv. Matrix religionis. Niceph. Lib. ii. cap. xl. Euseb. Lib. ii. cap. xxiv. Niceph. Lib. ii. cap. xliii. August. Epist. 170. et Epist. 178. Græcia, unde fides orta est.

Further this author saith, that "in all cases there lay appeals from the metropolitan to the bishop of Rome; and that by the authority of the Nicene council[19]." But that thing in the council of Carthage, St Augustine being then present, was utterly denied by all the bishops of Africa, Numidia, Mauritania, Byzancena, and Tripolis, to the number of two hundred and seventeen; and by the witness of the three patriarchs of Antiochia, Constantinopolis, and Alexandria, was found untrue[20]. Concil. Carth. vi.

This author saith: *Fuit semper vestræ sanctæ et apostolicæ sedi licentia, injuste damnatos vel excommunicatos potestative sua auctoritate restituere, et sua eis omnia reddere*[21]: "Your holy apostolic see had evermore a special prerogative, by your own authority, and by way of power, to relieve men unjustly condemned or excommunicate, and to restore them to their own." But it shall hereafter appear that the bishop of Rome at that time had no such power; and that it was not he that restored any man in that case by his power, but only the emperor.

St Paul saith: "Other foundation none can be laid, but only that is laid already, which is Christ Jesus;" and findeth great fault with the Corinthians that said: "I hold of Apollo, I hold of Paul, I hold of Peter." But M. Harding's Athanasius saith: *Tu es... Petrus, et super fundamentum tuum ecclesiæ columnæ, hoc est, episcopi,... sunt confirmatæ*[22]: "Thou art Peter; and upon thy foundation 1 Cor. iii.

[[11] Id. ibid.]

[[12] Avancing, 1565.]

[[13] Id. ibid. p. 357; where *unde*.]

[[14] Tertull. Op. Lut. 1641. Adv. Marcion. Lib. IV. 35. p. 562. See before, page 280, note 4.]

[[15] Niceph. Call. Hist. Eccles. Lut. Par. 1630. Lib. II. cap. xl. Tom. I. p. 202.]

[[16] Euseb. in Hist. Eccles. Script. Amst. 1695–1700. Lib. II. capp. xvi. xxiv. pp. 42, 53.]

[[17] Niceph. Call. Hist. Eccles. Lib. II. cap. xliii. Tom. I. p. 209.]

[[18] August. Op. Par. 1679-1700. Ad Severin. Epist. lii. 2. Tom. II. col. 119. Id. Alterc. cum Pascent. seu Epist. xx. 6. Tom. II. Append. col. 41.]

[[19] See before, note. 8.]

[[20] Concil. Carthag. VI. in Crabb. Concil. Tom. I. pp. 494, &c.]

[[21] Epist. Ægypt. ad Felic. in eod. Tom. I. p. 356.]

[[22] Id. ibid.; where *id* for *hoc*.]

Athanasius forged.

the pillars of the church, which are the bishops, are surely set." And thus he deviseth another foundation besides Christ, and contrary to St Paul's doctrine would have all the bishops of the world to hold of Peter.

But to leave all other untruths wherewith these epistles be stuffed full, mark, gentle reader, only this oversight, and thou shalt plainly see with thine eyes, that M. Harding's doctor is an impudent and an open liar. For the true Athanasius himself, of whom we make no doubt, saith that the Arians at Alexandria burnt the catholic men's books, and therewithal the canons of the council of Nice, in the time of the emperor Constantius, Julius being then bishop of Rome[1]. Which observation of time appeareth also by Socrates in his story[2]. But M. Harding's Athanasius is either so forgetful of his lies, or so impudent and careless what he say, that he maketh piteous complaint of the said burning unto Marcus, that was bishop in Rome before Julius, and was dead at the least nine years before the canons were burnt. By such doctors M. Harding upholdeth the state of Rome.

Athanas. in Epist. ad Orthod.

Socrat. Lib. ii. cap. viii.

As for Athanasius himself, he never understood the bishop of Rome had any such prerogative power, nor never named him by greater title than the bishop of Rome. And whereas this epistle, alleged in the name of Athanasius, soundeth far otherwise, it is no marvel; for it was dated at Alexandria, and made in Rome.

Now, if the decretal epistle, which M. Harding hath brought in under the name of Anacletus, be nothing else but forged evidence, as it is sufficiently declared—if M. Harding have uncourteously used St Gregory, cutting off his tale in the midst, and purposely leaving out those words: *Tamen [Petrus] universalis apostolus non vocatur*[3]: "Yet is not Peter called the universal apostle:" which was the only matter that St Gregory had then in hand—if St Gregory say: "None of my predecessors, bishops of Rome, would ever take upon him the name of universal bishop[4]"—if St Gregory say: "It is the puff of arrogancy; the word of pride; a new, a pompous, a perverse, a foolish, a rash, a superstitious, a profane, an ungodly, and a wicked name; a name of singularity; a name of error; a name of hypocrisy; a name of vanity, and a name of blasphemy; and that whosoever calleth himself, or desireth to be called by that arrogant name, in the pride of his heart is the forerunner of antichrist; and that the quiet and indifferent bearing of the same is the destruction of the faith of the universal church[5]"—if M. Harding have wittingly and openly falsified the words of St Cyprian[6], and that twice together in one sentence, as he himself cannot deny—if the epistle, that he allegeth under the title of Athanasius, be nothing else but a shameless counterfeit, full of vile flattering and apparent lies—then is this former part hitherto but weakly proved; neither can M. Harding truly say his doctrine standeth upon good and sure ground.

Gregor. Lib. iv. Epist. 32.

Gregor. Lib. iv. Epist. 36.

Gregor. Lib. vi. Epist. 30. Gregor. Lib. vi. Epist. 24.

Cypr. Lib. i. Epist. 3.

O what luck hath M. Harding to such authorities, having choice, as he saith, of so many, and tripping over so lightly, to speed so ill! His Amphilochius lieth at Verona; his Clemens in Candy; his Martial in a cave under ground: his canon of the council of Ephesus against Nestorius was never seen, and others otherwise miscarried: the council of Nice, wherein was the whole stay of the primacy of Rome, is burnt by the Arians, and, saving only in Rome, nowhere else in the world to be found.

For answer hereunto, methinketh these words, spoken generally by St Cyprian, had then, and have yet a special place in the see of Rome: *Ambitio dormit in sinu sacerdotum*[7]: "Ambition sleepeth in the bosom of priests." For, to pass over the great contention that even at the beginning happened there between

Cypr. de Jej. et Tent.

[1 Athanasius relates the burning of the books, and immediately after says that the incendiary calumniated him to Constantius.—Athanas. Op. Par. 1698. Encycl. ad Episc. Epist. Tom. I. pp. 113, 5.]

[2 Socrat. in Hist. Eccles. Script. Amst. 1695–1700. Lib. II. cap. viii. p. 70; where the council at Antioch is said to have been held in the reign of Constantius, Julius being bishop of Rome.]

[3 Gregor. Magni Papæ I. Op. Par. 1705. Epist. Lib. V. Indict. XIII. ad Mauric. August. Epist. xx. Tom. II. col. 748.]

[4 Id. ibid. Ad Eulog. et Anastas. Episc. Epist. xliii. col. 771. See before, page 346.]

[5 Id. Lib. VII. Indict. XV. Ad Mauric. August. Epist. xxxiii. col. 881.

Id. ibid. Ad Anastas. Episc. Epist. xxvii. col. 873. See before, page 345.]

[6 Cypr. Op. Oxon. 1682. Ad Cornel. Epist. lix. p. 129. See before, page 347, note 13.]

[7 Etiam in sinu sacerdotum ambitio dormit.—Id. De Jejun. et Tent. (Arnold.) p. 38.]

Damasus and Ursinus, whether of them two should be bishop, in which contention a great number of either part was slain[8]; St Augustine also complaineth that even the deacons of Rome in his time advanced[9] themselves far above their estate. These be his words: *Falcidius duce stultitia, et civitatis Romanæ jactantia,... diaconos presbyteris æquare contendit*[10]: "Falcidius, led by folly, and by the courage of the city of Rome, would have deacons to be nothing inferior unto priests." Likewise St Hierome saith: "The Romans are noted of courtesy and stoutness of mind[11]." And therefore St Paul gave this advertisement specially unto them above all others: "*Noli altum sapere, sed time:* "Be not high-minded, but stand in awe." Wherefore it is the less to be marvelled, if they have so ambitiously at all times attempted dominion over others.

The pride of Rome.

Ammi. Mar. Socrat. Lib. iv. cap. xxiv. August. in Quæst. Veteris et Novi Test. Quæst. ci. Hieron. in Præfat. ad Galat.

Rom. xi.

But M. Harding saith, the pre-eminence of power and authority of the bishop of Rome is commended to the world by many and sundry councils. Wherein I marvel he allegeth not the council of Carthage, of Hippo Regius, and of Africa, in which it was decreed thus: *Ut primæ sedis episcopus non appelletur princeps sacerdotum, aut summus sacerdos, aut aliquid hujusmodi, sed tantum primæ sedis episcopus*[12]: "That the bishop of the first see be not called the chief of priests, or the highest priest, or by any other like name; but only the bishop of the first see;" or the council of Africa, where, touching appeal to Rome, it was specially provided thus: *Si... provocandum putaverint, non provocent, nisi ad Africana concilia, vel ad primates provinciarum suarum. Ad transmarina... qui putaverit appellandum, a nullo intra Africam in communionem suscipiatur*[13]: "If they think it needful to appeal from their own bishops, let them not appeal but only unto councils to be holden within the country of Africa. But whosoever shall think it needful to appeal to the judgment of any beyond the sea (that is, to the bishop of Rome), let no man within Africa receive him to his communion." Why doth M. Harding so warily leave these councils that be extant, and to be seen, the authority whereof was never doubted of, and allege only a patch of the council of Nice, which he himself confessed[14] was burnt; and all the bishops of the east part, who are supposed to have made it, protest openly, under their hands and seals, it was never made? But M. Harding herein doth much like unto the Arians, that accused Athanasius, who were not ashamed to bring in the names of certain men, as being alive, to witness against him; and yet, notwithstanding, charged Athanasius with the same men, that he had slain them[15].

Concil. Carth. iii. can. 26. Concil. Hipp. can. 27. Concil. Aphr. cap. 6.

Concil. Aphr. cap. 92.

Synod. Alex. adversus Accusatores Athanasii.

Neither do I see wherefore M. Harding should need in this case to lean to the authority of any council. For his Anacletus thought it better to make men believe he had his superiority, "not from the apostles, but from Christ himself[16]." And Faustinus Episcopus Potentinus, claiming for the bishop of Rome in the council of Carthage, and finding himself to have small hold in this canon of the Nicene council, alleged rather custom and prescription. These be his words: *Tractandum est cum vestra beatitudine... de Nicenis canonibus, ut conserventur et constituta eorum et consuetudo; quia aliqua ordine et canone tenentur, aliqua consuetudine firmata sunt*[17]: "We must deal with your holiness of the canons of the council of Nice, that they may be kept, both the constitutions thereof, and also the custom. For certain things are holden by order and by canon; and certain things are made good by custom." But pope Nicolas the first utterly refuseth, not only the council of Nice, and all other councils in this behalf, but also the authority of prescription and custom. For thus he saith: *Animadver-*

Anacl. Epist. 1.

Concil. Carth. vi. can. 2.

Nicol. I. ad Michael. Imperatorem.

[8 Amm. Marcell. Op. Par. 1681. Lib. XXVII. cap. iii. pp. 480, 1.
Socrat. in Hist. Eccles. Script. Lib. IV. cap. xxix. p. 202.]

[9 Avanced, 1565.]

[10 Quidam igitur qui nomen habet Falcidii, duce &c. coæquare &c. — August. Op. Par. 1679-1700. Quæst. ex Utroq. Mixt. Quæst. ci. Tom. III. Append. col. 92.]

[11 ...facilitatis et superbiæ arguuntur.—Hieron. Op. Par. 1693-1706. Comm. Lib. II. in Epist. ad Gal. Præf. Tom. IV. Pars I. cols. 255, 6.]

[12 Concil. Carthag. III. cap. 26. in Crabb. Concil. Col. Agrip. 1551. Tom. I. p. 428.
Concil. Hippon. Abbrev. cap. 27. in eod. Tom. I. p. 434.
Concil. Afric. cap. 6. in eod. Tom. I. p. 503.]

[13 Id. cap. 92. in eod. Tom. I. p. 517.]

[14 Confesseth, 1565.]

[15 Concil. Alex. Epist. Synod. in Concil. Stud. Labb. et Cossart. Lut. Par. 1671-2. Tom. II. col. 552.]

[16 Anaclet. Epist. i. in Crabb. Concil. Tom. I. p. 58. See also Epist. iii. p. 63. See before, page 341, note 15.]

[17 Faustin. in Concil. Carthag. VI. cap. 2. in eod. Tom. I. p. 494; where *cum vestra beatitudine tractanda*, and in the text *constitutio*.]

The Pope a forger. *tendum est, quia non Nicena, non denique ulla synodus quicquam Romanæ contulit ecclesiæ privilegii; quæ in Petro noverat eam totius jura potestatis pleniter meruisse, et cunctarum Christi ovium regimen accepisse*[1]: "Ye must consider that neither the council of Nice, nor any other council, ever gave any privilege to the church of Rome: for this church knoweth that in Peter she hath fully deserved the right of all power, and hath attained the government of all the sheep of Christ."

But touching the forgery of this council of Nice, the very beginning of the quarrel, and the whole story standeth thus: One Apiarius, a priest of the church of Sicca in Africa, as it appeareth, a very ill man, being justly excommunicate, both by his own bishop, and also by a great number of other bishops together in the council there, appealed from them all unto Zosimus then bishop of Rome. Zosimus, without further knowledge of the cause, never hearing the other party, pronounced Apiarius to be innocent, and restored him to the communion; and, understanding there was a council gathered in Africa touching the same, sent thither Faustinus the bishop of Potentia, with two other priests of Rome, Philippus and Asellus, not only to see that the said Apiarius, without any further trial, might be restored unto his right, but also to make plea in the open council, that it should be lawful for any priest to appeal from his own ordinary, or metropolitan, or council, unto the apostolic see of Rome. The bishops of Africa
Concil. Carth. vi. cap. 3. answered, there was no law it should be so[2]. Faustinus laid forth this canon of the council of Nice, not made by the authority of the bishops there, but only devised by the bishop of Rome. The bishops there, among whom was St Au-
cap. 4. gustine, that famous learned father, thought it was a forged matter[3], and there-
They would not thus have done, if they had thought all the originals and copies had been burnt. fore said, they would send unto Alexandria, Antioch, and Constantinople, for the very original copies of the said council, and desired the bishop of Rome to do the same, and said that in the mean while they would do as they had done before. Upon this message, and return of the answer with the true authentic copies, from
cap. 7. Cyrillus the bishop of Alexandria, and Atticus the bishop of Constantinople[4], it
Concil. Aphr. cap. 102. appeared plainly unto the world, that the canons were corrupted, and that the pope had falsified that holy council; and, to the intent to advance[5] his apostolic see of Rome, had devised privileges and prerogatives of his own. Here might M. Harding well bestow his terms; here might he truly say: The pope coggeth and foisteth the die; the pope bombasteth the canons of councils, and the decrees of holy fathers, with his counterfeit stuffing. The bishops in the council of Africa, having thus thoroughly examined the truth hereof, wrote unto Cœles-
Concil. Aphr. cap. 105. tinus, being then bishop of Rome, in this wise: *Decreta Nicena, &c.*[6]: "The decrees of the council of Nice have committed both the inferior clerks, and also the bishops, unto their metropolitans. For it was discreetly and rightly considered that all matters are to be determined in the places where they began,

---

[[1] Nicol. Papæ I. Epist. ad Michael. Imp. in eod. Tom. II. p. 758; where in the text *privilegium*.]

[[2] Ita enim dixerunt ... in concilio Niceno, cum de episcoporum appellatione decernerent. Placuit autem, ut si episcopus accusatus fuerit, et judicaverint congregati episcopi regionis ipsius...et appellasse episcopus videatur, et confugerit ad beatissimum ecclesiæ Romanæ episcopum...ut renovetur examen.—Zosim. Common. recit. in Concil. Carthag. vi. cap. 3. in eod. Tom. I. p. 494.]

[[3]. Alyp. in eod. cap. 4. ibid. See below, page 358. See also cap. 7. p. 495.]

[[4] Rescr. Cyril. Alex. in Concil. Afric. cap. 102. in eod. Tom. I. p. 520.]

[[5] Avance, 1565.]

[[6] ... decreta Nicena sive inferioris gradus clericos, sive ipsos episcopos, suis metropolitanis apertissime commiserunt. Prudentissime enim justissimeque providerunt, quæcunque negocia in suis locis, ubi orta sunt, finienda: nec unicuique provinciæ gratiam sancti Spiritus defuturam, qua æquitas a Christi sacerdotibus et prudenter videatur, et constantissime teneatur: maxime, quia unicuique concessum est, si judicio offensus fuerit cognitorum, ad concilia suæ provinciæ vel etiam universale provocare. Nisi forte quisquam est, qui credat, uni cuilibet posse Deum nostrum examinis inspirare justitiam, et innumerabilibus congregatis in concilium sacerdotibus denegare. Aut quomodo ipsum transmarinum judicium ratum erit, ad quod testium necessariæ personæ, vel propter sexus vel propter senectutis infirmitatem, vel multis aliis intercurrentibus impedimentis, adduci non poterunt? Nam ut aliqui, tanquam a tuæ sanctitatis latere, mittantur, nulla invenimus patrum synodo constitutum; quia illud quod pridem per eundem coepiscopum nostrum Faustinum, tanquam ex parte Niceni concilii, exinde transmisistis: in conciliis verioribus, quæ accipiuntur Nicena, a sancto Cyrillo coepiscopo nostro Alexandrinæ ecclesiæ, et a venerabili Attico Constantinopolitano antistite, ex authentico missis...a nobis transmissa sunt, in quibus tale aliquid non potuimus reperire. Executores etiam clericos vestros quibusque petentibus nolite mittere, nolite concedere, ne fumosum typhum seculi in ecclesiam Christi... videamur inducere.—Epist. Concil. ad Cælestin. cap. 105. in eod. p. 521.]

and that no province can lack the Holy Ghost, whereby the bishops of Christ may be able both wisely to see, and also constantly to maintain the right; and specially for that it is lawful for every man, that shall mislike the discretion of his judges, to appeal either to a particular council within the same realm, or else to the universal council of the whole world: unless perchance some man will say, God is able to inspire the trial of justice into one man alone (because he is bishop of Rome), and will not inspire the same into a great number of bishops meeting together in council. And how may such beyond-sea judgment be thought good, whereunto the persons of the witnesses, which in trial of truth are thought necessary, either for that they be women, or for the infirmity of their age, or for many other incident lets, cannot be brought? Now that any should be sent abroad, as it were, from your holiness' side, we find it not decreed in any council. As for that you sent us lately by our brother Faustinus, as part of the council of Nice, we must do you to wit, that in the true councils, which we have received from our holy fellow-bishop Cyrillus of Alexandria, and the reverend father Atticus the bishop of Constantinople, taken out of the very originals, it cannot be found. And send you not any your clerks hither to execute justice at any man's request, lest we seem to bring the smoky puff of the world into the church of Christ." Thus far the words of the council.

The Pope a forger.

The pope taken in manifest forgery.

Fumosum typhum.

The bishop of Rome, when he saw he was taken with the manner, and found an open falsary, (for that the canons of his making disagreed from the very originals,) thought it good policy to say, the originals were burnt by the Arians, and so no true copy now remaining, but his only. And therefore he imagined a letter to be written in the name of Athanasius, and other bishops of Egypt, unto Marcus the bishop of Rome, wherein they besought him a copy of the Nicene council, for that all their books were utterly destroyed[7]. But this shift was too simple. For it were hard for M. Harding to shew, what help Athanasius could have found in any of those canons that are now presumed to be burnt, wherewith either to relieve himself in that case, or else to molest and grieve his adversaries.

But both Julius the bishop of Rome, and also Athanasius the bishop of Alexandria, make mention hereof. Therefore there is no cause, saith M. Harding, why this matter should be suspected of any untruth. This removing of suspicion, I know not how, seemeth somewhat to increase suspicion. If there were not a sore, what should it thus need to be salved? Indeed Julius allegeth a canon of the council of Nice; but M. Harding's canon he allegeth not. And the compiler of the councils gave this note in the margin touching the same: *Hoc statutum solum reducibile est ad quintum et sextum caput Niceni concilii; verum aperte non invenitur*[8]: "This decree may only be reduced to the fifth and sixth chapter of the council of Nice; but expressly it is not found." Such credit is to be given to this Julius in his allegations.

In Epist. Decret. Julii.

As for M. Harding's Athanasius, his tale is so simple, that it will soon bewray itself. For, as I noted before, he writeth unto Marcus the bishop of Rome, of the burning of the books; and yet Athanasius himself certainly knew that Marcus was dead at the least nine years before that burning happened[9].

Manifest forgery.

Athan. in Epist. ad Orthodox. Socrat. Lib. ii. cap. viii.

Even so the vain forger of the emperor Constantine's great donation[10] imagineth him to decree, that the bishop of Constantinople should be subject unto the see of Rome[11]. And yet neither was the city of Constantinople at that time built, nor any such name yet known in the world, nor any bishopric there erected. A man might say: *Non satis commode divisa sunt temporibus tibi, Dave, haec*[12].

Again, the same Athanasius, writing unto Felix, saith: "The Arians had falsified the Nicene council[13]." But writing unto Marcus of the same matter, as a man

Athan. in Epist. ad Fœl.

[[7] Epist. Ægypt. ad Marc. Papam, in eod. Tom. I. p. 299.]

[[8] Jul. Papæ I. Epist. in eod. Tom. I. p. 305; where (in the marginal note) *in Niceni 5 & 6 capi.*]

[[9] See before, page 354.] [[10] Dotation, 1565.]

[[11] Edict. Constant. in eod. Tom. I. p. 226.]

[[12] Ter. Andr. III. i. 17, 8.]

[[13] ...ut...legem, quæ in memorata Nicena synodo est promulgata, licet prædictorum insidiatorum...depravatione sit suffocata, reparetis.—Epist. Ægypt. ad Felic. in Crabb. Concil. Col. Agrip. 1551. Tom. I. p. 357. In an earlier part of the same epistle complaint is made that the Nicene canons were incensa, nobisque sublata. p. 356.]

The Pope a forger.

that had utterly forgotten himself, he saith: "The Arians had burnt the council of Nice[1]." But if it were burnt, how was it falsified? If it were falsified, how was it burnt? These tales hang not well together. But forasmuch as M. Harding would so fain have the pope to hold by burnt evidence, if it may please thee, gentle reader, discreetly to weigh the whole circumstance of the matter, thou shalt soon find that all this great ado was nothing else but a great fable. For first, it appeareth by Theodoretus, that the whole acts and copies of the council of Nice were sent abroad unto all bishops that were away[2]. And Marius Victorinus, writing against Arius, saith that the same acts were sent abroad into the whole world, and that "many thousand bishops" subscribed and agreed unto them[3]. Which thing being undoubtedly true, it were very much for M. Harding to say, that all these copies, in all parts of the world, could be destroyed upon the sudden, and that all together, in one place, and with one fire, and at one commandment. The Arians neither were so mighty to achieve it, nor so foolish to attempt it. Certainly the like never happened to any other council. But what needeth words, where the matter is plain? The bishops of Africa had the very copies of these canons. Alypius, the bishop of Tagasta, in this conference with Faustinus said: *Adhuc tamen me movet, quoniam cum inspiceremus Græca exemplaria hujus synodi Nicenæ, ista ibi, nescio qua ratione, minime invenimus*[4]: "But this one thing much moveth me, that, conferring and examining the Greek examples of this Nicene council, these matters (of the superiority of the see of Rome that is alleged), I know not how, we found not there." And Cyrillus the bishop of Alexandria, being desired for trial of this matter to send the true original of this council, made answer in this sort: *Necesse habui...fidelissima exemplaria ex authentica synodo...vestræ caritati dirigere*[5]: "I thought it needful to send unto you the true example[6] of the very authentic council." Likewise Atticus, the bishop of Constantinople, to the same request answereth thus: *Canones sicut statuti sunt in Nicæa civitate a patribus, in integro...[ad vos] direxi*[7]: "I have sent unto you the canons in the whole, even as they were made and ratified by the fathers in the city of Nice." Now if these canons were quite burnt, as M. Harding saith, how were they afterward found whole, as the godly father Atticus and the learned bishop Cyrillus saith? And if they were afterward found whole, how then were they quite burnt before? Or how is it, that no man, neither in Africa, nor in Europa, nor in Asia, neither in the east church, nor in the west, was ever able to see these canons, but only the bishop of Rome, that so ambitiously claimeth by them? And if he have them indeed, and that of such authentic record, under the hands of the three hundred and eighteen bishops, as it is boldly avouched, why are they not shewed? Why have they been, for the space of these thirteen hundred years, still kept invisible? Verily the council of Nice were well worth the shewing.

Athan. in Epist. ad Marc.

Theodor. Lib. i. cap. ix. et Lib. ii. cap. viii. Mar. Victor. adversus Arium, Lib. ii.

Concil. Carth. vi. cap 4.

Concil. Carth. vi. cap. 102.

Concil Carth. vi. cap. 103.

All these things rightly weighed may seem sufficient to descry a forger. Yet, gentle reader, the better to satisfy thy mind, mark how earnestly and with what cunning M. Harding's Athanasius forceth on his fable. He thought it not sufficient to say, "The canons all were quite burnt," which thing he only saith, and no man else; but, because he saw wise men would reply, There were no such canons ever made, therefore he took pains further to shew the considerations and causes, and the whole order and circumstance of the making, whereat, he saith, he himself was present. "Four-score canons," saith he[8], "were devised in the whole, whereof forty were laid in in Latin by the Latins, and forty other in

Athan. in Epist. ad Marc.

[[1] Libros ... nostros ... etiam Nicenam synodum... incenderunt.—Epist. Ægypt. ad Marc. in eod. Tom. I. p. 299.]

[[2] Theodor. in Hist. Eccles. Script. Amst. 1695-1700. Lib. I. cap. ix. Lib. II. cap. viii. pp. 29 &c., 74 &c. The former chapter contains a synodic epistle from the council of Nice, the latter one from that of Sardica.]

[[3] ...multi orbis episcopi trecenti quindecim in civitate Nicæa quam per totum orbem decretam fidem mittentes, episcoporum millia in eadem habuerunt, &c.—Mar. Victorin. adv. Ar. Lib. II. 9. in Biblioth. Vet. Patr. Stud. Galland. Venet. 1765-81. Tom. VIII. p. 178.]

[[4] Alyp. in Concil. Carthag. VI. cap. 4. in Crabb. Concil. Col. Agrip. 1551. Tom. I. p. 494.]

[[5] Rescr. Cyril. Alex. in Concil. Afric. cap. 102. in eod. Tom. I. p. 520.]

[[6] Examples, 1565, 1609.]

[[7] Epist. Attic. cap. 103. in eod. ibid.; where *canones* precedes *in integro*.]

[[8] He saith, 1565.]

Greek by the Grecians. Of this whole number of canons," saith he, "the fathers there took off ten canons, and divided them as they might most handsomely among the rest, and so made up only the number of three-score and ten canons, thereby mystically to represent the three-score and ten disciples; or else the number of the three-score and ten tongues that be known in the world[9]." Thus of wholesome and godly rules of faith and manners, M. Harding's Athanasius hath leisure to fancy pretty mysteries. The Pope a forger.

But for better view hereof, I remember, cardinal Cusanus, touching the famous donation of Constantine, writeth thus: *In ipsa scriptura reperi manifesta argumenta falsitatis*[10]: "Even in the writing of it I have found manifest tokens of falsehood." The like may be said of these M. Harding's new canons: Even in the utterance and writing of them we may find plain contrariety, and therefore undoubted tokens of untruth. For the former twenty canons, whereof there is no question, were made in the council of Nice; but the rest, whereof St Augustine and the bishops of Africa moved doubt, and whereby the bishop of Rome would seem to claim, were devised at Rome, and not at Nice. This new canon, here alleged, saith: "The bishop of Rome hath the rule and sovereignty over all patriarchs." But the very true and undoubted council of Nice saith far otherwise: *Antiqua consuetudo servetur per Ægyptum, Libyam, et Pentapolim:... ut Alexandrinus episcopus horum omnium habeat potestatem; quia et urbis Romæ episcopo parilis mos est*[11]: "Let the ancient custom be kept throughout Egypt, Libya, and Pentapolis; that the bishop of Alexandria have the government over all these: for the bishop of the city of Rome hath the like order." By this canon the bishop of Rome hath no sovereignty over the[12] other patriarchs, as M. Harding fantasieth, but only a fellowship and equality with the rest, to walk carefully within his own division, as others were bound to do within theirs. And in this canon these two words, *parilis mos*, are specially to be noted, which cannot otherwise be expounded, but only of like manner, order, and authority of jurisdiction. M. Harding's canon saith: "St Peter was master and ruler over all christian princes." And yet is not M. Harding able to prove that, while St Peter lived, there was any one prince christened in the whole world. And if Peter had had power over kings and princes, it is not likely he would have taken up his lodging with Cornelius[13] the poor tanner. In the end he concludeth with a terror: "If any man repine against this statute, accursed be he." Wherein he doth great wrong both to St Augustine, and also to all the bishops of Africa, Numidia, Mauritania, Pentapolis, and Bizancena; who not only repined openly against this canon, but also said it was falsified, and rebuked the pope of pride and ambition for the same. Nicol. Cusan. de Donat. Constan. Concil. Nic. can. 6. Parilis mos Acts x.

To be short, what leadeth M. Harding to say, "The bishop of Rome hath these three-score and ten canons in safe keeping?" Why doth he thus dissemble, and mock the world? Certainly the bishop of Rome himself utterly disclaimeth it, and saith, he hath them not. For thus he writeth touching the same: *Viginti tantum capitula Nicenæ synodi in sancta Romana ecclesia habentur; sed quo neglectu alia defecerint, ambiguum est*[14]: "There are in the church of Rome only twenty canons of the council of Nice. But by what negligence the rest are lost, it is not known." The pope saith, there are but twenty canons extant: M. Harding saith, there are three-score and ten canons. I trow, it is no reason we should believe M. Harding and leave the pope. Dist. 16. Vigint. Steph. Pap.

But Steven the bishop of Rome saith, there were sometime in Rome the full three-score and ten canons; which thing he gathereth only upon this forgery of

[9 Sane præsentibus nobis octoginta capitula in memorata tractata sunt synodo, scilicet quadraginta a Græcis, Græca edita lingua, et quadraginta a Latinis, similiter Latina edita lingua. Sed visum est trecentis decem et octo patribus,...ut decem capitula adunarentur aliis, atque congruis locis insererentur, et ad formam septuaginta discipulorum, vel totius orbis terræ linguarum, septuaginta tanti et tam excellentis concilii fierent capitula.—Epist. Ægypt. ad Marc. in eod. Tom. I. p. 299.]

[10 ... repperi ex ipsamet scriptura argumenta manifesta confictionis et falsitatis.—Nic. de Cusa, Op. Basil. 1565. De Concord. Cathol. Lib. III. cap. ii. Tom. II. p. 781.]

[11 Concil. Nicen. can. 6. in Concil. Stud. Labb. et Cossart. Lut. Par. 1671-2. Tom. II. cols. 32, 40, 1.]

[12 1565 omits *the*.]

[13 Simon.]

[14 Steph. Pap. in Corp. Jur. Canon. Lugd. 1624. Decret. Gratian. Decr. Prim. Pars, Dist. XVI. can. 13. col. 67.]

The Pope a forger.

M. Harding's Athanasius[1]. And the same being the evidence whereby he holdeth his whole title, and such evidence as was not to be found elsewhere in all the world, yet cannot he tell neither how he came by it, nor how long he kept it, nor how he lost it. But a thing is well lost that cannot be avouched and shewed without shame.

Cypr. de Simplicitate Prælator.

M. Harding's Athanasius saith: "Power to bind and loose is given to the holy see of Rome by special privilege above all other[2]." And yet the old catholic fathers could never understand any such special privilege. St Cyprian saith: *Quamvis [Dominus] apostolis omnibus post resurrectionem suam parem potestatem tribuat,... tamen ut unitatem manifestaret, unitatis ejusdem originem ab uno incipientem sua auctoritate disposuit. Hoc erant utique et ceteri apostoli, quod fuit Petrus, pari consortio prœditi et honoris et potestatis*[3]: "The Lord, after his resurrection, gave unto his apostles like power: yet, to declare unity, he disposed by his authority the original of unity, beginning of one. The rest of the apostles were even the same that Peter was, endued with like fellowship, both of honour and of power."

Et honoris, et potestatis.

Orig. in Matt. Tract. i.

Origen saith: *An vero soli Petro dantur a Christo claves regni cœlorum, nec alius beatorum quisquam eas accepturus est? Hoc dictum, Tibi dabo claves regni cœlorum, ceteris quoque est commune*[4]: "What, hath Christ given the keys of the kingdom of heaven unto Peter only? and shall no holy man else receive them? Verily this saying, 'To thee will I give the keys of the kingdom of heaven,' is common also to the rest." St Cyril saith: *Apostolis, et eorum in ecclesiis successoribus, plenam concessit potestatem*[5]: "Christ gave full power unto the apostles, and unto others that succeeded them in the churches." And St Basil saith: *Christus Petrum post se suæ ecclesiæ pastorem constituit, et consequenter omnibus pastoribus et doctoribus eandem tribuit potestatem: cujus signum est, quod omnes ex æquo et ligant, et absolvunt, quemadmodum ille*[6]: "Christ appointed Peter to be pastor of his church after him, and so consequently gave the same power unto all pastors and doctors: a token whereof is this, that all pastors do equally both bind and loose as well as he."

Cyril. in Johan. Lib. iii. cap. xx.

Basil. in Libello de Vita Solitaria, cap. xxiii.

Now, if Christ gave like power to all his apostles—if the rest of the apostles were the same that Peter was, endued all with like honour and like power—if Christ's words were common to all the rest—if all pastors do equally both bind and loose, as well as Peter; what a fable then is this, that M. Harding with his Athanasius hath brought in, that "power to bind and loose is given to the holy see of Rome, by special privilege above all others!"

Now, gentle reader, shortly and simply to lay all the effect hereof before thine eyes; M. Harding's canons were burnt before they were ever made. They were burnt, and yet were they falsified. They were falsified, and yet were they burnt too. This Athanasius informeth Marcus the bishop of Rome of the burning of them, nine years before the fire was made.

The pope is found in manifest forgery, and that by the witness of the patriarchs of Constantinople, and Antioch, and of all the bishops, and the whole council of Africa, St Augustine himself being present.

M. Harding saith, the pope hath the custody of these invisible canons.

The pope himself saith, he hath none of them.

These canons be plain contrary, not only to the old catholic fathers, but also to other canons of the same council.

The bishops in the council of Africa openly mislike the pope's attempt in this behalf, and call it worldly pride and vain ambition.

Such warrant hath M. Harding to advance[7] the state of the see of Rome.

[1 Id. ibid. col. 68, as the canon is quoted by Ivo.]

[2 Others, 1565.]

[3 Cypr. Op. Oxon. 1682. De Unit. Eccles. pp. 107, 8; where the words *post resurrectionem suam* precede the rest.]

[4 Orig. Op. Par. 1733-59. Comm. In Matt. 11. Tom. XII. Tom. III. pp. 524, 5.]

[5 Ποὸς δὲ τούτοις ὅτι καὶ τὸν τῆς εἰς ἡμᾶς διακονίας καρπὸν πλούσιον κομιεῖται παρὰ Θεοῦ τῶν μαθητῶν ὁ χορὸς, καὶ μετ' ἐκείνους οἱ τῶν ἁγίων τοῦ Θεοῦ προεστῶτες ἐκκλησιῶν.—Cyril. Alex. Op. Lut. 1638. Comm. in Joan. Lib. III. cap. iv. Tom. IV. p. 288.]

[6 Basil. Op. Par. 1721-30. Const. Monast. cap. xxii. 5. Tom. II. p. 573.]

[7 Avance, 1565.]

M. HARDING. THE SEVENTH DIVISION.

For further declaration of this matter, it were easy here to allege the council of The Pope a forger.
Can. 4. *Sardica*[8], *the council of Chalcedon*[9], *certain councils of Africa, yea, some*
Can. 9. *councils also holden by heretics, and sundry other; but, such store of authorities commonly known, these may suffice.*

THE BISHOP OF SARISBURY.

These councils are brought forth, all in a mummery, saying nothing. Therefore I might safely pass them over, until they had learned to speak somewhat. Yet, forasmuch as these men think it good policy to huddle up their matters in the dark, it will not be amiss to rip them abroad, and to bring them forth into the light.

In the council of Chalcedon it is decreed thus: *Teneat... et Ægyptus, ut episcopus Alexandriæ omnium habeat potestatem: quoniam et Romano episcopo hæc est consuetudo. Similiter... et qui in Antiochia constitutus est*[10]: "Let Egypt hold this order, that the bishop of Alexandria have the jurisdiction of all things there; for the bishop of Rome holdeth the same order (within his division). So likewise let the bishop of Antioch." By this council every of these patriarchs had his power limited within himself, and none of them to have dominion over other. Concil. Chalc. Actio. xvi.

The fathers in the council of Africa, wherein M. Harding would seem to have some affiance, have decreed thus: *Ne primæ sedis episcopus appelletur princeps sacerdotum, aut summus sacerdos, aut aliquid hujusmodi; sed tantum primæ sedis episcopus*[11]: "That the bishop of the first see be not called the chief of priests, or the highest priest, or by any other like title; but only the bishop of the first see." And again: "If any shall think it good to appeal, let them appeal only to councils to be holden within Africa, or else to the primates of their own provinces. But whosoever shall appeal beyond the seas (that is, to the bishop of Rome), let no man within Africa receive him to his communion[12]." Thus much only for a taste. I think M. Harding will not gather hereof, that the bishop of Rome was called universal bishop, or the head of the universal church. Concil. Aphr. cap. 6. Can. 102.

M. HARDING. THE EIGHTH DIVISION.

[*The* 3. *proof, edicts of emperors,* H. A. 1564.] *The christian princes, that ratified and confirmed with their proclamations and edicts the decrees of the canons concerning the pope's primacy, and gave not to him first that authority, as the adversaries do untruly report, were* (99) *Justinian and Phocas the emperors. The words of Justinian's edict be these:* Sancimus, secundum canonum definitiones, sanctissimum senioris Romæ papam primum esse omnium sacerdotum[14]: "*We ordain, according to the determinations of the canons, that the most holy pope, of the elder Rome, be foremost and chief of all priests.*" *In Authen. De Eccles. Tit.* The ninety-ninth untruth. For[13] Phocas gave this title to the bishop of Rome; but Justinian gave it never.

About three-score and ten years after Justinian, Phocas the emperor, in the time of Bonifacius, to repress the arrogancy of the bishop of Constantinople, as Paulus Diaconus writeth, who vainly, and, as Gregory saith, contrary to our Lord's teachings and the decrees of the canons, and for that wickedly, took upon him the name of the universal or œcumenical bishop, and wrote himself chief of all bishops, made the like decree and ordinance, that the holy see of the Roman and apostolic church should be holden for the head of all churches[15]. *Lib. iv. Hist. Longobardicæ, c. xxxvi.*

[[8] Concil. Sardic. can. 4. in Concil. Stud. Labb. et Cossart. Lut. Par. 1671-2. Tom. II. col. 629.]

[[9] The ninth canon of Chalcedon here referred to does not appear to contain any thing to the point. It directs an appeal to Constantinople, rather than to Rome.—Concil. Calched. can. 9. in eod. Tom. IV. col. 759.]

[[10] Id. Act. XVI. in eod. col. 811. See also Chalced. Concil. Act. XVI. in Crabb. Concil. Col. Agrip. 1551. Tom. I. p. 938.]

[[11] Concil. Afric. cap. 6. in Crabb. Concil. Tom. I. p. 503. See before, page 355.]

[[12] Id. cap. 92. in eod. p. 517. See before, page 355.]

[[13] 1565 omits *for.*]

[[14] Corp. Jur. Civil. Amst. 1663. Auth. Coll. IX. Tit. xiv. Novell. cxxxi. cap. 2. Tom. II. p. 184; where for *canonum* we find *earum: αὐτῶν.*]

[[15] Hic [Phocas] rogante papa Bonifacio statuit sedem Romanæ et apostolicæ ecclesiæ primam esse, cum prius Constantinopolitana se primam omnium ecclesiarum scriberet.—Paul. Diac. De Gest. Langob. Basil. 1532. Lib. IV. cap. xi. p. 401.]

THE BISHOP OF SARISBURY.

Papa.

Theodor. Lib. v. cap. xviii. Sozom. Lib. vii. cap. xxiv. Socrat. Lib. i. cap. xxiv.

Emperors, princes, and others, have been favourably inclined sometime to the parties, in respect of their places; sometime to the places, for the admiration and reverence of the parties. Theodosius the emperor said, "he never saw bishop that bare himself as a bishop indeed, but only St Ambrose[1]." Constantinus the emperor said of Eusebius the bishop of Cæsaria: *Dignus est qui sit episcopus, non tantum unius civitatis, sed etiam prope universi orbis*[2]: "He is worthy to be the bishop, not only of one city, but also in a manner of the whole world."

Authen. de Eccles. Tit. Collat. ix. Ideoque sancimus. Cod. de Sacrosanct. Eccles. Decernimus sacrosanctam. Authen. Collat. ix. de Eccles. Tit.

In respect of places, they were moved either for their antiquity, or for their authority and civil power, or for the commodity of the situation, or for some other good consideration and circumstance, to favour them, and to grant them privileges above others. Thus the emperor Justinian had a special inclination to the city of Constantinople, for that it was now grown in wealth and puissance, and, for the state and nobility thereof, called *nova Roma*[3], "new Rome;" and for that it was, as he saith, *mater pietatis nostræ, et Christianorum orthodoxæ religionis omnium*[4]: that is, "the mother of his majesty, and of all christian men of the catholic faith." For like consideration the emperor gave out this special privilege in favour of the see of Rome: *Sancimus, secundum canonum definitiones, sanctissimum senioris Romæ papam primum esse omnium sacerdotum*[5]: "We decree, according to the determination[6] of the canons, that the most holy pope of the elder Rome be the first or foremost of all priests." And, by the way, lest any error happen to grow of this word *papa*, it behoveth thee, good reader, to understand that *papa*, in old times, in the Greek tongue, signified a father, as appeareth by that Jupiter, the great idol that was honoured as God in Bithynia, was called *papa*, *ὁ ζεὺς, ὁ πάππας*[7], *Jupiter papa*: and further, that in St Augustine's time, and before, the same name was given, not only or specially to the bishop of Rome, but also generally to all bishops. The priests and deacons of Rome write thus unto St Cyprian the bishop of Carthage: *Cypriano papæ*[8]: "Unto pope Cyprian." And Galerius, the judge, having St Cyprian in examination for the christian faith, said thus unto him: *Tu es, quem Christiani papam suum nominant*[9]? "Art thou he, whom the Christians call their pope?" So likewise St Hierome intitleth his epistles unto St Augustine, being bishop of Hippo: *Hieronymus beatissimo papæ Augustino*[10]: "Hierome unto Augustine the most holy pope." Thus much only by the way.

Cœlius Rhodig. Lib. xi. cap. xxi. Jupiter papa.

Cypr. Lib. ii. Epist. 7. Pontius in Passione Cypr.

Inter Epist. August. Epist. 11.

But to return to the matter: M. Harding may not of every thing that he readeth conclude what he listeth. This privilege granted unto the bishop of Rome, to be the first of all priests, was not to bear the whole sway, and to overrule all the world; but only in general meetings and councils to sit in place above all others; and for avoiding of confusion, to direct and order them in their doings. The emperor's words be plain: *Prærogativa in episcoporum concilio, vel extra concilium ante alios residendi*[11]: "A prerogative in the council of bishops, or without the council to sit in order above others." This prerogative in Greek is called *προεδρία*, that is, "the privilege of the first place." And these phrases in that tongue be known and common, *τὰ πρωτεῖα ἔχειν, τὰ δευτερεῖα, τὰ τριτεῖα*, like as also these in the Latin tongue, *obtinere primas, secundas, tertias*; that is, "to have the pre-eminence of the first, second, or third place." And that the emperor Justinian meant only thus, and none otherwise, it is manifest even by the self-

Cod. de Sacrosanct. Eccles. Decernimus.

[[1] Ἀμβρόσιον γὰρ οἶδα μόνον ἐπίσκοπον ἀξίως καλούμενον.—Theodor. in Hist. Eccles. Script. Amst. 1695-1700. Lib. v. cap. xviii. p. 223. See also Sozom. in eod. Lib. VII. cap. xxv. pp. 603, 4.]

[[2] Socr. in eod. Lib. I. cap. xxiv. p. 49.]

[[3] Corp. Jur. Civil. Amst. 1663. Auth. Coll. IX. Tit. xiv. Novell. cxxxi. cap. 2. Tom. II. p. 184.]

[[4] Id. Cod. Lib. I. Tit. ii. 16. Tom. II. p. 8; where *matrem nostræ pietatis*.]

[[5] Id. Auth. Coll. IX. Tit. xiv. Novell. cxxxi. cap. 2. Tom. II. p. 184.]

[[6] Determinations, 1565, 1609.]

[[7] Cœl. Rhodig. Lect. Antiq. 1599. Lib. XI. cap. xxi. col. 515.]

[[8] Cypr. Op. Oxon. 1682. Ad Cypr. Epist. xxx. p. 56.]

[[9] Tu papam te sacrilegæ mentis hominibus præbuisti?—Cypr. Pass. in eod. p. 13.]

[[10] Hieron. ad August. Epist. lxxv. 1. in August. Op. Par. 1679-1700. Tom. II. col. 168; where the words are transposed.]

[[11] Corp. Jur. Civil. Cod. Lib. I. Tit. ii. 16. Tom. II. p. 8.]

same place that M. Harding hath here alleged. His words stand thus: *Sancimus, &c., senioris Romæ papam primum esse omnium sacerdotum: beatissimum autem archiepiscopum Constantinopoleos, novæ Romæ, secundum habere locum*[12]: "We ordain that the pope of the elder Rome shall be the first of all priests; and that the most holy archbishop of Constantinople, which is named new Rome, have the second place." Hereby it is plain that this privilege standeth only in placing the bishop of Rome in the first seat above others. But I beseech thee, gentle reader, weigh well the words that follow in the same law, and thou shalt see, both that M. Harding's dealing herein is not upright, and also that the bishop of Rome was then excluded by plain words from that universal power which he now so deeply dreameth of. It followeth immediately: *Beatissimum archiepiscopum primæ Justinianæ patriæ nostræ habere semper sub sua jurisdictione episcopos provinciarum Daciæ, et Daniæ, et Dardaniæ, et Mysiæ, ... atque Pannoniæ: et ab eo hos ordinari: ipsum vero a proprio ordinari concilio: et in subjectis sibi provinciis locum obtinere eum sedis apostolicæ Romæ*[13]: "We ordain that the most holy archbishop of Justiniana the first, which is in our country, shall have for ever under his jurisdiction the bishops of the provinces of Dacia, Dania, Dardania, Mysia, and Pannonia; and that they shall be invested by him; and he only by his own council; and that he, in the provinces subject unto him, shall have the place of the apostolic see of Rome." Here we see the bishop of Justiniana set in as high authority and power, within his own jurisdiction, as the bishop of Rome within his. In like sort the emperor Justinian saith: *Ecclesia urbis Constantinopolitanæ ... Romæ veteris prærogativa lætatur*[14]: "The church of the city of Constantinople enjoyeth now the prerogative of Rome the elder."

The first Bishop.

τὴν δευτέραν τάξιν.

Cod. de Sacrosanct. Eccles. Omni innovatione.

Now, if the bishop of Justiniana and the bishop of Rome, in their several divisions, have like authority; and if the church of Constantinople in all prerogatives and privileges be made equal with the city of Rome; then is not the bishop of Rome's power universal; neither can he justly be called the head of the universal church. Verily Justinian himself, writing unto Epiphanius the bishop of Constantinople, calleth him "the universal patriarch[15]:" which thing he would not have done, if he had thought that title of right had belonged to the bishop of Rome.

Authen. Ut determinatus sit numerus clericorum.

The argument that M. Harding gathereth of Justinian's words is this: The bishop of Rome had the first place in general councils; *ergo*, he was an universal bishop. Which argument, what weight it beareth, I leave to M. Harding to consider.

ὁ...βασιλεὺς Ἐπιφανίῳ... οἰκουμενικῷ πατριάρχῃ.

But the emperor Phocas gave this special grant to the see of Rome, that the bishop there should be called "the head of all churches." But M. Harding knoweth this grant was made unto Bonifacius the third, which was bishop in Rome in the year of our Lord six hundred and eight, even at the same very time that Mahomet first began to plant his doctrine in Arabia; and therefore maketh nothing to this purpose, as being without the compass of six hundred years. Notwithstanding both Platina[16] and Sabellicus[17] say, that Bonifacius hardly and with much ado got the same then to be granted. Howbeit, forasmuch as M. Harding would seem to found his supremacy upon some godly man, it may please thee, good reader, to understand that this Phocas, being but a soldier, by treason and conspiracy laid hands upon his liege lord and master, the emperor Mauritius, and in cruel sort did him to death. The manner whereof was this: first he commanded forth the emperor's youngest son, and caused him to be slain, even in the sight of his father, and so the second, and then the third, and afterward the wife; Mauritius heavily looking on, and lamenting, and saying unto God: "O Lord, thou art just; and just is thy judgment." Last of all, he used the like tyranny upon him

Anno Dom. 608.

Platina. Sabellicus.

Abbas Ursperg. in Maurit.

[[12] Id. Auth. Coll. IX. Tit. xiv. Novell. cxxxi. cap. 2. Tom. II. p. 184.]

[[13] Id. ibid. cap. 3; where *primæ Justinianæ nostræ patriæ archiepiscopum*, and *Daciæ mediterraneæ et Daciæ Ripensis et Privalis*: Δακίας μεδιτερρανέας καὶ Δακίας ῥιπενσίας, Τριβαλλέας, κ.τ.λ.]

[[14] Id. Cod. Lib. I. Tit. ii. 6. Tom. II. p. 6.]

[[15] Id. Auth. Coll. I. Tit. iii. Novell. iii. Tom. II. p. 6.]

[[16] Bonifacius ... a Phoca imperatore obtinuit, magna tamen contentione, &c.—Plat. De Vit. Pont. Col. 1551. Bonifac. III. p. 75.]

[[17] Estque id ægre, nec sine multa contentione, apostolicæ sedi datum.—Sabell. Rapsod. Hist. Par. 1509. Ennead. VIII. Lib. VI. Pars III. fol. 37, 2.]

also, and laid the emperor, his wife, and his children in a heap together[1]. Afterward, during the time of this Phocas, God seemed utterly to withdraw his blessing: France, Spain, Germany, Lombardy, and the greatest part of the east, fell from the empire for ever—such a wreck to the state as never had been seen before[2]. After that[3] he had thus lived, and committed sundry murders and other great mischiefs (*post multa homicidia et alia malefacta*), the people took him, and slew him, and threw him into the fire[4]. This was he that first proclaimed the bishop of Rome to be head of the universal church.

Carion. in Chronic.

Abbas Ursperg.

M. HARDING. THE NINTH DIVISION.

Of the doctors what shall I say? Verily, this matter is so often and so commonly reported of them, that their sayings laid together would scantly be comprised within a great volume. The recital of a few shall here give a taste, as it were, of the whole, and so suffice.

[*The 4. proof, doctors.* H.A. 1564.]

Irenæus, having much praised the church of Rome, at length uttereth these words, by which the sovereignty thereof is confessed: Ad hanc... ecclesiam propter potentiorem principalitatem necesse est omnem convenire ecclesiam, hoc est, eos qui undique sunt fideles[5]: "*To this church (of Rome) it is necessary all the church, that is to say, all that be faithful any where, to repair and come together, for the mightier principality of the same," that is to wit, for that it is of mightier*[6] *power and authority than other churches, and the principalest of all.*

Lib.iii.cap.iii.

THE BISHOP OF SARISBURY.

Touching the doctors, M. Harding findeth himself much troubled with the number of them: yet can he not find any one of them all that calleth the bishop of Rome the universal bishop, or head of the universal church.

Irenæus speaketh neither of supremacy, nor of headship of the church, nor of any other universal power. Therefore M. Harding mistelleth his author's tale, and avoucheth that he never meant. For Irenæus in that place writeth only against Valentinus, Cerdon, and Marcion, which, contrary to the doctrine of the apostles, had devised sundry strange heresies and fantasies of their own: for trial whereof, he biddeth them to behold the churches which the apostles had planted. "The church of Ephesus," saith he, "first instructed by St Paul, and afterward continued by St John, is a sufficient witness of the apostles' learning. Polycarpus, being converted, and taught by the apostles, instructed the church of Smyrna; and all the churches of Asia follow it. Yet none of all these churches ever allowed or received your strange doctrine[7]." "Yea, the very wild barbarous nations, that have received the faith of Christ at the apostles' hands only by hearing, without any book or letter, if they should hear of these heresies, they would stop their ears[8]." Thus Irenæus calleth forth these heretics, as we do now our adversaries, to be tried by the doctrine and churches of the apostles. But he saith: *Valde longum est in hoc tali volumine omnium ecclesiarum enumerare*

Irenæus, Lib. iii. cap. iii.

Irenæus, Lib. iii. cap. iv.

[1 At Phocas ... imperator efficitur: a quo Mauritius cum uxore ac filiis penes Calcedonem missus decollatur. Verum Mauritius patienter infelicitatem sustinuit, Deum in omnibus invocans, et crebro pronuncians: Justus es, Domine, et rectum judicium tuum.—Chronic. Abbat. Ursperg. Argent. 1537. Hist. Maurit. p. 157. The empress was not put to death at this time.]

[2 Defecerunt jam prorsus ab imperio Gallia, Hispania, Germania et Lombardi: præterea et Persarum rex Cosroa multas regiones et civitates pariter in Oriente occupavit.—Carion. Chronic. Lib. Par. 1543. Lib. III. fol. 82. 2.]

[3 1565 omits *that*.]

[4 Phocas ... cum homicidia ceteraque mala multa fecisset in populo... vulgus... apprehensum interfecit, et in igne apud Taurum cremavit.—Chronic. Abbat. Ursperg. Hist. Phoc. p. 158.]

[5 Iren. Op. Par. 1710. Contr. Hær. Lib. III. cap. iii. 2. pp. 175, 6. See below, note 10.]

[6 Greater, H.A. 1564.]

[7 *Καὶ Πολύκαρπος δὲ οὐ μόνον ὑπὸ ἀποστόλων μαθητευθεὶς ... ἀλλὰ καὶ ὑπὸ ἀποστόλων κατασταθεὶς εἰς τὴν Ἀσίαν, ἐν τῇ ἐν Σμύρνῃ ἐκκλησίᾳ, ἐπίσκοπος ... ταῦτα διδάξας ἀεὶ ... μαρτυροῦσιν τούτοις αἱ κατὰ τὴν Ἀσίαν ἐκκλησίαι πᾶσαι, κ.τ.λ. ἀλλὰ καὶ ἡ ἐν Ἐφέσῳ ἐκκλησία ὑπὸ Παύλου μὲν τεθεμελιωμένη, Ἰωάννου δὲ παραμείναντος αὐτοῖς... μάρτυς ἀληθής ἐστι τῆς ἀποστόλων παραδόσεως.*—Id. ibid. 4. pp. 176-8.]

[8 Hanc fidem qui sine literis crediderunt .... quibus si aliquis annunciaverit ea quæ ab hæreticis adinventa sunt ... statim concludentes aures, longo longius fugient.—Id. ibid. cap. iv. 2. p. 178.]

successiones[9]: "It would be very long in such a book as this is, to reckon up the successions of all churches." Therefore he resteth specially upon the example of the church of Rome, which he calleth *maximam, antiquissimam, et omnibus cognitam*[10], "the greatest, most ancient, and known to all men;" and saith: "By the example of this church we confound all perverse doctrine;" and addeth further: *Ad hanc...ecclesiam, propter potentiorem principalitatem, necesse est omnem ecclesiam convenire, quia in hac semper conservata est ea quæ est ab apostolis traditio*[10]: "Unto this church of Rome every other church must agree." The reason is: "For that in this church the tradition of the apostles hath ever been kept." So the emperors Gratian, Valentinian, and Theodosius commanded all them to be called catholics that follow the faith that St Peter delivered unto[11] the see of Rome[12]. For the apostles' doctrine is the trial and rule of faith. This doctrine at the beginning was exactly observed in Rome without corruption; and therefore was that church in reverence and estimation above others.

Cod. de Sum. Trin. Cunctos Popul. Sozom. Lib. vii. cap. iv.

But they will reply, Irenæus saith, *Propter potentiorem principalitatem.* Of these words groweth their error. They dream of a kingdom and principality. But Christ saith to his disciples: "The kings of nations rule over them:" *vos autem non sic:* "but you may not so." And Origen saith: *Qui vocatur...ad episcopatum, non vocatur ad principatum, sed ad servitutem totius ecclesiæ*[13]: "He that is called to be a bishop is not called to a principality, but unto the service of the whole church." The principality that Irenæus meant was the civil dominion and temporal state of the city of Rome, in which God had then planted the empire of the world, and made all nations subject unto it. And therefore the church of God, being once enkindled there, was more notable and better known unto all nations. As for the bishops of Rome that then were, they had neither lands nor rents, but lived still under the sword in continual persecution; as St Paul saith, "the off-shaving of the world, and the vilest of all people," far from any shew or colour of principality. Yet, that notwithstanding, the church there was called a principal and a chief church above others, because of the dominion and principality of the city. And in this sense *ecclesia principalis* is sometimes used in the old fathers. In the council of Carthage it is written thus: *Placuit ut nemini sit facultas, relicta principali cathedra, ad aliquam ecclesiam in diœcesi constitutam se conferre*[14]: "We think it good it be lawful for no man, leaving the principal chair or church, to go to any other church within the diocese." Likewise Paulinus unto Alypius: *Dominus in suis te civibus principalem cum principibus populi sui sede apostolica merito collocavit*[15]: "The Lord hath worthily placed thee in the see apostolic, a principal one among his citizens, with the princes of his people." Thus the principality, that Irenæus meaneth, stood not in the preaching of the gospel, but in the civil estate and worldly dominion; not in the bishop that professed Christ, but in the emperor that was an heathen; not in the church, but in the persecutors and enemies of the church. Therefore M. Harding, reasoning thus, Rome had the power and princehood of the world; *ergo*, the bishop there was head of the universal church, seemeth not well to weigh his own conclusion. For of the same grounds we might well reason thus: Rome now hath lost that power and princehood of the world; *ergo*, the bishop there is not now the head of the universal church.

Matt. xx. Luke xxii. Orig. in Esai. cap. vi. 1 Tim. iii.

vii. Quæst. 1. Placuit.

Inter Epist. August. Epist. 35.

To be short, if the church of Rome would now faithfully keep the traditions and doctrine of the apostles, we would frankly yield her all that honour that Irenæus giveth her. But she hath shaken off the yoke of Christ, and wilfully

---

[9 Id. ibid. cap. iii. 2. p. 175.]

[10 Id. Lib. III. cap. iii. 2. pp. 175, 6; where *maximæ et antiquissimæ et omnibus cognitæ, potiorem,* and *convenire ecclesiam, hoc est, eos qui sunt undique fideles, in qua semper ab his, qui sunt undique, conservata, &c.*]

[11 To, 1565, 1609.]

[12 Grat. Valent. et Theod. Edict. in Corp. Jur. Civil. Amst. 1663. Cod. Lib. I. Tit. i. 1. Tom. II. p. 1. See before, page 80, note 2. Sozom. in Hist. Eccles. Script. Amst. 1695-1700, Lib. VII. cap. iv. p. 575.]

[13 Orig. Op. Par. 1733-59. In Isai. Hom. vi. 1. Tom. III. p. 116; where *non ad principatum vocatur.*]

[14 Concil. Carthag. v. can. 5. in Corp. Jur. Canon. Lugd. 1624. Decret. Gratian. Decr. Sec. Pars, Caus. VII. Quæst. i. can. 21. col. 830.]

[15 In cujus te civibus, &c.—Paul. et Theras. ad Alyp. Epist. xxiv. 1. in August. Op. Par. 1679-1700. Tom. II. col. 34.]

Primatus.

breaketh God's commandments, to the intent to uphold her own traditions. For proof whereof, to pass over an infinite number of other disorders, the bishop there presumeth now to intitle himself "the universal bishop." But St Gregory saith: *Nemo...decessorum meorum hoc tam profano vocabulo uti consensit*[1]: "None of my predecessors ever consented to use this ungodly name." Therefore like as Irenæus saith of his time, "The church of Rome hath ever hitherto kept the tradition and doctrine of the apostles; *ergo*, all churches ought to take her for an example, and to agree unto her;" so may we in contrariwise say of our time: The church of Rome hath now broken the traditions and doctrine of the apostles; *ergo*, no church ought to follow her example, and to agree unto her.

Gregor. Lib. iv. Epist. 36.

M. HARDING. THE TENTH DIVISION.

Andrew followed our Saviour before that Peter did; et tamen primatum non accepit Andreas, sed Petrus[2]: *"and yet Andrew received not the primacy, but Peter," saith Ambrose.*

In 2 Cor. xi.

THE BISHOP OF SARISBURY.

This error holdeth only of the misunderstanding of this word, *primatus;* which, by M. Harding's judgment, must needs signify an universal power over the whole world. But it is easy to be shewed that *primatus*, among the old fathers, is far otherwise used; I mean, for any superiority or preferment before others. And first, to begin with St Ambrose, thus he writeth: *Esau per lentem honorem primatus amisit*[3]: "Esau by a dish of rice-pottage lost the honour of his primacy." In like sort writeth St Augustine: *Esau primatus suos, non propter gallinam, sed propter lenticulam perdidit*[4]. Likewise the council of Chalcedon, in the condemnation of the heretic abbat Eutyches, useth these words: *Decernimus... eum extraneum esse ab omni officio sacerdotali, et a nostra communione, et a primatu monasterii*[5]: "We decree that he shall be removed from his office of priesthood, and from our communion, and from the primacy of his abbey." So the council of Toledo: *Primatu dignitatis...honorabiles habentur in palatio*[6]: "They are counted honourable in the court for the primacy of their dignity." In these places, I reckon, we need not to take *primatus* for an universal or infinite government.

In Serm. 35. De Jejunio.

August. in Evang. Johan. Tract. lxxiii.

Concil. Chalc. Act. prima.

Concil. Tol. vi. cap. 13.

Likewise the same word *primatus* is often taken for the superiority of every of the four patriarchs, and not only for the dominion that is claimed by the bishop of Rome. In the council of Constantinople it is written thus: "*Alexandriæ...episcopi solius orientis curam gerant, servatis honoribus primatus ecclesiæ Antiochenæ*[7]: "Let the bishops of Alexandria have the charge only of the east, the honour of primacy ever reserved to the church of Antioch." In like manner it is written in the council of Chalcedon: *Episcopus qui in Antiochia constitutus est, et qui in ceteris provinciis, habeant primatus ecclesiæ civitatum ampliorum*[8]: "The bishop that is appointed for Antioch, and likewise others in other provinces, let them have the primacies of the greater cities." So the emperors Theodosius and Valentinian wrote unto Dioscorus the bishop of Alexandria, as it is reported in the council of Chalcedon: *Auctoritatem et primatum tuæ præbemus beatitudini*[9].

Concil. Const. i. can. 2.

Concil. Chalc. Act. xvi.

Concil. Chalc. Act. i.

Now, if this word *primatus* must needs signify that power and government that M. Harding fantasieth, then must it follow of necessity, that Esau, Eutyches,

[1 Gregor. Magni Papæ I. Op. Par. 1705. Epist. Lib. v. Indict. XIII. Ad Eulog. et Anastas. Epist. xliii. Tom. II. col. 771. See before, page 346.]

[2 Ambros. Op. Par. 1686-90. Comm. in Epist. II. ad Cor. cap. xii. v. 11. Tom. II. Append. col. 205.]

[3 Id. Serm. xxvii. 5. Tom. II. col. 429. This is not genuine.]

[4 August. Op. Append. Par. 1679-1700. In Johan. Evang. cap. xiv. Tractat. lxxiii. 1. Tom. III. Pars II. col. 689.]

[5 Concil. Calched. Act. I. in Concil. Stud. Labb. et Cossart. Lut. Par. 1671-2. Tom. IV. col. 229.]

[6 Concil. Tolet. VI. cap. 13. in eod. Tom. V. col. 1746; where *primatum dignitate*, and *in palatio honorabiles*.]

[7 Concil. Constant. I. can. 2. in eod. Tom. II. col. 947; where the primacy of Egypt alone is assigned to the bishop of Alexandria, and of the east to the prelates of the east. See, however, the canon in Crabb. Concil. Col. Agrip. 1551. Edit. i. Tom. I. p. 411; where it stands as Jewel has cited it.]

[8 Concil. Calched. Act. XVI. in Concil. Stud. Labb. et Cossart. Tom. IV. col. 811.]

[9 Imp. Epist. ad Diosc. in eod. Act. I. in eod. col. 109.]

the bishop of Antioch, and the bishop of Alexandria, had the universal power and government of the whole world. But if it may well be taken for any manner preferment, or pre-eminence, or priority before others, then is M. Harding's argument much acrased[10], and concludeth not so much as is pretended. Verily Tertullian saith: *Tot ac tantæ ecclesiæ, una est illa ab apostolis prima, ex qua omnes. Sic omnes primæ, et [omnes] apostolicæ, dum unam omnes probant unitatem*[11]: "So many and so great churches are all that first one church erected by the apostles, from whence came all. And so are all churches both the first, and also the apostolic churches, forasmuch as they all allow one truth." Primatus.

Tertul. de Præscrip. contr. Hæret.

As touching St Peter's pre-eminence, Cyprian saith: *Hoc erant alii, quod ...Petrus, pari consortio præditi et honoris et potestatis*[12]: "The rest of the disciples were even the same that Peter was, all endued with like fellowship, both of honour and also of power." Even so saith St Ambrose too, and that in the very same place that M. Harding hath alleged: *Inter Petrum et Paulum, quis cui præponatur, incertum est*[13]: "Of Peter and Paul, whether ought to be preferred before other, it is not known." Certainly, if Peter had had the universal sovereignty over all the apostles, he should have had the like over St Paul. And so perhaps M. Harding will say, notwithstanding St Ambrose by plain words denieth it; and although St Gregory say: *[Petrus] universalis apostolus non vocatur*[14]: "Peter is not called an universal apostle."

Cypr. de Simplicit. Prælat.

Gregor. Lib. iv. Epist. 32.

Of St Ambrose' words M. Harding reasoneth thus: Peter was the chiefest of the apostles; *ergo*, the pope is head of the universal church. This argument would be better considered; for, as it is, it holdeth but weakly.

M. HARDING. THE ELEVENTH DIVISION.

In the epistle of Athanasius and the bishops of Egypt to Liberius the pope, in which they sue for help against the oppressions of the Arians, we find these words: Hujus rei gratia, universalis vobis a Christo Jesu commissa est ecclesia[15], &c.: "*Even for this cause the universal church hath been committed to you of Christ Jesus, that you should travail for all, and not be negligent to help every one. For whiles the strong man being armed keepeth his house, all things that he possesseth are in peace.*"

This epistle is forged, and not written by Athanasius.

Luc. xi.

THE BISHOP OF SARISBURY.

This epistle under the name of Athanasius, besides that it is vain and childish, and full of needless and idle talk, hath also evident tokens of manifest forgery. For further answer hereunto, I refer myself[16] unto that is before answered unto the epistle written under the name of Athanasius unto Felix.

M. HARDING. THE TWELFTH DIVISION.

De Trinit. Lib. vi. [Matt. xvi. H. A. 1564.]

Hilarius, speaking much to the extolling of Peter and his (100) *successor in that see, saith:* Supereminentem beatæ fidei suæ confessione [locum] promeruit[17]: "*That for the confession of his blessed faith, he deserved a place of pre-eminence* (101) *above all other.*"

The hundredth untruth. For Hilary speaketh not one word of Peter's successor.

The hundred and first untruth, standing in false translation.

THE BISHOP OF SARISBURY.

Hilarius, by M. Harding's report, speaketh much to the extolling of St Peter and his successor in that see. Here is first a great untruth. For Hilarius, in that whole place, speaketh not one word neither of Rome, nor of the see, nor of the successor of Peter. Only he commendeth St Peter's faith, wherein he con-

[10 Acrased: crazed.]

[11 Tertull. Op. Lut. 1641. De Præscr. Hæret. 20. p. 238; where *prima*, and *una*.]

[12 Cypr. Op. Oxon. 1682. De Unit. Eccles. pp. 107, 8. See before, page 360.]

[13 Inter ipsos qui, &c.—Ambros. Op. Par. 1614. Serm. in Fest. SS. Petr. et Paul. Tom. V. col. 142. This is not genuine.]

[14 Gregor. Magni Papæ I. Op. Epist. Lib. v. Indict. XIII. Ad Mauric. August. Epist. xx. Tom. II. col. 748.]

[15 Epist. Ægypt. ad Liber. in Crabb. Concil. Tom. I. p. 353. These epistles of Athanasius are given up as forgeries by Labbe and Cossart.]

[16 Meself, 1565.]

[17 Hilar. Op. Par. 1693. De Trin. Lib. VI. 37, col. 904; where *supereminentem gloriam beatæ*.]

De Trin. Lib. vi. fessed that Christ is the Son of the living God, and saith: "*Hæc fides est fundamentum ecclesiæ: super hanc...confessionis petram ecclesiæ edificatio est*[1]: "This faith is the foundation of the church: upon this rock of confession the church[2] is built." And addeth further: "By the confession of his blessed faith he obtained a place of pre-eminence," as M. Harding addeth of his own, "above all other." Wherein also he committeth another untruth. For Hilarius saith only: "He obtained a special place," and speaketh not one word of any other. St Augustine August. in Johan. Tract. xi. et cxxiv. saith: *Petrus pro omnibus dixit, et cum omnibus accepit*[3]: "Peter spake for all the rest, and received promise with all the rest." As the confession was one, so the place of pre-eminence was all one. The pre-eminence was, that they should be 1 Cor. xv. 1 Cor. iv. Rom. ix. Matt. v. 1 Tim. iii. Luke xxii. Acts vii. Acts vi. Rev. i. Rev. ii. the first-fruits of God's saints, the vessels of election, the fathers of the people, the light of the world, the pillars of the church, and the angels of God; that they should sit upon twelve seats, and judge the twelve tribes of Israel. This was the special pre-eminence of the apostles of Christ, and was equally given unto them all.

But M. Harding cannot believe there is any place of pre-eminence, but only in Rome; and therefore imagineth that upon this confession Christ said unto Peter: "Blessed art thou, Simon Barjona, for thou shalt be pope, and shalt be exalted above thy brethren, and shalt be furnished with all worldly power; and all the princes of the world shall stoop unto thee." This is the pre-eminence that, by M. Harding's fantasy, Christ promised unto St Peter.

Of these words of Hilary M. Harding seemeth to reason thus: Peter obtained a place of pre-eminence; *ergo*, the bishop of Rome is head of the universal church. This argument is open, and sheweth itself.

M. HARDING. THE THIRTEENTH DIVISION.

St Ambrose, confessing himself to believe that the largeness of the Roman empire was by God's providence prepared, that the gospel might have his course, and be spread abroad the better, saith thus of Rome: Quæ tamen per apostolici sacerdotii principatum amplior facta est arce religionis quam solio potestatis[4]: "*Which for all that hath been advanced more by the chiefty of the apostolic priesthood in the tower of religion than in the throne of temporal power.*" *De Vocatione Gentium, Lib. ii. cap. vi.*

THE BISHOP OF SARISBURY.

These words of St Ambrose be true, and not denied, and further no part of M. Harding's purpose. But here is a whole sentence overhipped[5], that quite overthroweth his whole purpose. The words that immediately go before are these: *Quamvis gratia christiana non contenta sit eosdem limites habere, quos Roma, multosque jam populorum sceptro crucis Christi illi subdiderit, quos armis suis ista non domuit*[6]: "Howbeit the grace of Christ is not content to have the same limits that Rome hath; but hath subdued more nations by the sceptre of Christ's cross, than Rome ever subdued by force of war." If the grace and salvation of God have larger limits, and reach further than the power of Rome, how then claimeth the bishop of Rome his universal power? Many that live without the compass or obedience of Rome are notwithstanding partakers of the grace of Extra. de Major. et Obed. Unam sanctam. Christ. How then is it that Bonifacius the bishop there saith, *Subesse Romano pontifici omni humanæ creaturæ declaramus, dicimus, definimus,...pronuntiamus, omnino esse de necessitate salutis*[7]; "We declare, say, determine, and pronounce, that to be subject unto the bishop of Rome is undoubtedly of the necessity of salvation?"

[[1] Id. ibid. 36, 7. cols. 903, 4; where *ecclesiæ fundamentum est.*] [[2] Christ, 1611.]

[[3] Respondit Petrus, petra illa, voce omnium, &c. —August. Op. Par. 1679-1700. In Johan. Evang. cap. iii. Tractat. xi. 5. Tom. III. Pars II. col. 378.

Ecclesia ergo ... claves ... accepit in Petro, &c.—Id. ibid. cap. xxi. Tractat. cxxiv. 5. col. 822. See also ibid. 7. col. 824.]

[[4] Ambros. Op. Par. 1614. De Voc. Gent. Lib. II. cap. vi. Tom. IV. col. 543. This treatise, not being genuine, is not included in the Benedictine edition.]

[[5] Overhipped: passed by, skipped over.]

[[6] Id. ibid.; where *illa* for *illi*.]

[[7] Bonifac. VIII. in Corp. Jur. Canon. Lugd. 1624. Extrav. Comm. Lib. I. De Major. et Obed. cap. i. col. 212.]

St Ambrose, that the glory of the gospel of Christ might the better appear, compareth it with the power and puissance of the empire of Rome, which then overreached a great part of the world. One said: *Romanos rerum dominos.* St Ambrose saith: *Roma principatum et caput obtinet nationum*[8]*:* "Rome hath the empire and sovereignty of all nations." Thus he seemeth to compare the church with the city; the power of the gospel with the power of the empire; the sceptre of the cross with the sceptres of the prince; and the glory of the one side with the glory of the other. Although Rome were glorious for the empire, yet was she much more glorious for the gospel. The emperor there with his power subdued nations; but the gospel of Christ subdued the emperor. Constantinus, Theodosius, Valentinianus, and other emperors of Rome, with all their power, confessed themselves to be subjects unto Christ. And St Ambrose writeth unto Valentinian the emperor: *Quid...honorificentius, quam ut imperator dicatur filius ecclesiæ*[9]*?* "What can be more honourable, than that the emperor be called a child of the church?" This was the whole and only meaning of St Ambrose. And in that sense St Augustine saith: *Ostendatur mihi Romæ in honore tanto templum Romuli, in quanto [ego] ibi ostendo memoriam Petri. In Petro quis honoratur, nisi ille defunctus pro nobis? Sumus enim Christiani, non Petriani*[10]*:* "Shew me the temple of Romulus in Rome, in so great honour as I will shew you there the memory of Peter. And who is honoured in Peter, but he that died for us? For we are christian men, and not Peter's men." So likewise Chrysostom: *Contigit primum Antiochiæ discipulos appellari Christianos. Hoc autem civitatum quæ sunt in mundo cunctarum habet nulla, nec ipsa Romuli civitas*[11]*:* "It chanced that the disciples in this city of Antioch were first called Christians. Of all the cities that be in the world, none ever had this gift, no, not the city of Romulus." Therefore St Ambrose's meaning is, that Rome was never so noble before for the empire of the world, as it was afterward for the gospel of Christ. But St Ambrose saith, *Apostolici sacerdotii principatum:* "The principality of the apostolic priesthood." With which words worldly eyes may soon be dazzled. But M. Harding knoweth that St Peter being in Rome had no manner shew or state of princehood. His whole power was spiritual, and stood only in the preaching of the gospel, with which armour God is able to pull down kings and princes to the obedience of his Christ. Thus saith God unto Hieremy: *Constitui te super gentes et regna:* "I have set thee over nations and kingdoms." And St Peter, speaking generally unto all christian people, saith: *Vos estis regale sacerdotium:* "You are that kingly priesthood." This principality and tower of religion was not only in Rome, but also in every place where the name of Christ was received. Albeit I grant, both for the multitude of idols that there had been honoured, and also for the nobility of the empire, the victory of Christ in Rome appeared most glorious.

Ambros. in Serm. 66. | Ambros. Epist. 32. | August. in Psal. xliv. | Ad Populum Antioch. Hom. 17. | 2 Cor. x. | Jer. i. | 1 Pet. ii.

Now let us consider M. Harding's reasoning: The state of Rome was more famous for the gospel than ever it had been before for the empire; *ergo*, the pope was called the head of the universal church. This argument is such as needeth no answer.

M. HARDING. THE FOURTEENTH DIVISION.

Lib. i. contra 2. Epistolas Pelagianorum.

St Augustine, in his 162nd epistle, saith: In ecclesia Romana semper apostolicæ cathedræ viguit principatus[12]: "*The primacy or principality of the apostolic chair hath evermore been in force in the Roman church." The same St Augustine, speaking to Bonifacius bishop of Rome: "This care," saith he, complaining of the Pelagians, "is common to us all that have the office of a bishop, albeit therein thou thyself hast the pre-eminence over*

Ad Bonifacium, cap. i.

Quamvis ipse in eo præemineas celsiore fastigio speculæ pastoralis.

[8 In urbe Roma, quæ, &c.—Ambros. Op. Par. 1614. Serm. in Fest. SS. Petr. et Paul. Tom. V. col. 142.]

[9 Id. Op. Par. 1686-90. Serm. contr. Auxent. de Basil. Trad. 36. Tom. II. col. 873; where *ecclesiæ filius esse dicatur.*]

[10 August. Op. Enarr. in Psalm. xliv. 23. Tom. IV. col. 394.]

[11 Chrysost. Op. Par. 1718-38. Ad Pop. Ant. Hom. xvii. Tom. II. p. 176.]

[12 August. Op. Ad Glor. et cet. Epist. xliii. 7. Tom. II. col. 91. See below, page 371, note 15.]

The hundred and second untruth, standing in the false translation and corruption of St Augustine's words.

all, being on the top of the pastoral watch-tower[1]." *In another place he hath these words:* Ceterum magis vereri debeo, ne in Petrum contumeliosus existam. Quis enim nescit, illum apostolatus principatum cuilibet episcopatui præferendum[2]? "*But I ought rather to be afraid, lest I be reproachful toward Peter. For who is he that knoweth not that that principality of apostleship is to be preferred before any bishopric that is?*" *Another most evident place he hath in his book* De Utilitate Credendi ad Honoratum: Cum tamen[3] auxilium Dei, &c.[4]: "*Whereas,*" *saith he,* "*we see so great help of God, so great profit and fruit, shall we stand in doubt whether we may hide ourselves in the lap of that church, which (though heretics bark at it in vain round about, condemned partly by the judgment of the people themselves, partly by the sadness of councils, and partly by the majesty of miracles even to the confession of mankind,) for*[5] *the apostolic see, by successions of bishops, hath obtained the top or highest degree of authority? To which church if we will not give and grant the primacy, soothly it is a point either of most high wickedness, or of headlong arrogancy.*"

Lib. ii. de Baptismo contra Donatistas, cap. xvii.

Culmen auctoritatis obtinuit. Cui primas dare nolle, vel summæ profecto impietatis est, vel præcipitis arrogantiæ.

THE BISHOP OF SARISBURY.

These places of St Augustine may soon be answered. For here is neither universal bishop, nor head of the universal church, nor superiority or dominion over all others, nor any other word tending to that end. M. Harding knoweth that St Augustine was present at the council of Carthage, and gave his consent, that "the bishop of the first see should not be called neither the prince or chief of priests, nor the highest priest, nor by any other like title[6]."

Concil. Carth. iii. cap. 26.

He knoweth also that St Augustine afterward confirmed the same in a council holden at Hippo Regius in his own diocese[7]. Likewise he knoweth that the same St Augustine decreed among other bishops, to the number of two hundred and seventeen, in the council of Africa, that it should not be lawful for any man of those countries to seek for aid over the seas, and to appeal to the bishop of Rome; and that whosoever so appealed should stand excommunicate[8]; and so utterly condemned that infinite dominion, and universal power, that so many have sithence dreamed of. Again, writing upon the gospel of St John, he saith: *Petrus erat oculus in capite*[9]: "Peter was an eye in the head." He saith not, Peter was the head. In these words appeareth plainly St Augustine's certain and undoubted judgment touching this matter. The rest that is here brought in standeth only upon M. Harding's gathering.

Concil. Hipp. cap. 27.

Concil. Aphr. cap. 92.

August. in Johan. Tract. xiii.

It is true that as well St Augustine, as also other godly fathers, rightly and well in old times yielded great reverence to the see of Rome, both for the antiquity of the church, and for the honour and memory of St Peter, and for the constancy of the holy martyrs that there had suffered, and also for the purity of religion, which was preserved there a long time without spot, and might be a standard unto others. But the greatest increase of outward estimation in the world unto that see was the imperial seat and presence of the prince, as notably appeareth by the first council of Constantinople[10]. For these causes St Augustine saith: "The see of Rome had the highest place and chief pre-eminence above others."

Concil. Const. i. cap. 5. Dist. 22. Constantinopolitanæ.

[[1] Id. Contr. Du. Epist. Pelag. Lib. I. cap. i. 2. Tom. X. col. 412. See below, page 371, note 18.]

[[2] Id. De Bapt. contr. Donatist. Lib. II. 2. Tom. IX. cols. 96, 7.]

[[3] Tantum, H. A. 1564.]

[[4] Cum igitur tantum auxilium Dei, tantum profectum fructumque videamus, dubitabimus nos ejus ecclesiæ condere gremio, quæ usque ad confessionem generis humani ab apostolica sede per successiones episcoporum, frustra hæreticis circumlatrantibus, et partim plebis ipsius judicio, partim conciliorum gravitate, partim etiam miraculorum majestate damnatis, culmen, &c.? Cui nolle primas dare, vel &c.—Id. Lib. de Util. Credend. cap. xvii. 35. Tom. VIII. col. 69.]

[[5] From, H. A. 1564.]

[[6] Concil. Carthag. III. cap. 26. in Crabb. Concil. Col. Agrip. 1551. Tom. I. p. 428. See before, page 355.]

[[7] Concil. Hippon. Abbrev. cap. 27. in eod. Tom. I. p. 434.]

[[8] Concil. Afric. cap. 92. in eod. Tom. I. p. 517. See before, page 355.]

[[9] Petrus in corpore oculus est.—August. Op. Par. 1679-1700. In Johan. Evang. cap. iii. Tractat. xiv. 17. Tom. III. Pars II. col. 399.]

[[10] Constantinopolitanæ civitatis episcopum habere oportet primatus honorem post Romanum episcopum, propterea quod sit nova Roma.—Concil. Constant. I. cap. 5. in Corp. Jur. Canon. Lugd. 1624. Decret. Gratian. Decr. Prim. Pars, Dist. xxii. can. 3. col. 102.]

Perhaps M. Harding will press me further with this word *principatus*, which he expoundeth "the principality." Howbeit, I believe he will not say *principatus* signifieth an universal power or supreme government; and so his advantage of this word is not so great. Verily *princeps*, in the Latin tongue, is often used for a man that for his virtue or room, or any singular quality, is to be had in estimation above others. So Cicero saith: *Socrates princeps philosophorum: Gravitate dicendi princeps Plato: Princeps orbis terrarum Pompeius.* Like as also Chrysostom saith: *Caput prophetarum Elias*[11]: "Elias the head of the prophets." In these places *princeps* is taken, not for a prince or governor, but only for a man that for his qualities is to be esteemed above the rest. And in this sense St Augustine calleth the see of Rome, as it was in his time, *principatus*[12] *sedis apostolicæ*, and not in respect of any supreme government; for that he himself in the council of Africa, as it is already proved, utterly denied him. I grant, as St Augustine saith, the bishop of Rome truly and diligently doing the part of a bishop, he, that then would have denied him the chief pre-eminence for the respects above touched, had been wicked or arrogant. But the same bishop of Rome now claiming to himself the title of universal bishop, as St Gregory saith, "is the forerunner of antichrist[13];" and the consenting to the same, as the same Gregory saith, "is the renouncing and forsaking of the faith[14]."

De Natura Deorum. De Oratore. Pro Domo sua. Chrysost. ad Rom. Hom. 18.

Gregor. Lib. vi. Epist. 30. et Lib. iv. Epist. 39.

I could further say, that M. Harding in these authorities of St Augustine hath left out and transposed what he thought good; and so hath shewed no simple dealing. In the first place, St Augustine's words be these: *Episcopus videbat se Romanæ ecclesiæ, in qua semper apostolicæ cathedræ viguit principatus,... per communicatorias literas esse conjunctum*[15]: "He saw himself by letters of conference to be joined with the church of Rome, in which church the chief pre-eminence of the apostolic see had ever flourished." St Augustine saith, the bishop there was joined with the church of Rome, not by way of obedience or subjection, but by letters of conference; wherein is implied an equality or a fellowship. And afterward in the same epistle St Augustine saith that Meltiades the bishop of Rome, with certain other bishops, heard the matter between Cæcilianus and Donatus a Casis Nigris[16], not by any his universal or supreme power, as M. Harding imagineth, but by special commission from the emperor[17]. And so was the bishop of Rome the emperor's delegate; and that, not in any sovereign authority, but fellow-like, and equally joined with other bishops; and that afterward the same cause, upon complaint and misliking of Donatus, was by the emperor taken out of the bishop of Rome's hands, and by a new commission was put over to the hearing of the bishop of Arle in France[18]. But where was then the bishop of Rome's supreme government?

August. Epist. 162.

In the second place, M. Harding hath notably falsified both St Augustine's words in the Latin, and also his own translation in the English. St Augustine's words be these: *Communis est nobis omnibus, qui fungimur episcopatus officio, quamvis ipse in eo præemineas celsiore fastigio, specula pastoralis*[19]. Which words M. Harding by wilful depravation hath altered thus: *Celsiore fastigio speculæ pastoralis*; and so hath left the adjective *communis* without a substantive, and the principal verb, *est*, without a nominative case; and, to serve his turn, hath caused St Augustine to speak false Latin. This place of St Augustine may be Englished thus: "The pastoral watch-tower is common to us all that bear the office of

August. Lib. i. contra Epist. Pelag. cap. i.

[11 Chrysost. Op. Par. 1718-38. In Epist. ad Rom. Hom. xviii. Tom. IX. p. 636.]

[12 Principatum, 1565.]

[13 Gregor. Magni Papæ I. Op. Par. 1705. Epist. Lib. VII. Indict. XV. Ad Mauric. August. Epist. xxxiii. Tom. II. col. 881.]

[14 Id. Lib. V. Indict. XIII. Ad Sabin. Diac. Epist. xix. col. 747.]

[15 August. Op. Ad Glor. et cet. Epist. xliii. 7. Tom. II. col. 91; where *cum se videret et Romanæ*, &c.]

[16 He was bishop of Casæ Nigræ.]

[17 ... judicante Melchiade tunc Romanæ urbis episcopo cum collegis suis, quos ad preces Donatistarum miserat imperator.—Id. ibid. 4. col. 90. This passage however, it will be seen, precedes that previously cited.]

[18 ... post apud Arelatum memoratum imperatorem eandem caussam diligentius examinandam terminandamque curasse.—Id. ibid. The Benedictine editors attach the following note to the passage: In concilio I. Arelatensi, anno 314.]

[19 Id. Contr. Du. Epist. Pelag. Lib. I. cap. i. 2. Tom. X. col. 412; where *communisque sit omnibus nobis*, and *in ea*. It appears by a note that some editions exhibit Harding's reading.]

bishops: albeit thy pre-eminence is greater, as sitting in the higher room." M. Harding's translation is thus: "Thou thyself hast the pre-eminence over all, being in the top of the pastoral tower." Wherein these words, "over all," are not found in St Augustine, but only devised at pleasure by M. Harding. In the third place, besides other corruption, he dissembleth the words that St Augustine in the very same place allegeth out of St Cyprian, very well serving to this purpose. The words be these: *Nec Petrus....vendicavit sibi aliquid...aut arroganter assumpsit, ut diceret se primatum tenere, et obtemperari [sibi] a novellis et posteris...potius debere*[1]: "Neither did Peter challenge any thing, or proudly presume of himself to say that he had the primacy, and that therefore others as novices and underlings should be obedient unto him." All these things M. Harding dissembleth; and so, to furnish out his matter, and to smoothe his reader, he leaveth out what he listeth.

De Baptis. contr. Donat. Lib. ii. cap. i. Cypr. ad Quirinum.

M. HARDING. THE FIFTEENTH DIVISION.

The notable saying of St Hierome may not be let pass: Ecclesiæ salus a summi sacerdotis dignitate pendet; cui si non exsors quædam et ab omnibus eminens detur potestas, tot in ecclesiis efficiuntur[2] schismata, quot sacerdotes[3]: "*The safety of the church hangeth of the worship of the high priest* (103) (*he meaneth the pope, Peter's successor*), *to whom if there be not given a power peerless, and surmounting all others in the churches, we shall have so many schisms as there be priests.*"

Contra Luciferianos.

The hundred and third untruth. For[4] St Hierome meaneth not the pope, but any other several bishop.

THE BISHOP OF SARISBURY.

This place of St Hierome is notably well noted. But if it might have pleased M. Harding to note but the two lines that went before, he should soon have seen that this note was not worth the noting. For it is certain that St Hierome there speaketh generally of all bishops, and not one word specially of the bishop of Rome. He entreateth there of the order of confirmation, which, he saith, by the usage of the church, for quietness and unity, in many places was ministered only by the bishop, and not by any other priest, and that, he saith, *ad honorem magis sacerdotii, quam ad necessitatem legis*[5], "more for the honour of the state of bishops, than for the necessity of the law." And this, as I said, he speaketh generally of all bishops. Immediately after he addeth these words that M. Harding here allegeth: *Ecclesiæ salus, &c.*: "The safety of the church hangeth of the dignity of the high priest." Herein St Hierome agreeth thoroughly with St Cyprian, that is, "that, for avoiding of sects and schisms, one high priest, that is to say, one bishop, was by good policy appointed in every diocese[6], to whose doings and doctrine the rest of the clergy should conform themselves." And by this order the unity of the church was well preserved. St Cyprian saith: *Ecclesia... cohærentium sibi invicem sacerdotum glutino copulatur*[7]: "The church is joined together by the consent of bishops agreeing in one." So saith St Hierome: *Singuli ecclesiarum episcopi, singuli archiepiscopi, singuli archidiaconi, et omnis ordo ecclesiasticus suis rectoribus nititur*[8]: "There be several bishops of churches, several archbishops, and several archdeacons; and all the ecclesiastical order is stayed by the governors." And the gloss thereupon saith thus: *Hieronymus probat hic,...plures prælatos non debere esse in una ecclesia; sed singulos... debere esse in singulis ecclesiis*[9]: "St Hierome here proveth that there may not be two

Cypr. Lib. iv. Epist. 9.

Hieron. ad Nepotian. vii. Quæst. 1. In apibus.

[1 Id. De Bapt. contr. Donatist. Lib. II. 2. Tom. IX. col. 96. Cypr. Op. Oxon. 1682. Ad Quint. Epist. lxxi. pp. 194, 5; in both which places we find *oportere.*]

[2 Efficientur, 1565, and H. A. 1564.]

[3 Hieron. Op. Par 1693-1706. Adv. Lucifer. Tom. IV. Pars II. col. 295; where *in summi,* and *efficientur.*]

[4 1565 omits *for.*]

[5 Id. ibid.; where *potius* for *magis,* and *ad legem necessitatis.*]

[6 Division, 1565, 1609.]

[7 Cypr. Op. ad Florent. Pup. Epist. lxvi. p. 168. See before, page 349, note 8.]

[8 Hieron. in Corp. Jur. Canon. Lugd. 1624. Decret. Gratian. Decr. Sec. Pars, Caus. VII. Quæst. i. can. 41. col. 837; where we find *archipresbyteri.* Op. Ad Rust. Mon. Epist. xcv. Tom. IV. Pars II. col. 775.]

[9 Gloss. in eod. ibid.; where *eadem,* and *singuli ... debent esse.*]

or more bishops in one church; but that a several bishop must be in every several church." To the like purpose St Hierome writeth upon the epistle unto Titus: *Hæc propterea, ut ostenderemus, apud veteres eosdem fuisse presbyteros, quos et episcopos; paulatim vero, ut dissensionum plantaria evellerentur, ad unum omnem sollicitudinem esse delatam*[10]: "These things have I spoken, to the intent to shew that in old time priests and bishops were all one; and that in process, and by degrees, the whole charge was brought unto one man (he meaneth within one diocese), that the occasions of dissension might be rooted out." And therefore, as it is before declared, St Cyprian saith: "Hereof spring schisms, for that the priest of the Lord is not obeyed[11]." And therefore also saith St Hierome: "Unless the bishop have a special power above others, there will be as many schisms in the church as there be priests[12]." But all these things, thus uttered generally of all bishops, M. Harding wresteth and forceth only unto one bishop; and thus, that is general he maketh special, and that is special he maketh general, at his pleasure; and, as before he misreported St Cyprian, even so doth he now likewise misreport St Hierome, and so shoreth up a ruinous matter with the falsification of his doctors.

Hieron. ad Titum, cap. i.

Cypr. Lib. i. Epist. 3.

Hieron. contra Luciferian.

But M. Harding will say, St Hierome useth these special words, *summus sacerdos*, "the highest priest;" which cannot otherwise be taken, but only of the pope. And therefore he gave this note with a special parenthesis: ("He meaneth the pope, Peter's successor.") Yet M. Harding knoweth there is no such necessity wherefore these words should be so[13] taken. His own Amphilochius calleth St Basil *summus sacerdos*[14]; and yet he knoweth St Basil was never bishop of Rome. Every bishop within his own diocese may be called the highest priest, in respect of other priests that live under him. And in this sense Lactantius seemeth to call every bishopric *maximum sacerdotium*[15].

Amphilochius.

Lact. Lib. iv. cap. xxx.

As for the bishop of Rome, St Hierome advanceth[16] him not so high as M. Harding would seem, but rather maketh him equal and level with all other bishops. For thus he writeth unto Evagrius: *Si auctoritas quæritur, orbis major est urbe. Ubicunque fuerit episcopus, sive Romæ, sive Eugubii, sive Constantinopoli, sive Rhegii, &c., ejusdem [est] meriti, ejusdem...sacerdotii*[17]: "If we seek for authority, the world is greater than the city of Rome. Wheresoever there is a bishop, whether he be at Rome, or at Eugubium, or at Constantinople, or at Rhegium, &c., he is of like worthiness, and of like priesthood."

Hieron. ad Evag.

Here St Hierome specially and by name reckoneth the bishop of Rome among others, and maketh him equal to[18] the rest. And again he saith: *Quid mihi profers unius urbis consuetudinem*[17]? "What shewest thou me the order or manner of one city?" So much St Hierome seemeth to set by the see of Rome. And to this end St Cyprian saith: *Hoc erant...ceteri apostoli, quod fuit Petrus, pari consortio præditi et honoris et potestatis*[19]: "The rest of the apostles were the same that Peter was, all endued with like fellowship, both of honour, and also of power." And so St Cyprian calleth Cornelius bishop of Rome "his brother[20];" and Cyrillus calleth Cœlestinus, likewise bishop of Rome, "his fellow-servant[21]." And therefore when I hear M. Harding, by his strange interpretation, give unto the bishop of Rome "a power peerless, and surmounting all others," methinketh I hear doctor Durandus say: *Hic est Melchisedech, cujus sacerdotium non est ceteris comparatum:... [ille] est caput omnium pontificum, a quo illi, tanquam a capite membra, descendunt, et de cujus plenitudine omnes accipiunt*[22]: "This is Melchise-

Cypr. de Simplicit. Prælat.

Cypr. Lib. i. Epist. 3.

Cyril. in Epist. ad Cœlest.

Durand. Lib. ii.

[10 Hieron. Op. Comm. in Epist. ad Tit. cap. I. Tom. IV. Pars I. col. 413.]

[11 Cypr. Op. Ad Cornel. Epist. lix. p. 129. See before, page 347, note 13.]

[12 See before, page 372, note 3.]

[13 So be, 1565.]

[14 Βασίλειος, ὁ πάνσοφος ἀρχιερεύς ... μέγας ἱεράρχης Βασίλειος.—Amphiloch. Op. Par. 1644. In Vit. S. Basil. pp. 156, 224. See also p. 225.]

[15 Sed ii quorum fides fuit lubrica ... augendis opibus et honori studentes, affectabant maximum sacerdotium.—Lactant. Op. Lut. Par. 1748. Div. Inst. Lib. IV. cap. xxx. Tom. I. p. 353.]

[16 Avanceth, 1565.]

[17 Hieron. Op. Ad Evang. Epist. ci. Tom. IV. Pars II. col. 803.]

[18 Unto, 1565.]

[19 Cypr. Op. De Unit. Eccles. pp. 107, 8. See before, page 360.]

[20 Id. ad Cornel. Epist. lix. p. 126.]

[21 ... οὐδὲν ὅλως οὔτε πρὸς τὴν σὴν θεοσέβειαν γέγραφα ... οὔτε μὴν πρὸς ἕτερον τῶν συλλειτουργῶν.—Cyril. Alex. Op. Lut. 1638. Ad Cœlest. Epist. Tom. V. Pars II. p. 36.]

[22 Durand. Rat. Div. Offic. Lugd. 1565. Lib. II. cap. i. 17. fol. 46; where *caput est*.]

dech, whose priesthood is not comparable unto others. He is the head of all bishops, from whom all they grow, as members grow from the head, and of whose fulness all they receive." Methinketh I hear that is written by the canonists: **Dominus Deus noster papa*[1]: "Our Lord God the pope." And whereas he further saith, the safety of the church hangeth of the high priest, whom he supposeth to be the bishop of Rome, verily St Gregory saith: *Quando is, qui appellatur universalis, cadet, universa ecclesia a statu suo corruit*[2]: "Whensoever he that is called the universal bishop falleth, the whole church from her state must needs fall to the ground."

*Extravag. Johan. xxii. Cum inter. In Glossa. Impr. Lugd. anno 1556. et antea Lugd. anno 1513.

Gregor. Lib. iv. Epist. 76.

M. HARDING. THE SIXTEENTH DIVISION.

There is an epistle of Theodoretus bishop of Cyrus extant in Greek, written to Leo bishop of Rome, wherein we find a worthy witness of the primacy of the see apostolic. His words may thus be Englished: "If Paul," saith he, "the preacher of the[3] *truth, and trumpet of the Holy Ghost, ran to Peter to bring from him a determination and declaration for them who at Antioch were in argument and contention concerning living after Moses' law; much more we, who are but small and vile, shall run unto your throne apostolic, that of you we may have salve for the sores of the churches." There follow these words:* Διὰ πάντα γὰρ ὑμῖν τὸ πρωτεύειν ἁρμόττει: id est, Per omnia enim vobis convenit primas tenere. *That is to say: "For in all things (pertaining to faith or religion, so he meaneth) it is meet that you have the chief doings, or that you have the primacy. For your high seat or throne is endued with many prerogatives and privileges*[4]*."*

πολλοῖς γὰρ ὁ ὑμέτερος θρόνος κοσμεῖται πλεονεκτήμασι.

THE BISHOP OF SARISBURY.

Here might I say, that this Theodoret was a deadly enemy of St Cyrillus, and a Nestorian heretic, and condemned by that name in the general council of Constantinople, as appeareth by Evagrius[5], Nicephorus[6], and others. Verily, although he were brought into the council of Chalcedon by the authority and favour of the emperor Martianus, yet the bishops of Illyricum, Egypt, and Palestine, cried out against him: *Fides perit: Istum canones ejiciunt: Mitte hunc foras, magistrum Nestorii: Nolite istum dicere episcopum: Non est episcopus: Impugnatorem Dei foras mitte: Hæreticum foras mitte: Judæum foras mitte*[7]: "The faith is lost: This man the canons throw out: Out with this fellow: Out with Nestorius' schoolmaster: Call him not bishop: He is no bishop: Out with him that fighteth against God: Out with this heretic: Out with this Jew."

Concil. Const. Act. v. Evag. Lib. iv. cap. xxxviii. Niceph. Lib. xvii. cap. xxvii.

Concil. Chalc. Act. i.

But I will not use this advantage. I judge rather that this Theodoretus, as he was a man of deep learning and great renown, so he was also a careful and godly bishop. As for the Nestorian heresy, he defied it in the council of Constantinople, and openly pronounced: *Anathema Nestorio*[8]: "Accursed be Nestorius."

Concil. Const. Act. viii.

In these words that M. Harding hath here alleged, he saith nothing that of our part is denied. Certainly here is not one word, neither of the head of the church, nor of universal bishop.

But if Theodoretus think St Paul went up to Hierusalem, either to visit Peter as the head of the church, as M. Harding seemeth to guess, or else to be better resolved of his doctrine, as standing in some doubt whether he had thitherto

[1 Extrav. Joan. XXII. ad calc. Sext. Decretal. Par. 1585. Tit. xiv. Gloss. in cap. 4. col. 153. See before, page 96, note 4.]

[2 Universa ergo ecclesia ... a statu suo corruit, quando is, &c. — Gregor. Magni Papæ I. Op. Par. 1705. Epist. Lib. v. Indict. XIII. Ad Mauric. August. Epist. xx. Tom. II. col. 749.]

[3 H. A. 1564, omits *the*.]

[4 Εἰ Παῦλος τῆς ἀληθείας ὁ κήρυξ, ἡ τοῦ ἁγίου Πνεύματος σάλπιγξ, πρὸς τὸν μέγαν ἔδραμε Πέτρον, ὥστε τοῖς ἐν Ἀντιοχείᾳ περὶ τῆς κατὰ νόμον πολιτείας ἀμφισβητοῦσι παρ' αὐτοῦ κομίσαι τὴν λύσιν, πολλῷ μᾶλλον ἡμεῖς οἱ εὐτελεῖς καὶ σμικροὶ, πρὸς τὸν ἀποστολικὸν ὑμῶν τρέχομεν θρόνον, ὥστε παρ' ὑμῶν λαβεῖν τοῖς τῶν ἐκκλησιῶν ἕλκεσι θεραπείαν. διὰ κ. τ. λ.—Theodor. Op. Lut. Par. 1642-84. Ad Leon. Epist. cxiii. Tom. III. p. 984.]

[5 Evagr. Scholast. in Hist. Eccles. Script. Amst. 1695-1700. Lib. IV. cap. xxxviii. pp. 412, &c.]

[6 Niceph. Call. Hist. Eccles. Lut. Par. 1630. Lib. XVII. cap. xxvii. Tom. II. p. 776.]

[7 Concil. Calched. Act. I. in Concil. Stud. Labb. et Cossart. Lut. Par. 1671-2. Tom. IV. cols. 101, 4.]

[8 Id. Act. VIII. in eod. col. 622. The council of Chalcedon seems to be that intended by the author.]

preached the truth or no; then doth he quite overthrow St Paul's whole meaning. For it is plain that St Paul knoweth not Peter for his head, but, contrariwise, taketh him as his equal. For thus he saith: *Videbant mihi concreditum esse evangelium præputii, sicut Petro circumcisionis:* "They saw that I was put in trust with the gospel over the heathens, even as Peter was over the Jews." And again: "James, Peter, and John, that seemed to be the pillars, gave unto me and Barnabas the right hands of fellowship." Here we see between Peter and Paul a covenant of equality, and neither superiority nor subjection. Gal. ii. Dextras dederunt societatis.

And therefore St Ambrose saith, as it is before noted: *Inter Petrum et Paulum, quis cui præponatur, incertum est*[9]*:* "Between Peter and Paul, whether ought to be preferred before other, I cannot tell." Ambros. Serm. 66.

Neither went he up to be better informed of the truth, as being doubtful of his own doctrine. All his reasoning, and the whole drift of that epistle, is to the contrary. For thus lie his words: "I never conferred with flesh and blood (that is to say, with any man), neither did I return to Hierusalem to them that had been apostles before me." "I received not the gospel that I have preached of any man, but by the revelation of Jesus Christ." "If any preach unto you any other gospel than that I have preached, accursed be he." "They that were in chief regard among the apostles,... touching the truth of the gospel, added nothing unto me." "I withstood Peter, even in the face, and spake unto him before all the people; for he walked not uprightly, but was worthy to be blamed." Hereby it may sufficiently appear, that St Paul's going to Hierusalem was not to bring from Peter a determination of any matter of truth that lay in question, as it is here supposed. And therefore St Hierome saith: *Ad hoc ivit Hierosolymam, ut videret apostolum (Petrum) non discendi studio, qui et ipse eundem prædicationis haberet auctorem; sed honoris priori apostolo deferendi*[10]*:* "Paul went to Hierusalem, to the intent to see Peter the apostle, not to learn any thing of him, as having the same author of his preaching that Peter had, but to shew reverence unto him that had been apostle before him." And again: *Propterea quindecim ponit dies, ut ostendat non fuisse grande tempus, quo potuerit aliquid a Petro discere: ut ad illum sensum, a quo cœpit, cuncta referantur, se non ab homine doctum esse, sed a Deo*[11]*:* "Therefore he nameth fifteen days, to shew that he had no long time that he might learn any thing of Peter; to the intent to drive all his words to that sense wherewith he began, that he was taught not by man, but by God." Likewise saith Hugo Cardinalis, a barbarous writer: *Secundum literam instruimur de mutua dilectione, quam deberent habere prædicatores et doctores; quia Paulus venit videre Petrum, quoniam bona audierat de ejus doctrina*[12]*:* "According to the letter, we are here instructed of mutual love, which ought to be between all preachers and doctors. For Paul went to visit Peter, because he had heard good of his doctrine." But what can be so plain as that is written by Chrysostom touching the same? His words be these: *Paulus nihil opus habebat Petro, nec ejus egebat voce: sed honore par erat illi: nihil enim hic dicam amplius*[13]*:* "Paul had no need of Peter; neither needed he to be taught at his mouth; but he was equal to him in honour. I will say no more." And immediately after: *Sicut nunc multi fratrum nostrorum ad viros sanctos proficiscuntur, eodem affectu tunc Paulus ad Petrum profectus est*[14]*:* "Like as now-a-days many of our brethren go to holy men, so then with like affection went Paul unto Peter." Acts xv. Gal. i. Gal. ii. Hieron. in Epist. ad Gal. i. cap. Hieron. eodem loco. Gal. i. Hugo Cardinalis in Epist. ad Gal. cap. i. Chrysost. in Epist. ad Gal. cap. i.

As for the rest, that the bishop of Rome had an estimation, and a credit, and a prerogative before others, it is not denied. For of the four patriarchs he had the first place, both in council and out of council, and therefore the greatest authority and direction of matters in all assemblies. And this was τὸ πρωτεύειν, "to have the first or highest room;" and πλεονέκτημα, "a dignity or privilege:" which words M. Harding hath noted in the margin.

[[9] Ambros. Op. Par. 1614. Serm. in Fest. SS. Petr. et Paul. Tom. V. col. 142. See before, page 367, note 12.]

[[10] Hieron. Op. Par. 1693-1706. Comm. Lib. I. in Epist. ad Gal. cap. i. Tom. IV. Pars I. col. 236; where *ad hoc isse ut videret.*]

[[11] Id. ibid.]

[[12] Hugon. de S. Charo Op. Col. Agrip. 1621. Epist. ad Gal. cap. i. Tom. VII. fol. 149.]

[[13] Chrysost. Op. Par. 1718-38. In cap. i. Epist. ad Gal. Comm. Tom. X. p. 677.]

[[14] Id. ibid.]

Here M. Harding seemeth to reason thus:

The bishop of Rome had a privilege or dignity above others;

Ergo, he was an universal bishop.

This argument concludeth *a genere ad speciem affirmative;* and, as M. Harding knoweth, was never allowed in any schools.

Likewise he seemeth to say:

Paul went up to Hierusalem to visit Peter;

Ergo, the bishop of Rome is head of the church.

Such weak gear M. Harding hath brought forth; and yet with his furniture of words it seemeth somewhat. By the same reason he may prove that St James also was head of the church, as well as Peter: for Paul saith he visited him as well as Peter. And St Hierome saith of himself, that he purposely went to Alexandria to see Didymus[1]; yet was not Didymus therefore head of the church.

Gal. i.

Hieron. in Prooemio in Epist. ad Ephesios.

Indeed Hugo Cardinalis saith: "Hereof it first began that bishops and archbishops made a vow to visit the pope, because Paul went to Hierusalem to see Peter;" and saith further that "custom hath added to the same this commandment, written in the Deuteronomy: *Non apparebis in conspectu Domini vacuus*[2]: 'Thou shalt not appear in the presence of the Lord without somewhat.'"

Hugo Cardin. in Epist. ad Gal.

Deut. xvi.

M. Harding, tripping, as he saith, so nicely over the doctors, hath not yet once touched that thing that was looked for, and that he hath only and with such affiance taken in hand. For, notwithstanding a great pomp of words, and the names of many holy fathers, yet hath he not hitherto shewed that the bishop of Rome, within the space of six hundred years after Christ, was ever called the universal bishop, or the head of the universal church; which thing if he could have shewed, I believe he would not so lightly have tripped it over.

M. HARDING. THE SEVENTEENTH DIVISION.

Now let us see whether this chief authority may be found necessary by reason. That a multitude, which is in itself one, cannot continue one, unless it be contained and holden in by one, both learned philosophers have declared, and the common nature of things teacheth. For every multitude of their own nature goeth asunder into many; and from another it cometh that it is one, and that it continueth one. And that whereof it is one, and is kept in union or oneness, it is necessary that it be one; else that self also shall need the help of another, that it be one. For which cause that saying of Homer was alleged by Aristotle, as most notable: "It is not good to have many rulers: let one be ruler[3]*." Whereby is meant, that plurality of sovereign rulers is not fit to contain and keep unity of a multitude of subjects. Therefore sith that the church of Christ is one (for, as there is one faith, one baptism, one calling, so there is one church, yea, all we are one body, and "members one of another," as St Paul saith, and in our creed we all profess to believe one holy catholic and apostolic church), therefore, I say, it hath need of one prince and ruler, to be kept and holden in. If it be otherwise, unity must needs forthwith be sparkled and broken asunder. And therefore it behoved that the rule and government of the church should be committed to one.*

[*The 5. proof. Reason.* H. A. 1564.]

οὐκ ἀγαθὸν πολυκοιρανίη, εἷς κοίρανος ἔστω.

THE BISHOP OF SARISBURY.

All this is proved by Aristotle the philosopher, by one verse of the poet Homer, and by M. Harding's drift of reason, and none otherwise. Aristotle's and Homer's authority in this case cannot be great. And yet they spake[4] only of one captain-general in one field, and of one king in one realm, where as number or fellowship must of necessity breed confusion. But neither of them ever dreamed this new fantasy, that one king should rule over the whole world.

[1 ... Alexandriam perrexi, ut viderem Didymum.—Hieron. Op. Par. 1693-1706. Comm. in Epist. ad Ephes. Præf. Tom. IV. Pars I. cols. 319, 20.]

[2 Hinc ortum habet, quod episcopi et archiepiscopi profitentur de visitatione papæ ... Hinc autem adjecit consuetudo illud Deut. 16. d. et Eccl. 35. a. Non apparebis ante conspectum Domini vacuus.—Hugon. de S. Charo Op. Col. Agrip. 1621. Epist. ad Gal. cap. i. Tom. VII. fol. 149.]

[3 Hom. Il. B. 204.]

[4 Speak, 1565, 1609.]

M. Harding's reasons would weigh the more, if either Christ, or Peter, or Paul, or any old doctor or catholic father, had ever used the same. Otherwise St Augustine, speaking of discourse of reason in the understanding of the scriptures, saith thus: *Hæc consuetudo periculosa est. Per scripturas enim divinas multo tutius ambulatur*[5]: "This manner of expounding is very dangerous. The safer way is to walk by the scriptures." The force of M. Harding's reason caused Alexander, the ambitious king of Macedony, to say: "As the heavens can have but one sun, so may the whole world have but one king;" and likewise pope Bonifacius the eighth to say, as is before: *In principio creavit Deus cœlum et terram, non in principiis*[6]: "In the beginning, as in one, God made heaven and earth, and not in the beginnings, as in many; *ergo*, the pope is head of the church."

August. de Doctrina Christian. Lib. iii. cap. xxviii.

Quintus Curtius.

De Major. et Obed. Unam sanctam.

"But," saith M. Harding, "every multitude naturally goeth asunder; and the thing that keepeth it together must needs be one." That is to say, it is the pope only that preserveth the unity of the church and maketh it one: and therefore the pope himself must needs be one: otherwise, being two or more, saith M. Harding, they should need some other thing to make them one. And yet he remembereth that the council of Syrmium, to take up the contention between Felix and Liberius, that ambitiously strove together for the see of Rome, willed them to be bishops there both together[7]: which thing notwithstanding they meant not therefore neither to dissolve the unity of the church, nor to make the church a monster with two heads. And so Roffensis saith: "The church is one, not because of Christ, but because of the pope that keepeth it in one[8]." This reason, that M. Harding useth, is newly devised, and was never remembered of any of the old fathers. St Gregory saith: "None of my predecessors would ever take upon him to use this ungodly name, to be called the universal bishop[9]." And yet it appeareth not but the church was then kept in unity.

Sozom. Lib. iv. cap. xv. κοινῇ ἱερᾶσθαι.

Roffensis.

Gregor. Lib. iv. Epist. 32.

Neither can this infinite power, that is imagined, stand without infinite great dangers. And forasmuch as it pleaseth M. Harding to avouch the government of Christ's church by philosophers and poets, that never knew Christ; it may also please him to remember that his poets likewise say, that when Phaeton, an undiscreet and a fond young man, would needs leap into Phœbus his father's chariot, to carry the sun-beams about the heavens, for lack of skill, he soon set a-fire the whole world. It may not much displease M. Harding, that I compare the bishop of Rome with Phaeton, a rash young man: for St Gregory, for the same attempt and enterprise, as it plainly appeareth by his words, compareth him with Lucifer and with antichrist[10]; and further saith: *Si hanc [causam] æquanimiter portamus, universæ ecclesiæ fidem corrumpimus*[11]: "If we take this matter quietly, we destroy the faith of the whole church."

Gregor. Lib. iv. Epist. 34. et Epist. 38. Gregor. Lib. vii. Epist. 69. Lib. vi. Epist. 24.

This reason standeth thus: The church of Christ is one;

Ergo, the pope is an universal bishop.

If any man deny this sequel, I marvel by what logic M. Harding will ever be able to make it good.

M. HARDING. THE EIGHTEENTH DIVISION.

And whereas these gospellers say that Christ is the governor of the church, and that he being one keepeth the church in unity; we answer that, although the church be first and principally governed by Christ, as all other things are, yet God's high goodness hath so ordained, as each thing may be provided for, according to his own

---

[5 August. Op. Par. 1679-1700. De Doctr. Christ. Lib. III. cap. xxviii. 39. Tom. III. Pars I. col. 56.]

[6 Bonifac. VIII. in Corp. Jur. Canon. Lugd. 1624. Extrav. Comm. Lib. I. De Major. et Obed. cap. 1. col. 212. See before, page 14, note 2.]

[7 Sozom. in Hist. Eccles. Script. Amst. 1695-1700. Lib. IV. cap. xv. p. 454.]

[8 Hæc ecclesia est una, unum habens caput, hoc est papam, qui est vicarius Christi, a quo una vocatur.—Joan. Roffens. Episc. Op. Wirceb. 1597. Conc. De Libr. Luth. Crem. col. 1389.]

[9 Gregor. Magni Papæ I. Op. Par. 1705. Epist. Lib. v. Indict. XIII. Ad Mauric. August. Epist. xx. col. 749. See before, page 346, note 1.]

[10 Id. ibid. Ad Constant. August. Epist. xxi. col. 751.

Id. ibid. Ad Johan. Episc. Epist. xviii. cols. 742, 3, 4.

Id. Lib. IX. Indict. II. Ad Euseb. Thess. Epist. lxviii. col. 984.]

[11 Id. Lib. VII. Indict. XV. Ad Anastas. Epist. xxvii. col. 873.]

Christ's Vicar.

condition and nature. Therefore, whereas mankind dependeth most of sense, and receiveth all learning and institution of sensible things, therefore it hath need of a man to be a governor and ruler, whom it may perceive by outward sense. And even so the sacraments, by which the grace of God is given unto us, in consideration of man's nature, being so made of God as it is, are ordained in things sensible. Therefore it was behoveful this government of the church to be committed to one man, which at the first was Peter, and afterward each successor of Peter for his time, as is afore declared. Neither can this one man have this power of any consent, or company of men, but it is necessary he have it of God. (104) *For to ordain and appoint the vicar of Christ, it pertaineth to none other than to Christ. For whereas the church, and all that is of the church, is Christ's, as well for other causes, as specially for that we are bought with a great price, even with his blood, as St Paul saith; how can it pertain to any other than to him, to institute and appoint to himself a vicar, that is, one to do his stead?*

The hundred and fourth untruth. For Christ never appointed any such vicar.

[1 *Cor.* iii. 1565, 1609, and H. A. 1564.]

THE BISHOP OF SARISBURY.

M. Harding standeth very long in discoursing this matter by natural reason. And for that he knew St Augustine saith: *Si... ratio contra divinarum scripturarum auctoritatem redditur, quamlibet acuta sit, fallit verisimilitudine: nam vera esse non potest*[1]: "If natural reason be alleged against the authority of the holy scriptures, be it never so subtle, it beguileth men by a likeness or colour of the truth; for true it cannot be:" and for that he also saw the reasons he hath brought are very simple, and carry no weight; he hath therefore thrust a great many of them in a throng together, both to fill the hearers' senses, and also that the one might the better aid the other.

August. ad Marcellin. Epist. 7.

For his entry in mirth and game he calleth us gospellers. God open the eyes of his heart, that he may see the brightness of God's gospel, and consider what it is that he hath refused! Surely it is an horrible thing for a christian man thus to make mockery of the gospel of Christ. St Paul saith: *Si opertum est evangelium, in illis qui pereunt est opertum:* "If the gospel be covered, it is covered from them that perish."

2 Cor. iv.

It misliketh him that we build the unity of the church upon Christ only, and not also upon the pope; and this he calleth these new gospellers' doctrine. God be thanked, these gospellers have good warrant for their doctrine. St Paul saith: *Eum dedit caput super omnia ipsi ecclesiæ, quæ est corpus ejus:* "God hath given Christ to be head over all, even to the church, which is his body." And again: *Ille est caput, qui dat salutem corpori:* "Christ is the head, that giveth health unto the body." "Christ is our peace: all we are one in Christ Jesus[2]." Therefore St Gregory saith: *Nos quoque a vobis non longe sumus, quoniam in illo, qui ubique est, unum sumus. Agamus ergo ei gratias, qui, solutis inimicitiis in carne sua, fecit ut in omni orbe terrarum unus esset grex, et unum ovile, sub se uno Pastore*[3]: "We are not far away from you, because in him that is every where we are all one. Therefore let us give him thanks, that, enmity being broken in his flesh, hath caused that in all the world there should be one flock, and one fold, under himself, being the one Shepherd." These places, and infinite other like, are good warrants of our doctrine.

Eph. i.

Eph. v.

Eph. ii.

Gregor. Lib. iv. Epist. 36. ad Eulogium.

John x.

Now, if M. Harding be able by the scriptures, or holy doctors, to say as much for the bishop of Rome, that he is the head of the church, that is to say, the head of Christ's body; or, that the church receiveth influence or health from him; or, that he is our peace; or, that we are all one in him; or, that all the world is one flock, and one fold, and he the one shepherd; or, that St Paul, as he said, "There is one Lord, one faith, one baptism," so he said also, There is one pope; then have we some cause to think, according to M. Harding's fantasy, that the unity of the whole church is founded and built upon the pope. Certainly it seemeth St Augustine would not give this privilege unto St Paul. His words be

Eph. iv.

[1 August. Op. Par. 1679-1700. Ad Marcellin. Epist. cxliii. 7. Tom. II. col. 466.]

[2 Jesu, 1565.]

[3 Gregor. Magni Papæ I. Op. Par. 1705. Epist. Lib. v. Indict. XIII. Ad Eulog. et Anastas. Episc. Epist. xliii. Tom. II. col. 772; where *quia* for *quoniam*.]

plain: *Nec Paulus radix eorum erat, quos plantaverat; sed ille potius, qui ait, Ego sum vitis: vos estis sarmenta. Caput etiam eorum quomodo esse poterat, cum dicat, Nos omnes unum esse corpus in Christo, ipsumque Christum caput esse universi corporis*[4]? "Neither was Paul the root of them whom he had planted, but rather he that saith, 'I am the vine; and you are the sprigs.' But the head of them how could he be, seeing he himself saith, 'All we in Christ are one body;' and that of that whole body Christ himself is the head?" If St Paul, as St Augustine saith, could not be head of the church, how may we then think that the bishop of Rome may be head of the church?

Christ's Vicar.

August. contra Lit. Petilian. Lib. iii. cap. xlii. John xv. Eph. i. Eph. iv.

But mankind, saith M. Harding, dependeth most of sense: therefore the whole church must have one man to rule and govern over it; and that man is Peter's successor, and Christ's vicar in earth. I marvel that none of the old fathers could ever understand either the necessity of this reason, or this special name and title of Christ's vicar. Howbeit, one true word M. Harding hath uttered amongst many others, that is, that to appoint Christ's vicar, it pertaineth only unto Christ, and to none other. Of which ground we may well reason thus: Christ never ordained, nor appointed, nor once named, the bishop of Rome, or his successor, to be his vicar, that is, to be an universal bishop over the whole church. Therefore, by M. Harding's own position, the bishop of Rome hath of long time usurped a power against Christ without commission, and indeed is not Christ's vicar. St Hierome saith generally of all bishops: *Noverint episcopi, se magis consuetudine, quam dispositionis dominicæ veritate, presbyteris esse majores*[5]: "Let bishops understand that they be greater than the priests by order and custom (of the church), and not by the truth of God's ordinance." If Christ, as St Hierome saith, appointed not one priest above another, how then is it likely he appointed one priest to be, as M. Harding saith, prince and ruler over all priests throughout the whole world?

Hieron. in Epist. ad Titum.

As for the universal supplying of Christ's room, Tertullian saith, the Holy Ghost is Christ's vicar. For thus he writeth: *Sedet ad dextram [Dei] Patris: misit vicariam vim Spiritus sancti, qui credentes agat*[6]: "Christ sitteth at the right hand of God the Father; and, instead of himself, sent the power of the Holy Ghost, as his vicar, to direct them that believe."

Tertul. de Præscript. contr. Hæret.

But because we are not only led inwardly by God's Spirit, but also outwardly by our senses, therefore hath Christ appointed, not one man to be his vicar-general over all, but every of his apostles, and so every priest, to be his vicar within his division. So saith Eusebius bishop of Rome: *Caput...ecclesiæ Christus est: Christi autem vicarii sacerdotes sunt, qui vice Christi legatione funguntur in ecclesia*[7]: "Christ is the head of the church; and his vicars be the priests that do their message in the church in the stead of Christ." Therefore saith St Hierome: *Potentia divitiarum et paupertatis humilitas vel sublimiorem vel inferiorem episcopum non facit. Ceterum omnes apostolorum successores sunt*[8]: "The stoutness of riches, or the humility of poverty, maketh a bishop neither higher nor lower; but all bishops be the apostles' successors." Other universal vicar of Christ there is none named in the scriptures, unless it be he of whom St Paul forewarneth us: *Homo ille sceleratus, filius perditus, &c.*: "That wicked man, that child of perdition, that setteth himself up against God, and that so far forth, that he will sit in the temple of God, and shew himself as if he were God." But this vicar Christ shall destroy with the spirit of his mouth.

Euseb. Episc. Rom. Epist. 3. 2 Cor. v.

Hieron. ad Evag Tom. ii. p. 329.

2 Thess. ii.

To conclude, M. Harding seemeth to reason thus: Mankind dependeth most of sense; *ergo*, the pope is the head of the universal church. Here is a very unsensible argument: nor sense nor reason can make it good. By as good sequel he might say: Mankind dependeth most of sense; *ergo*, one king must rule over the whole world.

[4 Nec radix eorum erat ipse, sed ille, &c., nos multos, &c.—August. Op. Contr. Lit. Petil. Lib. III. cap. xlii. 51. Tom. IX. col. 322.]

[5 Hieron. Op. Par. 1693-1706. In Epist. ad Tit. cap. i. Tom. IV. Pars I. cols. 413, 4. See before, page 340, note 11.]

[6 Tertull. Op. Lut. 1641. De Præscr. Hæret. 13. p. 235; where *sedisse* and *misisse*.]

[7 Euseb. Papæ Epist. iii. in Crabb. Concil. Col. Agrip. 1551. Tom. I. p. 215.]

[8 Hieron. Op. Ad Evang. Epist. ci. Tom. IV. Pars II. col. 803.]

M. HARDING. THE NINETEENTH DIVISION.

Wherefore, to conclude, except we would wickedly grant that God's providence hath lacked, or doth lack to his church, for love of which he hath given his only-begotten Son, and which he hath promised never to forget, so as the woman cannot forget the child she bare in her womb; reason may soon induce us to believe that to one man, one bishop, the chief and highest of all bishops, the successor of Peter, the rule and government of the church by God hath been deferred. For else, if God had ordained that in the church should be sundry heads and rulers, and none constituted to be over other, but all of equal power, each one among their people, then he should seem to have set up so many churches as he hath appointed governors. And so he shall appear to have brought in among his faithful people that unruly confusion, the destruction of all commonweals, so much abhorred of princes, which the Greeks call anarchian, *which is a state, for lack of order in governors, without any government at all. Which thing, sith that the wise and politic men of this world do shun and detest in the government of these earthly kingdoms, as most pernicious and hurtful, to attribute to the high wisdom of God, and to our Lord Christ, who is the author of the most ordinate disposition of all things in earth and in heaven, it were heinous and profane impiety. Wherefore, if the state of a kingdom cannot continue safe unless one have power to rule, how shall not the church, spread so far abroad, be in danger of great disorders, corruption, and utter destruction, if, as occasion shall be given, among so great strifes and debates of men, among so many firebrands of discord, tossed to and fro by the devils, enemies of unity, there be not one head and ruler, of all to be consulted, of all to be heard, of all to be followed and obeyed? If strife and contention be stirred about matters of faith, if controversy happen to arise*[1] *about the sense of the scriptures, shall it not be necessary there be one supreme judge, to whose sentence the parties may stand? If need require (as it hath been often seen) that general councils be kept, how can the bishops, to whom the*[2] *matter belongeth, be brought together, but by the commandment of one head governor, whom they owe their obedience unto? For else, being summoned, perhaps they will not come. Finally, how shall the contumacy and pertinacy of mischievous persons be repressed, specially if the bishops be at dissension within themselves, if there be not a supreme power, who towards some may use the rod, towards other some the spirit of lenity, with such discreet temperament, as malice be vanquished, right defended, and concord procured, lest, if the small sparks of strife be not quenched by authority at the beginning, at length a great flame of schisms and heresies flash abroad, to the great danger of a multitude? Therefore, as there is one body of Christ, one flock, one church, even so is there one head of that his mystical body, one shepherd, and one chief servant, made steward, overseer, and ruler of*[3] *Christ's household in his absence, until his coming again.*

A sort of simple reasons.

THE BISHOP OF SARISBURY.

Whoso denieth the bishop of Rome's supreme government, saith M. Harding, he utterly denieth God's providence; and thus the great providence of God is brought forth to serve M. Harding's simple reason. The like consideration, as may be supposed, moved Petrus Bertrandus to write this special gloss upon the decretals: *Non videretur Dominus discretus fuisse, ut cum reverentia ejus loquar, nisi unicum post se talem vicarium reliquisset*[4]*:* "Otherwise Christ should not seem to have dealt discreetly, saving his reverence, unless he had left some one such vicar behind him." And therefore he saith further: *Christo data est omnis potestas in cœlo et in terra: ergo summus pontifex, qui est ejus vicarius, habet eandem potestatem*[5]*:* "All manner power both in heaven and earth is given to Christ; therefore the highest bishop, which is his vicar, hath the same power." Likewise they say: [a]*Papa potest facere omnia quæ Christus ipse potest*[6]*:* "The

De Major. et Obed. Unam sanctam. In Glossa.

[a] De Sentent. Excom. cap. Si aliquid. Hostien.

[[1] Rise, H. A. 1564.]

[[2] That, 1565, and H. A. 1564.]

[[3] Over, H. A. 1564.]

[[4] Corp. Jur. Canon. Lugd. 1624. Extrav. Comm. Lib. I. De Major. et Obed. Gloss. in cap. i. col. 212.]

[[5] Id. ibid.; where we have *data erat,* and *habebit hanc.*]

[[6] Hostiens. Op. Par. 1512. Super Quint. Decretal. De Sent. Excomm. foll. 115, 6. The words there, however, are: *Papa non subjacet legibus.*]

pope may do whatsoever Christ himself may do." And, [b] *Papæ et Christi est unum tribunal*[7]: "The pope and Christ have one consistory, and keep one court."

b De Trans. Episc. cap. Quanto Innocen. iii.

Upon occasion hereof, M. Harding seemeth to reason in this sort: Unless there be one appointed by God to be the universal bishop of the world, having *omnia jura in scrinio* [c] *pectoris sui*[8], "all manner law and right in the closet of his breast;" [d] *cui sit pro ratione voluntas*[9], "whose pleasure may stand instead of law;" unto whom, whatsoever he do, no man may say, [e] *Domine, cur ita facis*[10]? "Sir, why do you so?" and the same neither exhort, nor teach, nor minister sacrament, nor exercise discipline, nor do the duty either of bishop, or of priest, or of deacon, or any other the meanest officer of the church, but only take upon him to rule and govern the whole church; unless there be some such one, then, saith M. Harding, God hath no providence, neither is careful for his church.

c Extr. de Const. Licet Romanus.
d De Trans. Episc. cap. Quanto in Gloss.
e De Conces. Præbendæ. Ad Apost. in Gloss.

If controversy grow about the understanding and sense of God's word; if it be necessary that a council be called; if contention fall out between any other inferior bishops; then, saith M. Harding, it is necessary there be one supreme judge, that may infallibly declare God's meaning, that may summon the council, that may hear and determine matters between the bishops. Touching the searching out of the sense of the scriptures, St Augustine giveth sundry good rules[11]: but this strange rule of recourse to the pope he toucheth not, nor taketh it for any rule.

De Doctr. Christ. Lib. iii.

But they say, the scriptures be dark; therefore we must seek the meaning of them in the doctors. The doctors agree not; then must we weigh and try them by the Master of the Sentences. The Master of the Sentences himself sometimes is not holden; then must we seek further to the school-doctors. The school-doctors can in no wise agree: there is Scotus against Thomas, and Occam against Scotus, and Alliacensis against Occam, the nominals against the reals, the scholasticals against the canonists: the contention is greater, and the doubts darker, than ever they were before. Neither is there any resolution to be hoped for, but only of the bishop of Rome, whom M. Harding calleth the supreme judge; who, as one saith, is *doctor utriusque legis, auctoritate, non scientia*[12]: "doctor of both laws, by authority, not by knowledge." Howbeit it appeareth his knowledge and authority in such cases are both like. For notwithstanding any his determination, the contention standeth still as it did before. Truly Alphonsus de Castro, a doctor of the same side, saith: *Cum constet plures papas adeo illiteratos esse, ut grammaticam penitus ignorent, qui fit, ut sacras literas interpretari possint*[13]? "Seeing it is well known that many popes be so void of learning, that they be utterly ignorant of their grammar, how may it be, that they can expound the holy scriptures?" Thus that supreme judge, at whose only hands M. Harding would have all the world to seek for the very sense of God's word, as Alphonsus saith, may go to school to learn his grammar. And what if the pope be an heretic? as Liberius was an Arian, Honorius an Eunomian, Anastasius was a Photinian[14], and as Lyra saith: *Multi papæ inventi sunt apostatæ*[15]: "Many popes have been runagates of the faith." Or what if he be a sorcerer, and have league and conference with the devil, as had Sylvester the second[16]?

Magister non tenetur.
Baldus
Alphon. de Castr. Lib. i. cap. iv.
Alphon. de Castr. Lib. i. cap. iv.
Nicol. Lyra in Matt. xvi. cap.
Platin. in Sylvest.

[7 Corp. Jur. Canon. Lugd. 1624. Decretal. Gregor. IX. Lib. III. Tit. vii. Gloss. in cap. 3. col. 217.]

[8 Bonifac. VIII. in eod. Sext. Decretal. Lib. I. Tit. ii. cap. 1. col. 11. See before, page 68, note 3.]

[9 Ibid. Decretal. Gregor. IX. Lib. I. De Transl. Episc. Tit. vii. Gloss. in cap. 3. col. 217. See before, page 69, note 14.]

[10 Ibid. Extrav. Joan. XXII. De Conc. Preb. Tit. iv. Gloss. in cap. 2. col. 56.]

[11 August. Op. Par. 1679-1700. De Doctr Christ. Lib. III. capp. x. &c. Tom. III. Pars I. cols. 49, &c.]

[12 Not. hic, quod papa est doctor utriusque juris eo ipso quod est papa: et non est dubium quod est doctor auctoritate, sed non scientia, quia multi sunt qui jus civile ignorant.—Bald. super Decretal. De Confessis. *Cum monasterium.* n. 6. fol. 234. col. 4. Lugd. 1551.]

[13 Alfons. de Castro Adv. Hær. Col. 1539. Lib. I. cap. iv. fol. 8. 2; where *plures eorum*, and *possent.*]

[14 Nam de Liberio papa constat fuisse Arrianum, et Anastasium papam favisse Nestorianis.—Id. ibid. fol. 8.]

[15 ... multi principes et summi pontifices...inventi sunt apostasse a fide.—Bibl. cum Gloss. Ord. et Expos. N. de Lyra, Basil. 1502. Matt. cap. xvi. Pars V. fol. 52.]

[16 Plat. De Vit. Pont. Col. 1551. Sylvest. II. p. 139.]

Yet must we needs have recourse unto such an[1] one, as unto the mouth of God, for the certain sense and meaning of God's word? Verily, in the old times, men that stood in doubt of any matter of learning, and would gladly be resolved, sought unto the best learned, and not unto the pope. Pope Leo himself, in a case of doubt, thought it good to confer with other bishops[2]. The bishops of Numidia sent, not to the bishop of Rome to be resolved, but unto St Cyprian, and other bishops within Africa[3]. So likewise St Hierome writeth of himself: *Ob hanc causam vel maxime Alexandriam nuper perrexi, ut viderem Didymum, et ab eo in scripturis omnibus, quæ habebam, dubia omnia exquirerem*[4]: "For this cause chiefly I went of late to Alexandria, to the intent I might see Didymus, and be resolved by him in all such doubts as I had found in the scriptures." And St Ambrose saith, that certain learned men, in matter of question, having received answer and determination from the bishop of Rome, yet notwithstanding, for their better satisfaction, sought further unto him. Thus he writeth: *Post Romanæ ecclesiæ definitionem meam adhuc exspectant sententiam*[5]: "After the discussing of the church of Rome, they yet look for my sentence."

Leo. Epist. 37. ad Episc. Raven.

Cypr. Lib. i. Epist. 4.

Hieron. in Procemio in Epist. ad Eph.

Ambr. Lib. x. Epist. 83.

As for general councils, it is well known, and, God willing, shall appear hereafter more at large, that they were called and summoned by the emperors only, and not by the bishops of Rome. Sozomenus saith: *Imperator præceperat, concilium Mediolani celebrari*[6]: "The emperor had commanded a council to be kept at Milan."

Sozom. citat. inter Act. Liber.

Matters of variance between bishops were taken up, not only by the bishop of Rome, whose greatest practice these many years hath been to inflame and maintain discord among princes; but also sometimes by the prince, sometimes by councils, sometimes by other bishops, sometimes by some inferior persons, that were no bishops. St Ambrose was sent for into France, to pacify the bishops there[7]. Bernard, being but an abbat, compounded that great dissension that was between pope Innocentius and Peter in the church of Rome[8]. Therefore to these purposes it is nothing needful to erect a new vicar-general, or to give any man this universal power over the church of God.

Ambr. de Obit. Valent.

Bernard. in Cantic. Cant. Serm. 22.

M. Harding's reasons proceed thus: God is careful, and hath a special providence for his church; doubtful places of the scripture must be expounded; general councils must be summoned; bishops being at variance must be reconciled; *ergo*, the bishop of Rome is Christ's universal vicar, and head of the universal church. Otherwise, saith he, the church can never be rightly governed, nor preserved in unity. But, God's name be blessed for ever, God is able to govern his church, not only without such a vicar, but also maugre such a vicar. Miserable were God's church, if it stood only at the bishop of Rome's government. Long it were to open the looseness and dissolution of his own church, that lieth before him. St Bernard, speaking of the same, saith thus: *Mali ibi proficiunt: boni deficiunt*[9]: "Ill men there go forward; but good men go backward." *A planta pedis usque ad verticem capitis non est in ea sanitas*[10]: "From the sole of the foot unto the crown of the head there is no whole part in it." And again: *Servi Christi serviunt antichristo*[11]: "They would be called the servants

Bernard. ad Eug. Lib. iv.

Bernard. de Conv. Paul. Isai. i.

Bernard. in Cantic. Cant.

[[1] A, 1565.]

[[2] Leon. Magni Op. Lut. 1623. Ad Leon. Raven. Episc. Epist. xxxvii. cols. 349-51.]

[[3] Cypr. Op. Oxon. 1682. Ad Cler. et Pleb. Hisp. Epist. lxvii. pp. 170, &c. They were Spaniards, as the letter referred to indicates, who had applied to Cyprian.]

[[4] Hieron. Op. Par. 1693-1706. Comm. in Epist. ad Ephes. Præf. Tom. IV. Pars I. cols. 319, 20; where *nuper ob hanc vel maxime caussam Alexandriam perrexi*, and *dubia sciscitarer*.]

[[5] ... post ... Alexandrinæ ecclesiæ definitiones, episcopi quoque Romanæ ecclesiæ, per literas plerique meam adhuc exspectant sententiam.—Ambros. Op. Par. 1686-90. Ad Episc. per Æmil. Epist. xxiii. 8. Tom. II. col. 882.]

[[6] ... convenerunt episcopi...ut præcepto principis concilium Mediolani celebraretur.—Sozom. in Decret. Liber. Papæ in Crabb. Concil. Col. Agrip. 1551. Tom. I. p. 347. See also in Hist. Eccles. Script. Amst. 1695-1700. Lib. IV. cap. ix. p. 445.]

[[7] Ambros. Op. De Obit. Valent. Cons. 25. Tom. II. col. 1181.]

[[8] Hoc demum tertio...reditum ab urbe nostrum clementior oculus e cœlo respexit ... Quievit Leonina rabies ... ecclesia pacem recepit.—Bernard. Op. Par. 1690. In Cant. Serm. xxiv. i. Vol. I. Tom. IV. col. 1346.]

[[9] Perhaps the following is the passage meant: ...plures in ea [curia] defecisse bonos, quam malos profecisse probavimus.—Id. De Consid. Lib. IV. cap. iv. 11. Vol. I. Tom. II. col. 439.]

[[10] Id. in Convers. S. Paul. Serm. i. 3. Vol. I. Tom. III. col. 956; where *non est sanitas ulla*.]

[[11] Ministri Christi sunt, et serviunt antichristo.—Id. in Cant. Serm. xxxiii. 15. Vol. I. Tom. IV. col. 1393.]

of Christ; and yet indeed they serve antichrist." If the bishop of Rome can no better rule a few churches in one city, how then is he able to rule the infinite multitude of the whole universal church of God?

But God hath other ways and means whereby he hath ever governed his church. St Cyprian saith: *Ideo plures sunt in ecclesia sacerdotes, ut, uno hæresim faciente, ceteri subveniant*[12]: "Therefore there be many bishops in the church, that, one running into heresy, the rest may help." And again: "The church is preserved in unity by the consent of bishops agreeing in one[13]." And to this end St Hierome saith, as is before alleged: *Noverint episcopi ... se debere in commune ecclesiam regere*[14]: "Let bishops understand that they ought to rule the church as all in one."

Cypr. ad Steph. Lib. iii. Epist. 13.

Cypr. Lib. iv. Epist. 9.

Hieron. in Epist. ad Tit. cap. i.

As for the unity that M. Harding meaneth, it is a vile subjection and servitude: it is no unity. St Hierome saith: *Nomine unitatis et fidei infidelitas scripta est: nam illo tempore nihil tam pium, nihil tam conveniens servo Dei videbatur, quam unitatem sequi, et a totius mundi communione non scindi*[15]: "Infidelity hath been written under the name of faith and unity. For at that time nothing seemed either so godly, or so meet for the servant of God, as to follow unity, and not to be divided from the communion of the whole world." They seemed, saith St Hierome, to follow unity, and yet notwithstanding they hung in infidelity. So likewise saith the wise man: *In tanto viventes ignorantiæ bello, tot et tanta mala pacem appellabant:* "Whereas they lived in such a war of ignorance, so many and so great mischiefs they called unity."

Hieron. contra Lucif.

Wisd. xiv.

M. HARDING. THE TWENTIETH DIVISION.

[*The 6. proof, Practice of the church six-fold,* H. A. 1564.]

But here perhaps some will say, it cannot appear by the event of things, and practice of the church, that the pope had this supreme power and authority over all bishops, and over all Christ's flock in matters touching faith, and in cases[16] *ecclesiastical. Verily, whosoever peruseth the ecclesiastical stories, and vieweth the state of the church of all times and ages, cannot but confess this to be most evident. And here I might allege first certain places of the new testament, declaring that Peter practised this pre-eminence among the disciples at the beginning, and that they yielded the same, as of right appertaining unto him. As when he first and only moved them to choose one in the stead of Judas, and demeaned himself as the chief author of all that was done therein; when he made answer for all, at what time they were gazed and wondered at, and of some mocked, as being drunken with new wine, for that in the fiftieth day they spake with tongues of so many nations; when he used that dreadful severity in punishing the falsehood*[17] *and hypocrisy of Ananias and Saphira his wife; when, variance being risen about the observation of certain points of Moses' law, he, as chief and head of the rest, said his mind before all others. Among many other places, left out for brevity, that is not of least weight, that Paul, being returned to Damasco out of Arabia, after three years went to Jerusalem to see Peter, and abode with him fifteen days.*

Acts i. *Acts ii.* *Acts v.* *Acts xv.* *Gal. i.*

(105) *But because our adversaries do wreathe and wrest the scriptures, be they never so plain, by their private and strange constructions, to an understanding quite contrary to the sense of the catholic church, I will refer the reader, for further proof of this matter, to the stories bearing faithful witness of the whole state and condition of the church in all ages: in which stories the practice of the church is plainly reported to have been such, as thereby the primacy of Peter's successor may seem to all men sufficiently declared. For, perusing the ecclesiastical stories with writings of the fathers, beside many other things pertaining hereto, we find these*
1. *practices, for declaration of this special authority and power: first, that bishops*
(106) *of every nation have made their appeal in their weighty affairs to the pope,*

The hundred and fifth untruth, joined with a slander.

The hundred and sixth untruth, as afterward it shall appear.

[[12] Iccirco...copiosum corpus est sacerdotum...ut si quis ... hæresin facere ... tentaverit, subveniant ceteri.—Cypr. Op. Ad Steph. Epist. lxviii. p. 178.]

[[13] Id. Ad Florent. Pup. Epist. lxvi. p. 168. See before, page 349, note 8.]

[[14] Hieron. Op. Comm. in Epist. ad Tit. cap. i. Tom. IV. Pars I. cols. 413, 4.]

[[15] Id. Adv. Lucif. Tom. IV. Pars II. col. 299.]

[[16] Causes, 1565, 1609, and H. A. 1564.]

[[17] Falsehead, 1565, and H. A. 1564.]

Peter head.

and always have sued to the see apostolic, as well for succour and help against
violence, injuries, and oppressions, as for redress of other disorders. Also, that the 2.
malice of wicked persons hath been repressed and chastised of that authority by
excommunication, ejection, and expulsion out of their dignities and rooms, and by
other censures of the church. Furthermore, that the ordinances and elections of 3.
bishops of all provinces have been confirmed by the pope. Beside this, that the 4.
approving and disallowing of councils have pertained to him. Item, that bishops, 5.
wrongfully condemned and deprived by councils, by him have been assoiled and
restored to their churches again. Lastly, that bishops and patriarchs, after long 6.
strifes and contentions, have at length, upon better advice, been reconciled unto him
again.

THE BISHOP OF SARISBURY.

Here M. Harding assayeth to prove the possession and occupation of this universal authority, by the practice both of St Peter himself, and also of other bishops in Rome, that followed after him. And touching St Peter, he thinketh it sufficient to say thus: Peter, being among the rest, shewed his advice first before all others, and at the sound of his words Ananias and Saphira fell down dead; *ergo*, Peter was the head, and had an universal power over the whole church. Here be very weak proofs to maintain so great a title. I think M. Harding himself doth not believe that whosoever first uttereth his mind in any council, or worketh any strange miracle by the power of God, is therefore the head of all the world. For oftentimes in great councils the youngest or lowest beginneth first, and the eldest and head of all speaketh last. Certainly, in this assembly of the apostles, after that St Peter had opened his mind, and all the rest had done, last of all, not St Peter, but St James pronounced the sentence; which thing belonged only to the head and president of that council. He must be very simple, that will be led with such simple guesses.

Acts xv.

But whosoever well and thoroughly considereth St Peter's whole dealing at all times among his brethren, shall soon see that neither he bare himself, nor the rest received or used him, as the head of the universal church. He calleth the rest of the disciples his brethren: he calleth himself *compresbyterum*, fellow-elder. He commandeth not, nor chargeth any man, but heareth and entreateth others as his equals and fellows: being sent into Samaria by his brethren, he repined not, as being their head and governor, but went his way as their messenger; and, being reproved for going to Cornelius, and dealing with heathens, he excused himself, and came to his answer.

Acts xv. 1 Pet. v. Acts viii. Acts xi.

The rest of the apostles, no doubt, honoured St Peter, as the special member of Christ's body, with all reverence. But it appeareth not that any of them ever took him or used him as their head, or yielded him this infinite or universal power. St Paul compareth himself with him in apostleship, and saith: *Mihi concreditum est evangelium præputii, sicut Petro circumcisionis:* "To me is committed the gospel among the heathens, even as unto Peter among the Jews." And, "James, Peter, and John, which seemed to be pillars[1], gave unto me and Barnabas the right hands of fellowship." And afterward he saith: "I withstood Peter even unto the face; for that he was worthy to be rebuked." And again unto the Corinthians: *Arbitror me nihil inferiorem esse eximiis apostolis:* "I take myself[2] to be nothing inferior unto the chief apostles." Hereby it plainly appeareth that Paul esteemed and took Peter as his fellow, and not as his head.

Gal. ii. 2 Cor. xii.

Whereas it liketh M. Harding to say that we wreathe and wrest the scriptures; if it would have pleased him also particularly to shew how and wherein, he might have had the more credit. But it is commonly said: *Dolosus versatur in generalibus:* "He that walketh in generalities meaneth not plainly." I trust the indifferent reader seeth the scriptures are plain enough of our side, and need no wresting. And therefore touching this case St Cyprian saith, as is before alleged: *Idem erant alii, quod Petrus*[3]: "The rest were the same that Peter was." And

Cypr. de Simplicit. Prælat.

[1 The pillars, 1565, 1609.]
[2 Meself, 1565.]
[3 Cypr. Op. Oxon. 1682. De Unit. Eccles. p. 167. See before, page 360.]

Origen likewise: *Nos quoque efficimur Petrus; et nobis dicetur illud, quod hunc sermonem sequitur: Tu es Petrus, et super hanc petram ædificabo ecclesiam meam. Petra enim est, quisquis est discipulus Christi*[4]: "Even we are become Peter; and unto us the same shall be said that followeth these words: 'Thou art Peter; and upon this rock I will build my church.' For he is the rock whosoever is Christ's disciple." And so it is written in St Augustine against the Donatists: *Clarus a Mascula dixit, Manifesta est sententia Domini nostri Jesu Christi apostolos... mittentis, et ipsis solis potestatem a Patre sibi datam permittentis: quibus nos successimus, eadem potestate ecclesiam Domini gubernantes*[5]: "The saying of our Lord Jesus Christ, sending out his apostles, and giving unto them only the same power that he had received of his Father, is plain: into which apostles' rooms we have succeeded, governing the church with the same power that they did." These be good witnesses that we wrest not God's words, but use them simply as they were spoken.

Orig. in Matt. Tract. i.

August. de Baptis. contr. Donat. Lib. vii. cap. xliii.

Now it were a long labour to shew at full how M. Harding, with others of that side, have dealt herein. The words that be specially and only spoken of God himself, and of his Christ, it is lawful for them to apply the same unto the pope without any wreathing or wresting of the scriptures. Cornelius, a bishop in the last council of Trident, useth these words: *Papa lux venit in mundum; sed dilexerunt homines magis tenebras, quam lucem*[6]: "The pope, being the light, is come into the world; but men loved the darkness more than the light." And Stephanus, the archbishop of Patraca, in the council of Lateran directeth these words unto the pope: *Tibi data est omnis potestas in cœlo et in terra*[7]: "Unto thee is all power given both in heaven and earth." Likewise saith pope Bonifacius: *Spiritualis... a nemine judicatur*[8]: "The man that is spiritual is judged of no man; *ergo*, no man may judge the pope." And again: *Quæ sunt potestates, a Deo ordinatæ sunt*[9]: "The powers that be are ordained of God; *ergo*, the pope is above the emperor." Now, to pass by other like places, which are innumerable, whether this be wresting of the scriptures or no, I leave to[10] the discreet reader to consider. Verily, as I have said before, Camotensis thus reporteth of them: *Vim faciunt scripturis, ut habeant plenitudinem potestatis*[11]: "To the intent they may have the fulness of power, they do violence to the scriptures, and devise strange constructions, contrary to the sense of the church of God."

Corn. Episc. Bitont. in Orat. ad Synod.

Steph. Archiepisc. Patrac. in Concil. Later. sub Leon. Session. 10.

De Major. et Obed. Unam sanctam.

1 Cor. ii.

Rom. xiii.

Citat. a Corn. Agrip. de Vanit. Scien.

But forasmuch as M. Harding utterly leaveth the scriptures, wherein he seeth he hath so simple hold, and referreth the whole right of his cause to the continual practice of the church, I trust it shall not seem neither tedious nor unprofitable unto the reader, only for a taste, and by the way, to touch somewhat concerning the same; nothing doubting, but even thereby it shall well appear that, within the compass of six hundred years after Christ, the bishop of Rome was never neither named nor holden for the head of the universal church.

First of all, the bishops of other countries, writing to the bishop of Rome, call him not their head, but their brother or fellow. St Cyprian unto Cornelius writeth thus: *Cyprianus Cornelio fratri*[12]: "Cyprian unto Cornelius my brother." The bishops in the council of Carthage unto Innocentius: *Honoratissimo fratri*[13]: "To our most honourable brother." And John the bishop of Constantinople unto Hormisda: *Frater in Christo carissime*[14]: "My dear brother in Christ." So likewise Dionysius the bishop of Alexandria calleth Stephanus and Sistus, bishops

Cypr. Lib. i. Epist. 3.

Concil. Carth. v.

In Decret. Hormis.

Euseb. Lib. vii. cap. iv.

[[4] Orig. Op. Par. 1733-59. Comm. in Matt. Tom. XII. 10. Tom. III. pp. 523, 4.]

[[5] August. Op. Par. 1679-1700. De Bapt. cont. Don. Lib. VII. cap. xliii. 84. Tom. IX. col. 197. This was the sentence of one of the bishops at the council of Carthage under Cyprian.—Cypr. Op. lxxix. pp. 241, 2.]

[[6] Orat. Corn. Episc. Bitont. ad Trident. Synod. in Concil. Stud. Labb. et Cossart. Lut. Par. 1671-2. Tom. XIV. col. 996; where *papæ*.]

[[7] Orat. Steph. Arch. Patrac. in Sess. x. Concil. Later. v. in eod. Tom. XIV. col. 269. See before, pp. 93, 4, note 2.]

[[8] Bonifac. VIII. in Corp. Jur. Canon. Lugd. 1624. Extrav. Comm. Lib. I. De Major. et Obed. cap. 1. col. 211.]

[[9] Non est potestas nisi a Deo; quæ autem sunt, a Deo ordinata sunt.—Id. ibid. col. 209.]

[[10] It to, 1565.]

[[11] Corn. Agrippa repeatedly cites Camotensis [Carnotensis], De Incert. et Vanit. Scient. Col. 1584. cap. lxi. foll. N. 6, 7; and from him Jewel declares he took his quotations. The sense of the words here alleged may be found Joan. Sarisb. Polycr. L. Bat. 1595. Lib. VIII. cap. xvii. pp. 546, 7. Further reference to this author will occur hereafter.]

[[12] Cypr. Op. Ad Cornel. Epist. lix. p. 126.]

[[13] Concil. Carthag. Epist. ad Innoc. in Crabb. Concil. Col. Agrip. 1551. Tom. I. p. 469.]

[[14] Lib. Fid. Joan. Constant. ad Hormisd. in eod. Tom. I. p. 1036; where *in Christo frater*.]

Euseb. Lib. vii. cap. viii. In Concil. Aphric. In Concil. Ephes. Epiph. Lib. iii. Tom. i. Hæres. 72.

of Rome, "his loving brethren[1]." So the bishops of Africa call Anastasius *consacerdotem*[2], "their fellow-bishop:" like as Cyrillus also calleth Cœlestinus[3]; and Marcellus, the bishop of Ancyra, calleth Julius *comministrum*[4], "his fellow-servant." These words, "brother" and "fellow," seem rather to signify an equality between bishops, than any such sovereign power or universal authority as the bishop of Rome now claimeth.

Concil. Nicen. cap. 6. Concil. Aphr. cap. 92. Liter. Synod. Gregor. Lib. i. Epist. 25. et Lib. vi. Epist. 24. Ruffin. Lib. i. cap. xxix. Æn. Sylv.

Further, touching the order of outward government, the council of Nice limiteth unto the bishop of Rome not the jurisdiction of the whole world, but his own several portion among other patriarchs[5]. The council of Africa straitly forbiddeth any man out of that country to appeal to Rome[6]. The four patriarchs, of Rome, of Constantinople, of Antioch, and Alexandria, used to write letters of conference between themselves, thereby to profess their religion one to another[7]; which was a token of fellowship, and not of dominion. The council of Alexandria committed full authority to Asterius to visit and to redress all the churches in the east part of the world, and to Eusebius, to do the like in the west[8]; and so seemed to have small regard to the bishop of Rome, or to acknowledge him as the universal bishop. And what needeth many words? Æneas Sylvius, being himself afterward bishop of Rome, for certain proof hereof writeth thus: *Ad episcopos Romanos aliquis sane, sed tamen parvus, ante Nicenum concilium respectus erat*[9]: "Some regard there was unto the bishops of Rome before the council of Nice, although but small." To be short, I trust it shall appear, even by M. Harding's own proofs, that is to say, by the order of appeals, by excommunications, by the allowance of elections, by the approving of councils, by restoring of bishops, and by receiving of schismatics into favour, that the bishop of Rome was not taken for the head of the church, nor had any such absolute authority as is supposed. And so M. Harding's six-fold proof, which is noted in the margin, in conclusion will appear but single-soled.

M. HARDING. THE TWENTY-FIRST DIVISION.

[1. *Appellations the pope.* H. A. 1564.]

First, for the appellation of bishops to the see apostolic, beside many other, we have the known examples of Athanasius, that worthy bishop of Alexandria and light of the world; who, having sustained great and sundry wrongs at the Arians, appealed first to Julius the pope, and after his death to Felix; of Chrysostom, who appealed to Innocentius against the violence of Theophilus; of Theodoretus, who appealed to Leo. Neither made bishops only their appeal to the pope by their delegates, but also in certain cases, being cited, appeared[10] *before him in their own persons. Which is plainly gathered of Theodoretus his ecclesiastical story, who writeth thus: "Eusebius, bishop of Nicomedia (who was the chief pillar of the Arians), and they that joined with him in that faction, falsely accused Athanasius to Julius the bishop of Rome. Julius, following the ecclesiastical rule, commanded them to come to Rome, and caused the reverend Athanasius to be cited to judgment,* regulariter, *after the order of the canons. He came: the false accusers went not to Rome, knowing right well that their forged lie might easily be deprehended*[11]."

[1 Euseb. in Hist. Eccles. Script. Amst. 1695-1700. Lib. VII. capp. v. ix. pp. 205, 8.]

[2 Recitatis epistolis ... consacerdotis nostri Anastasii, &c.—Concil. Afric. cap. 32. in Crabb. Concil. Col. Agrip. 1551. Tom. I. p. 507.]

[3 Cyril. Alex. ad Cœlest. Epist. in Concil. Ephes. in Concil. Stud. Labb. et Cossart. Lut. Par. 1671-2. Tom. III. col. 342. See before, page 373, note 21.]

[4 ... συλλειτουργῷ, κ.τ.λ.—Epiph. Op. Par. 1622. Lib. III. Hær. lxxii. Epist. Marcell. ad Jul. Tom. I. p. 834.]

[5 Concil. Nic. can. 6. in Concil. Stud. Labb. et Cossart. Tom. II. col. 32.]

[6 Concil. Afric. cap. 92. in Crabb. Concil. Tom. I. p. 517.]

[7 Gregor. Magni Papæ I. Op. Par. 1705. Epist. Lib. I. Indict. IX. Ad Anastas. Patr. Epist. xxvi. Tom. II. cols. 516, 7. Id. Lib. VII. Indict. xv. Ad Anastas. Episc. Epist. xxvii. cols. 873, 4.

These are the epistles noted in the margin: others as much in point might readily be mentioned. See below, page 404.]

[8 Hist. Eccles. Par. Lib. x. cap. xxix. foll. 116, 7.]

[9 Quemadmodum factum esse videmus ante concilium Nicænum, dum sibi quisque vivebat, et ad Romanam ecclesiam parvus habebatur respectus.—Æn. Sylv. Op. Basil. 1571. Ad Mart. Mayer. Epist. cclxxxviii. p. 802.]

[10 Appear, 1611.]

[11 Καὶ γὰρ τῷ Ῥώμης ἐπισκόπῳ, Ἰούλιος δὲ τηνικαῦτα τὴν ἐκκλησίαν ἐκείνην ἐποίμαινεν, οἱ περὶ Εὐσέβιον τὰς κατὰ Ἀθανασίου συντεθείσας συκοφαντίας ἐξέπεμψαν. ὁ δὲ τῷ τῆς ἐκκλησίας ἑπόμενος νόμῳ, καὶ αὐτοὺς καταλαβεῖν τὴν Ῥώμην

In this[12] *cause and defence of John Chrysostom, these bishops came from Constantinople to Innocentius the pope, Pansophus bishop of Pisidia, Pappus of Syria, Demetrius of the second Galatia, and Eugenius of Phrygia. These were suitors for Chrysostom. He himself treated his matter with Innocentius by writing. In his epistle, among other things, he writeth thus: "Lest this outrageous confusion run over all, and bear rule every where, write, I pray you, and determine by your authority, such wicked acts done in our absence, and when we withdrew not ourselves from judgment, to be of no force, as by their own nature truly they be void and utterly none. Furthermore, who have committed these evils* (107), *put you them under the censure of the church. And as for us, sith that we are innocent, neither convict, neither found in any default, nor proved guilty of any crime, give commandment that we be restored to our churches again, that we may enjoy the accustomed charity and peace with our brethren*[13]*." Innocentius, after that he understood the whole matter, pronounced and decreed the judgment of Theophilus, that was against Chrysostom, to be void and of no force. This whole tragedy is at large set forth by Palladius bishop of Helenopolis,* In Vita Johannis Chrysostomi, *who lived at that time*[14]. *By this appeal of Chrysostom, and by the whole handling of the matter, and specially by the purport of his epistle to Innocentius, the superiority of the pope is evidently acknowledged. And so is it plainly confessed by Athanasius and the bishops of Egypt, Thebais, and Lybia, assembled in council at Alexandria, by these words of their epistle to Fœlix:* Vestrum est enim nobis manum porrigere[15], &c.: *"It is your part," say they, "to stretch forth your helping hand unto us, because we are committed unto you. It is your part to defend us and deliver us: it is our part to seek help of you, and to obey your commandments." And a little after: "For we know that you bear the cure and charge of the universal church, and specially of bishops, who, in respect of their contemplation and speculation, are called the eyes of our Lord; as always the prelates of your see, first the apostles, then their successors, have done."*

The hundred and seventh untruth. St Chrysostom's words untruly reported.

Theodoretus, that learned bishop of Cyrus, beside the epistle he wrote to Leo for succour and help in his troubles, in another that he wrote to Renatus, a priest near about Leo, saith thus: Spoliarunt me sacerdotio, &c.: *"They have violently robbed me of my bishopric; they have cast me forth of the cities; neither having reverenced mine age spent in religion, nor my hoar hairs. Wherefore, I beseech thee, that thou persuade the most holy archbishop* (he meaneth Leo) *to use his apostolic authority, and to command us to come unto your council or consistory. For this holy see holdeth the rudder, and hath the government of the churches of the whole world, partly for other respects, but specially for that it hath evermore continued clear from stench of heresy, and that none ever sat in it who was of contrary opinion, but rather hath ever kept the apostolic grace undefiled*[16]*." In which words of Theo-*

ἐκέλευσε, καὶ τὸν Ἀθανάσιον εἰς τὴν δίκην ἐκάλεσε. καὶ οὗτος μὲν ἐξώρμησεν εὐθὺς τὴν κλῆσιν δεξάμενος. οἱ δὲ τὸ δρᾶμα συντεθεικότες εἰς μὲν τὴν Ῥώμην οὐκ ἀπῆλθον, εὐφώρατον εἰδότες τὸ ψεῦδος.—Theod. in Hist. Eccles. Script. Lib. II. cap. iv. p. 71. See also Hist. Tripart. Par. Lib. IV. cap. vi. fol. F. 3; where the word *regulariter* occurs.]

[12 The, 1565, 1609, and H. A. 1564.]

[13 Ἵνα οὖν μὴ τοσαύτη σύγχυσις καταλάβῃ τὴν ὑφ' ἥλιον πᾶσαν, ἐπιστεῖλαι παρακλήθητε τὰ μὲν οὕτω παρανόμως γεγενημένα ἀπόντων ἡμῶν, καὶ ἐκ μιᾶς μοίρας, καὶ οὐ παραιτησαμένων κρίσιν, μηδεμίαν ἔχειν ἰσχὺν, ὥσπερ οὖν οὐδὲ ἔχει τῇ οἰκείᾳ φύσει· τοὺς δὲ τοιαῦτα παρανομήσαντας ἐλεγχομένους τῷ ἐπιτιμίῳ ὑποβάλλεσθαι τῶν ἐκκλησιαστικῶν νόμων· ἡμᾶς δὲ τοὺς οὐχ ἁλόντας, οὐκ ἐλεγχομένους, οὐκ ἀποδειχθέντας ὑπευθύνους, τῶν γραμμάτων τῶν ὑμετέρων δότε ἀπολαύειν συνεχῶς, καὶ τῆς ἀγάπης, καὶ πάντων τῶν ἄλλων, ὧνπερ καὶ ἔμπροσθεν.—Chrysost. Op. Par. 1718-38. Ad Innoc. Epist. i. Tom. III. p. 520.]

[14 Pallad. Dial. De Vit. Chrysost. in eod. Tom. XIII. pp. 20, &c. 84, 5.]

[15 Vestrum, &c., quia vobis commissi sumus. Vestrum est nos defendere atque liberare, nostrumque est, a vobis auxilium expetere, vestris parere jussionibus......Scimus enim (ut semper vestræ sedis præsules, primo apostoli, deinde successores eorum, fecerunt) vos universalis ecclesiæ, et maxime episcoporum, qui oculi, propter contemplationem et speculationem, vocantur Domini, curam gerere, &c.—Epist. Ægypt. ad Felic. in Crabb. Concil. Tom. I. p. 357.]

[16 ... ἐγύμνωσαν μὲν ἱερωσύνης, ἐξελαύνουσι δὲ καὶ πόλεως, οὐδὲ τὸ γῆρας αἰδεσθέντες, οὐδὲ τὴν πολιὰν τὴν ἐν εὐσεβείᾳ τραφεῖσαν. διά τοι τοῦτο τὴν ὑμετέραν ἁγιωσύνην παρακαλῶ, πεῖσαι τὸν ἁγιώτατον καὶ ὁσιώτατον ἀρχιεπίσκοπον τῇ ἀποστολικῇ χρήσασθαι ἐξουσίᾳ, καὶ εἰς τὸ ὑμέτερον ἀναδραμεῖν κελεῦσαι συνέδριον. ἔχει γὰρ ὁ πανάγιος θρόνος ἐκεῖνος τῶν κατὰ τὴν οἰκουμένην ἐκκλησιῶν τὴν ἡγεμονίαν διὰ πολλὰ, καὶ πρὸ τῶν ἄλλων ἁπάντων, ὅτι αἱρετικῆς μεμένηκε δυσωδίας ἀμύητος, καὶ οὐδεὶς τἀναντία φρονῶν εἰς ἐκεῖνον ἐκάθισεν, ἀλλὰ τὴν ἀποστολικὴν χάριν ἀκήρατον διεφύλαξε.—Theod. Op. Lut. Par. 1642-84. Ad Renat. Epist. cxvi. Tom. III. Pars II. p. 989.]

Appeals. *doretus this chiefly is*[1] *to be marked, that the holy see of Rome, as he saith, hath the government of the churches of all the world, most for this cause, that it was never infected with heresy, as all other churches founded by the apostles were.*

THE BISHOP OF SARISBURY.

It is certain that the bishops of Rome, to attain the pre-eminence and fulness of power over all the world, letted not to use many ambitious and importune means, and manifestly to falsify the canons of the holy council of Nice. Sithence which time they have not been idle, but have forged new canons to this purpose under the name of Clemens, Anacletus, Evaristus, Telesphorus, Higinus, and other martyrs; and besides have devised other like canons of their own. The decretal epistle that is abroad under the name of Julius seemeth to savour of some corruption, both for sundry other causes, and also for that it agreeth not with the very true epistle of Julius, which Athanasius allegeth in his apology[2]; and yet ought both these epistles to be all one without difference. Wherefore we have good cause to think that "all is not gospel that cometh from Rome."

Athanas. in Apolog. ii.

Thus ambitiously to advance[3] themselves under pretence of such appeals, oftentimes not understanding the case, (as it well appeareth by that is written of Apiarius, and by the story of Flavianus and Eutyches,) they found fault with good catholic bishops, and received heretics into their favour; wherewithal the bishops in the general council of Africa find themselves much grieved.

First, therefore, I must shew that there lay no such ordinary appeal from all countries of the world to the bishop of Rome, and that therefore the same is by M. Harding untruly avouched. That done, I trust it shall not be hard to answer these places of Chrysostom, Athanasius, and Theodoretus here alleged.

And that there lay not any such appeal to Rome, it is plain by consent of general councils; by the authority of holy fathers; and by the laws and ordinances of emperors and princes: by which grounds it is easy to understand the practice and order of the church in those days.

Concil. Nic. i. cap. 5.

In the council of Nice it is decreed thus: *Ab aliis excommunicati ab aliis ad communionem ne recipiantur*[4]: "Let not them, that stand excommunicate by one bishop, be received again to the communion by any other." M. Harding's appeals and these words cannot well stand together. But he will say, the bishop either of ignorance or of malice may excommunicate the party wrongfully. In this case the same council hath provided remedy of appeal, not unto the bishop of Rome, but unto a provincial synod within the country. These be the words: *Ergo, ut hæc possint digna examinatione perquiri, recte visum est, per singulos annos, in singulis provinciis, bis in anno, episcoporum concilium fieri, ut simul in unum convenientes ex communi provincia hujusmodi quæstiones examinent*[5]: "Therefore, that these things may be well examined, it is well provided, that every year in every province, at two several times, there be holden a council of bishops[6], that they, meeting together out of all parts of the province, may hear and determine such complaints."

Concil. Nic. i. can. 5.

Concil. Telen. tempore Zosim. can. 17.

The bishops in the council holden at Tela in Spain ordained thus: *Presbyteri et clerici ne appellent, nisi ad Africana concilia*[7]: "Let it not be lawful for priests or clerks to appeal (to Rome) but only to the councils holden in Africa."

Concil. Milev. can. 22.

So in the Milevitane council: *Si ab episcopis appellandum putaverint, non provocent, nisi ad Africana concilia, vel ad primates provinciarum suarum. Ad transmarina autem qui putaverint appellandum, a nullo intra Africam in communionem recipiantur*[8]: "If they think it meet to appeal from their bishops, let them

[1 This is chiefly, H. A. 1564.]

[2 Athanas. Op. Par. 1698. Epist. Jul. in Apol. contr. Arian. Tom. I. pp. 141, &c.]

[3 Avance, 1565.]

[4 Concil. Nic. can. 5. in Concil. Stud. Labb. et Cossart. Lut. Par. 1671-2. Tom. II. col. 32.]

[5 Id. ibid.] [6 Bishop, 1611.]

[7 Crabb. Concil. Col. Agrip. 1551. Tom. I. p. 489; where the council of Tela is referred to; but neither here nor p. 420, where a fuller account of it is given, is any thing to the point. In the same page, however, p. 489, are the titles of the canons of a council said to be held at Carthage; and the 17th of these is: De presbyteris et clericis, ut non appellent nisi ad Aphricana concilia.]

[8 Concil. Milev. cap. 22. in eod. Tom. I. p. 484; where *si et ab eis provocandum, qui putaverit,* and *suscipiatur.*]

not appeal, but only to the councils of Africa, or unto the primates of their own provinces. But if they shall make their appeal beyond the seas (that is, to Rome), let no man in Africa receive them to the communion." Appeals.

So likewise in the council of Africa: *Si...fuerit provocatum, eligat [is] qui provocaverit judices, et cum eo et ille, contra quem provocaverit, ut ab ipsis deinceps nulli liceat provocare*[9]: "If appeal be made, let him that shall appeal choose other judges of his side; and likewise let the other do the same against whom he appealeth; that from them afterward it be lawful for neither of them to appeal." Concil. Aphr. can. 63.

And again in the same council: *Non provocent nisi ad Africana concilia*[10]: "Let them not appeal, but only unto the councils holden within Africa;" and so forth word by word, as is alleged out of the council of Milevita. But here I may not well pass over Gratian's gloss touching this matter. For whereas the council hath determined that, if any man appeal beyond the seas, he stand excommunicate, Gratian hath expounded and salved it with this pretty exception: *Nisi forte Romanam sedem* [11] *appellaverit*[12]: "Unless they appeal to the see of Rome." And so, by his construction, he excepteth that only thing out of the law, for which only thing the whole law was made. For it is plain and without all question, that the council of Africa specially and namely meant to cut off all appeals to the see of Rome. And yet those only appeals Gratian by his construction would have to be saved. Concil. Aphr. can. 92. ii. Quæst. vi. can. Placuit.

But what can be so plain as the epistle of the two hundred and seventeen bishops in the council of Africa, sent unto Cœlestinus bishop of Rome, declaring at length both the state and conveyance of the cause, and also their grief and misliking of the whole matter? The words lie thus: *Decreta Nicena sive inferioris gradus clericos*[13], *&c.*: "The decrees of the council of Nice have evidently committed both the clerks of inferior rooms, and also the bishops themselves, unto their metropolitans. For both justly and discreetly they provided, that all manner actions should be determined in the same places where they began; and likewise thought[14] that no province should want the grace of the Holy Ghost, whereby christian bishops might be able both wisely to consider, and also constantly to maintain the right: and specially seeing that liberty is given that, if either party mislike his judges' order, he may lawfully appeal either to a convocation of bishops within the same country, or else to a general council. Unless any man will think that God is able to inspire the justice of trial into one man alone (meaning thereby the bishop of Rome), and will deny the same to a great number of bishops, being in council all together. And how can your beyond-sea judgment appear good, seeing that the witnesses, which be parties necessary, either for that they be women, or for that they be aged and weak, or for many other incident impediments, cannot come unto it? As for any delegates that should be sent, as from your side, we find no such matter determined in any council. And touching that you sent us of late by Faustinus, our fellow-bishop, as part of the Nicene council, in the very true councils of Nice, which we have received from holy Cyrillus the bishop of Alexandria, and from Atticus the bishop of Constantinople, &c. we find no such matter. Neither send ye, nor grant ye, your clerks to execute causes at any man's request, lest we seem to bring a smoky puff of worldly pride into the church of Christ, which, unto them that desire to see God, sheweth the light of simplicity and humility," &c. Epist. Aphr. Concil. ad Cœlest. Justitiam examinis unicuilibet. Executores clericos vestros.

The bishops of the east part of the world, being Arians, writing unto Julius the bishop of Rome, took it grievously that he would presume to over-rule them; and shewed him, it was not lawful for him, by any sleight or colour of appeal, to undo that thing that they had done[15]. Sozom. Lib. iii. cap. vii.

St Cyprian, finding fault with such running to Rome, and defeating of justice, writeth unto Cornelius the bishop there in this sort: *Cum...æquum justumque sit,* Cypr. Lib. i. Epist. 3.

[9 Concil. Afric. cap. 63. in eod. Tom. I. p. 513.]

[10 Ibid. cap. 92. ibid. p. 517.]

[11 Appellaverint, 1565.]

[12 Corp. Jur. Canon. Lugd. 1624. Decret. Gratian. Decr. Sec. Pars, Caus. II. Quæst. vi. ad calc. can. 35. col. 675.]

[13 Epist. Concil. Afric. ad Cœlestin. cap. 105. in Crabb. Concil. Tom. I. p. 521. See before, page 356, note 6.]

[14 Though, 1611.]

[15 Sozom. in Hist. Eccles. Script. Amst. 1695-1700. Lib. III. cap. viii. p. 414.]

Appeals.

ut uniuscujusque causa illic audiatur, ubi crimen est admissum, et singulis pastoribus portio gregis sit adscripta, quam regat unusquisque et gubernet, rationem sui actus Domino redditurus; oportet utique eos, quibus præsumus, non circumcursare, nec episcoporum concordiam cohærentem sua subdola et fallaci temeritate collidere, sed agere illic causam suam, ubi et accusatores habere et testes sui criminis possint: nisi ...paucis desperatis et perditis minor videtur esse auctoritas episcoporum in Africa constitutorum, qui jam de illis judicaverunt[1], *&c.*: "Seeing it is meet and right that every man's cause be heard there where the fault was committed, and seeing that every bishop hath a portion of the flock allotted unto him, which he must rule and govern, and yield account unto the Lord for the same; therefore it is not meet that they whom we are appointed to oversee do thus run about (with their appeals), and so, with their subtle and deceitful rashness, break that concord and consent of bishops: but there ought they to plead their cause, where they may have both accusers and witnesses of the fault; unless perhaps a few desperate and lewd fellows think the authority of the bishops of Africa, which have already judged and condemned them, to be less than is the authority of other bishops."

Lewd and desperate.

Hereby it is clear that the godly fathers and bishops, in old times, misliked much this shifting of matters to Rome, for that they saw it was the hindrance of right, the increase of ambition, and the open breach of the holy canons.

And therefore the emperor Justinian, foreseeing the disorders that hereof might grow, to bridle this ambitious outrage, thought it necessary for his subjects, to provide a strait law in this wise to the contrary: *Si quis ... sanctissimorum episcoporum ejusdem synodi dubitationem aliquam adinvicem habeat, sive pro ecclesiastico jure, sive pro aliis quibusdam rebus, prius metropolita eorum, cum aliis de sua synodo episcopis, causam examinet et judicet. Quod si utraque pars rata non habuerit ea quæ judicata sunt, tunc beatissimus patriarcha dioceseos illius inter eos audiat, et illa determinet quæ ecclesiasticis canonibus et legibus consonant, nulla parte ejus sententiæ contradicere valente*[2]: "If any of the most holy bishops, being of one synod, have any matter of doubt or question among themselves, whether it be for ecclesiastical right, or any other matters, first let their metropolitan, with other bishops of the same synod, examine and judge the cause. But if both the parties stand not to his and their judgments, then let the most holy patriarch of the same province hear and determine their matters[3], according to the ecclesiastical laws and canons. And neither of the parties may withstand his determination." And immediately after: *Patriarcha secundum canones et leges ... præbeat finem*[4]: "Let the patriarch according to the laws and canons make an end." By these words all appeals be quite cut off from the see of Rome.

Auth. de Sanct. Episc. Collat. ix. Si quis vero.

οὐδενὸς μέρους ... ἀντιλέγειν δυναμένου.

In eodem.

παρεχέτω πέρας.

Likewise the emperors Honorius and Theodosius have taken appeals away from the bishops of Rome, and have commanded the same to be entered before the bishop and synod of Constantinople. The law is written thus: *Omni innovatione cessante, vetustatem, et canones pristinos ecclesiasticos, qui usque tunc tenuerunt, . . . per omnes Illyrici provincias servari præcipimus: ut si quid dubietatis*[5] *emerserit, id oporteat, non absque sententia viri reverendissimi sacrosanctæ legis antistitis ecclesiæ urbis Constantinopolitanæ, quæ Romæ veteris prærogativa lætatur, conventui sacerdotali et sancto judicio reservari*[6]: "All innovation set apart, we command that the old order, and the ancient ecclesiastical canons, which hitherto have holden, be kept still through all the provinces of Illyricum; that, if any matter of doubt happen to arise, it be put over to be determined by the holy judgment and assembly of bishops, not without the discretion of the most

Cod. de Sacrosanct. Eccles. Omni.

Cod. de Episc. et Clericis. Actor in nullo alio foro, vel apud quenquam alterum judicem, clericos (ecclesiæ Constantinopolitanæ) litibus tentet irretire.[7]

[1 Cypr. Op. Oxon. 1682. Ad Cornel. Epist. lix. pp. 136, 7; where we find *æquum sit pariter ac justum*, and *est crimen*.]

[2 Corp. Jur. Civil. Amst. 1663. Auth. Coll. IX. Tit. VI. Novell. cxxiii. cap. 22; where *et si non rata habuerit utraque pars quæ*.]

[3 Matter, 1565, 1609.]

[4 Id. ibid.; where for *patriarcha* we find *et ille: κἀκεῖνος*.]

[5 Dubitatis, 1609, 1611.]

[6 Id. Cod. Lib. I. Tit. ii. 6. Tom. II. p. 6; where *usque nunc, scientia*, and *sanctoque*.]

[7 Id. ibid. Lib. I. Tit. iii. 25. Tom. II. p. 13; where for *actor* we have *qui*, and *eosdem clericos litibus irretire...tentet*.]

reverend the bishop of the city of Constantinople, which city now enjoyeth the prerogative of old Rome." Here M. Harding may not forget that the church of Constantinople had as great prerogative in all respects, of pre-eminence, superiority, and universality of charge, as ever had the church of Rome. Wherefore, if the bishop of Rome were head of the universal church, it must needs follow that the bishop of Constantinople was likewise head of the universal church. Appeals.

And again, the emperor Leo in plainer words: *Omnes qui ubicunque sunt, vel posthac fuerint, orthodoxæ fidei sacerdotes, et cleri*[8], *cujuscunque gradus sint, monachi quoque, in causis civilibus, ex nullius penitus majoris minorisve sententia judicis commonitoria ad extranea judicia pertrahantur; aut provinciam, vel locum, vel regionem quam habitant, exire cogantur*[9]: "All that be, or hereafter shall be, priests or clerks of the catholic faith, of what degree soever they be, monks also, let them not in any civil actions be drawn forth to foreign judgment, by the summon or commandment of any judge, more or less; neither let them be driven to come forth of either the province, or the place, or the country, where they dwell." Thus, whether the action were ecclesiastical or civil, the party was to be heard within his own province, and could not be forced to appear abroad. Cod. de Episc. et Cleric. Omnes.

Certainly, what good liking St Bernard had herein, it appeareth by his words. For thus he writeth to Eugenius the bishop of Rome: *Quousque non evigilat consideratio tua ad tantam appellationum confusionem?... Ambitio in ecclesia per te regnare molitur:... præter jus et fas, præter morem et ordinem, fiunt.... Repertum ad remedium, reperitur ad mortem:... antidotum versum [est] in venenum.... Murmur loquor et querimoniam [communem] ecclesiarum. Truncari se clamant et demembrari. Vel nullæ, vel paucæ admodum sunt, quæ plagam istam aut non doleant, aut non timeant*[10]: "When will thy consideration awake, to behold this so great confusion of appeals? Ambition and pride striveth through thee to reign in the church. These appeals be made beside all law and right, beside all manner and good order. It was devised for a remedy: it is found turned to death. That was triacle[11] is changed into poison. I speak of the murmuring and common complaint of the churches. They complain they be maimed and dismembered. There be either no churches, or very few, but either smart at this plague, or stand in fear of it." This is that worthy ground, whereupon M. Harding hath laid the first foundation of his supremacy: a confusion, a death, a poison, a terror, and dismembering of the churches; practised against law, against right, against manner, and against good order; misliked by the holy fathers, disallowed by godly councils, and utterly abrogated and abolished by sundry worthy and noble princes. This is M. Harding's principal foundation of his primacy. Bernard. ad Eugen. de Considerat. Lib. iii.

But yet these men will say, Chrysostom, Athanasius, and Theodoretus, being godly fathers and holy bishops, appealed to Rome, and acknowledged the pope's authority, and besought him to use the same. For the true understanding hereof, it shall be necessary to consider the state that these godly fathers then stood in, and the miserable confusion of the east part of the world in those days. Chrysostom thereof writeth thus: *Certamen est totius orbis; ecclesiæ usque ad genua humiliatæ sunt, populi dispersi, clerus divexatus, episcopi exules, constitutiones patrum violatæ*[12]: "It is the contention of the whole world; the churches are brought upon their knees; the people is scattered; the ministry is oppressed; the bishops are banished; the constitutions of our fathers are broken." The emperor's captain with a band of soldiers beset the church where Athanasius was praying. Of the people that was with him, some were spoiled and banished, some trodden under the soldiers' feet, some slain where they went. Paulus the bishop of Constantinople was hanged: Marcellus the bishop of Ancyra was deprived: Lucius the bishop of Adrianopolis died in prison: Theodulus and Olympius, two bishops of Thracia, were commanded to be murdered. The Epist. 2. Chrysost. ad Innocent. Socrat. Lib. ii. cap. xi. Sozom. Lib. iii. cap. vi. Athan. in Epist. ad solitariam vitam agentes. Theodor. Lib. ii. cap. xiv.

[8 Clerici, 1565, 1609.]

[9 Id. ibid. Lib. I. Tit. iii. 33. Tom. II. p. 17; where *ubique, clerici*, and *aut locum aut regionem.*]

[10 Bernard. Op. Par. 1690. De Consid. Lib. III. capp. ii. 7. i. 5. ii. 7, 8. iv. 14. Vol. I. Tom. II. cols. 428-31; where *ne quod repertum ad remedium fuit reperiatur ad mortem*, and *clamitant.*]

[11 Triacle: treacle.]

[12 Chrysost. Op. Par. 1718-38. Ad Innoc. Epist. ii. Tom. III. p. 522.]

Appeals. emperor had commanded Athanasius to be brought unto him, either dead or alive[1].

These godly fathers, being thus in extreme misery, and seeing their whole church in the east part so desolate, were forced to seek for comfort wheresoever they had hope to find any; and specially they sought to the church of Rome, which then, both for multitude of people, and for purity of religion and constancy in the same, and also for helping of the afflicted, and entreating for them, was most famous above all others. In like sort sometimes they fled for help unto the emperor. So Athanasius, being condemned in the council at Tyrus, fled to Constantinus the emperor[2]; Flavianus unto the emperors Theodosius and Valentinianus[3]; Donatus a Casis Nigris unto Constantinus[4]. And the emperors sometimes called the parties, and heard the matter themselves; sometimes they wrote favourable letters in their behalf. The emperor Constans wrote unto his brother Constantius to call before him the bishops of the east part, to yield a reckoning of their doings against Athanasius[5]. The emperor Honorius gave his endeavour that Athanasius might be restored[6]. Constantinus the emperor, upon Athanasius' complaint, commanded the bishops of the council of Tyrus to appear before him. The words of his summon be these: *Quotquot synodum Tyri habitam complevistis, sine mora ad pietatis nostræ castra properetis, ac re ipsa, quam sincere ac recte judicaveritis, ostendatis: idque coram me, quem sincerum esse Dei ministrum ne vos quidem ipsi negabitis*[7]: "As many of you as were at the council of Tyrus, hie you unto our camp or court without delay, and shew us how sincerely and uprightly ye have dealt; and that even *before me*, whom you yourselves cannot deny to be the sincere servant of God."

Athan. Apol. 2. Socrat. Lib. i. cap. xx. Cassiod. Lib. iv. cap. xx. Ambros. Lib. x. Epist. 78. August. Epist. 162. Inter Decret. Julii, e Sozom. Sozom. Lib. viii. cap. xxviii. Socrat. Lib. i. cap. xxii. Coram me.

Thus holy men, being in distress, sought help wheresoever they had hope to find it. This seeking of remedy by way of complaint, as it declareth their misery, so it is[8] not sufficient to prove an ordinary appeal.

But it is most certain, and without all question, that Chrysostom appealed unto Innocentius. For M. Harding hath here alleged his own words. I grant M. Harding hath here alleged Chrysostom, but in such faithful and trusty sort as pope Zosimus sometimes alleged the council of Nice. Good christian reader, if thou have Chrysostom, peruse this place, and weigh well his words; if thou have him not, yet be not over-hasty of belief. M. Harding's dealing with thee herein is not plain. The very words of Chrysostom in Latin stand thus: *Ne confusio hæc omnem, quæ sub cœlo est, nationem invadat, obsecro ut scribas, quod hæc tam inique facta, et absentibus nobis, et non declinantibus judicium, non habeant robur: sicut neque natura sua habent. Illi autem, qui inique egerunt, pœnæ ecclesiasticarum legum subjaceant. Nobis vero, qui nec convicti, nec redarguti, nec habiti ut rei [sumus], literis vestris, et caritate vestra, aliorumque omnium quorum... ante societate fruebamur, frui concedite*[9]. Which words into English may truly be translated thus: "Lest this confusion overrun all nations under heaven, I pray thee write (or signify) unto them, that these things so unjustly done, I being absent, and yet not flying[10] judgment, be of no force, as indeed of their own nature they be of none; and (write) that they that have done these things so

Epist. Chrysost. ad Innocent. in Tom. v. Epist. 1.

[1 Socrat. in Hist. Eccles. Script. Amst. 1695-1700. Lib. II. cap. xi. p. 74.
Sozom. in eod. Lib. II. cap. vi. p. 411.
Athanas. Op. Par. 1698. Hist. Arian. ad Monach. 6. 7. 19. Tom. I. pp. 347, 8, 354, 5.
Theodor. in Hist. Eccles. Script. Lib. II. cap. xiv. pp. 88, &c.]

[2 Athanas. Op. Apol. contr. Arian. 9. Tom. I. Pars I. p. 131.
Socrat. in Hist. Eccles. Script. Lib. I. capp. xxxi. xxxii. p. 56.
Hist. Tripart. Par. Lib. III. cap. v. fol. E. 6.
It is not easy to tell to what events in the text each particular marginal reference is made. The editor has given those which he supposed to be intended.]

[3 Ambros. Op. Par. 1686-90. Ad Theoph. Epist. lvi. 3. Tom. II. col. 1006.]

[4 August. Op. Par. 1679-1700. Ad Glor. et cet. Epist. xliii. 4. Tom. II. col. 90.]

[5 Sozom. in Decret. Jul. Papæ I. in Crabb. Concil. Col. Agrip. 1551. Tom. I. p. 314.]

[6 There is evidently an error here. For Athanasius probably Chrysostom is meant. The place referred to in Sozomen mentions the petition to the emperors Honorius and Arcadius for a synod with the view of obtaining the restoration of Chrysostom. Sozom. in Hist. Eccles. Script. Lib. VIII. cap. xxviii. p. 645.]

[7 Socrat. in eod. Lib. I. cap. xxxiv. p. 58.]

[8 Is it, 1565.]

[9 Chrysost. Op. Lat. Basil. 1547. Ad Innoc. Epist. i. Tom. V. cols. 972, 3; where *sua natura* and *antea*.]

[10 Fleeing, 1565.]

wrongfully be punished by the laws of the church; and grant you that we, that are neither convicted, nor reproved, nor found guilty, may enjoy your letters and your love, and likewise the letters and love of all others whose fellowship we enjoyed before." In these few words M. Harding hath notably falsified three places, quite altering the words that he found, and shuffling in and interlacing other words of his own. For these words in M. Harding's translation, that seem to signify authority in the bishop of Rome, and to import the appeal:

Appeals.

"Write, and determine by your authority: Put you them under the censure of the church:

"Give commandment that we be restored to our churches;"

these words, I say, are not to be found in Chrysostom, neither in the Greek nor in the Latin, but only are prettily conveyed in by M. Harding, the better to furnish and fashion up his appeal. He seeth well this matter will not stand upright without the manifest corruption and falsifying of the doctors. This therefore is M. Harding's appeal, and not Chrysostom's.

M. Harding falsifieth and untruly translateth St Chrysostom.

For that Chrysostom made no such appeal to the bishop of Rome, it may sufficiently appear, both by Chrysostom's own epistles, and by the bishop of Rome's dealing herein, and by the end and conclusion of the cause. Touching Chrysostom himself, he maketh no mention of any appeal, nor desireth the parties to be cited to Rome, nor taketh Innocentius for the bishop of the whole church, or for the universal judge of all the world, but only saluteth him thus: *Innocentio episcopo Romæ Johannes*[11]: "John to Innocentius bishop of Rome sendeth greeting." And again, in the same epistle, he utterly avoideth all such foreign judgments, according to the determinations of the councils of Carthage, Milevitum, and Africa. These be his words: *Neque ... congruum est, ut hi, qui in Ægypto sunt, judicent eos qui [sunt] in Thracia*[12]: "It is not meet that they that be in Egypt should be judges over them that be in Thracia."

Ad Innocent. Epist. priore.

Neither do the bishop of Rome's own words import any appeal, but rather the contrary: for he used[13] not his familiar words of bidding or commanding, but only in gentle and friendly manner exhorteth them to appear; and that not before himself, but only before the council of sundry bishops, summoned specially for that purpose. For thus Julius writeth unto the bishops of the east: *Quæ est causa offensionis? ... An quia adhortati vos sumus, ut ad synodum occurreretis*[14]? "What is the cause of your displeasure? Is it because we exhorted you to come to the council?" Here he exhorteth and entreateth them: he commandeth them not: he calleth them to come, not before himself, but before the council. Again he saith: *Legati vestri, Macarius presbyter, et Hesychius diaconus, ... concilium indici postulaverunt*[15]: "Your own ambassadors, Macarius being a priest, and Hesychius being a deacon, required that a council might be summoned." And again: *Vellem... vos magis ad jam dictam canonicam convenire vocationem, ut coram universali synodo reddatis rationem*[16]: "I would you rather to come to this canonical calling, that ye may yield your account of your doings before the general council." So likewise St Basil writeth to Athanasius, by way of counsel, in that heavy time of trouble: *Viros igitur ecclesiæ tuæ potentes ad occidentales episcopos mitte, qui, quibus calamitatibus premamur, illis exponant*[17]: "Send some worthy men of your churches (not unto the bishop of Rome, but) unto the bishops of the west, that may let them understand with what miseries we are beset." Likewise again he saith: *Visum mihi est consentaneum, ut scribatur episcopo Romæ, ut ea, quæ hic geruntur, consideret, detque concilium*[18]: "I think it good ye write to the bishop of Rome, that he may consider that is here done, and may appoint us a council."

Epist. Julii in Athan. Apol. 2.

In Apol. 2.

Epist. Julii ad Oriental. inter Decret. Julii.

Basil. Epist. 48. ad Athan.

Basil. ad Athan. Epist. 52.

[11 This is the address in the second epistle—Id. ibid.; in the first these words are added: domino meo reverendissimo, pientissimoque.—Ibid. cols. 969, 70.]

[12 Id. ibid. col. 970.]

[13 Useth, 1565.]

[14 Epist. Jul. in Athanas. Op. Apol. contr. Arian. 22. Tom. I. Pars I. p. 142.]

[15 Id. ibid.]

[16 Rescr. Jul. contr. Orient. in Crabb. Concil. Tom. I. p. 309; where *concilio redderetis.*]

[17 Basil. Op. Par. 1721-30. Ad Athanas. Epist. lxvi. Tom. III. p. 159.]

[18 Id. ad eund. Epist. lxix. p. 162; where however the Greek text has δοῦναι γνώμην, and a little below αὐτὸν αὐθεντῆσαι περὶ τὸ πρᾶγμα.]

Appeals.

Athan. in Epist. ad solitariam vitam agentes.

Neither did the bishop of Rome by his own authority summon the bishops of the east, but by the counsel and conference of other bishops. For so Athanasius saith: *Misit omnium Italicorum episcoporum consilio Julius ad episcopos orientales, certum illis synodi diem denuntians*[1]: "Julius sent unto the bishops of the east, by the counsel of all the bishops of Italy, giving them to understand the certain day of the council." Which thing Julius also himself avoucheth by these words: *Tametsi solus sim, qui scripsi, tamen non meam solius sententiam, sed omnium Italorum et omnium in his regionibus episcoporum scripsi*[2]: "Notwithstanding I alone wrote, yet it was not mine own mind only that I wrote, but also the mind of the bishops of Italy, and of all other bishops of these countries."

Epist. Julii in Apol. Athan. 2.

Niceph. Lib. xiii. cap. xxxiii.

So likewise Innocentius the bishop of Rome, being very desirous to restore Chrysostom, and to recover the unity of the church, not of himself, or by his own authority, but by the decree and consent of a council holden in Italy, sent messengers into the east[3]. And, sitting with others in the council, he took not upon him that universal power that is now imagined, but had his voice equal with his brethren, as it appeareth by Miltiades bishop of Rome, that sat with three bishops of Gallia, and fourteen other bishops of Italy, to determine the controversy between Cæcilianus and Donatus a Casis Nigris[4].

Optat. Lib. i.

Now, to come to the prosecution of the matter, M. Harding knoweth that the bishops of the east understood not this singular authority or prerogative of the bishop of Rome; and therefore, being called, obeyed not the summon, nor had any regard unto his sentence, as it is many ways easy to be seen. Therefore they returned unto Julius this answer: *Si nostris placitis...assentiri...volueritis,... pacem vobiscum et communionem habere volumus. Sin vero aliter egeritis, et eis amplius quam nobis assentiri judicaveritis, contraria celebrabimus: et deinceps nec vobiscum congregari, nec vobis obedire, nec vobis vestrisve favere volumus*[5]: "If you will agree unto our orders, we will have peace and communion with you; but, if you will otherwise do, and rather agree unto our adversaries than unto us, then will we publish the contrary; and henceforth neither will we sit in council with you, nor obey you, nor bear good-will either to you or to any of yours."

Inter Decret. Julii Concil. Tom. i.

This imperfection and weakness of their own doings the bishops of Rome themselves understood and confessed. For thus Innocentius writeth unto St Augustine, Alypius, and others in Africa, touching Pelagius: *Si adhuc taliter sentit, cum sciat se damnandum esse; quibus acceptis literis, aut quando se nostro judicio committet? Quod si accersendus esset, id ab illis melius fieret, qui magis proximi, et non longo terrarum spatio videntur esse disjuncti*[6]: "If he continue still in one mind, knowing that I will pronounce against him; at what request of letters, or when will he commit himself to our judgment? If it be good he were called to make answer, it were better some others called him, that are near at hand," &c.

Inter Decret. Innocent. Epist. 27.

Sozom. Lib. iii. cap. x.

And therefore Julius the bishop of Rome, finding his own infirmity herein, wrote unto the emperor Constans, and opened unto him the whole matter, and besought him to write unto his brother Constantius, that it might please him to send the bishops of the east, to make answer to that they had done against Athanasius[7]. Even so the clergy of the city of Antioch, in the like case of trouble and spoil, wrote unto John the patriarch of Constantinople, to entreat the emperor in their behalf[8]. It appeareth hereby, that this infinite authority and prerogative power over all the world in those days was not known.

Concil. Constant. quintum. Actio. 1.

[[1] Mention is made of the announcement by Julius that a council should be summoned, Athanas. Op. Par. 1698. Hist. Arian. ad Monach. 9, 11. Tom. I. Pars I. pp. 349, 50; but nothing is there said of the counsel of all the bishops of Italy.]

[[2] Epist. Jul. in eod. Apol. contr. Arian. 26. Tom. I. Pars I. p. 146.]

[[3] Niceph. Call. Hist. Eccles. Lut. Par. 1630. Lib. XIII. cap. xxxiii. Tom. II. p. 417.]

[[4] Optat. De Schism. Donatist. Lut. Par. 1700. Lib. I. cap. xxiii. p. 20. Optatus enumerates fifteen Italian bishops besides Miltiades.]

[[5] Epist. Orient. ad Jul. in Crabb. Concil. Col. Agrip. 1551. Tom. I. p. 307; where we find *assentire, eligitis, si vero, nobis assentire, vobiscum deinceps nec,* and *vestrisque.*]

[[6] ...si adhuc, &c., quando se nostro judicio, quibusvis acceptis literis, quum sciat damnandum se esse, committet? Quod si accersiendus esset, ab his melius, &c.—Rescr. Innoc. ad Aur. &c. Epist. xxvii. in eod. Tom. I. p. 480.]

[[7] Sozom. in Hist. Eccles. Script. Amst. 1695-1700. Lib. III. cap. x. p. 416.]

[[8] Suppl. Cler. Ant. ad Joan. Patr. et Syn. in Quint. Syn. Const. in Crabb. Concil. Tom. II. pp. 34, 5. See also Concil. Stud. Labb. et Cossart. Lut. Par. 1671-2. Tom. V. cols. 157, &c.]

I think it hereby plainly and sufficiently proved, first, that the bishop of Rome had no authority to receive appeals from all parts of the world, and that by the councils of Nice, of Tele, of Milevitum, and of Africa, by St Cyprian, and by the emperors Martian and Justinian. Next, that M. Harding, the better to furnish his matter, hath notoriously falsified Chrysostom's words three times in one place. Thirdly, that Chrysostom's letter unto Innocentius contained matter of complaint, but no appeal: which thing is also proved by the very words and tenor of the letter, by the bishops of Rome's own confession, and by the imperfection and weakness of their doings. For the law saith: *Jurisdictio sine modica coertione nulla est*[9]: "Jurisdiction without some compulsion is no jurisdiction." Appeals. De Officio ejus cui mandata est jurisdictio. Mandatam.

Indeed, by way of compromise and agreement of the parties, matters were sometimes brought to be heard and ended by the bishop of Rome, as also by other bishops, but not by any ordinary process or course of law. And so it appeareth this matter between Athanasius and the Arians was first brought unto Julius; for that the Arians willingly desired him, for trial thereof, to call a council. For thus Julius himself writeth unto the bishops of the east, as it is before alleged: *Si Macario et Hesychio nullam synodum postulantibus adhortator fuissem, ut ad synodum, qui ad me scripsissent, convocarentur, idque in gratiam fratrum, qui se injuriam pati conquerebantur, etiam ita justa fuisset mea cohortatio:...jam vero, ubi iidem illi, qui a vobis pro gravibus viris et fide dignis habiti sunt, auctores mihi fuerint, ut vos convocarem, certe id a vobis ægre*[10] *ferri non debuit*[11]: "If I had given advice unto (your messengers) Macarius and Hesychius, that they that had written unto me might be called to a council, and that in consideration of our brethren, which complained they suffered wrong, although neither of them had desired the same, yet had mine advice been void of injury. But now, seeing the same men, whom you took to be grave and worthy of credit, have made suit unto me that I should call you, verily ye should not take it in ill part." Epist. Julii in Apol. Athan. 2.

Hereby it is plain that Julius took upon him to call these parties, not by any such universal jurisdiction, as M. Harding fancieth, but only by the consent and request of both parties. And therefore Julius saith, he caused Athanasius to be cited *regulariter*, that is, according to order; for the order of judgment is that a man be first called, and then accused, and last of all condemned: but he meaneth not thereby the order of the canons, as M. Harding expoundeth it. For, touching appeals to Rome, there was no canon yet provided. The counterfeit epistle of Athanasius to Felix is answered before. Regulariter.

Theodoretus was deposed and banished and cruelly entreated, as it appeareth by his letters unto Renatus[12]; and therefore the words that he useth are rather tokens of his miseries and want of help, than certain testimonies of his judgment. For every man is naturally inclined to extol him, and to advance[13] his power, at whose hands[14] he seeketh help. Theodoretus.

But, if it were granted it was lawful then for the bishop of Rome to receive all manner appeals, in such order as it is pretended, yet cannot M. Harding thereof necessarily conclude, that the bishop of Rome was the head of the universal church. For Ostiensis saith: "Appeals may be made, not only from the lower judge unto the higher, but also from equal to equal." And in this order, as it shall afterward be shewed more at large, Donatus a Casis Nigris was by the emperor lawfully removed from the bishop of Rome to the bishop of Arle in France[15]. Ostiensis' words be these: *Non nocebit error, si appelletur ad majorem quam debuerit, vel ad parem*[16]: "The error shall not hurt, if the appeal be made August. Epist. 162. Extra. de Appellat. in Sext. Roman. Eccles. in Gloss.

[[9] Paul. in Corp. Jur. Civil. Amst. 1663. Digest. Lib. I. Tit. xxi. 5. Tom. I. p. 87; where *coercitione.*]

[[10] *Ægri*, 1611.]

[[11] Epist. Jul. in Athanas. Op. Apol. contr. Arian. 22. Tom. I. Pars I. pp. 142, 3. The Greek text for *qui ad me scripsissent convocarentur* is σκύλαι τοὺς γράψαντας.]

[[12] See before, page 387.] [[13] Avance, 1565.]

[[14] Hand, 1565, 1609.]

[[15] August. Op. Par. 1679-1700. Ad Glor. et cet. Epist. xliii. 4. Tom. II. col. 90. See before, page 371, note 17. See also Cler. Hippon. ad Januar. Epist. lxxxviii. 3. col. 214; where the same words *episcopale judicium* are used of the cause at Arles, as at Rome.]

[[16] Hostiens. Op. Par. 1512. In Extrav. Decr. Innoc. IV. De Appellat. fol. 151. See also Corp. Jur. Canon. Lugd. 1624. Sext. Decretal. Lib. II. Tit. xv. Gloss. in cap. iii. col. 402; where the words of Hostiensis are quoted, and the gloss proceeds: Valeat ergo consuetudo quoad parem; but the marginal note mentioned does not appear.]

Appeals. either to a higher judge than was meet, or to an equal." Where also it is thus noted in the margin: *Appellari potest ad parem, si de hoc sit consuetudo:* "Appeal may be made unto the equal, if there be a custom of it." Hereby it is plain that the right of appeal, by fine force of law, concludeth not any necessary superiority, much less this infinite power over the whole universal church.

But M. Harding might soon have foreseen that this his first principle of appeals would easily be turned against himself:

1. First, for that it is well known that appeals then, even in the ecclesiastical causes, were made unto the emperors and civil princes.

2. Secondly, for that the bishop of Rome determined such cases of appeal by warrant and commission from the emperor.

3. Thirdly, for that matters, being once heard and determined by the bishop of Rome, have been by appeal from him removed further unto others.

As touching the first, that appeals in ecclesiastical causes were lawfully made unto the prince, it is clear by Eusebius[1], by Socrates[2], by Nicephorus[3], and by St Augustine, in sundry places. Donatus, being condemned by three-score and ten bishops in Africa, appealed unto the emperor Constantinus, and was received[4]. St Augustine saith: *Parmenianus ultro passus est suos adire Constantinum*[5]: "Parmenianus willingly suffered his fellows to go unto the emperor Constantinus." Again he saith: *Infero adhuc et verba Constantini ex literis ejus,...ubi se inter partes cognovisse, et innocentem Cæcilianum comperisse, testatur*[6]: "Here I bring in the words of Constantine out of his own letters, wherein he confesseth that he heard the parties, and found Cæcilianus to be innocent." Likewise he saith: *An forte de religione fas non est ut dicat imperator, vel quos miserit imperator? Cur ergo ad imperatorem legati vestri venerunt*[7]*?* "What, is it not lawful for the emperor, or for such as shall be sent by the emperor, to pronounce sentence of religion? Wherefore then came your ambassadors unto the emperor?" And so likewise again: *Si nihil debent in his causis imperatores jubere, si ad imperatores christianos hæc cura pertinere non debet, quis urgebat majores vestros causam Cæciliani ad imperatorem mittere*[8]*?* "If emperors have nothing to command in these cases, or if this matter nothing touch a christian emperor's charge, who then forced your predecessors to remove Cæcilianus' matter unto the emperor?" Therefore the emperor Constantinus summoned the bishops of the east, that had been in the council of Tyrus, to appear before him, to render account of their doings. His words be these: *Ut re ipsa quam sincere ac recte judicaveritis, ostendatis; idque coram me*[9]: "I will you to make your appearance, and to shew indeed how sincerely and justly ye have dealt; and that even before me." By these few examples it may well appear that appeals in ecclesiastical causes in those days were made unto the prince, and that it was thought lawful then for the prince to have the hearing of the same. Yet was not the prince therefore the head of the universal church. Certainly St Gregory thought it not amiss to commit a spiritual matter, touching the purgation of a bishop, to Brunichilda the French queen[10]. Notwithstanding it be noted thus in the gloss: *Fuit tamen hic nimium papaliter dispensatum*[11].

Euseb. Lib. x. cap. v. Socrat. Lib. i. cap. xxi. Niceph. Lib. vii. cap. xliii. August. Epist. 162. Contra Epist. Parm. Lib. i. cap. v. Contra Cresc. Gram. Lib. iii. cap. lxxi. Contra Epist. Parm. Lib. i. cap. vii.

August. Epist. 68.

Socrat. Lib. i. cap. xxii.

Gregor. Lib. ii. Epist. 8. ii. Quæst. v. Mennam.

As touching the bishop of Rome's power herein, it is certain he heard such matters of appeal by warrant of the emperor's commission, and not as having authority of himself. St Augustine, opening the contention between Cæcilianus and Donatus a Casis Nigris, uttereth this matter at large in this wise:

[1 Euseb. in Hist. Eccles. Script. Amst. 1695-1700. Lib. x. cap. v. pp. 319, &c.]

[2 Socrat. in eod. Lib. I. capp. xxxiii. xxxiv. pp. 57, &c.]

[3 Niceph. Call. Hist. Eccles. Lut. Par. 1630. Lib. VII. cap. xliii. Tom. I. pp. 507, &c.]

[4 August. Op. Par. 1679-1700. Ad Glor. et cet. Epist. xliii. 4. Tom. II. col. 90.]

[5 ...ultro fassus est suos ipsos adiisse etiam Constantinum.—Id. Contr. Epist. Parm. Lib. I. cap. v. 10. Tom. IX. col. 17.]

[6 Id. Contr. Cresc. Donatist. Lib. III. cap. lxxi. 82. Tom. IX. col. 476; where *insero.*]

[7 Id. Contr. Epist. Parm. Lib. I. cap. ix. 15. Tom. IX. col. 20; where we find *vestri venere legati.*]

[8 Id. Cler. Hippon. ad Januar. Epist. lxxxviii. 5. Tom. II. col. 215.]

[9 Socrat. in Hist. Eccles. Script. Lib. I. cap. xxxiv. p. 58.]

[10 Gregor. in Corp. Jur. Canon. Lugd. 1624. Decret. Gratian. Decr. Sec. Pars, Caus. II. Quæst. v. can. 7. cols. 641, 2. A part only of this canon is found in Gregory's works, Par. 1705. Epist. Lib. XIII. Indict. VI. Ad Brunich. Reg. Epist. vi. Tom. II. col. 1219.]

[11 Gloss. in eod. ibid. col. 642.]

An forte non debuit Romanæ ecclesiæ episcopus Miltiades cum collegis transmarinis episcopis illud sibi usurpare judicium, quod ab Afris septuaginta, ubi primas Tigisitanus præsedit, fuerat terminatum? Quid, quod nec ipse usurpavit? Rogatus quippe imperator judices misit episcopos, qui cum eo sederent[12]: "But should not the bishop of Rome, Miltiades, with other his fellows, bishops beyond the seas, joined together in commission, take upon him the judgment of that thing that was determined before by three-score and ten bishops of Africa, amongst whom the primate of Tigisita sat as president? And what if he never took it upon him (as of himself)? For the emperor, being entreated by the party, sent other bishops to sit with him." The very copy of this commission is yet to be seen, both in Eusebius, and also in Nicephorus. Neither was the bishop of Rome alone in that commission, but joined together with Rheticius, Maternus, Marinus, and Marcus, whom the emperor calleth his commission-fellows. The words of the commission be these: *Constantinus imperator Miltiadi episcopo Romano, et Marco, &c.*[13]: "Constantinus emperor[14] unto Miltiades the bishop of Rome, and unto Marcus. Forasmuch as sundry letters have been sent unto me from Anilinus our most noble president of Africa, wherein Cæcilianus the bishop of Carthage is accused of many matters by certain his fellows of the same country, &c. Therefore I have thought it good that the said Cæcilianus, together with ten bishops his accusers, and other ten, such as he shall think meet, sail to Rome, that there in your presence, together with Rheticius, and Maternus, and Marinus, your fellow-commissioners, whom for that cause I have willed to travel to Rome, he may be heard," &c.

Appeals.

August. Epist. 162.

Euseb. Lib. x. cap. v. Niceph. Lib. vii. cap. xliii. Collegas.

Here it is evident to be seen, that the bishop of Rome was the emperor's delegate, and in ecclesiastical jurisdiction had his authority and power, not from St Peter, but from the emperor. Whereby it is easy to be gathered, that the bishop of Rome's power was not so universal then as M. Harding would seem now to make it; and that the world then understood not this decree of pope Clemens the fifth, which, as it is reported, he afterward published in the council of Vienna: *Omne jus regum pendet a papa*[15]: "All the right of the prince is derived from the pope."

Clemens v.

Neither was the bishop of Rome's determination of such force, but that it was lawful then for the party grieved to refuse his judgment, and to appeal further. And therefore Donatus, being condemned before Miltiades, appealed from him, and, upon his complaint unto the emperor, was put over unto the bishop of Arle, in France, and to certain others[16]. And in conclusion, understanding that judgment there would pass against him, last of all he appealed to the emperor's own person. And the emperor himself confesseth by his letters, that he sat in judgment, and heard both parties[17].

August. Epist. 68.

August. contra Cresc. Gram. Lib. iii. cap. lxxi.

Now, if receiving of appeals necessarily import this universal power, then was the emperor's power universal; for he received all appeals, out of all countries, without exception, and that even in causes ecclesiastical. Again, then was the bishop of Rome's power not universal; for it was lawful then to refuse him, and to appeal to some other. And thus M. Harding's reasons run roundly against himself.

[12 August. Op. Ad Glor. et cet. Epist. xliii. 14. Tom. II. col. 94; where *Melchiades episcopus*.]

[13 Κωνσταντῖνος σεβαστὸς Μιλτιάδῃ ἐπισκόπῳ Ῥωμαίων καὶ Μάρκῳ. ἐπειδὴ τοιοῦτοι χάρται παρὰ Ἀνυλίνου τοῦ λαμπροτάτου ἀνθυπάτου τῆς Ἀφρικῆς πρός με πλείους ἀπεστάλησαν, ἐν οἷς ἐμφέρεται Καικιλιανὸν τὸν ἐπίσκοπον τῆς Καρταγεννησίων πόλεως παρὰ τινῶν κολλήγων αὐτοῦ τῶν κατὰ τὴν Ἀφρικὴν καθεστώτων ἐν πολλοῖς πράγμασιν εὐθύνεσθαι· κ. τ. λ. ἔδοξέ μοι ἵν' αὐτὸς ὁ Καικιλιανὸς μετὰ δέκα ἐπισκόπων, τῶν αὐτῶν εὐθύνειν δοκούντων, καὶ δέκα ἑτέρων οὓς αὐτὸς τῇ ἑαυτοῦ δίκῃ ἀναγκαίους ὑπολάβοι, εἰς τὴν Ῥώμην πλῷ ἀπιέναι· ἵν' ἐκεῖσε ὑμῶν παρόντων, ἀλλὰ μὴν καὶ Ῥετεκίου καὶ Ματέρνου καὶ Μαρίνου τῶν κολλήγων ὑμῶν, οὓς τούτου ἕνεκεν εἰς τὴν Ῥώμην προσέταξα ἐπισπεῦσαι, δυνηθῇ ἀκουσθῆναι, κ. τ. λ.—Euseb. in Hist. Eccles. Script. Lib. x. cap. v. pp. 319, 20.

Niceph. Call. Hist. Eccles. Lib. VII. cap. xliii. Tom. I. p. 507.]

[14 The emperor, 1565.]

[15 Pretensions of this kind are asserted by Clement, Corp. Jur. Canon. Clementin. Lib. II. Titt. ix. xi. cap. 2. cols. 114, &c. 128, &c.]

[16 August. Op. Cler. Hippon. ad Januar. Epist. lxxxviii. 3. Tom. II. col. 214.]

[17 Id. Contr. Cresc. Donatist. Lib. III. cap. lxxi. 82. Tom. IX. cols. 476, 7.]

M. HARDING. THE TWENTY-SECOND DIVISION.

For which cause that see hath ever hitherto of all christian nations, and now also ought to be heard and obeyed in all points of faith. For that see, though it hath failed sometimes in charity, and hath been in case as it might truly say the words of the gospel, spoken by the foolish virgins, "Our lamps be without light;" yet it never failed in faith, as Theodoretus[1] *witnesseth, and St Augustine affirmeth the same: which special grace and singular privilege is to be imputed unto the prayer of Christ, by which he obtained of God, for Peter and his successors,* (108) *that their faith should not fail. Therefore the evil life of the bishops of Rome ought not to withdraw us from believing and following the doctrine preached and taught in the holy church of Rome.*

Matt. xxv.

[*Evil life of the B. of Rome ought not to sever us from the faith of the church of Rome.* H.A. 1564.]

The hundred and eighth untruth. For many popes have erred in faith, as shall appear.

For better credit hereof, that is earnestly to be considered which St Augustine writeth, epistola clxv, *where, after that he hath rehearsed in order all the popes that succeeded Peter, even to him that was pope in his time, he saith thus:* In illum... ordinem episcoporum, &c.[2] *"Into that rew*[3] *of bishops, that reacheth from Peter himself to Anastasius, which now sitteth in the same chair, if any traitor had crept in, it should nothing hurt the church and the innocent christian folk, over whom our Lord having providence saith of evil rulers, 'What they say unto you, do ye; but what they do, do ye not; for they say, and do not;' to the intent the hope of a faithful person may be certain, and such as being set, not in man, but in our Lord, be never scattered abroad with tempest of wicked schism." And in his* 166*th epistle he saith: "Our heavenly Master hath so far forewarned us to beware of all evil of dissension, that he assured the people also of evil rulers, that for their sakes the seat of wholesome doctrine should not be forsaken, in which seat even the very evil men be compelled to say good things. For the things which they say be not theirs, but God's, who in the seat of unity hath put the doctrine of verity*[4]*."*

Matt. xxiii.

St Augustine speaketh generally of all bishops, and not one word namely of the bishop of Rome.

By this we are plainly taught, that albeit the successors of Peter, Christ's vicars in earth, be found blame-worthy for their[5] *evil life, yet we ought not to dissent from them in doctrine, nor sever ourselves from them in faith, forasmuch as, notwithstanding they be evil, by God's providence, for the surety of his people, they be compelled to say the things that be good, and to teach the truth; the things they speak not being theirs, but God's, who hath put the doctrine of verity in the seat or chair of unity: which singular grace cometh specially to the see of Peter, either of the force of Christ's prayer, as is said before, or in respect of place and dignity, which the bishops of that see hold for Christ, as Balaam could be brought by no means to curse that people whom God would have*[6] *to be blessed. And Caiphas also prophesied, because he was high bishop of that year, and prophesied truly, being a man otherwise most wicked. And therefore the evil doings of the bishops*[7] *of Rome make no argument of discrediting their doctrine. To this purpose the example of Gregory Nazianzene may very fitly be applied, of the golden, silvern, and leaden seal*[8]*. As touching the value of metals, gold and silver are better; but, for the goodness of the seal, as well doth lead imprint a figure in wax as silver or gold. For this cause, that the see of Rome hath never been defiled with stinking heresies*[9]*, as Theodoretus saith, and God hath*

M. Harding compareth the pope with Balaam and Caiphas.

[[1] See before, page 387.]

[[2] In illum, &c. qui ducitur ab ipso Petro usque ad Anastasium, qui nunc eamdem cathedram sedet, etiam si quisquam traditor per illa tempora subrepsisset, nihil præjudicaret ecclesiæ et innocentibus Christianis: quibus Dominus providens, ait de præpositis malis: Quæ dicunt, facite; quæ autem faciunt, facere nolite: dicunt enim, et non faciunt. Ut certa sit spes fidelis, quæ non in homine, sed in Domino collocata, numquam tempestate sacrilegi schismatis dissipetur.—August. Op. Par. 1679-1700. Ad Gener. Epist. liii. 3. Tom. II. col. 121.]

[[3] Rew: row.]

[[4] Quod usque adeo cœlestis magister cavendum præmonuit, ut etiam de præpositis malis plebem securam faceret, ne propter illos doctrinæ salutaris cathedra desereretur, in qua coguntur etiam mali bona dicere. Neque enim sua sunt quæ dicunt, sed Dei, qui in cathedra unitatis doctrinam posuit veritatis.—Id. ad Donatist. Epist. cv. 16. Tom. II. col. 303.]

[[5] H. A. 1564, omits *their*.]

[[6] H. A. 1564, omits *have*.]

[[7] Of bishops, 1565, and H.A. 1564.]

[[8] Ἔστω χρυσὸς, ἔστω σίδηρος, δακτύλιοι δὲ ἀμφότεροι, καὶ τὴν αὐτὴν ἐγκεχαράχθωσαν εἰκόνα βασιλικὴν, εἶτα κηρὸν ἐντυπούτωσαν· τί διοίσει ἡ σφραγὶς αὕτη τῆς σφραγῖδος ἐκείνης; οὐδέν.—Gregor. Nazianz. Op. Par. 1778-1840. Orat. xl. 26. Tom. I. p. 712.]

[[9] See before, page 387, note 16.]

always kept in the[10] *chair of unity the doctrine of verity, as Augustine writeth; for this cause, I say, it sitteth at the stern, and governeth the churches of the whole world; for this cause bishops have made their appellations thither; judgment in doubts of doctrine, and determination in all controversies and strifes, hath been from thence always demanded.* Whether the Pope may err.

THE BISHOP OF SARISBURY.

This is a very poor help indeed. M. Harding here is fain to resemble the bishops of Rome, touching their doctrine, to Balaam, to Caiphas, and to a leaden seal; and, touching their lives, to confess they are lamps without light. "Yet," saith he, "all this notwithstanding, we may not therefore depart from them. For Christ saith, 'The scribes and Pharisees sit in Moses' chair: do ye that they say; but that they do, do ye not; for they say, and do not.'" Forasmuch as it liketh M. Harding to use these comparisons, it may not much mislike him, if some man upon occasion hereof happen to say, as Christ said in the like case: "Wo be unto you, ye scribes and Pharisees! ye blind guides! ye painted graves! ye shut up the kingdom of heaven before men: ye neither enter yourselves, nor suffer others that would enter: ye have made the house of God a cave of thieves." Matt. xxiii. Luke xi.

Certainly Balaam, notwithstanding he were a false prophet, yet he opened his mouth, and blessed the people of God. Caiphas, although he were a wicked bishop, yet he prophesied, and spake the truth. A seal, although it be cast in lead, yet it giveth a perfit print. The scribes and Pharisees, although they were hypocrites, and lived not well, yet they instructed the congregation, and said well. The Manichees, although they were heretics, and taught not well, yet outwardly, in the conversation and sight of the world, as St Augustine saith, they lived well[11]. But these, unto whom M. Harding claimeth the universal power over all the world, neither bless the people of God, nor preach God's truth, nor give any print of good life or doctrine, nor instruct the congregation, nor say well, as the scribes and Pharisees did, nor, by M. Harding's own confession, live well, as the Manichees did. St Augustine saith: *Qui nec regiminis in se rationem habet, nec sua crimina detersit, nec filiorum culpam correxit, canis impudicus dicendus est magis quam episcopus*[12]: "He that neither regardeth to rule himself, nor hath washed off his own sins, nor corrected the faults of his children, may rather be called a filthy dog than a bishop." Num. xxiii. & xxiv. John xi. August. Confes. Lib. iii. cap. vi. Retract. Lib. i. cap. vii. ii. Quæst. vii. Qui nec.

Yet, all this corruption of life notwithstanding, M. Harding saith the see of Rome can never fail in faith: for Christ said unto Peter: "I have prayed for thee, that thy faith may not fail." The like confidence and trust in themselves the priests had in the old times, as it may appear by these words of the prophet Micheas: *Sacerdotes in mercede docuerunt, et prophetæ in pecunia prophetaverunt, et super Dominum requiescebant, dicentes, Nonne Dominus est in medio nostri?* "The priests taught for hire, and the prophets prophesied for money; and yet they rested themselves upon the Lord and said, Is not the Lord in the midst amongst us?" With like confidence the priests said, as it is written in the prophet Hieremy: *Non peribit lex a sacerdote, nec consilium a seniore:* "The law shall not decay in the priest, nor counsel in the elder." But God answereth them far otherwise: *Nox vobis erit pro visione, et tenebræ pro divinatione:* "Ye shall have dark night instead of a vision; and ye shall have darkness instead of prophecy." Certainly the very gloss upon the decretals putteth this matter utterly out of doubt. These be the words: *Certum est, quod papa errare potest*[13]: "It is certain that the pope may err." And Alphonsus de Castro: *Omnis...homo errare potest in fide, etiamsi papa sit:* "Every man may err in the faith; yea, although it be the pope." And for proof hereof he saith: *De Liberio papa, constat fuisse Arianum*[14]: "Touching pope Liberius, it is certain he was an Arian heretic." Pope Honorius was an heretic of the sect of them that were called Monothelitæ, Luke xxii. Mic. iii. Jer. xviii. Mic. iii. xxiv. Quæst. i. in Gloss. Alphon. contra Hæres. Lib. i. cap. iv.

[10 That, 1565, and H. A. 1564.]

[11 August. Op. Confess. Lib. III. cap. vi. 10. Tom. I. col. 91.
Id. Retract. Lib. I. cap. vii. 1. Tom. I. col. 9.]

[12 Id. in Corp. Jur. Canon. Lugd. 1624. Decret. Gratian. Decr. Sec. Pars, Caus. II. Quæst. vii. can. 32; where *habuit, sua delicta,* and *filiorum crimen.*]

[13 Ibid. Caus. XXIV. Quæst. i. Gloss. in can. 9. col. 1387.]

[14 Alfons. de Castr. Adv. Hær. Col. 1539. Lib. I. cap. iv. fol. 8.]

Whether the Pope may err.

condemned for the same in the sixth council holden at Constantinople[1]. Pope Marcellinus openly made sacrifice unto an idol[2]. Pope John the twenty-second held a wicked heresy against the immortality of the soul, and for the same was reproved, not by his cardinals, but by Gerson, and the school of Sorbona in Paris[3].

Concil. Constan. vi. Act. 12. Concil. Tom. i. in Vita Marcel. Gerson. Holcot. in Lib. Sapien. Lect. 189. Dist. 19. Anastasius. Abbas Ursp. in Chron.

Pope Sylvester the second was a sorcerer, and had familiar conference with the devil, and by his procurement was made pope. Pope Anastasius communicated with Photinus the heretic, and therefore was forsaken of his clergy[4]. Pope Hildebrand, that first of all others in these countries forbade the lawful marriage of priests, both for his life, and also for his religion, is set out at large in a council holden at Brixia; where he is called and published to the world to be a vicious man, a burner of houses, a robber of churches, a maintainer of murders and perjuries, an heretic against the apostolic doctrine, the old disciple of Berengarius, a sorcerer, a necromancer, a man possessed with the devil, and therefore out of the catholic faith[5]. The fathers in the council of St Basil say: *Multi pontifices in errores et hæreses lapsi esse leguntur*[6]: "We read that many bishops of Rome have fallen into errors and heresies." And the bishop of Rome himself saith: "Notwithstanding the pope draw innumerable companies of people by heaps with him into hell, yet let no mortal man once dare to reprove him;" *nisi deprehendatur a fide devius*: "unless it be found that he stray from the faith[7]." To conclude, Nicolas Lyra is driven to say: *Multi papæ inventi sunt apostatæ*[8]: "We find that many popes have forsaken the faith."

Concil. Basil. in Epist. Synod.

Dist. 40. Si papa.

Nic. Lyra in xvi. cap. Matt.

All this notwithstanding, by M. Harding's resolution, the see of Rome never failed from the faith, nor never can fail. The Valentinian heretics, as Irenæus reporteth, were wont to say of themselves, that they were naturally made of an[9] heavenly substance, and therefore needed not to flee from sin, as[10] others needed. For, lived they never so wickedly, yet said they: "We are spiritual still: no sin can hurt us. For we are as pure tried gold, which notwithstanding it be laid in a heap of dung, yet keepeth it still the brightness and nature of gold, and receiveth no corruption of the dung[11]." Even so these men seem to say, that whatsoever the pope either believe, or speak, or do, his faith still remaineth sound, and can never fail, because he sitteth in Peter's chair; as if he had a lease of the church of God, without any manner impeachment of waste. And therefore they say: *Quod si totus mundus sentiet*[12] *in aliquo adversus papam, tamen videtur, quod magis standum est sententiæ papæ*[13]: "If all the world give sentence in any thing contrary to the pope, it seemeth we ought rather to stand to the pope's judgment than to the judgment of all the world." Again they say: *In papa si desint bona acquisita per meritum, sufficiunt* [ea] *quæ a loci* [*præ*]*decessore præ-*

Iren. Lib. i. cap. i.

De Elect. et Elect. Potestate. Significasti. In Gloss. Idem Albert. Pighius, Lib. vi. cap. xiii.

[1 Sext. Synod. Constant. Act. xiii. in Crabb. Concil. Col. Agrip. 1551. Tom. II. p. 373.]

[2 Ex Libr. Pontif. in eod. Tom. I. p. 184.]

[3 The passage referred to may be seen, Joan. Gerson. Op. Antw. 1736. Serm. in Fest. Pasch. Tom. III. Pars III. col. 1205. More upon this matter will occur in the Defence of the Apology.

Holkoth. in Lib. Sap. Prælect. 1586. Lect. clxxxix. p. 623.]

[4 Corp. Jur. Canon. Lugd. 1624. Decret. Gratian. Decr. Prim. Pars, Dist. xix. can. 9. cols. 86, 7. A note is added declaring this canon *omnino confictum.*]

[5 Chronic. Abbat. Ursperg. Argent. 1537. Anni Henr. IV. p. 237.]

[6 ...pontificibus, quorum nonnulli in hæreses et errores lapsi esse dicuntur et leguntur.—Concil. Basil. in Crabb. Concil. Resp. Synod. Tom. III. p. 146.]

[7 Si papa...nihilominus innumerabiles populos catervatim secum ducit, primo mancipio gehennæ.... Hujus culpas istic redarguere præsumit mortalium nullus:...nisi &c.—Ex Dict. Bonifac. Mart. in Corp. Jur. Canon. Decret. Gratian. Decr. Prim. Pars, Dist. xl. can. 6. cols. 194, 5.]

[8 Bibl. cum Gloss. Ord. et Expos. N. de Lyra, Basil. 1502. Matt. cap. xvi. Pars V. fol. 52. See before, page 381, note 15.]

[9 A, 1565.] [10 As as, 1565.]

[11 ...οὕτως πάλιν τὸ πνευματικὸν θέλουσιν οἱ αὐτοὶ εἶναι, ἀδύνατον φθορὰν καταδέξασθαι, κἂν ὁποίαις συγκαταγένωνται πράξεσιν· ὃν γὰρ τρόπον χρυσὸς ἐν βορβόρῳ κατατεθεὶς οὐκ ἀποβάλλει τὴν καλλονὴν αὐτοῦ, ἀλλὰ τὴν ἰδίαν φύσιν διαφυλάττει, τοῦ βορβόρου μηδὲν ἀδικῆσαι δυναμένου τὸν χρυσόν· οὕτω δὲ καὶ αὐτοὺς λέγουσι, κἂν ἐν ποίαις ὑλικαῖς πράξεσι καταγένωνται, μηδὲν αὐτοὺς παραβλάπτεσθαι, μηδὲ ἀποβάλλειν τὴν πνευματικὴν ὑπόστασιν.—Iren. Op. Par. 1710. Contr. Hær. Lib. I. cap. vi. 2. pp. 29, 30.]

[12 Sententiet, 1565.]

[13 Corp. Jur. Canon. Decret. Gratian. Decr. Sec. Pars, Caus. IX. Quæst. iii. Gloss. in can. 13. col. 877. See before, page 68, note 5. See also Alb. Pigh. Hierarch. Eccles. Col. 1538. Lib. VI. cap. xiii. foll. 245, &c.]

[Whether the Pope may err.]

stantur[14]: "If there want in the pope good things gotten by merit, yet the things that he hath of (Peter) his predecessor in that place are sufficient." Likewise again: *Papa sanctitatem recepit*[15] *a cathedra*[16]: "The pope receiveth his holiness of his chair." [a]And pope Sixtus saith that "St Peter dwelleth in the bishop of Rome, and directeth him in his doings, and beareth all burdens[17]." [Dist. 40. Non nos.]

Thus they feast and cheer themselves, and smooth the world with vain talk. [Dist. 40. Si papa. Dist. 19. Sic omnes. In Gloss. ἐν ὀλβίῳ ὄλβια πάντα. a Epist. Sixt. ii.] But St John saith: *Nolite dicere, Patrem habemus Abraham:* "Never say (Peter or) Abraham was our father." [Matt. iii.] St Paul, speaking of his successors, saith thus: *Equidem scio quod post discessum meum ingressuri sint ad vos lupi graves, non parcentes gregi:* "I know that, after my departure from you, there shall ravening wolves come amongst you, that shall not spare the flock." [Acts xx.] And St Hierome saith: *Non sunt sanctorum filii, qui tenent loca sanctorum*[18]: "They be not evermore the children of holy men, that sit in the rooms of holy men." [Dist. 40. Non est facile.]

Now, whereas M. Harding saith, Christ prayed for Peter that his faith should not fail, that prayer pertained to all the rest of the apostles, and not only unto Peter. Origen saith: *Num audebimus dicere, &c.*: "Shall we dare to say that the gates of hell prevailed not only against Peter, but shall prevail against the rest? [Orig. in Matt. Tract. 1.] Why may we not rather say that the words that Christ spake were verified in every of them of whom they were spoken?" *Nam et quæ prius dicta sunt, et quæ sequuntur, velut ad Petrum dicta, sunt omnium communia*[19]: "For both the things that were spoken of before, and also the things that follow, as spoken unto Peter, are common to all." So likewise Beda expoundeth the same generally of all the faithful[20], and not of Peter only. [Beda in Luc. cap. xxii.] And so Christ himself expoundeth his own words. For thus he prayeth unto his Father: *Pater sancte, serva eos per nomen tuum, &c.*: [John xvii.] "O holy Father, save them for thy name's sake.... I pray not for them only, but for all them that by their preaching shall believe in me."

But, saith M. Harding, be the bishop of Rome's life never so wicked, yet may we not sever ourselves from the church of Rome. Howbeit St Cyprian saith otherwise: *Plebs obsequens præceptis dominicis, et Deum metuens, a peccatore præposito separare se debet*[21]: [Cypr. Lib. i. Epist. 4.] "The people obeying God's commandments, and fearing God, must sever themselves from the wicked that ruleth over them." And pope Nicolas hath straitly commanded, upon pain of excommunication, that no man should be present to hear mass said by a priest that he knoweth undoubtedly to live in advoutry[22]. [Dist. 32. Nullus.] Howbeit indeed it is not their life only that the church of God is offended withal, but also and specially the filth and corruption of their religion, the oppressing of God's word, the open deceiving of the people, and the manifest maintenance of idolatry. And what if the silver of Rome be turned into dross? [Isai. i.] What if the city that was faithful be become an harlot? What if they can abide no sound doctrine? [2 Tim. iv.] What if they have made the house of God a cave of thieves? [Jer. vii. Matt. xxi.] What if Rome be become the great Babylon, the mother of fornication, imbrued and drunken with the blood of the saints of God? [Rev. xvii.] And what if abomination sit in the holy place, even in the temple of God? [Dan. ix. 2 Thess. ii.] Yet may we not depart from thence? Yet must that be the rule and standard of God's religion? Truly Christ saith: "Take heed of the leaven of the scribes and Pharisees." [Matt. xvi.] And God himself saith: *Exite de illa, populus meus, ne participes sitis delictorum ejus, et de plagis ejus ne accipiatis:* [Rev. xviii.] "O my people, come away from her, lest ye be partakers of her sins, and so receive part of her plagues." Irenæus

[14 Symmach. Papa in Corp. Jur. Canon. Decret. Gratian. Decr. Prim. Pars, Dist. xl. can. 1. col. 193; where *in quo si desunt bona.*]

[15 Recipit, 1565, 1609.]

[16 Ibid. Dist. xix. Gloss. in can. 2. col. 81; where *recipit.*]

[17 Portemus onera omnium qui gravantur; quinimo hæc portat in nobis beatus apostolus Petrus, cujus vice fungimur legatione, et cujus regula informamur.—Sixt. Papæ II. Epist. ii. in Crabb. Concil. Tom. I. p. 163.]

[18 Hieron. in Corp. Jur. Canon. Decret. Gratian. Decr. Prim. Pars, Dist. xl. can. 2. col. 194; where *non sanctorum filii sunt.*]

[19 Orig. Op. Par. 1733-59. Comm. in Matt. Tom. XII. 11. Tom. III. pp. 524, 5. See before, page 340.]

[20 Ven. Bed. Op. Col. Agrip. 1612. In Luc. Evang. cap. xxii. Lib. VI. Tom. V. col. 426. Bede here declares that Christ intended to teach all the apostles by what he said to Peter; but he does not say that he prayed for all. See also in Matt. Evang. cap. xvi. Lib. III. Tom. V. col. 52.]

[21 Cypr. Op. Oxon. 1682. Ad Cler. et Pleb. Hisp. Epist. lxvii. p. 171.]

[22 Nicol. Papa in Corp. Jur. Canon. Decret. Gratian. Decr. Prim. Pars, Dist. xxxii. can. 5. col. 156. See before, page 70, note 5.]

Whether the Pope may err.

Iren. Lib. iv. cap. xliii.

saith: *Presbyteris illis, qui sunt in ecclesia, obaudire oportet,... qui successionem, habent ab apostolis; qui cum episcopatus successione charisma veritatis certum secundum placitum Patris acceperunt*[1]: "We ought to obey the bishops in the church, that have their succession from the apostles; which, together with the succession of the bishopric, have received the certain gift of the truth, according to the will of the Father." This holy father saith bishops must be heard and obeyed with a limitation; that is, not all, whatsoever they be, or whatsoever they say, but that have the undoubted gift of God's truth. And, for that M. Harding seemeth to claim by the authority of the scribes and Pharisees, saying, "They sit in Moses' chair; and that therefore we ought to do that they say;" St Augustine expoundeth the same place in this sort: *Sedendo in cathedra legem Dei docent: ergo per illos Deus docet. Sua vero si illi docere velint, nolite audire, nolite facere*[2]: "By sitting in the chair (is meant) they teach the law of God; therefore it is God that teacheth by them. But if they will teach any thing of their own (as the church of Rome had[3] done, and yet doth above number), then," saith St Augustine, "hear it not, then do it not."

August. in Johan. Tract. 46.

M. HARDING. THE TWENTY-THIRD DIVISION.

The hundred and ninth untruth. For the bishops of the east never yielded such subjection to the pope.

Now, that the bishop of Rome had always cure and rule over all other bishops, (109) *specially them of the east (for touching them of the west church it is generally confessed), beside a hundred other evident arguments, this is one very sufficient, that he had in the east, to do his stead, three delegates or vicars; now commonly they be named legates: and this for the commodity of the bishops there, whose churches were far distant from Rome. The one was the bishop of Constantinople, as we find it mentioned* In Epistola Simplicii ad Achatium Constantinopolitanum[4]. *The second was the bishop of Alexandria, as the epistle of Bonifacius the second to Eulalius recordeth*[5]. *The third was the bishop of Thessalonica, as it is at large declared in the* 82nd *epistle of Leo,* Ad Anastasium Thessalonicensem[6]. *By perusing these epistles every man may see, that all the bishops of Greece, Asia, Syria, Egypt, and, to be short, of all the orient, rendered and exhibited their humble obedience to the bishop of Rome, and to his arbitrement referred their doubts, complaints, and causes, and to him only made their appellations.*

THE BISHOP OF SARISBURY.

What we may think of the other hundred proofs, which M. Harding, as he saith, hath left untouched, it may the sooner appear, for that this one proof, that is here brought forth instead of all, is not only untrue, but also utterly without any shadow or colour of truth. These authorities of Leo, Symmachus[7], and Bonifacius, forasmuch as they are alleged without words, may likewise be passed over without answer. Howbeit this Bonifacius the second, in defence of this quarrel, is forced to say that St Augustine, that godly father, and all other the bishops of Africa, Numidia, Pentapolis, and other countries adjoining, that withstood the proud attempt of the bishops of Rome, and found out their open forgery in falsifying the Nicene council, were altogether inflamed and led by the devil[8].

But how doth this appear to M. Harding, that the bishop of Rome had all the bishops of the east in subjection, to use and command them as his servants? In what council was it ever decreed it should be so? who subscribed it? who recorded it? who ever saw such canons? The best plea that pope Nicolas can

---

[[1] Iren. Op. Par. 1710. Contr. Hær. Lib. IV. cap. xxvi. 2. p. 262; where *quapropter eis qui in ecclesia sunt presbyteris obaudire.*]

[[2] August. Op. Par. 1679-1700. In Johan. Evang. cap. x. Tractat. xlvi. 6. Tom. III. Pars II. col. 604; where *sedendo enim cathedram Moysi legem,* and *illi si velint docere.*]

[[3] Hath, 1565, 1609.]

[[4] Simpl. ad Acac. Epist. iv. in Crabb. Concil. Col. Agrip. 1551. Tom. I. p. 957. There is little or nothing to the point in this epistle. See however Ad Zenon. Spalens. Epist. i. ibid. pp. 956, 7.]

[[5] Bonifac. II. ad Eulal. Epist. in eod. Tom. I. pp. 1057, 8.]

[[6] Leon. Magni Op. Lut. 1623. Ad Anastas. Thessal. Epist. lxxxiv. cap. i. cols. 446, &c.]

[[7] A mere mistake for Simplicius.]

[[8] Aurelius... cum collegis suis (instigante diabolo) superbire... cœpit.—Bonifac. II. ad Eulal. Epist. in Crabb. Concil. Tom. I. p. 1058.]

make in this behalf is, that Peter was first bishop of Antioch, and after Rome[9]; and St Mark, his scholar, bishop of Alexandria. Hereof he thinketh it may very well and substantially be gathered, that the bishops of Rome ought to have all the world in subjection[10]. Indeed in the counterfeit charter or donation of the emperor Constantine authority is given to the bishop of Rome over the other four patriarchs, of Antioch, of Alexandria, of Constantinople, and of Hierusalem[11]. But the bishops of Rome themselves and of themselves devised and forged this charter, and that so fondly that a very child may easily espy the folly. For, beside a great number of other untruths, at that very time, when it is imagined that charter was drawn, there was neither patriarch, nor bishop, nor priest, nor church in Constantinople, nor the city itself yet built, nor known to the world by that name. This notwithstanding, the bishop of Rome upon this simple title hath beset his mitre with three crowns, in token that he hath the universal power over the three divisions of the world, Europa, Asia, and Africa. And so, as the king of Persia in old times entitled himself *frater solis et lunæ;* even so pope Nicolas calleth himself "the prince of all lands and countries[12]."

Nicol. Papa ad Michael. Imper.

Nicol. Papa ad Michael. Imper. Princeps super omnem terram.

But what duty the bishops of the east parts owed to the bishops of Rome, whosoever hath read and considered the story and practice of the times may soon perceive. First, the council of Nice appointed every of the three patriarchs to his several charge[13], none of them to interrupt or trouble other, and willed the bishop of Rome, as Rufinus reporteth the story, to oversee *ecclesias suburbanas*[14], which were the churches within his province; and therefore Athanasius calleth Rome the chief or mother-city of the Roman jurisdiction[15]. And for that cause the bishops of the east, in their epistle unto Julius, call him their fellow-servant[16]; and Cyrillus the bishop of Alexandria, writing unto Cœlestinus, calleth him his brother[17]. Fellows and brothers be titles of equality, and not of subjection.

Concil. Nicen. can. 6.

Rufin. Lib. i. cap. vi.

Athan. in Epist. ad solitariam vitam agentes. Metropolis Romanæ ditionis.

Cassiod. Lib. iv. cap. xxiv.

Cyril. Epist. 27. p. 294.

Certain it is that sundry of the bishops of Rome began very rathe to seek this pre-eminence, even with manifest forgery and corruption of councils, as is already proved. But the bishops of other countries never yielded unto them, nor understood these vain titles. The bishops of the east, writing unto Julius, allege that the faith that then was in Rome came first from them, and that their churches, as Sozomenus writeth, "ought not to be accounted inferior to the church of Rome[18];" and, as Socrates further reporteth, "that they ought not to be ordered by the Roman bishop[19]." Gennadius the bishop of Constantinople, together with the council there, thus writeth unto the bishop of Rome: *Curet sanctitas tua universas tuas custodias, tibique subjectos episcopos*[20]: "Let thy holiness see unto thine own charge, and unto the bishops appointed unto thee."

Sozom. Lib. iii. cap. viii. οὐ παρὰ ταῦτα τὰ δευτερεῖα φέρειν ἠξίουν.

Socrat. Lib. ii. cap. xv. μὴ δεῖν κανονίζεσθαι παρ' αὐτοῦ.

The council of Alexandria committed the visitation and reforming of all the churches in the east unto Asterius, and of all the churches in the west unto Eusebius the bishop of Vercellæ[21]: by authority of which commission, Eusebius, together with Hilarius, visited and corrected all the churches of Illyricum, France, and Italy[22]. A man might say, Where was then the universal power of the bishop of Rome? St Basil saith: "The state and safety of the church of Antioch dependeth of Athanasius the bishop of Alexandria[23];" and not (as M. Harding

Rufin. Lib. i. cap. xxix.

Rufin. Lib. i. cap. xxx. et xxxi.

Basil. Epist. 48.

[9 Of Rome, 1565, 1609.]

[10 Nicol. Papæ I. ad Michael. Imp. Epist. in eod. Tom. II. p. 758.]

[11 Edict. Constant. Imp. in eod. Tom. I. p. 226.]

[12 Nicol. Papæ I. ad Michael. Imp. in eod. Tom. II. p. 758; where *principes*.]

[13 Concil. Nic. can. 6. in Concil. Stud. Labb. et Cossart. Lut. Par. 1671-2. Tom. II. col. 32.]

[14 ...hic suburbigarum ecclesiarum sollicitudinem gerat.—Hist. Eccles. Par. Lib. x. cap. vi. fol. 107. 2.]

[15 ...μητρόπολις ἡ 'Ρώμη τῆς 'Ρωμανίας ἐστίν.—Athanas. Op. Par. 1698. Hist. Arian. ad Monach. 35. Tom. I. Pars I. p. 364.]

[16 ...scripserunt Julio comministro nostro, ecclesiæ Romanæ pontifici, &c.—Litt. Sard. Concil. in Hist. Tripart. Par. Lib. IV. cap. xxiv. fol. F. 8. 2.]

[17 Cyril. Alex. Op. Lut. 1638. Ad Cœlest. Epist. Tom. V. Pars II. p. 36. Cyril does not, it would seem, use the word brother; but he addresses Cœlestine as one τῶν συλλειτουργῶν.]

[18 Sozom. in Hist. Eccles. Script. Amst. 1695-1700. Lib. III. cap. viii. p. 414; where τοῦτο δὲ τά.]

[19 Socrat. in eod. Lib. II. cap. xv. p. 76.]

[20 Epist. Synod. Concil. Constant. in Concil. Stud. Labb. et Cossart. Tom. IV. col. 1030. This is stated to have been a circular letter.]

[21 Hist. Eccles. Lib. x. cap. xxix. fol. 116. 2.]

[22 Id. ibid. capp. xxx. xxxi. fol. 117.]

[23 'Η μέντοι τῆς κατὰ τὴν Ἀντιόχειαν ἐκκλη-

here saith) of the bishop of Rome. And therefore he desireth Athanasius to see unto it.

Cod. De Sacrosanct. Eccl. Leg. 6. The emperors Honorius and Theodosius appointed over all matters of doubt, arising within the country of Illyricum, to be heard and ended before the bishop of Constantinople, and not before the bishop of Rome[1]. And the very gloss upon the decrees, expounding that same law of Honorius and Theodosius, hath these words: *Imperator dicit, quod [patriarcha Constantinopolitanus] habet idem in suis subditis, quod papa [habet] in suis*[2]*:* "The emperor saith, the patriarch of Constantinople hath the same authority over the people of his province, that the pope hath over his." The emperor's words be these: *Constantinopolitana ecclesia Romæ veteris prærogativa lætatur*[3]*:* "The church of Constantinople enjoyeth now the prerogative of old Rome." And therefore, for more proof hereof, whensoever any patriarch, in any of these four principal sees, was newly chosen, he wrote letters of conference and friendship unto the other patriarchs; wherein every of them declared unto other their religion and consent of faith. Thus did the bishop of Rome unto others, and thus did others unto him[4]. This is an infallible[5] token that their authority was equal, and none of them had power and government over his fellows. And therefore, when Eulogius the bishop of Alexandria had written thus unto Gregory, being then bishop of Rome, *Sicut jussistis*, "As ye commanded;" Gregory utterly shunned and refused that kind of writing; for thus he answereth him: *Hoc verbum jussionis, quæso, a meo auditu removete. Scio enim quis sim, et qui sitis. Loco ... mihi fratres estis; moribus patres. Non ergo jussi, sed quæ utilia visa sunt indicare curavi*[6]*:* "I pray you, have away this word of commanding from my hearing. For I know both what I am, and also what you are. Touching your place, you are my brethren: touching manners, you are my fathers. Therefore I commanded you not, but only shewed you what I thought good."

(Margin notes: Dist. 22. Renov. in Gloss. — Cod De Sacros. Eccl. Leg. 6. — Liter. Synod. — Gregor. Lib. i. Epist. 24, 25. et Lib. vi. Epist. 5. — Gregor. Lib. vii. Epist. 30.)

Paul. Æmil. in Hist. Gall. Lib. viii. Finally, for that Michael Palæologus, the emperor of the east parts, in the council holden at Lyons, about the year of our Lord 1442, after great entreaty made unto him by the bishop of Rome, had acknowledged the bishops of the east to be subject unto him; after he returned home again into his empire, and was dead, his clergy would not suffer him to be buried[7]. Yet, saith M. Harding, "all the bishops of Græcia, Asia, Syria, Ægypt, and, to be short, all the orient, rendered and exhibited their humble obedience to the bishop of Rome."

M. HARDING. THE TWENTY-FOURTH DIVISION.

[2. Corrections from the pope. H. A. 1564.]

Of the bishop of Rome his punishing of offenders by censures of the church and otherwise, as by excommunication[8]*, ejection, deposition, and enjoining penance for transgressions, we have more examples than I think good to recite here. They that have knowledge of the ecclesiastical stories may remember, how Timotheus bishop of Alexandria was excommunicated with Peter his deacon by Simplicius the pope*[9]*, Nestorius bishop of Constantinople by Cœlestinus, Theophilus bishop of Alexandria, with Arcadius the emperor and Eudoxia the empress, by Innocentius, for their wicked demeanour toward Chrysostom; how Dioscorus bishop of Alexandria was deposed, though the whole second Ephesine council stood in his defence; how Peter bishop of Antioch was not only put out of his bishopric, but also of all priestly honour; how Photius was put out of the patri-*

σίας εὐταξία προδήλως τῆς σῆς ἤρτηται θεοσεβείας.—Basil. Op. Par. 1721-30. Ad Athanas. Epist. lxvi. Tom. III. p. 159.]

[1 Corp. Jur. Civil. Amst. 1663. Cod. Lib. I. Tit. ii. 6. Tom. II. p. 6. See before, page 390.]

[2 Corp. Jur. Canon. Lugd. 1624. Decret. Gratian. Decr. Prim. Pars, Dist. xxii. Gloss. in can. 6. col. 103; where *idem juris habet*.]

[3 See before, page 390.]

[4 Gregor. Magni Papæ I. Op. Par. 1705. Epist. Lib. I. Indict. IX. Ad Johan. Episc. et cet. Patr. Epist. xxv. Tom. II. cols. 507, &c. Ad Anastas. Patr. Epist. xxvi. cols. 516, 7.

Id. Lib. VII. Indict. XV. Ad Cyriac. Episc. Epist. v. cols. 851, 2. See before, page 386, note 7.]

[5 Unfallible, 1565.]

[6 Id. Lib. VIII. Indict. I. Ad Eulog. Episc. Epist. xxx. Tom. II. col. 919. See before, page 346, note 5.]

[7 Paul. Æmyl. De Reb. Gest. Franc. Par. 1544. Lib. VIII. fol. 166. 2.]

[8 Excommunications, H. A. 1564.]

[9 Decr. Simplic. Ex Libr. Pontif. in Crabb. Concil. Col. Agrip. 1551. Tom. I. p. 956.]

archship of Constantinople, into which he was intruded by favour of Michael the emperor at the suit of his wicked uncle, by Nicolas the first[10].

[Lib. iii. Epist. 13. H. A. 1564.] *For proof of this authority, the epistle of Cyprian, which he wrote to Stephanus, pope in his time, against Martianus the bishop of Arelate in Gallia, maketh an evident argument. For that this Martianus became a maintainer of the heresy of Novatianus, and therewith seduced the faithful people, Cyprian, having intelligence of it by Faustinus from Lyons, advertised Stephanus of it, and moved him earnestly to direct his letters to the people of Arle, by authority of which Martianus should be deposed and another put in his room, "to the intent (saith he there) the flock of Christ, which, hitherto by him scattered abroad and wounded, is contemned, may be gathered together*[11]*." Which St Cyprian would not have written, had the bishop of Rome had no such authority.*

THE BISHOP OF SARISBURY.

This reason maketh no great proof. For it was ever lawful, not only to the bishop of Rome, but also to all other bishops, both to rebuke, and also to excommunicate wicked doers. Anthymus with his fellows was excommunicate by every of the patriarchal sees[12]; Paulus Samosatenus, as Nicephorus saith, by all the bishops under heaven[13]; Auxentius and Jovinianus by St Ambrose[14]; Dioscorus and Eutyches by the council of Constantinople[15]; Cyrillus, albeit he were a catholic and a godly bishop, by all the bishops of the east[16]. Yet were none of these, that thus used the right of excommunication, either bishops of Rome, or heads of the universal church. And, whereas M. Harding saith, we may remember by the ecclesiastical stories, that Innocentius the bishop of Rome excommunicated Arcadius the emperor[17], it may please him also to remember, by the same ecclesiastical stories, that St Ambrose excommunicated the emperor Theodosius[18]; and Anastasius the bishop of Antioch both by private letters reproved the emperor Justinian for his heresy, and also oftentimes said of him openly in the church: "Whosoever followeth[19] any other gospel, accursed be he[20]." Yet was neither St Ambrose nor Anastasius the bishop of Rome. [Concil. Constant. v. Act i. Niceph. Lib. vi. cap. xxviii. Ambros. Lib. x. Epist. 81. Concil. Constant. v. Act. v. Concil. Chalc. Act. x. Niceph. Lib. xiii. cap. xxiv. Theod. Lib. v. cap. xviii. Evag. Lib. iv. cap. xl.]

As for the execution of sentence, and depriving, or deposing of bishops, M. Harding knoweth the bishop of Rome's authority was too weak. And therefore Innocentius saith of Pelagius: *Quibus acceptis literis, aut quando committet se nostro judicio*[21]*?* "Upon what letters, or when will he yield himself to my judgment?" For this cause Felix the bishop of Rome prayed aid of the emperor Zeno; and the emperor answered: *Admisimus depositionem Anthymi*[22]*:* "We have admitted the deposition of Anthymus:" otherwise the pope's sentence had been in vain. And therefore the emperor Constantinus saith of himself: *Si quis episcoporum inconsulte tumultuatus sit, ministri Dei, hoc est, mea executione illius audacia coercebitur*[23]*:* "If any bishop undiscreetly rear tumult, his rashness shall be repressed by the hands of God's minister, that is, by my execution." And [Inter Decret. Innocent. Concil. Constant. v. Act. 1. Concil. Constant. v. Act. iv. Theod. Lib. i cap. xix.]

[10 Nearly all these are, with others, enumerated by Pighius.—Pigh. Hierarch. Eccles. Assert. Col. 1538. Lib. VI. cap. xiii. foll. 250, 1.]

[11 Cypr. Op. Oxon. 1682. Ad Steph. Epist. lxviii. pp. 176, &c.]

[12 Concil. Constant. sub Menna, Act. IV. in Concil. Stud. Labb. et Cossart. Lut. Par. 1671-2. Tom. V. cols. 85, &c., 89, &c. Concil. Hieros. in eod. Tom. V. cols. 280, &c. See also Crabb. Concil. Quint. Synod. Constant. Act. IV. Tom. II. pp. 85, &c.; where are recorded the sentences against Anthimus by the council of Constantinople and the patriarchs of Constantinople and Jerusalem.]

[13 ...τῆς ὑπὸ τὸν οὐρανὸν καθολικῆς ἐκκλησίας ἐκκήρυκτος γίνεται.—Niceph. Call. Hist. Eccles. Lut. Par. 1630. Lib. VI. cap. xxviii. Tom. I. p. 422.]

[14 Ambros. Op. Par. 1686-90. Ad Syric. Epist. xlii. 14. Tom. II. col. 969.]

[15 Constant. Concil. in Concil. Calched. Act. I. in Concil. Stud. Labb. et Cossart. Tom. IV. cols. 243, 5. See also Concil. Calched. Act. III. in eod. cols. 423, &c.]

[16 Concil. Calched. Act. x. in eod. Epist. Ib. Episc. Edess. Tom. IV. col. 663.]

[17 Niceph. Call. Hist. Eccles. Lib. XIII. cap. xxxiv. Tom. II. pp. 419, 20.]

[18 Theodor. in Hist. Eccles. Script. Amst. 1695-1700. Lib. v. cap. xviii. pp. 220, &c.]

[19 Follow, 1565.]

[20 Evagr. in eod. Lib. IV. cap. xl. p. 416.]

[21 Rescr. Innoc. ad Aurel. et cet. Epist. xxvii. in Crabb. Concil. Tom. I. p. 480. See before, page 394, note 6.]

[22 There was an epistle of Felix written to Zeno, praying him to confirm the deposition of Petrus Fullo, bishop of Antioch, in eod. Tom. II. pp. 18, 19. But see Const. Justin. contr. Antim. &c. in Quint. Synod. Constant. Act. I. in eod. Tom. II. pp. 61, &c. See also Concil. Stud. Labb. et Cossart., Tom. IV. cols. 1069, &c., Tom. V. cols. 264, &c.]

[23 Theodor. in Hist. Eccles. Script. Lib. I. cap. xx. p. 51.]

likewise the emperor Justinian hath set out a law in this sort: *Si quis episcopus* Authen. De Eccles. *definitum tempus emanserit, &c.*[1]: "If any bishop tarry out his time appointed, and being called home refuse to come, let him be deprived and put from his Divers. Capit. κατὰ τὴν τοῦ παρόντος νόμου δύναμιν. church, and another better chosen in his room:" he addeth, "by the virtue of this present law." By the force of this law bishops were deposed; for without it the pope was not able to put his sentence in execution.

Now, if M. Harding will reason thus:

The pope excommunicated other bishops;

Ergo, he was head of the church:

then of the same principle we may well to the contrary reason thus:

The pope himself was excommunicate by other bishops;

Ergo, the pope was not the head of the church.

For the antecedent, that the pope was pronounced excommunicate by other bishops, it is out of question. For it is recorded in the ecclesiastical story, that Sozom. Lib. iii. cap. xi. Julius, being bishop of Rome, was excommunicate by the bishops of the east[2]; Dist. 21. In tantum. pope Leo was excommunicate by Dioscorus[3]; [a] Niceph. Lib. xvii. cap. xxvi. [a]pope Vigilius was excommunicate by Menna the bishop of Constantinople[4]; and pope Honorius was excommunicate Concil. Constant. vi. Act. xiii. by the sixth council holden at Constantinople[5].

Or, if M. Harding repose more force in deposing of bishops than in excommunication, then let him likewise remember, that pope Julius was deposed by the Sozom. Lib. iii. cap. xi. καθεῖλον Ἰούλιον τὸν Ῥώμης ἐπίσκοπον. bishops of the east, as it is recorded by Sozomenus[6]; pope Hildebrand by the council of Brixia[7]; pope John by the council of Constance; pope Eugenius by the council of Basil; and two popes together, Sylverius and Vigilius, by the In Vita Vigil. emperor Justinian[8]. Thus M. Harding's own grounds overthrow his whole building, and conclude plainly against himself.

M. HARDING. THE TWENTY-FIFTH DIVISION.

For the pope's authority concerning confirmation of the ordinances[9] [3. *Confirmations by the pope.* H. A. 1564.] *and elections of* (110) *all bishops, many examples might easily be alleged; as the request made to Julius by the ninety Arian bishops assembled in council at*[10] *Antioch against Athanasius, that he would vouchsafe to ratify and confirm those that they had chosen in place of Athanasius, Paulus, Marcellus, and others, whom*[11] *they had condemned and deprived*[12].

The hundred and tenth untruth. For the bishop of Rome confirmed the bishops of his own province, but not all bishops throughout the world.

Also the earnest suit which Theodosius the emperor made to Leo for confirmation of Anatolius, and likewise that Martianus the emperor made to him for confirmation of Proterius, both bishops of Alexandria, as it appeareth by their letters written to Leo in their favour. And as for Anatolius, Leo would not in any wise order and confirm him, unless he would first profess that he believed and held the doctrine which was contained in Leo his epistle to Flavianus, and would further by writing witness that he agreed with Cyrillus and the other catholic fathers against Nestorius[13]. [*Vide Leonis Epist.* 13. H. A. 1564.] *For this, if nothing else could be alleged, the testimony of holy Gregory were sufficient to make good credit; who, understanding that Maximus was ordered bishop of Salonæ, a city in Illyrico, without the authority and confirmation of the see apostolic, standing in doubt lest perhaps that had been done by commandment of Mauritius the emperor, who did many other things wickedly, thereof writeth to Constantina the empress thus:* Salonitanæ... civitatis episcopus me ac responsali meo nesciente ordinatus est; et facta est

[1 ...*καὶ εἰ μὴ ἐντὸς τοῦ ὁριζομένου παρὰ τῶν ἱερέων χρόνου ὑποστρέψουσιν εἰς τὰς ἰδίας ἐκκλησίας, αὐτοὺς μὲν τῆς ἐπισκοπῆς ἐξωθεῖσθαι, ἑτέρους δὲ ἀντ' αὐτῶν καλλίονας χειροτονεῖσθαι, κατὰ κ. τ. λ.*—Corp. Jur. Civil. Amst. 1663. Auth. Coll. IX. Tit. vi. Novell. cxxiii. 9. Tom. II. p. 170.]

[2 Sozom. in Hist. Eccles. Script. Amst. 1695-1700. Lib. III. cap. xi. p. 417.]

[3 Nicol. Papa in Corp. Jur. Canon. Lugd. 1624. Decret. Gratian. Decr. Prim. Pars, Dist. xxi. can. 9. col. 99.]

[4 Niceph. Call. Hist. Eccles. Lut. Par. 1630. Lib. XVII. cap. xxvi. Tom. II. p. 774.]

[5 Concil. Constant. III. Act. XIII. in Concil. Stud. Labb. et Cossart. Lut. Par. 1671-2. Tom. VI. col. 943.]

[6 Sozom. in Hist. Eccles. Script. Lib. III. cap. xi. p. 417.]

[7 Concil. Brix. in Concil. Stud. Labb. et Cossart. Tom. X. col. 389.]

[8 Ex Libr. Pontif. in Crabb. Concil. Col. Agrip. 1551. Tom. II. pp. 1, &c., 4, &c.]

[9 Ordinations, 1565, and H. A. 1564.]

[10 As, H. A. 1564.]

[11 to whom, 1611.]

[12 Epist. Orient. ad Jul. in Crabb. Concil. Tom. I. p. 307.]

[13 Leon. Magni Op. Lut. 1623. Ad Theodos. August. Epist. xxxiii. cols. 344, &c.]

res, quæ sub nullis anterioribus principibus evenit[14]: "*The bishop of the city of Salonæ (saith he) is ordered, neither I nor my deputy*[15] *made privy to it. And herein that thing hath been done, which never happened in the time of any princes before our days." Thus it appeareth that, before a thousand years past, bishops had their ordination and election confirmed by the see apostolic.*

THE BISHOP OF SARISBURY.

If this reason may stand for good, and whosoever hath the allowing of the election or consecration of bishops must therefore be taken as head of the church, then must the church of necessity have many heads. For it is certain, the allowance hereof pertaineth to many. [a]St Ambrose saith that "all the bishops, both of the east and of the west, gave their consent and allowance to his election[16]." Theodosius the emperor, standing in the defence of Flavianus the bishop of Constantinople, saith "[b]that all the bishops of the east, of Asia, Pontus, Thracia, and Illyricum, had allowed his election[17]." [c]Eudoxius entered into the bishopric of Antioch without the allowance and consent of Gregorius[18] the bishop of Laodicea, and of Marcus the bishop of Arethusa, and of other bishops that had interest therein; and is reproved for the same[19]. [d]Gregorius Presbyter saith: For that the election and installation of Gregory Nazianzene was past before the bishops of Egypt and Macedonia were come, and so made without their consent, that therefore they utterly refused to allow him, or to admit him as bishop there, not for any misliking in the party, but for that they thought themselves defrauded of their voices[20].

[a] Ambros. Lib. x. Epist. 82.

[b] Theod. Lib. v. cap. xxiii. αἱ τῆς ἑῴας ἐκκλησίαι τῆς Φλαβιανοῦ προεδρίας ἀντέχονται.

[c] Sozom. Lib. iv. cap. xii. μήτε τῶν ἄλλων οἷς ἡ χειροτονία διέφερε συνθεμένων.

[d] Gregor. Presb. in Vita Naz. Ἀντέλεγον τῇ ψήφῳ.

Anacletus decreeth thus: *Episcopus non minus quam a tribus episcopis, reliquisque omnibus assensum præbentibus, ullatenus ordinetur*[21]: "Let a bishop in no wise be ordered of less than three bishops, all the rest giving their assent to the same." Anacl. Epist. 2.

Hereby it appeareth that, to the ratifying of the election of any one bishop, the consent of all other bishops within that province was thought necessary: which consent they testified among themselves, by writing letters of conference one to another. And therefore, when John the bishop of Constantinople had entitled himself the universal bishop, Gregory counselled Eulogius the bishop of Alexandria, and other bishops of the east, neither to write to him, nor to receive letters from him by that title[22]. (Gregor. Lib. iv. Epist. 36.) Likewise the bishops of the east, when they had excommunicate Julius the bishop of Rome, gave commandment that no man should either receive his letters or write unto him, in token they held him for no bishop[23]. (Sozom. Lib. iii. cap. xi.)

Neither did only bishops allow such elections, but also both the prince and the people. When St Ambrose, being once chosen and appointed bishop of Milan, began roughly to deal with the nobles of the court, and to rebuke their faults, the emperor Valentinian said: "All this I knew before; and therefore I not only said not nay, but also gave my voice and assent to his election[24]."

Theod. Lib. iv. cap. vii. καὶ σύμψηφος τῆς χειροτονίας γεγένημαι.

Touching the election of Nectarius, Sozomenus writeth in this wise: The bishops that were present at the election gave unto the emperor in writing sundry

Sozom. Lib. vii. cap. viii. τὸν δακτύλιον ἐπιθεὶς τῇ τελευταίᾳ γραφῇ.

[14 Gregor. Magni Papæ I. Op. Par. 1705. Epist. Lib. v. Indict. XIII. Ad Constant. August. Epist. xxi. Tom. II. col. 752; where *facta res est.*]

[15 Depute, H. A. 1564.]

[16 Tamen ordinationem meam occidentales episcopi judicio, orientales etiam exemplo probarunt.—Ambros. Op. Par. 1686-90. Ad Eccles. Vercell. Epist. lxiii. 65. Tom. II. col. 1037.]

[17 ...καὶ τῆς ἑῴας αἱ κ. τ. λ. πρὸς δὲ τῇ ἑῴᾳ καὶ τὴν Ἀσιανὴν ἅπασαν καὶ Ποντικὴν, καὶ μέντοι καὶ τὴν Θρᾳκικὴν κοινωνούσας ἔχει καὶ συνημμένας· καὶ τὸ Ἰλλυρικὸν δὲ ἅπαν ἐκεῖνον οἶδε τῶν κατὰ τὴν ἀνατολὴν ἐπισκόπων ἡγούμενον.—Theodor. in Hist. Eccles. Script. Lib. v. cap. xxiii. p. 231.]

[18 Georgius, 1565, and 1609.]

[19 ... Εὐδοξιος...καταλαμβάνει τὴν Ἀντιόχειαν, καὶ περιποιεῖται ἑαυτῷ τὴν ἐνθάδε ἐπισκοπὴν, μήτε Γεωργίου τοῦ Λαοδικείας ἐπισκόπου, μήτε Μάρκου τοῦ Ἀρεθούσης...μήτε κ. τ. λ.—Sozom. in eod. Lib. IV. cap. xii. p. 450.]

[20 Gregor. Nazianz. Op. Par. 1778-1840. Vit. S. Gregor. Tom. I. p. clv.]

[21 ...episcopus...est ordinandus...nullatenus minus quam a tribus, ceteris consentientibus cunctis, &c. —Anaclet. Epist. ii. in Crabb. Concil. Tom. I. p. 61.]

[22 State fortes, state securi: scripta cum universalis nominis falsitate nec dare umquam, nec suscipere præsumatis.—Gregor. Magni Papæ I. Op. Epist. Lib. v. Indict. XIII. Ad Eulog. et Anastas. Epist. xliii. Tom. II. col. 773.]

[23 Sozom. in Hist. Eccles. Script. Lib. III. cap. xi. p. 417.]

[24 Ταύτην σου, ἔφη ὁ βασιλεὺς, καὶ πάλαι ᾔδει τὴν παῤῥησίαν· καὶ σαφῶς ἐπιστάμενος οὐ μόνον οὐκ ἀντεῖπον, ἀλλὰ καὶ κ. τ. λ.—Theodor. in eod. Lib. IV. cap. vii. p. 158.]

names of such as they thought meet for that room: the emperor, weighing the persons, set his seal upon Nectarius' name, and elected him[1].

Gregor. Presb. in Vita Naz. ἐγκαθεδρῆσαι τὸν ἀρχιερέα τῷ θρόνῳ.

Gratianus the emperor at his coming to Constantinople embraced Gregory Nazianzene, and, after some conference with him had, said unto him: "O father, unto thee, and unto thy labours, God through us committeth this church. Behold, I give unto thee this holy house, and the stall. And the people besought the emperor to set the bishop in his chair[2]."

Anacl. Epist. 2.

The like might be said of the consent and allowance of the people. Anacletus, as he is commonly alleged, writeth thus: *Sacerdotes a proprio ordinentur episcopo, ita ut cives et alii sacerdotes assensum præbeant*[3]: "Let priests be ordered by their own several bishops, so that the people and other priests give their assent thereto." St Cyprian saith likewise: "The people, being obedient unto God's commandments, hath power especially[4] either to choose worthy priests or to refuse the unworthy[5]."

Cypr. Lib. i. Epist. 4.

Thus many voices were then thought necessary to the admission of any bishop. Therefore this seemeth no sufficient ground to prove that the bishop of Rome is head of the church. For M. Harding might soon have seen that the bishop of Rome himself, touching his own election, was wont to be allowed by other bishops. Verily, St Cyprian writeth thus of the allowance of Cornelius, bishop there: *Ut Cornelium . . . noveris . . . coepiscoporum testimonio, quorum numerus universus per . . . mundum concordi unanimitate consensit*[6]: "That thou mayest know Cornelius by the testimony of his fellow-bishops, the whole number of whom throughout the world hath agreed (to the allowing of his election) with one consent." Afterward, in an epistle unto Cornelius himself, he writeth thereof more at large: *Ad comprobandam ordinationem tuam, facta auctoritate majore, placuit ut per episcopos omnes omnino in ista provincia positos literæ fierent, . . . ut te universi collegæ nostri, et communicationem tuam, id est, ecclesiæ catholicæ unitatem, pariter et caritatem probarent, pariter et tenerent*[7]: "To allow thy consecration, more authority being gathered, I thought it good that letters should be sent unto all the bishops of this province, that all our brethren might both allow and hold both thee and thy communion, that is to say, the unity of the catholic church." If M. Harding will say, this was not the confirmation of the election of Cornelius, it followeth immediately: *Sic . . . episcopatus tui . . . veritas, pariter et dignitas, apertissima luce et manifestissima et firmissima confirmatione fundata est*[8]: "This is the truth and dignity of thy bishopric, founded in the open light, and with most manifest and most certain confirmation." Thus, whensoever any bishop was either installed or deposed, knowledge thereof was given unto the other bishops, and the same either allowed or disallowed by his brethren.

Cypr. Lib. iv. Epist. 2.

Cypr. Lib. iv. Epist. 8.

But that the bishop of Rome ordered and admitted all the bishops throughout the world, besides that it hath no possibility, or colour of truth in itself, it is also easy by good record and authority to be reproved. Agapetus bishop of Rome, about the year of our Lord 540, after he had, upon occasion, consecrate Menna the bishop of Constantinople, he uttered these words in commendation of the party: *Et hoc dignitati ejus (Mennæ) accidere*[9] *credimus, quod a temporibus Petri apostoli nullum alium unquam orientalis ecclesia suscepit episcopum manibus nostræ*

Concil. Constant. v. Act. ii.

[1 ...ἄλλοι μὲν ἄλλους ἐνέγραψαν...ἀναγνοὺς δὲ ὁ βασιλεὺς τῶν ἐγγραφέντων τὸν κατάλογον, ἔστη ἐπὶ Νεκταρίῳ· καὶ σύννους γενόμενος, σχολῇ καθ' ἑαυτὸν ἐβουλεύετο, τὸν κ. τ. λ. καὶ ἀναδραμὼν εἰς τὴν ἀρχὴν, αὖθις πάντας ἐπανῆλθε. καὶ Νεκτάριον αἱρεῖται.—Sozom. in eod. Lib. VII. cap. viii. p. 579.]

[2 Καὶ τηνικαῦτα προσδέξασθαι τὸν ἀρχιερέα Γρηγόριον ἐντίμως...καὶ τέλος εἰπεῖν· ὦ πάτερ, σοί τε καὶ τοῖς ἱδρῶσι τοῖς σοῖς δι' ἡμῶν ὁ Θεὸς ἐγχειρίζει τὴν ἐκκλησίαν. ἰδοὺ δίδωμί σοι τὸν οἶκον τὸν ἱερὸν, καὶ τὸν θρόνον......τόν τε βασιλέα ἱκέτευον ἐγκαθιδρῦσαι τὸν ἀρχιερέα τῷ θρόνῳ.—Gregor. Nazianz. Op. Par. 1778-1840. Vit. S. Gregor. Tom. I. pp. cli. clii. The emperor was Theodosius.]

[3 Anaclet. Epist. ii. in Crabb. Concil. Col. Agrip. 1551. Tom. I. p. 59.]

[4 Specially, 1565, 1609.]

[5 ...plebs obsequens præceptis dominicis...habeat potestatem vel eligendi dignos sacerdotes, vel indignos recusandi.—Cypr. Op. Oxon. 1682. Ad Cler. et Pleb. Hisp. Epist. lxvii. p. 171.]

[6 Id. ad Anton. Epist. lv. p. 103.]

[7 ...placuit ut per episcopos...ad comprobandam ordinationem tuam facta auctoritate majore... per omnes omnino istic positos &c....catholicæ ecclesiæ &c., probarent firmiter ac &c.—Id. ad Cornel. Epist. xlviii. p. 91.]

[8 Id. ibid.; where *comprobatione* for *confirmatione*.]

[9 Accedere, 1565, 1609.]

sedis ordinatum[10]: "And this is an augmentation of Menna's dignity, that, sithence the time of Peter the apostle, the east church never received any other bishop consecrate by the hands of our see." Now advise thyself[11], good reader, whether thou wilt believe pope Agapetus or M. Harding.

And let not M. Harding find fault, for that I place the ordering of bishops instead of their confirmation. For he himself seemeth to make confirmation and ordering both one thing, or at least to join them both together. These be his words: "Leo would not in any wise order and confirm Anatolius."

Liberat. cap. xx.

Truly Liberatus saith, the manner was in Alexandria, that whosoever was chosen bishop there should come to the bier, and lay his predecessor's hand upon his head, and put on St Mark's cloke, and then was he sufficiently confirmed bishop, without any mention made of Rome[12]. And St Cyprian writeth unto the bishops of Spain, that Sabinus, whom they had lawfully chosen bishop, should so continue still, yea, notwithstanding Cornelius, being then bishop of Rome, misliked him, and would not confirm him[13]. And that very counterfeit decree of Anacletus, that requireth all bishops once in the year to present themselves in Rome, extendeth not his commandment throughout all the world, but only to the bishops of the province of Rome. Thus stand the words: *Omnes episcopi, qui hujus apostolicæ sedis ordinationi subjacent, &c.*[14]: "All bishops that be bound to have their orders confirmed by this apostolic see, &c." Whereby it may be gathered, that other bishops were not subject to the ordinance of that see. And this was the fault that Gregory found in the bishop of Salonæ, that, being within the jurisdiction of his province, he was consecrate without his knowledge. And that Gregory meant it not of all bishops, but only of the bishops within his own charge, it is evident by his words. For thus he writeth: *Episcopi mei: episcopi mihi commissi*[15]: "My bishops: bishops being within my cure." And that the city of Salonæ, standing in Illyricum, was sometime within the province of Rome, it is plain by the epistle that Damasus the bishop of Rome sent unto the bishops of Illyricum. These be his words: *Par est, omnes qui sunt in orbe Romano magistros consentire*[16]: "It is meet that all the teachers that be within the precincts of the Roman jurisdiction agree together."

Cypr. Lib. i. Epist. 4.

Anacl. Epist. 3. Dist. 93. Juxta sanct.

Gregor. Lib. iv. Epist. 34.

Sozom. Lib. vi. cap. xxiiii. πάντας τοὺς ἐν τῷ Ῥωμαίων κόσμῳ διδασκάλους.

Whereas it is alleged, that the bishop of Rome was required to ratify the election of Flavianus, Anatolius, and of the Arian bishops; that was meant of a general allowance, such as was common to all bishops, specially to the four principal patriarchs, and not only to the bishop of Rome. Neither was the bishop of Rome's admission thought so necessary, as if he only had a voice negative, to take in and put[17] out whom he listed; but only of congruity and consent, that it might appear, there was no bishop in the church but was liked and allowed of all his brethren. For otherwise the bishops of the east wrote thus unto Julius: *Si... ordinatos [a nobis] episcopos, &c.*[18]: "If you will allow the bishops that we have ordered, we will be at peace, and communicate with you; if not, we will proclaim the contrary." And the emperor Gratian made Nectarius bishop of Constantinople contrary to the minds of the most part of the bishops[19]. Therefore M. Harding's argument might better have been framed thus: The bishop of Rome confirmed the bishops within his own province, and had no other special authority to confirm all other bishops in the world, no more than others had to confirm him; therefore he was not then taken for the head of the church, nor was thought to have this universal power.

Sozom. Lib. iii. cap. viii.

Sozom. Lib. vii. cap. viii.

[10 Concil. Constant. sub Menna, Act. ii. in Concil. Stud. Labb. et Cossart. Lut. Par. 1671-2. Tom. V. col. 46.]

[11 Theeself, 1565.]

[12 Liberat. Breviar. Par. 1675. cap. xx. p. 142.]

[13 Quod et apud vos factum videmus in Sabini collegæ nostri ordinatione...episcopatus ei deferretur. ...Nec rescindere ordinationem jure perfectam potest, quod Basilides...Romam pergens, Stephanum collegam nostrum longe positum...fefellit &c.—Cypr. Op. Ad Cler. et Pleb. Hisp. Epist. lxvii. pp. 172, 3.]

[14 Anaclet. et Zach. in Corp. Jur. Canon. Lugd. 1624. Decret. Gratian. Decr. Prim. Pars, Dist. xciii. can. 4. col. 441. See also in Crabb. Concil. Tom. I. p. 65.]

[15 Gregor. Magni Papæ I. Op. 1705. Epist. Lib. v. Indict. XIII. Ad Constant. August. Epist. xxi. Tom. II. col. 752.]

[16 Sozom. in Hist. Eccles. Script. Amst. 1695-1700. Lib. VI. cap. xxiii. p. 542.]

[17 To put, 1565, 1609.]

[18 Epist. Orient. ad Jul. in Crabb. Concil. Tom. I. p. 307. See also Sozom. in Hist. Eccles. Script. Lib. III. cap. viii. p. 414.]

[19 Id. Lib. VII. cap. viii. pp. 579, 80.]

M. HARDING. THE TWENTY-SIXTH DIVISION.

Confirmation of Councils.

That the bishops of Rome, by accustomed practice of the church, had authority to approve or disprove councils, I need to say nothing for proof of it, seeing that the ecclesiastical rule (as we read in the tripartite story) commandeth (111) *that no council be celebrate and kept without the advice and authority of the pope*[1]. *Verily the councils holden at Ariminum, at Seleucia, at Syrmium, at Antiochia, and the*[2] *second time at Ephesus, for that they were* (112) *not summoned nor approved by the authority of the bishop of Rome, have not been accounted for lawful councils; but as well for that rejected, as also for their heretical determinations. The fathers assembled in the council of Nice sent their epistle to Sylvester the pope, beseeching him with his consent to ratify and confirm whatsoever they had ordained*[3]. *Isidorus witnesseth that the Nicene council had set forth rules, the which (saith he) the church of Rome received and confirmed*[4]. *The second general council holden at Constantinople was likewise allowed and approved by Damasus, specially requested by the fathers of the same thereto. So was the third council holden at Ephesus ratified and confirmed by Cœlestinus, who had there for his vicars or deputies*[5] *Cyrillus the famous bishop of Alexandria, and one Arcadius a bishop out of Italy. As for the fourth council kept at Chalcedon, the fathers thereof also, in their epistle to Leo the pope, subscribed with the hands of forty-four bishops, made humble request unto him to establish, fortify, and allow the decrees and ordinances of the same. This being found true for the four first chief councils, we need not to say any thing of the rest that followed. But for the sure proof of all this, that chiefly is to be alleged, that Constantius the Arian emperor made so importune and so earnest suit to Liberius the pope, to confirm the acts of the council holden at Antioch by the ninety Arian bishops, wherein Athanasius was deprived and put out of his bishopric. For he believed, as Ammianus Marcellinus writeth, that what had been done in that council should not stand and take effect, unless it had been approved and confirmed by the authority of the bishop of Rome, which he termeth the eternal city*[6].

[4. The pope's approving of councils. H. A. 1564.] *Lib. iv. cap. xix.*

The hundred and eleventh untruth, standing in the wilful falsifying of the text.

The hundred and twelfth untruth. For in those days the bishop of Rome had no authority to summon councils.

Quas Romana suscipiens confirmavit ecclesia. In præfatione Niceni Concilii.

Lib. xv.

THE BISHOP OF SARISBURY.

Here M. Harding hath avouched two great untruths, the one in his translation in the English, the other in the allegation of the story. Touching the first, Cassiodorus in his Latin translation writeth thus: *Canones jubent, extra Romanum nihil decerni pontificem*[7]: Socrates in the Greek, out of which the Latin was taken, writeth thus: μὴ δεῖν παρὰ γνώμην τοῦ ἐπισκόπου Ῥώμης κανονίζειν τὰς ἐκκλησίας[8]. The English hereof is this: "It is provided by the canons, that rules to bind the church be not made without the consent of the bishop of Rome." Wherein M. Harding hath purposely corrupted and falsified altogether both the Greek and the Latin, not reporting one word that he found in the original: κανονίζειν, or *decernere*, he Englisheth "to keep," or, as he termeth it, "to celebrate" a council; παρὰ γνώμην, which is, *præter sententiam*, or, as Cassiodorus turneth it, *extra*, he Englisheth "without the advice and authority." No, he would not suffer, no not him in whose quarrel he thus fighteth, to pass without a venew[9]: for, where he saw him named in the Greek, ἐπίσκοπον Ῥώμης, and in the Latin, *Romanum pontificem*, "the Roman bishop," he thought it best to leave both the Greek and the Latin, and to call him the pope. And thus, to increase the pope's authority, he hath altered and corrupted the whole place, and not translated one word as he found it.

Cassiod. Lib. iv. cap. xix. Socrat. Lib. ii. cap. xvii.

Touching the story, he saith the Arians' councils were not allowed, for that

[1 See below, note 7.]

[2 And at the, H. A. 1564.]

[3 Epist. Synod. Nic. ad Sylvestr. in Crabb. Concil. Col. Agrip. 1551. Tom. I. p. 270. Little credit is to be attached to this epistle.]

[4 Nam et nonnullæ regulæ subnexæ sunt, quas memorata suscipiens, &c.—Præfat. in Concil. Nic. in eod. Tom. I. p. 234.]

[5 Deputes, 1565, and H. A. 1564.]

[6 Id enim ille [imperator], Athanasio semper infestus, licet sciret impletum, tamen auctoritate quoque, qua potiores æternæ urbis episcopi, firmari desiderio nitebatur ardenti. — Amm. Marcell. Op. Par. 1681. Lib. xv. cap. vii. p. 92.]

[7 Hist. Tripart. Par. Lib. IV. cap. xix. fol. F. 7.]

[8 Socrat. in Hist. Eccles. Script. Amst. 1695-1700. Lib. II. cap. xvii. p. 79.]

[9 Venew or venue: a bout in fencing.]

they were not summoned by the pope. And yet he knoweth right well, it was no part of the pope's office in those days to summon councils. For it is evident, even by the policy and practice of that time, that Constantinus the emperor summoned the council of Nice; Theodosius the first the council of Constantinople; Theodosius the second the council of Ephesus; and Marcianus the council of Chalcedon. And Socrates in his story saith thus: *Idcirco imperatores in historia complexus sum, quia ex quo tempore cœperunt esse christiani, ecclesiastica negotia pendent ab illis, et maxima concilia de illorum sententia et facta sunt, et fiunt*[10]: "Therefore I have comprised the emperors within my story; for that, sithence they began to be christened, the state of the church dependeth of them, and the greatest councils have been kept, and be still kept by their advice." And the bishops in the council of Constantinople witness, that they were summoned to come to the Roman council by Damasus the bishop of Rome; but they add withal, "by warrant of the emperor's letters[11]," not by any his own authority. And likewise in their epistle to the emperor Theodosius they write thus: *Literis, quibus nos convocasti, ecclesiam honore prosecutus es*[12]: "Your majesty hath honoured the church by the letters wherewith ye summoned us together."

Confirmation of Councils.

Socrat. Lib. v. in Procemio. τὰ τῆς ἐκκλησίας πράγματα ἤρτητο ἐξ αὐτῶν.

Theod. Lib. v. cap. ix. διὰ τῶν τοῦ θεοφιλεστάτου βασιλέως γραμμάτων. Inter Acta Concil. Constant. v.

As for the bishop of Rome, he was not yet of authority able to call a general council. For the world as yet had no skill of his universal power over all others, neither would they have appeared upon his summon. Gregorius, being bishop of Rome, could not cause the bishop of Salonæ, being but one man, to come before him. Thus he writeth by way of complaint unto the empress Constantia: *Contempto me atque despecto, ... ad me venire secundum jussionem dominorum noluit*[13]: "He despised me, and set me at nought, and would not come unto me, according to my lords the emperors' commandment." Therefore Leo, finding this weakness in himself, wrote unto the clergy and people of Constantinople, and willed them to crave a general council at the emperor's hand: *Exposcite, ut petitioni nostræ, qua plenariam indici synodum postulamus, clementissimus imperator dignetur annuere*[14]: "Make your request, that the emperor's majesty would vouchsafe to grant my humble petition, wherein I besought him to summon a general council." Liberatus said[15] that Leo the bishop of Rome, with other more bishops of Italy, fell upon their knees, and desired the emperor Valentinian, and the empress Eudoxia, to appoint a council, and yet could not obtain it[16]. Afterward he desired the emperor Theodosius, that he would call a council to some place within Italy[17]; and the emperor, contrary to the bishop of Rome's petition, appointed it to be holden at Ephesus. After that, he made the same request to the emperor Martianus[18]; and the emperor likewise, contrary to the bishop's humble request, commanded the council to be kept at Chalcedon. And whereas Leo had besought both these emperors, that it might please them to take a longer day for the council, for that the time of the summon seemed very short, and the ways were laid with enemies, and therefore dangerous for the bishops to travel[19]; yet would neither of them alter one day, but charged each man to appear as they were summoned. And Leo the bishop of Rome, with all his universal power, was fain to yield. Hereby we may soon conjecture how true it is, either that pope Gelasius writeth, that "only the apostolic see of Rome decreed by her authority that the council of Chalcedon should be summoned[20];" or else that M. Harding would have us believe, that "all councils were summoned by the pope."

Gregor. Lib. iv. Epist. 34.

Leo, Epist. 23

Liberat. cap. xii. Genibus provolutis. Leo, Epist. 11. ad Theod. August. Leo, Epist. 13. Leo, Epist. 50. Leo, Epist. 13. 44. 58.

Epist. Gelas. ad Episc. Dardan.

Neither was the bishop of Rome, nor his legate in his absence, evermore the

[10 Sozom. in eod. Lib. v. Procem. p. 212.]

[11 Theodor. in eod. Lib. v. cap. ix. p. 209.]

[12 Concil. Constant. I. in Concil. Stud. Labb. et Cossart. Lut. Par. 1671-2. Tom. II. col. 946.]

[13 Gregor. Magni Papæ I. Op. Par. 1705. Epist. Lib. v. Indict. XIII. Ad Constant. August. Epist. xxi. Tom. II. col. 752.]

[14 Leon. Magni Op. Lut. 1623. Ad Cler. Constant. Epist. xxiii. col. 332.]

[15 Saith, 1565, 1609.]

[16 Liberat. Breviar. Par. 1675. cap. xii. p. 78; where *provolutus*.]

[17 Leon. Magni Op. Ad Theod. August. Epist. ix. col. 303; Epist. xxiv. cols. 333, 4; Epist. xxxiii. col. 345.]

[18 Id. Ad Mart. August. Epist. l. col. 366.]

[19 Id. Ad Pulch. August. Epist. xiii. col. 318; ad Mart. August. Epist. xliv. col. 360; Epist. xlix. col. 365; Epist. l. col. 366.]

[20 ... auctoritate, ut synodus Chalcedonensis fieret, sola decrevit.—Gelas. Epist. ad Episc. Dardan. in Crabb. Concil. Tom. I. p. 980.]

Confirmation of Councils.

president or chief of the council. For it is known that, in the council of Nice, Eustathius the patriarch of Antioch was the president, and the bishop of Rome's legates, Vitus and Vincentius, sat in the fourth room beneath. In the council of Constantinople Menna was the chief; in the council of Sardica, Osius of Corduba in Spain; in the council of Aquileia, St Ambrose of Milan; in the council of Carthage, Aurelius the bishop there: in the council of Chalcedon Leo the bishop of Rome's legate had chief room, but by way of entreaty only, and by the emperor's special grant, and not of due right or universal authority.

But, saith M. Harding, the bishop of Rome allowed general councils. This is not denied. So did others, not only patriarchs, or bishops, but also civil princes. In the council of Chalcedon it is written thus: *Divæ memoriæ Theodosius confirmavit omnia, quæ judicata sunt a sancta et universali synodo generali lege*[1]: "Theodosius the emperor, of godly memory, hath confirmed all things by a general law, that were determined in the universal council." So likewise the emperor Martianus: *Sacro nostræ serenitatis edicto venerandam synodum confirmamus*[2]: "By the holy edict of our majesty we confirm that reverend council." So Eusebius witnesseth, that the emperor Constantinus confirmed the determinations of the council of Nice[3]. So the bishops in the council of Constantinople wrote unto the emperor Theodosius by these words: *Rogamus tuam clementiam, ut per literas tuæ pietatis ratum esse jubeas confirmesque concilii decretum*[4]: "We desire your favour, by your highness' letters, to ratify and confirm the decree of the council."

(Concil. Chalc. Act. i.) (Concil. Chalc. Act. iii.) (Euseb. in Vita Constant.) (Inter Act. Concil. Constant. v.)

Now, seeing it was lawful for princes and civil governors to confirm the decrees and determinations of councils, how can we doubt, but it was lawful for bishops also to do the same? Therefore Theodoretus saith: "The conclusions of the council of Nice were sent abroad to other bishops that were away[5]." And Victorinus saith that "many thousands of bishops allowed that same council, and agreed unto it[6]."

(Theod. Lib. i. cap. ix. et Lib. ii. cap. viii. Victor. Lib. ii.)

Above all others, the subscription and confirmation of the four principal patriarchs was specially required; for that both their charge, and also their countenance and credit, was greater than others. Among which four, the bishop of Rome was ever the first; and therefore his consent seemed to bear greatest weight. And for that cause the emperor Martianus required Leo the bishop of Rome to write unto the council of Chalcedon, and to declare that he gave his consent to the rule of faith that was there determined[7]. And in like sort the emperor Theodosius requireth all bishops to subscribe and to give their assent to the council of Nice[8]. For it is a rule agreeable unto law and reason: *Quod omnes tangit, ab omnibus debet approbari*[9]: "The thing that toucheth all ought to be allowed by all." And therefore Julius, being bishop of Rome, pronounced that all the acts of the council of Antioch were void, and of no force, for that he, being one of the four patriarchs, was not called thither, as well as others[10]. For it appeareth by Eusebius, Theodoretus, and others, that to all general councils all primates and metropolitans were specially summoned[11]. And this seemeth to be that canon that Julius allegeth, that it was not lawful to make rules and orders

(Leo, Epist. 60.) (Inter Act. Concil. Chalc. Regula Juris.) (Euseb. Orat. iii. de Vita Constan. Theod. Lib. i. cap. vii. τὰς ἐκκλησίας κανονίζειν.)

[1 Concil. Calched. in Concil. Stud. Labb. et Cossart. Lut. Par. 1671-2. Tom. IV. col. 112. See before, page 66, note 8.]

[2 Id. in eod. Pars III. cap. iv. Tom. IV. col. 842.]

[3 Euseb. De Vit. Constant. in Hist. Eccles. Script. Amst. 1695-1700. Lib. III. capp. xvii. &c. pp. 405, &c.]

[4 Concil. Constant. I. in Concil. Stud. Labb. et Cossart. Tom. II. col. 946.]

[5 Theodor. in Hist. Eccles. Script. Lib. I. cap. ix. Lib. II. cap. viii. pp. 29, &c. 74, &c. See before, page 358, note 2.]

[6 Mar. Victorin. adv. Ar. Lib. II. 9. in Biblioth. Vet. Patr. Stud. Galland. Venet. 1765-81. Tom. VIII. p. 178. See before, page 358, note 3.]

[7 Quod vero piisimus imperator ad omnes episcopos, qui Chalcedonensi synodo interfuere, voluit me scripta dirigere, quibus quæ illic de fidei sunt regula definita firmarem, libenter implevi.—Leon. Magni Op. Lut. 1623. Ad Pulch. August. Epist. lx. col. 394.]

[8 Imp. Epist. ad Diosc. Alex. in Concil. Calched. in Concil. Stud. Labb. et Cossart. Tom. IV. col. 109.]

[9 Corp. Jur. Canon. Lugd. 1624. De Reg. Jur. ad calc. Sext. Decretal. Reg. xxix. col. 812; where *debet ab omnibus*.]

[10 Perhaps the reference is to the Epist. Increp. ad Orient. Episc. in Crabb. Concil. Col. Agrip. 1551. Tom. I. pp. 304, &c.]

[11 Euseb. in Hist. Eccles. Script. De Vit. Const. Lib. III. cap. vii. p. 401.]

for the whole church, without the consent of the bishop of Rome, being one of the four chief patriarchs, and having in his province one great portion of the church[12]. And therefore Leo bishop of Rome testifieth his consent to the council of Chalcedon by these words: *Fraternitas vestra novit, me definitionem sanctæ synodi... toto corde complexum esse*[13]: "Your brotherhood knoweth that I have embraced with my whole heart the determination of that holy council." And likewise unto the emperor Martianus he writeth thus: *Contitutionibus synodalibus... libens adjeci sententiam meam*[14]: "Unto these constitutions of the council I have gladly given my assent." The end hereof was not to shew his sovereign power above all others, but that the decrees, so ratified by him and others, might be had in more estimation. So Leo himself writeth: *Clementia vestra arbitratur, malum facilius delendum, si per universas ecclesias definitiones sanctæ synodi... apostolicæ sedi placuisse doceantur*[15]: "Your highness thinketh this evil will the rather be suppressed, if it be declared throughout all churches, that the decrees of the holy council be well liked of the apostolic see."

Confirmation of Councils.

Leo, Epist. 61.

Leo, Epist. 59.

Leo, Epist. 59.

But that the whole ratification of councils depended, not only of the bishop of Rome, but also of others no less than of him, it is easy to be proved. The bishops in the Roman council, in the time of Damasus, condemned the council of the Arians holden at Ariminum, for that neither the bishop of Rome, whose mind should have been known before all others, nor Vincentius, nor any of the rest had agreed unto it[16]. Likewise the council of Carthage and of Africa are allowed for good, notwithstanding the bishop of Rome would not allow them. The council of Chalcedon decreed, that the bishop of Constantinople should be in dignity next unto the bishop of Rome, and should consecrate the metropolitans of Asia, Pontus, and Thracia. This decree Leo the bishop of Rome very much misliked, and would never assent unto it[17]: yet, that notwithstanding, it is in force and continueth still. Liberatus thereof writeth thus: *Cum Anatolius consentiente concilio primatum obtinuisset, legati vero Romani episcopi contradicerent, a judicibus et episcopis omnibus illa contradictio suscepta non est. Et licet sedes apostolica nunc usque contradicat,* [*tamen*] *quod a synodo firmatum est, imperatorio patrocinio permanet*[18]: "When Anatolius by consent of the council had obtained the primacy, and the bishop of Rome's legates stood against it, their gainsaying of the judges and bishops there was not received. And albeit the apostolic see of Rome even hitherto stand against it, yet the decree of the council by the maintenance of the emperor standeth still in force." Which thing seemeth agreeable to that St Hierome writeth: *Major est auctoritas orbis, quam urbis*[19]: "The authority of the world is greater than the authority of one city;" meaning thereby the city of Rome.

Sozom. Lib. vi. cap. xxiii.

Leo, Epist. 13.

Liberat. cap. xiii.

Hieron. ad Evag.

It may appear by that I have thus shortly touched, that the bishop of Rome had authority neither to summon councils, nor to be president or chief in councils, nor to ratify and confirm the decrees of councils, more than any other of the four patriarchs; and last of all, that councils may stand in force, although the pope mislike them and allow them not. I think it will be hard hereof to gather M. Harding's conclusion, "that the bishop of Rome was head to[20] the universal church."

M. HARDING. THE TWENTY-SEVENTH DIVISION.

Now what authority the bishops of Rome have ever had and exercised in the assoiling of bishops unjustly condemned, and in restoring of them

[5. *Absolutions from the pope.* H. A. 1564.]

[[12] Theodoret. in eod. Lib. I. cap. vii. pp. 24, 5.]

[[13] Omnem ... fraternitatem vestram nosse non ambigo, definitionem, &c. me fuisse complexum.—Leon. Magni Op. Ad Sanct. Synod. Epist. lxi. col. 394.]

[[14] Id. Ad Mart. August. Epist. lix. col. 393.]

[[15] Quod facilius clementia vestra arbitretur implendum, si, &c.—Id. ibid. col. 392.]

[[16] Sozom. in Hist. Eccles. Script. Lib. VI. cap. xxiii. pp. 542, 3.]

[[17] Leoni Magni Op. Ad Anatol. Constant. Episc. Epist. liii. cols. 377, &c This is most probably the epistle intended.]

[[18] ... legati papæ Leonis ... cognoverunt, quid Anatolius, consentiente concilio, egerat et obtinuerat: quibus ejus præsumptioni contradicentibus, a, &c.... imperatoris, &c.—Liberat. Breviar. Par. 1675. cap. xiii. pp. 93, 4.]

[[19] Hieron. Op. Par. 1693-1706. Ad Evang. Epist. cci. Tom. IV. Pars II. col. 803. See before, page 373, note 17.]

[[20] Of, 1565, 1609.]

again to their churches, of which they were wrongfully thrust out by heretics or other disorder, it is a thing so well known of all that read the stories in which the ancient state of the church is described, that I need not but rehearse the names only. Athanasius of Alexandria, and Paulus of Constantinople, deprived and thrust out of their bishoprics by the violence of the Arians, assisted with the emperor Constantius, appealed to Rome, to Julius the pope and bishop there, and by his (113) *authority were restored to their rooms again. So Leo assoiled Flavianus the bishop of Constantinople, excommunicated by Dioscorus. So Nicolaus the first restored Ignatius to the see of Constantinople, though Michael the emperor wrought all that he could against it. Many other bishops have been in all ages assoiled, and restored to their churches by the authority of the see apostolic, who have been, without desert, excommunicated, deprived, and put from all their dignities. But to have rehearsed these few, it may suffice.*

The hundred and thirteenth untruth. For the emperor restored Athanasius, and not the pope. Pope Nicolas died in the year of our Lord 868.

THE BISHOP OF SARISBURY.

Athanasius and Paulus, saith M. Harding, being deposed by the Arians, assisted with the emperor Constantius, appealed to the pope, and by the pope's authority were restored. Here I appeal unto the judgment and discretion of the reader, that can consider the state of that time, how likely it may seem, either that Athanasius should appeal from the emperor to the pope, or that the pope's commandment should be of sufficient force and authority against the emperor. For neither was pope Bonifacius the eighth yet born, that determined that the emperor should be inferior to the pope[1]; nor pope Innocentius the third, or his gloss, that rated the matter by good geometrical proportion, and pronounced that the pope is fifty and seven degrees above the emperor, even just as much as the sun is above the moon[2]; nor pope Alexander the third, that set his foot in the emperor's neck[3].

De Major. et Obed. Unam sanctam. Extr. de Major. et Obed. Sol. Et in Gloss. Carion in Frederico.

Verily the pope then by his authority was able neither to depose, nor to restore, nor to call before him any bishop; as appeareth by that I have already alleged of pope Innocentius[4], and pope Gregory[5], by their own confessions. No, pope Leo himself confesseth that he was not able to remove a poor monk, abbat Eutyches, from his abbey, but was fain to desire the empress Pulcheria to see him removed[6].

Epist. Decret. Innoc. xxvii. Gregor. Lib. iv. Epist. 34. Leo, Epist. 45.

As touching Athanasius, it was the emperor Constantinus the great that by his authority removed and banished him, as it appeareth by Socrates[7]; and therefore the emperor Justinian saith: "If any bishop offend herein, let him be deprived by force of this law[8]." And, as he was banished by the emperor Constantinus the father, so by his son Constantinus the emperor, and not by the pope, he was restored: which thing is testified, not only by Socrates[9], that wrote the story, but also by sundry epistles and letters, taken out of the emperor's records, concerning the same.

Socr. Lib. i. cap. xxiii. De Eccles. Diver. Capit. κατὰ τὴν τοῦ παρόντος νόμου δύναμιν. Socr. Lib. ii. cap. ii.

First it is known that the emperor Constans, that ruled the west part of the world, unto whom Athanasius, being deposed, fled for aid, wrote in his behalf unto his brother Constantius, that then was the emperor of the east, and besought him to see Athanasius restored unto his room: otherwise he threatened that he himself would come with his power to Alexandria and restore him[10]. Upon the sight of which letters, the emperor Constantius wrote unto Athanasius, and willed him to repair with speed unto his court, that he might be

Sozom. Lib. iii. cap. xix.

[1 Bonifac. VIII. in Corp. Jur. Canon. Lugd. 1624. Extrav. Comm. Lib. I. De Major. et Obed. cap. 1. col. 212. See before, page 14.]

[2 Innoc. III. in eod. Decretal. Gregor. IX. Lib. I. Tit. xxxiii. cap. 6. et Gloss. in eod. col. 426. See before, page 14, note 1.]

[3 Carion. Chronic. Lib. Par. 1543. Lib. III. Frideric. I. fol. 109.]

[4 Rescr. Innoc. Epist. xxvii. in Crabb. Concil. Col. Agrip. 1551. Tom. I. p. 480. See before, page 394, note 6.]

[5 Gregor. Magni Papæ I. Op. Par. 1705. Epist. Lib. v. Indict. XIII. Ad Constant. August. Epist. xxi. Tom. II. col. 752.]

[6 Leon. Magni Op. Lut. 1623. Ad Pulch. August. Epist. xlv. col. 361.]

[7 Socrat. in Hist. Eccles. Script. Amst. 1695-1700. Lib. I. cap. xxxv. p. 59.]

[8 Corp. Jur. Civil. Amst. 1663. Auth. Coll. IX. Tit. vi. Novell. cxxiii. 9. Tom. II. p. 170. See before, pages 405, 6, note 24.]

[9 Socrat. in Hist. Eccles. Script. Lib. II. capp. ii. iii. pp. 68, 9.]

[10 Sozom. in eod. Lib. III. cap. xx. p. 433.]

restored unto his country[11]; and at his coming he directed out his letters unto the clergy and people of Alexandria, commanding them to receive him with favour, and to abolish all such acts as they had before made against him[12]. To report the whole letters at large, it would be tedious. Among other words, the emperor Constantius writeth thus: *Recipiat voluntate Dei, nostroque judicio, patriam suam, pariter et ecclesiam*[13]. And again: *Omnes episcopum, superno judicio nostraque sententia destinatum, libenter et pie suscipite*[14]: "Let him, both by God's appointment, and by our decree, recover both his country and his church, &c."[15] Further saith Cassiodorus: *His... literis confidens Athanasius, rediit in orientem*[16]: "Athanasius, upon trust of these letters, returned again into the east." Likewise the bishops in the council of Hierusalem wrote abroad letters of gratulation upon his return in this form: *Debetis ergo etiam, &c.*[17]: "You ought also continually to pray for the emperors' majesties, for that, understanding your desires, they have restored Athanasius again unto you." And Theodoretus touching the same writeth thus: *Procerum senatorumque conjuges, &c.*[18]: "The lords' and counsellors' wives besought their husbands to entreat the emperor's majesty, that he would restore Athanasius unto his flock; and said further, unless they would so do, they would forsake them, and go to him."

Theod. Lib. ii. cap. viii.

Theod. Lib. ii. cap. xi.

Cassiod. Lib. iv. cap. xxxi.

Cassiod. Lib. iv. cap. xxx.

Cassiod. Lib. iv. cap. xxxvi.

Theod. Lib. ii. cap. xvii.

So likewise the bishops, that the Arians had deposed with Flavianus, were restored again by the emperor, and not by the pope. For pope Leo himself thereof writeth thus unto the empress Pulcheria: [*Vos*] *sacerdotes catholicos, qui de ecclesiis suis injusta fuerunt ejecti sententia, reduxistis*[19]: "Your majesties have restored home again the catholic bishops, which by wrongful sentence were thrust from their churches."

Leo, Epist. 39.

Pope Nicolas, as upon occasion I said before, was the second bishop in Rome, after pope Joan the woman, which was almost nine hundred years after Christ. Wherefore his authority might well have been spared. It is well known, that as the pope's power increased, so the empire abated. Therefore was Platina forced to say: *Periit et potestas imperatorum, et virtus pontificum*[20]: "Now the emperors have lost their civil power; and the popes have lost their holiness." In old times the emperor confirmed the pope; now the pope confirmeth the emperor. In old times the emperor called the pope to the council; now contrariwise the pope calleth the emperor.

Platina in Adriano ii.

As touching the restoring of Athanasius, pope Julius entreated the emperor in his behalf, which, as it appeareth, was his greatest request. For thus he writeth unto Liberius: *Precamur ut vestris exhortationibus, tam per vos, quam ... per apocrisiarios vestros adjuvemur*[21]: "We beseech you that, through your good exhortations, both by yourself, and by other your agents, we may be holpen." Moreover, for that he was a patriarch, he summoned a particular council, and laboured the bishops. For the Arians said: "There was an ecclesiastical canon, that no man being once deposed should be restored again, unless he had first cleared himself before a council; and that the bishops, that would restore him, ought to be more in number than were they that had deposed him[22]." And therefore Chrysostom was much blamed of his adversaries, for that he, being once

Epist. Athan. ad Liberium.

Sozom. Lib. iv. cap. viii. Orient. Epist. ad Julium.

[11 Theodor. in eod. Lib. II. cap. viii. p. 83.]

[12 Id. in eod. Lib. II. cap. xi. p. 86.]

[13 Hist. Tripart. Par. Lib. IV. cap. xxxi. fol. G. 6; where *recipiens voluntatem.*]

[14 Id. ibid. cap. xxxii. ibid.; where *decreto superno*, and *suscipiatis.*]

[15 1565 omits *&c.*]

[16 Id. ibid. cap. xxx. fol. G. 5; where *ad orientem venit.*]

[17 Debetis ergo etiam pro pietate Deo amabilium nostrorum imperatorum incessanter Deo orare: quoniam et ipsi cognoscentes vestrum desiderium vobis restituere destinaverunt.—Id. ibid. cap. xxxvi. fol. G. 7.]

[18 Theodor. in Hist. Eccles. Script. Lib. II. cap. xvii. p. 95. The intercession here spoken of was to Constantius in behalf of Liberius.]

[19 Leon. Magni Op. Ad Pulch. August. Epist. xxxix. col. 352.]

[20 The passage intended is probably the following: Verum nescio quo fato accidisse dicam, ut una cum industria imperatorum, simul etiam pontificum virtus et integritas defecerit.—Plat. De Vit. Pont. Col. 1551. Formosus I. p. 125.]

[21 Athanas. Epist. ad Liber. in Crabb. Concil. Tom. I. p. 352.]

[22 Sozom. in Hist. Eccles. Script. Lib. IV. cap. viii. p. 444.

... cum dudum decretum fuisset, nullum a pauciore numero restitui debere, quam depositum fuisse constaret. — Orient. Epist. ad Jul. in Crabb. Concil. Tom. I. p. 308.]

Socrat. Lib. vi. cap. xviii. deposed, had recovered his room without a council of other bishops[1]. And therefore Flavianus, being wrongfully put from his bishopric, offered up his bill of appeal, not unto the bishop of Rome alone, but unto him with other bishops. The truth hereof may well appear by these words of Leo, bishop of Rome, unto Leon. Epist. 24. the emperor Theodosius: *Omnes partium nostrarum ecclesiæ, omnes mansuetudini vestræ cum gemitibus et lacrymis supplicant sacerdotes, ut quia ... eisdem libellum appellationis Flavianus episcopus dedit, generalem synodum jubeatis intra Italiam celebrari*[2]: "All the churches of these our countries, and all the priests with sighs and tears beseech your highness, that, forasmuch as Flavianus hath offered up his bill of appeal unto them, it may please you to command a general council to be kept in Italy."

In such councils the bishop of Rome, being sometimes the chief, pronounced the party worthy either to be restored, or to be deposed. But that sentence was Sozom. Lib. iii. cap. xi. καθεῖλον. not always put in execution. The council of Antioch deposed pope Julius[3]; yet was not Julius therefore deposed. The council of Basil deposed pope Eugenius; Concil. Basil. yet Eugenius continued pope still. The decree of bishops in such cases without Athan. in Apol. ii. Cassiod. Lib. iv. cap. xxxiv. the emperor's authority was then of small force. And therefore Athanasius himself reporteth, that the emperor gave his consent to the determination of the council of Sardica, and so commanded him to be sent for home[4].

Sozom. Lib. iii. cap. viii. But M. Harding will say the words be plain, that Julius restored Athanasius[5]. It is true, and not denied. But the meaning of these words is, that Julius pronounced him clear in that he was accused of, and therefore worthy to be restored. For it is certain, and M. Harding well knoweth, that Athanasius upon pope Julius' letters was not restored. The like is also written of others. Cassiod. Lib. iv. cap. xxxiv. Cassiodorus saith: *Maximus ... [quoque] restituit ... beato Athanasio et communionem et dignitatem*[6]: "Maximus also restored unto Athanasius both his communion and also his dignity; that is to say, pronounced him worthy to be restored." For Maximus was not the bishop of Rome.

These things considered, M. Harding may make up his reason thus: The pope had no authority to restore them that were deposed; *ergo*, the pope was not head of the church.

Or thus: The emperor restored such as were deposed; *ergo*, the emperor was head of the church.

M. HARDING. THE TWENTY-EIGHTH DIVISION.

Concerning the reconciliation of the prelates of the church, both bishops and patriarchs, to the bishop of Rome, (114) *whereby his primacy is acknowledged and confessed, I need not say much, the matter being so evident. After that the whole church*[7] *of Africa had continued in*[a] *schism, and withdrawn themselves from the obedience of the see apostolic, through the enticement of Aurelius archbishop of Carthago, for the space of one hundred years*[b], *during which time by God's punishment they came into captivity of the barbarous and cruel Vandals, who were Arians; at the length, when it pleased God of his goodness to have pity on his people of that province, sending them Belisarius, the valiant captain that vanquished and destroyed the Vandals, and likewise Eulalius, that godly archbishop of Carthago, that brought the church*[7] *home again, and joined the divided members unto the whole body, the catholic church; a public instrument, containing the form of their repentance and of their humble submission, was offered and exhibited solemnly to Bonifacius the second, then pope, by Eulalius, in the name of that whole province, which was joyfully received, and he thereupon forthwith reconciled. Of this reconciliation and restoring of the African*

[6. Reconciliations to the pope. H. A. 1564.]

The hundred and fourteenth untruth. For reconciliation is no necessary token neither of primacy nor of subjection.

[a] St Augustine was one of these schismatics.

[b] During the same time Rome itself was six times sacked: which thing M. Harding hath quite forgotten.

[1 Socrat. in Hist. Eccles. Script. Amst. 1695-1700. Lib. VI. cap. xviii. p. 267.]

[2 Leon. Magni Op. Lut. 1623. Ad Theodos. August. Epist. xxiv. col. 334.]

[3 Sozom. in Hist. Eccles. Script. Lib. III. cap. xi. p. 417. See before, page 406.]

[4 Athanas. Op. Par. 1698. Apol. contr. Arian. 51. Tom. I. Pars I. pp. 169, &c. Hist. Tripart. Par. Lib. IV. cap. xxxiv. foll. G. 6, 7.]

[5 ... ὁ Ῥωμαίων ἐπίσκοπος ... αὐτοὺς εἰς κοινωνίαν προσήκατο. — Sozom. in Hist. Eccles. Script. Lib. III. cap. viii. p. 413.]

[6 Hist. Tripart. Lib. IV. cap. xxxiv. fol. G. 7.]

[7 Churches, H. A. 1564.]

churches to the catholic church, the mystical body of Christ, Bonifacius writeth his letters to Eulalius bishop of Thessalonica, requiring him with the churches thereabout to give Almighty God thanks for it[8]. Reconciliation.

But here if I would shew what bishops, dividing themselves through heresy, schism, or other enormity, from the obedience of the see of Rome, have upon better advice submitted themselves to the same again, and thereupon have been reconciled, I had a large field to walk in. As inferior bishops of sundry provinces have done it, so have the great patriarchs done likewise. Among them that, to satisfy the malicious mind of Eudoxia the empress, practised their wicked conspiracy against Chrysostom, through which he was deposed and carried away into banishment, Alexander, bishop of Antioch and primate of the orient, was one; (115) *who at length, stricken*[9] *with repentance for that he had been both a consenter and a promoter of that wicked act, submitted himself humbly to Innocentius the pope, and by all means sought to be assoiled and reconciled; and therefore sent his legate*[11] *to Rome, to exhibit to Innocentius a solemn instrument of his repentance and lowly submission, and to accept what should be enjoined. By which his humbleness Innocentius moved granted to his petitions, received him into the lap of the catholic church again; and thus was he reconciled. Sundry the like reconciliations of the patriarchs of Alexandria and Hierusalem to the see of Rome in like cases might easily be recited; which, for avoiding of tediousness, I pass over, as likewise of the patriarchs of Constantinople, which, as we read in ancient stories, have forsaken the church of Rome twelve times, and have been reconciled*[12] *to the same again.* The hundred and fifteenth untruth. For[10] this story is here interlaced with many untruths.

THE BISHOP OF SARISBURY.

First, M. Harding supposeth that this Latin word, *reconciliatio*, can in no wise stand amongst equals; and besides that, touching the reconciliation of the church of Antioch, as it shall appear, he misreporteth the whole story. Upon such grounds these proofs be builded. For M. Harding knoweth that, as submission is made by the subject towards the[13] prince, so reconciliation, in proper manner of speech, is made between equal friends.

Concerning that is here touched of Eulalius, the matter needeth no long answer. The story being truly known is sufficient to answer itself. It is certain, as we have before declared more at large, and as it plainly appeareth by the acts of the council of Africa, that Zosimus the bishop of Rome, to the intent to advance[14] himself over all other bishops, manifestly falsified the Nicene council. This forgery in the council of Africa was disclosed and laid abroad to the eyes of all the world. The bishops there, being in number two hundred and seventeen, saw that one Apiarius a priest, whom they for his open outrage and wickedness had excommunicate, was, without any further examining of the matter, only upon his bare complaint, admitted again unto the communion, and received into favour in despite of all their doings, by the bishop of Rome.

They saw that the accusers and witnesses, without whom no ordinary judgment can proceed, either for age or for sickness and other causes, could not well travel so far: therefore they desired the bishop of Rome by their letters, that he would bring no such ambitious puff of vanity into the church; and made a strait decree in the council among themselves, that it should not be lawful for any man to appeal out of Africa to any foreign bishop[15]. An hundred years after that, this Eulalius the bishop of Carthage, if it be true that is reported of him, and not forged at Rome, as were many things more, reconciled himself to the church of Rome in the time of Bonifacius the second, as it is recorded in the Pontifical; for other record thereof, to my remembrance, there is none. The words of the reconciliation be these: *Hanc professionem meam manu mea sub-* Fumosum seculi typhum. Inter Decret. Bonif. ii.

[8 Bonifac. Papæ II. Epist. ad Eulal. Alex. Episc. in Crabb. Concil. Col. Agripp. 1551. Tom. I. pp. 1057, 8.]

[9 Stroken, 1565, strooken, H. A. 1564.]

[10 1565 omits *for*.]

[11 Legates, 1565, 1609, and H. A. 1564.]

[12 Reconcilied, H. A. 1564.]

[13 His, 1565, 1609.]

[14 Avance, 1565.]

[15 Concil. Afric. Epist. ad Cœlestin. cap. 105. in Crabb. Concil. Tom. I. p. 521. See before, page 356, note 6.]

Reconciliation.

scripsi, &c.[1]: "This profession I have subscribed with mine own hand, and have directed the same to Bonifacius the holy and reverend pope of the city of Rome, utterly condemning my predecessors and successors, and all others that shall go about to frustrate the privileges of the apostolic see of Rome." Likewise Bonifacius writeth hereof unto Eulalius the bishop of Alexandria in this wise: *Aurelius . . . Carthaginensis ecclesiæ olim episcopus cum collegis suis, instigante diabolo, superbire temporibus prædecessorum nostrorum ... contra Romanam ecclesiam cœpit*[2]: "Aurelius sometime bishop of Carthage, together with his fellows (his fellows were St Augustine, Alypius, and two hundred and fifteen other bishops), being set on by the devil, in the time of my predecessors, began to bear himself disdainfully against the church of Rome." The one of these, by a public instrument under his hand and seal, utterly condemneth and accurseth St Augustine, with two hundred and sixteen other godly bishops, together with four general councils, of Africa, Carthage, Milevitum, and Hippo: the other saith, they were all set a-work and pricked forth by the devil, and lived out of the church of God, and died in schism.

Epist. Bonif. 2. ad Eulal.

St Augustine condemned and accursed, and set on by the devil.

If this be true, then ought St Augustine no longer to be holden for a saint, neither to have any room in the calendar.

But if all these godly fathers, that justly and truly defended the holy council of Nice, were led with the devil, with what spirit then was he led, that openly and in the sight of all the world durst to corrupt and falsify the same council? Verily, Dionysius the bishop of Corinth complaineth thus: *Rogatu fratrum meorum scripsi epistolas: sed illas apostoli diaboli, alia eximentes, alia interserentes, impleverunt zizaniis: quibus væ reponitur*[3]: "At the request of my brethren I wrote certain epistles; but the devil's apostles, by putting to and taking fro, have filled them full of tares and cockle. But wo be unto them!"

PopeZosimus a forger of councils.

Euseb. Lib. iv. cap. xxiii. *οἱ τοῦ διαβόλου ἀπόστολοι ζιζανίων γεγέμηκαν.*

But in the mean while, saith M. Harding, the country of Africa even by the punishment of God was brought into subjection and spoiled by the Vandals. Here M. Harding entereth into God's judgments, and pronounceth that all this misery happened unto that country for leaving the see of Rome; which thing he reckoneth all one with the leaving and forsaking of God himself. Howbeit M. Harding might soon know that about the very same time, while Africa was thus afflicted, the city of Rome itself was six times taken by wild and barbarous enemies, the Visigothi, Ostrogothi, Heruli, Vandali, Hunni, and Longobardi, within the space of an hundred and forty years. The walls were rased; the towers thrown down; the houses burnt; the nobility taken captive; the people spoiled and banished; the city itself a long time left waste and desolate without inhabiter[4]. If M. Harding can guess so rightly of the miseries of Africa, how happeneth it that he can guess nothing of six-fold greater miseries, that at the same time befel upon Rome? If the bishops and people of Africa were thus plagued for their schism, wherefore then were the bishops and people of[5] Rome plagued, that (as it is supposed) continued still without schism? Notwithstanding, Possidonius saith that God of special mercy granted St Augustine, who then was besieged by the enemies, that during his life his city of Hippo should not be taken[6]. And yet was the same St Augustine the greatest discloser of the forgery and pride of the bishop of Rome, that is to say, the greatest author and maintainer of all this schism.

Rome six times taken by enemies and sacked, within the space of one hundred and forty years.

Gregor. Lib. iv. Epist. 32.

Touching the reconciliation of Alexander the bishop of Antioch, M. Harding, for the better furniture of the tale, hath woven in and interlaced many words of his own. For in all that is written thereof by Innocentius, there is no manner mention, neither of solemn instrument of repentance, nor of accepting of penance,

---

[[1] Hanc autem &c., et Bonifacio sancto et venerabili papæ urbis Romæ direxi, damnans et antecessores et successores meos, et omnes qui sanctæ Romanæ et apostolicæ ecclesiæ privilegia cassare nituntur.—Exempl. Prec. Eulal. et Justin. in Decret. Bonifac. Papæ II. in eod. Tom. I. p. 1058.]

[[2] Bonifac. Papæ II. Epist. ad Eulal. in eod. ibid.]

[[3] Euseb. in Hist. Eccles. Script. Amst. 1695-1700. Lib. IV. cap. xxiii. p. 118; where γεγέμικαν.]

[[4] Gregor. Magni Papæ I. Op. Par. 1705. Epist. Lib. v. Indict. XIII. Ad Mauric. August. Epist. xx. Tom. II. cols. 747, &c. In this epistle Gregory, describing the miseries of the empire, regards them as the divine judgments on the pride of churchmen.]

[[5] *Of* is repeated, 1565.]

[[6] August. Op. Par. 1679-1700. August. Vit. auct. Possid. cap. xxix. Tom. X. Post-Append. cols. 278, 9.]

nor of subjection or humble submission. Indeed this Alexander, at his first entry into the bishopric of Antioch, finding his church full of division by mean of one Eustathius, by his wisdom and godly exhortations brought the whole people there unto unity; and afterward wrought the like godly policy in other churches, and ceased all the strife that had long continued for the condemnation of Chrysostom, and caused his name, that his enemies had rased out, to be enrolled again among other catholic bishops; and likewise wrote unto the emperor Theodosius the younger, and to the bishops of other countries, to do the like[7]. In the end, having appeased all contentions, in token, not of subjection, as M. Harding surmiseth, but of full consent and agreement, he desired that his church might be joined in communion and fellowship with the church of Rome and other churches of the west, from whence before, by reason of their dissensions, they had been divided. Which thing also appeareth by the words of Innocentius himself unto Alexander touching the same: *Gratias agens Domino, communionem ecclesiæ vestræ ita recepi, ut præ me feram apostolicæ sedis condiscipulos primos dedisse ceteris viam pacis*[8]: "I, giving God thanks, so received the communion and fellowship of your church, that I profess that you, being our school-fellows of the apostolic see, have first opened unto others the way of peace." Here Innocentius calleth Alexander his school-fellow, not his subject or underling. And therefore he calleth him his school-fellow of the apostolic see, for that St Peter sat first at Antioch, and after that in Rome; and for that cause, both these sees of Peter the apostle were called apostolic.

Reconciliation.

Theod. Lib. v. cap. xxxv. Niceph. Lib. xiv. cap. xxvi.

Innocent. Epist. 17. ad Alexandrum.

Again, in another epistle unto the same Alexander, he writeth thus: *Voluit... compresbyter noster Cassianus, hanc amicitiarum nostrarum paginulam...quasi primitias pacis nostræ conscribi, &c.*[9]: "Cassianus, our fellow-priest, would have this instrument of our friendship to be written, as the first-fruits of our peace. Therefore I greet well your brotherhood, and all others of that church that are of your mind." Here Innocentius himself calleth this composition an instrument of friendship or fellowship, not of repentance or humble submission, as it pleaseth M. Harding untruly to translate it. Neither doth this word, "reconciliation," necessarily import a superiority or a mastership; but also, and that most commonly, a fellowship or equality, as it is said before. So saith St Paul: "Christ hath reconciled both the Jew and the gentile in one body." And what is meant by that reconciliation, he expoundeth thus: *Omnes unum sumus in Christo Jesu:* "We are all one in Christ Jesu." So saith Pliny the younger: *Principis est reconciliare æmulas civitates*[10]: "It is a prince's part to reconcile cities that contend for the sovereignty:" not that the one may be brought into subjection to the other; but that they may be made friends, and live in peace. So likewise saith Christ: *Vade, reconcilieris fratri tuo:* "Go, and be reconciled to[11] thy brother."

Innocent. Epist. 15.

Eph. ii.

Gal. iii.

Plin. in Panegyrico.

Matt. v.

Thus therefore was the patriarch of Antioch reconciled to the bishop of Rome, not as a subject unto his prince, but as in a body one member unto another; and (forasmuch as Innocentius himself useth this word *condiscipuli*[12]) as in a school one scholar unto his fellow.

Innocent. Epist. 17.

So, whereas there was matter of dissension between the church of Rome and the church of Alexandria, it seemed good to the fathers in the council of Africa, to entreat between them, not that the church of Alexandria should submit herself, as unto her head, and live in subjection, but that they might be reconciled, and live in peace together[13]. So Liberatus saith, Petrus Moggus was reconciled unto Asatius[14], not as unto his superior, but as unto his brother. In this sense writeth

Concil. Aphr. cap. 68.

Liberat. cap. xviii.

[7 Theodor. in Hist. Eccles. Script. Lib. v. cap. xxxv. p. 241.

Niceph. Call. Hist. Eccles. Lut. Par. 1630. Lib. XIV. cap. xxv. pp. 489, 90.]

[8 Innoc. Papæ I. ad Alex. Antioch. Episc. Epist. xvii. in Crabb. Concil. Col. Agrip. 1551. Tom. I. p. 463.]

[9 Id. ad eund. Epist. xv. in eod. p. 462. The epistle proceeds: Saluto itaque et tuam mihi in Christo germanitatem, et omnem illam, quæ tecum tam bene sentit, ecclesiam.]

[10 O vere principis, atque etiam consulis, reconciliare æmulas civitates.—C. Plin. Cœcil. Secund. Op. Basil. 1552. Panegyr. p. 479.]

[11 Unto, 1565, 1609.]

[12 See before, note 8.]

[13 Placuit etiam, ut de dissensione Romanæ atque Alexandrinæ ecclesiæ ad sanctum papam Innocentium scribatur, quo utraque ecclesia intra se pacem, quam præcepit Dominus, teneat.—Concil. Afric. cap. 68. in Crabb. Concil. Tom. I. p. 514.]

[14 Acacius...rescripsit...quia...Petrum...Moggum suscepisset in communionem.—Liberat. Breviar. cap. xviii. in eod. Tom. II. p. 115.]

Reconciliation.

Concil. Const. v. Act. 2.

Hormisda bishop of Rome unto Epiphanius the bishop of Constantinople: *Æquale studium et æqualem curam suscipiamus, quibus una est in communione et fide amicitia*[1]: "Seeing we have one friendship in communion and in faith, let us therefore take like study and like care."

Socrat. Lib. iv. cap. xi.

This manner of reconciliation is largely set forth by Socrates in his story, and may be abridged in this sort: The Macedonian heretics, having forsaken their heresies, sent their messengers Eustathius, Sylvanus, and Theophilus unto Liberius the bishop of Rome, and to other the bishops of the west. Liberius, understanding that their faith agreed fully with the council of Nice, and with the faith that he himself and all the other bishops of the west church professed, received them unto the communion, and wrote favourably unto the bishops of the east in their behalf. These messengers, departing thence, went into Sicily, and, in a council of the bishops there, likewise reconciled themselves unto them; and, being returned home, they sent abroad into all the churches of those countries, and willed them to consider the letters sent from Liberius the bishop of Rome, and from other bishops of Italy, Africa, France, Sicily, and all the west, and to agree, and to communicate together with them[2].

Athan. Apol. Sec.

Another like example of reconciliation we have made by one Arsenius the bishop of Hipsilitæ unto Athanasius the bishop of Alexandria. The words of the reconciliation are these: *Nos volentes ecclesiastico canoni, &c.*: "We, desiring to be subject to the ecclesiastical canon, according to the ancient order, do write these unto you, *dilecte papa*, beloved pope, and likewise do promise in the name of our Lord, that we henceforth will not communicate with any schismatics, or with any that have not peace with the catholic church, whether they be bishops, priests, or deacons[3]." This submission or reconciliation was made unto Athanasius; yet was not Athanasius bishop[4] of Rome.

This then was the manner of reconciliation of churches, without any such humble subjection as M. Harding fancieth, or knowledge or token of supremacy, or any manner universal power.

M. HARDING. THE TWENTY-NINTH DIVISION.

The hundred and sixteenth untruth. For many great questions were never removed to Rome.

The hundred and seventeenth untruth. For Rome itself had her light from Græcia.

Thus, having declared the supreme authority and primacy of the pope by the common practice of the church, I need not to shew further, how in (116) *all questions, doubts, and controversies touching faith and religion the see of Rome hath always been consulted; how the decision of all doubtful cases hath been referred to the judgment of that see; and, to be short,* (117) *how all the world hath ever fetched light from thence. For proof*[5] *whereof, because it cannot be here declared briefly, I remit the learned reader to the ecclesiastical stories, where he shall find this matter amply treated.*

THE BISHOP OF SARISBURY.

Ἑλλὰς Ἑλλάδος. Cœl. Rhod. Lib. xviii. cap xxv.

As Rome, having achieved the empire of the whole world, both for renown and honour, and also for wisdom and learning, which commonly follow the empire, was the noblest and most famous of all other cities; so for commodity of access out of all kingdoms and countries, both of the east and of the west, and also out of Africa and Egypt, and other countries of the south, and also for receiving of questions, and resolution of doubts, it seemed to be planted in the fittest place of all the world. For as Thucydides calleth the city of Athens "Græcia of all Græcia;" so some called the city of Rome, in those days of her honour, *epitome orbis terrarum*[6], "the abridgment of the whole world." The admiration of this

---

[1 Hormisd. Epist. in Concil. Constant. sub Menna, Act. v. in Concil. Stud. Labb. et Cossart. Lut. Par. 1671-2. Tom. V. col. 152.]

[2 Socrat. in Hist. Eccles. Script. Amst. 1695-1700. Lib. IV. cap. xii. pp. 180, &c.]

[3 ...προῃρημένοι τε τῷ ἐκκλησιαστικῷ κανόνι κατὰ τὸν παλαιὸν τύπον ὑποτάσσεσθαι, γράφομέν σοι, ἀγαπητὲ πάπα, ὁμολογοῦντες ἐν ὀνόματι Κυρίου τοῦ λοιποῦ μὴ κοινωνήσειν τοῖς ἔτι σχίζουσι, καὶ μηδέπω εἰρηνεύουσι πρὸς τὴν καθολικὴν ἐκκλησίαν, ἐπισκόποις τε καὶ πρεσβυτέροις καὶ διακόνοις.—Athanas. Op. Par. 1698. Apol. contr. Arian. 69. Tom. I. Pars I. p. 185.]

[4 The bishop, 1565, 1609.]

[5 For the proof, H. A. 1564.]

[6 Cœl. Rhodig. Lect. Antiq. 1599. Lib. XVIII. cap. xxv. cols. 858, 9.]

glory drew such resort of people thither, that Beda, a learned man of this country, being there, and seeing the multitude of strangers that came only to gaze and to see news, expounded these four solemn letters, S. P. Q. R. in this wise: *Stultus populus quærit Romam*[7]: "Foolish folk fly[8] to Rome." Therefore for opportunity of the place, and expedition of answer, many matters of question and doubtful cases were brought thither. Many, I say, but not all. For men, that wanted counsel, wrote and sought unto them that had the fame of learning, and were thought best able to make them answer. So Marcellinus, Dulcitius, Bonifacius, Euodius, and others, sent their questions to St Augustine, and desired his counsel. St Ambrose saith, as it is before alleged, that many that had been with the bishop of Rome would afterward for their better satisfaction send to him[9]. And Leo himself, being bishop of Rome, and therefore, as M. Harding thinketh, the oracle of all the world, thought it not amiss to submit himself, and to ask counsel of other bishops[10]. Therefore this saying of M. Harding's neither is universally true, nor proveth his purpose. For if he will say, Some men in cases of doubt sought to Rome for counsel; *ergo*, the bishop there was called the head of the church; this conclusion will hardly follow.

Ambros. Lib. x. Epist. 83.

Leo, Epist. 27.

King Josias, in a great case of religion, sent to a woman named Olda, the wife of Sellum, to know her counsel; and it was a proverb among the Jews: *Qui interrogat, interroget in Abila*: "Whoso will seek counsel, let him seek it in Abila." Yet neither was Olda the head of the church, nor Abila the chief town in Israel or Juda.

2 Kings xxii. 2 Chron. xxxiv. 2 Sam. xx.

"But all the world," saith M. Harding, "hath received light from Rome." But all the world seeth this is another manifest untruth; and nevertheless, being granted, yet would it not conclude of his side.

Indeed in a kind of speech both Rome, and Antioch, and Alexandria, and any other great city famous for religion, may be called the head or spring of the gospel. So St John calleth Babylon *magna mater fornicationum et abominationum terræ*, "the great mother of the fornications and of the abominations of the earth." And so Arnobius calleth Hetruria[11], which is the country wherein Rome standeth; and St Ambrose calleth Rome itself *caput superstitionis*[12], "the head of superstition."

Rev. xvii.

Arnob. Lib. ii. adversus Gentes.

Ambros. Serm. 66.

But if we seek the place itself from whence the light of religion first sprang forth, we must needs confess it was Hierusalem, and not Rome. For so it is written in the prophet Esay: *De Sion exibit lex, et verbum Domini de Hierusalem*: "The law shall proceed from Sion, and the word of God from Hierusalem." And therefore the bishops of the east, being in a convocation at Constantinople, call Hierusalem "the mother of all churches[13]." Yet nevertheless, every great metropolitan city within her own province may be honoured with the like title. So saith Nazianzenus of the city of Cæsarea, where St Basil was bishop: *Cæsarea prope mater omnium*[14] *ecclesiarum*[15], *&c.*: "Cæsarea is in a manner the mother of all churches; and the whole christian commonwealth so embraceth and beholdeth it, as the circle embraceth and beholdeth the center." So Chrysostom likewise advanceth[16] the city of Antioch: *Cogita urbis magnitudinem, quod non de una vel de duabus, vel de tribus, vel de decem animabus, nunc nobis est consideratio; sed de millibus infinitis, de totius orbis capite*[17]: "Consider the greatness of this city: we have to deal not for one, two, three, or ten souls; but for infinite thousands, even

Isai. ii.

Theod. Lib. v. cap. ix.

Gregor. Naz. in Epist. ad Cæsar.

Ad Pop. Ant. Hom. 3.

[7 The editor can give no authority for what is here said. There is, however, a story told of Bede, that he interpreted PPP. SSS. RRR. FFF. as meaning Pater patriæ perditus est. Salus secum sublata est. Ruet regnum Romæ, Ferro, flamma, fame.—Vit. Bed. ad calc. Hist. Eccles. Cant. 1722. p. 800.]

[8 Flee, 1565.]

[9 Ambros. Op. Par. 1686-90. Ad Episc. per Æmil. Epist. xxiii. 8. Tom. II. col. 882. See before, page 382, note 5.]

[10 Leon. Magni Op. Lut. 1623. Ad Leon. Raven. Episc. Epist. xxxvii. cols. 349-51.]

[11 ...genitrix et mater superstitionis Hetruria.—Arnob. Op. Par. 1580. Adv. Gent. Lib. VII. p. 209.]

[12 Ambros. Op. Par. 1614. Serm. in Fest. SS. Petr. et Paul. Tom. V. col. 142.]

[13 Τῆς δέ γε μητρὸς ἁπασῶν τῶν ἐκκλησιῶν τῆς ἐν Ἱεροσολύμοις, κ. τ. λ.—Theodor. in Hist. Eccles. Script. Lib. v. cap. ix. p. 211.]

[14 Mater est omnium, 1565, 1609.]

[15 Gregor. Nazianz. Op. Par. 1778-1840. Ad Cæsar. Epist. xli. Tom. II. p. 36.]

[16 Avanceth, 1565.]

[17 Chrysost. Op. Par. 1718-38. Ad Pop. Ant. Hom. iii. Tom. II. col. 36.]

for the head of the world." Thus Chrysostom calleth Antioch "the head of the world," for that in that province of Syria it was the head; like as Rome also was the head city and principal church of the west.

M. HARDING. THE THIRTIETH DIVISION.

Now for a brief answer to M. Jewel, who denieth that within 600 *years after Christ the bishop of Rome was ever called an universal bishop or head*[1] *of the universal church, and maketh himself very sure of it; although it be a childish thing to stick at the name any thing is called by, the thing by the name signified being sufficiently proved; yet to the intent good folk may understand that all is not truth of the old gospel, which our new gospellers either affirm or deny, I will bring good and sufficient witness, that the bishop of Rome was then called both universal bishop, or œcumenical patriarch, which is one; to wit, bishop or principal father of the whole world, and also head of the church. Leo, that worthy bishop of Rome, was called the universal bishop, and universal patriarch, of six hundred and thirty fathers assembled together from all parts of the world in a general*[2] *council at Chalcedon; which is both* (118) *expressed in that council, and also clearly affirmed by St Gregory in three sundry epistles, to Mauritius the emperor, to Eulogius patriarch of Alexandria, and to Anastasius patriarch of Antioch*[4]. *Thus that name was deferred unto the pope by the fathers of that great council; which by them had not been done, had it been unlawful. In very deed neither Leo himself, nor any other his successor, ever called or wrote himself by that name, as St Gregory saith, much less presumed they to take it unto them; but rather used the name of humility, calling themselves each one* servum servorum Dei, "*the servant of the servants of God." Yet sundry holy martyrs, bishops of Rome, used to call themselves bishops of the universal church,* (119) *which in effect is the same, as the fathers of Chalcedon understood.* * *So did Sixtus in the time of Adrianus the emperor, in his epistle to the bishops of all the world*[5]. *So did Victor writing to Theophilus of Alexandria*[6]. *So did Pontianus writing to all that believed in Christ*[7], *before* 1300 *years past. So did Stephanus in his epistle to all bishops of all provinces*[8], *in the time of St Cyprian. And all*[9] *these were before Constantine the great, and before the council of Nice, which times our adversaries acknowledge and confess to have been without corruption. The same title was used likewise after the Nicene council by Felix*[10], *by* (120) *Leo, and by divers others, before the* 600[11] *years after Christ were expired. Neither did the bishops of Rome use this title and name only themselves to their own advancement, as the adversaries of the church charge them, but they were honoured therewith also by others; as namely Innocentius by the fathers assembled in council at Carthago*[12], *and Marcus by Athanasius and the bishops of Egypt*[13].

[*The pope above a thousand years sithence called universal bishop, and head of the universal church.* H. A. 1564.]

The hundred and eighteenth untruth. For[3] there is no mention made hereof in any canon in that council.

The hundred and nineteenth untruth. For these names import not one thing, as shall appear.

* All these be bastard epistles, without credit.

The hundred and twentieth untruth. For immediately before M. Harding confesseth that Leo never wrote himself by that name.

THE BISHOP OF SARISBURY.

Here M. Harding secretly confesseth that, in all he hath hitherto alleged, he hath not yet found that the bishop of Rome was known in the world, within the space of the first six hundred years after Christ, by the name either of the universal bishop, or of the head of the universal church; notwithstanding he hath much guessed about the matter, both by misreporting the practice of government that then was used, and also by wresting and misconstruing the words of the holy fathers. Thus hitherto he hath taken great pains to small purpose.

[1 The head, H. A. 1564.]

[2 In general, 1565, 1609, and H. A. 1564.]

[3 1565 omits *for*.]

[4 Gregor. Magni Papæ I. Op. Par. 1705. Epist. Lib. v. Indict. XIII. Ad Mauric. August. Epist. xx. Tom. II. col. 749. Ad Eulog. et Anastas. Episc. Epist. xliii. col. 771. Lib. VIII. Indict. I. Ad Eulog. Episc. Epist. xxx. col. 919. There are also other epistles in which Gregory affirms the same thing.]

[5 Sixt. Papæ I. Epist. ii. in Crabb. Concil. Col. Agrip. 1551. Tom. I. p. 79.]

[6 Victor. Papæ ad Theoph. Alex. Epist. i. in eod. p. 93.]

[7 Pontian. Papæ Epist. ii. in eod. p. 108.]

[8 Steph. Papæ I. Epist. ii. in eod. p. 157.]

[9 Also, 1611.]

[10 Felic. Papæ II. Rescr. ad Synod. Alex. in eod. p. 358.]

[11 The first six hundred, H. A. 1564.]

[12 See below, page 425.]

[13 Ægypt. Epist. ad Marc. in eod. p. 299.]

But hereunto he putteth his rhetorical correction, and saith: "It is a childish thing to stick at the name of any thing." And so all this long talk is driven in the end to a childish conclusion. Howbeit it appeareth St Gregory was not so persuaded of it, nor thought the matter to be so childish. For after that John of Constantinople had entitled himself the universal bishop, Gregory, being then bishop of Rome, withstood him earnestly, and wrote against him in this wise: "*Deus...ab unitate atque humilitate ecclesiæ hoc malum superbiæ et confusionis avertat*[14]: "God turn away this mischief of pride and confusion from the unity and humility of the church." Again: *Omnibus viribus...providendum [est], ne in unius veneno sermonis viventia in Christi corpore membra moriantur*[15]: "We must labour and provide, with all that we can do, lest the members, that live in Christ's body, happen to perish in the poison of one word." Moreover, as it is before at large declared, he calleth it a new, a perverse, a superstitious, an arrogant, an ungodly, an antichristian name, a name of singularity, a name of error, a name of confusion, a name of blasphemy, against the canons, against the whole church, against St Peter, and against the gospel. Yet, saith M. Harding, to stick at this name it is but a childish matter. Howbeit, if the thing itself, that this name importeth, had been lawful, then had this name not been so horrible. But contrariwise, the very usurpation of the name is horrible; therefore the thing itself thereby signified must of necessity be much more horrible.

Gregor. Lib. iv. Epist. 36.

Now for a brief answer: M. Harding hath found six hundred and thirty bishops, that gave this title to Leo bishop of Rome in the council of Chalcedon, and called him the universal bishop; which thing, as he saith, is recorded by St Gregory in three sundry places. Here, good christian reader, by the way, this one thing, I trust, thou wilt consider of thyself[16]. If the name of universal bishop were given to the bishop of Rome in the council of Chalcedon, which was holden in the year of our Lord 488[17]; then, by M. Harding's own grant, and by the witness of this council, the bishop of Rome before that time had not the name of universal bishop. Otherwise, how could either they give that they had not to bestow, or he receive that he had already? Indeed such bestowing of gifts had been very childish. Thus, of the whole number of six hundred years, M. Harding freely, even at the sight, hath yielded us back four hundred four-score and eight years towards the reckoning.

Before we pass further, let us see what credit the pope himself giveth to this council of six hundred and thirty fathers holden at Chalcedon. Pope Gelasius saith: "The apostolic see of Rome in part allowed it not; for that things were there borne out by inordinate presumption[18]." Pope Leo accuseth the whole council of "ambition and wilful rashness[19]." And St Hierome, in the case of matrimony *inter raptorem et raptam*, is received against all those six hundred and thirty bishops, and against the determination of that whole council[20]. In such regard they have the councils when they list! But the law saith: *Absurdum videtur, licere eidem partim comprobare judicium defuncti, partim evertere*[21]: "It is against reason that one man should in part allow the will of the dead (so far forth as it maketh for him), and in part overthrow it (where it seemeth to make against him)."

Gelasius inter Acta Concil. Tarracon. Per incompetentem præsumptionem ventilata. Leo, Ambitionem et inconsultam temeritatem. xxxvi. Quæst. ii. Tria legitima. Pan. de Bonis Libertor. Nam absurdum. Caius.

But M. Harding will say: Of what credit soever this council ought to be, it gave Leo the name of universal bishop. And what if all this be utterly untrue? What if there were no such title either given or offered in the council?

[14 Gregor. Magni Papæ I. Op. Epist. Lib. v. Indict. XIII. Ad Eulog. et Anastas. Episc. Epist. xliii. Tom. II. col. 773; where *hoc* precedes *ab unitate*.]

[15 Id. ibid.]

[16 Theeself, 1565.]

[17 This is the date erroneously given in Crabb. Concil. The council is usually assigned to the year 451.]

[18 ...alia autem, quæ per incompetentem præsumptionem illic perlata sunt, vel potius ventilata... quæ sedes apostolica...nullatenus approbavit, &c.—Gelas. Papæ Tom. de Anathem. Vinc. in Crabb. Concil. Tom. I. pp. 969, 70.]

[19 Leon. Magni Op. Lut. 1623. Ad Anatol. Const. Episc. Epist. liii.; ad Pulcher. August. Epist. lv.; ad Maxim. Antioch. Episc. Epist. lxii. cols. 378, 80, 5, 6, 97, 8. The exact words as they are here alleged are not found; but Leo in the places referred to again and again censures the council.]

[20 Hieron. in Corp. Jur. Canon. Lugd. 1624. Decret. Gratian. Decr. Sec. Pars, Caus. XXXVI. Quæst. ii. can. 8. col. 1882. An attempt is made to reconcile the opinion of Jerome with the decree of Chalcedon. See Not. and gloss. in loc.]

[21 Gaius in Corp. Jur. Civil. Amst. 1663. Digest. Lib. XXXVIII. Tit. ii. 7. Tom. I. p. 543.]

Pope not universal.

Certainly, the whole council of Chalcedon is extant abroad both written and printed, and may soon be seen. Why doth not M. Harding allege either the place, or the canon, or the words? At the least, why giveth he no note in the margin, where this authority may be found?

Perhaps he will say, this canon was burnt by some heretics, as he said before of the council of Nice. Howbeit, it were much for him to say, that of that whole council only six lines should be burnt, and that in all the examples throughout the world, and yet all the rest of the same council remain safe; or that the words, whereby the pope claimeth his title, should so negligently be lost, and that in Rome itself, in the pope's own library; and yet the words that the pope reproveth and condemneth should stand whole. M. Harding hath no other council within six hundred years after Christ to hold by, but only this; and yet the same cannot be found. But St Gregory is witness sufficient: he saith that six hundred and thirty bishops in the council of Chalcedon named the bishop of Rome the universal bishop. This is an untruth to beguile the reader. For Gregory saith not, the bishops in that council saluted, entitled, proclaimed, or called the bishop of Rome by that name. Only he saith: *Romano pontifici... universitatis nomen oblatum est*[1]: "The name of universal bishop was offered by the council of Chalcedon to the bishop of Rome." He saith they offered to call him so; but that they called him so indeed, he saith not. Therefore M. Harding herein overreacheth and mistelleth his author's tale. But St Gregory saith further that "neither Leo nor any other of his predecessors bishops of Rome would ever receive that arrogant and ungodly name, or suffer himself to be so called," notwithstanding it were offered by the council. The bishops of Rome never so[2] used that name, notwithstanding it were offered them. Therefore they ought to lose it by non-usure.

Gregor. Lib. iv. Epist. 32, et 36.

Superbum prophanum nomen.

M. Harding will say: This was only their humility, and not want of right: and therefore they chose rather to be called *servi servorum Dei*, "the servants of God's servants." Verily it may well be thought that Gregory, who first used these words, as his familiar style, named himself so without hypocrisy, only in respect of his intolerable pains and continual travails. For so he himself complaineth: *Veni in altitudinem maris, et tempestas demersit me*[3]: "I am come into the deep of the sea; and the rage of tempest hath drowned me up." So St Augustine long before St Gregory's time, for that he was likewise troubled, used sometimes the like style. For thus he writeth of himself: *Augustinus episcopus servus Christi servorumque Christi*[4]: "Augustine, bishop, the servant of Christ, and the servant of Christ's servants." But he that neither feedeth the flock, nor plougheth the Lord's ground, nor dresseth his vine, nor ministereth the sacraments, nor comforteth, nor exhorteth, nor teacheth; that is carried on high through the streets on noblemen's backs, and may not touch the ground for holiness; that causeth that noble prince the French king to hold his stirrup, the emperor of all Christendom to lead his horse by the rein, and the princes and governors of the world to kiss his shoe; that doth no manner of service or ministery in Christ's church; how can he call himself either the servant of Christ, or the servant of Christ's servants, without hypocrisy? This indeed is open dissimulation, and a childish playing with words, and an open mocking of the world. So one writeth of Julius Cæsar: *Deposuit nomen dictaturæ, at vim retinuit*: "He refused the name of dictator, but the power and force thereof he kept still." So likewise saith Appianus: "The princes of Rome name themselves *imperatores*, emperors," which was a name of government in the field, and lasted but for the while; but kings they will in no wise be called, for that the name of a king among them then was odious. "Howbeit," he saith, "indeed they are very kings." So Augustus Cæsar, notwithstanding he were a tyrant, and had oppressed the people, yet he chose to be called *tribunus plebis*, "the defender and patron of the people." And Verres, notwithstanding he had miserably wasted and consumed the whole

Gregor. Lib. i. Epist. 7, et 25.

De Meritis et Remissione Pec. ad Mar. Lib. iii. cap. i.

Dion.

Appianus.

εἰσὶ δὲ τὰ ἔργα βασιλεῖς. Cornelius Tacitus in Augusto. Cicero in Verrem.

[1 Gregor. Magni Papæ I. Op. Par. 1705. Epist. Lib. v. Indict. XIII. Ad Mauric. August. Epist. xx. Tom. II. col. 749. Ad Eulog. et Anastas. Episc. Epist. xliii. col. 771.] [2 1565 omits *so*.]

[3 Id. Lib. I. Indict. IX. Ad Anastas. Episc. Epistt. vii. xxvi. Tom. II. cols. 494, 516.]

[4 August. Op. Par. 1679-1700. De Pecc. Mer. et Rem. Lib. III. cap. i. Tom. X. col. 71.]

island of Sicily, yet in his title he would be called σωτὴρ, that is, the keeper and saviour of that island. Thus they dissemble openly, and, as one saith, "with fair names they cover foul faults." But it was not any such dissimulation or countenance of humility that moved Leo, Gregory, or any other godly bishop of Rome, to refuse this name, as M. Harding imagineth, but the very iniquity and injury therein contained. For thus saith St Gregory: *Si unus patriarcha universalis dicitur, patriarcharum nomen ceteris derogatur*[5], *&c.*: "If one be called the universal patriarch, then is the name of patriarchs taken from others. But God keep it far from any christian mind, that any man should take so much upon him." "The consenting unto this wicked name is the losing of the faith[6]." Therefore in the council of Carthage it is decreed thus: *Primæ sedis episcopus ne appelletur princeps sacerdotum, vel summus sacerdos, vel aliquid hujusmodi; sed tantum primæ sedis episcopus. Universalis autem nec etiam Romanus pontifex appelletur*[7]*:* "Let not the bishop of the first see be called the chief of bishops, or the highest bishop, or by any other like name. But the bishop of Rome himself may not be called the universal bishop." This latter clause of that canon (*universalis autem* [*episcopus*] *nec etiam Romanus pontifex appelletur*) one Peter Crabbe, the setter forth of the councils, of purpose, and contrary to good faith, dissembled and left out. Howbeit the fraud is soon discovered. For the same clause is to be found whole, both in written examples of the councils, and also in Gratian, that compiled the decrees, and in the very barbarous gloss upon the the same, by these words: *Hic dicitur, quod papa non debet vocari universalis*[8]*:* "Here it is said, that the pope may not be called the universal bishop." M. Harding saith: "The pope was called by that name:" and for proof thereof allegeth a council without a canon. But the whole general council of Carthage saith: "The bishop of Rome may not in any wise be so called;" and the canon thereof is apparent and may be seen. Now let the christian reader judge to whether he will give greater credit.

[Margin: Pope not universal.]

[Margin: τῷ ὀνόματι περιπέπτουσι τὴν μοχθηρίαν. Gregor. Lib. iv. Epist. 36.]

[Margin: Gregor. Lib. iv. cap. xxxix. Concil. Carth. iii. can. 26.]

[Margin: The bishop of Rome may not be called the universal bishop.]

[Margin: Dist. 99. Primæ sedis.]

"This council," saith M. Harding, "would not have offered this name unto Leo, unless it had been lawful." Yet he knoweth all is not law that is moved in council. Leo and Gelasius, as it is before said, condemned certain decrees of this same council of Chalcedon, as unlawful[9], notwithstanding the determination of six hundred and thirty bishops. The fathers in the council of Nice attempted, contrary to God's commandments, to break the lawful matrimony of priests and bishops: but their attempt, because it was unlawful, was reproved and stayed by Paphnutius[10]. M. Harding therefore might better conclude thus: Leo, Gregory, and other holy fathers, bishops of Rome, refused the name of universal bishop, as it appeareth by their words, for that it was injurious unto other bishops, and a corruption of the faith; and for the same cause the general council of Carthage determined, that the bishop of Rome should not, ne might not so be called: therefore that name was not lawful.

[Margin: Inter Decret. Concil. Tarr.]

[Margin: Socrat. Lib. i. cap. xi.]

All this notwithstanding, true it is that M. Harding saith: Leo in that council of Chalcedon was thus called. The places be known, and may not be denied. He is so saluted in three sundry epistles; the one sent by one Athanasius a priest; the other by one Ischyrion a deacon; the third by one Theodorus, likewise a deacon[11]. But of that whole number of six hundred and thirty bishops there assembled, I trow, M. Harding is not well able to shew that any one ever saluted or called him so.

[Margin: Concil. Chalc. Act. 3.]

[5 ...si unus, &c. Sed absit hoc, absit a Christiani mente id sibi velle quempiam arripere, &c.—Gregor. Magni Papæ I. Op. Epist. Lib. v. Indict. XIII. Ad Eulog. et Anastas. Episc. Tom. II. col. 771.]

[6 Id. ibid. Ad Sabin. Diac. Epist. xix. col. 747.]

[7 Concil. Carthag. III. cap. 26. in Crabb. Concil. Col. Agrip. 1551. Tom. I. p. 428. See before, page 355, note 12.]

[8 Corp. Jur. Canon. Lugd. 1624. Decret. Gratian. Decr. Prim. Pars, Dist. xcix. Gloss. in can. 3. col. 479; where *hæc est 3 pars distin. in qua dicitur, &c.*]

[9 See before, page 423, notes 17, 8.]

[10 Socrat. in Hist. Eccles. Script. Amst. 1695-1700. Lib. I. cap. xi. p. 33.]

[11 Τῷ...οἰκουμενικῷ πατριάρχῃ...Λέοντι, κ.τ.λ.—Lib. Athanas. in Concil. Calched. Act. III. in Concil. Stud. Labb. et Cossart. Lut. Par. 1671-2. Tom. IV. col. 406.

Lib. Ischyr. in eod. col. 399.

Lib. Theodor. in eod. col. 395.

See also Lib. Sophron. in eod. col. 411.]

Bishop of the universal church.

Therefore, whereas M. Harding, the better to put his reader in remembrance, hath set this note in the margin, that the bishop of Rome was called the universal bishop, and head of the church, above a thousand years sithence; he might with more truth, and much better have noted his book thus: ST GREGORY'S WORDS MISALLEGED, THE COUNCIL FALSIFIED, THIS ONLY CANON LOST, ALL THE REST WHOLE AND SAFE, A STRANGE PRIEST AND TWO POOR DEACONS, IN THEIR PRIVATE SUITS FOR THEIR GOODS AND LEGACIES, NAMED LEO THE UNIVERSAL BISHOP. BUT OF THE SIX HUNDRED AND THIRTY BISHOPS, THAT HAD VOICES IN THE COUNCIL, NOT ONE EVER NAMED HIM SO. Thus much M. Harding might truly have noted in the margin.

Yet, saith M. Harding, the bishops of Rome, that were godly fathers and holy martyrs, used this name, as it appeareth by their epistles. And here are brought in the titles of letters under the names of Sixtus, Pontianus, and certain others, written, as it is before declared, a long time after the writers were dead. Such ruinous foundations M. Harding hath chosen to build upon.

But what are these old fathers taught to say? Or how is M. Harding relieved by their words? In their[1] salutation before their letters they write thus: "Sixtus, Pontianus, Victor, bishop of the universal church." This, saith M. Harding, is even all one thing with *universalis episcopus:* there is no manner difference. O what ranging and hunting here is, to beat up that thing that will not be found! M. Harding, because he cannot find the universal bishop that he sought for, therefore he hath sought out the next of kin, that is, the bishop of the universal church; and these two, he saith, be both one. Howbeit this matter needed no great seeking: every child might soon have found it. But if an universal bishop and a bishop of the universal church be all one thing, how then is it true, that St Gregory saith, *Nemo [præ]decessorum*[2], *&c.*[3]*:* "None of my predecessors would ever consent to this name?" Or how can he find such fault with the name of universal bishop, and bear so easily with the name of bishop of the universal church, which he knew his predecessors had used, if he took them both for one thing, without difference? To be short, if these names, as M. Harding assureth himself, be both one, how is the one godly, the other ungodly; the one arrogant, the other not arrogant; the one blasphemous, the other not blasphemous?

Gregor. Lib. iv. Epist. 32. et 36.

This error riseth of misunderstanding these words, *universalis ecclesia.* For the church universal and the church catholic, the one being Greek, the other Latin, are both one, and are commonly used of the learned fathers, as contrary to a particular church, as be the churches of heretics and schismatics. In this sense every godly bishop is a bishop of the catholic or universal church; like as also every godly man is a member of the same. Thus writeth Calixtus: *Calixtus archiepiscopus ecclesiæ catholicæ urbis Romæ*[4]. Thus Marcellus: *Marcellus episcopus sanctæ et apostolicæ et catholicæ urbis Romæ*[5]. In these places Rome is called a catholic, that is to say, an universal city; partly to exclude the churches of heretics, which were mere particular; and partly also to signify that the church there was then a church of the catholic and universal doctrine. So likewise it is written in the council of Constantinople: *Clerici et monachi apostolici throni Antiochenæ magnæ civitatis, catholicæ, sanctæ ecclesiæ Dei*[6]*:* "The clerks and monks of the apostolic throne of the great city of Antioch, of the catholic or universal holy church of God."

Calixti Epist. Decret. 1. Marcel. Epist. 2.

Concil. Const. v. Act. 1.

Again, every bishop may be called the bishop of the universal church; for that it is his duty to care, not only for his own flock, but also for all others of the whole church of God. So saith Origen: *Qui vocatur...ad episcopatum,...vocatur ...ad servitutem totius ecclesiæ*[7]*:* "Whoso is called to a bishopric is called to the service of the whole church." So Chrysostom, exhorting the whole people together,

Orig. in Esai. Hom. 6.

[1 The, 1565.]

[2 Decessorum, 1565, 1609.]

[3 Gregor. Magni Papæ I. Op. Par. 1705. Epist. Lib. v. Indict. XIII. Ad Mauric. August. Epist. xx. Tom. II. col. 749. Ad Eulog. et Anastas. Episc. Epist. xliii. col. 771.]

[4 Callixt. Papæ I. ad Benedict. Epist. i. in Crabb. Concil. Col. Agrip. 1551. Tom. I. p. 100.]

[5 Marcell. Papæ ad Maxent. Epist. ii. in eod. Tom. I. p. 207.]

[6 Suppl. Cler. et Monach. Antioch. in Concil. Constant. sub Menna, Act. v. in Concil. Stud. Labb. et Cossart. Lut. Par. 1671-2. Tom. V. col. 157.]

[7 Orig. Op. Par. 1733-59. In Isai. Hom. vi. 1. Tom. III. p. 116.]

saith unto them: *Universæ ecclesiæ...curam geramus*[8]: "Let every one of us take the care of the universal church." So likewise pope Eleutherius writeth unto the bishops of France: *Hujus rei gratia universalis vobis a Christo...commissa est ecclesia, ut pro omnibus laboretis, et cunctis opem ferre non negligatis*[9]: "For that cause the whole universal church is committed unto you, that you should travail for all, and not be negligent to help all." Thus many ways the bishops both of Rome, and of Antioch, and of France, were called the bishops of the universal church. But the universal bishop none of them all was ever called. Of John of Constantinople, that first began to usurp that name, Gregory the bishop of Rome writeth thus: *Despectis omnibus,... solus conatur appellari episcopus*[10]: "Despising all other bishops, he would only be called a bishop." So likewise saith pope Pelagius: "If the chief patriarch be called universal, then the rest have lost the name of patriarchs[11]."

Bishop of the universal church.

Chrysost. in 2 Cor. Hom. 18.

Epist. Eleuth. ad Episc. Galliæ.

Gregor. Lib. iv. Epist. 34.

Pelag. ii. Epist. 1. Dist. 99. Nullus.

This is the meaning of an universal bishop, and the very self-same infinite and immoderate power that M. Harding claimeth for the bishop of Rome. For so he hath already said, that the other three patriarchs are no patriarchs indeed, but only his delegates and servants to do that shall please him to command them[12]. Instead hereof, M. Harding hath found out a bishop of the universal church: and so, leaving the thing that is demanded, he answereth to that is not in question; and privily confesseth, by his silence, that hitherto he hath not found nor can find his universal bishop.

Fol. 86. Div. 23.

This answer may serve to that is here alleged of the council of Africa, and the epistle of Athanasius; saving that the epistle bearing that holy father's name, as it is already proved[13], is nothing else but apparent forgery. The bishops in the council of Africa, besides that they utterly denied the pope's universal power, forbidding their clerks upon pain of excommunication to appeal to him, sundry times in the same council writing unto him, they use the name of familiarity and equality, and call him their brother[14].

Concil. Aphr. can. 12.

Can. 101, et 105.

Now for a surplusage, forasmuch as M. Harding, with all his study and conference with his friends, cannot yet find out his universal bishop in the church of Rome, let us see whether we may find him in some other place, and that not by the witness of a simple priest or a deacon, but by the authority of catholic emperors and councils, and of the bishop of Rome himself; and that not by shifting of terms one for another, as M. Harding is driven for want, instead of an universal bishop, to bring in a bishop of the universal church, but in plain, manifest, express words, and such as in nowise may be denied.

In the council of Constantinople, the bishop there is scarcely saluted or entitled by other name. For this is his common style: *Œcumenico patriarchæ Johanni*[15]: "To John the universal patriarch." "To John the father of fathers, and universal bishop." "The holy universal archbishop, and patriarch Mennas."

Concil. Const. v. Act. 1.

Nicephorus saith, the bishop of Alexandria was entitled *judex universi orbis*[16], "the judge of the whole world." Clement unto St James the bishop of Hierusalem writeth thus: *Clemens Jacobo fratri Domini,...episcopo episcoporum, regenti Hebræorum sanctam ecclesiam Hierosolymis, sed et omnes ecclesias, quæ ubique Dei providentia fundatæ sunt*[17]: "Clement unto James the brother of our Lord, the bishop of bishops, governing the holy church of the Jews at Hierusalem, and besides that, all the churches that be founded every where by God's providence."

Niceph. Lib. xiv. cap. xxxiv.

Clem. Epist. 1.

[8 Chrysost. Op. 1718-38. In Epist. II. ad Cor. Hom. xviii. Tom. X. p. 568.]

[9 Eleuth. Papæ ad Gall. Prov. Epist. in Crabb. Concil. Tom. I. p. 92.]

[10 Gregor. Magni Papæ I. Op. Epist. Lib. v. Indict. XIII. Ad Constant. August. Epist. xxi. Tom. II. col. 751; where *conetur*.]

[11 ...si unus patriarcha universalis dicitur, patriarcharum nomen ceteris derogatur. — Pelag. II. Epist. in Corp. Jur. Canon. Lugd. 1624. Decret. Gratian. Decr. Prim. Pars, Dist. xcix. can. 4. col. 479.]

[12 See before, page 402.]

[13 See before, page 354.]

[14 There is nothing to the point in cap. 12. Perhaps the following is meant: Recitatis epistolis beatissimi fratris et consacerdotis nostri Anastasii, ecclesiæ Romanæ episcopi, &c.—Concil. Afric. cap. 32. in Crabb. Concil. Tom. I. p. 507. See also capp. 101, 105. pp. 518, &c.]

[15 Relat. ad Johan. in Concil. Constant. sub Menna, Act. v. in Concil. Stud. Labb. et Cossart. Tom. V. col. 161.]

[16 Niceph. Call. Hist. Eccles. Lut. Par. 1630. Lib. XIV. cap. xxxiv. Tom. II. p. 512.]

[17 Clement. ad Jacob. Epist. i. in Crabb. Concil. Tom. I. p. 31.]

Peter chief.

The emperor Justinian writeth thus: "Unto Epiphanius the archbishop of this imperial city (Constantinople) and universal patriarch[1]." To conclude, the bishop of Rome himself thus saluteth the bishop of Constantinople: *Therasio generali patriarchæ Adrianus servus servorum Dei*[2]: "Unto Therasius the general patriarch, Adrian the servant of God's servants." And in the last council holden at Florence, Joseph the bishop of Constantinople, being there, used the same title, and wrote himself "the archbishop of new Rome, and the universal patriarch[3]." If M. Harding had so good evidence for the bishop of Rome, I believe he would not thus pass it away in silence.

Authen. Const. 3. οἰκουμενικῷ πατριάρχῃ. Conc. Nicen. ii. Act. 2.

M. HARDING. THE THIRTY-FIRST DIVISION.

Concerning the other name, "head of the church," I marvel not a little that M. Jewel denieth that the bishop of Rome was then so called. Either he doth contrary to his own knowledge, wherein he must needs be condemned in his own judgment, and of his own conscience; or he is not so well learned as of that side he is thought to be. For whosoever travaileth in the reading of the ancient fathers, findeth that name almost every where attributed to Peter the first bishop of Rome, (121) *and consequently to the successor of Peter, that name, I say, either in terms equivalent, or expressly. First the scripture calleth Peter* primum, *"the first among the apostles." The names of the twelve apostles, saith Matthew, are these:* * Primus Simon, qui dicitur Petrus: *"First Simon, who is called Peter." And yet was not Peter first called of Christ, but his brother Andrew before him, as is before said. Dionysius, that ancient writer, calleth Peter sometime* supremum decus, *"the highest honour," for that he was most honourable of all the apostles; sometime* summum; *sometime* verticalem, *the chiefest and the highest apostle*[4]. *Origen upon the beginning of John saith: "Let no man think that we set John before Peter. Who may so do? for who should be higher of the apostles than he who is and is called the top of them?" Cyprian calleth the church of Rome, in consideration of that bishop's supreme authority,* ecclesiam principalem, unde unitas sacerdotalis exorta est[5], *"the principal or chief church, from whence the unity of priests is sprung." Eusebius Cæsariensis, speaking of Peter sent to Rome by God's providence to vanquish Simon Magus, calleth him* potentissimum et maximum apostolorum, et reliquorum omnium principem[6], *"the mightiest of power, and greatest of the apostles, and prince of all the rest." Augustine commonly calleth Peter* primum apostolorum[7], *"first or chief of the apostles:" Hierome, Ambrose, Leo, and other doctors, "prince of the apostles." Chrysostom upon the place of John cap. xxi.,* Sequere me, *"Follow me," among other things saith thus:* **"If any would demand of me, how James took the see of Hierusalem, that is to say, how he became bishop there; I would answer, that this (he meaneth Peter) master of the whole world made him governor there*[8]." *And in another place, bringing in that God said to Hieremy, "I have set thee like an iron pillar, and like a brasen wall;" but "the Father", saith he, "made him over one nation, but Christ made this man (meaning Peter) ruler*

This is a fresh kind of rhetoric.

The hundred and twenty-first untruth. For Peter only is so called, yet was not Peter then bishop of Rome.

* These terms be not equivalent.

*These words are craftily added to Chrysostom, as to the discreet reader may soon appear.

[Head of the church. H. A. 1564.]

[Peter, and consequently the pope, Peter's successor, called head of the church, both in terms equivalent, and also expressly. H. A. 1564.]

Matt. x.

De Divinis Nominibus, cap. iii.

Lib. i. Epist. 3.

τὸν καρτερὸν καὶ μέγαν τῶν ἀποστόλων,[καὶ] τῶν λοιπῶν ἁπάντων προήγορον.

Homil. 87.

In Matt. Hom. 55. Jer. i.

[[1] ...Ἀνθεμίῳ τῷ θειοτάτῳ καὶ μακαριωτάτῳ ἀρχιεπισκόπῳ, καὶ, κ.τ.λ.—Corp. Jur. Civil. Amst. 1663. Auth. Coll. III. Tit. iii. Novell. xvi. Tom. II. p. 34. See also Auth. Coll. I. Tit. iii. Novell. iii. p. 6.]

[[2] Hadr. ad Taras. Epist. in Concil. Nic. II. Act. II. in Concil. Stud. Labb. et Cossart. Lut. Par. 1671-2. Tom. VII. col. 700. But the word *generali* is not in the Greek text. See ibid. col. 121.]

[[3] Joseph miseratione divina Constantinopolis et novæ Romæ archiepiscopus, ac œcumenicus patriarcha.—Gen. VIII. Synod. Florent. Sess. Ult. in Crabb. Concil. Tom. III. p. 474.]

[[4] ...Πέτρος, ἡ κορυφαία καὶ πρεσβυτάτη τῶν θεολόγων ἀκρότης.—Dionys. Areop. Op. Antv. 1634. De Div. Nom. cap. iii. 2. Tom. I. p. 539.]

[[5] Cypr. Op. Oxon. 1682. Ad Cornel. Epist. lix. pp. 135, 6.]

[[6] Euseb. in Hist. Eccles. Script. Amst. 1695-1700. Lib. II. cap. xiv. p. 41; where we find τὸν ἀρετῆς ἕνεκα τῶν λοιπῶν.]

[[7] In ... Petro, in ordine apostolorum primo et præcipuo, &c.—August. Op. Par. 1679-1700. Serm. lxxvi. 4. De Verb. Evang. Matt. xiv. Tom. V. col. 416.]

[[8] Εἰ δὲ λέγοι τις, πῶς οὖν ὁ Ἰάκωβος τὸν θρόνον ἔλαβε τῶν Ἱεροσολύμων; ἐκεῖνο ἂν εἴποιμι, ὅτι τοῦτον οὐ τοῦ θρόνου, ἀλλὰ τῆς οἰκουμένης ἐχειροτόνησε διδάσκαλον.—Chrysost. Op. Par. 1718-38. In Joan. Hom. lxxxviii. Tom. VIII. p. 527.]

of[9] the whole world, &c."[10] And lest these places should seem to attribute this supreme authority to Peter only, and not also to his successors, it is to be remembered, that Irenæus[11] and Cyprian acknowledge and call the church of Rome chief and principal. And Theodoretus in an epistle to Leo calleth the same, in consideration of the bishop of that see his primacy, orbi terrarum præsidentem[12], *"president, or (122) bearing rule over the world." Ambrose, upon that place of Paul, 1 Tim. iii., where the church is called the pillar and stay of the truth, saith thus:* Cum totus mundus Dei sit, ecclesia tamen domus ejus dicitur: cujus hodie rector est Damasus[13]: *"Whereas the whole world is God's, yet the church is called his house, the ruler whereof at these days is Damasus."*

Peter chief.

τῆς οἰκουμένης προκαθημένην.

The hundred and twenty-second untruth, standing in untrue translation.

**I would not weary and trouble the reader with such a number of allegations, were it not that M. Jewel beareth the world in hand, we have not one sentence or[14] clause for us, to prove either this or any other of all his articles.*

* All these words notwithstanding, M. Harding hath not yet found the head of the universal church.

*But perhaps some one will say[15], Yet I hear not the bishop of Rome called head of the universal church. What forceth it whether that very term be found in any ancient writer, or no? Other terms of the same virtue and power be oftentimes found. Is it not one to say, head of the universal church, and to say, ruler of God's house, which Ambrose saith? Whereof this argument may be made: *The church, yea, the universal church is the house of God: but Damasus bishop of Rome is ruler of the house of God, after Ambrose;* ergo, *Damasus is ruler of the universal church. And by like right and title is the pope, who is bishop of Rome, now also ruler of the same. What other is it to call the church of Rome the principal church, respect had to the bishop there, and not otherwise (wherein a figure of speech is used) as Irenæus and Cyprian do, and president, or (123) set in authority over the whole world[16], as Leo doth; than to call the bishop of Rome head of the universal church? What meaneth Chrysostom calling Peter* totius orbis magistrum, *"the master and teacher of all the world;" and saying in another place *that Christ made Peter, not ruler over one nation, as the Father made Jeremy over the Jews, but over the whole world? what other, I say, meaneth he thereby, than that he is head of the whole world, and therefore of the universal church?*

* A miserable syllogism. It concludeth "in secunda figura affirmative."

In locum Joh. xxi. Hom. 87.

Exponens illud, Sequere me. In Matt. Hom. 55.

The hundred and twenty-third untruth. For Leo hath not one such word.

* Even so Gregory[17] saith of Paul: "Obtinuit totius ecclesiæ principatum," in 1 Reg. Lib. iv. cap. IV.[18]

THE BISHOP OF SARISBURY.

Touching the name of the universal bishop, M. Harding hath but one authority; and yet the same cannot be found. Touching the other name, of head of the church, he cometh in only with jolly brags and great vaunts, as if he were playing at post[19], and should win all by vying. He saith, if M. Jewel know this, then he speaketh against his conscience; if he know it not, then is he not learned. To contend for learning, it were a childish folly. He is sufficiently learned, that saith the truth. But if M. Harding with all his learning be able to find out his head of the church, he shall have his request: I will grant him to be learned.

He saith: "The bishop of Rome is so named, either in terms equivalent or expressly." Thus he doubteth at the matter, and stammereth, and faltereth at the beginning. But if the bishop of Rome were the head of the church indeed, and so allowed and taken in the world, why was he never expressly and plainly named

[9 Over, 1565, 1609, and H. A. 1564.]

[10 Καθάπερ ὁ Πατὴρ πρὸς τὸν Ἱερεμίαν διαλεγόμενος ἔλεγεν· ὡς στῦλον χαλκοῦν, καὶ ὡσεὶ τεῖχος τίθημιν αὐτόν· ἀλλ' ἐκεῖνον μὲν ἑνὶ ἔθνει, τοῦτον δὲ [Πέτρον] πανταχοῦ τῆς οἰκουμένης.—Id. in Matt. Hom. liv. Tom. VII. p. 548.]

[11 Iren. Op. Par. 1710. Contr. Hær. Lib. III. cap. iii. 2. p. 175. See before, page 364.]

[12 Ἡ γὰρ αὐτὴ πασῶν μεγίστη ... καὶ τῆς οἰκουμένης προκαθημένη, κ. τ. λ.—Theodor. Op. Lut. Par. 1642-84. Ad Leon. Epist. cxiii. Tom. III. Pars II. p. 985.]

[13 Ambros. Op. Par. 1686-90. Comm. in Epist. I. ad Tim. cap. iii. Tom. II. Append. col. 296; where *dicatur.*]

[14 Nor, H. A. 1564.]

[15 Reply and say, H. A. 1564.]

[16 There is a passage ... sicut per beatissimum Petrum apostolorum principem sacrosancta ecclesia Romana teneret supra omnes totius mundi ecclesias principatum, ita, &c., to be found among the works of Leo, which may be that intended. But it was written to, not by, Leo.—Leon. Magni Op. Lut. 1623. Ad Leon. Epist. Comprov. Episc. Metrop. Arel. col. 525.]

[17 St Gregory, 1565.]

[18 See below, page 431, note 11.]

[19 Probably a game at cards. See Brand's Pop. Antiq. by Sir H. Ellis, Vol. II. p. 266.]

Paul chief.

so? Was there no man then in the world, for the space of six hundred years, able to express his name? His terms of like force and meaning, which he calleth equivalent, must needs import thus much: That the bishop of Rome is above all general councils; that he only hath power to expound the scriptures, and cannot err, nor be judged of any man; and that without him there is no health; and that all the world ought to know him for the universal head, upon pain of damnation. Thus much the pope himself claimeth by that name. If M. Harding's terms sound not thus, they are not equivalent. It had been the simpler and plainer dealing for M. Harding to have said, This name cannot yet be found; and so to have taken a longer day.

Terms equivalent.

As for the matter, the question is moved of the bishop of Rome: the answer is made of St Peter; as if St Peter continued there bishop still until this day. But it is presumed that, whatsoever privilege was in Peter, the same must needs be in the bishop of Rome by succession, yea, although he have not one spark of Peter. St Peter in the old fathers is diversly called, the first, the chief, the top, the high honour of the apostles; and in Eusebius and St Augustine, προήγορος, and *princeps apostolorum*. In which last words of St Augustine and Eusebius, I must do thee, good reader, to understand, that *princeps* is not always taken for a prince or governor[1] endued with power, but oftentimes for the first man, or best of a company. So we read in the scriptures, *princeps familiæ, princeps legationis, princeps coquorum*[2]; that is, "the chief of the house or stock, the chief of the embassage, the chief of the cooks." In this sense Cicero saith: *Servius princeps in jure civili; philosophorum princeps Aristippus:* "Servius the chief in the civil law; Aristippus the chief of philosophers." So is St Peter called *princeps apostolorum;* and therefore St Augustine calleth him *primum, et præcipuum*[3], that is, "the first, and the chief of the apostles."

Exod. vi. Num. x. 2 Kings xxv. Dist. 44. Cum autem. In Bruto. Tuscul. ii.

August. de Verbis Dom. in Evang. Matt. cap. xiv.

We may not imagine, as M. Harding seemeth to do, that Peter was made a lord, or prince, and had power and dominion over his brethren. St Ambrose, as it is before alleged, comparing Peter and Paul together, saith thus: *Inter ipsos quis cui præferatur, incertum est*[4]: "Whether of these two I may set before the other, I cannot tell." Likewise St Cyprian saith: *Hoc erant...ceteri apostoli, quod fuit Petrus, pari consortio prædìti et honoris et potestatis*[5]: "The rest of the apostles were the same that Peter was, endued with like fellowship both of honour and of power." St Ambrose saith: "He cannot discern between Peter and Paul, whether he may set before other." St Cyprian saith: "All the apostles had like honour, and like power." Yet, by M. Harding's fantasy, Peter only was the prince; and all the rest were subjects and underlings unto him.

Ambros. Ser. 66.

Cypr. de Simplicitate Prælatorum.

But Chrysostom saith: "Christ made Peter ruler over the whole world[6]." I know not what special power M. Harding will gather of these words. For the same commission that was given to Peter, in as large and as ample sort was given also to the rest of the apostles. Christ said unto them all: *Ite in universum mundum, &c.:* "Go into the whole world and preach the gospel." And St Paul saith it was prophesied of them before: *In omnem terram exivit sonus eorum:* "The sound of them went out into all the world." Therefore, that St Chrysostom speaketh here of St Peter, the same other where he speaketh in like form of words of all the apostles. Thus he writeth upon St John: *Apostoli suscipiunt curam totius mundi*[7]: "The apostles receive the charge of all the world." Likewise he writeth of St Paul: *Michaeli gens commissa est Judæorum: Paulo vero terræ, ac maria, atque universi orbis habitatio*[8]: "Unto Michael is committed the nation of the Jews; but land and sea and all the habitation of the world is com-

Chrysost. in Matt. Hom. 55.

Matt. xxviii. Mark xvi.

Psal. xix. Rom. x.

Chrysost. in Johan. Hom. 87.

Chrysost. in Act. Hom. iii.

[1 A governor, 1565.]

[2 ...Nabuzardam principem coquorum, &c.—Corp. Jur. Canon. Lugd. 1624. Decret. Gratian. Decr. Prim. Pars, Dist. xliv. col. 209.]

[3 August. Op. Par. 1679-1700. Serm. lxxvi. 4. De Verb. Evang. Matt. xiv. Tom. V. col. 416. See before, page 428, note 8.]

[4 Ambros. Op. Par. 1614. Serm. in Fest. SS. Petr. et Paul. Tom. V. col. 142. See before, page 367, note 12. It may be added that this is really a homily of Maximus.—Op. Lut. 1623. col. 664.]

[5 Cypr. Op. Oxon. 1682. De Unit. Eccles. pp. 107, 8.]

[6 See before, page 429, note 11.]

[7 ...ἔμελλον τῆς οἰκουμένης τὴν ἐπιτροπὴν ἀναδέξασθαι.—Chrysost. Op. Par. 1718-38. In Joan. Hom. lxxxviii. Tom. VIII. p. 528.]

[8 Id. De Laud. Paul. Apost. Hom. iii. Tom. II. p. 486.]

mitted unto Paul." And again: *Paulo Deus omnem prædicationem, et res orbis, et mysteria cuncta, universamque dispensationem concessit*[9]: "God hath given unto Paul all manner preaching, the matters of the world, all mysteries, and the ordering of all." So likewise saith St Gregory: *Paulus catenis vinctus Romam petit occupaturus mundum*[10]: "Paul, being bound with chains, went to Rome, to conquer the whole world." And again he saith: [*Paulus*] *ad Christum conversus, caput effectus est nationum; quia obtinuit totius ecclesiæ principatum*[11]: "Paul, being converted unto Christ, was made the head of nations, because he obtained the chiefty of all the church." This was that universal power that Chrysostom saith was given unto St Peter; and that not severally unto him alone, but jointly and together with all the rest of Christ's apostles. Which thing the same Chrysostom other where plainly declareth by these words: *Apostoli universum orbem terrarum pervaserunt, et omnibus principibus fuerunt magis proprie principes, regibus potentiores*[12]: "The apostles ranged over the whole world, and were more like princes than the princes indeed, and more mighty than the kings." Thus was not only Peter, but also all the rest and every of the apostles, made rulers over the whole world.

Paul chief.

Chrysost. in Epist. ad Rom. Hom. 18.

Greg. in Job. Lib. xxvii. cap. vi.

Greg. in 1 Reg. Lib. iv. cap. iv.

Chrysost. in Psal. xliv.

It is further alleged, that "Peter appointed James bishop of Hierusalem," and the same avouched by Chrysostom[13]. Although this place of Chrysostom import not greatly, yet being well sifted and considered, it may seem very suspicious, as nothing agreeing either with that went before, or with that followeth afterward, but altogether savouring of some corruption. If M. Harding himself would consider the words with indifferent judgment, I doubt not but he would marvel how they came thither.

Chrysost. in Johan. Hom. 87.

Neither is it likely that James took authority of Peter, having before taken sufficient authority of Christ himself. For this commission Christ gave to every of his apostles all alike: "As my living Father sent me, so do I send you; ye shall be witnesses to me, even to the ends of the world." And if Peter gave authority unto James, who then gave authority unto Paul? Certainly St Paul dwelt in no peculiar, but was as much subject to jurisdiction as St James. But St Paul saith "he was an apostle, *non ab hominibus, neque per hominem*, neither of men nor by man, but by Jesus Christ, and God the Father." "They that were the chief of the apostles gave nothing unto me." "The preaching of the gospel among the gentiles was committed unto me, even as unto Peter the preaching of the gospel among the Jews." And Chrysostom expounding the same place saith thus: *Paulus nihil opus habebat Petro, nec illius egebat voce, sed honore par erat illi: nihil hic dicam amplius*[14]: "Paul had no need of Peter's help, nor stood in need of his voice, but was in honour as good as he: I will say no more." Hereby it may appear, that the rest of the apostles took not their apostleship or authority of St Peter.

Luke xxiv. John xv. Acts i. John xvii. John xx.

Gal. i.

Gal. ii.

Chrysost. in Epist. ad Gal. cap. ii.

But being granted that Peter appointed James to preach in Hierusalem, yet will it not follow therefore that Peter had rule and dominion over the apostles. For thereof would follow this great inconvenience: The apostles at Hierusalem appointed Peter to go and to preach in Samaria; *ergo*, the apostles had rule and dominion over Peter. Which were an overthrow of M. Harding's greatest principle.

Acts viii.

But let us grant that Peter was the head of the apostles, as a matter nothing pertaining to this question; will M. Harding thereof conclude, that the pope is therefore the head of the universal church? For what is there in the pope that was in Peter? Preaching of the gospel? He preacheth not. Feeding of the flock? He feedeth not. He will say: Succession, and sitting in Peter's chair, which is in Rome. A man may answer: "The scribes and Pharisees sat in Moses' chair."

Matt. xxiii.

[9 Id. in Epist. ad Rom. Hom. xviii. Tom. IX. p. 635.]

[10 Idem rursus dum catenis vinctus Romam peteret Paulus occupaturus mundum, &c.—Gregor. Magni Papæ I. Op. Par. 1705. Lib. xxxvii. in cap. xxxvi. B. Job. cap. xi. Tom. I. col. 861.]

[11 Id. Lib. iv. in i. Reg. cap. v. 28. Tom. III. Pars ii. col. 250.]

[12 Chrysost. Op. Expos. in Psalm. xliv. Tom. V. p. 181.]

[13 See before, page 428.]

[14 Id. in cap. i. Epist. ad Gal. Tom. X. p. 677.]

Paul chief.

But M. Harding knoweth that Peter, when he received this privilege, was in Hierusalem, and not in Rome. Therefore this argument would better stand thus: Peter neither had dominion over the rest of the apostles, nor was bishop of Rome when Christ spake unto him; therefore the bishop of Rome cannot justly claim hereby the universal power and dominion over all the world. Verily St Augustine saith: *Paulus ipse non poterat esse caput eorum, quos plantaverat*[1], *&c.*: "Paul himself could not be the head of them that he had planted; for he saith that we being many are one body in Christ, and that Christ himself is the head of that universal body." Of these words of St Augustine we may gather this reason: St Paul could not be the head of them that he had planted; therefore much less may the pope be the head of them that he never planted.

August. contra Lit. Petil. Lib. i.

1 Cor. xii. Rom. xii. Eph. i.

Yet reply will be made, that Theodoretus calleth the church of Rome τῆς οἰκουμένης προκαθημένην, which words M. Harding untruly translateth "president, or bearing rule over the world." For he knoweth that the Greek word προκάθημαι signifieth, sitting in the first place, and forceth not of necessity any rule or government over others. He might better have turned it *ecclesiam orbis terrarum primariam*, "the most notable or chief church of the world." And so would his translation have well agreed with the constitutions of the emperor Justinian; wherein the pre-eminence of sitting in the first place in all councils and assemblies is by special privilege granted to the bishop of Rome[2].

Auth. Coll. ix. De Eccles. Tit. i.

Cod. de Sacrosanct. Eccl. cap. Decernimus.

Likewise it will be replied, that Cyprian calleth the church of Rome *ecclesiam principalem*[3], "the principal church;" whereof it were much for M. Harding to reason thus:

The church of Rome is a principal church;

Ergo, the bishop of Rome is head of the universal church.

Cypr. Lib. i. Epist. 3.

For Cyprian himself in the same epistle in plain express words saith: "The authority of the bishops of Africa is as good as the authority of the bishop of Rome[4]."

Cicero in Catil. Orat. iv.

Cicero, to blaze the nobility of that city, calleth it *lucem orbis terrarum, atque arcem omnium gentium*, "the light of the world, and the castle of all nations."

Petr. Crinit. Lib. i. cap. xviii.

Hieron. ad Algas. Quæst. xi.

Concil. Chalced. Act. 1.

Frontinus likewise: *Roma urbs indiges, terrarumque dea*[5]: "Rome is a wantless city, and the goddess of the world." And St Hierome of the same in his time saith: *Romanum imperium ... nunc universas gentes tenet*[6]: "The empire of Rome now possesseth all nations." And in[7] the council of Chalcedon the emperor of Rome is called *dominus omnis terræ*, and *dominus universi mundi*[8], "the lord of all the earth," and "the lord of the whole world." In consideration as well of this worldly state and majesty, as also of the number and constancy of martyrs, of the place of Peter's travail, of the antiquity of the church, and of the purity of doctrine, the church of Rome was called the principal church of all others.

But he addeth further: *Unde unitas sacerdotalis exorta est*: "From whence the unity of the priesthood first began." For that these words seem to weigh much, I think it good herein to hear the judgment of some other man that may seem indifferent. Polydorus Vergilius, expounding the same words of Cyprian, writeth thus: *Ne quis erret, nulla alia ratione sacerdotalis ordo a Romano episcopo profectus esse dici potest, nisi apud Italos duntaxat id factum [esse] intelligatur: cum perdiu ante adventum Petri in urbem Romam apud Hierosolymos sacerdotium rite institutum fuisse, liquido liqueat*[9]: "Lest any man hereby deceive himself, it cannot

Polyd. Verg. De Invent. Rer. Lib. iv.

[1 August. Op. Par. 1679-1700. Contr. Lit. Petil. Lib. I. cap. v. 6. Lib. III. cap. xlii. 51. Tom. IX. cols. 208, 322. See before, page 379, note 4.]

[2 Corp. Jur. Civil. Amst. 1663. Auth. Coll. IX. Tit. xiv. Novell. cxxxi. 2. Tom. II. p. 184. Id. Cod. Lib. I. Tit. ii. 16. Tom. II. p. 8. But this last, a constitution of Leo and Anthemius, seems rather to intend the see of Constantinople.]

[3 Cypr. Op. Oxon. 1682. Ad Cornel. Epist. lix. pp. 135, 6.]

[4 ... nisi si paucis desperatis et perditis minor videtur esse auctoritas episcoporum in Africa constitutorum, &c.—Id. ibid. pp. 136, 7.]

[5 Frontinus urbem Romam veteri verbo indigetem vocavit: Romana, inquit, urbs, &c.—Petr. Crinit. De Honest. Discipl. Lugd. 1585. Lib. I. cap. xviii. p. 96.]

[6 Hieron. Op. Par. 1693-1706. Ad Algas. Lib. Quæst. Quæst. xi. Tom. IV. Pars I. col. 209.]

[7 And therefore in, 1565.]

[8 Concil. Chalced. Act. I. in Crabb. Concil. Col. Agrip. 1551. Tom. I. pp. 813, &c. See also Concil. Stud. Labb. et Cossart. Lut. Par. 1671-2. Tom. IV. cols. 113, 395.]

[9 Polyd. Verg. De Invent. Rer. Amst. 1671. Lib. IV. cap. vi. pp. 250, 1.]

in any other wise be said that the order of priesthood grew first from the bishop of Rome, unless we understand it only within Italy. For it is clear and out of question, that priesthood was orderly appointed at Hierusalem a good while before Peter ever came to Rome." This commendation therefore, by the judgment of Polydore, was given by St Cyprian to the church of Rome in respect of Italy, and not in respect of the whole world. And therefore St Augustine saith: *Civitas, quasi mater et caput est ceterarum: unde etiam metropolis appellatur*[10]: "The city is as the mother and the head of other towns; and thereof (in respect of such towns) it is called the mother-city." And in this sense Chrysostom calleth the city of Antioch *metropolim fidei*[11], "the mother of the faith."

August. de Con. Evang. Lib. iii.

Ad Pop. Antioch. Hom. 17.

M. Harding saith further: "The church is called the house of God; the ruler whereof," saith St Ambrose, "in these days is Damasus[12]." Here is narrow seeking to find out somewhat; and yet the same somewhat will be worth nothing. First, what opinion St Ambrose had herein, it is easy elsewhere of other his words to be seen. In his epistle unto the emperor Valentinian he calleth Damasus, not prince of the people, nor head of the church, nor universal bishop, but only bishop of the church of Rome[13]. And, writing unto Siricius the bishop of Rome, he calleth him his brother[14].

Ambros. Lib. v. Epist. 30.

Ambros. Lib. x. Epist. 81.

But he calleth Damasus by express words, the ruler of God's church. He might have had the like witness of St Hierome: [*Damasus*] *virgo ecclesiæ virginis doctor* [*est*][15]: "Damasus, being a virgin, is the teacher of the church, that is a virgin." And what will M. Harding gather hereof? Or what thinketh he of Ambrose himself and of other bishops? was not every of them the ruler of the church of God? Verily St Paul thus exhorteth the clergy of Ephesus at his departing thence: "Take heed to yourselves, and to the whole flock, wherein the Holy Ghost hath made you overseers, to rule the church of God, which he hath gotten with his blood." There appeareth no other difference between these words of St Paul, and the other of St Ambrose, saving only that St Ambrose saith, *Rector ecclesiæ;* and St Paul saith, *Regere ecclesiam.* Yet did not St Paul by his words appoint the ministers of Ephesus to rule over the whole church of God. Thus St Hierome calleth Origen *magistrum ecclesiarum*[16], "the master or teacher of the churches." Thus Theodoretus calleth Chrysostom *doctorem orbis terrarum*[17], "the teacher of all the world." Thus Nazianzene calleth St Basil "the pillar and buttress of the church[18]."

De Apol. adv. Jov.

Acts xx.

Hieron. de Locis Heb.

Theod. Lib. v. cap. xxxii.

Nazianz. in Laudem Patris sui.

στύλον καὶ ἑδραίωμα.

But mark well, gentle reader, and thou shalt[19] see that M. Harding hath prettily wrested up this place of St Ambrose quite out of tune, and of an indefinite or a particular proposition, contrary to his rules of logic, will needs conclude an universal, the better to maintain the pope's universal power. For that St Ambrose speaketh indefinitely of a church, without limitation of one or other, that M. Harding stretcheth and forceth to the whole universal church; as if the whole church of God had been at Rome. The like kind of error led Bonifacius the eighth to reason thus: *Dominus dixit generaliter, Pasce oves meas, non singulariter, has, aut illas; ergo commisisse intelligitur universas*[20]: "The Lord said generally unto Peter, Feed my sheep: he said not specially, Feed these or them; therefore we must understand that he committed them unto Peter altogether." If M. Harding

De Major. et Obed. Unam sanctam.

John xxi.

[10 ...extra civitatem, quæ caput et quasi mater est ceterarum, unde metropolis appellatur.—August. Op. De Consens. Evang. Lib. III. cap. xxv. 71. Tom. III. Pars II. col. 141.]

[11 These words are not found in the homily cited. See, however, Chrysost. Op. Par. 1718-38. Ad Pop. Ant. Hom. xvii. Tom. II. p. 176; where Chrysostom shews that the events narrated in scripture as having occurred at Antioch bestow on it the true honour of a metropolis, though deprived by the emperor of that name.]

[12 See before, page 429.]

[13 ... Damasus Romanæ ecclesiæ sacerdos, &c.—Ambros. Op. Par. 1686-90. Ad Valent. Epist. xvii. 10. Tom. II. col. 826.]

[14 Id. ad Syric. Epist. xlii. 2. Tom. II. col. 966.]

[15 Hieron. Op. Ad Pammach. Epist. xxx. pro Libr. adv. Jovin. Apol. Tom. IV. Pars II. col. 240.]

[16 ...Origenem, quem post apostolos, ecclesiarum magistrum.—Id. Præf. in Lib. de Int. Nom. Hebr. Tom. II. cols. 3, 4.]

[17 Theodor. in Hist. Eccles. Script. Amst. 1695-1700. Lib. V. cap. xxxii. p. 238.]

[18 Gregor. Nazianz. Op. Par. 1778-1840. In Patr. Fun. Orat. xviii. 1. Tom. I. p. 330.]

[19 Shall, 1611.]

[20 ... dicente Domino ipsi Petro, 'Pasce oves meas'—meas, inquit, et generaliter, non singulariter has, vel illas; per quod commisisse sibi intelligitur universas.—Bonifac. VIII. in Corp. Jur. Canon. Lugd. 1624. Extrav. Comm. Lib. I. De Major. et Obed. cap. 1. col. 207.]

had not taken St Ambrose up so short by the words that immediately follow, he might well have known his meaning. For thus he openeth what he meant by the house of God: *Ibi necesse est dicatur esse domus Dei et veritas, ubi secundum voluntatem suam timetur*[1]: "There we must needs say God's house and truth is, wheresoever God is feared according to his will." This house was in all places where God was known and served; and not only in the church of Rome.

Ambros. in 1 Tim. cap. iii.

Yet will M. Harding say: These be evasions. For St Ambrose seemeth to acknowledge a special rule and government in Damasus that was not common unto others. Certainly his words import not so. And how can we know his meaning but by his words? But to put the matter out of doubt, let us consider whether the self-same form of speech have been applied unto any others in like sort. Arsenius in his submission writeth thus unto Athanasius: *Nos quoque diligimus pacem, et unitatem*[2] *cum ecclesia catholica, cui tu per Dei gratiam præfectus es*[3]: "We also love peace and unity with the catholic church, over which you by the grace of God are made governor." Here Athanasius is pronounced governor of the catholic church; yet was he not the bishop of Rome. So likewise saith St Cyprian: *Hæc ecclesia una est, quæ tenet et possidet omnem sponsi sui in gratiam: hac*[4] *præsidemus*[5]: "This church is one that keepeth and holdeth the grace of her spouse: in this church we are the rulers." Here St Cyprian calleth himself the president or ruler of God's church; yet was he the bishop of Carthage, and not of Rome. To be short, in like sort Origen pronounceth generally of all priests: *Si tales fuerint, ut a Christo super illos ædificetur ecclesia*[6]: "If they be such as upon them the church of God may be built." Here Origen imagineth that every priest is the foundation of God's church; yet were it hard to say every priest is bishop of Rome. St Ambrose's meaning therefore is, that every bishop or patriarch within his precincts or province is the ruler of the whole church. And this is it that Cyprian seemeth to say: *Episcopatus unus est, cujus a singulis in solidum pars tenetur*[7]: "The bishopric is one, a portion whereof is possessed in whole of every bishop." Therefore M. Harding seemeth to do wrong to St Ambrose, thus violently to abuse his words to prove the bishop of Rome's universal power.

Athanas. in Apol. ii.

Cypr. ad Jub. de Hær. Bapt.

Orig. in Matt. Tract. 1.

Cypr. de Sim. Prælat.

Here M. Harding, doubting lest his reader, being weary of these cold slender shifts, and looking for some other more substantial and formal reasons, would say, "I hear not yet the head of the universal church," purposely preventeth the matter, and saith: "What forceth that, whether that very term be used in any ancient writers[8] or no?" Gentle reader, I beseech thee, mark well this dealing. This name, "the head of the universal church," is the very thing that we deny, and that M. Harding hath taken in hand to prove, and boldly avoucheth that he hath already plainly shewed and proved the same. Yet now in the end, finding himself destitute, he turneth it off as a thing of nought, and saith: What forceth that, whether he were called by that very name or no? As though he would say: All the old fathers of the church, both Greeks and Latins, wanted words and eloquence, and either they could not, or they durst not call the head of the church by his own peculiar name. Howbeit, if the bishop of Rome be so called, it may be shewed; if not, then is my first assertion true. Verily, touching the title of universal bishop, St Gregory calleth it *novum nomen*[9], "a new name, unacquainted, and unknown unto the world;" and saith further: "If we quietly take this matter, we destroy the faith of the universal church[10]." This therefore was the cause, that the ancient doctors never called the bishop of Rome the head

Gregor. Lib. iv. Epist. 32. Gregor. Lib. vi. Epist. 24. Universæ ecclesiæ fidem corrumpimus.

[1 Ambros. Op. Par. 1686-90. Comm. in Epist. I. ad Tim. cap. iii. Tom. II. Append. col. 296; where *illic* for *ibi*.]

[2 Unanimitatem, 1565.]

[3 Athanas. Op. Par. 1698. Apol. contr. Arian. 69. Tom. I. Pars I. p. 185.]

[4 Sui gratiam: in hac, 1565.]

[5 Hæc est una quæ tenet et possidet omnem Sponsi sui et Domini potestatem; in hac præsidemus. —Cypr. Op. Oxon. 1682. Ad Jubai. Epist. lxxiii. p. 203.]

[6 Orig. Op. Par. 1733-59. Comm. in Matt. Tom. XII. 14. Tom. III. p. 531. Origen speaks of those οἳ τὸν τόπον τῆς ἐπισκοπῆς ἐκδικοῦντες χρῶνται τῷ ῥητῷ.]

[7 Cypr. Op. De Unit. Eccles. p. 108.]

[8 Writer, 1565, 1609.]

[9 Gregor. Magni Papæ I. Op. Par. 1705. Epist. Lib. V. Indict. XIII. Ad Mauric. August. Epist. xx. Tom. II. col. 748.]

[10 Id. Lib. VII. Indict. XV. Ad Anastas. Episc. Epist. xxvii. col. 873.]

of the church; for that they knew he was neither reputed nor taken so, nor was indeed the head of the church. M. Harding, having not yet found the thing that he so long sought for, at the last is fain to make it up by shift of reason: "The universal church," saith he, "is the house of God."

"Damasus is the ruler of the house of God; *ergo*, Damasus is ruler of the universal church."

This *syllogismus* is a manifest *fallax*, and hath as many faults as lines.

First, there is an equivocation or double understanding of these words, "the 1.
house of God:" for both the universal church, and also every particular church,
is God's house. Again, there is another *fallax*, which they call *ex meris particu-* 2.
laribus, or *a non distributo ad distributum*.

Thirdly, there is another foul fault in the very form of the syllogism, easy for 3.
any child to espy. For, contrary to all logic and order of reason, he concludeth *in secunda figura affirmative;* whereas M. Harding knoweth, all the moods or forms of the second figure must needs conclude *negative*. The weakness hereof will the better appear by the like: The universal church is the catholic church. But Arsenius saith: Athanasius the bishop of Alexandria was ruler of the catholic church; *ergo*, Athanasius the bishop of Alexandria was ruler of the universal church.

Thus hitherto M. Jewel may truly say, M. Harding hath yet brought neither clause nor sentence sufficient to prove that the bishop of Rome was called either the universal bishop, or the head of the universal church.

M. HARDING. THE THIRTY-SECOND DIVISION.

[*Peter and his successor called head of the church expressly.* H. A. 1564.]

But to satisfy these men, and to take away occasion of cavil, I will allege a few places where the express term "head" is attributed to Peter the first bishop of Rome, and by like right to his successors, and to the see apostolic. Chrysostom, speaking of the virtue and power of Peter, and of the stedfastness of the church, in the 55th Homily upon Matthew hath these words among other: Cujus pastor et caput homo piscator, atque ignobilis, &c.[11] *By which words he affirmeth that the pastor and head of the church, being but a fisher, a man, and one of base parentage, passeth in firmness the nature of the diamond. Again, in an homily of the praises of Paul, he saith thus: "Neither was this man only such a one, but he also which was the head of the apostles, who oftentimes said he was ready to bestow his life for Christ, and yet was full sore afraid of death[12]." If he were head of the apostles, then was he head of the inferior people, and so head of the universal church.*

A head for worthiness and boldness of spirit. So St Gregory saith: Paulus caput effectus est nationum. In 1 Regum, Lib. iv. cap. iv[13].

Hierome, writing against Jovinian, saith: Propterea inter duodecim unus eligitur, ut capite constituto schismatis tollatur occasio[14]: *"For that cause among the twelve one[15] is specially chosen out, that, the head being ordained, occasion of schism may be taken away." Whereby it appeareth that Peter was constituted head for avoiding of division and schism. Now the danger of the inconvenience remaining still, yea, more than at that time, for the greater multitude of the church, and for sundry other imperfections, the same remedy must be thought to continue, unless we would say that Christ hath less care over[16] his church now that it is so much increased, than he had at the beginning, when his flock was small. For this cause, except we deny God's providence toward his church, there is one head for avoiding of schism also now, as well as in the apostles' time: which is[17] the successor of him that was head by Christ's appointment then, the bishop of Rome sitting in the seat that Peter sat in.*

[11 The words as alleged do not appear in the homily referred to: Peter is, however, repeatedly termed τῶν ἀποστόλων κορυφαῖος.—Chrysost. Op. Par. 1718-38. In Matt. Hom. liv. (*al.* lv.) Tom. VII. pp. 547, 9. But see Op. Lat. Basil. 1547. In cap. Matt. xvi. Hom. lv. Tom. II. col. 460; where *piscator homo*, and *ignobilis terrarum orbe reluctante adamantis naturam firmitate superet.*]

[12 Οὐχ οὗτος δὲ μόνον τοιοῦτος ἦν, ἀλλὰ καὶ ὁ κορυφαῖος αὐτῶν πολλάκις εἰπὼν, ὅτι ἕτοιμός ἐστι τὴν ψυχὴν ἐπιδοῦναι, σφόδρα ἐδεδοίκει θάνατον.—Id. De Laud. Paul. Hom. vi. Tom. II. p. 508.]

[13 See before, page 431.]

[14 Hieron. Op. Par. 1693-1706. Adv. Jovin. Lib. I. Tom. IV. Pars II. col. 168.]

[15 On, H. A. 1564.]

[16 Of, H. A. 1564.]

[17 Which head is, H. A. 1564.]

Head.

Cyrillus saith: Petrus ut princeps caputque ceterorum primus exclamavit, Tu es Christus Filius Dei vivi[1]: "*Peter, as prince and head of the rest, first cried out, 'Thou art Christ, the Son of the living God.'" Augustine also, in a sermon to the people, calleth him head of the church, saying:* Totius corporis membrum in ipso capite curat ecclesiæ, et in ipso vertice componit omnium membrorum sanitatem[2]: "*He healeth the member of the whole body in the head itself of the church, and in the top itself he ordereth the health of all the members." And in another place:* Salvator quando pro se et Petro exsolvi jubet, pro omnibus exsolvisse videtur; quia sicut in Salvatore erant omnes causa magisterii, ita ... post Salvatorem in Petro omnes continentur: ipsum enim constituit caput (124) omnium[3]: "*Our Saviour," saith Augustine, "when as he commanded payment (for the emperor) to be made for himself and for Peter, he seemeth to have paid for all; because, as all were in our Saviour for cause of teaching, so after our Saviour all are contained in Peter; for he ordained him head of all." Here have these men the plain and express term, head of the rest, head of the church, head* of all, and therefore of the universal church. What will they have more? Neither here can they say, that, although this title*[4] *of the head be given to Peter, yet it is not derived and transferred from him to his successors. For this is manifest, that Christ instituted his church, so as it should continue to the world's end, according to the saying of Esay the prophet:* Super solium David, &c.: "*Upon the seat of David, and upon his kingdom, shall Messias sit to strengthen it, and to establish it in judgment and righteousness, from this day for evermore." And thereof it is evident that he ordained those who then were in ministry, so as their authority and power should be derived unto their after-comers for the utility of the church for ever; specially whereas he said: "Behold, I am with you until the end of the world." And therefore, as Victor writeth in his story of persecution of the Vandals, Eugenius bishop of Carthago, convented of Obadus a great captain of Hunerick king of the Vandals, about a council to be kept in Africa for matters of the faith, betwixt the Arians, supported by the king and the catholics, said in this wise:* Si nostram fidem, &c.: "*If the king's power desire to know our faith, which is one and the true, let him send to his friends. I will write also to my brethren, that my fellow-bishops come, who may declare the faith that is common to you and us;" (there he hath these words:)* et præcipue ecclesia Romana, quæ caput est omnium ecclesiarum: "*and specially the church of Rome, which is the head of all the churches*[5]." *Naming the church of Rome, he meaneth the bishop there, or his legates to be sent in his stead.*

Serm. 124. [de tempore. H. A. 1564.]

Lib. Quæst. Vet. et Nov. Test. Quæst. 75.

The hundred and twenty-fourth untruth, standing in the wilful falsifying of St Augustine.

*St Augustine saith, Caput eorum, not Caput omnium.

Cap. ix.

Matt. ult.

Lib. ii.

Thus it is proved by good and ancient authorities, that the name and title of the head, ruler, president, chief and principal governor of the church, is of the fathers attributed, not only to Peter, but also to his successors, bishops of the see apostolic. And therefore M. Jewel may think himself by this charitably admonished to remember his promise of yielding and subscribing.

THE BISHOP OF SARISBURY.

I might well pass all these authorities over without answer, as being no part of this question. For I trust the indifferent reader of himself will soon believe, we seek no quarrel against St Peter, nor go about to scan his titles, or to abridge him of his right. It is known that St Peter, by these fathers here alleged, Augustine, Hierome, Chrysostom, and Cyril, is called the top and head of the apostles. And, if need so required, the same might be avouched by authorities many more. For who is he that knoweth not this?

[1 Cyril. Alex. Op. Lut. 1638. Comm. in Joan. Evang. Lib. XII. Tom. IV. p. 1118.]

[2 August. Op. Par. 1679-1700. Serm. lxxix. 2. Tom. V. Append. col. 145; where *corporis morbum*, and *membrorum omnium*. This sermon is most probably not genuine.]

[3 Id. Quæst. ex Nov. Test. Quæst. lxxv. Tom. III. Append. col. 73; where *Salvator autem cum pro se et Petro dari*, and *esse caput eorum*.]

[4 This authority and title, 1565, and H. A. 1564.]

[5 Si nostram fidem, quæ una et vera est, potestas regis cognoscere desiderat, mittat ad amicos suos: scribam et ego fratribus meis, ut veniant coepiscopi mei, qui vobis nobiscum communem fidem nostram valeant demonstrare, et præcipue, &c.—Vict. Utic. De Persec. Wand. Lib. II. in Biblioth. Vet. Patr. per M. de la Bigne, Par. 1624. Tom. VII. col. 602.]

But M. Harding knoweth the case is moved, not of St Peter, but specially and namely of the bishops of Rome. And of them he knoweth he should have answered, if his mind had been to deal plainly, and, as he saith, fully to satisfy his reader. Within the space of the first six hundred years there were in Rome sixty-eight bishops, for their constancy in the faith, for their virtue and learning far exceeding the rest, that have been sithence. The number of them being so great, their learning so notable, their life so holy, it is marvel M. Harding should not be able to shew, that any one of them all, in so long a time, was once called the head of the church, and therefore should thus rest only upon St Peter, who, when he received these titles, was not bishop of Rome; and of whom there is no question moved. Wherefore M. Harding may better consider his note in the margin; and, whereas he hath written thus, "Peter and his successors called the head of the church expressly;" he may rather amend it, and make it thus: Only Peter, and not one of his successors, called head of the church expressly. So should his note and his text agree together; and so should he not deceive his reader. Head.

Here, by the way, I must put M. Harding in remembrance, notwithstanding, for his estimation's sake, he would fain have his forth in these matters, yet should he not therefore thus beguile the eyes of the simple, and thus misreport and falsify the words of the ancient fathers. For alleging St Hierome, he leaveth out words, and altogether dissembleth the whole meaning. In St Augustine he hath shifted and placed one word for another. St Hierome in that place, with great contention of words, commendeth St John above St Peter, namely, for that St Peter was a married man, and St John a virgin. In the heat of his talk he layeth this objection against himself: *At dices, super Petrum fundatur ecclesia: licet id ipsum in alio loco super omnes apostolos fiat, et cuncti claves regni cœlorum accipiant, et ex æquo super eos ecclesiæ fortitudo solidetur*[6]: "But thou wilt say, the church was built upon Peter (and not upon John). Albeit in another place the same is done (that is, the church is built) upon all the apostles; and all receive the keys of the kingdom of heaven; and the strength of the church is built equally upon them all." M. Harding thought it good to skip and dissemble these words, notwithstanding they be joined all together in one sentence with the rest. It followeth: *Tamen propterea inter duodecim unus eligitur, ut capite constituto, schismatis tollatur occasio. Sed cur non Johannes electus est virgo? Ætati delatum est, quia Petrus senior erat: ne adhuc adolescens, et pene puer progressæ ætatis hominibus præferretur*[6]: "Notwithstanding the disciples were all equal, yet therefore one is chosen among the twelve, that, a head being appointed, occasion of schism might be taken away. Thou wilt say again, And why was not John, being a virgin, chosen to be this head?" He answereth: "Christ gave the preeminence unto age; for Peter was an aged man; lest that John, being a young man, and in manner a child, should be placed before men of years." This therefore is St Hierome's meaning, that Christ, to avoid confusion, which lightly happeneth in all companies where as is none order, appointed St Peter, for that he was the eldest man, to speak and to deal for the rest, as the chief and head of all his brethren. Which order also was afterward universally taken throughout the world, that, in every congregation of priests, one should have a special preeminence above others, and be called *episcopus*, "the bishop[7]." This was thought a good politic way to avoid contention in the church; and not, as M. Harding imagineth, to make one man the universal ruler over all the world. But touching this whole matter I have answered more at large in the fifteenth division of this article.

M. Harding misallegeth the old doctors.

Hieron. adv. Jovin. Lib. i.

The apostles all equal.

Hieron. ad Nepot. vii. Quæst. i. In apibus. Hieron. in Epist. ad Tit cap. 1. Hieron. contr. Lucif.

In the allegation of St Augustine's words M. Harding, for his pleasure, hath uttered manifest corruption, in the stead of this word *eorum* purposely using this word *omnium*. For whereas St Augustine saith, *Ipsum constituit caput eorum*[8], "Christ appointed him to be the head of them;" M. Harding thought it better to allege it thus: *Ipsum constituit caput omnium*: "Christ appointed him to be

M. Harding misreporteth St Augustine.

August. in Quæst. Vet. et Nov. Test. Quæst. 75.

[[6] Hieron. Op. Par. 1693-1706. Adv. Jovin. Lib. Tom. IV. Pars II. col. 168; where *dicis*, and *ac pene puer*.]

[[7] Id. Ad Rust. Mon. Epist. xcv. Tom. IV. Pars II. col. 775; Comm. in Epist. ad Tit. cap. i. Tom. IV. Pars I. col. 413; Adv. Lucifer. Tom. IV. Pars II. col. 295. See before, pages 372, 3.]

[[8] See before, page 436, note 3.]

Head.

head of all." He saw right well that corrupt doctrine would not stand without some corruption.

Further, I doubt not but M. Harding doth well remember, that the question that lieth between us riseth not of any extraordinary name, once or twice given upon some special affection, but of the usual and known style of the bishops of Rome. For Theophrastus saith: *Quæ semel aut bis accidunt, contemnunt legislatores*[1]: "The law-makers have no regard to such things as never happen but once or twice." Neither whatsoever name is given to any man, of favour or admiration of his virtue, is therefore to be reckoned as his ordinary title. St Chrysostom writeth thus of the emperor Theodosius: *Læsus est, qui non habet parem ullum super terram, summitas, et caput omnium super terram hominum*[2]: "He is offended that in the earth hath no peer, the top and the head of all men in the world." Eleutherius the bishop of Rome gave this title unto Lucius the king of this island: *Vos estis vicarius Christi*[3]: "You (being the king) are Christ's[4] vicar." Chrysostom, speaking of Elias, calleth him *prophetarum caput*[5], "the head of the prophets." The council of Ephesus, writing unto the emperors Theodosius and Valentinianus, expresseth Cyrillus the bishop of Alexandria by this title: "*Caput...episcoporum congregatorum Cyrillus*[6]: "Cyrillus the head of the bishops there assembled." Likewise Gregory entitleth St Paul in this wise: [*Paulus*] *ad Christum conversus caput effectus est nationum*[7]: "Paul, being converted unto Christ, was made the head of nations." And to take nearer view of the bishop of Rome's own special titles, pope Nicolas thereof writeth thus: *Constat* [*pontificem*] *a pio principe Constantino...Deum appellatum*[8]: "It is well known that the pope of that godly prince Constantinus was called God." And further they say: *Papa est in primatu Abel, in zelo Elias, in mansuetudine David, in potestate Petrus, in unctione Christus*[9]: "The pope in primacy is Abel, in zeal is Elias, in mildness is David, in power is Peter, in anointing is Christ." These names, as I have said, of affection and favour have been given: yet will not M. Harding therefore say, that either the emperor ought to be called the head of all men upon earth, or the king Christ's vicar, or Elias the head of the prophets, or Cyrillus the head of the council, or St Paul the head of nations, or the bishop of Rome God or Christ, as by an usual and ordinary title. And although, as I have said, St Peter's titles be nothing incident to this question, yet we may examine M. Harding's argument touching the same: "Peter," saith he, "was head of the apostles;"

(Pan. de Leg. et Senat. et Long. Con. Nam ad ea.)
(Chrysost. ad Pop. Antioch. Hom. 2.)
(Chrysost. in Epist. ad Rom. xi. Hom. 18.)
(Cyril. Tom. iv. Epist. 5.)
(Gregor. in 1 Reg. Lib. iv. cap. iv.)
(Dist. 96. Satis evidenter.)

Ergo, he was head of other inferior people, and so head of the universal church.

This is a deceitful kind of argument, and riseth by degrees and steps, and in the schools is called *sorites*. In like sort M. Harding might conclude thus:

Elias, as Chrysostom saith, was "head of the prophets;"

Ergo, he was head of the inferior people, and so of the whole universal church.

But the error hereof will better appear by that argument that Themistocles the governor of Athens sometimes made of himself, his wife, and his child. Thus he said:

The people of Athens is ruled by me: I am ruled by my wife:

My wife is ruled by my child;

Ergo, the people of Athens is ruled by my child.

In this reason this one word "rule" hath three significations. For Themistocles ruled as a governor, his wife as a shrew, his child as a wanton. And therein

[1 Τὸ γὰρ ἅπαξ ἢ δὶς, id est, Quod enim semel aut bis existit, ut ait Theophrastus, παραβαίνουσιν οἱ νομοθέται, id est, prætereunt legislatores.—Paulus in Corp. Jur. Civil. Amst. 1663. Digest. Lib. I. Tit. iii. 6. Tom. I. p. 78. See also ibid. 3, 4, 5.]

[2 Chrysost. Op. Par. 1718-38. Ad Pop. Ant. Hom. ii. Tom. II. p. 23.]

[3 See before, page 306.] [4 Gods, 1565.]

[5 Chrysost. Op. in Epist. ad Rom. Hom. xviii. Tom. IX. p. 636.]

[6 Concil. Ephes. Relat. ad Imp. in Concil. Stud. Labb. et Cossart. Lut. Par. 1671-2. Tom. III. col. 656.]

[7 Gregor. Magni Papæ I. Op. Par. 1705. Lib. IV. in I. Reg. cap. v. 28. Tom. III. Pars II. col. 250.]

[8 Nicol. Papa in Epist. ad Michael. Imp. in Corp. Jur. Canon. Lugd. 1624. Decret. Gratian. Decr. Prim. Pars, Dist. xcvi. can. 7. col. 467.]

[9 Bernard uses the following expressions:...tu primatu Abel, gubernatu Noe, patriarchatu Abraham, ordine Melchisedech, dignitate Aaron, auctoritate Moyses, judicatu Samuel, potestate Petrus, unctione Christus.—Bernard. Op. Par. 1690. De Consid. Lib. II. cap. viii. Vol. I. Tom. II. col. 422.]

standeth the error of the argument. So likewise this word "head" signifieth sometime the chief in learning, sometime the chief in dignity, sometime the chief in government. And hereof also in reasoning riseth great error. For it were great folly to reason thus: Paul in learning and dignity was the head of all others; *ergo*, he was the head in government over all others. Peter not Head.

Touching Victor, that wrote the story of the Vandals, he is neither scripture, nor council, nor doctor, nor writeth the order or practice of the primitive church; nor is it well known either of what credit he was, or when he lived; nor doth he call the bishop of Rome the head of the universal church: only he saith: "Rome is the chief or head church of all others." Which thing of our part for that time is not denied; as may better appear by that is written before in sundry places of this article. So doth Prudentius call Bethleem the head of the world: *Sancta Bethlem caput est orbis*[10]. So likewise Chrysostom, giving instructions unto Flavianus touching the city of Antioch, saith unto him: *Cogita...de totius orbis capite*[11]: "Think thou of (Antioch, that is) the head of all the world." Hereby is meant a head of dignity or honour, and not of rule. Prudent. in Enchir. Chrysost. ad Pop. Antioch. Hom. 3.

M. Harding, finding not one of the whole number of the bishops of Rome once named the head of the whole church, therefore thought it best to found his proof upon St Peter. And for that cause others of his side have advanced[12] St Peter above all creatures. Bonifacius saith that God took Peter *in consortium individuæ Trinitatis*, "into the fellowship even of the indivisible Trinity;" and that "from him, as from the head, he poureth all his gifts into the body[13]." Hereof M. Harding forceth his argument thus: Peter was the head of the apostles, and so of all other inferiors; Extr. de Elect. et Elect. Potest. Bonif. viii. Fundamenta. Ab ipso, quasi quodam capite, dona sua omnia diffundit in corpus.

Ergo, the bishop of Rome is the head of the universal church.

Thus, as Julianus the emperor in his frenzy sometime[14] imagined that the great Alexander's soul was come by succession to dwell in him[15]; even so now the bishops of Rome imagine, by like phantasy or frenzy, that St Peter's soul cometh by succession to dwell in them; and that therefore they ought to have whatsoever title or interest Peter had. And for that cause they say, "We are Peter's successors:" even as the Pharisees sometime said, "We be the children of Abraham." But St John the Baptist said unto them: "Put not your affiance in such succession. For God is able even of the stones to raise up children unto Abraham." And when the children of Scæva, being sorcerers and infidels, began to practise in the name of Christ and Paul, the man possessed made them answer: "Christ I know, and Paul I know; but what are you?" Surely Peter was not the head of the apostles, because he was bishop of Rome. For he was so appointed by Christ in consideration of age and boldness of spirit, long before he came to Rome; yea, and had so been, and so had continued, although he had never come to Rome. Therefore M. Harding's argument is a *fallax*, and in the schools is called *fallacia accidentis*. Socrat. Lib. iii. cap. xxi. Matt. iii. Acts xix.

Thus, notwithstanding St Peter were head of the church, yet cannot the bishop of Rome therefore of right claim the same title. And albeit St Peter, of special reverence, and admiration of his spirit and virtues, were sometimes so called, as St Paul sometimes also[16] was; yet, understanding this chiefty for universal power, and government, and authority to command, St Peter neither was the head of the universal church indeed, nor was so esteemed or taken among his brethren, as many ways it may well appear. And therefore St Gregory saith: *Paulus membra dominici corporis certis extra Dominum quasi capitibus, et ipsis quidem apostolis subjici particulariter evitavit*[17]: "St Paul forbade Paul the head as well as Peter. Gregor. Lib. iv. Epist. 38.

[10 Aur. Prudent. Enchir. in Biblioth. Vet. Patr. per M. de la Bigne, Par. 1624. Nov. Test. 2. Tom. VIII. p. 561.]

[11 Chrysost. Op. Ad Pop. Ant. Hom. iii. Tom. II. p. 36.]

[12 Avanced, 1565.]

[13 ... ut ab ipso [Petro], quasi quodam capite, dona sua velut in corpus omne diffunderet. Hunc enim in consortium individuæ unitatis assumptum, id quod ipse erat, Dominus voluit nominari, &c.—Nicol. III. in Corp. Jur. Canon. Sext. Decretal. Lib. I. Tit. vi. cap. 17. col. 131.]

[14 Sometimes, 1565.]

[15 Socrat. in Hist. Eccles. Script. Amst. 1695-1700. Lib. III. cap. xxi. p. 159.]

[16 Upon like consideration also, 1565.]

[17 Gregor. Magni Papæ I. Op. Epist. Lib. v. Indict. XIII. Ad Johan. Episc. Epist. xviii. Tom. II. col. 742; where we find *ille* for *Paulus, extra Christum*, and *partialiter*.]

that the members of Christ's body should not be subject particularly unto any certain heads besides the Lord; no, not unto the apostles themselves." So saith St Augustine, as it is before alleged: [*Nec*] *apostolus Paulus caput est et origo eorum, quos plantaverat*[1]*:* "Neither is Paul himself the head of them whom he planted." Likewise again he saith: *Paulus...apostolus, quanquam sub capite præcipuum membrum,...tamen...membrum est corporis Christi*[2]*:* "Paul the apostle, although he be a special member under (Christ) the head, yet is he a member (and not the head) of Christ's body." To conclude, St Gregory saith: *Certe Petrus apostolus primum membrum sanctæ et universalis ecclesiæ* [*est*]. *Paulus, Andreas, Johannes, quid aliud quam singularium sunt plebium capita? Et tamen sub uno capite omnes membra* [*sunt ecclesiæ*]. *Atque, ut cuncta brevi cingulo locutionis astringam, sancti ante legem, sancti in lege, sancti sub gratia, omnes hi perficientes corpus Domini, in membris sunt ecclesiæ constituti: et nemo se unquam universalem vocari voluit*[3]*:* "Indeed Peter the apostle is the chief member of the holy universal church. Paul, Andrew, and John, what are they else, but the heads of several people[4]? Yet notwithstanding under one head they are all members of the church. To be short, the saints before the law, the saints in the law, the saints under grace, all accomplishing the Lord's body, are placed among the members of the church; and there was never yet none that would call himself universal."

August. contr. Lit. Pet. Lib. i. cap. v.

August. contr. Epist. Parm. Lib. ii. cap. viii.

Gregor. Lib. iv. Epist. 38.

Hereof we may well conclude thus: St Peter, touching government and ordinary rule, was not the head of the universal church; *ergo*, much less is the pope the head of the universal church.

M. HARDING. THE THIRTY-THIRD DIVISION.

I will add to all that hath been hitherto said of this matter a saying of Martin Luther, that such as do little regard the gravity of ancient fathers of the old church may yet somewhat be moved with the lightness of the young father Luther, patriarch and founder of their new church. Lightness I may well call it; for in this saying, which I shall here rehearse, he doth not so soberly allow the pope's primacy, as in sundry other treatises he doth rashly and furiously inveigh against the same. In a little treatise intituled, Resolutio Lutheriana super Propositione sua 13, De Potestate Papæ, *his words be these:* Primum quod me movet Romanum pontificem esse aliis omnibus, quos saltem noverimus se pontifices gerere, superiorem, est ipsa voluntas Dei, quam in ipso facto videmus. Neque enim sine voluntate Dei in hanc monarchiam unquam venire potuisset Romanus pontifex. At voluntas Dei, quoquo modo nota fuerit, cum reverentia suscipienda est; ideoque non licet temere Romano pontifici in suo primatu resistere. Hæc autem ratio tanta est, ut si etiam nulla scriptura, nulla alia causa esset, hæc tamen satis esset ad compescendam temeritatem resistentium. Et hac sola ratione gloriosissimus martyr Cyprianus per multas epistolas confidentissime gloriatur contra omnes episcoporum quorumcunque adversarios: sicut 3 Regum legimus, quod decem tribus Israel discesserunt a Roboam filio Salomonis; et tamen quia voluntate Dei sive auctoritate factum est, ratum apud Deum fuit. Nam et apud theologos omnes voluntas signi, quam vocant operationem Dei, non minus quam alia signa voluntatis Dei, ut præcepta prohibitiva, etc. metuenda est. Ideo non video quomodo sint excusati a schismatis reatu, qui huic voluntati contravenientes, sese a Romani pontificis auctoritate subtrahunt. Ecce hæc est una prima mihi insuperabilis ratio, quæ me subjicit Romano pontifici, et primatum ejus confiteri cogit[5]: *"The first thing, that moveth me to think the bishop of Rome to be over all other that we know to be bishops, is the very will of God, which we see in the fact or deed itself. For without the will of God the*

[*The pope's primacy acknowledged by Martin Luther.* H. A. 1564.]

[1 August. Op. Par. 1679-1700. Contr. Lit. Petil. Lib. I. cap. v. 6. Tom. IX. col. 208. See before, page 379, note 4.]

[2 Id. Contr. Epist. Parmen. Lib. II. cap. viii. 16. Tom. IX. col. 34.]

[3 Gregor. Magni Papæ I. Op. Par. 1705. Epist. Lib. V. Indict. XIII. Ad Johan. Episc. Epist. xviii. Tom. II. col. 743; where *Petrus apostolorum primus,* and *sub lege.*]

[4 Peoples, 1565.]

[5 Luth. Op. Witeb. 1554-83. Resol. sup. Prop. xiii. de Potest. Papæ, Tom. I. fol. 312; where 3 *Regum* 12, and *prohibita.*]

bishop of Rome could never have been[6] *comen unto this monarchy. But the will of God, by what mean soever it be known, is to be received reverently: and therefore it is not lawful rashly to resist the bishop of Rome in his primacy. And this is so great a reason for the same, that, if there were no scripture at all, nor other reason, yet this were enough to stay the rashness of them that resist. And through this only reason the most glorious martyr Cyprian in many of his epistles vaunteth himself very boldly against all the adversaries of bishops, whatsoever they were. As in the third book of the Kings we read that the ten tribes of Israel departed from Roboam, Salomon's son: yet, because it was done by the will or authority of God, it stood in effect with God. For among all the divines the will of the sign, which they call the working of God, is to be feared no less than other signs of God's will, as commandments prohibitive, &c. Therefore I see not how they may be excused of the guilt of schism, which, going against this will, withdraw themselves from the authority of the bishop of Rome. Lo, this is one chief invincible reason that maketh me to be under the bishop of Rome, and compelleth me to confess his primacy." Thus*[7] *far Luther.*

Thus I have briefly touched some deal of the scriptures, of the canons and councils, of the edicts of emperors, of the fathers' sayings, of the reasons, and of the manifold practices of the church, which are wont to be alleged for the pope's primacy and supreme authority. Withal I have proved that which M. Jewel denieth, (125) *that the bishop of Rome, within six hundred years after Christ, hath been called the universal bishop of no small number of men of great credit, and very oftentimes head of the universal church, both in terms equivalent, and also expressly. Now to the next article.*

The hundred and twenty-fifth untruth. For, Peter only excepted, either of these titles resteth yet unreproved[8].

THE BISHOP OF SARISBURY.

The case goeth somewhat hardly of M. Harding's side, when he is thus driven for want of other authorities to crave aid at Luther's hand. Touching alteration in religion, which it pleaseth him to name lightness, if he would soberly remember his own often changes, and the light occasions of the same, he should find small cause to condemn others. Certainly D. Luther, after God had once called him to be a minister of his truth, never looked backward from the plough, nor refused the grace that God had offered him, notwithstanding he saw all the powers of the world were against him. His argument is taken of the effects or tokens of God's will. The pope, said he, is advanced[9] unto a monarchy or imperial state of a kingdom: but he could never be so advanced[9] without God's will; *ergo*, it was God's will it should be so.

Arguments that be taken of God's permission, or of the tokens of his will, make no necessary proof, either that the things in themselves be good, or that God is pleased with them. For God suffered Nabuchodonozor, Sennacherib, Pharao, and others; and their very estates and proceedings were evident tokens of God's will. For if his will had been otherwise, they could not have reigned: yet neither were they good men, nor was God pleased with their doings. So shall God suffer antichrist to sit even in the holy place. Daniel saith: *Faciet, et prosperabitur:* "He shall take his pleasure and shall prosper." And again: *Roboratitur fortitudo ejus, et non in viribus suis:* "His power shall be confirmed, but not through his own strength," but through the strength of God. Yet shall not God therefore love or favour antichrist, or delight in his wickedness. For St Paul saith: "The Lord shall kill him with the spirit of his mouth, and shall destroy him with the brightness and glory of his coming.

Isai. xxxvi. Dan. vii. Matt. xxiv. Dan. viii. 2 Thess. ii.

Now, forasmuch as it hath pleased M. Harding, for the conclusion hereof, to touch the effects of God's will, I trust it shall not be painful to thee, gentle reader, likewise shortly to consider the effects and sequels of this universal power. It is granted that the church of Rome, for sundry causes before alleged, was evermore from the beginning the chief and most notable above all others. Notwithstanding, Æneas Sylvius, being himself a bishop of Rome, saith: *Ad Romanos pontifices ante Nicenum concilium aliquis sane, etsi non magnus, respectus*

Æn. Sylv.

[6 H. A. 1564, omits *been*.]
[7 This, 1565, and H. A. 1564.]
[8 Unproved, 1565.]
[9 Avanced, 1565.]

fuit[1]: "Verily there was some respect had to the bishops of Rome before the council of Nice, although it were not great." St Cyprian in his time complained that "pride and ambition seemed to lodge in priests' bosoms[2]." Origen in his time complained that the ministers of Christ seemed even then to pass the outrage of worldly princes[3]. Yet was the church of God in those days every where under cruel and vehement persecution. Therefore, to abate this ambitious courage, order was afterward taken in the council of Carthage, that "no man should be entitled the highest bishop, or the prince of bishops, or by any other like name[4]." The Greek bishops in the council of Antioch[5], and the bishops of Africa, being in number two hundred and seventeen, in the council there[6] found themselves grieved with the pride and arrogancy of the see of Rome. For that John the bishop of Constantinople took upon him to be called the universal bishop, therefore Gregory the bishop of Rome called him Lucifer and the messenger of antichrist, and said, he had chosen unto him a proud, an arrogant, a pompous, and a blasphemous name[7]. But after that, by great suit made unto the emperor Phocas, the bishops of Rome themselves had once obtained the same title, and had possessed and enjoyed the same a long while, in the end, their pride was such, that it seemed intolerable. Then they began to decree and determine, that every mortal man is bound to be subject to the see of Rome, and that upon pain of damnation; and that, without the obedience of that see, no man is saved[8]; that the bishop of Rome is an universal judge over all men[9]; and that he himself may be judged by no man, neither by emperor, nor by king, nor by all the clergy, nor by the whole people[10], for that it is written by the prophet Esay, "The axe shall not glory against him that heweth with it[11];" that, whatsoever he do, no man may presume to say unto him, *Domine, cur ita facis*[12]? "Sir, why do you thus?" that he hath all manner law and right *in scrinio pectoris sui*[13], "in the closet of his breast;" that "all other bishops receive of his fulness[14];" [a]that no councils can make laws for the church of Rome, and that the bishop of Rome's authority is plainly excepted out of all councils[15]; [b]that, notwithstanding the pope draw innumerable companies of people after him into hell, "yet no mortal man may dare to reprove him[16];" [c]that the pope's will or pleasure standeth as a law: *In illis quæ vult, est ei pro ratione voluntas*[17]; and that there is none other reason to be yielded of his doings but only this: *Quia ipse voluit:* "For he would." [d]For of that that is nothing he is able to make something: *Quia de eo, quod nihil est, potest facere aliquid*[18]; [e]that he hath the right of both swords, as well of the temporal, as of the spiritual; that the temporal prince may not draw his sword, but only at his beck and sufferance, *ad nutum et patien-*

Cypr. in Serm. De Jej. et Tent.
Orig. in Matt. Tract. 12.
Dist. 99. Primæ sedis.
Soz. Lib. iii. cap. viii.
Concil. Afric. Epist. ad Cœl.
Gregor. Lib. iv. Epist. 34, 38, &c.
Anno Dom. 602.
De Major. et Obed. Unam sanctam.
Ibidem in Gloss.
ix. Quæst. 3. Nemo.
Dist. 21. Inferior sedes.
Isai. x.
De Conc. Præbendæ, in Gloss.
Extr. de Con. Licet.
Duran. Lib. ii.
[a] De Elect. et Elect. Potest. Significasti.
[b] Dist. 40. Si papa.
[c] De Trans. Epis. Quanto in Gloss.
[d] De Conc. Præb. Proposuit, in Gloss.
[e] De Major. et Obed. Unam sanctam.

[1 Æn. Sylv. Op. Basil. 1571. Ad Mart. Mayer. Epist. cclxxxviii. p. 802. See before, p. 386, note 9.]

[2 Cypr. Op. Oxon. 1682. De Jejun. et Tent. (Arnold.) p. 38. See before, page 354, note 7.]

[3 ... ἡμεῖς δὲ ... τοιοῦτοί ἐσμεν ὡς ἐνίοτε καὶ τὸν τῶν κακῶς ἀρχόντων ἐν τοῖς ἔθνεσιν ὑπερβάλλειν τύφον.—Orig. Op. Par. 1733-59. Comm. in Matt. Tom. XVI. 8. Tom. III. p. 723.]

[4 Ex Concil. Afric. c. 6. in Corp. Jur. Canon. Lugd. 1624. Decret. Gratian. Decr. Prim. Pars, Dist. xcix. can. 3. col. 479. See before, pp. 355, 425.]

[5 Sozom. in Hist. Eccles. Script. Amst. 1695-1700. Lib. III. cap. viii. pp. 413, 4.]

[6 Concil. Afric. Epist. ad Cœlestin. cap. 105. in Crabb. Concil. Col. Agrip. 1551. Tom. I. p. 521. See before, page 356.]

[7 Gregor. Magni Papæ I. Op. Par. 1705. Epist. Lib. V. Indict. XIII. Ad Constant. August. Epist. xxi. Ad Johan. Episc. Epist. xviii. Tom. II. cols. 751, 742, 3.]

[8 Bonifac. VIII. in Corp. Jur. Canon. Extrav. Comm. Lib. I. De Major. et Obed. cap. 1. col. 212.]

[9 Gloss. in eod. ibid. col. 211.]

[10 Innoc. Papa in Corp. Jur. Canon. Decret. Gratian. Decr. Sec. Pars, Caus. IX. Quæst. iii. can. 13. col. 877.]

[11 Nicol. Papa ad Michael. Imp. in eod. Decr. Prim. Pars, Dist. xxi. can. 4. col. 96.]

[12 Extrav. Joan. XXII. in eod. De Conc. Preb. Tit. iv. Gloss. in cap. 2. col. 56.]

[13 Bonifac. VIII. in eod. Sext. Decretal. Lib. I. Tit. ii. cap. 1. col. 11.]

[14 ... de cujus [papæ] plenitudine omnes accipiunt.—Durand. Rat. Div. Offic. Lugd. 1565. Lib. II. cap. i. 17. fol. 46.]

[15 ... cum omnia concilia per Romanæ ecclesiæ auctoritatem et facta sint, et robur acceperint, et in eorum statutis Romani pontificis patenter excipiatur auctoritas.—Paschal. in Corp. Jur. Canon. Decretal. Gregor. IX. Lib. I. Tit. vi. cap. 4. col. 112.]

[16 Ex Dict. Bonifac. Mart. in eod. Decret. Gratian. Decr. Prim. Pars, Dist. xl. can. 6. cols. 194, 5.]

[17 Decretal. Gregor. IX. in eod. Lib. I. Tit. vii, Gloss. in cap. 3. col. 217; where *ei est*.]

[18 Non est alia ratio, nisi quia ipse voluit, quia de eo, quod nihil est, potest aliquid facere.—Ibid. Lib. III. Tit. viii. Gloss. in cap. 4. col. 1071.]

tiam ecclesiæ[19]; [f]that he is *hæres imperii*, "the heir apparent of the empire[20]," [g]and is seven and fifty degrees greater than the emperor; and that because in such proportion the sun is greater than the moon[21]; [h]that it is lawful for him to depose kings and emperors[22]; as he did the emperor Henry the sixth, and Childericus the French king.

[f] Clem. de Appel. Pastoral.
[g] De Major. et Obed. Solitæ in Gloss.
[h] De Senten. et Re Jud. Ad Apost.

Then he made the emperor of Christendom to lie down flat before him, and spared not to set his foot upon his neck[23], adding withal these words of the prophet David, "[i]Thou shalt walk over the asp and the cockatrice:" [k]then he was content that the emperor should be called *procurator ... ecclesiæ Romanæ*[24], "the proctor or steward of the church of Rome: [l]then, as if he had been Nabuchodonozor, or Alexander, or Antiochus, or Domitian, he claimed unto himself the name and title of Almighty God; and said further that, being God, he might not be judged of any mortal man[25]: [m]then he suffereth[26] men to say, *Dominus Deus noster papa*[27]: "Our Lord God the pope:" [n]*Tu es omnia, et super omnia*[28]: "Thou art all, and above all. All power is given unto thee, as well in heaven as in earth." I leave the miserable spoil of the empire, the losing of sundry great countries and nations that sometimes were christened, the weakening of the faith, the encouraging of the Turk, the ignorance and blindness of the people. These and other like be the effects of the pope's universal power. Would to God he were indeed that he would so fain be called, and would shew himself in his own particular church to be Christ's vicar, and the [o]dispenser of God's mysteries! Then should godly men have less cause to complain against him: as now, although that he claimeth were his very right, yet by his own judgment he is worthy to lose it. [p]For pope Gregory saith: *Privilegium ... meretur amittere, qui ... abutitur potestate*[29]: "He that abuseth his authority is worthy to lose his privilege." And pope Sylverius saith: [q]*[Etiam] quod habuit, amittat, qui, ... quod non accepit, usurpat*[30]: "He that usurpeth that he received not, let him lose that he had."

[i] Psal. xci.
[k] Dist. 96. Si imperator, in Gloss.
[l] Dist. 96. Satis evidenter.
[m] Johan. xxii. De Verb. Sig. in Gloss. Cum inter.
[n] In Conc. Later. sub Julio.
[o] 1 Cor. iv.
[p] xi. Quæst. 2. Privilegium.
[q] xxv. Quæst. 2. Sic decet.

Now briefly to lay abroad the whole contents of this article:

1. First, M. Harding hath wittingly alleged such testimonies under the names of Anacletus, Athanasius, and other holy fathers, as he himself knoweth undoubtedly to be forged, and with manifest absurdities and contradictions do betray themselves, and have no manner colour or shew of truth.
2. He hath made his claim by certain canons of the council of Nice, and of the council of Chalcedon; and yet he knoweth that neither there are, nor never were any such canons to be found.
3. He hath dismembered and mangled St Gregory's words, and, contrary to his own knowledge, he hath cut them off in the midst, the better to beguile his reader.
4. He hath violently and perforce drawn and racked the old godly fathers Irenæus, Cyprian, Ambrose, Cyrillus, Augustine, Theodoretus, Hierome, and others, contrary to their own sense and meaning.
5. Touching appeals to Rome, the government of the east part of the world, excommunications, approbations of orders, allowance of councils, restitutions, and reconciliations, he hath openly misreported the whole universal order and practice of the church.

[[19] Bonifac. VIII. in eod. Extrav. Comm. Lib. I. De Major. et Obed. cap. 1. col. 208; where *sacerdotis* for *ecclesiæ*.]

[[20] ... vacante imperio imperatori succedimus.—Clemens V. in eod. Clementin. Lib. II. Tit. xi. cap. 2. col. 136.]

[[21] Decretal. Gregor. IX. in eod. Lib. I. Tit. xxxiii. Gloss. in cap. 6. col. 426.]

[[22] Innoc. IV. in eod. Sext. Decretal. Lib. II. Tit. xiv. cap. 2. cols. 376, &c.]

[[23] See before, page 414, note 3.]

[[24] Decret. Gratian. in eod. Decr. Prim. Pars, Dist. xcvi. Gloss. in cap. 11. col. 469; where *Romanæ ecclesiæ*.]

[[25] Nicol. Papa in eod. ibid. Dist. xcvi. can. 7. col. 467.]

[[26] Suffered, 1565.]

[[27] Extrav. Joan. XXII. ad calc. Sext. Decretal. Par. 1585. Tit. xiv. Gloss. in cap. 4. col. 153. See before, page 96, note 4.]

[[28] Orat. Steph. Arch. Patrac. in Concil. Later. v. Sess. x. in Concil. Stud. Labb. et Cossart. Lut. Par. 1671-2. Tom. XIV. col. 269. See before, pp. 93, 4, note 2. See also Zanæ Orat. ibid. cols. 49, &c. and Marcell. Orat. ibid. cols. 108, &c.]

[[29] Gregor. in Corp. Jur. Canon. Decret. Gratian. Decr. Sec. Pars, Caus. XI. Quæst. iii. can. 63. col. 943.]

[[30] Silver. Papa in eod. ibid. Caus. XXV. Quæst. ii. can. 22. col. 1453; where *assumpserit* for *usurpat*.]

All this notwithstanding, he hath as yet found neither of these two glorious 6.
titles that he hath so narrowly sought for; notwithstanding great pains taken, and great promises and vaunts made touching the same.

Therefore to conclude, I must subscribe, and rescribe, even as before, that, albeit M. Harding have travailed painfully herein, both by himself, and also with conference of his friends, yet cannot he hitherto find, neither in the scriptures, nor in the old councils, nor in any one of all the ancient catholic fathers, that the bishop of Rome, within the space of the first six hundred years after Christ, was ever entitled either the universal bishop or the head of the universal church.

OF REAL PRESENCE.

THE FIFTH ARTICLE.

THE BISHOP OF SARISBURY.

OR that the people was then taught to believe that Christ's body is really, substantially, corporally, carnally, or naturally in the sacrament.

[OF THE TERMS REALLY, SUBSTANTIALLY, CORPORALLY, CARNALLY, NATURALLY, FOUND IN THE DOCTORS TREATING OF THE TRUE BEING OF CHRIST'S BODY IN THE BLESSED SACRAMENT. —ARTICLE V. H. A. 1564.]

M. HARDING. THE FIRST DIVISION.

(126) *Christian people hath ever been taught that the body and blood of Jesus Christ, by the unspeakable working of the grace of God and virtue of the Holy Ghost, is present in this most holy sacrament, and that verily and indeed. This doctrine is founded upon the plain words of Christ, which he uttered in the institution of this sacrament, expressed by the evangelists and by St Paul. As they were at supper, saith Matthew, Jesus took bread and blessed it, and brake it, and gave it to his disciples, and said*[1]*: "Take ye, eat ye, this is my body;" and, taking the cup, he gave thanks, and gave it to them, saying: "Drink ye all of this; for this is my blood of the new testament, which shall be shed for many in remission of sins." With like words almost Mark, Luke, and Paul do describe this divine institution. Neither said our Lord only, "This is my body;" but, lest some should doubt how his words are to be understanded, for a plain declaration of them, he addeth this further, "which is given for you." Likewise of the cup he saith not only, "This is my blood;" but also, as it were to put it out of all doubt, "which shall be shed for many."*

The hundred and twenty-sixth untruth. For M. Harding is not able to prove that the people in the primitive church was thus taught.

Matt. xxvi.

Mark xiv. *Luke xxii.* *1 Cor. xi.* *Luke xxii.*

Now, as faithful people do believe that Christ gave not a figure of his body, but his own true and very body in substance; and likewise not a figure of his blood, but his very precious blood itself at his passion and death on the cross for our redemption; so they believe also that the words of institution[2] *of this sacrament admit no other understanding, but that he giveth unto us in these holy mysteries his self-same body and his self-same blood in truth of substance, which was crucified and shed forth for us. Thus to the humble believers scripture itself ministereth sufficient argument of the truth of Christ's body and blood in the sacrament, against the sacramentaries, who hold opinion, that it is there but in a figure, sign, or token* (127) *only.*

The hundred and twenty-seventh untruth. For this is no part of our doctrine.

THE BISHOP OF SARISBURY.

I know not well whether M. Harding do this of purpose, or else it be his manner of writing. But this I see, that, being demanded of one thing, he always turneth his answer to another. The question is here moved, "whether Christ's body be really and corporally[3] in the sacrament." His answer is, that Christ's body is joined and united really and corporally unto us. And herein he bestoweth his whole treaty, and answereth not one word unto the question.

In the former articles he was able to allege some forged authorities, some counterfeit practice of the church, some words of the ancient doctors, although mistaken, some shew of natural and worldly reason, or, at the least wise, some

[1 Saith, 1565, and H. A. 1564.] [2 The institution, 1565, 1609, and H. A. 1564.] [3 Corporal, 1611.]

Dissension and contradiction of M. Harding's side.

colour or shift of words. But in this matter, for direct proof he is able to allege nothing; no, not so much as the help and drift of natural reason.

Where he saith, "Christian people hath ever been thus taught from the beginning," it is great marvel that either they should be so taught without a teacher; or their teacher should thus instruct them, without words; or such words should be spoken, and never written. Verily M. Harding, by his silence and want herein, secretly confesseth that these words, really, carnally, &c. in this matter of the sacrament, were never used of any ancient writer; for if they were, either he or his fellows would have found them.

But Christ saith: "This is my body;" "this is my blood;" and to put the matter out of doubt, he addeth, "which is given for you;" "which shall be shed for you." Hereupon M. Harding foundeth his carnal presence; notwithstanding Christ himself useth not any of these words, nor any other word leading thereunto. And doctor Fisher, sometime bishop of Rochester, a famous man of M. Harding's side, saith expressly, that this sense cannot in any wise be gathered of the bare words of Christ. For thus he writeth: *Hactenus Matthæus; qui et solus testamenti novi meminit. Neque ullum hic verbum positum est, quo probetur, in nostra missa veram fieri carnis et sanguinis Christi præsentiam*[1]: "Hitherto St Matthew; who only maketh mention of the new testament. Neither are there any words here written, whereby it may be proved that in our mass is made the very presence of the body and blood of Christ." And further he avoucheth it thus: *Non potest igitur per ullam scripturam probari*[2]: "Therefore it cannot be proved by any scripture." Here we see great variety of judgment in M. Harding's own side, and that in matters of greatest weight. M. Harding thinketh his carnal presence is proved sufficiently by these words of Christ, "This is my body:" Doctor Fisher contrariwise saith: "It cannot be proved, neither by these words of the scripture, nor by any other." And yet it was ever thought M. Fisher was as learned in every respect as M. Harding.

Jo. Fisherus contra Captiv. Bab. N. 8. et O.

And, albeit M. Harding lay such hold upon these words of Christ, as if they were so plain, yet others of his friends, by their diverse and sundry constructions touching the same, have made them somewhat dark and doubtful, and cannot yet throughly agree upon them. Some of them say, "Christ's natural body is in the sacrament, howbeit not naturally:" some others say, "It is there both naturally, and also sensibly:" some of them say precisely, "Never man used either of these two terms, naturally or sensibly, in this case of Christ's presence in the sacrament." Yet others of them put the matter out of doubt, and say, "Christ is there present naturally[3]." And in the council holden in Rome under pope Nicolas the second, it was determined, and Berengarius forced to subscribe, that Christ is in the sacrament sensibly; or, as they then grossly uttered it in Latin, *sensualiter*[4]. Some of them say: "Christ's body is not divided or broken in the sacrament, but only the accidents[5]." But pope Nicolas with his whole council saith: "Christ's body itself is touched with fingers, and divided, and broken, and rent with teeth, and not only the accidents[4]." Thus, to leave other more contrarieties, it is plain hereby that the best learned of that side are not yet fully agreed upon the sense of Christ's words, notwithstanding their suitors and well-willers are otherwise persuaded of them. And doth M. Harding believe that christian people were thoroughly resolved herein, when their doctors and teachers were not resolved; or that the scholars were better instructed than their masters?

D. Smyth, de Eucharist. Steph. Gardinerus. D. Smyth.

Steph. Gardiner in the Devil's Soph. fol. 6. De Con. Dist. 2. Ego Berengar. Steph. Gardiner in the Devil's Soph. fol. 15. EgoBerengar. Manibus tractari, frangi, dentibus atteri.

Now, if this article cannot be proved, neither by any words of the scriptures, as doctor Fisher saith, and as it further appeareth by the dissension of the teachers; nor by any one of all the old doctors and fathers, as M. Harding granteth

---

[1 Joan. Roffens. Def. Reg. Assert. contr. Babyl. Captiv. Col. 1525. cap. x. 2. fol. 80.

[2 Id. ibid. fol. 80. 2.]

[3 A Detection of the Deuil's Sophistrie, Lond. 1546. fol. 14. 2.]

[4 Ego Berengarius...anathematizo omnem hæresim, præcipue eam ... quæ astruere conatur panem et vinum ... post consecrationem solummodo sacramentum, et non verum corpus et sanguinem Domini nostri Jesu Christi esse, nec posse sensualiter, nisi in solo sacramento manibus sacerdotum tractari, vel frangi, aut fidelium dentibus atteri.—Confess. Bereng. in Corp. Jur. Canon. Lugd. 1624. Decret. Gratian. Decr. Tert. Pars, De Consecr. Dist. ii. can. 42. col. 1932.]

[5 A Detection of the Deuil's Sophistrie, foll. 15, 6.]

by his silence; then may godly and catholic christian people well stay their judgments, and stand in doubt of this carnal and fleshly presence. Indeed the question between us this day is not of the letters or syllables of Christ's words, for they are known and confessed of either party; but only of the sense and meaning of his words, which, as St Hierome saith, is the very pith and substance of the scriptures[6]. And the law itself saith: *In fraudem [legis facit],... qui salvis verbis legis sententiam ejus circumvenit*[7]: "He committeth fraud against the laws, that, saving the words of the law, overthroweth the meaning." And St Augustine seemeth herein to find fault with certain in his time. His words be these: *Cum in unam partem procliviter ire cœperint, non respiciunt divinæ auctoritatis alia testimonia, quibus possint ab illa intentione revocari, et in ea, quæ ex utrisque temperata est, veritate ac moderatione consistere*[8]: "When they once begin to run headlong of one side, they never consider other testimonies of divine authority, whereby they might be withdrawn from their purpose, and so might rest in that truth and measure that is tempered and tuned of both." If it be true that M. Harding saith, that this is the only sense and meaning of Christ's words, that his body is in such gross sort really and fleshly in the sacrament, and that, unless Christ mean so, he meaneth nothing; it is great wonder that none of the ancient catholic doctors of the church, no, not one, could ever see it; or, if they saw it, yet, being so eloquent, lacked words, and were never able to express it.

Figure.

Hieron. ad Galat. cap. i.

Pan. de Leg. et Senat. et Long. Cons. Contra Legem.

August. de Fide et Oper. cap. iv.

But he saith, "It is no bare figure, as the sacramentaries hold opinion;" and therefore he thinketh he may conclude that Christ's body is really present. So might he also say: The sacrament of baptism is no bare figure; therefore Christ is therein really present. Certainly St Augustine, speaking of the rock in the wilderness, writeth thus: *Hinc est, quod dictum est, Petra erat Christus. Non enim dixit, Petra significat Christum, sed tanquam hoc esset: quod utique per substantiam non hoc erat, sed per significationem*[9]: "Therefore it is written, 'The rock was Christ.' For St Paul saith not, The rock signified Christ, but as though it had been Christ indeed; whereas it was not Christ in substance, but by way of signification, or by a figure." St Paul saith not, The rock was a figure of Christ, but, "The rock was Christ." And St Basil in the[10] like sort saith: *Christus revera petra est immobilis, et inconcussa*[11]: "Christ indeed is the sure and the firm rock." Yet I trow M. Harding will not therefore say, Christ was really or carnally in the rock.

August. sup. Levit. Quæst. 57.

1 Cor. x.

Basil. de Pœnit.

Neither can I think M. Harding is such a deadly enemy unto figures as he would now seem to be. For he himself in these few words of Christ, touching the institution of this holy sacrament, as it shall be shewed hereafter more at large, is fain to seek help of sixteen or more sundry figures; and the same so strange, so gross, and so insensible, that neither St Augustine, nor St Hierome, nor any other old divine ever knew them, nor any good grammarian would allow them. So many, and such figures, it is lawful for him to devise and use, to maintain the falsehood; but for us, in defence of the truth, it may not be lawful to use one.

Verily the old catholic fathers were never so curious in this behalf, nor thought it such heresy, to expound Christ's words by a figure. Briefly for a taste hereof, St Augustine saith: [*Christus*] *adhibuit* [*Judam*] *ad convivium, in quo corporis et sanguinis sui figuram discipulis* [*suis*] *commendavit, et tradidit*[12]: "Christ received Judas to his banquet, wherein he gave unto his disciples the figure of his body and blood." Likewise Tertullian saith: [*Christus*] *acceptum panem, et distributum discipulis, corpus suum illum fecit, dicendo, Hoc est corpus meum, hoc est, figura corporis mei*[13]: "Christ, receiving the bread, and the same being divided unto

August. in Psal. iii.

Tertul. contra Marcion. Lib. iv.

[6 Nec putemus in verbis scripturarum esse evangelium; sed in sensu: non in superficie; sed in medulla.—Hieron. Op. Par. 1693-1706. Comm. Lib. I. in Epist. ad Gal. cap. i. Tom. IV. Pars I. col. 230.]

[7 Paul. in Corp. Jur. Civil. Amst. 1663. Digest. Lib. I. Tit. iii. 29. Tom. I. p. 78.]

[8 August. Op. Par. 1679-1700. Lib. de Fid. et Oper. cap. iv. 5. Tom. VI. col. 167.]

[9 Id. Quæst. in Hept. Lib. III. In Levit. Quæst. lvii. 3. Tom. III. Pars I. col. 516.]

[10 1565 omits *the*.]

[11 Basil. Op. Par. 1721-30. Hom. in Pœnit. Tom. II. p. 606. The Benedictine editor doubts the genuineness of this homily.]

[12 August. Op. Enarr. in Psalm. iii. 1. Tom. IV. col. 7.]

[13 Tertull. Op. Lut. 1641. Adv. Marcion. Lib. IV. 40. p. 571; where *illum suum fecit, Hoc est corpus meum dicendo, id est*.]

Figure. his disciples, made it his body, saying, 'This is my body,' that is to say, the figure of my body." St Ambrose saith: *Ante benedictionem verborum cælestium alia species nominatur: post consecrationem corpus [Christi] significatur*[1]: "Before the blessing of the heavenly words it is called another kind: after the consecration the body of Christ is signified." Here I must protest, that, as M. Harding is troubled with want of witness in this case, so am I oppressed with multitude. If I should allege all the rest of the ancient godly fathers that write the like, I should be over tedious to the reader. And another place, hereafter following, will serve more aptly to this purpose. But by the way, gentle reader, I must give thee to understand that St Augustine hereof writeth thus: *Ea demum est miserabilis animæ servitus, signa pro rebus accipere, et supra creaturam corpoream oculum mentis ad hauriendum æternum lumen levare non posse*[2]: "Indeed this is a miserable bondage of the soul to take the signs in the stead of things that be signified; and not to have power to lift up the eye of the mind above the bodily creature, to receive the light that is everlasting." And again: *In principio cavendum est, ne figuratam locutionem ad literam accipias. Et ad hoc enim pertinet, quod ait apostolus, Litera occidit; Spiritus autem vivificat. Cum enim figurate dictum sic accipitur, tanquam proprie dictum sit, carnaliter sapitur. Neque ulla mors animæ congruentius appellatur*[3]: "First of all, thou must beware that thou take not a figurative speech according to the letter. For thereunto also it appertaineth that the apostle saith, 'The letter killeth; the Spirit giveth life.' For, when the thing that is spoken in a figure is so taken as if it were plainly spoken (without figure), there is fleshly understanding; neither is there any death more fitly called the death of the soul." By these words, good reader, St Augustine stirreth up thy senses, to consider well what thou doest, lest perhaps thou be deceived.

Ambros. de illis qui initiantur Myst. cap. ultimo.

August. de Doct. Christ. Lib. iii. cap. v.

The bondage of the soul.

Ibidem.

The death of the soul.

And whereas M. Harding thus unjustly reporteth of us, that we maintain a naked figure and a bare sign or token only, and nothing else; if he be of God, he knoweth well he should not thus bestow his tongue or hand to bear false witness. It is written: "God will destroy them all that speak untruth." He knoweth well we feed not the people of God with bare signs and figures, but teach them that the sacraments of Christ be holy mysteries, and that in the ministration thereof Christ is set before us even as he was crucified upon the cross; and that therein we may behold the remission of our sins, and our reconciliation unto God; and, as Chrysostom briefly saith, "Christ's great benefit, and our salvation[4]." Herein we teach the people, not that a naked sign or token, but that Christ's body and blood indeed and verily is given unto us; that we verily eat it; that we verily drink it; that we verily be relieved and live by it; that we are bones of his bones, and flesh of his flesh; that Christ dwelleth in us, and we in him. Yet we say not, either that the substance of the bread or wine is done away; or that Christ's body is let down from heaven, or made really or fleshly present in the sacrament. We are taught, according to the doctrine of the old fathers, to lift up our hearts to heaven, and there to feed upon the Lamb of God. Chrysostom saith: "*Ad alta contendat oportet, qui ad hoc corpus accedit*[5]: "Whoso will reach to that body must mount on high." St Augustine likewise saith: *Quomodo tenebo absentem? Quomodo in cœlum manum mittam, ut ibi sedentem teneam? Fidem mitte, et tenuisti*[6]: "How shall I take hold of him, being absent? How shall I reach up my hand into heaven, and hold him sitting there? Send up thy faith, and thou hast taken him." Thus spiritually and with the mouth of our faith we eat the body of Christ and drink his blood, even as verily as his body was verily broken, and his blood verily shed upon the cross. And thus St Augustine, and St Chrysostom, and other holy fathers taught the people in their time

Deut. v. Exod. xx. Psal. v. Gal. iii. Rom. v.

Chrysost. ad Pop. Antioch. Hom. 60.

Eph. v. 1 John iv.

Sursum corda.

Chrysost. in 1 Cor. x Hom. 24.

August. in Joh. Tract. 50.

[1 Ambros. Op. Par. 1686-90. Lib. de Myst. cap. ix. 54. Tom. II. col. 339.]

[2 August. Op. Par. 1679-1700. De Doctr. Christ. Lib. III. cap. v. 9. Tom. III. Pars I. col. 47.]

[3 Id. ibid.]

[4 It is possible that the following passage may have been in the author's mind: ... hoc est enim bonorum caput, quoniam Filio suo non pepercit, ut servos alienatos salvaret. — Chrysost. Op. Lat. Basil. 1547. Ad Pop. Ant. Hom. lx. Tom. V. col. 398. See also Hom. lxi. col. 401; where, speaking of the blood of Christ in the sacrament, Chrysostom says: Hic est salus animarum nostrarum, &c.]

[5 Chrysost. Op. Par. 1718-38. In Epist. I. ad Cor. Hom. xxiv. Tom. X. p. 216.]

[6 August. Op. In Johan. Evang. cap. xi. Tractat. l. 4. Tom. III. Pars II. col. 630.]

to believe. Indeed the bread that we receive with our bodily mouths is an earthly thing, and therefore a figure, as the water in baptism is likewise also a figure; but the body of Christ that thereby is represented, and there is offered unto our faith, is the thing itself, and no figure. And in respect of the glory thereof, we have no regard unto the figure. Therefore St Bernard, alluding to the same, saith thus: *Annulus non valet quicquam:...hæreditas est quam quærebam*[7]: "The sealing-ring is nothing worth: it is the inheritance that I sought for."

Figure.

Bernard. de Cœna Domini.

1. To conclude, three things herein we must consider: first, that we put a difference between the sign and the thing itself that is signified.

2. Secondly, that we seek Christ above in heaven, and imagine not him to be present bodily upon the earth.

3. Thirdly, that the body of Christ is to be eaten by faith only, and none otherwise.

And in this last point appeareth a notable difference between us and M. Harding. For we place Christ in the heart, according to the doctrine of St Paul: M. Harding placeth him in the mouth. We say, Christ is eaten only by faith: M. Harding saith, he is eaten with the mouth and teeth. But, God's name be blessed! a great number of godly people doth already perceive the uncomfortable and unsavoury vanity of this doctrine. For they have learned of St Cyprian, that Christ's blessed body is *cibus mentis, non ventris*[8], "meat for the mind, not for the belly;" and they have heard St Augustine say: *Quid paras dentem et ventrem? Crede, et manducasti*[9]: "What preparest thou thy tooth and thy belly? Believe, and thou hast already eaten."

Eph. iii.

Now consider thou, good christian reader, with thyself[10], whether it be better to use this word "figure," which word hath been often used of Tertullian, St Augustine, and of all the rest of the ancient fathers, without controlment; or else these new-fangled words, "really," "corporally," "carnally," &c. Which words M. Harding is not able to shew that, in this case of being really in the sacrament, any one of all the old fathers ever used.

M. HARDING. THE SECOND DIVISION.

Again (128), *we cannot find where our Lord performed the promise he had*[11] *made in the sixth chapter of John, "The bread which I will give is my flesh, which I will give for the life of the world," but only in his last supper: where if he gave his flesh to his apostles, and that none other but the very same which he gave for the life of the world, it followeth that in the blessed sacrament is not mere bread, but that same his very body in substance. For it was not mere bread, but his very body, that was given and offered up upon the cross.*

The hundred and twenty-eighth untruth, joined with dangerous doctrine.

THE BISHOP OF SARISBURY.

This principle is not only false in itself, but also full of dangerous doctrine, and may soon lead to desperation. For if no man may eat the flesh of Christ, but only in the sacrament, as here by M. Harding it is supposed; then all christian children, and all others whosoever that depart this life without receiving the sacrament, must needs be damned, and die the children of God's anger. For Christ's words be plain and general: "Unless ye eat the flesh of the Son of man, ye shall have no life in you." Whereunto we may add this minor: Christian children receive not the sacrament; and therefore, by M. Harding's judgment, "eat not the flesh of the Son of man." Hereof it must needs follow, that christian children have no life in them, but are the children of damnation. This is the conclusion of M. Harding's doctrine. But little care these men who or how many perish, so their fantasies may stand upright. But our doctrine, grounded upon God's holy word, is this, that as certainly as Christ gave his body upon the cross, so certainly he giveth now the self-same body unto the faithful; and

John vi.

[7 Bernard. Op. Par. 1690. In Cœn. Dom. Serm. 2. Vol. I. Tom. III. col. 890.]

[8 Cypr. Op. Oxon. 1682. De Cœn. Dom. (Arnold.) p. 44. See before, page 141, note 11.]

[9 August. Op. In Johan. Evang. cap. vi. Tractat. xxv. 12 Tom. III. Pars II. col. 489.]

[10 Theeself, 1565.]

[11 1565, and H. A. 1564, omit *had*.]

Figure. that, not only in the ministration of the sacrament, as M. Harding untruly imagineth, but also at all times, whensoever we be able to say with St Paul, "I think I know nothing but Jesus Christ, and the same Christ crucified upon the cross." Therefore St Ambrose writeth thus: *Quid petis, O Judæe? ut tribuat tibi panem, quem dat omnibus, dat quotidie, dat semper*[1]: "O thou Jew, what desirest thou? That Christ should give thee bread? He giveth it to all men: he giveth it daily: he giveth it at all times." If it be true that St Ambrose saith, that Christ giveth that bread, which is his body, at all times, then is it false that M. Harding saith, that Christ performeth his promise, and giveth his body only at the ministration of the sacrament. And therefore St Augustine saith: *Non tantum in sacramento, sed etiam re ipsa comedunt corpus Christi*[2]: "They eat Christ's body, not only in the sacrament, but also in very deed." Here St Augustine saith, contrary to M. Harding's doctrine, that we eat Christ's body, not only in the sacrament, but also otherwise; yea, and so far he forceth this difference, that he maketh the eating of Christ's body in the sacrament to be one thing, and the very true eating thereof indeed to be another thing. Again, touching the fathers of the old law, he saith that Abraham, Moses, Aaron, and others, received the body of Christ truly and effectually, long time before that Christ either had received flesh of the blessed virgin, or had ordained the sacrament; and that even the self-same body that is received now of the faithful[3]. To be short, of christian children, and other faithful that never received the sacrament, he writeth thus: *Nulli est aliquatenus ambigendum, tunc unumquemque fidelium corporis sanguinisque Domini participem fieri, quando in baptismate efficitur membrum Christi, &c.*[4]: "No man may in any wise doubt, but that every faithful man is then made partaker of the body and blood of Christ, when in baptism he is made a member of Christ; and that he is not without the fellowship of that bread and of that cup, although, before he eat of that bread, and drink of that cup, he depart this world, being in the unity of Christ's body. For he is not made frustrate of the communion and benefit of that sacrament, while he findeth that thing which is signified by the sacrament." So far St Augustine. By these we may see, it is not all true that M. Harding so constantly avoucheth. If it might have pleased him to take advice of Beda, St Augustine, St Ambrose, and other godly fathers, he should soon have found that the faithful may otherwise eat Christ's body, and that verily and indeed, and not only in the sacrament.

1 Cor. ii.

Ambros. in Psal. cxviii. Serm. 18.

August de Civ. Lib. xxi. cap. xx.

Non solum.

August. de Util. Pœnit. cap. i. Manducaverunt eundem cibum quem nos.

August. in Serm. ad Inf. Citat. a Beda. 1 Cor. x.

Quando ipse hoc, quod illud sacramentum significat, invenit.

M. HARDING. THE THIRD DIVISION.

If the words spoken by Christ in St John of promise, that he performed in his holy supper, "The bread that I will give is my flesh," had been to be taken, not as they seem to mean, plainly and truly, but metaphorically, tropically, symbolically, and figuratively, so as the truth of our Lord's flesh be excluded, (129) *as our adversaries do understand them, then the Capernaites had not*[5] *any occasion at all of their great offence. Then should not they have had cause to murmur against Christ, as the evangelist sheweth: "The Jews," saith St John, "strove among themselves, saying, How can he give us his flesh to eat?" And much less his dear disciples, to whom he had shewed so many and so great miracles, to whom he had before declared so many parables, and so high secrets, should have had any occasion of offence. And doubtless, if Christ had meant they should eat but the sign or figure of his body, they would not have said,* Durus est hic sermo: *"This is a hard saying; and who can abide to hear it?" For then should they have done no greater thing, than they had done oftentimes before in eating the Easter lamb. And how could it seem a hard word or saying, if Christ had meant nothing else but this: The bread that I will give is a figure of my body, that shall cause you to remember me?*

The hundred and twenty-ninth untruth, joined with untrue report. For we understand these words of Christ's very flesh and blood.

Chap. vi.

[[1] Ambros. Op. Par. 1686-90. In Psalm. cxviii. Expos. Serm. xviii. 28. Tom. I. col. 1203.]

[[2] ... non solo sacramento, sed re ipsa manducaverunt corpus Christi.—August. Op. Par. 1679-1700. De Civ. Dei, Lib. XXI. cap. xx. Tom. VII. col. 639.]

[[3] Id. Serm. ccclii. De Util. Agend. Pœn. ii. cap. i. 3. Tom. V. cols. 1364, 5.]

[[4] Ven. Bed. Col. Agrip. 1612. Ad Cor. I. cap. x. Tom. VI. col. 365. See before, page 132, note 2.]

[[5] Had not had, H. A. 1564.]

Spiritual eating.

THE BISHOP OF SARISBURY.

This reason holdeth only of the ignorance of the Capernaites, and hangeth thus: The Capernaites mistook Christ's words, and understood not what he meant; *ergo*, Christ's body is really and carnally in the sacrament. And thus M. Harding, as his manner is, buildeth one error upon another.

For understanding hereof it shall be necessary, first, to open the very sense and meaning of Christ's words; next, to shew how perversely and grossly the Capernaites were deceived; and, last of all, to consider M. Harding's conclusion.

First of all, the Jews desired Christ to give them bread in the wilderness, as Moses had given before unto their fathers. Christ, to pull them from the gross and material cogitations of their bellies, promised them another kind of bread,
that should be spiritual, and last for ever. Thus he said unto them: "My Father John vi.
giveth you true bread from heaven. Whoso eateth of this bread shall live for ever." And that they might understand what he meant, he saith[6] further: "I am the bread that came from heaven. The bread that I will give you is my flesh, which I shall give for the life of the world." Thus he spake of the spiritual eating and digesting of his flesh in the hearts of the faithful. And so immediately after he opened his own mind. For when he saw the Jews, for that they understood him not, were offended, he said further unto them: "It is the Spirit that giveth life; the flesh profiteth nothing. The words that I speak are spirit and
life." Which words St Augustine in plain[7] sort expoundeth thus: *Spiritualiter* August. in Psal. xcviii.
intelligite, quod locutus sum. Non hoc corpus, quod videtis, manducaturi estis, et bibituri illum sanguinem, quem fusuri sunt, qui me crucifigent. Sacramentum aliquod vobis commendavi: spiritualiter intellectum vivificat vos[8]: "Understand ye spiritually that I have spoken. Ye shall not eat (with your bodily mouth) this body that you see; nor shall ye (with your bodily mouth) drink that blood which they shall shed, that shall crucify me. I give you a certain sacrament. The same being
spiritually understanded giveth you life." So saith St Basil: *Gustate, et videte, quo-* Basil. in Psal. xxxiii.
niam suavis est Dominus: "Taste ye, and see, that the Lord is gracious." And
further he saith: "We have oftentimes marked (in the scriptures), that the ἀνάγκη τὴν
inward powers of the mind have their names of the outward members of the ἡδονὴν...
body. Therefore, forasmuch as our Lord is the true bread, and his flesh the τοῦ ἄρτου διὰ γεύσε-
true food, it must needs be that the delectation and pleasure of the same be ως ἡμῖν
moved and caused within us by a spiritual kind of taste[9]." Again he saith: νοητῆς ἐγγίγνεσθαι.
"Further we say, that there is a certain spiritual mouth of the inner man, where- ἐστὶ μέν τι
with he is fed, receiving the word of life, which is the bread that came from καὶ νοητὸν στόμα τοῦ
heaven[10]." Likewise saith St Augustine: *Fides habet oculos suos*[11]: "Faith hath ἔνδον ἀν-
eyes of her own to see withal." Again: *Intus bibendo felix sum*[12]: "Happy am θρώπου. August.
I when I drink (in my heart) within." And again: *Panis... iste interioris hominis* Epist. 95.
quærit esuriem[13]: "This bread seeketh the hunger of the inner man." So saith August. in Johan. Tract. 26.
Leo: *Circa hoc corpus aquilæ sunt, quæ alis circumvolant spiritualibus*[14]: "About Ibidem.
this body be eagles, that flee about it with spiritual wings." So likewise Origen: De Consec. Dist. 2. In quibus.
Idcirco... et verum lumen dicitur, ut habeant oculi animæ, quo illuminentur: idcirco Origen. in
et verbum, ut habeant aures, quod audiant: et idcirco panis vitæ, ut habeat gustus Cant. Cantic. Hom. 2.

[6 Said, 1565, 1609.] [7 Plainer, 1565.]

[8 August. Op. In Psalm. xcviii. Enarr. 9. Tom. IV. col. 1066; where *vivificabit*.]

[9 Πολλαχοῦ τετηρήκαμεν, ὅτι τοῖς ἔξωθεν μέλεσιν ὁμωνύμως αἱ τῆς ψυχῆς προσαγορεύονται δυνάμεις. ἐπεὶ δὲ ἄρτος ἐστὶν ἀληθινὸς ὁ Κύριος ἡμῶν, καὶ ἡ σὰρξ αὐτοῦ ἀληθής ἐστι βρῶσις, ἀνάγκη κ.τ.λ.—Basil. Op. Par. 1721-30. Hom. in Psalm. xxxiii. Tom. I. pp. 148, 9.]

[10 Πρὸς δὴ τοῦτο λέγομεν, ὅτι ἐστὶ κ.τ.λ., ᾧ τρέφεται μεταλαμβάνων τοῦ λόγου τῆς ζωῆς, ὅς ἐστιν ἄρτος ἐκ τοῦ οὐρανοῦ καταβάς.—Id. ibid. p. 144.]

[11 It does not seem that the passage is in the epistle indicated. It may be found August. Op. Ad Consent. Epist. cxx. 8. Tom. II. col. 349; where *habet namque fides*.]

[12 Id. In Johan. Evang. cap. vi. Tractat. xxv. 17. Tom. III. Pars II. col. 493.]

[13 Id. ibid. Tractat. xxvi. 1. col. 494.]

[14 Leo in Corp. Jur. Canon. Lugd. 1624. Decret. Gratian. Decr. Tert. Pars, De Consecr. Dist. xxxviii. col. 1931; where *circumvolitant*. But the passage seems really to belong to Ambrose. See Op. Expos. Evang. sec. Luc. Lib. VIII. cap. xvii. 56. Tom. I. col. 1484.]

Spiritual eating.

animæ, quod degustet[1]: "Therefore is Christ called the light, that the eyes of the soul may have whereby they may be lightened: therefore he is called the word, that the ears of the soul may have what to hear; and therefore he is called the bread of life, that the sense of the soul may have what to taste." So Tertullian: *Auditu devorandus est, intellectu ruminandus, et fide digerendus*[2]: "Christ by hearing must be devoured, by understanding must be chewed, and by faith must be digested." In like sort Chrysostom: *Magnus iste panis, qui replet mentem,...non ventrem*[3]: "This is that great bread, that feedeth not the belly, but the mind." Therefore St Augustine saith: [*Christus*] *dixit, se* [*esse*] *panem qui de cœlo descendit, hortans ut credamus in ipsum. Credere enim in eum, hoc est manducare panem vivum*[4]: "Christ named himself the bread that came from heaven, exhorting us to believe in him. For believing in him is the eating of the bread of life."

Tertul. de Resur. Carn.

Chrysost. ex variis locis in Matt. Hom. 9.

August. in Johan. Tract. 26.

Hereby it is plain that Christ's meaning is spiritual, as Christ himself and all the old fathers and doctors of the church have expounded it; not real, carnal, gross, and fleshly, as M. Harding imagineth. M. Harding will say, that the eating with the mouth and the grinding with the teeth is a work spiritual. By this sense he is a good proctor for the Capernaites, and must needs say, that they had a spiritual understanding. Howbeit Chrysostom will not well suffer this evasion. His words be plain: *Quid est carnaliter intelligere? Simpliciter, ut res dicuntur; neque aliud quippiam cogitare*[5]: "What is it to understand carnally? It is to understand plainly, even as the things be uttered, and to think upon nothing else." Therefore St Augustine saith: *Figura est,... præcipiens passioni Domini communicandum* [*esse*], *et suaviter atque utiliter recondendum in memoria, quod Christus pro nobis mortuus sit*[6]: "The saying of Christ touching the eating of his flesh is a figure or manner of speech, commanding us to be partakers of Christ's passion, and with comfort and profit to lay up in our memory, that Christ hath suffered death for us." This, therefore, was Christ's meaning, and this is the very eating of his flesh.

Chrysost. in Johan. Hom. 47.

August. de Doct. Christ. Lib. iii. cap. xvi.

Now let us see what sense the Capernaites gathered hereof. Origen saith: *Accidit, ut simpliciores...nescientes distinguere,... quæ sint, quæ in scripturis divinis interiori homini, quæ... exteriori deputanda sint, vocabulorum similitudinibus falsi, ad ineptas quasdam fabulas et figmenta inania se contulerint*[7]: "It happeneth sometime that simple men, being not able to put difference between those things in the scriptures that pertain to the inner man, and those things that pertain to the outer[8] man, are deceived by the likeness of words, and so fall into foolish fables and vain fantasies." So saith St Hierome: *Cum seniores putentur in ecclesia et principes sacerdotum, simplicem sequendo literam occidunt Filium Dei*[9]: "Whereas they are taken for the elders in the church, and the chief of the priests, by following the plain letter, they kill the Son of God." Even thus it happened unto the Capernaites: that Christ spake spiritually of eating with faith, they understood grossly of eating with the teeth; as though they should swallow down his flesh into their bodies, as other meats[10]; even in such gross sort as M. Harding would now teach the people to eat Christ's body.

Orig. in Prol. in Cant. Cantic.

Hieron. Lib. iii. in Matt. cap. xvi.

August. in Johan. Tract. 11.

Tertullian openeth their error in this wise: *Durum et intolerabilem existimarunt sermonem ejus; quasi vere carnem suam illis edendam determinasset*[11]: "They thought his speech was hard and intolerable; as though he had determined to give them his flesh verily and indeed to be eaten" (with their mouths). Therein, saith Tertullian, stood their error.

Tertul. de Resur. Carn.

[[1] Orig. Op. Par. 1733-59. In Cantic. Canticor. Lib. II. Tom. III. p. 66; where *idcirco et panis*.]

[[2] ... devorandus auditu, et ruminandus intellectu, et &c.—Tertull. Op. Lut. 1641. De Resur. Carn. 37. p. 406.]

[[3] Chrysost. Op. Lat. Basil. 1547. Ex Matt. cap. v. De Orat. Domin. Hom. Tom. V. col. 716.]

[[4] August. Op. Par. 1679-1700. In Johan. Evang. cap. vi. Tractat. xxvi. 1. Tom. III. Pars II. col. 494; where *credamus in eum*.]

[[5] Chrysost. Op. Par. 1718-38. In Joan. Hom. xlvii. Tom. VIII. p. 278.]

[[6] August. Op. De Doctr. Christ. Lib. III. cap. xvi. 24. Tom. III. Pars I. col. 52; where *dominicæ*, and *pro nobis caro ejus crucifixa et vulnerata sit*.]

[[7] Orig. Op. Par. 1733-59. In Cantic. Canticor. Prolog. Tom. III. p. 28.] [[8] Utter, 1565.]

[[9] Hieron. Op. Par. 1693-1706. Comm. Lib. III. in Matt. cap. xvi. Tom. IV. Pars I. col. 75.]

[[10] August. Op. In Johan. Evang. cap. iii. Tractat. xi. 5. Tom. III. Pars II. col. 377.]

[[11] Tertull. Op. De Resur. Carn. 37. p. 406.]

Now, to consider M. Harding's guesses: first he saith: The Capernaites were offended with Christ's words; *ergo*, it is likely Christ meant, he would give his body really and carnally in the sacrament. First, Nicolas Lyra, M. Harding's own doctor, saith that "these words of Christ in the sixth of John pertain not unto the sacrament[12]." Again, it is but a simple guess to build religion upon an error. He might rather say thus: The Capernaites thought they should eat Christ's flesh really and fleshly with their mouths; but that was not Christ's meaning, as it well appeareth; for they were deceived; *ergo*, Christ meant not they should eat his flesh really and fleshly with their mouths. Nicol. Lyra in Psal. cx.

He addeth further: If Christ had meant he would give them only a figure of his body in his remembrance, there had been no cause why either the Capernaites or any other should be offended. Neither do we say that Christ, in the sixth chapter of John, speaking of the spiritual eating by faith, made mention of any figure, but only of his very flesh and very blood, indeed and verily to be eaten and drunken. Notwithstanding we say that Christ, afterward in his last supper, unto the same spiritual eating added also an outward sacrament, which of the old fathers is oftentimes and commonly called a figure. But hereof groweth M. Harding's error, for that, as Origen saith, "he putteth no difference between the body and the spirit, and things severally pertaining to them both[13]." The bread is a figure; but Christ's body is the thing itself, and no figure. The bread is in the earth; Christ's body is in heaven. The bread is subject to corruption; Christ's body is immortal, and glorious, and subject to no corruption. Therefore Rabanus Maurus saith: *Sacramentum... ore percipitur; virtute sacramenti interior homo satiatur. Sacramentum... in alimentum corporis redigitur; virtute...sacramenti æternam vitam adipiscimur*[14]*:* "The sacrament is received with the mouth; by the virtue of the sacrament the inner man is repaired. The sacrament is turned into the nourishing of the body; by the virtue of the sacrament we get everlasting life." And St Augustine saith: *Sacramentum... de mensa dominica sumitur, quibusdam ad vitam, quibusdam ad exitium: res vero ipsa, cujus sacramentum est, omni homini ad vitam, nulli ad exitium, quicunque ejus particeps fuerit*[15]*:* "The sacrament is received from the Lord's table, of some unto life, of some unto destruction: but the thing itself whereof it is a sacrament (that is, the body of Christ) is received of every man unto life, and of no man unto destruction, whosoever be partaker of it." Orig. in Prol. in Cant. Cantic. Raban. Maur. Lib. i. cap. xxxi. August. in Johan. Tract. 26.

M. HARDING. THE FOURTH DIVISION.

To conclude shortly: if Christ would so have been understanded, as though he had meant to give but a figure only of his body, it had been no need for him to have alleged his omnipotency and almighty power to his disciples, thereby the rather to bring them to belief of his true body to be given them to eat. Hoc vos scandalizat? *"Doth this offend you?" saith he. "What if you*[16] *see the Son of man ascend where he was before? It is the Spirit that giveth life," &c. As though he had said: Ye consider only my humanity, that seemeth weak and frail, neither do you esteem my divine power by the great miracles I have wrought. But when as ye shall see me by power of my Godhead ascend into heaven, from whence I came unto you, will you*[16] *then also stand in doubt whether ye may believe that I give you my very body to be eaten? Thus by signifying his divine power, Christ confounded their unbelief touching the verity and substance of his body, that he promised to give them in meat.* A simple proof. For Christ likewise sheweth his omnipotent power in the water of baptism.

[12 ... quia in eodem contextu litteræ declaratur: de qua manducatione et potatione intelligi debet, videlicet de spirituali.—Bibl. cum Gloss. Ord. et Expos. N. de Lyra, Basil. 1502. Psalm. cx. Repl. Pars III. fol. 254.]

[13 Orig. Op. In Cantic. Canticor. Prolog. Tom. III. p. 28. See the last page.]

[14 Raban. Maur. Op. Col. Agrip. 1626. De Inst. Cler. Lib. I. cap. xxxi. Tom. VI. p. 11; where *æternæ vitæ dignitas adipiscitur.*]

[15 August. Op. In Johan. Evang. cap. vi. Tractat. xxvi. 15. Tom. III. Pars II. col. 500.]

[16 Ye, H. A. 1564.]

THE BISHOP OF SARISBURY.

M. Harding wandereth still about his figures, and out of God's omnipotent power deviseth a very feeble argument. For thus he reasoneth:

Christ maketh mention of his ascension into heaven;

Ergo, his body is really in the sacrament.

He hath no just cause to be offended, for that I lay his logic thus abroad. It behoveth the reader to see by what force each thing is proved. Verily, if he conclude not thus, he runneth at riot, and concludeth nothing.

As touching Christ's ascension into heaven, St Augustine and other ancient fathers seem to use the same, to prove that there is no such gross presence in the sacrament. St Augustine thereof writeth thus: *Si ergo videritis Filium hominis ascendentem*[1], *&c.*: "'If you shall see the Son of man ascending up where he was before,' &c. And what is this? Hereby he openeth that thing wherewith they were offended. For they thought he would give them his body; but he told them that he would ascend into heaven, and that whole as he was. When ye shall see the Son of man ascend thither, where he was before, then shall you see that he giveth not his body in such sort as you imagine; then shall you perceive that his grace is not consumed or wasted by morsels."

August. in Johan. Tract. 27.

Illi enim putabant eum erogaturum corpus suum. Certe vel tunc intelligetis, quod gratia ejus non consumitur morsibus.

St Chrysostom saith, as it is before alleged: *Ad alta oportet eum contendere, qui ad hoc corpus accedit. Aquilarum, non graculorum, est hæc mensa*[2]: "He must mount on high, that will come to this body. For this table serveth for eagles, and not for jays." So saith St Hierome: *Ascendamus cum Domino [in] cœnaculum, magnum, stratum, et mundatum; et accipiamus ab eo sursum calicem novi testamenti*[3]: "Let us go up with the Lord (into heaven) into that great parlour, spread and clean; and let us receive of him above the cup of the new testament." The like might be alleged of other more catholic and ancient fathers. For Cyrillus saith in most plain words: *Sacramentum nostrum hominis manducationem non asserit, mentes credentium ad crassas cogitationes irreligiose inducens*[4]: "Our sacrament avoucheth not the eating of a man, leading the minds of the faithful in ungodly manner to gross (or fleshly) cogitations."

Chrysost. in 1 Cor. x. Hom. 24.

Hieron. ad Hedib. Quæst. 2.

Cyril. ad Object. Theod. Anath. 11. Ἀνθρωποφαγία.

Doubtless it seemeth to make very simple proofs[5] of M. Harding's side, to say thus:

Christ's body is ascended into heaven;

Ergo, the same body is really and fleshly in the sacrament.

But M. Harding will say: Christ, speaking to the Capernaites, made mention of his omnipotent power; therefore in the sacrament there must needs be a fleshly presence. First, as it is before alleged, Nicolas Lyra saith: "Christ's words to the Capernaites pertain nothing to the sacrament, but only unto the spiritual eating of Christ's body, which indeed is the omnipotent work of the Spirit of God[6]."

Nicol. Lyra in Psal. cx.

And again, would M. Harding make all the world believe, if Christ's body be not fleshly and grossly in the sacrament, according to his fantasy, that then God therefore is not omnipotent? Verily, the old catholic fathers acknowledge God's omnipotency in the water of baptism; yet is not Christ therefore really present in the water. St Chrysostom saith: *Cum baptizatis*[7], *sacerdos te non baptizat; sed Deus est, qui caput tuum invisibili potentia continet; et nec angelus, nec archangelus, nec ullus alius audet accedere et tangere*[8]: "When thou art baptized, it is not the

Chrysost. in Matt. Hom. 51.

[1 Si, &c. ubi erat prius? Quid est hoc? Hinc solvit quod illos moverat: hinc aperuit unde fuerant scandalizati ... Illi enim, &c., ille autem dixit se adscensurum in cœlum, utique integrum. Cum videritis Filium hominis adscendentem ubi erat prius; certe vel tunc videbitis, quia non eo modo quo putatis erogat corpus suum; certe, &c. quia, &c.—Id. ibid. Tractat. xxvii. 3. col. 502.]

[2 Chrysost. Op. Par. 1718-38. In Epist. I. ad Cor. Hom. xxiv. Tom. X. p. 216.]

[3 Hieron. Op. Par. 1693-1706. Ad Hedib. Epist. Quæst. ii. Tom. IV. Pars I. col. 172. See before, page 12, note 5.]

[4 Cyril. Alex. Op. Lut. 1638. Apolog. adv. Orient. Anath. xi. Def. Cyril. Tom. VI. p. 193.]

[5 Proof, 1565.]

[6 Bibl. cum Gloss. Ord. et Expos. N. de Lyra, Basil. 1502. Psalm. cx. Repl. Pars III. fol. 254. See before, page 453, note 12....quoniam eucharistia est opus Dei mirabilissimum.—Id. ibid. fol. 253.]

[7 Baptizaris, 1565.]

[8 Chrysost. Op. In Matt. Hom. l. Tom. VII. p. 517.]

priest that dippeth thee, but it is God, that by his invisible power holdeth thy head; and neither angel, nor archangel, nor any other power dareth to approach and touch thee." St Augustine saith: *Paulus baptizavit tanquam minister;...Dominus baptizavit tanquam potestas*[9]: "Paul baptized as a servant; the Lord baptized as the power itself." Again: *Nec...jam baptizare cessavit [Dominus]; sed adhuc id agit, non ministerio corporis, sed invisibili opere majestatis*[10]: "The Lord letteth not yet to baptize; but continueth baptizing still; not by the ministry of his body, but by the invisible work of his majesty." So likewise saith Leo the bishop of Rome: *[Christus] dedit aquæ, quod dedit matri. Virtus enim Altissimi et obumbratio Spiritus sancti, quæ fecit ut Maria pareret Salvatorem, eadem facit ut regeneret unda credentem*[11]: "Christ gave unto the water the same that he gave unto his mother. For the power of the Highest and the overshadowing of the Holy Ghost, that caused Mary to bear the Saviour, the same causeth that water doth regenerate the believer." It appeareth by these authorities, that Christ in the water of baptism sheweth his invisible and omnipotent power. Yet will not M. Harding say that Christ is therefore really and fleshly present in the water of baptism.

August. in Johan. Tract. 5.

August. contr. Lit. Petil. Lib. iii. cap. xlix.

Leo de Nativ. Serm. 4.

Therefore it was but vain labour to allege Christ's omnipotent power to prove this fleshly presence in the sacrament.

M. HARDING. THE FIFTH DIVISION.

[*What occasioned the fathers to use these terms, really, substantially, corporally, &c.* H. A. 1564.]

These places of the scripture, and many other reporting plainly that Christ at his supper gave to his disciples his very body, even that same which the day following suffered death on the cross, have ministered just cause to the (130) *godly and learned fathers of the church to say, that Christ's body is present in this sacrament really, substantially, corporally, carnally, and naturally. By use of which adverbs they have meant only a truth of being, and not a way or mean of being. And though this manner of speaking be not thus expressed in the scripture, yet is it deduced out of the scripture. For if Christ spake plainly,* (131) *and used no trope, figure, nor metaphor, as the scripture itself sufficiently declareth to an humble believer, and would his disciples to understand him, so as he spake in manifest terms when he said, "This is my body which is given for you;" then may we say, that in the sacrament his very body is present, yea, really, that is to say, indeed, substantially, that is, in substance, and corporally, carnally, and naturally; by which words is meant that his very body, his very flesh, and his very human nature, is there, not after corporal, carnal, or natural wise, but invisibly, unspeakably, miraculously, supernaturally, spiritually, divinely, and by way to him only known.*

The hundred and thirtieth untruth. For not one of the ancient fathers ever used any of these terms, touching Christ's presence in the sacrament.

The hundred and thirty-first untruth. For M. Harding himself is forced in the same words to acknowledge a great many figures.

THE BISHOP OF SARISBURY.

By these words that Christ at his last supper spake unto his disciples, "This is my body," it is plain, saith M. Harding, that he gave unto them the very same body that was crucified the next day upon the cross; and upon occasion thereof the learned fathers had just cause to say, that Christ's body is really and carnally in the sacrament. This argument is called *petitio principii*, which is, when a thing is taken to make proof that is doubtful, and standeth in question, and ought itself to be proved. This *fallax* may well beguile children; but among the learned it is counted in reasoning a great folly. The order or form hereof is naught; the antecedent unproved; the consequent false, as shall appear.

M. Harding saith these words, "This is my body," must needs be taken without metaphor, trope, or figure, even as the plain letter lieth, and none otherwise. So saith M. Harding only upon his own credit. But the old catholic doctors of the church, of whom, he saith, he hath such store, say not so. St Augustine, St

[9 Baptizavit ergo Paulus tamquam minister ... baptizavit autem Dominus tamquam potestas.—August. Op. Par. 1679-1700. In Johan. Evang. cap. i. Tractat. v. 7. Tom. III. Pars II. col. 323.]

[10 Id. Contr. Lit. Petil. Lib. III. cap. xlix. 59. Tom. IX. col. 327.]

[11 Leon. Magni Op. Lut. 1623. In Nativ. Serm. v. cap. v. col. 52.]

According to the letter.

Ambrose, St Hierome, St Chrysostom, St Basil, Tertullian, and others call the sacrament a figure, a token, a sign, an example, an image, a similitude, a remembrance; as hereafter, God willing, shall be shewed more at large upon better occasion, in an article specially touching the same. Even Duns himself, with sundry others of that side, saw that, following the very bare letter, we must needs say that "the bread itself is Christ's body[1]." For so the words stand: "This (bread) is my body:" which were a great inconvenience, and a repugnance in nature. For salving whereof they are driven to say that Christ, when he pointed to the bread, and said, "This," meant not "this bread," but, as they call it, *individuum vagum*, which is one certain thing in general; but what one thing, they cannot tell: but sure they be it was no bread. *Est* they expound *erit*, that is to say, "this shall be." Again, *erit, hoc est, transubstantiabitur*, that is, "the substance of this uncertain general one thing, that no man knoweth, shall be changed into the substance of my body." "Is given," they expound, "shall be given:" "is broken," they expound, "shall be broken:" "do ye this," they expound, "sacrifice ye this." "This bread," they expound thus, "this that was bread." And whereas these verbs stand together in order and construction, and rule all one case, *accepit, benedixit, fregit, dedit*, "he took, he blessed, he brake, he gave;" they are fain to shift it thus: "He took the bread; he blessed it away, and in place of it put another substance; he brake the accidents or shews of bread; he gave his body." Upon these few words of Christ thus many figures have they imagined; and besides these, a great many more, as in place more convenient it shall be declared: yet saith M. Harding, these words of Christ must of fine force be taken even according to the order and nature of the bare letter. "And this," he saith, "is sufficient to the humble believer." Howbeit, christian humility standeth not in error, but in truth; and St Augustine saith, as it is before alleged: *Ea demum est miserabilis animæ servitus, signa pro rebus accipere*[2]: "To take the signs instead of the things that thereby be signified is (not the humility of a christian faith, but) the miserable servitude of the soul." And Origen, that old learned father, saith: *Si...secundum literam sequaris id quod dictum est, Nisi manducaveritis carnem Filii hominis, non habebitis vitam in vobis, litera illa occidit*[3]: "If you follow these words of Christ according to the letter, 'Unless ye eat the flesh of the Son of man, ye shall have no life in you,' this letter killeth."

Hoc. Est. Erit. Traditur. Frangitur. Facite. Panis. Accepit. Benedixit. Fregit. Dedit.

August. de Doct. Christ. Lib. iii. cap. v.

Orig. Hom. 7. In Levit.

Upon these grounds of his own M. Harding reareth up this conclusion: "Then," saith he, "may we say, that Christ is in the sacrament really," &c. Indeed a man may say much, that hath no regard what he say. But if he will say, as the old godly fathers said, then must he say: *Hoc est corpus meum, hoc est, figura corporis mei*[4]: "This is my body, that is to say, a figure of my body." For so the old learned father Tertullian saith. Then must he say: [*Christus*] *corporis...sui figuram discipulis* [*suis*] *commendavit*[5]: "Christ delivered unto his disciples a figure of his body." For so the old learned father St Augustine saith. Then must he say: *Sacramentum corporis Christi secundum quendam modum corpus Christi est*[6]: "The sacrament of Christ's body after a certain phrase, or manner, or trope, or figure of speech, is the body of Christ." For so again St Augustine saith.

Tertull. contr. Marcion. Lib. iv.

August. in Psal. iii.

August. ad Bonifac. Epist. 23.

Here M. Harding, seeing the inconveniences and absurdities of his doctrine, thought good to heal it up with some plaister. By these words, really, carnally, &c., "the godly learned fathers," saith he, "meant that Christ's very body and flesh is there, but not in any natural or carnal wise." And thus M. Harding's doctors

---

[1 See Joan. Duns Scot. Op. Lugd. 1639. In Sentent. Lib. IV. Dist. viii. Quæst. 2. Dist. xi. Quæst. 3. Tom. VIII. pp. 422, 38, 606, 9, 16, 8, 9. Also Tom. XI. pp. 627, 8, 70.]

[2 August. Op. Par. 1679-1700. De Doctr. Christ. Lib. III. cap. v. 9. Tom. III. Pars I. col. 47.]

[3 Si enim secundum literam sequaris hoc ipsum quod dictum est, Nisi manducaveritis carnem meam ... occidit hæc litera.—Orig. Op. Par. 1733-59. In Levit. Hom. vii. Tom. II. p. 225.]

[4 Tertull. Op. Lut. 1641. Adv. Marcion. Lib. IV. 40. p. 571. See before, page 447, note 13.]

[5 August. Op. In Psalm. iii. Enarr. 1. Tom. IV. col. 7.]

[6 Id. ad Bonifac. Epist. xcviii. 9. Tom. II. col. 267; where the words *secundum quemdam modum* come first.]

wrote one thing, and meant another. For M. Harding knoweth that all adverbs, taken of nouns, signify evermore a quality, and never the substance; which thing children are taught to know in the grammar school; and may be resolved thus: *Viriliter, virili modo: muliebriter, muliebri modo.* And therefore his very canonists say in their manner of eloquence: *Deus non est remunerator nominum, sed adverbiorum:* "God rewardeth not nouns, but adverbs:" that is to say, God regardeth not the doing of any thing, but the manner of the doing. But M. Harding thinketh he may take upon him to overlook and to master the grammar rules. For unless we make nouns adverbs, and adverbs nouns, these men's divinity cannot stand. Therefore, as they have devised a new divinity, so must our children learn for their pleasure a new grammar.

Berengarius.

But what are these old learned fathers, that say Christ's body is thus really and fleshly in the sacrament? Where be their words? What be their names? If they have neither names nor words, how can they be allowed for sufficient witnesses? M. Harding well knoweth that the old learned fathers never said so: yet must he needs imagine both causes that moved them so to say, and also expositions, what they meant by so saying. So Montanus, the blind senator, being at supper with the emperor Tiberius, highly commended the great mullet, that he heard say was set on the table before them, and shewed how round, how fair, how fat it was, how it filled the charger, and how it lay, and evermore turned his face, and pointed with his finger to the higher end of the table; and yet was not the mullet there, but far beneath at the lower end[7]. Reason would that M. Harding had first been sure of the effect, before he had thus gone about to guess the causes.

M. HARDING. THE SIXTH DIVISION.

(132) *And the fathers have been driven to use these terms for the*[8] *more ample and full declaration of the truth, and also for withstanding and stopping objections made by heretics. And because the catholic faith, touching the verity of Christ's body in the sacrament, was not impugned by any man for the space of a thousand years after Christ's being in earth, and about that time* (133) *Berengarius first began openly to sow the wicked seed of the sacramentary heresy, which, then soon confuted by learned men, and by the same first author abjured and recanted, now is with no less wickedness, but more busily and more earnestly set forth again; the doctors, that sithence have written in the*[8] *defence of the true and catholic faith herein, have* (134) *more often used the terms before*[9] *mentioned, than the old and ancient fathers that wrote within M. Jewel's six hundred years after Christ; who doubtless would no less have used them, if that matter had been in question or doubt in their time. And albeit these terms were strange and new, as used within these five hundred years only, and that the people were never taught for six hundred years after Christ, as M. Jewel saith more boldly than truly, and therefore more rashly than wisely; yet the faith by them opened and declared is universal and old, verily no less old than is our Lord's supper, where this sacrament was first instituted.*

[*Berengarius.* H.A. 1564.]

The hundred and thirty-second untruth. For the fathers never used these terms.

The hundred and thirty-third untruth. For beside St Augustine, St Hierome, St Ambrose and others, Johan. Scotus and Bertramus wrote hereof 200 years before Berengarius.

The hundred and thirty-fourth untruth. For the old writers in this case used them never.

THE BISHOP OF SARISBURY.

M. Harding thinketh he may lead along his simple reader, and easily carry away the matter under the bare titles and names of the learned fathers. But what privy mystery is this? As I said before, have M. Harding's doctors no names? Or is not he able to name his own fathers? He should have set them out, as his wont is, with all their circumstances, what they were, when and where they lived, what they wrote, and how they have been ever and are now esteemed among the learned. But he well knew that these good fathers lived all within the compass of two hundred or three hundred years past, as Thomas, Duns, Ockam, Henricus de Gandavo, Robertus de Collo Torto, and such others. These be M. Harding's great fathers, by whom he claimeth his new

[7 Juv. Sat. iv. 119-21. The emperor was Domitian, and the blind flatterer Catullus.]

[8 H. A. 1564, omits *the*.]

[9 Afore, H. A. 1564.]

Berengarius.

doctrine; in respect of St Augustine, St Hierome, St Chrysostom, St Ambrose, and others, not worthy to have the name of children.

"But the catholic faith touching the sacrament," saith M. Harding, "for the space of a thousand years stood upright. Berengarius was the first that began to sow the seed of the sacramentary heresy." It is likely M. Harding hath no great regard how his tales hang together. For before, in the first article, to serve his turn, he said, the Messalians were the first fathers of this heresy[1]. Now he seemeth to be otherwise advised, and saith, this heresy was never heard of within six hundred years after the Messalians were repressed; and that the first founder of it was Berengarius. Yet M. Harding might soon have known that one Johannes Scotus[2], a famous learned man, and scholar unto Beda, and one Bertramus, as appeareth by his book, held and maintained the same doctrine in the time of the emperor Lotharius, two hundred years and more before Berengarius. Wherefore it seemeth not to be so true as M. Harding assureth it, that Berengarius was the first author of this doctrine.

The thirty-third division.

Johannes Scotus. Bertramus.

But, for further declaration hereof, it shall be necessary to open Berengarius' whole judgment in this matter, and afterward to consider the confutation of the same. Thus therefore Berengarius wrote, as his greatest adversary Lanfrancus reporteth of him: *Per consecrationem altaris panis et vinum fiunt sacramentum religionis: non ut desinant esse quæ erant, &c.*[3]: "By the consecration of the altar the bread and the wine are made a sacrament of religion, not that they leave to be the same they were before, but that 'they be altered into another thing,' and become that they were not before, as St Ambrose writeth. And the sacrifice of the church standeth of two things, the one visible, the other invisible; that is to say, the sacrament, and the matter or substance of the sacrament. Which substance notwithstanding, that is to say, the body of Christ, if it were before our eyes, it should be visible. But being taken up into heaven, and sitting at the right hand of the Father, until all things be restored, according to the words of the apostle St Peter, it cannot be called thence. Therefore St Augustine saith, 'When Christ is eaten, life is eaten; and when we eat him, we make no parts of him.' And again, St Augustine saith: *Sacramentum est sacrum signum:* 'A sacrament is a holy token.' And what this word *signum* meaneth, he declareth in his book, De Doctrina Christiana: *Signum est res præter speciem quam ingerit sensibus, aliud quiddam faciens in cogitationem venire:* 'A sign is a thing that, besides the sight that it offereth unto the eyes, causeth another thing to come into our mind.' Again, unto Bonifacius: 'Unless sacraments had some likeness of the things whereof they be sacraments, then were they no sacraments at all.' And again: 'Sacraments be visible signs of heavenly things; but the things themselves, being invisible, are honoured in them: neither is that element, being consecrate by the blessing, so to be taken, as it is in other uses.'" This is the judgment of Berengarius, agreeing thoroughly with the words and sense of the holy fathers, and confirmed and avouched by the same.

Lanfranc. de Sacram. Euchar.

Ambros. de Sacram. Lib. iv. cap. iv.

Sacramentum et res sacramenti.

Acts iii.

August. de Con. Dist. 2. Qui manducas.

August. de Doctr. Christ.

August. ad Bonifac. Epist. 23.

August. de Catech. Rudib.

Now let us see the confutation hereof. In a council holden at Rome under

[1 See before, page 188.]

[2 Scotus Erigena.]

[3 Per consecrationem altaris fiunt panis et vinum, &c., sed ut sint quæ erant, et in aliud commutentur, quod dicit beatus Ambrosius in libro de Sacramentis. [Ambros. Op. Par. 1686-90. De Sacram. Lib. IV. cap. iv. 15. Tom. II. col. 369.] ... Sacrificiumque ecclesiæ duobus constat, duobus conficitur, visibili sacramento et re sacramenti. Quæ tamen res, id est Christi corpus, si esset præ oculis, visibilis esset: sed elevata in cœlum, sedensque ad dexteram Patris usque in tempora restitutionis omnium, quod scribit apostolus Petrus, cœlo devocari non poterit ... Unde B. Augustinus in evangelio: Quando Christus manducatur, vita manducatur; nec quando manducamus, partes de illo facimus. [August. in Corp. Jur. Canon. Lugd. 1624. Decret. Gratian. Decr. Tert. Pars, De Consecr. Dist. ii. cans. 58, 75, cols. 1943, 55.] ... Unde beatus Augustinus in libro de Civitate Dei, Sacramentum, &c. [August. Op. Par. 1679-1700. De Civ. Dei, Lib. x. cap. v. Tom. VII. col. 241.] Signum diffinit in libro de Doctrina Christiana. Signum, &c. aliud aliquid ex se faciens, &c. [De Doctr. Christ. Lib. II. cap. i. 1. Tom. III. Pars I. col. 19.] ... Augustinus in epistola ad Bonifacium episcopum: Si sacramenta rerum, quarum sacramenta sunt, similitudinem non haberent, omnino sacramenta non essent. [Ad Bonifac. Epist. xcviii. 9. Tom. II. col. 267.] Idem de Cathechizandis Rudibus: Signacula quidem rerum divinarum sunt visibilia, sed res invisibiles in eis honorantur; nec sic habenda est species benedictione sanctificata, quemadmodum habetur in usu quolibet. [Lib. de Catech. Rud. cap. xxvi. 50. Tom. VI. col. 293.]—Lanfranc. De Euchar. Sacram. Lib. in Biblioth. Patr. per M. de la Bigne, Par. 1624. Tom. VI. cols. 197-200.]

pope Nicolas the second, Berengarius was forced to recant in this wise: [*Credo*] *corpus*... *Domini nostri Jesu Christi*... *sensualiter*,... [*et*] *in veritate, manibus sacerdotum tractari*, [*et*] *frangi, et fidelium dentibus atteri*[4]: "I believe that the body of our Lord Jesus Christ sensibly, and in very deed, is touched with the hands of the priests, and broken, and rent, and ground with the teeth of the faithful." This was the consent and judgment of that council. And what thinketh M. Harding of the same? Certainly the very rude gloss findeth fault herewithal, and giveth this warning thereof unto the reader: *Nisi sane intelligas verba Berengarii, &c.*[5]: "Unless you warily understand these words of Berengarius, you will fall into a greater heresy than ever he held any." Thus these fathers, by their own friend's confession, redress the less error by the greater; and in plain words in general council, by solemn way of recantation, profess a greater heresy than by their own judgment ever was defended by Berengarius.

Berengarius.

De Consecr. Dist. 2. Ego Berengar.

This is an horrible blasphemy.

Gloss. ibid.

Further, if this be indeed the catholic faith, as M. Harding would so fain have all the world to believe, and Bertramus and Johannes Scotus, both very famous and great learned men, wrote openly against it, with the good contentation of the world, and without the apparent controlment of any man, two hundred years or more before Berengarius was born; let him better advise himself, whether these words were truly, or boldly, or rashly, or wisely, with such affiance uttered and avouched of his side, that this his faith was never impugned by any man before the time of Berengarius.

But that M. Harding calleth the catholic faith is indeed a catholic error, the contrary whereof hath evermore been taught and defended by all the old learned catholic fathers, as may well appear by that is already, and hereafter shall be, alleged of their writings. Certainly they, that now condemn Berengarius for using the plain words and expositions of the old fathers, would as well condemn St Augustine, St Hierome, St Ambrose, and the rest, were it not for the credit and authority of their names.

"The doctors that have been sithence the time of Berengarius," saith M. Harding, "have more often used these terms, 'really,' 'carnally,' &c. than other old doctors within six hundred years after Christ." In these few words M. Harding hath handsomely conveyed in a great untruth: for this comparative, "more often," presupposeth the positive. Therefore the sense hereof must be this: The old doctors often used these terms, "really," "fleshly," &c. albeit not so often as others of the latter[6] years. But M. Harding knoweth this is untrue. For neither hath he here yet shewed, nor is he able to shew, that, in this case of the sacrament, any of these terms was ever used by any one of all the old ancient writers. Whereof we may well reason thus: The old catholic fathers, in treating of the substance of the sacrament, never used any of these words, "really," "carnally," &c. Therefore it is likely, they never taught the people to believe that Christ's body is present really and fleshly in the sacrament. Contrariwise, they in their sermons called the sacrament "a figure," "a sign," "a remembrance of Christ's body:" therefore it is likely, they would have the catholic people so to judge and believe of the sacrament.

M. HARDING. THE SEVENTH DIVISION.

Here, before that I bring in places of ancient fathers, reporting the same doctrine, and in like terms as the catholic church doth hold concerning this article, lest our opinion herein might happily appear over carnal and gross, I think it necessary briefly to declare what manner a true body and blood[7] *is in the sacrament. Christ in himself hath but one flesh and blood in substance, which his Godhead took of the virgin Mary once, and never afterward left it off. But this one flesh and blood, in respect of double quality, hath a double consideration. For at what time Christ lived here in earth among men, in the shape of*

[*The flesh and blood of Christ is of double consideration.* H. A. 1564.]

[4 Confess. Berengar. in Corp. Jur. Canon. Decret. Gratian. Decr. Tert. Pars, De Consecr. Dist. ii. can. 42. col. 1932.]

[5 Gloss. in eod. ibid.; which proceeds: in majorem incides hæresim, quam ipse habuit.]

[6 Later, 1565, 1609.]

[7 Blood of Christ, H. A. 1564.]

man, his flesh was thrall, and subject to the frailty of man's nature, sin and ignorance excepted. That flesh, being passible unto[1] *death, the soldiers at the procurement of the Jews crucified. And such manner blood was at his passion shed forth of his body, in sight of them which were then present. But, after that Christ rose again from the dead, his body from that time forward ever remaineth immortal, and lively, in danger no more of any infirmity or suffering, much less of death; but is become, by divine gifts and endowments, a spiritual and a divine body, as to whom the Godhead hath communicated divine and godly properties and excellencies, that been above all man's capacity of understanding. This flesh and body thus considered, which sundry doctors call* corpus spirituale, et deificatum, "*a spiritual, and a*[2] *deified body," is given to us in the blessed sacrament. This is*[3] *the doctrine of the church, uttered by St Hierome in his commentaries upon the epistle to the Ephesians, where he hath these words:* Dupliciter vero sanguis ... *Lib. i. cap. i.* et caro intelligitur, vel spiritualis illa atque divina, de qua ipse dixit, Caro mea vere est cibus, et sanguis meus vere est potus; et, Nisi manducaveritis carnem meam, et sanguinem meum biberitis, non habebitis vitam æternam; vel caro quæ crucifixa est, et sanguis, qui militis effusus est lancea[4]. *That is: "The blood and flesh of Christ is understanded two ways; either that it is that spiritual and divine flesh, of which he spake himself, 'My flesh is verily meat, and my blood is verily drink;' and, 'Except ye eat my flesh, and drink my blood, ye shall not have life in you;' or that flesh which was crucified, and that blood which was shed by piercing of the soldier's spear." And to the intent a man should not take this difference according to the substance of Christ's flesh and blood, but according to the quality only, St Hierome bringeth a similitude of our flesh, as of which it hath been in double respect said:* Juxta hanc divisionem et in sanctis etiam diversitas sanguinis et carnis accipitur; ut alia sit caro, quæ visura est salutare Dei, alia *Luke iii.* caro et sanguis[5], quæ regnum Dei non queant possidere[6]: "*According to this division, diversity of blood and flesh is to be understanded in saints also; so as there is one flesh which shall see the salvation of God, and another flesh and blood, which may not possess the kingdom of God." Which two states of flesh and blood seem (as it appeareth to the unlearned) quite contrary.*

But St Paul dissolveth this doubt, in the fifteenth chapter of his first epistle to the Corinthians, saying, that flesh of such sort as we bear about us in *1 Cor. xv.* *this life, earthly, mortal, frail, and burdenous to the soul, cannot possess the kingdom of God, because corruption shall not possess incorruption. But after resurrection we shall have a spiritual, glorious, incorruptible, and immortal flesh, and like in figure to the glorious body of Christ, as St Paul saith: "This corruptible body must put on incorruption, and this mortal, immortality." Then such flesh, or our flesh of that manner and sort, shall possess the kingdom of God, and shall behold God himself. And yet our flesh, now corruptible, and then incorruptible, is but one flesh in substance, but diverse in quality and property. Even so it is to be thought of our Lord's flesh, as is afore said. The due weighing of this difference giveth much light to this matter, and ought to stay many horrible blasphemies, wickedly uttered against this most blessed sacrament.*

THE BISHOP OF SARISBURY.

Here M. Harding much troubleth his head with a needless labour, and in the end concludeth against himself. For that the Son of God was made man, even like unto one of us, thrall and subject to the infirmities and miseries of this Psal. xxii. mortal life; and that, as he himself complaineth in the psalm, he seemed a vile worm and no man, the shame of the world, and the outcast of the people; and Eph. i. Phil. ii. that God the Father afterward advanced[7] him with glory, and set him at his right hand, above all powers and principalities, and gave him a name above all names, and endued him with a spiritual and a glorious body, and united the same unto

---

[[1] Until, H. A. 1564.]
[[2] H. A. 1564, omits *a*.] [[3] *Is*, omitted, 1611.]
[[4] Hieron. Op. Par. 1693-1706. Comm. Lib. I. in Epist. ad Ephes. cap. i. Tom. IV. Pars I. col. 328; where *vel caro et sanguis quæ crucifixa est et qui.*]
[[5] Sanguinis, 1611.]
[[6] Id. ibid.; where *ejus* for *etiam.*]
[[7] Avanced, 1565.]

the Godhead, and crowned him with honour and glory—all these things are known even unto babes and children, that have been godly brought up, and have learned the principles of their faith; and are so far from all doubt amongst us, that we believe Christ "shall transform our mortal bodies, and make them like unto the body of his glory." And therefore St Augustine saith: *Corpus Domini pro ipsa cœlesti habitatione cœlestem accepit mutationem: et hoc [nos] sperare in die ultimo jussi sumus. Ideo dicit apostolus,... qualis cœlestis, tales et cœlestes, id est, immortales, non solum animis, sed etiam corporibus*[8]: "The body of our Lord, according to that heavenly habitation, hath received an[9] heavenly change; and we ourselves are commanded at the last day to hope for the same. Therefore the apostle saith: 'As he is that is heavenly, so are they that are heavenly,' that is to say, immortal, and that not only in soul, but also in body." This is the comfortablest article of our belief; and therefore with us, and with all other faithful, it is out of all doubt and question.

Christ's body deified.

Phil. iii.

August. contr. Adimant. cap. xii.

1 Cor. xv.

Only Stephen Gardiner, who, for his constancy and fastness in his religion, would needs be called Constantius, hath given the world to understand by public writing, that Christ is not yet fully possessed in this glory. These be his words: *Tempus humilitatis Christi in conversatione visibili et terrena præstandæ plane præteriit: sed humilis dispensationis tempus eo usque manet, donec tradiderit regnum Deo [et] Patri*[10]: "The time of Christ's humility in visible and earthly conversation is undoubtedly past: but the time of the dispensation or service of his humility remaineth still, until he deliver up the kingdom unto God his Father." Thus one of them saith, Christ's body is deified and become God: another saith, it is yet still in the dispensation and service of humility, and therefore is not yet deified. It seemeth they be not yet well resolved of Christ's glory, how much or how little they may allow him. Neither indeed have they any certain direction to guide themselves herein; but only, as occasion is offered, to shift off objections, they are fain to take hold in any thing, true or false, to serve their turn. A man may well say unto them, as St Augustine sometime said unto the heretic Faustus Manicheus: *[Dices,] Hoc pro me facit: illud contra me. Tu es*[11] *ergo regula veritatis. Quicquid contra te fuerit, non est verum*[12]: "Thou wilt say, This thing is for me: that thing is against me. Then art thou the rule of truth. Whatsoever is against thee is not true."

Marc. Anton. Constant. Ad Object. 144.

August. contr. Faust. Manich. Lib. xi. cap. ii.

But to what end allegeth M. Harding the spiritual state of Christ's glorious body? Doth he not remember that the old heretic abbat Eutyches maintained his fantasies by the same, and was deceived? "Christ's body," said he, "is glorious; therefore it is changed into the very substance and nature of God, and hath now no shape or proportion of a body[13]." This is an old heresy, long sithence reproved by Leo, Gelasius, and other old fathers, and condemned by the council of Chalcedon; very much like unto this of M. Harding's, if it be not fully the same. We believe the body of Christ's[14] is endued with immortality, brightness, light, and glory: yet is it nevertheless the same body it was before. And therefore St Augustine saith: *Corpus Domini secundum substantiam etiam post resurrectionem caro appellata est*[15]: "The body of our Lord in respect of the substance of it, yea, after it is risen again, is called flesh." And again: *Dominus corpori suo immortalitatem dedit, naturam non abstulit*[16]: "The Lord gave to his body immortality; but he took not away the nature or substance of it."

Eutych. in Conc. Chal.

August. Retract. Lib. i. cap. xxii.

August. in Epist. 57. ad Dard.

And, notwithstanding certain of the old fathers call the body of Christ *corpus deificatum*, as M. Harding allegeth; yet it is not their meaning, that the same body, according to the natural signification and sound of that word, is changed

[8 Nam quoniam Domini nostri corpus...sic levatum est ... ut pro, &c. Ideo dixit, &c.—August. Op. Par. 1679-1700. Lib. contr. Adimant. cap. xii. 4. Tom. VIII. col. 125.]

[9 A, 1565.]

[10 Confut. Cavill. in Sacros. Euch. Sacr. Par. 1552. fol. 103.]

[11 Est, 1611.]

[12 August. Op. Contr. Faust. Lib. xi. cap. ii. Tom. VIII. col. 219; where *sonat* for *facit*.]

[13 The opinions of Eutyches may be found Flav. et Leon. Epistt. in Concil. Calched. Pars i. in Concil. Stud. Labb. et Cossart. Lut. Par. 1671-2. Tom. IV. cols. 13, &c. See below, page 481, note 5.]

[14 Christ, 1565, 1609.]

[15 ... substantiam, secundum quam Domini corpus etiam, &c.—August. Op. Retract. Lib. i. cap. xxii. 3. Tom. I. col. 33.]

[16 ... cui profecto [carni] immortalitatem, &c.—Id. Lib. ad Dard. seu Epist. clxxxvii. 10. Tom. II. col. 681.]

Christ's body deified.

and transformed into a divine nature, and made God, and so is no longer a natural body. For, as it is true that God was made man, even so, and in like sense, it is also true that man was made God, without any change of substance of either nature. And therefore the fathers say, Christ's body is deified, or made God, for that it is united in person and glory with the nature of God. To this purpose, although not altogether in like sense, St Augustine seemeth to say, that men are deified and made gods. Thus he writeth: *Homines dixit deos, et*[1] *gratia sua deificatos; non de substantia sua natos*[2]*:* "He called men gods, as being deified, and so made by his grace; but not as born so of his substance." So saith Dionysius: *Pontifex ipse mutatur in Deum*[3]*:* "The bishop himself is turned into God." Likewise St Cyprian calleth the scriptures *scripturas deificas*[4], "the scriptures that make men gods." And Clemens Alexandrinus saith: *Sacræ literæ nos deificant*[5]*:* "The holy scriptures make us gods." By these and other like words is meant, not that men are changed from their own natural substance, and indeed become gods, as the letter seemeth to import; but only that men are endued with godly virtues and qualities, and so made the children of God. And so Dionysius himself[6] saith: *Hæc mutatio nostri in Deum, est Dei in nobis similitudo, quantam capere natura potest*[7]*:* "This changing of us into God is the likeness or image of God within us, as far as nature can receive."

August. in Psal. xlix.

Dionys. de Eccles. Hierarch. cap. i. ἔχει θεωθῆναι.

Cypr. de Zel. et Livor. et Lib. ii. Epist. 8.

Clemens in Protrept.

Dionys. de Eccles. Hierarch. cap. i.

But St Hierome saith: "Christ's flesh hath double understanding, and may be taken either for his spiritual or divine flesh, or else for his mortal flesh, as it was crucified;" and is thought to make much for M. Harding. For answer hereunto, first of all, this one thing I pray thee, good reader, to consider, that St Hierome in that whole place speaketh not one word, neither of the sacrament, nor of any real or fleshly presence. Therefore M. Harding can have but very poor help hereof to prove his purpose. Only he expoundeth what St Paul meant by these words, "We have redemption by his blood:" and his meaning, as it appeareth by the whole drift of his words, is this, that the salvation, which we have in Christ, standeth not in that he was a mere natural man, as were Codrus, Decius, Curtius, or such others, that died for the safety and delivery of their countries; but in that his humanity was united and joined in one person with the nature of God. His words be these: *Quis iste, aiunt, tantus ac talis, qui possit pretio suo totum orbem redimere? Jesus Christus Filius Dei proprium sanguinem dedit, et nos de servitute eripiens libertate donavit. Et revera, si historiis gentilium credimus, quod Codrus, et Curtius, et Decii Mures pestilentias urbium, et fames, et bella suis mortibus represserint; quanto magis hoc in Dei Filio possibile judicandum est, quod cruore suo non urbem unam purgaverit, sed totum orbem*[8]*?* "They say, what was he, such a one, and so mighty, that by his price was able to redeem the whole world? Jesus Christ the Son of God gave his own blood, and, delivering us from bondage, hath made us free. And indeed, if we believe the heathen story[9], that Codrus, Curtius, and Decii Mures removed pestilences, famines, and wars from their cities by their death; how much more may we judge the same possible in the Son of God, that he by his blood hath purged, not only one city, but also the whole world!" Immediately after this follow the words that M. Harding hath here alleged: *Dupliciter vero, &c.:* "For the blood and flesh of Christ hath double understanding." By the whole course of these words thus going before, it is easy to perceive St Hierome's meaning: that is, that we have our salvation in Christ, and do eat him, and drink him, and live by him, not for that his flesh was mortal

Eph. i.

Hieron. ad Ephes. cap. i.

[1 Ex, 1565.]

[2 August. Op. Par. 1679-1700. In Psalm. xlix. Enarr. 2. Tom. IV. col. 444; where *ex gratia*.]

[3 ... *αὐτόν τε τὸν Ἱεράρχην ... θεωθῆναι.*—Dionys. Areop. Op. Antv. 1634. De Eccles. Hierarch. cap. i. 2. Tom. I. pp. 231, 2.]

[4 Cypr. Op. Oxon. 1682. De Zel. et Livor. p. 226; Id. ad Cornel. Epist. lii. p. 97. The expression in these places is *deifica disciplina*. But see the opinion of Crescens in the Council of Carthage, ibid. p. 232; where we find...*ex scripturis deificis*.]

[5 ... *τὰ ἱεροποιοῦντα καὶ θεοποιοῦντα γράμματα.*—Clement. Alex. Op. Oxon. 1715. Cohort. ad Gent. 9. Tom. I. p. 71.]

[6 Himself also, 1565.]

[7 *Ἡ δὲ θέωσίς ἐστιν ἡ πρὸς Θεὸν ὡς ἐφικτὸν ἀφομοίωσίς τε καὶ ἕνωσις.*—Dionys. Areop. De Eccles. Hierarch. cap. i. 3. Tom. I. p. 233.]

[8 Hieron. Op. Par. 1693-1706. Comm. Lib. I. in Epist. ad Ephes. cap. i. Tom. IV. Pars I. col. 328; where *et talis*, and *unam sed totum purgarit orbem*.]

[9 Stories, 1565.]

only, and crucified upon the cross; but for that it was spiritual and divine, that is to say, the flesh of the Son of God. And herein stood that great contention, that Cyrillus and other godly fathers had against Nestorius; as it is well known unto the learned. And therefore St Paul saith: "That I live now, I live in the flesh[10] of the Son of God." Christ's body deified. Gal. ii.

Therefore, notwithstanding St Augustine say, *Christus crucifixus est lac sugentibus, et cibus proficientibus*[11], "Christ crucified is milk unto the sucklings, and harder meat unto the strong;" and notwithstanding Angelomus say, "Christ's body is hay, whereby the gentiles are fed[12];" yet must both these, and also all other like places be taken, not of bare mortal flesh alone, but of the flesh of the Son of God; which St Hierome calleth divine and spiritual, for that it is personally and inseparably joined with the Godhead. August. in Johan. Tractat. 88. Angelom. in 1 Reg. cap. i.

Again, St Hierome's meaning is that the same flesh of Christ, being thus divine and spiritual, must also spiritually be received, and not in any such carnal or fleshly wise as it[13] is here imagined by M. Harding. For notwithstanding Christ's body be spiritual, yet is that no sufficient warrant to prove that therefore M. Harding's opinion is not, as he saith, over gross and carnal. For the Manichees and the Messalian heretics had gross and carnal imaginations of God himself, notwithstanding God be only spirit, and most spiritual. And therefore St Augustine saith of them: *Ecce ego.... derideo carnales homines, qui nondum possunt spiritualia cogitare*[14]: "Behold, I laugh to scorn these carnal and fleshly men, that are not yet able to conceive things spiritual." August. contr. Epist. Fund. cap. xxiii.

For proof hereof St Hierome himself saith: *De hac quidem hostia, quæ in Christi commemoratione mirabiliter fit, edere licet; de illa vero, quam Christus in ara crucis obtulit, secundum se nulli edere licet*[15]: "Of this oblation, which is marvellously made in the remembrance of Christ, it is lawful to eat; but of that oblation, which Christ offered upon the altar of the cross, according to itself (that is to say, in gross and fleshly manner) it is lawful for no man to eat." By these words St Hierome also sheweth a great difference between the sacrifice that is made in the remembrance of Christ, and the very sacrifice indeed that Christ made upon the cross. So St Chrysostom saith: *Si carnaliter quis accipiat, nihil lucratur*[16]: "If a man take it fleshly, he gaineth nothing." So likewise St Augustine saith, as it is alleged before: "It is a figure or form of speech, willing us to be partakers of Christ's passion, and comfortably to remember that Christ hath died for us[17]." This St Hierome calleth the eating of the divine and spiritual flesh of Christ. Therefore Clemens Alexandrinus saith, not only in like sense, but also in like form of words: *Duplex est sanguis Domini: alter carnalis, quo redempti sumus; alter spiritualis, quo uncti sumus. Et hoc est bibere Jesu sanguinem, participem esse incorruptionis Domini*[18]: "There are two sorts of Christ's blood: the one fleshly, wherewith we are redeemed; the other spiritual, wherewith we are anointed. And this is the drinking of the blood of Christ, to be partakers[19] of his immortality." In like sort St Augustine saith: *Judas Christum carnalem tradidit, tu spiritualem; furens evangelium sanctum flammis sacrilegis tradidisti*[20]: "Judas betrayed Christ carnal; but thou hast betrayed Christ spiritual: for in thy fury thou betrayedst the holy gospel to be burnt in wicked fire." Here St Augustine calleth Christ spiritual, for that the manner of the betraying was spiritual. Likewise that ancient father Clemens calleth Christ's blood spiritual, not in respect of difference in itself, but only in respect of the spiritual receiving. De Consecr. Dist. 2. De hac. Chrysost. in Johan. Hom. 47. August. de Doctr. Christ. Lib. iii. cap. xvi. Clement. Alex. in Pædag. Lib. ii. cap. ii. August. contr. Lit. Petil. Lib. ii. cap. viii.

[10 Now in the flesh I live in the faith, 1565.]

[11 Christus crucifixus...illis [parvulis] ergo tamquam lacteus potus; istis [capacioribus] tamquam solidus cibus.—August. Op. In Johan. Evang. cap. xvi. Tractat. lxxxviii. 2. Tom. III. Pars II. col. 739.]

[12 Herba ergo onagri est, hæc ipsa Mediatoris incarnatio, per quam ipsa gentilitas jam satiatur.—Angelom. Strom. in Lib. Reg. I. cap. i. in Mag. Biblioth. Vet. Patr. Col. Agrip. 1618-22. Tom. IX. p. 704.]

[13 1565 omits *it*.]

[14 August. Op. Lib. Contr. Epist. Manich. Fund. cap. xxiii. 25. Tom. VIII. col. 165.]

[15 Hieron. in Corp. Jur. Canon. Lugd. 1624. Decret. Gratian. Decr. Tert. Pars, De Consecr. Dist. ii. can. 76. col. 1955.]

[16 Chrysost. Op. Par. 1718-38. In Joan. Hom. xlvii. Tom. VIII. p. 278.]

[17 August. Op. De Doctr. Christ. Lib. III. cap. xvi. 24. Tom. III. Pars I. col. 52. See before, page 452.]

[18 Clement. Alex. Op. Pædag. Lib. II. cap. ii. Tom. I. p. 177.] [19 Partaker, 1565.]

[20 August. Op. Contr. Lit. Petil. Lib. II. cap. viii. 17. Tom. IX. col. 221; where *carnaliter tradidit*, and *spiritaliter furens*. They are the words of Petilian.]

Christ's body deified.

And I think M. Harding will not deny but these words of Clemens and Augustine, agreeing so near both in sense and phrase with the words of Hierome, may stand for sufficient exposition to the same. Certainly, as Christ's blood is not really or bloodily present to anoint us, so is it not really or bloodily present to nourish us: for this nourishing and this anointing are both spiritual. And therefore the old learned father Athanasius writeth thus: *Quomodo unum unius hominis corpus universo mundo sufficeret? quod, tanquam in illorum cogitationibus versatum, Christus commemorat. A quibus cogitationibus ut eos avocaret, quemadmodum paulo ante sui descensus e cœlis, ita nunc reditus sui in cœlum mentionem facit*[1]: "The Capernaites demanded, how one body of one man might suffice the whole world; which thing, as being in their cogitations, Christ calleth to remembrance. To remove them from which cogitations (of gross and fleshly eating), as he before made mention of his coming down from heaven, so now likewise he maketh mention of his repair again into heaven."

Athanas. de Pec. in Spirit. Sanct.

To conclude, once again, gentle reader, I must do thee to remember, that St Hierome in this whole place never spake one word, neither of any real or fleshly presence, nor of the sacrament. Yet notwithstanding, M. Harding, as though St Hierome had plainly and undoubtedly spoken of both, hereof gathereth his reason thus: St Hierome saith, We eat not the flesh of Christ that was crucified; *ergo*, Christ's flesh is really and fleshly in the sacrament. This argument is evident to the eye, and needeth no answer.

His reason would better have framed thus: St Hierome saith, We cannot eat the flesh of Christ that was crucified; *ergo*, we cannot really and carnally eat the flesh of Christ. Whereof it must necessarily follow, even by the authority that M. Harding hath here alleged, that Christ's body is not really and fleshly in the sacrament. Such relief hath M. Harding found in these words of St Hierome.

M. HARDING. THE EIGHTH DIVISION.

Now, whereas M. Jewel denieth that christian people were of old time taught to believe that Christ's body is really, substantially, corporally, carnally, or naturally in the sacrament, I do plainly affirm the contrary. Yet I acknowledge, that the learned fathers (135) *which have so taught would not thereby seem to make it here outwardly sensible or perceptible. For they confess all with St Chrysostom, that the thing which is here given us is not sensible, but that under visible signs invisible things be delivered unto us*[2]. *But they thought good* to use the aforesaid terms, to put away all doubt of the being of his very body in these holy mysteries, and to exclude the only imagination, fantasy, figure, sign, token, virtue, or signification thereof. For in such wise the sacramentaries have uttered their doctrine in this point, as they may seem by their manner of speaking and writing here to represent our Lord's body only, indeed being absent; as kings oftentimes are represented in a tragedy, or mean persons in a comedy. Verily, the manner and way by which it is here present, and given to us and received of us, is secret, not human ne natural; true for all that. And we do not attain it by sense, reason, or nature, but by faith. For which cause we do not over basely consider and attend the visible elements; but, as we are taught by the council of Nice, lifting up our mind and spirit, we behold by faith on that holy table put and laid* (*so for the better signification of the real presence their term soundeth*) *the Lamb of God that taketh away the sins of the world. And here, say they, we receive his precious body and blood* ἀληθῶς[3], *that is to say, verily and indeed: which is no otherwise nor less than this term really importeth.*

The hundred and thirty-fifth untruth. For the old fathers never taught us so.

* Another untruth, as afore.

Homil. 83. in Matth. et 60. ad Pop. Antioch.

Lifting up the mind. Behold by faith.

κεῖσθαι.

[1 Athanas. Op. Par. 1698. Epist. iv. ad Serapion. 19. Tom. I. Pars II. p. 710.]

[2 ...ἐν αἰσθητοῖς τὰ νοητά σοι παραδίδωσι.—Chrysost. Op. Par. 1718-38. In Matt. Hom. lxxxii. Tom. VII. p. 787. Op. Lat. Basil. 1547. Ad Pop. Ant. Hom. lx Tom. V. col. 395.]

[3 Ἐπὶ τῆς θείας τραπέζης πάλιν κἀνταῦθα μὴ τῷ προκειμένῳ ἄρτῳ καὶ τῷ ποτηρίῳ ταπεινῶς προσέχωμεν· ἀλλ' ὑψώσαντες ἡμῶν τὴν διάνοιαν, πίστει νοήσωμεν κεῖσθαι ἐπὶ τῆς ἱερᾶς ἐκείνης τραπέζης τὸν Ἀμνὸν τοῦ Θεοῦ, τὸν αἴροντα τὴν ἁμαρτίαν τοῦ κόσμου, ἀθύτως ὑπὸ τῶν ἱερέων θυόμενον· καὶ τὸ τίμιον αὐτοῦ σῶμα καὶ αἷμα ἀληθῶς λαμβάνοντας ἡμᾶς, πιστεύειν ταῦτα εἶναι τὰ τῆς ἡμετέρας ἀναστάσεως σύμβολα.—Gelas. Cyz. Hist. Concil. Nic. cap. xxx. in Concil. Stud. Labb. et Cossart. Lut. Par. 1671-2. Tom. II. col. 233.]

THE BISHOP OF SARISBURY.

Here M. Harding once again, as before, will teach us what the old fathers meant by those words that they never uttered. I trow, he hath some privy divination, that thus taketh upon him to know what men mean before they speak. Cicero saith: *Peritum esse necesse est eum, qui, silentium quid sit, intelligat*: "It must needs be some cunning fellow that understandeth what silence meaneth, and knoweth what they speak that speak nothing." He saith: "The fathers thought good to use the aforesaid term[4], to put away all doubt of the being of Christ's very body in these holy mysteries." Verily, this is a marvellous boldness, so often and with such confidence and countenance to say the old fathers used these terms, and yet not once to shew any one of them all that ever used them. It may be thought that he hath either too great affiance in himself, or too little regard unto his reader. As for this vain muster of names, of Chrysostom, Hilary, Gregory Nyssene, and Cyril, as it shall appear by the view, it helpeth him nothing. Cic. de Divin. 2.

The sacramentaries, saith M. Harding, utter their doctrine by these terms, figure, sign, token, signification, and virtue. I may not answer this discourtesy of talk with like discourtesy. Only I will say of these men, as St Augustine sometime said of the Arians: *Cum se tanta...voragine impietatis immergant, nos, tanquam opprobrio novi nominis, homousianos vocant,...quia contra illorum errorem homousion defendimus*[5]: "Whereas they have drowned themselves in such a dungeon of wickedness, now they call us homousians, to reproach us with a new name, because we defend the unity of the holy Trinity against their error." But if they be all sacramentaries that use these terms, then must St Augustine, St Hierome, St Chrysostom, St Ambrose, and all other the holy fathers that used the same, needs be condemned for sacramentaries. But if they be sacramentaries that shamefully abuse and corrupt the holy sacraments, then may M. Harding and his friends rightly be called sacramentaries. M. Harding addeth: "Chrysostom saith, In visible signs things invisible be delivered;" *ergo*, the body of Christ is really and fleshly in the sacrament. First, if M. Harding had well considered that whole homily, happily he would have charged Chrysostom himself with his sacramentary quarrel, as now he doth others. For, touching the sacrament, Chrysostom even there writeth thus: *Quando dicunt, Unde patet Christum fuisse immolatum? hæc afferentes mysteria ora ipsorum consuimus. Si enim mortuus Jesus non est, cujus symbolum ac signum hoc sacrificium est*[6]? "When they say, How may we know that Christ was offered? bringing forth these mysteries, we stop their mouths. For if Christ died not, whose sign and token is this sacrifice?" But to return to the matter: O how light occasions these men take to deceive the simple! M. Harding knoweth that Chrysostom speaketh not these words only of the sacrament of Christ's body, but also generally of all other mysteries. For he addeth immediately: *Sic et in baptismo per aquam, quæ res sensibilis est, donum illud conceditur. Quod autem in ea conficitur, regeneratio scilicet et renovatio, intelligibile quiddam est*[7]: "Even so in baptism the gift is granted by water, which is a thing sensible. But the regeneration and renovation that therein is wrought is a thing spiritual." Wherefore, if M. Harding upon occasion of these words will force his real and fleshly presence in the one sacrament, he must likewise force the same in the other. August. contr. Serm. Arian. cap. xxxvi. Chrysost. in Matt. Hom. 83.

And forasmuch as, these two sacraments being both of force like, these men, to advance[8] their fantasies in the one, by comparison so much abase the other; and specially for the better opening of Chrysostom's mind, I think it good briefly and by the way somewhat to touch what the old catholic fathers have written of God's invisible working in the sacrament of baptism. Dionysius generally of all mysteries writeth thus: *Angeli Deum, &c.*[9]: "The angels, being creatures spiritual, Dionys. Eccles. Hierarch. cap. i.

[4 Terms, 1565.]

[5 August. Op. Par. 1679-1700. Lib. contr. Serm. Arian. cap. xxxvi. 34. Tom. VIII. cols. 646, 7; where *quia contra eorum errorem Græco vocabulo ὁμοούσιον defendimus.*]

[6 Chrysost. Op. In Matt. Hom. lxxxii. Tom. VII. p. 783.]

[7 Id. ibid. p. 787.]

[8 Avance, 1565.]

[9 Αἱ μὲν, ὡς νόες, νοῦσι [Θεόν τε καὶ θείαν

Laid on the table. so far forth as it is lawful for them, behold God and his godly power. But we are led as we may, by sensible outward tokens (which he calleth images), unto the contemplation of heavenly things." The fathers in the council of Nice say thus: Concil. Nic. πλήρη τοῦ θείου πυρὸς νόει τὰ ὕδατα. "Baptism must be considered not with our bodily eyes, but with the eyes of our mind. Thou seest the water: think thou of the power of God that in the water is hidden. Think thou that the water is full of heavenly fire, and of the sanctification of the Holy Ghost[1]." Chrysostom, speaking likewise of baptism, saith Chrysost. in 1 Cor. cap. ii. Hom. 7. thus: *Ego non aspectu judico ea, quæ videntur, sed mentis oculis, &c.*[2]: "The things that I see I judge not by sight, but by the eyes of my mind. The heathen, when he heareth the water of baptism, taketh it only for plain water; but I Ego non simpliciter video, quod video. see not simply or barely that I see: I see the cleansing of the soul by the Spirit Nazianz. de Sanct. Baptis. of God." So likewise saith Nazianzenus: *Mysterium (baptismi) majus est, quam* μεῖζον τῶν ὁρωμένων ἐστὶ τὸ μυστήριον. *ea quæ videntur*[3]: "The mystery of baptism is greater than it appeareth to the eye." So St Ambrose: *Aliud est, quod visibiliter agitur; aliud, quod invisibiliter celebratur*[4]: "In baptism there is one thing done visibly to the eye: another Ambros. de Spirit. Sanct. Lib. iii. cap. xi. thing is wrought invisibly to the mind." Again he saith: *Ne solis corporis tui oculis credas: magis videtur, quod non videtur, &c.*[5]: "Believe not only the[6] bodily Ambros. de his qui initiantur Myst. cap. iii. eyes (in this sacrament of baptism): the thing that is not seen is better seen: the thing that thou seest is corruptible; the thing that thou seest not is for ever." Tertull. de Baptism. To be short, in consideration of these invisible effects Tertullian saith: "The Basil. de Sanct. Baptism. Holy Ghost cometh down, and halloweth the water[7]." St Basil saith: "The kingdom of heaven is there set open[8]." Chrysostom saith: "God himself in Chrysost. in Matt. Hom. 51. baptism by his invisible power holdeth thy head[9]." St Ambrose saith: "The Ambros. de Sacram. Lib. i. cap. v. water hath the grace of Christ: in it is the presence of the Trinity[10]." St Bernard saith: *Lavemur in sanguine ejus*[11]: "Let us be washed in his blood."

Bernard. sup. Missus est Gabriel. Serm. 3. By the authorities of thus many ancient fathers it is plain that, in the sacrament of baptism, by the sensible sign of water the invisible grace of God is given unto us. Wherefore, as M. Harding by force of Chrysostom's words proveth his fleshly presence in the one sacrament, so may he by the force of the same words as well prove that the power of God, the heavenly fire, the grace, and the blood of Christ is really and fleshly present in the other.

All this notwithstanding, he hopeth to find some help in two words, uttered, κεῖσθαι. ἀληθῶς. as he saith, in the council of Nice, κεῖσθαι and ἀληθῶς; one of which words, either of forgetfulness or of purpose, he hath devised and set to of himself. For as this whole Greek authority, alleged here by M. Harding, was never found in the old allowed Nicene council, but only hath been sought out and published of late years; even so this word κεῖσθαι was never found in the Greek[12], neither De Euchar. Lib. i. as it is commonly set abroad, nor as it is alleged by D. Cuthbert Tonstal[13].

ἀρετὴν] κατὰ τὸ αὐταῖς θεμιτόν· ἡμεῖς δὲ αἰσθηταῖς εἰκόσιν ἐπὶ τὰς θείας, ὡς δυνατόν, ἀναγόμεθα θεωρίας.—Dionys. Areop. Op. Antv. 1634. De Eccles. Hierarch. cap. i. 2. Tom. I. p. 232.]

[1 Τὸ βάπτισμα ἡμῶν οὐ τοῖς αἰσθητοῖς ὀφθαλμοῖς κατανοητέον, ἀλλὰ τοῖς νοεροῖς. ὕδωρ ὁρᾷς, νόησον τὴν ἐν τοῖς ὕδασι κρυπτομένην τοῦ Θεοῦ δύναμιν·...πλήρη τοῦ ἁγιασμοῦ τοῦ Πνεύματος καὶ τοῦ θείου, κ.τ.λ.—Gelas. Cyz. Hist. Concil. Nic. cap. xxx. in Concil. Stud. Labb. et Cossart. Lut. Par. 1671-2. Tom. II. p. 233.]

[2 Ἀκούων λουτρὸν ἐκεῖνος [ὁ ἄπιστος] ἁπλῶς ὕδωρ νομίζει· ἐγὼ δὲ οὐ τὸ ὁρώμενον ἁπλῶς βλέπω, ἀλλὰ τὸν τῆς ψυχῆς καθαρμὸν τὸν διὰ τοῦ Πνεύματος...οὐ γὰρ τῇ ὄψει κρίνω τὰ φαινόμενα, ἀλλὰ τοῖς ὀφθαλμοῖς τῆς διανοίας.—Chrysost. Op. Par. 1718-38. In Epist. I. ad Cor. Hom. vii. Tom. X. p. 51.]

[3 Gregor. Nazianz. Op. Par. 1778-1840. In Sanct. Baptism. Orat. xl. 25. Tom. I. p. 711.]

[4 Perhaps the following may be the passage intended: Alterum igitur invisibile, alterum visibile testimonium sacramento consequimur spiritali.—Ambros. Op. Par. 1686-90. De Spirit. Sanct. Lib. III. cap. x. 68. Tom. II. col. 678.]

[5 Non ergo solis corporis tui credas oculis: magis videtur quod non videtur; quia istud temporale, illud æternum adspicitur, quod oculis non comprehenditur.—Id. Lib. de Myst. cap. iii. 15. Tom. II. col. 328.]

[6 Thy, 1565, 1609.]

[7 Supervenit enim statim Spiritus de cœlis, et aquis superest, sanctificans eas de semetipso.—Tertull. Op. Lut. 1641. De Baptism. 4. p. 257.]

[8 Βασιλεία οὐρανῶν ἤνοικται.—Basil. Op. Par. 1721-30. Hom. in Sanct. Baptism. Tom. II. p. 114.]

[9 Chrysost. Op. In Matt. Hom. l. Tom. VII. p. 517.]

[10 ...aqua sanat, quæ habet gratiam Christi... sanctificetur fons, et adsit præsentia Trinitatis æternæ.—Ambros. Op. De Sacram. Lib. II. cap. v. 15, 8. Tom. II. col. 352, 3.]

[11 Bernard. Op. Par. 1690. Sup. Missus est, Hom. iii. 14. Vol. I. Tom. III. col. 748.]

[12 It appears as given in Labbe and Cossart. See before, page 464, note 3.]

[13 Tonst. De Verit. Corp. et Sang. Dom. in Euchar. Lut. 1554. Lib. I. fol. 40.]

But let it be lawful for M. Harding to use some corruption, and to do in this place as he commonly doth in other, the better to furnish out the matter. Yet must this word κεῖσθαι, which signifieth "to be set" or "placed," needs sound a real presence? Or when St Paul saith, *Christus habitat in cordibus nostris per fidem*, "Christ dwelleth in our hearts by faith;" must he needs mean that Christ is really and fleshly placed within our hearts? Verily, St Hierome, writing unto Marcella of the holy grave, wherein Christ's body sometime was laid, hath these words: *Quoties ingredimur in sepulchrum Domini, toties jacere in sindone cernimus Salvatorem*[14]: "As often as we enter into the sepulchre of the[15] Lord, so often we see our Saviour lying in his shroud." And in the council of Chalcedon it is written thus: *In qua scriptura duæ naturæ jacent*[16]? "In what scripture lie these two natures of Christ?" Here is the self-same word that M. Harding hath added of his own to the council of Nice. Yet, I think, he will not therefore say that either the two natures of Christ are really contained in the scriptures, or the very body of Christ lieth still shrouded fleshly and really in the grave. Again, this word κεῖσθαι, which signifieth "to be laid" or "placed," in the natural signification requireth both situation of place, and also a bodily description, and order of parts. But M. Harding himself in the next article following saith: "Christ's body is not here by local presence, either by filling or by changing of place;" therefore it followeth that Christ's body is not laid on the table by any natural or fleshly presence.

Laid on the table.

Eph. iii.

Hieron. ad Marcell.

Concil. Chalced. Act. 1. κεῖνται.

In the next Article, Division 1.

The words of the council of Nice only withdraw us from the natural and visible elements of the bread and the wine, and require our inner spiritual sight, and the contemplation of the mind. The words be plain: *Ne proposito pani et poculo humiliter intenti simus*[17]: "That we consider not basely the bread and the wine that are set before us." And therefore St Augustine saith: *In sacramentis fidelium dicitur, Sursum corda*[18]: "In the sacraments of the faithful it is said, 'Lift up your hearts.'" By which words we are put in remembrance that there is nothing in the action to be considered, but only Christ the Lamb of God, that hath taken away the sins of the world. And therefore Chrysostom saith: "We must become eagles, and soar above, if we list to come near to that body[19]." Thus with the spiritual eyes of our hearts we see the Lamb of God. And as St Ambrose saith: *Magis videtur quod non videtur*[20]: "The thing is better seen that (with our bodily eyes) is not seen." For the same cause St Augustine saith: *In sacramentis videndum est, non quid sint, sed quid ostendant. Signa enim rerum sunt, aliud existentia, et aliud significantia*[21]: "In sacraments we must consider not what they be indeed, but what they represent. For they are tokens of things, being one thing in themselves[22], and signifying another." And as touching our beholding of Christ in the sacrament, in most plain wise he writeth thus: *Sic nos facit moveri, tanquam videamus præsentem Dominum in cruce*[23]: "It worketh such motions in us, as if we saw our Lord himself present upon the cross." And this is it that Eusebius Emissenus writeth, as he is alleged of Gratian, *ut coleretur jugiter per mysterium;... et perennis illa victima viveret in memoria, et semper præsens esset in gratia*[24]: "that the body (that was once offered for our price) should evermore be worshipped by a mystery; and that that everlasting sacrifice should live in remembrance, and be present in grace for ever." In this spiritual

τῷ προκειμένῳ ἄρτῳ, καὶ τῷ ποτηρίῳ.

August. de Bono Persev.

Chrysost. 1 Cor. Hom. 24.

Ambros. de his qui init. Myst. cap. iii.

August. contr. Max. Lib. iii. cap. xxii.

De Consecr. Dist. 2. Semel Christus. Et in Psal. xx.

De Consecr. Dist. 2. Quia corpus.

[14 Quod quotiesquumque ingredimur, toties, &c.—Hieron. Op. Par. 1693-1706. Paul. et Eustoch. ad Marcell. Epist. xliv. Tom. IV. Pars II. col. 548.]

[15 Our, 1565, 1609.]

[16 Ὅτι ἐν ποίᾳ γραφῇ κεῖται, δύο φύσεις;—Concil. Constant. Act. VI. in Concil. Calched. Act. I. in Concil. Stud. Labb. et Cossart. Tom. IV. col. 213.]

[17 Gelas. Cyz. Hist. Concil. Nic. cap. xxx. in Concil. Stud. Labb. et Cossart. Tom. II. col. 233. See before, page 464, note 3.]

[18 August. Op. Par. 1679-1700. De Don. Persev. cap. xiv. 33. Tom. X. col. 839; where *ut sursum cor habeamus*.]

[19 Chrysost. Op. In Epist. I. ad Cor. Hom. xxiv. Tom. X. p. 216.]

[20 Ambros. Op. Lib. de Myst. cap. iii. 15. Tom. II. col. 328.]

[21 Hæc enim sacramenta sunt, in quibus non quid sint, sed quid ostendant semper adtenditur: quoniam signa sunt rerum, aliud, &c.—August. Op. Contr. Max. Arian. Lib. II. cap. xxii. 3. Tom. VIII. col. 725.]

[22 Themself, 1565.]

[23 Id. in Corp. Jur. Canon. Lugd. 1624. Decret. Gratian. Decr. Tert. Pars, De Consecr. Dist. ii. can. 51. col. 1938; where *videamus in cruce pendentem Dominum*. Op. In Psalm. xxi. Enarr. ii. 1. Tom. IV. col. 93.]

[24 Euseb. Emiss. in eod. ibid. can. 35. col. 1927; where *victima illa*.]

Laid on the table. sort is Christ laid present upon the table; but not in M. Harding's gross and fleshly manner. And therefore St Augustine saith in like sense unto the faithful communicants: *Vos estis in mensa,.....vos estis in calice*[1]: "You are upon the table, you are in the cup." As St Augustine saith the people is laid upon the table, even so, and none otherwise, the council of Nice saith the Lamb of God is laid upon the table.

August. in Serm. ad Infant. citat. a Bed. in 1 Cor. x.

ἀληθῶς. The other Greek word that M. Harding holdeth by is ἀληθῶς, which is, "verily" or "truly;" and that in his judgment soundeth no less than really or fleshly. And thus, although he hunt like a wanton spaniel, and range at riot, and beat up butterflies, yet at the last he thinketh he hath found somewhat. Howbeit, I marvel he seeth no better his own error. For he might soon have known that these two words "truly" and "fleshly" have sundry meanings; and that, in the sense that Christ spake unto the Jews, the one of them doth utterly exclude the other. For neither doth he that eateth grossly and sensibly with his teeth eat "truly" and "verily," as Christ meant; nor doth he that eateth spiritually with his faith eat grossly and fleshly, as the Capernaites meant. Therefore it is great folly to say, "verily" and "fleshly" are all one thing. Indeed, the spiritual eating of Christ's body by faith is the true eating; and he that eateth the same most spiritually eateth most truly. Otherwise Christ saith: *Ego sum vitis vera:* "I am the true vine." St Hierome calleth the faithful people *vitem veram*[2], "the true vine." Cyrillus calleth Christ *verum manna*[3], "the true manna." St Hierome saith: *Nos vere sumus unus*[4] *panis*[5]: "We are verily one bread." Origen saith: *Apostoli vere erant cœli*[6]: "The apostles verily were the heavens." And to be short, they were wont to sing at the blessing of the paschal taper: *Hæc sunt ... festa paschalia, in quibus vere ... Agnus occiditur*[7]: "This is the paschal feast, wherein verily and indeed the Lamb is slain." By these few examples, both the difference between these two words "truly" and "fleshly," and also the slenderness of M. Harding's collection, may soon appear. For, notwithstanding we do verily eat Christ, yet it followeth not that we do grossly and naturally eat him with our bodily mouths; and, although Christ be verily meat, yet it followeth not that he is therefore really and fleshly in the sacrament. And therefore St Augustine in this respect utterly removeth the natural office of the body. His words be plain: *Quid paras dentem aut ventrem? Crede, et manducasti*[8]: "What preparest thou thy tooth or thy belly? Believe, and thou hast eaten." Again: *Credere in eum, hoc est manducare panem vivum*[9]: "Believing in him is the eating of the bread of life."

John xv. Hieron. in ii. cap. Hier. Lib. i. Cyril. Lib. iii. cap. xxiv. in Johan. Hieron. ad Gal. cap. iv. Orig. in Gen. cap. i. Hom. i. In Manuali. August. in Johan. Tractat. 26.

M. HARDING. THE NINTH DIVISION.

The hundred and thirty-sixth untruth. For these terms are not all one.

And touching these terms; first, verily, or (136) *which is all one, really and substantially, methinketh M. Jewel should bear the more with us for use of the same, sith that Bucer himself, one of the greatest learned men of that side, hath allowed them; yea, and that after much writing against Luther in defence of Zwinglius and Œcolampadius by him set forth, and after that he had assured himself of the truth in this article by divine inspiration; as most constantly he affirmeth with these words:* Hæc non dubitamus divinitus nobis et per scripturam revelata de hoc sacramento: *"We doubt not," saith he, "but these things, concerning the*[10] *sacrament, be revealed unto us from God, and by the scripture." If you demand where this may be found, in the acts of a council holden between the Lutherans and Zwinglians for this very purpose in Martin Luther's house at Wittenberg, in the year of our Lord* 1536, *you shall find these words:* Audivimus D. Bucerum explicantem

In responsione ad Luther.

[1 Ven. Bed. Op. Col. Agrip. 1612. Ad Cor. I. cap. X. Tom. VI. col. 365. See August. Op. Par. 1679-1700. Serm. ccxxix. Tom. V. col. 976.]

[2 ... ut vitis electa vel vera sit.—Hieron. Op. Par. 1693-1706. Comm. Lib. I. in Jer. Proph. cap. ii. Tom. III. col. 537.]

[3 Cyril. Alex. Op. Lut. 1638. Comm. in Joan. Evang. Lib. III. cap. vi. Tom. IV. p. 319.]

[4 Vnis, 1565.]

[5 Vere in Christo omnes unus panis sumus.—Hieron. Op. Comm. Lib. II. in Epist. ad Gal. cap. iv. Tom. IV. Pars I. col. 265.]

[6 ... apostoli qui erant cœli.—Orig. Op. Par. 1733-59. In Gen. Hom. i. Tom. II. p. 57.]

[7 Missal. ad Us. ac Consuet. Sar. Par. 1527. Bened. Cer. Paschal. fol. 92.]

[8 August. Op. In Johan. Evang. cap. vi. Tractat. xxv. 12. Tom. III. Pars II. col. 489; where *dentes*.]

[9 Id. ibid. Tractat. xxvi. 1. col. 494.]

[10 This, 1565, and H. A. 1564.]

suam sententiam de sacramento corporis et sanguinis Domini, hoc modo: Cum pane et vino vere et substantialiter adest, exhibetur, &c.[11] sumitur corpus Christi, et sanguis. Et sacramentali unione panis est corpus Christi; et porrecto pane, vere adest, et vere exhibetur corpus Christi[12]: "*We have heard M. Bucer declaring*[13] *his mind touching the sacrament of the body and blood of our Lord, in this sort: With the bread and wine the body of Christ and his blood is present, exhibited and received verily and substantially. And by sacramental union the bread is the body of Christ; and, the bread being given, the body of Christ is verily present and verily delivered.*"

Though this opinion of Bucer, by which he recanted[14] *his former Zwinglian heresy, be in sundry points false and heretical, yet in this he agreeth with the catholic church against M. Jewel's negative assertion, that the body and blood of Christ is present in the sacrament verily, that is, truly and really, or indeed and substantially;* (137) *wherein he speaketh as the ancient fathers spake long before, a thousand years past.*

The hundred and thirty-seventh untruth. For the ancient fathers in this matter of the sacrament spake not so.

THE BISHOP OF SARISBURY.

Hitherto M. Harding hath alleged neither ancient doctor nor old council to serve his purpose. The first that he can find is Doctor Bucer, that died in Cambridge the fourth year of king Edward the sixth, in the year of our Lord 1551. Of his judgment herein I will say nothing. What reasons led him to yield to the other side for quietness' sake, I remit it wholly unto God. But thus much I may well and justly say: If M. Harding could have found any other doctor, he would not thus have made his entry with M. Bucer.

Touching that brotherly and sober conference that was between D. Luther and D. Bucer, Philip Melancthon, and other godly-learned men of Germany in the university of Wittenberg, I see no great cause why M. Harding should thus sport himself with it, and call it a council. He might rather and more justly have scoffed at the vain council of the eight special chosen cardinals holden in Rome under pope Paulus the third, Anno Domini 1538[15], two years after that conference at Wittenberg. For if he will compare voices, they of Wittenberg were more in number; if knowledge, they were better learned; if purposes, they sought peace in truth, and the glory of God; if issue, God hath blessed their doings, and given force and increase unto his word, as it appeareth this day. His holy name be praised therefore for ever! But these eight picked cardinals, after great study and long debating of the matter, espied out only such faults as every child might have soon found without study; and yet never redressed any of the same.

Concil. Select. Card. Romæ, Anno 1538.

If master Harding had been in the apostles' times, perhaps he would have made some sport at their councils. For where or in what house assembled they together? What bishop or Pharisee was among them? Certainly St Augustine had conference and disputation with Pascentius the Arian at Hippo in the private house of one Anitius[16], and yet was never scoffed at for his doing. Thus there be ever some that laugh and scorn at the repairing of Hierusalem. Origen saith: *Inimici veritatis... videntes sine philosophia consurgere muros evangelii,... cum irrisione... dicunt, Hoc facile posse destrui calliditate sermonum,* [*et*] *per astutas fallacias*[17]: "The enemies of the truth, seeing the walls of the gospel rise without worldly policy, say scornfully among themselves, All this by our crafty speech and falsehood will soon be overthrown." But he that sitteth in heaven will laugh them to scorn.

August. Epist. 178. in Dom. Anit.

Orig. in Cant. Cantic. Hom. 4.

[11 Et, 1565, and H. A. 1564.]

[12 Audiamus D. Bucerum explicantem suam... sententiam de sacramento corporis et sanguinis Jesu Christi, hoc modo...cum pane et vino vere et substantialiter adesse, exhiberi et sumi corpus Christi et sanguinem...sacramentali unione panem esse corpus Christi, hoc est....porrecto pane simul adesse, et vere exhiberi corpus Christi.—Seckendorf. Comm. Hist. de Lutheranism. Lips. 1694. Lib. III. sect. xv. 47. Addit. p. 132.]

[13 Declare, H. A. 1564.]

[14 Received, 1609, 1611.]

[15 Crabb. Concil. Col. Agrip. 1551. Tom. III. pp. 819, &c.]

[16 August. Op. Alterc. cum Pascent. seu Epist. xx. Tom. II. Append. cols. 41, &c.]

[17 Orig. Op. In Cant. Canticor. Lib. IV. Tom. III. p. 93; where *absque arte grammatica et peritia philosophica,* and *perfacile hoc posse destrui.*]

M. HARDING. THE TENTH DIVISION.

Let Chrysostom for proof of this be instead of many that might be alleged. His words be these: Nos secum in unam, ut ita dicam, massam reducit, neque id fide solum, sed re ipsa corpus[1] suum efficit[2]: "*By this sacrament,*" *saith he,* "*Christ reduceth us, as it were, into one lump with himself, and that not by faith only, but he maketh us his own body in very deed,*" re ipsa, *which is no other to say than* "*really.*" **The other adverbs, corporally, carnally, naturally, be found in the fathers not seldom, specially where they dispute against the Arians. And therefore it had been*[3] *more convenient for M. Jewel to have modestly interpreted them, than utterly to have denied them. The old fathers of the Greek and Latin church deny that faithful people have an habitude or disposition, union or conjunction with Christ only by faith and charity, or that we are spiritually joined and united to him only by hope, love, religion, obedience, and will. Yea, further they affirm, that by the virtue and efficacy of this sacrament duly and worthily received Christ is really and indeed communicated by true communication, and participation of the nature and substance of his body and blood, and that he is and dwelleth in us truly, because of our receiving the same in this sacrament. The benefit whereof is such as we be in Christ and Christ in us, according to that he saith:* Qui manducat meam carnem, manet in me, et ego in illo: "*Who eateth my flesh, he dwelleth in me, and I in him.*" *The which dwelling, union, and joining together of him with us, and of us with him, that it might the better be expressed and recommended unto us, they thought good in their writings to use the aforesaid adverbs.*

In xxvi. cap. Matt. Homil. 83.

Christ maketh himself one with us, not with the sacrament.

* Untruth, as afore.

For[4] they proved the same by the sacrament of baptism, by faith, by the birth of Christ, &c.

[John vi. 1565, and H.A. 1564.]

Hilarius, writing against the Arians, alleging the words of Christ, 17th John, Ut omnes unum sint, sicut tu, Pater, in me, et ego in te, ut et ipsi in nobis unum sint; "*That all*[5] *may be one, as thou, Father, art in me, and I in thee, they also may be one in us,*" *going about by those words to shew that the Son and the Father were not one in nature and substance, but only in concord and unity of will; among other many and long sentences for proof of unity in substance, both between Christ and the Father, and also between Christ and us, hath these words:* Si enim vere Verbum caro factum est, et nos vere Verbum carnem cibo dominico sumimus, quomodo non naturaliter manere in nobis existimandus est, qui et naturam carnis nostræ jam inseparabilem sibi homo natus assumpsit, et naturam carnis suæ ad naturam æternitatis sub sacramento nobis communicandæ carnis admiscuit?[6] "*If the Word be made flesh verily, and we receive the Word being flesh in our Lord's meat verily; how is it*[7] *to be thought not to dwell in us naturally, who both hath taken the nature of our flesh now inseparable to himself, in that he is born man, and also hath mingled the nature of his own flesh to the nature of his everlastingness under the sacrament of his flesh to be received of us in the communion?*" *There afterward this word* naturaliter, *in this sense, that by the sacrament worthily received Christ is in us and we in Christ naturally, that is, in truth of nature, is sundry times put and rehearsed. Whoso listeth to read further his eighth book* De Trinitate, *he shall find him agnise,* *manentem in nobis carnaliter Filium[8], *that* "*the Son of God (through the sacrament) dwelleth in us carnally,*" *that is, in truth of flesh; and that by the same sacrament we with him and he with us are united and knit together* corporaliter et inseparabiliter, "*corporally and inseparably;*" *for they be his very words.*

[De Trinitate, Lib. viii. 1565, and H.A. 1564.]

St Hilary saith Christ dwelleth naturally in us, but not in the sacrament.

* Not in the sacrament, but in us.

Gregory Nyssene, speaking to this purpose, saith: Panis qui de cœlo descendit, ... non incorporea quædam res est. Quo enim pacto res incorporea corpori cibus fiet? Res vero quæ incorporea non est, corpus omnino est. Hujus corporis panem non aratio, non satio, non agricolarum opus efficit[9]: sed terra intacta permansit; et tamen pane plena fuit, quo famescentes, mysterium

In Lib. de Vita Mosis.

[1 Nos corpus, H. A. 1564.]

[2 Chrysost. Op. Par. 1718-38. In Matt. Hom. lxxxii. Tom. VII. p. 788. The qualification, however, *ut ita dicam,* has nothing corresponding to it in the Greek text, nor is it found Op. Lat. Basil. 1547. In cap. Matt. xxvi. Hom. lxxxiii. Tom. II. col. 670.]

[3 Be, H. A. 1564.] [4 1565 omits *for.*]

[5 That they all, H. A. 1564.]

[6 Hilar. Op. Par. 1693. De Trin. Lib. VIII. 13. cols. 954, 5; where *vere nos verbum.*]

[7 He, H. A. 1564.] [8 Id. ibid. 17. col. 957.]

[9 Effecit, 1565, and H. A. 1564.]

virginis perdocti, facile saturantur[10]: (138) *which words report so plainly the truth of Christ's body in the sacrament, as all manner of figure and signification must be excluded. And thus they may be Englished: "The bread that came down from heaven is not a bodiless thing. For by what mean shall a bodiless thing be made meat to a body? And the thing which is not bodiless is a body, without doubt. It is not earing*[11]*, nor*[12] *sowing, not the work of tillers, that hath brought forth the bread of this body; but the earth which remained untouched, and yet was full of the bread, whereof they that wax hungry, being thoroughly taught the mystery of the virgin, soon have their fill." Of these words may easily be inferred a conclusion, that in the sacrament is Christ, and that in the same we receive him corporally, that is, in verity and substance of his body; forasmuch as that is there, and that is of us received, which was brought forth and born of the virgin Mary.*

The hundred and thirty-eighth untruth. For Gregory Nyssenus in this place speaketh not one word of the sacrament.

In Johan. Lib. x. cap. xiii.

Cyrillus, that ancient father and worthy bishop of Alexandria, for confirmation of the catholic faith in this point, saith thus: Non... negamus recta nos fide caritateque sincera Christo spiritualiter conjungi: sed nullam nobis conjunctionis rationem secundum carnem cum illo esse, id profecto pernegamus, idque a divinis scripturis omnino alienum dicimus[13]: "*We deny not but that we are joined spiritually with Christ, by right faith and pure charity; but that we have no manner of joining with him according to the flesh* (*which is one as to say* carnaliter, '*carnally*') *that we utterly deny*[14]*, and say, that it is not agreeable with the scriptures." Again, lest any man should think this joining of us and Christ together to be* (139) *by other means than by the participation of his body in the sacrament, in the same place afterward he saith further:* An fortassis putat ignotam nobis mysticæ benedictionis virtutem esse? Quæ cum in nobis fiat, nonne corporaliter quoque facit communicatione corporis Christi Christum in nobis habitare[15]? "*What, troweth this Arian heretic perhaps that we know not the virtue of the mystical blessing,* (*whereby is meant this sacrament*)*? which when it is become to be in us, doth it not cause Christ to dwell in us corporally by receiving of Christ's body in the communion?" And after this he saith as plainly that Christ is in us,* non habitudine solum, quæ per caritatem intelligitur... verumetiam et participatione naturali[16]; "*not by charity only, but also by natural participation.*"

The hundred and thirty-ninth untruth. For Christ dwelleth in us, and we are incorporate into him by baptism, &c. as shall appear.

In us.

The same Cyril saith in another place, that through the holy communion of Christ's body we are joined to him in natural union: Quis enim eos, qui unius sancti corporis unione in uno Christo uniti sunt, ab hac naturali unione alienos putabit[17]? "*Who will think,*" *saith he,* "*that they, which be united together by the union of that one holy body in one Christ, be not of this natural union?" He calleth this also a corporal union in the same book, and at length after large discussion how we be united unto*[18] *Christ, not only by charity and obedience of religion, but also in substance, concludeth thus:* Sed de unione corporali satis: "*But we have treated enough of the corporal union." Yet afterward in divers sentences he useth these adverbs* (140) *for declaring of the verity of Christ's body in the sacrament,* naturaliter, substantialiter, secundum carnem, *or* carnaliter, corporaliter, *as most manifestly in the twenty-seventh chapter of the same book:* Corporaliter... Filius per benedictionem mysticam nobis ut homo unitur, spiritualiter autem ut Deus[19]: "*The Son of God is united unto us corporally as man, and spiritually as God.*"

Lib. in Johan. xi. cap. xxvi.

The hundred and fortieth untruth. For here is not one word of presence in the sacrament.

Again, whereas he saith there: Filium... Dei natura Patri unitum corporaliter substantialiterque... accipientes, clarificamur, glorificamurque[20], &c.: "*We, re-*

[10 Gregor. Nyss. Op. Par. 1638. De Vit. Mos. Tom. I. p. 214.] [11 Earing: ploughing.]

[12 Not, 1565, 1609, and H. A. 1564.]

[13 Cyril. Alex. Op. Lut. 1638. Comm. in Joan. Evang. Lib. x. cap. ii. Tom. IV. p. 862.]

[14 Deny utterly, H. A. 1564.]

[15 Λεγέτω γάρ τις ἡμῖν τὴν αἰτίαν, καὶ διδασκέτω παρελθὼν τῆς μυστικῆς εὐλογίας τὴν δύναμιν. γίνεται γὰρ ἐν ἡμῖν διατί; ἆρ' οὐχὶ καὶ σωματικῶς ἡμῖν ἐνοικίζουσα τὸν Χριστὸν τῇ μεθέξει καὶ κοινωνίᾳ τῆς ἁγίας αὐτοῦ σαρκός;—Id. ibid.]

[16 Ἐν γὰρ δὴ τούτῳ μάλιστα κατιδεῖν ἄξιον, ὡς οὐ κατὰ σχέσιν τινὰ μόνην, τὴν ἐν διαθέσει νοουμένην, ἐν ἡμῖν ἔσεσθαί φησιν ὁ Χριστὸς, ἀλλὰ καὶ κατὰ μέθεξιν [φυσικὴν] ἤτοι φυσικήν.—Id. ibid. p. 860.]

[17 Id. ibid. Lib. XI. cap. xi. pp. 998, 9.]

[18 To, H. A. 1564.]

[19 Id. ibid. cap. xii. p. 1001.]

[20 Id. ibid. p. 1002. See also Lib. XII. pp. 1104, 5. It may be observed that these quotations seem to have been made from the Latin version. See therefore Op. Insig. Cyril. Alex. in Evang. Joan. a G. Trapezont. traduct. Par. 1508. Lib. X. cap. xiii. fol. 151; Lib. XI. cap. xxvi. fol. 181. cap. xxvii. fol. 182; Lib. XII. cap. lviii. fol. 216; where in the second quotation *communicatione carnis Christi.*]

Christ dwelleth in us.

ceiving the Son of God, united to the Father by nature corporally and substantially, are clarified and glorified, or made glorious, being made partakers of the supreme nature." *The like saying he hath* Lib. xii. cap. 58. *Now this being and remaining of Christ in us, and of us in Christ naturally and carnally, and this uniting of us and Christ together corporally, presupposeth a participation of his very body,* (141) *which body we cannot truly participate but in this blessed sacrament. And therefore Christ is in the sacrament naturally, carnally, corporally, that is to say, according to the truth of his nature, of his flesh, and of his body.* (142) *For were not he so in the sacrament, we could not be joined unto him, nor he and we could not be joined and united together corporally.*

The hundred and forty-first untruth, joined with pernicious and dangerous doctrine.

The hundred and forty-second untruth. For Christ is likewise joined corporally to us by the sacrament of baptism.

Divers other ancient fathers have used the like manner of speech; but none so much as Hilarius and Cyrillus; (143) *whereby they understand that Christ is present in the*[1] *sacrament, as we have said, according to the truth of his substance, of his nature, of his flesh, of his body and blood.*

The hundred and forty-third untruth. For they neither understand so, nor write so.

THE BISHOP OF SARISBURY.

Now at the last M. Harding draweth near the matter, and bringeth forth the old fathers with these very terms, "really," "substantially," "corporally," "carnally," &c. and allegeth these few, as he saith, instead of many, having indeed no more to bring. And although these fathers speak not any one word that is either denied by us or any wise serveth to this purpose, yet he cunningly leadeth away the eyes of the ignorant with the shew of old names, and, like a juggler, changeth the natural countenance of things, and maketh them appear what him listeth.

For whereas he hath taken in hand to prove that Christ's body is really and fleshly in the sacrament, he, finding his weakness and want therein, altereth the whole case, and proveth that Christ's body is really, fleshly, and naturally within us. But this matter was not in question, and therefore needeth[2] no proof at all. Herein standeth the whole guile; and thus the simple is deceived. To this end M. Harding so useth the words and witness of these holy fathers, as Cacus the outlaw sometime used Hercules' kine[3]: because he cannot handsomely drive them forward, he taketh them by the tails, and pulleth them backward.

But because M. Harding will hereof reason thus, If Christ's body by mean of the sacrament be really and carnally in us, it is likely the same body is also really and carnally in the sacrament: for answer hereunto, it shall be necessary first to understand how many ways Christ's body dwelleth in our bodies, and thereby afterward to view M. Harding's reason. Four special means there be whereby Christ dwelleth in us and we in him: his nativity, whereby he embraced us; our faith, whereby we embrace him; the sacrament of baptism; and the sacrament of his body. By every of these means Christ's body dwelleth in our bodies; and that not by way of imagination, or by figure or fantasy; but really, naturally, substantially, fleshly, and indeed.

Bernard. de Epiph. Serm. i.

And touching Christ's nativity, St Bernard saith: [*Corpus Christi*] *de meo est, et meum est: parvulus enim natus est nobis, et filius datus est nobis*[4]*:* "The body of Christ is of my body, and is now become mine; for a Babe is born unto us, and a Son is given unto us." So saith St Basil: *Participes facti sumus Verbi et Sapientiæ per incarnationem et sensibilem vitam. Carnem enim et sanguinem appellavit omnem illam mysticam conversationem*[5]*:* "We are partakers of the Word and of the Wisdom (which is Christ) by his incarnation, and by his sensible life. For flesh and blood he called all his mystical conversation." *So saith Gregorius Nyssenus: *Corpus Christi ... est omnis humana natura, cui admixtus est*[6]*:* "His body is all mankind, whereunto he is mingled." And thus Christ, being in the womb of the blessed virgin, became flesh of our flesh, and bone of our bones. And in that sense St John saith: *Verbum caro factum est, et habitavit in nobis:* "The Word was made flesh, and dwelt in us." And therefore Christ calleth him-

Basil. in Apol. ad Cæsar. σάρκα γὰρ καὶ αἷμα πᾶσαν... τὴν μυστικὴν ἐπιδημίαν ὠνόμασε.

* In dictum apostoli, Tunc etiam ipse filius subjicietur ei. Eph. v.

[1 This, H. A. 1564.]
[2 Needed, 1565, 1609.] [3 Keene, 1565.]
[4 Bernard. Op. Par. 1690. In Epiph. Serm. i. 4. Vol. I. Tom. III. col. 797.]
[5 Basil. Op. Par. 1721-30. Ad Cæsar. Apol. Epist. viii. Tom. III. p. 84.]
[6 Gregor. Nyss. Op. Par. 1638. In illud, Quando sibi, &c. Orat. Tom. II. p. 17.]

self the vine, and us the branches: St Paul calleth Christ the head, and us the body; which be names of most near and natural conjunction.

Christ dwelleth in us.

Touching faith, St Paul saith: *Christus habitat in cordibus nostris per fidem:* "Christ by faith dwelleth in our hearts." And St Peter saith: "Hereby we are made partakers of the divine nature." So saith Ignatius: "By his passion and resurrection (that is, by our faith in the same) we are made the members of his body[7]."

John i. John xv. Eph. iv. Col. ii. Eph. iii. 2 Pet. i. Ignat. ad Trall.

And notwithstanding by these means Christ be in us, and we in him, yet forasmuch as both our life and faith is unperfect[8], as we daily desire God to amend our life, and to augment our faith, even so we daily pray that this conjunction between Christ and us may be increased, that Christ may come nearer[9] and nearer[9] into us, and that we may grow into a perfect[10] man in him. And to this end God hath specially appointed us his holy sacraments. And therefore St Paul saith concerning the sacrament of baptism: "They that are baptized are planted into Christ;" "they have put Christ upon them;" "by one Spirit they are baptized into one body." St Augustine saith: *Ad hoc baptismus valet, ut baptizati Christo incorporentur*[11]*:* "This is the use of baptism, that they that be baptized may be incorporate into Christ." Which word *incorporari* he useth also in sundry other places, speaking of baptism. In this respect Dionysius saith: *Baptizati transimus in Deum*[12]*:* "Being baptized, we are turned into God." And Pachymeres saith: "We are graft into Christ, and made one nature with him by holy baptism[13]."

Eph. iv. Rom. vi. Gal. iii. 1 Cor. xii. De Consecr. Dist. 4. Ad hoc. De Eccles. Hierarch. cap. i. Pachym. in Dionys. cap. iv. σύμφυτοι γεγονότες αὐτῷ διὰ τοῦ θείου βαπτίσματος.

Thus much may suffice to descry M. Harding's slender argument. For, notwithstanding by the sacrament of baptism Christ be naturally in us, yet may not he therefore conclude that Christ is naturally in the sacrament of baptism. Bonaventura saith well: *Non est aliquo modo dicendum, quod gratia continetur in ... sacramentis essentialiter, tanquam aqua in vase.... hoc enim dicere est erroneum. Sed dicuntur continere gratiam, quia eam significant*[14]*:* "We may not in any wise say, that the grace of God is contained in the sacraments, as water in a vessel. For so to say, it were an error. But they are said to contain God's grace, because they signify God's grace."

Bonavent. in iv. Sent. Dist. 1. Quæst. 3.

But Chrysostom saith: "Christ mingleth his body with our bodies, and driveth us, as it were, into one lump of dough with himself." This place would have stood[15] M. Harding in better stead, if Chrysostom had said, Christ mingleth his body with the sacrament, and driveth himself and it into one lump. For this is it that should be proved. Neither will M. Harding say, that either Christ mingleth himself with us, or we are made one lump of dough with him, simply and according to the letter, and without figure. Whereof he seeth it must needs follow, that much less is Christ's body in the sacrament, according to that he would have the letter to sound, plainly, simply, or, as he saith, really and fleshly, and without figure. It is a vehement and a hot kind of speech, such as Chrysostom was most delighted with, far passing the common sense and course of truth; and therefore he himself thought it necessary to correct and to qualify the rigour of the same by these words, *Ut ita dicam;* which is, "As it were," or "If I may be bold so to say." In such phrase of talk Anacletus saith: *In oleo virtus Spiritus sancti invisibilis permista est*[16]*:* "The invisible power of the Holy Ghost is mingled with the oil." And Alexander saith: *In sacramentorum ... obla-*

Anaclet. Epist. 2. Inter Decret. Alex. i.

[7 ... δι' οὗ, ἐν τῷ πάθει αὐτοῦ, προσκαλεῖται ὑμᾶς, ὄντας μέλη αὐτοῦ.—Ignat. ad Trall. Epist. cap. xi. in Patr. Apostol. Oxon. 1838. Tom. II. p. 338. See also Interp. Epist. in Coteler. Patr. Apostol. Amst. 1724. Tom. II. p. 67.]

[8 Unperfite, 1565.]

[9 Neare, 1565.]

[10 Perfite, 1565.]

[11 August. in Corp. Jur. Canon. Lugd. 1624. Decret. Gratian. Decr. Tert. Pars, De Consecr. Dist. iv. can. 143. col. 2030. See Op. Par. 1679-1700. De Pecc. Mer. et Rem. Lib. I. cap. xxvi. 39. Tom. X. col. 22.]

[12 The exact words have not been found; but the idea frequently occurs: thus ... ἡ δὲ [σωτηρία] οὐχ ἑτέρως γενέσθαι δύναται, μὴ θεουμένων τῶν σωζομένων.—Dionys. Areop. Op. Antv. 1634. De Eccles. Hierarch. cap. i. Tom. I. p. 233. See also cap. ii. 3. pp. 257, 9.]

[13 Pachym. Paraphr. cap. iv. in eod. Tom. I. p. 354; where συμφύτους γεγονότας.]

[14 Bonavent. Op. Mogunt. 1609. In Lib. IV. Sentent. Dist. i. Quæst. 3. Tom. V. p. 7; where we have *contineatur*, *intelligere* for *enim dicere*, and *ipsam* for *eam*.]

[15 Stand, 1565.]

[16 ... omnis sanctificatio constat in Spiritu sancto, cujus virtus invisibilis sancto chrismati est permixta. —Anaclet. Epist. ii. in Crabb. Concil. Col. Agrip. 1551. Tom. I. p. 59.]

Christ mingled with us.

tionibus ... passio Domini miscenda est[1]: "The passion of Christ must be mingled with the oblations of the sacraments." So saith Gregorius Nyssenus of St Stephen: *Gratia sancti Spiritus permixtus et contemperatus, per illum sublatus et evectus est ad contemplationem Dei*[2]: "St Stephen, being mingled and tempered with the grace of the Holy Ghost, was by him advanced[3], and taken up to the sight of God." These and other such-like sayings of holy fathers may not be hardly pressed according to the sound of the letter; but rather must be gently expounded and qualified, according to the sense and meaning of the writer.

Gregor. Nyss. de S. Steph.

Chrysostom's purpose was, by this word *massa*, which in this place signifieth a lump of dough, to make resemblance unto these words of St Paul, "We are one loaf, and one body;" and by such majesty of speech the more to quicken and lift up our spirits, and to cause us thereby the better to consider that wonderful conjunction and knitting that is between Christ and us, whereby either is in other, he in us, and we in him; and that even in one person; in such sort as he is neither in the angels, nor in the archangels, nor in any other power in heaven. And therefore St Paul saith: "The angels he took not, but he took the seed of Abraham." But this wonderful conjunction, and (as Chrysostom calleth it) this "mixture," is wrought, not only in the holy mysteries, but also in the sacrament of baptism. And in that sense Leo saith: *Susceptus a Christo, Christumque suscipiens, non est idem post lavacrum, qui ante baptismum fuit; sed corpus regenerati fit caro crucifixi*[4]: "A man received of Christ, and receiving Christ (in baptism), is not the same after baptism that he was before; but the body of him that is regenerate is made the flesh of him that was crucified." Likewise St Augustine saith: *Ergo gratulemur et agamus gratias, non solum nos Christianos factos esse, sed [etiam] Christum. Intelligitis, fratres, gratiam Dei super nos; capitis; admiramini; gaudete; Christus facti sumus. Si enim ille caput est, et nos membra, totus ille homo, et nos*[5]: "Let us rejoice and give thanks that we are not only made christian men, but also made Christ. Brethren, ye understand the grace of God that is upon us; ye understand it; ye wonder at it; rejoice ye; we are made Christ. For if he be the head, and we the members, both he and we are one whole man."

[1] Cor. x.

Heb. ii.

Leo, Serm. 14. De Passione.

August. in Joh. Tract. 21.

Now, gentle reader, as Leo saith, our bodies by baptism are made Christ's flesh; as St Augustine saith, we are made Christ himself; and as Gregory Nyssene saith, St Stephen was tempered and mingled with the grace of the Holy Ghost; even so, and in the same sense Chrysostom saith, we are made one lump of dough with Christ; and Christ hath tempered and mingled himself with us. These things considered, the force of M. Harding's reason must needs fail. Certainly Primasius saith: "As the breaking of this bread is the partaking of the body of our Lord, even so the bread of idols is the partaking of devils." And addeth further: *Si de eodem pane manducamus, quo idololatræ, unum cum illis corpus efficimur*[6]: "If we eat of one bread with idolaters, we are made one body with them."

Prim. in 1 Cor. xi.

These other three authorities, of Hilary, Gregory Nyssene, and Cyril, may well be discharged with one answer, saving that Gregory Nyssene, an old writer newly set abroad with sundry corruptions, is brought in only to make a shew, not speaking any one word, neither of Christ's natural dwelling in us, nor of the sacrament. His purpose was only to speak of Christ's birth, and of that body which he received of the blessed virgin, which was not a shadow, or a fantasy, but real, fleshly, and indeed. And in like manner of speech St Hierome saith: *Triticum, ... de quo panis cœlestis efficitur, illud est, de quo loquitur Dominus, Caro mea vere est cibus*[7]: "The wheat whereof the heavenly bread is made is that of which our Lord saith, 'My flesh is meat indeed'." And to this purpose Amphilochius saith,

Gregor. Nyss.

Hieron. in Esai. cap. lxii.

[1 Alexandr. I. Epist. i. in eod. Tom. I. p. 73.]

[2 Gregor. Nyss. Op. Par. 1638. In S. Stephan. Encom. Tom. III. p. 364.]

[3 Avanced, 1565.]

[4 Leon. Magni Op. Lut. 1623. Serm. xiv. De Pass. Dom. col. 176; where we have *non idem sit*, and *fiat caro*.]

[5 August. Op. Par. 1679-1700. In Johan. Evang. cap. v. Tractat. xxi. 8. Tom. III. Pars II. col. 459; where *si enim caput ille, nos membra; totus homo, ille et nos*.]

[6 Et panis quem frangimus, nonne participatio corporis Domini est? Sic et idolorum panis dæmonum participatio est... Sic et si de &c. unde idololatræ, &c.—Primas. Comm. in Epist. ad Cor. I. cap. x. in Mag. Biblioth. Vet. Patr. Col. Agrip. 1618-22. Tom. VI. Pars II. p. 60.]

[7 Hieron. Op. Par. 1693-1706. Comm. Lib. XVII. in Isai. Proph. cap. lxii. Tom. III. col. 461.]

as he is alleged by Cyrillus: *Nisi Christus natus fuisset carnaliter, tu natus non fuisses spiritualiter*[8]: "Unless Christ had been born carnally, thou hadst not been born spiritually." (Cyril. in Apol.) Touching Gregorius Nyssenus, as he saith, "Christ is made our bread;" (Gregor. Nyss. in Vita Mosis.) so he saith likewise in the same place: *Quicquid assumenti conveniens sit,... in id mutatur. Fit perfectioribus solidus cibus, inferioribus olus, infantibus lac*[9]: "Whatsoever thing is convenient for the receiver, into the same thing Christ turneth himself. He becometh strong meat unto the perfect[10], herbs unto the weaker[11], and milk unto children." And as Christ is herbs or milk, even so, and none otherwise, he is bread or flesh. Neither will this ancient father agree unto M. Harding's error, that we cannot receive Christ's body but only in the sacrament; for even in the same place he holdeth the contrary. His words be these: *Qui abundanter ex apostolicis fontibus biberit, is jam totum recepit Christum*[12]: (Ibidem.) "Whoso hath abundantly drunken of the apostles' springs, hath already received whole Christ." The argument that M. Harding gathereth hereof must needs stand thus: Christ was born of the virgin; *ergo*, his body is really and fleshly in the sacrament. This conclusion is but childish; yet, if he conclude not thus, he concludeth nothing.

The greatest weight of this matter lieth upon two old fathers, Cyril and Hilary. For Hilary saith: "We receive Christ *vere sub mysterio*[13], verily under a mystery;" (Hilar. de Trin. Lib. viii.) and either of them useth these terms, carnally, corporally, naturally; and that not once or twice, but in sundry places. The authorities be great: the words be plain. But, God be thanked! these places be common, and not unknown. And for answer of the same, once again remember, good christian reader, that, notwithstanding M. Harding have found in these two fathers that Christ's body is corporally and naturally in us, yet hath he not hitherto found that thing that he sought for, neither in these fathers, nor in any other; that is, that Christ's body is naturally or corporally in the sacrament. Wherefore I much marvel that either he would avouch this matter so strongly, finding himself so weak; or else thus vainly dally, and shew one thing for another, and deceive his reader.

That we verily and undoubtedly receive Christ's body in the sacrament, it is neither denied, nor in question. St Augustine saith: *Panis est cordis:...intus esuri: intus siti*[14]: (August. in Psal. ciii.) "It is the bread of the heart: hunger thou within: thirst thou within." And the thing that is inwardly received in faith, and in spirit, is received verily and indeed. St Bernard meant no falsehood[15] when he said: *Lavemur in sanguine ejus*[16]: (Bern. sup. Missus est Gab. Serm. 3.) "Let us be washed in the blood of Christ." Notwithstanding, he meant not that our bodies really and indeed should be washed with the blood of Christ. And whereas St Augustine saith, *Quid paras dentem et ventrem? Crede, et manducasti*[17], (August. in Joh. cap. vi. Tract. 26.) "What preparest thou thy tooth and thy belly? Believe, and thou hast eaten;" we may not think that he meant any fantastical or false eating; notwithstanding he utterly refuseth, in this behalf, both the teeth and the belly, and all other office of the body. And therefore Cyrillus saith: *Sacramentum nostrum hominis manducationem non asserit, mentes credentium ad crassas cogitationes irreligiose introducens*[18]: (Cyril. ad Object. Theod.) "Our sacrament teacheth us not to eat a man (with the material mouth of our body), in ungodly sort leading the minds of the faithful unto gross cogitations." It is a holy mystery, and a heavenly action, forcing our minds up into heaven, and there teaching us to eat the body of Christ, and to drink his blood; not outwardly by the service of our bodies, but inwardly by our faith, and that verily and indeed. The truth hereof standeth not in any real or

[8 Cyril. Alex. Op. Lut. 1638. Apolog. adv. Orient. Anath. I. Tom. VI. p. 163.]

[9 Gregor. Nyss. Op. De Vit. Mos. Tom. I. p. 215. The Greek text of the latter part of the quotation is, ὡς διδάσκει ὁ τὴν τοιαύτην τοῖς αὐτοῦ παρατιθεὶς ἡμῖν τράπεζαν, Παῦλος...ὁ τοῖς τελειοτέροις στεῤῥοτέραν τὲ καὶ κρεώδη βρῶσιν τὸν Λόγον ποιῶν, καὶ λάχανον τοῖς ἀσθενεστέροις, καὶ γάλα τοῖς νηπιάζουσι.]

[10 Perfite, 1565.] [11 Weak, 1565.]

[12 Ὁ γὰρ ... ταῖς ἀποστολικαῖς ἐντρυφήσας πηγαῖς...οὗτος ἤδη καὶ τοῦ Θεοῦ δεκτικὸς γίνεται. ἡ γὰρ πέτρα...ὁ Χριστός ἐστιν.—Id. ibid. p. 214.]

[13 Vere sub mysterio carnem corporis sui sumimus.—Hilar. Op. Par. 1693. De Trin. Lib. VIII. 13. col. 955.]

[14 August. Op. In Psalm. ciii. Enarr. Serm. iii. 14. Tom. IV. col. 1160.] [15 Falsehead, 1565.]

[16 Bernard. Op. Par. 1690. Sup. Missus est, Hom. iii. 14. Vol. I. Tom. III. col. 748.]

[17 August. Op. In Johan. Evang. cap. vi. Tractat. xxv. 12. Tom. III. Pars II. col. 489.]

[18 Cyril. Alex. Op. Apolog. adv. Orient. Anath. xi. Def. Cyril. Tom. VI. p. 193.]

Corporally, naturally.

corporal presence, but, as Hilarius saith, in a mystery, which is, in a sacrament: whereby outwardly and unto our senses we express that thing in our bodies that must be wrought inwardly in our minds. For this cause Dionysius saith: [*Regeneratio*] *naturali illa purgatione, quæ fit per aquam, corporali quodam modo denuntiat animæ purgationem*[1]: "Our regeneration which we have in baptism, by that natural purgation that is wrought by water in a certain bodily sort, teacheth us the purgation of the mind." Thus are we truly washed with Christ's blood in the holy mystery of baptism: thus are we truly and indeed fed with Christ's body in the holy mystery of his supper. And albeit Christ be in neither of these mysteries in bodily and fleshly presence, yet doth not that thing any wise hinder either the substance of the holy mystery, or the truth of our receiving. And for that cause St Augustine saith: *Non fallit nos apostolus, qui dicit, Christum habitare in cordibus nostris per fidem. In te est, quia ipsa fides in te est*[2]: "The apostle deceiveth us not in saying that Christ dwelleth in our hearts by faith. He is in thee (not really or bodily, but) because his faith is within thee." M. Harding will reply: This cannot suffice: for Cyril and Hilary say that "Christ, not only by faith, but also corporally, carnally, and naturally is within us." These words in their own rigour, without some gentle construction, seem very hard. Even so Hilarius, in the same book of the Trinity, saith that "we are one with God the Father, and the Son, not only by adoption or consent of mind, but also by nature[3]." Which saying, according to the sound of the letter, cannot be true. Therefore the fathers have been fain to expound and to mollify such violent and excessive kinds of speech. Chrysostom, where he saith, "We are made one lump with Christ[4]," addeth, as it is said before, his correction withal, *ut ita dicam*, "as it were," or "if I may use such manner of speech." In like manner saith St Augustine: *Qui . . . in Christum credit, credendo in Christum venit, [et] in eum Christus, et quodammodo unitur in eum, et membrum in corpore ejus efficitur*[5]: "He that believeth in Christ, by believing cometh into Christ, and Christ into him, and, after a certain manner, is united unto him, and made a member in his body." "In a manner," he saith, but not according to the force of the letter. Again, he expoundeth this word *corporaliter* in this wise: *Non umbraliter, sed vere, et solide*[6]: "Not as in a shadow, but truly and perfectly[7]." So Cyrillus expoundeth his own meaning: *Naturalis unio non aliud est, quam vera: . . . natura sumus filii iræ, id est, vere*[8]: "Natural union is nothing else but a true union. We are by nature the children of anger, that is, we are indeed and truly the children of anger." In which sense St Paul saith: *Gentes factæ sunt cohæredes, et concorporales, et comparticipes promissionis in Christo Jesu*: "The heathens are become coinheritors, concorporal, and partakers of the promise in Christ Jesus." Thus much of these words corporally, naturally, &c.: whereby is meant a full perfect[9] spiritual conjunction, excluding all manner of imagination or fantasy; not a gross and fleshly being of Christ's body in our bodies, according to the appearance of the letter. Otherwise there must needs follow this great inconvenience, that our bodies must be in like manner corporally, naturally, and fleshly in Christ's body. For Hilarius saith: *Nos quoque in eo sumus naturaliter*[10]: "We also are naturally in him." And Cyrillus, as he saith, "Christ is corporally in us;" so he saith, "We are corporally in Christ[11]."

Dion. Eccles. Hier. cap. ii. σωματικώτερον αὐτοῦ διαγγέλλει.

August. de Verbis Apost. Serm. 16.

Hilar. Lib. viii. De Trin. Non tantum adoptione, aut consensu, sed etiam natura.

Chrysost. in Matt. Hom. 83.

August. de Verbis Dom. sec. Joh. Serm. 60.

August. in Psal. lxvii.

Cyril. in Apol. ad Anath. iii.

Eph. iii. συσσώματοι.

Hilar. de Trin. Lib. viii. Cyril. in Joh. Lib. x. cap. xiii.

[1 Dion. Areop. Op. Antv. 1634. De Eccles. Hierarch. cap. ii. 3. Tom. I. p. 255; where αὐτῷ διαγγέλλουσα.]

[2 Ecce ubi est, in te est, quia et fides ipsa in teipso est. An fallit nos apostolus, qui dicit habitare Christum per fidem in cordibus nostris?—August. Op. Par. 1679-1700. De Verb. Apost. Serm. clviii. 8. Tom. V. col. 764.]

[3 Perhaps the following may be the passage intended: . . . hæretici mentientes unitatis nostræ ad Deum utebantur exemplo, tamquam nobis ad Filium, et per Filium ad Patrem, obsequio tantum ac voluntate religionis unitis, nulla per sacramentum carnis et sanguinis naturalis communionis proprietas indulgeretur.—Hilar. Op. Par. 1693. De Trin. Lib. VIII. 17. col. 957.]

[4 Chrysost. Op. Par. 1718-38. In Matt. Hom. lxxxii. Tom. VII. p. 788. See before, page 470, note 2.]

[5 August. Op. De Verb. Evang. Johan. Serm. cxliv. 2. Tom. V. col. 694.]

[6 . . . non umbraliter . . . sed corporaliter, id est, solide atque veraciter.—Id. in Psalm. lxvii. Enarr. 23. Tom. IV. col. 677.]

[7 Perfitely, 1565.]

[8 Cyril. Alex. Op. Lut. 1638. Apolog. adv. Orient. Anath. iii. Def. Cyril. Tom. VI. p. 167.]

[9 Perfit, 1565.]

[10 . . . nos quoque in eo naturaliter inessemus, &c. —Hilar. Op. De Trin. Lib. VIII. 15. col. 956.]

[11 . . . διὰ τῆς μεταλήψεως τοῦ σώματος τοῦ Χριστοῦ, καὶ τοῦ τιμίου αἵματος, αὐτὸς μὲν ἐν ἡμῖν, ἡμεῖς δὲ αὖ πάλιν ἐν αὐτῷ συνενούμεθα. οὐ γὰρ ἦν

Corporally, naturally.

Further, that we be thus in Christ, and Christ in us, requireth not any corporal or local being, as in things natural. We are in Christ sitting in heaven, and Christ sitting in heaven is here in us, not by a natural, but by a spiritual mean of being. St Augustine saith: *Postquam ex mortuis resurrexit, et ascendit ad Patrem, est in nobis per Spiritum*[12]: "After that Christ is risen from the dead, and ascended unto his Father, he is in us by his Spirit." Which saying agreeth well with these words of St Basil: *Paulus ait, Si quis Spiritum Christi non habet, hic non est ejus. Deinde addit, Si tamen Christus sit in vobis; ac si diceret, Si Spiritus Christi sit in vobis*[13]: "St Paul saith, 'If any man have not the Spirit of Christ, he is not of him.' He addeth further these words, 'If Christ be in you;' which is as much as if he had said, If the Spirit of Christ be within you." So likewise St Augustine imagineth Christ to say unto Mary Maudlen: *Ascendam ad Patrem meum; tum tange me*[14]: "I will ascend up unto my Father; then touch thou me;" meaning thereby, that distance of place cannot hinder spiritual touching. Again St Augustine imagineth Christ thus to say unto the people: *Qui venit ad me, incorporatur mihi*: "He that cometh unto me is incorporate into me." He addeth of his own: *Veniamus ad eum; intremus ad eum; incorporemur ei*[15]: "Let us go unto him; let us enter unto him; let us be incorporate into him." Thus, notwithstanding Christ were in heaven, and distant in place, yet was he present in St Paul; for so St Paul saith[16]: "Will ye have a trial of Christ, that speaketh within me?" This conjunction is spiritual, and therefore needeth not neither circumstance of place nor corporal presence. Likewise St Cyprian saith: *Nostra et Christi conjunctio nec miscet personas, nec unit substantias; sed affectus consociat, et confœderat voluntates*[17]: "The conjunction that is between Christ and us neither doth mingle persons, nor unite substances; but it doth knit our affects together, and join our wills." Yet notwithstanding, the same conjunction, because it is spiritual, true, full, and perfect[18], therefore is expressed of these holy fathers by this term corporal, which removeth all manner light and accidental joining; and natural, whereby all manner imagination or fantasy, and conjunction only of will and consent, is excluded: not that Christ's body is corporally or naturally in our body, as is before said, no more than our bodies are corporally or naturally in Christ's body; but that we have life in us, and are become immortal, because by faith and spirit we are partakers of the natural body of Christ.

August. de Trin. Lib. vi.

Basil. de Sanct. Baptism.

εἰ δὲ Χριστὸς ἐν ὑμῖν, ἀντὶ τοῦ λέγειν,...εἰ δὲ τὸ Πνεῦμα ἐν ὑμῖν.

August. Serm. de Temp. 153.

August. in Joh. Tract. 25.

2 Cor. xiii.

Cypr. de Cœna Domini.

M. Harding saith: We are thus joined unto Christ, and have him corporally within us, only by receiving the sacrament, and by none other means. This is utterly untrue, as it is already proved by the authorities of St Augustine, St Basil, Gregory Nazianzene, Leo, Ignatius, Bernard, and other holy fathers; neither doth either Cyrillus or Hilary so avouch it. Certainly, neither have they all Christ dwelling in them that receive the sacrament, nor are they all void of Christ that never received the sacrament. Besides the untruth hereof, this doctrine were also many ways very uncomfortable. For what may the godly father think of his child, that, being baptized, departeth this life, without receiving the sacrament of Christ's body? By M. Harding's construction, he must needs think his child is damned, for that it had no natural participation of Christ's flesh, without which there is no salvation; which participation, as M. Harding assureth us, is had by none other means, but only by receiving of the sacrament. Yet St Chrysostom saith: "In the sacrament of baptism we are made flesh of Christ's flesh, and bone of his bones[19]."

Chrysost. in Epist. ad Ephes. Hom. 20.

ἑτέρως ζωοποιηθῆναι δύνασθαι...εἰ μὴ συνεπλάκη σωματικῶς τῷ σώματι τῆς κατὰ φύσιν ζωῆς.—Cyril. Alex. Op. Comm. in Joan. Evang. Lib. x. cap. ii. Tom. IV. p. 863.]

[12 This passage is not found in the book indicated. But for a somewhat similar notion see August. Op. De Trin. Lib. xv. 31. Tom. VIII. col. 989.]

[13 Basil. Op. Par. 1721-30. Hom. de Spirit. Sanct. Tom. II. p. 584. The Benedictine editor doubts whether this homily be genuine.]

[14 Adscendam ad Patrem, et tunc tange.—August. Op. In dieb. Pasch. Serm. ccxlv. 2. Tom. V. col. 1020.]

[15 Id. In Johan. Evang. cap. vi. Tractat. xxv. 16, 8. Tom. III. Pars II. cols. 492, 3; where *qui ad. me venit.*]

[16 Himself saith, 1565.]

[17 Cypr. Op. Oxon. 1682. De Cœn. Dom. (Arnold.) p. 40; where *nostra vero et ipsius conjunctio.*]

[18 Perfite, 1565.]

[19 Πῶς οὖν ἐκ τῆς σαρκὸς αὐτοῦ ἐσμεν, καὶ ἐκ τῶν ὀστῶν αὐτοῦ;...ἡμεῖς γεννώμεθα ἐν τῷ λουτρῷ.—Chrysost. Op. In Epist. ad Ephes. cap. v. Hom. xx. Tom. XI. p. 147.]

Naturally, corporally.

For better trial hereof, understand thou, gentle reader, that both Cyrillus and Hilarius in those places dispute against the Arians, whose error was this, that God the Father and the Son are one, not by nature, but only by will and consent. Against them Hilarius reasoned thus:

Christ is as really joined unto the Father as unto us:
But Christ is joined unto us by nature;
Therefore Christ is joined to God the Father by nature.

Hilar. de Trin. Lib. viii. Per naturam unius fidei, id est, naturaliter. Ejusdem regeneratione naturæ. Per naturam ejusdem baptismi.

The minor, that is, that "Christ is joined unto us by nature," he proveth thus: "We are joined unto Christ by faith," that is, "by the nature of one faith, and that is to say, naturally." Likewise he saith: "We are joined unto Christ by the regeneration of one nature." And again: "We are joined to Christ by the nature of one baptism." Hereof he concludeth: "Therefore are we naturally joined unto him[1]." Thus it appeareth by St Hilary, we may have Christ naturally within us by three other sundry means; and therefore not only, as M. Harding holdeth, by receiving of the sacrament. And like as Christ is naturally, corporally, and carnally in us by faith, by regeneration, and by baptism; even so, and none otherwise, he is in us by the sacrament of his body. In which holy mystery Christ is joined unto us corporally, as being man, because we are fed indeed and verily with his flesh; and spiritually is joined to us, as God.

Thus much unto Cyrillus and Hilarius, in whom M. Harding is not yet able to find that Christ's body is either corporally received into our bodies, or corporally present in the sacrament; which was the only thing that M. Harding hath here taken in hand, and should have proved; and now, not having proved that, notwithstanding all this great ado, hath proved nothing.

But he saith: "It had been more convenient rather modestly to have interpreted these words, than thus utterly to have denied them." Verily, perhaps it were so for him, that can make somewhat of nothing, and devise a commentary without a text, and imagine constructions, as M. Harding doth, of words that were never spoken.

Hereof M. Harding guesseth thus:

These fathers say that Christ is naturally and corporally in us; *ergo*, it is likely their meaning was, that Christ is naturally and corporally present in the sacrament. This reason is very simple; for, notwithstanding Christ were naturally within our bodies, yet the like being in the sacrament would not follow. But this argument would conclude the contrary, and hold better in this wise:

Christ's body is not naturally or corporally present within us;
Therefore much less it is corporally present in the sacrament.

M. HARDING. THE ELEVENTH DIVISION.

All these were very young fathers.

And the catholic fathers, that sithence the time of Berengarius have written in defence of the truth in this point, using these terms sometimes for excluding of metaphors, allegories, figures, and significations only, whereby the sacramentaries would defraud faithful people of the truth of Christ's precious body in this sacrament, do not thereby mean that the manner, mean, or way of Christ's presence, dwelling, union, and conjunction with us, and of us with him, is therefore natural, substantial, corporal, or carnal; but they and all other catholic men confess the contrary, that it is far higher and worthier, supernatural, supersubstantial, invisible, unspeakable, special, and proper to this sacrament, true, real, and in deed notwithstanding; and not only tropical, symbolical, metaphorical, allegorical; not spiritual only, and yet spiritual; not figurative or significative only. And likewise concerning the manner of the presence and being of that body and blood in the sacrament, they and we acknowledge and confess that it is not local, circumscriptive, diffinitive, or subjective, or natural; but such as is known to God only.

[1 ...quomodo non naturalem in his intelligis unitatem, qui per naturam unius fidei unum sunt? ...cessat in his assensus unitas, qui unum sunt in ejusdem regeneratione naturæ?...quid...hic animorum concordia faciet, cum per id unum sint, quod uno Christo per naturam unius baptismi induantur? ...Eos nunc, qui inter Patrem et Filium voluntatis ingerunt unitatem, interrogo utrumne per naturæ veritatem hodie Christus in nobis sit, an per concordiam voluntatis?—Hilar. Op. Par. 1693. De Trin. Lib. VIII. 7, 8, 13. cols. 951, 2, 4.]

THE BISHOP OF SARISBURY.

These doctors lived within these two or three hundred years, and are such as M. Harding thought not worth the naming. Their doctrine in these cases is very unsavoury and without comfort. Generally, they hold that Christ's body remaineth no longer in our bodies, but only until the forms of the bread and wine begin to alter. Some others say that, as soon as our teeth touch the bread, straightways Christ's body is taken up into heaven. The words be these: *Certum est, quod quam cito species dentibus teruntur, tam cito in cœlum rapitur corpus Christi*[2]. This doctrine notwithstanding, they say that Christ is naturally and corporally within us. Here a man may[3] say unto M. Harding, as he did before to the Arian heretic: What, troweth M. Harding, or his new doctors, that Christ cometh to us from heaven, and by and by forsaketh us? Or, that we eat Christ, and yet receive him not? Or, that we receive Christ, and yet have him not? Or, that Christ is corporally within us, and yet entereth not? Is this Christ's natural being in us? Is this the virtue of the mystical benediction? Is this the meaning of these holy fathers? Or troweth M. Harding, that, holding and maintaining such absurdities, his reader, be he never so simple, will believe him?

De Consecr. Dist. 2. Tribus gradibus. In Glossa.

The absurdities of M. Harding's doctrine.

Last of all, to declare the manner of Christ's presence in the sacrament, he saith, it is not local, not circumscriptive, not diffinitive, not subjective. By these terms his reader may rather wonder at his strange divinity and eloquence, than well conjecture what he meaneth. And, as it appeareth, he himself is not yet able to conceive his own meaning. For thus he saith: "This presence is known to God only." Then it followeth: M. Harding knoweth it not. And so this article at last is concluded with an *ignoramus*. Howbeit, the old learned fathers never left us in such doubts. Emissenus saith, as it is before alleged: *Præsens est in gratia*[4]: "Christ is present by his grace." St Augustine saith: *Est in nobis per Spiritum*[5]: "Christ is in us by his Spirit." Likewise again he saith: "*Non hoc corpus, quod videtis, manducaturi estis;... sacramentum aliquod vobis trado*[6]: "Ye shall not eat this body that ye see. It is a certain sacrament that I deliver you." Thus the holy fathers say Christ is present, not corporally, carnally, naturally; but, as in a sacrament, by his Spirit, and by his grace.

De Consecr. Dist. 2. Quia corpus. August. de Trin. August. in Psal. xcviii.

[2 Corp. Jur. Canon. Lugd. 1624. Decret. Gratian. Decr. Tert. Pars, De Consecr. Dist. ii. Gloss. in can. 23. col. 1922; where *species quam cito.*]

[3 May a man, 1565.]

[4 Euseb. Emiss. in eod. ibid. can. 35. col. 1927; where *esset.*]

[5 See before, page 477, note 12.]

[6 Id. in Psalm. xcviii. Enarr. 9. Tom. IV. col. 1066; where *commendavi* for *trado.*]

OF BEING IN MANY PLACES.

THE SIXTH ARTICLE.

THE BISHOP OF SARISBURY.

Or, that Christ's[1] body is or may be in a thousand places or more at one time.

[OF THE BEING OF CHRIST'S BODY IN MANY PLACES AT ONE TIME.—ARTICLE VI. H. A. 1564.]

M. HARDING. THE FIRST DIVISION.

The hundred and forty-fourth untruth. For none of the ancient fathers ever knew this miracle.

The hundred and forty-fifth untruth. And a doctrine hitherto seldom heard of.

The hundred and forty-sixth untruth. For, notwithstanding the body of Christ be joined with the Godhead, yet it remaineth still a creature.

(144) *Among the miracles of this blessed sacrament one is, that one and the same body may be in many places at once, to wit, under all consecrated hosts. As for God, it is agreeable to his Godhead to be every where* simpliciter et proprie; *but as for a creature, to be but in one place only. But as for the body of Christ,* (145) *it is after a manner between both. For, whereas it is a creature, it ought not to be made equal with the Creator in this behalf, that it be every where: but, whereas it is united to the Godhead, herein it ought to excel other bodies, so as it may in one* (146) *time be in more places under this holy sacrament*[2]*. For the uniting of Christ's natural body unto the almighty Godhead, duly considered, bringeth a true christian man in respect of the same to forsake reason and to lean to faith, to put apart all doubts and discourses of human understanding, and to rest in reverent simplicity of belief.*

Matt. xiv. Luke xxiv. Matt. xvii. Luke xxiv. Acts i. Matt. xxviii. John xx.

The hundred and forty-seventh untruth. For Christ uttereth no such word; and faith without God's word is no faith.

Thereby through the Holy Ghost persuaded, he knoweth that, although the body of Christ be natural and human indeed, yet, through the union and conjunction, many things be possible to the same now, that to all other bodies be impossible; as to walk upon waters, to vanish away out of sight, to be transfigured and made bright as the sun, to ascend up through the clouds; and, after it became immortal, death being conquered, to rise up again out of the grave, and to enter through doors fast shut. Through the same faith he believeth and acknowledgeth that, (147) *according unto his word, by his power it is made present in the blessed sacrament of the altar, under the form of bread and wine, wheresoever the same is duly consecrated, according unto his institution in his holy supper; and that not after a gross or carnal manner, but spiritually and supernaturally, and yet substantially; not by local, but by substantial presence; not by manner of quantity, or filling of a place, or by changing of place, or by leaving his sitting on the right hand of the Father, but in such a manner as God only knoweth, and yet doth us to understand by faith the truth of his very presence, far passing all man's capacity to comprehend the manner how.*

[*Christ's being in heaven and in the sacrament at one time implieth no contradiction.* H. A. 1564.]

Whereas some against this point of belief do allege the article of Christ's ascension, and of his being in heaven at the right hand of God the Father, bringing certain texts of the[3] *scriptures pertaining to the same, and testimonies of ancient doctors signifying Christ's absence from the earth; it may be rightly understanded, that he is verily both in heaven at the right hand of his Father, in his visible and corporal form, very God and man, after which manner he is there, and not here; and also in the sacrament invisibly*

[1 His, H. A. 1564.]

[2 Deo convenit esse ubique simpliciter, proprie; creaturæ convenit esse in uno loco tantum; corpus Christi autem medio modo se habet de corpore Christi: cum enim sit creatura, non debet æquari Creatori in hoc, quod ubique est; in hoc vero, quod est unitum divinitati, debet excellere alia corpora, ut simul in locis plurimis possit esse sub sacramento altaris.—Floret. Lugd. 1499. Lib. IV. fol. 96. 2.]

[3 H. A. 1564, omits *the*.]

and spiritually, both God and man in a mystery; so as the granting of the one may stand without denial of the other, no contradiction found in these beings, but only a distinction in the way and manner of being.

Errors touching Christ's body.

THE BISHOP OF SARISBURY.

Having somewhat largely answered the five first articles, wherein seemed to lie the greatest weight, I trust I may now the more slightly pass over the rest. Herein M. Harding seemeth in words thoroughly to yield unto us without exception. For, whereas the question is moved of the being of Christ's body in a thousand places, or more, his answer is, that Christ's body is local only in one place, and so cannot be in a thousand places, but only in one place at one time. Howbeit, thus saying, he swerveth much from the old fathers, whose words, as it shall appear, sound far otherwise.

Further, for the better understanding hereof, it shall behove thee, gentle reader, to understand that, touching the body of Christ, there have been sundry great errors raised and maintained in the church of old time, and that not only by heretics, but also by holy learned fathers. The Manichees held that Christ had only a fantastical body, without any material flesh, blood, or bone, in appearance and in sight somewhat, but in very deed and in substance nothing[4]. Eutyches held that Christ's body, after his incarnation, was made equal with his divinity[5]; an error much like unto this that is now maintained by M. Harding. St Hilary held that Christ received no flesh of the blessed virgin, but brought the same from heaven; and that his body was impassible, and felt no more grief when it was stricken, than water, fire, or air, when it is divided with a knife[6]. Theodoretus saith that the heretics called *Helcesæi* held that there be sundry Christs, two at the least; the one dwelling in heaven above, the other in the world here beneath[7]. All these, and other such-like errors and heresies, grew only of admiration and reverence towards Christ's divine nature; and the authors and maintainers of the same, leaving reason, according to M. Harding's counsel, and cleaving wholly to their imagination, which they called faith, were far deceived.

August. ad Quod-vult-Deum. Leon. Epist. 95. Epist. Flav. ad Leon. Hilar. de Trin. Lib. x. Theodor. de Fab. Hæret. Lib. ii.

But M. Harding layeth the foundation hereof upon a miracle; whereof, notwithstanding, touching this gross and fleshly presence, he hath no manner warrant, neither in the scriptures, nor in any of the holy fathers. As for that is alleged of Chrysostom and Basil, it is to a far other purpose, as shall appear, and may soon be answered. St Augustine wrote three special books namely of the miracles of the old and new testament[8]; and Gregory Nazianzene wrote in like sort of the same: yet did neither of them both ever make mention of this miracle. And albeit this kind of reasoning, *ab auctoritate negative*, in such cases imply no great necessity; yet must it needs be thought either great negligence or great forgetfulness, writing purposely and namely of miracles, to leave out untouched the greatest miracle. Certainly, St Augustine hereof writeth thus: *Quia hæc hominibus nota sunt, quia per homines fiunt, honorem, tanquam religiosa, habere possunt; stuporem, tanquam mira, non possunt*[9]: "These things (speaking of the sacrament of Christ's body), because they are known unto men, and by men are wrought, may have honour, as things appointed to religion; but wonder, as things marvellous, they cannot have." Thus St Augustine overthroweth M. Harding's whole foundation, and saith that in his great miracle there is no wonder or miracle at all.

August. de Mirab. Sacræ Script. Tom. 3. Nazianzen. August. de Trin. Lib. iii. cap. x.

He saith further: "It is agreeable to the Godhead to be every where, *simpliciter* and *proprie*. For a creature it is agreeable to be in one place. But as for the body of Christ," he saith, "it is after a manner between both." This is

[4 August. Op. Par. 1679-1700. Ad Quodvultd. Lib. de Hær. 46. Tom. VIII. col. 16.]

[5 Leon. Magni Op. Lut. 1623. Ad Leon. August. Epist. xcvii. cap. i. cols. 495, 6.

Flavian. ad Leon. Epist. cap. iii. in eod. cols. 299, 300.]

[6 Hilar. Op. Par. 1693. De Trin. Lib. x. 16, 20, 3. cols. 1045, 8, 50, 1, &c.]

[7 Χριστὸν δὲ οὐχ ἕνα λέγουσιν, ἀλλὰ τὸν μὲν ἄνω, τὸν δὲ κάτω.—Theodor. Op. Lut. Par. 1642-84. Hær. Fab. Lib. II. 7. Tom. IV. p. 221.]

[8 August. Op. De Mirab. Sacr. Script. Libr. Tres, Tom. III. Append. cols. 1, &c. This work is considered spurious.]

[9 Id. De Trin. Lib. III. cap. x. 20. Tom. VIII. col. 803; where *possunt habere*.]

A mean between both. the whole countenance of this matter. And this whole place M. Harding hath borrowed, even word by word, out of Gerson[1]. But, whereas he addeth that the body of Christ, as it is united unto the Godhead, may be at one time in sundry places, he should have remembered that this is an old error, long sithence Gers. contr. Flor. reproved and condemned by St Augustine and other learned fathers. St Augus- August. ad Dard. Epist. 57. tine saith thus: *Cavendum est,... ne ita divinitatem astruamus hominis, ut veritatem corporis auferamus. Non est autem consequens, ut, quod in Deo est, ita sit ubique, ut Deus*[2]*:* "We must beware that we do not so maintain the divine nature of Christ being man, that we take away the truth of his body. Neither doth it follow that the thing that is in God is therefore every where, as God is." St Augustine's words be plain, that whoso saith the body of Christ is every where (or in infinite places at one time, which is all one thing, the reason and miracle being like) utterly denieth the verity of Christ's body.

But what a fantasy is this, that "Christ's body is neither the Creator nor a creature, but," as it is here avouched, "after a manner between both?" Who ever would warrant this doctrine, but that old heretic abbat Eutyches? Verily St In Lib. Sent. Prosp. Augustine saith: *Omnis substantia, quæ Deus non est, creatura est; et quæ creatura non est, Deus est*... [*et*] *quod Deo minus est, Deus non est*[3]*:* "Every substance that is not God is a creature; and that is not a creature is God; and whatsoever is less than God is not God." Here St Augustine knoweth a Creator and a creature; but M. Harding's mean between both he knoweth not. Leo, writing against Eutyches, of whom M. Harding seemeth to have received this learning, Leon. Epist. 95, ad Leon. August. writeth thus: *Emergunt alii, qui carnem Domini et divinitatem dicunt unius esse naturæ. Quæ tantum sacrilegium inferna vomuere?... Tolerabiliores sunt Ariani,* &c.[4]: "Up there start others, that say the flesh of Christ and his divinity are both of one nature. What hell hath poured us out such wicked sacrilege? The very Arians are more to be borne withal than these men." St Augustine saith: August. Epist. 57. De Verb. Dom. in Evang. sec. Johan. cap. lviii. *Quod ad hominem attinet, creatura est Christus*[5]*:* "Christ, as concerning his manhood, is (not a mean between both, but) a creature." Again he saith: *Duas ... substantias, id est, naturas esse fatemur; divinitatis scilicet et humanitatis; ... creatricis et creatæ: quæ tamen substantiæ, non ... confusæ, sed unitæ, atque in una eademque persona inseparabiles, et in sua semper proprietate manentes*[6]*:* "We confess there are in Christ two substances or natures; the one of the Godhead, the other of the manhood[7]; the one of the Creator, the other of the creature: which substances notwithstanding are not confused, but united, and in one selfsame person inseparable, and remaining evermore in their own properties." The like writeth Leo, Cyrillus, Gelasius, and all the rest of the old learned fathers. Therefore M. Harding was much overseen, either to teach the people that Christ's body is neither the Creator nor the creature, but a mean between both; or else to say that the same body, being united unto the Godhead, may therefore be in sundry places at one time. Herein rested the old heresy of Eutyches: for thus Flavian. ad Leon. Flavianus writeth of him: *Corpus Domini ... humanum quidem ... vocat; tamen negat esse nobis consubstantiale*[8]*:* "He calleth the body of our Lord a man's body; but yet he saith it is not one in substance with our bodies."

But M. Harding replieth: Christ's body is now become immortal and glorious. This is most true, and without all question. Howbeit, it may please him to remember, that when Christ ministered the holy communion to his disciples, his body was then mortal, and subject to death and other injuries, and not glorious. Therefore, if Christ's body in the sacrament be immortal and glorious, it must follow that for that present Christ had two manner bodies; the one mortal, the

[1 See before, page 480, note 2.]

[2 August. Op. 1679-1700. Lib. ad Dard. seu Epist. clxxxvii. 10. Tom. II. col. 681.]

[3 Id. Prosp. Lib. Sentent. 55. Tom. X. Append. col. 227.]

[4 Leon. Magni Op. Ad Leon. August. Epist. xcvii. cap. v. col. 505. Leo, however, is quoting the words of Ambrose. See Ambros. Op. Par. 1686-90. Lib. de Incarn. Dom. Sacram. cap. vi. 49. Tom. II. col. 714; where *dicant*, and *vomuerunt*. As cited by Leo there are other slight variations.]

[5 Quod vero ad hominem, creatus est Christus. —August. Op. Lib. ad Dard. seu Epist. clxxxvii. 8. Tom. II. col. 680.]

[6 Id. de Myst. Trin. Serm. ccxlvi. 1. Tom. V. Append. col. 403.]

[7 Manhead, 1565.]

[8 Flavian. ad Leon. Epist. in Leon. Magni Op. col. 301; where *non tamen nobis*.]

other immortal; the one glorious, the other not glorious. Thus M. Harding's rules and examples match not together. A mean between both.

He addeth further: "Christ's body walked upon the waters, vanished out of sight, ascended through the clouds, and entered through the doors, being fast shut," &c. These were the reasons that deceived the old Manichees. I marvel that M. Harding, being (as he saith) lately become a professor of the catholic faith, would found the whole substance of his doctrine upon heretics. Touching the special trust that the Manichees reposed in this argument, St Hierome writeth thus: *Cum dicit Manichæus, et similis Manichæorum, Dominus non resurrexit in corporis veritate, et, ut scias non fuisse verum corpus, clausis ingressus est ostiis, nos quid dicemus? Domine, libera animam meam a labiis iniquis, et a lingua dolosa*[9]: "When the Manichee, or any other like the Manichees, saith, The Lord arose not again in the truth of his body; and for proof thereof saith thus, He entered in when the doors were shut; what then shall we say? Even thus: O Lord, deliver my soul from wicked lips and deceitful tongues." Here we see M. Harding is driven to seek upon old condemned heretics, and to borrow their weapons; wherefore it shall be good to follow St Hierome's counsel, and to say: "O Lord, deliver my soul from wicked lips and deceitful tongues." Hieron. in Psal. cxix.

Likewise St Ambrose saith the apostles of Christ, by the same manner of reasoning, were deceived. For upon that, "Christ entered, the gates being shut," he writeth thus: *Denique conturbati discipuli æstimabant se spiritum videre. Et ideo Dominus, ut speciem nobis resurrectionis ostenderet, Palpate, inquit, et videte: quia spiritus carnem et ossa non habet, sicut me videtis habere*[10]: "The disciples, being astonied, thought they saw a spirit or a fantasy. Therefore the Lord, to shew a token of his resurrection, said unto them, 'Feel, and see; for a spirit or fantasy hath not flesh and bone, as you see that I have'." Now, if these arguments were able to deceive the apostles of Christ, it is not impossible but they may likewise deceive M. Harding. Chrysostom saith: *Clausa erant ostia, et ingressus est Jesus: ... non erat phantasma: non erat spiritus: vere corpus erat: habebat carnes, et ossa*[11]: "The doors were shut; and Jesus entered: it was no fantasy: it was no spirit: it was verily a body: it had flesh and bones." Thus, notwithstanding these marvellous effects, yet the ancient godly fathers said, Christ's body nevertheless is, and continueth still a creature, not a mean between both, as M. Harding here strangely hath imagined. Now let us consider M. Harding's arguments: Ambros. in Luc. Lib. x. cap. xxiv. Chrysost. in Hom. de Johan. Bapt.

Christ's body walked upon the waters:
It entered through the doors being shut:
It ascended through the clouds;
Ergo, it may be at one time in sundry places.

Although this argument may soon be espied, having utterly no manner sequel in reason, yet the folly thereof may the better appear by the like:

St Peter walked upon the water: Matt. xiv.
Elias was taken up into the clouds: 2 Kings ii.
St Bartholomew entered through the doors being shut[12];
Ergo, St Peter, Elias, and St Bartholomew may be at one time in sundry places.

And that I allege here of St Bartholomew, although it be but a vain fable, yet it may not easily be denied. For it is recorded by Abdias the bishop of Babylon[12], who, as Master Harding supposeth, saw Christ in the flesh, and was one of the apostles' fellows. Abd. in Barthol.

Over all this M. Harding throweth a sweet mist, to carry away the simple in the dark: Christ's body, saith he, is in the sacrament, not by local, but by substantial presence; carnally, but not in carnal manner; placed in the pix, in the hand, in the mouth, and yet in no place at all; a very natural body, even as

---

[9 This passage does not appear in the place referred to.]

[10 Ambros. Op. Expos. Evang. sec. Luc. Lib. x. cap. xxiv. 169. Tom. I. col. 1540.]

[11 Chrysost. Op. Lat. Bas. 1547. De Joan. Bapt. Hom. Tom. III. col. 426; where *habebat ossa.*]

[12 ...apparuit regi apostolus, ostio clauso, in cubiculo ipsius, &c.—Abd. Apost. Hist. Par. 1571. Lib. VIII. fol. 97. 2.]

it was upon the cross, yet without all manner quantity and dimensions or proportions of a body, that is, neither thick, nor broad, nor short, nor long; there now where before it was not, and yet without any shifting or change of places. Unless this man were fast asleep, he could never fall into so deep a dream. In these fantasies he seemeth well to agree with the old heretics Eutyches and Manichee. For even such a body they imagined that Christ received of the blessed virgin; and yet were they heretics notwithstanding. For which of all the old learned fathers ever taught us this strange doctrine? Who ever durst to spoil Christ of his place, of his quantity, and of the natural proportions of his body? If the doctors of the church say thus, why are they not alleged? If they say not thus, why is this matter carried away with such countenance of antiquity? Or why doth M. Harding thus avouch this unsensible and unsavoury learning, only upon his own credit, without the authority of any doctor? The Manichees in old times, the better to maintain their error, and to avoid absurdities, were driven to say there were two Gods; the one good, the other ill[1]. Even so M. Harding, to maintain his errors, and to avoid infinite absurdities, is driven to say: There are two Christs; the one local, the other not local; the one above, the other beneath; the one with proportion of body, the other without proportion. Howbeit, he seemeth to publish this principle unawares against himself. For if Christ's body in the sacrament be not local, as he saith, then is it no natural or real body. This rule St Augustine taketh to be infallible. His words be these: *Tolle loca corporibus, et nusquam erunt; et quia*[2] *nusquam erunt, nec erunt*[3]*:* "Take away the places from the bodies, and the bodies shall be no where; and, because they shall be no where, they shall have no being;" and so shall be no bodies at all. And he speaketh not thus only of other natural bodies, but specially and namely of the body of Christ.

Epiphan. August. ad Quod-vult-Deum.

August. Epist. 57.

Certainly, the more spiritual a thing is, the more it is void from the circumstance and necessity of place. Wherefore, when M. Harding saith the body of Christ is in heaven as in a place, and in the sacrament without place; he seemeth secretly to say that Christ's body in the sacrament is more glorious, more spiritual, and divine, than[4] is the very body of Christ indeed that is in heaven, in the glory of God the Father. Which conclusion, how well it may stand either with the rest of his own doctrine, or with the truth of our christian religion, I leave it in consideration to the reader.

Christ's body more glorious in the sacrament, than in heaven.

But what needeth this new-devised difference of Christ's body local, and Christ's body not local? Or what forceth these men to say that only the bare substance of Christ's body is in the sacrament, without length, breadth, or any other respect of quantity? Will M. Harding now at the last forsake the reverend simplicity of his belief, and lean to reason? Or will he in God's secret mysteries give credit to his eyes, and hearken to the course of nature? Verily God, as he is able by his omnipotent power to make Christ's body present without place and quantity; so is he likewise able to make the same body present in place, and with quantity, and all other natural dimensions. If M. Harding will say nay, Duns himself, his own doctor, will reprove him. His words be plain: *Idem corpus localiter et dimensive potest esse in diversis locis. Et Deus potest quodcunque corpus universi convertere in corpus Christi, sicut panem; et facere corpus Christi ubique esse, non solum sacramentaliter, sed etiam localiter et dimensionaliter*[5]*:* "One body, both locally and with the natural dimensions of a body, may be in sundry places. And God is able to turn any body in the world into the body of Christ, as well as bread; and to cause Christ's body to be every-where, not only by way of sacrament, but also by way of place and dimensions." Which saying seemeth

Scot. iv. Sent. Dist. 10. Quæst. 2.

[[1] Epiphan. Op. Par. 1622. Adv. Hær. Lib. II. Hær. lxvi. 8. Tom. I. p. 625.

August. Op. Par. 1679-1700. Lib. de Hær. 46. Tom. VIII. col. 13.]

[[2] Qui, 1565.]

[[3] Id. Lib. ad Dard. seu Epist. clxxxvii. 18. Tom. II. col. 683; where *spatia locorum tolle corporibus, nusquam.*]

[[4] That, 1611.]

[[5] ...dico, idem corpus simul esse localiter in diversis locis, &c.......ipsi concedunt, quod corpus Christi posset ubique esse sacramentaliter: posset enim Deus quodcumque corpus universi convertere in corpus Christi, sicut panem; et ego dico, quod non est major limitatio ad esse alicubi localiter quam sacramentaliter, comparando ad potentiam Dei.—Joan. Duns Scot. Op. Lugd. 1639. In Lib. IV. Sentent. Dist. x. Quæst. 2. Tom. VIII. pp. 513, 9.]

also to be well liked and allowed of Durandus[6]. Therefore M. Harding should not thus nicely shrink back, and so dissemble in dark speeches; but should rather boldly and plainly say, Christ's body is in the sacrament, not only substantially, but also locally and by way of place; as having as good warrant for the one as for the other. For it is a catholic man's part to be bold of God's omnipotent power; and whatsoever God, being omnipotent, is able to do, to believe it is already done, without any regard had to his will or promise. If he think it lawful for him without cause to deny this manner of Christ's presence, let him not be offended, if we upon good and just cause deny the other. Verily Alexander de Hales, a great doctor of that side, reckoneth M. Harding to be in a great error in this behalf. This is his resolution: *Quidam ponebant corpus Christi esse sub sacramento, non secundum quantitatem, &c.... Sed hæc positio est erronea*[7]*:* "Some hold[8] that Christ's body is under the sacrament, not according unto quantity; but this opinion is erroneous." Thus much I thought good only to touch; not so much for any great credit of the author, but that it may appear that, notwithstanding all these men would so fain have Christ really and fleshly present, yet they reprove one another of error and ignorance, and cannot agree among themselves in what sort they may have him present. Howbeit, the ancient fathers of the church have written far otherwise in this behalf. For like as Athanasius saith, *Æqualis Patri secundum divinitatem; minor Patre secundum humanitatem*[9]; "Christ, according to his divine nature, is equal unto the Father; and according to his manhood[10] is inferior unto the Father;" even so saith Gregory Nazianzene: "Christ, according to his body, is within the limitation of place: according to his spirit and Godhead, he is without the limits of any place[11]." But, that any one of all the old fathers ever said, "Christ's body is sometime in one place and sometime in many, sometime limited and sometime not limited;" I think it not easy for M. Harding well to prove.

Lib. iv. de 6 parte Can.

Alex. de Hales. iv. Quæst. 40. Memb. 3.

Gregor. Nazianz. contr. Apoll. περίγραπτος σώματι, ἀπερίγραπτος πνεύματι... χωρητὸς, καὶ ἀχώρητος.

As for the difference that he hath devised, of visible and unvisible, local and not local, which is both trench and bulwark to maintain this piece[12], it is a very toy, only meet to beguile children; as neither having foundation in the scriptures or holy fathers, nor effectually serving to prove his purpose. For we reason not of respects and qualities; but, as St Augustine, St Cyril, and other catholic doctors do, of the very nature and substance of Christ's body. Neither can M. Harding well maintain that whatsoever is invisible is therefore of nature infinite, or may be at one time in a thousand places. As touching Christ's being in a mystery, as it requireth no local presence, according to M. Harding's own confession, so likewise it requireth no natural or real body; as hereafter, God willing, it shall be shewed more at large.

M. HARDING. THE SECOND DIVISION.

And how the ancient fathers of the church have confessed and taught both these beings, of Christ in heaven and in the sacrament together, contrary to M. Jewel's negative, by witness of their own words we may perceive. Basil in his liturgy, that is to say, service of mass[13]*, saith thus in a prayer: "Look down upon us, Lord Jesus Christ, our God, from thy holy tabernacle, and from the throne of glory of thy kingdom, and come to sanctify us, which sittest above with thy Father, and art* conversant here invisibly; and vouchsafe to impart unto us thine undefiled body and precious blood, and by us to all thy people*[14]*."*

[*Qui supra cum Patre sedes, et hic invisibiliter versaris.* H. A. 1564.]

* Not bodily, but by Spirit and grace.

[6 ...idem corpus totum simul in diversis locis consistit, et a diversis percipitur, &c.—Durand. Rat. Div. Offic. Lugd. 1565. Lib. IV. cap. xli. 25. fol. 164. 2.]

[7 Alex. Ales. Summ. Theol. Col. Agrip. 1622. Pars IV. Quæst. x. Membr. vii. Art. iii. 4. p. 352.]

[8 Held, 1565.]

[9 Athanas. Op. Par. 1698. Symb. de Fid. Cathol. Tom. II. p. 729.]

[10 Manhead, 1565.]

[11 Gregor. Nazianz. Op. Par. 1778-1840. Ad Cledon. contr. Apoll. Epist. ci. Tom. II. p. 85; where περίγραπτον, ἀπερίγραπτον, χωρητὸν, and ἀχώρητον.]

[12 Piece: castle.]

[13 Of his mass, H. A. 1564.]

[14 Πρόσχες Κύριε Ἰησοῦ Χριστὲ ὁ Θεὸς ἡμῶν ἐξ ἁγίου κατοικητηρίου σου, καὶ ἀπὸ θρόνου δόξης τῆς βασιλείας σου, καὶ ἐλθὲ εἰς τὸ ἁγιάσαι ἡμᾶς, ὁ ἄνω τῷ Πατρὶ συγκαθήμενος, καὶ ὧδε ἡμῖν ἀοράτως συνών· καὶ καταξίωσον τῇ κραταιᾷ σου χειρὶ

THE BISHOP OF SARISBURY.

Touching these ancient fathers that here be alleged, notwithstanding the credit of some of them might well come in question, as namely that Chrysostom in his liturgy prayeth for the emperor of[1] Alexius, which was not born within five hundred years after that Chrysostom was dead[2]; yet will I spare both this, and also all other like advantages, and receive all these authorities as if they were good and perfect[3] without exception.

But first, for the clearer conceiving of the answer hereunto, understand, good christian reader, that by the record of the old fathers Christ is present amongst us sundry ways: by his holy Spirit, as Cyrillus saith[4]; by his grace, as Eusebius Emissenus saith[5]; by his divinity and majesty, as St Augustine saith[6]; by faith dwelling in our hearts, as St Paul saith. Thus is Christ most comfortably present in his holy word, in the mystery of baptism, and in the sacrament of his body. We deny only that gross and fleshly presence that M. Harding here defendeth; wherein we have the authority and consent of the old learned fathers. For, to allege one instead of many, St Augustine saith: *Corpus....in quo resurrexit,* [*in*] *uno loco esse oportet*[7]*:* "The body wherein Christ rose again must be in one place."

Cyril. in Joh. Lib. viii. cap. vii. Emiss. de Consecr. Dist. 2. Quia corpus. August. in Tract. in Joh. 50. Eph. iii.

August. de Consecr. Dist. 2. Prima.

Here M. Harding, as his manner is, taketh one thing in hand, and proveth another. For to prove that Christ is really and fleshly present in the sacrament, he allegeth the old fathers, that never spake one word of this real or fleshly presence. And therefore, setting such countenance upon the matter with the names of holy fathers, and not once coming near that thing wherein standeth the whole question, he dallieth vainly and abuseth the simplicity of the people. For touching Chrysostom and Basil, we grant that Christ, being in heaven in his humanity and in the substance of his body, is nevertheless by his Spirit and grace invisibly present in his sacraments. Which answer, notwithstanding it might serve generally to all these authorities here brought in, yet I have thought it not amiss to consider them all severally as they come.

M. HARDING. THE THIRD DIVISION.

St Chrysostom prayeth with the very same words also in his liturgy or mass: where we read further, that "the priest and the deacon do adore and worship, saying three times secretly, 'God be merciful to me a sinner;' and that the people do all likewise devoutly adore"[9]*. Now, sith he will adoration to be made, he acknowledgeth Christ present, whom he granteth to be also at the same time in heaven.*

Et populus similiter omnis[8] ***cum pietate adorant.***

THE BISHOP OF SARISBURY.

It is likely, saith Master Harding, that Christ is fleshly present in the sacrament, for that the priest and the people adoreth him. This guess hath very slender hold. For would he that the people should never worship Christ, but only when they have him present before their face? Certainly St Hierome writeth thus of a gentlewoman named Melania: *Ad Christi pedes provoluta est*[10]*:*

Hieron. ad Paul. de Ob. Blesil.

μεταδοῦναι ἡμῖν τοῦ ἀχράντου σώματός σου, καὶ τοῦ τιμίου αἵματος, καὶ δι' ἡμῶν παντὶ τῷ λαῷ.—Basil. Lit. in Lit. Sanct. Patr. Par. 1560. pp. 66, 7.]

[1 1565 omits *of*.]

[2 See before, page 114, note 4.]

[3 Perfit, 1565, 1609.]

[4 ...*ἐναυλίζεται τοῖς ἀξίοις διὰ τοῦ Πνεύματος.*—Cyril. Alex. Op. Lut. 1638. Comm. in Joan. Evang. Lib. XI. cap. ii. Tom. IV. p. 933.]

[5 Euseb. Emiss. in Corp. Jur. Canon. Lugd. 1624. Decret. Gratian. Decr. Tert. Pars, De Consecr. Dist. ii. can. 35. col. 1927. See before, page 467.]

[6 August. Op. Par. 1679-1700. In Johan. Evang. cap. xii. Tractat. l. 13. Tom. III. Pars II. col. 634.]

[7 Id. in Corp. Jur. Canon. Decret. Gratian. Decr. Tert. Pars, De Consecr. Dist. ii. can. 44. col. 1935.]

[8 Omnes, H. A. 1564.]

[9 *Πρόσχες, κ.τ.λ. Εἶτα προσκυνεῖ ὁ ἱερεὺς καὶ ὁ διάκονος ἐν ᾧ ἐστὶ τρόπῳ, λέγοντες μυστικῶς τρὶς, Ὁ Θεὸς ἱλάσθητί μοι τῷ ἁμαρτωλῷ. Καὶ ὁ λαὸς ὁμοίως, πάντες μετὰ εὐλαβείας προσκυνοῦσιν.*—Chrysost. Lit. in Lit. Sanct. Patr. p. 103.]

[10 ...ad pedis advoluta Christi, quasi ipsum teneret, arrisit.—Hieron. Op. Par. 1693-1706. Ad Paul. sup. Ob. Blesil. Epist. xxii. Tom. IV. Pars II. col. 58.]

"She fell down and worshipped at Christ's feet:" notwithstanding she had not Christ there bodily present. Likewise Chrysostom teacheth us to worship Christ in the sacrament of baptism. For thus he saith unto the people: *Et vos, qui accepturi estis baptisma,...tenete pedes Salvatoris: lavate lacrymis: crine tergite*[11]: "You that will receive baptism, hold the feet of our Saviour: wash them with your tears: wipe them with your hair." Yet will not M. Harding therefore say that Christ is bodily and carnally present in the water of baptism. Thus the faithful then were taught to worship Christ, although they had him not corporally in real presence. The idolaters worshipped the sun and the moon; yet they pulled them not down from heaven to receive their worship. Therefore M. Harding's argument of adoration can stand him but in little stead. For we are taught to worship Christ sitting in heaven, not lying bodily present before our eyes.

Miracle.

Chrysost. in Marc. Hom. 14.

M. HARDING. THE FOURTH DIVISION.

Which he uttereth more plainly in these words: O miraculum, O Dei benignitatem, &c.: *"O miracle, O the goodness of God, who sitteth above with the Father, at that very instant of time is handled with the hands of all, and giveth himself to those that will receive and embrace him. And that is done by no crafty slightness*[12]*, but openly in the sight of all that stand about. How sayest thou, seem these things no better to thee*[13] *than to be contemned and despised*[14]*?" By which words of St Chrysostom we may see that Christ's being in heaven maketh no proof that he is not in earth, sith both these verities may well stand together.*

Chrysostom. de Sacerdotio, Lib. iii.

THE BISHOP OF SARISBURY.

This argument would serve well, if there were none other miracle but carnal presence. But if M. Harding had conferred with the old catholic fathers, he should have found miracles in the sacrament of baptism, no less than in this sacrament of Christ's body. Leo saith: *[Deus] mirabile nobis sacramentum regenerationis indulsit*[15]: "God hath granted us the marvellous sacrament of regeneration." So saith Eusebius Emissenus: *Veniant [nunc] qui futuræ resurrectionis gloriam sitiunt: jam nunc de...remissione peccatorum digno miraculo reficiant fidem suam. Homo [in] fonte tingitur, &c.*[16]: "Let them draw near that thirst after the glory of the resurrection that is to come: even now let them refresh their faith with that worthy miracle of remission of sin. A man is washed in the font," &c. In like sort writeth Chrysostom touching the same: *Nullo pacto de intellectuali per baptismum regeneratione et admirabili partu rationem reddemus. Nam et angeli, qui adfuerunt, tam inenarrabilis operis modum minime possunt enarrare. Adfuerunt tantum, et viderunt; nihil autem operati sunt: sed Pater tantum, et Filius, et Spiritus sanctus*[17]: "We are never able to yield a reason of the spiritual regeneration and miraculous birth that we have by baptism. The very angels that were present are not able to utter the manner of that unspeakable work. They were present only, and saw; but they wrought nothing; but only the Father, the Son, and the Holy Ghost." Here we see a miracle in baptism, and such a miracle as the angels of God are not able to utter it. Yet will not M. Harding say that Christ's body is therefore really present in the water of baptism. So weakly these proofs hang together.

Leon. Epist. 13.

Hom. Sext. Fer. de Baptism.

Chrysost. in Joh. Hom. 24.

But Chrysostom's words are very vehement: That Christ is present at the

[11 Chrysost. Op. Lat. Basil. 1547. In Marc. Hom. xiv. Tom. II. col. 1284.]

[12 Sleights, H. A. 1564.]

[13 To thee no better, H. A. 1564.]

[14 Ὢ τοῦ θαύματος· ὢ τῆς τοῦ Θεοῦ φιλανθρωπίας· ὁ μετὰ τοῦ Πατρὸς ἄνω καθήμενος, κατὰ τὴν ὥραν ἐκείνην τῶν ἁπάντων κατέχεται χερσὶ, καὶ δίδωσιν αὑτὸν τοῖς βουλομένοις περιπτύξασθαι καὶ περιλαβεῖν. ποιοῦσι δὲ τοῦτο πάντες διὰ τῶν ὀφθαλμῶν τῆς πίστεως. ἆρά σοι τοῦ καταφρονεῖσθαι ταῦτα ἄξια καταφαίνεται;—Chrysost. Op. Par. 1718-38. De Sacerdot. Lib. III. 4. Tom. I. p. 382.]

[15 Leon. Magni Op. Lut. 1623. Ad Pulch. August. Epist. xiii. col. 317; where *sacramentum nobis.*]

[16 Euseb. Emis. Hom. Lut. Par. 1547. Hom. vii. de Pasch. fol. 51. 2; where *jam tunc.*]

[17 Chrysost. Op. In Joan. Hom. xxv. Tom. VIII. p. 145.]

holy ministration; that every man both toucheth him with his fingers, and also seeth him with his eyes, and that clearly and openly, without guile or error. I grant these words be very vehement, and much exceed the common sense. But here would I learn of master Harding, whether he will take these words plainly and simply as they lie, or else will rather qualify them with a courteous and gentle interpretation. If he follow the rigour of the words, then appeareth there a manifest contradiction; and Chrysostom in uttering one sentence is found clean contrary to himself. For first he saith, "Christ is there invisibly, in such sort as no man can see him;" and yet immediately after, with one breath he saith, "Every man seeth him with his eyes plainly, and without guile or error." Again, by the rigour of the same words, we must needs grant that the people both verily and indeed seeth Christ's very body, and also handleth and toucheth it with their fingers; which is not only a manifest untruth, but also a greater heresy than ever was defended by Berengarius, as it is confessed by the doctors of M. Harding's own side[1]. Indeed, the marvellous effects that God worketh in the faithful, in that dreadful time of the holy communion, wherein the whole mystery of our redemption that we have in the blood of Christ is expressed, Chrysostom calleth a miracle; and therefore the more to stir the people's minds to the consideration of the same, he inflameth his speech with rhetorical amplifications and heat of words. He saith: "Christ is crucified before our eyes: his blood gusheth out of his side, and streameth and floweth over the holy table; and the people is therewith made red and bloody[2]." This advancing[3] and ravishing of the mind he calleth a miracle; but of any corporal or fleshly presence he speaketh nothing. By such figurative and fiery speech he meant not that we should understand him precisely according to the sound of his words, but sought only to lift up and enkindle his hearers' minds. So St Paul saith to the Galathians: "Christ was crucified before your eyes." So St Hierome: "Our faces are marked in baptism with the blood of Christ[4]." So saith Tertullian: "We are washed in the passion of our Lord[5]." So St Gregory saith: *Eundem Agnum Johannes ostendendo, Esaias prævidendo, Abel offerendo locutus est: et quem Johannes in ostensione, quem Esaias in locutione, hunc Abel significando in manibus tenuit*[6]: "St John the Baptist spake of the same Lamb by pointing, Esaias by seeing, Abel by offering. And the Lamb that John held in his hand by pointing, and Esay by speaking, the same Lamb Abel held in his hand by signifying." These sayings, and other like, are vehement, as is that of Chrysostom; and, as M. Harding knoweth, may not be taken as they lie, but must be mollified with a gentle construction.

De Consecr. Dist. 2. Ego Berengarius. In Gloss.

Gal. iii.

Hieron. in Psal. lxxxv. Tertull. de Baptism. Gregor. in Job. Lib. xxix. cap. xvi.

M. HARDING. THE FIFTH DIVISION.

The same father confesseth the body of Christ to be in divers places likewise in his homilies ad Populum Antiochenum, *most plainly alluding to Elias.* Elias, *saith he,* melotem quidem discipulo reliquit: Filius autem Dei ascendens suam nobis carnem dimisit. Sed Elias quidem exutus: Christus autem et nobis reliquit, et ipsam habens ascendit[7]: "*Elias (when he was carried up in the fiery chariot) left to his disciple Elizeus his mantle of sheep's skins: but the Son of God, when he ascended, left to us his flesh. But Elias did put off his mantle; and Christ both left his flesh to us, and also ascended having it with him." Nothing can be spoken more plainly, whereby to shew that we have the same*

[*Christ's body in many places at once.* H.A. 1564.]

Hom. 2.

Chrysostom's words not justly and fully reported.

[1 Corp. Jur. Canon. Lugd. 1624. Decret. Gratian. Decr. Tert. Pars, De Consecr. Dist. ii. Gloss. in can. 42. col. 1932. See before, page 459, note 4.]

[2 Ὅταν γὰρ ἴδῃς τὸν Κύριον τεθυμένον, καὶ κείμενον, καὶ τὸν ἱερέα ἐφεστῶτα τῷ θύματι, καὶ ἐπευχόμενον· καὶ πάντας ἐκείνῳ τῷ τιμίῳ φοινισσομένους αἵματι· κ.τ.λ.—Chrysost. Op. Par. 1718-38. De Sacerdot. Lib. III. 4. Tom. I. p. 382. See also In Matt. Hom. lxxxii. Tom. VII. p. 788.]

[3 Avancing, 1565.]

[4 Perhaps the reference is to the following passage: Ergo post lepram sanari non poteris nisi per passionem Christi et per baptismum...Exterminator quum viderit sanguinem in fronte tua, accedere non poterit.—Hieron. Op. Par. 1693-1706. Breviar. in Psalt. Psalm. lxxxiv. Tom. II. Append. col. 344.]

[5 ...passio Domini, in quam tinguimur.—Tertull. Op. Lut. 1641. De Baptism. 19. p. 264.]

[6 Gregor. Magni Papæ I. Op. Par. 1705. Lib. XXIX. in cap. xxxviii. B. Job. cap. xxxi. 69. Tom. I. col. 948.]

[7 Chrysost. Op. Ad Pop. Ant. Hom. ii. Tom. II. p. 34.]

flesh here in earth that was received into heaven, which Christ hath not put off to give it to us. By which doctrine of St Chrysostom (148) *we are taught to believe, that Christ's flesh or his body is both in heaven and also in the earth, in how many places soever this blessed sacrament is rightly celebrated.* The hundred and forty-eighth untruth. For the very order of the comparison plainly concludeth the contrary.

THE BISHOP OF SARISBURY.

This place well considered both openeth itself, and also giveth light unto other like. Chrysostom sheweth in what sort Christ hath both taken up his flesh into heaven, and also left the same here amongst the faithful in the earth; and to that end compareth Elias and Christ together. The story is known, that, when Elias was taken up in a fiery chariot, he let down his coat unto Elizeus 2 Kings ii. that stood beneath; who took it up, and by the power of the same divided the water of Jordan. Upon occasion hereof Chrysostom saith: *Tanquam maximam* Chrysost. ad Pop. Ant. Hom. 2. *hæreditatem Elizæus melotem suscepit. Etenim vere maxima fuit hæreditas omni auro pretiosior. Et erat postea duplex Elias: et erat sursum Elias, et deorsum Elias*[8]*:* "Elizeus received the coat made of sheep's skins as a great inheritance. And doubtless it was an inheritance more precious than any gold. After that time Elias was double: for there was Elias above, and Elias beneath." Above was the very true Elias in the natural substance and presence of his body; beneath was nothing else but Elias' coat; which coat notwithstanding, because of the powers that were wrought with it, he calleth Elias. Thus Chrysostom compareth Elias with Christ, and Elias' coat with the sacrament; and thus he saith, Christ is above, and Christ is beneath; as he saith, Elias is above, and Elias is beneath. For, as Elias' coat was called Elias, even so the sacrament of Christ's body is called Christ's body. Which saying agreeth well with these words of St Augustine: *Sacramentum corporis Christi secundum quendam modum corpus* August. Epist. 23. ad Bonifac. *Christi est*[9]*:* "The sacrament of Christ's body, after a certain manner, is the body of Christ;" not substantially or really or indeed, but as Elias' coat is Elias.

Hereof M. Harding might well have formed this argument:

Elias, being above, was not verily and indeed present beneath in his coat;

Therefore by Chrysostom's comparison Christ's body is not indeed really and fleshly present in the sacrament.

M. HARDING. THE SIXTH DIVISION.

(149) *And whereas many, measuring all things by the common order and laws of nature, believe nothing can be done above nature, and therefore think that the body of Christ, forasmuch as it is of nature finite, cannot by power of God be in many places at once, of which opinion M. Jewel seemeth to be himself; it shall not be beside the purpose, though the places already alleged prove the contrary, to recite the testimonies of an old doctor or two, wherein they confess most plainly that which by this article is most untruly denied.* The hundred and forty-ninth untruth, joined with a slander.

THE BISHOP OF SARISBURY.

M. Harding hopeth to win the victory by untrue reports. For with what truth or modesty can he say that we measure all things by the laws of nature, and believe nothing above the judgment of our senses? He knoweth well our doctrine is according to the doctrine of St Cyprian[10], St Augustine, and other old fathers, Cyprian. de Cœn. Dom. Cibus mentis, non ventris. that Christ's body is meat for our minds, and not for our bellies; and that the same cannot be eaten with our mouth or teeth, or by any other natural or material means, but only spiritually by faith, which is the mouth of the inner man. He knoweth we teach the people to lift up their hearts, and, as St Chrysostom saith, "to become eagles in this life, and to mount up unto the gates of heaven, Chrysost. 1 Cor. Hom. 24. even unto the heaven[11] of heavens, and so to draw near to Christ's body[12]." He

[8 Id. ibid.]

[9 August. Op. Par. 1679-1700. Ad Bonifac. Epist. xcviii. 9. Tom. II. col. 267; where the words are transposed.]

[10 Cypr. Op. Oxon. 1682. De Cœn. Dom. (Arnold.) p. 44. See before, page 141, note 11.]

[11 Heavens, 1565, 1609.]

[12 Chrysost. Op. In Epist. I. ad Cor. Hom. xxiv. Tom. X. p. 218.]

knoweth we say Christ is present by his Godhead, by his Spirit, and by his grace, and worketh miraculously in the sacrament of his body, as he doth in the sacrament of baptism. All this it pleaseth M. Harding to call the law of nature and the judgment of our senses. Verily we yield no more unto nature than it is meet we should. Neither do we abridge God's omnipotent power. But all vain fantasies of man's head may not be measured by the power of God. This argument the heretic Praxeas used against Tertullian. For thus he said: God is omnipotent, and can do it; therefore we must believe that he doth it. But Tertullian answereth him: *Si tam abrupte in præsumptionibus nostris hac sententia utamur, quidvis de Deo confingere poterimus: quasi fecerit, quia facere potuerit. Non autem, quia omnia potest facere, ideo ... credendum est illum fecisse: ... sed an fecerit, requirendum*[1]: "If we use this saying so rashly in our presumptions, we may imagine of God what we list; as though, because God can do it, that therefore indeed he hath done it. But we may not believe that God hath done every thing, because he is able to do it; but rather we must search out whether he have done it or no." Thus M. Harding's new catholic faith is called of Tertullian a vain presumption.

Tertull. adv. Prax.

M. HARDING. THE SEVENTH DIVISION.

St Ambrose speaketh only of the spiritual sight and fruition of the mind, and requireth no manner gross or corporal presence.

St Ambrose hath these words: Etsi ... Christus nunc non videtur offerre, tamen ipse offertur in terris, quando Christi corpus offertur. Imo ipse offerre manifestatur in nobis, cujus sermo sanctificat sacrificium quod offertur[2]: *"If Christ now be not seen to offer, yet he is offered in earth, when the body of Christ is offered. Yea, it is manifest that himself offereth in us, whose word sanctifieth and consecrateth the sacrifice that is offered." Now, if Christ's body be offered in earth, as this father affirmeth, and that of Christ himself, in respect that the sacrifice which is offered is by his word consecrated; then it followeth, Christ's body to be in so many places as it is offered in. Where by the way this may be noted, that the sacrifice of the church* (150) *is not thanksgiving (as our new masters do teach), but the body of Christ itself, which of the fathers is called "an unbloody and quickening or life-giving sacrifice*[3]."

In Psal. xxxviii.

Sacrificium incruentum et vivificum.

The hundred and fiftieth untruth. For St Augustine calleth it the sacrifice of praise and thanksgiving.

THE BISHOP OF SARISBURY.

In all these words there is no mention of carnal presence; and therefore M. Harding's purpose is hereby but weakly furthered. But, good christian reader, to put thee out of all doubt of St Ambrose's judgment in this behalf, I beseech thee to consider these words that he writeth upon the gospel of St Luke: *Quæ sursum sunt, sapite, non quæ supra terram. Ergo non supra terram, nec in terra, nec secundum carnem te quærere debemus, si volumus invenire*[4]: "Seek the things that be above, not the things that be upon earth. Therefore we must seek thee neither upon the earth, nor in the earth, nor according to the flesh, if we list to find thee." This is St Ambrose's undoubted and most certain judgment; from which we may not be removed by any amplification or shew of words. If M. Harding will needs force and press the bare letter, as I said before of St Chrysostom, he will make St Ambrose in one sentence plain contrary to himself. For first he saith: *Vidimus Principem sacerdotum*[5], *&c.*: "We have seen (Christ) the Prince of priests coming unto us: we have seen him and heard him offering up for us his blood." He addeth immediately: *Etsi nunc Christus non videtur offerre, &c.*: "Although Christ be not seen to offer, yet is he offered in the earth." If we follow the very force and sound of the words, this contradiction of seeing and not seeing cannot be salved. Wherefore, to avoid this inconvenience, we must say that St Ambrose speaketh of the spiritual eyes of our faith, with which eyes we see Christ indeed offering up himself upon the cross. And thus, as St Ambrose saith, *magis videtur, quod non videtur*[6]: "the thing is the better seen

Col. iii. Ambros. in Luc. Lib. x. cap. xxiv.

De iis qui init. Myst. cap. iii.

[[1] Tertull. Op. Lut. 1641. Adv. Prax. 10. p. 641.]

[[2] Ambros. Op. Par. 1686-90. In Psalm. xxxviii. Enarr. 25. Tom. I. col. 853; where *nunc Christus.*]

[[3] See before, page 108.]

[[4] Id. Expos. Evang. sec. Luc. Lib. x. cap. xxiv. 159, 60. Tom. I. col. 1538; where *quæ super terram.*]

[[5] Vidimus Principem sacerdotum ad nos venientem, vidimus et audivimus offerentem pro nobis sanguinem suum.—Id. in Psalm. xxxviii. Enarr. 25. Tom. I. col. 853.]

[[6] Id. Lib. de Myst. cap. iii. 15. Tom. II. col. 328.]

that is not seen." It is best seen with our faith that is least seen with our body; for our faith is sharper than our eye. And in like sense St Augustine saith: *Non vides, quomodo rubeat pars Christi? Interroga oculos fidei. Si crucem vides, attende et cruorem. Si vides quod pendet, attende quod fudit*[7]: "Seest thou not how Christ's portion is red with blood? Ask the eyes of thy faith. If thou see the cross, behold also the blood. If thou see that hangeth, behold also that is[8] shed." Of these eyes and of this sight St Ambrose speaketh; unto which is required neither circumstance of place, nor any manner corporal or fleshly presence. In this sense St Ambrose writeth unto certain holy virgins: *Vestras mentes confidenter altaria dixerim, in quibus quotidie pro redemptione corporis Christus offertur*[9]: "I may boldly call your minds altars; for that in them Christ is daily offered for the redemption of the body."

August. Serm. 119. De Tempore.

Ambros. de Virg. Lib. ii.

Hereof M. Harding reasoneth thus:

Christ is offered in the earth;

Ergo, Christ's body is at one time in many places.

If this argument were good, then would this argument likewise be good:

The Lamb, that is, Christ, was offered from the beginning of the world; Rev. v.

Ergo, Christ's body was really in sundry places before it was born in the world.

M. Harding might better have reasoned thus, and have concluded the contrary:

Christ is not now really and fleshly offered in the earth;

Ergo, Christ's body is not really and fleshly present in many places.

But M. Harding saith: "The sacrifice of the church is not thanksgiving, as our new masters teach us." Certainly our sacrifice is the very body of Christ, and that for ever, according to the order of Melchisedech, evermore standing in God's presence, and evermore obtaining pardon for us; not offered up by us, but offering us up unto God the Father. For the same it is our part to offer unto God our sacrifice of praise and thanksgiving. And this is the doctrine, not only of them whom it liketh M. Harding to call new masters, but also of the oldest and most catholic doctors of the church. And, to allege one instead of many, St Augustine hereof writeth thus: *In illis...carnalibus victimis figuratio fuit carnis,...quam [Christus]...fuerat oblaturus....In isto autem sacrificio [est] gratiarum actio, et commemoratio carnis,...quam pro nobis obtulit*[10]: "In those fleshly sacrifices (of the Jews) there was a figure of the flesh that Christ afterward would offer; but in this sacrifice of the church there is thanksgiving, and a remembrance of that flesh which Christ hath already offered for us." If M. Harding will happily refuse St Augustine, as mistrusted for one of these new masters, yet he may not well[11] refuse his own mass-book. There he himself even at his mass is taught to say: [*Qui*] *tibi offerimus...hoc sacrificium laudis*[12]: "We that do offer up to thee this sacrifice of praise." Wherefore, unless M. Harding will leave his mass, he himself must needs pass in the number of these new masters.

Heb. vi. vii. x. Rom. viii.

August. ad Petr. Diac. cap. xix.

But to conclude, who can better expound St Ambrose's meaning than St Augustine, that was sometime his scholar? He sheweth us by how many ways we may have Christ present among us. His words be these: *Habes Christum et in præsenti, et in futuro: in præsenti per fidem; in præsenti per signum; in præsenti per baptismatis sacramentum; in præsenti per altaris cibum et potum*[13]: "Thou hast Christ both in the time present, and also in the time to come. In the time present thou hast Christ by faith; in the time present by his token; in the time present by the sacrament of baptism; in the time present by the meat and drink of the altar." The like hereof is written also by Origen,

August. in Joh. Tract. 50.

[7 August. Op. Par. 1679-1700. Serm. ccxiii. 8. Tom. V. col. 942.]

[8 It, 1565, 1609.]

[9 Ambros. Op. De Virgin. Lib. II. cap. ii. 18. Tom. II. col. 166; where *quarum mentes altaria confidenter dixerim,* and *Christus immolatur.*]

[10 Fulgent. Op. Par. 1623. Lib. de Fid. ad Petr. Diac. col. 356; where *atque commemoratio est.*]

[11 Will, 1611.]

[12 Missal. ad Us. ac Consuet. Sar. Par. 1527. fol. 156. 2.]

[13 August. Op. In Johan. Evang. cap. xii. Tractat. l. 12. Tom. III. Pars II. col. 633.]

and that in like order and form of words; saving that he addeth, By the preaching of the apostles; and instead of *signum* hath these words: *Per gloriosum crucis signaculum*[1]. Verily the same Origen saith: *Si...virtus Jesu una sit cum eis qui congregantur in nomine ejus, non peregrinatur a suis, sed semper præsto est eis*[2]: "If the power of Jesus be together with them that be assembled in his name, he is not away from his own, but is still present with them." And again he saith: *Nihil [est] contrarium...ipsum Jesum secundum quendam...intellectum esse ubique; secundum alium [intellectum]...peregrinari*[3]: "It is no inconvenience nor contrariety, that Christ in one sense be every where, and in another sense be a stranger and absent from us." Thus many ways, saith St Augustine and Origen, we have Christ present amongst us; and even thus, saith St Ambrose, "Christ is offered in the earth." Whereupon we may conclude thus: We have Christ in faith, in the sign and in the sacrament of baptism, without real or fleshly presence; therefore, we have him likewise without any such real presence in the sacrament of his body.

Orig. in Div. Hom. 1. Orig. in Matt. Tract. 33.

Orig. eodem Tract.

M. HARDING. THE EIGHTH DIVISION.

Chrysostom expoundeth himself. He calleth it a commemoration, a figure, a remembrance; whereunto is required no corporal presence.

We find in Chrysostom a most manifest place for the being of Christ's body in many places at once; so as, though he be offered in many places, yet is he but one Christ, not many Christs. His words be these: Unum est hoc sacrificium: alioquin hac ratione, quoniam multis in locis offertur, multi Christi sunt? Nequaquam; sed unus ubique est Christus, et hic plenus existens, et illic plenus. Unum corpus. Sicut enim qui ubique offertur, unum corpus est, et non multa corpora; ita etiam et unum sacrificium[4]: "*This sacrifice is one; else by this reason, sith it is offered in many places, be there many Christs? Not so; but there is but one Christ every where, being here both*[5] *fully, and there fully also; one body. For as he that is offered every where is but one body, and not many bodies, so likewise it is but one sacrifice." By this place of Chrysostom we see what hath been the faith of the old fathers touching this article; even the same which the catholic church professeth at these days, that one Christ is offered in many places, so as he be fully and perfectly*[6] *here, and fully and perfectly*[6] *there. And thus we perceive what force their arguments have in the judgment of the learned fathers, by which they take away from Christ power to make his body present in many places at once. St Bernard uttereth the faith of the church in his time, agreeable with this, in these words:* Sed unde hoc nobis, piissime Domine, ut nos vermiculi reptantes, &c.[7]: "*From whence cometh this, most loving Lord, that we silly*[8] *worms, creeping on the face of the earth, yea, we that are but dust and ashes, be admitted to have thee present in our hands, and before our eyes, which all and whole sittest at the right hand of thy Father, which also art present all*[9] *in one moment of time from the east to the west, from the north to the south; one in many, the same in divers places; from whence, I say, cometh this? Soothly, not of our duty or desert, but of thy good-will, and of the good pleasure of thy sweetness; for thou hast prepared in thy sweetness for the poor one, O God." In the same sermon, exhorting the church to rejoice of the presence of Christ, he saith:* In terra sponsum habes in sacramento, in cœlis habitura es sine velamento: et hic et ibi veritas; sed hic palliata, ibi manifestata[10]: "*In the earth thou hast thy spouse in the sacrament, in heaven*

In Epist. ad Heb. Hom. 17.

Bernard lived after Christ Anno 1120.

Sermo in Cœna Domini.

[[1] Orig. Op. Lat. Basil. 1545. In Divers. Hom. i. Tom. II. p. 291. See below, page 499, note 11.]

[[2] Id. Op. Par. 1733-59. In Matt. Comm. Ser. 65. Tom. III. p. 882; where *congregatur cum his qui.*]

[[3] Id. ibid. p. 883.]

[[4] Chrysost. Op. Par. 1718-38. In Epist. ad Hebr. cap. x. Hom. xvii. Tom. XII. pp. 168, 9.]

[[5] Both here, 1565, and H. A. 1564.]

[[6] Perfitely, 1565, and H. A. 1564.]

[[7] Sed, &c. piissime Jesu, ut &c. super faciem terræ; nos, inquam, qui pulvis et cinis sumus, te præsentem habere mereamur præ manibus, præ oculis, qui totus et integer sedes ad dexteram Patris? Qui etiam unius horæ momento ab ortu solis usque ad occasum, ab aquilone usque ad austrum præsto es omnibus, unus in multis, idem in diversis locis. Unde hoc, inquam? Certe non ex debito, vel ex merito nostro; sed ex voluntate tua, et dulcedinis tuæ beneplacito. Parasti enim in dulcedine tua pauperi, Deus. —Bernard. Op. Par. 1690. Serm. de Excell. Sacram. 3. Vol. II. Tom. v. col. 669.]

[[8] Seely, 1565, and H. A. 1564.]

[[9] To all, 1565, and H. A. 1564.]

[[10] Id. ibid. 7. col. 671; where *manifesta.*]

thou shalt have him without veil or covering: both here and there[11] *is the truth* (*of his presence*)*; but here covered, there opened.*"

Christ whole here, and whole there.

THE BISHOP OF SARISBURY.

This place is uttered by St Ambrose, Primasius, Remigius, Haimo, Sedulius, in like manner and form of words, and hath been often alleged and often answered. If it had pleased M. Harding to suffer St Chrysostom to tell out his own tale, the place had been plain of itself. For thus he saith: *Offerimus quidem, sed recordationem facientes mortis ejus. Hoc sacrificium exemplar illius est. Hoc, quod nos facimus, in commemorationem fit ejus, quod factum est. Christus enim ait, Hoc facite in meam commemorationem....Id ipsum semper offerimus: magis autem sacrificii recordationem operamur*[12]: "We offer indeed, but we do it in remembrance of his death. This sacrifice is an exemplar or figure of that sacrifice. The thing that we do is done in remembrance of that thing that was done before. For Christ saith, 'Do this in my remembrance.' We offer up the same thing; nay, rather we work the remembrance of a sacrifice." By thus many sundry ways Chrysostom opened his own meaning. Yet all this M. Harding thought best to dissemble closely, and to pass it in silence. Certainly, the commemoration or figure or remembrance of Christ's death maketh small proof for corporal or fleshly presence. True it is that whole Christ is fully at every communion, as Chrysostom saith: not that he is there in fleshly or bodily presence; for so St Chrysostom saith not; but for that by his grace and holy Spirit he worketh wholly and effectually in the hearts of the faithful. Chrysost. in Epist. ad Heb. Hom. 17.

St Augustine and other learned fathers have used the like manner of speech, and in the same seem fully to express Chrysostom's mind. St Augustine writeth thus: *Veritas una est, qua illustrantur animæ sanctæ: sed quoniam multæ sunt animæ, in ipsis multæ veritates dici possunt; sicut ab una facie multæ in speculis imagines apparent*[13]: "There is but one truth wherewith the blessed souls are lightened. But, forasmuch as the souls be many, it may be said, that in the same are many truths; as sundry images appear in sundry glasses, notwithstanding the face be one." Again, St Augustine saith: *Sapientia Dei, Verbum Dei, Dominus Jesus Christus ubique præsens est: quia ubique est veritas, ubique est sapientia. Intelligit quis in oriente justitiam: intelligit quis in occidente justitiam. Nunquid alia est justitia, quam ille intelligit, alia, quam iste*[14]*?* "The Wisdom of God, the Word of God, our Lord Jesus Christ, is every where present; for the truth is every where, and wisdom is every where. One man understandeth righteousness in the east, another understandeth righteousness in the west; and doth the one of them understand one righteousness, and the other another?" So likewise, and somewhat near to the manner of Chrysostom's speech, Origen speaketh: *Et hodie in hac congregatione Dominus loquitur; et non solum in hac, sed etiam in alio cœtu, et in toto orbe docet Jesus, quærens organa, per quæ doceat*[15]: "And even this day, in this congregation, the Lord speaketh; and not only in this, but also in another company, and in the whole world, Jesus teacheth, seeking instruments by which he may teach." In this sort is Christ present at the holy ministration, because his truth, his wisdom, his righteousness, his word is there present, as the face is present in the glass; not by any bodily or fleshly presence. In this manner St Ambrose writeth: *Cœlum aspice: Jesus illic est. Terram intuere: Jesus adest....Si ascenderis in cœlum, Jesus illic est: si descenderis ad infernum, adest. Hodie, cum loquor, mecum est: intra hunc punctum, intra hoc momentum. Et si in Armenia nunc loquatur Christus*[16]*, Jesus adest. Nemo enim dicit Dominum Jesum, nisi in Spiritu sancto*[17]: "Look up into the heaven: there is Jesus. Behold the earth: Jesus is there.

August. in Psal. xi.

August. in Joh. Tract. 35.

Orig. in Luc. Hom. 32.

Ambros. in Luc. Lib. ii. cap. i.

[11 Also there, H. A. 1564.]

[12 Chrysost. Op. In Epist. ad Hebr. cap. x. Hom. xvii. Tom. XII. pp. 168, 9.]

[13 August. Op. Par. 1679-1700. In Psalm. xi. Enarr. 2. Tom. IV. col. 65.]

[14 Id. in Johan. Evang. cap. viii. Tractat. XXXV. 4; where *alius in occidente*.]

[15 Orig. Op. In Luc. Hom. xxxii. Tom. III. p. 970.]

[16 Christianus, 1565.]

[17 Ambros. Op. Par. 1686-90. Expos. Evang. sec. Luc. Lib. II. cap. i. 13. Tom. I. col. 1286; where *in infernum, hoc punctum,* and *loquitur Christianus.*]

Arguments taken of Christ's humanity.

If thou mount up into heaven, there is Jesus: if thou go down into hell, Jesus is present. Even now while I speak, Jesus is with me, even at this hour, even at this minute. And if any christian man speak now in Armenia, so far hence Jesus is with him. 'For no man saith, The Lord Jesus, but in the Holy Ghost'."

Chrysost. ad Pop. Ant. Hom. 51.

And such kind of presence at one time in sundry places is avouched by St Chrysostom, not only of Christ's body, which is immortal and glorious, but also of any other godly mortal man. For thus he writeth: *Vidistis caritatis excellentiam, quemadmodum unum hominem inexpugnabilem reddat, et multiplicet; et quemadmodum unus in multis locis esse possit; idem et in Perside, et Romæ. Nam quod natura non potest, potest caritas. Nam ejus hoc quidem hic erit, hoc autem illic. Quin potius integer hic, et integer illic. Itaque si mille habeas amicos, vel duo millia, perpende quorsum possit potentia pervenire. Vides quemadmodum caritas res sit augmentativa. Hoc enim est mirabile, quod unum facit millecuplum*[1]: "Thou hast seen the excellent working of charity, how it fortifieth a man, as it were in a castle, and multiplieth him, and, being one man, maketh him many. Thou hast seen how one man may be in many places; one man in Persia, and the same man in Rome. For charity can do that nature cannot do. Of one man one portion shall be here, and another portion there. Nay rather, he shall be whole here, and whole there. Therefore, if one man have a thousand friends, or two thousand, consider, how far he may reach by his[2] power. Thou seest how that charity is a matter of increase. And this is a wonder, it maketh one man to be a thousand-fold more than he is, and as if he were a thousand men."

The same answer may serve also for St Bernard; howbeit his authority in this case is not great, as living in the very time of corruption, at the least eleven hundred years after Christ, and so five hundred years at the least without the compass of the first six hundred years.

M. HARDING. THE NINTH DIVISION.

Thus all these fathers, as likewise the rest, confess as it were with one mouth, that Christ sitteth at the right hand of his Father, and yet[3] *is here present in the sacrament the same time; that he is in heaven and in earth at once, in many and divers places, one, and the same*[4] *is every where offered, the one true sacrifice of the church. And this article is by them so clearly and plainly uttered, that* (151) *figures, significations, tropes, and metaphors, can find no appearance or*[5] *colour at all. Whereby the new masters' reasons seem very peevish: Christ is ascended;* ergo, *he is not in the sacrament. Christ is in heaven sitting at the right hand of his Father;* ergo, *he is not in earth. Christ's body is of nature finite;* ergo, *it is contained in a place circumscriptively;* ergo, *it is not in many places.*

The hundred and fifty-first untruth. For these very words of Ambrose and Chrysostom are full of figures, as shall appear.

THE BISHOP OF SARISBURY.

M. Harding needeth no great study to answer our arguments. It is sufficient for him to pronounce by authority, "these new masters' arguments be all peevish." Verily, it appeareth by the whole substance and course of M. Harding's book, that he hath some good pretty skill in peevish arguments; otherwise he could not have them and use them in such plenty. But the old learned fathers oftentimes and commonly used such arguments of Christ's humanity; and yet were they never reproved as peevish for the same, but only by heretics. St Augustine saith: *Donec seculum finiatur, sursum est Dominus; sed tamen etiam hic nobiscum est veritas Domini. Corpus enim,... in quo resurrexit, [in] uno loco esse oportet*[6]: "Until

De Consecr. Dist. ii. Prima.

[[1] Vidisti caritatis excellentiam, qualiter unum inexpugnabilem, &c. qualiter unus et multis in locis esse potest, idem, &c.: et quod, &c. mille habeat, &c. perpende quo rursum potentia perveniet. Vides quomodo caritas sit res, &c. facit millenum.—Chrysost. Op. Lat. Basil. 1547. Ad Pop. Ant. Hom. li. Tom. V. col. 350.]

[[2] This, 1565.]

[[3] H. A. 1564, omits *yet*.]

[[4] That the same, H. A. 1564.]

[[5] Nor, 1565, 1609, and H. A. 1564.]

[[6] August. in Corp. Jur. Canon. Lugd. 1624. Decret. Gratian. Decr. Tert. Pars, De Consecr. Dist. ii. can. 44. col. 1935; where *hic etiam*, and *veritas Dominus*.]

Arguments taken of Christ's humanity.

the world be ended, the Lord is above; yet notwithstanding, even here is the truth of the Lord. For the body wherein he rose again must needs be in one place." St Cyrillus saith: *Christus non poterat in carne versari cum apostolis, postquam ascendisset ad Patrem*[7]: "Christ could not be conversant with his apostles in his flesh, after that he had ascended unto his Father." So St Augustine, writing against the heretic Manichee, that seemed much to savour of M. Harding's error, saith: [*Christus*] *secundum præsentiam.... corporalem, simul et in sole, et in luna, et in cruce esse non potuit*[8]: "Christ, according to the presence of his body, could not be both in the sun, and in the moon, and upon the cross at one time." Again he saith: [*Christus*] *venturus est, illa angelica voce testante, quemadmodum ire visus est in cœlum, id est, in eadem carnis forma atque substantia; cui profecto immortalitatem dedit, naturam non abstulit*[9]: "Christ shall come again, as it is witnessed by the angel, even as he was seen to go into heaven; that is, in the same shape and substance of his flesh; unto which flesh as he hath given immortality, so hath he left unto it the same nature that it had before." Thus St Augustine. And further he saith, that "whoso holdeth that Christ's body is both in heaven and in earth at one time, utterly dissolveth and destroyeth the nature of the body of Christ[10]." To be short, and not to overcharge the reader with allegations, St Augustine seemeth to give a special note by way of prophecy touching the[11] same. For thus he saith: *His... dictis mox ascendit in cœlum: præmunire voluit aures nostras adversus eos, quos, procedentibus temporibus, exsurrecturos esse prædixerat, et dicturos, Ecce hic... Christus, ecce illic: quibus ne crederemus, admonuit. Nec ulla nobis excusatio est, si crediderimus adversus vocem Pastoris* [*nostri*] *tam claram, tam apertam, tam manifestam, ut nemo vel obtusus, et tardus corde, possit dicere, Non intellexi*[12]: "These words spoken, he ascended into heaven. Hereby he gave our ears a *præmunire* against them, which he foretold us would rise in process of time, and say: 'Behold, here is Christ; behold, there is Christ.' Unto whom he warned us we should give no credit. Neither have we now any manner excuse, if we believe them against the voice of our Shepherd, being so clear, so open, and so plain, that no man, be he never so heavy or dull of heart, can justly say, I understood him not." Thus the old catholic doctors thought they might warrant the arguments for good and effectual, that they took of Christ's humanity, and of the natural substance of his body. But perhaps they must all go for new masters, and their arguments likewise be condemned for peevish.

Cyril. in Joh. Lib. xi. cap. iii.
August. contr. Faust. Manich. Lib. xx. cap. xi.
August. Epist. 57.
August. de Unit. Eccles. cap. x.
Matt. xxiv. Luke xvii.

Let us therefore consider the arguments that M. Harding and his company have founded hereupon. Thus therefore reason they: Christ is ascended into heaven in his humanity: "the heavens must hold his body," as St Peter saith, "until all things be restored." St Paul saith, "Our conversation is in heaven, from whence we look for our Saviour Jesus Christ." Christ saith, "I leave the world, and go to my Father:" "the poor ye shall still have among you, but me ye shall not have;" *ergo*, say they, Christ is still here in the world in his corporal and fleshly presence. Christ's body is of nature and substance finite; *ergo*, it is in places infinite. Christ hath two sorts of bodies: one only local; all the rest of the other sort not local. It is in place, yet it occupieth or filleth no place. It is a very natural man's body; yet is it neither round, nor square, nor thick, nor broad, nor short, nor long. It hath in it no distance or difference of parts, as between eye and eye, or eye and ear, or head and foot; but eye, ear, arm, hand, heel, toe, head, and foot are all together, and each is other, and all is one. In ten thousand several places Christ's body is full and whole; and yet all these are but one

Acts i.
Acts iii.
Phil. iii.
John xvi.
Matt. xxvi.
Thom. in iii. Quæst. 76. Art. 30.

[7 Εἰ γὰρ καὶ ἀποδημεῖ σαρκὶ παραστήσας ἑαυτὸν ὑπὲρ ἡμῶν τῷ Πατρὶ, κ.τ.λ.—Cyril. Alex. Op. Lut. 1638. Comm. in Joan. Lib. xi. cap. ii. Tom. IV. p. 933.]

[8 August. Op. Par. 1679-1700. Contr. Faust. Lib. xx. cap. xi. Tom. VIII. col. 341; where *posset.*]

[9 Id. Lib. ad Dard. seu Epist. clxxxvii. 10. Tom. II. col. 681.]

[10 Secundum hanc formam non est putandus ubique diffusus. Cavendum est enim, ne ita divinitatem adstruamus hominis, ut veritatem corporis auferamus.—Id. ibid. See also ibid. 9, 18, 41. cols. 680, 3, 92.]

[11 This, 1565.]

[12 Id. Contr. Donat. Epist. vulg. Lib. de Unit. Eccles. cap. xi. 28. Tom. IX. col. 355; where *contra vocem.*]

Arguments taken of Christ's humanity. body[1]. Thus one is many, and many are one: above is beneath, and beneath is above: local is not local, and not local is local; and all this without the authority either of God's holy word, or of any one old catholic father. These be M. Harding's catholic conclusions; even the very same that were used and avouched by Eutyches, Apollinarius, Manichæus, and other like heretics in old times; and therefore they may not now be counted peevish. And that thou mayest the better feel the savour and soundness of these men's doctrine, I beseech thee, gentle reader, to consider these words of Robert Holcot, a great doctor of that side: *Si fuissent mille hostiæ in mille locis* [*eo tempore, quo Christus pependit in cruce,*] *Christus fuisset crucifixus in mille locis*[2]: "If there had been a thousand hosts in a thousand places at that very time when Christ hung upon the cross, then had Christ been crucified in a thousand places." Again he saith: *Pono, quod tempore illo*[3], *&c.*[4]: "I suppose that at the same time the soul of Christ, departing from his body upon the cross, had come unto and rested at one[5] of the said hosts. If so, then had Christ's body been both quick and dead in one[6] time." Thus much D. Holcot. Here hast thou, good reader, a taste of M. Harding's doctrine, in respect whereof all other doctrine must needs be condemned and cast as peevish. Alas! they wander up and down in mere vanities, and, as St Paul saith, they would be the[7] doctors of the law, "not understanding neither what they say, nor what they affirm." Verily, St Augustine saith: *Quando ... de forma servi cogitas in Christo, humanam effigiem cogita, si est in te fides*[8]: "When thou thinkest of the form of a servant in Christ, think of the form of a man, if thou have any faith in thee."

Holcot. in iv. Sent. Quæst. 3.

1 Tim. i.

August. in Joh. Tract. 40.

This matter, saith M. Harding, is so clearly uttered by these fathers, that figures, significations, tropes, and metaphors can have no place. M. Harding would not thus have said, if he had any regard unto his reader. By the very order and tenor of these fathers' words, Christ cometh, and yet cometh not. Christ is not seen, and yet is seen. Christ is touched with hands, yet no man can touch him. Every man seeth him without guile or error, yet no man seeth him. Elias is above, and, at the same time, the same Elias is beneath. Elias' coat is called Elias. Chrysostom and Ambrose are fain both to correct the rigour of their speech, and to use these words, memory, exemplar, commemoration, and remembrance. And what is there here else but figures? Yet, saith M. Harding, "significations and figures here can have no place." It is too great tyranny, so much to mock and abuse God's people.

M. HARDING. THE TENTH DIVISION.

In making of which slender arguments, they will not seem to acknowledge whose body it is, even that which is proper to God, whose power is over all, and to whom all things obey.

THE BISHOP OF SARISBURY.

Yes, undoubtedly, we acknowledge the body of Christ to be the body of the Son of God, and therefore the body of very God. Yet nevertheless we know, and M. Harding also ought to know, that the same body of Christ is a creature, and therefore no God. And surely, if M. Harding had well considered the principles of his own doctrine, he might soon have found out the folly of this reason. For Albertus Magnus, his own doctor, is full against him. Thus he writeth: *Corpus Christi non est in pluribus locis ratione unionis, sed ratione consecrationis, quia consecratur in pluribus locis*[9]: "The body of Christ is not in many places by

Albert. Magn. in Dion. Eccles. Hierarch.

[1 Aquinat. Op. Venet. 1595. Summ. Theolog. Tert. Pars, Quæst. lxxvi. Art. 3. Tom. XII. fol. 246.]

[2 Holkot. sup. Quat. Lib. Sentent. Lugd. 1497. Lib. IV. Quæst. iii. fol. m. vii. 2.]

[3 Illos, 1611.]

[4 ...pono quod tempore illo quo anima Christi fuit separata a corpore venisset sponte ad species illas existentes in a domo et fuisset simul cum corpore sub istis speciebus: tunc autem corpus Christi fuit animatum in a vel non? &c.—Holkot. ubi supr.]

[5 In one, 1565, 1609.]

[6 At one, 1565, 1609.] [7 1565 omits *the*.]

[8 August. Op. Par. 1679-1700. In Johan. Evang. cap. viii. Tractat. xl. 4. Tom. III. Pars II. col. 566.]

[9 ... corpori Christi non convenit esse in pluribus sacramentaliter secundum unionem ad divinam naturam ... sed in quantum est cibus spiritualis: et ideo est in omnibus speciebus significantibus spiritualiter refectionem, ubicunque consecrentur, &c.—Albert. Magni Op. Lugd. 1651. In Lib. de Eccles. Hierarch. cap. iii. Tom. XIII. p. 45.]

mean of the union it hath with the Godhead, but by mean of the consecration, because it is consecrate in many places." Thus Albertus wrote of Christ's body, contrary to M. Harding's meaning, notwithstanding he was not ignorant whose body it was.

Eutych. Pap. Epist. 1.

Indeed Eutychianus saith: *Hæc...fallendi simplices atque ignorantes hæreticis occasio est, &c.*[10]: "This occasion heretics have to beguile the simple and the ignorant, that the things that are spoken of Christ according to his manhood[11], they imagine the same to be spoken according to the infirmity of the divine nature; and because Christ, being one person, speaketh all things of himself, they say he spake all things of his Godhead." Thus Eutychianus saith M. Harding's reason served well heretics in old times, therewith to beguile the people then, as he doth now. So the old heretics Saturninus, Manichæus, and Marcion denied the verity of Christ's flesh, because it is joined and united to the Godhead. So Athanasius and Epiphanius say that the heretic Apollinarius held and taught the people, that Christ's body was of one substance with the deity[12].

Athanas. de Incarn. Christi. Epiph. de Ebion. *τὸ σῶμα Χριστοῦ ὁμοούσιον εἶναι τῇ θεότητι.*

In consideration of the same union, the emperor Justinian was led into the heresy of certain that were called *ἀφθαρτοδοκηταὶ*, and held that Christ's body was evermore glorious, and without corruption[13]. So likewise was Eutyches deceived; likewise the godly learned father St Hilary[14], as it is said before. All these heresies and errors sprang only of M. Harding's reason, for that the authors and maintainers thereof, yielding reverence unto Christ's body as duty required, overmuch considered whose body it was.

Evagr. Lib. iv. cap. xxxix. Niceph. Lib. xvii. cap. xxix. Hilar. Lib. x. de Trin.

It is indeed, as I said before, the body of God. But St Augustine saith: *Non...quod in Deo est, est ubique, ut Deus*[15]: "Whatsoever is in God is not therefore every where, as God is." And again: *Cavendum est,...ne ita divinitatem astruamus hominis, ut veritatem corporis auferamus*[16]: "We must beware that we do not so defend the Godhead of the man, that we destroy the truth of his body." And therefore Epiphanius, expressing the state of Christ's immortal body as it is now in heaven, writeth thus: *Sedet ad dextram Patris, &c.*[17]: "He sitteth at his Father's right hand in glory, not putting away his body, but joining the same in spiritual condition in the perfection of one Godhead; even as our bodies, that now are sown according to the flesh, shall be raised again according to the spirit." So saith the godly martyr Vigilius: [*Caro Christi,*] *quando in terra fuit, non erat...in cœlo; et nunc, quia est in cœlo, non est utique in terris*[18]: "The flesh of Christ, when it was in the earth, was not in heaven; and now, because it is in heaven, is not verily in the earth." This holy father assureth it and avoucheth it for true, and saith: "Verily it is not in the earth;" and his reason is only this: "Because it is in heaven." And he concludeth thus at the last: *Hæc est fides, et professio catholica, quam apostoli tradiderunt, martyres roboraverunt, et fideles hucusque custodiunt*[18]: "This is the catholic profession and faith, which the apostles have delivered, the martyrs have confirmed, and the faithful hitherto do continue." Thus the old catholic fathers in old times believed and wrote of Christ's body; and yet they had not forgotten whose body it was.

August. Epist. 57. ad Dard. Epiph. Lib. iii. In brevi declaratione de fide catholica. *ὡς καὶ τὰ ἡμῶν σώματα μέλλει, &c.* Vigil. contr. Eutych. Lib. i. Quia est in cœlo. The catholic faith.

[10 Hæc itaque fallendi, &c. ut quæ ab eo secundum hominem dicta sunt, dicta esse secundum divinæ naturæ infirmitatem mentiantur; et quia unus atque idem est, loquens omnia, quæ loquitur de semetipso, omnia eum de divinitate loquutum esse contendant.—Eutych. ad Joan. et Bœt. Episc. Epist. i. in Crabb. Concil. Col. Agrip. 1551. Tom. I. p. 175.]

[11 Manhead, 1565.]

[12 ...λέγοντες τὴν τοῦ Χριστοῦ σάρκα...ὁμοούσιον τῆς θεότητος.—Athanas. Op. Par. 1698. De Incarn. Christ. contr. Apoll. Lib. I. 2. Tom. I. Pars II. p. 923.

...ἵνα δείξῃ ὡς οὐκ ἦν ὁμοούσιον τὸ σῶμα τῇ θεότητι, ὡς φησὶν Ἀπολινάριος.—Epiph. Op. Par. 1622. Adv. Hær. Lib. I. Hær. xxx. 28. Tom. I. p. 153.]

[13 Evagr. in Hist. Eccles. Script. Amst. 1695-1700. Lib. IV. cap. xxxix. p. 415.

Niceph. Call. Lut. Par. 1630. Lib. XVII. Tom. II. pp. 780, &c.]

[14 Hilar. Op. Par. 1693. De Trin. Lib. x. 16, &c. cols. 1045, &c.]

[15 August. Op. Lib. ad Dard. seu Epist. clxxxvii. 10. Tom. II. col. 681; where *ita sit ubique.*]

[16 Id. ibid.]

[17 ...ἐκάθισεν ἐν δεξιᾷ τοῦ Πατρὸς ἐν δόξῃ, οὐκ ἀποθέμενος τὸ σῶμα, ἀλλὰ συνενώσας εἰς πνευματικὸν, ἐν τελειότητι μιᾶς θεότητος· ὡς καὶ τὰ ἡμῶν σώματα μέλλει, τὰ νῦν σπειρόμενα ψυχικῶς, ἐγείρεσθαι πνευματικῶς.—Epiph. Op. Adv. Hær. Lib. III. Expos. Fid. Cath 17. Tom. I. p. 1100.]

[18 Vigil. adv. Eutych. in Cassandr. Op. Par. 1616. Lib. IV. pp. 546, 7; where *in cœlo est, utique in terra, confessio,* and *nunc usque.*]

M. HARDING. THE ELEVENTH DIVISION.

But because M. Jewel, and they of that sect, seem to set little by these fathers, though very ancient, St Bernard excepted, and of the church holden for saints, I will bring forth the authority of Martin Bucer, a late doctor of their[1] *side, though not canonizate for a saint as yet, for that I know. This new father, whom they esteem so much, and was the reader of divinity in Cambridge in king Edward's time, very vehemently, and for so much truly, affirmeth the true real presence of Christ's body in the sacrament. For he saith: "Christ said not, This is my spirit, this is my virtue; but, 'This is my body.' Wherefore we must believe," saith he, "Christ's body to be there, even the same that did hang upon the cross, our Lord himself." Which in some part to declare, he useth the similitude of the sun for his purpose, contrary to M. Jewel's negative, to prove Christ's body present, and that really and substantially, in what places soever the sacrament is rightly ministered. His words be these:* Ut sol vere uno in loco cœli visibilis circumscriptus est, radiis tamen suis præsens vere et substantialiter exhibetur ubilibet orbis; ita Dominus, etiamsi circumscribatur uno loco cœli arcani et divini, id est, gloriæ Patris, verbo tamen suo et sacris symbolis, vere et totus ipse Deus et homo, præsens exhibetur in sacra cœna, eoque substantialiter: quam præsentiam non minus certo agnoscit mens credens verbis his Domini et symbolis, quam oculi vident et habent solem præsentem demonstratum, et exhibitum sua corporali luce. Res ista arcana est, et novi testamenti, res fidei: non sunt igitur huc admittendæ cogitationes de præsentatione corporis, quæ constat ratione hujus vitæ etiam patibilis et fluxæ[2]. Verbo Domini simpliciter inhærendum est, et debet fides sensuum defectui præbere supplementum[3]. *Which may thus be Englished: "As the sun is truly placed determinately in one place of the visible heaven, and yet is exhibited truly and substantially by his beams every where abroad in the world; so our Lord, although he be contained in one place of the secret and divine heaven, that is to wit, the glory of his Father, yet for all that, by his word and holy tokens, he is exhibited present in his holy supper truly, and himself whole, God and man, and therefore substantially or in substance. Which presence, the mind giving credit to these our Lord's words and tokens, doth no less certainly acknowledge, than our eyes see, and have the sun present shewed and exhibited with his corporal light. This is a secret matter, and of the new testament; a matter of faith: therefore herein thoughts be not to be admitted of such presentation*[4] *of the body, as consisteth in the manner of this life, passible and transitory. We must simply cleave to the word of our Lord; and, where our senses fail, there must faith help to supply." Thus we see how Bucer, in sundry other points of faith both deceived and also a deceiver, confirmeth the truth of this article pithily and plainly. Such is the force of truth, that oftentimes it is confessed by the very enemies of truth.*

[*Truth confessed by the enemy of truth.* H. A. 1564.]

This similitude of the sun clearly openeth the whole matter. For the substance or body of the sun is really present only in one place.

In Comment. in xvi. cap. Matt.

Fight not with the church, M. Jewel, but fight with the enemy of the church. Fight with him whom you have followed in departing from the church, who nevertheless, by force of truth, is driven against you to confess the truth in those most plain words: Vere et totus ipse Deus et homo, præsens exhibetur in sacra cœna, eoque substantialiter: "*In this holy supper himself, God and man, is exhibited present truly and whole, and therefore substantially.*"

THE BISHOP OF SARISBURY.

God's name be praised! neither do we refuse the judgment of the ancient fathers in these cases; neither hath Master Harding, for ought that may yet appear, any just cause thus to vaunt himself of the same. Here he allegeth the authority of Doctor Bucer, even as the heretic Eutyches sometime, to maintain his heresy, alleged St Cyprian[5], or as the Nestorian heretics alleged the authority

In Concil. Chalced. Act. I. Concil. Tom. i.

[1 Their own, H. A. 1564.]

[2 Fluxa, 1611.]

[3 Bucer. in Quat. Evang. Enarr. 1553. In Matt. cap. xxvi. fol. 185. 2; where *vitæ etiamnum*.]

[4 A presentation, 1565, 1609, and H. A. 1564.]

[5 Perhaps Cyprian is an error for Cyril. Eutyches repeatedly alleged the authority of Cyril, Athanasius, and other fathers, as making for him.—Libell. Confess. Eutych. in Concil. Calched. Act. I. in Concil. Stud. Labb. et Cossart. Lut. Par. 1671-2. Tom. IV. col. 136. Concil. Constant. Act. VII. in eod. cols. 228, &c.]

of the Nicene council[6]. For notwithstanding Doctor Bucer, to avoid contention as a man desirous of peace, was content to yield unto certain indifferent terms, as Osius that learned father sometime did in the council of Ariminum to the Arians[7], yet was his resolution herein evermore thoroughly and fully known. And the very similitude or example that he useth of the sun putteth the matter out of all question. For like as the body or compass of the sun, being in one certain place of the heavens, reacheth out his beams, and giveth influence into the world; even so Christ, the sun of justice, being in heaven in one place at the right hand of God, likewise reacheth out his beams, and giveth his influence into the faithful, and so feedeth them, not by bare imagination or fantasy, but truly, substantially, and indeed. And as the sun is more comfortable, and more refresheth the world, being absent, by his beams, than if his very natural substance and compass lay here upon the earth; even so the body of Christ, being in the glory of his Father, in the very substance and nature of our flesh, and there evermore entreating mercy for our sins, is much more comfortable unto us, and more quickeneth both our bodies and souls by his heavenly and spiritual influence, than if it were here present fleshly before our eyes. And as the sun, not coming down from heaven, nor leaving his place, is nevertheless present with us in our houses, in our faces, in our hands, and in our bosoms; even so Christ, being in heaven, not coming down, nor leaving his room there, yet nevertheless is present with us in our congregations, in our hearts, in our prayers, in the mystery of baptism, and in the sacrament of his body and blood. Therefore St Ambrose saith: *Maria,... quia quærebat in terra, tangere non potuit: Stephanus tetigit, quia quærebat in cœlo*[8]*:* "Mary could not touch Christ, because she sought him upon the earth; but Stephen touched him, because he sought him in heaven." And again he saith: *Non enim corporali tactu,... sed fide tangimus*[9]*:* "For we touch not Christ by any bodily mean, but by our faith." And therefore again he saith: *Stephanus intra cœlos Dominum cernit absentem*[10]*:* "Stephen seeth Christ, being absent, within the heavens." So saith Origen: *Per evangelistarum et apostolorum prædicationem, per sui sancti corporis et sanguinis sacramentum, per gloriosum crucis signaculum... nobiscum Deus*[11]*:* "God is with us by the preaching of the evangelists and apostles, by the sacrament of his body and blood, and by the glorious sign of his cross." So St Augustine: *O stulta infidelitas persequentis! Si quæris exilium, quo Christianus jubeatur ire, prius si potes inveni, quo Christus cogatur exire*[12]*:* "O the fond infidelity of this persecutor! If thou seek a place of banishment, whither thou mayest command a christian man to go; first, if thou can, find a place from whence thou mayest command Christ to depart." And again thus he writeth unto the godly widow Italica: *Non debes te desolatam arbitrari, cum in interiore homine habeas Christum præsentem per fidem in corde tuo*[13]*:* "Thou mayest not think thyself[14] to be desolate, while thou hast Christ present in thy heart, in the inner man, by faith." So again: *Non... est Judæus, non est Græcus, &c. Sed omnia et in omnibus Christus*[15]*:* "There is no Jew, there is no gentile; but Christ is all and in all." In like sense St Hierome saith: *Tangat... digitulo; et ultro exibimus. Domini est terra, et plenitudo ejus. Christus loco non tenetur inclusus*[16]*:* "Let him push us with his finger; and we will forth willingly. The earth is the Lord's and the fulness thereof. Christ is not holden prisoner in any place."

In Apolog. Cyril. In Præfat. Conc. I. Sard. Hilarius.

The sun.

Ambros. in Luc. Lib. x. cap. xxiv.

Ibid.

Ambros. Serm. 58. de Maria Magdal.

Orig. in Div. Evang. Locos. Hom. 1.

August. de Nat. B. Cypr. Serm. 12.

August. Epist. 6.

August. de Serm. Dom. in Mont. Lib. i.

Hieron. adv. Error. Joh. Hieros.

[6 Exempl. Relat. Orient. ad calc. Cyril. Lib. Apolog. in Crabb. Concil. Col. Agrip. 1551. Tom. I. p. 586.]

[7 Præfat. Concil. Sard. in Crabb. Concil. Col. Agrip. 1551. Tom. I. p. 328.

Hilar. Op. Par. 1693. Lib. de Synod. seu de Fid. Oriental. 63. cols. 1186, 7. Hilary says it was at Sirmium that Osius yielded.]

[8 Ambros. Op. Par. 1686-90. Expos. Evang. sec. Luc. Lib. x. cap. xxiv. 160. Tom. I. col. 1538; where *quia quæsivit.*]

[9 Id. ibid. 155. col. 1537.]

[10 Maxim. Taur. Hom. ad calc. Leon. Magni Op. Lut. 1623. De Sep. Dom. et de Mar. Magdal. Hom. iv. col. 612. This homily was improperly attributed to St Ambrose.]

[11 Orig. Op. Lat. Basil. 1545. In Divers. Hom. i. Tom. II. p. 291; where *gloriosæ.*]

[12 August. Op. Par. 1679-1700. In Nat. Cypr. I. Serm. cccix. 2. Tom. V. col. 1247; where *unde Christus.*]

[13 Non enim te desolatam putare debes, cum, &c. præsentem Christum, &c.—Id. ad Ital. Epist. xcii. 1. Tom. II. col. 227.]

[14 Theeself, 1565.]

[15 Id. de Serm. Dom. in Mont. Lib. I. cap. xv. 40. Tom. III. Pars II. col. 182; where *neque Græcus.*]

[16 Hieron. Op. Par. 1693-1706. Adv. Johan. Jerosol. Epist. xxxix. Tom. IV. Pars II. col. 338.]

Thus is Christ present among[1] us: thus we feel him: thus we see him. But all this is the work of faith: it needeth no fleshly or local presence. Therefore St Augustine saith: *Non recte tangitur, id est, ... non recte in illum creditur*[2]: "He is not touched well: that is to say, he is[3] not believed well." So saith St Bernard: [*Tangitur*], *sed affectu, non manu; voto, non oculo; fide, non sensibus*[4]: "He is touched, but with devotion, not with hand; with zeal, not with eye; with faith, not with sense." And thus we say, we have Christ present, not, as M. Harding saith, only for a minute of an hour, wherein is neither savour nor comfort; but verily, effectually, and, if he be delighted with that word, substantially, and for ever, even unto the consummation of the world. Neither doth he deny that Christ is present, that denieth this imagination of gross and fleshly presence. Origen saith: *Si ... virtus Jesu congregatur cum his, qui congregantur in nomine ejus, non peregrinatur a suis, sed semper præsto est eis*[5]: "If the power of Jesus be together with them that are gathered in his name, then is not he absent from his own, but is evermore present with them."

August. in Joh. Tract. 121.

Bernard. in Cant. Cantic. Serm. 26.

Orig. in Matt. Tract. 33.

By these few I trust it may appear that we neither are departed from the church of God, nor fight against the church. But you, M. Harding, under this glorious title of the church, think to carry yourself invisible. Howbeit, as there be two sorts of faiths, so are there two sorts of churches; the one true, the other false. Your church, being as now utterly void of God's word, is as a lantern without light. Leo, writing against such as you be, saith thus: *Ecclesiæ nomine armamini, et contra ecclesiam dimicatis*[6]: "Ye arm yourselves[7] with the name of the church, and yet ye fight against the church." St John in his Revelations saith: "They name themselves Jews," that is, the people of God, "but they are the synagogue of Satan." O fight not, M. Harding, thus against God: fight not against your own conscience. It is hard for you thus to kick against the prick. The more ye fight, the more ye bewray your own nakedness. These colours and shadows must needs fade[8]; God with his truth will have the victory. Amen.

Leon. ad Palæst.

Rev. ii.

Acts ix.

M. HARDING. THE TWELFTH DIVISION.

Now to be short, whereas the chief arguments that be made against the being of Christ's body in many places at once be deduced of nature, in respect that this article seemeth to them to abolish nature; it may please them to understand that God, who is author of nature, can by his power do with a body that which is above the nature of a body, nature not destroyed, but kept and preserved whole. Which Plato the heathen philosopher would soon have been induced to believe, if he were alive; who, asked what was nature, answered: Quod Deus vult: "*That which God will.*" *And therefore we believe that Enoch and Elias, yet mortal by nature, do by power of God live in body, and that above nature. Abacuc was by the same power caught up, and in a moment carried from Jewry to Babylon, his nature reserved whole. St Peter by God according to nature walked on the earth; the same by God besides*[9] *nature walked upon the waters. Christ, after condition of nature assumpted, suffered death in body; the same Christ by his divine power entered with his body in to his disciples through doors closed.*

[*God working above nature destroyeth not nature.* H. A. 1564.]

M. Harding seemeth not well to consider what Plato meant.

THE BISHOP OF SARISBURY.

Our proofs are grounded, not only upon natural reason, but also upon the express and known will of God. And by such arguments the learned fathers were wont in old times to dispute of Christ's humanity against Apollinarius, Manicheus, Eutyches, and other like heretics, without controlment. For natural reason, holden within her bands, is not the enemy, but the daughter of God's

[1 Amongst, 1565, 1609.]

[2 August. Op. Par. 1679-1700. In Johan. Evang. cap. xx. Tractat. cxxi. 3. Tom. III. Pars II. col. 808; where *in eum*.]

[3 It, 1611.]

[4 Bernard. Op. Par. 1690. In Cant. Serm. xxviii. 9. Vol. I. Tom. IV. col. 1369.]

[5 Orig. Op. Par. 1733-59. In Matt. Comm. Ser. 65. Tom. III. p. 882.]

[6 Leon. Magni Op. Lut. 1623. Ad Palæst. Episc. Epist. lxxxiii. 8. col. 444.]

[7 Yourself, 1565.]

[8 Vade, 1565.]

[9 Beside, H. A. 1564.]

truth. And therefore he must be very unreasonable that will thus without cause be angry with reason. But it appeareth that M. Harding, as he is utterly without scriptures and doctors in these cases, so is he also void of reason. As touching Plato, it seemeth there was hard hold, when a natural philosopher must stand forth to prove Christ's mysteries. This matter, within these few hundred years, hath been attempted many ways, by logic, by philosophy, by the metaphysics, and by the names of old fathers. But when none of all these helps would serve, they imagined and brought forth *animosam fidem*, a faith without any word of God, bold to believe they knew not what. In the end, finding their want and weakness herein, for that this faith had no ground, they devised miracles, and fires enow[10], and joined them with it: then was the matter sufficiently and fully proved.

But Plato saith: *Natura est, quod Deus vult:* "Nature is that thing that God will." First, what if M. Harding understand not what Plato meant? And what if Plato never understood what M. Harding meaneth? Yet must Plato's name serve to prove all M. Harding's fantasies? Plato saith: "Nature is whatsoever God will." Must we therefore conclude that cold is hot, white is black, accident without subject, subject without accident, a body is no body, a nature finite is infinite? What a strange kind of philosophy hath M. Harding found out! It is a simple weapon that these men will refuse to serve their turn.

The philosophers called *Epicuræi* held this fantasy, that God sitteth in heaven idly and at ease, never encumbering or troubling himself with the rule of the world; and that therefore nature ruleth itself only by chance, and at adventure, without any certain direction of God's government; and that whatsoever is done therein is no part of God's doing. Contrariwise, the philosophers called *Stoici* held another fantasy, that God himself is nothing else but nature, and that therefore all things are wrought by necessity and force of destiny, and that God is able to work no miracle, nor to do any thing contrary to the common course of nature. Both these follies Plato reproved by this short answer: *Natura est, quod Deus vult.* His meaning is, that nature is subject and obedient unto God, and that there is neither chance nor necessity in the course of nature; but all things are ordered by God's appointment, and natural causes are only the instruments of God's will. And therefore some compare nature to the horse, and God to the horseman, that bridleth her and turneth her whither he listeth. And for the same cause Origen saith: *Anima mundi est virtus Dei*[11]: "The soul of the world is the power of God." And St Basil saith: "The world is the school of our souls, to lead us to know God[12]." Therefore God was able by his power to divide the sea, to pull back and to stay the sun, to open the earth, to make the water of Jordan to stand as a wall, to stay the fire from burning and the water from drowning. If any man list to know the cause hereof, there is none other but God's will. In this sense the philosopher Simonides was wont to say: *Solus Deus est metaphysicus:* "God alone is supernatural." And Pindarus for the same called God ἀριστότεχνον, "the best or skilfullest artificer." Likewise St Augustine saith: *Quomodo est... contra naturam, quod Dei fit voluntate, cum voluntas tanti... Conditoris sit cujuscunque rei natura*[13]*?* "How is it against nature, that is done by God's will, seeing the will of so noble a Creator is the nature of every thing?" This undoubtedly was Plato's meaning. Now let us examine M. Harding's reasons.

Origen. περὶ ἀρχῶν. Lib. ii. cap. i.

Basil. Hex. Hom. 1. ψυχῶν... διδασκαλεῖον, καὶ θεογνωσίας... παιδευτήριον.

August. de Civit. Dei, Lib. xxi. cap. viii.

Nature is whatsoever God will: Elias and Enoch are yet alive in their bodies: Abacuc was caught and carried to Babylon: St Peter walked upon the sea; *ergo*, Christ's body is at one time in a thousand places. These arguments hold *a posse ad esse*, and might have stood[14] the heretics Manichæus and Eutyches in some good stead; but in catholic schools they have no place.

[[10] Enough, 1565.]

[[11] ...universum mundum velut animal quoddam ...puto, quod quasi ab una anima, virtute Dei,...teneatur.—Orig. Op. De Princip. Lib. II. cap. i. 3. Tom. I. pp. 77, 8.]

[[12] Basil. Op. Par. 1721-30. In Hexaem. Hom. i. Tom. I. p. 6.]

[[13] August. Op. De Civ. Dei, Lib. XXI. cap. viii. 2. Tom. VII. col. 628; where *conditæ rei cujusque natura sit.*]

[[14] Stand, 1565.]

Christ in his own hands.

But how is M. Harding so well assured of God's will? How knoweth he that God will have Christ's body to be in a thousand places at one time, to be every where, to be infinite, to be no body? Verily, the ancient fathers, for any thing that may appear, never knew it. Contrariwise he might have said, God's holy will was that Christ should take the natural substance of a man's body, and that "in all things he should be like unto his brethren," and that his body should be a creature, and, as St Augustine saith, should be in one place[1]. This is God's known and express will; therefore by Plato's judgment this is nature. Certainly St Augustine saith, as it is before alleged: *Christus corpori suo immortalitatem dedit, naturam non abstulit*[2]: "Christ gave immortality to his body; but he took not from it the former nature of a body." Thus much hath M. Harding gotten by the authority of Plato.

Heb. ii.

August. de Consec. Dist. 2. Prima.

August. Epist. 57.

M. HARDING. THE THIRTEENTH DIVISION.

Christ at his last supper according to nature sat down with his twelve disciples, and among them occupied a place at the table visibly; by his divine power there he held his body in his hands invisibly: (152) *for, as St Augustine saith,* ferebatur... manibus suis[3], *"he was borne in his own hands:" where nature gave place, and his own*[4] *body was in more places than one. Verily,* non est abbreviata manus Domini, *"the hand of our Lord is not shortened:" his power is as great as ever it was. And therefore let us not doubt but he is able to use nature finite infinitely; specially now, the nature of his body being glorified after his resurrection from the dead. And as the living is not to be sought among the dead, so the things that be done by the power of God above nature are not to be tried by the*[5] *rules of nature.*

The hundred and fifty-second untruth, standing in unsufficient reporting and misconstruing St Augustine's words.

In Expositione Psal. xxxiii.

THE BISHOP OF SARISBURY.

St Augustine saith: *Christus ferebatur in manibus suis*[3]: "Christ was borne in his own hands." These words are often alleged, and seem at the view to sound somewhat of M. Harding's side: but, being well weighed and considered, they discharge themselves[6], and are soon answered. First, it is known and confessed that St Augustine, in reporting these words, either by mean of the translation, or by some other error, was much overseen, and alleged that for scripture that indeed neither is any portion of the scripture, nor elsewhere to be found. For where he saith David was borne in his own hands, the very text is this: *Collabebatur in manibus eorum*: "He went reeling in their hands." And so St Basil allegeth and expoundeth the same place: παραφερόμενος ἐν ταῖς χερσὶ τῶν οἰκετῶν[7]: "Carried along in the servants' hands." And thus St Augustine, being deceived in the text, was fain to force the same to some violent construction.

1 Sam. xxi.

Basil. in Psal. xxxiii.

Yet, saith M. Harding, St Augustine's words be plain: "Christ was borne in his own hands." It is neither indifferent nor true dealing thus to nip and to proine[8] the doctors' sayings; and, alleging a few words, to leave out the rest, and especially such words as be material, and able to give light unto the whole. For St Augustine saith not, Christ bare himself really, substantially, and indeed in his own hands, as it is here untruly supposed; neither, as Master Harding hath added of his own, "by his divine power, or invisibly;" but contrariwise he expoundeth himself by these words: *Ipse se quodammodo portabat*[9]: "In a manner and after a sort he carried himself." This word *quodammodo* in the schools is called *terminus diminuens*, which oftentimes in reasoning breedeth error. For these words, *quodammodo*, "after a sort," and *vere*, "verily or indeed," are ever contrary. So saith St Augustine: *Sacramentum corporis Christi secundum quendam modum*

Quodammodo.

August. Epist. 23. ad Bonifac.

[1 August. in Corp. Jur. Canon. Lugd. 1624. Decret. Gratian. Decr. Tert. Pars, De Consecr. Dist. ii. can. 44. col. 1935. See before, page 486.]

[2 Id. Op. Par. 1679-1700. Lib. ad Dard. seu Epist. clxxxvii. 10. Tom. II. col. 681. See before, page 461, note 16.]

[3 Id. in Psalm. xxxiii. Enarr. ii. 2. Tom. IV. col. 215.]

[4 One, H. A. 1564.]

[5 H. A. 1564, omits *the*.]

[6 Themself, 1565.]

[7 Basil. Op. Par. 1721-30. Hom. in Psalm. xxxiii. Tom. I. p. 143.]

[8 Proine: prune.]

[9 August. Op. In Psalm. xxxiii. Enarr. ii. 2. Tom. IV. col. 216; where *portabat quodammodo*.]

corpus Christi est[10]: "The sacrament of Christ's body in a certain sort is the body of Christ." And this sort or manner he expoundeth thus: *Nisi enim sacramenta similitudinem quandam earum rerum, quarum sacramenta sunt, haberent, omnino sacramenta non essent*[11]: "Unless sacraments had some likeness of those things whereof they be sacraments, they should utterly be no sacraments." Christ in his own hands. Ibid.

Likewise saith Bertramus: *Secundum quendam modum corpus Christi est. Modus hic in figura est, et [in] imagine*[12]: "The sacrament after a certain manner is the body of Christ: this manner standeth in a figure and in a representation." So likewise the very barbarous gloss upon the decrees expoundeth the same: *Cœleste sacramentum, quod vere repræsentat corpus Christi, dicitur corpus Christi, sed improprie. Unde dicitur, suo modo: sed non rei veritate, sed significante mysterio; ut sit sensus, Vocatur corpus Christi; id est, significat [corpus Christi]*[13]: "The heavenly sacrament, which verily doth represent the flesh of Christ, is called Christ's body; but not in plain kind of speech. Therefore St Augustine saith, *suo modo*, 'after a sort;' which is not in the very truth of the matter, but by a mystery signifying, that the meaning be thus: It is called the body of Christ, because it signifieth the body of Christ." Touching the thing that Christ held in his hand, St Augustine confesseth it was bread; for thus he writeth: *Quamvis ... panem, quem Dominus gestavit in manibus, oculis suis [non] aspexerint*[14]: "Albeit they never saw with their eyes the bread that the Lord held in his hands." Yet the same bread, because it is a sacrament of Christ's body, "after a sort," as St Augustine saith, is also called Christ's body. Thus doth St Augustine oftentimes use this word *quodammodo*. For example, he writeth thus: *Ecclesia, ... quos lucrata fuerit aliquo modo, [eos] manducat quodammodo*[15]: "The church after a sort eateth them whom by any mean she hath gotten." And again upon the same psalm: *Quid est ... hærere cornibus, nisi quodammodo crucifigi? Figura est ista de Christo*[16]: "What was it else that the wether was tied by the horns, but after a sort to be crucified? Therefore this is a figure of Christ." In this sense St Augustine saith Christ, *quodammodo*, "after a sort," not verily or indeed, but in a sacrament or in a figure, bare himself in his hands. Bertram. de Sacr. Euch. De Consecr. Dist. 2. Hoc est, in Glossa. August. de Verb. Dom. in Evang. Matt. Serm. 33. August. in Psal. xxx.

But M. Harding will reply, St Augustine saith thus: *[Hoc] quomodo intelligatur in ipso Davide*[17] *secundum literam, non invenimus; in Christo autem invenimus*[18]: "How this may be taken in David himself, according to the letter, we find not; but in Christ we find it." Therefore he will say, this must be verified in Christ, "even according to the letter." This error riseth of the misunderstanding of these words of St Augustine, *secundum literam;* which sometime are used for the literal sense, or the very sound of the bare words; sometime for the historical sense, that is to say, for the course and tenor of the story. Now saith St Augustine, that David should any way bear himself, *secundum literam*, "according to the story written of him," it doth not appear; but that Christ, "after a sort," that is, by way of a sacrament, thus carried himself, even in the story of the gospel, which is to say, *secundum literam*, it doth appear. And that these words *secundum literam* be oftentimes thus used, any man may soon perceive that shall diligently note and consider the ancient fathers. First, St Augustine in the place alleged, uttereth this matter of David in this sort: *In Regnorum libris, ubi omnia nobis scripta sunt, quæ pertinent ad res gestas Davidis*[17] *... non invenimus hoc*[19]: "In the books of the Kings, where as all things are written to us that pertain to the doings of David, this thing we find not." And again in the same place: *[Christus] cum commendaret corpus et sanguinem suum, humilitatem suam commendavit, in eo,* August. in Psal. xxxiii. Secundum literam. August. in Psal. xxxiii. Ibid. Conc. 2.

[10 Id. Ad Bonifac. Epist. xcviii. 9. Tom. II. col. 267; where *secundum quemdam modum* are the first words.]

[11 Si enim sacramenta quamdam similitudinem, &c. non haberent, &c.—Id. ibid.]

[12 Ratramn. Lib. de Corp. et Sang. Dom. Oxon. 1838. cap. lxxxiv. p. 42; where *Christi esse cognoscitur et modus iste.*]

[13 Corp. Jur. Canon. Decret. Gratian. Decr. Tert. Pars, De Consecr. Dist. ii. Gloss. in can. 48. col. 1937; where *repræsentat Christi carnem, significati mysterio,* and *vocatur Christi corpus.*]

[14 August. Op. De Verb. Evang. Luc. xiv. Serm. cxii. 4. Tom. V. col. 566; where *nec panem.*]

[15 Id. in Psalm. xxx. Enarr. iii. 5. Tom. IV. col. 156.]

[16 Id. ibid. 9. col. 159.]

[17 David, 1565, 1609.]

[18 Id. in Psalm. xxxiii. Enarr. i. 10. Tom. IV. col. 214; where *David.*]

[19 Id. ibid. 2. col. 209; where *David.*]

Being in a mystery.

quod in ipsa historia scriptum est in illo quasi furore Davidis[1]: "When Christ recommended unto us his body and blood, he recommended unto us his humility in that thing that is written in the very story touching that madness of David." This is that[2] St Augustine meant by these words, *secundum literam*. Now that this word *litera* is often taken for the story, it doth many ways appear. St Augustine saith thus: *Ambrosius cum tractaret [hunc locum] ait: Nec historia nec litera docet, Mariam gladio finivisse vitam*[3]: "Ambrose, writing hereof, saith thus: Neither the story nor the letter doth teach us that Mary was slain with a sword." So St Hierome: *Escam dedit timentibus se*: "He gave food to them that fear him." In the time of hunger he fed Elias; in the wilderness he rained manna unto the Jews: he addeth, [*et*] *hoc secundum literam*[4], "and this according to the letter;" which is, according to the story. So likewise St Gregory: *Subditur, quod de eo minime scriptum legitur; effudit in terram viscera mea: ex qua re necesse est, ut, dum hæc juxta literam invenire non possumus, ea quæ in verbis ejus secundum historiam sonant, juxta spiritum inquiramus*[5]. Thus St Augustine useth these words *secundum literam*, not for the literal sense, as these men would fain have it, but for the record and knowledge of the story written of David. M. Harding should have remembered, that misunderstanding of his doctor maketh no sufficient proof. Howbeit, it is much to be feared that M. Harding of purpose left out this word *quodammodo*; and not of ignorance, but wittingly and willingly misreported and falsified St Augustine's meaning. Certainly St Augustine hath not one of all these words, neither "by divine power," nor "invisibly," nor "nature gave place," nor "Christ's body was in more places than one."

August. de Sanct. Serm. 35.

Hieron. in Psal. cx. et cxi.

Gregor. in Jobum, Lib. xiii. cap. vi.

M. HARDING. THE FOURTEENTH DIVISION.

And that all absurdities and carnal grossness be severed from our thoughts, where true christian people believe Christ's body to be in many places at once, they understand it so to be in a mystery. Now to be in a mystery is not to be comprehended in a place, but by the power of God to be made present in sort and manner as he[6] *himself knoweth, verily so as no reason of man can attain it, and so as it may be shewed by no examples in nature. Whereof that notable saying of St Augustine may very well be reported:* O homo, si rationem a me poscis, non erit mirabile:... exemplum quæritur, non erit singulare[7]: *that is, "O man, if* (153) *(herein) thou require reason, it shall not be marvellous: seek for the like example, and then it shall not be singular." "If God's working be comprehended by reason," saith holy Gregory, "it is not wondrous: neither faith hath meed, whereto man's reason giveth proof*[8]*."*

[*Being in a mystery.* H.A. 1564.]

Being in a mystery requireth no corporal or real presence.

August. in Epist. ad Volusianum. Item Ser. 159. De Tempore.

The hundred and fifty-third untruth. For these words of Augustine and Gregory pertain nothing to the sacrament.

[*Gregorius in Homil.* H.A. 1564.]

THE BISHOP OF SARISBURY.

Being in a mystery, as it is before answered, like as it requireth no circumstance or necessity of place, so it requireth no bodily or real presence. Contrariwise, if Christ's body were present indeed, and that in such gross and fleshly sort as is here conceived, then were it no mystery. For to be present in a mystery, and to be bodily and fleshly present, are taken for contraries. And therefore the gloss saith, as is before alleged: *Sacramentum dicitur corpus Christi, non rei veritate, sed significante mysterio*[9]: "The sacrament of Christ's body is called Christ's body, not in truth of the matter, but by a mystery signifying."

De Consecr. Dist. 2. Hoc est, in Gloss.

[1 Id. Enarr. ii. 4. col. 216; where we find *commendat* occurring twice, and *David*.]

[2 Is it that, 1565, 1609.]

[3 Id. in Fest. Assumpt. B. Mar. Serm. ccviii. 3. Tom. V. Append. col. 344; where *litteræ docent*, and *vitam finisse*. This is not a genuine sermon of Augustine.]

[4 Hieron. Op. Par. 1693-1706. Brev. in Psalt. Psalm. cx. Tom. II. Append. col. 425.]

[5 ...nisi subderetur quod de, &c. ut dum hoc, &c. —Gregor. Magni Papæ I. Op. Par. 1705. Lib. XIII. in cap. xvi. B. Job. cap. xvi. 19. Tom. I. col. 424.]

[6 H. A. 1564, omits *he*.]

[7 August. Op. Par. 1679-1700. Ad Volus. Epist. cxxxvii. 8. Tom. II. col. 405. Id. in Pasch. xi. Serm. clxix. 2. Tom. V. Append. col. 294. The words as here cited are from the last-named place: in the former they somewhat differ. The sermon is not really by Augustine.]

[8 Sed sciendum nobis est, quod divina operatio si ratione comprehenditur, non est admirabilis: nec fides habet meritum, cui humana ratio præbet experimentum.—Gregor. Magni Papæ I. Op. In Evang. Lib. II. Hom. xxvi. 1. Tom. I. col. 1552.]

[9 Corp. Jur. Canon. Lugd. 1624. Decret. Gratian. Decr. Tert. Pars, De Consecr. Dist. ii. Gloss. in can. 48. col. 1937. See before, page 503, note 13.]

But, whereas it is further said that this mystical presence is known only unto God, and, I trow, to M. Harding, and to no man beside; all this is nothing else but religious[10] folly, imagined only to astonne and amaze the simple. For the scriptures and holy fathers are acquainted with no such mystery. The sacrament of baptism is a mystery, even as is the sacrament of Christ's body; and, as Christ is present in the one, so is he also present in the other; that is to say, truly, verily, effectually, and indeed; howbeit, not in this gross manner of M. Harding's fleshly presence. The places of St Augustine and St Gregory concern only Christ's incarnation, the union of the divinity and the humanity, and other such articles and grounds of christian religion, wherein nature and reason utterly have no place; and therefore, being spoken of one thing, are applied by M. Harding unto another. Neither is M. Harding able truly to say, that in any of all those places there is either mention once made or one word spoken of the sacrament. Wherefore it seemeth M. Harding would purposely mislead his reader, and teach him to reason in this sort: Being in a mystery.

Christ was miraculously incarnate of the blessed virgin;
Ergo, Christ's body is really and fleshly in the sacrament.

True it is that the faith of our religion cannot be proved by discourse of reason. But every fantasy may not go for christian faith. St Paul saith: *Fides ex auditu; auditus ex verbo Dei*: "Faith cometh by hearing; hearing cometh by the word of God." Certainly M. Harding's new faith or fantasy in the time of the old catholic fathers was neither christened nor known in the world; as may appear by their own witness of good record. For besides others, whom in this treatise I have touched upon occasion by the way, St Augustine writeth purposely hereof unto Dardanus in this wise: *Noli... dubitare, ibi nunc esse hominem Christum Jesum, unde venturus est*[11], *&c.*: "Doubt thou not but Christ Jesus, as man, is there from whence he shall come; and have thou in remembrance, and faithfully hold the christian confession, that he is risen from the dead; that he is ascended into heaven; that he sitteth at the right hand of his Father; and that from thence, and from no where else, he shall come to judge the quick and the dead, even as he was seen going into heaven; that is, in the same form and substance of his body; to which body undoubtedly he hath given immortality, but hath not taken from the same the nature of a body. According to this form (of man) we may not think that Christ is poured abroad into all places. For we must beware we do not so defend the Godhead of the man, that we destroy the truth of his body." Again: *Unus Christus Jesus; ubique, per id quod Deus est; in cœlo autem, per id quod homo*[12]: "Christ Jesus is one person, and the same every where, in that he is God; but he is in heaven, in that he is man." Again he saith: *Semper quidem divinitate nobiscum est: sed, nisi corporaliter abiret a nobis, semper ejus corpus carnaliter videremus*[13]: "Christ by his Godhead is ever with us; but, unless he had departed away bodily from us, we should evermore carnally see his body." These words are specially to be noted. If Christ were bodily here, he should carnally be seen: therefore, by St Augustine's judgment, if Christ were bodily present in the sacrament, we should see him carnally in the sacrament. Again: *Et abiit, et hic est; et rediit, et nos non deseruit. Corpus enim suum intulit cœlo; majestatem* [*autem*] *non abstulit mundo*[14]: "He is gone, and yet is here. He is returned to his Father, and yet hath not forsaken us. For he hath carried his body into heaven; but he hath not taken his majesty from the world." Again: *Pauperes semper habebitis vobiscum*[15], *&c.*: "'The poor ye shall have ever-

Rom. x.

August. Epist. 57.

Cui profecto immortalitatem dedit; naturam non abstulit. Cavendum est, ... ne ita divinitatem astruamus hominis, ut veritatem corporis auferamus.

August. de Verb. Dom. in Evang. secund. Joh. Serm. 60.

August. in Johan. Tract. 50.

Ibid.

[10 A religious, 1565.]

[11 Noli, &c. memoriterque recole, et fideliter tene christianam confessionem, quoniam resurrexit a mortuis, adscendit in cœlum, sedet ad dexteram Patris, nec aliunde quam inde venturus est ad vivos mortuosque judicandos...quemadmodum ire visus est in cœlum, id est, in eadem carnis forma atque substantia; cui profecto, &c. Secundum hanc formam non est putandus ubique diffusus. Cavendum, &c.—August. Op. Lib. ad Dard. seu Epist. clxxxvii. 10. Tom. II. col. 681.]

[12 Id. ibid.]

[13 Id. de Verb. Evang. Johan. xvi. Serm. cxliii. 4. Tom. V. col. 692.]

[14 Id. in Johan. Evang. cap. xi. Tractat. l. 4. Tom. III. Pars II. col. 631; where *deserit*.]

[15 Pauperes, &c., me autem non semper habebitis. Accipiant hoc et boni, sed non sint solliciti: loquebatur enim de præsentia corporis sui. Nam secundum majestatem suam, secundum providentiam, secundum ineffabilem et invisibilem gratiam, impletur quod ab eo dictum est, Ecce ego

Christ's body in one place.

more[1] with you, but me ye[2] shall not have.' Let good men hear this, and not be careful. For this he spake of the presence of his body. For according to his majesty, according to his providence, according to his unspeakable and invisible grace, it is fulfilled that he said, 'I am with you always until the consummation of the world.' But according to the flesh that the Word received, according to that he was born of the virgin, according to that he was taken of the Jews, according to that he was nailed to the cross, according to that he was taken down, and lapped in a shroud, and laid in the grave, and rose again, and shewed himself; in this respect it is true that he said, 'Ye shall not evermore have me with you.'"

August. in Epist. Johan. Tract. 1.

Likewise again: *Dominus consolatur nos, qui ipsum jam in cœlo sedentem manu contrectare non possumus, sed fide contingere*[3]: "The Lord doth comfort us, that cannot touch him with our hand, sitting now in heaven, but may touch him notwithstanding with our faith." And again: *Si illi propterea crediderunt, quia tenuerunt et palpaverunt, nos quid facimus? Jam Christus ascendit in cœlum, et non est venturus, nisi in fine, ut judicet de vivis et mortuis*[4]: "If they therefore believed in Christ, because they held him and touched him, what do we then? For Christ is now ascended into heaven, and will not come again, but in the end, to judge the quick and the dead." So saith Origen: [*Christus*] *secundum... divinitatis suæ naturam non peregrinatur* [*a nobis*]; *sed peregrinatur secundum dispensationem corporis, quod suscepit*[5]: "Christ, according to the nature of his Godhead, is not a stranger unto us; but he is a stranger to us touching the dispensation of the body, which he hath received." Again: *Nec... est homo qui est, ubicunque duo vel tres in ejus nomine fuerint congregati, &c.*[6]: "It is not Christ, as man, that is wheresoever two or three be gathered in his name; neither is Christ, as man, with us always until the consummation of the world." So likewise saith St Hierome: *Christus non est corporaliter in ecclesia: surgens enim a mortuis, ascendit in cœlum*[7]: "Christ is not now bodily in the church; for, being risen from the dead, he is ascended into heaven."

August. in Epist. Johan. Tract. 2.

Orig. in Matt. Tract. 33.

Orig. in eadem Hom.

Hieron. in Prov. Lib. i. cap. viii.

I pass over St Ambrose, St Gregory, St Cyril, St Basil, Vigilius, Fulgentius, Didymus, Beda, and other like ancient fathers. Thus were they then resolved of Christ's body, and this they took to be the catholic faith.

Yet neither were they therefore condemned for new masters, nor followed they only the judgment of nature, nor led they the world with peevish reasons, nor, touching Christ's body, had they forgotten whose body it was, nor were they counted the enemies of God's omnipotent power, nor were they then thought to fight against the church. But M. Harding, with his new-devised fantasy, is a patron and a maintainer of the Manichees, of the Apollinarists, of the Eutychians, and other more horrible and old condemned heretics.

vobiscum sum usque in consummationem seculi. Secundum carnem vero quam Verbum assumsit, secundum id quod de virgine natus est, secundum id quod a Judæis prehensus est, quod ligno confixus, quod de cruce depositus, quod linteis involutus, quod in sepulchro conditus, quod in resurrectione manifestatus, non semper habebitis vobiscum.—Id. ibid. cap. xii. Tractat. l. 13. cols. 633, 4.]

[1 Evermore have, 1565.]

[2 You, 1565, 1609.]

[3 Id. in Epist. Johan. cap. i. Tractat. i. 3. Tom. III. Pars II. col. 828; where *consolans*.]

[4 Id. ibid. cap. ii. Tractat. ii. 1. col. 836; where *si enim propterea illi*, and *faciemus*.]

[5 Orig. Op. Par. 1733-59. In Matt. Comm. Ser. 65. Tom. III. p. 883.]

[6 Nec, &c. in nomine ejus, &c. Neque homo nobiscum est omnibus diebus usque ad consummationem seculi.—Id. ibid.]

[7 Non est, inquiunt, Christus corporaliter.—Hieron. Op. Par. 1693-1706. Comm. Lib. I. in Proverb. cap. vii. Tom. V. col. 538. This is not a genuine work of Jerome.]

OF ELEVATION.

THE SEVENTH ARTICLE.

THE BISHOP OF SARISBURY.

Or that the priest did then hold up the sacrament over his head.

[OF THE ELEVATION OR LIFTING UP OF THE SACRAMENT.—
Article VII. H. A. 1564.]

M. HARDING.

*Of what weight this ceremony is to be accounted, catholic christian men, whom you call your adversaries, M. Jewel, know no less than you. Verily, whereas it pleaseth you thus to jest, and, like a Lucian, to scoff at the sacraments of the church, and the reverent use of the same, calling all these articles in general the highest mysteries and greatest keys of our religion, without which our doctrine cannot be maintained and stand upright; understand you that this, as sundry other articles which you deny and require proof of, is not such, ne never was so esteemed. * The priest's lifting up or shewing of the sacrament is not one of the highest mysteries or greatest keys of our religion; and the doctrine of the catholic church may right well be maintained and stand without it. But it appeareth you regard not so much what you say, as how you say somewhat for colour of defacing the church: which whiles you go about to do, you deface yourself more than you seem to be ware of, and do that thing whereby among good christian men, specially the learned, you may be ashamed to shew your face. For as you have over rashly, yea, I may say, wickedly affirmed the negative of sundry other articles, and stoutly cracked of your assurance thereof, so you have likewise of this. For, perusing the ancient fathers' writings, we find record of this ceremony used even* (154) *from the apostles' time forward. St Dionyse, that was St Paul's scholar, sheweth that the priest at his time, after the consecration, was wont to* (155) *hold up the dreadful mysteries, so as the people might behold them. His words be these, according to the Greek:* Pontifex divina munera laude prosecutus, sacrosancta et augustissima mysteria conficit, et collaudata in conspectum agit per symbola sacre proposita[8]: "*The bishop, after that he hath done his service of praising the divine gifts, consecrateth the holy and most worthy mysteries, and bringeth them so praised into the sight of the people, by the tokens set forth for that holy purpose." On which place the ancient Greek writer of the scholies upon that work saith thus:* τὸν κουφισμὸν καὶ τὴν ὕψωσιν τῆς μιᾶς εὐλογίας τοῦ θείου ἄρτου φησὶ, ὃν ὑψεῖ ἱερεὺς λέγων, Τὰ ἅγια τοῖς ἁγίοις[9]: Loquitur de unius benedictionis, nimirum panis divini, elevatione, quem pontifex (156) in sublime attollit, dicens, Sancta sanctis: "*This father speaketh in this place of the lifting up of the one blessing (that is to say, of the one form or kind of the sacrament), even of that divine bread which the bishop lifteth up on high, saying, Holy things for the holy." * In St Basil's and Chrysostom's*[10] *mass we find these words:* Sacerdos elevans sacrum panem, dicit, Sancta sanctis[11]: "*The priest, holding up that sacred bread, saith, Holy things for the holy." In St Chrysostom's mass we read that, as the people is kneeling down after the example of the priest and of the deacon, the deacon, seeing*

* The elevation of the sacrament is now no article of religion; yet in the late time of tyranny it was more looked unto than any one article of the Trinity.

The hundred and fifty-fourth untruth, as shall appear.

[*Elevation of the sacrament.* H.A. 1564.]

The hundred and fifty-fifth untruth; for Dionysius hath no such words.

Eccles. Hier. cap. iii.

The hundred and fifty-sixth untruth, standing in false translation. He meaneth lifting up a little from the table; not over the head.

Chrysostom saith, "modicum."

* Here is no mention of lifting over the head. M. Harding mistaketh one thing for another.

[8 Dionys. Areop. Op. Antv. 1634. De Eccles. Hierarch. cap. iii. 2. Tom. I. p. 284.]

[9 Max. Schol. in eod. p. 306; where φησὶν ὃν ὑψοῖ ὁ ἱερεύς.]

[10 Chrysostom, 1611.]

[11 Pontifex exaltans panem, orat secrete...voce sublata dicit, Sancta sanctis.—Basil. Lit. in Cassandr. Op. Par. 1616. Liturg. cap. viii. p. 23.]

the priest stretching forth his hands, and taking up that holy bread, πρὸς τὸ ποιῆσαι τὴν ἁγίαν ὕψωσιν, ἐκφωνεῖ, πρόσχωμεν, ad sacram elevationem peragendam palam edicit, Attendamus [1], "*to do the holy elevation, speaketh out aloud, Let us be attent; and* (*then*) *the priest saith* (*as he holdeth up the sacrament*), *Holy things for the holy.*"

A fable. *Amphilochius, of whom mention is made before*[2] *in the life of St Basil, speaking of his wondrous celebrating the mass, among other things saith thus:* Et post finem orationum exaltavit panem, sine intermissione orans, et dicens, Respice, Domine Jesu Christe, &c.[3]: "*And, after that he had done the prayers of consecration, he lifted up the bread, without ceasing praying, and saying, Look upon us, Lord Jesus Christ, &c.*" *The same St Basil meant likewise of the elevation and holding up of the sacrament after the custom of the occidental church, in his book* de Spiritu Sancto, *where he saith thus:* Invocationis *cap. xxvii.* verba, dum ostenditur panis eucharistiæ et calix benedictionis, quis sanctorum nobis scripto reliquit[4]? "*Which of the saints hath left unto us in writing the words of invocation, whiles the bread of* eucharistia (157) (*that is to wit, the blessed sacrament, in form of bread*), *and the consecrated chalice, is shewed in sight?*" *He speaketh there of many things that be of great authority and weight in the church, which we have by tradition only, and cannot be avouched by holy scripture. Of shewing the holy mysteries to them that be present in the sacrifice the old doctors make mention not seldom.*

The hundred and fifty-seventh untruth, standing in false construction.

St Chrysostom declareth the manner of it, saying, that such as were *In Epist. ad Ephes. Serm. 3. in Moral.* *accounted unworthy and heinous sinners were put forth of the church whiles the sacrifice was offered, whiles Christ and that Lamb of our Lord was sacrificed*[5]. *Which being put out of the church, then were the vails* (*of the altar*) *taken away, to the intent the holy mysteries might be shewed in sight, doubtless to stir the people to more devotion, reverence,* (158) *and to the adoration of Christ's body in them present. And thus for the elevation or holding up of the sacrament we have said enough.*

The hundred and fifty-eighth untruth. For the Grecians knew neither this kind of adoration nor real presence.

THE BISHOP OF SARISBURY.

M. Harding seemeth in part to disclaim this article, as a matter of small weight, and none of the principal keys of his religion; wherein I see not but I may safely and easily grant unto him, adding notwithstanding thus much withal, that the less it is the less hurt is in it. Yet notwithstanding, of late days it was otherwise esteemed, and most severely exacted, as the thing wherein stood their adoration, which was the whole price and beauty of their mass. The priest was wicked that would not use it: the people was wicked that would not allow it: their greatest doctors have travailed painfully to know the cause and signification of this mystery, and yet cannot find it. All this notwithstanding, it is now confessed to be a small matter, of no great weight, and such as the church may well spare without hindrance. But, as M. Harding here saith his doctrine may sufficiently be maintained, and stand upright without this ceremony of elevation; even so may we truly and justly say, that the heavenly and infallible doctrine of the gospel of Christ may likewise stand upright, and be maintained, not only without this new ceremony, but also without their private mass, without their half communion, without their strange unknown prayers, without their supremacy of Rome, without their transubstantiation, and other like fantasies by them devised.

Yet are not they all of that side hitherto fully resolved touching their own elevation, neither when, nor where, nor wherefore it first came in use, nor what it meaneth. Some of them say the lifting up of the sacramental bread signifieth Christ's incarnation: some of them say it signifieth Christ hanging upon the cross; some of them that it signifieth the taking down of his body from the

---

[1 Sacerdos sustollens modicum portionem, quæ est in sancta patina, dicit, Sancta sanctis.—Chrysost. Lit. in eod. ibid. cap. vii. p. 19. See also below, page 512, note 2.]

[2 Afore, H. A. 1564.]

[3 Amphiloch. Op. Par. 1644. In Vit. S. Basil. pp. 175, 6. See before, page 188.]

[4 Basil. Op. Par. 1721-30. Lib. de Spirit. Sanct. cap. xxvii. Tom. III. pp. 54, 5.]

[5 ...οὕτω δὴ καὶ ἐνταῦθα, ἐκφερομένης τῆς θυσίας, καὶ τοῦ Χριστοῦ τεθυμένου, καὶ τοῦ προβάτου τοῦ δεσποτικοῦ, κ. τ. λ.—Chrysost. Op. Par. 1718-38. In Epist. ad Ephes. cap. i. Hom. iii. Tom. XI. p. 23.]

cross; some his resurrection; some his ascension into heaven; some that it signifieth a sacrifice special, above all sacrifices: some others say that the priest lifteth up the chalice, to signify that Christ, crying out with a loud voice, gave up the spirit[6]. M. Harding saith: "It is lifted up doubtless to the intent the people may adore." Thus many and more mysteries they have imagined in one thing, and yet the same, as it is confessed, no key of their religion. Disagreement evermore argueth ignorance. St Augustine saith: *Si vix aut omnino nunquam inveniri possint caussæ, quas in istis rebus instituendis homines sequuti sunt, ubi facultas tribuitur, sine ulla dubitatione resecanda existimo*[7]: "If the causes which men followed in devising such things can hardly or never be found, I think it best, when opportunity and occasion is given, they be abolished and put away without scruple or staggering."

Ger. Lorich. Lib. iii. Durand. Lib. iv. de sexta parte Canon. Titil. de Offic. Missæ.

August. ad Januar. Epist. 119.

They have assayed earnestly to prove this ceremony by the warrant of God's word, as if God himself had commanded it. Gerardus Lorichius saith: *Hunc ritum David videtur prævidisse in spiritu*[8]: "David seemeth to have foreseen this order in the spirit." And to this purpose he allegeth the authority of Rabbi Johai, whom I marvel M. Harding had forgotten. Durandus, for the same, allegeth the words of Christ: *Ego si exaltatus fuero a terra, omnia traham ad meipsum*[9]: "If I be once lifted up from the earth, I shall draw all things to myself[10]." And to speed the matter the better forward, Linwood saith: "The pope hath given liberal dole of pardons[11];" and the more to astonne the simple people, Alexander of Hales saith: "They have of themselves invented and devised many strange miracles[12]." They have earnestly and sadly disputed whether the cup should be holden up open or covered[13]. They say: "It is a matter of special meed, and able to confound heresies[14]." They have wrested and corrupted the scriptures, and falsified the rabbins for the same. M. Harding also would seem to allege a multitude of old doctors, and long continuance, even from the apostles' time. To be short, they have holden them for heretics, and burned them, that durst to speak against it. Yet now in the end M. Harding saith: "It is but a small matter, and the rest of their religion may well stand without it." I wonder he proceedeth not herein with as good courage as in the rest.

Ger. Lorich. Lib. iii.

Rab. Johai.

Durand. Lib. iv. de sexta parte Canon. John xii.

Linwood de Celeb. Miss. Altis.

Alexand. de Hales, iv. Quæst. 53. Memb. 4. Art. 3.

Durand. Lib. iv.

Ger. Lorich. Lib. iii.

Neither did I scoff hereat as a Lucian, as it pleaseth M. Harding in his choler to report, but reverently and soberly spake the truth, even as in the presence of God. It pitied me to see God's people so deceived, and that even by such as had taken upon them to be the fathers and guiders of the people. But, O merciful God! what religion may this be that no man may touch or truly report of it, without surmise or suspicion of scoffing? And whereas M. Harding, as a man somewhat overmuch subject to his passions, saith further, "I may be ashamed to

---

[6 Elevatio hostiæ videtur respicere ad hoc Christi, Cum exaltatus fuero, omnia traham ad me ipsum. Significat Christum in cruce exaltatum... Sublevatur salutaris hostia ut populus catholicus veneretur et adoret. Elevatio enim...in missa Christi significat passionem, &c.—Ger. Lorich. De Miss. Pub. Prorogand. 1536. Lib. III. cap. iii. pp. 277, 8, 80.

Sacerdos elevat corpus Christi: primo, ut cuncti astantes illud videant, et petant quod proficit ad salutem; juxta illud: Ego si exaltatus fuero a terra, &c. Joan. xii. Secundo ad notandum, quod non est aliud dignum sacrificium: imo est super omnes hostias. Tertio, exaltatio eucharistiæ...signat Christum verum panem, per prophetas in scripturis exaltatum: quando scilicet ejus incarnationem prophetizabant. Unde Esa. Ecce virgo concipiet...Quarto, significat resurrectionem.—Durand. Rat. Div. Offic. Lugd. 1565. Lib. iv. cap. xli. 51. fol. 169. 2. Sacerdos ergo elevans Nicodemum repræsentat: ipsa vero elevatio, Christi depositionem de cruce.—Id. ibid. cap. xlvi. 22. fol. 1842.]

[7 August. Op. Par. 1679-1700. Ad Inq. Januar. Lib. II. seu Epist. lv. 35. Tom. II. col. 142; where *ita ut vix* and *in eis instituendis*.]

[8 Hunc, &c. quod ex hoc psalmi 72 conjicere possumus: Et erit fundamentum in terra, in summis montum superextolletur, &c....Accedit huc quod Rabbi Johai, qui Christum diu antecessit, hunc versum magis de eucharistiæ sacramenti institutione, et de elevationis hostiæ mysterio intelligit: legit enim, Et erit placenta frumenti in terra in capite montium. —Ger. Lorich. de Miss. Pub. Prorogand. Lib. III. cap. iii. p. 278.]

[9 See above, note 6.]

[10 Meself, 1565.]

[11 ...ut populares...flectant genua, indulgentias concessas a pluribus episcopis habituri.—Pecch. in Lyndw. Provinc. Oxon. 1679. Lib. III. Tit. xxiii. pp. 231, 2. See also Annot. in loc. ibid.]

[12 These words have not been met with in Hales. The following, however, is a passage nearly similar: Notandum est autem, quod in corpore Christi undecim miracula considerantur, de quibus expressa reddi ratio non potest.—Durand. Rat. Div. Offic. Lib. IV. cap. xli. 16. fol. 164.]

[13 Id. ibid. cap. xlii. 30. fol. 166. 2.]

[14 ...quod ritus ille vere est salutaris, quippe qui occasio est maximi meriti, et simul errorum multorum obstructio quædam.—Ger. Lorich. De Miss. Pub. Prorogand. Lib. III. cap. iii. p. 279.]

shew my face among learned men;" if he mean the learned of his own side, verily, it can be no great glory for me to behold those faces that have been so often turned. O M. Harding! we have no cause to be ashamed of the gospel of Christ: "it is the mighty power of God unto salvation." I pray God, that both
Rom. i. you and I may leave these worldly respects and faces of men, and so use the gifts that God hath lent us, and so freely discharge our consciences in this life, that Christ be not ashamed of us before his Father, but we may come to see God
Luke ix. face to face.

Touching the matter itself, M. Harding thinketh it best to claim his elevation even from the apostles' time. So the Romans in old times, because they
Tit. Liv. Lib. i. knew not from whence their *ancilia* came unto them, they thought it not amiss, for the more credit of the matter, to say they were sent to them from heaven.
Plut. in Num. So Romulus and Theseus, because they were base-born, and no man knew their fathers, therefore were reckoned to be the children of the gods. Dionysius, Chrysostomus, and Basil, as they are worthy of much credit for their antiquity, so in this case they say nothing that of our part is denied. The question is, whether the priest did then hold up the sacrament over his head, or no. This thing M. Harding dissembleth and passeth by, and turneth his whole proof to another thing, that neither is doubted of nor denied. First, whereas Dionysius
Dion. Eccles. Hier. cap. iii. saith, *In conspectum agit*[1]; "He bringeth the mysteries into sight;" this maketh very small proof of M. Harding's side, except happily he will say, no man can bring a thing to sight, unless he hold it over his head. But that thou mayest thoroughly and fully see both the very ground and sense of these words of Dionysius, and also M. Harding's perverse and strange construction touching the same, it may please thee, gentle reader, to understand that in those days the manner was, that the sacrament, being all in one whole loaf or cake, undivided, should remain still upon the holy table, covered under a fair cloth, until the time of the distribution thereof unto the people. Touching which ceremony Pachy-
Pachym. in tert. caput Eccles. Hier. meres the Greek paraphrast writeth thus: Ἀποκαλυπτομένων τῶν παναγίων δώρων μετὰ τὰς εὐχὰς, μενόντων δὲ κεκαλυμμένων ἕως καιροῦ μεταλήψεως[2]: "The holy gifts being
Maximus: ὅτι κεκαλυμμένον ἔμενε τὸ θεῖον δῶρον ἕως καιροῦ μεταλήψεως. opened after the prayers or consecration, and yet remaining still covered until the time of the distribution, &c." So likewise saith Maximus in his scholy upon the same place; and addeth further: Not only the holy bread was set forth covered, but also the holy cup, which thing, he saith, now is not done[3].

This order or ceremony to[4] the church then well considered, Dionysius is plain enough of himself without other commentary. For thus stand his words:
Dion. Eccles. Hierar. cap. iii. εἰς ὄψιν ἄγει. *Profert ea, quæ laudavit, in conspectum,... per symbola reverenter proposita: et dona sacrificiorum commonstrans, ad sacram illorum communionem et ipse accedit, et hortatur alios*[5]: "The priest bringeth forth the things that he hath praised into sight, by the tokens reverently set before him; and, shewing forth the gifts of the mysteries, both he himself draweth near to the holy communion of the same, and also exhorteth others." This shewing and bringing into sight was nothing else but the uncovering and laying abroad of the mysteries.

If M. Harding will say this exposition is wrested or violent, let him then hear Dionysius expound himself: thus he writeth afterward in the speculation or exposition of the same: *In conspectum profert, &c.*: "He bringeth forth the
τὸν γὰρ ἐγκεκαλυμμένον καὶ ἀδιαίρετον ἄρτον ἀνακαλύψας, καὶ εἰς πολλὰ διελών. εἰς τὸ ἐμφανὲς ἄγει. things that he hath praised into sight," &c. It followeth: *Nam opertum et indivisum panem aperiens, et in multas partes dividens, et unitatem poculi omnibus impertiens, symbolice implet unitatem*[6]: "For uncovering the bread that was covered, and stood whole and undivided, and cutting it into many parts, and parting the unity of the cup unto all the people, by way of a sacrament he fulfilleth unity." If all this will not content M. Harding, yet Dionysius saith again in plainer sort: τὰ μὲν ἐγκεκαλυμμένα δῶρα εἰς τὸ ἐμφανὲς ἄγει[7]: *Munera quæ tecta*

[1 Dionys. Areop. Op. Antv. 1634. De Eccles. Hierarch. cap. iii. 2. Tom. I. p. 284.]

[2 Pachym. Paraphr. in eod. p. 316.]

[3 Max. Schol. in eod. p. 306; also p. 312; where μᾶλλον τότε ἔμενον κεκαλυμμένα τὰ θεῖα δῶρα, ἕως καιροῦ τῆς ἁγίας μεταλήψεως.]

[4 Of, 1565, 1609.]

[5 Dionys. Areop. Op. De Eccles. Hierarch. cap. iii. 2. Tom. I. p. 284; where ὑπ' ὄψιν.]

[6 Id. ibid. 3. p. 299.]

[7 Id. ibid. pp. 299, 300; where πρὸς τὸ ἐμφανὲς ἄγων.]

fuerant, in apertum profert: "He bringeth forth into open sight the gifts or sacraments that before were covered." This undoubtedly was the meaning of these words; unless perhaps M. Harding will say, Dionysius understood not his own meaning. Verily Pachymeres the paraphrast expoundeth it thus: *Profert in conspectum, ostendens hæc esse Christi symbola*[8]*:* "He bringeth these things into sight, shewing that they be tokens and signs of Christ." Hitherto there is no manner mention of holding the sacrament over the head.

Pachym. σαφηνίζων ὡς Χριστοῦ εἰσὶ τὰ τοιαῦτα σύμβολα.

But M. Harding replieth: Maximus saith, Dionysius meant the holding up of the one part of the sacrament. This may easily be granted. But the same Maximus, whatsoever he were, or whensoever he lived, saith not, the same one part was holden over the priest's head; and therefore M. Harding is but weakly relieved by his authority. And again, the same Maximus, as a man not very certain what to say, deviseth two other expositions of Dionysius' words, besides this[9]. But let this exposition of Maximus stand for good. The priest held up from the table, and shewed forth the sacrament, to declare that the holy communion was ready, that the people might prepare themselves and draw near. And therefore he spake aloud: "Holy things for the holy." Which words Chrysostom expoundeth thus: *Quando sacerdos dicit, Sancta sanctis, hoc dicit: Si quis non est sanctus, non accedat*[10]*:* "When the priest saith, Holy things unto the holy, thus he saith: If any man be not holy, let him not come near." So likewise Nicolaus Cabasilas, a Greek writer of late days: [*Sacerdos clamat*], *Sancta sanctis, propemodum dicens, Ecce panis vitæ:... accurrite...participes futuri: sed non omnes; verum si quis est sanctus*[11]*:* "The priest speaketh aloud, Holy things for the holy: as though he should say, Behold the bread of life: come near and take part; howbeit not all, but if any man be holy." And lest he should seem to discourage any man in respect of his unworthiness, he saith further: *Sanctos autem vocat, non virtute perfectos, sed quicunque ad illam tendunt perfectionem:* "He calleth them holy, not that be full perfect[12] in virtue, but that be inclined to perfection." To this end therefore the minister shewed forth the bread, that the people might prepare themselves to the distribution; and therefore it is written thus in Chrysostom's liturgy: *Sacerdos ostendit calicem populo, dicens, Cum timore Dei,* [*et fide,*] *et dilectione accedite*[13]*:* "The priest sheweth the cup unto the people, saying unto them, Draw near with the fear of God, and with faith and love:" and the people answereth: "Blessed is he that cometh in the name of the Lord." This same was St Basil's meaning in his book *de Spiritu Sancto*[14]. The words of invocation that there are spoken of were of such authority in the church, and of such weight, that neither M. Harding, nor, I believe, any other of that side, is able now to shew us what they were. In the liturgy that beareth St Basil's name, it is only noted thus: "When the priest saith, *Sancta sanctis*, the people answereth, *Unus sanctus: unus Pater: unus Filius*[15]." The very same was Chrysostom's meaning upon the epistle to the Ephesians[16]. The curtains of the holy communion-table were drawn, that the mysteries prepared for the people might be seen upon the table, not that the priest should lift them up over his head. The vain fable of M. Harding's Amphilochius, so often repeated, is not worth the answering.

Sancta sanctis. Chrysost. in Epist. ad Hebr. Hom. 17.

Nicol. Cabas.

Basil. de Spirit. Sanct. cap. xxvii.

Liturg. Basil.

Chrysost. in Epist. ad Ephes. Hom. 3.

All this notwithstanding, M. Harding doubteth not to make us believe that all these fathers spake plainly of the elevation of the sacrament over the priest's head; and that, as he saith, according to the custom of the occidental church. And to that end he hath prettily falsified the words of Maximus. For whereas Maximus in the Greek writeth thus, ὃν [ἄρτον] ὑψοῖ ὁ ἱερεύς[17]; M. Harding hath

[8 Pachym. Paraphr. in eod. p. 316.]

[9 Max. Schol. in eod. pp. 306, 12.]

[10 Chrysost. Op. Par. 1718-38. In Epist. ad Hebr. cap. x. Hom. xvii. Tom. XII. p. 171.]

[11 Nic. Cabas. Lit. Expos. cap. xxxvi. in Mag. Biblioth. Vet. Patr. Col. Agrip. 1618-22. Tom. XIV. p. 153; where *sancta inquit sanctis*, and *sed si quis*.]

[12 Perfite, 1565.]

[13 Chrysost. Lit. in Lit. Sanct. Patr. Par. 1560. p. 106.]

[14 Basil. Op. Par. 1721-30. Lib. de Spirit. Sanct. cap. xxvii. Tom. III. pp. 54, 5.]

[15 Ὁ ἱερεὺς...τὰ ἅγια τοῖς ἁγίοις. ὁ λαὸς λέγει...εἷς Πατὴρ ἅγιος, εἷς Υἱὸς ἅγιος, ἓν Πνεῦμα ἅγιον. Ἀμήν.—Id. Lit. Alex. Tom. II. Append. p. 684. See also Basil. Lit. qua Syri utuntur in Cassandr. Op. Par. 1616. Liturg. cap. ix. p. 26. Other copies differ.]

[16 See before, page 508, note 5.]

[17 Max. Schol. in Dionys. Areop. Op. Tom. I. p. 306.]

translated it in this wise: *Quem panem pontifex in sublime attollit:* "Which bread the bishop lifteth on high." And so it were easy to deceive the simple, unless the fathers had otherwise declared their own meaning. Pachymeres expoundeth

Pachym.

that word thus: *ὑποδείκνυσιν, ἤγουν ἀνυψοῖ*[1]: "He sheweth or lifteth up." He saith not, The priest lifted the sacrament above his head, or on high, as M. Harding hath turned it; but, He shewed the sacrament a little up from the table, that it might

Chrysost. in Liturg. Modicum.

be seen of the people. And so saith Chrysostom touching the same: *Sacerdos modicum tollens portionem, quæ est in sancta patena, dicit, Sancta sanctis*[2]: "The priest, a little lifting up the portion that is in the holy dish, saith, Holy things for

Claudius du Sainctes. Cassander.

the holy." And so likewise Claudius du Sainctes readeth it. And in St Basil's liturgy it is thus noted in the margin: *Hic sacerdos hostiam fractam in patena jacentem una cum patena sublevat, et ostendit populo*[3]: "Here the priest lifteth up the host or sacrament lying broken in the dish, and together with the dish sheweth it unto the people." Yet must all these be brought forth to prove this new manner of elevation now used in the church of Rome. So bold is M. Harding of the simplicity of the people.

But one strange thing, among others, I note by the way in M. Harding's answer; that, being demanded of this late-devised ceremony in the church of Rome, he foundeth his whole answer upon the east church of Græcia, and sheweth not one example, nor moveth one word of the church of Rome; and yet notwithstanding he knoweth right well, that this kind of elevation, from the beginning until this day, was never used in the church of Græcia.

It seemeth likely that as well this usage, as also sundry others, of apparel, of oil, &c., grew first from the imitation of the ceremonies of the Jews; among whom the priest, in the time of their sacrifices, held up the oblation before his breast.

Terumali.

So in the primitive church, whatsoever was offered by any man to the relief of the poor, it was taken by the priest, and holden up, and presented in the church, as a pleasant sacrifice before God. So Chrysostom saith, the priest in the time

In Liturg.

of the holy ministration lifted up the gospel. His words be these: *Sacerdos in*

Nicol. Cabas. in Expos. Liturg.

altum tollit evangelium[4]. And Nicolas Cabasilas likewise saith: *His...peractis, sacerdos stans super altare, in altum tollit evangelium, et ostendit*[5]: "These things being done, the priest, standing over the altar, lifteth the gospel on high, and sheweth it."

But, that the holding up of the sacrament should import adoration to the same, as M. Harding surmiseth, neither is it thought true by all others of that side, nor hath it any good savour or shew of truth. Indeed great pardons and charters have been liberally given of late years for the better maintenance

Durand. Lib. iv.

thereof. And Durandus saith, therefore elevation is made, *ut populus intelligat, Christum venisse super altare*[6], "that the people may understand that Christ is come down upon the altar." But the old learned fathers, both Greeks and Latins, when they held up a little, or shewed the sacrament, evermore they called the people to draw near, to receive, to be partakers of the holy mysteries, and to lift up their hearts; but in the time of the same ceremony they never spake one

Pachym. in Eccles. Hier. cap. iii.

word of adoration. Pachymeres saith: *Sacerdos ostendit, hæc esse Christi symbola*[7]: "The priest sheweth that these be tokens or signs of Christ." He saith not, the sacraments be Christ himself, but tokens and signs of Christ. Maximus

Max. in Schol.

saith, *ὅτι σύμβολα ταῦτα, καὶ οὐκ ἀλήθεια*: *Symbola ista sunt, non autem veritas*[8]: "These be tokens (of the truth), but not the truth itself." And perhaps upon

[1 Ὑποδείκνυσι δὲ, κ. τ. λ.—Pachym. Paraphr. in eod. p. 316.]

[2 Ὅταν δὲ ἴδῃ ὁ διάκονος τὸν ἱερέα ἐκτείνοντα τὰς χεῖρας, καὶ ἀπτόμενον τοῦ ἁγίου ἄρτου πρὸς τὸ ποιῆσαι τὴν ἁγίαν ὕψωσιν, ἐκφωνεῖ, κ. τ. λ. The Latin version is: Et sacerdos se inclinans suscipit portionem quæ est in sancta patena, et modicum sustollens dicit, Sancta sanctis.—Chrysost. Lit. in Lit. Sanct. Patr. Par. 1560. p. 103. and fol. 20, 2.]

[3 Ὁ ἱερεὺς ὑψοῖ τὸ σπουδικόν.—Basil. Op. Par. 1721-30. Lit. Alex. Tom. II. Append. p. 684. τὸ σπουδικὸν is explained, majorem hostiæ partem.]

[4 ...ἀνυψοῖ μικρὸν τὰς χεῖρας, καὶ δεικνύων τὸ ἅγιον εὐαγγέλιον, κ. τ. λ.—Chrysost. Op. Par. 1718-38. Lit. Tom. XII. p. 783.]

[5 Nic. Cabas. Lit. Expos. cap. xx. in Mag. Biblioth. Vet. Patr. col. 1618-22. Tom. XIV. p. 146.]

[6 Quinto, hostia elevatur, ut populus non præveniens consecrationem, sed ex hoc cognoscens illam factam esse, et Christum super altare venisse, reverenter ad terram prosternantur.—Durand. Rat. Div. Offic. Lugd. 1565. Lib. IV. cap. xli. 51. fol. 169. 2.]

[7 Pachym. Paraphr. in Dionys. Areop. Op. Antv. 1634. Tom. I. p. 316.]

[8 Max. Schol. in eod. p. 306.]

this occasion Beguinæ and Beguardi held, that no man ought to rise up or to give reverence at the elevation of the sacrament[9]. Clement. Lib. v. Ad nostrum.

To conclude, Gerardus Lorichius, in his book that he writeth in the defence of the private mass, hath these words: *Ex hoc ritu [elevationis] inferimus, missam neutiquam rite celebrari, nisi in usum publicum ecclesiæ, hoc est, propter populum, vel sacramentum eucharistiæ sumentem, vel sacrificium laudis votis et encomiis celebrantem; siquidem propter eum usum hostia elevatur. Missæ igitur privatæ, quæ absente populo catholico fiunt, abominatio verius quam oblatio dicendæ [sunt]*[10]: "By this very usage of elevation we conclude that no mass is rightly said, but for the public use of the church, that is to say, for the people, either receiving the sacrament, or else advancing[11] the sacrifice of praise with heart and devotion: for to this end (and not to be adored) the sacrament is holden up. Therefore private masses, which are said without catholic people being present, may rather be called an abomination than an oblation." Thus much Gerardus Lorichius, a doctor of M. Harding's own side. Ger. Lorich. Lib. iii.

[[9] Clemens V. in Corp. Jur. Canon. Lugd. 1624. Clement. Lib. v. Tit. iii. cap. 3. col. 277.]

[[10] Ger. Lorich. De Miss. Pub. Prorogand. 1536. Lib. III. cap. iii. pp. 279, 80.]

[[11] Avancing, 1565.]

OF ADORATION.

THE EIGHTH ARTICLE.

THE BISHOP OF SARISBURY.

Or that the people did then fall down and worship the sacrament with godly honour.

[OF THE WORSHIPPING OR ADORATION OF THE SACRAMENT.—
Article VIII. H. A. 1564.]

M. HARDING. THE FIRST DIVISION.

If the blessed sacrament of the altar were no other than M. Jewel and the rest of the sacramentaries think of it, then were it not well done the people to bow down to it, and to worship it with godly honour. (159) *For then were it but bare bread and wine, how honourably soever they speak of it, calling it symbolical, that is, tokening, and sacramental bread and wine.*

The hundred and fifty-ninth untruth, joined with a slander.

THE BISHOP OF SARISBURY.

M. Harding, as a man overmuch obedient unto his affections, in the beginning hereof calleth us sacramentaries, by which word he understandeth schismatics, heretics, and the enemies of God; and so breaketh up his way into this treatise with unsavoury and bitter talk; and, as a cock that is well pampered with garlic before the fight, he seeketh to overmatch his fellow rather with rankness of breath than with might of body.

And, forasmuch as he striveth to make the world think our doctrine is injurious to the Godhead and glory of Christ; first, we protest that, as we believe that Christ "is the Lamb of God that hath taken away the sins of the world," and that "there is none other name under heaven whereby we can be saved;" and that, as the prophet Esay saith, "he is the mighty God, the Father of the world, that was to come;" and that, as St Paul saith, "he is God revealed in the flesh:" even so we yield unto him the very honour that is due unto God; and that not only to his Godhead alone, but also to his humanity inseparably joined with his Godhead in one person, sitting now at the right hand of God. Thus we teach the people that "God hath advanced[1] him into all height, and hath given him a name above all names, that at the name of Jesus every knee shall be bowed, all[2] things in heaven, in the earth, and under the earth; and that every tongue shall confess that Jesus Christ is the Lord, in the glory of God the Father."

John i. Acts iv. Isai. ix. 1 Tim. iii. Phil. ii.

Neither do we only adore Christ as very God, but also we worship and reverence the sacrament and holy mystery of Christ's body; and, as St Augustine teacheth us, *baptismum... Christi, ubicunque* [*est*], *veneramur*[3], "we worship the baptism of Christ, wheresoever it be." We worship the word of God, according to this counsel of Anastasius: *Dominica verba attente audiant, et fideliter adorent*[4]: "Let them diligently hear and faithfully worship the words of God." Briefly, we worship all other like things in such religious wise unto Christ belonging. But these things we use and reverence as holy, and appointed or commanded by Christ; but we adore them not with godly honour, as Christ himself.

August. Epist. 146. De Consecr. Dist. 1. Apostol.

[1 Avanced, 1565.] [2 Of, 1565.]
[3 August. Op. Par. 1679-1700. Ad Emerit. Epist. lxxxvii. 9. Tom. II. col. 212; where *ubique*.]
[4 Anastas. Epist. i. cap. 1. in Corp. Jur. Canon. Lugd. 1624. Decret. Gratian. Decr. Tert. Pars, De Consecr. Dist. i. can. 68. col. 1909.]

St Ambrose saith of the wise men: *Cognoverunt hanc stellam esse, quæ hominem Deumque signabat; [sed] adoraverunt parvulum*[5]: "They knew this was the star that signified him unto them that was both man and God; but they adored the little one (and not the star)."

Sacramental sign.

Ambros. in Luc. Lib. ii. cap. ii.

And whereas M. Harding, as well herein, as also in the rest, untruly and unjustly defameth us, as making the sacraments of Christ nothing else but bare tokens; let him well understand that we do both think and speak soberly and reverently of Christ's sacraments, as knowing them to be the testimonies of God's promises, and the instruments of the Holy Ghost. And, as we make not the sacrament of baptism bare water, notwithstanding the nature and substance of water remain still; so we make not the sacrament of Christ's body and blood bare bread and wine. We use the same words and definitions that St Augustine, and other ancient fathers, and Peter Lombard, and Gratian, M. Harding's own doctors, have used before us: *Sacramentum est signum rei sacræ*[6]: *Sacramentum est invisibilis gratiæ visibilis forma*[7]: "A sacrament is a token of a holy thing: A sacrament is a form visible of grace invisible." Neither do we hereof make a bare or naked token, as M. Harding imagineth; but we say, as St Paul saith, "it is a perfect[8] seal, and a sufficient warrant of God's promises, whereby God bindeth himself unto us, and we likewise stand bounden unto God, so as God is our God, and we are his people." This I reckon is no bare or naked token. And touching this word *signum*, what it meaneth, St Augustine sheweth in this sort: *Signum est, quod præter speciem, quam ingerit sensibus, aliud quiddam facit ex se in cognitionem venire*[9]: "A sign is a thing that, besides the form or sight that it offereth to our senses, causeth of itself some other thing to come to our knowledge." And hereof it is called a mystery, or a holy secrecy; for that our eye beholdeth one thing, and our faith another. For example, in baptism our bodily eye seeth water; but our faith, which is the eye of our mind, seeth the blood of Christ, which, as St John saith, "hath washed us from all our sins." Therefore Chrysostom saith: *Incredulus, cum baptismatis lavacrum audit, persuadet sibi, simpliciter esse aquam. Ego vero non simpliciter video quod video, sed animæ per Spiritum purgationem; et sepulturam, resurrectionem, sanctificationem, justitiam, redemptionem, adoptionem, hæreditatem, regnum cœlorum, Spiritus satietatem considero. Non enim aspectu judico ea, quæ videntur, sed mentis oculis*[10]: "The infidel, when he heareth of the water of baptism, thinketh it to be only plain water; but I, that believe in Christ, do not only and simply see water, but I see the cleansing of the soul by the Spirit of God: I consider Christ's burial, his resurrection, our sanctification, our righteousness, our redemption, our adoption, our inheritance, the kingdom of heaven, and the fulness of the Spirit. For the things that I see I judge not with my bodily eyes, but with the eyes of my mind." Now, will M. Harding say that Chrysostom only for a countenance speaketh thus honourably of the sacrament of baptism, meaning notwithstanding it is nothing else but bare water? Certainly St Augustine saith: *In sacramentis videndum est, non quid sint, sed quid significent*[11]: "In sacraments we must consider, not what they be indeed, but what they signify." If that every thing, according to M. Harding's judgment, must needs be accounted bare wherein Christ's body is not really present, then is the sacrament of baptism a bare sacrament; and M. Harding's book must likewise of necessity seem a very bare book: unless perhaps he will say, Christ's body is really inclosed in it. Plato saith: It is the greatest part of wisdom to discern *aliud* and *idem*, one and the same thing from another thing:

De Consecr. Dist. 2. Sacrif. Pet. Lomb. Lib. iv. Dist. 1. Samaritanus. Rom. iv. Signaculum justitiæ fidei.

August. de Doctr. Christ. Lib. ii. cap. i. De Consecr. Dist. 2. Signum.

1 John i.

Chrysost. in 1 Epist. ad Cor. Hom. 7.

August. contr. Max. Lib. iii. cap. xxii.

Plato.

[5 Ambros. Op. Par. 1686-90. Expos. Evang. sec. Luc. Lib. II. cap. ii. 48. Tom. I.; where *cognoverunt hanc esse stellam*, and *significat* for *signabat*.]

[6 Pet. Lomb. Libr. Sentent. Col. Agrip. 1576. Lib. IV. Dist. i. B. fol. 330. 2; where *sacræ rei signum*.]

[7 August. in Corp. Jur. Canon. Decret. Gratian. Decr. Tert. Pars, De Consecr. Dist. ii. can. 32. col. 1926.]

[8 Perfite, 1565, 1609.]

[9 Id. in eod. ibid. Op. De Doctr. Christ. Lib. II. cap. i. 1. Tom. III. Pars I. col. 19. See before, page 458, note 3.]

[10 Chrysost. Op. Par. 1718-38. In Epist. I. ad Cor. Hom. vii. Tom. X. p. 51. See before, page 466, note 2.]

[11 August. Op. Contr. Max. Arian. Lib. II. cap. xxii. 3. Tom. VIII. col. 725. See before, page 467, note 21.]

August. in Joh. Tract. 26. for of error herein evermore riseth all confusion. But St Augustine saith: *Aliud est sacramentum, aliud res sacramenti*[1]: "The sacrament is one thing; and the substance of the sacrament (which is Christ's body) is another thing." And, lest M. Harding should shift off this matter and say, as his manner is, that the sacrament is nothing else but the outward form and appearance or shew of bread and wine, Raban.Maur. Lib. i. cap. xxxi. Rabanus Maurus hath prevented him in this wise: *Sacramentum ... in alimentum corporis redigitur*[2]: "The sacrament is turned into the nourishment of the body." Therefore, these two things being diverse and sundry, the one the token, the other the thing tokened; the one Christ's body, and the other the sacrament of the same body; the one naturally feeding the body, the other supernaturally feeding the soul; it were great confusion either to make them both one, or else by error to take the one for the other. And for that cause St August. de Doctr. Christ. Lib. iii. cap. v. Augustine saith, as it is before alleged: *Ea demum est miserabilis animæ servitus, signa pro rebus accipere*[3]: "That indeed is a miserable servitude of the soul, to take signs[4] instead of the things that be signified."

Now, touching the adoration of the sacrament, M. Harding is not able to shew neither any commandment of Christ, nor any word or example of the apostles or ancient fathers concerning the same. It is a thing very lately devised by pope Extr. de Celeb. Miss. Honorius, about the year of our Lord 1226[5]; afterward increased by the new solemn feast of *Corpus Christi* day, by pope Urbanus, anno 1264; and last of all confirmed for ever by multitudes of pardons in the council of Vienna by pope Clement. Lib. iii. Tit. xvi. cap. Si Dominum. Clement the fifth, anno 1310[6]. The church of Asia and Græcia never received it until this day. The matter is great, and cannot be attempted without great danger. To give the honour of God to a creature that is no God, it is manifest Rev. xxi. idolatry. And "all idolaters," as St John saith, "shall have their portion in the lake burning with fire and brimstone, which is the second death."

M. HARDING. THE SECOND DIVISION.

But now, this being that very bread which God the Father gave us from heaven, as Christ saith: This bread being the flesh of Christ, which he gave for the life of the world. John vi.

THE BISHOP OF SARISBURY.

M. Harding would seem to have trained all the ancient doctors unto his side, and to that end hath mustered them here in an army all together. Howbeit, of them all there is not one that teacheth us one word of the adoration of the sacrament. Wherefore, if he bring them forth only for a shew, they are too many; but, if he bring them as witnesses, they are too few; for touching the case they say nothing. Yet M. Harding, as a man much doubting his reader's memory, whatsoever he hath shortly alleged here, hath elsewhere repeated, and doubled the same in other places of his book; so that, if I would answer all in particular, I should be over tedious. For avoiding whereof, it shall be sufficient to refer myself[7] over to such places, where as these authorities are answered severally more at large.

First, as I have said before, there is not one of all these fathers that willeth us to adore the sacrament with godly honour. Which thing, notwithstanding, they were able to have written, if it had been then either used or thought convenient; and M. Harding was able to have found it, if it had been written. The bread of the sacrament is not that bread of which Christ speaketh in the sixth of St John; Cypr. Lib. i. Epist. 6. but very material bread indeed, and, as St Cyprian saith, *ex multorum granorum*

[1 Id. in Johan. Evang. cap. vi. Tractat. xxvi. 11. Tom. III. Pars II. col. 498; where *virtus sacramenti*.]

[2 Raban. Maur. Op. Col. Agrip. 1626. De Inst. Cler. Lib. I. cap. xxxi. Tom. VI. p. 11. See before, page 453.]

[3 August. Op. Par. 1679-1700. De Doctr. Christ. Lib. III. cap. v. 9. Tom. III. Pars I. col. 47. See before, page 448.] [4 The signs, 1565, 1609.]

[5 Honor. III. in Corp. Jur. Canon. Lugd. 1624. Decretal. Gregor. IX. Lib. III. Tit. xli. cap. x. col. 1378.]

[6 Clemens V. in eod. Clement. Lib. III. Tit. xvi. cols. 240, &c.] [7 Meself, 1565.]

adunatione congestus[8], "moulded together of the mingling of many corns;" and a sacrament of that bread that came from heaven. But this matter is answered in the fifth article, and in the first, second, and third division.

M. HARDING. THE THIRD DIVISION.

[1 Cor. xi. H. A. 1564.] *This being that bread and that cup, whereof whosoever eateth or drinketh unworthily shall be guilty of the body and blood of our Lord.*

THE BISHOP OF SARISBURY.

St Hierome saith: *Dum... sacramenta violantur, ipse, cujus sacramenta sunt, violatur*[9]: "When the sacraments be misused, God himself, whose sacraments they be, is misused." And the greatest abuse and villany that can happen to any sacrament is, contrary to Christ's institution and the nature of a sacrament, to be honoured instead of God. And St Augustine saith: *Qui indigne accipit baptisma, judicium accipit, non salutem*[10]: "Whoso receiveth baptism unworthily receiveth his judgment, and not his health." Wherefore, if M. Harding think this warrant sufficient to prove adoration, then must he also adore the water of baptism.

Hieron. in Malach. cap. i.

August. contr. Fulgent. cap. vi.

M. HARDING. THE FOURTH DIVISION.

(160) *In this sacrament being contained the very real and substantial body and blood of Christ, as himself saith expressly in the three first evangelists, and in St Paul.*

The hundred and sixtieth untruth[11], five together in the report of four words.

THE BISHOP OF SARISBURY.

It is a bold enterprise, in the report of these four plain words of Christ, *hoc est corpus meum*, to commit[12] five manifest untruths, and that all together with one breath. Certainly M. Harding well knoweth that neither Christ, nor Paul, nor any of the evangelists, I add further, nor any of the catholic doctors, in this case of the sacrament, ever used any of these terms, either carnally contained, or expressly, or very, or real, or substantial. Only they say, "This is my body;" which words the ancient father Tertullian expoundeth thus: "This is a figure of my body[13]."

Tertull. contr. Marc. Lib. iv.

M. HARDING. THE FIFTH DIVISION.

In epistola quadam ad Smyrnenses, ut citatur a Theodoreto in Polymorph. Lib. iv. contra Hæreses, cap. xxxiv.

This being that holy eucharistia *which Ignatius calleth "the flesh of our Saviour Jesus Christ, that hath suffered for our sins, which the Father by his goodness hath raised up to life again*[14]*:" this being not common bread, but the* eucharistia, *after consecration "consisting of two things, earthly and heavenly*[15]*," as Irenæus saith, meaning by the one* (161) *the outward form*[16]*, by the other the very body and blood of Christ, who, partly for the Godhead inseparably thereto united, and partly for that they were conceived of the Holy Ghost, in the most holy virgin Mary, are worthily called heavenly.*

The hundred and sixty-first untruth. For Irenæus meaneth not the forms or shews of bread, but the substance of very bread itself.

THE BISHOP OF SARISBURY.

What Theodoretus thought in this behalf, it is plain by his own words. For thus he writeth: *Signa mystica post sanctificationem non recedunt a natura sua*[17]: "The mystical tokens, after the sanctification or consecration, go not from their

Theodor. Dial. 2.

[[8] Cypr. Op. Oxon. 1682. Ad Magn. Epist. lxix. p. 182; where *de* for *ex*.]

[[9] Hieron. Op. Par. 1693-1706. Comm. in Malach. Proph. cap. i. Tom. III. col. 1811; where *cujus sunt sacramenta*.]

[[10] August. Op. Lib. contr. Fulgent. Donat. cap. vi. Tom. IX. Append. col. 6; where *accipit indigne baptisma*. This book is not genuine.]

[[11] Untruths, 1565, 1609.]

[[12] Of four plain words to commit, 1565.]

[[13] Tertull. Op. Lut. 1641. Adv. Marcion. Lib. IV. 40. p. 571. See before, page 447.]

[[14] Εὐχαριστίας ... ἀπέχονται, διὰ τὸ μὴ ὁμολογεῖν τὴν εὐχαριστίαν σάρκα εἶναι τοῦ Σωτῆρος ἡμῶν Ἰησοῦ Χριστοῦ, τὴν ὑπὲρ τῶν ἁμαρτιῶν ἡμῶν παθοῦσαν, ἣν τῇ χρηστότητι ὁ Πατὴρ ἤγειρεν.—Ignat. ad Smyrn. Epist. cap. vi. in Patr. Apostol. Oxon. 1838. Tom. II. p. 412. See also Theodor. Op. Lut. Par. 1642-84. Impat. Dial. III. Tom. IV. p. 154, where οὐκ ἀποδέχονται, and ἣν χρηστότητι.]

[[15] ...οὐκέτι κοινὸς ἄρτος ἐστίν, ἀλλ' εὐχαριστία, ἐκ δύο πραγμάτων συνεστηκυῖα, ἐπιγείου τε καὶ οὐρανίου.—Iren. Op. Par. 1710. Lib. IV. cap. xviii. 5. p. 251.] [[16] Forms, 1565, and H. A. 1564.]

[[17] Theodor. Op. Inconfus. Dial. II. Tom. IV. p. 85.]

own nature:" that is to say, remain in substance and nature, as they were before. By these words we may plainly see Theodoretus' judgment. Howbeit, in all sacraments two things must be considered, whereof, as Irenæus saith, they do consist. The one is earthly, the other is heavenly: the one we see with our bodily eyes, the other we see with the eyes of our faith: the one is in the earth, the other is in heaven. These parts because they are joined in one mystery, therefore oftentimes they scorce[1] names, the one interchangeably with the other. For as Christ's very body is called bread, although indeed it be not[2] bread; so the sacramental bread is called Christ's body, although indeed it be not Christ's body. Therefore, as the sacrament is called Christ's body, even so, according to the saying of Ignatius, it is the flesh of Christ[3], even the same that hath suffered for our sins, and that the Father hath raised again to life; that is to say, a sacrament of that flesh. In like sort St Chrysostom writeth of the sacrament of baptism: *Ostendit hoc loco, idem esse sanguinem, et aquam. Baptisma enim ejus etiam passio ejus est*[4]*:* "St Paul sheweth in this place that the blood (of Christ) and the water (of baptism) are both one. For Christ's baptism is Christ's passion." He saith, The water and the blood of Christ are both one thing; and that, he saith, was St Paul's meaning. Yet notwithstanding, neither is the water Christ's blood indeed, neither is Christ's blood indeed material water. But thus they borrow each of them the other's name, because they are joined together in one mystery. So is the blood of Christ called water, because it cleanseth: so is the water called Christ's blood, because it is a sacrament of that blood. And, as St Chrysostom saith, "The water of baptism is Christ's blood;" even so Ignatius saith, "The bread is the flesh[5]," and none otherwise. These things are plain, and without cavil.

Theod. in Polym.

Chrysost. in Epist. ad Heb. Hom. 16.

Therefore St Augustine saith: [*Sacramenta*] *ex... similitudine plerunque etiam rerum ipsarum nomina accipiunt.... Ergo secundum quendam modum sacramentum corporis Christi corpus Christi est;* [*et*] *sacramentum sanguinis Christi sanguis Christi est*[6]*:* "Sacraments, because of a certain likeness, oftentimes receive the names of the things themselves[7] (whereof they be sacraments). And therefore the sacrament of Christ's body after a certain manner (of speech) is the body of Christ; and the sacrament of Christ's blood is likewise (after a certain manner) the blood of Christ."

August. Epist. 23. Secundum quendam modum.

But here hath M. Harding taken great pains to wrest and to falsify the plain words of that holy father Irenæus. For that part of the mystery that Irenæus calleth *rem terrenam*[8], "an earthly thing," that is to say, bread, the same M. Harding, contrary to his author's meaning, calleth "forms," or "accidents," or "shews of bread." For this fond and heathenish kind of speech was not heard of in the church in that holy father's days, but was brought in well near a thousand years afterward, to accompany transubstantiation. But Irenæus in plain wise calleth it a creature. Thus he saith: *Sanctificamus creaturam*[9]*:* "We do sanctify a creature." *Offerimus ei... ex creatura ejus*[10]*:* "We offer up unto him of his creature." And that he meaneth not a miraculous creature, as is *accidens sine subjecto*, the like whereof was never seen; but he saith simply: *Creaturam, quæ est secundum nos*[11]*:* "Such a creature as we have in common use:" such as we see, such as we feel, such as we eat, such as we drink; and, utterly to cut off M. Harding's shifts, he saith: *Ex illa augetur et consistit carnis nostræ substantia*[12]*:* "Of the same the substance of our flesh is increased and standeth." Therefore it is certain and most manifest by Irenæus, that, as Christ's body is the

Iren. Lib. iv. cap. xxxiv.

Irenæus eodem loco.

Ibidem.

Secundum nos. καθ' ἡμᾶς.

Iren. Lib. v.

[1 Scorce or scorse: exchange.] [2 No, 1565.]

[3 See above, page 517, note 14.]

[4 Chrysost. Op. Par. 1718-38. In Epist. ad Hebr. cap. ix. Hom. xvi. Tom. XII. p. 159. The Greek text has, τὸ γὰρ βάπτισμα αὐτοῦ τοῦ πάθους ἐστὶ σύμβολον. But see the version of Mutianus, ibid. where the clause is exactly as Jewel has cited it.]

[5 Flesh of Christ, 1565.]

[6 August. Op. Par. 1679-1700. Ad Bonifac. Epist. xcviii. 9. Tom. II. col. 267; where *ipsarum rerum.*]

[7 Themself, 1565.]

[8 Iren. Op. Par. 1710. Contr. Hær. Lib. iv. cap. xviii. 5. p. 251.]

[9 Id. ibid. 6; where *sanctificantes.*]

[10 Id. ibid. 4; where *offerens.*]

[11 Alii enim alterum præter fabricatorem dicentes Patrem, ea quæ secundum nos creata sunt offerentes ei, cupidum alieni ostendunt eum, et aliena concupiscentem.—Id. ibid.]

[12 Id. ibid. Lib. v. cap. ii. 3. p. 294.]

one part of the sacrament, so is material bread the other. Likewise in baptism, as the one part of that holy mystery is Christ's blood, so is the other part the material water. Neither are these parts joined together in place, but in mystery; and therefore they be oftentimes severed, and the one is received without the other. And for that cause St Augustine saith: *Qui discordat a Christo, nec panem ejus manducat, nec sanguinem bibit; etiam si tantæ rei sacramentum ad judicium suæ præsumptionis quotidie indifferenter accipiat*[13]: "Whoso disagreeth from Christ neither eateth his bread nor drinketh his blood, although he daily receive the sacrament of so great a thing without difference to the judgment of his presumption." August. In Lib. Sententiarum, Sent. 338. et in Johan. Tract. 26.

If any man think it strange that the sacrament is called the body and the flesh of Christ, being not so indeed, let him understand that the written word of God is likewise called Christ's body and Christ's flesh, even the same that was born of the virgin, and that the Father raised again to life, although indeed it be not so. So saith St Hierome: *Quando dicit, Qui non comederit carnem meam, et biberit sanguinem meum, [&c.] licet... in mysterio possit intelligi, tamen verius corpus Christi et sanguis ejus sermo scripturarum est*[14]: "When Christ saith, 'He that eateth not my flesh, and drinketh not my blood, &c.;' notwithstanding it may be taken of the mystery, yet the word of God is more truly the body of Christ, and his blood." Here note, good reader, that by these words of St Hierome the word of God is the body and blood of Christ, and that more truly than is the sacrament. Hieron. in Psal. cxlvii. Verius.

M. HARDING. THE SIXTH DIVISION.

In Serm. de Cœna Domini. *This being that bread, which, "of our Lord given to his disciples, not in shape, but in nature changed, by the almighty power of the Word is made flesh*[15]*," as St Cyprian termeth it.*

THE BISHOP OF SARISBURY.

This authority is answered more at large in the tenth article, and in the second division.

M. HARDING. THE SEVENTH DIVISION.

Hom. 5. De Pascha. *This being that holy mystery wherein "the invisible priest turneth the visible creatures (of bread and wine) into the substance of his body and blood, by his word, with secret power*[16]*," as Eusebius Emissenus reporteth.*

THE BISHOP OF SARISBURY.

This authority is answered in the tenth article, and in the sixth[17] division.

M. HARDING. THE EIGHTH DIVISION.

Lib. viii. De Trinitate. *This being that holy food, by worthy receiving whereof Christ dwelleth in us naturally, that is to wit, in us*[18] *"by truth of nature, and not by concord of will only*[19]*," as Hilarius affirmeth.* • So St Hilary saith Christ dwelleth in us naturally by the water of baptism[20]. De Trin. Lib. viii.

[[13] August. Op. Prosp. Lib. Sentent. 341. Tom. X. Append. col. 247; where *carnem ejus*. See also In Johan. Evang. cap. vi. Tractat. xxvi. 18. Tom. III. Pars II. col. 501.]

[[14] Hieron. Op. Par. 1693-1706. Brev. in Psalt. Psalm. cxlvii. Tom. II. Append. col. 504.]

[[15] Panis iste quem Dominus discipulis porrigebat, non effigie, sed natura mutatus, omnipotentia Verbi factus est caro.—Cypr. Op. Oxon. 1682. De Cœn. Dom. (Arnold.) p. 40.]

[[16] Nam invisibilis sacerdos visibiles creaturas in substantia corporis et sanguinis sui verbo suo secreta potestate convertit.—Euseb. Emis. Hom. Lut. Par. 1547. Hom. v. de Pasch. fol. 44. 2. See also Corp. Jur. Canon. Lugd. 1624. Decret. Gratian. Decr. Tert. Pars, De Consecr. Dist. ii. can. 35. col. 1927; where *substantiam*.]

[[17] Seventh, 1565.] [[18] Is in us, H. A. 1564.]

[[19] Hilar. Op. Par. 1693. De Trin. Lib. VIII. 13. col. 954.]

[[20] Id. ibid. 8. col. 952. See before, page 478, note 1.]

THE BISHOP OF SARISBURY.

This authority is answered before, in the fifth article, and the tenth division[1].

M. HARDING. THE NINTH DIVISION.

Again, this being that table whereat "in our Lord's meat we receive the Word truly made flesh of the most holy virgin Mary[2]," as the same Hilary saith.

THE BISHOP OF SARISBURY.

This authority, as it nothing hindereth us, so it nothing furthereth M. Harding. We say that at that holy table our faith is directed, not unto a fantasy, but unto the very body and blood of Christ, and tasteth it, and feedeth on it; and that as verily and as effectually as our body feedeth upon material food. And John vi. we add further, that whosoever eateth not Christ's flesh, nor drinketh his blood, shall not have everlasting life. But the thing that we receive with our mouth is not the same thing that we receive with our faith. For, as it is before alleged August. in Joh. Tractat. 26. out of St Augustine, *aliud est sacramentum, aliud res sacramenti*[3]*:* "the sacrament is one thing; and the matter or substance of the sacrament (which is Christ's very body) is another thing."

But, being granted that Christ's body is verily and really in the sacrament, yet cannot M. Harding thereof conclude his purpose. His argument standeth thus:

Christ's body ought to be adored with godly honour:
Christ's body is in the sacrament;
Ergo, the sacrament ought to be adored with godly honour.

This argument is made up of four terms; and therefore in the schools would be counted childish. The error whereof[4] will the better appear by the like:

Christ's body ought to be adored with godly honour:
Christ's body is in heaven;
Ergo, heaven ought to be adored with godly honour.

M. HARDING. THE TENTH DIVISION.

This being that bread which "neither earing, nor sowing, nor work of tillers hath brought forth, but that earth which remained untouched, and was full of the same," that is, the blessed virgin Mary[5], as Gregory Nyssene describeth. [*Lib. de Vita Mosis, cap. xlviii.* H. A. 1564.]

THE BISHOP OF SARISBURY.

Gregory Nyssene in this whole place speaketh not one word, neither of any adoration, nor of the sacrament, but only of Christ's birth of the blessed virgin. These words are alleged and answered before, in the fifth article, and tenth division[1]. Yet shortly, and by the way, these words yield us one good reason against M. Harding. For, whereas Gregory Nyssene saith, the bread of Christ's body cometh not of the labour of tillers, that is to say, of material corn; and Cyprian. Lib. i. Epist. 6. August. in Joh. Tractat. 26. nevertheless St Cyprian[6] and St Augustine[7] say, the sacrament is wrought of many corns; of these fathers thus considered together we may conclude that Christ's body and the sacrament are sundry things. The argument that M. Harding can gather hereof standeth thus:

Christ was born of the blessed virgin;
Ergo, we ought to adore the sacrament. For other necessity of sequel out of these words there is none.

[1 See before, pages 474, &c.]

[2 Id. ibid. 13. cols. 954, 5.]

[3 August. Op. Par. 1679-1700. In Johan. Evang. cap. vi. Tractat. xxvi. 11. Tom. III. Pars II. col. 498.]

[4 Thereof, 1565.]

[5 Τὸ δὲ *σῶμα τούτου τοῦ ἄρτου οὔτε ἄροσις οὔτε σπορὰ ἐγεώργησεν· ἀλλ' ἡ γῆ οἵα ἐστὶ μείνασα, πλήρης εὑρίσκεται τῆς θείας ταύτης τροφῆς, ἧς οἱ πεινῶντες μετέχουσι, τὸ κατὰ τὴν παρθένον μυστήριον διὰ τῆς θαυματοποιΐας ταύτης προπαιδευόμενοι.*—Gregor. Nyss. Op. Par. 1638. De Vit. Mos. Tom. I. p. 214.]

[6 Cypr. Op. Oxon. 1682. Ad Magn. Epist. xlix. p. 182. See before, pages 516, 7.]

[7 ...aliud in unum ex multis granis confit.—August. Op. In Johan. Evang. cap. vi. Tractat. xxvi. 17. Tom. III. Pars II. col. 500.]

M. HARDING. THE ELEVENTH DIVISION.

Constitut. Apostolicorum, Lib. viii. cap. ult.
In Levit. Lib. i. cap. iv.

This being that supper in the which Christ sacrificed himself, as Clemens Romanus[8]*, and as Hesychius*[9] *declareth; who furthermore in another place writeth most plainly that "these mysteries," meaning the blessed sacrament of the altar, "are* sancta sanctorum, *'the holiest of all holy things,' because it is the body of himself, of whom Gabriel said to the virgin, 'The Holy Ghost shall come upon thee, and the power of the Highest shall overshadow thee; therefore that holy thing which shall be born of thee shall be called the Son of God;' and of whom also Esay spake, 'Holy is our Lord, and dwelleth on high,' verily in*[10] *the bosom of the Father*[11]*."*

Hesychius speaketh these words, not of the sacrament, but of Christ himself.

[*Luke* i. H. A. 1564.]

THE BISHOP OF SARISBURY.

Christ, as he had shewed his disciples before, that he must go up to Hierusalem, and there be crucified; so, being at that his last mournful supper, he ordained a sacrament of his death, and took bread, and brake it, and described and expressed before their eyes the whole order and manner of his passion: as if he should have said: Thus shall my body be broken; thus shall my blood be shed. This description of Christ's death, so plain and so lively, Hesychius calleth a sacrifice, that is to say, an exemplar or resemblance of that sacrifice, which he had to offer the day following upon the cross. And indeed, as the bread was Christ's body, so the breaking of the same was Christ's passion. And in this manner of speech the ancient fathers seem to call baptism a sacrifice. Chrysostom saith: *Baptisma Christi passio Christi est*[12]: "The baptism of Christ is Christ's passion." So Tertullian: *Tingimur in passione Domini*[13]: "We be washed in the passion of our Lord." So likewise again Chrysostom saith: *Quod crux et sepulchrum fuit Christo, id nobis baptismus factus est*[14]: "That is baptism unto us, that the cross and grave was unto Christ." In this sense Hesychius saith: "Christ offered himself at his last supper;" that is to say, by way of a sacrament, and in a mystery, but not indeed, to take away the sins of the world. In like sense the same Hesychius calleth the birth of Christ a sacrifice. These be his words: *Sacrificium ... coctum Christi appellat incarnationem*[15]: "The baked sacrifice he calleth the incarnation of Christ."

Chrysost. in Epist. ad Heb. Hom. 16.
Tertull. de Baptism.
Chrysost. in Epist. ad Rom. Hom. 10.
Isych. in Levit. Lib. i. cap. ii.

Touching this word *sancta sanctorum*, it is not the outward sacrament that Hesychius calleth by that name, but the very body of Christ itself; which, as St Augustine saith, is *res sacramenti*[16]: "the substance and matter of the sacrament." So writeth Origen upon Leviticus: *Quæ est hostia, quæ pro peccatis offertur, et est sancta sanctorum, nisi unigenitus Filius Dei, Dominus meus Jesus Christus? Ipse solus est hostia pro peccatis, et ipse est hostia, sancta sanctorum*[17]: "What is that sacrifice that is offered up for sin, and is the holy of the holy, but the only-begotten Son of God, my Lord Jesus Christ? He only is the sacrifice for sin; and he is the sacrifice, of holy things the most holy." And this he speaketh of the sacrifice that Christ made upon the cross. And therefore he added[18] thus: *Quod uno verbo apostolus explicavit, cum dicit, Qui seipsum obtulit Deo*[19]: "Which thing the apostle expressed in one word, saying thus: 'Which hath offered up himself unto God'."

August. in Johan. Tract. 26.
Orig. in Levit. Hom. 7.

Howbeit, not only the sacrament, but also other things appointed unto godly

---

[[8] Const. Apost. Lib. VIII. cap. xlvi. in Concil. Stud. Labb. et Cossart. Lut. Par. 1671, 2. Tom. I. col. 509. See below, page 522.]

[[9] ... semetipsum in cœna apostolorum immolavit.—Isych. in Levit. Basil. 1527. Lib. I. cap. iv. fol. 20.]

[[10] Even in, H. A. 1564.]

[[11] Sancta sanctorum sunt proprie Christi mysteria, quia ipsius est corpus, de quo Gabriel ad virginem dicebat: Spiritus sanctus superveniet in te, et virtus Altissimi obumbrabit tibi; ideo quod nascetur ex te, sanctum vocabitur Filius Dei. Sed et Esaias: Sanctus Dominus, et in altis habitat, in sinu videlicet Patris.—Id. ibid. Lib. VI. cap. xxii. fol. 132.]

[[12] Chrysost. Op. Par. 1718-28. In Epist. ad Hebr. Hom. xvi. Tom. XII. p. 159. See before, page 518, note 4.]

[[13] Tertull. Op. Lut. 1641. De Baptism. 19. p. 264. See before, page 488, note 5.]

[[14] Chrysost. Op. In Epist. ad Rom. Hom. x. Tom. IX. p. 525.]

[[15] Isych. in Levit. Lib. I. cap. ii. fol. 13. 2.]

[[16] August. Op. In Johan. Evang. cap. vi. Tractat. xxvi. 15. 18. Tom. III. Pars II. cols. 500, 1.]

[[17] Orig. Op. Par. 1733-59. In Levit. Hom. v. 3. Tom. II. p. 207.]

[[18] Addeth, 1565.]

[[19] Id. ibid.]

Inter Decret. Bonifac. I. Decret. 3. xii. Quæst. 2. Nulli liceat. Lev. xxvii.

use, may be called *sancta sanctorum*. So it is written and determined by Bonifacius the first: *Omne quod Domino consecratur, sive fuerit homo, sive animal, sive ager, vel quicquid fuerit semel consecratum, sanctum sanctorum erit Domino*[1]: "Every thing that is consecrate unto the Lord, be it man, or beast, or lands, or whatsoever, being consecrate, it is holy of the holy unto the Lord." Neither doth he call the holy mysteries *sancta sanctorum* in that sense that M. Harding meaneth, for that they are the holiest of all holy thiugs, but because they are appointed for holy people. For thus he expoundeth it himself: [*Panis iste, et calix*] *sancta . . . sanctorum sunt. Vides, quomodo non dixerit, sancta tantummodo, sed sancta sanctorum. Ac si diceret, panis iste . . . non est communis omnium, nec cujusque indigni, sed sanctorum est. Quanto magis hoc et de verbo Dei . . . dicemus, Hic sermo non est omnium, nec cujuscunque, sed sanctorum est*[2]*!* "This bread and this cup are the holy things of the holy. You see that he saith not only, they are holy things, but he addeth besides, of the holy. As if he would say, This bread is not common to all men, nor to every unworthy; but it is the bread of the holy. How much more may we say the same of God's word, This word is not of all men, or of every body, but of the holy!" Therefore St Chrysostom saith, The priest was wont to shew forth the bread in the time of the holy mysteries, and to say, *Sancta sanctis*[3], "Holy things for the holy." And this is the meaning of *sancta sanctorum*.

Orig. in Levit. Hom. 13.

As for Clemens of Rome, the apostles' fellow, as M. Harding every where calleth him, he saith not that Christ offered himself at his last supper, but rather far otherwise. Thus he saith: *Propter nos homo factus, et spirituale sacrificium offerens Deo*[4]: "Christ being made man for us, and offering unto God a spiritual sacrifice." And in plainer sort he maketh this prayer unto God touching the same: *Offerimus tibi Regi et Deo, juxta Christi institutionem, hunc panem et hoc poculum*[5]: "We offer up unto thee, O King and God, this bread and this cup." He saith not, We offer up really the body of thy Son; but, this bread and this cup. Which also he calleth *antitypa*, that is to say, *signa corporis et sanguinis Christi*[6], "the tokens or pledges of Christ's body and blood." And so Theodoretus writeth hereof: *Ecclesia offert corporis et sanguinis ejus symbola*[7]: "The church offereth the tokens or signs of his body and blood."

Lib. viii. cap. xiii.

Theodor. in Psal. cx.

M. HARDING. THE TWELFTH DIVISION.

On the holy table, where these mysteries are celebrated, the "Lamb of God being laid, and sacrificed of priests unbloodily," as that most ancient and worthy council of Nice reporteth[8].

THE BISHOP OF SARISBURY.

As the council of Nice saith, "The Lamb is laid upon the altar," alluding unto the sacrifices of the old law; even so doth St Augustine say unto the people: *Vos estis in mensa . . . vos estis in calice*[9]: "You are upon the table: you are in the cup." As the people is laid upon the table, so is Christ laid upon the table. But this authority is answered more at large in the fifth article, and the eighth division[10].

August. in Serm. ad Infant. citat. a Bed. 1 Cor. x.

M. HARDING. THE THIRTEENTH DIVISION.

Briefly, in this highest sacrament under visible shape invisible things, soothly the very true, real, lively, natural, and substantial body and blood of our Saviour

[1 Bonifac. I. Decret. 3. in Crabb. Concil. Col. Agrip. 1551. Tom. I. p. 493. See also Corp. Jur. Canon. Lugd. 1624. Decret. Gratian. Decr. Sec. Pars, Caus. XII. Quæst. ii. can. 3. col. 980; where the order of the words is slightly varied.]

[2 Orig. Op. Par. 1733-59. In Levit. Hom. xiii. 5, 6. Tom. II. pp. 257, 8; where *non dixit, ut si, cibus iste*, and *cujuscumque indigni*.]

[3 See before, page 512, note 2.]

[4 Const. Apost. Lib. VIII. cap. xlvi. in Concil. Stud. Labb. et Cossart. Lut. Par. 1671-2. Tom. I. col. 509.]

[5 Id. ibid. cap. xii. col. 482.]

[6 Id. ibid. Lib. v. cap. xiii. col. 358.]

[7 Theodor. Op. Lut. Par. 1642-84. Interp. Psalm. cix. Tom. I. p. 852.]

[8 Gelas. Cyz. Hist. Concil. Nic. cap. xxx. in Concil. Stud. Labb. et Cossart. Tom. II. col. 233. See before, page 464, note 3.]

[9 Ven. Bed. Op. Col. Agrip. 1612. Ad Cor. I. cap. x. Tom. VI. col. 365. See before, page 468, note 1.]

[10 See before, pages 465, &c.]

Christ being contained, as (162) *the scriptures, doctors, councils, yea, and the best learned of Martin Luther's school, do most plainly and assuredly affirm.* Constancy.

THE BISHOP OF SARISBURY.

The hundred and sixty-second untruth, misreporting the scriptures, the councils, and ancient fathers.

Now soothly, if M. Harding could have found any of all these terms, real, lively, natural, or substantial, either in the scriptures, or in the doctors, or in any council, he would not have spared the allegation. But thus avouching these terms, and so constantly assuring us thereof by these authorities, being nevertheless not able any where to find the same, we must needs think he misreporteth the scriptures, the doctors, and the councils, and much abuseth the simple credulity of the people.

M. HARDING. THE FOURTEENTH DIVISION.

This, I say in conclusion, being so, as it is undoubtedly so, we, that remain in the catholic church, and can by no persecution be removed from the catholic faith, whom it liketh M. Jewel and his fellows to call papists, believe verily that it is our bounden duty to adore the sacrament, and to worship it with all godly honour. By which word sacrament, notwithstanding, in this respect we mean not the outward forms, (163) *that properly are called the sacrament, but the thing of the sacrament, the invisible grace and virtue therein contained, even the very body and blood of Christ.*

The hundred and sixty-third untruth. For these speeches were never known nor heard of in any time of the ancient fathers.

[*What christian people adore in the sacrament.* H. A. 1564.]

And when we adore and worship this blessed sacramant, we do not adore and worship the substance itself of bread and wine, (164) *because after consecration none at all remaineth. Neither do we adore the outward shapes and forms of bread and wine which remain; for they be but creatures, that ought not to be adored; but the body itself and blood of Christ,* (165) *under those forms verily and really contained, lowly and devoutly do we adore. And therefore, to speak more properly, and according to skill, lest our adversaries might take advantage against us through occasion of terms, where right sense only is meant, we protest and say, that we do and ought to adore and worship the body and blood of Christ in the sacrament.*

The hundred and sixty-fourth untruth. For the bread and wine remain still, as shall appear in the tenth article.

The hundred and sixty-fifth untruth. As may more largely appear by the fifth and sixth[11] article.

THE BISHOP OF SARISBURY.

If M. Harding be persecuted, as he saith, verily it seemeth a delicate kind of persecution. They of his side did not so persecute others. But Salomon saith: "There be certain that flee when no man followeth them." Thus did Arius the heretic sometimes complain of his persecutors: Ἄρειος ὁ διωκόμενος . . . ἀδίκως διὰ τὴν πάντα νικῶσαν ἀλήθειαν[12]: "Arius, that wrongfully suffereth persecution for the truth's sake, that conquereth all things." Prov. xxviii. Epiph. Lib. ii. De Ariomanitis.

As for M. Harding's constancy, which is here brought in as instead of some proof, I will say nothing. Howbeit his friends think so many, so light, and so sudden changes, can scarcely stand well with the title of constancy. Certainly the maintenance of open and known error should rather have some other name. The prophet Zachary saith: *Posuerunt ut adamantem cor suum:* "They have set their hearts[13] as the adamant stone." Job saith: *Stetit cor ejus sicut incus:* "His heart stood as a steady[14]." Yet might not they therefore be called constant. St Hilary saith: *Gravis et periculosus est lapsus in multis. Etsi enim se intelligant, tamen pudor exsurgendi auctoritatem sibi præsumit; ut, quod errant, prudentiam velint existimari; quod cum multis errant, intelligentiam esse asserant veritatis*[15]: "Falling from God in many men is grievous and dangerous. For albeit

Zech. vii. Job xli. Hilar. de Trin. Lib. vi. cap. lxxxiv.

[[11] The sixth, 1565.]

[[12] Epiph. Op. Par. 1622. Adv. Hær. Lib. II. Hær. lxix. 6. Tom. I. p. 731.]

[[13] Heart, 1565.] [[14] Steady: an anvil.]

[[15] Gravis enim et periculosus est error in plurimis: et multorum lapsus, etiamsi se intelligat, tamen exsurgendi pudore auctoritatem sibi præsumit, ex numero habens hoc impudentiæ, ut quod errat, prudentiam velit existimari; et quod cum multis errat, intelligentiam esse asserat veritatis, dum minus erroris esse existimatur in multis.—Hilar. Op. Par. 1693. De Trin. Lib. VI. 1. col. 879.]

they understand themselves[1], yet, for that they are ashamed to rise again, they therefore take upon them some authority, and will have their error counted wisdom; and that they are deceived with many, they call it the understanding of the truth." Touching the purpose, it appeareth this matter cannot stand without the disordering and confounding of the natural course and sound of words. Sometimes the accidents and shews of bread must be the sacrament, sometimes Christ's body; which, as M. Harding confesseth, indeed is not the sacrament, yet, to maintain this new adoration, must needs become the sacrament. And thus now we have two sacraments together in one sacrament. And yet, in the conclusion, we may not worship the very sacrament, but only Christ's body in the sacrament. And this, as M. Harding telleth us, is a proper, plain, familiar kind of speech, and according unto skill. Thus he teacheth us to lift up our hearts, and to worship God in spirit and truth. Unless the simple people go to the universities, and learn this new skill, what is *accidens absque subjecto, corpus sine loco, locus sine corpore, quantitas sine modo quanti,* they cannot skilfully worship Christ's body. Or if they worship without this skill, they worship one thing for another, and become idolaters.

M. HARDING. THE FIFTEENTH DIVISION.

And here thus[2] *much is further to be said, that in the sacrament of the altar the body of Christ is not adored by thought of mind sundered from the Word, but being inseparably united to the Word. For this is specially to be considered, that in the*[3] *most holy sacrament the body and blood of Christ are not present by themselves alone, as being separated from his soul and from the Godhead; but that there is* (166) *here his true and living flesh and blood joined together with his Godhead inseparably, and that they be as himself is, perfect*[4], *whole, and inseparable. Which is sufficiently confirmed by sundry his own words in St John. "I am," said*[5] *he, "the bread of life." Again: "This is bread coming down from heaven, that if any eat of it he die not. I am the lively bread that came down from heaven; if any eat of this bread, he shall live everlastingly." And, to shew what bread he meant, he concludeth with these words: "And the bread which I shall give is my flesh, which I shall give for the life of the world." By which words he assureth us plainly that his flesh which he giveth us to eat is full of life and joined with his Godhead, which bringeth to the worthy receivers thereof immortality as well of body as of soul. Which thing flesh and blood of itself could not perform; as our Lord himself declareth plainly, where he saith, as there it followeth: "It is the Spirit that quickeneth or giveth life: the flesh profiteth nothing. The words which I have spoken to you be Spirit and life." As though he had said thus: The flesh of itself profiteth nothing; but my flesh, which is full of Godhead and Spirit, bringeth and worketh immortality and life everlasting to them *that receive it worthily. Thus we understand in this blessed sacrament not only the body and blood of Christ, but all and whole Christ, God and man, to be present in substance, and that for the inseparable unity of the person of Christ; and for this cause we acknowledge ourselves bounden to adore him as very true God and man.*

The hundred and sixty-sixth untruth, often avouched, and never proved. For[6] these words pertain only to Christ himself, and nothing at all unto the sacrament.

* A vain addition. For St Augustine saith, the body of Christ itself is received of all men unto life, and of no man unto judgment[7].

For a clearer declaration hereof I will not let to recite a notable sentence out of St Augustine, where he expoundeth these words of Christ: "Then if ye see the Son of man go up where he was before." "There had been no question," saith he, "if he had thus said: If ye see the Son of God go up where he was before. But whereas he said, 'The Son of man go up where he was before;' what, was the Son of man in heaven before that he began to be in earth? Verily here he said, 'Where he was before;' as though then he were not there when he spake these words. And in another place he saith: 'No man hath ascended into heaven but he that descended from heaven, the Son of man which is in heaven.' He said not was; *but 'the Son of*

In Johan. Tract. 27.

[1 Themself, 1565.]
[2 This, 1565 and H. A. 1564.]
[3 This, H. A. 1564.]
[4 Perfite, 1565 and H. A. 1564.]
[5 Saith, 1565, 1609, and H. A. 1564.]
[6 1565 omits *for*.]
[7 ...res vero ipsa...omni homini ad vitam, nulli ad exitium.—August. Op. Par. 1679-1700. In Johan. Evang. cap. vi. Tractat. xxvi. 15. Tom. III. Pars II. col. 500.]

man,' saith he, 'which is in heaven.' In earth he spake and said himself to be in heaven. To what pertaineth this, but that we understand Christ to be one person, God and man, not two; lest our faith be not a Trinity, but a quaternity? Wherefore Christ is one, the Word, the soul, and the flesh, one Christ; the Son of God and the Son of man, one Christ: the Son of God ever, the Son of man in time; yet one Christ, according to the unity of person, was in heaven, when he spake in earth. So was the Son of man in heaven, as the Son of God was in earth. The Son of God in earth in flesh taken, the Son of man in heaven in unity of person[8]." *Thus*[9] *far St Augustine.*

THE BISHOP OF SARISBURY.

It is true that Christ's body and his Godhead are joined inseparably, and therefore must be adored both together. For we may not divide the Godhead from the manhead, and so imagine two sundry Christs, the one to be honoured, the other to stand without honour, as did the heretic Nestorius. But as the body and soul of man, being joined both in one, are honoured both together; so must Cyril.in Apol.
the humanity and divinity of Christ, being joined both in one, likewise be honoured both together[10]. Otherwise to say, as the heretic Nestorius said, "Thomas touched In edicto imperatoris
him that was risen again, and honoured him that raised him up[11]," it were great Justin. Inter Decret.
blasphemy. Nevertheless, notwithstanding the body and Godhead of Christ be Johan. ii. Concil.
joined in one person, yet are they distinct and sundry natures[12]; the one finite, Chalced. Act. 1.
the other infinite; the one in place, the other incomprehensible without place; the one a creature, the other the Creator. Neither is there any godly honour due unto the body of Christ in respect of itself, but only for that it is joined in one person with the divinity. All these things be true and out of question.

Likewise, the words, that Christ spake in the sixth chapter of St John, and are here alleged by M. Harding, are undoubtedly true; howbeit, not according to the simple sound and tenor of the letter; for that, as St Augustine saith, were *flagitium et facinus*[13], "an heinous wickedness." And, as Origen saith: "It would August. de Doct. Christ.
kill the soul[14]." And therefore Christ himself expoundeth his own meaning touch- Lib. iii. cap. xvi.
ing the same: "It is the Spirit that giveth life: the flesh profiteth nothing. The Orig.in Levit.
words that I have spoken be Spirit and life." Which words St Augustine ex- Hom. 7.
poundeth thus: *Spiritualiter intelligite, quæ locutus sum. Non hoc corpus quod* August. in
videtis, manducaturi estis[15]: "Understand ye spiritually the things that I have Psal. xcviii.
spoken. Ye shall not eat this body that ye see." Likewise Chrysostom: *Secun-* Chrysost. in
dum spiritum verba mea audienda sunt: qui secundum carnem audit, nihil lucratur, Joh. Hom. 47.
nihil utilitatis accipit[16]: "My words must be heard spiritually; whoso heareth

---

[8 Nulla enim esset quæstio si ita dixisset, Si videritis Filium Dei adscendentem ubi erat prius: cum vero Filium hominis dixit adscendentem ubi erat prius, numquid Filius hominis in cœlo erat prius, quando in terra esse cœpit? Hic quidem dixit, ubi erat prius, quasi tunc non ibi esset quando hæc loquebatur. Alio autem loco ait, Nemo adscendit in cœlum, nisi qui de cœlo descendit, Filius hominis qui est in cœlo: non dixit erat, sed Filius, inquit, hominis qui est in cœlo. In terra loquebatur, et in cœlo se esse dicebat....Quo pertinet, nisi ut intelligamus...unam personam esse Christum Deum et hominem, non duas; ne fides nostra non sit Trinitas, sed quaternitas? Christus ergo unus est: Verbum, anima et caro unus Christus: Filius Dei et Filius hominis unus Christus: Filius Dei semper, Filius hominis ex tempore; tamen unus Christus secundum unitatem personæ. In cœlo erat, quando in terra loquebatur. Sic erat Filius hominis in cœlo, quomodo Filius Dei erat in terra: Filius Dei in terra in suscepta carne, Filius hominis in cœlo in unitate personæ.—Id. ibid. Tractat. xxvii. 4. col. 503.]

[9 This, H. A. 1564.]

[10 ...ὁ σαρκωθεὶς τοῦ Θεοῦ Λόγος...οὐχὶ δίχα τῆς ἑαυτοῦ σαρκὸς, μετὰ ταύτης δὲ μᾶλλον, ἐστὶ προσκυνητός· καθάπερ ἀμέλει καὶ ἡ τοῦ ἀνθρώπου ψυχὴ μετὰ τοῦ ἰδίου τιμᾶται σώματος.—Cyril. Alex. Op. Lut. 1638. Apol. adv. Orient. Anath. viii. Def. Cyril. Tom. VI. p. 179.]

[11 ...de quo blasphemans dixit, quod palpavit Thomas eum qui resurrexit, et adoravit eum qui resuscitavit.—Justin. Fid. temp. Joan. ii. in Crabb. Concil. Col. Agrip. 1551. Tom. I. p. 1068.]

[12 ...διάφοροι μὲν αἱ πρὸς ἑνότητα τὴν ἀληθινὴν συνενεχθεῖσαι φύσεις, εἷς δὲ ἐξ ἀμφοῖν Χριστὸς, καὶ υἱός· οὐχ ὡς τῆς τῶν φύσεων διαφορᾶς ἀνῃρημένης διὰ τὴν ἕνωσιν, ἀποτελεσασῶν δὲ μᾶλλον ἡμῖν τὸν ἕνα Κύριον, καὶ Χριστὸν, καὶ υἱὸν, θεότητός τε καὶ ἀνθρωπότητος, κ. τ. λ.—Cyril. Rescr. ad Nestor. in Concil. Calched. Act. i. in Concil. Stud. Labb. et Cossart. Lut. Par. 1671-2. Tom. IV. col. 160.]

[13 Facinus vel flagitium videtur jubere.—August. Op. De Doctr. Christ. Lib. III. cap. xvi. 24. Tom. III. Pars I. col. 52.]

[14 Orig. Op. Par. 1733-59. In Levit. Hom. vii. 5. Tom. II. p. 225. See before, page 456, note 3.]

[15 August. Op. In Psalm. xcviii. Enarr. 9. Tom. IV. col. 1066; where *quod* for *quæ*.]

[16 Chrysost. Op. Par. 1718-38. In Joan. Hom. xlvii. Tom. VIII. p. 277.]

them carnally, or according to the flesh, getteth nothing, nor hath any profit by them." He saith further by way of objection against himself: *Quid ergo est carnaliter intelligere? Simpliciter, ut res dicuntur; neque aliud quicquam cogitare*[1]: "And what is meant by these words, To understand according to the flesh?" He answereth: "It is to understand simply and plainly, even as things be spoken, and to think upon nothing else." Thus therefore Christ said, to cut off their carnal cogitations: "The words that I spake are Spirit and life." As if he should say: Neither is my flesh meat, nor my blood drink, to enter into your mouths and to feed your bodies. But if your souls be hungry, I am spiritual meat to feed you; if your souls be thirsty, I am spiritual drink to refresh you. To this purpose St Chrysostom saith thus: *Omnia tibi Christus factus est; mensa, vestimentum, domus, caput, et radix*[2], *&c.*: "Christ is become all things unto thee; thy table, thy apparel, thy house, thy head, and thy root, &c.[3] St Paul saith, 'As many of you as are baptized in Christ, ye have put on Christ:' behold, how Christ is made thy apparel. And wilt thou learn how he is become thy table? He saith, 'Whoso eateth me shall live through me:' and that he is thy house, he saith, 'Whoso eateth my flesh dwelleth in me, and I in him:' and that he is thy root, again he saith, 'I am the vine, and you are the branches.'" So saith Gregorius Nyssenus: "Christ unto the strong is strong meat; unto the weaker sort he is herbs; and unto infants he is milk[4]." So saith Origen: *Ne mireris: quia verbum Dei et caro dicitur, et panis, et lac, ... et olera, ... et pro mensura credentium, vel possibilitate sumentium diverse nominatur*[5]: "Marvel not; for the word of God is called both flesh, and bread, and milk, and herbs; and, according to the measure of the believers, and the possibility of the receivers, is diversely named." And likewise Gregory Nazianzene: *Quemadmodum Dominus noster Jesus Christus appellatur vita, via, panis, vitis, lux vera, et mille alia, sic etiam appellatur gladius*[6]: "Like as our Lord Jesus Christ is called the life, the way, the bread, the wine[7], the true light, and a thousand things else, so is he also called the sword." Now as Christ is bread, even so in like manner of speech he is a sword, and none otherwise. Thus is Christ unto us a spiritual table, a spiritual apparel, a spiritual house, a spiritual head, a spiritual root, spiritual meat, spiritual herbs, spiritual milk, spiritual flesh, life, way, bread, wine[7], and light. And to this end Christ saith: "My words be Spirit and life."

Chrysost. ad Popul. Ant. Hom. 21.

Gal. iii.

John vi.

John xv.

Gregor. Nyss. In Vita Mosis.

Origen. in Exod. cap. xv. Hom. 7.

Nazianz. in Psal. xliv.

Hitherto the words of Christ, that be here alleged, weigh very little of M. Harding's side.

Besides all this, he saith that whole Christ, both God and man, is really, substantially, and carnally in the sacrament. This thing, because he is not able any way to prove, he presumeth of himself by authority, as though it were already proved. It shall be good to give him a day to consider the matter and to prove it better. In the mean season the substance of his reason standeth thus:

The humanity and divinity of Christ are joined together in one person;

Ergo, we must adore the sacrament with godly honour.

M. HARDING. THE SIXTEENTH DIVISION.

Hereupon he expoundeth these words, "It is the Spirit that quickeneth or giveth life; the flesh availeth nothing," thus: "The flesh profiteth nothing, but the only flesh. Come the Spirit to the flesh, and it profiteth very much. For if the flesh should profit nothing, the Word should not be made flesh to dwell among[8] *us*[9]." "*For this*

[1 Id. ibid. p. 278.] [2 1565 omits *&c.*]

[3 ...πάντα σοι ὁ Χριστὸς γίνεται, καὶ τράπεζα, καὶ ἱμάτιον, καὶ οἶκος, καὶ κεφαλὴ, καὶ ῥίζα. ὅσοι γὰρ εἰς Χριστὸν ἐβαπτίσθητε, Χριστὸν ἐνεδύσασθε· ἰδοὺ πῶς ἱμάτιόν σοι γέγονε. βούλει μαθεῖν, πῶς καὶ τράπεζά σοι γίνεται; ὁ τρώγων με, φησὶ, κἀκεῖνος ζήσεται δι' ἐμέ. ὅτι δὲ καὶ οἶκός σοι γίνεται, ὁ τρώγων μου τὴν σάρκα ἐν ἐμοὶ μένει, κἀγὼ ἐν αὐτῷ. καὶ ὅτι ῥίζα, πάλιν φησὶν, ἐγὼ ἡ ἄμπελος, ὑμεῖς τὰ κλήματα.—Id. ad Illum. Catech. ii. Tom. II. p. 236.]

[4 Gregor. Nyss. Op. Par. 1638. De Vit. Mos. Tom. I. p. 215. See before, page 475, note 9.]

[5 Orig. Op. Par. 1733-59. In Exod. Hom. vii. 8. Tom. II. p. 155; where *nec* for *ne*.]

[6 There is a passage in which many appellations of Christ are enumerated, and among others, that of sword, but it is in an oration or homily on Matt. xix. See Gregor. Nazianz. Op. Par. 1778-1840. Orat. xxxvii. 4. Tom. I. pp. 647, 8.]

[7 Vine, 1565, 1609.]

[8 Amongst, H. A. 1564.]

[9 Sic etiam nunc, Caro non prodest quidquam, sed sola caro: accedat spiritus ad carnem...et prodest plurimum. Nam si caro nihil prodesset, Verbum caro non fieret, ut inhabitaret in nobis.—August. Op. Par. 1679-1700. In Johan. Evang. cap. vi. Tractat. xxvii. 5. Tom. III. Pars II. col. 503.]

unity of person to be understanded in both natures (saith the great learned father Leo), we read that both the Son of man came down from heaven, when as the Son of God took flesh of that virgin of whom he was born; and again, it is said that the Son of God was crucified and buried, whereas he suffered these things not in the Godhead itself, in which the only-begotten is coeverlasting and consubstantial with the Father, but in the infirmity of human nature. Wherefore we confess all in the creed also, the only-begotten Son of God crucified and buried, according to that saying of the apostle: 'For if they had known, they would never have crucified the Lord of majesty'[10]."

Epist. ad Flavianum Constantinopol. Episc. cap. v.

1 Cor. ii.

According to this doctrine, Cyrillus writing upon St John saith: "He that eateth the flesh of Christ hath life everlasting. For this flesh hath the Word of God, which naturally is life. Therefore he saith: 'I will raise him again in the last day.' For I, said he, that is my body, which shall be eaten, will raise him again. For he is not other than his flesh. I say not this because by nature he is not other, but because, after incarnation, he suffereth not himself to be divided into two sons[11]." By which words he reproveth the heresy of wicked Nestorius, that went about to divide Christ, and of Christ to make two sons; the one the Son of God, the other the son of Mary, and so two persons. For which Nestorius was condemned in the first Ephesine council, and also specially for that he said (167) *we receive in this sacrament only the flesh of Christ in the bread, and his blood only in the wine, without the Godhead; because Christ said, 'He that eateth my flesh,' and said not, he that eateth or drinketh my Godhead, because his Godhead cannot be eaten, but his flesh only. Which heretical cavil Cyrillus doth thus avoid. "Although (saith he) the nature of the Godhead be not eaten, yet we eat the body of Christ, which verily may be eaten. But this body is the Word's own proper body, which quickeneth all things; and, inasmuch as it is the body of life, it is quickening or life-giving[12]." Now he quickeneth us, or giveth us life, as God, the only fountain of life. Wherefore such speeches uttered in the scriptures of Christ, whereby that appeareth to be attributed to the one nature which appertaineth to the other, and contrariwise, according to that incomprehensible and unspeakable conjunction and union of the divine and human nature in one person, are to be taken of him inseparably, inasmuch as he is both God and man; and not of this or that other nature only, as being severed from the other. For through cause of this inseparable union, whatsoever is appertaining or peculiar to either nature, it is rightly ascribed, yea, and it ought to be ascribed to the whole person: and this done[13], as the learned divines term it,* per communicationem idiomatum. *And thus Cyrillus teacheth how Christ may be eaten, not according to the divine, but human nature, which he took of us; and so likewise he is of christian people adored in the sacrament according to his divine nature. And yet not according to his divine nature only, as though that were separated from his human nature, but his whole person together, God and man. And his precious flesh and blood are adored for the inseparable conjunction of both natures into one person, which is Jesus Christ, God and man: "whom God hath exalted (as St Paul saith) and hath given him a name which is above all names[14], that at[15] the name*

In Johan. Lib. iv. cap. xv.

The hundred and sixty-seventh untruth. For neither was there any such error defended by Nestorius, nor any such canon ever moved in that council.

Vide Anathematismum, 11. Item ad Theodos. de Recta Fide, et Lib. ii. ad Reginas de Recta Fide.

Phil. ii.

[10 Propter hanc ergo unitatem personæ, in utraque natura intelligendam, et Filius hominis legitur descendisse de cœlo, cum Filius Dei carnem de ea virgine, de qua est natus, assumpserit. Et rursus, Filius Dei crucifixus dicitur ac sepultus, cum hæc non in divinitate ipsa, qua unigenitus, consempiternus, et consubstantialis est Patri, sed in naturæ humanæ sit infirmitate perpessus. Unde unigenitum Filium Dei crucifixum et sepultum omnes etiam in symbolo confitemur, secundum illud apostoli, Si enim cognovissent, nunquam Dominum majestatis crucifixissent.—Leon. Magni Op. Lut. 1623. Ad Flavian. Constant. Episc. Epist. x. cap. v. cols. 308, 9.]

[11 Οὐκοῦν ὁ τρώγων τὴν ἁγίαν σάρκα Χριστοῦ ζωὴν αἰώνιον ἔχει· ἔχει γὰρ ἡ σὰρξ ἐν ἑαυτῇ τὸν Λόγον, κατὰ φύσιν ὄντα ζωήν. διὰ γὰρ τοῦτό φησιν, ὅτι ἐγὼ ἀναστήσω αὐτὸν ἐν τῇ ἐσχάτῃ ἡμέρᾳ. ἀντὶ δὲ τοῦ εἰπεῖν, ὅτι περ αὐτὸν, τὸν ἐσθίοντα δηλονότι, τὸ ἐμὸν ἀναστήσει σῶμα, τὸ ἐγὼ τέθεικεν, οὐχ ὡς ἕτερος ὢν παρὰ τὴν ἰδίαν σάρκα, καὶ οὐ πάντως τῇ φύσει· διατέμνεσθαι γὰρ εἰς υἱῶν δυάδα μετὰ τὴν ἕνωσιν οὐκ ἀνέχεται.—Cyril. Alex. Op. Lut. 1638. Comm. in Joan. Evang. Lib. IV. cap. ii. Tom. IV. p. 363.]

[12 Οὐ γὰρ ἐπειδήπερ οὐκ ἐσθίεται θεότητος φύσις, διὰ τοῦτο κοινὸν εἶναι φαίη τις ἂν τὸ ἅγιον σῶμα Χριστοῦ. εἰδέναι δὲ ἀναγκαῖον, ὅτι...ἴδιόν ἐστι σῶμα τοῦ τὰ πάντα ζωοποιοῦντος Λόγου· ἐπειδὰν δέ ἐστι σῶμα ζωῆς, ζωοποιόν ἐστι.—Id. Apol. adv. Orient. Anath. xi. Def. Cyril. Tom. VI. p. 193. Id. De Rect. Fid. ad Theod. 48. Tom. V. Pars II. p. 35. Id ad Regin. Lib. II. 56. Tom. V. Pars II. p. 177.]

[13 This is done, H. A. 1564.]

[14 Name, H. A. 1564.]

[15 In, 1565, 1609, and H. A. 1564.]

of Jesus every knee be bowed, of the heavenly and the earthly things, and of things beneath, and that every tongue confess that our Lord Jesus Christ is in glory of God the Father," that is, of equal glory with the Father. And "when God (saith St Paul) bringeth his first-begotten into the world, he saith, And let all the angels of God adore him." Heb. i. Psal. xcvii. *St John writeth in his Revelation,* Rev. v. *that he heard all creatures say, "Blessing, honour, glory, and power, be to him which sitteth in the throne, and to the Lamb for ever. And the four and twenty elders fell down on their faces, and adored him that liveth until worlds of worlds."*

THE BISHOP OF SARISBURY.

I marvel M. Harding would bestow so many waste words to so small purpose. These authorities be all true, and, saving only that of the council of Chalcedon[1], touching Nestorius, all truly alleged. But every thing that is true maketh not by and bye proof sufficient in every case. Plin. Sæpe respiciendum est ad titulum. Pliny the second giveth good sad[2] counsel, that whosoever will take in hand to write a book have evermore a good eye unto his title, or to the purpose whereof he writeth, lest he happen to wander and to run at random. As now M. Harding seemeth to shoot fair, although a great way from the mark. For in all these words there is no manner mention, neither of the sacrament, nor of the adoration thereof, nor of any other thing thereto belonging: unless M. Harding upon occasion of these words will reason thus:

The Son of man came down from heaven;

Ergo, we must adore the sacrament.

The words of Cyrillus be likewise true. "Christ's flesh is joined with the Godhead, and therefore it naturally giveth life." John vi. And when Christ said, "I will raise him up at the last day;" he meant, even as Cyrillus saith, that his flesh that we eat shall raise us up at the last day. For whatsoever favour or mercy we have from God, we have it only by the flesh of Christ. St Augustine saith: August. in Psal. cix. *Mortalis factus est immortalis, ut, peracta sua morte, [nos] faceret* [3]*immortales*[4]*:* "He that is immortal became mortal, that through his death he might make us immortal." August. in Psal. cxviii. Again he saith: *Nos non efficeremur participes divinitatis ejus, nisi ipse factus fuisset particeps mortalitatis nostræ*[5]*:* "We could not be partakers of his Godhead, unless he had been partaker of our mortality." All these words be true, as containing nothing else but the exposition of these words of Christ: "He that eateth my flesh and drinketh my blood shall live for ever."

But M. Harding, to make these words of Cyrillus to serve his turn, hath imagined two great errors: the one is that Christ's body cannot be eaten, but only in the sacrament; the other is that, unless we receive Christ's body with our mouth, and swallow it down into our belly, we eat it not: as though either Christ or these holy fathers had meant a carnal or fleshly eating. This whole doctrine is horrible and full of desperation. For M. Harding's position being true, that no man shall be partaker of that blessed resurrection, but only such as have eaten Christ's body in the sacrament, what then shall become of christian children that have departed this life, never having received the sacrament? Who shall raise them up again at the last day? Or doth M. Harding believe, that such little ones, being baptized, and so the members of Christ, shall never rise again, but lie damned for ever, only because they have not received the sacrament?

Verily, Christ in these words, as it is witnessed by all the holy fathers, speaketh not of the sacrament, but of the spiritual eating with our faith; and in this behalf utterly excludeth the corporal office of our body. Therefore St Augustine saith: August. in sext. caput Johannis. *Crede, et manducasti*[6]*:* "Believe, and thou hast eaten." And again: August. de Verb. Apost. Serm. 2. *Illud manducare, refici est:... illud bibere, quid est nisi vivere*[7]*?* "That

[1 An error for Ephesus.] [2 Sad: grave.]

[3 Immortalis, 1611.]

[4 August. Op. Par. 1679-1700. In Psalm. cix. Enarr. 12. Tom. IV. col. 1236.]

[5 Neque enim efficeremur, &c. ipse mortalitatis nostræ particeps fieret.—Id. in Psalm. cxviii. Serm. xvi. 6. Tom. IV. col. 1319.]

[6 Id. In Johan. Evang. cap. vi. Tractat. xxv. 12. Tom. III. Pars II. col. 489.]

[7 Id. Serm. cxxxi. 1. Tom. V. col. 641.]

eating is to be refreshed; and that drinking, what is it else, but to live?" Likewise St Basil saith: *Est spirituale os interni hominis, quo recipitur verbum vitæ, quod est panis qui de cœlo descendit*[8]: "There is a spiritual mouth of the inner man, wherewith is received the Word of life, which is that bread that came down from heaven." Spiritual eating. Basil. in Psal. xxxiii.

And touching our rising again from the dead he saith: τὸ...βάπτισμα δύναμις ἐστὶ πρὸς...ἀνάστασιν[9]: "Our baptism is a strength or power to resurrection." So St Augustine: *Nemini dubitandum est, &c.*[10]: "No man may doubt, but every man is then made partaker of the body and blood of Christ, when in baptism he is made the member of Christ's body." Likewise St Chrysostom: "In baptism we are incorporate unto Christ, and made flesh of his flesh, and bone of his bones[11]." Thus by faith we eat the body of Christ, and that not by way of imagination or fantasy, but effectually, verily, and indeed; and therefore Christ shall raise us up again at the last day. Basil. in Exhort. ad Sanct. Baptism. August. citat. a Beda in 1 Cor. x. Chrysost. in Epist. ad Ephes. Hom. 20.

M. Harding's error, as I have said, resteth herein, that he imagineth that Christ's body cannot be eaten, but only in the sacrament, and that by mean[12] and office of our bodily mouth. But, as it is before alleged out of Rabanus Maurus: "The sacrament is received outwardly with the mouth of our body; but the body of Christ is received into the inner man, and that with the spiritual mouth of our soul[13]." And thus both may the sacrament be received without Christ's body, and also the body of Christ may be received without the sacrament. Rab. Maur. Lib. i. cap. xxxi.

Hitherto M. Harding hath not once touched one word of adoration.

Concerning Nestorius, M. Harding in the drift of his tale hath handsomely couched in a great untruth. For, whereas he saith Nestorius held this opinion, that in the sacrament of the bread we receive only Christ's body without his blood, and in the cup the blood of Christ alone without the body; neither did Nestorius, notwithstanding he were an heretic, ever hold this peevish error, nor is there any such record either in the council of Ephesus, that here untruly is alleged, or in any other old council or ancient father. M. Harding untruly allegeth the council of Ephesus.

But the right of M. Harding's cause hangeth of such evidence as never was found in any record. If there be any such canon to be found in that whole council, or any mention thereof made in any of all the ancient doctors, let M. Harding shew it, that we may believe him. If, having alleged it so constantly and so often, he be able utterly to shew nothing, let him give men leave to think that he abuseth the world with vain titles, and meaneth no truth.

Although he might be bold freely to devise matter against Nestorius, as being an heretic, yet he should not thus report untruth of a general council.

But Cyrillus saith further: "We cannot eat the Godhead of Christ; it is his manhood[14] only that is eaten." Hereby M. Harding thinketh he is able to overthrow our whole doctrine of spiritual eating, that is wrought by faith. For thus he will reason:

By your doctrine eating of Christ's body is believing:
But Cyrillus saith we cannot eat God;
Ergo, by your doctrine we cannot believe in God.

Thus he thinketh we are driven to confess a great inconvenience. This reason seemeth to have some shew. And therefore I beseech thee, good reader, to consider both the parts thereof, and also the answer.

Eating, in common use of speech, is the receiving of food and sustenance, and the turning of the same into the substance of our bodies; and by a metaphor, or an extraordinary kind of speech, is often used for the spiritual eating and turning of heavenly food to the refreshing and nourishing of our souls. By neither of these ways it can rightly be said that we eat the Godhead. For neither can we receive the majesty of God's divine nature, neither turn the same into the

[8 Basil. Op. Par. 1721-30. Hom. in Psalm. xxxiii. Tom. I. p. 144.]

[9 Id. Hom. in Sanct. Baptism. Tom. II. p. 114.]

[10 See before, page 132, note 2.]

[11 Chrysost. Op. Par. 1718-38. In Epist. ad Ephes. cap. v. Hom. xx. Tom. XI. p. 147. See before, page 477, note 19.]

[12 By the mean, 1565.]

[13 Rab. Maur. Op. Col. Agrip. 1626-7. De Inst. Cler. Lib. I. cap. xxxi. Tom. VI. p. 11. See before, page 453, note 14.]

[14 Manhead, 1565.]

To eat God.

substance of our nature. But we may receive and eat and feed upon the humanity and body of Christ, and become bone of his bones and flesh of his flesh, so as he may dwell in us and we in him. Wherefore, notwithstanding Christ be both God and man, yet we have not our feeding and life of Christ in respect of his Godhead alone, but first and principally in respect of his humanity, in that he was made man, and became "partaker of flesh and blood," and was crucified, and shed his blood, and yielded up his spirit upon the cross. This is our spiritual feeding: herein standeth our whole life. Therefore St Paul saith: *Quod nunc vivo in carne, in fide vivo Filii Dei, qui dedit semetipsum pro me:* "That I live now in the flesh, I live in the faith of the Son of God, that hath given himself for me." And again: "God forbid that I should rejoice in any thing, saving only in the cross of Jesus Christ." Likewise St Peter: "There is none other name given unto men under heaven whereby they may be saved, but only the name of Christ Jesus." Thus, as Cyrillus saith, "we have our life and feeding, not of the Godhead, but of the manhood[1] of Christ."

Eph. v. Heb. ii. Gal. ii. Gal. vi. Acts iv.

De Consecr. Dist. 2. Christus. In margine.

And therefore it is very well noted upon the decrees: [*Christus*] *per hoc est factus noster panis, et sustentatio, et vita...quia assumsit carnem nostram*[2]*:* "Christ in this is become our bread, and our sustenance, and our life, because he hath taken our flesh."

But M. Harding will say: According to the judgment of Cyrillus, "we cannot eat the Godhead;" yet nevertheless we do believe in God; *ergo*, contrary to your doctrine, believing and eating are not both one. Verily, it appeareth both by Cyrillus himself, and also by a general consent of other old learned fathers, that we cannot neither know God, nor believe in God, nor call upon God, as he is in himself in his divine majesty, but only as it pleased him to become like unto us, and to take upon him our mortal nature. St Chrysostom saith: *Illum, si in nuda deitate venisset, non cœlum, non terra, non maria, non ulla creatura sustinere potuisset*[3]*:* "If God had come in his manifest divinity, neither the heaven, nor the earth, nor the sea, nor any creature could have borne his presence." So St Hilary: *Cognitus fieri Deus homini, nisi assumpto homine, non potuit. Quia incognoscibilem cognoscere, nisi per naturam nostram, natura nostra non potuit*[4]*:* "Unless God had taken man, he could never have been known unto man. For him that cannot be known, our nature, saving only by mean of our own nature, could never have known." Likewise saith Cyrillus: "*Christus non aliter erit adorabilis, nisi credamus, quod ipsum Verbum... caro factum sit*[5]*:* "Christ is not otherwise to be adored, unless we believe that the very Word was made flesh." Likewise saith St Augustine: *Respice altitudinem ipsius: In principio erat Verbum, &c.*[6]*:* "Behold the highness of him: 'In the beginning was the Word, and the Word was with God, and God was that Word.' Behold the everlasting meat: but the angels and high powers and the heavenly spirits feed upon it. But what man can attain unto that meat? What heart can be meet for it? Therefore it was necessary that the[7] meat should turn into milk, and so should come unto us little ones." It followeth: *Quomodo ergo de ipso pane pavit nos Sapientia Dei? Quia Verbum caro factum est, et habitavit in nobis*[8]*:* "How then did the Wisdom of God feed us with that bread?" He answereth: "Because the Word was made flesh and dwelled in us." Again he saith: *Ita Verbum incarnatum factum est nobis receptibile; quod recipere non valeremus, si Filius æqualis Deo non se exinaniret formam servi accipiens*[9]*:* "Thus were we able to receive the Word incarnate, which we could not receive unless the Son, being equal unto the Father,

Chrysost. citat a Cassiod. in Psal. xvii.

Hilar. in Psal. cxliii.

Cyril. ad Reg.

August. in Psal. xxxiii. John i.

August. in Psal. cix.

[1 Manhead, 1565.]

[2 Corp. Jur. Canon. Lugd. 1624. Decret. Gratian. Decr. Tert. Pars, De Consecr. Dist. ii. Not. in can. 57. col. 1943.]

[3 Chrysost. in Cassiodor. Op. Rotom. 1679. Expos. in Psalm. xvii. Tom. II. p. 59; where *illum quem si nuda.*]

[4 Hilar. Op. Par. 1693. In Psalm. cxliii. Tractat. 8. col. 556.]

[5 Cyril. Alex. Op. Lut. 1638. Lib. de Rect. Fid. ad Regin. 6. Tom. V. Pars II. p. 45.]

[6 Respice, &c. et Verbum erat apud Deum, et Deus erat Verbum. Ecce cibus sempiternus: sed manducant angeli, manducant supernæ virtutes, manducant cœlestes spiritus......Quis autem homo posset ad illum cibum? Unde cor tam idoneum illi cibo? Oportebat ergo ut mensa illa lactesceret, et ad parvulos perveniret.—August. Op. Par. 1679-1700. In Psalm. xxxiii. Enarr. i. 6. Tom. IV. col. 211.]

[7 That, 1565.]

[8 Id. ibid.]

[9 Id. in Psalm. cix. Enarr. 12. Tom. IV. col. 1236; where *ita nobis Verbum.*]

had abased himself, receiving the form of a servant." I pass over other allegations to like purpose. This therefore is the meaning of Cyrillus: We are not able neither to receive, nor to know, nor to believe in, nor to adore, nor to eat, not[10] to feed upon the divine majesty of God, being pure and simple in itself; but our knowledge, our faith, our food, and our life is in this, that Christ hath taken our mortal nature, and joined the same inseparably in one person to his Godhead. Dissension.

M. HARDING. THE SEVENTEENTH DIVISION.

[*Contrariety in the first devisers of the new gospel.* H. A. 1564.] *But it shall be more tedious than needful to recite places out of the scriptures for proof of the adoration of Christ, there may of them be found so great plenty: yet, because Luther was either so blind, or rather so devilish, as to deny the adoration, where notwithstanding he confessed the presence of Christ's true and natural body in the sacrament, I will here recite what the sacramentaries of Zurich have written against him therefore. "What (say they), is the bread the true and natural body of Christ, and is Christ in the supper (as the pope and Luther do teach) present? Wherefore then ought not the Lord there to be adored, where ye say him to be present? Why shall we be forbidden to adore that which is not only sacramentally, but also corporally, the body of Christ? Thomas toucheth the true body of Christ raised up from the dead, and falling down on his knees, adoreth, saying, 'My God, and my Lord.' The disciples adore the Lord as well before as after his ascension.* Matt. xxviii. Acts i. *And the Lord in St John saith to the blind man: "Believest thou in the Son of God? and he answereth*[11] *him, saying, Lord, who is he, that I may believe in him? And Jesus said to him, Thou hast both seen him, and who speaketh with thee, he it is. Then he saith, Lord, I believe; and he adored him.' Now if we were*[12] *taught our Lord's bread to be the natural body of Christ, verily we would adore it also faithfully with the papists." Thus*[13] *much the Zwinglians against Luther: whereby they prove sufficiently the adoration of Christ's body in the sacrament, and so consequently of Christ himself, God and man, because of the inseparable conjunction of his divine and human nature in unity of person, so as, where his body is, there it is*[14] *joined and united also unto his Godhead; and so there Christ is present perfectly*[15]*, wholly, and substantially, very God and man.* John ix.

For the clear understanding whereof the better to be attained, the scholastical divines have profitably devised the term concomitantia, *plainly and truly teaching, that in this sacrament, after consecration, under the form of bread is present the body of Christ, and under the form of wine his blood,* ex vi sacramenti; *and with the body, under form of bread, also the blood, the soul, and Godhead of Christ; and likewise with the blood, under the form of wine, the body, soul, and Godhead,* ex concomitantia, *as they term it, in shorter and plainer wise uttering the same doctrine of faith,* (168) *which the holy fathers did in the Ephesine council against Nestorius. Whereby they mean that where the body of Christ is present, by necessary sequel, because of the indivisible copulation of both natures in the unity of person, (forasmuch as the Word made flesh never left the human nature), there is also his blood, his soul, his Godhead, and so whole and perfect*[16] *Christ, God and man. And in this respect the term is not to be misliked of any godly-learned man, though some new masters scoff at it, who fill the measure of their predecessors, that likewise have been offended with terms for the apter declaration of certain necessary articles of our faith, by holy and learned fathers in general councils wholesomely devised. Of which sort been these,* homousion, humanatio, incarnatio, transubstantiatio, &c. *Now here is to be noted how the Zwinglians, whom M. Jewel followeth, in the article of adoration confute the Lutherans; as, on the other side, the Lutherans in the article of the presence confute the Zwinglians. As though it were by God's special providence, for the better stay of his church, so wrought, that both the truth should be confessed by the enemies*

The hundred and sixty-eighth untruth. For there was no such doctrine moved in the council of Ephesus. Transubstantiation was but lately found, in the council of Lateran in Rome, Anno 1215.

[10 Nor, 1565.]
[11 Answered, 1565, and H. A. 1564.]
[12 H. A. 1564, omits *were*.]
[13 This, 1565, and H. A. 1564.]
[14 Is it, 1565, and H. A. 1564.]
[15 Perfitely, 1565, and H. A. 1564.]
[16 Perfite, 1565, and H. A. 1564.]

Dissension. *of truth, and also for uttering of untruth the one should be condemned of the other; that by the war of heretics the peace of the church might be established, and by their discord the catholic people might the faster grow*[1] *together in concord.*

Now, having sufficiently proved by the scriptures, and that with the Zwinglians also, adoration and godly honour to be due unto Christ's body, wheresoever it please his divine majesty to exhibit the same present; let us see whether we can find the same doctrine affirmed by the holy and ancient fathers.

THE BISHOP OF SARISBURY.

Whereas M. Harding thus checketh us with some dissension that hath been between Doctor Luther and Doctor Zwinglius, touching this matter of adoration, I may justly say unto him, as one sometime said unto Philippus the king of Macedony, entreating a peace between Peloponnesus and the rest of Græcia: "Go first and conclude a peace in thine own house at home." For at the same time his own wife Olympias and his own son Alexander were known to live in deadly dissension; and therefore he seemed no fit instrument to conclude a peace between others. (Demaratus.)

M. Harding should have remembered that the greatest buttresses and pillars of his gospel, sithence the first beginning of his new doctrine, have evermore lived in contradiction, and could never yet be reconciled. He should have remembered that his own doctors, and chiefest doctors, pope Innocentius and Scotus, teach contrary doctrines; that Scotus is against Thomas; Ockam against Scotus; Petrus de Alliaco against Ockam; and the nominals against the reals; and not only thus, but also Scotists against Scotists, and Thomists against Thomists, at civil war within one band; and that touching the very words of consecration and other like matters, both great and many, whereof to shew the particulars it would be tedious. But the matters hang still in mortal enmity, and are never like to be reconciled. Having such bloody fields at home, M. Harding should not be so ready to reproach others for some one or other matter of dissension.

It were much to be wished, (and God of his mercy so grant it, if it be his holy will!) that the gospel of Christ may pass forth freely without any such occasion of offence or hindrance. Howbeit, from the beginning it hath been otherwise. For even at the first planting of the gospel, whiles the martyrs' blood was yet warm, there were some that said, "I hold of Paul; some others that said, I hold of Peter;" and thus were they divided among themselves. St Paul "withstood and gainsayed Peter unto his face." St Hierome chargeth St Augustine with heresy; St Augustine willeth St Hierome to recant[2]; St Hierome despiseth St Ambrose, and findeth fault with St Basil; St Cyprian in judgment is contrary to St Cornelius; Pope Sabinianus would have burned all St Gregory's his predecessor's books[3]. Hereby it appeareth that saints have been against saints, and martyrs against martyrs, even in matters and cases of religion. (1 Cor. i. Gal. ii. August. Epist. 19.)

And hereof heretics and other wicked and godless people have evermore taken occasion to slander the gospel. Marcion the heretic thought he had found contrarieties between the new testament and the old[4]; and therefore said, he was able to prove falsehood[5] in the scriptures. St Hierome saith: *Hunc locum nobis objecit Julianus Augustus, de dissonantia evangelistarum*[6]*:* "This place, of the disagreeing of the evangelists, the heathen emperor Julianus charged us withal." Again he saith: *Sceleratus Porphyrius in primo libro, quem scripsit adversus nos, objecit, Petrum a Paulo esse reprehensum, quod non recto pede incederet ad evangelium*[7]*:* "That wicked man Porphyrius, in the first book that (Tertull. Lib. iv. contr. Marcion. Hieron. in Matt. Lib. i. cap. i. Hieron. in Proœm. in Epist. ad Gal.)

[[1] Grewe, 1565, and H. A. 1564.]

[[2] August. Op. Par. 1679-1700. Ad Hieron. Epist. xl. 7. Tom. II. col. 86.]

[[3] Plat. De Vit. Pontif. Col. 1551. Sabin. I. p. 75.]

[[4] Tertull. Op. Lut. 1641. Adv. Marcion. Lib. IV. 1, 6, 9, &c. pp. 501, 6, 10, &c.]

[[5] Falsehead, 1565.]

[[6] Hoc loco objecit nobis Julianus Augustus dissonantiam evangelistarum.—Hieron. Op. Par. 1693-1706. Comm. Lib. I. in Matt. cap. i. Tom. IV. Pars I. col. 7.]

[[7] ...sceleratus ille Porphyrius, in primo operis sui adversum nos libro, Petrum a Paulo objecit esse, &c. ad evangelizandum.—Id. Comm. in Epist. ad Gal. Lib. I. Præf. Tom. IV. Pars I. cols. 223, 4.]

he wrote against us, laid to our charge that Peter was rebuked of Paul, for that he walked not uprightly towards the gospel." So Socrates[8] and Sozomenus[9] say, that the Christians because of their dissensions were scorned at of the infidels in open assemblies and market-places, and pointed at with their fingers.

Dissension. Concomitantia.

Notwithstanding, such diversity of judgment, as it is an offence unto the weak, and an occasion of ill unto the wicked that seek occasions against God; even so unto the godly it is occasion of much good. For unto them that God hath called according to his purpose, all things help and further unto good. Nicholas Lyra saith: *Expositorum diversitas excitat attentionem*[10]: "The diversity of expositors stirreth up attention in the hearers, and causeth them to consider that men be men, and see unperfitly, as in a glass, as having received faith only by measure; and therefore to search and examine the scriptures, and not to glory in men; that whoso will glory may glory in the Lord."

Socrat. Lib. i. cap. vi. Sozom. Lib. i. cap. xvi. 2 Cor. xi. Rom. viii. Nic. Lyra in Prol. in Gen. 1 Cor. xiii. 2 Cor. x. 1 Cor. iii. 1 Cor. x.

These two worthy members of God's church, whom it liketh M. Harding thus to control, never differed or dissented in any foundation or principle of the christian faith, but only of one certain conclusion and phrase of the scriptures.

Either of them knew and confessed that Christ's body ought to be adored with godly honour, for that it is joined in one person with the divinity. But the one of them saith, notwithstanding Christ's body be present in the sacrament, yet it is not there to that use and purpose to be honoured; neither have we any warrant of God's word so to honour it. So is Christ's body in us naturally, really, corporally, carnally, substantially, and indeed. Yet may we not therefore one kneel down to another, so to adore Christ, being there present, with godly honour. Thus the whole disagreement of these two learned fathers stood only in this one point, of the manner of Christ's presence. Otherwise their whole hearts were joined and bent together to the disclosing of falsehood[11] and hypocrisy, and to the advancing[12] of God's glory.

We wonder not, as M. Harding thinketh, at his strange term, *concomitantia*, which he hath here brought in as a special stay of his ruinous doctrine; notwithstanding St Paul hath charged us to beware of such new-fangled wicked words: but we wonder to see the same term so childishly applied to so vain a purpose. Indeed these terms, *homousios, humanatio, incarnatio*, are not found expressed in the scriptures. Yet is the sense and meaning of the same terms, as Epiphanius saith, easy every where to be found[13].

1 Tim. vi. Profanas verborum novitates. βεβήλους κενοφωνίας. Epiph. contr. Semiar. Lib. iii. ὁ δὲ νοῦς πανταχοῦ.

Neither was that name first devised in the council of Nice. For long before the time of that council it[14] was used by Origen, and by other ancient learned bishops; as appeareth well by Socrates, whose words be these: *Doctos quosdam ex veteribus et illustres episcopos . . . homousii dictione usos esse cognovimus*[15]: "We know that of the old writers certain learned men and notable bishops have used this word *homousion*." And therefore St Augustine saith not, This name *homousios* was invented or devised; but, "This name was confirmed and stablished in the council of Nice[16]." Therefore M. Harding, as well herein as also elsewhere, hath reported untruth.

Socrat. Lib. i. cap. viii. August. contr. Max. Lib. iii. cap. xiv. Firmatum est.

As for transubstantiation, it is numbered here among these words, *homousios, humanatio*, and *incarnatio*, as Judas is numbered among the apostles. God wot, a very young name, newly brought at last into the world about twelve hundred years after the birth of Christ, at what time king John was king of England; neither had it any manner face or foundation in the word of God. Yet was the same name given a long while before any such child was thoroughly born. For, as it appeareth by the council of Florence, the east church of Græcia and Asia

Concil. Flor. sessione ultima.

[8 Socrat. in Hist. Eccles. Script. Amst. 1695-1700. Lib. I. cap. vi. p. 12.]

[9 Sozom. in eod. Lib. I. cap. xvi. p. 349.]

[10 ...expositorum diversitas non omnino inutilis est: quinimo per eam pigritia studentium excutitur: &c.—Prolog. in Replic. Def. Postill. ed. a M. Doring, in Bibl. cum Gloss. Ord. et Expos. N. de Lyra, Basil. 1502. Pars I. fol. 8. 2.]

[11 Falsehead, 1565.]

[12 Avancing, 1565.]

[13 Τὸ τῆς οὐσίας ὄνομα γυμνῶς μὲν ἐν παλαιᾷ καὶ καινῇ οὐ κεῖται γραφῇ, ὁ νοῦς δὲ πανταχοῦ φέρεται.—Epiph. Op. Par. 1622. Adv. Hær. Lib. III. Hær. lxxiii. 12. Tom. I. p. 859.]

[14 Is, 1611.]

[15 Socrat. in Hist. Eccles. Script. Lib. I. cap. viii. p. 22.]

[16 Hoc est illud *homousion*, quod in concilio Niceno...firmatum est.—August. Op. Contr. Maxim. Arian. Lib. II. cap. xiv. 3. Tom. VIII. col. 704.]

received it not, nor never would receive it until this day[1]; neither be the first inventers and devisers of it fully resolved upon the same.

For this word *transubstantiatio* signifieth a passing or turning of one substance into another. But that, they think, were not tolerable to say, that the substance of bread is changed into the substance of Christ's body. And therefore Duns himself utterly refuseth and shunneth it; and thinketh it better to hold, that the bread departeth and getteth itself away, and that then in place of it succeedeth Christ's body[2]. And this is now the common opinion of the schools. But this kind of change cannot in any wise be called *transubstantiatio*, but rather *cessio, annihilatio, successio*, or *substitutio*. Therefore M. Harding must go and seek a new name; for transubstantiation will not serve so well. Thus, after twelve hundred years' study, they have found out a thing, and yet cannot hitherto tell what to make of it. Yet must their determination herein be compared even with the council of Nice. Verily, cardinal Beno, that was then alive, saith that pope Gregory the seventh appointed three days' fast, and a solemn procession, to the end he might have some sign from heaven for the certainty hereof; and yet in the end concluded without any revelation at all[3].

Beno in Vita Hildebr.

Now, touching this new fantasy of *concomitantia*, after they had once devised a new religion, it was necessary, for aid of the same, to devise also new words. Whereas Christ saith, "This is my body;" they say, "This is my body and my blood." Where Christ saith, "This is my blood," they say, "This is my blood and my body;" and in either part, they say, is whole Christ, God and man. If ye demand how they know it, they say, not by the word of God, but by this new imagination of *concomitantia*. So likewise M. Harding here confesseth that he cannot prove the adoration of the sacrament by any warrant of the scriptures, but only, I trow, by his *concomitantia*.

M. HARDING. THE EIGHTEENTH DIVISION.

What the apostles taught in their time concerning this article, we may judge by that we read in Dionysius, that was St Paul's scholar, and for that it is to be believed[4]. *He adoreth and worshippeth this holy mystery with these very words:* Sed, O divinum penitus sanctumque mysterium, &c.[5]: *"But, O divine and holy mystery, which vouchsafest to open the coverings of signs laid over thee, utter thy light to us openly and plainly, and fill our spiritual eyes with the singular and evident brightness of thy light."*

Eccles. Hierarch. cap. iii.

THE BISHOP OF SARISBURY.

I marvel M. Harding would ever allege this place for the adoration of the sacrament. For doth he think that whatsoever thing is so called upon is therefore adored with godly honour? Or hath he forgotten that in his church of Rome they use thus to salute the holy oil, *Ave, sanctum oleum?* "All hail, O holy oil?" Or hath he forgotten that he himself in his church thus saluteth a cross of wood, *Ave, rex noster?* "All hail, our king?" Or that he maketh his prayer and petition to the same material wooden cross in this wise: *O crux, ave, spes unica, hoc passionis tempore: auge piis justitiam, reisque dona veniam*[6]: "All hail, O cross, our only hope, in this time of the passion; give thou increase of righteousness unto the godly, and give thou pardon unto sinners?" Or shall we think therefore, either that he giveth godly honour unto a corruptible creature,

[1 Gen. VIII. Synod. Sess. Ult. Sanct. Union. Litt. in Crabb. Concil. Col. Agrip. 1551. Tom. III. p. 476; where all that is said on the eucharist is, that the body of Christ is truly consecrated in both leavened and unleavened bread, and that either may be used according to the respective practice of churches.]

[2 Joan. Duns Scot. Op. Lugd. 1639. In Lib. IV. Sentent. Dist. xi. Quæst. 4. Tom. VIII. pp. 657, &c.; where the question is discussed at length.]

[3 Ben. Vit. Hild. in Fascic. Rer. Expet. et Fug. Lond. 1690. Tom. I. p. 79.]

[4 That is to believed, H. A. 1564; that it is to believed, 1611.]

[5 Ἀλλ' ὦ θειοτάτη καὶ ἱερὰ τελετὴ, τὰ περικείμενά σοι συμβολικῶς ἀμφιέσματα τῶν αἰνιγμάτων ἀποκαλυψαμένη, τηλαυγῶς ἡμῖν ἀναδείχθητι, καὶ τὰς νοερὰς ἡμῶν ὄψεις ἑνιαίου καὶ ἀπερικαλύπτου φωτὸς ἀποπλήρωσον.—Dionys. Ar. Op. Antv. 1634. De Eccles. Hierarch. cap. iii. 3. Tom. I. p. 286.]

[6 Hymns to the cross are of frequent occurrence in the Romish services. See Missal. ad Us. ac Consuet. Sar. Par. 1527. In Die Parasc. fol. 89. 2; In Invent. Sanct. Cruc. iii. Maii; In Exalt. Sanct. Cruc. xiv. Sept. See also in Dom. in Ramisp. fol. 79. 2. See also Portifor. seu Breviar. ad Us. Eccles. Sarisb. Par. 1510. In Exalt. Sanct. Cruc. &c.]

or that Christ is there present hidden under the form of wood? This might suffice to answer this place of Dionysius. I think M. Harding doth remember that Epiphanius saith: "The sacrament is a thing unsensible[7]," that can neither (Epiph. in Anchorat.) see us nor hear our prayer. And he knoweth that Pachymeres, the Greek paraphrast, in this sense expoundeth the words of Dionysius: *O divinum et sacrum* (Pachym. ὡς ἐμψύχῳ αὐτῇ διαλέγεται.) *mysterium. Affatur illud, tanquam rem animatam, &c.*[8]: "He speaketh unto the sacrament, as if it were a thing endued with sense and life. And well. For so Gregory the great divine saith: *O magnum et sanctum pascha:* 'O great and holy passover.' For our Lord Jesus Christ, as he is our passover, so is he that holy mystery. And unto him the bishop directeth his speech." Unto him, being in heaven, not unto the thing that presently lieth before him upon the table. And that this was Dionysius' very meaning, it appeareth by that immediately went before: *Ingrediamur ab effectis ad causas*[9]: "Let us enter from these outward effects into the causes;" that is to say, let us withdraw our eyes from the visible sacraments, and spiritually let us behold Christ, whose sacraments they be, and who by the same is represented. In like manner Dionysius speaketh of the consecration of the oil: *Adducamus vela, &c.*[10]: "Let us remove the vails, and behold that spiritual brightness itself," &c. By which spiritual brightness doubtless he meant Christ. Thus he teacheth us with our bodily eyes to see one thing, and with our spiritual eyes to see another; with our bodily eyes the things that be present; with our spiritual eyes the things that be absent. For the more likelihood hereof let us consider what words St Andrew useth to the very material wooden cross of his execution. *Salve crux, &c.*[11]: "All hail, thou cross, that here standest (Abdias in Andrea.) thus long looking for me. I come merrily unto thee. For I know thy secresy: I know thy mystery: I see in thee the things that are promised unto me of my Lord. Receive thou me, O thou chosen cross, that am thus humble for my God; and help the poor servant unto his Master." Here are plain words of invocation; here is manifest adoration. Yet may the force of these words make us believe that St Andrew indeed gave godly honour to a cross of tree?

But, because M. Harding seemeth to make some account of this place of Dionysius, let us answer one mystery by another. St Ambrose speaketh thus to the water of baptism: *O aqua, quæ humano aspersum sanguine, &c.*[12]: "O (Ambros. in Luc. Lib. x. cap. xxii.) thou water that hast washed the world, stained with man's blood. O thou water that deservedst to be a sacrament of Christ. Thou beginnest, thou fulfillest the perfit mysteries," &c. Must we needs think, because St Ambrose thus speaketh unto, and calleth upon the water, that therefore either the water had ears, and heard him, or Christ himself was there corporally present in the water? Doubtless, both bread and water are material elements, and void of life: therefore, as St Ambrose spake unto the one, even so and none otherwise did Dionysius speak unto the other. But forasmuch as M. Harding seemeth for Amphilochius' sake to brook well all news that come from Verona, let us see with what devotion they teach us there to call upon our lady's girdle. The words of the prayer are these: *O veneranda zona,...fac nos hæredes æternæ et beatæ vitæ: et hanc nostram vitam [ab] interitu...conserva.... Tuam hæreditatem, tuum populum O intemeratæ zona intemerata conserva....Habeamus te vires et auxilium; murum et propugnaculum; portum et salutare refugium*[13]: "O blessed girdle, make us the inheritors of ever-

[7 Τὸ μὲν γάρ ἐστι στρογγυλοειδὲς καὶ ἀναίσθητον, κ.τ.λ.—Epiph. Op. Par. 1622. Ancorat. 57. Tom. II. p. 60.]

[8 Pachym. Paraphr. in Dionys. Areop. Op. Tom. I. p. 318. Pachymeres proceeds: τὸ ἡμέτερον γὰρ πάσχα, καὶ ἡ τοιαύτη ἱερὰ τελετὴ, αὐτός ἐστιν ὁ Κύριος ἡμῶν Ἰησοῦς Χριστὸς, πρὸς ὃν ποιεῖται τὸν λόγον ὁ ἅγιος.]

[9 Dionys. De Eccles. Hierarch. cap. iii. 3. p. 286.]

[10 ...εἰς τὸ θειότερον αὐτῆς ἀποβλέψωμεν κάλλος, αὐτὴν ἐφ' ἑαυτῆς ἀποκαλυψαμένην τὰ περιπετάσματα, θεώμενοι τὴν μακαρίαν ἀποστίλβουσαν ἐμφανῶς αἴγλην.—Id. ibid. cap. iv. 3. p. 332.]

[11 Salve crux, quæ diu fatigata requiescis, tanto tempore expectans me...lætus pergo ad te: quia secretum tuum cognosco, et mysterium novi...Video enim in te, quæ a Domino mihi sunt promissa. Suscipe itaque electa crux humilem propter Deum, et transfer servum ejus ad Dominum suum.—Abd. Apost. Hist. Par. 1571. Lib. III. fol. 43. 2.]

[12 O aqua, quæ humano adspersum sanguine... orbem terrarum lavisti! O aqua, quæ sacramentum Christi esse meruisti...Tu incipis prima, tu comples perfecta mysteria. — Ambros. Op. Par. 1686-90. Expos. Evang. sec. Luc. Lib. x. cap. xxii. 48. Tom. I. col. 1514.]

[13 German. Encom. in Ador. Vener. Zon. Deip. in Lipom. Sanctor. Hist. Lov. 1565. Pars Prim. pp. 282, 3. A similar encomium attributed to Euthymius succeeds.]

lasting and blessed life; and keep our present life from destruction. O unspotted girdle of the unspotted virgin, save thine inheritance; O save thy people. Be thou our strength, our help, our wall, our fort, our haven, our refuge." This prayer beareth the name of one Euthymius, as it is supposed, an ancient learned Greek father, set forth this last year by Aloysius Lipomanus the bishop of Verona, and printed both in Venice and in Lovaine in two great huge volumes of like stuff. And lest the matter should seem to want earnest, the good catholic father and learned bishop of Verona, Lipomanus, hath specially marked the place in the margin in this sort: *O quam magna et mira petit a veneranda zona*[1]*!* "O how great, and how marvellous things he desireth of this blessed girdle!" All this notwithstanding, I trow M. Harding will not say that either Euthymius or Lipomanus would have us to worship our lady's girdle with godly honour.

M. HARDING. THE NINETEENTH DIVISION.

Origen teacheth us how to adore and worship Christ in the sacrament before we receive it, after this form of words: Quando sanctum cibum, &c.[2]: *"When thou receivest the holy meat, and that uncorrupt banquet, when thou enjoyest the bread and cup of life, thou eatest and drinkest the body and blood of our Lord: then our Lord entereth in under thy*[3] *roof. And therefore thou also, humbling thyself, follow this centurion or captain, and say: 'Lord, I am not worthy that thou enter under my roof.' For where he entereth in unworthily, there he entereth in to the condemnation of the receiver."* *Hom. 5. in Diversos Evangelii locos.*

THE BISHOP OF SARISBURY.

O how easy a matter it is to deceive the ignorant! Origen in that whole place speaketh not one word, neither of worshipping the sacrament, nor of Christ's real or corporal being therein, nor of material[4] entering into our bodies. But, taking occasion of the centurion, that thought himself unworthy to receive Christ into his house, he sheweth by what ways and means Christ useth to enter into the faithful. And two special ways he expressly nameth in that place: the one when any godly man cometh to us; the other when we receive the holy communion. His words be these: *Quando sancti et Deo acceptabiles*[5] *ecclesiarum antistites, &c.*[2]*:* "When holy bishops, acceptable unto God, enter into thy house, then by them the Lord doth enter. And be thou persuaded that thou receivest God himself. Another mean is, when thou receivest that incorruptible and holy banquet." Thus, by this holy father's judgment, as Christ entereth into us by a bishop or holy man, even so he entereth into us by the receiving of the holy mysteries. And so likewise he saith in the first homily of the same book: *Per evangelistarum et apostolorum prædicationem, &c.*[6]*:* "God is with us by the preaching of the evangelists and apostles, by the sacrament of his holy body and blood, and by the sign of the glorious cross. By all these things God cometh to us, and is in us; as he himself saith: 'Behold, I am with you all days, until the consummation of the world.'" Thus in the old testament, when the ark of God was lifted up, it seemed God himself was lifted up. And therefore, in lifting up thereof, the priests said, *Exsurgat Deus:* "Let the Lord arise;" and when the ark was brought into the camp, they said, "God himself was come;" and, when the ark was taken, they said, "The glory of Israel was taken."

Matt. viii. Luke vii.

Origen. in Div. Evang. locos, Hom. 1.

Cometh to us.

Matt. xxviii.

Num. x.

1 Sam. iv.

[1 Id. ibid. p. 282; where *quam mira et magna*.]

[2 Nunc enim quando sancti et Deo acceptabiles ecclesiarum antistites sub tectum tuum intrant, tunc ibidem per eos Dominus ingreditur. Et tu sic existimes tanquam Dominum suscipiens. Et aliud: quando sanctum cibum illudque incorruptum accipis epulum, quando vitæ pane et poculo frueris, manducas et bibis corpus et sanguinem Domini, tunc Dominus sub tectum tuum ingreditur. Et tu ergo humilians temetipsum imitare hunc centurionem, et dicito: Domine, non sum dignus ut intres sub tectum meum. Ubi enim indigne ingreditur, ibi ad judicium ingreditur accipienti.—Orig. Op. Lat. Basil. 1545. In Divers. Hom. v. Tom. II. p. 308.]

[3 They, 1565.]

[4 His material, 1565.]

[5 Acceptabilis, 1611.]

[6 Id. ibid. Hom. i. p. 291. See before, page 499. The author proceeds: Per ista ergo omnia nobiscum Deus, et ad nos atque in nobis, sicut ipse ait: Ecce ego vobiscum sum omnibus diebus usque ad consummationem seculi.]

Neither may we think that Origen meant any corporal or real entering of Christ into our houses. His own words and exposition are to the contrary. For thus he writeth in the same place: *Tantum dic verbo:... tantum veni verbo: verbum aspectus tuus est, opusque est consummatum:... ostende absens corpore, quod præsens spiritu consummare potes*[7]: "Only, O Lord, speak thou the word: only come by the[8] word: thy word is thy sight, and a perfite work: being absent in thy body, shew that thou art able to make perfite, being present in spirit." So saith Christ: "I and my Father will come unto him, and will make our abode in him." In which words we may not conceive any material or corporal coming. Therefore, whensoever Christ entereth thus into our house, whether it be by some holy man, or by the sacrament of his body, or by the sign of the cross, or, as St Augustine saith, by faith, or by the sacrament of baptism[9], Origen teacheth us to humble our hearts, and to say at every such coming or presence: "O Lord, I am not worthy that thou shouldest thus enter into my house." If M. Harding will gather hereof that Origen teacheth us to adore the sacrament, then must he also say that Origen likewise teacheth us to adore the bishop, or any other godly man, and that even as God, and with godly honour.

Origen. in Div. Evang. locos, Hom. 5. Absens corpore.

John xiv.

August. in Johan. Tract. 50.

M. HARDING. THE TWENTIETH DIVISION.

What can be thought of St Cyprian, but that he adored the invisible thing of this sacrament, which is the body and blood of Christ, seeing that he confesseth the Godhead to be in the same, no less than it was in the person of Christ, which he uttereth by these words? Panis iste quem Dominus discipulis porrigebat, &c.[10]: "*This bread, which our Lord gave to his disciples, changed not in shape, but in nature, by the almighty power of God, is made flesh. And as in the person of Christ the manhood was seen, and the Godhead was hidden; even so the divine essence hath unspeakably infused itself into the visible sacrament.*"

In Sermone de Cœna Domini.

The invisible thing of the sacrament is the body and blood of Christ being in heaven.

THE BISHOP OF SARISBURY.

This place of St Cyprian is often alleged by M. Harding as matter invincible; and to answer it severally in every place it would be tedious. Wherefore I thought it good to refer thee, gentle reader, to the second division of the tenth article, and to the fourth division of the twenty-first article, where it shall be answered more at large. Howbeit, thus much we may note by the way, that St Cyprian in this place speaketh not one word of the adoration of the sacrament. As for M. Harding's guesses, they import no proof. By the way, as St Cyprian saith the divine essence, as M. Harding turneth it, infuseth itself into the visible sacrament; so doth Paulinus say of the water of baptism: *Concipit unda Deum*[11]: "The water conceiveth or receiveth God." And St Augustine, speaking likewise of baptism: *Sacramento suo divina virtus assistit*[12]: "The divine power of God is assistant unto the sacrament."

August. contr. Donat. Lib. iii. cap. x.

M. HARDING. THE TWENTY-FIRST DIVISION.

In x. cap. prioris ad Corinth.

Chrysostom hath a notable place for the adoration of Christ's body in the sacrament, in his commentaries upon St Paul, where he affirmeth also the (169) *real presence and the sacrifice.* "*Let us not, let us not,*" *saith he,* "*be willing impudently to kill ourselves. And when thou seest that body set forth, say with thyself*[13]: '*For cause of this body I am no longer earth and ashes; no*

The hundred and sixty-ninth untruth. For St Chrysostom affirmeth no real presence; but only advanceth[14] our minds into heaven.

[7 Id. ibid. Hom. v. p. 308.]

[8 Thy, 1565, 1609.]

[9 ...habes Christum ... in præsenti per fidem, in præsenti per signum, in præsenti per baptismatis sacramentum, in præsenti per altaris cibum et potum.—August. Op. Par. 1679-1700. In Johan. Evang. cap. xii. Tractat. l. 12. Tom. III. Pars II. col. 633.]

[10 Panis, &c., non effigie, sed natura mutatus, omnipotentia verbi factus est caro: et sicut in persona Christi humanitas videbatur, et latebat divinitas; ita sacramento visibili ineffabiliter divina se infudit essentia.—Cypr. Op. Oxon. 1682. De Cœn. Dom. (Arnold.) p. 40.]

[11 Paulin. Op. Antv. 1622. Ad Sever. Epist. xii. p. 144.]

[12 August. Op. De Bapt. contr. Donatist. Lib. III. cap. x. 15. Tom. IX. col. 113.]

[13 Theeself, 1565.] [14 Avanceth, 1565.]

longer captive, but free. This body, fastened (on the cross) and beaten, was not overcome with death.'" After this he exhorteth all to adore and worship our Lord's body in the sacrament. * *"This body," saith he, "the wise men worshipped in the stall; and having taken a long journey, being both wicked and aliens, with very great fear and trembling adored him. Wherefore let us follow at least those aliens—us, I say, that are citizens of heaven. For they, whereas they saw but that stall and cabin only, and none of all the things thou seest now, came, notwithstanding, with the greatest reverence and fear that was possible. But thou seest it not in a stall of beasts, but on the altar; not a woman to hold it in her arms, but a priest present, and the Holy Ghost plentifully spread upon the sacrifice[1]." This father in his mass maketh a prayer in presence of the blessed sacrament, almost with the same words that St Basil did:* Attende, Domine Jesu Christe, Deus noster, &c.[2]: *"Look upon us, O Lord Jesus Christ, our God, from thy holy habitacle, and from the throne of the glory of thy kingdom, and come to sanctify us; who sittest on high with the Father, and art here invisibly with us; and make us worthy by thy mighty hand, that we may be partakers of thy unspotted body and precious blood, and through us all the people."*

* This body here represented by this sacrament.

In the presence of the sacrament, but not to the sacrament.

In the same Chrysostom's liturgy or mass a most evident testimony of adoration of the sacrament is thus uttered: Sacerdos adorat, et diaconus in eo quo[3] est loco, ter secreto dicentes: Deus propitius esto, &c.[4]: *"The priest adoreth, and the deacon likewise in the place he standeth in, saying three times secretly: 'God be merciful to me a sinner.' So the people, and likewise all, make their adoration devoutly and reverently."*

In the same father is another prayer, which the Greek priests do use to this day at their adoration of Christ's body in the sacrament, and it is expressed in these words: *Domine, non sum dignus, &c.[5]: *"Lord, I am not worthy that thou enter under the filthy roof of my soul. But as thou tookest in good part to lie in the den and stall of brute beasts, and, in the house of Simon the leprous, receivedst also a harlot and a sinner like me coming unto thee; vouchsafe also to enter into the stall of my soul, void of reason,* *and into my filthy body, being dead and leprous. And as thou didst not abhor the foul mouth of a harlot, kissing thine undefiled feet; so, my Lord God, abhor not me, though a sinner, but vouchsafe of thy goodness and benignity that I may be made partaker of thy most holy body and blood."*

* This prayer is directed unto Christ himself; not unto the sacrament, nor to any thing really contained in the sacrament.

* By a mystical manner of speech Christ entereth into our bodies, when we receive the sacrament of Christ into our bodies.

THE BISHOP OF SARISBURY.

The answer that is already made unto Dionysius and Origen may also serve to that is here alleged of Chrysostom. Yet, for some further declaration of Chrysostom's meaning, it may please thee, good christian reader, to understand that Chrysostom, in the very same homily here alleged, writeth thus: *Quid significat panis? Corpus Christi*[6]: "What doth the bread signify? The body of Christ." And in his homilies upon St Matthew he writeth thus: *In istis vasis non est verum corpus*

Chrysost. in 1 Cor. Hom. 24.

Chrysost. in Oper. Imperf. Hom. 11.

[1 Μὴ, παρακαλῶ, μὴ κατασφάξωμεν ἑαυτοὺς διὰ τῆς ἀναισχυντίας, ἀλλὰ μετὰ φρίκης καὶ καθαρότητος ἁπάσης αὐτῷ προσίωμεν· καὶ ὅταν αὐτὸ προκείμενον ἴδῃς, λέγε πρὸς σεαυτόν· διὰ τοῦτο τὸ σῶμα οὐκέτι γῆ καὶ σποδὸς ἐγὼ, οὐκέτι αἰχμάλωτος, ἀλλ' ἐλεύθερος...τοῦτο τὸ σῶμα προσηλούμενον καὶ μαστιζόμενον οὐκ ἤνεγκεν ὁ θάνατος...τοῦτο τὸ σῶμα καὶ ἐπὶ φάτνης κείμενον ᾐδέσθησαν μάγοι· καὶ ἄνδρες ἀσεβεῖς καὶ βάρβαροι τὴν πατρίδα καὶ τὴν οἰκίαν ἀφέντες, καὶ ὁδὸν ἐστείλαντο μακρὰν, καὶ ἐλθόντες μετὰ φόβου καὶ τρόμου πολλοῦ προσεκύνησαν. μιμησώμεθα τοίνυν κἂν τοὺς βαρβάρους ἡμεῖς οἱ τῶν οὐρανῶν πολῖται. ἐκεῖνοι μὲν γὰρ καὶ ἐπὶ φάτνης ἰδόντες, οἷον σὺ νῦν, μετὰ πολλῆς τῆς φρίκης προσῄεσαν. σὺ δὲ οὐκ ἐν φάτνῃ ὁρᾷς, ἀλλ' ἐν θυσιαστηρίῳ, οὐ γυναῖκα κατέχουσαν, ἀλλ' ἱερέα παρεστῶτα, καὶ Πνεῦμα μετὰ πολλῆς τῆς δαψιλείας τοῖς προκειμένοις ἐφιπτάμενον.—Chrysost. Op. Par. 1718-38. In Epist. I. ad Cor. Hom. xxiv. Tom. X. pp. 216-8.]

[2 Chrysost. Lit. in Lit. Sanct. Patr. Par. 1560. p. 103. See before, pages 485, 6.]

[3 In quo, H. A. 1564.]

[4 Id. ibid.]

[5 Κύριε, οὐκ εἰμὶ ἄξιος, ἵνα ὑπὸ τὴν ῥυπαρὰν στέγην τῆς ψυχῆς μου εἰσέλθῃς· ἀλλ' ὡς κατεδέξω ἐν σπηλαίῳ καὶ φάτνῃ ἀλόγων ἀνακλιθῆναι, καὶ ἐν τῇ οἰκίᾳ Σίμωνος τοῦ λεπροῦ, καὶ τὴν ὁμοίαν μοι πόρνην τὴν ἁμαρτωλὸν προσερχομένην σοι καταδεξάμενος, αὐτὸς καταξίωσον καὶ ἐν τῇ φάτνῃ τῆς ἀλόγου μου ψυχῆς, καὶ ἐν τῷ ἐσπηλωμένῳ μου σώματι εἰσελθεῖν τοῦ νεκροῦ καὶ λεπροῦ. καὶ ὡς οὐκ ἐβδελύξω τὸ στόμα τὸ ῥυπαρὸν τῆς πόρνης καταφιλούσης τοὺς ἀχράντους σου πόδας, οὕτω, Δέσποτα Θεέ μου, μὴ βδελύξῃ καὶ ἐμὲ τὸν ἁμαρτωλὸν, ἀλλ' ὡς ἀγαθὸς καὶ φιλάνθρωπος ἀξίωσόν με κοινωνὸν γενέσθαι τοῦ παναγίου σώματος καὶ αἵματός σου.—Id. ibid. pp. 104, 5.]

[6 Id. in Epist. I. ad Cor. Hom. xxiv. Tom. X. p. 213. The Greek text is, τί γάρ ἐστιν ὁ ἄρτος;]

Christi, sed mysterium corporis ejus continetur[7]: "In these vessels is not the very body of Christ, but a mystery of his body is therein contained." And therefore, in the same homily upon the epistle to the Corinthians, he withdraweth the minds of the people from the sensible elements of the bread and the wine, and lifteth them up by spiritual cogitations into heaven. Thus he speaketh unto the people: *Ubi cadaver, ibi aquilæ. Cadaver est Domini corpus propter mortem.... Aquilas autem appellat, ut ostendat, ad alta eum oportere contendere, qui ad hoc corpus accedit*[8]: "Where as the carcase is, there are the eagles. The carcase is the Lord's body, because of his death. But eagles he nameth to shew, that he must flee on high that will come near to that body." Afterward he addeth thus: *Ascende ergo ad cœli portas, et diligenter attende; imo non cœli, sed cœli cœlorum: et tunc, quod dicimus, intueberis*[9]: "Therefore go up unto the gates of heaven, and mark diligently; nay, I say not to the gates of heaven, but of the heaven of heavens: then shalt thou see the things that I speak of." Thus therefore that godly father Chrysostom dealeth with his people, as if they were already in heaven, and willeth them to behold, not the bread and wine, which are things corruptible, but the very body and blood of Christ; not the outward sacrament, but the substance of the sacrament; not the things that lie present before them, but the things that, touching bodily presence, are away. For in the holy communion there is none other sight laid before us, but only the cross and death of Christ, and that Lamb of God that taketh away the sins of the world. "And the very cogitation hereof," saith St Augustine, "so moveth our hearts, as if we saw Christ hanging presently before us upon his cross[10]."

Chrysost. in 1 Cor. Hom. 24.

De Consecr. Dist. 2. Semel mortuus.

In this wise therefore, having removed the people's hearts into heaven, and placed them even in the sight of Christ, he saith further unto them: For this body's sake thou art no longer dust and ashes; this body hath made thee free; this body was broken for thee upon the cross; this body must we adore, as the wise men did; this body not now upon the earth, but at the right hand of God in heaven; this body that thou seest with thy spirit, and touchest with thy faith, whereof the sacrament that thou receivest is a mystery. So saith Emissenus: *Sacrum Dei tui corpus ... fide respice, ... mente continge, cordis manu* [11]*suspice*[12]: "With thy faith behold the holy body of thy God, touch it with thy mind, receive it with the hand of thy heart."

De Consecr. Dist. 2. Quia corpus.

But M. Harding will reply, Chrysostom saith: "As Christ was in the stall, so he is now upon the altar; and as he was sometimes in the woman's arms, so he is[13] now in the priest's hands." True it is Christ was there, and Christ is here; but not in one or like sort of being. For he was in the stall by bodily presence; upon the holy table he is by way of a sacrament. The woman in her arms held him really; the priest in his hands holdeth him only in a mystery. So saith St Paul: "Christ dwelleth in our hearts;" and no doubt[14] the same Christ that lay in the stall. It is one and the same Christ; but the difference standeth in the manner of his being there: for in the stall he lay by presence of his body; in our hearts he lieth by presence of faith.

Eph. iii.

If this exposition seem to M. Harding over exquisite or curious, then will I say further: Christ is so upon the table as the faithful people is upon the table. St Augustine, speaking to the people, saith thus: *Vos estis in mensa, ... vos estis in calice*[15]: "You are upon the table, you are in the cup." But the people is not there grossly, really, and indeed, but in a mystery. Even so is Christ's body upon the table, not grossly, not really, or indeed, but in a mystery. And as Chrysostom saith, "The priest holdeth Christ in his hand;" even so St Gregory saith, "Abel held Christ in his hand," and that four thousand years before Christ was born; and yet, not a bare sign, or a naked token, but the very same Christ

August. citat. a Beda in 1 Cor. x.

[7 Id. Op. Imperf. in Matt. Hom. xi. Tom. VI. p. lxiii.; where *in quibus non*.]

[8 Id. in Epist. I. ad Cor. Hom. xxiv. Tom. X. p. 216.]

[9 Id. ibid. p. 218.]

[10 ...recordatio...sic nos, &c.—August. in Corp. Jur. Canon. Lugd. 1624. Decret. Gratian. Decr. Tert. Pars, De Consecr. Dist. ii. can. 51. col. 1938. See before, page 467.]

[11 Suscipe, 1565.]

[12 Euseb. Emiss. in eod. ibid. can. 35. col. 1928; where *suscipe*.]

[13 Is he, 1565.] [14 Doubts, 1565, 1609.]

[15 Ven. Bed. Op. Col. Agrip. 1612. Ad Cor. I. cap. x. Tom. VI. col. 365. See before, page 468, note 1.]

that Esay saw, and that John Baptist pointed with his finger. For thus stand his words: *Quem Johannes in ostensione, quem Esaias in locutione, hunc Abel significando in manibus tenuit*[1]. Thus Chrysostom saith the priest holdeth Christ in his hand, as John Baptist held him, as Esay held him, as Abel held him.

Gregor. in Job. Lib. xxix. cap. xxxviii.

And that this was Chrysostom's meaning, it appeareth by the very form and order of his words; for he saith: Thou seest the Holy Ghost: thou seest and touchest that princely body. Thus he speaketh of a spiritual seeing and touching, wherewith we see and touch things, be they never so far absent from us. For otherwise, touching bodily sight, M. Harding knoweth the Holy Ghost cannot be seen; and by his own doctrine the body of Christ is there invisible.

But lest M. Harding take occasion hereof to say, This is a fantastical and a vain kind of seeing; let him remember the words that St Hierome writeth to Paula and Eustochium, touching their abode at Bethleem: *Magos . . . tria deferentes munera in visione beatis oculis vidisti. Ipsa eadem munera . . . fide Deo obtulisti; . . . cum iisdem magis Deum puerum in præsepio adorasti*[2]: "Thou sawest with thy happy eyes the wise men carrying their three sorts of presents: thou tookest the same presents and offeredst them unto God by faith: with the same wise men thou adoredst God being a child in the manger." She saw the wise men, and yet saw them not: she received their presents, and yet received them not: she adored the child in the manger, and yet the child was not there. Thus she did, not verily or indeed, and yet not vainly, nor by way of fantasy notwithstanding; but truly and effectually, by presence of faith.

Hieron. ad Paul. et Eustoch.

Thus did the wise men see Christ: thus do we now see Christ. Thus did they worship him: thus do we worship him. They saw him and worshipped him, being in earth: we see him and worship him, being in heaven. They had him bodily present: we have him bodily absent, and present only to our faith.

And in this behalf St Ambrose saith: *Magis videtur, quod non videtur*[3]: "It is best seen that is not seen." That is to say, we see more certainly with our faith than we can see with the eyes of our body. For our bodily eye may deceive us; but the eye of our soul, which is faith, cannot deceive us.

Ambros. de his qui initiantur Myst. cap. iii.

M. Harding's reason hereof standeth thus: The priest at the time of the holy ministration said, "O God, be merciful to me, being a sinner:" and, "Look upon us, O Lord Jesus Christ our God, from thy holy tabernacle, and from the throne of thy glory;" *ergo* he made his prayers and gave adoration to the sacrament. Of the same premises he might much better conclude the contrary: The priest withdrew his mind from these sensible and corruptible elements, and adored Christ being in heaven in his tabernacle, and in the throne of his glory; *ergo*, he did not adore the sacrament.

M. HARDING. THE TWENTY-SECOND DIVISION.

St Ambrose, after long search and discussion how that saying of the prophet might be understanded, "Adore and worship ye his footstool, because it is holy," at length concludeth so as by the footstool he understandeth the earth; because it is written, "Heaven is my seat, and the earth is my footstool:" and because the earth is not to be adored, for that it is a creature, by this earth he understandeth that earth which our Lord Jesus took in the assumption of his flesh of the virgin Mary; and hereupon he uttereth those plain words for testimony of the adoration: Itaque per scabellum terra intelligitur, per terram autem caro Christi, quam hodie quoque in mysteriis adoramus; et quam apostoli in Domino Jesu . . . adorarunt[4]: "*And thus by the footstool earth may be*

De Spiritu Sancto, Lib. iii. cap. xii.

Psal. xcix. Isai. lxvi.

[[1] Gregor. Magni Papæ I. Op. Par. 1705. Lib. XXIX. in cap. xxxviii. B. Job. cap. xxxi. 69. Tom. I. col. 948.]

[[2] Hieron. Op. Par. 1693-1706. Ad Paul. et Eustoch. de Assumpt. Mar. Virg. Serm. Tom. V. col. 83; where *conspexisti* and *eisdem*. This piece is spurious.]

[[3] Ambros. Op. Par. 1686-90. Lib. de Myst. cap. iii. 15. Tom. II. col. 328.]

[[4] Non mediocris igitur quæstio, et ideo diligentius consideremus quid sit scabellum. Legimus enim alibi: Cœlum mihi thronus, terra autem scabellum pedum meorum. Sed nec terra adoranda est nobis, quia creatura est Dei. Videamus tamen ne terram illam dicat adorandam propheta, quam Dominus Jesus in carnis adsumptione suscepit. Itaque, &c. hodieque, &c.—Id. De Spirit. Sanct. Lib. III. cap. xi. 78, 9. Tom. II. cols. 680, 1.]

understanded, and by earth the flesh of Christ, which even now-a-days also we adore in the mysteries, and the apostles adored in our Lord Jesus."

St Augustine's learned handling of this place of the psalm, "Adore ye his footstool, because it is holy," maketh so evidently for this purpose, that of all other authorities, which in great number might be brought for proof of the same, it ought least to be omitted. The place being long, I will recite it in English only. His In Psal. xcviii. *words be these: "'Adore ye his footstool, because it is holy.' See ye, brethren, what that is he biddeth us to adore. In another place the scripture saith:* Isai. lxvi. *'Heaven is my seat, and the earth is my footstool.' What, doth he then bid us adore and worship the earth, because he said in another place, that it is the footstool of God? And how shall we adore the earth, whereas the scripture saith* Deut. vi. x. *plainly, 'Thou shalt adore thy Lord thy God;' and here he saith,* Matt. iv. *'Adore ye his footstool?' But he expoundeth to me what his footstool is, and saith: 'And the earth is my footstool.' I am made doubtful; afraid I am to adore the earth, lest he damn me that made heaven and earth. Again, I am afraid not[5] to adore the footstool of my Lord, because the psalm saith to me: 'Adore ye his footstool.' I seek what thing is his footstool, and the scripture telleth me: 'The earth is my footstool.' Being thus wavering, I turn me to Christ, because him I seek here, and I find how without impiety the earth may be adored. For he took of earth earth, because flesh is of earth, and of the flesh of Mary he took flesh. And because he walked here in flesh, and that very flesh he gave us to eat to salvation, and no man eateth that flesh except first he adore it; it is found out how such a footstool of our Lord may be adored, and how we not only sin not by adoring, but sin by not adoring. Doth not the flesh quicken and give life? Our Lord himself said, when he* John vi. *spake of the commendation[6] itself of that earth: 'It is the Spirit that quickeneth; but the flesh profiteth nothing.' Therefore, when thou bowest thyself[7], and fallest down to every such earth, behold it not as earth, but that holy One, whose footstool it is that thou dost adore, for because of him thou dost adore. And therefore here he added: 'Adore ye his footstool, because it is holy.' Who is holy? He for whose love thou adorest his footstool. And when thou adorest him, remain not by cogitation in flesh, that thou be not quickened of the Spirit. For 'the Spirit,' saith he, 'quickeneth; and the flesh profiteth nothing.' And then, when our Lord commended this unto us, he had spoken of his flesh, and had said: 'Except a man eat my flesh, he shall not have in him life everlasting[8].'"*

We eat Christ sitting in heaven; and so we adore him, not lying under accidents, but sitting in heaven.

THE BISHOP OF SARISBURY.

St Ambrose and St Augustine, as they agree together for the exposition of the psalm, so, touching the matter itself, neither do they any wise disagree from

[5 1611 omits *not.*]

[6 Condemnation, 1609, and 1611.]

[7 Theeself, 1565.]

[8 Et adorate scabellum pedum ejus, quoniam sanctus est....videte fratres, quid nos jubeat adorare. Alio loco scripturarum dicitur, Cœlum mihi sedes est, terra autem scabellum pedum meorum. Ergo terram nos jubet adorare, quia dixit alio loco quod sit scabellum pedum Dei? Et quomodo adorabimus terram, cum dicat aperte scriptura, Dominum Deum tuum adorabis? Et hic dicit, Adorate scabellum pedum ejus: exponens autem mihi quod sit scabellum pedum ejus, dicit, Terra autem scabellum pedum meorum. Anceps factus sum: timeo adorare terram, ne damnet me qui fecit cœlum et terram: rursus timeo non adorare scabellum pedum Domini mei, quia psalmus mihi dicit, Adorate scabellum pedum ejus. Quæro quod sit scabellum pedum ejus; et dicit mihi scriptura, Terra scabellum pedum meorum. Fluctuans converto me ad Christum, quia ipsum quæro hic; et invenio quomodo sine impietate adoretur terra, sine impietate adoretur scabellum pedum ejus. Suscepit enim de terra terram; quia caro de terra est, et de carne Mariæ carnem accepit. Et quia in ipsa carne hic ambulavit, et ipsam carnem nobis manducandam ad salutem dedit; nemo autem illam carnem manducat, nisi prius adoraverit; inventum est quemadmodum adoretur tale scabellum pedum Domini, et non solum non peccemus adorando, sed peccemus non adorando. Numquid autem caro vivificat? Ipse Dominus dixit, cum de ipsa commendatione ejusdem terræ loqueretur, Spiritus est qui vivificat, caro autem nihil prodest. Ideo et ad terram quamlibet cum te inclinas atque prosternis, non quasi terram intuearis, sed illum sanctum, cujus pedum scabellum est quod adoras; propter ipsum enim adoras; ideo et hic subjecit, Adorate scabellum pedum ejus, quoniam sanctus est. Quid sanctus est? In cujus honore adoras scabellum pedum ejus. Et cum adoras illum, ne cogitatione remaneas in carne, et ab Spiritu non vivificeris: Spiritus est enim, inquit, qui vivificat; caro autem nihil prodest. Tunc autem, quando hoc Dominus commendavit, de carne sua locutus erat, et dixerat, Nisi quis manducaverit carnem meam, non habebit in se vitam æternam.—August. Op. Par. 1679–1700. In Psalm. xcviii. Enarr. 9. Tom. IV. cols. 1064, 5.]

us, nor any wise agree with M. Harding. They teach us humbly to adore Christ's flesh; but they teach us not to adore the sacrament of Christ's flesh. Thus M. Harding hath taken a needless labour to prove a matter that is already proved; but the thing that he should have proved he toucheth not. This is too bold abusing of the simple reader, to bear him in hand that these godly fathers teach us to adore the sacrament, that spake not one word of adoring the sacrament.

But M. Harding will say: We must adore the flesh of Christ. We grant; we believe it; it is our faith; we teach the people, as the old learned fathers did, that no man eateth that flesh but first he adoreth it; and that he deadly offendeth God, and is wicked, and guilty of the Lord's body, that adoreth it not.

But, as we eat it, so we adore it. We eat it sitting in heaven at the right hand of God: thither we lift up our hearts, and there we adore it. St Ambrose Ambros. in Serm. 58. De Maria Magd. saith: *Stephanus in terris positus, Christum tangit in cœlo*[1]: "Stephen, standing in the earth, toucheth Christ being in heaven." Again he saith: *Non ... corporali* Ambros. in Luc. Lib. x. cap. xxiv. *tactu Christum, sed fide tangimus*[2]: "We touch Christ by faith, and not by corporal touching." And, as we touch Christ, so we see him; that is, with the spiritual eyes of our faith, and not otherwise. So St Ambrose saith in the place Ambros. in Serm. 58. De Maria Magd. before alleged: *Stephanus intra cœlos Dominum cernit absentem*[3]: "Stephen seeth Christ being absent within the heavens." And for proof hereof, that all that glorious sight was mere spiritual, and not offered to the corporal eye of the body, August. de Cog. Veræ Vitæ, cap. xlii. St Augustine saith that St Stephen stood then under a roof before the judges, and saw the heavens open, when with his bodily eyes he was not able to look up and to see the heavens[4]. There we see Christ's body; there we approach unto it; there we touch it; there we taste it; there we eat it; there we adore it. And doth M. Harding think that the religion of Christ is so gross and so sensible that we cannot eat or adore his body, unless it lie corporally present before our eyes? August. in Psal. xxxix. Col. iii. Verily St Augustine saith: *Si resurrexistis cum Christo, dicit fidelibus, dicit corpus et sanguinem Domini accipientibus, Si resurrexistis cum Christo, quæ sursum sunt sapite, ubi Christus est in dextra Dei sedens: quæ sursum sunt quærite, non quæ super terram*[5]: "If ye be risen again with Christ, St Paul saith unto the faithful, and unto them that receive the body and blood of Christ, 'If ye be risen again with Christ, savour the things that be above, where Christ is sitting at the right hand of God: seek the things that be above, and not the things that be upon the August. in Psal. xcviii. earth'." And in this very place by M. Harding alleged he saith: *Spiritualiter intelligite, quod locutus sum. Non hoc corpus, quod videtis, manducaturi estis*[6]: "Understand you spiritually that I have said unto you. You shall not eat (with your bodily mouths) this body of mine that ye see." Thus St Augustine in the same place expoundeth and openeth his own meaning. Doubtless, as the wicked may dishonour Christ, so may the godly honour him. But the wicked, as St Paul Heb. vi. saith, do crucify the Son of God being in heaven; and Christ, being in heaven, Acts ix. saith unto Paul being in the earth beneath, 'Saul, Saul, why dost thou persecute me?' Therefore the godly, being in earth, may likewise adore and honour Christ being in heaven.

But they will reply, St Ambrose saith: "We do adore Christ's flesh in the mysteries." Hereof groweth their whole error. For St Ambrose saith not, We do adore the mysteries, or the flesh of Christ really present, or materially contained in the mysteries; as it is supposed by M. Harding. Only he saith: "We adore Christ's flesh in the mysteries," that is to say, in the ministration of the mysteries. And doubtless it is our duty to adore the body of Christ in the word of God, in the sacrament of baptism, in the mysteries of Christ's body and blood, and wheresoever we see any step or token of it, but specially in the holy

---

[1 Maxim. Taur. Hom. ad calc. Leon. Magni Op. Lut. 1623. De Sep. Dom. et de Mar. Magdal. Hom. iv. col. 612. See before, page 499, note 10.]

[2 Ambros. Op. Par. 1686-90. Expos. Evang. sec. Luc. Lib. x. cap. xxiv. 155. Tom. I. col. 1537.]

[3 Maxim. Taur. De Sep. Dom. et de Mar. Magdal. Hom. iv. col. 612.]

[4 Sed et concio illa, in qua Stephanus stans Christum conspexit, in domo aliqua fuit: cujus tecti culmen ipsius corporeus oculus penetrare minime potuit.—August. Op. Par. 1679-1700. De Cogn. Ver. Vit. cap. xlii. Tom. VI. Append. col. 181. The Benedictine editors ascribe this treatise to Honorius of Autun.]

[5 Id. in Psalm. xxxix. Enarr. 28. Tom. IV. col. 343; where *dicit* follows *accipientibus*.]

[6 Id. in Psalm. xcviii. Enarr. 9. Tom. IV. col. 1066.]

mysteries; for that there is lively laid forth before us the whole story of Christ's conversation in the flesh. But this adoration, as it is said before, neither is directed to the sacraments, nor requireth any corporal or real presence. So St Hierome saith: "Paula adored Christ in the stall[7]," and that he himself adored Christ in the grave. And St Chrysostom teacheth us to adore Christ's body in the sacrament of baptism[8]. Yet neither was Christ's body then really present in the stall, or grave; nor is it now present in the water of baptism. Thus St Ambrose saith: "We adore the flesh of Christ in the mysteries."

Hieron. ad Paul. et Eust. Chrysost. in Marc. Hom. 14.

M. HARDING. THE TWENTY-THIRD DIVISION.

Again, St Augustine sheweth the manner and custom of his time touching the adoration of Christ in the sacrament, writing thus ad Honoratum *upon the verse of the 21st Psalm,* Edent pauperes, et saturabuntur, *that is, " The poor shall eat, and be filled;" and upon that other,* Manducaverunt et adoraverunt omnes divites terræ, *"All the rich of the earth have eaten, and adored." " It is not without cause," saith he, " that the rich and the poor be so distincted, that of the poor it was said before, ' The poor shall eat, and be filled;' and here (of the rich), ' They have eaten, and adored, all that be the rich of the earth.' For they have been brought to the table of Christ, and do take of his body and blood; but they do adore only, and be not also filled, forasmuch as they do not follow him[9]."*

Epist. 120. *cap. xxi.*

In Psal. xxi.

Likewise in his exposition upon that psalm: "All the rich also," saith he there, "of the earth have eaten the body of the humbleness of their Lord; neither have they been filled as the poor, until the following. But yet they have adored and worshipped (170) *it[10]," that is, by adoration they have acknowledged Christ their Lord there present.*

The hundred and seventieth untruth, standing in untrue interpretation. M. Harding addeth " it" of his own.

THE BISHOP OF SARISBURY.

This place may be passed over with the former answer. St Augustine here speaketh of the adoring of Christ, and not one word of the adoring of the sacrament. The whole drift of his talk standeth in an allegory of hungering, eating, filling, and adoring. We hunger Christ; we eat Christ; we be filled with Christ sitting in heaven; and likewise we adore and worship Christ sitting in heaven.

But St Augustine saith: *Comedunt pauperem:* "They eat Christ being poor." We know that Christ is now no longer in the dispensation of his poverty. " God hath exalted him, and given him a name above all names, and made all things subject to his feet." But St Augustine calleth him poor, for that he so humbled himself, and became obedient unto the death, even unto the death of the cross. In this respect of his cross, of his death, of his poverty we embrace him; we live by that body that was broken for us; we be refreshed by that blood that was shed for us. And thus we eat Christ, and be relieved, and have our life by him only in respect of his blood-shedding, and of his poverty.

Phil. ii. Heb. ii. Eph. i.

The poor that have refused and forsaken themselves eat Christ sitting in heaven, and are filled with him. But the rich eat him and adore him likewise sitting in heaven; but they are not filled. They see that Christ is the very true Messias that was looked for; they see that all things are fulfilled that were written of him in the prophets, and that his name is published unto the ends of the world; they believe that there is none other name under heaven whereby they can be saved. Therefore they profess his name; they believe in him; they eat him and adore him. But they make some account of the world; they forsake

Acts xiii. Rom. x. Acts iv

[7 See before, page 540, note 2.]

[8 Chrysost. Op. Lat. Basil. 1547. In Marc. Hom. xiv. Tom. II. col. 1284. See before, page 487.]

[9 Neque enim frustra ita distincti sunt, ut de pauperibus supra diceretur, Edent pauperes, et saturabuntur; hic vero, Manducaverunt et adoraverunt omnes divites terræ. Et ipsi quippe adducti sunt ad mensam Christi, et accipiunt de corpore et sanguine ejus: sed adorant tantum, non etiam saturantur; quoniam non imitantur.—August. Op. Lib. ad Honorat. seu Epist. cxl. cap. xxvii. 66. Tom. II. col. 447.]

[10 Manducaverunt corpus humilitatis Domini sui etiam divites terræ, nec sicut pauperes saturati sunt usque ad imitationem; sed tamen adoraverunt.—Id. in Psalm. xxi. Enarr. i. 30. Tom. IV. col. 93.]

not themselves; they follow not Christ; and therefore they are not filled with him. Thus doth St Augustine expound his own meaning: *Inde erat piscator*[1], *&c.* "Of those poor was Peter, and John, and James, and Matthew the publican. They did eat and were filled; for they suffered the same things that they had eaten. Christ gave to them his supper; he gave to them his passion: he is filled that followeth the same." Hitherto St Augustine speaketh not one word of adoration, either of the sacrament, or of Christ's body, as being really present in the sacrament. Therefore M. Harding was the more blame-worthy thus to add words of his own unto St Augustine, and so utterly to falsify and to corrupt his meaning. It is no good catholic point so to use the old fathers. Verily, whereas St Augustine writeth thus: *Nec sicut pauperes saturati sunt usque ad imitationem; sed tamen adoraverunt*[2]: "Neither were they filled as the poor, even unto the following; and yet notwithstanding they adored;" M. Harding addeth thereto of his own a pretty little "it," which he found not in St Augustine; and so maketh it up thus: "But yet they have[3] adored and worshipped it:" and, as if it were good text of St Augustine, afterward he furnisheth it out with this exposition or commentary of his own: that is, "They have acknowledged by adoration Christ their Lord there present." His friends will hardly think there is so much cunning in his dealing. He cannot lightly lack authorities, as long as he can thus shape them of his own. But St Augustine knoweth not neither this commentary, nor this text, nor ever gave M. Harding to understand of this corporal presence. As it is said and proved before, we see Christ, and worship Christ sitting in heaven. Certainly St Augustine, who best knew his own mind, saith thus: *Habes aurum; sed nondum tenes præsentem Christum*[4]: "Thou hast gold; but thou holdest not yet Christ present." St Augustine saith: "Christ is not here present." M. Harding's commentary saith: "Christ is here present." Now let the reader consider whether of these two he will believe.

August. in Psal. xxii.

August. in eundem Psal.

It.

August. Dom. quinta post Trin. Serm. 1.

M. HARDING. THE TWENTY-FOURTH DIVISION.

Furthermore, writing against Faustus, the heretic of the Manichees' sect, amongst other things he sheweth how the ethnicks thought that christian people for the honour they did before the blessed sacrament, that is, of bread and wine consecrated, did honour Bacchus and Ceres[5], *which were false gods honoured of the gentiles for the invention of wine and corn. Whereof may justly be gathered an argument, that in those days faithful people worshipped the body and blood of Christ in the sacrament, under the forms of bread and wine. For else the infidels could not have suspected them of doing idolatry to Bacchus and Ceres.*

This conclusion is not well considered. For the heathens never worshipped Bacchus and Ceres under the forms of bread and wine.

THE BISHOP OF SARISBURY.

This guess hath neither sense nor savour in it; and therefore I marvel that M. Harding, being learned, and having, as he saith, such store and choice of other, would ever use this for an argument. For the very children in grammar-schools can tell him that the heathens, that adored Bacchus and Ceres as their gods, yet notwithstanding never gave godly honour to bread and wine. And Cicero himself, being an heathen, was able to say: *Quis tam stultus est, ut id quo vescitur, credat esse deum?* "Who is so very a fool that will believe the thing that he eateth to be his god?" And in like sort Juvenal, an heathen poet, scorneth at this folly: *O sanctas gentes, quibus hæc nascuntur in agris numina*[6]! "O happy is that people that hath gods growing in their fields!" The heathens in their rude gentility[7] thought that Bacchus and Ceres had first found out and taught them the use of

Cic. de Nat. Deor.

Juvenal.

[1 Inde, &c. ille Petrus, inde erat alius piscator Johannes et Jacobus frater ipsius, inde erat etiam publicanus Matthæus. De pauperibus ipsi erant, qui comederunt et saturati sunt, talia passi, qualia manducaverunt. Cœnam suam dedit, passionem suam dedit: ille saturatur, qui imitatur.—August. Op. Par. 1679-1700. In Psalm. xxi. Enarr. ii. 27. Tom. IV. col. 100.]

[2 Id. ibid. Enarr. i. 30. col. 93.]

[3 Have they, 1565.]

[4 Id. De Verb. Evang. Matt. xix. Serm. lxxxv. 4. Tom. V. col. 454.]

[5 ...nonnulli, qui nos propter panem et calicem Cererem ac Liberum colere existimant.—Id. Contr. Faust. Lib. xx. cap. xiii. Tom. VIII. col. 342.]

[6 Juv. Sat. xv. 10, 1; where *hortis*.]

[7 Gentility: heathenism.]

bread and wine, whereas before they fed of acorns, and drank water; and therefore, in remembrance and witness of so great a benefit, they honoured the one with bread and the other with wine. But that they ever honoured the elements of bread and wine, I think M. Harding is not able well to shew; therefore he might have formed his argument in this sort: The Christians were thought to honour their sacraments, as the heathens honoured bread and wine: but the heathens never honoured bread and wine with godly honour;

Ergo, the Christians never honoured their sacraments with godly honour.

M. HARDING. THE TWENTY-FIFTH DIVISION.

De Consecr. Dist. 2. can. Nos autem.

One other most evident place touching this honour and adoration we find in him rehearsed by Gratian, Lib. Sentent. Prosp. "*We do honour,*" *saith he,* "** in form of bread and wine which we see, things invisible, that is to say, flesh and blood. * Neither take we likewise these two forms as we took them before consecration: sith that we do faithfully grant that before consecration it is bread and wine, which nature hath shaped; but after consecration flesh and blood of Christ, which the blessing* (*of the priest*) *hath consecrated*[8]."

* By this word "form" St Augustine meaneth the substance and kind of bread.

* The accidents of the bread are after consecration as they were before.

THE BISHOP OF SARISBURY.

First, this authority here alleged is not to be found, neither in St Augustine, in whose name it is brought, nor in the Sentences of Prosper. As for Gratian, M. Harding knoweth he is a common falsifier of the doctors; and therefore his credit in such cases cannot be great. Notwithstanding, touching the matter, we know that bread, wine, and water, of themselves[9] be nothing else but corruptible and simple creatures. If we conceive none otherwise of them than they be of themselves[9], then all our sacraments be in vain. Therefore the godly fathers labour evermore to draw us from the outward visible creatures to the meaning and substance of the sacraments. And to that end St Augustine saith: *In sacramentis videndum est, non quid sint, sed quid significent*[10]: "In sacraments we must consider, not what they be indeed, but what they signify." So it is written in the council of Nice: *Vides aquam? Cogita divinam vim quæ in aqua latet*[11]: "Seest thou the water of baptism? (it is not that it was before). Consider thou that heavenly power that lieth hidden in the water." So Chrysostom saith: *Antequam sanctificetur panis, panem nominamus: divina autem sanctificante illum gratia, mediante sacerdote, liberatus est quidem ab appellatione panis; dignus autem habitus* [*est*] *dominici corporis appellatione; etiamsi natura panis in illo remanserit*[12]: "The bread, before it is sanctified, is called bread; but, being sanctified by the heavenly grace, by mean of the priest, it is delivered from the name of bread, and thought worthy of the name of the Lord's body, notwithstanding the nature of bread remain in it still." Thus, as Chrysostom saith, the bread remaineth still bread, in his former kind and substance, without any such transubstantiation or change of nature as is now imagined. The words be plain: M. Harding cannot deny them. And yet, notwithstanding, it is not the thing it was before, because it is also called the Lord's body. So likewise saith St Augustine: *Quicunque in manna Christum intellexerunt, eundem quem nos spiritualem cibum manducarunt*[13]: "As many as in manna understood Christ, they did eat the same

August. contr. Max. Lib. iii.

Concil. Nicen. κρυπτομένην.

Chrysost. ad Cæsar. Monach.

August. de Util. Pœnit. 1 Cor. x.

[8 Nos autem in specie panis et vini, quam videmus, res invisibiles, id est, Christi carnem et sanguinem honoramus: nec similiter comprehendimus has duas species, ex quibus consecratur dominicum corpus, quemadmodum ante consecrationem comprehendebamus; cum fideliter fateamur ante consecrationem esse panem et vinum, quod natura formavit; post consecrationem vero Christi carnem et sanguinem, quod benedictio consecravit.—August. in Lib. Sentent. Prosp. in Corp. Jur. Canon. Lugd. 1624. Decret. Gratian. Decr. Tert. Pars, De Consecr. Dist. ii. can. 41. col. 1932.]

[9 Themself, 1565.]

[10 Id. Op. Contr. Maxim. Arian. Lib. II. cap. xxii. 3. Tom. VIII. col. 725. See before, page 467, note 21.]

[11 Gelas. Cyz. Hist. Concil. Nic. cap. xxx. in Concil. Stud. Labb. et Cossart. Lut. Par. 1671-2. Tom. II. col. 233.]

[12 Chrysost. Op. Par. 1718-38. Epist. ad Cæsar. Monach. Tom. III. p. 744; where *illum sanctificante*, and *in ipso permansit*.]

[13 August. Op. Serm. ccclii. 3. De Util. Agend. Pœnit. ii. Tom. V. col. 1365; where *cibum spiritalem manducaverunt*.]

spiritual meat that we eat" (that is, the very body of Christ): and so unto them manna was Christ's body, and not the same thing it was before. And for better declaration hereof, Bertramus saith: *Christus ut nunc panem convertit in corpus suum, ita tum manna de cœlo datum suum corpus invisibiliter operatus est*[1]: "Christ, as he now turneth the bread into his body, even so then in like sort the manna that fell from heaven, invisibly he made his body." Thus, as the bread is Christ's body, even so was manna Christ's body; and that invisibly, and by the omnipotent power of God. Thus are the elements of manna, of the bread, of the wine, and of the water, changed, and are not as they were before; and therefore in every of the same we honour the body of Christ invisible, not as really and fleshly present, but as being in heaven. This whole matter, and the causes thereof, St Augustine seemeth to open in this wise: *Signacula quidem rerum divinarum esse visibilia, &c.*[2]: "Let the new-christened man be taught that sacraments be visible signs of heavenly things, and that the things themselves[3] that he seeth not must be honoured in them, and that the same kind and element (bread, wine, or water) is not so to be taken as it is in daily use. Let him also be taught, what the words mean that he hath heard, and what is hidden (and to be believed) in Christ, whose image or likeness that thing (that is, that sacrament) beareth." He addeth further: *Deinde monendus est ex hac occasione, ut si quid etiam in scripturis audiat, quod carnaliter sonet, etiamsi non intelligat, credat tamen spirituale aliquid significari*[4]: "Moreover, upon occasion hereof he must be taught that, if he hear any thing even in the scriptures that sound carnally, yet he think there is some spiritual thing meant by it."

Bert. de Sac. Eucharist.

August. de Catech. Rud. cap. xxvi.

M. HARDING. THE TWENTY-SIXTH DIVISION.

Leaving a number of places that might be alleged out of the ancient fathers for the confirmation of this matter, to avoid tediousness, I will conclude with that most plain place of Theodoretus, who, speaking of the outward signs of the sacrament, saith, that notwithstanding they remain after the mystical blessing (171) *in the propriety of their former nature, as those that may be seen and felt no less than before; yet they are understanded and believed to be the things which they are made by virtue of consecration, and are worshipped with godly honour. His words be these:* Intelliguntur ea esse, quæ facta sunt, et creduntur, et adorantur, ut quæ illa sint, quæ creduntur[5]: *"These mystical signs," saith he, "are understanded to be those things which they are made; and so they are believed and are adored as being the things which they are believed to be." With which words Theodoretus affirmeth both the real presence, and also the adoration: the real presence, in that he saith these outward signs or tokens after consecration to be made things which are not seen, but understanded and believed; whereby he signifieth the invisible thing of this sacrament, the body and blood of Christ: adoration he teacheth with express terms, and that because, through power of the mystical blessing, the signs be in existence and in deed the things which they are believed to be, soothly the body and blood of Christ. For, otherwise, God forbid that christian people should be taught to adore and worship the insensible creatures, bread and wine! Of which he saith that they are adored, not as signs, not so in nowise, but as being the things which they are believed to be. Now I report me to the christian reader, whether this adoration of the sacrament, whereby we mean the godly worship of Christ's body in the sacrament, be a new device, or no, brought into the church but lately, about three hundred years past, as M. Jewel maketh himself sure of it in his sermon*[6].

The hundred and seventy-first untruth. For Theodoretus saith: Manent in priori substantia. By M. Harding's construction, the outward signs are Christ's body, and must be worshipped with godly honour.

Dialog. 2.

[*Fol.* 20. H. A. 1564.]

[1 Ipse...qui nunc...panem...in sui corporis carnem...convertit, ipse tunc quoque manna de cœlo datum corpus suum ... invisibiliter operatus est.—Ratramn. Lib. de Corp. et Sang. Dom. Oxon. 1838. cap. xxv. p. 14.]

[2 Signacula &c., sed res ipsas invisibiles in eis honorari; nec sic habendam esse illam speciem benedictione sanctificatam, quemadmodum habetur in usu quolibet: dicendum etiam quid significet et sermo ille quem audivit, quid in illo condiat, cujus illa res similitudinem gerit.—August. Op. Par. 1679-1700. Lib. de Catech. Rud. cap. xxvi. 50. Tom. VI. col. 293.]

[3 Themself, 1565.]

[4 Id. ibid.; where *intelligit*, and *spiritale*.]

[5 Theodor. Op. Lut. Par. 1642-84. Inconfus. Dial. II. Tom. IV. p. 85.]

[6 See before, page 10.]

THE BISHOP OF SARISBURY.

By these words of Theodoret, M. Harding thinketh himself able to prove both real presence and also adoration of the sacrament; and I doubt not but the discreet reader shall soon perceive he hath proved as well the one as the other. Touching real presence, Theodoretus speaketh nothing; no, not one word. His manner of speech seemeth rather to incline to transubstantiation; whereunto notwithstanding Theodoretus is an enemy, and thinketh it a great folly, proceeding of ignorance, as it shall appear. And whereas Theodoretus imagineth two men to reason together by way of a dialogue, a catholic man and an heretic, M. Harding is fain, for defence of his doctrine, to take part with the heretic, and to use his arguments as if they were catholic. For thus the heretic there saith, even as M. Harding now saith: *Symbola dominici corporis et sanguinis alia quidem sunt ante* Theodor. Dial. ii. Inconfus. *invocationem sacerdotis; sed post invocationem mutantur, et alia fiunt*[7]: "The sacraments or signs of Christ's body and blood are one thing before the blessing of the priest; but after the blessing they are changed, and made other things." And he speaketh of the change of substance as[8] M. Harding doth. The catholic man maketh answer: *Signa mystica post sanctificationem non recedunt a natura sua. Manent enim in priori substantia, et figura, et forma*[9]: "Nay, marry, the mystical signs after the blessing (of the priest) depart not from their own nature. For they remain in their former substance, and figure, and form." He saith further: "Yet the same bread and wine, remaining as they were before, are understanded and believed and adored as the things that they are believed." Ut quæ sint illa quæ creduntur.

Here, good christian reader, note by the way, M. Harding saith: The nature and substance of the bread and wine is utterly abolished and done away; but the catholic man saith: "The same nature and substance remaineth still as it was before." If the catholic man's saying be catholic, then M. Harding's saying is not catholic.

M. Harding will reply: But these signs are honoured. Even so St Augustine saith: *Baptisma, ubicunque est, veneramur*[10]: "We honour baptism, wheresoever it be." August. Epist. clxiv. But for answer[11] hereto, understand thou, good reader, that Theodoret was a Greek bishop, and that the Grecians never used to give godly honour to the sacrament until this day. Further understand thou, that St Ambrose touching the sacrament writeth thus: *Venisti ad altare: vidisti sacramenta posita super* Ambros de Sacr. Lib. iv. cap. iii. *altare: et ipsam quidem miratus es creaturam. Tamen creatura solennis et nota*[12]: "Thou camest to the altar: thou sawest the sacraments laid upon the same, and didst marvel at the very creature. Yet is it a creature used and known."

Here St Ambrose calleth the sacrament a creature, and that twice together in one place. I think M. Harding will not have us believe that Theodoretus, being so godly a man, gave godly honour unto a creature.

But Theodoretus saith they are honoured. This is already answered in the last objection. For, as St Augustine teacheth us, "in sacraments we must consider, not what they be indeed, but what they signify[13]." August. contr. Max. Lib. iii. And in this sense they are understanded and believed and adored, as by signification being or representing the things that are believed. St Augustine saith: *Sacramenta* [*sunt*] . . . August. contr. Faust. Manich. Lib. xix. cap. xv. *verba visibilia*[14]: "Sacraments be visible words." But words are oftentimes put for the things that are signified by the words. So saith St Hilary: *Verba Dei* Hilar. de Trin. Lib. vi. *sunt illa quæ enuntiant*[15]: "The words of God be the very things that they utter or signify." So Christ saith: "My words be spirit and life;" John vi. because they be instruments of spirit and life. And so Origen saith: *Hoc quod modo loquimur* Origen. in Num. Hom. 23.

[7 Id. ibid.]

[8 Even as, 1565.]

[9 Id. ibid.]

[10 August. Op. Ad Emer. Epist. lxxxvii. 9. Tom. II. col. 212. See before, page 514, note 3.]

[11 Further answer, 1565.]

[12 Ambros. Op. Par. 1686-90. De Sacram. Lib. IV. cap. iii. 8. Tom. II. cols. 366, 7; where *creaturam solemnem et notam.*]

[13 August. Op. Contr. Maxim. Arian. Lib. II. cap. xxii. 3. Tom. VIII. col. 725. See before, page 467, note 21.]

[14 Id. Contr. Faust. Lib. XIX. cap. xvi. Tom. VIII. col. 321.]

[15 ...vim verbis Dei affers, ne sint quod enuntiant.—Hilar. Op. Par. 1693. De Trin. Lib. VI. 25. col. 895.]

sunt carnes Christi[1]: "The very words that I now speak are the flesh of Christ." Even in this sort the sacraments are the flesh of Christ, and are so understanded and believed and adored. But the whole honour resteth not in them, but is passed over from them to the things that be signified.

M. Harding will say, by this construction *adorantur* is as much to say as *non adorantur;* "they are honoured," that is, they are not honoured, but only lead us to those things that must be honoured. Herein is none inconvenience. For so it appeareth Theodoretus expoundeth his own meaning. His words immediately following are these: *Confer ergo imaginem cum exemplari, et videbis similitudinem. Oportet enim figuram esse veritati similem*[2]: "Compare therefore the image (that is, the sacrament) with the pattern (that is, with Christ's body). For the figure must be like unto the truth." Theodoretus calleth the sacrament an image, a resemblance, and a figure. I think M. Harding will not say that images, resemblances, and figures, be worthy of godly honour. And hereunto very aptly agreeth St Augustine's lesson touching the same: *Qui ... adorat utile signum divinitus institutum, cujus vim significationemque intelligit, non hoc veneratur, quod videtur et transit, sed illud potius, quo talia cuncta referenda sunt*[3]: "He, that worshippeth a profitable sign appointed by God, and understandeth the power and signification of the same, doth not worship that thing that is seen with the eye and passeth away, but rather he worshippeth that thing unto which all such things have relation." Here St Augustine thinketh it no inconvenience to say, we worship the sign, and yet worship it not. And this he speaketh, not only of the sacrament of Christ's body, but also of the sacrament of baptism. For so he saith further in the same place: *Sicuti est baptismi sacramentum, &c.*[4]: "As is the sacrament of baptism and the celebration of the body and blood of the Lord: which sacraments every man, when he receiveth them, being instructed, knoweth whereto they belong, that he may worship them, not with carnal bondage, but with the freedom of the Spirit." I might add hereto the words of that most fond and lewd second council of Nice: *Venerandas imagines perfecte adoramus; et eos, qui secus confitentur, anathematizamus*[5]: "We do perfectly[6] adore the reverend images, and do accurse them that profess otherwise." And yet afterward they say: "*Honor imagini exhibitus refertur ad prototypum*[5]: "The honour given to the image [(is not given to the image, but)[7]] redoundeth unto the pattern." Thus that council saith: "Images are honoured:" that is to say, they are not honoured.

August. de Doctr. Christ. Lib. iii. cap. ix.

August. in eodem capite.

To worship baptism.

Now let us examine what construction M. Harding maketh upon these words:

1. Theodoretus saith: "The bread and the wine leave not, or be not changed from, their former nature:" that is to say, by this new exposition, they utterly leave their former nature.

2. "They remain still in their substance:" that is to say, saith M. Harding, they remain not in their substance.

Further M. Harding saith:

3. The accidents of bread and wine be the signs of Christ's body: the bread and the wine be no signs.

4. The visible accidents are made the invisible body and blood of Christ: the bread and wine are made nothing.

5. The signs be made the very self thing that is signified, and that in existence, and in deed. And so one thing at one time and in one respect is substance and accident, visible and invisible, and, as they term it in the schools, *fundamentum* and *terminus;* which was ever wont to be called a monster in nature. So many errors are scarcely sufficient to maintain one error.

[[1] Orig. Op. Par. 1733-59. In Num. Hom. xxiii. 6. Tom. II. p. 359; where *carnes sunt Verbi Dei.*]

[[2] Theodor. Op. Lut. Par. 1642-84. Inconfus. Dial. II. Tom. IV. p. 85.]

[[3] August. Op. Par. 1679-1700. De Doctr. Christ. Lib. III. cap. ix. 13. Tom. III. Pars I. col. 49; where *veneratur* for *adorat.*]

[[4] Sicuti est baptismi sacramentum, et celebratio corporis et sanguinis Domini: quæ unusquisque cum percipit, quo referantur imbutus agnoscit, ut ea non carnali servitute, sed spiritali potius libertate veneretur.—Id. ibid.]

[[5] Concil. Nic. II. Def. Act. VII. in Crabb. Concil. Col. Agrip. 1551. Tom. II. pp. 599, 603. See also in Concil. Stud. Labb. et Cossart. Lut. Par. 1671-2. Tom. VII. cols. 556, 76.]

[[6] Perfitely, 1565.]

[[7] This clause is inserted from 1565.]

Now I trust the christian reader will soon consider how soundly M. Harding hath discharged his promise, and proved the adoration of the sacrament. Verily, of all these doctors that he hath here alleged (Theodoretus only excepted, in whom he would seem to have some colour of aid, who also is already clearly answered), there is not one that any way may be thought to touch, either the worshipping of the outward sacrament itself, or of Christ, as present in the sacrament.

The greatest doctors of that side say that, unless transubstantiation be concluded, the people cannot freely worship the sacrament without occasion of idolatry. Now it is known that transubstantiation is a new fantasy, newly devised in the council of Lateran in Rome: and D. Tonstal saith that, before that time, it was free and lawful for any man to hold the contrary[8]. Wherefore it is likely that before that time there was no such adoration: otherwise it must needs have been with great danger of idolatry. But after that, as it is said before, pope Honorius took order, and gave commandment that the people should adore[9]; pope Urbanus added thereto a new solemn feast of *Corpus Christi* day; and pope Clement confirmed the same with great store of pardons[10]. This is the antiquity and petite degree of this kind of adoration.

Ann. Dom. 1215.

Tonst. Lib. i. de Sacr. Euch. fol. 46.

Extra. de Celeb. Miss. Clemen. Lib. iii. Tit. 16. Si Dominum.

M. HARDING. THE TWENTY-SEVENTH DIVISION.

[*Fol.* 26. H. A. 1564.]

And whereas, utterly to abolish this adoration, he allegeth great danger of idolatry, in case the priest do not truly consecrate[11]*; thereto may be answered, that Jacob stood in no danger of conscience for that, by the procurement of Laban, he lay with Lea instead of Rachel; neither for the same was he to be charged with advoutery, because he meant good faith, and thought himself to have had the company of his wife Rachel. So idolatry is not to be imputed unto him that worshippeth Christ with godly honour in the bread not consecrate, which of good faith he thinketh to be consecrate. Touching this case, St Augustine hath this notable saying: "We have need," saith he, "to put a difference in our judgment, and to know good from evil; forasmuch as Satan, changing his shape, sheweth himself as an angel of light, lest through deceit he lead us aside to some pernicious things. For, when he deceiveth the senses of the body, and removeth not the mind from true and right meaning, wherein each man leadeth a faithful life, there is no peril in religion. Or if when he feigneth himself good, and doth or saith those things that of congruence pertain to good angels, although he be thought to be good, this is not a perilous or sickly error of christian faith. But when as by these things he beginneth to bring us to things quite contrary, then to know him from the good Spirit, and not to go after him, it standeth us much upon diligently to watch and take heed*[12]*." Thus St Augustine. Thus*[13] *much for the adoration of the sacrament, or rather of Christ in the sacrament, may suffice.*

Gen. xxix.

Enchir. 60.

A very simple defence of manifest idolatry. Even so the idolaters thought their idol of good faith to be very God.

THE BISHOP OF SARISBURY.

The great danger and horror of idolatry that hereof riseth, M. Harding thinketh may easily be salved by the example of Rachel and Lea: and thus he bringeth in God's mystical providence for defence of open error; and thus teacheth us instead of Rachel to take Lea, and to honour a creature instead of

[8 Porro ante Innocentium tertium Romanum episcopum, qui in Lateranensi concilio præsedit, tribus modis id posse fieri curiosius scrutantibus visum est: &c.—Tonst. De Verit. Corp. et Sang. Dom. in Euch. Lut. 1554. Lib. I. fol. 46.]

[9 Honor. III. in Corp. Jur. Canon. Lugd. 1624. Decretal. Gregor. IX. Lib. III. Tit. xli. cap. 10. col. 1378.]

[10 Clemens V. in eod. Clement. Lib. III. Tit. xvi. cols. 240, &c.]

[11 See before, page 13.]

[12 Magis opus est dijudicare atque dignoscere, cum se Satanas transfigurat velut angelum lucis, ne fallendo ad aliqua perniciosa seducat. Nam quando sensus corporis fallit, mentem vero non movet a vera rectaque sententia, qua quisque vitam fidelem gerit, nullum est in religione periculum: vel cum se bonum fingens, ea facit sive dicit quæ bonis angelis congruunt, etiam si credatur bonus, non est error christianæ fidei periculosus aut morbidus. Cum vero per hæc aliena ad sua incipit ducere, tunc eum dignoscere, nec ire post eum, magna et necessaria vigilantia est. —August. Op. Enchirid. cap. lx. 16. Tom. VI. cols. 218, 9.]

[13 This, 1565, and H. A. 1564.]

Doubts touching Consecration.

God. Wherein it shall be necessary briefly to touch how many ways, even by their own doctrine, the poor simple people may be deceived, and yield the honour of God to that thing that in their own judgment is no God.

Thom. Par. iii. Quæst. 83. Thus therefore they say: If the priest chance to forget to put wine into the cup, and so pass over the consecration without wine[1];

Johan. de Burg. Pup. Ocul. cap. iii. Or if the bread be made of any other than wheaten flour, which may possibly happen[2];

Idem. Or if there be so much water in quantity, that it overcome and alter the nature of the wine;

Idem. Gers. contr. Flor. Lib. iv. Or if the wine be changed into vinegar, and therefore cannot serve to consecration;

Or if there be thirteen cakes upon the table, and the priest for his consecration determine only upon twelve, in which case, they say, not one of them all is consecrate[3];

Extra. de Celeb. Miss. De homine. Or if the priest dissemble or leave out the words of consecration; or if he forget it, or mind it not, or think not of it—in every of these, and other like defects, there is nothing consecrate; and therefore the people, in these cases honouring the sacrament, by their own doctrine giveth the glory of God to a creature[4], which is undoubted idolatry.

And, that the folly hereof may the better appear, one of them writeth thus: Summa Ang. Euch. 26. *Quod si sacerdos, &c.*[5]: "If the priest, having before him sundry cakes at the time of consecration, do mind only and precisely to consecrate that only cake that he holdeth in his hand, some say the rest be not consecrate; but say thou, as Duns saith, they be all consecrate." Yea, further he saith: "If the priest do precisely determine to consecrate only the one half part of the cake, and not likewise the other half, that then, the cake being whole, that one part only is consecrate, and not the other[6]."

Dist. 81. Si qui. Pope Gregory saith: "If the priest be a known adulterer[7] or fornicator, and continue still in the same, that his blessing shall be turned into cursing; and that the people obeying not this most wholesome precept commit[8] idolatry[9]."

In this case standeth the simple people: so many ways and so easily they may be deceived. For notwithstanding they may in some part know the priest's life and open dealing, yet how can they be assured of his secret words, of his

---

[1 Contingit quandoque quod per negligentiam ministri aut aqua non ponitur in calice, aut etiam nec vinum, &c.—Thom. Aquinat. Op. Venet. 1595. Summ. Theol. Tert. Pars, Quæst. lxxxiii. Art. 6. fol. 280, 2.]

[2 Possibly and easily happen, 1565.]

[3 Materia necessaria eucharistiæ est panis frumentarius: quia sine illo non potest fieri consecratio...Quæritur hic utrum possit confici ab aceto... Dicendum quod si sit jam perfecte acetum, quod non potest confici ex aceto...alioquin enim si vinum ab aqua vinceretur, consecratio impeditur...Quæritur si sint quindecim hostiæ consecrandæ supra altare, et sacerdos non credat esse nisi duodecim; utrum illæ quindecim erunt consecratæ. Berengarius archiepiscopus Compostelanus...ad istud dubium respondet cum distinctione tali...aut intendit præcise consecrare duodecim et non plures, et non determinat quæ sunt illæ duodecim. Et tunc dicit idem Berengarius quod nulla est consecrata.—Floret. Lib. Lugd. 1499. Lib. IV. foll. 94, 5, 6.

Materia congrua, immo necessaria, hujus sacramenti est panis et vinum...Panis enim consecrandus debet esse triticius....Materia calicis necessaria est vinum de vite: quia sanguis Christi de alia materia quam de vino vitis confici non potest...Si enim tantum apponitur de aqua quod substantia vini absorbeatur...de illa mixtura non potest confici sanguis Christi.—Joan. de Burg. Pup. Ocul. Argent. 1514. Pars IV. De Sacram. Euch. fol. 16, 7.]

[4 Quæsivistis quid de incauto presbytero videatur, qui...missam celebrare se fingit...gravius... videtur offendere...cum...non solum Deo...sed populo, quem decipit, se astringat.—Innoc. III. in Corp. Jur. Canon. Lugd. 1624. Decretal. Gregor. IX. Lib. III. Tit. xli. cap. 7. col. 1374.]

[5 Quid si sacerdos acceptis pluribus hostiis consecrandis: quando venit ad actum consecrationis non advertit nisi ad eam quam habet in manu?...quidam dicunt quod non sunt aliæ consecratæ. Sed tu dic cum Scoto quod omnes sunt consecratæ.—Clavas. Summ. Angel. Argent. 1513. Euchar. i. 27. fol. 85.]

[6 Utrum sacerdos virtute verborum præfatorum possit unam partem ipsius hostiæ consecrare sine alia hostia continua remanente. Resp. Rich. in iv. di. x. quod sic: si intenderet determinate ad alteram partem: puta dexteram, vel a tali signo citra.—Id. ibid. 26.] [7 Advouterer, 1565, 1609.]

[8 People knowing his life, and nevertheless hearing his mass, commit, 1565.]

[9 Si qui sunt presbyteri...qui in crimine fornicationis jaceant, interdicimus eis...Si qui vero in suo peccato perseverare maluerint ... benedictio eorum vertitur in maledictionem...Qui vero huic saluberrimo præcepto obedire noluerit, idololatriæ peccatum incurrit.—Gregor. VII. in Corp. Jur. Canon. Decret. Gratian. Decr. Prim. Pars, Dist. lxxxi. can. 15. cols. 388, 9.]

intention, of his mind, and of his will? Or if they cannot, how can they safely adore the sacrament without doubt and danger of idolatry?

But they themselves see well it cannot be; and therefore have devised a simple poor help of their own. They say: We may not adore the sacrament, but under a condition, that is to say, if it be consecrate[10]. And so saith Thomas Sarisburiensis: *Nullus, quantumcunque sit simplex, vel quantumcunque sit discretus, debet præcise credere, hoc esse corpus Domini; sed cum hac conditione, si in consecratione rite sint acta omnia. Aliter enim asseret de creatura, quod ipsa sit Creator; et ita esset idololatria*[11]: "No man, be he never so simple, or never so wise, ought precisely to believe that this is the body of our Lord that the priest hath consecrate, but only under this condition, if all things concerning the consecration be done as appertaineth. For otherwise he shall avouch a creature to be the Creator: which were idolatry." By this doctrine M. Harding teacheth the people thus to kneel down and to adore the sacrament: "If thou be God indeed, then I worship thee; but, if thou be not God, then I will not worship thee." Thus, Arnobius saith, the heathens in old time were wont to call upon Jupiter: *Sive tu deus es, sive tu dea* [*es*][12]: "Whether thou be a god or a goddess, we call upon thee." Thus God's people is led to give the honour of God they cannot tell unto what, and to honour a creature instead of God.

Thom. in Lib. iii. Sent. Dist. 9.

Thom. Sarisb. de Arte Præd. cap. xxv.

Arnob. Lib. iii.

Yet must all this be excused by the example of Rachel and Lea. As if M. Harding would reason thus: Jacob, by God's special providence, knew Lea instead of Rachel;

Gen. xxix.

Ergo, we may safely adore a bare creature with godly honour, and say unto it, Thou art our God: thou madest heaven and earth: we have none other God but thee; and all this without peril of idolatry. He would not thus dally, if he knew what it were to bestow God's glory upon that thing that is no God. Certainly, this is not the worshipping of God "in spirit and truth."

John iv.

St Martin was much more circumspect in this case, as may well appear by that is written of him. For when the devil came unto him, and took upon him to be Christ, and therefore required him to bow down, and to give him honour; "No," said St Martin, "I cannot tell whether thou be Christ or no. Unless I see Christ in the same shape and form that he was crucified in upon the cross, I will not adore him in any wise[13]." St Augustine saith: *Audistis quia Messias Christus est: audistis quia Christus unctus est. Non ... sic posuit* [*Jacob*] *lapidem unctum, ut veniret et adoraret: alioqui idololatria est, non significatio Christi*[14]: "Ye have heard that Messias is Christ: ye have heard that Christ is the Anointed. Jacob did not erect the anointed stone to the intent to come and to adore it. Otherwise, it is idolatry, and not a signification of Christ." Theophilus, being sometime demanded wherefore he would not adore the emperor, as the manner then was, with godly honour, made answer thus: *Quia non ad hoc institutus est imperator, ut adoretur, sed ut legitimo honore honoretur*[15]: "Because the emperor is not appointed to the end we should honour him as God, but that we should give him that honour that unto him appertaineth." So, if M. Harding will likewise demand wherefore we adore not the sacrament with godly honour, the godly simple man may make him this answer: Because it was ordained reverently to be received, and not to be adored, as a sacrament, and not as God. For in all the scriptures and holy fathers we have neither commandment to force us

Sulpit. in Vita Martin.

August. in Johan. Tract. 7.

Theoph. contr. Autol. Lib. i.

[10 Thom. Aquinat. Op. In Lib. III. Sent. Dist. ix. Quæst. 1. Art. 2. Tom. VII. fol. 37.]

[11 Thomas Sarisburiensis theologus Anglus scripsit quoddam opus *De Arte Prædicandi, Librum Unum* MS. Cantabrigiæ in Collegio S. Benedicti. De aliis ejus scriptis, et de tempore, quo vixit, nihil...—Joan. Pitsei Relat. Hist. de Reb. Angl. Par. 1619. Append. 65. Tom. I. p. 916.—The MS. here referred to is No. CCCCLV. of the C.C.C.C. MSS. where the passage occurs as quoted by Jewel, with the following unimportant variations: *nullus quantumcunque discretus vel quantumcunque sit simplex, hoc* est *corpus*, sunt *acta omnia* quæ agi debuerant, assereret, esset Creator, idolatria.]

[12 Arnob. Op. Par. 1580. Adv. Gent. Lib. III. p. 167.]

[13 Ego Christum, nisi in eo habitu formaque qua passus est, nisi crucis stigmata proferentem, venisse non credam.—Sulpit. Div. Mart. Vit. Lib. I. ad calc. Abd. Apost. Hist. Par. 1571. p. 203.]

[14 August. Op. Par. 1679-1700. In Johan. Evang. cap. i. Tractat. vii. 23. Tom. III. Pars II. col. 352; where *unctus Christus*, and *alioquin idololatria esset*.]

[15 Theophil. Ant. ad Autol. Lib. I. 11. ad calc. Just. Mart. Op. Par. 1742. p. 344.]

hereto, nor example to lead us hereto. We adore the body of Christ, not only for the turning of an hand, while the priest is able to hold up the sacrament, and that with doubt of ourselves, whether we do well or no; which thing is utterly uncomfortable, and dangerous, and full of terror to the conscience; but we worship that blessed and glorious body, as that blessed martyr St Stephen did, being in heaven at the right hand of the power of God, and therefore without doubt and danger; and that at all times and for ever; and we believe and confess that Jesus Christ, even in the nature and substance of our flesh, is the Lord in the glory of God the Father.